SO-BYX-194

EXPLORING LITERATURE

THROUGH READING AND WRITING

Bernard A. Drabeck

Helen E. Ellis

Hartley A. Pfeil

Greenfield Community College

HOUGHTON MIFFLIN COMPANY   Boston

Dallas   Geneva, Illinois   Hopewell, New Jersey,   Palo Alto   London

Printed in the U.S.A.

Library of Congress Catalog Card Number: 81-82566

ISBN: 0-395-31694-4

Text Credits: **Aiken, Conrad.** "The Quarrel," from *Collected Poems* by Conrad Aiken. Copyright © 1953, 1970 by Conrad Aiken. Reprinted by permission of Oxford University Press, Inc.   **Anderson, Sherwood.** "The Egg," reprinted by permission of Harold Ober Associates Incorporated. Copyright © 1921 by B. W. Huebsch, Inc. Renewed 1948 by Eleanor Copenhaver Anderson.   **Arrabel, Fernando.** *Picnic on the Battlefield,* from *Guernica and Other Plays,* reprinted by permission of Grove Press, Inc. Translated from the French by Barbara Wright. Copyright © 1967 by Calder & Boyars, Ltd. CAUTION: This play is fully protected, in whole, in part, or in any form under the copyright laws of the United States of America, the British Empire including the Dominion of Canada, and all other countries of the Copyright Union, and is subject to royalty. All rights, including professional, amateur, motion picture, radio, television, recitation, public reading, and any method of photographic reproduction, are strictly reserved. For professional and amateur rights in Great Britain, all inquiries should be addressed to Margaret Ramsay Ltd., 14a Goodwin's Court, London W.C.2, England; for American rights, all inquiries should be addressed to Samuel French, Inc., 25 W. 45th Street, New York, New York 10036.   **Auden, W. H.** "Musée des Beaux Arts" and "The Unknown Citizen," copyright 1940 and renewed 1968 by W. H. Auden. Reprinted from *W. H. Auden: Collected Poems* by W. H. Auden, edited by Edward Mendelson, by permission of Random House, Inc.; "Musée des Beaux Arts" reprinted from *Collected Shorter Poems* by permission of Faber and Faber Ltd.   **Austin, Mary Hunter.** "Papago Wedding," from *One-Smoke Stories* by Mary Austin. Copyright, 1934, by Mary Austin. Copyright © renewed 1962 by Kenneth M. Chapman and Mary C. Wheelwright. Reprinted by permission of Houghton Mifflin Company.   **Bierce, Ambrose.** "Oil of Dog," from the book *Complete Short Stories of Ambrose Bierce,* compiled with commentary by Ernest Jerome Hopkins. Copyright © 1970 by Ernest Jerome Hopkins. Reprinted by permission of Doubleday & Company, Inc.   **Bontemps, Arna.** "A Summer Tragedy," reprinted by permission of Dodd, Mead & Company, Inc., from *The Old South* by Arna Bontemps. Copyright 1933 by Arna Bontemps. Copyright renewed 1961 by Arna Bontemps.   **Bradbury, Ray.** "There Will Come Soft Rains," copyright © 1950 by Crowell Collier Publishing Company, copyright © renewed 1977 by Ray Bradbury. Reprinted by permission of the Harold Matson Company, Inc.   **Brooks, Gwendolyn.** "An Aspect of Love, Alive in the Ice and Fire" (p. 778), by Gwendolyn Brooks, from *Riot.* Reprinted with permission from Broadside/Crummell Press, Detroit, Michigan. "The Ballad of Rudolph Reed" (p. 364) and "The Chicago *Defender* Sends a Man to Little Rock: Fall, 1957" (p. 532), from *The World of Gwendolyn Brooks* by Gwendolyn Brooks. Copyright © 1960 by Gwendolyn Brooks. Reprinted by permission of Harper & Row, Publishers, Inc.   **Callaghan, Morley.** "The Faithful Wife," copyright © 1929 by The New Yorker, copyright © renewed 1957 by Morley Callaghan. Reprinted

ACKNOWLEDGMENTS

by permission of the Harold Matson Company, Inc.   **Cary, Joyce.** "A Special Occasion," from *Spring Song and Other Stories*, reprinted by permission of Curtis Brown, Ltd. Copyright © 1951, 1952, 1953, 1954, 1955, 1956, 1957, 1958, 1960 by Arthur Lucius Michael Cary and David Alexander Ogilvie, executors of the Estate of Joyce Cary. **Clarke, Arthur C.** "The Nine Billion Names of God," copyright 1953 by Ballantine Books, Inc. Reprinted from *The Nine Billion Names of God* by Arthur C. Clarke, by permission of Harcourt Brace Jovanovich, Inc.   **Connor, Tony.** "Elegy for Alfred Hubbard" from *With Love Somehow*, Oxford University Press (London) 1962 by permission of the author.   **cummings, e. e.** " 'next to of course god america i" is reprinted from *IS 5 poems* by permission of Liveright Publishing Corporation. Copyright 1926 by Horace Liveright. Copyright renewed 1953 by E. E. Cummings. "who's most afraid of death? thou," reprinted from *Tulips & Chimneys* by E. E. Cummings, by permission of Liveright Publishing Corporation. Copyright 1923, 1925 and renewed 1951, 1953 by E. E. Cummings. Copyright © 1973, 1976 by Nancy T. Andrews. Copyright © 1973, 1976 by George James Firmage. "i thank You God for most this amazing," copyright 1947 by E. E. Cummings, copyright 1975 by Nancy T. Andrews; and "when serpents bargain for the right to squirm," copyright 1948 by E. E. Cummings, both reprinted from *Complete Poems, 1913–1962* by E. E. Cummings, by permission of Harcourt Brace Jovanovich, Inc.   **DeVries, Peter.** "Pizzicato on the Heartstrings," copyright 1936 Story Magazine, renewed 1963, reprinted by permission of A. Watkins, Inc. **Dickinson, Emily.** "Exultation is the Going," " 'Hope' is the thing with feathers," "I heard a Fly Buzz—when I died," "It dropped so low—in my Regard," "The lightning is a Yellow Fork," "The Soul selects her own Society—" and "Success is counted sweetest," reprinted by permission of the publishers and the Trustees of Amherst College from *The Poems of Emily Dickinson*, edited by Thomas H. Johnson, Cambridge, Mass.: The Belknap Press of Harvard University Press, copyright 1951, © 1955, 1979 by the President and Fellows of Harvard College.   **Duerrenmatt, Friedrich.** *The Visit*, adapted and translated by Maurice Valency. Copyright © 1956 by Maurice Valency, as an unpublished work entitled "The Old Lady's Visit," adapted by Maurice Valency from *Der Besuch der alten Dame* by Friedrich Duerrenmatt. Copyright © 1958 by Maurice Valency. Reprinted by permission of Random House, Inc. CAUTION: Professionals and amateurs are hereby warned that this play, being fully protected under the Copyright Laws of the United States of America, the British Commonwealth, including the Dominion of Canada, and all other countries of the Berne and Universal Copyright Conventions, is subject to royalty. All rights, including professional, amateur, motion picture, recitation, lecturing, public reading, radio and television broadcasting, and the rights of translation into foreign languages, are strictly reserved. Particular emphasis is laid on the question of readings, permission for which must be secured in writing from the author's agent, International Creative Management, Inc., 40 West 75th Street, New York, New York 10019.   **Dugan, Alan.** "Love Song: I and Thou," reprinted by permission of the author from *Collected Poems* (New Haven: Yale University Press, 1970).   **Eliot, T. S.** "Preludes," from *Collected Poems, 1909–1962* by T. S. Eliot, copyright, 1936, by Harcourt Brace Jovanovich, Inc.: copyright © 1963, 1964, by T. S. Eliot. Reprinted by permission of the publisher and Faber and Faber Limited.   **Faulkner, William.** "That Evening Sun," copyright 1931 and renewed 1959 by William Faulkner. Reprinted from *Collected Stories of William Faulkner* by William Faulkner, by permission of Random House, Inc.   **Ferlinghetti, Lawrence.** "Constantly Risking Absurdity," from *A Coney Island of the Mind* by Lawrence Ferlinghetti. Copyright © 1958 by Lawrence Ferlinghetti. Reprinted by permission of New Directions.   **Field, Edward.** "Unwanted," from *Stand Up Friend with Me*, reprinted by permission of Grove Press, Inc. Copyright © 1963 by Edward Field.   **Finkel, Donald.** "Hunting Song," reprinted by permission of the author.   **Freeman, Mary E. Wilkins.** "A New

ACKNOWLEDGMENTS

England Nun" (p. 56), from *A New England Nun and Other Stories* by Mary E. Wilkins Freeman, Harper & Row, reprinted by permission of Harper & Row, Publishers, Inc. **Frost, Robert.** "Design," "Directive," "Fire and Ice," "Provide, Provide," "The Vanishing Red," and "The Wood Pile" from *The Poetry of Robert Frost*, edited by Edward Connery Lathem. Copyright 1916, 1923, 1930, 1939, 1947, © 1969 by Holt, Rinehart and Winston. Copyright 1936, 1944, 1951, © 1958 by Robert Frost. Copyright © 1964, 1967, 1975 by Lesley Frost Ballantine. Reprinted by permission of Holt, Rinehart and Winston, Publishers. **Glaspell, Susan.** *Trifles*, reprinted by permission of Dodd, Mead & Company, Inc., from *Plays* by Susan Glaspell. Copyright 1920 by Dodd, Mead & Company, Inc. Copyright renewed 1948 by Susan Glaspell. **Gorki, Maxim.** "Twenty-six Men and a Girl," from *Twenty-six Men and a Girl and Other Stories*, tr. Jakowleff and Montefiore. (London: Duckworth, 1902.) **Greene, Graham.** "Brother" from *Collected Stories of Graham Greene*. Copyright 1947 by Graham Greene. Copyright © renewed 1975 by Graham Greene. Reprinted by permission of Viking Penguin Inc., The Bodley Head, and William Heinemann. **Hardy, Thomas.** "The Curate's Kindness," "The Man He Killed," "Neutral Tones," "The Ruined Maid," and "The Slow Nature" from *The Complete Poems of Thomas Hardy*, edited by James Gibson (New York: Macmillan, 1978), reproduced by permission of the Trustees of the Hardy Estate and Macmillan, London, as publishers. **Hayden, Robert.** "The Whipping," reprinted from *Angle of Ascent: New and Selected Poems* by Robert Hayden, with the permission of Liveright Publishing Corporation. Copyright © 1975, 1972, 1970, 1966 by Robert Hayden. **Hemingway, Ernest.** "Old Man at the Bridge," from *The Short Stories of Ernest Hemingway* by Ernest Hemingway. Copyright 1938 by Ernest Hemingway; Copyright renewed. Reprinted with the permission of Charles Scribner's Sons. **Henry, O.** "The Cop and the Anthem," from *The Four Million* by O. Henry, which appears in *The Complete Works of O. Henry*. Reprinted by permission of Doubleday & Company, Inc. **Hopkins, Gerard Manley.** "(Carrion Comfort)" and "God's Grandeur," from *Poems of Gerard Manley Hopkins*, 4th ed., edited by W. H. Gardner and N. H. Mackenzie (New York: Oxford University Press, 1970). **Housman, A. E.** "Is My Team Ploughing," from "A Shropshire Lad" — Authorised Edition — from *The Collected Poems of A. E. Housman*. Copyright 1939, 1940, © 1965 by Holt, Rinehart and Winston. Copyright © 1967, 1968 by Robert E. Symons. Reprinted by permission of Holt, Rinehart and Winston, Publishers, and The Society of Authors as the literary representative of the Estate of A. E. Housman, and Jonathan Cape Ltd., publishers of A. E. Housman's *Collected Poems*. **Hughes, Langston.** "The Ballad of the Landlord," reprinted by permission of Harold Ober Associates Incorporated. Copyright © 1949 by the Curtis Publishing Company. Renewed 1976 by George H. Bass as Executor for the Estate of Langston Hughes. **James, Henry.** "Paste," from *The Novels and Tales of Henry James*, New York Edition (New York: Charles Scribner's Sons, 1907–1909). Reprinted with the Permission of Charles Scribner's Sons. **Jarrell, Randall.** "Second Air Force," reprinted with permission of Farrar, Straus and Giroux, Inc. "Second Air Force" from *Complete Poems* by Randall Jarrell. Copyright 1944 by Mrs. Randall Jarrell. Copyright renewed © 1971 by Mrs. Randall Jarrell. **Jong, Erica.** "The Man Under the Bed," from *Fruits & Vegetables* by Erica Jong. Copyright © 1968, 1970, 1971 by Erica Mann Jong. Reprinted by permission of Holt, Rinehart and Winston, Publishers. **Joyce, James.** "Counterparts," from *Dubliners* by James Joyce. Copyright © 1967 by the Estate of James Joyce. Reprinted by permission of Viking Penguin Inc. **Kipling, Rudyard.** "Danny Deever," from *Barrack Room Ballads*, reprinted by permission of The National Trust of Great Britain and Eyre Methuen Limited; "The Gardener," from *Debits and Credits* by Rudyard Kipling. Copyright 1926 by Rudyard Kipling. Reprinted by permission of Doubleday & Company, Inc., The National Trust of Great Britain, and Macmillan London Ltd. **Lawrence, D. H.** "The Rocking-Horse

ACKNOWLEDGMENTS

Winner," from *The Complete Short Stories of D. H. Lawrence*, Vol. III. Copyright 1934 by Frieda Lawrence. Copyright © renewed 1962 by Angelo Ravagli and C. M. Weekley, Executors of the Estate of Frieda Lawrence Ravagli. Reprinted by permission of Viking Penguin Inc.   **Lee, Don.** "Big Momma," from *We Walk the Way of the New World* by Don L. Lee, copyright 1970. Reprinted with permission from Broadside/Crummel Press, Detroit, Michigan.   **Lester, Julius.** "Parents," excerpted from the book *Search for the New Land* by Julius Lester. Copyright © 1969 by Julius Lester. Reprinted by permission of The Dial Press.   **Locke, William J.** "The Adventure of the Kind Mr. Smith," from *Far Away Stories* (New York: Dodd, Mead, 1919).   **Lowell, Amy.** "Patterns," from *The Complete Poetical Works of Amy Lowell*, published by Houghton Mifflin Company. Copyright 1955 by Houghton Mifflin Company. Reprinted by permission.   **Lowell, Robert.** "The Drunken Fisherman," from *Lord Weary's Castle*, copyright 1946, 1974 by Robert Lowell. Reprinted by permission of Harcourt Brace Jovanovich.   **MacLeish, Archibald.** "The End of the World" and "Memorial Rain," from *New & Collected Poems, 1917–1976*, by Archibald MacLeish. Copyright © 1976 by Archibald MacLeish. Reprinted by permission of the publisher, Houghton Mifflin Company. *The Fall of the City*, from *Six Plays* by Archibald MacLeish. Copyright © 1980 by Archibald MacLeish. Reprinted by permission of Houghton Mifflin Company. **Mahon, Derek.** "My Wicked Uncle," from *Poems, 1962–1978* by Derek Mahon, © Derek Mahon 1979. Reprinted by permission of Oxford University Press.   **Malamud, Bernard.** "The Jewbird," reprinted by permission of Farrar, Straus and Giroux, Inc. "The Jewbird" from *Idiots First* by Bernard Malamud. Copyright © 1963 by Bernard Malamud.   **Manifold, John.** "The Griesly Wife" (p. 223), from *Selected Verse* by John Manifold (The John Day Company). Copyright, 1946, by The John Day Company. Reprinted by permission of Harper & Row, Publishers, Inc.   **Mansfield, Katherine.** "The Fly," copyright 1922 by Alfred A. Knopf, Inc., and renewed 1950 by John Middleton Murry. Reprinted from *The Short Stories of Katherine Mansfield* by Katherine Mansfield, by permission of Alfred A. Knopf, Inc.   **Maricopa Indian Tale.** "The Creator, the Snake, and the Rabbit," from *Yuman Tribes of the Gila River*, edited by Leslie Spier. *University of Chicago Publications in Anthropology, Ethnological Series*. Copyright 1933 by The University of Chicago, all rights reserved. Published September 1933. Reprinted by permission of The University of Chicago Press.   **Masters, Edgar Lee.** "Barry Holden," "Eugene Carman," "Fiddler Jones," "Harry Wilmans," "Judge Selah Lively," "Mrs. Charles Bliss," "Nancy Knapp," "Rev. Lemuel Wiley," "Walter Simmons," "Wendell P. Bloyd," and "Willie Metcalf," from *Spoon River Anthology* by Edgar Lee Masters (New York: Macmillan, 1962). Reprinted by permission of Ellen C. Masters.   **Montale, Eugenio.** "The Man in Pyjamas," reprinted by permission of London Magazine Editions. This story first appeared in *London Magazine*.   **Muro, Amado Jesus.** "Mala Torres," from the *Arizona Quarterly*, Summer, 1968, reprinted by permission of the *Arizona Quarterly* and Mrs. Chester Seltzer.   **Nemerov, Howard.** "The Vacuum," from *The Collected Poems of Howard Nemerov*, The University of Chicago Press, 1977, reprinted by permission of the author.   **O'Connor, Flannery.** "Everything That Rises Must Converge," reprinted by permission of Farrar, Straus & Giroux, Inc., from *Everything That Rises Must Converge* by Flannery O'Connor. Copyright © 1961, 1965 by the Estate of Flannery O'Connor.   **Papago Indian Lyric.** "War Song," from *Singing for Power: The Song Magic of the Papago Indians of Southern Arizona*, edited by Ruth Underhill (Berkeley: University of California Press, 1938, pp. 193–194). Reprinted by permission.   **Peretz, I. L.** "If Not Higher" by I. L. Peretz, from *A Treasure of Yiddish Stories*, edited by Irving Howe and Eliezer Greenberg. Copyright 1953, 1954 by The Viking Press, Inc. Used by permission of Viking Penguin Inc.   **Petry, Ann.** "Like a Winding Sheet," originally published in *The Crisis*, November, 1945. Copyright 1945 by the Crisis Publishing Company, Inc.

Reprinted by permission. **Piercy, Marge.** "The Crippling," from *To Be of Use* (New York: Doubleday & Company, 1973), used by permission of the author. Copyright © 1973 by Marge Piercy. **Plath, Sylvia.** "The Colossus" and "Spinster," copyright © 1961 by Sylvia Plath. Reprinted from *The Colossus and Other Poems*, by permission of Alfred A. Knopf, Inc., and Faber and Faber, London (Olwyn Hughes, Literary Agent). Copyright Ted Hughes 1967. **Pound, Ezra.** "Salutation," from *Personae* by Ezra Pound. Copyright 1926 by Ezra Pound. Reprinted by permission of New Directions. **Purdy, James.** "Daddy Wolf," from *Children Is All* by James Purdy. Copyright © 1960 by James Purdy. Reprinted by permission of New Directions. **Ransom, John Crowe.** "Bells for John Whiteside's Daughter," "Parting, Without a Sequel," and "Piazza Piece," copyright 1927 by Alfred A. Knopf, Inc., and renewed 1955 by John Crowe Ransom. Reprinted from *Selected Poems, Third Edition, Revised and Enlarged* by John Crowe Ransom, by permission of Alfred A. Knopf, Inc. **Reed, Henry.** "Naming of Parts," from *A Map of Verona*, reprinted by permission of Jonathan Cape Ltd. **Rich, Adrienne.** "Living in Sin," reprinted from *Poems, Selected and New* by Adrienne Rich, with the permission of W. W. Norton & Company, Inc. Copyright © 1975, 1973, 1971, 1969, 1966 by W. W. Norton & Company, Inc. Copyright © 1955 by Adrienne Rich. **Robinson, Edwin Arlington.** "Aaron Stark" and "Richard Cory," from *The Children of the Night* by Edwin Arlington Robinson. Copyright under the Berne Convention. Reprinted with the permission of Charles Scribner's Sons. "Uncle Ananias," from *The Town Down the River* by Edwin Arlington Robinson. Copyright 1910 by Charles Scribner's Sons; copyright renewed. Reprinted with the permission of Charles Scribner's Sons. "John Gorham" and "Mr. Flood's Party," reprinted with permission of Macmillan Publishing Company, Inc., from *Collected Poems* by Edwin Arlington Robinson. Copyright 1916 by Edwin Arlington Robinson, renewed 1944 by Ruth Nivison. Copyright 1921 by Edwin Arlington Robinson, renewed 1945 by Ruth Nivison. **Roethke, Theodore.** "The Waking," from *Collected Poems of Theodore Roethke*. Copyright 1953 by Theodore Roethke. Reprinted by permission of Doubleday & Company, Inc. **Roth, Philip.** "The Conversion of the Jews," from *Goodbye, Columbus* by Philip Roth. Copyright © 1959 by Philip Roth. Reprinted by permission of Houghton Mifflin Company. **Russell, Norman.** "indian school," copyright © 1974 by Norman Russell, reprinted by permission of the author. **Sexton, Anne.** "Ringing the Bells," from *To Bedlam and Partway Back* by Anne Sexton. Copyright © 1960 by Anne Sexton. Reprinted by permission of the publisher, Houghton Mifflin Company. **Shakespeare, William.** All selections from W. A. Neilson and C. J. Hill, *The Complete Plays and Poems of William Shakespeare* (Boston, 1942). Copyright 1942 by William Allan Neilson and Charles Jarvis Hill. Used by permission of Houghton Mifflin Company. **Sophocles.** *Antigone*, from *The Complete Greek Tragedies*, Volume II, edited by David Grene and Richard Lattimore. Tr. Elizabeth Wyckoff. Copyright 1954 by The University of Chicago. Used by permission of The University of Chicago Press. **Stephens, James.** "A Glass of Beer," reprinted with permission of Macmillan Publishing Co., Inc., Mrs. Iris Wise, and Macmillan, London and Basingstoke, from *Collected Poems* by James Stephens. Copyright 1918 by Macmillan Publishing Co., Inc., renewed 1946 by James Stephens. **Stuart, Jesse.** "Dawn of Remembered Spring," copyright Jesse Stuart, reprinted with permission of the author. **Stuart, Muriel.** "In the Orchard," from *Collected Poems*, reprinted by permission of the Executors of the Muriel Stuart Estate and Jonathan Cape Ltd. **Teasdale, Sara.** "There Will Come Soft Rains," reprinted with permission of Macmillan Publishing Co., Inc., from *Collected Poems* by Sara Teasdale. Copyright 1920 by Macmillan Publishing Co., Inc., renewed 1948 by Mamie T. Wheless. **Thomas, Dylan.** "Do Not Go Gentle into That Good Night," from *The Poems of Dylan Thomas*. Copyright 1952 by Dylan Thomas. Reprinted by permission of New Directions and David Higham Associates Limited. **Vonnegut, Kurt, Jr.** "Harrison Bergeron," excerpted from the book *Welcome to the Monkey House* by Kurt Vonnegut, Jr. Copyright © 1961 by Kurt Vonnegut, Jr. Originally published in *Fantasy and Science Fiction.* Reprinted by permission of Delacorte Press/Seymour Lawrence.   **Welty, Eudora.** "A Worn Path," copyright 1941, 1969 by Eudora Welty. Reprinted from her volume *A Curtain of Green and Other Stories* by permission of Harcourt Brace Jovanovich, Inc.   **Wilbur, Richard.** "Mind," from *Things of This World,* © 1956 by Richard Wilbur. Reprinted by permission of Harcourt Brace Jovanovich, Inc. "To an American Poet Just Dead," from *Ceremony and Other Poems,* copyright 1950, 1978 by Richard Wilbur. Reprinted by permission of Harcourt Brace Jovanovich, Inc.   **Williams, Tennessee.** *27 Wagons Full of Cotton.* Copyright 1945 by Tennessee Williams. Reprinted by permission of New Directions. CAUTION: Professionals and amateurs are hereby warned that *27 Wagons Full of Cotton,* being fully protected under the copyright laws of the United States of America, the British Commonwealth including the Dominion of Canada, and all other countries of the Copyright Union, is subject to royalty. All rights, including professional, amateur, motion picture, recitation, lecturing, public reading, radio and television broadcasting, and the rights of translation into foreign languages, are strictly reserved. Particular emphasis is laid on the question of readings, permission for which must be secured from the author's agent, Mitch Douglas, c/o International Creative Management, 40 West 57th St., New York 10019. Inquiries concerning the amateur acting rights should be directed to The Dramatists' Play Service, Inc., 440 Park Avenue South, New York 10016, without whose permission in writing no amateur performance may be given.   **Williams, William Carlos.** "The Use of Force," from *The Farmers' Daughters* by William Carlos Williams. Copyright 1938 by William Carlos Williams. Reprinted by permission of New Directions.   **Wodehouse, P. G.** "Honeysuckle Cottage," from *Meet Mr. Mulliner* (New York: Doubleday & Co., 1928). Copyright 1925, 1926, 1927, 1928 by Pelham Grenville Wodehouse. Copyright renewed 1952, 1953, 1954, 1955 by Pelham Grenville Wodehouse. Reprinted by permission of the author and the author's agents, Scott Meredith Literary Agency, Inc., 845 Third Avenue, New York, New York 10022.   **Woolf, Virginia.** "The Legacy," from *A Haunted House and Other Stories* by Virginia Woolf, copyright 1944, 1972 by Harcourt Brace Jovanovich. Reprinted by permission of the publisher, the author's Literary Estate, and The Hogarth Press Ltd.   **Wylie, Elinor.** "Velvet Shoes," copyright 1921 by Alfred A. Knopf, Inc., and renewed 1949 by William Rose Benet. Reprinted from *Collected Poems of Elinor Wylie,* by permission of Alfred A. Knopf, Inc.   **Yamamoto, Hisaye.** "Seventeen Syllables," reprinted by permission of the author, Hisaye Yamamoto DeSoto. This story first appeared in *Partisan Review,* 1949, Vol. XVI, No. 11, November.   **Yeats, William Butler.** "The Wild Swans at Coole," reprinted by permission of Macmillan Publishing Co., Inc., Michael B. Yeats, Anne Yeats, and Macmillan London Limited, from *Collected Poems* by William Butler Yeats. Copyright 1919 by Macmillan Publishing Co., Inc., renewed 1947 by Bertha Georgie Yeats.

Art Credits: **Chapter 1.** *Sentimental Yearner* by Grant Wood. The Minneapolis Institute of Arts.   **Chapter 2.** *St. George and the Dragon* by Raphael. National Gallery of Art.   **Chapter 3.** *London Visitors* by James-Jacques-Joseph Tissot. The Toledo Museum of Art; gift of Edward Drummond Libbey.   **Chapter 4.** *The Blind Girl* by J. E. Millais. By courtesy of Birmingham Museums and Art Gallery.   *The Fall of Icarus* by Pieter Brueghel. Musée des Beaux Arts, Brussels, Belgium.   **Chapter 5.** *Romeo and Juliet* by Ford Maddox Brown. BBC Hulton Picture Library.   **Cover.** *London Visitors* (detail) by James-Jacques-Joseph Tissot. The Toledo Museum of Art; gift of Edward Drummond Libbey.

CONTENTS

CONTENTS

PREFACE

This text focuses on the elements from which imaginative literary works are built: character, conflict, and setting, all expressed in carefully chosen special language. These elements, viewed singly or in combination, provide one perspective through which a reader can discover not only how an author constructs and communicates his or her vision of the world but also what that vision might mean.

The first four chapters of this book investigate in close detail these four elements of literature—character, conflict, setting, and language. In each an introductory section defines and examines the element being discussed. This section also presents a method for close reading and analyzes several literary works in depth. It is followed by suggested assignments for writing about literature and detailed writing instructions for completing these assignments. Writing options in each chapter include a critical essay as well as other creative responses. Finally, at the end of each chapter a number of reading selections are presented for discussion and study.

Chapter 5 presents one play by Shakespeare, *Romeo and Juliet*. In this chapter we discuss the interrelationship of character, conflict, setting, and language in one work, to discover how this interrelationship produces meaning in a rich and complex work. Such understanding will provide students with deeper and more lasting rewards in all their subsequent reading. And that, we believe, should be the purpose of any introduction to literature: to help students become more expert readers and, as they increase in skill, knowledge, and understanding, to help them find greater enjoyment in what can be a lifelong source of pleasure and enlightenment.

We are pleased to acknowledge the advice and suggestions of several colleagues in the preparation of this book: Jean M. English, Tallahassee Community College; Michael Flachmann, California State College, Bakersfield; Joan E. Hartman, The College of Staten Island; A. L. Hough, Murray State University; Lawrence E. Hussman, Jr., Wright State University; Walter Klarner, Johnson County Community College; Joanne M. McCarthy, Tacoma Community College; and Mary Rohrberger, Oklahoma State University.

B.A.D.
H.E.E.
H.A.P.

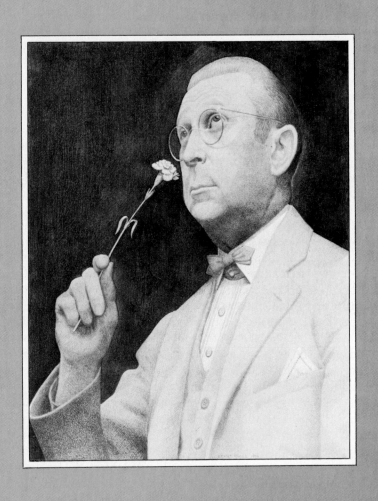

CHAPTER 1

CHARACTER AND MEANING

PERSONS AND CHARACTERS

When we are asked who someone is, we generally begin by listing observable facts. We describe height, weight, sex, color of skin, hair, and eyes, and other body features. If we know the person well we might add address, age, job, education, family background, community activities, and hobbies. For most people, such information is a matter of record.

When we are asked not just *who* someone is but also *what kind* of person he or she is, we need to go beyond appearances and public records. We have to identify inner qualities—emotional, mental, and moral traits—that make up personality. Those inner qualities control a person's behavior (past, present, or future) and describe what a person was, is, or can be like. Although most traits are common to many people, no two people ever share precisely the same cluster of traits; nor do two people display a single trait to the same degree. Traits, singly or in combination, help define the uniqueness of an individual. However, since people are continually influenced or modified by their experiences, character traits do not remain constant within a person. The personality of every individual can, and often does, change over a period of time, just like physical and social attributes. A criminal, for example, may become an upright and honest citizen, and vice versa. Sometimes a lazy, undependable worker will become efficient and reliable. Because people change, we can define them only as we know them at a particular time. Furthermore, our ability to know or describe people is limited because they tend to try to control what others know or think about them. As a result, most people may spend their entire lives trying to discover the real nature of the people around them, just as they search for their own identity.

Characters in literature are usually easier to know, since the purpose of most authors is to reveal, not conceal. Thus a writer acquaints us with an individual in prose or poetry through a variety of means—what we are told by words and actions and even occasionally what is left out. Created characters therefore have an existence that is confined to the work in which they appear, but somehow, if the proper literary magic is at work, these characters appear real to us nonetheless. They will also be believable if the author endows them with traits that are capable of motivating their behaviors.

The amount and nature of information given about a character's biography and traits will vary. Minor characters are usually treated very differently from those who play a major role; usually, the less important the role, the fewer details used to reveal character traits. Other considerations can also affect characterization. Is the character flat (one-dimensional) or rounded (true to life, three-dimensional)? Is the character an individual or a stereotype? Is the focus of the work itself on character, or is the meaning of the work conveyed largely through some other literary element (conflict, setting, or language)? If an author's primary interest is character development, he or she will attempt to provide enough information to make at least the major characters rounded individuals whose shape and substance are sharply etched and richly detailed.

Because all fictional characters, no matter how real they seem, have a limited "life," they are not only easier to know but also more predictable than people. As we noted earlier, people comprise so many complex traits and are affected by so many experiences that their behavior is not always what we expect, and in time even their traits may change. Fictional characters, on the other hand, are permanently fixed within their literary environment. In addition, they are restricted by the number of their experiences. When characters do not alter in traits or behavior through these experiences, they are "static." Sometimes, however, the meaning of a work relates to the ability of a character to experience growth or deterioration in his or her traits. Such a character is "dynamic."

Whether characters are static or dynamic, mere sketches or fully detailed portraits, they are essential to the creation of literary meaning. By getting to know them and how they function, we learn something about people and life. Getting to know a real person can involve a great deal of time, energy, and even pain. If the person matters to us, we consider the effort worthwhile. The same holds true for fictional characters. If the author makes us care, then we are willing to go through the effort of getting to know the characters and understand them. When an author successfully shapes material, we meet characters who take life before our eyes. They have a definite past, present, and perhaps even future. And just as really knowing other people makes our lives fuller, knowing characters in literature that matters enriches us too.

The following poem introduces us to a fictional character. As you read it, think about what the writer tells us about him—how much the writer lets us know—and what you must do to interpret or expand on this information in order to know him.

Edgar Lee Masters (1869–1950)

WALTER SIMMONS

My parents thought that I would be
As great as Edison or greater:
For as a boy I made balloons
And wondrous kites and toys with clocks
And little engines with tracks to run on
And telephones of cans and thread.
I played the cornet and painted pictures,
Modeled in clay and took the part
Of the villain in the "Octoroon."

5

But then at twenty-one I married   10
And had to live, and so, to live
I learned the trade of making watches
And kept the jewelry store on the square,
Thinking, thinking, thinking, thinking,—
Not of business, but of the engine   15
I studied the calculus to build.
And all Spoon River watched and waited
To see it work, but it never worked.
And a few kind souls believed my genius
Was somehow hampered by the store.   20
It wasn't true. The truth was this:
I didn't have the brains.

In this poem, Edgar Lee Masters lets Simmons speak for himself. Simmons omits many biographical details, including those about his physical appearance. Yet as he describes certain experiences he has had and his responses to them, he gives us some clues to his background as well as his inner traits. Clearly a bright child, Simmons used to play cornet, paint, act, make mechanical toys, and study calculus. He placed a high value on creativity, primarily because his parents expected it (lines 1–2). When he married at twenty-one, however, he channeled his talent into "the trade of making watches" (line 12). His ready acceptance of responsibility seems to show that he is mature, but he is never satisfied with his life. The hopes of his parents that he would be "As great as Edison or greater" (line 2) and of the townspeople who all "watched and waited" (line 17) both exert pressure on him to create an engine that works. His desire to fulfill those expectations reveals his need for social approval. Because of that trait, he devotes years of his life to "Thinking, thinking, thinking, thinking,— / Not of business, but of the engine" (lines 14–15). In the end, he fails. Looking back at his life, he realizes he failed because he "didn't have the brains" (line 22). Although he was in many ways a successful and productive man, his need for approval caused him to devote much of his time to an impossible task and resulted in an unhappy life.

In Masters' poem, Simmons is allowed to speak for himself. Who narrates and how characters are thereby disclosed are related to a very important literary device called point of view.

MEETING CHARACTERS IN LITERATURE: POINT OF VIEW

The process of getting to know actual people depends in part on chance and in part on our own choices. We may meet someone new in class or on the job.

By chance we may encounter the same person again and plan to further our acquaintance. The process of getting to know characters in literature, on the other hand, depends on the author's choices and on the reader's awareness of how character is revealed in literature. The first and most fundamental choice an author makes affecting what we may learn about characters is this: Who shall tell the reader about the events in the narrative? In other words, what shall be the narrative point of view?

Point of view in literature determines much more than who is telling about characters and events. It also controls just what and how much is told. It affects the overall shape of the work and the ways in which the author's vision is communicated to the reader. In particular, as we shall see, it controls the kind of information given to the reader about characters in the work. There are many possible narrative points of view, but the outline below lists most of them:

    I. First-person point of view
      A. Major character
      B. Minor character
    II. Third-person point of view
      A. Omniscient
      B. Limited
      C. Objective
   III. Dialogue

While there are important differences among the three major types of literature—stories, poems, and plays—any work that introduces the reader to characters and events has some narrative point of view. Although the term is most often used in the discussion of prose fiction, that is, stories, it applies to other types of literature as well. In the following discussion, some short poems are used to illustrate the major points of view.

Suppose, for example, that an author considers writing about a farm couple who have experienced a series of problems. The couple is older; they have been married a long time. Relatives of the husband (one married brother and two sisters, one a widow and the other unmarried) live nearby and accuse the husband of acquiring their inheritance in an underhanded way, thereby taking upon himself what should also have been theirs. The couple has neighbor problems too—a boundary dispute with one, a problem over water rights with another. The couple work hard at their farm, but they are beset by a series of disasters: crop failures, diseased cattle, a granary struck by lightning. Throughout this difficult period, the wife feels a terrible sense of loss and failure; she also has to cope with the in-laws and neighbors, whom she believes to be partly responsible for the predicament. Ultimately, the ordeal is too much for her and she goes insane, finally setting fire to the house and dancing madly around the burning structure while her husband looks on in agonized shock.

An author might tell this story using a first-person point of view, with one of the characters as narrator—the wife, the husband, an in-law, or one of the neighbors. This choice would set limits on what the reader can learn; a brother-in-law, for example, will have observed only certain details and learned of others by hearsay. The husband, on the other hand, will have observed much more quite directly. At the same time, their attitudes toward events and toward the characters involved will differ greatly. Since everyone has some biases, any narrator who is also a character will describe people and their actions from a personal perspective and may even omit or distort material. Thus the character of the narrator will in many ways determine the content, style, and structure of the narrative. In addition to controlling what we learn about the events described, use of first-person narration will give the reader direct experience of the mind of the speaker in action. When fictional events are told in this way, the reader experiences a sense of immediacy and directness, as if hearing a story told aloud by someone who has witnessed the events at first hand.

An author might also choose a third-person point of view—an outside narrator who does not participate in the events. Such an unidentified narrator can move freely into the thoughts and feelings of various characters, giving the reader glimpses of a number of minds at work. This narrative point of view also allows for objective reporting of the fictional events: an outside narrator may state from an unbiased perspective what "happened" as opposed to what a given character thinks or feels about what happened. Telling the story of the farm couple from such a narrative point of view might allow the reader to gain more of an overview of the quarrels and their causes, but it would give a less direct sense of personal contact with characters as persons. Since third-person narrations are often somewhat leisurely and philosophical, they may, in effect, examine characters and events from a little distance.

The events sketched above concerning a farm couple are narrated in the following poem. As you read it, note Edgar Lee Masters' choice of narrative point of view and the effects that choice has on the poem.

Edgar Lee Masters (1869–1950)

NANCY KNAPP

Well, don't you see this was the way of it:
We bought the farm with what he inherited,
And his brothers and sisters accused him of poisoning
His father's mind against the rest of them.
And we never had any peace with our treasure.   5
The murrain took the cattle, and the crops failed.

And lightning struck the granary.
So we mortgaged the farm to keep going.
And he grew silent and was worried all the time.
Then some of the neighbors refused to speak to us,   10
And took sides with his brothers and sisters.
And I had no place to turn, as one may say to himself,
At an earlier time in life: "No matter,
So and so is my friend, or I can shake this off
With a little trip to Decatur."   15
Then the dreadfulest smells infested the rooms.
So I set fire to the beds and the old witch-house
Went up in a roar of flame,
As I danced in the yard with waving arms,
While he wept like a freezing steer.   20

    The first step toward understanding the fictional people in this poem lies in recognizing the point of view. Nancy Knapp, a major character, is the narrator, or speaker. She tells only those events that seem important to her; and naturally, she gives her own interpretation of those events. We may at first be tempted to take Nancy's side against what appear to be her jealous and interfering in-laws. Later in the poem, however, we experience the shock of realizing that she is insane, and that from the very beginning she may have suffered from delusions of persecution, and so misread the motives of others. We are given a chilling insight into what the world may look like from the perspective of a diseased mind. In this case, the first-person point of view enriches the poem's impact on the reader, but it also presents some puzzles for the reader to solve. If the narrator is insane, how can we be sure of what is "really" happening and what the other characters are "really" like?

    The first-person point of view has a number of variations. Nancy Knapp, like many other first-person narrators, seems to be addressing her remarks directly to the reader or perhaps to the world in general. Some other first-person narrations take place in a dramatic context, with the speaker addressing another identifiable character, who is presumably listening and reacting. (For an example of this type of narration, see "My Last Duchess," p. 16.) Frequently, a first-person narrator is, like Nancy Knapp or the Duke in "My Last Duchess," one of the principal characters in the work. Such a major character is very likely to have certain personal prejudices or a need for self-justification. Consequently, such a narrator may not always present an accurate picture of the events and people involved. On the other hand, some first-person narrators are only minor characters who observe the action without being central to it. Because they often lack essential information, the reader must make intelligent guesses about what is really happening. In either case, the reader must ask such questions as: How much does the narrator really know about events and the people experiencing them? What prejudices and personal needs may affect what the narrator says? Is the speaker a reliable observer and a trustworthy reporter?

The third-person point of view involves a speaker who is not a character in the work. The effect of such a point of view is to gain some distance: instead of being obliged to examine the people and events through the limitations of a particular character's perspective, the reader may look at them from the outside. This can be seen in Hardy's poem "The Slow Nature."

Thomas Hardy (1840–1928)

THE SLOW NATURE

(An incident of Froom Valley)

"Thy husband—poor, poor Heart!—is dead—
    Dead, out by Moreford Rise;
A bull escaped the barton-shed,
    Gored him, and there he lies!"

—"Ha, ha—go away! 'Tis a tale, methink,   5
    Thou joker Kit!" laughed she.
"I've known thee many a year, Kit Twink,
    And ever hast thou fooled me!"

—"But, Mistress Damon—I can swear
    Thy goodman John is dead!   10
And soon th'lt hear their feet who bear
    His body to his bed."

So unwontedly sad was the merry man's face—
    That face which had long deceived—
That she gazed and gazed; and then could trace   15
    The truth there; and she believed.

She laid a hand on the dresser-ledge,
    And scanned far Egdon-side;
And stood; and you heard the wind-swept sedge
    And the rippling Froom; till she cried: 20

"O my chamber's untidied, unmade my bed,
    Though the day has begun to wear;
'What a slovenly hussif!' it will be said,
    When they all go up my stair!"

She disappeared; and the joker stood   25
    Depressed by his neighbour's doom,

And amazed that a wife struck to widowhood
Thought first of her unkempt room.

But a fortnight thence she could take no food,
  And she pined in a slow decay;   30
While Kit soon lost his mournful mood
  And laughed in his ancient way.

Although Thomas Hardy's poem begins with dialogue between two characters, in stanza 2 a narrator remarks, "laughed she" (line 6), and in stanza 4 that same narrator begins telling the events. Who is that narrator? It is someone unidentified, for all practical purposes indistinguishable from the author. This outside narrator never intrudes into the poem as "I," but uses third-person pronouns ("he," "she") in referring to the characters. Since a third-person narrator is not identifiable as a character, it is pointless to ask about his or her prejudices, except as these may reflect the author's personal philosophy. The reader has no choice but to accept whatever such a narrator says as "true."

The objective facts in this poem are that the news of a man's death is brought to his wife by a person known to be a practical joker, and that after a few moments the wife hurries upstairs to tidy up her room and make the bed. However, in order to understand Mistress Damon's behavior, the reader must also learn what passes through her mind. A first-person narrator—for example, Kit—could recount the actual events and state his own feelings at the time; he could only guess at the thoughts and feelings of the other characters. However, a third-person narrator may, as in this poem, be *omniscient,* and so tell not only what happens but also what various characters think and how they feel. (*Omniscient* means "all-knowing": many people think of God as omniscient, knowing our thoughts as well as our actions.) Thus an omniscient third-person narrator knows and is able to report the feelings and responses of various characters, as well as events. The narrator of "The Slow Nature," for example, says that Mistress Damon at first laughs at Kit's news, but after a time "she believed" (line 16). Kit's reactions also are significant, and so are reported: failing to understand the defense mechanisms working in the woman, he is "Depressed . . . and amazed" (lines 26–27).

Not all third-person narrators are omniscient. The author may choose to focus on the thoughts and feelings of only one character. In this case, the third-person narration is spoken of as *limited.* A limited narrator may include an objective, "truthful," account of events or may report those events as they appear to a certain character. Other characters, on the other hand, are seen only from the outside. Their actions and remarks (but not their thoughts) may be reported objectively by the third-person narrator, or they may be commented on as they are perceived by the one character whose thoughts are revealed. Again, an author may choose an entirely *objective* third-person point of view, in which no thoughts or feelings are directly reported to the reader, although the narrator may objectively report conversations (in which thoughts and feelings may be revealed), describe the scene, and narrate events.

In any case, the reader must keep track of who is speaking at any given moment. What are that person's biases and perspective? What can he or she be counted on to know as well as to report reliably? To whom is the person speaking, and what are the motivations behind the remark? Read the following poem with these questions in mind.

Thomas Hardy (1840–1928)

THE RUINED MAID

"O 'Melia, my dear, this does everything crown!
Who could have supposed I should meet you in Town?
And whence such fair garments, such prosperi-ty?"—
"O didn't you know I'd been ruined?" said she.

—"You left us in tatters, without shoes or socks,   5
Tired of digging potatoes, and spudding up docks;
And now you've gay bracelets and bright feathers three!"—
"Yes: that's how we dress when we're ruined," said she.

—"At home in the barton you said 'thee' and 'thou,'
And 'thik oon,' and 'theas oon,' and 't'other'; but now   10
Your talking quite fits 'ee for high compa-ny!"—
"Some polish is gained with one's ruin," said she.

—"Your hands were like paws then, your face blue and bleak
But now I'm bewitched by your delicate cheek,
And your little gloves fit as on any la-dy!"—   15
"We never do work when we're ruined," said she.

—"You used to call home-life a hag-ridden dream,
And you'd sigh, and you'd sock; but at present you seem
To know not of megrims or melancho-ly!"—
"True. One's pretty lively when ruined," said she.   20

—"I wish I had feathers, a fine sweeping gown,
And a delicate face, and could strut about Town!"—
"My dear—a raw country girl, such as you be,
Cannot quite expect that. You ain't ruined," said she.

In "The Ruined Maid" the reader learns about the events in the lives of the two women entirely through their dialogue. This technique, used in most plays and in some stories and poems, gives the reader the feeling of actually listening in on the conversation of two or more characters. On the basis of the conversation, together with whatever information or stage directions are provided, the reader can imagine what the people look like, what they do, what tone of voice they use, and so on. Of course, a third-person objective narrator could describe the clothing worn by the two women in "The Ruined Maid," state what actions or facial expressions accompany the remarks, and otherwise explain to the reader what is happening. However, the dialogue in this poem provides ample clues: 'Melia is dressed in what her acquaintance from the country regards as high fashion, and she behaves in a lively, light-hearted way, quite well satisfied with having been "ruined." The other woman is at first surprised and perhaps shocked but later envious. The narrator's omission of any moral comment is important to the poem's effect. The irony of the situation, that the honest, hard-working woman still remains ill-dressed and ill-fed while the prostitute lives comfortably, allows us to make our own judgments about a society in which this can happen.

It is therefore important to discover the "point of view" as we first approach a work of literature. The whole shape of the narrative and its effect on the reader are directly connected to it. In particular, what the reader is able to learn about characters depends on who is describing the events. Understanding who the narrator is constitutes an important first step toward learning about fictional people and their traits. A second step is recognizing and interpreting the various clues to character that are presented in the work.

SECOND CLUES TO CHARACTER: HOW WE LEARN ABOUT PEOPLE

In life, we get to know people in a variety of ways. First of all, we usually are somewhat affected by their physical appearance. Then we get biographical information—either from the person or from someone who knows him or her. Next comes the more difficult process of becoming acquainted with the nature of the individual we have met. This we learn through what the person says and does. As we hear words, we can listen for tone of voice, watch facial expressions, and note gestures and body movements. All of these observations help us identify and interpret inner traits. Sometimes, we can learn about a person from what others say. We must be careful to assess the credibility of the witness, however, if we are to judge the truth of what is said. But whether we are learning about a person from his or her behavior or from what others say, we must avoid hasty judgments. A person who always seems to be totally at ease when performing before an audience may, in fact, be very nervous. Such apparent calm may result from strong self-discipline—mental control over fear. Moreover, people do not always tell the truth about how they feel or think. Thus, to understand the reasons for behavior, we need to see a person act in a number of situations. Only after repeated observations can we begin to identify the mental, emotional, and moral traits that motivate a person to behave in certain ways. Few of us categorize the various traits we recognize in others or in ourselves. Yet we recognize that some traits have to do with ways of thinking and reasoning and are, thus, mental; others reveal feelings or emotions; and still others reflect moral concepts of right and wrong. For example, thoughtlessness, obstinacy, arrogance, and creativity all relate to ways of thinking; jealousy, sympathy, and aggression have to do with emotions; and honesty, loyalty, greed, and patriotism reveal moral attitudes.

In literature, we can learn about a character's different mental, emotional, and moral traits in many of the same ways we learn about those of real people. We learn from either *direct* or *indirect* characterization. In *direct* characterization, either the narrator or one of the other characters in the work tells us outright what a person is like. For example, in "The Slow Nature," Kit is described as having a "merry man's face . . . which had long deceived" (lines 13–14). In his present situation, however, he is said to be "unwontedly sad" (line 13). These statements make it clear to us that Kit is a man whose inner qualities include cheerfulness and fondness for teasing people. Since the speaker is a third-person narrator, we have to accept the information as accurate—as a statement of fact. If another character makes statements directly labeling behavior—as when Mistress Damon calls Kit a "joker" (line 6)—we may need to be cautious about Mistress Damon's possible prejudices, but still accept her statement as direct evidence.

More often, however, writers rely on *indirect* methods of characterization, such as the following. These methods require readers to interpret clues in order to identify traits and thus understand causes of or motivations for behavior.

What a Character Says   In a first-person narration, much of the work involves the character's own words and thus provides insights into the inner qualities that make up his or her "character." For example, in "Walter Simmons," the first-person narrator tells us that as a child he made toys, acted in plays, played a musical instrument, and so on and that he later made watches and tried to make an engine. If we believe what he tells us (and we are not given any reason for disbelief), we use all these clues to discover the inner quality of "creativity." In a third-person narrative, we are given such clues whenever there is a dialogue in which a character takes part. Thus in "The Slow Nature," when Mistress Damon reacts to her husband's death by saying, "O my chamber's untidied, unmade my bed" (line 21), we can see that shock causes her to fall back on the habit of keeping an orderly house. Her words suggest that one of her traits is "orderliness." Of course, any time characters talk about others, they also give clues to their own traits. Thus, when Nancy Knapp talks about her in-laws' poor treatment of her, we, in fact, learn more about her than about them.

What a Character Does Walter Simmons, we saw, was a "mature" man because he entered into a business he really did not like in order to support a family. In "The Slow Nature," we are told that Kit "soon lost his mournful mood / And laughed in his ancient way" (lines 31–32). Kit's quick return to merriment reinforces the direct characterization that says he is "merry." And when Mistress Damon "could take no food, / And she pined in a slow decay" (lines 29–30), we realize that she is mourning for her husband so deeply she has lost interest in life.

What a Character Thinks In "The Slow Nature," for example, Kit is "amazed that a wife struck to widowhood / Thought first of her unkempt room" (lines 27–28). Kit thinks, in other words, "I can't believe that a woman who has just been told her husband is dead thinks first about the appearance of her bedroom!" Although this thought certainly tells us something about Mistress Damon, it also tells us something about Kit himself, perhaps that he is inexperienced in dealing with people in shock and is naive about how they react. Or when Nancy Knapp explains that at a younger age, when things went wrong, she would have thought, "No matter, / So and so is my friend, or I can shake this off / With a little trip to Decatur" (lines 13–15), she reveals that age has made her unable to accept diversion or comfort from usual sources.

Others' Statements About and Actions Toward a Character In "The Ruined Maid" the young lady who is admiring 'Melia's clothes, jewels, language, and overall appearance gives a number of clues to indicate that 'Melia, while recognizing that she's "ruined," feels no shame. In fact, 'Melia flaunts her position by the clothes and jewels she wears. Her own moral values appear to be different from society's, since she seems to be even proud of her station, which has lifted her out of a life "without shoes or socks" (line 5).

To understand what emotional, mental, and moral character traits a fictional person possesses, readers must watch for both direct statements and clues provided by the various methods of indirect characterization. Only by putting together all of these can we understand underlying causes of behavior. When we reach such understanding, we can discover something that helps us understand living people, and perhaps even ourselves, a little better.

How do we interpret clues to character? The following poem gives a detailed portrait of a man. In order to understand him and discover his traits, we must first read the poem through to gain a general idea of its contents.

Robert Browning (1812–1889)

MY LAST DUCHESS

Ferrara

That's my last duchess painted on the wall,
Looking as if she were alive. I call
That piece a wonder, now; Fra Pandolf's hands
Worked busily a day, and there she stands.
Will't please you sit and look at her? I said   5
"Fra Pandolf" by design, for never read
Strangers like you that pictured countenance,
The depth and passion of its earnest glance,
But to myself they turned (since none puts by
The curtain I have drawn for you, but I)   10
And seemed as they would ask me, if they durst,
How such a glance came there; so, not the first
Are you to turn and ask thus. Sir, 'twas not
Her husband's presence only, called that spot
Of joy into the Duchess' cheek; perhaps   15
Fra Pandolf chanced to say, "Her mantle laps
Over my lady's wrist too much," or, "Paint
Must never hope to reproduce the faint
Half-flush that dies along her throat." Such stuff
Was courtesy, she thought, and cause enough   20
For calling up that spot of joy. She had
A heart—how shall I say?—too soon made glad,
Too easily impressed; she liked whate'er
She looked on, and her looks went everywhere.
Sir, 'twas all one! My favor at her breast,   25
The dropping of the daylight in the West,
The bough of cherries some officious fool
Broke in the orchard for her, the white mule
She rode with round the terrace—all and each
Would draw from her alike the approving speech,   30
Or blush, at least. She thanked men—good! but thanked
Somehow—I know not how—as if she ranked
My gift of a nine-hundred-years-old name

With anybody's gift. Who'd stoop to blame
This sort of trifling? Even had you skill   35
In speech—which I have not—to make your will
Quite clear to such an one, and say, "Just this
Or that in you disgusts me; here you miss,
Or there exceed the mark"—and if she let
Herself be lessoned so, nor plainly set   40
Her wits to yours, forsooth, and made excuse—
E'en then would be some stooping; and I choose
Never to stoop. Oh, sir, she smiled, no doubt,
Whene'er I passed her; but who passed without
Much the same smile? This grew; I gave commands;   45
Then all smiles stopped together. There she stands
As if alive. Will 't please you rise? We'll meet
The company below, then. I repeat,
The Count your master's known munificence
Is ample warrant that no just pretense   50
Of mine for dowry will be disallowed;
Though his fair daughter's self, as I avowed
At starting, is my object. Nay, we'll go
Together down, sir. Notice Neptune, though,
Taming a sea-horse, thought a rarity,   55
Which Claus of Innsbruck cast in bronze for me!

Most readers will come to the following conclusions about the poem right
away:

1. A major character provides a first-person narrative point of view. That
   character is the only person who speaks, although he occasionally reports
   what others have said. The poem can properly be labeled a dramatic
   monologue.
2. The narrator, or speaker, of the poem is a Duke, probably the Duke of
   Ferrara, living in the Italian Renaissance.
3. Although his "last Duchess" is a major topic in the Duke's remarks, the
   character of the Duke himself is of primary interest to both the author
   and the reader. Since the Duke is also the only speaker, all the clues are
   examples of "what a character says," except for a few instances where
   we learn indirectly "what a character does." Since we can hardly expect
   him to be fully objective about himself, we have to be alert for evidence
   of his particular personal perspective so that we can truly understand
   what he says.

However much or little we initially understand of the poem, close, active
study, sentence by sentence, is certain to increase our comprehension. *Active* is the key word. We must look carefully for clues to character, and we

must constantly ask, *Why?* What motivation, attitude, or traits lead the character to make that remark or carry out that action?

Here is an example of how we might proceed with such a study of the poem:

That's my last duchess painted on the wall,
Looking as if she were alive.

> *"Last."* Have there been other duchesses, and will there be more in the future? She looks alive in the painting: Is she dead?

                               I call
That piece a wonder, now; Fra Pandolf's hands
Worked busily a day, and there she stands.

> The painting is "a wonder." What does the Duke mean? He mentions the artist by name. Is he proud of owning a "Pandolf"? He certainly likes the painting.

Will't please you sit and look at her?

> The Duke is talking to some other person. Who?

                              I said
"Fra Pandolf" by design, for never read
Strangers like you that pictured countenance,
The depth and passion of its earnest glance,

> "By design"—on purpose. What *are* the Duke's purposes? Is he showing off the beauty of the last Duchess or the artistic quality of the painting? Or is he simply a name dropper?

But to myself they turned (since none puts by
The curtain I have drawn for you, but I)
And seemed as they would ask me, if they durst,
How such a glance came there; so, not the first
Are you to turn and ask thus.

> He keeps the painting covered by a curtain and allows no one else to uncover it. Does he feel possessive toward it? Various people have noticed something special about the facial expression of the duchess. What is that expression, and what caused it?

                          Sir, 'twas not
Her husband's presence only, called that spot
Of joy into the Duchess' cheek;

> A "spot of joy." The duchess was extremely happy while posing. Why? *Not* because the Duke was present, he says. Is he complaining? Is he jealous of the painter?

SECOND CLUES TO CHARACTER: HOW WE LEARN ABOUT PEOPLE

perhaps
Fra Pandolf chanced to say, "Her mantle laps
Over my lady's wrist too much," or, "Paint
Must never hope to reproduce the faint
Half-flush that dies along her throat."

He quotes two remarks that the painter "perhaps" made. One is a routine comment about her pose and the arrangement of her clothes. The other is an elaborate and very personal compliment. Does the Duke feel the Duchess could not distinguish between the two?

Such stuff
Was courtesy, she thought, and cause enough
For calling up that spot of joy. She had
A heart—how shall I say?—too soon made glad,
Too easily impressed; she liked whate'er
She looked on, and her looks went everywhere.

Why does he criticize the Duchess? Is he jealous of her pleasure in life? Is he perhaps possessive toward her as well as toward the painting?

Sir, 'twas all one! My favor at her breast,
The dropping of the daylight in the West,
The bough of cherries some officious fool
Broke in the orchard for her, the white mule
She rode with round the terrace—all and each
Would draw from her alike the approving speech,
Or blush, at least.

A sunset, cherry blossoms, a pet animal—these please her as much as "my favor," a scarf or brooch he has given her. But a proud, possessive, and jealous husband might not want her to appreciate anything other than himself.

She thanked men—good! but thanked
Somehow—I know not how—as if she ranked
My gift of a nine-hundred-years-old name
With anybody's gift. Who'd stoop to blame
This sort of trifling?

He thinks a long family pedigree is more valuable than "anybody's gift." She does not seem to make distinctions of this kind. He seems angry, another example of his pride.

Even had you skill
In speech—which I have not—to make your will
Quite clear to such an one, and say, "Just this
Or that in you disgusts me; here you miss,
Or there exceed the mark"—and if she let
Herself be lessoned so, nor plainly set
Her wits to yours, forsooth, and made excuse—
E'en then would be some stooping; and I choose
Never to stoop.

In order to explain to her why she has displeased him, he would have to "stoop" and admit that he has unfulfilled needs. This is another way in which pride affects his behavior.

Oh, sir, she smiled, no doubt,
Whene'er I passed her; but who passed without
Much the same smile?

Here we find jealousy and possessiveness again.

This grew; I gave commands;
Then all smiles stopped together. There she stands
As if alive.

He gives orders for her death because she does not single him out for special affection! That sounds pretty arrogant. But why admit to—or is it boast of—murder?

Will 't please you rise? We'll meet
The company below, then. I repeat,
The Count your master's known munificence
Is ample warrant that no just pretense
Of mine for dowry will be disallowed;
Though his fair daughter's self, as I avowed
At starting, is my object.

Time to stop looking at the painting. There are other people downstairs. Who? "I repeat . . ." Here apparently he returns to a topic he was discussing before showing off the painting: marriage and dowry negotiations concerning the Count's daughter. And he has been talking all this time to an employee of the Count, someone responsible for negotiating a marriage contract. Why has he talked so much about his last Duchess? Pride and arrogance again— perhaps he wants a warning delivered, but he does not "choose to stoop" to give that warning directly.

Nay, we'll go
Together down, sir.

Don't follow behind me? Don't linger looking at *my* painting?

Notice Neptune, though,
Taming a sea-horse, thought a rarity,
Which Claus of Innsbruck cast in bronze for me!

The Duke points out another work of art, "thought a rarity." Another prized possession shown off, and another famous name dropped.

By this time, even though some questions about details remain unanswered, the general character of the Duke is quite clear. He can be seen as a complete person, with a definite biography or background and certain attitudes and habits of mind. Three qualities—pride, possessiveness, and arrogance—are central to his character, as we learn from the clues in the poem. These traits account for the Duke's monstrous behavior and tell us clearly what the poem is "about."

We have arrived at this clear awareness of the Duke's character by following a procedure that can and should be applied—in the study of all literature in which character is an important concern:

1. In an initial reading of the work, try to gain an overall sense of the events, determining the narrative point of view, and identifying the one or two most fully developed character(s).
2. Reread more carefully, sentence by sentence, noting any direct statements about character and attempting to interpret each indirect clue. Constantly ask, Why? What motivation, attitude, or trait might cause this behavior?
3. Add up the clues. Notice how often a given trait is implied by the evidence. Sometimes only one clue points to a given trait, and you must decide how important that trait is in relation to the character and what he or she does. The significance of a trait is more easily determined if it is suggested repeatedly in the work and is a motivating force for crucial behavior or events. Such a trait is obviously closely related to the author's ideas about character.

WRITING CRITICAL ESSAYS ABOUT LITERATURE

Literary criticism, the process of examining a work of literature, usually takes the form of a critical essay. Like most expository prose, such an essay develops an idea that must be presented to the reader in a well-organized way. However, literary criticism requires a particular method and approach because it deals with the analysis of a short story, poem, or play.

First of all, the reader should be aware that not all interpretations of fiction, poetry, or drama are equally valid; some interpretations are obviously better than others and are to be preferred. What makes for sound criticism? Any interpretation must be based on the *whole text,* not on bits and pieces of randomly selected material. In addition, the student should be familiar with methods of organizing a critical essay as well as with certain technical aspects of its composition.

1. The structure of a critical essay generally follows a simple pattern: introduction, body, and conclusion.
   a. The format of the introduction can vary greatly. Suggestions for appropriate ways to begin an essay on literature are contained in the guidelines for each of the chapters. However, any introduction must name the piece being analyzed and contain a main-idea sentence. The

main-idea sentence is a thesis or topic sentence that states the point of the essay and that indicates how the essay will be organized.

b. The body of the paper can also vary in both content and structure. Both the material used and its organization should be carefully planned, so that ideas are fully developed and clearly expressed. A very helpful way to organize is around the principle of division.

i. *Division* means breaking a topic into its parts or subtopics—related or principal groups, categories, characteristics, or kinds. Coins, for instance, are divided into the following units: dollar, half-dollar, quarter, dime, nickel, and penny. American psychologists divide conditioning into two types: operant and classical. Any division you make should be both complete and consistent, according to whatever basis of division you have established. With some topics, such as point of view in literature, completeness and consistency are easy to achieve. With other topics, such as an examination of a character in literature, the division is determined largely by the nature of the material in the text and the structure imposed on that material by the reader. One way to look at character is through the two major aspects of any person: biography and personality (although, of course, each reflects and influences the other). Personality traits can be subdivided into components of a principal characteristic (for instance, ways in which pride can be revealed: through attitudes toward things, toward other people, and toward the self); or into a group of related traits (pride, greed, and lust for power). Note that when the subgroups of a division are a related or contrasting pair, the structure of your paper can be built around a comparison of the similarities or differences between the two. Such a structure would be useful if you were to compare two characters in literature, or even the ways in which what a person appears to be is different from what he or she actually is. "The Ruined Maid" lends itself to this sort of comparison. Another kind of comparison can be made between contrasting states of being before and after a critical incident, as in "The Slow Nature."

ii. After the subtopics are decided upon, they must be arranged in a suitable order. For this purpose, an order of climax is useful and effective. To achieve this order, arrange the subtopics in an ascending order of importance, saving the most interesting and impressive one for the last section of the body. Another way of arranging the subgroups would be acceptable too, as long as some kind of order is imposed on them. If they are randomly arranged, the presentation will be unconvincing. The guidelines to each chapter offer directions on the use of division in organizing the body of the paper.

c. The conclusion of a critical essay can, like the introduction, take many forms. Again, the guidelines will suggest various possibilities for this section of your essay.

2. Writing about literature demands some knowledge of manuscript form and style, since the essay will be expected to include direct and indirect quotations from the work.

   a. Reference to the work itself:

      i. Name the author in your first paragraph. First reference usually includes the full name; subsequent references use the last name only.

     ii. Name the work in your first paragraph, *not* just in the title of your paper. Titles of short stories, one-act plays, and most poems are placed within quotation marks. Titles of very long poems, full-length plays, and novels are underlined.

    iii. If you are referring to a work within this text, you will not need a footnote. If, however, you use material from another source, be sure to footnote properly (see the appendix, "Guidelines for Documentation of Sources").

   b. Quotations and paraphrase:

      i. When you use a quotation from a story, poem, or play in your essay, be sure to quote accurately.

     ii. After quoting from a story or play, give the page number on which the quote appears in parentheses following the citation: "through the trees" (p. 32). If the quotation runs on from one page to another, use pp. as the abbreviation for the plural (pp. 32–33).

    iii. Give the line reference in parentheses following a quotation from a poem: "on the wall" (line 1). If the quotation runs to more than one line, use a slash to indicate line division and begin the next line with a capital letter: "on the wall / Looking as if she were alive" (lines 1–2).

    iv. When you are quoting more than three lines from a story or poem, use a block quotation form centered, single-spaced (if typed), and *without* quotation marks. Indicate a quotation within the passage cited by using *double* quotation marks. As before, cite page or line references at the end of the quotation, in brackets. Note the following example used to illustrate the Duke's outrage at his wife's willingness to be pleased even by the comments of the artist who painted her portrait:

> . . . perhaps
> Fra Pandolf chanced to say, "Her mantle laps
> Over my lady's wrist too much," or, "Paint
> Must never hope to reproduce the faint
> Half-flush that dies along her throat."
>
> [Lines 15–19]

v. When quoting a speech of three lines or more from a play, use block quotation form. If the passage includes more than one speaker, name the characters. At the end of the passage, provide act and scene numbers. For poetic drama, such as *Romeo and Juliet*, give act, scene, and line numbers. Here is an example, showing Romeo suffering from thwarted love but nevertheless exchanging puns with his friend Mercutio:

> **Rom.** I dream'd a dream to-night.
> **Mer.**   And so did I.
> **Rom.** Well, what was yours?
> **Mer.**   That dreamers often lie.
> **Rom.** In bed asleep, while they do dream things true.
>   [I, iv, 50–52]

vi. Use ellipses (three spaced periods; four if the omission includes end punctuation) to indicate material that has been left out of a quotation: "Notice Neptune, though, / Taming a sea-horse . . . / Which Claus of Innsbruck cast in bronze for me" (lines 54–56).

vii. If the quotation you use forms part of your own sentence, the first quoted word is not capitalized, unless it is the beginning of a line of poetry or unless the quotation follows a colon: "The Duke cannot forgive his late wife for ranking his 'gift of a nine-hundred-years-old name / With anybody's gift' (lines 33–34)." Here is another example: "The Duke cannot speak to the Duchess about her failings even if she were to allow 'Herself be lessoned so' (line 40)."

viii. Use paraphrase interwoven with quotations for some of your citations; that is, put material into your own words. "As the Duke recounts his wife's sins, he recalls that ' 'twas all one' to her, from his 'favor at her breast' to a 'bough of cherries' to 'the white mule' which she 'rode with round the terrace' (lines 25–29." Note that the quotations must be carefully worked into the structure of your own sentence. Since criticism usually employs the present tense, what you quote should not shift tenses to the past. In addition, avoid a shift in pronouns. "My Last Duchess" is a monologue with a first-person narrator. A paper that focuses on the Duke will need careful attention to keep pronoun references clear and consistent. In passages using paraphrase and quotations, quote only those portions that do not include the first person and supply the connecting links in your own words. "Ultimately, the Duke 'gave commands; / Then all smiles stopped together' (lines 45–46)."

ix. Finally, while a critical essay should make ample use of paraphrase or quoted material, it should not consist of a string of unrelated citations. In every case, when you quote or paraphrase, show how the citation fits into your exposition and analysis.

WRITING ABOUT CHARACTERS

Writing about characters in literature can take many forms, depending on the purpose of the paper. The primary goal of any assignment in this unit will be to examine a personality presented in a poem, story, or play. This requires a thorough knowledge of the character being studied as well as the work in which this fictional person appears. As your first step, undertake a careful reading of the kind presented in the detailed exploration of "My Last Duchess." After you have made such a reading, you are ready to prepare your paper by following the guidelines for whichever of the options you choose to write.

Option I: Analysis of a Character in a Story, Play, or Poem

Perhaps the most familiar assignment relating to the study of characterization in literature is an analysis of a character. In this kind of paper, the writer attempts to show understanding of a character and his or her behavior as they are revealed in a narrative. Usually, such a paper is divided into two parts: biographical information about a character, and an examination of the qualities of the person being discussed. Such an analysis requires command of material and control of its organization. This means that the focus and structure of the paper must be clear. In addition, the writer must use material from the text itself as the basis for interpretation. All three elements—focus, structure, and proper use of quoted material—are dealt with in the steps that follow.

1. Select a character from a work that interests you and reread the story, poem, or play carefully to learn (a) the outline of action: what happens; and (b) the function of your character in the narrative: what are this person's qualities and how do they influence what happens?

2. Accumulate biographical information about your character. Sometimes an author will supply a complete physical description of this person; at other times, such information is largely omitted. In any case, make detailed notes about background and history, using quotations from the text where appropriate. Quote precisely what is written in the work. If you are dealing with a short story or a play indicate the page number(s) where you obtained each item, so that you may properly document what you use in your paper. If the work you are examining is a poem, write down the line number(s) rather than the page.

3. Determine the principal trait or traits of your character. To do this, ask, What is the most important action committed by this person? and Why does that person do that? Write down the answers to both questions, again using appropriate quotations as evidence. Next, examine the story, poem, or play for any other examples of behavior that also reveal this aspect of

character and add them to your list, together with suitable evidence from the text.

4. Write an introduction to your paper. You might start with (a) an extended definition of the trait exemplified by your character or (b) a *brief* statement of the dramatic situation. What are the particular circumstances that mark the beginning of the story? This statement should be no more than two or three sentences long and does *not* constitute a plot summary. However you begin, your first paragraph must include (a) an identification of the work and the particular character you plan to discuss and (b) a main-idea sentence for the paper, in the form of a statement about the character's major trait and its impact on events. Also note that the work and its contents are referred to constantly in the present tense (present perfect where a completed "past" action precedes the present) because these fictional events never "happened." They are eternal and occur each time someone reads the work or comments about it.

5. Write the body of your paper. This section will consist of two paragraphs, the first giving biographical background of the character and the second developing information about the principal trait. The paragraph sketching the history of the character will be based on notes you made in step 2. Step 3 provides the basis for the paragraph on the principal trait and the action it brings about. In both paragraphs, begin with a topic sentence and proceed to details that support your assertions gathered from the text. Since the section on biography will be primarily descriptive, its structure will be flexible, but the following format might be helpful: What is the person's present status? How did he get that way? What is the significance of his position, particularly in reference to his major trait? The section on that trait will follow and should be constructed around the retelling of incidents that show the trait in operation. In both sections, be sure to show how your evidence is related to biography or trait and provide smooth transitions from one piece of evidence to another.

6. Write the conclusion. Like the introduction, the conclusion can focus on several considerations, but a broader examination of the principal trait and its implications in the work is usually a good device for a final paragraph. As you compose your conclusion think about questions like the following: How does the trait ultimately affect the character? Does the ending of the story indicate anything about the person's future? What do the character and his trait reveal about life in general?

7. Compose a title for your paper. You can use a word or phrase in your paper that will catch the reader's interest and hint at the paper's contents, summarize briefly the thematic material you are discussing, or describe the paper.

8. Revise and polish your paper carefully before making a fair copy to hand in. Here is a checklist to guide you in the preparation of your final draft:

a. Are your sentences as smooth and clear as you can make them?
b. Have you checked spelling, punctuation, and diction?

c. Have you quoted the work of literature accurately and properly anno-
tated all borrowed material?

OPTION I: SAMPLE ESSAY

Power and Pride

Identification of the work and character to be discussed	In "My Last Duchess," by Robert Browning, the principal character is the narrator, the Duke of Ferrara. As the poem begins, he and an unnamed companion have just entered an upper chamber in
Statement of dramatic situation	the ducal palace. After uncovering a painting, the Duke asks his listener to be seated and begins to talk about the subject of the portrait, his "last" Duchess. His remarks tell us something about her; but they tell us much more about the Duke himself. What we see is an arrogant, stubborn, and proud
Main-idea sentence	man. Pride in fact dominates his personality and seals the fate of his late wife.
Topic sentence paragraph on biography	Although the poem does not give us a great deal of biographical information about the Duke, we

learn enough to sketch the outlines of his character. First of all, he is the absolute ruler of a small
but powerful dukedom in Italy. He lives in a palace
filled with various art objects that he values not
only for what they are and who made them but
also because some were created just for him. We
also discover that he has been married at least once
and is currently negotiating for a new wife—the
daughter of a Count whose emissary is his audience.
Such negotiations, we are aware, were common
practice prior to any marriage, especially between
royalty, and they included a dowry settled on the
prospective wife by her family. Because of the
status of women in the Renaissance (when the action of the poem takes place), the dowry was intended to make the woman more worthy of her
husband; but the goods she brought with her to the
marriage were like her own person—considered to
be part of her husband's property. In those times,
the wife's principal duties were to be a decorative
addition to the palace furnishings and to please her
lord and master in every way. The Duke would

expect such behavior from a wife as a matter of course, especially in view of his wealth, position, and power.

Topic sentence provides transition into paragraph

The Duke's pride in his wealth, position, and power is a primary motivating force in his behavior. We see, in fact, that his last Duchess displeased him because she wounded that pride. Her crime, he says, was that she lacked discrimination. To her, it was "all one! My favor at her breast, / The dropping of the daylight in the West," or a "bough of cherries" (lines 25–26, 27). She smiles at the Duke, but unfortunately for her, she gives the same smile to others, even the painter (lines 43–45). Her fatal mistake is that she ranks his "gift of a nine-hundred-years-old name / With anybody's gift" (lines 33–34). Because she is unaware that she displeases him, she does not change her behavior on her own. He refuses to correct her because to do so would be "stooping," and he chooses "Never to stoop" (line 43). His anger grows until he "gave commands; / Then all smiles stopped together" (lines 45–46). She is murdered because she has failed to give him the honor his pride demands.

Conclusion: further implications of the effect of the character's major trait

Although the Duke never reveals why he tells his listener about his late wife, it seems totally within his character that he is delivering a warning to his next Duchess. If she values her life, she will not bestow on others the attentions that should be reserved for the Duke alone. Otherwise, she too will find herself living and smiling in a painting to which he controls the access. His attitude towards a wife is perhaps the clearest indication of the pride that is his controlling trait. He is puffed up with a sense of tremendous self-importance; he sees the world and the people in it only in relation to himself and his ego. The pride he exhibits is not, of course, an uncommon human failing; but he

Broader implications of the work's meaning

provides a particularly memorable example of what can happen when pride is allowed to dominate a person. Because he is in a position of unlimited power, the Duke is able to act on his pride, no matter how outrageous the deed or the reasons for it.

Option II: Director's Notes on a Character

One way to bring a character to life is to visualize the work in which he is found—that is, imagine rewriting or thinking about a short story or a poem as a play, and then plan it as a dramatic presentation.

Notes for a characterization in such a dramatization can be compiled from many points of view, but perhaps the most pertinent might be that of the director of the play. The director is the person in charge of the production; it is his or her function to interpret the script through visual and aural means. The director must decide, for instance, what the play is about (meaning). That decision will affect what the set looks like, how the costumes are designed, and how the characters behave by themselves and in relation to one another. What the director decides will be implemented through the cooperation of the various designers who work with him and the actors who take the roles.

For this assignment, you may examine a character in a story, poem or play by assuming the position of the director of the production. To compose notes on a character from that point of view, proceed as follows.

1. Select a character from a story, poem, or play that particularly interests you.

2. Think about a dramatized version of the work. Imagine how the character you have selected would appear on stage. What is the principal motivation for the behavior of the character, and what meaning in the work is implied? Your notes on general interpretation will provide the basis for the first section of your paper.

3. Write down your impressions of the character you are examining in relation to the following:

> a. Biographical information. What do you learn about the character's age, background, and situation in life?
>
> b. Stage appearance. What does the person look and sound like? How does he or she dress?
>
> c. Stage action. How does this person act on stage? How does he or she move? What kind of gestures would he or she use? How should an actor suggest the dominant characteristic of the person?
>
> d. Key scene. How does the character function in a climactic movement of the drama? Hemingway has said that a moment of stress reveals character. Since climax involves perhaps the greatest moment of stress, this point in the drama should offer the clearest exhibition of the character's nature.

To compile an adequate list, be sure you consider not only what the character does, but also *why*. That question will require you to think about motives for behavior. Use appropriate quotations as evidence, and annotate properly in your notes and in the essay itself (see Option I, step 2). Motivation must be clearly indicated by the director in relation to the overall meaning or effect of the work. Consistency of interpretation is especially important when you invent details of appearance or action that are not supplied by the text itself.

4. Construct the director's notes by expanding on steps 2 and 3, using the following division:

    a. Give a general interpretation of the character you are describing. How does the character's reason for behavior relate to the work as a whole?
    b. Provide a statement about the character's history or background.
    c. Describe the character's appearance.
    d. Discuss the character's behavior and the reasons for same.
    e. Describe an important scene that clearly shows what the character is like.

Each section will comprise one paragraph properly headed. Be sure your sentences are clear, complete, and suitably connected.

5. As the heading for your paper, name the character and work you are examining. A sample composition analyzing the character of the Duke in director's notes might be written as follows:

OPTION II: SAMPLE DIRECTOR'S NOTES

The Duke in "My Last Duchess"

1. General interpretation. The Duke in Browning's poem "My Last Duchess" reflects an old theme in literature—the evil of pride. The setting, the costumes, and the action combine to show how the Duke's sense of his own importance is the chief motivating force in the drama.

2. Biographical background. The Duke is the ruler of the powerful dukedom of Ferrara in Italy. It is a title he has inherited. As a Duke, he is the absolute and undisputed head of the state: his word and his whim are law. He has been married at least once, and is currently negotiating for a new wife, the daughter of a Count. In the Renaissance, when the poem takes place, wives were considered property, like lands and houses; and the negotiations for a marriage involved necessary settlements of wealth (dowry) on the bride by her family. In the poem, the Duke is speaking to the Count's emissary in an upper chamber of the ducal palace, prior to joining the rest of the party assembled in one of the large rooms on a lower level.

3. Stage appearance. The Duke is only of medium height, but he looks much taller because of the way he carries himself—always erect and unbending. He wears a doublet of blue velvet, trimmed with fur, blue tights,

and fur-trimmed slippers. A huge gold cross studded with jewels hangs from a massive gold chain, and he has several large rings on his fingers. Perhaps his most impressive features are his eyes, dark, beneath black hair, together with a black mustache and small, neatly trimmed beard. He speaks quietly, his voice resonant and intense.

4. Stage action. The Duke is obviously a man born to command, and his bearing exudes power. He strides into a room and immediately becomes the center of attention. He expects this and will not tolerate any other focus. As the Duke describes his last Duchess, he moves very little. His gestures are controlled, sometimes deliberate, calculated to produce a certain effect. That effect always relates to his vision of himself as absolute ruler in his world. The actor playing the Duke must concentrate his energies so that they dominate his immediate surroundings and suggest the power that goes beyond the room and into Ferrara itself. At the same time, however, the Duke must be seen as a person who derives great joy from his possessions. When he speaks of the portrait of the last Duchess, the tone conveys pride in the ownership of a fine work of art, but it also suggests pleasure in that ownership. Similarly, when he speaks of the bronze sculpture cast just for him, there is a hint of trying to impress with the beauty of his goods and their authorship. The note is that of a collector, and it must be made clear that the collecting impulse probably extends to duchesses too. Has he had more than one, for instance? And isn't the next one, the daughter of the Count, really nothing more to him than an object?

5. Key scene. The movement of the entire episode is built around two objects in the white, undecorated chamber: the painting and a little gold bench in front of it. Most of the time, the Duke appears to be addressing the painting itself, almost as if he were now free to tell his last Duchess how she went wrong; but his occasional glances at the listener seated on the bench make it clear that the Duke never for one moment forgets his audience. As the narrative reaches its climax, at the point when he admits to murder, he moves away from the bench and advances slowly to the portrait. He clenches his fists as his rage mounts, and his voice lowers to a snarl as he remembers how she had injured him because she had ranked his "gift of a nine-hundred-years-old name / With anybody's gift" (lines 33–34). After he utters "This grew; I gave commands; / Then all smiles stopped together" (lines 45–46), his rage relaxes into a smirk as if he were applauding himself for a noble act rather than telling a tale of petty revenge. The entire scene gives the effect of a performance rather than a spontaneous recital. He plays on his audience of one as if he himself were an artist—and achieves a great success. His listener is stunned into immobility, but we are sure that as soon as the pair leaves the room the emissary will deliver a warning to the Count's daughter so that she won't make the mistake the last Duchess did— not giving the Duke the respect and appreciation he demands as his due.

Option III: An Original Character Sketch Inspired by a Character Found in a Work of Literature

One of the important skills for the reader is noticing and understanding the clues left by the author as to the traits of characters. One way to strengthen that skill may be to try out various methods of characterization in your own writing. This assignment will involve you in two general steps: You will have to analyze a character in one of the works you have read, making sure you understand his or her principal traits and their relation to the character's behavior. You will have to make use of direct and indirect characterization to reveal a similar trait or set of traits in some person you know in real life.

Choosing the person to write about may at first seem a problem. However, one of the pleasures of reading is the shock of recognition we sometimes experience. As we become involved with a literary character and notice his or her traits in action we may exclaim, "Why, that's just what a friend of mine is like." If you have had such a moment of recognition in the course of your reading, you have at hand a natural choice for this assignment. Even without such an experience, however, you may think about the principal trait(s) of a given character who interests you, and ask yourself, Do I know someone who shares these traits? By these means you may arrive fairly easily at your topic.

If you decide to do an original character sketch as your paper for this chapter, follow the guidelines provided.

1. Choose from your reading a character whose principal trait or traits remind you of someone you know. You cannot of course expect to find an exact match between a literary character and one of your actual acquaintances, but you are very likely to find that certain literary characters and actual people you know share surprisingly similar principal traits.

2. Describe the trait or traits shared by the literary character and the actual person you know. (See Option I, step 2).

3. List additional details about your acquaintance. Include the following:

   a. Biographical information—such material as age, general appearance, occupation, and the impact of his or her personality on others
   b. The trait or traits you wish to explore and their effect on the person's life
   c. An incident in the person's life that clearly illustrates the trait or traits and their outcome(s).

4. Determine an appropriate narrative point of view for your character sketch. Note that while a first-person point of view in which you are narrator seems the most natural way to write about someone you know, a third-person point of view might enable you to gain more objectivity.

5. Introduce your character sketch with a paragraph in which you clearly identify the story, poem, or play that has inspired your work and the character who resembles your acquaintance. Provide evidence that reveals the character's principal trait and its effect on his or her behavior. Add a main-idea sentence identifying your acquaintance and showing his or her central resemblance to the literary character you have described.

6. Continue with general biographical information about your acquaintance and a brief description of that person's principal qualities.

7. Complete your character sketch with a narrative of the incident that shows his or her trait(s) in action. Make sure to use a variety of methods of characterization. Almost certainly some of your material will be direct characterization; however, in telling the incident rely as much as you can on indirect methods—what the person says or does, thinks or feels, and how others respond to him or her.

8. Conclude with an explanation of the results of the traits; their influence on the person or on others.

9. Reread your essay, revising as needed for smoothness and unity. Then prepare a clean copy for submission to your instructor.

OPTION III: SAMPLE ORIGINAL CHARACTER SKETCH

Identification of work
and character that are
basis for essay

Statement of major
trait and its effect

Main-idea sentence

Biographical
information

Description of
principal qualities

In "My Last Duchess" by Robert Browning, the principal character is the narrator, a Duke in Renaissance Italy. In the poem, he describes his previous wife to the emissary of a Count whose daughter is slated to be the next duchess. As he talks, he reveals that his wife displeased him so much that he had her killed. Her principal offense was that she did not appreciate him or his title sufficiently and thus offended his pride. It is also pride that keeps him from making his complaint known to her. To tell her what she was doing wrong would be "stooping," and he chooses "never to stoop" (line 43). This inability to communicate, which stems from an overpowering sense of pride, characterized one of the unhappiest people I ever knew.

John St. Germain was his name, and when I knew him he was in his thirties, of average height, with fair complexion, small, almost delicate features, deep blue eyes, and thin lips. The eyes and the lips gave him away, at least to those who knew him best, because usually when the lips smiled, the eyes were cold. And even when the temperature was warmer, there was something like a shield over them, so that he could not ever be discovered and risk being defeated or diminished in any way. On the surface, John was the most amiable of men, happy, even anxious to be helpful, ever pleasant, ever genial. He seemed to be a model of patience and courtesy. In his business, for instance (he made and sold leather goods at small craft shows throughout the area), he never tired of answering customers' questions, no matter how foolish or insignificant they were. And he was liked and respected by his fellow craftsmen because his willingness to assist them if they needed materials or time was remarkable. Nothing was ever too great an imposition or demand, it appeared. But very few people were ever really close to John. What they saw was apparently all they were allowed to know. I learned a very different side of him, however, when I talked to his wife, after their separation.

She was filled with love and admiration for the man, but she finally decided to let go of their relationship when she found that she could never really get beyond the surface. He wouldn't allow her to. In particular, he would not or could not tell her how his hurts could be healed, and she was never quite sure what those hurts were. He was bottled up, and instead of talking about injuries seemed to expect that she would somehow guess his needs and his feelings. She tried, she said, but told me that she usually guessed wrong. As she saw it, he may have felt that revealing dissatisfactions would recognize or affirm her power over his person. It would, to use the word of the Duke, be "stooping." This he could not do, so instead he built shells around himself that not even she could break down.

When I last saw him, he was living alone. He said to me, after a drink or two, that he had no friends. It was said defiantly, almost as if he were proud of the fact. Of course, he was wrong. Several people cared for him, some deeply. But the defenses he had set up would not permit him to recognize them

Transitional sentence

Incident to show trait in action

as such. He had made of himself a creature perfectly isolated, except for the most superficial social contacts, and he dwelt unhappily in his own marble walls.

READING SELECTIONS: STORIES

Langston Hughes (1902–1967)

ON THE WAY HOME

Carl was not what you would call a drinking man. Not that he had any moral scruples about drinking, for he prided himself on being broad-minded. But he had always been told that his father (whom he couldn't remember) was a drunkard. So in the back of his head, he didn't really feel it was right to get drunk. Except for perhaps a glass of wine on holidays, or a mug of beer if he was out with a party and didn't want to be conspicuous, he never drank. He was almost a teetotaler.

Carl had promised his mother not to drink *at all*. He was an only child, fond of his mother, but she had raised him with almost too much kindness. To adjust himself to people who were less kind had been hard. But since there were no good jobs in Sommerville, he went away to Chicago to work. Every month he went back home for a Sunday, taking the four o'clock bus Saturday afternoon, which put him off in front of the door of his boyhood home in time for supper—a supper with country butter, fresh milk, and homemade bread.

After supper he would go uptown with his mother in the cool of evening, if it was summer, to do her Saturday-night shopping. Or if it was winter, they might go over to a neighbor's house and pop corn or drink cider. Or friends might come to their house and sit around the parlor talking and playing old records on an old Victrola—Sousa's marches, Nora Bayes, Bert Williams, Caruso—records that most other people had long ago thrown away or forgotten. It was fun, old-fashioned, and very different from the rum parties most of his office friends gave in Chicago.

Carl had promised his mother and himself not to drink. But this particular afternoon, he stood in front of a long counter in a liquor store on Clark Street and heard himself say, strangely enough, "A bottle of wine."

"What kind of wine?" the clerk asked brusquely.

"That kind," Carl answered, pointing to a row of tall yellow bottles on the middle shelf. It just happened that his finger stopped at the yellow bottles. He did not know the names or brands of wines.

"That's sweet wine," the clerk told him.

"That's all right," Carl said, for he wanted to get the wine quickly and go.

The clerk wrapped the bottle, made change, and turned to another customer. Carl took the bottle and went out. He walked slowly, yet he could hardly wait to get to his room. He had never been so anxious to drink before. He might have stopped at a bar, since he passed many, but he was not used to drinking at bars. So he went to his room.

It was quiet in the big, dark old rooming house. There was no one in the hall as he went up the wide creaking staircase. All the roomers were at work. It was Tuesday. He would have been at work, too, had he not received at the office that noon a wire that his mother was suddenly very ill, and he had better come home. He knew there was no bus until four o'clock. It was one now. He would get ready to go soon. But he needed a drink. Did not men sometimes drink to steady their nerves? In novels, they took a swig of brandy—but brandy made Carl sick. Wine would be better—milder.

In his room he tore open the package and uncorked the bottle, even before he hung his hat in the closet. He took his toothbrush out of a glass on his dresser and poured the glass a third full of amber-yellow wine. He tried to keep himself from wondering if his mother was going to die.

"Please, no!" he prayed. He drank the wine.

He sat down on the bed to get his breath back. That climb up the steps had never taken his breath before, but now his heart was beating fast and sweat came out on his brow; so he took off his coat, tie, shirt, and got ready to wash his face.

But no, he would pack his bag first. Then, he suddenly thought, he had no present for his mother—but he caught himself in the middle of the thought. This was not Saturday, not one of his monthly Saturdays when he went home. This was Tuesday and there was this telegram in his pocket that had suddenly broken the whole rhythm of his life: YOUR MOTHER GRAVELY ILL COME HOME AT ONCE.

John and Nellie Rossiter had been neighbors since childhood. They would not frighten him needlessly. His mother must be very ill indeed; so he need not think of taking her a present. He went to the closet door to pull out the suitcase, but his hands did not move. The wine, amber-yellow in its tall bottle, stood on the dresser beside him. Warm, sweet, forbidden.

There was no one in the room. Nobody in the whole house, perhaps, except the landlady. Nobody really in all Chicago to talk to in his trouble. With a mother to take care of on a small salary, room rent, a class at business college, books to buy, there's not much time left to make friends, or take girls out. In a big city it's hard for a young man to know people.

Carl poured the glass full of wine again—drank it. Then he opened the top drawer, took out his toilet articles, and put them on the bed. From the second drawer he took a couple of shirts. Maybe three would be better, or four. This was not a week-end. Perhaps he had better take some extra clothing—in case his mother was ill long, and he had to stay a week or more. Perhaps he'd better take his dark suit in case she—

It hit him in the stomach like a fist. A pang of fear spread over his whole body. He sat down trembling on the bed.

"Buck up, old man." The sound of his own voice comforted him. He smiled weakly at his brown face in the mirror. "Be a man."

He filled the glass full this time and drank it without stopping. He had never drunk so much wine before, and this was warm, sweet, and palatable. He stood, threw his shoulders back, and felt suddenly tall as though his head were touching the ceiling. Then, for no reason at all, he looked at himself in the mirror and began to sing. He made up a song out of nowhere that repeated itself over and over:

> In the spring the roses
> In the spring begin to sing
> Roses in the spring
> Begin to sing . . .

He took off his clothes, put on his bathrobe, carefully drained the bottle, then went down the hall to the bathroom, still singing. He ran a tub full of water, climbed in, and sat down. The water in the tub was warm like the wine. He felt good, remembering a dark grassy slope in a corner of his mother's yard where he played with a little peach-colored girl when he was very young at home. His mother came out, separated them and sent the little girl away because she wasn't of a decent family. But now his mother would never dismiss another little girl be—

Carl sat up quickly in the tub, splashed water over his back and over his head. Drunk? What's the matter? What's the matter with you? Thinking of your mother that way and maybe she's dy— Say! Listen, don't you know you have to catch a four o'clock bus? And here he was getting drunk on the way home. He trembled. His heart beat very fast, so fast that he lay down in the tub to catch his breath, covered with the warm water—all but his head.

To lie quiet that way was fine. Still and quiet. Tuesday. Everybody working at the office. And here he was, Carl Anderson, lying quiet in a deep warm tub of water. Maybe someday after the war with a little money saved up, and no expenses at home, and a car to take girls out in the spring when the roses sing in the spring . . .

He had a good voice and the song that he had made up about the roses sounded good with that sweet wine on his breath; so he stood up in the tub, grabbed a towel, and began to sing quite loudly and lustily. Suddenly there was a knock at the door.

"What's going on in there?" It was the landlady's voice in the hall out-side. She must have heard him singing downstairs.

"Nothing, Mrs. Dyer! Nothing! I just feel like singing."

"Mr. Anderson? Is that you? What're you doing in the house this time of day?"

"I'm on the way home to see my mother. She's . . ."

"You sound happier than a lark about it. I couldn't imagine—"

He heard the landlady's feet shuffling off down the stairs.

"She's . . ." His head began to go round and round. "My mother's . . ." His eyes suddenly burned. To step out of the tub, he held tightly to the sides. Drunk, that's what he was! Drunk!

He lurched down the hall, fell across the bed in his room, and buried his head in the pillows. He stretched his arms above his head and held onto the rods of the bedstead. He felt ashamed.

With his head in the pillows all was dark. His mother dying? No! No! But he was drunk. In the dark he seemed to feel his mother's hand on his head when he was a little boy, and her voice saying, "Be sweet, Carl. Be a good boy. Keep clean. Mother loves you. She'll look out for you. Be sweet and remember what you're taught at home."

Then the roses in the song he had made up, and the wine he had drunk, began to go around and around in his head, and he felt as if he had betrayed his mother and home singing about roses and spring and dreaming of cars and pretty brown girls with that yellow telegram right there in his coat pocket on the back of the chair beside the bed that suddenly seemed to go around, too.

But when he closed his eyes, it stopped. He held his breath. He buried his head deeper in the pillows. He lay very still. It was dark and warm. And quiet, and darker than ever. A long time passed, a very long time, dark, and quiet, and peaceful, and still.

"Mr. Anderson! Hey, Mr. Anderson!"

In the darkness far off, somebody called, then nearer—but still very far away—then knocking on a distant door.

"Mr. Anderson!" The voice was quite near now, sharper. The door opened, light streamed in. A hand shook his shoulder. He opened his eyes. Mrs. Dyer stood there large and dark, looking down at him in indignant amazement. "Mr. Anderson, are you drunk?"

"No, Mrs. Dyer," he said in a daze, blinking at the landlady standing above him. The electric light bulb she had switched on hurt his eyes.

"Mr. Anderson, they's a long-distance call for you on the phone down-stairs in the hall. Get up. Button up that bathrobe. Hurry on down there and get it, will you? I've been yelling for five minutes."

"What time is it?" Carl sat bolt upright. The landlady stopped in the door.

"It's way after dinner time," she said. "Must be six-thirty, seven o'clock."

"Seven o'clock?" Carl gasped. "I've missed my bus!"

"What bus?"

"The four o'clock bus."

"I guess you have," said the landlady. "Alcohol and timetables don't mix, young man. That must be your mother on the phone now." Disgusted, she went downstairs, leaving his door open.

The phone! Carl jumped. He felt sick and unsteady on his legs. He pulled his bathrobe together, stumbled down the stairs. The telephone! A kind of weakness rushed through his veins. The telephone! He had promised his mother not to drink. She said his father—he couldn't remember his father. He died long ago. And now, his mother was . . . anyhow, he should have been home by now, by seven o'clock, at her bedside, holding her hand. He could have been home an hour ago. Now, maybe she . . .

He picked up the receiver. His voice was hoarse, frightened.

"Hello . . . Yes, this is Carl . . . Yes, Mrs. Rossiter . . ."

"Carl, honey, we kept looking for you on that six o'clock bus. My husband went out on the road a piece to meet you in his car. We thought it might be quicker. Carl, honey . . ."

"Yes, Mrs. Rossiter?"

"Your mother . . ."

"Yes, Mrs. Rossiter."

"Your mother just passed away. I thought maybe you ought to know in case you hadn't already started. I thought maybe . . ."

For a moment he couldn't hear what she said. Then he knew that she was asking him a question—that she was repeating it.

"I could have Jerry drive to Chicago and get you tonight. Would you like to have me do that, since there's no bus now until morning?"

"I wish you would, Mrs. Rossiter. But then, no—listen! Never mind! There's two or three things I ought to do before I come home. I ought to go to the bank. I must. But I'll catch that first bus in the morning. First thing in the morning, Mrs. Rossiter, I'll be home."

"We're your neighbors and your friends. You know *this* is your home, too, so come right here."

"Yes, Mrs. Rossiter, I know. I will, I'll be home."

He ran back upstairs, jumped into his clothes. He had to get out. Had to get out! His body burned. His throat was dry. He picked up the wine bottle and read the label. Good wine! Warm and easy on the throat! Hurry before the landlady comes. Hurry! She wouldn't understand this haste. I wonder— *did she die alone?* Quickly he put on his coat and plunged down the steps. Outside it was dark. The street lights seemed dimmer than usual. *Did she die alone?* At the corner there was a bar, palely lighted. He had never stopped there before, but this time he went in. He could drink all he wanted now. *Alone, at home, alone! Did she die alone?*

The bar was dismal, like a barn. A nickel machine played a raucous hit song. A brown-skinned woman stood near the machine singing to herself, her hair dark and curly under her little white cap.

Carl went up to the bar.

"What'll it be?" the bartender passed his towel over the counter in front of him.

"A drink," Carl said.

"Whiskey?"

"Yes."

"Can you make it two?" asked the curly-haired woman.

"Sure," Carl said. "Make it two."

"What's the matter? You're shivering!" she exclaimed.

"Cold," Carl said.

"You've been drinking?" the woman said, close beside him. "But it don't smell like whiskey."

"Wasn't," Carl said. "Was wine."

"Oh, so you mix your drinks, heh? O.K. But if that wine along with this whiskey knocks you out, I'll have to take you home to my house, little boy."

"Home?" he asked.

"Yes," the woman said, "home—with me. You and I alone—home."

She put her arm around his shoulders.

"Home?" Carl said.

"Home, sure, baby! Home to my house."

"Home?" Carl was about to repeat when suddenly a volley of sobs shook his body, choking the word "home." He leaned forward on the bar with his head in his arms and wept. The bartender and the woman looked at him in amazement.

Then the woman said gently, "You're drunk, kid! Come on, buck up. I'll take you home. It don't have to be my house, either, if you really want to go home."

STUDY QUESTIONS

1. Carl has had to cope with two divergent worlds: the old-fashioned, country world of his hometown Sommerville and the fast, city world of downtown Chicago where he works. How has balancing these two lifestyles affected his character development?
2. Why does the question of drinking pose such an intense moral dilemma for Carl? How has he dealt with this conflict emotionally and mentally?
3. Describe Carl's relationship with his mother. Cite examples from the story to support your conclusions.
4. Why does Carl sing in the bathtub after receiving the telegram about the state of his mother's health? Analyze his behavior in terms of his moral, mental, and emotional character traits.

5. The word *home* is frequently used in the story. Define the various meanings it has for Carl.
6. How does Carl behave in response to the news of his mother's illness and death? What clues to his moral, mental, and emotional characteristics does his behavior provide?

Amado Jesus Muro (1931–   )

MALA TORRES [1]

Now my old friend Memo Torres, once nicknamed La Malita, is different. He wears a black suit and a black hat and a Roman collar[2] whenever he appears in El Paso. He comes to El Paso once a year and that is the only time Salvador Zavala and I ever get to see him. He still calls Chava and I by our first names and jokes with us when we are on our lunch hour at the ice plant. But now we are always polite to him and wait until he has gone before we finish our stories about Mexico.

"Good afternoon, Padre Guillermo," the other icemen say to him.

"Good afternoon, Padre Guillermo," I say to him.

Chava and I were in Our Lady of the Thunderbolt Church in Parral, Chihuahua,[3] the day Memo said his first mass and became different. The church was crowded with people, relatives and friends, but Memo did not make a mistake. Chava knew because he was once an altar boy. Memo and Chava used to serve mass together when they went to Our Lady of the Thunderbolt School.

That was long ago—before Memo took the holy orders. He was like us then. He lived in our neighborhood La Primavera, and his father worked in La Prieta mine like ours. We played La Viborita[4] and the Burro[5] and the Rayuela[6] every day in the streets.

Memo Torres had big placid eyes and a round smooth face with freckles across the nose. He had a calm air which underlined his deep, slow voice, and his black hair was always combed flat with every strand in place. Broad-shouldered and compact with bulging biceps, he was stronger than any of us. When we went to the General Rodrigo Quevedo Gym, he bench-pressed more weight and punched the light bag faster than anyone. Skipping rope, shadow boxing, and working on the body bag, he looked so much like Carlos Malacara, the Chihuahua lightweight who once beat Champion Juan Zurita, that countrymen called him La Malita or Little Mala.

[1] Mala: bad.
[2] Roman collar: priest's circular collar.
[3] Chihuahua: province in Mexico.
[4] La Viborita: child's game of cracking the whip.
[5] Burro: child's game; literally, "donkey."
[6] Rayuela: child's game of hopscotch.

"The boy moves like the great Mala himself," they enthused. "He's muy Mexicanota." [7]

Memo was a year older, and we all tried to be like him. The boys in our neighborhood always let him be the leader. He had an air of importance which appealed to us in a way that more reasonable people had never done. We did everything he said. When he told Chava and I to play hooky with him, we carried out his order though our mothers called us vagos[8] for it. But Chava and I agreed a scolding was a small price to pay for a footloose day with Memo Torres.

Memo could think of more reasons for playing hooky than a country Mexican can for going to Chihuahua City. Memo and Chava and I lived within tobacco-spitting distance of school. But at least once a week we never got there. Memo led us down to the Street of the Crazy Women instead. Wandering up and down it was more fun than staying in a classroom.

"It's more educational too," Memo always insisted, and we couldn't help but agree. What we saw and heard there we never forgot. The classroom was different; what we heard there we never remembered.

The street that enthralled Memo so wasn't much to look at. It was just another broken-down street in a mining town that had many like it. But to Memo and Chava and I it was an exciting change from our own neighborhood with its poor homes on crooked streets that wound up hillsides.

Then, too, in those days the Street of the Crazy Women was a village in itself, northern as the nopal. One Viva Villa[9] was worth four Viva Zapatas[10] there, and its mariachis sang of Blondie Lopez instead of Gabino Barrera. Chihuahuenses[11] said this long, dusty street held more poor Mexicans than jails do. Its sights and sounds made them all feel at home. Mesquite[12] wood smoke fogged it. Bawling vendors filled it. Misty vapors from steaming cornmeal drifted down it. There, women vendors scrubbed griddles with maguey[13] fiber brushes, and countrymen scrubbed their teeth with their fingers in primitive Mexican village style.

Toward sidehills matted with chaparral, mesquite, and gobernadora,[14] stood adobe homes with blessed palms hanging over their doors to keep evil spirits and lightning away. Stumpy cottonwoods, misted with gray veils woven by caterpillars, leaned before them. On clear days, the gossiping housewives, whose doings gave the street its name, sat on rush-plaited chairs under the heavy-leafed trees where, wrapped in thick mantas[15] woven

[7] muy Mexicanota: like a distinguished Mexican.
[8] vagos: tramps or truants.
[9] Viva Villa: "Long live Villa"; reference to Pancho Villa, revolutionary leader in 1910.
[10] Viva Zapatas: "Long live Zapata" (revolutionary leader in 1910).
[11] Chihuahuenses: people from Chihuahua.
[12] mesquite: a desert plant.
[13] maguey: cactus from which tequila is made.
[14] gobernadora: a creeping bush.
[15] mantas: shawls or blankets.

by High Sierra Indians, they patched Tenancingo[16] rebozos[17] and Santa Maria prayer shawls in the sunshine.

Their conversations were famous. They talked mostly about their husbands. Some said they wished they had gone into the convent instead of getting married. Others disagreed, "Ay Madre, it's better to undress one-horned drunkards than dress plaster saints," they insisted. Sometimes we listened until they drove us away.

We liked the street vendor's crowing cries too. They merged into a boisterous tympany.[18] It was like Memo said. There was always something to see, something to listen to on the Street of the Crazy Women.

At one end of the street, near Jesus Maria Alley, was a rabbit warren[19] cluster of rickety puestos[20] that slumped and sagged like miniature Towers of Pisa. Robust women with nicknames like Maria la Bandida, La Trompitas, and La Chata Micaela, operated these foodstands popularly called agachados[21] because they are so lowslung.

When we got hungry, we went to the Pearls of Coyame puesto run by Petra Porras, a buxom, smiling woman nicknamed Petra la Pozolera.[22] In this little hut, made of rough boards so badly painted the wood's natural color showed through, we were always welcome.

Petra the Pozole Vendor, gray-haired with a broad, pleasant face, greeted us with a wide smile that showed the glittering gold fillings of her teeth.

"Mira no mas—pura raza," [23] she said when she saw us. "Ay, Jesus me valga.[24] What vagabond's faces you have."

Sometimes we helped her scrub with shuck brooms and a bucket of hot water and lye. Then, too, we carried water on shoulder yokes, emptied ash buckets, and brought ice cubes for tepache.

"Now we'll eat with the big spoon," Dona Petra promised after all the chores were done.

The Pozole Vendor worked a la Mexicana singing at the top of her lungs. While she cooked pozole in a big black cazuela,[25] we listened to her sing corridos[26] that exuded blood and gunpowder and watched Jesus Maria Alley's milling crowds.

Many of the men going past us trudged as if they were exhausted or sick, their bodies stooped as if bent by pain. Where they'd been and where they'd

[16] Tenancingo: village in Mexico.
[17] rebozos: shawls worn over the head.
[18] tympany: kettle drum.
[19] rabbit warren: the connected burrows that house a colony of rabbits.
[20] puestos: lean-tos.
[21] agachados: lowly.
[22] Pozolera: from *pozole*, a mixture of boiled barley and beans.
[23] Mira no mas—pura raza: "Just look at you—the pure race."
[24] Jesus me valga: "Jesus save me."
[25] cazuela: kettle.
[26] corridos: popular tunes.

yet to go, we couldn't tell. But many hungry men, broken by suffering, came to the Pozolera's puesto. Some, so weary they spoke in a whisper, told her they lived on mesquites, quelites,[27] and even sabandijas.[28] She never turned them away.

"Money is only a means of capping hunger," she said when she served them. "Eat, and may San Francisco give you his most sacred blessing."

The Pozolera's dark eyes were steady with hope and courage, and to us she was beautiful as an angel of Puebla. Many times this kindly woman told us about the destitute men who came to her puesto.

"They are men for whom a day without work is a tragedy—Ay Madre, the wind blows colder on them," she said. "Most don't have enough flesh on them for an albondiga,[29] and all have a hunger from here to Balleza. May Nuestro Senor[30] give them all a good place in the sky con todo y zapatos." [31]

After lunch, we camped on a grassy bank near the Guanajuato Bridge where the Parral River was brown and swift and deep with quicksands making little whirlpools on the surface. The river bank was a nice place to be. The sound of the wind in the cottonwoods was like a gentle rain, and doves teetered nimbly on the branches and opened and closed their wings. Beyond the stone bridge, Parral looked like a mirage city with its low-built homes and broad, quiet squares colored by stone-bordered flower beds.

We built a chunk fire on a patch of beaten, grassless earth, and then sat down on the ground with our backs against a big limestone rock. We talked of far-off places and read dog-eared copies of *El Ruedo*[32] and *Box y Lucha*[33] until the first stars appeared and were reflected in the quiet river.

When Memo wasn't poring over boxing and bullfighting magazines, he read poems by Juan de Dios Peza and Manuel Plaza. Their poems inspired him to write poetry too. One poem, about the San Jose Bakery, I remember especially. This was probably because Jacinto Turrieta, a spindly Southerner with a dark, scowling face, owned the bakery.

Don Chinto Turrieta came from Michoacan and his high-pitched voice was pleasant with the slurred, lilting drawl of Mexico's big harp country. His way of speaking was like a song in our ears. But he was high-strung and when he got mad his breath came with heavy, rasping gasps.

I remember the day Memo printed his poem on the San Jose Bakery's front window. It was pale and windy with the chilled tang of approaching winter, but Memo was bareheaded and the sleeves of his home-sewn shirt were rolled high on his biceps. With the incontrovertible assurance that

---

[27] quelites: birds.
[28] sabandijas: repulsive insects.
[29] albondiga: meatball.
[30] Nuestro Senor: "Our Father."
[31] con todo y zapatos: "with everything and shoes."
[32] *El Ruedo: The Wheel.*
[33] *Box y Lucha: Boxing and Wrestling.*

AMADO JESUS MURO

characterized him, he stepped up to the window and wrote boldly and legibly. When he finished printing with yellow chalk, he stood back and studied the poem which read:

> El que puso este letrero
> No supo lo que ponia
> San Jose fue carpintero
> No tuvo panaderia.

(The man who named this place didn't know what he was doing. Saint Joseph was a carpenter. He didn't have a bakery.)

Chava and I waited to see what would happen. We did not have to wait long. Soon grinning paisanos[34] gathered to read the verses. Their laughter filled Noche Triste Street like fresh notes on a musical scale, bringing Don Chinto out to see what the trouble was.

"¿Tengo monos?"[35] he snapped petulantly when countrymen smiled at him.

Don Chinto wrinkled his brows together, and read the poem. Then anger made him double up his fists, and he glared darkly at Memo.

"Son of the bad sleep, I'll make tortillas out of your snout," he shouted. "By the barricades of Guerrero I swear I'll carve a Viva Mexico on your face."

But Memo, resolute and composed, remained adamant.

"What I wrote is the truth as God lives," he maintained.

When Don Chinto's tantrum subsided, he rubbed out the poem and then was quiet again. But, not long after that, he changed the bakery's name to El Suriano.[36]

Now Memo is different. He has taken the holy orders. He wears a black suit, and we don't joke with him any more.

"Good morning, Padre," I say to him now.

STUDY QUESTIONS

1. This story is told from the first-person point of view. What effects does that have on the reader? Is it important for the "flavor" of the story?
2. In what way does the narrator stress the physical strength of "Mala Torres"? Why?
3. How does the narrator create a hero? Do authors create heroes in a similar way?

[34] paisanos: countrymen.
[35] ¿Tengo monos? "What's so funny?"
[36] El Suriano: The Southerner.

4. Memories of childhood are central to the story. How do those memories contribute to point of view? What childhood traits remain with the adults of the story?
5. What feelings does the narrator hold for his nationality? Is his nationality crucial to his characterization and experience?
6. What aspects of the narrator's character can we determine from what he chooses to tell us?
7. Discuss the contrasts in Memo's character. Are they credible? Do they make sense in light of his vocation? Consider in your answer his poem on the bakery window.
8. Who changes in this story? Is the change sufficiently motivated?
9. Discuss the change in the narrator's opinion of Memo from boyhood to adulthood.

Alexander Kuprin (1870–1938)

CAPRICE

Waves of light, from three gas chandeliers ornamented with crystal prisms, flooded the theatre-hall of the University. The stage was decorated with flags, palms, and ferns. Near the proscenium stood a highly-polished grand-piano, with open top.

Although the hall seemed quite full, yet people kept streaming in through the entrance-doors. One's eyes grew dizzy watching the seated throng of bald heads, chevelures,[1] black frock-coats, uniforms, ladies' bright dresses . . . slowly waving fans, slim white-gloved hands, agitated gestures . . . and coquettish, feminine, holiday-smiles. . . .

A handsome singer, with a self-assured, almost haughty air, climbed up on the stage and walked up to the proscenium. He wore a frock-coat, with a red gardenia in the lapel. His accompanist followed in his footsteps, un-observed, like a shadow.

The hall grew still. Several student-dandies with badges on their coat-fronts, evidently the arrangement committee, bustled about impatiently in the chill coat-room. They were anxiously awaiting the arrival of Henrietta Ducroix, prima-donna of the Parisian opera, who was a guest-singer in the city for the winter season. Although she had received the deputation of students with charming amiability, and assured them that she would deem it a great honour to sing at their entertainment, nevertheless, the number in which she was to appear had already begun, and she had not yet arrived. Was it possible that she had left them in the lurch? . . . This was the un-easy, though unspoken, thought that flitted through the minds of the half-frozen arrangement committee. They hurried incessantly to the window,

[1] chevelures: heads of hair.

pressing their faces against the panes, and staring into the darkness of the wintry night.

The grinding sound of an approaching carriage became audible, and two big carriage-lamps flashed by the window. The committee hurried to the doors, bumping and jostling one another in their eager haste.

It was indeed "the" Ducroix. She blew into the coat-room like a fragrant breeze, smiling to the students, and pointing significantly to her throat, which was wrapped in costly sables; the gesture meant that she wanted to explain why she was late, but could not speak,—the room was so chilly,—for fear of catching cold.

As the Ducroix number was long past, and the disappointed public had given up expecting her, her sudden appearance on the stage came as an overwhelming surprise. Hundreds of youthful throats, and twice as many strong palms, gave her such a long and deafening ovation, that even she, who was used to being idolised by the public, felt a flattered titillation.

She stood on the stage, bent slightly forward, her laughing black eyes slowly passing along the front rows of spectators. She wore a dress of shining white satin, the corsage suspended from her shoulders by narrow ribbons, showing her beautiful arms, her high full bosom,—cut quite low,—and her fair proud neck, looking as if chiselled from warm marble. . . .

Several times the applause subsided, but no sooner did she approach the piano, than a new wave of enthusiasm brought her back to the proscenium. Finally she made a pleading gesture, smiling bewitchingly, and motioned to the piano. The crying and applause gradually died down, while the whole hall gazed at her, fascinated. From the perfectly quiet, but living listening stillness issued the first notes of a Saint-Saëns[2] romance.

Alexei Sumiloff, a second-year medical student, stood near the stage leaning against a pillar, and listened to the singing with half-shut eyes. He loved music with a strange, profound, almost sickly passion, hearing it not only with his ears, but feeling it with all his nerves, with every fibre of his being. The sound of the beautiful voice penetrated into the depths of his soul, and reverberated with a sweet shiver through his whole body, so that for moments at a time it seemed to him the voice was singing within him, within his own heart. . . .

The shouting and clapping after every encore caused him almost physical pain. He looked at the audience with an expression of fear, pleading, and suffering.

The Ducroix began a new aria, and Alexei again lowered his eyes, abandoning himself utterly to the waves of glorious sound. He wished yearningly that the singing might never cease. . . .

They forced her to give almost a dozen encores, and let her go only when

[2] Camille Saint-Saëns (1835–1921): a prolific French composer of opera, symphonies, and many other sorts of music.

she put her hand to her throat, smiling sweetly, and shook her head in regretful protest.

Sumiloff heaved a deep, broken sigh, as if he had just awakened from a lovely day-dream.

As he was descending the stairs he felt a sudden tap on the shoulder. He turned around and saw the jurist-student Beeber, his former class-mate in the Gymnasium, the son of a well-known millionaire. Beeber was radiant with happy excitement. He put his arm around Sumiloff's waist and hugged him affectionately, whispering in his ear: "She has consented. The troikas[3] will be here in a few minutes". . . .

"Who has consented?" asked Sumiloff.

"She . . . the Ducroix. . . . We've ordered supper in the European. . . . She refused, at first—absolutely. . . . But she weakened, after a while. . . . The whole gang'll be there. . . . You're coming along, of course, aren't you?". . . .

"I? . . . No; I don't care to go". . . .

Sumiloff did not belong to Beeber's "crowd," which comprised the golden youth of the University, the sons of substantial proprietors, bankers, and merchants. Beeber was quite conscious of this, but he felt so elated that he wished to bestow his kindness on everybody. He therefore protested at Sumiloff's refusal.

"Oh, come, don't talk nonsense; you must come along. . . . What're your objections?" . . .

Sumiloff, with a rather embarrassed laugh, answered: "You see . . . well, —you know . . . my . . ."

"Oh, never mind! . . . You'll give me the details later. . . . All right, old boy, then you're with us". . . .

By this time the troikas had arrived. . . . The horses neighed and tossed their heads, causing the bells around their necks to jingle merrily. The students disposed themselves pell-mell in the troikas, their voices sounding rather shrill and strained through the frosty night-air.

Sumiloff sat next to Beeber. He was still under the influence of the music, his mind absorbed in a strange revery, while the troikas raced through the deserted streets. The whistling of the wind, the singing of the steel runners over the snow . . . the cries of the students, and the ceaseless jingle of the bells, blended in a wondrous harmony. . . . There were moments when he did not comprehend,—or forgot, rather,—what was happening to him, and where he was being taken.

At the supper-table all the students crowded around the Ducroix. They kept on kissing her hands, and paying her bold compliments in bad French. Her handsome, fascinating décolleté[4] person intoxicated them more than the

[3] troikas: horse-drawn Russian carriages.
[4] décolleté: having a low-cut neckline.

champagne . . . their eyes fairly gleamed with desire. . . . She was trying to answer them all at once . . . laughing uproariously as she leaned back on the satin-covered divan . . . slapping her young courtiers lightly on their too-free lips with her fan. . . .

Sumiloff was not used to wine . . . the two goblets he had drunk mounted to his head. He sat in a corner, shielding his eyes from the light of the candelabra, and looking at the Ducroix with enraptured eyes. Inwardly, he wondered at the audacity of his colleagues in behaving so familiarly with the great singer . . . at the same time he felt vexed, envious . . . and even jealous. . . .

Sumiloff was by nature timid, and his upbringing in a genteel, conservative family, had increased his bashfulness. His intimate friends called him "young lady." He was indeed, in many ways, quite naïve and child-like, with rare purity of thought and feeling. . . .

"Who is the gentleman over there in the corner?" asked the Ducroix pointing to Alexei. "He seems to be afraid of us, like a mouse. . . . Perhaps the gentleman is a poet. . . . Listen, Mr. Poet. . . . Come here!" exclaimed the singer.

Sumiloff approached with an embarrassed air, and stopped in front of the singer. . . . He felt the blood rushing to his cheeks.

"Mon dieu! Your poet is quite a handsome fellow" . . . laughed the Ducroix. "He looks like a high-school miss. . . . My word! he is actually blushing. . . . How pretty!" . . .

She looked with genuine pleasure at his straight, slim, flexible figure . . . his clear, rosy face covered with a light down . . . his fair, soft hair falling in disorder over his forehead. . . . Suddenly seizing his hand, the singer forced him to sit down near her on the divan.

"Why didn't you want to come over to me?" she asked. "You are too proud. . . . Do you expect a woman to make overtures to you . . . ?"

Alexei was dumb. One of the students, who had never seen him in their company, said, with a malicious little laugh: "Madam, our colleague doesn't understand French". . . .

The remark affected Alexei like the lash of a whip. He turned around sharply, and gazing at the speaker, answered curtly, but in most elegant French, the French which was once the pride of the Russian nobility, and still remains such in some families . . . : "It is quite unnecessary, Monsieur, that you should speak for me, particularly as I have not the honor of being acquainted with you."

While he spoke his brows contracted and his blue eyes flashed.

"Bravo! bravo!" cried the singer, without letting his hand go. "What is your name, mon poète?"

Sumiloff, whose anger had subsided, became bashful again, and blushed as he answered: "Alexei."

"How? how? . . . Ale,—"

Sumiloff repeated the name.

"Oh, that's the same as Alexis. Well, Monsieur Alexis, as a punishment for keeping distant, you'll have to escort me home. I want to take a walk . . . otherwise I'll get up with a headache to-morrow."

The carriage stopped in front of a first-class hotel. Sumiloff assisted her from the carriage and began to take leave of her. She looked at him with a seductive expression of tenderness, and asked: "Won't you see my little den?"

"I should be . . . very . . . happy," he stammered nervously; "but I'm afraid . . . it's so late". . . .

"Come!" she answered. "I want to punish you completely. . . ."

While she was changing her clothes Alexei gazed about the room. He observed that she had furnished the commonplace apartment with an elegant coquettish chic which only a Parisienne is capable of. The air was scented with a subtle perfume which he had first perceived when he sat beside her in the carriage.

She re-appeared in a loose, white, gold-clasped peignoir. She sat down on a low Turkish divan, arranging the folds of her gown about her feet, and with an imperative gesture motioned Alexei to sit down next to her. He obeyed.

"Closer, closer . . . still closer . . . so! Now, then, let's have a little chat, Monsieur Alexei. In the first place, where did you gain such mastery of the French tongue? You express yourself like a Marquis". . . .

Sumiloff told her that he had had French governesses from his earliest childhood, and that French was the language most spoken in his family.

She then began to overwhelm him with numerous questions about his family, his studies, his friends. . . . He had scarcely time to answer any of them. Suddenly, in a low, soft voice, she asked: "Tell me . . . have you ever loved any woman. . . ."

"Yes. . . . When I was fourteen I was in love with my cousin". . . .

"No one else? . . ."

"No."

"On your word of honour?"

"On my word of honour."

"And you have never loved a woman . . . altogether . . . ?"

He understood, and while he fingered the fringes of the table-cloth nervously, whispered, "No . . . never". . . .

"Don't you love me?" she asked in the same faint whisper, bending so close to him that he felt the warmth of her cheeks. . . . "Look into a person's face when you're spoken to," she exclaimed with playful vexation, seizing his head in her hands and causing him to look into her eyes. . . . Her passionate glance frightened him, at first . . . then saddened him . . . and finally awoke the same passion in him. . . . He bent closer to her . . . her lips were moist, burning. . . .

"Is Madame Ducroix at home?"
"No."
"Are you sure? . . . Perhaps she has returned by this time."
The fat, liveried footman, with his red, swollen, sleepy face rubbed his back against the door-jamb.
"What do you mean, am I sure . . . ? It's my business to know whether she's in or not. Why are you so all-fired anxious about her? . . . You've been running up here these last two weeks bothering me about her. . . . If I tell you she ain't home, she ain't home; that settles it. . . . She don't want to see you . . . d'you understand? . . . That's the whole story. . . ."
The whole story! . . . He felt his heart throbbing painfully, aching with vain longing . . . burning with anger. . . . Why had she done this to him? . . .

STUDY QUESTIONS

1. What is achieved by calling the soprano "the" Ducroix?
2. Is the soprano's behavior typical? Of what?
3. How do Ducroix's gestures contribute to her characterization?
4. Why does Sumiloff feel jealous at supper?
5. What does Sumiloff's nickname tell us about him or about how others see him?
6. What is the significance of Russians speaking French? Does it tell us anything about their status?
7. How would first-person narration change the effect of the story?
8. Are Ducroix's final two actions understandable, considering the earlier pages of the story?
9. Is Ducroix, do you think, a moral, an amoral, or an immoral woman? Defend your opinion.
10. Will Alexei's experience change him? What specific character traits might change?
11. Does the title of the story reveal information about a character?

Emile Zola (1840–1902)

THE MAID OF THE DAUBER

She is still in bed, half nude, smiling, her head sunk in the pillow and her eyes heavy with sleep. One of her arms is hidden in her hair, and the other dangles over the edge of the bed. The count, in his slippers, stands before one of the windows and pulls up the shade. He is smoking a cigar and seems absorbed in thought.

You all know her. She was twenty yesterday, but looks barely sixteen. She wears the most magnificent crown that heaven has ever granted to one of its angels, a crown of brown gold, soft and strong as a horse's mane, glossy as a skein of silk. The curling flame rolls, all about her neck. Each wisp straightens itself and then runs out very long. The curls fall, the tresses slide and roll; the entire mass glows resplendent. And under the burning mass, in the midst of its splendour, appears the nape of a white and delicate neck, creamy shoulders and full breasts. Irresistible seduction dwells on that snowy throat, peeping out discreetly from beneath the fiery red hair. Passion kindles and burns when your eyes explore that neck of tender lights and golden shadows. Here mingle wild beast and the child, boldness and innocence, intoxication invoking ardent kisses.

Is she beautiful? It is hard to say; her face is hidden by masses of hair. She must have a low forehead; greyish eyes, narrow and long. Her nose is doubtless irregular, capricious; her mouth somewhat large with rosy lips.

What matter for the rest? You could not analyse her features or determine the contour of her face. She intoxicates you at first sight, as a strong wine does at the first glass. All you see is a whiteness amidst a red flame, a rosy smile; and her eyes are like the flash of silver in the sunlight. She turns your head and you are already too captivated to study her perfections one by one. She is of medium height—a little slow and heavy in her movements. Her hands and feet are those of a little girl. Her whole body expresses indolent voluptuousness. One of her bare arms, rounded and dazzling, provokes a thrill of desire. She is queen of May evenings, queen of loves that last but for a day.

She reclines on her left arm, which is slightly bent. Presently she will rise. Meanwhile she half opens her eyelids to accustom them to the daylight, and looks at the pale blue bed-curtains.

She lies lost in the lace of her pillows. She seems engulfed in perspiration and the delicious lassitude of awakening. Her body is stretched out, white and motionless, barely stirring with gentle breathing. Rosy flesh appears here and there, where the batiste nightgown opens. Nothing could be more luxurious than this bed and the woman lying upon it. The divine swan has a nest worthy of her.

The chamber is a marvel of delicate blue. The colours and the perfume are refreshing. The air is enervating, thrilling and cool. The curtains hang in lazy folds. The carpet lies indolently on the floor, deaf and mute. The silence of this temple, the softness of the lights, the discreetness of the shadows, the purity of the furnishings remind one of a goddess, who unites in herself all the grace and elegance with the soul of an artist and that of a duchess. Surely she was reared on milk baths. Her delicate limbs bespeak the noble indolence of her life. It is amusing to fancy that her soul has all the purity of her body.

The count is finishing his cigar, deeply interested in a horse which has just fallen in the Champs Elysée[1] and which they are trying to set again on its legs. The poor beast has fallen on his left flank, and the shaft must be breaking his ribs.

At the back of the bedroom, on her perfumed bed, the beautiful creature is slowly awakening. Now she has her eyes wide open, but remains motionless. The mind is awake, the body asleep. She is dreaming. To what luminous space has she been soaring? What angelic legions are passing before her and bringing a smile to her lips? What project, what task is she pondering? What curious idea, dawn of her awakening, has just surprised her? Her wide-open eyes are fixed on the curtain. She has not yet stirred. She is absorbed in vagaries. She lies thus nursing her dreams.

Then briskly, as if obeying an irresistible call, she stretches forth her feet and leaps lightly to the carpet. She flings back her hair which tumbles in flaming curls about her snowy shoulders. She gathers up her laces, slips into her blue velvet slippers, crosses her arms in a graceful pose; then, half-stooping, her shoulders arched, pouting like a sullen child, she trots off swiftly, noiselessly, and opening a door, disappears.

The count throws away his cigar with a sigh of satisfaction. The horse in the street has been raised. A lash of a whip brought the poor beast to its feet. The count turns and sees the empty bed. He looks at it a moment; then advancing leisurely, and sitting on the edge, begins in his turn to contemplate the pale blue curtains.

The woman's face is brazen: a man's is like a clear spring which reveals all the secrets of its limpidity. The count is studying the curtain, and figures mechanically how much a yard it may have cost. He adds and multiplies and concludes with a huge figure. Then involuntarily, carried away by the chain of ideas, he proceeds to set a valuation on the whole bedchamber, and arrives at an enormous total.

His hand rests on the bed, elbow on the pillow. The spot is warm. The count becomes oblivious to the temple and begins to think of the idol. He examines the bed, that voluptuous disorder which every beautiful sleeper leaves behind her; and at the sight of a golden hair, glistening on the whiteness of the pillow, he grows absorbed in thought of this woman. Then two ideas unite: he thinks of the woman and of the chamber synchronously. In his fancy he compares the woman and the furniture, the draperies and the carpet. Everything is in harmony.

Here the count's revery strays, and by one of those inexplicable mysteries

[1] Champs Elysée: public avenue in Paris.

of human thought, his boots claim his attention. Suggested by nothing, the idea of boots suddenly invades his whole mind. He recalls that for about three months every morning when he has left this room he has found his boots cleaned and brilliantly polished. He ruminates over this recollection.

The chamber is magnificent. The woman simply divine. The count glances again at the sky-blue curtains and the single golden hair on the sheet. He compliments himself, declaring that he repaired an error of Providence when he clad in satin this queen of grace, whom destiny caused to be born to a sewer-cleaner and a concierge near Fontainebleau. He praises himself for having given a soft nest to this marvel for the insignificant sum of five or six hundred thousand francs. He rises and takes a few steps forward. He is alone. He recalls that he has been left alone thus every morning for a full quarter of an hour. And then, without curiosity, merely to be doing something, he opens the door and disappears in his turn.

The count passes through a long suite of rooms, without encountering anybody. But returning, he hears in a closet a violent and continued sound of brushing. Thinking that it is a servant, and wishing to question her as to her mistress' absence, he opens the door and puts his head in. And he stops on the threshold, gaping, stupefied.

The closet is small, painted yellow, with a brown base the height of a man. In one corner there is a pail and a large sponge, in another a broom and a duster. A bay-window throws an imperfect light on the bareness of this store-room, very high and narrow. The air is damp and chilly.

In the centre, on a door-mat, with her feet tucked under her, sits the beauty with golden hair. On her right is a pot of boot-blacking, with a brush blackened from use, still thick and damp. On her left is a boot, shining like a mirror, masterpiece of the bootblack's art. About her are spattered dabs of dirt and a fine grey dust. A little further off lies the knife used to scrape the mud off the soles. She is holding the other boot on her hand. One of her arms is quite lost in its interior. Her little fingers clutch an enormous brush with long, stiff bristles, and she is scrubbing furiously at the heel, which refuses to shine.

She has swathed her laces about her legs which she holds apart. Drops of perspiration roll down her cheeks and shoulders; and now and then she must stop to impatiently thrust back her tresses, which fall over her eyes. Her alabaster bosom and arms are covered with spots, some tiny as pin-heads, some large as lentils: the blacking, as it flies from the bristles, has flecked that dazzling whiteness with black stars. She compresses her lips, and her eyes are moist and smiling. She bends lovingly over the boot, appearing rather to caress than to brush it. She is absorbed in her task and forgets herself in her infinite pleasure, shaken by her rapid movements. Through the bay-window a cold light shines on her. A wide ray falls across her, kindling her hair, enhancing the rosy tint of her skin and turning her laces blue; and reveals this marvel of grace and delicacy in the mud.

She is eager and happy. She is the daughter of her father, the true child of her mother. Every morning, upon awakening, she thinks of her childhood spent on the filthy staircase, in the midst of the old shoes of all the lodgers. She dreams of them; and a wild desire possesses her to clean something, even if it is only a pair of boots. She has a passion for polishing, as other people have a passion for flowers. This is her secret, the thing of which she is ashamed, but in which she finds strange delights. And so, she rises and goes every morning in her luxury, in her immaculate beauty, to scrape the soles with the tips of her white fingers, and to bedraggle the delicacy of a great lady in the dirty task of a bootblack.

The count touches her lightly on the shoulder: and when she raises her head in surprise he takes his boots from her, puts them on, tosses her five sous and quietly withdraws.

Later in the day the maid of the dauber[2] is vexed and outraged. She writes to the count. She claims an indemnity of a hundred thousand francs. The count replies that he does recall owing her something. Polishing his boots at twenty-five centimes a day makes twenty-three francs at the end of three months. So he sends her twenty-three francs by his man.

STUDY QUESTIONS

1. On page 55, the maid is said to be "eager and happy. She is the daughter of her father, the true child of her mother." Knowing the background of the parents, explain what the statement means and what it discloses about the maid's character.

2. Reread the passage on page 52, beginning with "You all know her." What does it reveal about the moral character of the maid?

3. "He compliments himself. . . ." "He praises himself. . . ." What aspects of the count's character do these lines reveal?

4. "Indolent" is used in the beginning of the story to describe the maid. By the end of the story, however, does the term still seem applicable? Cite examples from the text to substantiate your argument.

5. When the maid of the dauber ceases to be an indolent lady of leisure, the count loses interest in her. What aspects of the count's personality and character cause his disdain for her?

6. The count's thoughts proceed from interest in the poor fallen horse in the street below to a calculation of the cost of the bedchamber. When he wanders from the room, he does so "without curiosity, merely to be do-

---

2 dauber: a brush.

ing something." What adjectives would you use to describe the count's actions and thoughts that morning? What impression do the adjectives give of his character?

Mary E. Wilkins Freeman (1852–1930)

A NEW ENGLAND NUN

It was late in the afternoon, and the light was waning. There was a difference in the look of the tree shadows out in the yard. Somewhere in the distance cows were lowing and a little bell was tinkling; now and then a farm-wagon tilted by, and the dust flew; some blue-shirted laborers with shovels over their shoulders plodded past; little swarms of flies were dancing up and down before the peoples' faces in the soft air. There seemed to be a gentle stir arising over everything for the mere sake of subsidence—a very premonition of rest and hush and night.

This soft diurnal commotion was over Louisa Ellis also. She had been peacefully sewing at her sitting-room window all the afternoon. Now she quilted her needle carefully into her work, which she folded precisely, and laid in a basket with her thimble and thread and scissors. Louisa Ellis could not remember that ever in her life she had mislaid one of these little feminine appurtenances, which had become, from long use and constant association, a very part of her personality.

Louisa tied a green apron round her waist, and got out a flat straw hat with a green ribbon. Then she went into the garden with a little blue crockery bowl, to pick some currants for her tea. After the currants were picked she sat on the back door-step and stemmed them, collecting the stems carefully in her apron, and afterwards throwing them into the hen-coop. She looked sharply at the grass beside the step to see if any had fallen there.

Louisa was slow and still in her movements; it took her a long time to prepare her tea; but when ready it was set forth with as much grace as if she had been a veritable guest to her own self. The little square table stood exactly in the centre of the kitchen, and was covered with a starched linen cloth whose border pattern of flowers glistened. Louisa had a damask napkin on her tea-tray, where were arranged a cut-glass tumbler full of teaspoons, a silver cream-pitcher, a china sugar-bowl, and one pink china cup and saucer. Louisa used china every day—something which none of her neighbors did. They whispered about it among themselves. Their daily tables were laid with common crockery, their sets of best china stayed in the parlor closet, and Louisa Ellis was no richer nor better bred than they. Still she would use the china. She had for her supper a glass dish full of sugared currants, a plate of little cakes, and one of light white biscuits. Also a leaf or two of lettuce, which she cut up daintily. Louisa was very fond of lettuce, which she raised to perfection in her little garden. She ate quite heartily, though in a delicate, pecking way; it seemed almost surprising that any considerable bulk of the food should vanish.

After tea she filled a plate with nicely baked thin corn-cakes, and carried them out into the back-yard.

"Cæsar!" she called. "Cæsar! Cæsar!"

There was a little rush, and the clank of a chain, and a large yellow-and-white dog appeared at the door of his tiny hut, which was half-hidden among the tall grasses and flowers. Louisa patted him and gave him the corn-cakes. Then she returned to the house and washed the tea-things, polishing the china carefully. The twilight had deepened; the chorus of the frogs floated in at the open window wonderfully loud and shrill, and once in a while a long sharp drone from a tree-toad pierced it. Louisa took off her green gingham apron, disclosing a shorter one of pink and white print. She lighted her lamp, and sat down again with her sewing.

In about half an hour Joe Dagget came. She heard his heavy step on the walk, and rose and took off her pink-and-white apron. Under that was still another—white linen with a little cambric edging on the bottom; that was Louisa's company apron. She never wore it without her calico sewing apron over it unless she had a guest. She had barely folded the pink and white one with methodical haste and laid it in a table-drawer when the door opened and Joe Dagget entered.

He seemed to fill up the whole room. A little yellow canary that had been asleep in his green cage at the south window woke up and fluttered wildly, beating his little yellow wings against the wires. He always did so when Joe Dagget came into the room.

"Good-evening," said Louisa. She extended her hand with a kind of solemn cordiality.

"Good-evening, Louisa," returned the man, in a loud voice.

She placed a chair for him, and they sat facing each other, with the table between them. He sat bolt-upright, toeing out his heavy feet squarely, glancing with a good-humored uneasiness around the room. She sat gently erect, folding her slender hands in her white-linen lap.

"Been a pleasant day," remarked Dagget.

"Real pleasant," Louisa assented, softly. "Have you been haying?" she asked, after a little while.

"Yes, I've been haying all day, down in the ten-acre lot. Pretty hot work."

"It must be."

"Yes, it's pretty hot work in the sun."

"Is your mother well to-day?"

"Yes, mother's pretty well."

"I suppose Lily Dyer's with her now?"

Dagget colored. "Yes, she's with her," he answered, slowly.

He was not very young, but there was a boyish look about his large face.

Louisa was not quite as old as he, her face was fairer and smoother, but she gave people the impression of being older.

"I suppose she's a good deal of help to your mother," she said, further.

"I guess she is; I don't know how mother'd get along without her," said Dagget, with a sort of embarrassed warmth.

"She looks like a real capable girl. She's pretty-looking too," remarked Louisa.

"Yes, she is pretty fair looking."

Presently Dagget began fingering the books on the table. There was a square red autograph album, and a Young Lady's Gift-Book which had belonged to Louisa's mother. He took them up one after the other and opened them; then laid them down again, the album on the Gift-Book.

Louisa kept eying them with mild uneasiness. Finally she rose and changed the position of the books, putting the album underneath. That was the way they had been arranged in the first place.

Dagget gave an awkward little laugh. "Now what difference did it make which book was on top?" said he.

Louisa looked at him with a deprecating smile. "I always keep them that way," murmured she.

"You do beat everything," said Dagget, trying to laugh again. His large face was flushed.

He remained about an hour longer, then rose to take leave. Going out, he stumbled over a rug, and trying to recover himself, hit Louisa's work-basket on the table, and knocked it on the floor.

He looked at Louisa, then at the rolling spools; he ducked himself awkwardly toward them, but she stopped him. "Never mind," said she; "I'll pick them up after you're gone."

She spoke with a mild stiffness. Either she was a little disturbed, or his nervousness affected her, and made her seem constrained in her effort to reassure him.

When Joe Dagget was outside he drew in the sweet evening air with a sigh, and felt much as an innocent and perfectly well-intentioned bear might after his exit from a china shop.

Louisa, on her part, felt much as the kind-hearted, long-suffering owner of the china shop might have done after the exit of the bear.

She tied on the pink, then the green apron, picked up all the scattered treasures and replaced them in her work-basket, and straightened the rug. Then she set the lamp on the floor, and began sharply examining the carpet. She even rubbed her fingers over it, and looked at them.

"He's tracked in a good deal of dust," she murmured. "I thought he must have."

Louisa got a dust-pan and brush, and swept Joe Dagget's track carefully.

If he could have known it, it would have increased his perplexity and uneasiness, although it would not have disturbed his loyalty in the least. He came twice a week to see Louisa Ellis, and every time, sitting there in her delicately sweet room, he felt as if surrounded by a hedge of lace. He was afraid to stir lest he should put a clumsy foot or hand through the fairy web, and he had always the consciousness that Louisa was watching fearfully lest he should.

Still the lace and Louisa commanded perforce his perfect respect and patience and loyalty. They were to be married in a month, after a singular courtship which had lasted for a matter of fifteen years. For fourteen out of the fifteen years the two had not once seen each other, and they seldom exchanged letters. Joe had been all those years in Australia, where he had gone to make his fortune, and where he had stayed until he made it. He would have stayed fifty years if it had taken so long, and come home feeble and tottering, or never come home at all, to marry Louisa.

But the fortune had been made in the fourteen years, and he had come home now to marry the woman who had been patiently and unquestioningly waiting for him all that time.

Shortly after they were engaged he had announced to Louisa his determination to strike out into new fields, and secure a competency before they should be married. She had listened and assented with the sweet serenity which never failed her, not even when her lover set forth on that long and uncertain journey. Joe, buoyed up as he was by his sturdy determination, broke down a little at the last, but Louisa kissed him with a mild blush, and said good-by.

"It won't be for long," poor Joe had said, huskily; but it was for fourteen years.

In that length of time much had happened. Louisa's mother and brother had died, and she was all alone in the world. But greatest happening of all —a subtle happening which both were too simple to understand—Louisa's feet had turned into a path, smooth maybe under a calm, serene sky, but so straight and unswerving that it could only meet a check at her grave, and so narrow that there was no room for any one at her side.

Louisa's first emotion when Joe Dagget came home (he had not apprised her of his coming) was consternation, although she would not admit it to herself, and he never dreamed of it. Fifteen years ago she had been in love with him—at least she considered herself to be. Just at that time, gently acquiescing with and falling into the natural drift of girlhood, she had seen marriage ahead as a reasonable feature and a probable desirability of life. She had listened with calm docility to her mother's views upon the subject. Her mother was remarkable for her cool sense and sweet, even temperament. She talked wisely to her daughter when Joe Dagget presented himself, and Louisa accepted him with no hesitation. He was the first lover she had ever had.

She had been faithful to him all these years. She had never dreamed of the possibility of marrying any one else. Her life, especially for the last seven years, had been full of a pleasant peace, she had never felt discontented nor impatient over her lover's absence; still she had always looked forward to his return and their marriage as the inevitable conclusion of things. However, she had fallen into a way of placing it so far in the future that it was almost equal to placing it over the boundaries of another life.

When Joe came she had been expecting him, and expecting to be married for fourteen years, but she was as much surprised and taken aback as if she had never thought of it.

Joe's consternation came later. He eyed Louisa with an instant confirmation of his old admiration. She had changed but little. She still kept her pretty manner and soft grace, and was, he considered, every whit as attractive as ever. As for himself, his stint was done; he had turned his face away from fortune-seeking, and the old winds of romance whistled as loud and sweet as ever through his ears. All the song which he had been wont to hear in them was Louisa; he had for a long time a loyal belief that he heard it still, but finally it seemed to him that although the winds sang always that one song, it had another name. But for Louisa the wind had never more than murmured; now it had gone down, and everything was still. She listened for a little while with half-wistful attention; then she turned quietly away and went to work on her wedding-clothes.

Joe had made some extensive and quite magnificent alterations in his house. It was the old homestead; the newly-married couple would live there, for Joe could not desert his mother, who refused to leave her old home. So Louisa must leave hers. Every morning, rising and going about among her neat maidenly possessions, she felt as one looking her last upon the faces of dear friends. It was true that in a measure she could take them with her, but, robbed of their old environments, they would appear in such new guises that they would almost cease to be themselves. Then there were some peculiar features of her happy solitary life which she would probably be obliged to relinquish altogether. Sterner tasks than these graceful but half-needless ones would probably devolve upon her. There would be a large house to care for; there would be company to entertain; there would be Joe's rigorous and feeble old mother to wait upon; and it would be contrary to all thrifty village traditions for her to keep more than one servant. Louisa had a little still, and she used to occupy herself pleasantly in summer weather with distilling the sweet and aromatic essences from roses and peppermint and spearmint. By-and-by her still must be laid away. Her store of essences was already considerable, and there would be no time for her to distil for the mere pleasure of it. Then Joe's mother would think it foolishness; she had already hinted her opinion in the matter. Louisa dearly loved to sew a linen seam, not always for use, but for the simple, mild pleasure which she took in it. She would have been loath to confess how more than once she had ripped a seam for the mere delight of sewing it together again. Sitting at her window during long sweet afternoons, drawing her needle gently through the dainty fabric, she was peace itself. But there was small chance of such foolish comfort in the future. Joe's mother, domineering, shrewd old matron that she was even in her old age, and very likely even Joe himself, with his honest masculine rudeness, would laugh and frown down all these pretty but senseless old maiden ways.

Louisa had almost the enthusiasm of an artist over the mere order and cleanliness of her solitary home. She had throbs of genuine triumph at the sight of the window-panes which she had polished until they shone like jewels. She gloated gently over her orderly bureau-drawers, with their exquisitely folded contents redolent with lavender and sweet clover and very purity. Could she be sure of the endurance of even this? She had visions, so startling that she half repudiated them as indelicate, of coarse masculine belongings strewn about in endless litter; of dust and disorder arising necessarily from a coarse masculine presence in the midst of all this delicate harmony.

Among her forebodings of disturbance, not the least was with regard to Cæsar. Cæsar was a veritable hermit of a dog. For the greater part of his life he had dwelt in his secluded hut, shut out from the society of his kind and all innocent canine joys. Never had Cæsar since his early youth watched at a woodchuck's hole; never had he known the delights of a stray bone at a neighbor's kitchen door. And it was all on account of a sin committed when hardly out of his puppyhood. No one knew the possible depth of remorse of which this mild-visaged, altogether innocent-looking old dog might be capable; but whether or not he had encountered remorse, he had encountered a full measure of righteous retribution. Old Cæsar seldom lifted up his voice in a growl or a bark; he was fat and sleepy; there were yellow rings which looked like spectacles around his dim old eyes; but there was a neighbor who bore on his hand the imprint of several of Cæsar's sharp white youthful teeth, and for that he had lived at the end of a chain, all alone in a little hut, for fourteen years. The neighbor, who was choleric and smarting with the pain of his wound, had demanded either Cæsar's death or complete ostracism. So Louisa's brother, to whom the dog had belonged, had built him his little kennel and tied him up. It was now fourteen years since, in a flood of youthful spirits, he had inflicted that memorable bite, and with the exception of short excursions, always at the end of the chain, under the strict guardianship of his master or Louisa, the old dog had remained a close prisoner. It is doubtful if, with his limited ambition, he took much pride in the fact, but it is certain that he was possessed of considerable cheap fame. He was regarded by all the children in the village and by many adults as a very monster of ferocity. St. George's dragon could hardly have surpassed in evil repute Louisa Ellis's old yellow dog. Mothers charged their children with solemn emphasis not to go too near him, and the children listened and believed greedily, with a fascinated appetite for terror, and ran by Louisa's house stealthily, with many sidelong and backward glances at the terrible dog. If perchance he sounded a hoarse bark, there was a panic. Wayfarers chancing into Louisa's yard eyed him with respect, and inquired if the chain were stout. Cæsar at large might have seemed a very ordinary dog and excited no comment whatever; chained, his reputation overshadowed him, so that he lost his own proper outlines and looked darkly vague and enormous. Joe Dagget, however, with his good-humored sense and shrewdness, saw him as he was. He strode valiantly up to him and patted him on the head, in spite of Louisa's soft clamor of warning, and even attempted to set him loose. Louisa grew so alarmed that he desisted, but kept announcing his opinion in the matter quite forcibly at intervals. "There ain't a better-natured dog in town," he would say, "and it's downright cruel to keep him tied up there. Some day I'm going to take him out."

Louisa had very little hope that he would not, one of these days, when their interests and possessions should be more completely fused in one. She pictured to herself Cæsar on the rampage through the quiet and unguarded village. She saw innocent children bleeding in his path. She was herself very fond of the old dog, because he had belonged to her dead brother, and he was always very gentle with her; still she had great faith in his ferocity. She always warned people not to go too near him. She fed him on ascetic fare of corn-mush and cakes, and never fired his dangerous temper with heating and sanguinary diet of flesh and bones. Louisa looked at the old dog munching his simple fare, and thought of her approaching marriage and trembled. Still no anticipation of disorder and confusion in lieu of sweet peace and harmony, no forebodings of Cæsar on the rampage, no wild fluttering of her little yellow canary, were sufficient to turn her a hair's-breadth. Joe Dagget had been fond of her and working for her all these years. It was not for her, whatever came to pass, to prove untrue and break his heart. She put the exquisite little stitches into her wedding-garments, and the time went on until it was only a week before her wedding-day. It was a Tuesday evening, and the wedding was to be a week from Wednesday.

There was a full moon that night. About nine o'clock Louisa strolled down the road a little way. There were harvest-fields on either hand, bordered by low stone walls. Luxuriant clumps of bushes grew beside the wall, and trees —wild cherry and old apple-trees—at intervals. Presently Louisa sat down on the wall and looked about her with mildly sorrowful reflectiveness. Tall shrubs of blueberry and meadow-sweet, all woven together and tangled with blackberry vines and horsebriers, shut her in on either side. She had a little clear space between them. Opposite her, on the other side of the road, was a spreading tree; the moon shone between its boughs, and the leaves twinkled like silver. The road was bespread with a beautiful shifting dapple of silver and shadow; the air was full of a mysterious sweetness. "I wonder if it's wild grapes?" murmured Louisa. She sat there some time. She was just thinking of rising, when she heard footsteps and low voices, and remained quiet. It was a lonely place, and she felt a little timid. She thought she would keep still in the shadow and let the persons, whoever they might be, pass her.

But just before they reached her the voices ceased, and the footsteps. She understood that their owners had also found seats upon the stone wall. She was wondering if she could not steal away unobserved, when the voice broke the stillness. It was Joe Dagget's. She sat still and listened.

The voice was announced by a loud sigh, which was as familiar as itself. "Well," said Dagget, "you've made up your mind, then, I suppose?"

"Yes," returned another voice; "I'm going day after to-morrow."

"That's Lily Dyer," thought Louisa to herself. The voice embodied itself in her mind. She saw a girl tall and full-figured, with a firm, fair face, looking fairer and firmer in the moonlight, her strong yellow hair braided in a close knot. A girl full of calm rustic strength and bloom, with a masterful way which might have beseemed a princess. Lily Dyer was a favorite with the village folk; she had just the qualities to arouse the admiration. She was good and handsome and smart. Louisa had often heard her praises sounded.

"Well," said Joe Dagget, "I ain't got a word to say."

"I don't know what you could say," returned Lily Dyer.

"Not a word to say," repeated Joe, drawing out the words heavily. Then there was a silence. "I ain't sorry," he began at last, "that that happened yesterday—that we kind of let on how we felt to each other. I guess it's just as well we knew. Of course I can't do anything any different. I'm going right on an' get married next week. I ain't going back on a woman that's waited for me fourteen years, an' break her heart."

"If you should jilt her to-morrow, I wouldn't have you," spoke up the girl, with sudden vehemence.

"Well, I ain't going to give you the chance," said he; "but I don't believe you would, either."

"You'd see I wouldn't. Honor's honor, an' right's right. An' I'd never think anything of any man that went against 'em for me or any other girl; you'd find that out, Joe Dagget."

"Well, you'll find out fast enough that I ain't going against 'em for you or any other girl," returned he. Their voices sounded almost as if they were angry with each other. Louisa was listening eagerly.

"I'm sorry you feel as if you must go away," said Joe, "but I don't know but it's best."

"Of course it's best. I hope you and I have got common-sense."

"Well, I suppose you're right." Suddenly Joe's voice got an undertone of tenderness. "Say, Lily," said he, "I'll get along well enough myself, but I can't bear to think—You don't suppose you're going to fret much over it?"

"I guess you'll find out I sha'n't fret much over a married man."

"Well, I hope you won't—I hope you won't, Lily. God knows I do. And —I hope—one of these days—you'll—come across somebody else—"

"I don't see any reason why I shouldn't." Suddenly her tone changed.

She spoke in a sweet, clear voice, so loud that she could have been heard across the street. "No, Joe Dagget," said she, "I'll never marry any other man as long as I live. I've got good sense, an' I ain't going to break my heart nor make a fool of myself; but I'm never going to be married, you can be sure of that. I ain't that sort of a girl to feel this way twice."

Louisa heard an exclamation and a soft commotion behind the bushes; then Lily spoke again—the voice sounded as if she had risen. "This must be put a stop to," said she. "We've stayed here long enough. I'm going home."

Louisa sat there in a daze, listening to their retreating steps. After a while she got up and slunk softly home herself. The next day she did her house-work methodically; that was as much a matter of course as breathing; but she did not sew on her wedding-clothes. She sat at her window and medi-tated. In the evening Joe came. Louisa Ellis had never known that she had any diplomacy in her, but when she came to look for it that night she found it, although meek of its kind, among her little feminine weapons. Even now she could hardly believe that she had heard aright, and that she would not do Joe a terrible injury should she break her troth-plight. She wanted to sound him without betraying too soon her own inclinations in the matter. She did it successfully, and they finally came to an understanding; but it was a difficult thing, for he was as afraid of betraying himself as she.

She never mentioned Lily Dyer. She simply said that while she had no cause of complaint against him, she had lived so long in one way that she shrank from making a change.

"Well, I never shrank, Louisa," said Dagget. "I'm going to be honest enough to say that I think maybe it's better this way; but if you'd wanted to keep on, I'd have stuck to you till my dying day. I hope you know that."

"Yes, I do," said she.

That night she and Joe parted more tenderly than they had done for a long time. Standing in the door, holding each other's hands, a last great wave of regretful memory swept over them.

"Well, this ain't the way we've thought it was all going to end, is it, Louisa?" said Joe.

She shook her head. There was a little quiver on her placid face.

"You let me know if there's ever anything I can do for you," said he. "I ain't ever going to forget you, Louisa." Then he kissed her, and went down the path.

Louisa, all alone by herself that night, wept a little, she hardly knew why; but the next morning, on waking, she felt like a queen who, after fearing lest her domain be wrested away from her, sees it firmly insured in her possession.

Now the tall weeds and grasses might cluster around Cæsar's little hermit hut, the snow might fall on its roof year in and year out, but he never would go on a rampage through the unguarded village. Now the little canary might turn itself into a peaceful yellow ball night after night, and have no need to wake and flutter with wild terror against its bars. Louisa could sew linen seams, and distil roses, and dust and polish and fold away in lavender, as long as she listed.[1] That afternoon she sat with her needle-work at the window, and felt fairly steeped in peace. Lily Dyer, tall and erect and blooming, went past; but she felt no qualm. If Louisa Ellis had sold her birthright she did not know it, the taste of the pottage was so delicious, and had been her sole satisfaction for so long. Serenity and placid narrowness had become to her as the birthright itself. She gazed ahead through a long reach of future days strung together like pearls in a rosary, every one like the others, and all smooth and flawless and innocent, and her heart went up in thankfulness. Outside was the fervid summer afternoon; the air was filled with the sounds of the busy harvest of men and birds and bees; there were halloos, metallic clatterings, sweet calls, and long hummings. Louisa sat, prayerfully numbering her days, like an uncloistered nun.

STUDY QUESTIONS

1. In the first two paragraphs we are presented with two major methods of characterization. What are they?
2. Enumerate the ways in which Louisa is described.
3. List the important adverbs and adjectives that the author uses to characterize Louisa. Can you detect a pattern in them?
4. Discuss the relationship of setting—interior and exterior—and characterization.
5. Discuss the meaning of "Louisa's feet had turned into a path" (paragraph 5, p. 59).
6. Does the characterization of Louisa represent a stereotyped view of women? Discuss.
7. A dog is characterized in this story. What does that have to do with the characterization of Louisa?
8. Discuss the function of dialogue in relation to characterization.
9. Joe and Louisa are afraid of "betraying" themselves. Discuss this fear in the context of their characters and of the general tone of the story.
10. Do any characters change in the story? Discuss.
11. What techniques does the author use to characterize Lily? Do you "see" her, or do you get the sense she is "hidden"? If she is hidden, how does the author manage this?
12. Conversation overheard is crucial to the story's plot. What function does the specific point of view play in regard to that incident?

[1] listed: wished, chose.

James Joyce (1882–1941)

COUNTERPARTS

The bell rang furiously and, when Miss Parker went to the tube, a furious voice called out in a piercing North of Ireland accent:

—Send Farrington here!

Miss Parker returned to her machine, saying to a man who was writing at a desk:

—Mr Alleyne wants you upstairs.

The man muttered *Blast him!* under his breath and pushed back his chair to stand up. When he stood up he was tall and of great bulk. He had a hanging face, dark wine-coloured, with fair eyebrows and moustache: his eyes bulged forward slightly and the whites of them were dirty. He lifted up the counter and, passing by the clients, went out of the office with a heavy step.

He went heavily upstairs until he came to the second landing, where a door bore a brass plate with the inscription *Mr Alleyne*. Here he halted, puffing with labour and vexation, and knocked. The shrill voice cried:

—Come in!

The man entered Mr Alleyne's room. Simultaneously Mr Alleyne, a little man wearing gold-rimmed glasses on a clean-shaven face, shot his head up over a pile of documents. The head itself was so pink and hairless that it seemed like a large egg reposing on the papers. Mr Alleyne did not lose a moment:

—Farrington? What is the meaning of this? Why have I always to complain of you? May I ask you why you haven't made a copy of that contract between Bodley and Kirwan? I told you it must be ready by four o'clock.

—But Mr Shelley said, sir—

—*Mr Shelley said, sir.* . . . Kindly attend to what I say and not to what *Mr Shelley says, sir.* You have always some excuse or another for shirking work. Let me tell you that if the contract is not copied before this evening I'll lay the matter before Mr Crosbie. . . . Do you hear me now?

—Yes, sir.

—Do you hear me now? . . . Ay and another little matter! I might as well be talking to the wall as talking to you. Understand once for all that you get a half an hour for your lunch and not an hour and a half. How many courses do you want, I'd like to know. . . . Do you mind me, now?

—Yes, sir.

Mr Alleyne bent his head again upon his pile of papers. The man stared fixedly at the polished skull which directed the affairs of Crosbie & Alleyne, gauging its fragility. A spasm of rage gripped his throat for a few moments and then passed, leaving after it a sharp sensation of thirst. The man recognised the sensation and felt that he must have a good night's drinking. The middle of the month was passed and, if he could get the copy done in time, Mr Alleyne might give him an order on the cashier. He stood still, gazing fixedly at the head upon the pile of papers. Suddenly Mr Alleyne began to upset all the papers, searching for something. Then, as if he had been unaware of the man's presence till that moment, he shot up his head again, saying:

—Eh? Are you going to stand there all day? Upon my word, Farrington, you take things easy!

—I was waiting to see . . .

—Very good, you needn't wait to see. Go downstairs and do your work.

The man walked heavily towards the door and, as he went out of the room, he heard Mr Alleyne cry after him that if the contract was not copied by evening Mr Crosbie would hear of the matter.

He returned to his desk in the lower office and counted the sheets which remained to be copied. He took up his pen and dipped it in the ink but he continued to stare stupidly at the last words he had written. *In no case shall the said Bernard Bodley be* . . . The evening was falling and in a few minutes they would be lighting the gas: then he could write. He felt that he must slake the thirst in his throat. He stood up from his desk and, lifting the counter as before, passed out of the office. As he was passing out the chief clerk looked at him inquiringly.

—It's all right, Mr Shelley, said the man, pointing with his finger to indicate the objective of his journey.

The chief clerk glanced at the hat-rack but, seeing the row complete, offered no remark. As soon as he was on the landing the man pulled a shepherd's plaid cap out of his pocket, put it on his head and ran quickly down the rickety stairs. From the street door he walked on furtively on the inner side of the path towards the corner and all at once dived into a doorway. He was now safe in the dark snug of O'Neill's shop, and, filling up the little window that looked into the bar with his inflamed face, the colour of dark wine or dark meat, he called out:

—Here, Pat, give us a g.p.,[1] like a good fellow.

The curate brought him a glass of plain porter. The man drank it at a gulp and asked for a caraway seed. He put his penny on the counter and, leaving the curate to grope for it in the gloom, retreated out of the snug as furtively as he had entered it.

Darkness, accompanied by a thick fog, was gaining upon the dusk of February and the lamps in Eustace Street had been lit. The man went up by the houses until he reached the door of the office, wondering whether he could finish his copy in time. On the stairs a moist pungent odour of perfumes

[1] g.p.: glass of porter (beer or ale).

saluted his nose: evidently Miss Delacour had come while he was out in O'Neill's. He crammed his cap back again into his pocket and re-entered the office, assuming an air of absent-mindedness.

—Mr Alleyne has been calling for you, said the chief clerk severely. Where were you?

The man glanced at the two clients who were standing at the counter as if to intimate that their presence prevented him from answering. As the clients were both male the chief clerk allowed himself a laugh.

—I know that game, he said. Five times in one day is a little bit. . . . Well, you better look sharp and get a copy of our correspondence in the Delacour case for Mr Alleyne.

This address in the presence of the public, his run upstairs and the porter he had gulped down so hastily confused the man and, as he sat down at his desk to get what was required, he realised how hopeless was the task of finishing his copy of the contract before half past five. The dark damp night was coming and he longed to spend it in the bars, drinking with his friends amid the glare of gas and the clatter of glasses. He got out the Delacour correspondence and passed out of the office. He hoped Mr Alleyne would not discover that the last two letters were missing.

The moist pungent perfume lay all the way up to Mr Alleyne's room. Miss Delacour was a middle-aged woman of Jewish appearance. Mr Alleyne was said to be sweet on her or on her money. She came to the office often and stayed a long time when she came. She was sitting beside his desk now in an aroma of perfumes, smoothing the handle of her umbrella and nodding the great black feather in her hat. Mr Alleyne had swivelled his chair round to face her and thrown his right foot jauntily upon his left knee. The man put the correspondence on the desk and bowed respectfully but neither Mr Alleyne nor Miss Delacour took any notice of his bow. Mr Alleyne tapped a finger on the correspondence and then flicked it towards him as if to say: *That's all right: you can go.*

The man returned to the lower office and sat down again at his desk. He stared intently at the incomplete phrase: *In no case shall the said Bernard Bodley be . . .* and thought how strange it was that the last three words began with the same letter. The chief clerk began to hurry Miss Parker, saying she would never have the letters typed in time for post. The man listened to the clicking of the machine for a few minutes and then set to work to finish his copy. But his head was not clear and his mind wandered away to the glare and rattle of the public-house. It was a night for hot punches. He struggled on with his copy, but when the clock struck five he had still fourteen pages to write. Blast it! He couldn't finish it in time. He longed to execrate aloud, to bring his fist down on something violently. He was so enraged that he wrote *Bernard Bernard* instead of *Bernard Bodley* and had to begin again on a clean sheet.

He felt strong enough to clear out the whole office single-handed. His body ached to do something, to rush out and revel in violence. All the indignities of his life enraged him. . . . Could he ask the cashier privately for an advance? No, the cashier was no good, no damn good: he wouldn't give an advance. . . . He knew where he would meet the boys: Leonard and O'Halloran and Nosey Flynn. The barometer of his emotional nature was set for a spell of riot.

His imagination had so abstracted him that his name was called twice before he answered. Mr Alleyne and Miss Delacour were standing outside the counter and all the clerks had turned round in anticipation of something. The man got up from his desk. Mr Alleyne began a tirade of abuse, saying that two letters were missing. The man answered that he knew nothing about them, that he had made a faithful copy. The tirade continued: it was so bitter and violent that the man could hardly restrain his fist from descending upon the head of the manikin before him.

—I know nothing about any other two letters, he said stupidly.

—*You—know—nothing*. Of course you know nothing, said Mr Alleyne. Tell me, he added, glancing first for approval to the lady beside him, do you take me for a fool? Do you think me an utter fool?

The man glanced from the lady's face to the little egg-shaped head and back again; and, almost before he was aware of it, his tongue had found a felicitous moment:

—I don't think, sir, he said, that that's a fair question to put to me.

There was a pause in the very breathing of the clerks. Everyone was astounded (the author of the witticism no less than his neighbours) and Miss Delacour, who was a stout amiable person, began to smile broadly. Mr Alleyne flushed to the hue of a wild rose and his mouth twitched with a dwarf's passion. He shook his fist in the man's face till it seemed to vibrate like the knob of some electric machine:

—You impertinent ruffian! You impertinent ruffian! I'll make short work of you! Wait till you see! You'll apologise to me for your impertinence or you'll quit the office instanter! You'll quit this, I'm telling you, or you'll apologise to me!

He stood in a doorway opposite the office watching to see if the cashier would come out alone. All the clerks passed out and finally the cashier came out with the chief clerk. It was no use trying to say a word to him when he was with the chief clerk. The man felt that his position was bad enough. He had been obliged to offer an abject apology to Mr Alleyne for his impertinence but he knew what a hornet's nest the office would be for him. He could remember the way in which Mr Alleyne had hounded little Peake out of the office in order to make room for his own nephew. He felt savage and thirsty and revengeful, annoyed with himself and with everyone else. Mr Alleyne would never give him an hour's rest; his life would be a hell to him. He had made a proper fool of himself this time. Could he not keep his tongue in his cheek? But they had never pulled together from the first, he and Mr Alleyne, ever since the day Mr Alleyne had overheard him mimicking his North of Ireland accent to amuse Higgins and Miss Parker: that had been the beginning of it. He might have tried Higgins for the money, but sure Higgins never had anything for himself. A man with two establishments to keep up, of course he couldn't. . . .

He felt his great body again aching for the comfort of the public-house. The fog had begun to chill him and he wondered could he touch Pat in O'Neill's. He could not touch him for more than a bob—and a bob was no use. Yet he must get money somewhere or other: he had spent his last penny for the g.p. and soon it would be too late for getting money anywhere. Suddenly, as he was fingering his watch-chain, he thought of Terry Kelly's pawn-office in Fleet Street. That was the dart! Why didn't he think of it sooner?

He went through the narrow alley of Temple Bar quickly, muttering to himself that they could all go to hell because he was going to have a good night of it. The clerk in Terry Kelly's said *A crown!* [2] but the consignor held out for six shillings; and in the end the six shillings was allowed him literally. He came out of the pawn-office joyfully, making a little cylinder of the coins between his thumb and fingers. In Westmoreland Street the footpaths were crowded with young men and women returning from business and ragged urchins ran here and there yelling out the names of the evening editions. The man passed through the crowd, looking on the spectacle generally with proud satisfaction and staring masterfully at the office-girls. His head was full of the noises of tram-gongs and swishing trolleys and his nose already sniffed the curling fumes of punch. As he walked on he preconsidered the terms in which he would narrate the incident to the boys.

—So, I just looked at him—coolly, you know, and looked at her. Then I looked back at him again—taking my time, you know. *I don't think that that's a fair question to put to me,* says I.

Nosey Flynn was sitting up in his usual corner of Davy Byrne's and, when he heard the story, he stood Farrington a half-one, saying it was as smart a thing as ever he heard. Farrington stood a drink in his turn. After a while O'Halloran and Paddy Leonard came in and the story was repeated to them. O'Halloran stood tailors of malt, hot, all round and told the story of the retort he had made to the chief clerk when he was in Callan's of Fownes's Street; but, as the retort was after the manner of the liberal shepherds in the eclogues, he had to admit that it was not so clever as Farrington's retort. At this Farrington told the boys to polish off that and have another.

Just as they were naming their poisons who should come in but Higgins! Of course he had to join in with the others. The men asked him to give his version of it, and he did so with great vivacity for the sight of five small hot

2 crown: a coin worth five shillings.

whiskies was very exhilarating. Everyone roared laughing when he showed the way in which Mr Alleyne shook his fist in Farrington's face. Then he imitated Farrington, saying, *And here was my nabs, as cool as you please,* while Farrington looked at the company out of his heavy dirty eyes, smiling and at times drawing forth stray drops of liquor from his moustache with the aid of his lower lip.

When that round was over there was a pause. O'Halloran had money but neither of the other two seemed to have any; so the whole party left the shop somewhat regretfully. At the corner of Duke Street Higgins and Nosey Flynn bevelled off to the left while the other three turned back towards the city. Rain was drizzling down on the cold streets and, when they reached the Ballast Office, Farrington suggested the Scotch House. The bar was full of men and loud with the noise of tongues and glasses. The three men pushed past the whining match-sellers at the door and formed a little party at the corner of the counter. They began to exchange stories. Leonard introduced them to a young fellow named Weathers who was performing at the Tivoli as an acrobat and knock-about *artiste.* Farrington stood a drink all round. Weathers said he would take a small Irish and Apollinaris. Farrington, who had definite notions of what was what, asked the boys would they have an Apollinaris too; but the boys told Tim to make theirs hot. The talk became theatrical. O'Halloran stood a round and then Farrington stood another round, Weathers protesting that the hospitality was too Irish. He promised to get them in behind the scenes and introduce them to some nice girls. O'Halloran said that he and Leonard would go but that Farrington wouldn't go because he was a married man; and Farrington's heavy dirty eyes leered at the company in token that he understood he was being chaffed. Weathers made them all have just one little tincture at his expense and promised to meet them later on at Mulligan's in Poolbeg Street.

When the Scotch House closed they went round to Mulligan's. They went into the parlour at the back and O'Halloran ordered small hot specials all round. They were all beginning to feel mellow. Farrington was just standing another round when Weathers came back. Much to Farrington's relief he drank a glass of bitter this time. Funds were running low but they had enough to keep them going. Presently two young women with big hats and a young man in a check suit came in and sat at a table close by. Weathers saluted them and told the company that they were out of the Tivoli. Farrington's eyes wandered at every moment in the direction of one of the young women. There was something striking in her appearance. An immense scarf of peacock-blue muslin was wound round her hat and knotted in a great bow under her chin; and she wore bright yellow gloves, reaching to the elbow. Farrington gazed admiringly at the plump arm which she moved very often and with much grace; and when, after a little time, she answered his gaze he admired still more her large dark brown eyes. The oblique staring expression in them fascinated him. She glanced at him once or twice and,

when the party was leaving the room, she brushed against his chair and said
O, *pardon!* in a London accent. He watched her leave the room in the hope
that she would look back at him, but he was disappointed. He cursed his
want of money and cursed all the rounds he had stood, particularly all the
whiskies and Apollinaris which he had stood to Weathers. If there was one
thing that he hated it was a sponge. He was so angry that he lost count of
the conversation of his friends.

When Paddy Leonard called him he found that they were talking about
feats of strength. Weathers was showing his biceps muscle to the company
and boasting so much that the other two had called on Farrington to uphold
the national honour. Farrington pulled up his sleeve accordingly and showed
his biceps muscle to the company. The two arms were examined and compared and finally it was agreed to have a trial of strength. The table was
cleared and the two men rested their elbows on it, clasping hands. When
Paddy Leonard said *Go!* each was to try to bring down the other's hand on
to the table. Farrington looked very serious and determined.

The trial began. After about thirty seconds Weathers brought his opponent's hand slowly down on to the table. Farrington's dark wine-coloured
face flushed darker still with anger and humiliation at having been defeated
by such a stripling.

—You're not to put the weight of your body behind it. Play fair, he said.

—Who's not playing fair? said the other.

—Come on again. The two best out of three.

The trial began again. The veins stood out on Farrington's forehead, and
the pallor of Weathers' complexion changed to peony. Their hands and
arms trembled under the stress. After a long struggle Weathers again
brought his opponent's hand slowly on to the table. There was a murmur of
applause from the spectators. The curate, who was standing beside the table,
nodded his red head towards the victor and said with loutish familiarity:

—Ah! that's the knack!

—What the hell do you know about it? said Farrington fiercely, turning
on the man. What do you put in your gab for?

—Sh, sh! said O'Halloran, observing the violent expression of Farrington's face. Pony up, boys. We'll have just one little smahan[3] more and then
we'll be off.

A very sullen-faced man stood at the corner of O'Connell Bridge waiting
for the little Sandymount tram to take him home. He was full of smouldering anger and revengefulness. He felt humiliated and discontented; he did
not even feel drunk; and he had only twopence in his pocket. He cursed
everything. He had done for himself in the office, pawned his watch, spent
all his money; and he had not even got drunk. He began to feel thirsty again

---

[3] smahan: small drink.

and he longed to be back again in the hot reeking public-house. He had lost his reputation as a strong man, having been defeated twice by a mere boy. His heart swelled with fury and, when he thought of the woman in the big hat who had brushed against him and said *Pardon!* his fury nearly choked him.

His tram let him down at Shelbourne Road and he steered his great body along in the shadow of the wall of the barracks. He loathed returning to his home. When he went in by the side-door he found the kitchen empty and the kitchen fire nearly out. He bawled upstairs:

—Ada! Ada!

His wife was a little sharp-faced woman who bullied her husband when he was sober and was bullied by him when he was drunk. They had five children. A little boy came running down the stairs.

—Who is that? said the man, peering through the darkness.

—Me, pa.

—Who are you? Charlie?

—No, pa, Tom.

—Where's your mother?

—She's out at the chapel.

—That's right. . . . Did she think of leaving any dinner for me?

—Yes, pa. I—

—Light the lamp. What do you mean by having the place in darkness? Are the other children in bed?

The man sat down heavily on one of the chairs while the little boy lit the lamp. He began to mimic his son's flat accent, saying half to himself: *At the chapel. At the chapel, if you please!* When the lamp was lit he banged his fist on the table and shouted:

—What's for my dinner?

—I'm going . . . to cook it, pa, said the little boy.

The man jumped up furiously and pointed to the fire.

—On that fire! You let the fire out! By God, I'll teach you to do that again!

He took a step to the door and seized the walking-stick which was standing behind it.

—I'll teach you to let the fire out! he said, rolling up his sleeve in order to give his arm free play.

The little boy cried *O, pa!* and ran whimpering round the table, but the man followed him and caught him by the coat. The little boy looked about him wildly but, seeing no way of escape, fell upon his knees.

—Now, you'll let the fire out the next time! said the man, striking at him viciously with the stick. Take that, you little whelp!

The boy uttered a squeal of pain as the stick cut his thigh. He clasped his hands together in the air and his voice shook with fright.

—O, pa! he cried. Don't beat me, pa! And I'll . . . I'll say a *Hail Mary* for you. . . . I'll say a *Hail Mary* for you, pa, if you don't beat me. . . . I'll say a *Hail Mary*. . . .

STUDY QUESTIONS

1. Does the title of the story refer to characters? Discuss.
2. What is credible about Farrington? Alleyne? What traits does Joyce give them to make them recognizable? Are they stereotypes?
3. What is this story's point of view? Is it effective?
4. How would the story change if it were told from Farrington's point of view?
5. Joyce uses minimal characterization to describe Miss Delacour, yet she seems credible. What does Joyce emphasize in characterizing her? Does her character serve a purpose?
6. Discuss the single character trait that motivates the important events of the story.
7. Discuss the "indignities" (p. 69) of Farrington's life. Do you consider them to be real or imagined, self- or outwardly inflicted?
8. How does Joyce infuse this story with the overwhelming sense of repressed violence?
9. This story ends in violent action. What in the story's characterizations makes this ending credible?

Morley Callaghan (1903–)

THE FAITHFUL WIFE

Until a week before Christmas George worked in the station restaurant at the lunch counter. The last week was extraordinarily cold, then the sun shone strongly for a few days, though it was always cold again in the evenings. There were three other men working at the counter. For years they must have had a poor reputation. Women, unless they were careless and easy-going, never started a conversation with them when having a light lunch at noontime. The girls at the station always avoided the red-capped porters and the countermen.

George, who was working there till he got enough money to go back home for a week and then start late in the year at college, was a young fellow with fine hair retreating far back on his forehead and rather bad upper teeth, but he was very polite and generous. Steve, the plump Italian, with the waxed black mustaches, who had charge of the restaurant, was very fond of George.

Many people passed the restaurant window on the way to the platform and the trains. The four men, watching them frequently, got to know some of them. Girls, brightly dressed and highly powdered, loitered in front of the open door, smiling at George, who saw them so often he knew their first names. At noontime, other girls, with a few minutes to spare before going back to work, used to walk up and down the tiled tunnel to the waiting-room, loafing the time away, but they never even glanced in at the counter-men. It was cold outside, the streets were slippery, and it was warm in the station, that was all. George got to know most of these girls too, and talked about them with the other fellows.

George watched carefully one girl every day at noon hour. The other men had also noticed her, and two or three times she came in for a cup of coffee, but she was so gentle, and aloofly pleasant, and so unobtrusively beyond them, they were afraid to try and amuse her with easy cheerful talk. George wished earnestly that she had never seen him there in the restaurant behind the counter, even though he knew she had never noticed him at all. Her cheeks were usually rosy from the cold wind outside. When she went out the door to walk up and down for a few minutes, an agreeable expression on her face, she never once looked back at the restaurant. George, following her with his eye while pouring coffee slowly, did not expect her to look back. She was about twenty-eight, pretty, rather shy, and dressed plainly and poorly in a thin blue-cloth coat without any fur on it. Most girls managed to have a piece of fur of some kind on their coats.

With little to do in the middle of the afternoon, George used to think of her because of seeing her every day and looking at her face in profile when she passed the window. Then, on the day she had on the light-fawn felt hat, she smiled politely at him, when having a cup of coffee, and as long as possible, he remained opposite her, cleaning the counter with a damp cloth.

The last night he worked at the station he went out at about half past eight in the evening, for he had an hour to himself, and then worked on till ten o'clock. In the morning he was going home, so he walked out of the station and down the side street to the docks, and was having only pleasant thoughts, passing the warehouses, looking out over the dark cold lake and liking the tang of the wind on his face. Christmas was only a week away. The snow was falling lazily and melting slowly when it hit the sidewalk. He was glad he was through with the job at the restaurant.

An hour later, back at the restaurant, Steve said, "A dame just phoned you, George, and left her number."

"Do you know who she was?"

"No, you got too many girls, George. Don't you know the number?"

"I never saw it before."

He called the number and did not recognize the voice that answered him. A woman was asking him pleasantly enough if he remembered her. He said he did not. She said she had had a cup of coffee that afternoon at noontime, and added that she had worn a blue coat and a tan-colored felt hat, and even though she had not spoken to him, she thought he would remember her.

"Good Lord," he said.

She wanted to know if he would come and see her at half past ten that evening. Timidly he said he would, and hardly heard her giving the address. Steve and the other boys started to kid him brightly, but he was too astonished, wondering how she had found out his name, to bother with them. The boys, saying good-bye to him later, winked and elbowed him in the ribs, urging him to celebrate on his last night in the city. Steve, who was very fond of him, shook his head sadly and pulled the ends of his mustaches down into his lips.

The address the girl had given him was only eight blocks away, so he walked, holding his hands clenched tightly in his pockets, for he was cold from nervousness. He was watching the automobile headlights shining on slippery spots on the sidewalk. The house, opposite a public-school ground on a side street, was a large old rooming house. A light was in a window on the second story over the door. Ringing the bell he didn't really expect anyone to answer, and was surprised when the girl herself opened the door.

"Good evening," he said shyly.

"Oh, come upstairs," she said, smiling and practical.

In the front room he took off his overcoat and hat and sat down slowly, noticing, out of the corner of his eye, that she was even slimmer, and had nice fair hair and lovely eyes. But she was moving very nervously. He had intended to ask at once how she found out his name, but forgot about it as soon as she sat down opposite him on a camp bed and smiled shyly. She had on a red woollen sweater, fitting her tightly at the waist. Twice he shook his head, unable to get used to having her there opposite him, nervous and expectant. The trouble was she had always seemed so aloof.

"You're not very friendly," she said awkwardly.

"Oh, yes, I am. Indeed I am."

"Why don't you come over here and sit beside me?"

Slowly he sat down beside her on the camp bed, smiling stupidly. He was even slow to see that she was waiting for him to put his arms around her. Ashamed of himself, he finally kissed her eagerly and she held on to him tightly. Her heart was thumping underneath the red woollen sweater. She just kept on holding him, almost savagely, closing her eyes slowly and breathing deeply every time he kissed her. She was so delighted and satisfied to hold him in her arms that she did not bother talking at all. Finally he became very eager and she got up suddenly, walking up and down the room, looking occasionally at the cheap alarm clock on a bureau. The room was clean but poorly furnished.

"What's the matter?" he said irritably.

"My girl friend, the one I room with, will be home in twenty minutes."

"Come here anyway."

"Please sit down, please do," she said.

Slowly she sat down beside him. When he kissed her she did not object, but her lips were dry, her shoulders were trembling, and she kept on watching the clock. Though she was holding his wrist so tightly her nails dug into the skin, he knew she would be glad when he had to go. He kissed her again and she drew her left hand slowly over her lips.

"You really must be out of here before Irene comes home," she said.

"But I've only kissed and hugged you and you're wonderful." He noticed the red ring mark on her finger. "Are you sure you're not waiting for your husband to come home?" he said a bit irritably.

Frowning, looking away vaguely, she said, "Why do you have to say that?"

"There's a ring mark on your finger."

"I can't help it," she said, and began to cry quietly. "Yes, oh, yes, I'm waiting for my husband to come home. He'll be here at Christmas."

"It's too bad. Can't we do something about it?"

"I tell you I love my husband. I do, I really do, and I'm faithful to him too."

"Maybe I'd better go," he said uncomfortably, feeling ridiculous.

"Eh, what's that? My husband, he's at a sanitarium. He got his spine hurt in the war, then he got tuberculosis. He's pretty bad. They've got to carry him around. We want to love each other every time we meet, but we can't."

"That's tough, poor kid, and I suppose you've got to pay for him."

"Yes."

"Do you have many fellows?"

"No. I don't want to have any."

"Do they come here to see you?"

"No. No, I don't know what got into me. I liked you, and felt a little crazy."

"I'll slide along then. What's your first name?"

"Lola. You'd better go now."

"Couldn't I see you again?" he said suddenly.

"No, you're going away tomorrow," she said, smiling confidently.

"So you've got it all figured out. Supposing I don't go?"

"Please, you must."

Her arms were trembling when she held his overcoat. She wanted him to go before Irene came home. "You didn't give me much time," he said flatly.

"No. Irene comes in at this time. You're a lovely boy. Kiss me."

"You had that figured out too."

"Just kiss and hold me once more, George." She held on to him as if she did not expect to be embraced again for a long time, and he said, "I think I'll stay in the city a while longer."

"It's too bad, but you've got to go. We can't see each other again."

In the poorly lighted hall she looked lovely. Her cheeks were flushed, and though still eager, she was quite satisfied with the whole affair. Everything had gone perfectly for her.

As he went out the door and down the walk to the street he remembered that he hadn't asked how she had found out his name. Snow was falling lightly and there were hardly any footprints on the sidewalk. All he could think of was that he ought to go back to the restaurant and ask Steve for his job again. Steve was fond of him. But he knew he could not spoil it for her. "She had it all figured out," he muttered, turning up his coat collar.

William J. Locke (1863–1930)

THE ADVENTURE OF THE KIND MR. SMITH

Aristide Pujol started life on his own account as a *chasseur*[1] in a Nice *café* —one of those luckless children tightly encased in bottle-green cloth by means of brass buttons, who earn a sketchy livelihood by enduring with cherubic[2] smiles the continuous maledictions[3] of the establishment. There he soothed his hours of servitude by dreams of vast ambitions. He would become the manager of a great hotel—not a contemptible hostelry where commercial travellers and seedy Germans were indifferently bedded, but one of those white palaces where milords (English) and millionaires (American) paid a thousand francs a night for a bedroom and five louis[4] for a glass of beer. Now, in order to derive such profit from the Anglo-Saxon a knowledge of English was indispensable. He resolved to learn the language. How he did so, except by sheer effrontery, taking linguistic toll of frequenters of the *café,* would be a mystery to anyone unacquainted with Aristide. But to his friends his mastery of the English tongue in such circumstances is comprehensible. To Aristide the impossible was ever the one thing easy of attainment; the possible the one thing he never could achieve. That was the paradoxical nature of the man. Before his days of hunted-little-devildom were over he had acquired sufficient knowledge of English to carry him, a few years later, through various vicissitudes in England, until, fired by new social ambitions and self-educated in a haphazard way, he found himself appointed Professor of French in an academy for young ladies.

One of these days, when I can pin my dragonfly friend down to a plain,

[1] *chasseur:* footman.
[2] cherubic: angelic.
[3] maledictions: curses.
[4] louis: French gold coin.

unvarnished autobiography, I may be able to trace some chronological sequence in the kaleidoscopic changes in his career. But hitherto, in his talks with me, he flits about from any one date to any other during a couple of decades, in a manner so confusing that for the present I abandon such an attempt. All I know of the date of the episode I am about to chronicle is that it occurred immediately after the termination of his engagement at the academy just mentioned. Somehow, Aristide's history is a category of terminations.

If the head mistress of the academy had herself played dragon at his classes, all would have gone well. He would have made his pupils conjugate irregular verbs, rendered them adepts in the mysteries of the past participle and the subjunctive mood, and turned them out quite innocent of the idiomatic quaintnesses of the French tongue. But *dis aliter visum.*[5] The gods always saw wrong-headedly otherwise in the case of Aristide. A weak-minded governess—and in a governess a sense of humour and of novelty is always a sign of a weak mind—played dragon during Aristide's lessons. She appreciated his method, which was colloquial. The colloquial Aristide was jocular. His lessons therefore were a giggling joy from beginning to end. He imparted to his pupils delicious knowledge. *En avez-vous des-z-homards? Oh, les sales bêtes, elles ont du poil aux pattes,* which, being translated, is: "Have you any lobsters? Oh, the dirty animals, they have hair on their feet"—a catch phrase which, some years ago, added greatly to the gaiety of Paris, but in which I must confess to seeing no gleam of wit— became the historic property of the school. He recited to them, till they were word-perfect, a music-hall ditty of the early eighties, *Sur le bi, sur le banc, sur le bi du bout du banc,*[6] and delighted them with dissertations on Mme. Yvette Guilbert's earlier *répertoire.*[7] But for him they would have gone to their lives' end without knowing that *pognon* meant money; *rouspétance,* assaulting the police; *thune,* a five-franc piece; and *boufler,* to take nourishment. He made (according to his own statement) French a living language. There was never a school in Great Britain, the Colonies, or America on which the Parisian accent was so electrically impressed. The retort, *Eh! ta sœur,*[8] was the purest Montmartre; also *Fich'-moi la paix, mon petit,*[9] and *Tu as un toupet, toi;*[10] and the delectable locution, *Allons étrangler un perroquet* (let us strangle a parrot), employed by Apaches when inviting each other to drink a glass of absinthe, soon became current French in the school for invitations to surreptitious cocoa-parties.

[5] *dis aliter visum:* "the gods see otherwise."
[6] *Sur le bi, . . . :* "On the slope, on the bench [or bank], on the slope at the end of the bench [or at the bottom of the bank]."
[7] *répertoire:* numbers ready to be performed.
[8] *Eh! ta sœur:* "So's your sister!" (sl.).
[9] *Fich' moi la paix, . . . :* "Get off my back!" (sl.).
[10] *Tu as un toupet, toi:* "You have a lot of guts" (sl.).

The progress that academy made in a real grip of the French language was miraculous; but the knowledge it gained in French grammar and syntax was deplorable. A certain mid-term examination—the paper being set by a neighbouring vicar—produced awful results. The phrase, "How do you do, dear?" which ought, by all the rules of Stratford-atte-Bowe, to be translated by *Comment vous portez-vous, ma chère?* was rendered by most of the senior scholars *Eh, ma vieille, ça boulotte?* [11] One innocent and anachronistic damsel, writing on the execution of Charles I, declared that he *cracha dans le panier* in 1649, thereby mystifying the good vicar, who was unaware that "to spit into the basket" is to be guillotined. This wealth of vocabulary was discounted by abject poverty in other branches of the language. No one could give a list of the words in *al* that took *s* in the plural, no one knew anything at all about the defective verb *échoir*,[12] and the orthography[13] of the school would have disgraced a kindergarten. The head mistress suspected a lack of method in the teaching of M. Pujol, and one day paid his class a surprise visit.

The sight that met her eyes petrified her. The class, including the governess, bubbled and gurgled and shrieked with laughter. M. Pujol, his bright eyes agleam with merriment and his arms moving in frantic gestures, danced about the platform. He was telling them a story—and when Aristide told a story, he told it with the eloquence of his entire frame. He bent himself double and threw out his hands.

"Il était saoûl comme un porc," [14] he shouted.

And then came the hush of death. The rest of the artless tale about the man as drunk as a pig was never told. The head mistress, indignant majesty, strode up the room.

"M. Pujol, you have a strange way of giving French lessons."

"I believe, madame," said he, with a polite bow, "in interesting my pupils in their studies."

"Pupils have to be taught, not interested," said the head mistress. "Will you kindly put the class through some irregular verbs?"

So for the remainder of the lesson Aristide, under the freezing eyes of the head mistress, put his sorrowful class through irregular verbs, of which his own knowledge was singularly inexact, and at the end received his dismissal. In vain he argued. Outraged Minerva[15] was implacable. Go he must.

We find him, then, one miserable December evening, standing on the arrival platform of Euston Station (the academy was near Manchester), an unwonted statue of dubiety. At his feet lay his meagre valise; in his hand

[11] *Eh, ma vieille,* . . . : (literally) "So, my old one, how does it jog along?"
[12] *échoir:* to fall due, to happen.
[13] orthography: spelling.
[14] *Il était saoûl* . . . : "He was drunk as a pig."
[15] Minerva: Roman goddess of wisdom.

was an enormous bouquet, a useful tribute of esteem from his disconsolate pupils; around him luggage-laden porters and passengers hurried; in front were drawn up the long line of cabs, their drivers' waterproofs glistening with wet; and in his pocket rattled the few paltry coins that, for Heaven knew how long, were to keep him from starvation. Should he commit the extravagance of taking a cab or should he go forth, valise in hand, into the pouring rain? He hesitated.

"*Sacré mille cochons! Quel chien de climat!*" [16] he muttered.

A smart footman standing by turned quickly and touched his hat.

"Beg pardon, sir; I'm from Mr. Smith."

"I'm glad to hear it, my friend," said Aristide.

"You're the French gentleman from Manchester?"

"Decidedly," said Aristide.

"Then, sir, Mr. Smith has sent the carriage for you."

"That's very kind of him," said Aristide.

The footman picked up the valise and darted down the platform. Aristide followed. The footman held invitingly open the door of a cosy brougham.[17] Aristide paused for the fraction of a second. Who was this hospitable Mr. Smith?

"Bah!" said he to himself, "the best way of finding out is to go and see."

He entered the carriage, sank back luxuriously on the soft cushions, and inhaled the warm smell of leather. They started, and soon the pelting rain beat harmlessly against the windows. Aristide looked out at the streaming streets, and, hugging himself comfortably, thanked Providence and Mr. Smith. But who was Mr. Smith? *Tiens*,[18] thought he, there were two little Miss Smiths at the academy; he had pitied them because they had chilblains, freckles, and perpetual colds in their heads; possibly this was their kind papa. But, after all, what did it matter whose papa he was? He was expecting him. He had sent the carriage for him. Evidently a well-bred and attentive person. And *tiens!* there was even a hot-water can on the floor of the brougham. "He thinks of everything, that man," said Aristide. "I feel I am going to like him."

The carriage stopped at a house in Hampstead, standing, as far as he could see in the darkness, in its own grounds. The footman opened the door for him to alight and escorted him up the front steps. A neat parlourmaid received him in a comfortably furnished hall and took his hat and great-coat and magnificent bouquet.

"Mr. Smith hasn't come back yet from the City, sir; but Miss Christabel is in the drawing-room."

"Ah!" said Aristide. "Please give me back my bouquet."

---

[16] *Sacré mille* . . . : "A thousand cursed pigs! What a dog of a climate!"
[17] brougham: a closed, horse-drawn carriage.
[18] *Tiens:* "Look here!" "Well!" "There!"

The maid showed him into the drawing-room. A pretty girl of three-and-twenty rose from a fender-stool and advanced smilingly to meet him.

"Good afternoon, M. le Baron. I was wondering whether Thomas would spot you. I'm so glad he did. You see, neither Father nor I could give him any description, for we had never seen you."

This fitted in with his theory. But why Baron? After all, why not? The English loved titles.

"He seems to be an intelligent fellow, mademoiselle."

There was a span of silence. The girl looked at the bouquet, then at Aristide, who looked at the girl, then at the bouquet, then at the girl again.

"Mademoiselle," said he, "will you deign to accept these flowers as a token of my respectful homage?"

Miss Christabel took the flowers and blushed prettily. She had dark hair and eyes and a fascinating, upturned little nose, and the kindest little mouth in the world.

"An Englishman would not have thought of that," she said.

Aristide smiled in his roguish way and raised a deprecating hand.

"Oh, yes, he would. But he would not have had—what you call the cheek to do it."

Miss Christabel laughed merrily, invited him to a seat by the fire, and comforted him with tea and hot muffins. The frank charm of his girl-hostess captivated Aristide and drove from his mind the riddle of his adventure. Besides, think of the Arabian Nights' enchantment of the change from his lonely and shabby bed-sitting-room in the Rusholme Road to this fragrant palace with princess and all to keep him company! He watched the firelight dancing through her hair, the dainty play of laughter over her face, and decided that the brougham had transported him to Bagdad instead of Hampstead.

"You have the air of a veritable princess," said he.

"I once met a princess—at a charity bazaar—and she was a most matter-of-fact businesslike person."

"Bah!" said Aristide. "A princess of a charity bazaar! I was talking of the princess in a fairy-tale. They are the only real ones."

"Do you know," said Miss Christabel, "that when men pay such compliments to English girls they are apt to get laughed at?"

"Englishmen, yes," replied Aristide, "because they think over a compliment for a week, so that by the time they pay it, it is addled, like a bad egg. But we of Provence pay tribute to beauty straight out of our hearts. It is true. It is sincere. And what comes out of the heart is not ridiculous."

Again the girl coloured and laughed. "I've always heard that a Frenchman makes love to every woman he meets."

"Naturally," said Aristide. "If they are pretty. What else are pretty women for? Otherwise they might as well be hideous."

WILLIAM J. LOCKE

"Oh!" said the girl, to whom this Provençal [19] point of view had not occurred.

"So, if I make love to you, it is but your due."

"I wonder what my fiancé would say if he heard you?"

"Your——?"

"My fiancé! There's his photograph on the table beside you. He is six foot one, and so jealous!" she laughed again.

"The Turk!" [20] cried Aristide, his swiftly conceived romance crumbling into dust. Then he brightened up. "But when this six feet of muscle and egotism is absent, surely other poor mortals can glean a smile?"

"You will observe that I'm not frowning," said Miss Christabel. "But you must not call my fiancé a Turk, for he's a very charming fellow whom I hope you'll like very much."

Aristide sighed. "And the name of this thrice-blessed mortal?"

Miss Christabel told his name—one Harry Ralston—and not only his name, but, such was the peculiar, childlike charm of Aristide Pujol, also many other things about him. He was the Honourable Harry Ralston, the heir to a great brewery peerage, and very wealthy. He was a member of Parliament, and but for Parliamentary duties would have dined there that evening; but he was to come in later, as soon as he could leave the House. He also had a house in Hampshire, full of the most beautiful works of art. It was through their common hobby that her father and Harry had first made acquaintance.

"We're supposed to have a very fine collection here," she said, with a motion of her hand.

Aristide looked round the walls and saw them hung with pictures in gold frames. In those days he had not acquired an extensive culture. Besides, who having before him the firelight gleaming through Miss Christabel's hair could waste his time over painted canvas? She noted his cursory glance.

"I thought you were a connoisseur?"

"I am," said Aristide, his bright eyes fixed on her in frank admiration. She blushed again; but this time she rose.

"I must go and dress for dinner. Perhaps you would like to be shown your room?"

He hung his head on one side.

"Have I been too bold, Mademoiselle?"

"I don't know," she said. "You see, I've never met a Frenchman before."

"Then a world of undreamed-of homage is at your feet," said he.

A servant ushered him up broad, carpeted staircases into a bedroom such as he had never seen in his life before. It was all curtains and hangings and

[19] Provençal: referring to Provence, a southeastern region of France.
[20] Turk: here, a brutal or tyrannical person.

rugs and soft couches and satin quilts and dainty writing-tables and subdued lights, and a great fire glowed red and cheerful, and before it hung a
clean shirt. His poor little toilet apparatus was laid on the dressing-table,
and (with a tact which he did not appreciate, for he had, sad to tell, no
dress-suit) the servant had spread his precious frock-coat and spare pair of
trousers on the bed. On the pillow lay his night-shirt, neatly folded.

"Evidently," said Aristide, impressed by these preparations, "it is expected that I wash myself now and change my clothes, and that I sleep here
for the night. And for all that the ravishing Miss Christabel is engaged to
her Honourable Harry, this is none the less a corner of Paradise."

So Aristide attired himself in his best, which included a white tie and a
pair of nearly new brown boots—a long task, as he found that his valise
had been spirited away and its contents, including the white tie of ceremony
(he had but one), hidden in unexpected drawers and wardrobes—and eventually went downstairs into the drawing-room. There he found Miss Christabel and, warming himself on the hearthrug, a bald-headed, beefy-faced
Briton, with little pig's eyes and a hearty manner, attired in a dinner-suit.

"My dear fellow," said this personage, with outstretched hand, "I'm delighted to have you here. I've heard so much about you; and my little girl
has been singing your praises."

"Mademoiselle is too kind," said Aristide.

"You must take us as you find us," said Mr. Smith. "We're just ordinary
folk, but I can give you a good bottle of wine and a good cigar—it's only in
England, you know, that you can get champagne fit to drink and cigars fit
to smoke—and I can give you a glimpse of a modest English home. I believe you haven't a word for it in French."

"Ma foi,[21] no," said Aristide, who had once or twice before heard this
lunatic charge brought against his country. "In France the men all live in
cafés, the children are all put out to nurse, and the women, saving the respect of mademoiselle—well, the less said about them the better."

"England is the only place, isn't it?" Mr. Smith declared, heartily. "I
don't say that Paris hasn't its points. But after all—the Moulin Rouge[22] and
the Folies Bergères[23] and that sort of thing soon pall, you know—soon
pall."

"Yet Paris has its serious side," argued Aristide. "There is always the tomb
of Napoleon."

"Papa will never take me to Paris," sighed the girl.

"You shall go there on your honeymoon," said Mr. Smith.

Dinner was announced. Aristide gave his arm to Miss Christabel, and
proud not only of his partner, but also of his frock-coat, white tie, and shiny

---

[21] *Ma foi:* "My word."
[22] Moulin Rouge: café in Paris.
[23] Folies Bergères: famous nightclub in Paris.

WILLIAM J. LOCKE

brown boots, strutted into the dining-room. The host sat at the end of the beautifully set table, his daughter on his right, Aristide on his left. The meal began gaily. The kind Mr. Smith was in the best of humours.

"And how is our dear old friend, Jules Dancourt?" he asked.

"*Tiens!*" said Aristide, to himself, "we have a dear friend Jules Dancourt." "Wonderfully well," he replied at a venture, "but he suffers terribly at times from the gout." [24]

"So do I, confound it!" said Mr. Smith, drinking sherry.

"You and the good Jules were always sympathetic," said Aristide. "Ah! he has spoken to me so often about you, the tears in his eyes."

"Men cry, my dear, in France," Mr. Smith explained. "They also kiss each other."

"*Ah, mais c'est un beau pays, mademoiselle!*" [25] cried Aristide, and he began to talk of France and to draw pictures of his country which set the girl's eyes dancing. After that he told some of the funny little stories which had brought him disaster at the academy. Mr. Smith, with jovial magnanimity, declared that he was the first Frenchman he had ever met with a sense of humour.

"But I thought, Baron," said he, "that you lived all your life shut up in that old château of yours?"

"*Tiens!*" thought Aristide. "I am still a Baron, and I have an old château."

"Tell us about the château. Has it a fosse[26] and a drawbridge and a Gothic chapel?" asked Miss Christabel.

"Which one do you mean?" inquired Aristide, airily. "For I have two."

When relating to me this Arabian Nights' adventure, he drew my special attention to his astuteness.

His host's eye quivered in a wink. "The one in Languedoc," [27] said he.

Languedoc! Almost Pujol's own country! With entire lack of morality, but with picturesque imagination, Aristide plunged into a description of that non-existent baronial hall. Fosse, drawbridge, Gothic chapel were but insignificant features. It had tourelles,[28] emblazoned gateways, bastions,[29] donjons,[30] barbicans;[31] it had innumerable rooms; in the *salle des chevaliers*[32] two hundred men-at-arms had his ancestors fed at a sitting. There was the room in which François Premier[33] had slept, and one in which Joan

---

[24] gout: inflammation of the joints.
[25] *Ah, mais c'est*...: "Ah, but it is a beautiful country, miss."
[26] fosse: ditch or moat.
[27] Languedoc: a region in southern France.
[28] tourelles: turrets.
[29] bastions: projecting parts of fortifications.
[30] donjons: fortified towers, dungeons.
[31] barbicans: towers for defense.
[32] *salle des chevaliers*: room for the knights.
[33] François Premier: Francis I, King of France from 1515 to 1547.

of Arc had almost been assassinated. What the name of himself or of his ancestors was supposed to be Aristide had no ghost of an idea. But as he proceeded with the erection of his airy palace he gradually began to believe in it. He invested the place with a living atmosphere; conjured up a staff of family retainers, notably one Marie-Joseph Loufoque, the wizened old major-domo, with his long white whiskers and blue and silver livery. There were also Madeline Mioulles the cook, and Bernadet the groom, and La Petite Fripette the goose girl. Ah! they should see La Petite Fripette! And he kept dogs and horses and cows and ducks and hens—and there was a great pond whence frogs were drawn to be fed for the consumption of the household.

Miss Christabel shivered. "I should not like to eat frogs."

"They also eat snails," said her father.

"I have a snail farm," said Aristide. "You never saw such interesting little animals. They are so intelligent. If you're kind to them they come and eat out of your hand."

"You've forgotten the pictures," said Mr. Smith.

"Ah! the pictures," cried Aristide, with a wide sweep of his arms. "Galleries full of them. Raphael, Michael Angelo, Wiertz, Reynolds——"

He paused, not in order to produce the effect of a dramatic aposiopesis, but because he could not for the moment remember other names of painters.

"It is a truly historical château," said he.

"I should love to see it," said the girl.

Aristide threw out his arms across the table. "It is yours, mademoiselle, for your honeymoon," said he.

Dinner came to an end. Miss Christabel left the gentlemen to their wine, an excellent port whose English qualities were vaunted by the host. Aristide, full of food and drink and the mellow glories of the castle in Languedoc, and smoking an enormous cigar, felt at ease with all the world. He knew he should like the kind Mr. Smith, hospitable though somewhat insular man. He could stay with him for a week—or a month—why not a year?

After coffee and liqueurs had been served Mr. Smith rose and switched on a powerful electric light at the end of the large room, showing a picture on an easel covered by a curtain. He beckoned to Aristide to join him and, drawing the curtain, disclosed the picture.

"There!" said he. "Isn't it a stunner?"

It was a picture all grey skies and grey water and grey feathery trees, and a little man in the foreground wore a red cap.

"It is beautiful, but indeed it is magnificent!" cried Aristide, always impressionable to things of beauty.

"Genuine Corot,[34] isn't it?"

"Without doubt," said Aristide.

---

[34] Corot: Jean Baptiste Camille Corot (1796–1875), French Impressionist painter.

His host poked him in the ribs. "I thought I'd astonish you. You wouldn't believe Gottschalk could have done it. There it is—as large as life and twice as natural. If you or anyone else can tell it from a genuine Corot I'll eat my hat. And all for eight pounds."

Aristide looked at the beefy face and caught a look of cunning in the little pig's eyes.

"Now are you satisfied?" asked Mr. Smith.

"More than satisfied," said Aristide, though what he was to be satisfied about passed, for the moment, his comprehension.

"If it was a copy of an existing picture, you know—one might have understood it—that, of course, would be dangerous—but for a man to go and get bits out of various Corots and stick them together like this is miraculous. If it hadn't been for a matter of business principle I'd have given the fellow eight guineas instead of pounds—hanged if I wouldn't! He deserves it."

"He does indeed," said Aristide Pujol.

"And now that you've seen it with your own eyes, what do you think you might ask me for it? I suggested something between two and three thousand—shall we say three? You're the owner, you know." Again the process of rib-digging. "Came out of that historic château of yours. My eye! you're a holy terror when you begin to talk. You almost persuaded me it was real."

"Tiens!" said Aristide to himself. "I don't seem to have a château after all."

"Certainly three thousand," said he, with a grave face.

"That young man thinks he knows a lot, but he doesn't," said Mr. Smith.

"Ah!" said Aristide, with singular laconicism.

"Not a blooming thing," continued his host. "But he'll pay three thousand, which is the principal, isn't it? He's partner in the show, you know, Ralston, Wiggins, and Wix's Brewery"—Aristide pricked up his ears—"and when his doddering old father dies he'll be Lord Ranelagh and come into a million of money."

"Has he seen the picture?" asked Aristide.

"Oh, yes. Regards it as a masterpiece. Didn't Brauneberger tell you of the Lancret we planted on the American?" Mr. Smith rubbed hearty hands at the memory of the iniquity. "Same old game. Always easy. I have nothing to do with the bargaining or the sale. Just an old friend of the ruined French nobleman with the historic château and family treasures. He comes along and fixes the price. I told our friend Harry——"

"Good," thought Aristide. "This is the same Honourable Harry, M.P., who is engaged to the ravishing Miss Christabel."

"I told him," said Mr. Smith, "that it might come to three or four thousand. He jibbed a bit—so when I wrote to you I said two or three. But you might try him with three to begin with."

Aristide went back to the table and poured himself out a fresh glass of his kind host's 1865 brandy and drank it off.

"Exquisite, my dear fellow," said he. "I've none finer in my historic château."

"Don't suppose you have," grinned the host, joining him. He slapped him on the back. "Well," said he, with a shifty look in his little pig's eyes, "let us talk business. What do you think would be your fair commission? You see, all the trouble and invention have been mine. What do you say to four hundred pounds?"

"Five," said Aristide, promptly.

A sudden gleam came into the little pig's eyes.

"Done!" said Mr. Smith, who had imagined that the other would demand a thousand and was prepared to pay eight hundred. "Done!" said he again.

They shook hands to seal the bargain and drank another glass of old brandy. At that moment, a servant, entering, took the host aside.

"Please excuse me a moment," said he, and went with the servant out of the room.

Aristide, left alone, lighted another of his kind host's fat cigars and threw himself in a great leathern armchair by the fire, and surrendered himself deliciously to the soothing charm of the moment. Now and then he laughed, finding a certain comicality in his position. And what a charming father-in-law, this kind Mr. Smith!

His cheerful reflections were soon disturbed by the sudden irruption of his host and a grizzled, elderly, foxy-faced gentleman with a white moustache, wearing the ribbon of the Legion of Honour[35] in the button-hole of his overcoat.

"Here, you!" cried the kind Mr. Smith, striding up to Aristide, with a very red face. "Will you have the kindness to tell me who the devil you are?"

Aristide rose, and, putting his hands behind the tails of his frock-coat, stood smiling radiantly on the hearthrug. A wit much less alert than my irresponsible friend's would have instantly appreciated the fact that the real Simon Pure had arrived on the scene.

"I, my dear friend," said he, "am the Baron de Je ne Sais Plus."

"You're a confounded impostor," spluttered Mr. Smith.

"And this gentleman here to whom I have not had the pleasure of being introduced?" asked Aristide, blandly.

"I am M. Poiron, monsieur, the agent of Messrs. Brauneberger and Compagnie, art dealers, of the Rue Notre-Dame des Petits Champs[36] of Paris," said the newcomer, with an air of defiance.

"Ah, I thought you were the Baron," said Aristide.

---

[35] Legion of Honour: highly distinguished French civilian and military decoration.
[36] Rue Notre-Dame . . . : Street of Our Lady of the Little Fields.

"There's no blooming Baron at all about it!" screamed Mr. Smith. "Are you Poiron, or is he?"

"I would not have a name like Poiron for anything in the world," said Aristide. "My name is Aristide Pujol, soldier of fortune, at your service."

"How the blazes did you get here?"

"Your servant asked me if I was a French gentleman from Manchester. I was. He said that Mr. Smith had sent his carriage for me. I thought it hospitable of the kind Mr. Smith. I entered the carriage—*et voilà!*" [37]

"Then clear out of here this very minute," said Mr. Smith, reaching forward his hand to the bell-push.

Aristide checked his impulsive action.

"Pardon me, dear host," said he. "It is raining dogs and cats outside. I am very comfortable in your luxurious home. I am here, and here I stay."

"I'm shot if you do," said the kind Mr. Smith, his face growing redder and uglier. "Now, will you go out, or will you be thrown out?"

Aristide, who had no desire whatever to be ejected from this snug nest into the welter of the wet and friendless world, puffed at his cigar, and looked at his host with the irresistible drollery of his eyes.

"You forget, *mon cher ami*," [38] said he, "that neither the beautiful Miss Christabel nor her affianced, the Honourable Harry, M.P., would care to know that the talented Gottschalk got only eight pounds, not even guineas, for painting that three-thousand-pound picture."

"So it's blackmail, eh?"

"Precisely," said Aristide, "and I don't blush at it."

"You infernal little blackguard!"

"I seem to be in congenial company," said Aristide. "I don't think our friend M. Poiron has more scruples than he has right to the ribbon of the Legion of Honour which he is wearing."

"How much will you take to go out? I have a cheque-book handy."

Mr. Smith moved a few steps from the hearthrug. Aristide sat down in the armchair. An engaging, fantastic impudence was one of the charms of Aristide Pujol.

"I'll take five hundred pounds," said he, "to stay in."

"Stay in?" Mr. Smith grew apoplectic.

"Yes," said Aristide. "You can't do without me. Your daughter and your servants know me as M. le Baron—by the way, what is my name? And where is my historic château in Languedoc?"

"Mireilles," said M. Poiron, who was sitting grim and taciturn on one of the dining-room chairs. "And the place is the same, near Montpellier."

"I like to meet an intelligent man," said Aristide.

"I should like to wring your infernal neck," said the kind Mr. Smith.

---

[37] *et voilà!:* "and behold!"
[38] *mon cher ami:* "my dear friend."

"But, by George, if we do let you in you'll have to sign me a receipt implicating yourself up to the hilt. I'm not going to be put into the cart by you, you can bet your life."

"Anything you like," said Aristide, "so long as we all swing together."

Now, when Aristide Pujol arrived at this point in his narrative, I, his chronicler, who am nothing if not an eminently respectable, law-abiding Briton, took him warmly to task for his sheer absence of moral sense. His eyes, as they sometimes did, assumed a luminous pathos.

"My dear friend," said he, "have you ever faced the world in a foreign country in December with no character and fifteen pounds five and threepence in your pocket? Five hundred pounds was a fortune. It is one now. And to be gained just by lending oneself to a good farce, which didn't hurt anybody. You and your British morals! Bah!" said he, with a fine flourish.

Aristide, after much parleying, was finally admitted into the nefarious brotherhood. He was to retain his rank as the Baron de Mireilles, and play the part of the pecuniarily inconvenienced nobleman forced to sell some of his rare collection. Mr. Smith had heard of the Corot through their dear old common friend, Jules Dancourt of Rheims, had mentioned it alluringly to the Honourable Harry, had arranged for the Baron, who was visiting England, to bring it over and dispatch it to Mr. Smith's house, and on his return from Manchester to pay a visit to Mr. Smith, so that he could meet the Honourable Harry in person. In whatever transaction ensued Mr. Smith, so far as his prospective son-in-law was concerned, was to be the purely disinterested friend. It was Aristide's wit which invented a part for the supplanted M. Poiron. He should be the eminent Parisian expert who, chancing to be in London, had been telephoned for by the kind Mr. Smith.

"It would not be wise for M. Poiron," said Aristide, chuckling inwardly with puckish glee, "to stay here for the night—or for two or three days—or a week—like myself. He must go back to his hotel when the business is concluded."

"*Mais, pardon!*" [39] cried M. Poiron, who had been formally invited, and had arrived late solely because he had missed his train at Manchester, and come on by the next one. "I cannot go out into the wet, and I have no hotel to go to."

Aristide appealed to his host. "But he is unreasonable, *cher ami*. He must play his *rôle*. M. Poiron has been telephoned for. He can't possibly stay here. Surely five hundred pounds is worth one little night of discomfort? And there are a legion of hotels in London."

"Five hundred pounds!" exclaimed M. Poiron. "*Qu'est-ce que vous chantez là?* [40] I want more than five hundred pounds."

"Then you're jolly well not going to get it," cried Mr. Smith, in a rage.

[39] *Mais, pardon!*: "But pardon!"
[40] *Qu'est-ce que vous . . .* : "What's that you're singing?"

"And as for you"—he turned on Aristide—"I'll wring your infernal neck yet."

"Calm yourself, calm yourself!" smiled Aristide, who was enjoying himself hugely.

At this moment the door opened and Miss Christabel appeared. On seeing the decorated stranger she started with a little "Oh!" of surprise.

"I beg your pardon."

Mr. Smith's angry face wreathed itself in smiles.

"This, my darling, is M. Poiron, the eminent Paris expert, who has been good enough to come and give us his opinion on the picture."

M. Poiron bowed. Aristide advanced.

"Mademoiselle, your appearance is like a mirage in a desert."

She smiled indulgently and turned to her father. "I've been wondering what had become of you. Harry has been here for the last half-hour."

"Bring him in, dear child, bring him in!" said Mr. Smith, with all the heartiness of the fine old English gentleman. "Our good friends are dying to meet him."

The girl flickered out of the room like a sunbeam (the phrase is Aristide's), and the three precious rascals put their heads together in a hurried and earnest colloquy. Presently Miss Christabel returned, and with her came the Honourable Harry Ralston, a tall, soldierly fellow, with close-cropped fair curly hair and a fair moustache, and frank blue eyes that, even in Parliament, had seen no harm in his fellow-creatures. Aristide's magical vision caught him wincing ever so little at Mr. Smith's effusive greeting and overdone introductions. He shook Aristide warmly by the hand.

"You have a beauty there, Baron, a perfect beauty," said he, with the insane ingenuousness of youth. "I wonder how you can manage to part with it."

"Ma foi," said Aristide, with his back against the end of the dining-table and gazing at the masterpiece. "I have so many at the Château de Mireilles. When one begins to collect, you know—and when one's grandfather and father have had also the divine mania——"

"You were saying, M. le Baron," said M. Poiron of Paris, "that your respected grandfather bought this direct from Corot himself."

"A commission," said Aristide. "My grandfather was a patron of Corot."

"Do you like it, dear?" asked the Honourable Harry.

"Oh, yes!" replied the girl, fervently. "It is beautiful. I feel like Harry about it." She turned to Aristide. "How can you part with it? Were you really in earnest when you said you would like me to come and see your collection?"

"For me," said Aristide, "it would be a visit of enchantment."

"You must take me, then," she whispered to Harry. "The Baron has been telling us about his lovely old château."

"Will you come, monsieur?" asked Aristide.

"Since I'm going to rob you of your picture," said the young man, with smiling courtesy, "the least I can do is to pay you a visit of apology. Lovely!" said he, going up to the Corot.

Aristide took Miss Christabel, now more bewitching than ever with the glow of young love in her eyes and a flush on her cheek, a step or two aside and whispered:

"But he is charming, your fiancé! He almost deserves his good fortune."

"Why almost?" she laughed, shyly.

"It is not a man, but a demi-god, that would deserve you, mademoiselle."

M. Poiron's harsh voice broke out.

"You see, it is painted in the beginning of Corot's later manner—it is 1864. There is the mystery which, when he was quite an old man, became a trick. If you were to put it up to auction at Christie's it would fetch, I am sure, five thousand pounds."

"That's more than I can afford to give," said the young man, with a laugh. "Mr. Smith mentioned something between three and four thousand pounds. I don't think I can go above three."

"I have nothing to do with it, my dear boy, nothing whatever," said Mr. Smith, rubbing his hands. "You wanted a Corot. I said I thought I could put you on to one. It's for the Baron here to mention his price. I retire now and for ever."

"Well, Baron?" said the young man, cheerfully. "What's your idea?"

Aristide came forward and resumed his place at the end of the table. The picture was in front of him beneath the strong electric light; on his left stood Mr. Smith and Poiron, on his right Miss Christabel and the Honourable Harry.

"I'll not take three thousand pounds for it," said Aristide. "A picture like that! Never!"

"I assure you it would be a fair price," said Poiron.

"You mentioned that figure yourself only just now," said Mr. Smith, with an ugly glitter in his little pig's eyes.

"I presume, gentlemen," said Aristide, "that this picture is my own property." He turned engagingly to his host. "Is it not, *cher ami?*"

"Of course it is. Who said it wasn't?"

"And you, M. Poiron, acknowledge formally that it is mine?" he asked, in French.

"*Sans aucun doute.*" [41]

"*Eh bien,*" [42] said Aristide, throwing open his arms and gazing round sweetly. "I have changed my mind. I do not sell the picture at all."

"Not sell it? What the—what do you mean?" asked Mr. Smith, striving to mellow the gathering thunder on his brow.

"I do not sell," said Aristide. "Listen, my dear friends!" He was in the

---

[41] *Sans aucun doute:* "Without any doubt."
[42] *Eh bien:* "Oh, well."

seventh heaven of happiness—the principal man, the star, taking the centre of the stage. "I have an announcement to make to you. I have fallen desperately in love with mademoiselle."

There was a general gasp. Mr. Smith looked at him, red-faced and openmouthed. Miss Christabel blushed furiously and emitted a sound half between a laugh and a scream. Harry Ralston's eyes flashed.

"My dear sir——" he began.

"Pardon," said Aristide, disarming him with the merry splendour of his glance. "I do not wish to take mademoiselle from you. My love is hopeless! I know it. But it will feed me to my dying day. In return for the joy of this hopeless passion I will not sell you the picture—I give it to you as a wedding present."

He stood, with the air of a hero, both arms extended towards the amazed pair of lovers.

"I give it to you," said he. "It is mine. I have no wish but for your happiness. In my Château de Mireilles there are a hundred others."

"This is madness!" said Mr. Smith, bursting with suppressed indignation, so that his bald head grew scarlet.

"My dear fellow!" said Mr. Harry Ralston. "It is unheard-of generosity on your part. But we can't accept it."

"Then," said Aristide, advancing dramatically to the picture, "I take it under my arm, I put it in a hansom cab, and I go with it back to Languedoc."

Mr. Smith caught him by the wrist and dragged him out of the room.

"You little brute! Do you want your neck broken?"

"Do you want the marriage of your daughter with the rich and Honourable Harry broken?" asked Aristide.

"Oh, damn! Oh, damn! Oh, damn!" cried Mr. Smith, stamping about helplessly and half weeping.

Aristide entered the dining-room and beamed on the company.

"The kind Mr. Smith has consented. Mr. Honourable Harry and Miss Christabel, there is your Corot. And now, may I be permitted?" He rang the bell. A servant appeared.

"Some champagne to drink to the health of the fiancés," he cried. "Lots of champagne."

Mr. Smith looked at him almost admiringly.

"By Jove!" he muttered. "You *have* got a nerve."

"*Voilà!*" said Aristide, when he had finished the story.

"And did they accept the Corot?" I asked.

"Of course. It is hanging now in the big house in Hampshire. I stayed with the kind Mr. Smith for six weeks," he added, doubling himself up in his chair and hugging himself with mirth, "and we became very good friends. And I was at the wedding."

"And what about their honeymoon visit to Languedoc?"

"Alas!" said Aristide. "The morning before the wedding I had a telegram—it was from my old father at Aigues-Mortes—to tell me that the historic Château de Mireilles, with my priceless collection of pictures, had been burned to the ground."

Rudyard Kipling (1865–1936)

THE GARDENER

One grave to me was given,
  One watch till Judgment Day;
And God looked down from Heaven
  And rolled the stone away.

One day in all the years,
  One hour in that one day,
His Angel saw my tears,
  And rolled the stone away!

Every one in the village knew that Helen Turrell did her duty by all her world, and by none more honourably than by her only brother's unfortunate child. The village knew, too, that George Turrell had tried his family severely since early youth, and were not surprised to be told that, after many fresh starts given and thrown away, he, an Inspector of Indian Police, had entangled himself with the daughter of a retired non-commissioned officer, and had died of a fall from a horse a few weeks before his child was born. Mercifully, George's father and mother were both dead, and though Helen, thirty-five and independent, might well have washed her hands of the whole disgraceful affair, she most nobly took charge, though she was, at the time, under threat of lung trouble which had driven her to the South of France. She arranged for the passage of the child and a nurse from Bombay, met them at Marseilles, nursed the baby through an attack of infantile dysentery due to the carelessness of the nurse, whom she had had to dismiss, and at last, thin and worn but triumphant, brought the boy late in the autumn, wholly restored, to her Hampshire[1] home.

All these details were public property, for Helen was as open as the day, and held that scandals are only increased by hushing them up. She admitted that George had always been rather a black sheep, but things might have been much worse if the mother had insisted on her right to keep the boy. Luckily, it seemed that people of that class would do almost anything for money, and, as George had always turned to her in his scrapes, she felt herself justified—her friends agreed with her—in cutting the whole non-commissioned officer connection, and giving the child every advantage. A christening, by the Rector, under the name of Michael, was the first step. So far as she knew herself, she was not, she said, a child-lover, but, for all his

[1] Hampshire: county in the south of England.

faults, she had been very fond of George, and she pointed out that little
Michael had his father's mouth to a line; which made something to build
upon.

As a matter of fact, it was the Turrell forehead, broad, low, and well-
shaped, with the widely spaced eyes beneath it, that Michael had most faithfully reproduced. His mouth was somewhat better cut than the family type.
But Helen, who would concede nothing good to his mother's side, vowed
he was a Turrell all over, and, there being no one to contradict, the likeness
was established.

In a few years Michael took his place, as accepted as Helen had always
been—fearless, philosophical, and fairly good-looking. At six, he wished to
know why he could not call her "Mummy," as other boys called their
mothers. She explained that she was only his auntie, and that aunties were
not quite the same as mummies, but that, if it gave him pleasure, he might
call her "Mummy" at bedtime, for a pet-name between themselves.

Michael kept his secret most loyally, but Helen, as usual, explained the
fact to her friends; which when Michael heard, he raged.

"Why did you tell? *Why* did you tell?" came at the end of the storm.

"Because it's always best to tell the truth," Helen answered, her arm
round him as he shook in his cot.

"All right, but when the troof's ugly I don't think it's nice."

"Don't you, dear?"

"No, I don't, and"—she felt the small body stiffen—"now you've told, I
won't call you 'Mummy' any more—not even at bedtimes."

"But isn't that rather unkind?" said Helen softly.

"I don't care! I don't care! You've hurted me in my insides and I'll hurt
you back. I'll hurt you as long as I live!"

"Don't, oh, don't talk like that, dear! You don't know what—"

"I will! And when I'm dead I'll hurt you worse!"

"Thank goodness, I shall be dead long before you, darling."

"Huh! Emma says, 'Never know your luck.' " (Michael had been talking
to Helen's elderly, flat-faced maid.) "Lots of little boys die quite soon. So'll I.
Then you'll see!"

Helen caught her breath and moved towards the door, but the wail of
"Mummy! Mummy!" drew her back again, and the two wept together.

At ten years old, after two terms at a prep. school, something or somebody gave him the idea that his civil status was not quite regular. He attacked Helen on the subject, breaking down her stammered defences with
the family directness.

" 'Don't believe a word of it," he said, cheerily, at the end. "People
wouldn't have talked like they did if my people had been married. But don't
you bother, Auntie. I've found out all about my sort in English Hist'ry and
the Shakespeare bits. There was William the Conqueror to begin with, and

—oh, heaps more, and they all got on first-rate. 'Twon't make any difference to you, my being *that*—will it?"

"As if anything could—" she began.

"All right. We won't talk about it any more if it makes you cry." He never mentioned the thing again of his own will, but when, two years later, he skilfully managed to have measles in the holidays, as his temperature went up to the appointed one hundred and four he muttered of nothing else, till Helen's voice, piercing at last his delirium, reached him with assurance that nothing on earth or beyond could make any difference between them.

The terms at his public school and the wonderful Christmas, Easter, and Summer holidays followed each other, variegated and glorious as jewels on a string; and as jewels Helen treasured them. In due time Michael developed his own interests, which ran their courses and gave way to others; but his interest in Helen was constant and increasing throughout. She repaid it with all that she had of affection or could command of counsel and money; and since Michael was no fool, the War took him just before what was like to have been a most promising career.

He was to have gone up to Oxford, with a scholarship, in October. At the end of August he was on the edge of joining the first holocaust of public-school boys who threw themselves into the Line; but the captain of his O.T.C., where he had been sergeant for nearly a year, headed him off and steered him directly to a commission in a battalion so new that half of it still wore the old Army red, and the other half was breeding meningitis through living overcrowdedly in damp tents. Helen had been shocked at the idea of direct enlistment.

"But it's in the family," Michael laughed.

"You don't mean to tell me that you believed that old story all this time?" said Helen. (Emma, her maid, had been dead now several years.) "I gave you my word of honour—and I give it again—that—that it's all right. It is indeed."

"Oh, *that* doesn't worry me. It never did," he replied valiantly. "What I meant was, I should have got into the show earlier if I'd enlisted—like my grandfather."

"Don't talk like that! Are you afraid of its ending so soon, then?"

"No such luck. You know what K. says."

"Yes. But my banker told me last Monday it couldn't *possibly* last beyond Christmas—for financial reasons."

" 'Hope he's right, but our Colonel—and he's a Regular—says it's going to be a long job."

Michael's battalion was fortunate in that, by some chance which meant several "leaves," it was used for coast-defence among shallow trenches on the Norfolk[2] coast; thence sent north to watch the mouth of a Scotch estuary, and, lastly, held for weeks on a baseless rumour of distant service. But,

[2] Norfolk: county in the south of England.

the very day that Michael was to have met Helen for four whole hours at a railway-junction up the line, it was hurled out, to help make good the wastage of Loos, and he had only just time to send her a wire of farewell.

In France luck again helped the battalion. It was put down near the Salient, where it led a meritorious and unexacting life, while the Somme[3] was being manufactured; and enjoyed the peace of the Armentières and Laventie[4] sectors when that battle began. Finding that it had sound views on protecting its own flanks and could dig, a prudent Commander stole it out of its own Division, under pretence of helping to lay telegraphs, and used it round Ypres[5] at large.

A month later, and just after Michael had written Helen that there was nothing special doing and therefore no need to worry, a shell-splinter dropping out of a wet dawn killed him at once. The next shell uprooted and laid down over the body what had been the foundation of a barn wall, so neatly that none but an expert would have guessed that anything unpleasant had happened.

By this time the village was old in experience of war, and, English fashion, had evolved a ritual to meet it. When the postmistress handed her seven-year-old daughter the official telegram to take to Miss Turrell, she observed to the Rector's gardener: "It's Miss Helen's turn now." He replied, thinking of his own son: "Well, he's lasted longer than some." The child herself came to the front-door weeping aloud, because Master Michael had often given her sweets. Helen, presently, found herself pulling down the house-blinds one after one with great care, and saying earnestly to each: "Missing *always* means dead." Then she took her place in the dreary procession that was impelled to go through an inevitable series of unprofitable emotions. The Rector, of course, preached hope and prophesied word, very soon, from a prison camp. Several friends, too, told her perfectly truthful tales, but always about other women, to whom, after months and months of silence, their missing had been miraculously restored. Other people urged her to communicate with infallible Secretaries of organisations who could communicate with benevolent neutrals, who could extract accurate information from the most secretive of Hun[6] prison commandants. Helen did and wrote and signed everything that was suggested or put before her.

Once, on one of Michael's leaves, he had taken her over a munition factory, where she saw the progress of a shell from blank-iron to the all but finished article. It struck her at the time that the wretched thing was never left alone for a single second; and "I'm being manufactured into a bereaved next of kin," she told herself, as she prepared her documents.

In due course, when all the organisations had deeply or sincerely regretted

[3] Somme: region in northern France, the scene of heavy fighting in World War I.
[4] Armentières, Laventie: communes in northern France.
[5] Ypres: town in northwestern Belgium.
[6] Hun: German.

their inability to trace, etc., something gave way within her and all sensation—save of thankfulness for the release—came to an end in blessed passivity. Michael had died and her world had stood still and she had been one with the full shock of that arrest. Now she was standing still and the world was going forward, but it did not concern her—in no way or relation did it touch her. She knew this by the ease with which she could slip Michael's name into talk and incline her head to the proper angle, at the proper murmur of sympathy.

In the blessed realisation of that relief, the Armistice with all its bells broke over her and passed unheeded. At the end of another year she had overcome her physical loathing of the living and returned young, so that she could take them by the hand and almost sincerely wish them well. She had no interest in any aftermath, national or personal, of the war, but, moving at an immense distance, she sat on various relief committees and held strong views—she heard herself delivering them—about the site of the proposed village War Memorial.

Then there came to her, as next of kin, an official intimation, backed by a page of a letter to her in indelible pencil, a silver identity-disc, and a watch, to the effect that the body of Lieutenant Michael Turrell had been found, identified, and re-interred in Hagenzeele Third Military Cemetery[7]—the letter of the row and the grave's number in that row duly given.

So Helen found herself moved on to another process of the manufacturer —to a world full of exultant or broken relatives, now strong in the certainty that there was an altar upon earth where they might lay their love. These soon told her, and by means of time-tables made clear, how easy it was and how little it interfered with life's affairs to go and see one's grave.

"So different," as the Rector's wife said, "if he'd been killed in Mesopotamia,[8] or even Gallipoli." [9]

The agony of being waked up to some sort of a second life drove Helen across the Channel, where, in a new world of abbreviated titles, she learnt that Hagenzeele Third could be comfortably reached by an afternoon train which fitted in with the morning boat, and that there was a comfortable little hotel not three kilometres from Hagenzeele itself, where one could spend quite a comfortable night and see one's grave next morning. All this she had from a Central Authority who lived in a board and tarpaper shed on the skirts of a razed city full of whirling lime-dust and blown papers.

"By the way," said he, "you know your grave, of course?"

"Yes, thank you," said Helen, and showed its row and number typed on Michael's own little typewriter. The officer would have checked it, out of one of his many books; but a large Lancashire woman thrust between them and bade him tell her where she might find her son, who had been corporal in

---

[7] Hagenzeele: locale in Belgium.

[8] Mesopotamia: part of modern Iraq.

[9] Gallipoli: port city in European Turkey.

the A.S.C. His proper name, she sobbed, was Anderson, but, coming of respectable folk, he had of course enlisted under the name of Smith; and had been killed at Dickiebush, in early 'Fifteen. She had not his number nor did she know which of his two Christian names he might have used with his alias; but her Cook's tourist ticket expired at the end of Easter week, and if by then she could not find her child she should go mad. Whereupon she fell forward on Helen's breast; but the officer's wife came out quickly from a little bedroom behind the office, and the three of them lifted the woman on to the cot.

"They are often like this," said the officer's wife, loosening the tight bonnet-strings. "Yesterday she said he'd been killed at Hooge. Are you sure you know your grave? It makes such a difference."

"Yes, thank you," said Helen, and hurried out before the woman on the bed should begin to lament again.

Tea in a crowded mauve and blue striped wooden structure, with a false front, carried her still further into the nightmare. She paid her bill beside a stolid, plain-featured Englishwoman, who, hearing her inquire about the train to Hagenzeele, volunteered to come with her.

"I'm going to Hagenzeele myself," she explained. "Not to Hagenzeele Third; mine is Sugar Factory, but they call it La Rosière now. It's just south of Hagenzeele Three. Have you got your room at the hotel there?"

"Oh yes, thank you. I've wired."

"That's better. Sometimes the place is quite full, and at others there's hardly a soul. But they've put bathrooms into the old Lion d'Or—that's the hotel on the west side of Sugar Factory—and it draws off a lot of people, luckily."

"It's all new to me. This is the first time I've been over."

"Indeed! This is my ninth time since the Armistice. Not on my own account. I haven't lost any one, thank God—but, like every one else, I've a lot of friends at home who have. Coming over as often as I do, I find it helps them to have some one just look at the—the place and tell them about it afterwards. And one can take photos for them, too. I get quite a list of commissions to execute." She laughed nervously and tapped her slung Kodak. "There are two or three to see at Sugar Factory this time, and plenty of others in the cemeteries all about. My system is to save them up, and arrange them, you know. And when I've got enough commissions for one area to make it worth while, I pop over and execute them. It *does* comfort people."

"I suppose so," Helen answered, shivering as they entered the little train.

"Of course it does. (Isn't it lucky we've got window-seats?) It must do or they wouldn't ask one to do it, would they? I've a list of quite twelve or fifteen commissions here"—she tapped the Kodak again—"I must sort them out to-night. Oh, I forgot to ask you. What's yours?"

"My nephew," said Helen. "But I was very fond of him."

"Ah, yes! I sometimes wonder whether *they* know after death? What do you think?"

"Oh, I don't—I haven't dared to think much about that sort of thing," said Helen, almost lifting her hands to keep her off.

"Perhaps that's better," the woman answered. "The sense of loss must be enough, I expect. Well, I won't worry you any more."

Helen was grateful, but when they reached the hotel Mrs. Scarsworth (they had exchanged names) insisted on dining at the same table with her, and after the meal, in the little, hideous salon full of low-voiced relatives, took Helen through her "commissions" with biographies of the dead, where she happened to know them, and sketches of their next of kin. Helen endured till nearly half-past nine, ere she fled to her room.

Almost at once there was a knock at her door and Mrs. Scarsworth entered; her hands, holding the dreadful list, clasped before her.

"Yes—yes—*I* know," she began. "You're sick of me, but I want to tell you something. You—you aren't married, are you? Then perhaps you won't ... But it doesn't matter. I've *got* to tell some one. I can't go on any longer like this."

"But please—" Mrs. Scarsworth had backed against the shut door, and her mouth worked dryly.

"In a minute," she said. "You—you know about these graves of mine I was telling you about downstairs, just now? They really *are* commissions. At least several of them are." Her eye wandered round the room. "What extraordinary wall-papers they have in Belgium, don't you think? ... Yes. I swear they are commissions. But there's *one*, d'you see, and—and he was more to me than anything else in the world. Do you understand?"

Helen nodded.

"More than any one else. And, of course, he oughtn't to have been. He ought to have been nothing to me. But he *was*. He *is*. That's why I do the commissions, you see. That's all."

"But why do you tell me?" Helen asked desperately.

"Because I'm *so* tired of lying. Tired of lying—always lying—year in and year out. When I don't tell lies I've got to act 'em and I've got to think 'em, always. *You* don't know what that means. He was everything to me that he oughtn't to have been—the one real thing—the only thing that ever happened to me in all my life; and I've had to pretend he wasn't. I've had to watch every word I said, and think out what lie I'd tell next, for years and years!"

"How many years?" Helen asked.

"Six years and four months before, and two and three-quarters after. I've gone to him eight times, since. Tomorrow'll make the ninth, and—and I can't—I *can't* go to him again with nobody in the world knowing. I want to be honest with some one before I go. Do you understand? It doesn't matter about *me*. I was never truthful, even as a girl. But it isn't worthy of *him*. So—so I—I had to tell you. I can't keep it up any longer. Oh, I can't!"

She lifted her joined hands almost to the level of her mouth, and brought them down sharply, still joined, to full arms' length below her waist. Helen reached forward, caught them, bowed her head over them, and murmured: "Oh, my dear! My dear!" Mrs. Scarsworth stepped back, her face all mottled.

"My God!" said she. "Is *that* how you take it?"

Helen could not speak, and the woman went out; but it was a long while before Helen was able to sleep.

Next morning Mrs. Scarsworth left early on her round of commissions, and Helen walked alone to Hagenzeele Third. The place was still in the making, and stood some five or six feet above the metalled road, which it flanked for hundreds of yards. Culverts across a deep ditch served for entrances through the unfinished boundary wall. She climbed a few woodenfaced earthen steps and then met the entire crowded level of the thing in one held breath. She did not know that Hagenzeele Third counted twenty-one thousand dead already. All she saw was a merciless sea of black crosses, bearing little strips of stamped tin at all angles across their faces. She could distinguish no order or arrangement in their mass; nothing but a waist-high wilderness as of weeds stricken dead, rushing at her. She went forward, moved to the left and the right hopelessly, wondering by what guidance she should ever come to her own. A great distance away there was a line of whiteness. It proved to be a block of some two or three hundred graves whose headstones had already been set, whose flowers were planted out, and whose new-sown grass showed green. Here she could see clear-cut letters at the ends of the rows, and, referring to her slip, realised that it was not here she must look.

A man knelt behind a line of headstones—evidently a gardener, for he was firming a young plant in the soft earth. She went towards him, her paper in her hand. He rose at her approach and without prelude or salutation asked: "Who are you looking for?"

"Lieutenant Michael Turrell—my nephew," said Helen slowly and word for word, as she had many thousands of times in her life.

The man lifted his eyes and looked at her with infinite compassion before he turned from the fresh-sown grass towards the naked black crosses.

"Come with me," he said, "and I will show you where your son lies."

When Helen left the Cemetery she turned for a last look. In the distance she saw the man bending over his young plants; and she went away, supposing him to be the gardener.

Virginia Woolf (1882–1941)

THE LEGACY

"For Sissy Miller." Gilbert Clandon, taking up the pearl brooch that lay among a litter of rings and brooches on a little table in his wife's drawing-room, read the inscription: "For Sissy Miller, with my love."

It was like Angela to have remembered even Sissy Miller, her secretary. Yet how strange it was, Gilbert Clandon thought once more, that she had left everything in such order—a little gift of some sort for every one of her friends. It was as if she had foreseen her death. Yet she had been in perfect health when she left the house that morning, six weeks ago; when she stepped off the kerb in Piccadilly and the car had killed her.

He was waiting for Sissy Miller. He had asked her to come; he owed her, he felt, after all the years she had been with them, this token of considera-tion. Yes, he went on, as he sat there waiting, it was strange that Angela had left everything in such order. Every friend had been left some little token of her affection. Every ring, every necklace, every little Chinese box— she had a passion for little boxes—had a name on it. And each had some memory for him. This he had given her; this—the enamel dolphin with the ruby eyes—she had pounced upon one day in a back street in Venice. He could remember her little cry of delight. To him, of course, she had left nothing in particular, unless it were her diary. Fifteen little volumes, bound in green leather, stood behind him on her writing table. Ever since they were married, she had kept a diary. Some of their very few—he could not call them quarrels, say tiffs—had been about that diary. When he came in and found her writing, she always shut it or put her hand over it. "No, no, no," he could hear her say. "After I'm dead—perhaps." So she had left it him, as her legacy. It was the only thing they had not shared when she was alive. But he had always taken it for granted that she would outlive him. If only she had stopped one moment, and had thought what she was doing, she would be alive now. But she had stepped straight off the kerb, the driver of the car had said at the inquest. She had given him no chance to pull up. . . . Here the sound of voices in the hall interrupted him.

"Miss Miller, Sir," said the maid.

She came in. He had never seen her alone in his life, nor, of course, in tears. She was terribly distressed, and no wonder. Angela had been much more to her than an employer. She had been a friend. To himself, he thought, as he pushed a chair for her and asked her to sit down, she was scarcely dis-tinguishable from any other woman of her kind. There were thousands of Sissy Millers—drab little women in black carrying attaché cases. But An-gela, with her genius for sympathy, had discovered all sorts of qualities in Sissy Miller. She was the soul of discretion; so silent; so trustworthy, one could tell her anything, and so on.

Miss Miller could not speak at first. She sat there dabbing her eyes with her pocket handkerchief. Then she made an effort.

"Pardon me, Mr. Clandon," she said.

He murmured. Of course he understood. It was only natural. He could guess what his wife had meant to her.

"I've been so happy here," she said, looking round. Her eyes rested on the writing table behind him. It was here they had worked—she and Angela. For Angela had her share of the duties that fall to the lot of a prominent politician's wife. She had been the greatest help to him in his career. He had often seen her and Sissy sitting at that table—Sissy at the typewriter, taking down letters from her dictation. No doubt Miss Miller was thinking of that, too. Now all he had to do was to give her the brooch his wife had left her. A rather incongruous gift it seemed. It might have been better to have left her a sum of money, or even the typewriter. But there it was—"For Sissy Miller, with my love." And, taking the brooch, he gave it her with the little speech that he had prepared. He knew, he said, that she would value it. His wife had often worn it. . . . And she replied, as she took it almost as if she too had prepared a speech, that it would always be a treasured possession. . . . She had, he supposed, other clothes upon which a pearl brooch would not look quite so incongruous. She was wearing the little black coat and skirt that seemed the uniform of her profession. Then he remembered—she was in mourning, of course. She, too, had had her tragedy—a brother, to whom she was devoted, had died only a week or two before Angela. In some accident was it? He could not remember—only Angela telling him. Angela, with her genius for sympathy, had been terribly upset. Meanwhile Sissy Miller had risen. She was putting on her gloves. Evidently she felt that she ought not to intrude. But he could not let her go without saying something about her future. What were her plans? Was there any way in which he could help her?

She was gazing at the table, where she had sat at her typewriter, where the diary lay. And, lost in her memories of Angela, she did not at once answer his suggestion that he should help her. She seemed for a moment not to understand. So he repeated:

"What are your plans, Miss Miller?"

"My plans? Oh, that's all right, Mr. Clandon," she exclaimed. "Please don't bother yourself about me."

He took her to mean that she was in no need of financial assistance. It would be better, he realized, to make any suggestion of that kind in a letter. All he could do now was to say as he pressed her hand, "Remember, Miss Miller, if there's any way in which I can help you, it will be a pleasure. . . ." Then he opened the door. For a moment, on the threshold, as if a sudden thought had struck her, she stopped.

"Mr. Clandon," she said, looking straight at him for the first time, and for the first time he was struck by the expression, sympathetic yet searching, in her eyes. "If at any time," she continued, "there's anything I can do to help you, remember, I shall feel it, for your wife's sake, a pleasure. . . ."

With that she was gone. Her words and the look that went with them were unexpected. It was almost as if she believed, or hoped, that he would need her. A curious, perhaps a fantastic idea occurred to him as he returned to his chair. Could it be, that during all those years when he had scarcely noticed her, she, as the novelists say, had entertained a passion for him? He caught his own reflection in the glass as he passed. He was over fifty; but he could not help admitting that he was still, as the looking-glass showed him, a very distinguished-looking man.

"Poor Sissy Miller!" he said, half laughing. How he would have liked to share that joke with his wife! He turned instinctively to her diary. "Gilbert," he read, opening it at random, "looked so wondeful. . . ." It was as if she had answered his question. Of course, she seemed to say, you're very attractive to women. Of course Sissy Miller felt that too. He read on. "How proud I am to be his wife!" And he had always been very proud to be her husband. How often, when they dined out somewhere, he had looked at her across the table and said to himself, "She is the loveliest woman here!" He read on. That first year he had been standing for Parliament. They had toured his constituency. "When Gilbert sat down the applause was terrific. The whole audience rose and sang: 'For he's a jolly good fellow.' I was quite overcome." He remembered that, too. She had been sitting on the platform beside him. He could still see the glance she cast at him, and how she had tears in her eyes. And then? He turned the pages. They had gone to Venice. He recalled that happy holiday after the election. "We had ices at Florians."[1] He smiled—she was still such a child; she loved ices. "Gilbert gave me a most interesting account of the history of Venice. He told me that the Doges[2] . . ." she had written it all out in her schoolgirl hand. One of the delights of travelling with Angela had been that she was so eager to learn. She was so terribly ignorant, she used to say, as if that were not one of her charms. And then—he opened the next volume—they had come back to London. "I was so anxious to make a good impression. I wore my wedding dress." He could see her now sitting next old Sir Edward; and making a conquest of that formidable old man, his chief. He read on rapidly, filling in scene after scene from her scrappy fragments. "Dined at the House of Commons. . . . To an evening party at the Lovegroves'. Did I realize my responsibility, Lady L. asked me, as Gilbert's wife?" Then, as the years passed—he took another volume from the writing table—he had become more and more absorbed in his work. And she, of course, was more often home. . . . It had been a great grief to her, apparently, that they had had no children. "How I wish," one entry read, "that Gilbert had a son!" Oddly enough he had never much regretted that himself. Life had been so full, so

[1] Florians: a very fashionable and elegant café in Venice.
[2] Doges: highest-ranking public officials in the former republic of Venice.

rich as it was. That year he had been given a minor post in the government. A minor post only, but her comment was: "I am quite certain now that he will be Prime Minister!" Well, if things had gone differently, it might have been so. He paused here to speculate upon what might have been. Politics was a gamble, he reflected; but the game wasn't over yet. Not at fifty. He cast his eyes rapidly over more pages, full of the little trifles, the insignificant, happy, daily trifles that had made up her life.

He took up another volume and opened it at random. "What a coward I am! I let the chance slip again. But it seemed selfish to bother him with my own affairs, when he had so much to think about. And we so seldom have an evening alone." What was the meaning of that? Oh, here was the explanation—it referred to her work in the East End. "I plucked up courage and talked to Gilbert at last. He was so kind, so good. He made no objection." He remembered that conversation. She had told him that she felt so idle, so useless. She wished to have some work of her own. She wanted to do something—she had blushed so prettily, he remembered, as she said it, sitting in that very chair—to help others. He had bantered her a little. Hadn't she enough to do looking after him, after her home? Still, if it amused her, of course he had no objection. What was it? Some district? Some committee? Only she must promise not to make herself ill. So it seemed that every Wednesday she went to Whitechapel. He remembered how he hated the clothes she wore on those occasions. But she had taken it very seriously, it seemed. The diary was full of references like this: "Saw Mrs. Jones. . . . She has ten children. . . . Husband lost his arm in an accident. . . . Did my best to find a job for Lily." He skipped on. His own name occurred less frequently. His interest slackened. Some of the entries conveyed nothing to him. For example: "Had a heated argument about socialism with B. M." Who was B. M.? He could not fill in the initials; some woman, he supposed, that she had met on one of her committees. "B. M. made a violent attack upon the upper classes. . . . I walked back after the meeting with B. M. and tried to convince him. But he is so narrow-minded." So B. M. was a man— no doubt one of those "intellectuals," as they call themselves, who are so violent, as Angela said, and so narrow-minded. She had invited him to come and see her apparently. "B. M. came to dinner. He shook hands with Minnie!" That note of exclamation gave another twist to his mental picture. B. M., it seemed, wasn't used to parlourmaids; he had shaken hands with Minnie. Presumably he was one of those tame working men who air their views in ladies' drawing-rooms. Gilbert knew the type, and had no liking for this particular specimen, whoever B. M. might be. Here he was again. "Went with B. M. to the Tower of London. . . . He said revolution is bound to come. . . . He said we live in a Fool's Paradise." That was just the kind of thing B. M. would say—Gilbert could hear him. He could also see him quite distinctly—a stubby little man, with a rough beard, red tie, dressed as they always did in tweeds, who had never done an honest day's work in his life.

Surely Angela had the sense to see through him? He read on. "B. M. said some very disagreeable things about ——." The name was carefully scratched out. "I told him I would not listen to any more abuse of ——" Again the name was obliterated. Could it have been his own name? Was that why Angela covered the page so quickly when he came in? The thought added to his growing dislike of B. M. He had had the impertinence to discuss him in this very room. Why had Angela never told him? It was very unlike her to conceal anything; she had been the soul of candour. He turned the pages, picking out every reference to B. M. "B. M. told me the story of his childhood. His mother went out charring. . . . When I think of it, I can hardly bear to go on living in such luxury. . . . Three guineas for one hat!" If only she had discussed the matter with him, instead of puzzling her poor little head about questions that were much too difficult for her to understand! He had lent her books. *Karl Marx, The Coming Revolution.* The initials B. M., B. M., B. M., recurred repeatedly. But why never the full name? There was an informality, an intimacy in the use of initials that was very unlike Angela. Had she called him B. M. to his face? He read on. "B. M. came unexpectedly after dinner. Luckily, I was alone." That was only a year ago. "Luckily"—why luckily?—"I was alone." Where had he been that night? He checked the date in his engagement book. It had been the night of the Mansion House dinner. And B. M. and Angela had spent the evening alone! He tried to recall that evening. Was she waiting up for him when he came back? Had the room looked just as usual? Were there glasses on the table? Were the chairs drawn close together? He could remember nothing —nothing whatever, nothing except his own speech at the Mansion House dinner. It became more and more inexplicable to him—the whole situation: his wife receiving an unknown man alone. Perhaps the next volume would explain. Hastily he reached for the last of the diaries—the one she had left unfinished when she died. There, on the very first page, was that cursed fellow again. "Dined alone with B. M. . . . He became very agitated. He said it was time we understood each other. . . . I tried to make him listen. But he would not. He threatened that if I did not . . ." the rest of the page was scored over. She had written "Egypt. Egypt. Egypt," over the whole page. He could not make out a single word; but there could be only one interpretation: the scoundrel had asked her to become his mistress. Alone in his room! The blood rushed to Gilbert Clandon's face. He turned the pages rapidly. What had been her answer? Initials had ceased. It was simply "he" now. "He came again. I told him I could not come to any decision. . . . I implored him to leave me." He had forced himself upon her in this very house. But why hadn't she told him? How could she have hesitated for an instant? Then: "I wrote him a letter." Then pages were left blank. Then there was this: "No answer to my letter." Then more blank pages; and then this: "He has done what he threatened." After that—what came after that? He turned page after page. All were blank. But there, on the very day before her death, was this entry: "Have I the courage to do it too?" That was the end.

Gilbert Clandon let the book slide to the floor. He could see her in front of him. She was standing on the kerb in Piccadilly. Her eyes stared; her fists were clenched. Here came the car. . . .

He could not bear it. He must know the truth. He strode to the telephone.

"Miss Miller!" There was silence. Then he heard someone moving in the room.

"Sissy Miller speaking"—her voice at last answered him.

"Who," he thundered, "is B. M.?"

He could hear the cheap clock ticking on her mantelpiece; then a long drawn sigh. Then at last she said:

"He was my brother."

He *was* her brother; her brother who had killed himself. "Is there," he heard Sissy Miller asking, "anything that I can explain?"

"Nothing!" he cried. "Nothing!"

He had received his legacy. She had told him the truth. She had stepped off the kerb to rejoin her lover. She had stepped off the kerb to escape from him.

Eudora Welty (1909–   )

A WORN PATH

It was December—a bright frozen day in the early morning. Far out in the country there was an old Negro woman with her head tied in a red rag, coming along a path through the pinewoods. Her name was Phoenix Jackson. She was very old and small and she walked slowly in the dark pine shadows, moving a little from side to side in her steps, with the balanced heaviness and lightness of a pendulum in a grandfather clock. She carried a thin, small cane made from an umbrella, and with this she kept tapping the frozen earth in front of her. This made a grave and persistent noise in the still air, that seemed meditative, like the chirping of a solitary little bird.

She wore a dark striped dress reaching down to her shoetops, and an equally long apron of bleached sugar sacks, with a full pocket; all neat and tidy, but every time she took a step she might have fallen over her shoelaces, which dragged from her unlaced shoes. She looked straight ahead. Her eyes were blue with age. Her skin had a pattern all its own of numberless branching wrinkles and as though a whole little tree stood in the middle of her forehead, but a golden color run underneath, and the two knobs of her cheeks were illuminated by a yellow burning under the dark. Under the red rag her hair came down on her neck in the frailest of ringlets, still black, and with an odor like copper.

Now and then there was a quivering in the thicket. Old Phoenix said,

"Out of my way, all you foxes, owls, beetles, jack rabbits, coons, and wild animals! . . . Keep out from under these feet, little bobwhites. . . . Keep the big wild hogs out of my path. Don't let none of those come running my direction. I got a long way." Under her small black-freckled hand her cane, limber as a buggy whip, would switch at the brush as if to rouse up any hiding things.

On she went. The woods were deep and still. The sun made the pine needles almost too bright to look at, up where the wind rocked. The cones dropped as light as feathers. Down in the hollow was the mourning dove—it was not too late for him.

The path ran up a hill. "Seem like there is chains about my feet, time I get this far," she said, in the voice of argument old people keep to use with themselves. "Something always take a hold on this hill—pleads I should stay."

After she got to the top she turned and gave a full, severe look behind her where she had come. "Up through pines," she said at length. "Now down through oaks."

Her eyes opened their widest and she started down gently. But before she got to the bottom of the hill a bush caught her dress.

Her fingers were busy and intent, but her skirts were full and long, so that before she could pull them free in one place they were caught in another. It was not possible to allow the dress to tear. "I in the thorny bush," she said. "Thorns, you doing your appointed work. Never want to let folks pass—no sir. Old eyes thought you was a pretty little green bush."

Finally, trembling all over, she stood free, and after a moment dared to stoop for her cane.

"Sun so high!" she cried, leaning back and looking, while the thick tears went over her eyes. "The time getting all gone here."

At the foot of this hill was a place where a log was laid across the creek.

"Now comes the trial," said Phoenix.

Putting her right foot out, she mounted the log and shut her eyes. Lifting her skirt, levelling her cane fiercely before her, like a festival figure in some parade, she began to march across. Then she opened her eyes and she was safe on the other side.

"I wasn't as old as I thought," she said.

But she sat down to rest. She spread her skirts on the bank around her and folded her hands over her knees. Up above her was a tree in a pearly cloud of mistletoe. She did not dare to close her eyes, and when a little boy brought her a little plate with a slice of marble-cake on it she spoke to him. "That would be acceptable," she said. But when she went to take it there was just her own hand in the air.

So she left that tree, and had to go through a barbed-wire fence. There she had to creep and crawl, spreading her knees and stretching her fingers like a baby trying to climb the steps. But she talked loudly to herself: she could not let her dress be torn now, so late in the day, and she could not pay for having her arm or her leg sawed off if she got caught fast where she was.

At last she was safe through the fence and risen up out in the clearing. Big dead trees, like black men with one arm, were standing in the purple stalks of the withered cotton field. There sat a buzzard.

"Who you watching?"

In the furrow she made her way along.

"Glad this not the season for bulls," she said, looking sideways, "and the good Lord made his snakes to curl up and sleep in the winter. A pleasure I don't see no two-headed snake coming around that tree, where it come once. It took a while to get by him, back in the summer."

She passed through the old cotton and went into a field of dead corn. It whispered and shook, and was taller than her head. "Through the maze now," she said, for there was no path.

Then there was something tall, black and skinny there, moving before her.

At first she took it for a man. It could have been a man dancing in the field. But she stood still and listened, and it did not make a sound. It was as silent as a ghost.

"Ghost," she said sharply, "who be you the ghost of? For I have heard of nary death close by."

But there was no answer, only the ragged dancing in the wind.

She shut her eyes, reached out her hand, and touched a sleeve. She found a coat and inside that an emptiness, cold as ice.

"You scarecrow," she said. Her face lighted. "I ought to be shut up for good," she said with laughter. "My senses is gone. I too old. I the oldest people I ever know. Dance, old scarecrow," she said, "while I dancing with you."

She kicked her foot over the furrow, and with mouth drawn down shook her head once or twice in a little strutting way. Some husks blew down and whirled in streamers about her skirts.

Then she went on, parting her way from side to side with the cane, through the whispering field. At last she came to the end, to a wagon track, where the silver grass blew between the red ruts. The quail were walking around like pullets, seeming all dainty and unseen.

"Walk pretty," she said. "This the easy place. This the easy going."

She followed the track, swaying through the quiet bare fields, through the little strings of trees silver in their dead leaves, past cabins silver from weather, with the doors and windows boarded shut, all like old women under a spell sitting there. "I walking in their sleep," she said, nodding her head vigorously.

In a ravine she went where a spring was silently flowing through a hollow log. Old Phoenix bent and drank. "Sweetgum makes the water sweet," she said, and drank more. "Nobody know who made this well, for it was here when I was born."

The track crossed a swampy part where the moss hung as white as lace from every limb. "Sleep on, alligators, and blow your bubbles." Then the track went into the road.

Deep, deep the road went down between the high green-colored banks. Overhead the live-oaks met, and it was as dark as a cave.

A black dog with a lolling tongue came up out of the weeds by the ditch. She was meditating, and not ready, and when he came at her she only hit him a little with her cane. Over she went in the ditch, like a little puff of milkweed.

Down there, her senses drifted away. A dream visited her, and she reached her hand up, but nothing reached down and gave her a pull. So she lay there and presently went to talking. "Old woman," she said to herself, "that black dog came up out of the weeds to stall you off, and now there he sitting on his fine tail, smiling at you."

A white man finally came along and found her—a hunter, a young man, with his dog on a chain.

"Well, Granny!" he laughed. "What are you doing there?"

"Lying on my back like a June-bug waiting to be turned over, mister," she said, reaching up her hand.

He lifted her up, gave her a swing in the air, and set her down. "Anything broken, Granny?"

"No sir, them old dead weeds is springy enough," said Phoenix, when she had got her breath. "I thank you for your trouble."

"Where do you live, Granny?" he asked, while the two dogs were growling at each other.

"Away back yonder, sir, behind the ridge. You can't even see it from here."

"On your way home?"

"No, sir, I going to town."

"Why, that's too far! That's as far as I walk when I come out myself, and I get something for my trouble." He patted the stuffed bag he carried, and there hung down a little closed claw. It was one of the bobwhites, with its beak hooked bitterly to show it was dead. "Now you go on home, Granny!"

"I bound to go to town, mister," said Phoenix. "The time come around."

He gave another laugh, filling the whole landscape. "I know you colored people! Wouldn't miss going to town to see Santa Claus!"

But something held Old Phoenix very still. The deep lines in her face went into a fierce and different radiation. Without warning she had seen with her own eyes a flashing nickel fall out of the man's pocket on to the ground.

"How old are you, Granny?" he was saying.

"There is no telling, mister," she said, "no telling."

Then she gave a little cry and clapped her hands, and said, "Git on away from here, dog! Look! Look at that dog!" She laughed as if in admiration. "He ain't scared of nobody. He a big black dog." She whispered, "Sick him!"

"Watch me get rid of that cur," said the man. "Sick him, Pete! Sick him!"

Phoenix heard the dogs fighting and heard the man running and throwing sticks. She even heard a gunshot. But she was slowly bending forward by that time, further and further forward, the lids stretched down over her eyes, as if she were doing this in her sleep. Her chin was lowered almost to her knees. The yellow palm of her hand came out from the fold of her apron. Her fingers slid down and along the ground under the piece of money with the grace and care they would have in lifting an egg from under a sitting hen. Then she slowly straightened up, she stood erect, and the nickel was in her apron pocket. A bird flew by. Her lips moved, "God watching me the whole time. I come to stealing."

The man came back, and his own dog panted about them. "Well, I scared him off that time," he said, and then he laughed and lifted his gun and pointed it at Phoenix.

She stood straight and faced him.

"Doesn't the gun scare you?" he said, still pointing it.

"No, sir. I seen plenty go off closer by, in my day, and for less than what I done," she said, holding utterly still.

He smiled, and shouldered the gun. "Well, Granny," he said, "you must be a hundred years old, and scared of nothing. I'd give you a dime if I had any money with me. But you take my advice and stay home, and nothing will happen to you."

"I bound to go on my way, mister," said Phoenix. She inclined her head in the red rag. Then they went in different directions, but she could hear the gun shooting again and again over the hill.

She walked on. The shadows hung from the oak trees to the road like curtains. Then she smelled wood-smoke, and smelled the river, and she saw a steeple and the cabins on their steep steps. Dozens of little black children whirled around her. There ahead was Natchez shining. Bells were ringing. She walked on.

In the paved city it was Christmas time. There were red and green electric lights strung and crisscrossed everywhere, and all turned on in the daytime. Old Phoenix would have been lost if she had not distrusted her eyesight and depended on her feet to know where to take her.

She paused quietly on the sidewalk, where people were passing by. A lady came along in the crowd, carrying an armful of red-, green-, and silver-wrapped presents; she gave off perfume like the red roses in hot summer, and Phoenix stopped her.

"Please, missy, will you lace up my shoe?" She held up her foot.

"What do you want, Grandma?"

"See my shoe," said Phoenix. "Do all right for out in the country, but wouldn't look right to go in a big building."

"Stand still then, Grandma," said the lady. She put her packages down carefully on the sidewalk beside her and laced and tied both shoes tightly.

"Can't lace 'em with a cane," said Phoenix. "Thank you, missy. I doesn't mind asking a nice lady to tie up my shoe when I gets out on the street."

Moving slowly and from side to side, she went into the stone building and into a tower of steps, where she walked up and around and around until her feet knew to stop.

She entered a door, and there she saw nailed up on the wall the document that had been stamped with a gold seal and framed in the gold frame which matched the dream that was hung up in her head.

"Here I be," she said. There was a fixed and ceremonial stiffness over her body.

"A charity case, I suppose," said an attendant who sat at the desk before her.

But Phoenix only looked above her head. There was sweat on her face; the wrinkles shone like a bright net.

"Speak up, Grandma," the woman said. "What's your name? We must have your history, you know. Have you been here before? What seems to be the trouble with you?"

Old Phoenix only gave a twitch to her face as if a fly were bothering her.

"Are you deaf?" cried the attendant.

But then the nurse came in.

"Oh, that's just old Aunt Phoenix," she said. "She doesn't come for herself—she has a little grandson. She makes these trips just as regular as clockwork. She lives away back off the Old Natchez Trace." She bent down. "Well, Aunt Phoenix, why don't you just take a seat? We won't keep you standing after your long trip." She pointed.

The old woman sat down, bolt upright in the chair.

"Now, how is the boy?" asked the nurse.

Old Phoenix did not speak.

"I said, how is the boy?"

But Phoenix only waited and stared straight ahead, her face very solemn and withdrawn into rigidity.

"Is his throat any better?" asked the nurse. "Aunt Phoenix, don't you hear me? Is your grandson's throat any better since the last time you came for the medicine?"

With her hand on her knees, the old woman waited, silent, erect and motionless, just as if she were in armour.

"You mustn't take up our time this way, Aunt Phoenix," the nurse said. "Tell us quickly about your grandson, and get it over. He isn't dead, is he?"

At last there came a flicker and then a flame of comprehension across her face, and she spoke.

"My grandson. It was my memory had left me. There I sat and forgot why I made my long trip."

"Forgot?" The nurse frowned. "After you came so far?"

Then Phoenix was like an old woman begging a dignified forgiveness for waking up frightened in the night. "I never did go to school—I was too old at the Surrender," she said in a soft voice. "I'm an old woman without an education. It was my memory fail me. My little grandson, he is just the same, and I forgot it in the coming."

"Throat never heals, does it?" said the nurse, speaking in a loud, sure voice to Old Phoenix. By now she had a card with something written on it, a little list. "Yes. Swallowed lye. When was it—January—two—three years ago—"

Phoenix spoke unasked now. "No, missy, he not dead, he just the same. Every little while his throat begin to close up again, and he not able to swallow. He not get his breath. He not able to help himself. So the time come around, and I go on another trip for the soothing-medicine."

"All right. The doctor said as long as you came to get it you could have it," said the nurse. "But it's an obstinate case."

"My little grandson, he sit up there in the house all wrapped up, waiting by himself," Phoenix went on. "We is the only two left in the world. He suffer and it don't seem to put him back at all. He got a sweet look. He going to last. He wear a little patch quilt and peep out, holding his mouth open like a little bird. I remembers so plain now, I not going to forget him again, no, the whole enduring time. I could tell him from all the others in creation."

"All right." The nurse was trying to hush her now. She brought her a bottle of medicine. "Charity," she said, making a check mark in a book.

Old Phoenix held the bottle close to her eyes and then carefully put it into her pocket.

"I thank you," she said.

"It's Christmas time, Grandma," said the attendant. "Could I give you a few pennies out of my purse?"

"Five pennies is a nickel," said Phoenix stiffly.

"Here's a nickel," said the attendant.

Phoenix rose carefully and held out her hand. She received the nickel and then fished the other nickel out of her pocket and laid it beside the new one. She stared at her palm closely, with her head on one side.

Then she gave a tap with her cane on the floor.

"This is what come to me to do," she said. "I going to the store and buy my child a little windmill they sells, made out of paper. He going to find it hard to believe there such a thing in the world. I'll march myself back where he waiting, holding it straight up in this hand."

She lifted her free hand, gave a little nod, turned round, and walked out of the doctor's office. Then her slow step began on the stairs, going down.

READING SELECTIONS: POEMS

Edgar Lee Masters (1869–1950)

FIDDLER JONES

The earth keeps some vibration going
There in your heart, and that is you.
And if the people find you can fiddle,
Why, fiddle you must, for all your life.
What do you see, a harvest of clover?   5
Or a meadow to walk through to the river?
The wind's in the corn; you rub your hands
For beeves hereafter ready for market;
Or else you hear the rustle of skirts
Like the girls when dancing at Little Grove.   10
To Cooney Potter a pillar of dust
Or whirling leaves meant ruinous drouth;
They looked to me like Red-Head Sammy
Stepping it off, to "Toor-a-Loor."
How could I till my forty acres   15
Not to speak of getting more,
With a medley of horns, bassoons and piccolos
Stirred in my brain by crows and robins
And the creak of a wind-mill—only these?
And I never started to plow in my life   20
That some one did not stop in the road
And take me away to a dance or picnic.
I ended up with forty acres;
I ended up with a broken fiddle—
And a broken laugh, and a thousand memories,   25
And not a single regret.

8. beeves: beef cattle.

STUDY QUESTIONS

1. Define the narrative point of view of the poem.
2. Jones establishes a series of contrasting attitudes in lines 5–12. What is the purpose of these comparisons? What do they reveal about Jones's character?
3. The narrator blames his failure at farming on the fact that people always

called him away from work to fiddle for a dance or picnic. On what personal trait does he also blame this failure?

4. What is the relationship between the statement made in the first two lines of the poem and the final statement?

Edgar Lee Masters (1869–1950)

EUGENE CARMAN

Rhodes' slave! Selling shoes and gingham,
Flour and bacon, overalls, clothing, all day long
For fourteen hours a day for three hundred and thirteen days
For more than twenty years,
Saying "Yes'm" and "Yes, sir" and "Thank you"   5
A thousand times a day, and all for fifty dollars a month.
Living in this stinking room in the rattle-trap "Commercial."
And compelled to go to Sunday School, and to listen
To the Rev. Abner Peet one hundred and four times a year
For more than an hour at a time,   10
Because Thomas Rhodes ran the church
As well as the store and the bank.
So while I was tying my neck-tie that morning
I suddenly saw myself in the glass:
My hair all gray, my face like a sodden pie.   15
So I cursed and cursed: You damned old thing!
You cowardly dog! You rotten pauper!
You Rhodes' slave! Till Roger Baughman
Thought I was having a fight with some one,
And looked through the transom just in time   20
To see me fall on the floor in a heap
From a broken vein in my head.

STUDY QUESTIONS

1. Although Eugene Carman is the narrator, you learn a good deal about the character of Mr. Rhodes as well. What biographical facts are you given? What character traits are revealed? Identify each as mental, moral, or emotional.
2. Explain the relationship between Rhodes and Carman. What is the effect of that relationship on Carman?
3. What does Carman's long servitude to Rhodes tell the reader about Carman's character?
4. What does his final act tell the reader about Carman's character?

Derek Mahon (1941–   )

MY WICKED UNCLE

It was my first funeral.
Some loss of status as a nephew since
Dictates that I recall
My numbness, my grandfather's hesitance,
My five aunts busy in the hall.   5

I found him closeted with living souls—
Coffined to perfection in the bedroom.
Death had deprived him of his mustache,
His thick horn-rimmed spectacles,
The easy corners of his salesman dash   10
(Those things by which I had remembered him)
And sundered him behind unnatural gauze.
His hair was badly parted on the right
As if for Sunday school. That night
I saw my uncle as he really was.   15

The narrative he dispensed was mostly
Wicked avuncular fantasy—
He went in for waistcoats and haircream.
But something about him
Demanded that you picture the surprise   20
Of the chairman of the board, when to
'What will you have with your whiskey?' my uncle replies—
'Another whiskey, please.'

Once he was jailed in New York
Twice on the same day—   25
The crookedest chief steward in the Head Line.
And once (he affected communism)
He brought the whole crew out on strike
In protest at the loss of a day's pay
Crossing the international date line.   30

They buried him slowly above the sea,
The young Presbyterian minister
Rumpled and windy in the sea air.
A most absorbing ceremony—
Ashes to ashes, dust to dust.   35
I saw sheep huddled in the long wet grass

---

17. avuncular: appropriate for an uncle.

Of the golf-course, and the empty freighters
Sailing for ever down Belfast Lough

In a fine rain, their sirens going,
As the gradual graph of my uncle's life and   40
Times dipped precipitately
Into the bowels of Carnmoney Cemetery.

His teenage kids are growing horns and claws—
More wicked already than ever my uncle was.

STUDY QUESTIONS

1. In what specific ways was the uncle "wicked"? How does the wickedness of his teenage children differ from his?
2. Why are the events in the poem told by "a nephew" instead of by an external narrator?
3. Explain "That night / I saw my uncle as he really was" (lines 14–15).

Edward Field (1924–   )

UNWANTED

The poster with my picture on it
Is hanging on the bulletin board in the Post Office.

I stand by it hoping to be recognized
Posing first full face and then profile

But everybody passes by and I have to admit   5
The photograph was taken some years ago.

I was unwanted then and I'm unwanted now
Ah guess ah'll go up echo mountain and crah.

I wish someone would find my fingerprints somewhere
Maybe on a corpse and say, You're it.   10

Description: Male, or reasonably so
White, but not lily-white and usually deep-red

Thirty-fivish, and looks it lately
Five-feet-nine and one-hundred-thirty pounds: no physique

Black hair going gray, hairline receding fast   15
What used to be curly, now fuzzy

Brown eyes starey under beetling brow
Mole on chin, probably will become a wen

It is perfectly obvious that he was not popular at school
No good at baseball, and wet his bed.   20

His aliases tell his story: Dumbell, Good-for-nothing,
Jewboy, Fieldinsky, Skinny, Fierce Face, Greaseball, Sissy.

Warning: This man is not dangerous, answers to any name
Responds to love, don't call him or he will come.

STUDY QUESTIONS

1. What parts of this poem are intended to be taken literally? What parts
   represent a fantasy on the part of the speaker?
2. What are the speaker's attitudes toward himself? What traits of character are implied by those attitudes?
3. If the contents of this poem were told by an acquaintance of the speaker,
   how would they be changed?

Don L. Lee (1942–   )

BIG MOMMA

finally retired   pensionless
from cleaning somebody else's house
she remained home to clean
the one she didn't own.

in her kitchen where we often talked   5
the *chicago tribune* served as a tablecloth
for the two cups of tomato soup that went
along with my weekly visit & talkingto.

she was in a seriously-funny mood
& from the get-go she was down, realdown: 10

    roaches around here are like
    letters on a newspaper
    or
    u gonta be a writer, hunh
    when u gone write me some writen   15
    or

the way niggers act around here
if talk cd kill we'd all be dead.

she's somewhat confused about all this *blackness*
but said that it's good when negroes start putting themselves 20
first and added: we've always shopped at the colored stores,
        & the way niggers cut each other up round
        here every weekend that whiteman don't
         haveta
        worry bout no revolution specially when he's
        gonta haveta pay for it too, anyhow all he's 25
        gotta do is drop a truck load of *dope* out
         there
        on 43rd st. & all the niggers & yr
         revolutionaries
        be too busy getten high & then they'll turn
         round
        and fight each other over who got the
         mostest.
we finished our soup and i moved to excuse myself, 30
as we walked to the front door she made a last comment:
        now *luther* i knows you done changed a lots but if
        you can think back, we never did eat too much pork
        round here anyways, it was bad for the belly.
i shared her smile and agreed. 35

touching the snow lightly i headed for 43rd st.
at the corner i saw a brother crying   while
trying to hold up a lamp post,
thru his watery eyes i cd see big momma's words.

at sixty-eight 40
she moves freely, is often right
and when there is food
eats   joyously with her own
real teeth.

STUDY QUESTIONS

1. List the biographical information that the poem gives about "Big Momma."
2. What are her attitudes toward the younger generation of blacks? What traits of character are implied by her life and her present philosophy?

3. Who is the speaker of the poem? Although he disagrees with "Big Momma" in many ways, he appears to respect her character and values. Why?

Robert Hayden (1913–1980)

THE WHIPPING

The old woman across the way
    is whipping the boy again
and shouting to the neighborhood
    her goodness and his wrongs.

Wildly he crashes through elephant ears,   5
    pleads in dusty zinnias,
while she in spite of crippling fat
    pursues and corners him.

She strikes and strikes the shrilly circling
    boy till the stick breaks   10
in her hand. His tears are rainy weather
    to woundlike memories:

My head gripped in bony vise
    of knees, the writhing struggle
to wrench free, the blows, the fear   15
    worse than blows that hateful

Words could bring, the face that I
    no longer knew or loved . . .
Well, it is over now, it is over,
    and the boy sobs in his room,   20

And the woman leans muttering against
    a tree, exhausted, purged—
avenged in part for lifelong hidings
    she has had to bear.

STUDY QUESTIONS

1. What is the narrative point of view? How does the speaker of the poem react to the actions of the woman and the boy?
2. Why does the woman whip the boy "again"? What past experiences and what present traits influence her behavior?

William Wordsworth (1770–1850)

LUCY GRAY
OR, SOLITUDE

Oft I had heard of Lucy Gray:
And, when I crossed the wild,
I chanced to see, at break of day,
The solitary child.

No mate, no comrade Lucy knew;   5
She dwelt on a wide moor,—
The sweetest thing that ever grew
Beside a human door!

You yet may spy the fawn at play,
The hare upon the green;   10
But the sweet face of Lucy Gray
Will never more be seen.

"To-night will be a stormy night,—
You to the town must go;
And take a lantern, Child, to light   15
Your mother through the snow."

"That, Father! will I gladly do:
'Tis scarcely afternoon,—
The minster-clock has just struck two,
And yonder is the moon!"   20

At this the father raised his hook,
And snapped a fagot-band;
He plied his work,—and Lucy took
The lantern in her hand.

Not blither is the mountain roe: 25
With many a wanton stroke
Her feet disperse the powdery snow,
That rises up like smoke.

The storm came on before its time:
She wandered up and down;   30
And many a hill did Lucy climb:
But never reached the town.

19. minster: church.   22. fagot-band: cord binding a bundle of sticks.

The wretched parents all that night
Went shouting far and wide;
But there was neither sound nor sight   35
To serve them for a guide.

At daybreak on the hill they stood
That overlooked the moor;
And thence they saw the bridge of wood,
A furlong from their door.   40

They wept,—and, turning homeward, cried,
"In heaven we all shall meet!"—
When in the snow the mother spied
The print of Lucy's feet.

Then downwards from the steep hill's edge   45
They tracked the footmarks small;
And through the broken hawthorn-hedge,
And by the long stone wall;

And then an open field they crossed:
The marks were still the same;   50
They tracked them on, nor ever lost;
And to the bridge they came.

They followed from the snowy bank
Those footmarks, one by one,
Into the middle of the plank;   55
And further there were none!

—Yet some maintain that to this day
She is a living child;
That you may see sweet Lucy Gray
Upon the lonesome wild.   60

O'er rough and smooth she trips along,
And never looks behind;
And sings a solitary song
That whistles in the wind.

STUDY QUESTIONS

1. Briefly summarize the action described in the poem.
2. How much information are you given about Lucy? Quote words or
   phrases that provide that information. Is the information simply biographical?

3. Who is the speaker of the poem? Why does he tell the story of Lucy? Does his telling her story relate to her character in any way? Does her character relate to the meaning of the poem? Explain your response and support it with references to the poem.

Edwin Arlington Robinson (1869–1935)

AARON STARK

Withal a meagre man was Aaron Stark,
Cursed and unkempt, shrewd, shrivelled, and morose.
A miser was he, with a miser's nose,
And eyes like little dollars in the dark.
His thin, pinched mouth was nothing but a mark;   5
And when he spoke there came like sullen blows
Through scattered fangs a few snarled words and close,
As if a cur were chary of its bark.

Glad for the murmur of his hard renown,
Year after year he shambled through the town,   10
A loveless exile moving with a staff;
And oftentimes there crept into his ears
A sound of alien pity, touched with tears,—
And then (and only then) did Aaron laugh.

1. meagre: thin.   8. chary: sorrowful.

STUDY QUESTIONS

1. The narrator explicitly mentions several traits of Stark's character. List as many as you can.
2. Why are Stark's teeth described as "scattered fangs" and his speech compared to barking of a "cur"?
3. Exactly what is it that makes Stark "glad"? At what does he laugh? What trait or traits, in addition to those explicitly mentioned by the narrator, do the last six lines of the poem suggest?

John Crowe Ransom (1888–   )

BELLS FOR JOHN WHITESIDE'S DAUGHTER

There was such speed in her little body,
And such lightness in her footfall,

It is no wonder her brown study
Astonishes us all.

Her wars were bruited in our high window.   5
We looked among orchard trees and beyond
Where she took arms against her shadow,
Or harried unto the pond

The lazy geese, like a snow cloud
Dripping their snow on the green grass,   10
Tricking and stopping, sleepy and proud,
Who cried in goose, Alas,

For the tireless heart within the little
Lady with rod that made them rise
From their noon apple-dreams and scuttle   15
Goose-fashion under the skies!

But now go the bells, and we are ready,
In one house we are sternly stopped
To say we are vexed at her brown study,
Lying so primly propped.   20

3. brown study: a state of deep meditation, reverie.   5. bruited: discussed.

STUDY QUESTIONS

1. What has happened to John Whiteside's daughter? Why are there bells? Why does the narrator say all are astonished and "vexed"? What is meant by saying she is "Lying so primly propped"?
2. *Brown study* is an old familiar expression referring to a deeply pensive or introspective mood. Which of the daughter's character traits make a "brown study" astonishing?
3. Why is the poem spoken by an anonymous outsider? How would it differ if John Whiteside himself were the narrator?

Robert Browning (1812–1889)

SOLILOQUY OF THE SPANISH CLOISTER

Gr-r-r—there go, my heart's abhorrence!
    Water your damned flower-pots, do!
If hate killed men, Brother Lawrence,
    God's blood, would not mine kill you!

What? your myrtle-bush wants trimming?   5
  Oh, that rose has prior claims—
Needs its leaden vase filled brimming?
  Hell dry you up with its flames!

At the meal we sit together:
  Salve tibi! I must hear   10
Wise talk of the kind of weather,
  Sort of season, time of year:
Not a plenteous cork-crop: scarcely
  Dare we hope oak-galls, I doubt:
What's the Latin name for "parsley"?   15
  What's the Greek name for Swine's Snout?

Whew! We'll have our platter burnished,
  Laid with care on our own shelf!
With a fire-new spoon we're furnished,
  And a goblet for ourself,   20
Rinsed like something sacrificial
  Ere 'tis fit to touch our chaps—
Marked with L for our initial!
  He-he! There his lily snaps!

Saint, forsooth! While brown Dolores   25
  Squats outside the Convent bank
With Sanchicha, telling stories,
  Steeping tresses in the tank,
Blue-black, lustrous, thick like horsehairs,
  —Can't I see his dead eye glow,   30
Bright as 'twere a Barbary corsair's?
  (That is, if he'd let it show!)

When he finishes refection,
  Knife and fork he never lays
Cross-wise, to my recollection,   35
  As do I, in Jesu's praise.
I the Trinity illustrate,
  Drinking watered orange-pulp—
In three sips the Arian frustrate;
  While he drains his at one gulp.   40

Oh, those melons! If he's able
  We're to have a feast! so nice!

10. *Salve tibi!*: "Hail to thee!"   14. oak-galls: growths on oak trees used in tanning
leather.   22. chaps: jaws.   31. Barbary corsair: pirate on the Barbary Coast, Africa.
33. refection: dinner.   39. Arian: follower of Arius, who denied the Trinity.

One goes to the Abbot's table,
   All of us get each a slice.
How go on your flowers? None double?   45
   Not one fruit-sort can you spy?
Strange!—And I, too, at such trouble
   Keep them close-nipped on the sly!

There's a great text in Galatians,
   Once you trip on it, entails   50
Twenty-nine distinct damnations,
   One sure, if another fails:
If I trip him just a-dying,
   Sure of heaven as sure can be,
Spin him round and send him flying   55
   Off to hell, a Manichee?

Or, my scrofulous French novel
   On gray paper with blunt type!
Simply glance at it, you grovel
   Hand and feet in Belial's gripe: 60
If I double down its pages
   At the woeful sixteenth print,
When he gathers his greengages,
   Ope a sieve and slip it in't?

Or, there's Satan!—one might venture   65
   Pledge one's soul to him, yet leave
Such a flaw in the indenture
   As he'd miss till, past retrieve,
Blasted lay that rose-acacia
   We're so proud of! *Hy, Zy, Hine* . . .   70
'St, there's Vespers! *Plena gratiâ,*
   Ave, Virgo! Gr-r-r—you swine!

56. Manichee: heretic.   71. *Plena gratiâ*: full of grace.   72. *Ave, Virgo!*: "Hail, Virgin!"

STUDY QUESTIONS

1. Define the narrative point of view of this poem. Is the speaker the principal character, or is Brother Lawrence?
2. What are the speaker's attitudes toward Brother Lawrence? What do those attitudes suggest to you about the speaker's own character traits?

3. What are the speaker's feelings about women? Table manners? Gardens and gardening? What can the reader learn, indirectly, about Brother Lawrence by carefully interpreting the speaker's remarks?
4. Compare this poem with "My Last Duchess." Is the narrator of "Soliloquy" in any way like the Duke? Explain your answer.

e e cummings (1894–1962)

"next to of course god america i

"next to of course god america i
love you land of the pilgrims' and so forth oh
say can you see by the dawn's early my
country 'tis of centuries come and go
and are no more what of it we should worry   5
in every language even deafanddumb
thy sons acclaim your glorious name by gorry
by jingo by gee by gosh by gum
why talk of beauty what could be more beautiful than these heroic happy dead   10
who rushed like lions to the roaring slaughter
they did not stop to think they died instead
then shall the voice of liberty be mute?"

He spoke. And drank rapidly a glass of water

STUDY QUESTIONS

1. The poem appears at first to be a monologue. Is it? If not, what is the point of view?
2. What is happening in the poem? List the clues to the situation that are given by the speaker in the first thirteen lines. List the clues given in the final line.
3. Quote examples of clichés and identify the sources of well-known phrases. Do these clichés and other phrases provide clues to the character of the speaker? If so, what traits do they reveal?
4. What is the speaker's topic? How sincere is he? Defend your answer by quoting lines or phrases he uses or by filling in missing words in his speech.

John Keats (1795–1821)

⁜ LA BELLE DAME SANS MERCI

"Ah, what can ail thee, Knight-at-arms,
    Alone and palely loitering?
The sedge has withered from the lake,
    And no birds sing.

"Ah, what can ail thee, Knight-at-arms,   5
    So haggard and so woe-begone?
The squirrel's granary is full,
    And the harvest's done.

"I see a lily on thy brow
    With anguish moist and fever-dew,   10
And on thy cheeks a fading rose
    Fast withereth too."

"I met a lady in the meads,
    Full beautiful—a faery's child;
Her hair was long, her foot was light,   15
    And her eyes were wild.

"I made a garland for her head,
    And bracelets too, and fragrant zone;
She looked at me as she did love,
    And made sweet moan.   20

"I set her on my pacing steed,
    And nothing else saw all day long;
For sidelong would she bend, and sing
    A faery's song.

"She found me roots of relish sweet,   25
    And honey wild and manna-dew;
And sure in language strange she said,
    'I love thee true.'

"She took me to her elfin grot,
    And there she gazed and sighed full sore,   30
And there I shut her wild, wild eyes—
    With kisses four.

3. sedge: grasslike plant.   13. meads: meadows.   14. faery: enchanted creature.
18. zone: belt or girdle.   26. manna: spiritual nourishment of divine origin.   29.
grot: grotto.

JOHN KEATS

"And there she lullèd me asleep,
  And there I dreamed—ah! woe betide!—
The latest dream I ever dreamed   35
  On the cold hill's side.

"I saw pale kings, and princes too,
  Pale warriors, death-pale were they all:
They cried—'La belle Dame sans Merci
  Hath thee in thrall!'   40

"I saw their starved lips in the gloam
  With horrid warning gapèd wide,
And I awoke, and found me here
  On the cold hill side.

"And this is why I sojourn here   45
  Alone and palely loitering,
Though the sedge is withered from the lake,
  And no birds sing."

39. La belle Dame sans Merci: the beautiful Lady without Pity.

STUDY QUESTIONS

1. A ballad is a verse narrative. The popular ballad is part of an oral, folk tradition ("Bonny Barbara Allan," for example). Ballads usually contain the following: little characterization or description, action developed through dialogue, simplicity of presentation, dramatic or exciting episodes, repetition of phrases or lines, and some sort of summary stanza. Keats' poem has been called an art ballad. What elements in "La Belle Dame" are similar to those in a folk ballad?
2. There are two major speakers in the poem: the knight and a stranger who questions him. What do the stranger's speeches contribute to characterization? To action?
3. The "femme fatale" is a traditional character in literature. Quote lines that reveal her traits and identify what those traits are.
4. Can you suggest legendary femmes fatales in films or in other literary genres? How does La belle Dame resemble or differ from them?
5. Most literary femmes fatales are the creations of men. How does this fact affect the nature and truth of their perceptions?
6. What does the knight's dream contribute to the story? Does it add to the emotion, to the suspense, or to characterization?
7. The final stanza repeats the first stanza, with several important differences. What are those differences? What is their effect on meaning?

Anonymous

ᛒ BONNY BARBARA ALLAN

In Scarlet town, where I was born,
   There was a fair maid dwelling,
Made every youth cry *Well-a-way!*
   Her name was Barbara Allan.

All in the merry month of May,   5
   When green buds they were swelling,
Young Jemmy Grove on his death-bed lay,
   For love of Barbara Allan.

O slowly, slowly rose she up,
   To the place where he was lying,   10
And when she drew the curtain by,
   "Young man, I think you're dying."

"O 'tis I'm sick, and very, very sick,
   And 'tis a' for Barbara Allan";
"O the better for me ye's never be,   15
   Tho your heart's blood were spilling.

"O dinna ye mind, young man," said she,
   "When ye was in the tavern drinking,
That ye made the healths go round and round,
   And slighted Barbara Allan?"   20

He turned his face unto the wall,
   And death was with him dealing:
"Adieu, adieu, my dear friends all,
   And be kind to Barbara Allan."

And slowly, slowly rose she up,   25
   And slowly, slowly left him,
And sighing said she could not stay,
   Since death of life had reft him.

She had not gane a mile but twa,
   When she heard the dead-bell knelling,   30
And every jow that the dead-bell gave
   Cried, "Woe to Barbara Allan!"

"O mother, mother, make my bed!
   O make it saft and narrow!
Since my love died for me today,   35
   I'll die for him tomorrow."

29. gane: gone; twa: two.   31. jow: sound.   34. saft: soft.

Edgar Lee Masters (1869–1950)

BARRY HOLDEN

The very fall my sister Nancy Knapp
Set fire to the house
They were trying Dr. Duval
For the murder of Zora Clemens,
And I sat in the court two weeks   5
Listening to every witness.
It was clear he had got her in a family way;
And to let the child be born
Would not do.
Well, how about me with eight children,   10
And one coming, and the farm
Mortgaged to Thomas Rhodes?
And when I got home that night,
(After listening to the story of the buggy ride,
And the finding of Zora in the ditch),   15
The first thing I saw, right there by the steps,
Where the boys had hacked for angle worms,
Was the hatchet!
And just as I entered there was my wife,
Standing before me, big with child.   20
She started the talk of the mortgaged farm,
And I killed her.

Edgar Lee Masters (1869–1950)

WENDELL P. BLOYD

They first charged me with disorderly conduct,
There being no statute on blasphemy.
Later they locked me up as insane
Where I was beaten to death by a Catholic guard.
My offense was this: 5
I said God lied to Adam, and destined him
To lead the life of a fool,
Ignorant that there is evil in the world as well as
    good.
And when Adam outwitted God by eating the
    apple
And saw through the lie,   10
God drove him out of Eden to keep him from
    taking

The fruit of immortal life.
For Christ's sake, you sensible people,
Here's what God Himself says about it in the book
   of Genesis:
"And the Lord God said, behold the man   15
Is become as one of us" (a little envy, you see),
"To know good and evil" (The all-is-good lie ex-
   posed):
"And now lest he put forth his hand and take
Also of the tree of life and eat, and live forever:
Therefore the Lord God sent Him forth from the
   garden of Eden."   20
(The reason I believe God crucified His Own Son
To get out of the wretched tangle is, because it
   sounds just like Him.)

Edgar Lee Masters (1869–1950)

JUDGE SELAH LIVELY

Suppose you stood just five feet two,
And had worked your way as a grocery clerk,
Studying law by candle light
Until you became an attorney at law?
And then suppose through your diligence,   5
And regular church attendance,
You became attorney for Thomas Rhodes,
Collecting notes and mortgages,
And representing all the widows
In the Probate Court? And through it all   10
They jeered at your size, and laughed at your clothes
And your polished boots? And then suppose
You became the County Judge?
And Jefferson Howard and Kinsey Keene,
And Harmon Whitney, and all the giants   15
Who had sneered at you, were forced to stand
Before the bar and say "Your Honor"—
Well, don't you think it was natural
That I made it hard for them?

Edgar Lee Masters (1869–1950)

WILLIE METCALF

I was Willie Metcalf.
They used to call me "Doctor Meyers"
Because, they said, I looked like him.
And he was my father, according to Jack McGuire.
I lived in the livery stable,   5
Sleeping on the floor
Side by side with Roger Baughman's bulldog,
Or sometimes in a stall.
I could crawl between the legs of the wildest horses
Without getting kicked—we knew each other.   10
On spring days I tramped through the country
To get the feeling, which I sometimes lost,
That I was not a separate thing from the earth.
I used to lose myself, as if in sleep,
By lying with eyes half-open in the woods.   15
Sometimes I talked with animals—even toads and snakes—
Anything that had an eye to look into.
Once I saw a stone in the sunshine
Trying to turn into jelly.
In April days in this cemetery   20
The dead people gathered all about me,
And grew still, like a congregation in silent prayer.
I never knew whether I was a part of the earth
With flowers growing in me, or whether I walked—
Now I know.   25

Marge Piercy (1936–   )

THE CRIPPLING

I used to watch
it on the ledge:
a crippled bird.
Surely it would
die soon.   5
Then I saw a man
at one of the windows
fed it a few seeds,
a crust from lunch.
Often he forgot   10

and it went hopping on the ledge
a starving scurvy sparrow.
Every couple of weeks
he caught it in his hand
and clipped back one wing.   15
I call it a sparrow.
The plumage was sooty.
Sometimes in the sun
the feathers might have
been scarlet like a tanager.   20
He never
let it fly.
He never took it in.
Perhaps he was starving himself.

Tony Connor (1930–   )

ELEGY FOR ALFRED HUBBARD

Hubbard is dead, the old plumber;
who will mend our burst pipes now,
the tap that has dripped all the summer,
testing the sink's overflow?

No other like him. Young men with knowledge   5
of new techniques, theories from books,
may better his work straight from college,
but who will challenge his squint-eyed looks

in kitchen, bathroom, under floorboards,
rules of thumb which were often wrong;   10
seek as erringly stopcocks in cupboards,
or make a job last half as long?

He was a man who knew the ginnels,
alleyways, streets—the whole district,
family secrets, minor annals,   15
time-honored fictions fused to fact.

Seventy years of gossip muttered
under his cap, his tufty thatch,
so that his talk was slow and clotted,
hard to follow, and too much.   20

As though nothing fell, none vanished,
and time were the maze of Cheetham Hill,

in which the dead—with jobs unfinished—
waited to hear him ring the bell.

For much he never got round to doing,   25
but meant to, when weather bucked up,
or worsened, or when his pipe was drawing,
or when he'd finished this cup.

I thought time, he forgot so often,
had forgotten him but here's Death's pomp   30
over his house, and by the coffin
the son who will inherit his blowlamp,

tools, workshop, cart, and cornet
(pride of Cheetham Prize Brass Band),
and there's his mourning widow, Janet,   35
stood at the gate he'd promised to mend.

Soon he will make his final journey;
shaved and silent, strangely trim,
with never a pause to talk to any-
body: how arrow-like, for him!   40

In St. Mark's church, whose dismal tower
he pointed and painted when a lad,
they will sing his praises amidst flowers
while, somewhere, a cellar starts to flood,

and the housewife banging his front-door knocker   45
is not surprised to find him gone,
and runs for Thwaite, who's a better worker,
and sticks at a job until it's done.

13. ginnels: archaic word referring to underground tunnels.

James Stephens (1882–1950)

A GLASS OF BEER

The lanky hank of a she in the inn over there
Nearly killed me for asking the loan of a glass of beer;
May the devil grip the whey-faced slut by the hair,
And beat bad manners out of her skin for a year.

That parboiled ape, with the toughest jaw you will see   5
On virtue's path, and a voice that would rasp the dead,

3. whey-faced: pale, pasty.

Came roaring and raging the minute she looked at me,
And threw me out of the house on the back of my head!

If I asked her master he'd give me a cask a day;
But she, with the beer at hand, not a gill would arrange!　　　10
May she marry a ghost and bear him a kitten, and may
The High King of Glory permit her to get the mange.

10. gill: quarter-pint.

Edwin Arlington Robinson (1869–1935)

UNCLE ANANIAS

His words were magic and his heart was true,
　　And everywhere he wandered he was blessed.
Out of all ancient men my childhood knew
　　I choose him and I mark him for the best.
Of all authoritative liars, too,　　　　　　　　　5
　　I crown him loveliest.

How fondly I remember the delight
　　That always glorified him in the spring;
The joyous courage and the benedight
　　Profusion of his faith in everything!　　　　10

9. benedight: archaic term meaning "blessed."

George Gordon, Lord Byron (1788–1824)

SHE WALKS IN BEAUTY

She walks in beauty, like the night
　　Of cloudless climes and starry skies;
And all that's best of dark and bright
　　Meet in her aspect and her eyes:
Thus mellowed to that tender light　　　　　5
　　Which heaven to gaudy day denies.

One shade the more, one ray the less,
　　Had half impaired the nameless grace
Which waves in every raven tress,
　　Or softly lightens o'er her face;　　　　10
Where thoughts serenely sweet express,
　　How pure, how dear their dwelling place.

And on that cheek, and o'er that brow,
    So soft, so calm, yet eloquent,
The smiles that win, the tints that glow,   15
    But tell of days in goodness spent,
A mind at peace with all below,
    A heart whose love is innocent!

2. climes: climates.

Alfred, Lord Tennyson (1809–1892)

ULYSSES

It little profits that an idle king,
By this still hearth, among these barren crags,
Match'd with an aged wife, I mete and dole
Unequal laws unto a savage race,
That hoard, and sleep, and feed, and know not me.   5
I cannot rest from travel; I will drink
Life to the lees. All times I have enjoy'd
Greatly, have suffer'd greatly, both with those
That loved me, and alone; on shore, and when
Thro' scudding drifts the rainy Hyades   10
Vext the dim sea. I am become a name;
For always roaming with a hungry heart
Much have I seen and known,—cities of men
And manners, climates, councils, governments,
Myself not least, but honor'd of them all,—   15
And drunk delight of battle with my peers,
Far on the ringing plains of windy Troy.
I am a part of all that I have met;
Yet all experience is an arch wherethro'
Gleams that untravell'd world whose margin fades   20
For ever and for ever when I move.
How dull it is to pause, to make an end,
To rust unburnish'd, not to shine in use!
As tho' to breathe were life! Life piled on life
Were all too little, and of one to me   25
Little remains; but every hour is saved
From that eternal silence, something more,
A bringer of new things; and vile it were
For some three suns to store and hoard myself,
And this gray spirit yearning in desire   30

To follow knowledge like a sinking star,
Beyond the utmost bound of human thought.
   This is my son, mine own Telemachus,
To whom I leave the sceptre and the isle,—
Well-loved of me, discerning to fulfil   35
This labor, by slow prudence to make mild
A rugged people, and thro' soft degrees
Subdue them to the useful and the good.
Most blameless is he, centred in the sphere
Of common duties, decent not to fail   40
In offices of tenderness, and pay
Meet adoration to my household gods,
When I am gone. He works his work, I mine.
   There lies the port; the vessel puffs her sail;
There gloom the dark, broad seas. My mariners,   45
Souls that have toil'd, and wrought, and thought with me,—
That ever with a frolic welcome took
The thunder and the sunshine, and opposed
Free hearts, free foreheads,—you and I are old;
Old age hath yet his honor and his toil.   50
Death closes all; but something ere the end,
Some work of noble note, may yet be done,
Not unbecoming men that strove with Gods.
The lights begin to twinkle from the rocks;
The long day wanes; the slow moon climbs; the deep   55
Moans round with many voices. Come, my friends,
'Tis not too late to seek a newer world.
Push off, and sitting well in order smite
The sounding furrows; for my purpose holds
To sail beyond the sunset, and the baths   60
Of all the western stars, until I die.
It may be that the gulfs will wash us down;
It may be we shall touch the Happy Isles,
And see the great Achilles, whom we knew.
Tho' much is taken, much abides; and tho'   65
We are not now that strength which in old days
Moved earth and heaven, that which we are, we are,—
One equal temper of heroic hearts,
Made weak by time and fate, but strong in will
To strive, to seek, to find, and not to yield.   70

Title: Ulysses: Greek king, hero of Homer's *Odyssey*.   3. mete: measure out.
10. Hyades: in Greek mythology, the five stars that controlled rain.   63. Happy
Isles: Greek Paradise.   64. Achilles: Greek prince, hero of Homer's *Iliad*.

Robert Browning (1812–1889)

CONFESSIONS

1

What is he buzzing in my ears?
   "Now that I come to die,
Do I view the world as a vale of tears?"
   Ah, reverend sir, not I!

2

What I viewed there once, what I view again   5
   Where the physic bottles stand
On the table's edge—is a suburb lane,
   With a wall to my bedside hand.

3

That lane sloped, much as the bottles do,
   From a house you could descry   10
O'er the garden wall: is the curtain blue
   Or green to a healthy eye?

4

To mine, it serves for the old June weather
   Blue above lane and wall;
And that farthest bottle labeled "Ether"   15
   Is the house o'ertopping all.

5

At a terrace, somewhere near the stopper,
   There watched for me, one June,
A girl: I know, sir, it's improper,
   My poor mind's out of tune.   20

6

Only, there was a way . . . you crept
   Close by the side to dodge
Eyes in the house, two eyes except:
   They styled their house "The Lodge."

7

What right had a lounger up their lane?   25
   But, by creeping very close,
With the good wall's help—their eyes might strain
   And stretch themselves to O's,

8

Yet never catch her and me together,
    As she left the attic, there,   30
By the rim of the bottle labeled "Ether,"
    And stole from stair to stair,

9

And stood by the rose-wreathed gate. Alas,
    We loved, sir—used to meet:
How sad and bad and mad it was—   35
    But then, how it was sweet!

Robert Browning (1812–1889)

THE LABORATORY

Ancien Régime

Now that I, tying thy glass mask tightly,
May gaze through these faint smokes curling whitely,
As thou pliest thy trade in this devil's-smithy—
Which is the poison to poison her, prithee?

He is with her; and they know that I know   5
Where they are, what they do: they believe my tears flow
While they laugh, laugh at me, at me fled to the drear
Empty church, to pray God in, for them!—I am here.

Grind away, moisten and mash up thy paste,
Pound at thy powder,—I am not in haste!   10
Better sit thus, and observe thy strange things,
Than go where men wait me and dance at the King's.

That in the mortar—you call it a gum?
Ah, the brave tree whence such gold oozings come!
And yonder soft phial, the exquisite blue   15
Sure to taste sweetly,—is that poison too?

Had I but all of them, thee and thy treasures,
What a wild crowd of invisible pleasures!
To carry pure death in an earring, a casket,
A signet, a fan-mount, a filigree-basket!   20

Soon, at the King's, a mere lozenge to give,
And Pauline should have just thirty minutes to live!
But to light a pastille, and Elise, with her head,
And her breast and her arms and her hands, should drop dead!

Quick—is it finished? The color's too grim!   25
Why not soft like the phial's, enticing and dim?
Let it brighten her drink, let her turn it and stir,
And try it and taste, ere she fix and prefer!

What a drop! She's not little, no minion like me!
That's why she ensnared him: this never will free   30
The soul from those masculine eyes,—say, "no!"
To that pulse's magnificent come-and-go.

For only last night, as they whispered, I brought
My own eyes to bear on her so, that I thought
Could I keep them one half minute fixed, she would fall,   35
Shriveled; she fell not; yet this does it all!

Not that I bid you spare her the pain!
Let death be felt and the proof remain;
Brand, burn up, bite into its grace—
He is sure to remember her dying face!   40

Is it done? Take my mask off! Nay, be not morose,
It kills her, and this prevents seeing it close:
The delicate droplet, my whole fortune's fee!
If it hurts her, beside, can it ever hurt me?

Now, take all my jewels, gorge gold to your fill,   45
You may kiss me, old man, on my mouth if you will!
But brush this dust off me, lest horror it brings
Ere I know it—next moment I dance at the King's!

Subtitle: ancien régime: the period during the monarchy in France before the Revolution.   20. signet: ring with compartment.   23. pastille: aromatic paste used to
scent a room.   29. minion: servant.

READING SELECTIONS: PLAYS

Tennessee Williams (1914–)

27 WAGONS FULL OF COTTON

CHARACTERS

Jake Meighan,   *a cotton-gin owner.*
Flora Meighan,   *his wife.*
Silva Vicarro,   *superintendent of the Syndicate Plantation.*

All of the action takes place on the front porch of the Meighans' residence near Blue Mountain, Mississippi.

Scene: *The front porch of the Meighans' cottage near Blue Mountain, Mississippi. The porch is narrow and rises into a single narrow gable. There are spindling white pillars on either side supporting the porch roof and a door of Gothic design and two Gothic windows on either side of it. The peaked door has an oval of richly stained glass, azure, crimson, emerald and gold. At the windows are fluffy white curtains gathered coquettishly in the middle by baby-blue satin bows. The effect is not unlike a doll's house.*

Scene I.   *It is early evening and there is a faint rosy dusk in the sky. Shortly after the curtain rises,* JAKE MEIGHAN, *a fat man of sixty, scrambles out the front door and races around the corner of the house carrying a gallon can of coal-oil. A dog barks at him. A car is heard starting and receding rapidly in the distance. A moment later* FLORA *calls from inside the house.*

Flora   Jake! I've lost m' white kid purse! (*closer to the door*) Jake? Look'n see 'f uh laid it on th' swing. (*There is a pause*). Guess I could've left it in th' Chevy? (*She comes up to screen door*). Jake. Look'n see if uh left it in th' Chevy. Jake? (*She steps outside in the fading rosy dusk. She switches on the porch light and stares about, slapping at gnats attracted by the light. Locusts provide the only answering voice.* FLORA *gives a long nasal call*). Ja-ay—a-a-ake! (*A cow moos in the distance with the same inflection. There is a muffled explosion somewhere about half a mile away. A strange flickering glow appears, the reflection of a burst of flame. Distant voices are heard exclaiming.*)

Voices (*shrill, cackling like hens*)

You heah that noise?

Yeah! Sound like a bomb went off!

Oh, look!

Why, it's a fire!

Where's it at? You tell?

Th' Syndicate Plantation!

Oh, my God! Let's go! (*A fire whistle sounds in the distance.*)

Henry! Start th' car! You all wanta go with us?

Yeah, we'll be right out!

Hurry, honey! (*A car can be heard starting up.*)

Be right there!

Well, hurry.

Voice (*just across the dirt road*)   Missus Meighan?

Flora   Ye-ah?

Voice   Ahn't you goin' th' fire?

Flora   I wish I could but Jake's gone off in th' Chevy.

Voice   Come awn an' go with us, honey!

Flora   Oh, I cain't an' leave th' house wide open! Jake's gone off with th' keys. What do you all think it is on fire?

Voice   Th' Syndicate Plantation!

Flora   Th' Syndicate Plan-*ta*-tion? (*The car starts off and recedes*). Oh, my Go-od! (*She climbs laboriously back up on the porch and sits on the swing which faces the front. She speaks tragically to herself*). Nobody! Nobody! Never! Never! Nobody!

(*Locusts can be heard. A car is heard approaching and stopping at a distance back of house. After a moment* JAKE *ambles casually up around the side of the house.*)

Flora (*in a petulant babyish tone*)   Well!

Jake   Whatsamatter, Baby?

Flora   I never known a human being could be that mean an' thoughtless!

Jake   Aw, now, that's a mighty broad statement fo' you to make, Mrs. Meighan. What's the complaint this time?

Flora   Just flew out of the house without even sayin' a word!

Jake   What's so bad about that?

Flora I told you I had a headache comin' on an' had to have a dope, there wassen a single bottle lef' in th' house, an' you said, Yeah, get into yuh things 'n' we'll drive in town right away! So I get into m' things an' I cain't find m' white kid purse. Then I remember I left it on th' front seat of th' Chevy. I come out here t' git it. Where are you? Gone off! Without a word! Then there's a big explosion! Feel my heart!

Jake Feel my baby's heart?

(*He puts a hand on her huge bosom.*)

Flora Yeah, just you feel it, poundin' like a hammer! How'd I know what happened? You not here, just disappeared somewhere!

Jake (*sharply*) Shut up!

(*He pushes her head roughly.*)

Flora Jake! What did you do that fo'?

Jake I don't like how you holler! Holler ev'ry thing you say!

Flora What's the matter with you?

Jake Nothing's the matter with me.

Flora Well, why did you go off?

Jake I didn' go off!

Flora You certainly *did* go off! Try an' tell me that you never went off when I just now seen an' heard you drivin' back in th' car? What uh you take me faw? No sense a-tall?

Jake If you got sense you keep your big mouth shut!

Flora Don't talk to me like that!

Jake Come on inside.

Flora I won't. Selfish an' inconsiderate, that's what you are! I told you at supper, There's not a bottle of Coca-Cola left on th' place. You said, Okay, right after supper we'll drive on over to th' White Star drugstore an' lay in a good supply. When I come out of th' house—

Jake (*he stands in front of her and grips her neck with both hands*) Look here! Listen to what I tell you!

Flora *Jake!*

Jake Shhh! Just listen, Baby.

Flora Lemme go! G'damn you, le' go my throat!

Jake Jus' try an' concentrate on what I tell yuh!

Flora Tell me what?

Jake I ain't been off th' po'ch.

Flora Huh!

Jake I ain't been off th' front po'ch! Not since supper! Understand that, now?

Flora Jake, honey, you've gone out of you' mind!

Jake Maybe so. Never you mind. Just get that straight an' keep it in your haid. I ain't been off the porch of this house since supper.

Flora But you sure as God *was* off it! (*He twists her wrist*). Ouuuu! Stop it, stop it, stop it!

Jake Where have I been since supper?

Flora Here, here! On th' porch! Fo' God's sake, quit that twistin'!

Jake Where have I been?

Flora Porch! Porch! Here!

Jake Doin' what?

Flora *Jake!*

Jake Doin' what?

Flora Lemme go! Christ, Jake! Let loose! Quit twisting, you'll break my wrist!

Jake (*laughing between his teeth*) Doin' what? What doin'? Since supper?

Flora (*crying out*) How in hell do I know!

Jake 'Cause you was right here with me, all the time, for every second! You an' me, sweetheart, was sittin' here together on th' swing, just swingin' back an' forth every minute since supper! You got that in your haid good now?

Flora (*whimpering*) Le'-go!

Jake Got it? In your haid good now?

Flora Yeh, yeh, yeh—leggo!

Jake What was I doin', then?

Flora Swinging! For Christ's sake—swingin'!

(*He releases her. She whimpers and rubs her wrist but the impression is that the experience was not without pleasure for both parties. She groans and whimpers. He grips her loose curls in his hand and bends her head back. He plants a long wet kiss on her mouth.*)

Flora (*whimpering*) Mmmmhmmmm! Mmmm! Mmmm!

Jake (*huskily*) Tha's my swee' baby girl.

Flora Mmmmm! Hurt! Hurt!

Jake Hurt?

Flora Mmmm! Hurt!

Jake Kiss?

Flora Mmmm!

Jake Good?

Flora Mmmm . . .

Jake Good! Make little room.

Flora Too hot!

Jake Go on, make little room.

Flora Mmmmm . . .

Jake Cross patch?

Flora Mmmmmm.

Jake Whose baby? Big? Sweet?

Flora   Mmmmm! Hurt!
Jake   Kiss!

(*He lifts her wrist to his lips and makes gobbling sounds*).

Flora (*giggling*)   Stop! Silly! Mmmm!
Jake   What would I do if you was a big piece of cake?
Flora   Silly.
Jake   Gobble! Gobble!
Flora   Oh, you—
Jake   What would I do if you was angel food cake? Big white piece with lots of nice thick icin'?
Flora (*giggling*)   Quit!
Jake   Gobble, gobble, gobble!
Flora (*squealing*)   Jake!
Jake   Huh?
Flora   You *tick*-le!
Jake   Answer little question!
Flora   Wh-at?
Jake   Where I been since supper?
Flora   Off in the Chevy!

(*He instantly seizes the wrist again. She shrieks.*)

Jake   Where've I been since supper?
Flora   Po'ch! Swing!
Jake   Doin' what?
Flora   *Swingin'!* Oh, Christ, Jake, let loose!
Jake   Hurt?
Flora   Mmmmm . . .
Jake   Good?
Flora (*whimpering*)   Mmmmm . . .
Jake   Now you know where I been an' what I been doin' since supper?
Flora   Yeah . . .
Jake   Case anybody should ask?
Flora   Who's going to ast?
Jake   Never mind who's goin' t' ast, just you know the answers! Uh-huh?
Flora   Uh-huh. (*Lisping babyishly*). This is where you been. Settin' on th' swing since we had supper. Swingin'—back an' fo'th—back an' fo'th. . . . You didn' go off in th' Chevy. (*Slowly.*) An' you was awf'ly surprised w'en th' syndicate fire broke out! (JAKE *slaps her*). Jake!
Jake   Everything you said is awright. But don't you get ideas.
Flora   Ideas?
Jake   A woman like you's not made to have ideas. Made to be hugged an' squeezed!
Flora (*babyishly*)   Mmmm. . . .

Jake But not for ideas. So don't you have ideas. (*He rises*). Go out an' get in th' Chevy.

Flora We goin' to th' fire?

Jake No. We ain' goin' no fire. We goin' in town an' get us a case a dopes because we're hot an' thirsty.

Flora (*vaguely, as she rises*) I lost m' white—kid—purse . . .

Jake It's on the seat of th' Chevy whe' you left it.

Flora Whe' *you* goin'?

Jake I'm goin' in t' th' toilet. I'll be right out.

(*He goes inside, letting the screen door slam.* FLORA *shuffles to the edge of the steps and stands there with a slight idiotic smile. She begins to descend, letting herself down each time with the same foot, like a child just learning to walk. She stops at the bottom of the steps and stares at the sky, vacantly and raptly, her fingers closing gently around the bruised wrist.* JAKE *can be heard singing inside.*)

> 'My baby don' care fo' rings
> or other expensive things—
> My baby just cares—fo'—me!'

(*Curtain*)

Scene II. *It is just after noon. The sky is the color of the satin bows on the window curtains—a translucent, innocent blue. Heat devils are shimmering over the flat Delta country and the peaked white front of the house is like a shrill exclamation.* JAKE'S *gin is busy; heard like a steady pulse across the road. A delicate lint of cotton is drifting about in the atmosphere.*

> JAKE *appears, a large and purposeful man with arms like hams covered with a fuzz of fine blond hair. He is followed by* SILVA VICARRO *who is the Superintendent of the Syndicate Plantation where the fire occurred last night.* VICARRO *is a rather small and wiry man of dark Latin looks and nature. He wears whipcord breeches, laced boots, and a white undershirt. He has a Roman Catholic medallion on a chain about his neck.*

Jake (*with the good-natured condescension of a very large man for a small one*) Well, suh, all I got to say is you're a mighty lucky little fellow.

Vicarro Lucky? In what way?

Jake That I can take on a job like this right now! Twenty-seven wagons full of cotton's a pretty big piece of bus'ness, Mr. Vicarro. (*Stopping at the steps.*) Baby! (*He bites off a piece of tobacco plug.*) What's yuh firs' name?

Vicarro Silva.

Jake How do you spell it?

Vicarro S-I-L-V-A.

Jake Silva! Like a silver lining! Ev'ry cloud has got a silver lining. What does that come from? The Bible?

Vicarro (*sitting on the steps*) No. The Mother Goose Book.

Jake Well, suh, you sure are lucky that I can do it. If I'd been busy like I was two weeks ago I would've turned it down. *BABY! COME OUT HERE A MINUTE!*

(*There is a vague response from inside.*)

Vicarro Lucky. Very lucky.

(*He lights a cigarette.* FLORA *pushes open the screen door and comes out. She has on her watermelon pink silk dress and is clutching against her body the big white kid purse with her initials on it in big nickel plate.*)

Jake (*proudly*) Mr. Vicarro—I want you to meet Mrs. Meighan. Baby, this is a very down-at-the-mouth young fellow I want you to cheer up fo' me. He thinks he's out of luck because his cotton gin burnt down. He's got twenty-seven wagons full of cotton to be ginned out on a hurry-up order from his most impo'tant customers in Mobile. Well, suh, I said to him, Mr. Vicarro, you're to be congratulated—not because it burnt down, but because I happen to be in a situation to take the business over. Now you tell him just how lucky he is!

Flora (*nervously*) Well, I guess he don't see how it was lucky to have his gin burned down.

Vicarro (*acidly*) No, ma'am.

Jake (*quickly*) Mr. Vicarro. Some fellows marry a girl when she's little an' tiny. They like a small figure. See? Then, when the girl gets comfo'tably settled down—what does she do? Puts on flesh—of cou'se!

Flora (*bashfully*) Jake!

Jake Now then! How do they react? Accept it as a matter of cou'se, as something which 'as been ordained by nature? Nope! No, suh, not a bit! They sta't to feeling abused. They think that fate must have a grudge against them because the little woman is not so little as she used to be. Because she's gone an' put on a matronly figure. Well, suh, that's at the root of a lot of domestic trouble. However, Mr. Vicarro, I never made that mistake. When I fell in love with this baby-doll I've got here, she was just the same size then that you see her today.

Flora (*crossing shyly to porch rail*) Jake . . .

Jake (*grinning*) A woman not large but tremendous! That's how I liked her—tremendous! I told her right off, when I slipped th' ring on her finger, one Satiddy night in a boathouse on Moon Lake—I said to her, Honey, if you take off one single pound of that body—I'm going to quit yuh! I'm going to quit yuh, I said, the minute I notice you've started to take off weight!

Flora Aw, Jake—please!

Jake I don't want nothing little, not in a woman. I'm not after nothing *petite*, as the Frenchmen call it. This is what I wanted—and what I *got!* Look at her, Mr. Vicarro. Look at her blush!

(*He grips the back of* FLORA's *neck and tries to turn her around.*)

Flora   Aw, quit, Jake! Quit, will yuh?

Jake   See what a doll she is? (FLORA *turns suddenly and spanks him with the kid purse. He cackles and runs down the steps. At the corner of the house, he stops and turns*). Baby, you keep Mr. Vicarro comfo'table while I'm ginnin' out that twenty-seven wagons full of cotton. Th' good-neighbor policy, Mr. Vicarro. You do me a good turn an' I'll do you a good one! Be see'n' yuh! So long, Baby!

(*He walks away with an energetic stride.*)

Vicarro   The good-neighbor policy!

(*He sits on the porch steps.*)

Flora (*sitting on the swing*)   Izzen he out-*ray*-juss!

(*She laughs foolishly and puts the purse in her lap.* VICARRO *stares gloomily across the dancing brilliance of the fields. His lip sticks out like a pouting child's. A rooster crows in the distance.*)

Flora   I would'n' dare to expose myself like that.
Vicarro   Expose? To what?
Flora   The sun. I take a terrible burn. I'll never forget the burn I took one time. It was on Moon Lake one Sunday before I was married. I never did like t' go fishin' but this young fellow, one of the Peterson boys, insisted that we go fishin'. Well, he didn't catch nothin' but jus' kep' fishin' an' fishin' an' I set there in th' boat with all that hot sun on me. I said, Stay under the willows. But he would'n' lissen to me, an' sure enough I took such an awful burn I had t' sleep on m' stummick th' nex' three nights.
Vicarro (*absently*)   What did you say? You got sun-burned?
Flora   Yes. One time on Moon Lake.
Vicarro   That's too bad. You got over it all right?
Flora   Oh, yes. Finally. Yes.
Vicarro   That must've been pretty bad.
Flora   I fell in the lake once, too. Also with one of the Peterson boys. On another fishing trip. That was a wild bunch of boys, those Peterson boys. I never went out with 'em but something happened which made me wish I hadn't. One time, sunburned. One time, nearly drowned. One time— poison ivy! Well, lookin' back on it, now, we had a good deal of fun in spite of it, though.
Vicarro   The good-neighbor policy, huh?

(*He slaps his boot with the riding crop. Then he rises from steps.*)

Flora   You might as well come up on th' po'ch an' make you'self as comfo'table as you can.

Vicarro Uh-huh.

Flora I'm not much good at—makin' conversation.

Vicarro (*finally noticing her*) Now don't you bother to make conversation for my benefit, Mrs. Meighan. I'm the type that prefers a quiet understanding. (FLORA *laughs uncertainly*). One thing I always notice about you ladies . . .

Flora What's that, Mr. Vicarro?

Vicarro You always have something in your hands—to hold onto. Now that kid purse . . .

Flora My purse?

Vicarro You have no reason to keep that purse in your hands. You're certainly not afraid that I'm going to snatch it!

Flora Oh, God, no! I wassen afraid of that!

Vicarro That wouldn't be the good-neighbor policy, would it? But you hold onto that purse because it gives you something to get a grip on. Isn't that right?

Flora Yes. I always like to have something in my hands.

Vicarro Sure you do. You feel what a lot of uncertain things there are. Gins burn down. The volunteer fire department don't have decent equipment. Nothing is any protection. The afternoon sun is hot. It's no protection. The trees are back of the house. They're no protection. The goods that dress is made of—is no protection. So what do you do, Mrs. Meighan? You pick up the white kid purse. It's solid. It's sure. It's certain. It's something to hold *on* to. You get what I mean?

Flora Yeah, I think I do.

Vicarro It gives you a feeling of being attached to something. The mother protects the baby? No, no, no—the baby protects the mother! From being lost and empty and having nothing but lifeless things in her hands! Maybe you think there isn't much connection!

Flora You'll have to excuse me from thinking. I'm too lazy.

Vicarro What's your name, Mrs. Meighan?

Flora Flora.

Vicarro Mine is Silva. Something not gold but—Silva!

Flora Like a silver dollar?

Vicarro No, like a silver dime! It's an Italian name. I'm a native of New Orleans.

Flora Then it's not sun-burn. You're natcherally dark.

Vicarro (*raising his undershirt from his belly*) Look at this!

Flora Mr. Vicarro!

Vicarro Just as dark as my arm is!

Flora You don't have to show me! I'm not from Missouri!

Vicarro (*grinning*) Excuse me.

Flora (*she laughs nervously*) Whew! I'm sorry to say we don't have a coke in the house. We meant to get a case of cokes las' night, but what with all the excitement going on—

Vicarro What excitement was that?

Flora Oh, the fire and all.

Vicarro (*lighting a cigarette*) I shouldn't think you all would of been excited about the fire.

Flora A fire is always exciting. After a fire, dogs an' chickens don't sleep. I don't think our chickens got to sleep all night.

Vicarro No?

Flora They cackled an' fussed an' flopped around on the roost—took on something awful! Myself, I couldn't sleep neither. I jus' lay there an' sweated all night long.

Vicarro On account of th' fire?

Flora An' the heat an' mosquitoes. And I was mad at Jake.

Vicarro Mad at Mr. Meighan? What about?

Flora Oh, he went off an' left me settin' here on this ole po'ch last night without a Coca-Cola on the place.

Vicarro Went off an' left you, did he?

Flora Yep. Right after supper. An' when he got back the fire 'd already broke out an' instead of drivin' in to town like he said, he decided to go an' take a look at your burnt-down cotton gin. I got smoke in my eyes an' my nose an' throat. It hurt my sinus an' I was in such a wo'n out, nervous condition, it made me cry. I cried like a baby. Finally took two teaspoons of paregoric. Enough to put an elephant to sleep. But still I stayed awake an' heard them chickens carryin' on out there!

Vicarro It sounds like you passed a very uncomfortable night.

Flora Sounds like? Well, it *was*.

Vicarro So Mr. Meighan—you say—disappeared after supper? (*There is a pause while* FLORA *looks at him blankly.*)

Flora Huh?

Vicarro You say Mr. Meighan was out of the house for a while after supper?

(*Something in his tone makes her aware of her indiscretion.*)

Flora Oh—uh—just for a moment.

Vicarro Just for a moment, huh? How long a moment?

(*He stares at her very hard.*)

Flora What are you driving at, Mr. Vicarro?

Vicarro Driving at? Nothing.

Flora You're looking at me so funny.

Vicarro He disappeared for a moment! Is that what he did? How long a moment did he disappear for? Can you remember, Mrs. Meighan?

Flora What difference does that make? What's it to you, anyhow?

Vicarro Why should you mind me asking?

Flora You make this sound like I was on trial for something!

Vicarro Don't you like to pretend like you're a witness?

Flora   Witness of what, Mr. Vicarro?

Vicarro   Why—for instance—say—a case of arson!

Flora (*wetting her lips*)   Case of—? What is—arson?

Vicarro   The willful destruction of property by fire. (*He slaps his boots sharply with the riding crop.*)

Flora (*startled*)   Oh! (*She nervously fingers the purse*).   Well, now, don't you go and be getting any—funny ideas.

Vicarro   Ideas about what, Mrs. Meighan?

Flora   My husband's disappearin'—after supper. I can explain that.

Vicarro   Can you?

Flora   Sure I can.

Vicarro   Good! How do you explain it? (*He stares at her. She looks down*). What's the matter? Can't you collect your thoughts, Mrs. Meighan?

Flora   No, but—

Vicarro   Your mind's a blank on the subject?

Flora   Look here, now—

(*She squirms on the swing.*)

Vicarro   You find it impossible to remember just what your husband disappeared for after supper? You can't imagine what kind of errand it was that he went out on, can you?

Flora   No! No, I can't!

Vicarro   But when he returned—let's see . . . The fire had just broken out at the Syndicate Plantation?

Flora   Mr. Vicarro, I don't have the slightest idear what you could be driving at.

Vicarro   You're a very unsatisfactory witness, Mrs. Meighan.

Flora   I never can think when people—stare straight at me.

Vicarro   Okay. I'll look away, then. (*He turns his back to her*). Now does that improve your memory any? Now are you able to concentrate on the question?

Flora   Huh . . .

Vicarro   No? You're not? (*He turns around again, grinning evilly*). Well . . . shall we drop the subject?

Flora   I sure do wish you would.

Vicarro   It's no use crying over a burnt-down gin. This world is built on the principle of tit for tat.

Flora   What do you mean?

Vicarro   Nothing at all specific. Mind if I . . . ?

Flora   What?

Vicarro   You want to move over a little an' make some room? (Flora *edges aside on the swing. He sits down with her*). I like a swing. I've always liked to sit an' rock on a swing. Relaxes you . . . You relaxed?

Flora   Sure.

Vicarro   No, you're not. Your nerves are all tied up.

Flora Well, you made me feel kind of nervous. All of them questions you ast me about the fire.

Vicarro I didn't ask you questions about the fire. I only asked you about your husband's leaving the house after supper.

Flora I explained that to you.

Vicarro Sure. That's right. You did. The good-neighbor policy. That was a lovely remark your husband made about the good-neighbor policy. I see what he means by that now.

Flora He was thinking about President Roosevelt's speech. We sat up an' lissened to it one night last week.

Vicarro No, I think that he was talking about something closer to home, Mrs. Meighan. You do me a good turn and I'll do you one, that was the way that he put it. You have a piece of cotton on your face. Hold still— I'll pick it off. (*He delicately removes the lint*). There now.

Flora (*nervously*) Thanks.

Vicarro There's a lot of fine cotton lint floating round in the air.

Flora I know there is. It irritates my nose. I think it gets up in my sinus.

Vicarro Well, you're a delicate woman.

Flora Delicate? Me? Oh, no. I'm too big for that.

Vicarro Your size is part of your delicacy, Mrs. Meighan.

Flora How do you mean?

Vicarro There's a lot of you, but every bit of you is delicate. Choice. Delectable, I might say.

Flora Huh?

Vicarro I mean you're altogether lacking in any—coarseness. You're soft. Fine-fibered. And smooth.

Flora Our talk is certainly taking a personal turn.

Vicarro Yes. You make me think of cotton.

Flora Huh?

Vicarro Cotton!

Flora Well! Should I say thanks or something?

Vicarro No, just smile, Mrs. Meighan. You have an attractive smile. Dimples!

Flora No . . .

Vicarro Yes, you have! Smile, Mrs. Meighan! Come on—smile! (FLORA *averts her face, smiling helplessly*). There now. See? You've got them!

(*He delicately touches one of the dimples*).

Flora Please don't touch me. I don't like to be touched.

Vicarro Then why do you giggle?

Flora Can't help it. You make me feel kind of hysterical, Mr. Vicarro. Mr. Vicarro—

Vicarro Yes?

Flora I hope you don't think that Jake was mixed up in that fire. I swear to goodness he never left the front porch. I remember it perfeckly now.

We just set here on the swing till the fire broke out and then we drove in town.

Vicarro To celebrate?

Flora No, no, no.

Vicarro Twenty-seven wagons full of cotton's a pretty big piece of business to fall in your lap like a gift from the gods, Mrs. Meighan.

Flora I thought you said that we would drop the subjeck.

Vicarro You brought it up that time.

Flora Well, please don't try to mix me up any more. I swear to goodness the fire had already broke out when he got back.

Vicarro That's not what you told me a moment ago.

Flora You got me all twisted up. We went in town. The fire broke out an' we didn't know about it.

Vicarro I thought you said it irritated your sinus.

Flora Oh, my God, you sure put words in my mouth. Maybe I'd better make us some lemonade.

Vicarro Don't go to the trouble.

Flora I'll go in an' fix it direckly, but right at this moment I'm too weak to get up. I don't know why, but I can't hardly hold my eyes open. They keep falling shut. . . . I think it's a little too crowded, two on a swing. Will you do me a favor an' set back down over there?

Vicarro Why do you want me to move?

Flora It makes too much body heat when we're crowded together.

Vicarro One body can borrow coolness from another.

Flora I always heard that bodies borrowed heat.

Vicarro Not in this case. I'm cool.

Flora You don't seem like it to me.

Vicarro I'm just as cool as a cucumber. If you don't believe it, touch me.

Flora Where?

Vicarro Anywhere.

Flora (*rising with great effort*) Excuse me. I got to go in. (*He pins her back down*). What did you do that for?

Vicarro I don't want to be deprived of your company yet.

Flora Mr. Vicarro, you're getting awf'ly familiar.

Vicarro Haven't you got any fun-loving spirit about you?

Flora This isn't fun.

Vicarro Then why do you giggle?

Flora I'm ticklish! Quit switching me, will yuh?

Vicarro I'm just shooing the flies off.

Flora Leave 'em be, then, please. They don't hurt nothin'.

Vicarro I think you like to be switched.

Flora I don't. I wish you'd quit.

Vicarro You'd like to be switched harder.

Flora No, I wouldn't.

Vicarro That blue mark on your wrist—
Flora What about it?
Vicarro I've got a suspicion.
Flora Of what?
Vicarro It was twisted. By your husband.
Flora You're crazy.
Vicarro Yes, it was. And you liked it.
Flora I certainly didn't. Would you mind moving your arm?
Vicarro Don't be so skittish.
Flora Awright. I'll get up then.
Vicarro Go on.
Flora I feel so weak.
Vicarro Dizzy?
Flora A little bit. Yeah. My head's spinning round. I wish you would stop the swing.
Vicarro It's not swinging much.
Flora But even a little's too much.
Vicarro You're a delicate woman. A pretty big woman, too.
Flora So is America. Big.
Vicarro That's a funny remark.
Flora Yeah. I don't know why I made it. My head's so buzzy.
Vicarro Fuzzy?
Flora Fuzzy an'—buzzy. . . Is something on my arm?
Vicarro No.
Flora Then what're you brushing?
Vicarro Sweat off.
Flora Leave it alone.
Vicarro Let me wipe it.

(*He brushes her arm with a handkerchief.*)

Flora (*laughing weakly*) No, please, don't. It feels funny.
Vicarro How does it feel?
Flora It tickles me. All up an' down. You cut it out now. If you don't cut it out I'm going to call.
Vicarro Call who?
Flora I'm going to call that nigger. The nigger that's cutting the grass across the road.
Vicarro Go on. Call, then.
Flora (*weakly*) Hey! Hey, boy!
Vicarro Can't you call any louder?
Flora I feel so funny. What is the matter with me?
Vicarro You're just relaxing. You're big. A big type of woman. I like you. Don't get so excited.
Flora I'm not, but you—

Vicarro   What am I doing?

Flora   Suspicions. About my husband and ideas you have about me.

Vicarro   Such as what?

Flora   He burnt your gin down. He didn't. And I'm not a big piece of cotton. (*She pulls herself up*). I'm going inside.

Vicarro (*rising*).   I think that's a good idea.

Flora   I said I was. Not you.

Vicarro   Why not me?

Flora   Inside it might be crowded, with you an' me.

Vicarro   Three's a crowd. We're two.

Flora   You stay out. Wait here.

Vicarro   What'll you do?

Flora   I'll make us a pitcher of nice cold lemonade.

Vicarro   Okay. You go on in.

Flora   What'll you do?

Vicarro   I'll follow.

Flora   That's what I figured you might be aiming to do. We'll both stay out.

Vicarro   In the sun?

Flora   We'll sit back down in th' shade. (*He blocks her*). Don't stand in my way.

Vicarro   You're standing in mine.

Flora   I'm dizzy.

Vicarro   You ought to lie down.

Flora   How can I?

Vicarro   Go in.

Flora   You'd follow me.

Vicarro   What if I did?

Flora   I'm afraid.

Vicarro   You're starting to cry.

Flora   I'm afraid!

Vicarro   What of?

Flora   Of you.

Vicarro   I'm little.

Flora   I'm dizzy. My knees are so weak they're like water. I've got to sit down.

Vicarro   Go in.

Flora   I can't.

Vicarro   Why not?

Flora   You'd follow.

Vicarro   Would that be so awful?

Flora   You've got a mean look in your eyes and I don't like the whip. Honest to God he never. He didn't, I swear!

Vicarro   Do what?

Flora The fire . . .
Vicarro Go on.
Flora Please don't!
Vicarro Don't what?
Flora Put it down. The whip, please put it down. Leave it out here on the porch.
Vicarro What are you scared of?
Flora You.
Vicarro Go on.

(*She turns helplessly and moves to the screen. He pulls it open.*)

Flora Don't follow. Please don't follow!

(*She sways uncertainly. He presses his hand against her. She moves inside. He follows. The door is shut quietly. The gin pumps slowly and steadily across the road. From inside the house there is a wild and despairing cry. A door is slammed. The cry is repeated more faintly.*)

(*Curtain*)

Scene III. *It is about nine o'clock the same evening. Although the sky behind the house is a dusky rose color, a full September moon of almost garish intensity gives the front of the house a ghostly brilliance. Dogs are howling like demons across the prostrate fields of the Delta.*
  The front porch of the MEIGHANS is empty.
  After a moment the screen door is pushed slowly open and FLORA MEIGHAN emerges gradually. Her appearance is ravaged. Her eyes have a vacant limpidity in the moonlight, her lips are slightly apart. She moves with her hands stretched gropingly before her till she has reached a pillar of the porch. There she stops and stands moaning a little. Her hair hangs loose and disordered. The upper part of her body is unclothed except for a torn pink band about her breasts. Dark streaks are visible on the bare shoulders and arms and there is a large discoloration along one cheek. A dark trickle, now congealed, descends from one corner of her mouth. These more apparent tokens she covers with one hand when JAKE comes up on the porch. He is now heard approaching, singing to himself.

Jake By the light—by the light—by the light—Of the sil-very mo-o-on! (*Instinctively FLORA draws back into the sharply etched shadow from the porch roof. JAKE is too tired and triumphant to notice her appearance*). How's a baby? (*FLORA utters a moaning grunt*). Tired? Too tired t' talk? Well, that's how I feel. Too tired t' talk. Too goddam tired t' speak a friggin' word! (*He lets himself down on the steps, groaning and without giving FLORA more than a glance*). Twenty-seven wagons full of cotton. That's how much I've ginned since ten this mawnin'. A man-size job.

Flora (*huskily*)   Uh-huh. . . . A man-size—job. . . .

Jake   *Twen*-ty *sev*-en *wa*-gons *full* of *cot*-ton!

Flora (*senselessly repeating*)   *Twen*-ty *sev*-en *wa*-gons *full* of *cot*-ton!

(*A dog howls.* FLORA *utters a breathless laugh.*)

Jake   What're you laughin' at, honey? Not at me, I hope.

Flora   No. . . .

Jake   That's good. The job that I've turned out is nothing to laugh at. I drove that pack of niggers like a mule-skinner. They don't have a brain in their bodies. All they got is bodies. You got to drive, drive, drive. I don't even see how niggers eat without somebody to tell them to put the food in their moufs! (*She laughs again, like water spilling out of her mouth*). Huh! You got a laugh like a—Christ. A terrific day's work I finished.

Flora (*slowly*)   I would'n' brag—about it. . . .

Jake   I'm not braggin' about it, I'm just sayin' I done a big day's work, I'm all wo'n out an' I want a little appreciation, not cross speeches. Honey. . . .

Flora   I'm not—(*she laughs again*)—makin' cross speeches.

Jake   To take on a big piece of work an' finish it up an' mention the fack that it's finished I wouldn't call braggin'.

Flora   You're not the only one's—done a big day's—work.

Jake   Who else that you know of? (*There is a pause.*)

Flora   Maybe you think that I had an easy time.

(*Her laughter spills out again.*)

Jake   You're laughin' like you been on a goddam jag. (FLORA *laughs*). What did you get pissed on? Roach poison or citronella? I think I make it pretty easy for you, workin' like a mule-skinner so you can hire you a nigger to do the wash an' take the house-work on. An elephant woman who acks as frail as a kitten, that's the kind of a woman I got on m' hands.

Flora   Sure. . . . (*She laughs*). You make it easy!

Jake   I've yet t' see you lift a little finger. Even gotten too lazy t' put you' things on. Round the house ha'f naked all th' time. Y' live in a cloud. All you can think of is "Give me a Coca-Cola!" Well, you better look out. They got a new bureau in the guvamint files. It's called U.W. Stands for Useless Wimmen. Tha's secret plans on foot t' have 'em shot! (*He laughs at his joke.*)

Flora   Secret—plans—on foot?

Jake   T' have 'em *shot.*

Flora   That's good. I'm glad t' hear it.

(*She laughs again.*)

Jake   I come home tired an' you cain't wait t' peck at me. What 're you cross about now?

Flora I think it was a mistake.

Jake What was a mistake?

Flora Fo' you t' fool with th' Syndicate—Plantation. . . .

Jake I don't know about that. We wuh kind of up-against it, honey. Th' Syndicate buyin' up all th' lan' aroun' here an' turnin' the ole croppers off it without their wages—mighty near busted ev'ry mercantile store in Two Rivers County! An' then they build their own gin to gin their own cotton. It looked for a while like I was stuck up high an' dry. But when the gin burnt down an' Mr. Vicarro decided he'd better throw a little bus'ness my way—I'd say the situation was much improved!

Flora (*she laughs weakly*) Then maybe you don't understand th' good-neighbor—policy.

Jake Don't understand it? Why, I'm the boy that invented it.

Flora Huh-huh! What an—*invention!* All I can say is—I hope you're satisfied now that you've ginned out—twenty-seven wagons full of—cotton.

Jake Vicarro was pretty well pleased w'en he dropped over.

Flora Yeah. He was—pretty well—pleased.

Jake How did you all get along?

Flora We got along jus' fine. Jus' fine an'—dandy.

Jake He didn't seem like such a bad little guy. He takes a sensible attitude.

Flora (*laughing helplessly*) He—sure—does!

Jake I hope you made him comfo'table in the house?

Flora (*giggling*) I made him a pitcher—of nice cold—lemonade!

Jake With a little gin in it, huh? That's how you got pissed. A nice cool drink don't sound bad to me right now. Got any left?

Flora Not a bit, Mr. Meighan. We drank it *a-a-ll* up!

(*She flops onto the swing.*)

Jake So you didn't have such a tiresome time after all?

Flora No. Not tiresome a bit. I had a nice conversation with Mistuh—Vicarro. . . .

Jake What did you all talk about?

Flora Th' good-neighbor policy.

Jake (*chuckling*) How does he feel about th' good-neighbor policy?

Flora Oh—(*She giggles*).—He thinks it's a—good idea! He says—

Jake Huh? (Flora *laughs weakly*). Says what?

Flora Says—

(*She goes off into another spasm of laughter.*)

Jake What ever he said must've been a panic!

Flora He says—(*controlling her spasm*)—he don't think he'll build him a new cotton gin any more. He's gonna let you do a-a-lll his ginnin'—fo' him!

Jake I told you he'd take a sensible attitude.

Flora Yeah. Tomorrow he plans t' come back—with lots more cotton. Maybe another twenty-seven wagons.

Jake Yeah?

Flora An' while you ginnin' it out—he'll have me entertain him with—nice lemonade!

(*She has another fit of giggles.*)

Jake The more I hear about that lemonade the better I like it. Lemonade highballs, huh? Mr. Thomas Collins?

Flora I guess it's—gonna go on fo'—th' rest of th'—summer. . . .

Jake (*rising and stretching happily*) Well, it'll . . . it'll soon be fall. Cooler nights comin' on.

Flora I don't know that that will put a—stop to it—though. . . .

Jake (*obliviously*) The air feels cooler already. You shouldn't be settin' out here without you' shirt on, honey. A change in the air can give you a mighty bad cold.

Flora I couldn't stan' nothin' on me—nex' to my—skin.

Jake It ain't the heat that gives you all them hives, it's too much liquor. Grog-blossoms, that's what you got! I'm goin' inside to the toilet. When I come out—(*He opens the screen door and goes in*).—We'll drive in town an' see what's at th' movies. You go hop in the Chevy!

(FLORA *laughs to herself. She slowly opens the huge kid purse and removes a wad of Kleenex. She touches herself tenderly here and there, giggling breathlessly.*)

Flora (*aloud*) I really oughtn't' have a white kid purse. It's wadded full of —Kleenex—to make it big—like a baby! Big—in my arms—like a baby!

Jake (*from inside*) What did you say, Baby?

Flora (*dragging herself up by the chain of the swing*) I'm not—Baby. Mama! Ma! That's—me. . . .

(*Cradling the big white purse in her arms, she advances slowly and tenderly to the edge of the porch. The moon shines full on her smiling and ravaged face. She begins to rock and sway gently, rocking the purse in her arms and crooning.*)

Rock-a-bye Baby—in uh treetops!
If a wind blows—a cradle will rock! (*She descends a step*).
If a bough bends—a baby will fall! (*She descends another step*).
Down will come Baby—cradle—an'—all! (*She laughs and stares raptly and vacantly up at the moon.*)

(*Curtain*)

Friedrich Duerrenmatt (1921–)
THE VISIT
Adapted by Maurice Valency

CHARACTERS

(In order of appearance)

Hofbauer (First Man)	**Second Grandchild**
Helmesberger (Second Man)	**Mike**
Wechsler (Third Man)	**Max**
Vogel (Fourth Man)	**First Blind Man**
Painter	**Second Blind Man**
Station Master	**Athlete**
Burgomaster	**Frau Burgomaster**
Teacher	**Frau Schill**
Pastor	**Daughter**
Anton Schill	**Son**
Claire Zachanassian	**Doctor Nüsslin**
Conductor	**Frau Block (First Woman)**
Pedro Cabral	**Truck Driver**
Bobby	**Reporter**
Policeman	**Townsman**
First Grandchild	

The action of the play takes place in and around the little town of Güllen,
somewhere in Europe.

There are three acts.

ACT I

A railway-crossing bell starts ringing. Then is heard the distant sound of
a locomotive whistle. The curtain rises.

The scene represents, in the simplest possible manner, a little town some-
where in Central Europe. The time is the present. The town is shabby

and ruined, as if the plague had passed there. Its name, Güllen, is inscribed on the shabby signboard which adorns the façade of the railway station. This edifice is summarily indicated by a length of rusty iron paling, a platform parallel to the proscenium, beyond which one imagines the rails to be, and a baggage truck standing by a wall on which a torn timetable, marked "Fahrplan," [1] *is affixed by three nails. In the station wall is a door with a sign: "Eintritt Verboten."* [2] *This leads to the* STATION MASTER's *office.*

Left of the station is a little house of gray stucco, formerly whitewashed. It has a tile roof, badly in need of repair. Some shreds of travel posters still adhere to the windowless walls. A shingle hanging over the entrance, left, reads: "Männer." [3] *On the other side of the shingle reads: "Damen."* [4] *Along the wall of the little house there is a wooden bench, backless, on which four men are lounging cheerlessly, shabbily dressed, with cracked shoes. A fifth man is busied with paintpot and brush. He is kneeling on the ground, painting a strip of canvas with the words: "Welcome, Clara."*

The warning signal rings uninterruptedly. The sound of the approaching train comes closer and closer. The STATION MASTER *issues from his office, advances to the center of the platform and salutes.*

The train is heard thundering past in a direction parallel to the footlights, and is lost in the distance. The men on the bench follow its passing with a slow movement of their heads, from left to right.

First Man The "Emperor." Hamburg-Naples.
Second Man Then comes the "Diplomat."
Third Man Then the "Banker."
Fourth Man And at eleven twenty-seven the "Flying Dutchman." Venice-Stockholm.
First Man Our only pleasure—watching trains.

(*The station bell rings again. The* STATION MASTER *comes out of his office and salutes another train. The men follow its course, right to left*)

Fourth Man Once upon a time the "Emperor" and the "Flying Dutchman" used to stop here in Güllen. So did the "Diplomat," the "Banker," and the "Silver Comet."

[1] Fahrplan: timetable.
[2] Eintritt Verboten: No Entrance.
[3] Männer: Men.
[4] Damen: Women.

Second Man Now it's only the local from Kaffigen and the twelve-forty from Kalberstadt.

Third Man The fact is, we're ruined.

First Man What with the Wagonworks shut down . . .

Second Man The Foundry finished . . .

Fourth Man The Golden Eagle Pencil Factory all washed up . . .

First Man It's life on the dole.

Second Man Did you say life?

Third Man We're rotting.

First Man Starving.

Second Man Crumbling.

Fourth Man The whole damn town.

(*The station bell rings*)

Third Man Once we were a center of industry.

Painter A cradle of culture.

Fourth Man One of the best little towns in the country.

First Man In the world.

Second Man Here Goethe[5] slept.

Fourth Man Brahms[6] composed a quartet.

Third Man Here Berthold Schwarz[7] invented gunpowder.

Painter And I once got first prize at the Dresden Exhibition of Contemporary Art. What am I doing now? Painting signs.

(*The station bell rings. The* STATION MASTER *comes out. He throws away a cigarette butt. The men scramble for it*)

First Man Well, anyway, Madame Zachanassian will help us.

Fourth Man If she comes . . .

Third Man If she comes.

Second Man Last week she was in France. She gave them a hospital.

First Man In Rome she founded a free public nursery.

Third Man In Leuthenau, a bird sanctuary.

Painter They say she got Picasso to design her car.

First Man Where does she get all that money?

Second Man An oil company, a shipping line, three banks and five railways—

Fourth Man And the biggest string of geisha houses in Japan.

(*From the direction of the town come the* BURGOMASTER,[8] *the* PASTOR, *the* TEACHER *and* ANTON SCHILL. *The* BURGOMASTER, *the* TEACHER *and* SCHILL *are*

[5] Goethe: Johann von Goethe (1749–1832), German poet, dramatist, and novelist.
[6] Brahms: Johannes Brahms (1833–1897), German composer.
[7] Berthold Schwarz: German monk of the fourteenth century.
[8] Burgomaster: mayor.

men in their fifties. The Pastor *is ten years younger. All four are dressed shabbily and are sad-looking. The* Burgomaster *looks official.* Schill *is tall and handsome, but graying and worn; nevertheless a man of considerable charm and presence. He walks directly to the little house and disappears into it)*

Painter Any news, Burgomaster? Is she coming?

All Yes, is she coming?

Burgomaster She's coming. The telegram has been confirmed. Our distinguished guest will arrive on the twelve-forty from Kalberstadt. Everyone must be ready.

Teacher The mixed choir is ready. So is the children's chorus.

Burgomaster And the church bell, Pastor?

Pastor The church bell will ring. As soon as the new bell ropes are fitted. The man is working on them now.

Burgomaster The town band will be drawn up in the market place and the Athletic Association will form a human pyramid in her honor—the top man will hold the wreath with her initials. Then lunch at the Golden Apostle. I shall say a few words.

Teacher Of course.

Burgomaster I had thought of illuminating the town hall and the cathedral, but we can't afford the lamps.

Painter Burgomaster—what do you think of this?

(He shows the banner)

Burgomaster *(Calls)* Schill! Schill!

Teacher Schill!

*(*Schill *comes out of the little house)*

Schill Yes, right away. Right away.

Burgomaster This is more in your line. What do you think of this?

Schill *(Looks at the sign)* No, no, no. That certainly won't do, Burgomaster. It's much too intimate. It shouldn't read: "Welcome, Clara." It should read: "Welcome, Madame . . ."

Teacher Zachanassian.

Burgomaster Zachanassian.

Schill Zachanassian.

Painter But she's Clara to us.

First Man Clara Wäscher.

Second Man Born here.

Third Man Her father was a carpenter. He built this.

(All turn and stare at the little house)

Schill All the same . . .

Painter If I . . .

FRIEDRICH DUERRENMATT

Burgomaster No, no, no. He's right. You'll have to change it.

Painter Oh, well, I'll tell you what I'll do. I'll leave this and I'll put "Welcome, Madame Zachanassian" on the other side. Then if things go well, we can always turn it around.

Burgomaster Good idea. (*To* SCHILL) Yes?

Schill Well, anyway, it's safer. Everything depends on the first impression.

(*The train bell is heard. Two clangs. The* PAINTER *turns the banner over and goes to work*)

First Man Hear that? The "Flying Dutchman" has just passed through Leuthenau.

Fourth Man Eleven twenty.

Burgomaster Gentlemen, you know that the millionairess is our only hope.

Pastor Under God.

Burgomaster Under God. Naturally. Schill, we depend entirely on you.

Schill Yes, I know. You keep telling me.

Burgomaster After all, you're the only one who really knew her.

Schill Yes, I knew her.

Pastor You were really quite close to one another, I hear, in those days.

Schill Close? Yes, we were close, there's no denying it. We were in love. I was young—good-looking, so they said—and Clara—you know, I can still see her in the great barn coming toward me—like a light out of the darkness. And in the Konradsweil Forest she'd come running to meet me —barefooted—her beautiful red hair streaming behind her. Like a witch. I was in love with her, all right. But you know how it is when you're twenty.

Pastor What happened?

Schill (*Shrugs*) Life came between us.

Burgomaster You must give me some points about her for my speech.

(*He takes out his notebook*)

Schill I think I can help you there.

Teacher Well, I've gone through the school records. And the young lady's marks were, I'm afraid to say, absolutely dreadful. Even in deportment. The only subject in which she was even remotely passable was natural history.

Burgomaster Good in natural history. That's fine. Give me a pencil.

(*He makes a note*)

Schill She was an outdoor girl. Wild. Once, I remember, they arrested a tramp, and she threw stones at the policeman. She hated injustice passionately.

Burgomaster Strong sense of justice. Excellent.

Schill   And generous . . .

All   Generous?

Schill   Generous to a fault. Whatever little she had, she shared—so good-hearted. I remember once she stole a bag of potatoes to give to a poor widow.

Burgomaster (*Writing in notebook*)   Wonderful generosity—

Teacher   Generosity.

Burgomaster   That, gentlemen, is something I must not fail to make a point of.

Schill   And such a sense of humor. I remember once when the oldest man in town fell and broke his leg, she said, "Oh, dear, now they'll have to shoot him."

Burgomaster   Well, I've got enough. The rest, my friend, is up to you.

(*He puts the notebook away*)

Schill   Yes, I know, but it's not so easy. After all, to part a woman like that from her millions—

Burgomaster   Exactly. Millions. We have to think in big terms here.

Teacher   If she's thinking of buying us off with a nursery school—

All   Nursery school!

Pastor   Don't accept.

Teacher   Hold out.

Schill   I'm not so sure that I can do it. You know, she may have forgotten me completely.

Burgomaster (*He exchanges a look with the* TEACHER *and the* PASTOR)   Schill, for many years you have been our most popular citizen. The most respected and the best loved.

Schill   Why, thank you . . .

Burgomaster   And therefore I must tell you—last week I sounded out the political opposition, and they agreed. In the spring you will be elected to succeed me as Burgomaster. By unanimous vote.

(*The others clap their hands in approval*)

Schill   But, my dear Burgomaster—!

Burgomaster   It's true.

Teacher   I'm a witness. I was at the meeting.

Schill   This is—naturally, I'm terribly flattered— It's a completely unexpected honor.

Burgomaster   You deserve it.

Schill   Burgomaster! Well, well—! (*Briskly*) Gentlemen, to business. The first chance I get, of course, I shall discuss our miserable position with Clara.

Teacher   But tactfully, tactfully—

Schill   What do you take me for? We must feel our way. Everything must be correct. Psychologically correct. For example, here at the railway station, a single blunder, one false note, could be disastrous.

Burgomaster   He's absolutely right. The first impression colors all the rest. Madame Zachanassian sets foot on her native soil for the first time in many years. She sees our love and she sees our misery. She remembers her youth, her friends. The tears well up into her eyes. Her childhood companions throng about her. I will naturally not present myself like this, but in my black coat with my top hat. Next to me, my wife. Before me, my two grandchildren all in white, with roses. My God, if it only comes off as I see it! If only it comes off. (*The station bell begins ringing*) Oh, my God! Quick! We must get dressed.

First Man   It's not her train. It's only the "Flying Dutchman."

Pastor (*Calmly*)   We have still two hours before she arrives.

Schill   For God's sake, don't let's lose our heads. We still have a full two hours.

Burgomaster   Who's losing their heads? (*To* First *and* Second Man) When her train comes, you two, Helmesberger and Vogel, will hold up the banner with "Welcome Madame Zachanassian." The rest will applaud.

Third Man   Bravo!

(*He applauds*)

Burgomaster   But, please, one thing—no wild cheering like last year with the government relief committee. It made no impression at all and we still haven't received any loan. What we need is a feeling of genuine sincerity. That's how we greet with full hearts our beloved sister who has been away from us so long. Be sincerely moved, my friends, that's the secret; be sincere. Remember you're not dealing with a child. Next a few brief words from me. Then the church bell will start pealing—

Pastor   If he can fix the ropes in time.

(*The station bell rings*)

Burgomaster   —Then the mixed choir moves in. And then—

Teacher   We'll form a line down here.

Burgomaster   Then the rest of us will form in two lines leading from the station—

(*He is interrupted by the thunder of the approaching train. The men crane their heads to see it pass. The* Station Master *advances to the platform and salutes. There is a sudden shriek of air brakes. The train screams to a stop. The four men jump up in consternation*)

Painter   But the "Flying Dutchman" never stops!

First Man   It's stopping.

Second Man   In Güllen!

Third Man   In the poorest—

First Man The dreariest—
Second Man The lousiest—
Fourth Man The most God-forsaken hole between Venice and Stockholm.
Station Master It cannot stop!

(*The train noises stop. There is only the panting of the engine*)

Painter It's stopped!

(*The* STATION MASTER *runs out*)

Offstage Voices What's happened? Is there an accident?

(*A hubbub of offstage voices, as if the passengers on the invisible train were alighting*)

Claire (*Offstage*) Is this Güllen?
Conductor (*Offstage*) Here, here, what's going on?
Claire (*Offstage*) Who the hell are you?
Conductor (*Offstage*) But you pulled the emergency cord, madame!
Claire (*Offstage*) I always pull the emergency cord.
Station Master (*Offstage*) I must ask you what's going on here.
Claire (*Offstage*) And who the hell are you?
Station Master (*Offstage*) I'm the Station Master, madame, and I must ask you—
Claire (*Enters*) No!

(*From the right* CLAIRE ZACHANASSIAN *appears. She is an extraordinary woman. She is in her fifties, red-haired, remarkably dressed, with a face as impassive as that of an ancient idol, beautiful still, and with a singular grace of movement and manner. She is simple and unaffected, yet she has the haughtiness of a world power. The entire effect is striking to the point of the unbelievable. Behind her comes her fiancé,* PEDRO CABRAL, *tall, young, very handsome, and completely equipped for fishing, with creel and net, and with a rod case in his hand. An excited* CONDUCTOR *follows*)

Conductor But, madame, I must insist! You have stopped "The Flying Dutchman." I must have an explanation.
Claire Nonsense. Pedro.
Pedro Yes, my love?
Claire This is Güllen. Nothing has changed. I recognize it all. There's the forest of Konradsweil. There's a brook in it full of trout, where you can fish. And there's the roof of the great barn. Ha! God! What a miserable blot on the map.

(*She crosses the stage and goes off with* PEDRO)

Schill My God! Clara!
Teacher Claire Zachanassian!

All Claire Zachanassian!

Burgomaster And the town band? The town band! Where is it?

Teacher The mixed choir! The mixed choir!

Pastor The church bell! The church bell!

Burgomaster (*To the* FIRST MAN) Quick! My dress coat. My top hat. My grandchildren. Run! Run! (FIRST MAN *runs off. The* BURGOMASTER *shouts after him*) And don't forget my wife!

(*General panic. The* THIRD MAN *and* FOURTH MAN *hold up the banner, on which only part of the name has been painted: "Welcome Mad—"* CLAIRE *and* PEDRO *re-enter, right*)

Conductor (*Mastering himself with an effort*) Madame. The train is waiting. The entire international railway schedule has been disrupted. I await your explanation.

Claire You're a very foolish man. I wish to visit this town. Did you expect me to jump off a moving train?

Conductor (*Stupefied*) You stopped the "Flying Dutchman" because you wished to visit the town?

Claire Naturally.

Conductor (*Inarticulate*) Madame!

Station Master Madame, if you wished to visit the town, the twelve forty from Kalberstadt was entirely at your service. Arrival in Güllen, one seventeen.

Claire The local that stops at Loken, Beisenbach, and Leuthenau? Do you expect me to waste three-quarters of an hour chugging dismally through this wilderness?

Conductor Madame, you shall pay for this!

Claire Bobby, give him a thousand marks.

(BOBBY, *her butler, a man in his seventies, wearing dark glasses, opens his wallet. The townspeople gasp*)

Conductor (*Taking the money in amazement*) But, madame!

Claire And three thousand for the Railway Widows' Relief Fund.

Conductor (*With the money in his hands*) But we have no such fund, madame.

Claire Now you have.

(*The* BURGOMASTER *pushes his way forward*)

Burgomaster (*He whispers to the* CONDUCTOR *and* TEACHER) The lady is Madame Claire Zachanassian!

Conductor Claire Zachanassian? Oh, my God! But that's naturally quite different. Needless to say, we would have stopped the train if we'd had the slightest idea. (*He hands the money back to* BOBBY) Here, please. I couldn't dream of it. Four thousand. My God!

Claire   Keep it. Don't fuss.

Conductor   Would you like the train to wait, madame, while you visit the town? The administration will be delighted. The cathedral porch. The town hall—

Claire   You may take the train away. I don't need it any more.

Station Master   All aboard!

(*He puts his whistle to his lips.* PEDRO *stops him*)

Pedro   But the press, my angel. They don't know anything about this. They're still in the dining car.

Claire   Let them stay there. I don't want the press in Güllen at the moment. Later they will come by themselves. (*To* STATION MASTER) And now what are you waiting for?

Station Master   All aboard!

(*The* STATION MASTER *blows a long blast on his whistle. The train leaves. Meanwhile, the* FIRST MAN *has brought the* BURGOMASTER'S *dress coat and top hat. The* BURGOMASTER *puts on the coat, then advances slowly and solemnly*)

Conductor   I trust madame will not speak of this to the administration. It was a pure misunderstanding.

(*He salutes and runs for the train as it starts moving*)

Burgomaster (*Bows*)   Gracious lady, as Burgomaster of the town of Güllen, I have the honor—

(*The rest of the speech is lost in the roar of the departing train. He continues speaking and gesturing, and at last bows amid applause as the train noises end*)

Claire   Thank you, Mr. Burgomaster.

(*She glances at the beaming faces, and lastly at* SCHILL, *whom she does not recognize. She turns upstage*)

Schill   Clara!

Claire (*Turns and stares*)   Anton?

Schill   Yes. It's good that you've come back.

Claire   Yes. I've waited for this moment. All my life. Ever since I left Güllen.

Schill (*A little embarrassed*)   That is very kind of you to say, Clara.

Claire   And have you thought about me?

Schill   Naturally. Always. You know that.

Claire   Those were happy times we spent together.

Schill   Unforgettable.

(*He smiles reassuringly at the* BURGOMASTER)

Claire   Call me by the name you used to call me.

Schill (*Whispers*)   My kitten.

Claire   What?

Schill (*Louder*)   My kitten.

Claire   And what else?

Schill   Little witch.

Claire   I used to call you my black panther. You're gray now, and soft.

Schill   But you are still the same, little witch.

Claire   I am the same? (*She laughs*) Oh, no, my black panther, I am not at all the same.

Schill (*Gallantly*)   In my eyes you are. I see no difference.

Claire   Would you like to meet my fiancé? Pedro Cabral. He owns an enormous plantation in Brazil.

Schill   A pleasure.

Claire   We're to be married soon.

Schill   Congratulations.

Claire   He will be my eighth husband. (PEDRO *stands by himself downstage, right*) Pedro, come here and show your face. Come along, darling —come here! Don't sulk. Say hello.

Pedro   Hello.

Claire   A man of few words! Isn't he charming? A diplomat. He's interested only in fishing. Isn't he handsome, in his Latin way? You'd swear he was a Brazilian. But he's not—he's a Greek. His father was a White Russian. We were betrothed by a Bulgarian priest. We plan to be married in a few days here in the cathedral.

Burgomaster   Here in the cathedral? What an honor for us!

Claire   No. It was my dream, when I was seventeen, to be married in Güllen cathedral. The dreams of youth are sacred, don't you think so, Anton?

Schill   Yes, of course.

Claire   Yes, of course. I think so, too. Now I would like to look at the town. (*The mixed choir arrives, breathless, wearing ordinary clothes with green sashes*) What's all this? Go away. (*She laughs*) Ha! Ha! Ha!

Teacher   Dear lady—(*He steps forward, having put on a sash also*) Dear lady, as Rector of the high school and a devotee of that noble muse, Music, I take pleasure in presenting the Güllen mixed choir.

Claire   How do you do?

Teacher   Who will sing for you an ancient folk song of the region, with specially amended words—if you will deign to listen.

Claire   Very well. Fire away.

(*The* TEACHER *blows a pitch pipe. The mixed choir begins to sing the ancient folk song with the amended words. Just then the station bell starts ringing.*

The song is drowned in the roar of the passing express. The STATION MAS-
TER *salutes. When the train has passed, there is applause*)

Burgomaster The church bell! The church bell! Where's the church bell?

(*The* PASTOR *shrugs helplessly*)

Claire Thank you, Professor. They sang beautifully. The big little blond
bass—no, not that one—the one with the big Adam's apple—was most
impressive. (*The* TEACHER *bows. The* POLICEMAN *pushes his way profes-
sionally through the mixed choir and comes to attention in front of*
CLAIRE ZACHANASSIAN) Now, who are you?

Policeman (*Clicks heels*) Police Chief Schultz. At your service.

Claire (*She looks him up and down*) I have no need of you at the moment.
But I think there will be work for you by and by. Tell me, do you know
how to close an eye from time to time?

Policeman How else could I get along in my profession?

Claire You might practice closing both.

Schill (*Laughs*) What a sense of humor, eh?

Burgomaster (*Puts on the top hat*) Permit me to present my grandchildren,
gracious lady. Hermine and Adolphine. There's only my wife still to
come.

(*He wipes the perspiration from his brow, and replaces the hat. The little
girls present the roses with elaborate curtsies*)

Claire Thank you, my dears. Congratulations, Burgomaster. Extraordinary
children.

(*She plants the roses in* PEDRO'S *arms. The* BURGOMASTER *secretly passes his
top hat to the* PASTOR, *who puts it on*)

Burgomaster Our pastor, madame.

(*The* PASTOR *takes off the hat and bows*)

Claire Ah. The pastor. How do you do? Do you give consolation to the
dying?

Pastor (*A bit puzzled*) That is part of my ministry, yes.

Claire And to those who are condemned to death?

Pastor Capital punishment has been abolished in this country, madame.

Claire I see. Well, it could be restored, I suppose.

(*The* PASTOR *hands back the hat. He shrugs his shoulders in confusion*)

Schill (*Laughs*) What an original sense of humor!

(*All laugh, a little blankly*)

Claire Well, I can't sit here all day—I should like to see the town.

(*The* Burgomaster *offers his arm*)

Burgomaster   May I have the honor, gracious lady?
Claire   Thank you, but these legs are not what they were. This one was broken in five places.
Schill (*Full of concern*)   My kitten!
Claire   When my airplane bumped into a mountain in Afghanistan. All the others were killed. Even the pilot. But as you see, I survived. I don't fly any more.
Schill   But you're as strong as ever now.
Claire   Stronger.
Burgomaster   Never fear, gracious lady. The town doctor has a car.
Claire   I never ride in motors.
Burgomaster   You never ride in motors?
Claire   Not since my Ferrari crashed in Hong Kong.
Schill   But how do you travel, then, little witch? On a broom?
Claire   Mike—Max! (*She claps her hands. Two huge bodyguards come in, left, carrying a sedan chair.*[9] *She sits in it*) I travel this way—a bit antiquated, of course. But perfectly safe. Ha! Ha! Aren't they magnificent? Mike and Max. I bought them in America. They were in jail, condemned to the chair. I had them pardoned. Now they're condemned to my chair. I paid fifty thousand dollars apiece for them. You couldn't get them now for twice the sum. The sedan chair comes from the Louvre.[10] I fancied it so much that the President of France gave it to me. The French are so impulsive, don't you think so, Anton? Go!

(Mike *and* Max *start to carry her off*)

Burgomaster   You wish to visit the cathedral? And the old town hall?
Claire   No. The great barn. And the forest of Konradsweil. I wish to go with Anton and visit our old haunts once again.
The Pastor   Very touching.
Claire (*To the butler*)   Will you send my luggage and the coffin to the Golden Apostle?
Burgomaster   The coffin?
Claire   Yes. I brought one with me. Go!
Teacher   Hip-hip—
All   Hurrah! Hip-hip, hurrah! Hurrah!

(*They bear off in the direction of the town. The* Townspeople *burst into cheers. The church bell rings*)

Burgomaster   Ah, thank God—the bell at last.

[9] sedan chair: enclosed, portable chair carried on poles.
[10] Louvre: Paris art museum.

(*The* POLICEMAN *is about to follow the others, when the two* BLIND MEN *appear. They are not young, yet they seem childish—a strange effect. Though they are of different height and features, they are dressed exactly alike, and so create the effect of being twins. They walk slowly, feeling their way. Their voices, when they speak, are curiously high and flutelike, and they have a curious trick of repetition of phrases*)

First Blind Man   We're in—
Both Blind Men   Güllen.
First Blind Man   We breathe—
Second Blind Man   We breathe—
Both Blind Men   We breathe the air, the air of Güllen.
Policeman (*Startled*)   Who are you?
First Blind Man   We belong to the lady.
Second Blind Man   We belong to the lady. She calls us—
First Blind Man   Kobby.
Second Blind Man   And Lobby.
Policeman   Madame Zachanassian is staying at the Golden Apostle.
First Blind Man   We're blind.
Second Blind Man   We're blind.
Policeman   Blind? Come along with me, then. I'll take you there.
First Blind Man   Thank you, Mr. Policeman.
Second Blind Man   Thanks very much.
Policeman   Hey! How do you know I'm a policeman, if you're blind?
Both Blind Men   By your voice. By your voice.
First Blind Man   All policemen sound the same.
Policeman   You've had a lot to do with the police, have you, little men?
First Blind Man   Men he calls us!
Both Blind Men   Men!
Policeman   What are you then?
Both Blind Men   You'll see. You'll see.

(*The* POLICEMAN *claps his hands suddenly. The* BLIND MEN *turn sharply toward the sound. The* POLICEMAN *is convinced they are blind*)

Policeman   What's your trade?
Both Blind Men   We have no trade.
Second Blind Man   We play music.
First Blind Man   We sing.
Second Blind Man   We amuse the lady.
First Blind Man   We look after the beast.
Second Blind Man   We feed it.
First Blind Man   We stroke it.
Second Blind Man   We take it for walks.
Policeman   What beast?

Both Blind Men   You'll see—you'll see.
Second Blind Man   We give it raw meat.
First Blind Man   —And she gives us chicken and wine.
Second Blind Man   Every day—
Both Blind Men   Every day.
Policeman   Rich people have strange tastes.
Both Blind Men   Strange tastes—strange tastes.

(*The* POLICEMAN *puts on his helmet*)

Policeman   Come along, I'll take you to the lady.

(*The two* BLIND MEN *turn and walk off*)

Both Blind Men   We know the way—we know the way.

(*The station and the little house vanish. A sign representing the Golden Apostle descends. The scene dissolves into the interior of the inn. The Golden Apostle is seen to be in the last stages of decay. The walls are cracked and moldering, and the plaster is falling from the ancient lath. A table represents the café of the inn. The* BURGOMASTER *and the* TEACHER *sit at this table, drinking a glass together. A procession of* TOWNSPEOPLE, *carrying many pieces of luggage, passes. Then comes a coffin, and, last, a large box covered with a canvas. They cross the stage from right to left*)

Burgomaster   Trunks. Suitcases. Boxes. (*He looks up apprehensively at the ceiling*) The floor will never bear the weight. (*As the large covered box is carried in, he peers under the canvas, then draws back*) Good God!
Teacher   Why, what's in it?
Burgomaster   A live panther. (*They laugh. The* BURGOMASTER *lifts his glass solemnly*) Your health, Professor. Let's hope she puts the Foundry back on its feet.
Teacher (*Lifts his glass*)   And the Wagonworks.
Burgomaster   And the Golden Eagle Pencil Factory. Once that starts moving, everything else will go. *Prosit.*[11]

(*They touch glasses and drink*)

Teacher   What does she need a panther for?
Burgomaster   Don't ask me. The whole thing is too much for me. The Pastor had to go home and lie down.
Teacher (*Sets down his glass*)   If you want to know the truth, she frightens me.
Burgomaster (*Nods gravely*)   She's a strange one.
Teacher   You understand, Burgomaster, a man who for twenty-two years has been correcting the Latin compositions of the students of Güllen is

[11] *Prosit:* "To your health."

not unaccustomed to surprises. I have seen things to make one's hair stand on end. But when this woman suddenly appeared on the platform, a shudder tore through me. It was as though out of the clear sky all at once a fury descended upon us, beating its black wings—

(*The* POLICEMAN *comes in. He mops his face*)

Policeman   Ah! Now the old place is livening up a bit!

Burgomaster   Ah, Schultz, come and join us.

Policeman   Thank you. (*He calls*) Beer!

Burgomaster   Well, what's the news from the front?

Policeman   I'm just back from Schiller's barn. My God! What a scene! She had us all tiptoeing around in the straw as if we were in church. Nobody dared to speak above a whisper. And the way she carried on! I was so embarrassed I let them go to the forest by themselves.

Burgomaster   Does the fiancé go with them?

Policeman   With his fishing rod and his landing net. In full marching order. (*He calls again*) Beer!

Burgomaster   That will be her seventh husband.

Teacher   Her eighth.

Burgomaster   But what does she expect to find in the Konradsweil forest?

Policeman   The same thing she expected to find in the old barn, I suppose. The—the—

Teacher   The ashes of her youthful love.

Policeman   Exactly.

Teacher   It's poetry.

Policeman   Poetry.

Teacher   Sheer poetry! It makes one think of Shakespeare, of Wagner.[12] Of Romeo and Juliet.

(*The* SECOND MAN *comes in as a waiter. The* POLICEMAN *is served his beer*)

Burgomaster   Yes, you're right. (*Solemnly*) Gentlemen, I would like to propose a toast. To our great and good friend, Anton Schill, who is even now working on our behalf.

Policeman   Yes! He's really working.

Burgomaster   Gentlemen, to the best-loved citizen of this town. My successor, Anton Schill!

(*They raise their glasses. At this point an unearthly scream is heard. It is the black panther howling offstage. The sign of the Golden Apostle rises out of sight. The lights go down. The inn vanishes. Only the wooden bench, on which the four men were lounging in the opening scene, is left on the stage, downstage right. The procession comes on upstage. The two bodyguards carry in* CLAIRE's *sedan chair. Next to it walks* SCHILL. PEDRO *walks*

---

[12] Wagner: Richard Wagner (1813–1883), German composer.

behind, with his fishing rod. Last come the two BLIND MEN *and the butler.*
CLAIRE *alights*)

Claire Stop! Take my chair off somewhere else. I'm tired of looking at
you. (*The bodyguards and the sedan chair go off*) Pedro darling, your
brook is just a little further along down that path. Listen. You can hear
it from here. Bobby, take him and show him where it is.

Both Blind Men We'll show him the way—we'll show him the way.

(*They go off, left.* PEDRO *follows.* BOBBY *walks off, right*)

Claire Look, Anton. Our tree. There's the heart you carved in the bark
long ago.

Schill Yes. It's still there.

Claire How it has grown! The trunk is black and wrinkled. Why, its limbs
are twice what they were. Some of them have died.

Schill It's aged. But it's there.

Claire Like everything else. (*She crosses, examining other trees*) Oh, how
tall they are. How long it is since I walked here, barefoot over the pine
needles and the damp leaves! Look, Anton. A fawn.

Schill Yes, a fawn. It's the season.

Claire I thought everything would be changed. But it's all just as we left
it. This is the seat we sat on years ago. Under these branches you kissed
me. And over there under the hawthorn, where the moss is soft and
green, we would lie in each other's arms. It is all as it used to be. Only
we have changed.

Schill Not so much, little witch. I remember the first night we spent together, you ran away and I chased you till I was quite breathless—

Claire Yes.

Schill Then I was angry and I was going home, when suddenly I heard
you call and I looked up, and there you were sitting in a tree, laughing
down at me.

Claire No. It was in the great barn. I was in the hayloft.

Schill Were you?

Claire Yes. What else do you remember?

Schill I remember the morning we went swimming by the waterfall, and
afterwards we were lying together on the big rock in the sun, when
suddenly we heard footsteps and we just had time to snatch up our
clothes and run behind the bushes when the old pastor appeared and
scolded you for not being in school.

Claire No. It was the schoolmaster who found us. It was Sunday and I
was supposed to be in church.

Schill Really?

Claire Yes. Tell me more.

Schill I remember the time your father beat you, and you showed me the cuts on your back, and I swore I'd kill him. And the next day I dropped a tile from a roof top and split his head open.

Claire   You missed him.

Schill   No!

Claire   You hit old Mr. Reiner.

Schill   Did I?

Claire   Yes. I was seventeen. And you were not yet twenty. You were so handsome. You were the best-looking boy in town.

(*The two* BLIND MEN *begin playing mandolin music offstage, very softly*)

Schill   And you were the prettiest girl.

Claire   We were made for each other.

Schill   So we were.

Claire   But you married Mathilde Blumhard and her store, and I married old Zachanassian and his oil wells. He found me in a whorehouse in Hamburg. It was my hair that entangled him, the old golden beetle.

Schill   Clara!

Claire (*She claps her hands*)   Bobby! A cigar.

(BOBBY *appears with a leather case. He selects a cigar, puts it in a holder, lights it, and presents it to* CLAIRE)

Schill   My kitten smokes cigars!

Claire   Yes. I adore them. Would you care for one?

Schill   Yes, please. I've never smoked one of those.

Claire   It's a taste I acquired from old Zachanassian. Among other things. He was a real connoisseur.

Schill   We used to sit on this bench once, you and I, and smoke cigarettes. Do you remember?

Claire   Yes. I remember.

Schill   The cigarettes I bought from Mathilde.

Claire   No. She gave them to you for nothing.

Schill   Clara—don't be angry with me for marrying Mathilde.

Claire   She had money.

Schill   But what a lucky thing for you that I did!

Claire   Oh?

Schill   You were so young, so beautiful. You deserved a far better fate than to settle for this wretched town without any future.

Claire   Yes?

Schill   If you had stayed in Güllen and married me, your life would have been wasted, like mine.

Claire   Oh?

Schill   Look at me. A wretched shopkeeper in a bankrupt town!

Claire   But you have your family.

Schill My family! Never for a moment do they let me forget my failure, my poverty.

Claire Mathilde has not made you happy?

Schill (*Shrugs*) What does it matter?

Claire And the children?

Schill (*Shakes his head*) They're so completely materialistic. You know, they have no interest whatever in higher things.

Claire How sad for you.

(*A moment's pause, during which only the faint tinkling of the music is heard*)

Schill Yes. You know, since you went away my life has passed by like a stupid dream. I've hardly once been out of this town. A trip to a lake years ago. It rained all the time. And once five days in Berlin. That's all.

Claire The world is much the same everywhere.

Schill At least you've seen it.

Claire Yes. I've seen it.

Schill You've lived in it.

Claire I've lived in it. The world and I have been on very intimate terms.

Schill Now that you've come back, perhaps things will change.

Claire Naturally. I certainly won't leave my native town in this condition.

Schill It will take millions to put us on our feet again.

Claire I have millions.

Schill One, two, three.

Claire Why not?

Schill You mean—you will help us?

Claire Yes.

(*A woodpecker is heard in the distance*)

Schill I knew it—I knew it. I told them you were generous. I told them you were good. Oh, my kitten, my kitten.

(*He takes her hand. She turns her head away and listens*)

Claire Listen! A woodpecker.

Schill It's all just the way it was in the days when we were young and full of courage. The sun high above the pines. White clouds, piling up on one another. And the cry of the cuckoo in the distance. And the wind rustling the leaves, like the sound of surf on a beach. Just as it was years ago. If only we could roll back time and be together always.

Claire Is that your wish?

Schill Yes. You left me, but you never left my heart. (*He raises her hand to his lips*) The same soft little hand.

Claire No, not quite the same. It was crushed in the plane accident. But they mended it. They mend everything nowadays.

Schill Crushed? You wouldn't know it. See, another fawn.
Claire The old wood is alive with memories.

(PEDRO *appears, right, with a fish in his hand*)

Pedro See what I've caught, darling. See? A pike. Over two kilos.

(*The* BLIND MEN *appear onstage*)

Both Blind Men (*Clapping their hands*) A pike! A pike! Hurrah! Hurrah!

(*As the* BLIND MEN *clap their hands,* CLAIRE *and* SCHILL *exit, and the scene dissolves. The clapping of hands is taken up on all sides. The townspeople wheel in the walls of the café. A brass band strikes up a march tune. The door of the Golden Apostle descends. The townspeople bring in tables and set them with ragged tablecloths, cracked china and glassware. There is a table in the center, upstage, flanked by two tables perpendicular to it, right and left. The* PASTOR *and the* BURGOMASTER *come in.* SCHILL *enters. Other townspeople filter in, left and right. One, the* ATHLETE, *is in gymnastic costume. The applause continues*)

Burgomaster She's coming! (CLAIRE *enters upstage, center, followed by* BOBBY) The applause is meant for you, gracious lady.
Claire The band deserves it more than I. They blow from the heart. And the human pyramid was beautiful. You, show me your muscles. (*The* ATHLETE *kneels before her*) Superb. Wonderful arms, powerful hands. Have you ever strangled a man with them?
Athlete Strangled?
Claire Yes. It's perfectly simple. A little pressure in the proper place, and the rest goes by itself. As in politics.

(*The* BURGOMASTER'S *wife comes up, simpering*)

Burgomaster (*Presents her*) Permit me to present my wife, Madame Zachanassian.
Claire Annette Dummermuth. The head of our class.
Burgomaster (*He presents another sour-looking woman*) Frau Schill.
Claire Mathilde Blumhard. I remember the way you used to follow Anton with your eyes, from behind the shop door. You've grown a little thin and dry, my poor Mathilde.
Schill My daughter, Ottilie.
Claire Your daughter . . .
Schill My son, Karl.
Claire Your son. Two of them!

(*The town* DOCTOR *comes in, right. He is a man of fifty, strong and stocky, with bristly black hair, a mustache, and a saber cut on his cheek. He is wearing an old cutaway*)

Doctor   Well, well, my old Mercedes got me here in time after all!

Burgomaster   Dr. Nüsslin, the town physician. Madame Zachanassian.

Doctor   Deeply honored, madame.

(*He kisses her hand.* CLAIRE *studies him*)

Claire   It is you who signs the death certificates?

Doctor   Death certificates?

Claire   When someone dies.

Doctor   Why certainly. That is one of my duties.

Claire   And when the heart dies, what do you put down? Heart failure?

Schill (*Laughing*)   What a golden sense of humor!

Doctor   Bit grim, wouldn't you say?

Schill (*Whispers*)   Not at all, not at all. She's promised us a million.

Burgomaster (*Turns his head*)   What?

Schill   A million!

All (*Whisper*)   A million!

(CLAIRE *turns toward them*)

Claire   Burgomaster.

Burgomaster   Yes?

Claire   I'm hungry. (*The girls and the waiter fill glasses and bring food. There is a general stir. All take their places at the tables*) Are you going to make a speech?

(*The* BURGOMASTER *bows.* CLAIRE *sits next to the* BURGOMASTER. *The* BURGO-MASTER *rises, tapping his knife on his glass. He is radiant with good will. All applaud*)

Burgomaster   Gracious lady and friends. Gracious lady, it is now many years since you first left your native town of Güllen, which was founded by the Elector Hasso and which nestles in the green slope between the forest of Konradsweil and the beautiful valley of Pückenried. Much has taken place in this time, much that is evil.

Teacher   That's true.

Burgomaster   The world is not what it was; it has become harsh and bitter, and we too have had our share of harshness and bitterness. But in all this time, dear lady, we have never forgotten our little Clara. (*Applause*) Many years ago you brightened the town with your pretty face as a child, and now once again you brighten it with your presence. (*Polite applause*) We haven't forgotten you, and we haven't forgotten your family. Your mother, beautiful and robust even in her old age—(*He looks for his notes on the table*)—although unfortunately taken from us in the bloom of her youth by an infirmity of the lungs. Your respected father, Siegfried Wäscher, the builder, an example of whose work next to our railway station is often visited—(SCHILL *covers his face*)—that is to say, admired

—a lasting monument of local design and local workmanship. And you, gracious lady, whom we remember as a golden-haired—(*He looks at her*) —little red-headed sprite romping about our peaceful streets—on your way to school—which of us does not treasure your memory? (*He pokes nervously at his notebook*) We well remember your scholarly attainments—

Teacher Yes.

Burgomaster Natural history . . . Extraordinary sense of justice . . . And, above all, your supreme generosity. (*Great applause*) We shall never forget how you once spent the whole of your little savings to buy a sack of potatoes for a poor starving widow who was in need of food. Gracious lady, ladies and gentlemen, today our little Clara has become the world-famous Claire Zachanassian who has founded hospitals, soup kitchens, charitable institutes, art projects, libraries, nurseries, and schools, and now that she has at last once more returned to the town of her birth, sadly fallen as it is, I say in the name of all her loving friends who have sorely missed her: Long live our Clara!

All Long live our Clara!

(*Cheers. Music. Fanfare. Applause.* CLAIRE *rises*)

Claire Mr. Burgomaster. Fellow townsmen. I am greatly moved by the nature of your welcome and the disinterested joy which you have manifested on the occasion of my visit to my native town. I was not quite the child the Burgomaster described in his gracious address . . .

Burgomaster Too modest, madame.

Claire In school I was beaten—

Teacher Not by me.

Claire And the sack of potatoes which I presented to Widow Boll, I stole with the help of Anton Schill, not to save the old trull from starvation, but so that for once I might sleep with Anton in a real bed instead of under the trees of the forest. (*The townspeople look grave, embarrassed*) Nevertheless, I shall try to deserve your good opinion. In memory of the seventeen years I spent among you, I am prepared to hand over as a gift to the town of Güllen the sum of one billion marks. Five hundred million to the town, and five hundred million to be divided per capita among the citizens.

(*There is a moment of dead silence*)

Burgomaster A billion marks?

Claire On one condition.

(*Suddenly a movement of uncontrollable joy breaks out. People jump on chairs, dance about, yell excitedly. The* ATHLETE *turns handsprings in front of the speaker's table*)

Schill Oh, Clara, you astonishing, incredible, magnificent woman! What a heart! What a gesture! Oh—my little witch!

(*He kisses her hand*)

Burgomaster (*Holds up his arms for order*) Quiet! Quiet, please! On one condition, the gracious lady said. Now, madame, may we know what that condition is?

Claire I will tell you. In exchange for my billion marks, I want justice.

(*Silence*)

Burgomaster Justice, madame?
Claire I wish to buy justice.
Burgomaster But justice cannot be bought, madame.
Claire Everything cán be bought.
Burgomaster I don't understand at all.
Claire Bobby, step forward.

(*The butler goes to the center of the stage. He takes off his dark glasses and turns his face with a solemn air*)

Bobby Does anyone here present recognize me?
Frau Schill Hofer! Hofer!
All Who? What's that?
Teacher Not Chief Magistrate Hofer?
Bobby Exactly. Chief Magistrate Hofer. When Madame Zachanassian was a girl, I was presiding judge at the criminal court of Güllen. I served there until twenty-five years ago, when Madame Zachanassian offered me the opportunity of entering her service as butler. I accepted. You may consider it a strange employment for a member of the magistracy, but the salary—

(CLAIRE *bangs the mallet on the table*)

Claire Come to the point.
Bobby You have heard Madame Zachanassian's offer. She will give you a billion marks—when you have undone the injustice that she suffered at your hands here in Güllen as a girl.

(*All murmur*)

Burgomaster Injustice at our hands? Impossible!
Bobby Anton Schill . . .
Schill Yes?
Bobby Kindly stand.

(SCHILL *rises. He smiles, as if puzzled. He shrugs*)

Schill Yes?
Bobby In those days, a bastardy case was tried before me. Madame Claire

Zachanassian, at that time called Clara Wäscher, charged you with being the father of her illegitimate child. (*Silence*) You denied the charge. And produced two witnesses in your support.

Schill That's ancient history. An absurd business. We were children. Who remembers?

Claire Where are the blind men?

Both Blind Men Here we are. Here we are.

(MIKE *and* MAX *push them forward*)

Bobby You recognize these men, Anton Schill?

Schill I never saw them before in my life. What are they?

Both Blind Men We've changed. We've changed.

Bobby What were your names in your former life?

First Blind Man I was Jacob Hueblein. Jacob Hueblein.

Second Blind Man I was Ludwig Sparr. Ludwig Sparr.

Bobby (*To* SCHILL) Well?

Schill These names mean nothing to me.

Bobby Jacob Hueblein and Ludwig Sparr, do you recognize the defendant?

First Blind Man We're blind.

Second Blind Man We're blind.

Schill Ha-ha-ha!

Bobby By his voice?

Both Blind Men By his voice. By his voice.

Bobby At that trial, I was the judge. And you?

Both Blind Men We were the witnesses.

Bobby And what did you testify on that occasion?

First Blind Man That we had slept with Clara Wäscher.

Second Blind Man Both of us. Many times.

Bobby And was it true?

First Blind Man No.

Second Blind Man We swore falsely.

Bobby And why did you swear falsely?

First Blind Man Anton Schill bribed us.

Second Blind Man He bribed us.

Bobby With what?

Both Blind Men With a bottle of schnapps.

Bobby And now tell the people what happened to you. (*They hesitate and whimper*) Speak!

First Blind Man (*In a low voice*) She tracked us down.

Bobby Madame Zachanassian tracked them down. Jacob Hueblein was found in Canada. Ludwig Sparr in Australia. And when she found you, what did she do to you?

Second Blind Man She handed us over to Mike and Max.

Bobby And what did Mike and Max do to you?

First Blind Man   They made us what you see.

(*The* BLIND MEN *cover their faces.* MIKE *and* MAX *push them off*)

Bobby   And there you have it. We are all present in Güllen once again. The plaintiff. The defendant. The two false witnesses. The judge. Many years have passed. Does the plaintiff have anything further to add?

Claire   There is nothing to add.

Bobby   And the defendant?

Schill   Why are you doing this? It was all dead and buried.

Bobby   What happened to the child that was born?

Claire (*In a low voice*)   It lived a year.

Bobby   And what happened to you?

Claire   I became a whore.

Bobby   Why?

Claire   The judgment of the court left me no alternative. No one would trust me. No one would give me work.

Bobby   So. And now, what is the nature of the reparation you demand?

Claire   I want the life of Anton Schill.

(FRAU SCHILL *springs to Anton's side. She puts her arms around him. The children rush to him. He breaks away*)

Frau Schill   Anton! No! No!

Schill   No— No— She's joking. That happened long ago. That's all forgotten.

Claire   Nothing is forgotten. Neither the mornings in the forest, nor the nights in the great barn, nor the bedroom in the cottage, nor your treachery at the end. You said this morning that you wished that time might be rolled back. Very well—I have rolled it back. And now it is I who will buy justice. You bought it with a bottle of schnapps. I am willing to pay one billion marks.

(*The* BURGOMASTER *stands up, very pale and dignified*)

Burgomaster   Madame Zachanassian, we are not in the jungle. We are in Europe. We may be poor, but we are not heathens. In the name of the town of Güllen, I decline your offer. In the name of humanity. We shall never accept.

(*All applaud wildly. The applause turns into a sinister rhythmic beat. As* CLAIRE *rises, it dies away. She looks at the crowd, then at the* BURGOMASTER)

Claire   Thank you, Burgomaster. (*She stares at him a long moment*) I can wait.

(*She turns and walks off*)

Curtain

ACT II

The façade of the Golden Apostle, with a balcony on which chairs and a table are set out. To the right of the inn is a sign which reads: "Anton Schill, Handlung." [13] Under the sign the shop is represented by a broken counter. Behind the counter are some shelves with tobacco, cigarettes, and liquor bottles. There are two milk cans. The shop door is imaginary, but each entrance is indicated by a doorbell with a tinny sound.

It is early morning.

SCHILL *is sweeping the shop. The* SON *has a pan and brush and also sweeps. The* DAUGHTER *is dusting. They are singing "The Happy Wanderer."*

Schill   Karl—

(KARL *crosses with a dustpan.* SCHILL *sweeps dust into the pan. The doorbell rings. The* THIRD MAN *appears, carrying a crate of eggs*)

Third Man   'Morning.
Schill   Ah, good morning, Wechsler.
Third Man   Twelve dozen eggs, medium brown. Right?
Schill   Take them, Karl. (*The* SON *puts the crate in a corner*) Did they deliver the milk yet?
Son   Before you came down.
Third Man   Eggs are going up again, Herr Schill. First of the month.

(*He gives* SCHILL *a slip to sign*)

Schill   What? Again? And who's going to buy them?
Third Man   Fifty pfennig a dozen.
Schill   I'll have to cancel my order, that's all.
Third Man   That's up to you, Herr Schill.

(SCHILL *signs the slip*)

Schill   There's nothing else to do. (*He hands back the slip*) And how's the family?
Third Man   Oh, scraping along. Maybe now things will get better.
Schill   Maybe.
Third Man (*Going*)   'Morning.
Schill   Close the door. Don't let the flies in. (*The children resume their singing*) Now, listen to me, children. I have a little piece of good news for you. I didn't mean to speak of it yet awhile, but well, why not? Who do you suppose is going to be the next Burgomaster? Eh? (*They look up at him*) Yes, in spite of everything. It's settled. It's official. What an honor

---

[13] Handlung: merchandise.

for the family, eh? Especially at a time like this. To say nothing of the salary and the rest of it.

Son Burgomaster!

Schill Burgomaster. (*The* SON *shakes him warmly by the hand. The* DAUGHTER *kisses him*) You see, you don't have to be entirely ashamed of your father. (*Silence*) Is your mother coming down to breakfast soon?

Daughter Mother's tired. She's going to stay upstairs.

Schill You have a good mother, at least. There you are lucky. Oh, well, if she wants to rest, let her rest. We'll have breakfast together, the three of us. I'll fry some eggs and open a tin of the American ham. This morning we're going to breakfast like kings.

Son I'd like to, only—I can't.

Schill You've got to eat, you know.

Son I've got to run down to the station. One of the laborers is sick. They said they could use me.

Schill You want to work on the rails in all this heat? That's no work for a son of mine.

Son Look, Father, we can use the money.

Schill Well, if you feel you have to.

(*The* SON *goes to the door. The* DAUGHTER *moves toward* SCHILL)

Daughter I'm sorry, Father. I have to go too.

Schill You too? And where is the young lady going, if I may be so bold?

Daughter There may be something for me at the employment agency.

Schill Employment agency?

Daughter It's important to get there early.

Schill All right. I'll have something nice for you when you get home.

Son *and* **Daughter** (*Salute*) Good day, Burgomaster.

(*The* SON *and* DAUGHTER *go out. The* FIRST MAN *comes into* SCHILL's *shop. Mandolin and guitar music are heard offstage*)

Schill Good morning, Hofbauer.

First Man Cigarettes. (SCHILL *takes a pack from the shelf*) Not those. I'll have the green today.

Schill They cost more.

First Man Put it in the book.

Schill What?

First Man Charge it.

Schill Well, all right, I'll make an exception this time—seeing it's you, Hofbauer.

(SCHILL *writes in his cash book*)

First Man (*Opening the pack of cigarettes*) Who's that playing out there?

Schill The two blind men.

First Man They play well.

Schill   To hell with them.

First Man   They make you nervous? (SCHILL *shrugs. The* FIRST MAN *lights a cigarette*) She's getting ready for the wedding, I hear.

Schill   Yes. So they say.

(*Enter the* FIRST *and* SECOND WOMAN. *They cross to the counter*)

First Woman   Good morning, good morning.

Second Woman   Good morning.

First Man   Good morning.

Schill   Good morning, ladies.

First Woman   Good morning, Herr Schill.

Second Woman   Good morning.

First Woman   Milk please, Herr Schill.

Schill   Milk.

Second Woman   And milk for me too.

Schill   A liter of milk each. Right away.

First Woman   Whole milk, please, Herr Schill.

Schill   Whole milk?

Second Woman   Yes. Whole milk, please.

Schill   Whole milk, I can only give you half a liter each of whole milk.

First Woman   All right.

Schill   Half a liter of whole milk here, and half a liter of whole milk here. There you are.

First Woman   And butter please, a quarter kilo.

Schill   Butter, I haven't any butter. I can give you some very nice lard?

First Woman   No. Butter.

Schill   Goose fat? (*The* FIRST WOMAN *shakes her head*) Chicken fat?

First Woman   Butter.

Schill   Butter. Now, wait a minute, though. I have a tin of imported butter here somewhere. Ah. There you are. No, sorry, she asked first, but I can order some for you from Kalberstadt tomorrow.

Second Woman   And white bread.

Schill   White bread.

(*He takes a loaf and a knife*)

Second Woman   The whole loaf.

Schill   But a whole loaf would cost . . .

Second Woman   Charge it.

Schill   Charge it?

First Woman   And a package of milk chocolate.

Schill   Package of milk chocolate—right away.

Second Woman   One for me, too, Herr Schill.

Schill   And a package of milk chocolate for you, too.

First Woman   We'll eat it here, if you don't mind.

Schill Yes, please do.

Second Woman It's so cool at the back of the shop.

Schill Charge it?

Women Of course.

Schill All for one, one for all.

(*The* SECOND MAN *enters*)

Second Man Good morning.

The Two Women Good morning.

Schill Good morning, Helmesberger.

Second Man It's going to be a hot day.

Schill Phew!

Second Man How's business?

Schill Fabulous. For a while no one came, and now all of a sudden I'm running a luxury trade.

Second Man Good!

Schill Oh, I'll never forget the way you all stood by me at the Golden Apostle in spite of your need, in spite of everything. That was the finest hour of my life.

First Man We're not heathens, you know.

Second Man We're behind you, my boy; the whole town's behind you.

First Man As firm as a rock.

First Woman (*Munching her chocolate*) As firm as a rock, Herr Schill.

Both Women As firm as a rock.

Second Man There's no denying it—you're the most popular man in town.

First Man The most important.

Second Man And in the spring, God willing, you will be our Burgomaster.

First Man Sure as a gun.

All Sure as a gun.

(*Enter* PEDRO *with fishing equipment and a fish in his landing net*)

Pedro Would you please weigh my fish for me?

Schill (*Weighs it*) Two kilos.

Pedro Is that all?

Schill Two kilos exactly.

Pedro Two kilos!

(*He gives* SCHILL *a tip and exits*)

Second Woman The fiancé.

First Woman They're to be married this week. It will be a tremendous wedding.

Second Woman I saw his picture in the paper.

First Woman (*Sighs*) Ah, what a man!

Second Man Give me a bottle of schnapps.

Schill   The usual?

Second Man   No, cognac.

Schill   Cognac? But cognac costs twenty-two marks fifty.

Second Man   We all have to splurge a little now and again—

Schill   Here you are. Three Star.

Second Man   And a package of pipe tobacco.

Schill   Black or blond?

Second Man   English.

Schill   English. But that makes twenty-three marks eighty.

Second Man   Chalk it up.

Schill   Now, look. I'll make an exception this week. Only, you will have to pay me the moment your unemployment check comes in. I don't want to be kept waiting. (*Suddenly*) Helmesberger, are those new shoes you're wearing?

Second Man   Yes, what about it?

Schill   You too, Hofbauer. Yellow shoes! Brand new!

First Man   So?

Schill (*To the women*)   And you. You all have new shoes! New shoes!

First Woman   A person can't walk around forever in the same old shoes.

Second Woman   Shoes wear out.

Schill   And the money. Where does the money come from?

First Woman   We got them on credit, Herr Schill.

Second Woman   On credit.

Schill   On credit? And where all of a sudden do you get credit?

Second Man   Everybody gives credit now.

First Woman   You gave us credit yourself.

Schill   And what are you going to pay with? Eh? (*They are all silent.* SCHILL *advances upon them threateningly*) With what? Eh? With what? With what?

(*Suddenly he understands. He takes his apron off quickly, flings it on the counter, gets his jacket, and walks off with an air of determination. Now the shop sign vanishes. The shelves are pushed off. The lights go up on the balcony of the Golden Apostle, and the balcony unit itself moves forward into the optical center.* CLAIRE *and* BOBBY *step out on the balcony.* CLAIRE *sits down.* BOBBY *serves coffee*)

Claire   A lovely autumn morning. A silver haze on the streets and a violet sky above. Count Holk would have liked this. Remember him, Bobby? My third husband?

Bobby   Yes, madame.

Claire   Horrible man!

Bobby   Yes, madame.

Claire   Where is Monsieur Pedro? Is he up yet?

Bobby   Yes, madame. He's fishing.

Claire Already? What a singular passion!

(PEDRO *comes in with the fish*)

Pedro Good morning, my love.
Claire Pedro! There you are.
Pedro Look, my darling. Four kilos!
Claire A jewel! I'll have it grilled for your lunch. Give it to Bobby.
Pedro Ah—it is so wonderful here! I like your little town.
Claire Oh, do you?
Pedro Yes. These people, they are all so—what is the word?
Claire Simple, honest, hard-working, decent.
Pedro But, my angel, you are a mind reader. That's just what I was going to say—however did you guess?
Claire I know them.
Pedro Yet when we arrived it was all so dirty, so—what is the word?
Claire Shabby.
Pedro Exactly. But now everywhere you go, you see them busy as bees, cleaning their streets—
Claire Repairing their houses, sweeping—dusting—hanging new curtains in the windows—singing as they work.
Pedro But you astonishing, wonderful woman! You can't see all that from here.
Claire I know them. And in their gardens—I am sure that in their gardens they are manuring the soil for the spring.
Pedro My angel, you know everything. This morning on my way fishing I said to myself, look at them all manuring their gardens. It is extraordinary—and it's all because of you. Your return has given them a new —what is the word?
Claire Lease on life?
Pedro Precisely.
Claire The town was dying, it's true. But a town doesn't have to die. I think they realize that now. People die, not towns. Bobby! (BOBBY *appears*) A cigar.

(*The lights fade on the balcony, which moves back upstage. Somewhat to the right, a sign descends. It reads:* "Polizei." [14] *The* POLICEMAN *pushes a desk under it. This, with the bench, becomes the police station. He places a bottle of beer and a glass on the desk, and goes to hang up his coat off-stage. The telephone rings*)

Policeman Schultz speaking. Yes, we have a couple of rooms for the night. No, not for rent. This is not the hotel. This is the Güllen police station.

(*He laughs and hangs up.* SCHILL *comes in. He is evidently nervous*)

[14] Polizei: police.

Schill Schultz.
Policeman Hello, Schill. Come in. Sit down. Beer?
Schill Please.

(*He drinks thirstily*)

Policeman What can I do for you?
Schill I want you to arrest Madame Zachanassian.
Policeman Eh?
Schill I said I want you to arrest Madame Zachanassian.
Policeman What the hell are you talking about?
Schill I ask you to arrest this woman at once.
Policeman What offense has the lady committed?
Schill You know perfectly well. She offered a billion marks—
Policeman And you want her arrested for that?

(*He pours beer into his glass*)

Schill Schultz! It's your duty.
Schultz Extraordinary! Extraordinary idea!

(*He drinks his beer*)

Schill I'm speaking to you as your next Burgomaster.
Policeman Schill, that's true. The lady offered us a billion marks. But that doesn't entitle us to take police action against her.
Schill Why not?
Policeman In order to be arrested, a person must first commit a crime.
Schill Incitement to murder.
Policeman Incitement to murder is a crime. I agree.
Schill Well?
Policeman And such a proposal—if serious—constitutes an assault.
Schill That's what I mean.
Policeman But her offer can't be serious.
Schill Why?
Policeman The price is too high. In a case like yours, one pays a thousand marks, at the most two thousand. But not a billion! That's ridiculous. And even if she meant it, that would only prove she was out of her mind. And that's not a matter for the police.
Schill Whether she's out of her mind or not, the danger to me is the same. That's obvious.
Policeman Look, Schill, you show us where anyone threatens your life in any way—say, for instance, a man points a gun at you—and we'll be there in a flash.
Schill (*Gets up*) So I'm to wait till someone points a gun at me?
Policeman Pull yourself together, Schill. We're all for you in this town.
Schill I wish I could believe it.

Policeman   You don't believe it?

Schill   No. No, I don't. All of a sudden my customers are buying white bread, whole milk, butter, imported tobacco. What does it mean?

Policeman   It means business is picking up.

Schill   Helmesberger lives on the dole; he hasn't earned anything in five years. Today he bought French cognac.

Policeman   I'll have to try your cognac one of these days.

Schill   And shoes. They all have new shoes.

Policeman   And what have you got against new shoes? I'm wearing a new pair myself.

(*He holds out his foot*)

Schill   You too?

Policeman   Why not?

(*He pours out the rest of his beer*)

Schill   Is that Pilsen you're drinking now?

Policeman   It's the only thing.

Schill   You used to drink the local beer.

Policeman   Hogwash.

(*Radio music is heard offstage*)

Schill   Listen. You hear?

Policeman   "The Merry Widow." [15] Yes.

Schill   No. It's a radio.

Policeman   That's Bergholzer's radio.

Schill   Bergholzer!

Policeman   You're right. He should close his window when he plays it. I'll make a note to speak to him.

(*He makes a note in his notebook*)

Schill   And how can Bergholzer pay for a radio?

Policeman   That's his business.

Schill   And you, Schultz, with your new shoes and your imported beer— how are you going to pay for them?

Policeman   That's my business. (*His telephone rings. He picks it up*) Police Station, Güllen. What? What? Where? Where? How? Right, we'll deal with it.

(*He hangs up*)

Schill (*He speaks during the* POLICEMAN's *telephone conversation*)   Schultz, listen. No. Schultz, please—listen to me. Don't you see they're all . . .

---

[15] "The Merry Widow": waltz by Franz Lehar (1870–1948).

Listen, please. Look, Schultz. They're all running up debts. And out of these debts comes this sudden prosperity. And out of this prosperity comes the absolute need to kill me.

Policeman (*Putting on his jacket*)   You're imagining things.

Schill   All she has to do is to sit on her balcony and wait.

Policeman   Don't be a child.

Schill   You're all waiting.

Policeman (*Snaps a loaded clip into the magazine of a rifle*)   Look, Schill, you can relax. The police are here for your protection. They know their job. Let anyone, any time, make the slightest threat to your life, and all you have to do is let us know. We'll do the rest . . . Now, don't worry.

Schill   No, I won't.

Policeman   And don't upset yourself. All right?

Schill   Yes. I won't. (*Then suddenly, in a low tone*) You have a new gold tooth in your mouth!

Policeman   What are you talking about?

Schill (*Taking the* Policeman's *head in his hands, and forcing his lips open*) A brand new, shining gold tooth.

Policeman (*Breaks away and involuntarily levels the gun at* Schill)   Are you crazy? Look, I've no time to waste. Madame Zachanassian's panther's broken loose.

Schill   Panther?

Policeman   Yes, it's at large. I've got to hunt it down.

Schill   You're not hunting a panther and you know it. It's me you're hunting!

(*The* Policeman *clicks on the safety and lowers the gun*)

Policeman   Schill! Take my advice. Go home. Lock the door. Keep out of everyone's way. That way you'll be safe. Cheer up! Good times are just around the corner!

(*The lights dim in this area and light up on the balcony.* Pedro *is lounging in a chair.* Claire *is smoking*)

Pedro   Oh, this little town oppresses me.

Claire   Oh, does it? So you've changed your mind?

Pedro   It is true, I find it charming, delightful—

Claire   Picturesque.

Pedro   Yes. After all, it's the place where you were born. But it is too quiet for me. Too provincial. Too much like all small towns everywhere. These people—look at them. They fear nothing, they desire nothing, they strive for nothing. They have everything they want. They are asleep.

Claire   Perhaps one day they will come to life again.

Pedro   My God—do I have to wait for that?

Claire   Yes, you do. Why don't you go back to your fishing?

Pedro I think I will.

(Pedro *turns to go*)

Claire Pedro.
Pedro Yes, my love?
Claire Telephone the president of Hambro's Bank. Ask him to transfer a billion marks to my current account.
Pedro A billion? Yes, my love.

(*He goes. The lights fade on the balcony. A sign is flown in. It reads: "Rathaus."* [16] *The* Third Man *crosses the stage, right to left, wheeling a new television set on a hand truck. The counter of* Schill's *shop is transformed into the* Burgomaster's *office. The* Burgomaster *comes in. He takes a revolver from his pocket, examines it and sets it down on the desk. He sits down and starts writing.* Schill *knocks*)

Burgomaster Come in.
Schill I must have a word with you, Burgomaster.
Burgomaster Ah, Schill. Sit down, my friend.
Schill Man to man. As your successor.
Burgomaster But of course. Naturally.

(Schill *remains standing. He looks at the revolver*)

Schill Is that a gun?
Burgomaster Madame Zachanassian's black panther's broken loose. It's been seen near the cathedral. It's as well to be prepared.
Schill Oh, yes. Of course.
Burgomaster I've sent out a call for all able-bodied men with firearms. The streets have been cleared. The children have been kept in school. We don't want any accidents.
Schill (*Suspiciously*) You're making quite a thing of it.
Burgomaster (*Shrugs*) Naturally. A panther is a dangerous beast. Well? What's on your mind? Speak out. We're old friends.
Schill That's a good cigar you're smoking, Burgomaster.
Burgomaster Yes. Havana.
Schill You used to smoke something else.
Burgomaster Fortuna.
Schill Cheaper.
Burgomaster Too strong.
Schill A new tie? Silk?
Burgomaster Yes. Do you like it?
Schill And have you also bought new shoes?
Burgomaster (*Brings his feet out from under the desk*) Why, yes. I

[16] Rathaus: City Hall.

ordered a new pair from Kalberstadt. Extraordinary! However did you guess?

Schill That's why I'm here.

(*The* THIRD MAN *knocks*)

Burgomaster Come in.

Third Man The new typewriter, sir.

Burgomaster Put it on the table. (*The* THIRD MAN *sets it down and goes*) What's the matter with you? My dear fellow, aren't you well?

Schill It's you who don't seem well, Burgomaster.

Burgomaster What do you mean?

Schill You look pale.

Burgomaster I?

Schill Your hands are trembling. (*The* BURGOMASTER *involuntarily hides his hands*) Are you frightened?

Burgomaster What have I to be afraid of?

Schill Perhaps this sudden prosperity alarms you.

Burgomaster Is prosperity a crime?

Schill That depends on how you pay for it.

Burgomaster You'll have to forgive me, Schill, but I really haven't the slightest idea what you're talking about. Am I supposed to feel like a criminal every time I order a new typewriter?

Schill Do you?

Burgomaster Well, I hope you haven't come here to talk about a new typewriter. Now, what was it you wanted?

Schill I have come to claim the protection of the authorities.

Burgomaster Ei! Against whom?

Schill You know against whom.

Burgomaster You don't trust us?

Schill That woman has put a price on my head.

Burgomaster If you don't feel safe, why don't you go to the police?

Schill I have just come from the police.

Burgomaster And?

Schill The chief has a new gold tooth in his mouth.

Burgomaster A new—? Oh, Schill, really! You're forgetting. This is Güllen, the town of humane traditions. Goethe slept here. Brahms composed a quartet. You must have faith in us. This is a law-abiding community.

Schill Then arrest this woman who wants to have me killed.

Burgomaster Look here, Schill. God knows the lady has every right to be angry with you. What you did there wasn't very pretty. You forced two decent lads to perjure themselves and had a young girl thrown out on the streets.

Schill That young girl owns half the world.

(*A moment's silence*)

Burgomaster   Very well, then, we'll speak frankly.

Schill   That's why I'm here.

Burgomaster   Man to man, just as you said. (*He clears his throat*) Now—after what you did, you have no moral right to say a word against this lady. And I advise you not to try. Also—I regret to have to tell you this —there is no longer any question of your being elected Burgomaster.

Schill   Is that official?

Burgomaster   Official.

Schill   I see.

Burgomaster   The man who is chosen to exercise the high post of Burgomaster must have, obviously, certain moral qualifications. Qualifications which, unhappily, you no longer possess. Naturally, you may count on the esteem and friendship of the town, just as before. That goes without saying. The best thing will be to spread the mantle of silence over the whole miserable business.

Schill   So I'm to remain silent while they arrange my murder?

(*The* BURGOMASTER *gets up*)

Burgomaster (*Suddenly noble*)   Now, who is arranging your murder? Give me the names and I will investigate the case at once. Unrelentingly. Well? The names?

Schill   You.

Burgomaster   I resent this. Do you think we want to kill you for money?

Schill   No. You don't want to kill me. But you want to have me killed.

(*The lights go down. The stage is filled with men prowling about with rifles, as if they were stalking a quarry. In the interval, the* POLICEMAN'S *bench and the* BURGOMASTER'S *desk are shifted somewhat, so that they will compose the setting for the sacristy. The stage empties. The lights come up on the balcony.* CLAIRE *appears*)

Claire   Bobby, what's going on here? What are all these men doing with guns? Whom are they hunting?

Bobby   The black panther has escaped, madame.

Claire   Who let him out?

Bobby   Kobby and Lobby, madame.

Claire   How excited they are! There may be shooting?

Bobby   It is possible, madame.

(*The lights fade on the balcony. The sacristan comes in. He arranges the set, and puts the altar cloth on the altar. Then* SCHILL *comes on. He is looking for the* PASTOR. *The* PASTOR *enters, left. He is wearing his gown and carrying a rifle*)

Schill   Sorry to disturb you, Pastor.

Pastor   God's house is open to all. (*He sees that* SCHILL *is staring at the gun*) Oh, the gun? That's because of the panther. It's best to be prepared.

Schill Pastor, help me.

Pastor Of course. Sit down. (*He puts the rifle on the bench*) What's the trouble?

Schill (*Sits on the bench*) I'm frightened.

Pastor Frightened? Of what?

Schill Of everyone. They're hunting me down like a beast.

Pastor Have no fear of man, Schill. Fear God. Fear not the death of the body. Fear the death of the soul. Zip up my gown behind, Sacristan.

Schill I'm afraid, Pastor.

Pastor Put your trust in heaven, my friend.

Schill You see, I'm not well. I shake. I have such pains around the heart. I sweat.

Pastor I know. You're passing through a profound psychic experience.

Schill I'm going through hell.

Pastor The hell you are going through exists only within yourself. Many years ago you betrayed a girl shamefully, for money. Now you think that we shall sell you just as you sold her. No, my friend, you are projecting your guilt upon others. It's quite natural. But remember, the root of our torment lies always within ourselves, in our hearts, in our sins. When you have understood this, you can conquer the fears that oppress you; you have weapons with which to destroy them.

Schill Siemethofer has bought a new washing machine.

Pastor Don't worry about the washing machine. Worry about your immortal soul.

Schill Stockers has a television set.

Pastor There is also great comfort in prayer. Sacristan, the bands. (SCHILL *crosses to the altar and kneels. The sacristan ties on the* PASTOR's *bands*) Examine your conscience, Schill. Repent. Otherwise your fears will consume you. Believe me, this is the only way. We have no other. (*The church bell begins to peal.* SCHILL *seems relieved*) Now I must leave you. I have a baptism. You may stay as long as you like. Sacristan, the Bible, Liturgy, and Psalter. The child is beginning to cry. I can hear it from here. It is frightened. Let us make haste to give it the only security which this world affords.

Schill A new bell?

Pastor Yes. Its tone is marvelous, don't you think? Full. Sonorous.

Schill (*Steps back in horror*)   A new bell! You too, Pastor? You too?

(*The* PASTOR *clasps his hands in horror. Then he takes* SCHILL *into his arms*)

Pastor Oh, God, God forgive me. We are poor, weak things, all of us. Do not tempt us further into the hell in which you are burning. Go, Schill, my friend, go my brother, go while there is time.

(*The* PASTOR *goes.* SCHILL *picks up the rifle with a gesture of desperation. He goes out with it. As the lights fade, men appear with guns. Two shots are fired in the darkness. The lights come up on the balcony, which moves forward)*

Claire   Bobby! What was that shooting? Have they caught the panther?
Bobby   He is dead, madame.
Claire   There were two shots.
Bobby   The panther is dead, madame.
Claire   I loved him. (*Waves* BOBBY *away*) I shall miss him.

(*The* TEACHER *comes in with two little girls, singing. They stop under the balcony*)

Teacher   Gracious lady, be so good as to accept our heartfelt condolences. Your beautiful panther is no more. Believe me, we are deeply pained that so tragic an event should mar your visit here. But what could we do? The panther was savage, a beast. To him our human laws could not apply. There was no other way—(SCHILL *appears with the gun. He looks dangerous. The girls run off, frightened. The* TEACHER *follows the girls*)— Children—children—children!
Claire   Anton, why are you frightening the children? (*He works the bolt, loading the chamber, and raises the gun slowly*)
Schill   Go away, Claire—I warn you. Go away.
Claire   How strange it is, Anton! How clearly it comes back to me! The day we saw one another for the first time, do you remember? I was on a balcony then. It was a day like today, a day in autumn without a breath of wind, warm as it is now—only lately I am always cold. You stood down there and stared at me without moving. I was embarrassed. I didn't know what to do. I wanted to go back into the darkness of the room, where it was safe, but I couldn't. You stared up at me darkly, almost angrily, as if you wished to hurt me, but your eyes were full of passion. (SCHILL *begins to lower the rifle involuntarily*) Then, I don't know why, I left the balcony and I came down and stood in the street beside you. You didn't greet me, you didn't say a word, but you took my hand and we walked together out of the town into the fields, and behind us came Kobby and Lobby, like two dogs, sniveling and giggling and snarling. Suddenly you picked up a stone and hurled it at them, and they ran yelping back into the town, and we were alone. (SCHILL *has lowered the rifle completely. He moves forward toward her, as close as he can come*) That was the beginning, and everything else had to follow. There was no escape.

(*She goes in and closes the shutters.* SCHILL *stands immobile. The* TEACHER *tiptoes in. He stares at* SCHILL, *who doesn't see him. Then he beckons to the children*)

Teacher   Come, children, sing. Sing.

(*They begin singing. He creeps behind* SCHILL *and snatches away the rifle.* SCHILL *turns sharply. The* PASTOR *comes in*)

Pastor Go, Schill—go!

(SCHILL *goes out. The children continue singing, moving across the stage and off. The Golden Apostle vanishes. The crossing bell is heard. The scene dissolves into the railway-station setting, as in Act One. But there are certain changes. The timetable marked "Fahrplan" is now new, the frame freshly painted. There is a new travel poster on the station wall. It has a yellow sun and the words: "Reist in den Süden."* [17] *On the other side of the Fahrplan is another poster with the words: "Die Passionsspiele Oberammergau."* [18] *The sound of passing trains covers the scene change.* SCHILL *appears with an old valise in his hand, dressed in a shabby trench coat, his hat on his head. He looks about with a furtive air, walking slowly to the platform. Slowly, as if by chance, the townspeople enter, from all sides.* SCHILL *hesitates, stops*)

Burgomaster (*From upstage, center*) Good evening, Schill.
Schill Good evening.
Policeman Good evening.
Schill Good evening.
Painter (*Enters*) Good evening.
Schill Good evening.
Doctor Good evening.
Schill Good evening.
Burgomaster So you're taking a little trip?
Schill Yes. A little trip.
Policeman May one ask where to?
Schill I don't know.
Painter Don't know?
Schill To Kalberstadt.
Burgomaster (*With disbelief, pointing to the valise*) Kalberstadt?
Schill After that—somewhere else.
Painter Ah. After that somewhere else.

(*The* FOURTH MAN *walks in*)

Schill I thought maybe Australia.
Burgomaster Australia!
All Australia!
Schill I'll raise the money somehow.
Burgomaster But why Australia?
Policeman What would you be doing in Australia?
Schill One can't always live in the same town, year in, year out.

[17] Reist in den Süden: travel in the South.
[18] "Die Passionsspiele Oberammergau": "The Oberammergau Passion Play," portraying the death of Jesus.

Painter But Australia—
Doctor It's a risky trip for a man of your age.
Burgomaster One of the lady's little men ran off to Australia . . .
All Yes.
Policeman You'll be much safer here.
Painter Much!

(SCHILL *looks about him in anguish, like a beast at bay*)

Schill (*Low voice*) I wrote a letter to the administration at Kaffigen.
Burgomaster Yes? And?

(*They are all intent on the answer*)

Schill They didn't answer.

(*All laugh*)

Doctor Do you mean to say you don't trust old friends? That's not very flattering, you know.
Burgomaster No one's going to do you any harm here.
Doctor No harm here.
Schill They didn't answer because our postmaster held up my letter.
Painter Our postmaster? What an idea.
Burgomaster The postmaster is a member of the town council.
Policeman A man of the utmost integrity.
Doctor He doesn't hold up letters. What an idea!

(*The crossing bell starts ringing*)

Station Master (*Announces*) Local to Kalberstadt!

(*The townspeople all cross down to see the train arrive. Then they turn, with their backs to the audience, in a line across the stage.* SCHILL *cannot get through to reach the train*)

Schill (*In a low voice*) What are you all doing here? What do you want of me?
Burgomaster We don't like to see you go.
Doctor We've come to see you off.

(*The sound of the approaching train grows louder*)

Schill I didn't ask you to come.
Policeman But we have come.
Doctor As old friends.
All As old friends.

(*The* STATION MASTER *holds up his paddle. The train stops with a screech of brakes. We hear the engine panting offstage*)

Voice (*Offstage*) Güllen!
Burgomaster A pleasant journey.

Doctor   And long life!

Painter   And good luck in Australia!

All   Yes, good luck in Australia.

(*They press around him jovially. He stands motionless and pale*)

Schill   Why are you crowding me?

Policeman   What's the matter now?

(*The* STATION MASTER *blows a long blast on his whistle*)

Schill   Give me room.

Doctor   But you have plenty of room.

(*They all move away from him*)

Policeman   Better get aboard, Schill.

Schill   I see. I see. One of you is going to push me under the wheels.

Policeman   Oh, nonsense. Go on, get aboard.

Schill   Get away from me, all of you.

Burgomaster   I don't know what you want. Just get on the train.

Schill   No. One of you will push me under.

Doctor   You're being ridiculous. Now, go on, get on the train.

Schill   Why are you all so near me?

Doctor   The man's gone mad.

Station Master   'Board!

(*He blows his whistle. The engine bell clangs. The train starts*)

Burgomaster   Get aboard man. Quick.

(*The following speeches are spoken all together until the train noises fade away*)

Doctor   The train's starting.

All   Get aboard, man. Get aboard. The train's starting.

Schill   If I try to get aboard, one of you will hold me back.

All   No, no.

Burgomaster   Get on the train.

Schill (*In terror, crouches against the wall of the* STATION MASTER's *office*) No—no—no. No. (*He falls on his knees. The others crowd around him. He cowers on the ground, abjectly. The train sounds fade away*) Oh, no —no—don't push me, don't push me!

Policeman   There. It's gone off without you.

(*Slowly they leave him. He raises himself up to a sitting position, still trembling. A* TRUCK DRIVER *enters with an empty can*)

Truck Driver   Do you know where I can get some water? My truck's boiling over. (SCHILL *points to the station office*) Thanks: (*He enters the office, gets the water and comes out. By this time,* SCHILL *is erect*) Missed your train?

Schill   Yes.

Truck Driver   To Kalberstadt?

Schill   Yes.

Truck Driver   Well, come with me. I'm going that way.

Schill   This is my town. This is my home. (*With strange new dignity*) No, thank you. I've changed my mind. I'm staying.

Truck Driver (*Shrugs*)   All right.

(*He goes out.* SCHILL *picks up his bag, looks right and left, and slowly walks off*)

Curtain

ACT III

Music is heard. Then the curtain rises on the interior of the old barn, a dim, cavernous structure. Bars of light fall across the shadowy forms, shafts of sunlight from the holes and cracks in the walls and roof. Overhead hang old rags, decaying sacks, great cobwebs. Extreme left is a ladder leading to the loft. Near it, an old haycart. Left, CLAIRE ZACHANASSIAN *is sitting in her gilded sedan chair, motionless, in her magnificent bridal gown and veil. Near the chair stands an old keg.*

Bobby (*Comes in, treading carefully*)   The doctor and the teacher from the high school to see you, madame.

Claire (*Impassive*)   Show them in.

(BOBBY *ushers them in as if they were entering a hall of state. The two grope their way through the litter. At last they find the lady, and bow. They are both well dressed in new clothes, but are very dusty*)

Bobby   Dr. Nüsslin and Professor Müller . . .

Doctor   Madame.

Claire   You look dusty, gentlemen.

Doctor (*Dusts himself off vigorously*)   Oh, forgive us. We had to climb over an old carriage.

Teacher   Our respects.

Doctor   A fabulous wedding.

Teacher   Beautiful occasion.

Claire   It's stifling here. But I love this old barn. The smell of hay and old straw and axle grease—it is the scent of my youth. Sit down. All this rubbish—the haycart, the old carriage, the cask, even the pitchfork —it was all here when I was a girl.

Teacher   Remarkable place.

(*He mops his brow*)

Claire   I thought the pastor's text was very appropriate. The lesson a trifle long.

Teacher   I Corinthians 13.[19]

Claire   Your choristers sang beautifully, Professor.

Teacher   Bach. From the *St. Matthew Passion.*

Doctor   Güllen has never seen such magnificence! The flowers! The jewels! And the people.

Teacher   The theatrical world, the world of finance, the world of art, the world of science . . .

Claire   All these worlds are now back in their Cadillacs, speeding toward the capital for the wedding reception. But I'm sure you didn't come here to talk about them.

Doctor   Dear lady, we should not intrude on your valuable time. Your husband must be waiting impatiently.

Claire   No, no, I've packed him off to Brazil.

Doctor   To Brazil, madame?

Claire   Yes. For his honeymoon.

Teacher *and* **Doctor**   Oh! But your wedding guests?

Claire   I've planned a delightful dinner for them. They'll never miss me. Now what was it you wished to talk about?

Teacher   About Anton Schill, madame.

Claire   Is he dead?

Teacher   Madame, we may be poor. But we have our principles.

Claire   I see. Then what do you want?

Teacher (*He mops his brow again*)   The fact is, madame, in anticipation of your well-known munificence, that is, feeling that you would give the town some sort of gift, we have all been buying things. Necessities . . .

Doctor   With money we don't have.

(*The* TEACHER *blows his nose*)

Claire   You've run into debt?

Doctor   Up to here.

Claire   In spite of your principles?

Teacher   We're human, madame.

Claire   I see.

Teacher   We have been poor for a long time. A long, long time.

Doctor (*He rises*)   The question is, how are we going to pay?

Claire   You already know.

Teacher (*Courageously*)   I beg you, Madame Zachanassian, put yourself in our position for a moment. For twenty-two years I've been cudgeling my brains to plant a few seeds of knowledge in this wilderness. And all this time, my gallant colleague, Dr. Nüsslin, has been rattling around in his ancient Mercedes, from patient to patient, trying to keep these wretches alive. Why? Why have we spent our lives in this miserable hole? For money? Hardly. The pay is ridiculous.

[19] I Corinthians 13:13: "But abideth faith, hope, love, these three; and the greatest of these is love."

Doctor And yet, the professor here has declined an offer to head the high school in Kalberstadt.

Teacher And Dr. Nüsslin has refused an important post at the University of Erlangen. Madame, the simple fact is, we love our town. We were born here. It is our life.

Doctor That's true.

Teacher What has kept us going all these years is the hope that one day the community will prosper again as it did in the days when we were young.

Claire Good.

Teacher Madame, there is no reason for our poverty. We suffer here from a mysterious blight. We have factories. They stand idle. There is oil in the valley of Pückenried.

Doctor There is copper under the Konradsweil Forest. There is power in our streams, in our waterfalls.

Teacher We are not poor, madame. If we had credit, if we had confidence, the factories would open, orders and commissions would pour in. And our economy would bloom together with our cultural life. We would become once again like the towns around us, healthy and prosperous.

Doctor If the Wagonworks were put on its feet again—

Teacher The Foundry.

Doctor The Golden Eagle Pencil Factory.

Teacher Buy these plants, madame. Put them in operation once more, and I swear to you, Güllen will flourish and it will bless you. We don't need a billion marks. Ten million, properly invested, would give us back our life, and incidentally return to the investor an excellent dividend. Save us, madame. Save us, and we will not only bless you, we will make money for you.

Claire I don't need money.

Doctor Madame, we are not asking for charity. This is business.

Claire It's a good idea . . .

Doctor Dear lady! I knew you wouldn't let us down.

Claire But it's out of the question. I cannot buy the Wagonworks. I already own them.

Doctor The Wagonworks?

Teacher And the Foundry?

Claire And the Foundry.

Doctor And the Golden Eagle Pencil Factory?

Claire Everything. The valley of Pückenried with its oil, the forest of Konradsweil with its ore, the barn, the town, the streets, the houses, the shops, everything. I had my agents buy up this rubbish over the years, bit by bit, piece by piece, until I had it all. Your hopes were an illusion, your vision empty, your self-sacrifice a stupidity, your whole life completely senseless.

Teacher Then the mysterious blight—

Claire The mysterious blight was I.

Doctor But this is monstrous!

Claire Monstrous. I was seventeen when I left this town. It was winter. I was dressed in a sailor suit and my red braids hung down my back. I was in my seventh month. As I walked down the street to the station, the boys whistled after me, and someone threw something. I sat freezing in my seat in the Hamburg Express. But before the roof of the great barn was lost behind the trees, I had made up my mind that one day I would come back...

Teacher But, madame—

Claire (*She smiles*) And now I have. (*She claps her hands*) Mike. Max. Take me back to the Golden Apostle. I've been here long enough.

(MIKE *and* MAX *start to pick up the sedan chair. The* TEACHER *pushes* MIKE *away*)

Teacher Madame. One moment. Please. I see it all now. I had thought of you as an avenging fury, a Medea,[20] a Clytemnestra[21]—but I was wrong. You are a warm-hearted woman who has suffered a terrible injustice, and now you have returned and taught us an unforgettable lesson. You have stripped us bare. But now that we stand before you naked, I know you will set aside these thoughts of vengeance. If we made you suffer, you too have put us through the fire. Have mercy, madame.

Claire When I have had justice. Mike!

(*She signals to* MIKE *and* MAX *to pick up the sedan chair. They cross the stage. The* TEACHER *bars the way*)

Teacher But, madame, one injustice cannot cure another. What good will it do to force us into crime? Horror succeeds horror, shame is piled on shame. It settles nothing.

Claire It settles everything.

(*They move upstage toward the exit. The* TEACHER *follows*)

Teacher Madame, this lesson you have taught us will never be forgotten. We will hand it down from father to son. It will be a monument more lasting than any vengeance. Whatever we have been, in the future we shall be better because of you. You have pushed us to the extreme. Now forgive us. Show us the way to a better life. Have pity, madame—pity. That is the highest justice.

(*The sedan chair stops*)

Claire The highest justice has no pity. It is bright and pure and clear. The world made me into a whore; now I make the world into a brothel.

[20] Medea: in Greek legend, a sorceress who killed her rival and her own children.
[21] Clytemnestra: in Greek legend, a queen who killed her husband, Agamemnon.

Those who wish to go down, may go down. Those who wish to dance with me, may dance with me. (*To her porters*) Go.

(*She is carried off. The lights black out. Downstage, right, appears* SCHILL'S *shop. It has a new sign, a new counter. The doorbell, when it rings, has an impressive sound.* FRAU SCHILL *stands behind the counter in a new dress. The* FIRST MAN *enters, left. He is dressed as a prosperous butcher, a few bloodstains on his snowy apron, a gold watch chain across his open vest*)

First Man   What a wedding! I'll swear the whole town was there. Cigarettes.

Frau Schill   Clara is entitled to a little happiness after all. I'm happy for her. Green or white?

First Man   Turkish. The bridesmaids! Dancers and opera singers. And the dresses! Down to here.

Frau Schill   It's the fashion nowadays.

First Man   Reporters! Photographers! From all over the world! (*In a low voice*) They will be here any minute.

Frau Schill   What have reporters to do with us? We are simple people, Herr Hofbauer. There is nothing for them here.

First Man   They're questioning everybody. They're asking everything. (*The* FIRST MAN *lights a cigarette. He looks up at the ceiling*) Footsteps.

Frau Schill   He's pacing the room. Up and down. Day and night.

First Man   Haven't seen him all week.

Frau Schill   He never goes out.

First Man   It's his conscience. That was pretty mean, the way he treated poor Madame Zachanassian.

Frau Schill   That's true. I feel very badly about it myself.

First Man   To ruin a young girl like that— God doesn't forgive it. (FRAU SCHILL *nods solemnly with pursed lips. The butcher gives her a level glance*) Look, I hope he'll have sense enough to keep his mouth shut in front of the reporters.

Frau Schill   I certainly hope so.

First Man   You know his character.

Frau Schill   Only too well, Herr Hofbauer.

First Man   If he tries to throw dirt at our Clara and tell a lot of lies, how she tried to get us to kill him, which anyway she never meant—

Frau Schill.   Of course not.

First Man   —Then we'll really have to do something! And not because of the money— (*He spits*) But out of ordinary human decency. God knows Madame Zachanassian has suffered enough through him already.

Frau Schill   She has indeed.

(*The* TEACHER *comes in. He is not quite sober*)

Teacher (*Looks about the shop*)   Has the press been here yet?

First Man   No.

Teacher   It's not my custom, as you know, Frau Schill—but I wonder if I could have a strong alcoholic drink?

Frau Schill   It's an honor to serve you, Herr Professor. I have a good Steinhäger.[22] Would you like to try a glass?

Teacher   A very small glass.

(FRAU SCHILL *serves bottle and glass. The* TEACHER *tosses off a glass*)

Frau Schill   Your hand is shaking, Herr Professor.

Teacher   To tell the truth, I have been drinking a little already.

Frau Schill   Have another glass. It will do you good.

(*He accepts another glass*)

Teacher   Is that he up there, walking?

Frau Schill   Up and down. Up and down.

First Man   It's God punishing him.

(*The* PAINTER *comes in with the* SON *and the* DAUGHTER)

Painter   Careful! A reporter just asked us the way to this shop.

First Man   I hope you didn't tell him.

Painter   I told him we were strangers here.

(*They all laugh. The door opens. The* SECOND MAN *darts into the shop*)

Second Man   Look out, everybody! The press! They are across the street in your shop, Hofbauer.

First Man   My boy will know how to deal with them.

Second Man   Make sure Schill doesn't come down, Hofbauer.

First Man   Leave that to me.

(*They group themselves about the shop*)

Teacher   Listen to me, all of you. When the reporters come I'm going to speak to them. I'm going to make a statement. A statement to the world on behalf of myself as Rector of Güllen High School and on behalf of you all, for all your sakes.

Painter   What are you going to say?

Teacher   I shall tell the truth about Claire Zachanassian.

Frau Schill   You're drunk, Herr Professor; you should be ashamed of yourself.

Teacher   I should be ashamed? You should all be ashamed!

Son   Shut your trap. You're drunk.

Daughter   Please, Professor—

Teacher   Girl, you disappoint me. It is your place to speak. But you are silent and you force your old teacher to raise his voice. I am going to

[22] Steinhäger: a strong alcoholic beverage.

speak the truth. It is my duty and I am not afraid. The world may not wish to listen, but no one can silence me. I'm not going to wait—I'm going over to Hofbauer's shop now.

All No, you're not. Stop him. Stop him.

(*They all spring at the* TEACHER. *He defends himself. At this moment,* SCHILL *appears through the door upstage. In contrast to the others, he is dressed shabbily in an old black jacket, his best*)

Schill What's going on in my shop? (*The townsmen let go of the* TEACHER *and turn to stare at* SCHILL) What's the trouble, Professor?

Teacher Schill, I am speaking out at last! I am going to tell the press everything.

Schill Be quiet, Professor.

Teacher What did you say?

Schill Be quiet.

Teacher You want me to be quiet?

Schill Please.

Teacher But, Schill, if I keep quiet, if you miss this opportunity—they're over in Hofbauer's shop now . . .

Schill Please.

Teacher As you wish. If you too are on their side, I have no more to say.

(*The doorbell jingles. A* REPORTER *comes in*)

Reporter Is Anton Schill here? (*Moves to* SCHILL) Are you Herr Schill?

Schill What?

Reporter Herr Schill.

Schill Er—no. Herr Schill's gone to Kalberstadt for the day.

Reporter Oh, thank you. Good day.

(*He goes out*)

Painter (*Mops his brow*) Whew! Close shave.

(*He follows the* REPORTER *out*)

Second Man (*Walking up to* SCHILL) That was pretty smart of you to keep your mouth shut. You know what to expect if you don't.

(*He goes*)

First Man Give me a Havana. (SCHILL *serves him*) Charge it. You bastard!

(*He goes.* SCHILL *opens his account book*)

Frau Schill Come along, children—

(FRAU SCHILL, *the* SON *and the* DAUGHTER *go off, upstage*)

Teacher They're going to kill you. I've known it all along, and you too, you must have known it. The need is too strong, the temptation too great. And now perhaps I too will join against you. I belong to them and, like them, I can feel myself hardening into something that is not human—not beautiful.

Schill It can't be helped.

Teacher Pull yourself together, man. Speak to the reporters; you've no time to lose.

(SCHILL *looks up from his account book*)

Schill No. I'm not going to fight any more.

Teacher Are you so frightened that you don't dare open your mouth?

Schill I made Claire what she is, I made myself what I am. What should I do? Should I pretend that I'm innocent?

Teacher No, you can't. You are as guilty as hell.

Schill Yes.

Teacher You are a bastard.

Schill Yes.

Teacher But that does not justify your murder. (SCHILL *looks at him*) I wish I could believe that for what they're doing—for what they're going to do—they will suffer for the rest of their lives. But it's not true. In a little while they will have justified everything and forgotten everything.

Schill Of course.

Teacher Your name will never again be mentioned in this town. That's how it will be.

Schill I don't hold it against you.

Teacher But I do. I will hold it against myself all my life. That's why—

(*The doorbell jingles. The* BURGOMASTER *comes in. The* TEACHER *stares at him, then goes out without another word*)

Burgomaster Good afternoon, Schill. Don't let me disturb you. I've just dropped in for a moment.

Schill I'm just finishing my accounts for the week. (*A moment's pause*)

Burgomaster The town council meets tonight. At the Golden Apostle. In the auditorium.

Schill I'll be there.

Burgomaster The whole town will be there. Your case will be discussed and final action taken. You've put us in a pretty tight spot, you know.

Schill Yes. I'm sorry.

Burgomaster The lady's offer will be rejected.

Schill Possibly.

Burgomaster Of course, I may be wrong.

Schill Of course.

Burgomaster In that case—are you prepared to accept the judgment of the town? The meeting will be covered by the press, you know.

Schill By the press?

Burgomaster Yes, and the radio and the newsreel. It's a very ticklish situation. Not only for you—believe me, it's even worse for us. What with the wedding, and all the publicity, we've become famous. All of a sudden our ancient democratic institutions have become of interest to the world.

Schill   Are you going to make the lady's condition public?

Burgomaster   No, no, of course not. Not directly. We will have to put the matter to a vote—that is unavoidable. But only those involved will understand.

Schill   I see.

Burgomaster   As far as the press is concerned, you are simply the intermediary between us and Madame Zachanassian. I have whitewashed you completely.

Schill   That is very generous of you.

Burgomaster   Frankly, it's not for your sake, but for the sake of your family. They are honest and decent people.

Schill   Oh—

Burgomaster   So far we've all played fair. You've kept your mouth shut and so have we. Now can we continue to depend on you? Because if you have any idea of opening your mouth at tonight's meeting, there won't be any meeting.

Schill   I'm glad to hear an open threat at last.

Burgomaster   We are not threatening you. You are threatening us. If you speak, you force us to act—in advance.

Schill   That won't be necessary.

Burgomaster   So if the town decides against you?

Schill   I will accept their decision.

Burgomaster   Good. (*A moment's pause*) I'm delighted to see there is still a spark of decency left in you. But—wouldn't it be better if we didn't have to call a meeting at all? (*He pauses. He takes a gun from his pocket and puts it on the counter*) I've brought you this.

Schill   Thank you.

Burgomaster   It's loaded.

Schill   I don't need a gun.

Burgomaster   (*He clears his throat*)   You see? We could tell the lady that we had condemned you in secret session and you had anticipated our decision. I've lost a lot of sleep getting to this point, believe me.

Schill   I believe you.

Burgomaster   Frankly, in your place, I myself would prefer to take the path of honor. Get it over with, once and for all. Don't you agree? For the sake of your friends! For the sake of our children, your own children —you have a daughter, a son—Schill, you know our need, our misery.

Schill   You've put me through hell, you and your town. You were my friends, you smiled and reassured me. But day by day I saw you change —your shoes, your ties, your suits—your hearts. If you had been honest with me then, perhaps I would feel differently toward you now. I might even use that gun you brought me. For the sake of my friends. But now I have conquered my fear. Alone. It was hard, but it's done. And now you will have to judge me. And I will accept your judgment. For me that will be justice. How it will be for you, I don't know. (*He turns away*) You may kill me if you like. I won't complain, I won't protest, I won't defend myself. But I won't do your job for you either.

Burgomaster (*Takes up his gun*) There it is. You've had your chance and you won't take it. Too bad. (*He takes out a cigarette*) I suppose it's more than we can expect of a man like you. (SCHILL *lights the* BURGO-MASTER's *cigarette*) Good day.

Schill Good day. (*The* BURGOMASTER *goes.* FRAU SCHILL *comes in, dressed in a fur coat. The* DAUGHTER *is in a new red dress. The* SON *has a new sports jacket*) What a beautiful coat, Mathilde!

Frau Schill Real fur. You like it?

Schill Should I? What a lovely dress, Ottilie!

Daughter *C'est très chic, n'est-ce pas?* [23]

Schill What?

Frau Schill Ottilie is taking a course in French.

Schill Very useful. Karl—whose automobile is that out there at the curb?

Son Oh, it's only an Opel. They're not expensive.

Schill You bought yourself a car?

Son On credit. Easiest thing in the world.

Frau Schill Everyone's buying on credit now, Anton. These fears of yours are ridiculous. You'll see. Clara has a good heart. She only means to teach you a lesson.

Daughter She means to teach you a lesson, that's all.

Son It's high time you got the point, Father.

Schill I get the point. (*The church bells start ringing*) Listen. The bells of Güllen. Do you hear?

Son Yes, we have four bells now. It sounds quite good.

Daughter Just like Gray's Elegy.

Schill What?

Frau Schill Ottilie is taking a course in English literature.

Schill Congratulations! It's Sunday. I should very much like to take a ride in your car. Our car.

Son You want to ride in the car?

Schill Why not? I want to ride through the Konradsweil Forest. I want to see the town where I've lived all my life.

Frau Schill I don't think that will look very nice for any of us.

Schill No—perhaps not. Well, I'll go for a walk by myself.

Frau Schill Then take us to Kalberstadt, Karl, and we'll go to a cinema.

Schill A cinema? It's a good idea.

---

[23] *C'est très chic, n'est-ce pas?* "It's very chic, isn't it?"

Frau Schill   See you soon, Anton.
Schill   Good-bye, Ottilie. Good-bye, Karl. Good-bye, Mathilde.
Family   Good-bye.

(*They go out*)

Schill   Good-bye. (*The shop sign flies off. The lights black out. They come up at once on the forest scene*) Autumn. Even the forest has turned to gold.

(SCHILL *wanders down to the bench in the forest. He sits.* CLAIRE'S *voice is heard*)

Claire   (*Offstage*)   Stop. Wait here. (CLAIRE *comes in. She gazes slowly up at the trees, kicks at some leaves. Then she walks slowly down center. She stops before a tree, glances up the trunk*) Bark-borers. The old tree is dying.

(*She catches sight of* SCHILL)

Schill   Clara.
Claire   How pleasant to see you here. I was visiting my forest. May I sit by you?
Schill   Oh, yes. Please do. (*She sits next to him*) I've just been saying good-bye to my family. They've gone to the cinema. Karl has bought himself a car.
Claire   How nice.
Schill   Ottilie is taking French lessons. And a course in English literature.
Claire   You see? They're beginning to take an interest in higher things.
Schill   Listen. A finch. You hear?
Claire   Yes. It's a finch. And a cuckoo in the distance. Would you like some music?
Schill   Oh, yes. That would be very nice.
Claire   Anything special?
Schill   "Deep in the Forest."
Claire   Your favorite song. They know it.

(*She raises her hand. Offstage, the mandolin and guitar play the tune softly*)

Schill   We had a child?
Claire   Yes.
Schill   Boy or girl?
Claire   Girl.
Schill   What name did you give her?
Claire   I called her Genevieve.
Schill   That's a very pretty name.
Claire   Yes.
Schill   What was she like?

Claire   I saw her only once. When she was born. Then they took her away from me.

Schill   Her eyes?

Claire   They weren't open yet.

Schill   And her hair?

Claire   Black, I think. It's usually black at first.

Schill   Yes, of course. Where did she die, Clara?

Claire   In some family. I've forgotten their name. Meningitis, they said. The officials wrote me a letter.

Schill   Oh, I'm so very sorry, Clara.

Claire   I've told you about our child. Now tell me about myself.

Schill   About yourself?

Claire   Yes. How I was when I was seventeen in the days when you loved me.

Schill   I remember one day you waited for me in the great barn. I had to look all over the place for you. At last I found you lying in the haycart with nothing on and a long straw between your lips . . .

Claire   Yes. I was pretty in those days.

Schill   You were beautiful, Clara.

Claire   You were strong. The time you fought with those two railway men who were following me, I wiped the blood from your face with my red petticoat. (*The music ends*) They've stopped.

Schill   Tell them to play "Thoughts of Home."

Claire   They know that too.

(*The music plays*)

Schill   Here we are, Clara, sitting together in our forest for the last time. The town council meets tonight. They will condemn me to death, and one of them will kill me. I don't know who and I don't know where. Clara, I only know that in a little while a useless life will come to an end.

(*He bows his head on her bosom. She takes him in her arms*)

Claire (*Tenderly*)   I shall take you in your coffin to Capri. You will have your tomb in the park of my villa, where I can see you from my bedroom window. White marble and onyx in a grove of green cypress. With a beautiful view of the Mediterranean.

Schill   I've always wanted to see it.

Claire   Your love for me died years ago, Anton. But my love for you would not die. It turned into something strong, like the hidden roots of the forest; something evil, like white mushrooms that grow unseen in the darkness. And slowly it reached out for your life. Now I have you. You are mine. Alone. At last, and forever, a peaceful ghost in a silent house.

(*The music ends*)

Schill The song is over.
Claire Adieu, Anton.

(CLAIRE *kisses* ANTON, *a long kiss. Then she rises*)

Schill Adieu.

(*She goes.* SCHILL *remains sitting on the bench. A row of lamps descends from the flies. The townsmen come in from both sides, each bearing his chair. A table and chairs are set upstage, center. On both sides sit the townspeople. The* POLICEMAN, *in a new uniform, sits on the bench behind* SCHILL. *All the townsmen are in new Sunday clothes. Around them are technicians of all sorts, with lights, cameras, and other equipment. The townswomen are absent. They do not vote. The* BURGOMASTER *takes his place at the table, center. The* DOCTOR *and the* PASTOR *sit at the same table, at his right, and the* TEACHER *in his academic gown, at his left*)

Burgomaster (*At a sign from the radio technician, he pounds the floor with his wand of office*) Fellow citizens of Güllen, I call this meeting to order. The agenda: there is only one matter before us. I have the honor to announce officially that Madame Claire Zachanassian, daughter of our beloved citizen, the famous architect Siegfried Wäscher, has decided to make a gift to the town of one billion marks. Five hundred million to the town, five hundred million to be divided per capita among the citizens. After certain necessary preliminaries, a vote will be taken, and you, as citizens of Güllen, will signify your will by a show of hands. Has anyone any objection to this mode of procedure? The pastor? (*Silence*) The police? (*Silence*) The town health official? (*Silence*) The Rector of Güllen High School? (*Silence*) The political opposition? (*Silence*) I shall then proceed to the vote—(*The* TEACHER *rises. The* BURGOMASTER *turns in surprise and irritation*) You wish to speak?
Teacher Yes.
Burgomaster Very well.

(*He takes his seat. The* TEACHER *advances. The movie camera starts running*)

Teacher Fellow townsmen. (*The photographer flashes a bulb in his face*) Fellow townsmen. We all know that by means of this gift, Madame Claire Zachanassian intends to attain a certain object. What is this object? To enrich the town of her youth, yes. But more than that, she desires by means of this gift to re-establish justice among us. This desire expressed by our benefactress raises an all-important question. Is it true that our community harbors in its soul such a burden of guilt?
Burgomaster Yes! True!
Second Man Crimes are concealed among us.
Third Man (*He jumps up*) Sins!

Fourth Man (*He jumps up also*)   Perjuries.

Painter   Justice!

Townsmen   Justice! Justice!

Teacher   Citizens of Güllen, this, then, is the simple fact of the case. We have participated in an injustice. I thoroughly recognize the material advantages which this gift opens to us—I do not overlook the fact that it is poverty which is the root of all this bitterness and evil. Nevertheless, there is no question here of money.

Townsmen   No! No!

Teacher   Here there is no question of our prosperity as a community, or our well-being as individuals—The question is—must be—whether or not we wish to live according to the principles of justice, those principles for which our forefathers lived and fought and for which they died, those principles which form the soul of our Western culture.

Townsmen   Hear! Hear!

(*Applause*)

Teacher (*Desperately, realizing that he is fighting a losing battle, and on the verge of hysteria*)   Wealth has meaning only when benevolence comes of it, but only he who hungers for grace will receive grace. Do you feel this hunger, my fellow citizens, this hunger of the spirit, or do you feel only that other profane hunger, the hunger of the body? That is the question which I, as Rector of your high school, now propound to you. Only if you can no longer tolerate the presence of evil among you, only if you can in no circumstances endure a world in which injustice exists, are you worthy to receive Madame Zachanassian's billion and fulfill the condition bound up with this gift. If not—(*Wild applause. He gestures desperately for silence*) If not, then God have mercy on us!

(*The townsmen crowd around him, ambiguously, in a mood somewhat between threat and congratulation. He takes his seat, utterly crushed, exhausted by his effort. The* BURGOMASTER *advances and takes charge once again. Order is restored*)

Burgomaster   Anton Schill—(*The* POLICEMAN *gives* SCHILL *a shove.* SCHILL *gets up*) Anton Schill, it is through you that this gift is offered to the town. Are you willing that this offer should be accepted?

(SCHILL *mumbles something*)

Radio Reporter (*Steps to his side*)   You'll have to speak up a little, Herr Schill.

Schill   Yes.

Burgomaster   Will you respect our decision in the matter before us?

Schill   I will respect your decision.

Burgomaster   Then I proceed to the vote. All those who are in accord with the terms on which this gift is offered will signify the same by raising their right hands. (*After a moment, the* POLICEMAN *raises his hand. Then one by one the others. Last of all, very slowly, the* TEACHER) All against? The offer is accepted. I now solemnly call upon you, fellow townsmen, to declare in the face of all the world that you take this action, not out of love for worldly gain . . .

Townsmen (*In chorus*)   Not out of love for worldly gain . . .

Burgomaster   But out of love for the right.

Townsmen   But out of love for the right.

Burgomaster (*Holds up his hand, as if taking an oath*)   We join together, now, as brothers . . .

Townsmen (*Hold up their hands*)   We join together, now, as brothers . . .

Burgomaster   To purify our town of guilt . . .

Townsmen   To purify our town of guilt . . .

Burgomaster   And to reaffirm our faith . . .

Townsmen   And to reaffirm our faith . . .

Burgomaster   In the eternal power of justice.

Townsmen   In the eternal power of justice.

(*The lights go off suddenly*)

Schill (*A scream*)   Oh, God!

Voice   I'm sorry, Herr Burgomaster. We seem to have blown a fuse. (*The lights go on*) Ah—there we are. Would you mind doing that last bit again?

Burgomaster   Again?

The Cameraman (*Walks forward*)   Yes, for the newsreel.

Burgomaster   Oh, the newsreel. Certainly.

The Cameraman   Ready now? Right.

Burgomaster   And to reaffirm our faith . . .

Townsmen   And to reaffirm our faith . . .

Burgomaster   In the eternal power of justice.

Townsmen   In the eternal power of justice.

The Cameraman (*To his assistant*)   It was better before, when he screamed "Oh, God."

(*The assistant shrugs*)

Burgomaster   Fellow citizens of Güllen, I declare this meeting adjourned. The ladies and gentlemen of the press will find refreshments served downstairs, with the compliments of the town council. The exits lead directly to the restaurant.

The Cameraman   Thank you.

(*The newsmen go off with alacrity. The townsmen remain on the stage.* SCHILL *gets up*)

Policeman (*Pushes* SCHILL *down*)   Sit down.

Schill   Is it to be now?

Policeman   Naturally, now.

Schill   I thought it might be best to have it at my house.

Policeman   It will be here.

Burgomaster   Lower the lights. (*The lights dim*) Are they all gone?

Voice   All gone.

Burgomaster   The gallery?

Second Voice   Empty.

Burgomaster   Lock the doors.

The Voice   Locked here.

Second Voice   Locked here.

Burgomaster   Form a lane. (*The men form a lane. At the end stands the* ATHLETE *in elegant white slacks, a red scarf around his singlet*) Pastor. Will you be so good?

(*The* PASTOR *walks slowly to* SCHILL)

Pastor   Anton Schill, your heavy hour has come.

Schill   May I have a cigarette?

Pastor   Cigarette, Burgomaster.

Burgomaster   Of course. With pleasure. And a good one.

(*He gives his case to the* PASTOR, *who offers it to* SCHILL. *The* POLICEMAN *lights the cigarette. The* PASTOR *returns the case*)

Pastor   In the words of the prophet Amos—

Schill   Please—

(*He shakes his head*)

Pastor   You're no longer afraid?

Schill   No. I'm not afraid.

Pastor   I will pray for you.

Schill   Pray for us all.

(*The* PASTOR *bows his head*)

Burgomaster   Anton Schill, stand up!

(SCHILL *hesitates*)

Policeman   Stand up, you swine!

Burgomaster   Schultz, please.

Policeman   I'm sorry. I was carried away. (SCHILL *gives the cigarette to the* POLICEMAN. *Then he walks slowly to the center of the stage and turns his back on the audience*) Enter the lane.

(SCHILL *hesitates a moment. He goes slowly into the lane of silent men. The* ATHLETE *stares at him from the opposite end.* SCHILL *looks in turn at the hard faces of those who surround him, and sinks slowly to his knees. The lane contracts silently into a knot as the men close in and crouch over. Complete silence. The knot of men pulls back slowly, coming downstage. Then it opens. Only the* DOCTOR *is left in the center of the stage, kneeling by the corpse, over which the* TEACHER's *gown has been spread. The* DOCTOR *rises and takes off his stethoscope)*

Pastor   Is it all over?
Doctor   Heart failure.
Burgomaster   Died of joy.
All   Died of joy.

(The townsmen turn their backs on the corpse and at once light cigarettes. A cloud of smoke rises over them. From the left comes CLAIRE ZACHANASSIAN, *dressed in black, followed by* BOBBY. *She sees the corpse. Then she walks slowly to center stage and looks down at the body of* SCHILL)

Claire   Uncover him. (BOBBY *uncovers* SCHILL's *face. She stares at it a long moment. She sighs)* Cover his face.

*(*BOBBY *covers it.* CLAIRE *goes out, up center.* BOBBY *takes the check from his wallet, holds it out peremptorily to the* BURGOMASTER, *who walks over from the knot of silent men. He holds out his hand for the check. The lights fade. At once the warning bell is heard, and the scene dissolves into the setting of the railway station. The gradual transformation of the shabby town into a thing of elegance and beauty is now accomplished. The railway station glitters with neon lights and is surrounded with garlands, bright posters, and flags. The townsfolk, men and women, now in brand new clothes, form themselves into a group in front of the station. The sound of the approaching train grows louder. The train stops)*

Station Master   Güllen-Rome Express. All aboard, please. *(The church bells start pealing. Men appear with trunks and boxes, a procession which duplicates that of the lady's arrival, but in inverse order. Then come the* Two Blind Men, *then* Bobby, *and* Mike *and* Max *carrying the coffin. Lastly* Claire. *She is dressed in modish black. Her head is high, her face as impassive as that of an ancient idol. The procession crosses the stage and goes off. The people bow in silence as the coffin passes. When* Claire *and her retinue have boarded the train, the* Station Master *blows a long blast)* 'Bo—ard!

(He holds up his paddle. The train starts and moves off slowly, picking up speed. The crowd turns slowly, gazing after the departing train in complete silence. The train sounds fade)

The curtain falls slowly

CHAPTER 2

CONFLICT
AND MEANING

To give readers pleasure and insight into human experience, literature must seem as real as life itself. The incidents within a story, play, or narrative poem should be logically connected both to one another and to the other elements in the work (character, setting, and language) in order to create an illusion of reality: of people involved in particular situations, occurring in specific places and times. Even in fantasies—where characters might be talking robots or animals, and the setting is an imaginary place—such logical relationships are essential to the success of a story, for they contribute to artistic unity as well as to meaning. The author's view of these connections and the effect that he or she strives for determine the selection of events and the way those events are organized. The result—the organization of the *action* of the work—is called *plot*.

Although sometimes used interchangeably, *plot* and *action* have different meanings. *Action* is the chronological sequence of events in the work. Sometimes these events may be incidents or adventures, such as fights, intrigues, escapes, and romance. Sometimes, however, the action consists of a series of thoughts, reflections, or imaginings. *Plot*, on the other hand, is the organization of the action, thus the sequence in which the various events or thoughts are presented to the reader. Often the plot and the action are essentially the same since the events are presented in order of their occurrence. At other times the plot may be quite different, with *flashbacks* (movements into an earlier time), or projections into the future, or any combination of before–now–after. In any case, the plot includes the following divisions: *the initial situation, rising action, the deciding factor, climax, denouement*, and *resolution*.

The initial situation usually introduces the reader to the central character and the dramatic context of the action. In the rising action, the author develops a series of episodes that complicate the situation for the central character (these episodes are sometimes called the complication). The deciding factor is the particular event that either forces the central character to make a decision, reverses the winning side, or in some other way brings everything to a head. The actual moment when the decisive action occurs, when the major decision is made, is the climax—the point at which the outcome is most in doubt and suspense is generally strongest for the reader. The climax is also most significant for the central character because what happens at this point—what decision is made—determines the outcome. The remainder of the work consists of the denouement—the untying of the complications—and the resolution—the ending. The resolution may be happy, sad, or tragic, but it concludes the work.

In the following ballad, John Manifold's "The Griesly Wife," which is a narrative in simple verse, the reader can easily recognize the various elements of plot.

John Manifold (1915–   )

THE GRIESLY WIFE

"Lie still, my newly married wife,
  Lie easy as you can.
You're young and ill accustomed yet
  To sleeping with a man."

The snow lay thick, the moon was full   5
  And shone across the floor.
The young wife went with never a word
  Barefooted to the door.

He up and followed sure and fast,
  The moon shone clear and white.   10
But before his coat was on his back
  His wife was out of sight.

He trod the trail wherever it turned
  By many a mound and scree,
And still the barefoot track led on   15
  And an angry man was he.

He followed fast, he followed slow,
  And still he called her name,
But only the dingoes of the hills
  Yowled back at him again.   20

His hair stood up along his neck,
  His angry mind was gone,
For the track of the two bare feet gave out
  And a four-foot track went on.

Her nightgown lay upon the snow   25
  As it might upon the sheet,
But the track that led on from where it lay
  Was never of human feet.

His heart turned over in his chest,
  He looked from side to side,   30
And he thought more of his gumwood fire
  Than he did of his griesly bride.

And first he started walking back
  And then began to run
And his quarry wheeled at the end of her track   35
  And hunted him in turn.

Oh, long the fire may burn for him
  And open stand the door,

And long the bed may wait empty:
He'll not be back any more.   40

Title: griesly: uncanny, ghastly.   14. scree: pile of broken rocks fallen from a moun-
tainside.   19. dingoes: wild dogs.

The first stanza of the poem introduces us to the principal characters, a newly married couple, and the initial situation: they are alone in their snow-surrounded house on their wedding night, and the husband tries to tell his bride not to be afraid. The rising action begins when the wife, without a word, leaves her husband and bed and goes coatless and barefooted out the door. This action continues as he follows her through the woods in the moonlit night, calling her name, growing more and more angry. Suddenly, however, he notices something in the snow that frightens him (deciding factor), for the barefoot tracks of his wife have been replaced by footprints that are not those of a human. He turns around (climax) and, first walking, then running, he returns home; but the creature that his wife has become turns, too, and hunts him down (denouement). Apparently she overtakes and kills him (resolution) because the scene switches back to the house where the door still stands open and the bed remains empty. We are told he will never return.

WHAT IS CONFLICT?

If we examine the action of "The Griesly Wife," we see that the center of the plot is a conflict—a struggle between two or more forces. It is conflict, in fact, that creates suspense in the work—the feeling of uncertainty or fear caused by anticipation as to the outcome of events, particularly as those events affect a character in the work for whom the reader has formed a sympathetic attachment. Obviously, suspense is a major device for capturing and holding interest in "who will win?" But conflict also affects literary quality, since the nature of the struggle contributes to the total impact of the work. Is the conflict superficial or does it have depth? Is the conflict too one-sided? Is it trumped-up, supported only by coincidence? Is the conflict too obvious or simply false? Are all elements of plot genuinely part of the struggle? The answers to these questions relate to the effect and artistic merit of a piece. The conflict may be highly accessible. It may, on the other hand, be both subtle and complex, so that the reader has difficulty identifying the nature of the conflicts and the various forces involved.

Conflicts are of two kinds: *external,* in which the central character (called the protagonist) contends with some other character or force (called the antagonist); or *internal,* in which the protagonist attempts to choose between contrary needs or impulses within himself or herself. Whether the conflict is external or internal, the protagonist's struggles provide the basic materials for the construction of plot. The parts of the plot are directly related to the *introduction* of the conflict (initial situation), its *growth* and *development* (rising action), a *dramatic reversal* in the struggle, usually brought on by the deciding factor, and its resolution. In "The Griesly Wife," the principal conflict is external. It is introduced in the initial situation, when the wife leaves her husband and walks into the night. It grows in the rising action as the husband/protagonist follows his wife/antagonist. The conflict is dramatically reversed when the wife's transformation into a beast causes the pursuer to become the pursued, and it is resolved and concluded when she captures her prey and dispatches him.

External conflicts do not, however, always involve a struggle of one character against another. Sometimes the conflict pits a character against nature, as in an outdoor adventure when the central character must fight an Arctic storm or the ocean for survival. A character may also attempt to survive in a hostile society or in the face of a fate that seems bent on destruction. When the protagonist is an obvious hero and the antagonist is an obvious villain, we may expect a resolution in which the hero wins and the villain loses. We look for the kind of satisfaction that follows a "happy" ending. Such a neat conclusion is not always possible or desirable, however. In some works, the hero loses; in others, neither protagonist nor antagonist can be appropriately designated hero or villain. Instead they are two characters of approximately equal merit or appeal. Their conflict may involve simple differences in personal goals and desires rather than a struggle between good and evil.

Similarly an *internal conflict* does not always involve choices that can clearly be labeled "good" or "bad." The choice may be between two legitimate desires, which simply cannot both be satisfied. Sometimes, as in the following poem, the internal conflict builds from discordant emotional states:

John Crowe Ransom (1888–   )

PARTING, WITHOUT A SEQUEL

She has finished and sealed the letter
At last, which he so richly has deserved,
With characters venomous and hatefully curved,
And nothing could be better.

But even as she gave it,   5
Saying to the blue-capped functioner of doom,
"Into his hands," she hoped the leering groom
Might somewhere lose and leave it.

Then all the blood
Forsook the face. She was too pale for tears,   10
Observing the ruin of her younger years.
She went and stood

Under her father's vaunting oak
Who kept his peace in wind and sun, and glistened
Stoical in the rain; to whom she listened   15
If he spoke.

And now the agitation of the rain
Rasped his sere leaves, and he talked low and gentle,
Reproaching the wan daughter by the lintel;
Ceasing, and beginning again.   20

Away went the messenger's bicycle,
His serpent's track went up the hill forever.
And all the time she stood there hot as fever
And cold as any icicle.

7. groom: messenger or servant.

In this poem, there are three characters: a woman who sends a letter, an unnamed "he," who is the eventual recipient of her message, and a postman or servant who comes on a bicycle to collect and deliver the letter. What action there is can be diagrammed as follows: the initial situation introduces the woman just after she has written a letter to a man. The rising action consists of her giving the letter to the postman. The aftermath is her complex reaction to what she has done. There is no deciding factor or climax. Although the initial situation in the poem does describe some kind of external conflict between the woman and the man, the primary experience revolves around the workings of her own mind as she copes with severe internal conflict. On the one hand, she feels that she has been terribly wronged, so the letter written in "characters venomous" (line 3) is richly "deserved" (line 2): "nothing could be better" (line 4). At the same time, however, she feels that she has thrown away her opportunity for love and happiness, that she is observing the "ruin of her younger years" (line 11). This struggle between self-satisfaction and despair is never resolved, and an important part of the poem's effect is the woman's apparent paralysis of will as she stands there "all the time" (line 23) both furious and afraid. If she could resolve her internal conflict, she would either dash after the postman to retrieve her letter or compose herself and prepare to find a new relationship. Thus conflicts are not always resolved in literature; in most works, however, the protagonist clearly chooses one set of alternatives, suppressing or eliminating one tendency in the self in order to support another.

INTERRELATIONSHIP OF CONFLICTS

Most stories, poems, and plays, especially longer ones, are built around a number of interconnected conflicts, both external and internal. Even the two short works we have examined contain subsidiary conflicts. In "The Griesly Wife," for instance, the husband pauses a moment in his pursuit of his wife when he notices the change in footprints. This action denotes an internal struggle—whether he should continue to follow her or return to his "gumwood fire." And in "Parting, Without a Sequel," the internal conflict follows the woman's external conflict with her lover. In works like these, however, the central conflict dominates the action so that examination of the principal struggle provides the clearest focus for analysis. In other works, several conflicts combine at once as the narration moves toward resolution. Study of conflict, then, means examining the interrelationships among the various struggles, as we see in the following short story:

Eugenio Montale (1896–   )

THE MAN IN PYJAMAS

I was walking up and down the corridor in slippers and pyjamas, stepping from time to time over a heap of dirty linen. It was an A class hotel. It had two lifts and one goods lift which were almost always out of order, but there was no store-room for sheets, pillow-slips and towels in temporary disuse, and the chambermaids had to pile them up where they could, that is, in all sorts of odd corners. Late at night I used to visit these corners and because of this the chambermaids never liked me. However, by tipping them I had, as it were, obtained their tacit approval to stroll wherever I wanted. It was past midnight and I heard the telephone ring softly. Could it be in my room? I glided stealthily towards it but noticed that it was ringing in a room adjacent to mine—room 22. As I was returning I overheard a woman's voice on the phone, saying: "Don't come yet, Attilio; there's a man in pyjamas walking through the corridor. He might see you."

From the other end of the line I heard an indistinct chatter. "Oh," she answered, "I don't know who he is—a poor wretch always hanging around. Please, don't come. In any case I'll let you know." She put the receiver down with a bang. I heard her footsteps in the room. I slipped hurriedly back towards the far end of the corridor where there was a sofa, another pile of linen and a wall. But I could hear the door of room 22 open and I gathered that the woman was watching me through the slit. I could not stay where I was for long, so I slowly returned. In something like ten seconds I was to pass her room and I considered the various alternatives: (1) to return to my room and lock myself up; (2) the same, but with a difference, that is to say, to inform the lady that I had overheard everything and that I intended to do her a favor by retiring; (3) to ask her if she was really all that keen on having Attilio, or if I was merely used as pretext to avoid a rather disagreeable nocturnal bullfight; (4) to ignore the telephonic conversation and carry on my stroll; (5) to ask if she might eventually care to substitute me for Attilio for the object referred to in alternative number 3; (6) to demand explanation for the nomenclature "poor wretch" with which she had chosen to designate me; (7) . . . there was some difficulty in formulating the seventh alternative. But by this time I was already in front of the slit. Two dark eyes, a crimson bed-jacket worn over a silk skirt, and short curly hair. Just a brief second and the opening shut again with a snap. My heart was beating fast as I entered my room and heard the telephone ring again next door. The woman was saying something in a soft voice which I did not catch. Like a wolf I shot back to the corridor and tried to make out what she was saying. "It's impossible, Attilio, I say it's impossible. . . ." And then the clack of the telephone followed by the sound of her footsteps nearing the door. I made a dash towards the second pile of dirty linen, turning over in my mind alternatives 2, 3 and 5. The door opened again narrowly and it was now impossible for me to stand still. . . . I said to myself: I *am* a poor wretch, but how could *she* know that? And what if by my walking up and down the corridor I may not have perhaps saved her from Attilio? Or saved Attilio from her? I am not born to be an arbiter of anything, much less an arbiter of the life of others. I returned to my room, kicking along a pillow-slip with a slipper. This time the door opened rather wider and the curly head projected a little further. I was just about a yard away from it so, having kicked off the slipper and come to attention, I bellowed out in a voice that could be heard right down the corridor: "I have finished walking up and down, Madam. But how do you know that I am a poor wretch?"

"We all are," she snapped and slammed the door. The telephone was ringing again.

To discover conflicts and determine how they are interrelated, ask the following questions:

a. Who is the protagonist?
b. Against whom or what is he or she struggling (who is the antagonist in external conflicts)?
c. What decisions is he or she faced with (internal conflict)?
d. How are his or her struggles and decisions connected (what is the interrelationship between external and internal conflicts in development)?
e. How are the struggles and the decision-making process concluded (what is the resolution of conflicts)?

In "The Man in Pyjamas," we see the following.

1. Apart from the chambermaids who are named but do not actually appear in the scene, there are only two characters: the unnamed narrator (the "man in pyjamas"), and the woman in room 22. Since the narrator appears in all of the action and is the most important character in the narrative, he is the protagonist.

2. The action involves a character struggling or at odds with some other person or force. These struggles involve disputes, different points of view, and contradictory purposes. For example, the narrator likes to explore the corners of the corridors that have been used for linen storage. The chambermaids prefer that he not do so. Therefore, the narrator and the maids are in conflict. Next, the woman in the adjoining room repeatedly tells a man named Attilio to stay away when he obviously wants to come, so they are in conflict. Again, the man in pyjamas seems to have distressed the woman

by roaming the corridor, and she disturbs him by calling him a "poor wretch." They too are in conflict; and since the principal conflict he experiences arises because of her, she is the antagonist.

3. At one point in the narrative, the protagonist considers "various alternatives" to her attack and names them for us. This list constitutes the nature of his chief internal conflict, as he contemplates seven things he might do, such as returning to his room, continuing his stroll, or demanding to know why she called him what she did.

4. As we trace the line of action from initial situation to climax, we see that one conflict grows out of another. Specifically, the protagonist insists on taking a habitual midnight corridor stroll, thus the conflict with the chambermaids. In the rising action, he walks the hall and overhears a telephone conversation, apparently a quarrel between the woman and Attilio in which she calls the narrator a "poor wretch." That conversation leads to his internal conflict and, when the telephone rings again, to his rushing out to the hall to confront the woman once more (the climax of the story), at which point the external and internal conflicts become explicitly connected and are finally dealt with in the falling action and denouement.

5. The conflicts are at least partially resolved, for when he faces his neighbor (principal external conflict), he chooses one of the alternatives (internal conflict) he has been considering—"to demand explanation for the nomenclature 'poor wretch' with which she had chosen to designate me." Her abrupt answer—"We all are"—and equally decisive action of slamming the door draws these conflicts to a close, even though the narrative does not indicate his response and concludes with the ringing of the telephone once again, which apparently means her quarrel with Attilio is not yet finished.

WHAT WE LEARN
FROM CONFLICTS

Finding conflicts in literature has no particular point unless the reader makes some attempt to discover not only what the different struggles in a narrative are but also what they might mean. Like most artists, writers use their craft to express their views about the world they see and the people who live in it. The struggles or conflicts of literary characters often constitute one way in which to make some point about life. Of course, some conflicts, like an unlucky husband's murder by a monster wife, are not particularly meaningful. But other kinds of struggles relate to attitudinal, psychological, or philosophical truths. A person's decision to end a relationship, for instance, can have great meaning, as "Parting, Without a Sequel" indicates. In the poem that decision causes such anxiety that the person who has made it is caught in a state of paralysis between feelings of satisfaction and feelings of despair. Similarly, a person's frustration and fury over a series of conflicts that confront him with the bleak reality of his existence are also meaningful. In "The Man in Pyjamas," the interaction among the successive conflicts gradually reveals a picture of the relatively wretched nature of much human life, an awareness that even generally fortunate people need to have.

How do we arrive at such an understanding of meaning? The discovery of meaning begins with a first reading to identify conflicts and their elements, a process already described. Next, the reader must choose whether to focus attention on a single major conflict or to examine the interaction among two or more related conflicts. Third, the reader must generalize elements of conflict into the larger concepts they embody. This step can be accomplished by direct substitution of class designations for the particular persons or objects that are part of the conflict. Fourth, the reader should note what element of conflict the author seems to focus on: development (rising action), turning point (climax), or resolution (denouement, conclusion). Finally, from the generalization and the focus the reader can state some of the meanings found in the work.

In "The Man in Pyjamas," for example, generalization of the elements of conflict reveals a person in conflict with a group of persons, but struggling against one person in particular. His struggles involve his desire to be undisturbed by other persons. The conflicts are resolved by explanation and compromise. The focus of the conflicts is the rising action, particularly the protagonist's disputes with the only persons he seems to relate to—the chambermaids and the neighbor—about the mean boundaries of his life.

Using this framework as the basis for exploration, we can see that the narrative presents a portrait of a life spent poking in corners of a hotel corridor. The central character leads a life without interpersonal relations or vital interests. His existence seems bounded by corridors and bribes, and he does not even mind seeing himself as a stand-in for someone else. His external and internal conflicts relate to his wish to live free from interference, but his disputes with the only persons he appears to relate to are as petty and restricted as the life he seems to lead. The neighbor's comment ("We all are") about general wretchedness is an explicit statement about the grubby, restricted lives many people lead, with desires limited to poking about dusty corridors or engaging in furtive meetings. The story also suggests that the desires of one poor wretch often come into conflict with those of another.

To arrive at any statement of meaning derived from conflict in a narrative involves careful reading, especially, as is usually the case, when the author makes no explicit statement about what the meanings might be. The procedure described can be used to arrive at a clear understanding of meaning as well as the function of conflict in a work of literature.

The entire process of first reading, identification of the elements of conflict, generalization, discovery of the author's focus, and exploration of meaning is illustrated in the analysis of the following poem:

Edwin Arlington Robinson (1869–1935)

JOHN GORHAM

"Tell me what you're doing over here, John Gorham,
Sighing hard and seeming to be sorry when you're not;
Make me laugh or let me go now, for long faces in the moonlight
Are a sign for me to say again a word that you forgot."—

"I'm over here to tell you what the moon already   5
May have said or maybe shouted ever since a year ago;
I'm over here to tell you what you are, Jane Wayland,
And to make you rather sorry, I should say, for being so."—

"Tell me what you're saying to me now, John Gorham,
Or you'll never see as much of me as ribbons any more;   10
I'll vanish in as many ways as I have toes and fingers,
And you'll not follow far for one where flocks have been before."—

"I'm sorry now you never saw the flocks, Jane Wayland,
But you're the one to make of them as many as you need.
And then about the vanishing. It's I who mean to vanish;   15
And when I'm here no longer you'll be done with me indeed."—

"That's a way to tell me what I am, John Gorham!
How am I to know myself until I make you smile?
Try to look as if the moon were making faces at you,
And a little more as if you meant to stay a little while."—   20

"You are what it is that over rose-blown gardens
Makes a pretty flutter for a season in the sun;
You are what it is that with a mouse, Jane Wayland,
Catches him and lets him go and eats him up for fun."—

"Sure I never took you for a mouse, John Gorham;   25
All you say is easy, but so far from being true
That I wish you wouldn't ever be again the one to think so;
For it isn't cats and butterflies that I would be to you."

"All your little animals are in one picture—
One I've had before me since a year ago to-night;   30
And the picture where they live will be of you, Jane Wayland,
Till you find a way to kill them or to keep them out of sight."—

"Won't you ever see me as I am, John Gorham,
Leaving out the foolishness and all I never meant?
Somewhere in me there's a woman, if you know the way to find her.   35
Will you like me any better if I prove it and repent?"—

"I doubt if I shall ever have the time, Jane Wayland;
And I dare say all this moonlight lying round us might as well
Fall for nothing on the shards of broken urns that are forgotten,
As on two that have no longer much of anything to tell."   40

After the first reading, we can say the following:

1. The protagonist is John Gorham.
2. The antagonist is Jane Wayland.
3. The external conflict involves a quarrel between the two that took place some time ago and continues into the present.
4. The internal conflicts within each character involve uncertainty about what to say or do when he comes to visit her.
5. The rising action is the quarrel, which grows in intensity.
6. The climax is the moment when she wavers and suggests a possible resumption of their relationship.
7. The resolution is John Gorham's statement that there is no chance that they could resume what has been destroyed.

Because external and internal conflicts are interrelated, both must be examined to define the struggles going on between the two and within each. Exactly how these conflicts are connected is clear after a *close second* reading of the work:

"Tell me what you're doing over here, John Gorham,
Sighing hard and seeming to be sorry when you're not;
Make me laugh or let me go now, for long faces in the moonlight
Are a sign for me to say again a word that you forgot."—

It is night time, a moonlit night. John Gorham pays an unexpected visit to Jane Wayland. He is sighing. Why? Does he want to apologize to her? Does he expect something from her? She is prompted by his long face to tell him again a "word" he seems to have forgotten.

"I'm over here to tell you what the moon already
May have said or maybe shouted ever since a year ago;
I'm over here to tell you what you are, Jane Wayland,
And to make you rather sorry, I should say, for being so."—

There was a quarrel a year ago, an external conflict; it is still in his mind. He says he is there to tell her what she is really like and to make her sorry for being that way.

"Tell me what you're saying to me now, John Gorham,
Or you'll never see as much of me as ribbons any more;
I'll vanish in as many ways as I have toes and fingers,
And you'll not follow far for one where flocks have been before."—

She demands to know what he wants to say, and threatens to vanish from his life. She won't even allow him to be one of a large number of suitors who follow her.

"I'm sorry now you never saw the flocks, Jane
    Wayland,
But you're the one to make of them as many as
    you need.
And then about the vanishing. It's I who mean to
    vanish;
And when I'm here no longer you'll be done with
    me indeed."—

He corrects her: she won't
vanish; he will. He sets
forth his position on their external conflict over which of
the two will have the final say.

"That's a way to tell me what I am, John Gorham!
How am I to know myself until I make you smile?
Try to look as if the moon were making faces at
    you,
And a little more as if you meant to stay a little
    while."—

She tries to lighten his mood
and perhaps resolve their argument from a year ago by
some kind of reconciliation.

"You are what it is that over rose-blown gardens
Makes a pretty flutter for a season in the sun;
You are what it is that with a mouse, Jane Way-
    land,
Catches him and lets him go and eats him up for
    fun."—

He doesn't respond to her
teasing; instead he tells her
what he thinks she is—a
butterfly fluttering for a time
over roses, or a cat that torments a helpless mouse. He
apparently experiences some
internal conflict between at-
traction to her and fear of her
cruelty.

"Sure I never took you for a mouse, John Gorham;
All you say is easy, but so far from being true
That I wish you wouldn't ever be again the one
    to think so;
For it isn't cats and butterflies that I would be to
    you."—

She denies the charge. It might
be easy for him to say; but
she doesn't want to be a cat or
butterfly to him.

"All your little animals are in one picture—
One I've had before me since a year ago to-night;
And the picture where they live will be of you,
    Jane Wayland,
Till you find a way to kill them or to keep them
    out of sight."—

He replies that her cruelty has
been in his mind for a year. It
will be with him forever unless she somehow changes.

"Won't you ever see me as I am, John Gorham,
Leaving out the foolishness and all I never meant?
Somewhere in me there's a woman, if you know
    the way to find her.
Will you like me any better if I prove it and re-
    pent?"—

She begs him to take her as
she is, a woman who may
have said something she didn't
mean. She reveals an internal
conflict of her own as she asks
him if her status in his eyes
will improve if she says she is
sorry for what she may have
said or done.

"I doubt if I shall ever have the time, Jane Wayland;
And I dare say all this moonlight lying round us
might as well
Fall for nothing on the shards of broken urns that
are forgotten,
As on two that have no longer much of anything
to tell."

He brings all conflicts to a resolution as he refuses the offer. He doesn't have the time or interest any more. Their affair is absolutely over, and they really don't have anything more to say to each other.

If we generalize the particulars of the poem, we find two persons in a conflict over a relationship. The principal interest in this conflict seems to be
the development of the argument (the rising action) as these two persons
meet again for the first time in a year, after a bitter quarrel. The deciding
factor, we learn, is also significant, since the poem is also centered on one
person's determination to have the last word and thereby rid himself of
the humiliation and self-doubt he has been suffering. The author's—and the
reader's—attention is therefore focused on the questions: What will a person do to achieve satisfaction after injury? More generally, how can a person deal with a complex pattern of unresolved conflicts? The answers to
these questions define some of the meanings of the poem, as we see a
person deeply hurt in the breakup of a relationship triumphing by returning
the hurt instead of making any attempt to restore what might have been.

WRITING ABOUT CONFLICT

Obviously, any paper that attempts to investigate conflict must include a
careful analysis of what that conflict is. If there is only one principal conflict,
the analysis should focus on both sides of that conflict. What two forces are
in opposition? Who is the protagonist? Who is the antagonist? How is the
conflict developed? What is the deciding factor? How is the conflict resolved? All this information must be presented as specifically as possible,
usually supported by quotations from the text. If a work contains two or
more conflicts, each must be examined in this way and the interrelationship
between them carefully worked out. The same requirement for a paper on
conflict holds true, whether you are writing a critical analysis, a personal
essay, or an examination essay.

Option I: Critical Analysis of Conflict

A paper that attempts to examine the function of conflict in a story, poem,
or play will necessarily focus on an extended examination of the forces
struggling against each other. This examination will be the heart of the

paper, preceded by an introduction in which the conflicts are named and followed by a conclusion that indicates the meaning derived from the conflict and its resolution. The purpose of such a paper is threefold. First, it allows you to show your understanding of conflict as it controls the development of the work. Such an understanding can be achieved only if you have a secure grasp of the critical principles involved and the ability to apply them to the work of your choice. In writing the paper, you must also demonstrate your skill in quoting material, since quotations will make what you are saying stronger and more convincing. Finally, this paper will offer you the opportunity to comment on the meaning of the work. To do this, you will have to know not only what the conflicts are but also what the conflicts/resolutions have to say about human existence and behavior. You will also have to reflect on what that meaning suggests to you and your understanding of life in general. All three purposes are explained in detail in the guidelines that follow:

1. Choose the work you wish to examine and reread it carefully, noting the dramatic situation and principal events.

2. List conflicts and identify the protagonist. Since by definition the protagonist is the person most centrally involved in the important conflicts in a work, the first step toward identifying the protagonist is to study the conflicts themselves. Examine the narrative and list those forces that are fighting against each other. Remember—sometimes these forces will be external (man or woman against man, nature, society, or fate) and sometimes the struggle will be internal, that is, within a single individual (two tendencies or emotional states at war with one another).

3. Decide whether to concentrate on a single conflict or to examine the interplay of two or more conflicts in the work. Remember that very frequently an external struggle grows out of or creates an internal conflict in the protagonist, but in some works only one of the two is adequately developed to provide a basis for meaning.

4. Write down details about the conflict(s) you have chosen to examine. Make sure to include information about *both sides* of any conflict you discuss, as well as the resolution and its deciding factor. Then consider meaning in the context of the narrative. To help you arrive at meaning, generalize by substituting larger, more inclusive terms for each specific detail. Finally, make some observations on the meaning of the work, as revealed by your analysis.

5. Find words and phrases in the work that illuminate the nature of the forces in conflict and the way in which the conflicts are resolved. Remember to quote accurately and to note a page or line number for each detail. List as many specific pieces of evidence as you can find. While you are unlikely to use all of these quotations in the actual paper, it is best to have ample material to choose from before you start to write.

6. Write an introduction for your paper, including at least the following

elements: (a) an identification of the work you intend to discuss, complete with a footnote at the bottom of the first page giving bibliographic facts; (b) a main-idea statement identifying the two sides of a single conflict or listing a group of related conflicts—this statement will serve as the basis of organization for the paper; and (c) a statement of the significance of the conflict(s) and resolution(s) to the meaning of the work as a whole. There are, of course, various ways to begin a paper analyzing a work of literature, one of which was discussed in the preceding chapter. Another way is to start with a discussion of the generalization explored by the work. Think about the significance of the experience you are meant to share in the poem, story, or play and describe briefly what the insights revealed mean to you. In this way, you will not only be providing an appropriate lead-in to a discussion of the work itself, you will also give the reader some indication of the thoughts you will be exploring in greater detail in the conclusion.

7. Write the body of your paper. The body may consist of one fairly long paragraph divided into two or more parts, or it may consist of several paragraphs. In either event, a typical division of your material can be

a. for dealing with *one* conflict:
   i. one force in the principal conflict,
   ii. the other force in the principal conflict;
b. for dealing with two or more conflicts:
   i. details about the first conflict,
   ii. details about the second conflict, including a statement about how it arises from the first.

Clearly identify each part of your division with a topic sentence. Then refer to your list of quotations and choose those that seem most supportive of and appropriate to your position. For each piece of evidence you give, state precisely how it relates to the topic under discussion and include a page or line reference in parentheses, immediately following the specific detail. You should also provide transitional material showing how the two forces in conflict or two different conflicts relate to each other.

8. Write a concluding paragraph. This paragraph should focus on the resolution of the single conflict or the outcomes of two or more struggles. Show how meaning is derived from one principal conflict or from the relationship between the interacting conflicts. While the concluding paragraph is general in nature and therefore does not need any direct specific evidence, the addition of some quotations from your source may strengthen it.

9. Read your first draft and rewrite it as necessary. Be sure that your sentences are correct and that your style is as smooth as you can make it. Also check to see that quoted material relates directly to your discussion of conflict, that you are quoting *exactly*, and that you are providing the correct page or line number for each quotation.

10. Write your final draft, choose a title, and proofread before you hand in the paper.

OPTION I: SAMPLE ESSAY

Getting Even

After a quarrel most people wish that they had said this or that, and they devote a lot of energy to recreating the dispute in their own minds and settling it in their own way. Most people, however, don't find the opportunity to act out their fantasy. John Gorham, in the poem by Edwin Arlington Robinson, is a man who does just that. The poem focuses on a lover's quarrel, one that took place a year ago. At that time, Jane Wayland apparently gave him the "word" and he has returned a year later not to seek reconciliation, as she at first thinks, but to conclude the argument that began that night. Their conversation reveals both the external conflict between them and the internal conflicts that are going on within each. The interrelationship between those conflicts relates directly to the emotional satisfaction that the protagonist seeks and finally gets.

The external conflict is simple to identify. It consists of the quarrel between the two, and we learn something about its substance as the poem progresses. By nature, Jane appears to be a flirt, taking advantage of her beauty to play with her suitors. At one time, John was one of those suitors, but a year ago she precipitated an argument that severed the relationship. During the year since, he has been thinking about their quarrel, and he decides to visit her for two purposes. First, he wants to tell her "what you are, Jane Wayland" (line 7) and second to play with her as she did with him, leaving his final intention unspoken until she hesitantly asks if he will like her any better "if I prove it and repent" (line 36). Then he has the last word —he is absolutely finished with her and will never more allow her to be part of his life.

The internal conflicts are perhaps not so obvious, but both parties seem to be undergoing some kind of struggle. John's "sighing hard" (line 2) and his long face indicate his agitation, even though she misreads his behavior and we ourselves do not discover what they mean until the end of the poem. Then, too, she changes her attitude, from uneasy playfulness at first to a guarded offer of repentance. It is that offer that gives John his complete triumph—when he rejects her firmly, without hesitation, comparing their present relationship to "shards of broken urns" (line 39) that lie scattered in the moonlight.

The meaning in the poem arises from the interaction of the external and internal conflicts. What we see in John Gorham is a person who comes to a decision that he must right the wrong he feels has been done to him. No matter how anxious he is about the confrontation, he returns, speaks his piece, and enjoys the satisfaction of winning. Sometimes that victory can be hollow, especially if the other person is apologetic and wishes to renew the relationship. But if the desire for vindication is strong enough, no apology will do and the original attractions that sparked the relationship are nothing compared to the pleasure of vengeance attempted and achieved.

Option II: The Personal Essay

Since literature presents fundamental conflicts of human experience, you will often discover that a story, poem, or play explores a conflict similar to one you experienced in your own life. Perhaps the protagonist must make, as you did, an important choice and is in mental conflict. Perhaps he or she is opposed by an antagonist, as you were, and is involved in an external conflict. Such similarity remains, even where the resolution of the struggle in the literary work may be quite different from that in your own situation. One way to show your understanding of both the work and your own experience is to write a personal essay comparing the two. In a personal essay you tell your story, usually in chronological order, using first-person narration. Although the purpose of such a paper is essentially the same as that of the analytical essay—to show your understanding of a work—the structure is much less formal, allowing a more free-flowing narrative.

The following guidelines outline a series of steps to follow in preparing and writing such a paper.

1. Choose a work that describes a conflict similar to one you have experienced. Reread the work carefully, making notes of the dramatic situation and the principal events.

2. Identify the protagonist, his or her external and/or internal conflicts, and the outcome or resolution. Although the protagonist is often involved in more than one significant conflict, select the chief one for this assignment.

3. Identify the principal conflict and write down details about *both sides* of it and the resolution. To help to arrive at the meaning of the conflict/resolution generalize by substituting a larger, more inclusive term for each item: protagonist, conflict, resolution. Finally, note how this meaning is revealed in the work.

4. Write down details about a situation you have experienced that parallels this conflict and illustrates the same meaning. Include such information as the following: (a) the forces in conflict with each other, (b) precisely how these forces are in opposition, (c) how long the conflict lasted, (d) how the conflict affected you, (e) the resolution of the conflict, (f) how the resolution affected you.

5. Write the introduction to your paper, including the following elements: (a) an identification of the work whose conflict you have examined; (b) a statement naming the principal conflict and specifying the two sides struggling against each other; (c) a brief discussion of the nature of the conflict, including reference to rising action, turning point, and resolution; (d) a statement of the meaning of the conflict and its resolution; (e) a transitional sentence in which you state how the conflict you have examined is related to a conflict in your own experience.

6. Write the body of your paper, in which you enlarge on the material you outlined in step 4. Since this section of your paper presents information about something that happened to you, remember to structure your organization around the chronology of your experience.

7. Write the conclusion of your paper. Include an explanation about the resolution of your experience, what you learned. Relate your insights to the work you discussed in the first paragraph.

8. Decide on a title. The title can simply be a short reference to the conflict, resolution, *or* meaning of the work. It can be also a one-word indication of the subject of the work you are analyzing. Another possibility is a brief reference to the significance of the personal material you are presenting.

9. After you have completed your first draft, set it aside for a day or two, so that you can look at your paper more objectively. Then rewrite as necessary. Be sure that your grammar and syntax are correct and that your style is smooth.

OPTION II: SAMPLE ESSAY

Ah! Sweet Vengeance!

Most people are hurt and angry when they feel that their worth, whether to a particular person or simply as human beings, is denied. Their one desire often is to "get even," either by making the person who rejected them feel the same hurt or by proving that they do, indeed, have value. In Edwin Arlington Robinson's "John Gorham," we see a desire for revenge translated into action. In that poem, Gorham converses with a former sweetheart, who apparently had said some terrible word to him a year before in an argument. Gorham has waited an entire year to have vengeance; he finally confronts her, prepared to make her "rather sorry" and tell her the kind of person she is (lines 7–8). Although the woman is surprised to see him and at first assumes he has forgotten what she said, she soon discovers he has not. His coldness toward her leads her to tease him and then to ask him not to go; it finally prevents his yielding. In the end he has the satisfaction of rejecting her, saying that they are "two that have no longer much of anything to tell" (line 40). With these words, he shows her that she no longer has any worth for him and thereby gets his revenge. Like Gorham, I have had my worth denied by someone who was important to me, and I also had the opportunity to even the score.

I was a sophomore in college and convinced that I wanted to be a writer. One of the professors who taught creative writing was an esteemed poet and I longed to take his course. From him I was sure I could learn the techniques and concepts needed to be successful. I was greatly excited and full of anticipation when I enrolled in the course and, on the basis of some sample poems, was accepted. For the first several weeks he assigned only exercises in the use of imagistic language and metaphors and discussed in detail well-known poems in class. I was happier in his class than in any other and listened to his words as if they were gospel. Finally he assigned each of his students to write four poems, saying that he would not grade them. I was nervous about such a close examination of my work by a person I considered to be a great man; but I was also eager and hopeful.

On the fateful day, I entered his office full of awe, but optimism, too. I sat in the chair opposite him and waited for him to speak. When he did, however, his words weren't at all what I'd expected: "no real talent . . . perhaps some flair for language, but not real creativity. . . ." Too hurt and angry to speak, I somehow sat through the rest of the meeting and left. My initial reaction was a feeling of tremendous dejection: I had been judged and found guilty; my sin was a lack of ability. My second reaction was scorn: This man was no god—how could I have so misjudged him? I wanted to drop the course, but a part of me insisted I shouldn't—that despite his lack of perception my poet-professor had something to teach me. Then, too, if I stayed in the class and persisted, perhaps I could prove him wrong. That would be the sweetest possible revenge.

A few weeks later the university magazine announced a contest: a first, second, and third prize would be given for the best student poems submitted. These would be published in the magazine and winners would read their poems to the combined creative writing classes. The judges were the editors of the university press, all English professors accustomed to making such judgments. The poems had to be submitted without the name of the poet on them; names of poets and poem titles were to be put into a separate envelope. After considering the possible results, and with some encouragement from my friends, I finally decided that I would submit one poem. It was a new one, written since the beginning of the course but never turned in.

The next few weeks I waited anxiously, alternating between hope and despair. Then, one Monday, just after the beginning of the class hour, the professor entered, glanced around the room, and announced that he had just learned the winners of the writing contest. My heart jumped and began to race. I held my breath and looked intently at the wall, keeping my face expressionless. He began by naming the third prize winner—no one I knew. Then he named the second prize winner—no one I knew. I glanced at him, just as he said my name. I had won first prize! I stared at his face. He smiled slightly (and it seemed to me, with great effort). Amid the applause of my classmates, I didn't need to say a word; I simply grinned triumphantly at him. No matter what he thought, I'd proved not only that I had worth as a writer but also that he wasn't infallible. Like John Gorham, I knew, finally, the satisfaction of having won the final victory. How sweet it was!

Option III: Examination Question

Essay questions usually serve two important purposes: in addition to revealing how much you know about a certain topic, they show how well you can organize and apply that knowledge in a sustained communication. How much you know will depend on how diligently you have prepared daily assignments and how actively you have listened to and participated in class discussions. Assuming you have command of the material, success in an essay test will require that you plan carefully *before* you write, to demonstrate your ability to handle the knowledge you have acquired.

One common type of essay question asks you to compare two items that you have previously explored separately. The guidelines and the sample below are intended to illustrate what might happen with such a question, requiring a comparison of the conflicts in two works of literature. The step-by-step procedures include advice that will serve you well in taking any exam in any subject and also some specific suggestions for dealing with a paper on literature. Your instructor may, of course, assign a similar topic for a paper to be written on your own time, and if so you should follow essentially the same steps. Here is a sample essay question:

Choose two works in which conflict is an important vehicle for developing meaning, and in which you find some basic similarities in either the nature of the conflict(s) or the theme that is explored. Write a brief essay discussing similarities and differences between the two works. In your answer demonstrate your understanding of how conflict relates to meaning.
(Suggested time: one hour.)

1. Read the examination question carefully, making sure you understand it clearly. As with all exam questions, it may be helpful to underline the key words and phrases in the directions. It is also wise to budget your time. Most students need between one-fifth and one-fourth of the total time for planning (12 to 15 minutes, if the question is designed for one hour). You should allow a few minutes, too, for proofreading and corrections before handing in your paper.

2. Choose two works for comparison. (If the question specifies the works to be compared, you will of course skip this step.) A successful comparison requires that there be some basic similarity against which differences may be discussed. Pairs of topics for comparison might include (a) two works that deal with conflicts growing out of similar problems in human experience (for example, the death of a loved one, rivalry and competition for a job or honors, a quarrel that ends a relationship) but resolve the conflicts in different ways and hence suggest different meanings; or, (b) two works that develop similar themes by examining conflicts that are in some ways quite different. In other words, choose works having both similarities and differences in the use of conflict to generate meaning. There is little point in comparing two works that are nearly identical in conflicts, resolutions, and meaning; and it would be almost impossible to organize a comparison of two works that have almost nothing at all in common.

3. Write a rough outline for your answer. Do not try to cover more than you have time for. If you normally require half an hour to write one paragraph, there is little point in planning to write a long essay in 40 minutes. Whether you have time for one paragraph, three, or even five, a typical outline for your paper might look like this:

a. introduction, naming works, protagonists, principal conflicts
b. external conflicts, similarities and differences
c. internal conflicts, similarities and differences
d. resolutions, similarities and differences
e. conclusion, including generalization to meaning

The nature and extent of the details you list under these topics will of course vary with the length and scope of the paper you plan to write and the time limits.

4. Write the introduction. Be sure to identify the two works you are comparing as well as the similarity that makes comparison possible. Include a summary of the main points you are going to develop in the body of your paper.

5. Write the body of your answer. If you have time enough, you may wish to devote a separate paragraph to each subtopic of your comparison. On the other hand, if time will allow you to write only one paragraph, try to make it a substantial one in which you link your subtopics together into a single unit. In an "open book" exam, you may use appropriate quotations from the two works in support of your comments. Even without access to the text, you may remember one or two brief quotations to enrich your paper.

6. Write your conclusion. Sum up the comparison you have made, generalizing on the principal similarities and differences you have discussed.

7. Proofread and correct your answer. In the timed conditions of an exam,

you will definitely not have time to prepare a fresh copy, but you may cross out minor mistakes and write corrections between the lines. While neatness is desirable, accuracy is more important.

OPTION III: SAMPLE ANSWER

Two short poems that examine the after-effects of a lovers' quarrel are John Crowe Ransom's "Parting, Without a Sequel" and "John Gorham" by Edwin Arlington Robinson. In both poems, the actual quarrel takes place before the action begins, but the two sets of conflicts are quite different, especially in how much is revealed of the external conflict, in the exact nature of the internal conflict experienced by the protagonist, and in the final resolution.

Both protagonists blame the other party for the quarrel that has already occurred, and therefore both take action to bring the external conflict to an end. The young woman in Ransom's poem feels that her anger is well justified, although we are given no hint as to the exact nature of the man's behavior. All we know is that to her mind he thoroughly deserves to be hurt by the bitter letter she writes to end their relationship. John Gorham, too, feels that the breakup of the relationship was mainly caused by some hateful word Jane Wayland said to him a year ago—which she now threatens to repeat. Far from feeling that her remark was justified, he wishes to point out to her that her behavior has been flirtatious and fickle, that the entire external conflict has been her fault, and that she deserves to be hurt as he has been hurt.

During the action in the poems, both protagonists experience internal conflicts, though these are very different. The young woman still feels the anger that prompted her letter, but she also feels regret at having sent it and a wish that her relationship might somehow be resumed in spite of her actions. John Gorham, on the other hand, has largely given up whatever regrets he may have initially experienced: he returns to Jane for the purpose of expressing his pent-up anger. He does so almost without hesitation, even though his long face at the start of the poem suggests to her that he has come to apologize. There is some emotional struggle at work in him, as his sighs suggest, but his desire for revenge is so strong as to overwhelm any conflicting feelings he may have.

Since John Gorham's inner conflict is much weaker than that of the young woman in the Ransom poem, he is able to achieve a much more satisfactory resolution of it. He is able to lead Jane Wayland from her initial assumption that he wants to apologize to a mood where she is ready to make such an apology herself. He is then in a position to gratify his anger fully: he can dismiss her finally from his life, leaving her with the sense of hurt he has suffered for a year. No such satisfaction is possible for the protagonist of the other poem: she has taken the action that expresses her anger, but she is so regretful that she cannot take pleasure in the end of the affair. She is in fact left with the feeling that she will never recover from her present anguish. Her internal conflict is not resolved, and she will probably suffer with it for some time.

Lovers' quarrels do not always end unhappily. Sometimes both parties are able to admit their mistakes and so reestablish trust and affection. Sometimes one party is so helplessly in love as to take all the blame and beg forgiveness—and this may occasionally lead to a renewal of the relationship. However, when one party has been deeply hurt or angered, there is not much hope for rebuilding a relationship. After a time, it may be possible for the wounded one, like John Gorham, to discharge his or her feelings and thereby get rid of the pain of the broken relationship. One can hope that this may in time happen to Ransom's protagonist, but for now she is unable to deal with her mixed feelings and remains "hot as fever / And cold as any icicle."

READING SELECTIONS: STORIES

Jesse Stuart (1907–   )

DAWN OF REMEMBERED SPRING

"Be careful, Shan," Mom said. "I'm afraid if you wade that creek that a water moccasin[1] will bite you."

"All right, Mom."

"You know what happened to Roy Deer last Sunday!"

"Yes, Mom!"

"He's nigh at the point of death," she said. "I'm going over there now to see him. His leg's swelled hard as a rock and it's turned black as black-oak bark. They're not looking for Roy to live until midnight tonight."

"All water moccasins ought to be killed, hadn't they, Mom?"

"Yes, they're pizen things, but you can't kill them," Mom said. "They're in all of these creeks around here. There's so many of them we can't kill 'em all."

Mom stood at the foot-log that crossed the creek in front of our house. Her white apron was starched stiff; I heard it rustle when Mom put her hand

---

[1] water moccasin: a common poisonous snake.

in the little pocket in the right upper corner to get tobacco crumbs for her pipe. Mom wore her slat bonnet that shaded her sun-tanned face—a bonnet with strings that came under her chin and tied in a bowknot.

"I feel uneasy," Mom said as she filled her long-stemmed clay-stone pipe with bright-burley crumbs, tamped them down with her index finger, and struck a match on the rough bark of an apple tree that grew on the creek bank by the foot-log.

"Don't feel uneasy about me," I said.

"But I do," Mom said. "Your Pa out groundhog huntin' and I'll be away at Deers'—nobody at home but you, and so many pizen snakes around this house."

Mom blew a cloud of blue smoke from her pipe. She walked across the foot-log—her long clean dress sweeping the weed stubble where Pa had mown the weeds along the path with a scythe so we could leave the house without getting our legs wet by the dew-covered weeds.

When Mom walked out of sight around the turn of the pasture hill and the trail of smoke that she left behind her had disappeared into the light blue April air, I crossed the garden fence at the wild-plum thicket.

Everyone gone, I thought. I am left alone. I'll do as I please. A water moccasin bit Roy Deer but a water moccasin will never bite me. I'll get me a club from this wild-plum thicket and I'll wade up the creek killing water moccasins.

There was a dead wild-plum sprout standing among the thicket of living sprouts. It was about the size of a tobacco stick. I stepped out of my path into the wild-plum thicket. Barefooted, I walked among the wild-plum thorns. I uprooted the dead wild-plum sprout. There was a bulge on it where roots had once been—now the roots had rotted in the earth. It was like a maul with this big bulge on the end of it. It would be good to hit water moccasins with.

The mules played in the pasture. It was Sunday—their day of rest. And the mules knew it. This was Sunday and it was my day of rest. It was my one day of freedom, too, when Mom and Pa were gone and I was left alone. I would like to be a man now, I thought, I'd love to plow the mules, run a farm, and kill snakes. A water moccasin bit Roy Deer but one would never bite me.

The bright sunlight of April played over the green Kentucky hills. Sunlight fell onto the creek of blue water that twisted like a crawling snake around the high bluffs and between the high rocks. In many places dwarf willows, horse-weeds, iron weeds, and wild grapevines shut away the sunlight and the creek waters stood in quiet cool puddles. These little puddles under the shade of weeds, vines, and willows were the places where the water moccasins lived.

I rolled my overall legs above my knees so I wouldn't wet them and Mom wouldn't know I'd been wading the creek. I started wading up the creek toward the head of the hollow. I carried my wild-plum club across my shoulder with both hands gripped tightly around the small end of it. I was ready to maul the first water moccasin I saw.

"One of you old water moccasins bit Roy Deer," I said bravely, clinching my grip tighter around my club, "but you won't bite me."

As I waded the cool creek waters, my bare feet touched gravel on the creek bottom. When I touched a wet water-soaked stick on the bottom of the creek bed, I'd think it was a snake and I'd jump. I'd wade into banks of quicksand. I'd sink into the sand above my knees. It was hard to pull my legs out of this quicksand and when I pulled them out they'd be covered with thin quicky mud that the next puddle of water would wash away.

"A water moccasin," I said to myself. I was scared to look at him. He was wrapped around a willow that was bent over the creek. He was sleeping in the sun. I slipped toward him quietly—step by step—with my club drawn over my shoulder. Soon as I got close enough to reach him, I came over my shoulder with the club. I hit the water moccasin a powerful blow that mashed its head flat against the willow. It fell dead into the water. I picked it up by the tail and threw it up on the bank.

"One gone," I said to myself.

The water was warm around my feet and legs. The sharp-edged gravels hurt the bottoms of my feet but the soft sand soothed them. Butterflies swarmed over my head and around me—alighting on the wild pink phlox that grew in clusters along the creek bank. Wild honey bees, bumble bees, and butterflies worked on the elder blossoms, the shoe-make blossoms and the beet-red finger-long blossoms of the ironweed and the whitish pink covered smart-weed blossoms. Birds sang among the willows and flew up and down the creek with four-winged snake-feeders in their bills.

This is what I like to do, I thought. I love to kill snakes. I'm not afraid of snakes. I laughed to think how afraid of snakes Mom was—how she struck a potato-digger tine through a big rusty-golden copperhead's skin just enough to pin him to the earth and hold him so he couldn't get under our floor. He fought the potato-digger handle until Pa came home from work and killed him. Where he'd thrown poison over the ground it killed the weeds and weeds didn't grow on this spot again for four years.

Once when Mom was making my bed upstairs, she heard a noise of something running behind the paper that was pasted over the cracks between the logs—the paper split and a house snake six feet long fell onto the floor with a mouse in his mouth. Mom killed him with a bed slat. She called me once to bring her a goose-neck hoe upstairs quickly. I ran upstairs and killed two cow snakes restin' on the wall plate. And Pa killed twenty-eight copperheads out of a two-acre oat field in the hollow above the house one spring season.

"Snakes—snakes," Mom used to say, "are goin' to run us out'n this Hollow."

"It's because these woods ain't been burnt out in years," Pa'd always answer. "Back when I's a boy the old people burnt the woods out every spring to kill the snakes. Got so anymore there ain't enough good timber for a board tree and people have had to quit burning up the good timber. Snakes are about to take the woods again."

I thought about the snakes Pa had killed in the cornfield and the tobacco patch and how nearly copperheads had come to biting me and how I'd always seen the snake in time to cut his head off with a hoe or get out of his way. I thought of the times I had heard a rattlesnake's warning and how I'd run when I hadn't seen the snake. As I thought these thoughts, plop, a big water moccasin fell from the creek bank into a puddle of water.

"I'll get you," I said. "You can't fool me! You can't stand muddy water."

I stirred the water until it was muddy with my wild-plum club. I waited for the water moccasin to stick his head above the water. Where wild ferns dipped down from the bank's edge and touched the water, I saw the snake's head rise slowly above the water—watchin' me with his lidless eyes. I swung sidewise with my club like batting at a ball. I couldn't swing over my shoulder, for there were willow limbs above my head.

I surely got him, I thought. I waited to see. Soon, something like milk spread over the water. "I got 'im." I raked in the water with my club and lifted from the bottom of the creek bed a water moccasin long as my club. It was longer than I was tall. I threw him up on the bank and moved slowly up the creek—looking on every drift, stump, log, and sunny spot. I looked for a snake's head along the edges of the creek bank where ferns dipped over and touched the water.

I waded up the creek all day killing water moccasins. If one were asleep on the bank, I slipped upon him quietly as a cat. I mauled him with the big end of my wild-plum club. I killed him in his sleep. He never knew what struck him. If a brush caught the end of my club and caused me to miss and let the snake get into a puddle of water, I muddied the water and waited for him to stick his head above the water. When he stuck his head above the water, I got him. Not one water moccasin got away from me. It was four o'clock when I stepped from the creek onto the bank. I'd killed fifty-three water moccasins.

Water moccasins are not half as dangerous as turtles, I thought. A water moccasin can't bite you under the water for he gets his mouth full of water. A turtle can bite you under water and when one bites you he won't let loose until it thunders, unless you cut his head off. I'd been afraid of turtles all day because I didn't have a knife in my pocket to cut one's head off if it grabbed my foot and held it.

When I left the creek, I was afraid of the snakes I'd killed. I didn't throw my club away. I gripped the club until my hands hurt. I looked below my path, above my path, and in front of me. When I saw a stick on the ground, I thought it was a snake. I eased up to it quietly as a cat trying to catch a bird. I was ready to hit it with my club.

What will Mom think when I tell her I've killed fifty-three water moccasins? I thought. A water moccasin bit Roy Deer but one's not going to bite me. I paid the snakes back for biting him. It was good enough for them. Roy wasn't bothering the water moccasin that bit him. He was just crossing the creek at the foot-log and it jumped from the grass and bit him.

Shadows lengthened from the tall trees. The Hollow was deep and the creek flowed softly in the cool recesses of evening shadows. There was one patch of sunlight. It was upon the steep broomsedge-covered [2] bluff above the path.

"Snakes," I cried, "snakes a-fightin' and they're not water moccasins! They're copperheads!"

They were wrapped around each other. Their lidless eyes looked into each other's eyes. Their hard lips touched each other's lips. They did not move. They did not pay any attention to me. They looked at one another.

I'll kill 'em, I thought, if they don't kill one another in this fight.

I stood in the path with my club ready. I had heard snakes fought each other but I'd never seen them fight.

"What're you lookin' at, Shan?" Uncle Alf Skinner asked. He walked up the path with a cane in his hand.

"Snakes a-fightin'."

"Snakes a-fightin'?"

"Yes."

"I never saw it in my life."

"I'll kill 'em both if they don't finish the fight," I said. "I'll club 'em to death."

"Snakes a-fightin', Shan," he shouted, "you are too young to know! It's snakes in love! Snakes in love! Don't kill 'em—just keep your eye on 'em until I bring Martha over here! She's never seen snakes in love!"

Uncle Alf ran around the turn of the hill. He brought Aunt Martha back with him. She was carrying a basket of greens on her arm and the case knife that she'd been cutting greens with in her hand.

"See 'em, Martha," Uncle Alf said. "Look up there in that broomsedge!"

"I'll declare," she said. "I've lived all my life and I never saw this. I've wondered about snakes!"

She stood with a smile on her wrinkled lips. Uncle Alf stood with a wide smile on his deep-lined face. I looked at them and wondered why they

[2] broomsedge: a kind of coarse grass.

looked at these copperheads and smiled. Uncle Alf looked at Aunt Martha. They smiled at each other.

"Shan! Shan!" I heard Mom calling.

"I'm here," I shouted.

"Where've you been?" she asked as she turned around the bend of the hill with a switch in her hand.

"Be quiet, Sall," Uncle Alf said. "Come here and look for yourself!"

"What is it?" Mom asked.

"Snakes in love," Uncle Alf said.

Mom was mad. "Shan, I feel like limbing you," [3] she said. "I've hunted everyplace for you! Where've you been?"

"Killin' snakes," I answered.

"Roy Deer is dead," she said. "That's how dangerous it is to fool with snakes."

"I paid the snakes back for him," I said. "I've killed fifty-three water moccasins!"

"Look, Sall!"

"Yes, Alf, I see," Mom said.

Mom threw her switch on the ground. Her eyes were wide apart. The frowns left her face.

"It's the first time I ever saw snakes in love," Aunt Martha said to Mom.

"It's the first time I ever saw anything like this," Mom said. "Shan, you go tell your Pa to come and look at this."

I was glad to do anything for Mom. I was afraid of her switch. When I brought Pa back to the sunny bank where the copperheads were loving, Art and Sadie Baker were there and Tom and Ethel Riggs—and there were a lot of strangers there. They were looking at the copperheads wrapped around each other with their eyes looking into each other's eyes and their hard lips touching each other's lips.

"You hurry to the house, Shan," Pa said, "and cut your stove wood for tonight."

"I'd like to kill these copperheads," I said.

"Why?" Pa asked.

"Fightin'," I said.

Uncle Alf and Aunt Martha laughed as I walked down the path carrying my club. It was something—I didn't know what—all the crowd watching the snakes were smiling. Their faces were made over new. The snakes had done something to them. Their wrinkled faces were as bright as the spring sunlight on the bluff; their eyes were shiny as the creek was in the noonday sunlight. And they laughed and talked to one another. I heard their laughter grow fainter as I walked down the path toward the house. Their laughter

[3] limbing: literally, the word means "tearing from limb to limb"; as a colloquialism, she may mean here "taking a switch [limb] to you."

was louder than the wild honey bees I had heard swarming over the shoe-make, alderberry, and wild phlox blossoms along the creek.

STUDY QUESTIONS

1. At the time of the incident, the narrator is a young boy. How important is this fact to the development of the story?
2. Describe the conflicts in the story. Are these conflicts external or internal? Identify the major conflict.
3. What is the climax of the story? The resolution?
4. Why don't the older people want Shan to kill the snakes? What is the difference between Shan's perception of the snakes and the older people's?
5. There are three main events in this story: Shan's killing of the fifty-three snakes, Roy Deer's death from snakebite, and the characters' reactions to the "snakes in love." How are these experiences related to one another? To the meaning of the story?

Hisaye Yamamoto (1921–   )

SEVENTEEN SYLLABLES

The first Rosie knew that her mother had taken to writing poems was one evening when she finished one and read it aloud for her daughter's approval. It was about cats, and Rosie pretended to understand it thoroughly and appreciate it no end, partly because she hesitated to disillusion her mother about the quantity and quality of Japanese she had learned in all the years now that she had been going to Japanese school every Saturday (and Wednesday, too, in the Summer). Even so, her mother must have been skeptical about the depth of Rosie's understanding, because she explained afterwards about the kind of poem she was trying to write.

See, Rosie, she said, it was a *haiku*, a poem in which she must pack all her meaning into seventeen syllables only, which were divided into three lines of five, seven, and five syllables. In the one she had just read, she had tried to capture the charm of a kitten, as well as comment on the superstition that owning a cat of three colors meant good luck.

"Yes, yes, I understand. How utterly lovely," Rosie said, and her mother, either satisfied or seeing through the deception and resigned went back to composing.

The truth was that Rosie was lazy; English lay ready on the tongue but Japanese had to be searched for and examined, and even then put forth tentatively (probably to meet with laughter). It was so much easier to say yes, yes, even when one meant no, no. Besides this was what was in her mind to say: I was looking through one of your magazines from Japan last night, Mother, and towards the back I found some *haiku* in English that delighted me. There was one that made me giggle off and on until I fell asleep—

> It is morning, and lo!
> I lie awake, comme il faut,[1]
> sighing for some dough.

Now, how to reach her mother, how to communicate the melancholy song? Rosie knew formal Japanese by fits and starts, her mother had even less English, no French. It was much more possible to say yes, yes.

It developed that her mother was writing the *haiku* for a daily newspaper, the *Mainichi Shinbun*, that was published in San Francisco. Los Angeles, to be sure, was closer to the farming community in which the Hayashi family lived and several Japanese vernaculars were printed there, but Rosie's parents said they preferred the tone of the northern paper. Once a week, the *Mainichi* would have a section devoted to *haiku*, and her mother became an extravagant contributor, taking for herself the blossoming pen name, Umé Hanazono.

So Rosie and her father lived for awhile with two women, her mother and Umé Hanazono. Her mother (Tomé Hayashi by name) kept house, cooked, washed, and, along with her husband and the Carrascos, the Mexican family hired for the harvest, did her ample share of picking tomatoes out in the sweltering fields and boxing them in tidy strata in the cool packing shed. Umé Hanazono, who came to life after the dinner dishes were done, was an earnest, muttering stranger who often neglected speaking when spoken to and stayed busy at the parlor table as late as midnight scribbling with pencil on scratch paper or carefully copying characters on good paper with her fat, pale green Parker.

This new interest had some repercussions on the household routine. Before, Rosie had been accustomed to her parents and herself taking their hot baths early and going to bed almost immediately afterwards, unless her parents challenged each other to a game of flower cards or unless company dropped in. Now, if her father wanted to play cards, he had to resort to solitaire (at which he always cheated fearlessly), and if a group of friends came over, it was bound to contain someone who was also writing *haiku*, and the small assemblage would be split in two, her father entertaining the non-literary members and her mother comparing ecstatic notes with the visiting poet.

If they went out, it was more of the same thing. But Umé Hanazono's life span, even for a poet's, was very brief—perhaps three months at most.

---

[1] *comme il faut:* "as is proper."

One night they went over to see the Hayano family in the neighboring town to the west, an adventure both painful and attractive to Rosie. It was attractive because there were four Hayano girls, all lovely and each one named after a season of the year (Haru, Natsu, Aki, Fuyu), painful because something had been wrong with Mrs. Hayano ever since the birth of her first child. Rosie would sometimes watch Mrs. Hayano, reputed to have been the belle of her native village, making her way about a room, stooped, slowly shuffling, violently trembling (*always* trembling), and she would be reminded that this woman, in this same condition, had carried and given issue to three babies. She would look wonderingly at Mr. Hayano, handsome, tall, and strong, and she would look at her four pretty friends. But it was not a matter she could come to any decision about.

On this visit, however, Mrs. Hayano sat all evening in the rocker, as motionless and unobtrusive as it was possible for her to be, and Rosie found the greater part of the evening practically anaesthetic. Too, Rosie spent most of it in the girls' room, because Haru, the garrulous one, said almost as soon as the bows and other greetings were over, "Oh, you must see my new coat!"

It was a pale plaid of gray, sand, and blue, with an enormous collar, and Rosie, seeing nothing special in it, said, "Gee, how nice."

"Nice?" said Haru, indignantly. "Is that all you can say about it? It's gorgeous! And so cheap, too. Only seventeen-ninety-eight, because it was a sale. The saleslady said it was twenty-five dollars regular."

"Gee," said Rosie. Natsu, who never said much and when she said anything said it shyly, fingered the coat covetously and Haru pulled it away.

"Mine," she said, putting it on. She minced in the aisle between the two large beds and smiled happily. "Let's see how your mother likes it."

She broke into the front room and the adult conversation, and went to stand in front of Rosie's mother, while the rest watched from the door. Rosie's mother was properly envious. "May I inherit it when you're through with it?"

Haru, pleased, giggled and said yes, she could, but Natsu reminded gravely from the door, "You promised me, Haru."

Everyone laughed but Natsu, who shamefacedly retreated into the bedroom. Haru came in laughing, taking off the coat. "We were only kidding, Natsu," she said. "Here, you try it on now."

After Natsu buttoned herself into the coat, inspected herself solemnly in the bureau mirror, and reluctantly shed it, Rosie, Aki, and Fuyu got their turns, and Fuyu, who was eight, drowned in it while her sisters and Rosie doubled up in amusement. They all went to the front room later, because Haru's mother quaveringly called to her to fix the tea and rice cakes and open a can of sliced peaches for everybody. Rosie noticed that her mother and Mr. Hayano were talking together at the little table—they were discussing a *haiku* that Mr. Hayano was planning to send to the *Mainichi,* while her father was sitting at one end of the sofa looking through a copy of *Life*, the new picture magazine. Occasionally, her father would comment on a photograph, holding it toward Mrs. Hayano and speaking to her as he always did—loudly, as though he thought someone such as she must surely be at least a trifle deaf also.

The five girls had their refreshments at the kitchen table, and it was while Rosie was showing the sisters her trick of swallowing peach slices without chewing (she chased each slippery crescent down with a swig of tea) that her father brought his empty teacup and untouched saucer to the sink and said, "Come on, Rosie, we're going home now."

"Already?" asked Rosie.

"Work tomorrow," he said.

He sounded irritated, and Rosie, puzzled, gulped one last yellow slice and stood up to go, while the sisters began protesting, as was their wont.

"We have to get up at five-thirty," he told them, going into the front room quickly, so that they did not have their usual chance to hang onto his hands and plead for an extension of time.

Rosie, following, saw that her mother and Mr. Hayano were sipping tea and still talking together, while Mrs. Hayano concentrated, quivering, on raising the handleless Japanese cup to her lips with both her hands and lowering it back to her lap. Her father, saying nothing, went out the door, onto the bright porch, and down the steps. Her mother looked up and asked, "Where is he going?"

"Where is he going?" Rosie said. "He said we were going home now."

"Going home?" Her mother looked with embarrassment at Mr. Hayano and his absorbed wife and then forced a smile. "He must be tired," she said.

Haru was not giving up yet. "May Rosie stay overnight?" she asked, and Natsu, Aki, and Fuyu came to reinforce their sister's plea by helping her make a circle around Rosie's mother. Rosie, for once having no desire to stay, was relieved when her mother, apologizing to the perturbed Mr. and Mrs. Hayano for her father's abruptness at the same time, managed to shake her head no at the quartet, kindly but adamant, so that they broke their circle to let her go.

Rosie's father looked ahead into the windshield as the two joined him. "I'm sorry," her mother said. "You must be tired." Her father, stepping on the starter, said nothing. "You know how I get when it's *haiku*," she continued, "I forget what time it is." He only grunted.

As they rode homeward, silently, Rosie, sitting between, felt a rush of hate for both, for her mother for begging, for her father for denying her mother. I wish this old Ford would crash, right now, she thought, then immediately, no, no, I wish my father would laugh, but it was too late: already the vision had passed through her mind of the green pick-up crumpled in the dark against one of the mighty eucalyptus trees they were just riding past, of the three contorted, bleeding bodies, one of them hers.

Rosie ran between two patches of tomatoes, her heart working more rambunctiously than she had ever known it to. How lucky it was that Aunt Taka and Uncle Gimpachi had come tonight, though, how very lucky. Otherwise, she might not have really kept her half-promise to meet Jesús Carrasco. Jesús, who was going to be a senior in September at the same school she went to, and his parents were the ones helping with the tomatoes this year. She and Jesús, who hardly remembered seeing each other at Cleveland high, where there were so many other people and two whole grades between them, had become great friends this Summer—he always had a joke for her when he periodically drove the loaded pick-up up from the fields to the shed where she was usually sorting while her mother and father did the packing, and they laughed a great deal together over infinitesimal repartee during the afternoon break for chilled watermelon or ice cream in the shade of the shed.

What she enjoyed most was racing him to see which could finish picking a double row first. He, who could work faster, would tease her by slowing down until she thought she would surely pass him this time, then speeding up furiously to leave her several sprawling vines behind. Once he had made her screech hideously by crossing over, while her back was turned, to place atop the tomatoes in her green-stained bucket a truly monstrous, pale green worm (it had looked more like an infant snake). And it was when they had finished a contest this morning, after she had pantingly pointed a green finger at the immature tomatoes evident in the lugs at the end of his row and he had returned the accusation (with justice), that he had startlingly brought up the matter of their possibly meeting outside the range of both their parents' dubious eyes.

"What for?" she had asked.

"I've got a secret I want to tell you," he said.

"Tell me now," she demanded.

"It won't be ready till tonight," he said.

She laughed. "Tell me tomorrow then."

"It'll be gone tomorrow," he threatened.

"Well, for seven hakes,[2] what is it?" she had asked, more than twice, and when he had suggested that the packing shed would be an appropriate place to find out, she had cautiously answered maybe. She had not been certain she was going to keep the appointment until the arrival of her mother's sister and her husband. Their coming seemed a sort of signal of permission, of grace, and she had definitely made up her mind to lie and leave as she was bowing them welcome.

So, as soon as everyone appeared settled back for the evening, she announced loudly that she was going to the privy outside, "I'm going to the *benjo!*" and slipped out the door. And now that she was actually on her

---

[2] for seven hakes: for heaven's sake (sl.).

way, her heart pumped in such an undisciplined way that she could hear it with her ears. It's because I'm running, she told herself, slowing to a walk. The shed was up ahead, one more patch away, in the middle of the fields. Its bulk, looming in the dimness, took on a sinisterness that was funny when Rosie reminded herself that it was only a wooden frame with a canvas roof and three canvas walls that made a slapping noise on breezy days.

Jesús was sitting on the narrow plank that was the sorting platform and she went around to the other side and jumped backwards to seat herself on the rim of a packing stand. "Well, tell me," she said without greeting, thinking her voice sounded reassuringly familiar.

"I saw you coming out the door," Jesús said. "I heard you running part of the way, too."

"Uh-huh," Rosie said. "Now tell me the secret."

"I was afraid you wouldn't come," he said.

Rosie delved around on the chicken-wire bottom of the slab for number two tomatoes, ripe, which she was sitting beside, and came up with a left-over that felt edible. She bit into it and began sucking out the pulp and seeds. "I'm here," she pointed out.

"Rosie, are you sorry you came?"

"Sorry? What for?" she said. "You said you were going to tell me something."

"I will, I will," Jesús said, but his voice contained disappointment, and Rosie, fleetingly, felt the older of the two, realizing a brand-new power which vanished without category under her recognition.

"I have to go back in a minute," she said. "My aunt and uncle are here from Wintersburg. I told them I was going to the privy."

Jesús laughed. "You funny thing," he said. "You slay me!"

"Just because you have a bathroom *inside*," Rosie said. "Come on, tell me."

Chuckling, Jesús came around to lean on the stand facing her. They still could not see each other very clearly, but Rosie noticed that Jesús became very sober again as he took the hollow tomato from her hand and dropped it back into the stall. When he took hold of her empty hand, she could find no words to protest; her vocabulary had become distressingly constricted and she thought desperately that all that remained intact now was yes and no and oh, and even these few sounds would not easily out. Thus, kissed by Jesús, Rosie fell, for the first time, entirely victim to a helplessness delectable beyond speech. But the terrible, beautiful sensation lasted no more than a second, and the reality of Jesús' lips and tongue and teeth and hands made her pull away with such strength that she nearly tumbled.

Rosie stopped running as she approached the lights from the windows of home. How long since she had left? She could not guess but gasping yet, she went to the privy in back and locked herself in. Her own breathing deafened her in the dark, close space, and she sat and waited until she could hear at last the nightly calling of the frogs and crickets. Even then, all she could think to say was oh, no, and the pressure of Jesús' face against her face would not leave.

No one had missed her in the parlor, however, and Rosie walked in and through quickly, announcing that she was next going to take a bath. "Your father's in the bathhouse," her mother said, and Rosie, in her room, recalled that she had not seen him when she entered. There had been only Aunt Taka and Uncle Gimpachi with her mother at the table, drinking tea. She got her robe and straw sandals and crossed the parlor again to go outside. Her mother was telling them about the *haiku* competition in the *Mainichi* and the poem she had entered.

Rosie met her father coming out of the bathhouse. "Are you through, Father?" she asked. "I was going to ask you to scrub my back."

"Scrub your own back," he said shortly, going toward the main house.

"What have I done now?" she yelled after him. She suddenly felt like doing a lot of yelling. But he did not answer, and she went into the bathhouse. Turning on the dangling light, she removed her denims and T-shirt and threw them in the big carton for dirty clothes standing next to the washing machine. Her other things she took with her into the bath compartment to wash after her bath. After she had scooped a basin of hot water from the square wooden tub, she sat on the grey cement of the floor and soaped herself at exaggerated leisure, singing, "Red Sails in the Sunset" at the top of her voice and using da-da-da where she suspected her words. Then, standing, still singing, for she was possessed by the notion that any attempt now to analyze would result in spoilage and she believed that the larger her volume the less she would be able to hear herself think, she obtained more hot water and poured it on until she was free of lather. Only then did she allow herself to step into the steam vat, one leg first, then the remainder of her body inch by inch until the water no longer stung and she could move around at will.

She took a long time soaking, afterwards remembering to go around outside to stoke the embers of the tin-lined fireplace beneath the tub and to throw on a few more sticks so that the water might keep its heat for her mother, and when she finally returned to the parlor, she found her mother still talking *haiku* with her aunt and uncle, the three of them on another round of tea. Her father was nowhere in sight.

At Japanese school the next day (Wednesday, it was), Rosie was grave and giddy by turns. Preoccupied at her desk in the row for students on Book Eight, she made up for it at recess by performing wild mimicry for the benefit of her friend Chizuko. She held her nose and whined a witticism or two in what she considered was the manner of Fred Allen; she assumed intoxication and a British accent to go over the climax of the Rudy Vallee recording of the pub conversation about William Ewart Gladstone; she was the child Shirley Temple piping, "On the Good Ship Lollipop"; she was the gentleman soprano of the Four Inkspots trilling, "If I Didn't Care." And she felt reasonably satisfied when Chizuko wept and gasped, "Oh, Rosie, you ought to be in the movies!"

Her father came after her at noon, bringing her sandwiches of minced ham and two nectarines to eat while she rode, so that she could pitch right into the sorting when they got home. The lugs were piling up, he said, and the ripe tomatoes in them would probably have to be taken to the cannery tomorrow if they were not ready for the produce haulers tonight. "This heat's not doing them any good. And we've got no time for a break today."

It *was* hot, probably the hottest day of the year, and Rosie's blouse stuck damply to her back even under the protection of the canvas. But she worked as efficiently as a flawless machine and kept the stalls heaped, with one part of her mind listening in to the parental murmuring about the heat and the tomatoes and with another part planning the exact words she would say to Jesús when he drove up with the first load of the afternoon. But when at last she saw that the pick-up was coming, her hands went beserk and the tomatoes started falling in the wrong stalls, and her father said, "Hey, hey! Rosie, watch what you're doing!"

"Well, I have to go to the *benjo*," she said, hiding panic.

"Go in the weeds over there," he said, only half-joking.

"Oh, Father!" she protested.

"Oh, go on home," her mother said. "We'll make out for awhile."

In the privy, Rosie peered through a knothole toward the fields, watching as much as she could of Jesús. Happily she thought she saw him look in the direction of the house from time to time before he finished unloading and went back toward the patch where his mother and father worked. As she was heading for the shed, a very presentable black car purred up the dirt driveway to the house and its driver motioned to her. Was this the Hayashi home, he wanted to know. She nodded. Was she a Hayashi? Yes, she said, thinking that he was a good-looking man. He got out of the car with a huge, flat package and she saw that he warmly wore a business suit. "I have something here for your mother then," he said, in a more elegant Japanese than she was used to.

She told him where her mother was and he came along with her, patting his face with an immaculate white handkerchief and saying something about the coolness of San Francisco. To her surprised mother and father, he bowed and introduced himself as, among other things, the *haiku* editor of the *Mainichi Shinbun*, saying that since he had been coming as far as Los Angeles anyway, he had decided to bring her the first prize she had won in the recent contest.

"First prize?" her mother echoed, believing and not believing, pleased and overwhelmed. Handed the package with a bow, she bobbed her head up and down numerous times to express her utter gratitude.

"It is nothing much," he added, "but I hope it will serve as a token of our great appreciation for your contributions and our great admiration of your considerable talent."

"I am not worthy," she said, falling easily into his style. "It is I who should make some sign of my humble thanks for being permitted to contribute."

"No, no, to the contrary," he said, bowing again.

But Rosie's mother insisted, and then saying that she knew she was being unorthodox, she asked if she might open the package because her curiosity was so great. Certainly she might. In fact, he would like her reaction to it, for personally, it was one of his favorite *Hiroshiges*.

Rosie thought it was a pleasant picture, which looked to have been sketched with delicate quickness. There were pink clouds, containing some graceful calligraphy, and a sea, that was a pale blue except at the edges, containing four sampans with indications of people in them. Pines edged the water and on the far-off beach there was a cluster of thatched huts towered over by pine-dotted mountains of grey and blue. The frame was scalloped and gilt.

After Rosie's mother pronounced it without peer and somewhat prodded her father into nodding agreement, she said Mr. Kuroda must at least have a cup of tea, after coming all this way, and although Mr. Kuroda did not want to impose, he soon agreed that a cup of tea would be refreshing and went along with her to the house, carrying the picture for her.

"Ha, your mother's crazy!" Rosie's father said, and Rosie laughed uneasily as she resumed judgment on the tomatoes. She had emptied six lugs when he broke into an imaginary conversation with Jesús to tell her to go and remind her mother of the tomatoes, and she went slowly.

Mr. Kuroda was in his shirtsleeves expounding some *haiku* theory as he munched a rice cake, and her mother was rapt. Abashed in the great man's presence, Rosie stood next to her mother's chair until her mother looked up inquiringly, and then she started to whisper the message, but her mother pushed her gently away and reproached, "You are not being very polite to our guest."

"Father says the tomatoes . . ." Rosie said aloud, smiling foolishly.

"Tell him I shall only be a minute," her mother said, speaking the language of Mr. Kuroda.

When Rosie carried the reply to her father, he did not seem to hear and she said again, "Mother says she'll be back in a minute."

"All right, all right," he nodded, and they worked again in silence. But suddenly, her father uttered an incredible noise, exactly like the cork of a bottle popping, and the next Rosie knew, he was stalking angrily toward the house, almost running, in fact, and she chased after him crying, "Father! Father! What are you going to do?"

He stopped long enough to order her back to the shed. "Never mind!" he shouted. "Get on with the sorting!"

And from the place in the fields where she stood, frightened and vacillating, Rosie saw her father enter the house. Soon Mr. Kuroda came out alone, putting on his coat. Mr. Kuroda got into his car and backed out down the driveway, onto the highway. Next her father emerged, also alone, something in his arms (it was the picture, she realized), and, going over to the bathhouse woodpile, he threw the picture on the ground and picked up the axe. Smashing the picture, glass and all (she heard the explosion faintly), he reached over for the kerosene that was used to encourage the bath fire and poured it over the wreckage. I am dreaming, Rosie said to herself, I am dreaming, but her father, having made sure that his act of cremation was irrevocable, was even then returning to the fields.

Rosie ran past him and toward the house. What had become of her mother? She burst into the parlor and found her mother at the back window, watching the dying fire. They watched together until there remained only a feeble smoke under the blazing sun. Her mother was very calm.

"Do you know why I married your father?" she said, without turning.

"No," said Rosie. It was the most frightening question she had ever been called upon to answer. Don't tell me now, she wanted to say, tell me tomorrow, tell me next week, don't tell me today. But she knew she would be told now, that the telling would combine with the other violence of the hot afternoon to level her life, her world (so various, so beautiful, so new?) to the very ground.

It was like a story out of the magazines, illustrated in sepia, which she had consumed so greedily for a period until the information had somehow reached her that those wretchedly unhappy autobiographies, offered to her as the testimonials of living men and women, were largely inventions: Her mother, at nineteen, had come to America and married her father as an alternative to suicide.

At eighteen, she had been in love with the first son of one of the well-to-do families in her village. The two had met whenever and wherever they could, secretly, because it would not have done for his family to see him favor her—her father had no money; he was a drunkard and a gambler besides. She had learned she was with child; an excellent match had already been arranged for her lover. Despised by her family, she had given premature birth to a stillborn son, who would be seventeen now. Her family did not turn her out, but she could no longer project herself in any direction without refreshing in them the memory of her indiscretion. She wrote to Aunt Taka, her favorite sister, in America, threatening to kill herself if Aunt Taka would not send for her. Aunt Taka hastily arranged a marriage with a young man, but lately arrived from Japan, of whom she knew, a young man of simple mind, it was said, but of kindly heart. The young man was never told why his unseen betrothed was so eager to hasten the day of meeting.

The story was told perfectly, with neither groping for words nor untoward passion. It was as though her mother had memorized it by heart, reciting it to herself so many times over that its nagging vileness had long since gone.

"I had a brother then?" Rosie asked, for this was what seemed to matter now; she would think about the other later, she assured herself, pushing back the illumination which threatened all that darkness that had hitherto been merely mysterious or even glamourous. "A half-brother?"

"Yes."

"I would have liked a brother," she said.

Suddenly, her mother knelt on the floor and took her by the wrists. "Rosie," she said urgently, "promise me you will never marry!" Shocked more by the request than the revelation, Rosie stared at her mother's face. Jesus, Jesus, she called silently, not certain whether she was invoking the help of the son of the Carrascos or of God, until there returned sweetly the memory of Jesús' hand, how it had touched her and where. Still her mother waited for an answer, holding her wrists so tightly that her hands were going numb. She tried to pull free. Promise, her mother whispered fiercely, promise. Yes, yes, I promise, Rosie said. But for an instant she turned away, and her mother, hearing the familiar glib agreement, released her. Oh, you, you, you, her eyes and twisted mouth said, you fool. Rosie, covering her face, began at last to cry, and the embrace and consoling hand came much later than she expected.

STUDY QUESTIONS

1. Identify some of the many conflicts in this story. Which do you think are the principal ones?
2. What is the importance of Rosie's inability to speak Japanese?
3. Describe the relationship between Rosie's parents. What is the subject of their conflict? Is there a deeper reason for their problems?
4. What are Rosie's feelings after Jesús kisses her? Does she experience an internal conflict? Cite evidence from the text to support your answer.
5. What conflict is generated in Rosie by her mother's request that she never marry?
6. Compare this story with "Living in Sin" (p. 351). After she learns the circumstances of her parents' marriage, how are Rosie's feelings similar to and different from the feelings of the woman in the poem?

Ann Petry (1912–   )

LIKE A WINDING SHEET

He had planned to get up before Mae did and surprise her by fixing breakfast. Instead he went back to sleep and she got out of bed so quietly he didn't know she wasn't there beside him until he woke up and heard the queer soft gurgle of water running out of the sink in the bathroom.

He knew he ought to get up but instead he put his arms across his forehead to shut the afternoon sunlight out of his eyes, pulled his legs up close to his body, testing them to see if the ache was still in them.

Mae had finished in the bathroom. He could tell because she never closed the door when she was in there and now the sweet smell of talcum powder was drifting down the hall and into the bedroom. Then he heard her coming down the hall.

'Hi, babe,' she said affectionately.

'Hum,' he grunted, and moved his arms away from his head, opened one eye.

'It's a nice morning.'

'Yeah,' he rolled over and the sheet twisted around him, outlining his thighs, his chest. 'You mean afternoon, don't ya?'

Mae looked at the twisted sheet and giggled. 'Looks like a winding sheet,' she said. 'A shroud—.' Laughter tangled with her words and she had to pause for a moment before she could continue. 'You look like a huckleberry —in a winding sheet—'

'That's no way to talk. Early in the day like this,' he protested.

He looked at his arms silhouetted against the white of the sheets. They were inky black by contrast and he had to smile in spite of himself and he lay there smiling and savouring the sweet sound of Mae's giggling.

'Early?' She pointed a finger at the alarm clock on the table near the bed, and giggled again. 'It's almost four o'clock. And if you don't spring up out of there you're going to be late again.'

'What do you mean "again"?'

'Twice last week. Three times the week before. And once the week before and—'

'I can't get used to sleeping in the day time,' he said fretfully. He pushed his legs out from under the covers experimentally. Some of the ache had gone out of them but they weren't really rested yet. 'It's too light for good sleeping. And all that standing beats the hell out of my legs.'

'After two years you oughtta be used to it,' Mae said.

He watched her as she fixed her hair, powdered her face, slipping into a pair of blue denim overalls. She moved quickly and yet she didn't seem to hurry.

'You look like you'd had plenty of sleep,' he said lazily. He had to get up but he kept putting the moment off, not wanting to move, yet he didn't dare let his legs go completely limp because if he did he'd go back to sleep. It was getting later and later but the thought of putting his weight on his legs kept him lying there.

When he finally got up he had to hurry and he gulped his breakfast so fast that he wondered if his stomach could possibly use food thrown at it at such a rate of speed. He was still wondering about it as he and Mae were putting their coats on in the hall.

Mae paused to look at the calendar. 'It's the thirteenth,' she said. Then a faint excitement in her voice. 'Why it's Friday the thirteenth.' She had one arm in her coat sleeve and she held it there while she stared at the calendar. 'I oughtta stay home,' she said. 'I shouldn't go otta the house.'

'Aw don't be a fool,' he said. 'To-day's payday. And payday is a good luck day everywhere, any way you look at it.' And as she stood hesitating he said, 'Aw, come on.'

And he was late for work again because they spent fifteen minutes arguing before he could convince her she ought to go to work just the same. He had to talk persuasively, urging her gently and it took time. But he couldn't bring himself to talk to her roughly or threaten to strike her like a lot of men might have done. He wasn't made that way.

So when he reached the plant he was late and he had to wait to punch the time clock because the day shift workers were streaming out in long lines, in groups and bunches that impeded his progress.

Even now just starting his work-day his legs ached. He had to force himself to struggle past the out-going workers, punch the time clock, and get the little cart he pushed around all night because he kept toying with the idea of going home and getting back in bed.

He pushed the cart out on the concrete floor, thinking that if this was his plant he'd make a lot of changes in it. There were too many standing up jobs for one thing. He'd figure out some way most of 'em could be done sitting down and he'd put a lot more benches around. And this job he had —this job that forced him to walk ten hours a night, pushing this little cart, well, he'd turn it into a sittin-down job. One of those little trucks they used around railroad stations would be good for a job like this. Guys sat on a seat and the thing moved easily, taking up little room and turning in hardly any space at all, like on a dime.

He pushed the cart near the foreman. He never could remember to refer to her as the forelady even in his mind. It was funny to have a woman for a boss in a plant like this one.

She was sore about something. He could tell by the way her face was red and her eyes were half shut until they were slits. Probably been out late and didn't get enough sleep. He avoided looking at her and hurried a little, head down, as he passed her though he couldn't resist stealing a glance at her out of the corner of his eyes. He saw the edge of the light colored slacks she wore and the tip end of a big tan shoe.

'Hey, Johnson!' the woman said.

The machines had started full blast. The whirr and the grinding made the building shake, made it impossible to hear conversations. The men and women at the machines talked to each other but looking at them from just a little distance away they appeared to be simply moving their lips because you couldn't hear what they were saying. Yet the woman's voice cut across the machine sounds—harsh, angry.

He turned his head slowly. 'Good Evenin', Mrs. Scott,' he said and waited.

'You're late again.'

'That's right. My legs were bothering me.'

The woman's face grew redder, angrier looking. 'Half this shift comes in late,' she said. 'And you're the worst one of all. You're always late. Whatsa matter with ya?'

'It's my legs,' he said. 'Somehow they don't ever get rested. I don't seem to get used to sleeping days. And I just can't get started.'

'Excuses. You guys always got excuses,' her anger grew and spread. 'Every guy comes in here late always has an excuse. His wife's sick or his grandmother died or somebody in the family had to go to the hospital,' she paused, drew a deep breath. 'And the niggers are the worse. I don't care what's wrong with your legs. You get in here on time. I'm sick of you niggers—'

'You got the right to get mad,' he interrupted softly. 'You got the right to cuss me four ways to Sunday but I ain't letting nobody call me a nigger.'

He stepped closer to her. His fists were doubled. His lips were drawn back in a thin narrow line. A vein in his forehead stood out swollen, thick.

And the woman backed away from him, not hurriedly but slowly—two, three steps back.

'Aw, forget it,' she said. 'I didn't mean nothing by it. It slipped out. It was a accident.' The red of her face deepened until the small blood vessels in her cheeks were purple. 'Go on and get to work,' she urged. And she took three more slow backward steps.

He stood motionless for a moment and then turned away from the red lipstick on her mouth that made him remember that the foreman was a woman. And he couldn't bring himself to hit a woman. He felt a curious tingling in his fingers and he looked down at his hands. They were clenched tight, hard, ready to smash some of those small purple veins in her face.

He pushed the cart ahead of him, walking slowly. When he turned his head, she was staring in his direction, mopping her forehead with a dark blue handkerchief. Their eyes met and then they both looked away.

He didn't glance in her direction again but moved past the long work benches, carefully collecting the finished parts, going slowly and steadily up and down, back and forth the length of the building and as he walked he forced himself to swallow his anger, get rid of it.

And he succeeded so that he was able to think about what had happened without getting upset about it. An hour went by but the tension stayed in his hands. They were clenched and knotted on the handles of the cart as though ready to aim a blow.

And he thought he should have hit her anyway, smacked her hard in the face, felt the soft flesh of her face give under the hardness of his hands. He tried to make his hands relax by offering them a description of what it would have been like to strike her because he had the queer feeling that his hands were not exactly a part of him any more—they had developed a separate life of their own over which he had no control. So he dwelt on the pleasure his hands would have felt—both of them cracking at her, first one and then the other. If he had done that his hands would have felt good now —relaxed, rested.

And he decided that even if he'd lost his job for it he should have let her have it and it would have been a long time, maybe the rest of her life before she called anybody else a nigger.

The only trouble was he couldn't hit a woman. A woman couldn't hit back the same way a man did. But it would have been a deeply satisfying thing to have cracked her narrow lips wide open with just one blow, beautifully timed and with all his weight in back of it. That way he would have gotten rid of all the energy and tension his anger had created in him. He kept remembering how his heart had started pumping blood so fast he had felt it tingle even in the tips of his fingers.

With the approach of night fatigue nibbled at him. The corners of his mouth dropped, the frown between his eyes deepened, his shoulders sagged, but his hands stayed tight and tense. As the hours dragged by he noticed that the women workers had started to snap and snarl at each other. He couldn't hear what they said because of the sound of machines but he could see the quick lip movements that sent words tumbling from the sides of their mouths. They gestured irritably with their hands and scowled as their mouths moved.

Their violent jerky motions told him that it was getting close to quitting time but somehow he felt that the night still stretched ahead of him, composed of endless hours of steady walking on his aching legs. When the whistle finally blew he went on pushing his cart, unable to believe that it had sounded. The whirring of the machines died away to a murmur and he knew then that he'd really heard the whistle. He stood still for a moment filled with a relief that made him sigh.

Then he moved briskly, putting the cart in the store room, hurrying to take his place in the line forming before the paymaster. That was another thing he'd change, he thought. He'd have the pay envelopes handed to the people right at their benches so there wouldn't be ten or fifteen minutes lost waiting for the pay. He always got home about fifteen minutes late on payday. They did it better in the plant where Mae worked, brought the money right to them at their benches.

He stuck his pay envelope in his pants' pocket and followed the line of workers heading for the subway in a slow moving stream. He glanced up at the sky. It was a nice night, the sky looked packed full to running over with stars. And he thought if he and Mae would go right to bed when they got home from work they'd catch a few hours of darkness for sleeping. But they never did. They fooled around—cooking and eating and listening to the radio and he always stayed in a big chair in the living room and went almost but not quite to sleep and when they finally got to bed it was five or six in the morning and daylight was already seeping around the edges of the sky.

He walked slowly, putting off the moment when he would have to plunge into the crowd hurrying toward the subway. It was a long ride to Harlem and to-night the thought of it appalled him. He paused outside an all-night restaurant to kill time, so that some of the first rush of workers would be gone when he reached the subway.

The lights in the restaurant were brilliant, enticing. There was life and motion inside. And as he looked through the window he thought that everything within range of his eyes gleamed—the long imitation marble counter, the tall stools, the white porcelain topped tables and especially the big metal coffee urn right near the window. Steam issued from its top and a gas flame flickered under it—a lively, dancing, blue flame.

A lot of the workers from his shift—men and women—were lining up near the coffee urn. He watched them walk to the porcelain topped tables carrying steaming cups of coffee and he saw that just the smell of the coffee lessened the fatigue lines in their faces. After the first sip their faces softened, they smiled, they began to talk and laugh.

On a sudden impulse he shoved the door open and joined the line in front of the coffee urn. The line moved slowly. And as he stood there the smell of the coffee, the sound of the laughter and of the voices, helped dull the sharp ache in his legs.

He didn't pay any attention to the girl who was serving the coffee at the urn. He kept looking at the cups in the hands of the men who had been ahead of him. Each time a man stepped out of the line with one of the thick white cups the fragrant steam got in his nostrils. He saw that they walked carefully so as not to spill a single drop. There was a froth of bubbles at the top of each cup and he thought about how he would let the bubbles break against his lips before he actually took a big deep swallow.

Then it was his turn. 'A cup of coffee,' he said, just as he had heard the others say.

The girl looked past him, put her hands up to her head and gently lifted her hair away from the back of her neck, tossing her head back a little. 'No more coffee for awhile,' she said.

He wasn't certain he'd heard her correctly and he said, 'What?' blankly. 'No more coffee for awhile,' she repeated.

There was silence behind him and then uneasy movement. He thought someone would say something, ask why or protest, but there was only silence and then a faint shuffling sound as though the men standing behind him had simultaneously shifted their weight from one foot to the other.

He looked at her without saying anything. He felt his hands begin to tingle and the tingling went all the way down to his finger tips so that he glanced down at them. They were clenched tight, hard, into fists. Then he looked at the girl again. What he wanted to do was hit her so hard that the scarlet lipstick on her mouth would smear and spread over her nose, her chin, out toward her cheeks; so hard that she would never toss her head again and refuse a man a cup of coffee because he was black.

He estimated the distance across the counter and reached forward, balancing his weight on the balls of his feet, ready to let the blow go. And then his hands fell back down to his sides because he forced himself to lower them, to unclench them and make them dangle loose. The effort took his breath away because his hands fought against him. But he couldn't hit her. He couldn't even now bring himself to hit a woman, not even this one, who had refused him a cup of coffee with a toss of her head. He kept seeing the gesture with which she had lifted the length of her blond hair from the back of her neck as expressive of her contempt for him.

When he went out the door he didn't look back. If he had he would have seen the flickering blue flame under the shiny coffee urn being extinguished. The line of men who had stood behind him lingered a moment to watch the people drinking coffee at the tables and then they left just as he had without having had the coffee they wanted so badly. The girl behind the counter poured water in the urn and swabbed it out and as she waited for the water to run out she lifted her hair gently from the back of her neck and tossed her head before she began making a fresh lot of coffee.

But he walked away without a backward look, his head down, his hands in his pockets, raging at himself and whatever it was inside of him that had forced him to stand quiet and still when he wanted to strike out.

The subway was crowded and he had to stand. He tried grasping an overhead strap and his hands were too tense to grip it. So he moved near the train door and stood there swaying back and forth with the rocking of the train. The roar of the train beat inside his head, making it ache and throb, and the pain in his legs clawed up into his groin so that he seemed to be bursting with pain and he told himself that it was due to all that anger-born energy that had piled up in him and not been used and so it had spread through him like a poison—from his feet and legs all the way up to his head.

Mae was in the house before he was. He knew she was home before he put the key in the door of the apartment. The radio was going. She had it tuned up loud and she was singing along with it.

'Hello, Babe,' she called out as soon as he opened the door.

He tried to say 'hello' and it came out half a grunt and half sigh.

'You sure sound cheerful,' she said.

She was in the bedroom and he went and leaned against the door jamb. The denim overalls she wore to work were carefully draped over the back of a chair by the bed. She was standing in front of the dresser, tying the sash of a yellow housecoat around her waist and chewing gum vigorously as she admired her reflection in the mirror over the dresser.

'Whatsa matter?' she said. 'You get bawled out by the boss or somep'n?'

'Just tired,' he said slowly. 'For God's sake do you have to crack that gum like that?'

'You don't have to lissen to me,' she said complacently. She patted a curl in place near the side of her head and then lifted her hair away from the back of her neck, ducking her head forward and then back.

He winced away from the gesture. 'What you got to be always fooling with your hair for?' he protested.

'Say, what's the matter with you, anyway?' she turned away from the mirror to face him, put her hands on her hips. 'You ain't been in the house two minutes and you're picking on me.'

He didn't answer her because her eyes were angry and he didn't want to quarrel with her. They'd been married too long and got along too well and so he walked all the way into the room and sat down in the chair by the bed and stretched his legs out in front of him, putting his weight on the heels of his shoes, leaning way back in the chair, not saying anything.

'Lissen,' she said sharply. 'I've got to wear those overalls again tomorrow. You're going to get them all wrinkled up leaning against them like that.'

He didn't move. He was too tired and his legs were throbbing now that he had sat down. Besides the overalls were already wrinkled and dirty, he thought. They couldn't help but be for she'd worn them all week. He leaned further back in the chair.

'Come on, get up,' she ordered.

'Oh, what the hell,' he said wearily and got up from the chair. 'I'd just as soon live in a subway. There'd be just as much place to sit down.'

He saw that her sense of humor was struggling with her anger. But her sense of humor won because she giggled.

'Aw, come on and eat,' she said. There was a coaxing note in her voice. 'You're nothing but a old hungry nigger trying to act tough and—' she paused to giggle and then continued, 'You—'

He had always found her giggling pleasant and deliberately said things that might amuse her and then waited, listening for the delicate sound to emerge from her throat. This time he didn't even hear the giggle. He didn't let her finish what she was saying. She was standing close to him and that funny tingling started in his finger tips, went fast up his arms and sent his fist shooting straight for her face.

There was the smacking sound of soft flesh being struck by a hard object and it wasn't until she screamed that he realized he had hit her in the mouth —so hard that the dark red lipstick had blurred and spread over her full lips, reaching up toward the tip of her nose, down toward her chin, out toward her cheeks.

The knowledge that he had struck her seeped through him slowly and he was appalled but he couldn't drag his hands away from her face. He kept striking her and he thought with horror that something inside him was holding him, binding him to this act, wrapping and twisting about him so that he had to continue it. He had lost all control over his hands. And he groped for a phrase, a word, something to describe what this thing was like that was happening to him and he thought it was like being enmeshed in a winding sheet—that was it—like a winding sheet. And even as the thought formed in his mind his hands reached for her face again and yet again.

STUDY QUESTIONS

1. The incident that begins the major conflict occurs at work. What, then, is the purpose of the beginning section of the story?
2. Who is the protagonist? What facts do you know about him or her?
3. Who or what is the antagonist? Explain your answer and support it with references to particular events in the story.
4. What is the point of climax? How does the climax relate to the title of the work?
5. The story seems to deal with several social issues: black/white relations; male/female roles; management/labor relations. What issue seems to be the writer's major concern? Explain your response.

Flannery O'Connor (1925–1964)

EVERYTHING THAT RISES MUST CONVERGE

Her doctor had told Julian's mother that she must lose twenty pounds on account of her blood pressure, so on Wednesday nights Julian had to take her downtown on the bus for a reducing class at the Y. The reducing class was designed for working girls over fifty, who weighed from 165 to 200 pounds. His mother was one of the slimmer ones, but she said ladies did not tell their age or weight. She would not ride the buses by herself at night since they had been integrated, and because the reducing class was one of her few pleasures, necessary for her health, and *free,* she said Julian could at least put himself out to take her, considering all she did for him. Julian did not like to consider all she did for him, but every Wednesday night he braced himself and took her.

She was almost ready to go, standing before the hall mirror, putting on her hat, while he, his hands behind him, appeared pinned to the door frame, waiting like Saint Sebastian[1] for the arrows to begin piercing him. The hat was new and had cost her seven dollars and a half. She kept saying, "Maybe I shouldn't have paid that for it. No, I shouldn't have. I'll take it off and return it tomorrow. I shouldn't have bought it."

[1] Saint Sebastian: third-century Christian martyr, shot with many arrows.

Julian raised his eyes to heaven. "Yes, you should have bought it," he said. "Put it on and let's go." It was a hideous hat. A purple velvet flap came down on one side of it and stood up on the other; the rest of it was green and looked like a cushion with the stuffing out. He decided it was less comical than jaunty and pathetic. Everything that gave her pleasure was small and depressed him.

She lifted the hat one more time and set it down slowly on top of her head. Two wings of gray hair protruded on either side of her florid face, but her eyes, sky-blue, were as innocent and untouched by experience as they must have been when she was ten. Were it not that she was a widow who had struggled fiercely to feed and clothe and put him through school and who was supporting him still, "until he got on his feet," she might have been a little girl that he had to take to town.

"It's all right, it's all right," he said. "Let's go." He opened the door himself and started down the walk to get her going. The sky was a dying violet and the houses stood out darkly against it, bulbous liver-colored monstrosities of a uniform ugliness though no two were alike. Since this had been a fashionable neighborhood forty years ago, his mother persisted in thinking they did well to have an apartment in it. Each house had a narrow collar of dirt around it in which sat, usually, a grubby child. Julian walked with his hands in his pockets, his head down and thrust forward and his eyes glazed with the determination to make himself completely numb during the time he would be sacrificed to her pleasure.

The door closed and he turned to find the dumpy figure, surmounted by the atrocious hat, coming toward him. "Well," she said, "you only live once and paying a little more for it, I at least won't meet myself coming and going."

"Some day I'll start making money," Julian said gloomily—he knew he never would—"and you can have one of those jokes whenever you take the fit." But first they would move. He visualized a place where the nearest neighbors would be three miles away on either side.

"I think you're doing fine," she said, drawing on her gloves. "You've only been out of school a year. Rome wasn't built in a day."

She was one of the few members of the Y reducing class who arrived in hat and gloves and who had a son who had been to college. "It takes time," she said, "and the world is in such a mess. This hat looked better on me than any of the others, though when she brought it out I said, 'Take that thing back. I wouldn't have it on my head,' and she said, 'Now wait till you see it on,' and when she put it on me, I said, 'We-ull,' and she said, 'If you ask me, that hat does something for you and you do something for the hat and besides,' she said, 'with that hat, you won't meet yourself coming and going.' "

Julian thought he could have stood his lot better if she had been selfish, if she had been an old hag who drank and screamed at him. He walked along, saturated in depression, as if in the midst of his martyrdom he had lost his faith. Catching sight of his long, hopeless, irritated face, she stopped suddenly with a grief-stricken look, and pulled back on his arm. "Wait on me," she said. "I'm going back to the house and take this thing off and tomorrow I'm going to return it. I was out of my head. I can pay the gas bill with that seven-fifty."

He caught her arm in a vicious grip. "You are not going to take it back," he said. "I like it."

"Well," she said, "I don't think I ought . . ."

"Shut up and enjoy it," he muttered, more depressed than ever.

"With the world in the mess it's in," she said, "it's a wonder we can enjoy anything. I tell you, the bottom rail is on the top."

Julian sighed.

"Of course," she said, "if you know who you are, you can go anywhere." She said this every time he took her to the reducing class. "Most of them in it are not our kind of people," she said, "but I can be gracious to anybody. I know who I am."

"They don't give a damn for your graciousness," Julian said savagely. "Knowing who you are is good for one generation only. You haven't the foggiest idea where you stand now or who you are."

She stopped and allowed her eyes to flash at him. "I most certainly do know who I am," she said, "and if you don't know who you are, I'm ashamed of you."

"Oh hell," Julian said.

"Your great-grandfather was a former governor of this state," she said. "Your grandfather was a prosperous landowner. Your grandmother was a Godhigh."

"Will you look around you," he said tensely, "and see where you are now?" and he swept his arm jerkily out to indicate the neighborhood, which the growing darkness at least made less dingy.

"You remain what you are," she said. "Your great-grandfather had a plantation and two hundred slaves."

"There are no more slaves," he said irritably.

"They were better off when they were," she said. He groaned to see that she was off on that topic. She rolled onto it every few days like a train on an open track. He knew every stop, every junction, every swamp along the way, and knew the exact point at which her conclusion would roll majestically into the station: "It's ridiculous. It's simply not realistic. They should rise, yes, but on their own side of the fence."

"Let's skip it," Julian said.

"The ones I feel sorry for," she said, "are the ones that are half white. They're tragic."

"Will you skip it?"

"Suppose we were half white. We would certainly have mixed feelings."

"I have mixed feelings now," he groaned.

"Well let's talk about something pleasant," she said. "I remember going to Grandpa's when I was a little girl. Then the house had double stairways that went up to what was really the second floor—all the cooking was done on the first. I used to like to stay down in the kitchen on account of the way the walls smelled. I would sit with my nose pressed against the plaster and take deep breaths. Actually the place belonged to the Godhighs but your grandfather Chestny paid the mortgage and saved it for them. They were in reduced circumstances," she said, "but reduced or not, they never forgot who they were."

"Doubtless that decayed mansion reminded them," Julian muttered. He never spoke of it without contempt or thought of it without longing. He had seen it once when he was a child before it had been sold. The double stairways had rotted and been torn down. Negroes were living in it. But it remained in his mind as his mother had known it. It appeared in his dreams regularly. He would stand on the wide porch, listening to the rustle of oak leaves, then wander through the high-ceilinged hall into the parlor that opened onto it and gaze at the worn rugs and faded draperies. It occurred to him that it was he, not she, who could have appreciated it. He preferred its threadbare elegance to anything he could name and it was because of it that all the neighborhoods they had lived in had been a torment to him— whereas she had hardly known the difference. She called her insensitivity "being adjustable."

"And I remember the old darky who was my nurse, Caroline. There was no better person in the world. I've always had a great respect for my colored friends," she said. "I'd do anything in the world for them and they'd . . ."

"Will you for God's sake get off that subject?" Julian said. When he got on a bus by himself, he made it a point to sit down beside a Negro, in reparation as it were for his mother's sins.

"You're mighty touchy tonight," she said. "Do you feel all right?"

"Yes I feel all right," he said. "Now lay off."

She pursed her lips. "Well, you certainly are in a vile humor," she observed. "I just won't speak to you at all."

They had reached the bus stop. There was no bus in sight and Julian, his hands still jammed in his pockets and his head thrust forward, scowled down the empty street. The frustration of having to wait on the bus as well as ride on it began to creep up his neck like a hot hand. The presence of his mother was borne in upon him as she gave a pained sigh. He looked at her bleakly. She was holding herself very erect under the preposterous hat, wearing it like a banner of her imaginary dignity. There was in him an evil urge to break her spirit. He suddenly unloosened his tie and pulled it off and put it in his pocket.

She stiffened. "Why must you look like *that* when you take me to town?" she said. "Why must you deliberately embarrass me?"

"If you'll never learn where you are," he said, "you can at least learn where I am."

"You look like a—thug," she said.

"Then I must be one," he murmured.

"I'll just go home," she said. "I will not bother you. If you can't do a little thing like that for me . . ."

Rolling his eyes upward, he put his tie back on. "Restored to my class," he muttered. He thrust his face toward her and hissed, "True culture is in the mind, the *mind*," he said, and tapped his head, "the mind."

"It's in the heart," she said, "and in how you do things and how you do things is because of who you *are*."

"Nobody in the damn bus cares who you are."

"I care who I am," she said icily.

The lighted bus appeared on top of the next hill and as it approached, they moved out into the street to meet it. He put his hand under her elbow and hoisted her up on the creaking step. She entered with a little smile, as if she were going into a drawing room where everyone had been waiting for her. While he put in the tokens, she sat down on one of the broad front seats for three which faced the aisle. A thin woman with protruding teeth and long yellow hair was sitting on the end of it. His mother moved up beside her and left room for Julian beside herself. He sat down and looked at the floor across the aisle where a pair of thin feet in red and white canvas sandals were planted.

His mother immediately began a general conversation meant to attract anyone who felt like talking. "Can it get any hotter?" she said and removed from her purse a folding fan, black with a Japanese scene on it, which she began to flutter before her.

"I reckon it might could," the woman with the protruding teeth said, "but I know for a fact my apartment couldn't get no hotter."

"It must get the afternoon sun," his mother said. She sat forward and looked up and down the bus. It was half filled. Everybody was white. "I see we have the bus to ourselves," she said. Julian cringed.

"For a change," said the woman across the aisle, the owner of the red and white canvas sandals. "I come on one the other day and they were thick as fleas—up front and all through."

"The world is in a mess everywhere," his mother said. "I don't know how we've let it get in this fix."

"What gets my goat is all those boys from good families stealing automobile tires," the woman with the protruding teeth said. "I told my boy, I said you may not be rich but you been raised right and if I ever catch you in any such mess, they can send you on to the reformatory. Be exactly where you belong."

"Training tells," his mother said. "Is your boy in high school?"

"Ninth grade," the woman said.

"My son just finished college last year. He wants to write but he's selling typewriters until he gets started," his mother said.

The woman leaned forward and peered at Julian. He threw her such a malevolent look that she subsided against the seat. On the floor across the aisle there was an abandoned newspaper. He got up and got it and opened it out in front of him. His mother discreetly continued the conversation in a lower tone but the woman across the aisle said in a loud voice, "Well that's nice. Selling typewriters is close to writing. He can go right from one to the other."

"I tell him," his mother said, "that Rome wasn't built in a day."

Behind the newspaper Julian was withdrawing into the inner compartment of his mind where he spent most of his time. This was a kind of mental bubble in which he established himself when he could not bear to be a part of what was going on around him. From it he could see out and judge but in it he was safe from any kind of penetration from without. It was the only place where he felt free of the general idiocy of his fellows. His mother had never entered it but from it he could see her with absolute clarity.

The old lady was clever enough and he thought that if she had started from any of the right premises, more might have been expected of her. She lived according to the laws of her own fantasy world, outside of which he had never seen her set foot. The law of it was to sacrifice herself for him after she had first created the necessity to do so by making a mess of things. If he had permitted her sacrifices, it was only because her lack of foresight had made them necessary. All of her life had been a struggle to act like a Chestny without the Chestny goods, and to give him everything she thought a Chestny ought to have; but since, said she, it was fun to struggle, why complain? And when you had won, as she had won, what fun to look back on the hard times! He could not forgive her that she had enjoyed the struggle and that she thought *she* had won.

What she meant when she said she had won was that she had brought him up successfully and had sent him to college and that he had turned out so well—good looking (her teeth had gone unfilled so that his could be straightened), intelligent (he realized he was too intelligent to be a success), and with a future ahead of him (there was of course no future ahead of him). She excused his gloominess on the grounds that he was still growing up and his radical ideas on his lack of practical experience. She said he didn't yet know a thing about "life," that he hadn't even entered the real world— when already he was as disenchanted with it as a man of fifty.

The further irony of all this was that in spite of her, he had turned out so well. In spite of going to only a third-rate college, he had, on his own initiative, come out with a first-rate education; in spite of growing up dominated by a small mind, he had ended up with a large one; in spite of all her foolish views, he was free of prejudice and unafraid to face facts. Most miraculous of all, instead of being blinded by love for her as she was for him, he had cut himself emotionally free of her and could see her with complete objectivity. He was not dominated by his mother.

The bus stopped with a sudden jerk and shook him from his meditation.

A woman from the back lurched forward with little steps and barely escaped falling in his newspaper as she righted herself. She got off and a large Negro got on. Julian kept his paper lowered to watch. It gave him a certain satisfaction to see injustice in daily operation. It confirmed his view that with a few exceptions there was no one worth knowing within a radius of three hundred miles. The Negro was well dressed and carried a briefcase. He looked around and then sat down on the other end of the seat where the woman with the red and white canvas sandals was sitting. He immediately unfolded a newspaper and obscured himself behind it. Julian's mother's elbow at once prodded insistently into his ribs. "Now you see why I won't ride on these buses by myself," she whispered.

The woman with the red and white canvas sandals had risen at the same time the Negro sat down and had gone further back in the bus and taken the seat of the woman who had got off. His mother leaned forward and cast her an approving look.

Julian rose, crossed the aisle, and sat down in the place of the woman with the canvas sandals. From this position, he looked serenely across at his mother. Her face had turned an angry red. He stared at her, making his eyes the eyes of a stranger. He felt his tension suddenly lift as if he had openly declared war on her.

He would have liked to get in conversation with the Negro and to talk with him about art or politics or any subject that would be above the comprehension of those around them, but the man remained entrenched behind his paper. He was either ignoring the change of seating or had never noticed it. There was no way for Julian to convey his sympathy.

His mother kept her eyes fixed reproachfully on his face. The woman with the protruding teeth was looking at him avidly as if he were a type of monster new to her.

"Do you have a light?" he asked the Negro.

Without looking away from his paper, the man reached in his pocket and handed him a packet of matches.

"Thanks," Julian said. For a moment he held the matches foolishly. A NO SMOKING sign looked down upon him from over the door. This alone would not have deterred him; he had no cigarettes. He had quit smoking some months before because he could not afford it. "Sorry," he muttered and handed back the matches. The Negro lowered the paper and gave him an annoyed look. He took the matches and raised the paper again.

His mother continued to gaze at him but she did not take advantage of his momentary discomfort. Her eyes retained their battered look. Her face seemed to be unnaturally red, as if her blood pressure had risen. Julian allowed no glimmer of sympathy to show on his face. Having got the advantage, he wanted desperately to keep it and carry it through. He would have liked to teach her a lesson that would last a while, but there seemed no way to continue the point. The Negro refused to come out from behind his paper.

Julian folded his arms and looked stolidly before him, facing her but as if he did not see her, as if he had ceased to recognize her existence. He visualized a scene in which, the bus having reached their stop, he would remain in his seat and when she said, "Aren't you going to get off?" he would look at her as at a stranger who had rashly addressed him. The corner they got off on was usually deserted, but it was well lighted and it would not hurt her to walk by herself the four blocks to the Y. He decided to wait until the time came and then decide whether or not he would let her get off by herself. He would have to be at the Y at ten to bring her back, but he could leave her wondering if he was going to show up. There was no reason for her to think she could always depend on him.

He retired again into the high-ceilinged room sparsely settled with large pieces of antique furniture. His soul expanded momentarily but then he became aware of his mother across from him and the vision shriveled. He studied her coldly. Her feet in little pumps dangled like a child's and did not quite reach the floor. She was training on him an exaggerated look of reproach. He felt completely detached from her. At that moment he could with pleasure have slapped her as he would have slapped a particularly obnoxious child in his charge.

He began to imagine various unlikely ways by which he could teach her a lesson. He might make friends with some distinguished Negro professor or lawyer and bring him home to spend the evening. He would be entirely justified but her blood pressure would rise to 300. He could not push her to the extent of making her have a stroke, and moreover, he had never been successful at making any Negro friends. He had tried to strike up an acquaintance on the bus with some of the better types, with ones that looked like professors or ministers or lawyers. One morning he had sat down next to a distinguished-looking dark brown man who had answered his questions with a sonorous solemnity but who had turned out to be an undertaker. Another day he had sat down beside a cigar-smoking Negro with a diamond ring on his finger, but after a few stilted pleasantries, the Negro had rung the buzzer and risen, slipping two lottery tickets into Julian's hand as he climbed over him to leave.

He imagined his mother lying desperately ill and his being able to secure only a Negro doctor for her. He toyed with that idea for a few minutes and then dropped it for a momentary vision of himself participating as a sympathizer in a sit-in demonstration. This was possible but he did not linger with it. Instead, he approached the ultimate horror. He brought home a beautiful suspiciously Negroid woman. Prepare yourself, he said. There is nothing you can do about it. This is the woman I've chosen. She's intelligent, dignified, even good, and she's suffered and she hasn't thought it *fun*. Now persecute us, go ahead and persecute us. Drive her out of here, but remember, you're driving me too. His eyes were narrowed and through the indignation he had generated, he saw his mother across the aisle, purple-faced, shrunken to the dwarf-like proportions of her moral nature, sitting like a mummy beneath the ridiculous banner of her hat.

He was tilted out of his fantasy again as the bus stopped. The door opened with a sucking hiss and out of the dark, a large, gaily dressed, sullen-looking colored woman got on with a little boy. The child, who might have been four, had on a short plaid suit and a Tyrolean[2] hat with a blue feather in it. Julian hoped that he would sit down beside him and that the woman would push in beside his mother. He could think of no better arrangement.

As she waited for her tokens, the woman was surveying the seating possibilities—he hoped with the idea of sitting where she was least wanted. There was something familiar-looking about her but Julian could not place what it was. She was a giant of a woman. Her face was set not only to meet opposition but to seek it out. The downward tilt of her large lower lip was like a warning sign: DON'T TAMPER WITH ME. Her bulging figure was encased in a green crepe dress and her feet overflowed in red shoes. She had on a hideous hat. A purple velvet flap came down on one side of it and stood up on the other; the rest of it was green and looked like a cushion with the stuffing out. She carried a mammoth red pocketbook that bulged throughout as if it were stuffed with rocks.

To Julian's disappointment, the little boy climbed up on the empty seat beside his mother. His mother lumped all children, black and white, into the common category, "cute," and she thought little Negroes were on the whole cuter than little white children. She smiled at the little boy as he climbed on the seat.

Meanwhile the woman was bearing down upon the empty seat beside Julian. To his annoyance, she squeezed herself into it. He saw his mother's face change as the woman settled herself next to him and he realized with satisfaction that this was more objectionable to her than it was to him. Her face seemed almost gray and there was a look of dull recognition in her eyes, as if suddenly she had sickened at some awful confrontation. Julian saw that it was because she and the woman had, in a sense, swapped sons. Though his mother would not realize the symbolic significance of this, she would feel it. His amusement showed plainly on his face.

The woman next to him muttered something unintelligible to herself. He was conscious of a kind of bristling next to him, a muted growling like that of an angry cat. He could not see anything but the red pocketbook upright on the bulging green thighs. He visualized the woman as she had stood wait-

[2] Tyrolean: in the style of the Tyrol, a region of western Austria known for brightly-colored peasant costume.

ing for her tokens—the ponderous figure, rising from the red shoes upward over the solid hips, the mammoth bosom, the haughty face, to the green and purple hat.

His eyes widened.

The vision of the two hats, identical, broke upon him with the radiance of a brilliant sunrise. His face was suddenly lit with joy. He could not believe that Fate had thrust upon his mother such a lesson. He gave a loud chuckle so that she would look at him and see that he saw. She turned her eyes on him slowly. The blue in them seemed to have turned a bruised purple. For a moment he had an uncomfortable sense of her innocence, but it lasted only a second before principle rescued him. Justice entitled him to laugh. His grin hardened until it said to her as plainly as if he were saying aloud: Your punishment exactly fits your pettiness. This should teach you a permanent lesson.

Her eyes shifted to the woman. She seemed unable to bear looking at him and to find the woman preferable. He became conscious again of the bristling presence at his side. The woman was rumbling like a volcano about to become active. His mother's mouth began to twitch slightly at one corner. With a sinking heart, he saw incipient signs of recovery on her face and realized that this was going to strike her suddenly funny and was going to be no lesson at all. She kept her eyes on the woman and an amused smile came over her face as if the woman were a monkey that had stolen her hat. The little Negro was looking up at her with large fascinated eyes. He had been trying to attract her attention for some time.

"Carver!" the woman said suddenly. "Come heah!"

When he saw that the spotlight was on him at last, Carver drew his feet up and turned himself toward Julian's mother and giggled.

"Carver!" the woman said. "You heah me? Come heah!"

Carver slid down from the seat but remained squatting with his back against the base of it, his head turned slyly around toward Julian's mother, who was smiling at him. The woman reached a hand across the aisle and snatched him to her. He righted himself and hung backwards on her knees, grinning at Julian's mother. "Isn't he cute?" Julian's mother said to the woman with the protruding teeth.

"I reckon he is," the woman said without conviction.

The Negress yanked him upright but he eased out of her grip and shot across the aisle and scrambled, giggling wildly, onto the seat beside his love.

"I think he likes me," Julian's mother said, and smiled at the woman. It was the smile she used when she was being particularly gracious to an inferior. Julian saw everything lost. The lesson had rolled off her like rain on a roof.

The woman stood up and yanked the little boy off the seat as if she were snatching him from contagion. Julian could feel the rage in her at having no weapon like his mother's smile. She gave the child a sharp slap across his leg. He howled once and then thrust his head into her stomach and kicked his feet against her shins. "Be-have," she said vehemently.

The bus stopped and the Negro who had been reading the newspaper got off. The woman moved over and set the little boy down with a thump between herself and Julian. She held him firmly by the knee. In a moment he put his hands in front of his face and peeped at Julian's mother through his fingers.

"I see yoooooooo!" she said and put her hand in front of her face and peeped at him.

The woman slapped his hand down. "Quit yo' foolishness," she said, "before I knock the living Jesus out of you!"

Julian was thankful that the next stop was theirs. He reached up and pulled the cord. The woman reached up and pulled it at the same time. Oh my God, he thought. He had the terrible intuition that when they got off the bus together, his mother would open her purse and give the little boy a nickel. The gesture would be as natural to her as breathing. The bus stopped and the woman got up and lunged to the front, dragging the child, who wished to stay on, after her. Julian and his mother got up and followed. As they neared the door, Julian tried to relieve her of her pocketbook.

"No," she murmured, "I want to give the little boy a nickel."

"No!" Julian hissed. "No!"

She smiled down at the child and opened her bag. The bus door opened and the woman picked him up by the arm and descended with him, hanging at her hip. Once in the street she set him down and shook him.

Julian's mother had to close her purse while she got down the bus step but as soon as her feet were on the ground, she opened it again and began to rummage inside. "I can't find but a penny," she whispered, "but it looks like a new one."

"Don't do it!" Julian said fiercely between his teeth. There was a streetlight on the corner and she hurried to get under it so that she could better see into her pocketbook. The woman was heading off rapidly down the street with the child still hanging backward on her hand.

"Oh little boy!" Julian's mother called and took a few quick steps and caught up with them just beyond the lamp-post. "Here's a bright new penny for you," and she held out the coin, which shone bronze in the dim light.

The huge woman turned and for a moment stood, her shoulders lifted and her face frozen with frustrated rage, and stared at Julian's mother. Then all at once she seemed to explode like a piece of machinery that had been given one ounce of pressure too much. Julian saw the black fist swing out with the red pocketbook. He shut his eyes and cringed as he heard the woman shout, "He don't take nobody's pennies!" When he opened his eyes, the woman was disappearing down the street with the little boy staring wide-eyed over her shoulder. Julian's mother was sitting on the sidewalk.

"I told you not to do that," Julian said angrily. "I told you not to do that!"

He stood over her for a minute, gritting his teeth. Her legs were stretched out in front of her and her hat was on her lap. He squatted down and looked her in the face. It was totally expressionless. "You got exactly what you deserved," he said. "Now get up."

He picked up her pocketbook and put what had fallen out back in it. He picked the hat up off her lap. The penny caught his eye on the sidewalk and he picked that up and let it drop before her eyes into the purse. Then he stood up and leaned over and held his hands out to pull her up. She remained immobile. He sighed. Rising above them on either side were black apartment buildings, marked with irregular rectangles of light. At the end of the block a man came out of a door and walked off in the opposite direction. "All right," he said, "suppose somebody happens by and wants to know why you're sitting on the sidewalk?"

She took the hand and, breathing hard, pulled heavily up on it and then stood for a moment, swaying slightly as if the spots of light in the darkness were circling around her. Her eyes, shadowed and confused, finally settled on his face. He did not try to conceal his irritation. "I hope this teaches you a lesson," he said. She leaned forward and her eyes raked his face. She seemed trying to determine his identity. Then, as if she found nothing familiar about him, she started off with a headlong movement in the wrong direction.

"Aren't you going on to the Y?" he asked.

"Home," she muttered.

"Well, are we walking?"

For answer she kept going. Julian followed along, his hands behind him. He saw no reason to let the lesson she had had go without backing it up with an explanation of its meaning. She might as well be made to understand what had happened to her. "Don't think that was just an uppity Negro woman," he said. "That was the whole colored race which will no longer take your condescending pennies. That was your black double. She can wear the same hat as you, and to be sure," he added gratuitously (because he thought it was funny), "it looked better on her than it did on you. What all this means," he said, "is that the old world is gone. The old manners are obsolete and your graciousness is not worth a damn." He thought bitterly of the house that had been lost for him. "You aren't who you think you are," he said.

She continued to plow ahead, paying no attention to him. Her hair had come undone on one side. She dropped her pocketbook and took no notice. He stooped and picked it up and handed it to her but she did not take it.

"You needn't act as if the world had come to an end," he said, "because it hasn't. From now on you've got to live in a new world and face a few realities for a change. Buck up," he said, "it won't kill you."

She was breathing fast.

"Let's wait on the bus," he said.

"Home," she said thickly.

"I hate to see you behave like this," he said. "Just like a child. I should be able to expect more of you." He decided to stop where he was and make her stop and wait for a bus. "I'm not going any farther," he said, stopping. "We're going on the bus."

She continued to go on as if she had not heard him. He took a few steps and caught her arm and stopped her. He looked into her face and caught his breath. He was looking into a face he had never seen before. "Tell Grandpa to come get me," she said.

He stared, stricken.

"Tell Caroline to come get me," she said.

Stunned, he let her go and she lurched forward again, walking as if one leg were shorter than the other. A tide of darkness seemed to be sweeping her from him. "Mother!" he cried. "Darling, sweetheart, wait!" Crumpling, she fell to the pavement. He dashed forward and fell at her side, crying, "Mamma, Mamma!" He turned her over. Her face was fiercely distorted. One eye, large and staring, moved slightly to the left as if it had become unmoored. The other remained fixed on him, raked his face again, found nothing and closed.

"Wait here, wait here!" he cried and jumped up and began to run for help toward a cluster of lights he saw in the distance ahead of him. "Help, help!" he shouted, but his voice was thin, scarcely a thread of sound. The lights drifted farther away the faster he ran and his feet moved numbly as if they carried him nowhere. The tide of darkness seemed to sweep him back to her, postponing from moment to moment his entry into the world of guilt and sorrow.

STUDY QUESTIONS

1. How does the first sentence of the story relate to the final incident of the stroke? List other sentences in the story that foreshadow Julian's mother's collapse.
2. What are Julian's feelings toward his mother? Are those feelings ambivalent? If so, what is the nature of his internal conflict? How do his daydreams reveal his internal conflict?
3. How does Julian's internal conflict relate to the external conflict between himself and his mother?
4. Both Julian and his mother seem to experience a conflict with their environment. Find examples in the story that reveal such a conflict.
5. Trace the development of the external conflict between Julian and his mother from the initial situation; through the rising action; to the climax, falling action, and resolution.

6. Reread the paragraph beginning "the further irony of all this was that in spite of her, he had turned out so well" (p. 273). Is the point of view here Julian's or the third person narrator's? Defend your answer.
7. Suggest all the possible meanings of the story implied by the title.

Graham Greene (1904–   )

BROTHER

The Communists were the first to appear. They walked quickly, a group of about a dozen, up the boulevard which runs from Combat to Ménilmontant;[1] a young man and a girl lagged a little way behind because the man's leg was hurt and the girl was helping him along. They looked impatient, harassed, hopeless, as if they were trying to catch a train which they knew already in their hearts they were too late to catch.

The proprietor of the café saw them coming when they were still a long way off; the lamps at that time were still alight (it was later that the bullets broke the bulbs and dropped darkness all over that quarter of Paris), and the group showed up plainly in the wide barren boulevard. Since sunset only one customer had entered the café, and very soon after sunset firing could be heard from the direction of Combat; the Métro[2] station had closed hours ago. And yet something obstinate and undefeatable in the proprietor's character prevented him from putting up the shutters; it might have been avarice; he could not himself have told what it was as he pressed his broad yellow forehead against the glass and stared this way and that, up the boulevard and down the boulevard.

But when he saw the group and their air of hurry he began immediately to close his café. First he went and warned his only customer, who was practising billiard shots, walking round and round the table, frowning and stroking a thin moustache between shots, a little green in the face under the low diffused lights.

"The Reds are coming," the proprietor said, "you'd better be off. I'm putting up the shutters."

"Don't interrupt. They won't harm me," the customer said. "This is a tricky shot. Reds in baulk.[3] Off the cushion. Screw[4] on spot." He shot his ball straight into a pocket.

"I knew you couldn't do anything with that," the proprietor said, nodding his bald head. "You might just as well go home. Give me a hand with the

---

[1] Combat, Ménilmontant: streets in Paris.
[2] Métro: Paris subway system.
[3] baulk: space between the cushion and the baulk line on a billiard table from which opening shots are made.
[4] screw: to put spin on the cue ball by hitting it low and to one side.

shutters first. I've sent my wife away." The customer turned on him maliciously, rattling the cue between his fingers. "It was your talking that spoilt the shot. You've cause to be frightened, I dare say. But I'm a poor man. I'm safe. I'm not going to stir." He went across to his coat and took out a dry cigar. "Bring me a bock."[5] He walked round the table on his toes and the balls clicked and the proprietor padded back into the bar, elderly and irritated. He did not fetch the beer but began to close the shutters; every move he made was slow and clumsy. Long before he had finished the group of Communists was outside.

He stopped what he was doing and watched them with furtive dislike. He was afraid that the rattle of the shutters would attract their attention. If I am very quiet and still, he thought, they may go on, and he remembered with malicious pleasure the police barricade across the Place de la République. That will finish them. In the meanwhile I must be very quiet, very still, and he felt a kind of warm satisfaction at the idea that worldly wisdom dictated the very attitude most suited to his nature. So he stared through the edge of a shutter, yellow, plump, cautious, hearing the billiard balls crackle in the other room, seeing the young man come limping up the pavement on the girl's arm, watching them stand and stare with dubious faces up the boulevard towards Combat.

But when they came into the café he was already behind the bar, smiling and bowing and missing nothing, noticing how they had divided forces, how six of them had begun to run back the way they had come.

The young man sat down in a dark corner above the cellar stairs and the others stood around the door waiting for something to happen. It gave the proprietor an odd feeling that they should stand there in his café not asking for a drink, knowing what to expect, when he, the owner, knew nothing, understood nothing. At last the girl said "Cognac," leaving the others and coming to the bar, but when he had poured it out for her, very careful to give a fair and not a generous measure, she simply took it to the man sitting in the dark and held it to his mouth.

"Three francs," the proprietor said. She took the glass and sipped a little and turned it so that the man's lips might touch the same spot. Then she knelt down and rested her forehead against the man's forehead and so they stayed.

"Three francs," the proprietor said, but he could not make his voice bold. The man was no longer visible in his corner, only the girl's back, thin and shabby in a black cotton frock, as she knelt, leaning forward to find the man's face. The proprietor was daunted by the four men at the door, by the knowledge that they were Reds who had no respect for private property, who would drink his wine and go away without paying, who would rape his women (but there was only his wife, and she was not there), who

---

[5] bock: a heavy, dark beer.

would rob his bank, who would murder him as soon as look at him. So with fear in his heart he gave up the three francs as lost rather than attract any more attention.

Then the worst that he contemplated happened.

One of the men at the door came up to the bar and told him to pour out four glasses of cognac. "Yes, yes," the proprietor said, fumbling with the cork, praying secretly to the Virgin to send an angel, to send the police, to send the Gardes Mobiles,[6] now, immediately, before the cork came out, "that will be twelve francs."

"Oh, no," the man said, "we are all comrades here. Share and share alike. Listen," he said, with earnest mockery, leaning across the bar, "all we have is yours just as much as it's ours, comrade," and stepping back a pace he presented himself to the proprietor, so that he might take his choice of stringy tie, of threadbare trousers, of starved features. "And it follows from that, comrade, that all you have is ours. So four cognacs. Share and share alike."

"Of course," the proprietor said, "I was only joking." Then he stood with bottle poised, and the four glasses tingled upon the counter. "A machine-gun," he said, "up by Combat," and smiled to see how for the moment the men forgot their brandy as they fidgeted near the door. Very soon now, he thought, and I shall be quit of them.

"A machine-gun," the Red said incredulously, "they're using machine-guns?"

"Well," the proprietor said, encouraged by this sign that the Gardes Mobiles were not very far away, "you can't pretend that you aren't armed yourselves." He leant across the bar in a way that was almost paternal. "After all, you know, your ideas—they wouldn't do in France. Free love."

"Who's talking of free love?" the Red said.

The proprietor shrugged and smiled and nodded at the corner. The girl knelt with her head on the man's shoulder, her back to the room. They were quite silent and the glass of brandy stood on the floor beside them. The girl's beret was pushed back on her head and one stocking was laddered and darned from knee to ankle.

"What, those two? They aren't lovers."

"I," the proprietor said, "with my bourgeois notions would have thought . . ."

"He's her brother," the Red said.

The men came clustering round the bar and laughed at him, but softly as if a sleeper or a sick person were in the house. All the time they were listening for something. Between their shoulders the proprietor could look out across the boulevard; he could see the corner of the Faubourg du Temple.[7]

6 Gardes Mobiles: police cruisers.
7 Faubourg du Temple: district of Paris.

"What are you waiting for?"

"For friends," the Red said. He made a gesture with open palm as if to say, You see, we share and share alike. We have no secrets.

Something moved at the corner of the Faubourg du Temple.

"Four more cognacs," the Red said.

"What about those two?" the proprietor asked.

"Leave them alone. They'll look after themselves. They're tired."

How tired they were. No walk up the boulevard from Ménilmontant could explain the tiredness. They seemed to have come farther and fared a great deal worse than their companions. They were more starved; they were infinitely more hopeless, sitting in their dark corner away from the friendly gossip, the amicable desperate voices which now confused the proprietor's brain, until for a moment he believed himself to be a host entertaining friends.

He laughed and made a broad joke directed at the two of them; but they made no sign of understanding. Perhaps they were to be pitied, cut off from the camaraderie round the counter; perhaps they were to be envied for their deeper comradeship. The proprietor thought for no reason at all of the bare grey trees of the Tuileries[8] like a series of exclamation marks drawn against the winter sky. Puzzled, disintegrated, with all his bearings lost, he stared out through the door towards the Faubourg.

It was as if they had not seen each other for a long while and would soon again be saying good-bye. Hardly aware of what he was doing he filled the four glasses with brandy. They stretched out worn blunted fingers for them.

"Wait," he said. "I've got something better than this"; then paused, conscious of what was happening across the boulevard. The lamplight splashed down on blue steel helmets; the Gardes Mobiles were lining out across the entrance to the Faubourg, and a machine-gun pointed directly at the café windows.

So, the proprietor thought, my prayers are answered. Now I must do my part, not look, not warn them, save myself. Have they covered the side door? I will get the other bottle. Real Napoleon brandy. Share and share alike.

He felt a curious lack of triumph as he opened the trap of the bar and came out. He tried not to walk quickly back towards the billiard room. Nothing that he did must warn these men; he tried to spur himself with the thought that every slow casual step he took was a blow for France, for his café, for his savings. He had to step over the girl's feet to pass her; she was asleep. He noted the sharp shoulder blades thrusting through the cotton, and raised his eyes and met her brother's, filled with pain and despair.

He stopped. He found he could not pass without a word. It was as if he needed to explain something, as if he belonged to the wrong party. With

_____
[8] Tuileries: a park in Paris.

false bonhomie[9] he waved the corkscrew he carried in the other's face. "Another cognac, eh?"

"It's no good talking to them," the Red said. "They're German. They don't understand a word."

"German?"

"That's what's wrong with his leg. A concentration camp."

The proprietor told himself that he must be quick, that he must put a door between him and them, that the end was very close, but he was bewildered by the hopelessness in the man's gaze. "What's he doing here?" Nobody answered him. It was as if his question were too foolish to need a reply. With his head sunk upon his breast the proprietor went past, and the girl slept on. He was like a stranger leaving a room where all the rest are friends. A German. They don't understand a word; and up, up through the heavy darkness of his mind, through the avarice and the dubious triumph, a few German words remembered from very old days climbed like spies into the light: a line from the *Lorelei*[10] learnt at school, *Kamerad* [11] with its war-time suggestion of fear and surrender, and oddly from nowhere the phrase *mein Bruder*.[12] He opened the door of the billiard room and closed it behind him and softly turned the key.

"Spot in baulk," the customer explained and leant across the great green table, but while he took aim, wrinkling his narrow peevish eyes, the firing started. It came in two bursts with a rip of glass between. The girl cried out something, but it was not one of the words he knew. Then feet ran across the floor, the trap of the bar slammed. The proprietor sat back against the table and listened and listened for any further sound; but silence came in under the door and silence through the keyhole.

"The cloth. My God, the cloth," the customer said, and the proprietor looked down at his own hand which was working the corkscrew into the table.

"Will this absurdity ever end?" the customer said. "I shall go home."

"Wait," the proprietor said. "Wait." He was listening to voices and footsteps in the other room. These were voices he did not recognize. Then a car drove up and presently drove away again. Somebody rattled the handle of the door.

"Who is it?" the proprietor called.

"Who are you? Open that door."

"Ah," the customer said with relief, "the police. Where was I now? Spot in baulk." He began to chalk his cue. The proprietor opened the door. Yes, the Gardes Mobiles had arrived; he was safe again, though his windows were smashed. The Reds had vanished as if they had never been. He looked

[9] bonhomie: good-natured friendliness.
[10] *Lorelei*: poem by Heinrich Heine (1797–1856), a German poet and critic.
[11] *Kamerad*: comrade.
[12] *mein Bruder*: "my brother."

at the raised trap, at the smashed electric bulbs, at the broken bottle which dripped behind the bar. The café was full of men, and he remembered with odd relief that he had not had time to lock the side door.

"Are you the owner?" the officer asked. "A bock for each of these men and a cognac for myself. Be quick about it."

The proprietor calculated: "Nine francs fifty," and watched closely with bent head the coins rattle down upon the counter.

"You see," the officer said with significance, "we pay." He nodded towards the side door. "Those others: did they pay?"

No, the proprietor admitted, they had not paid, but as he counted the coins and slipped them into the till, he caught himself silently repeating the officer's order—"A bock for each of these men." Those others, he thought, one's got to say that for them, they weren't mean about the drink. It was four cognacs with them. But, of course, they did not pay. "And my windows," he complained aloud with sudden asperity, "what about my windows?"

"Never you mind," the officer said, "the government will pay. You have only to send in your bill. Hurry up now with my cognac. I have no time for gossip."

"You can see for yourself," the proprietor said, "how the bottles have been broken. Who will pay for that?"

"Everything will be paid for," the officer said.

"And now I must go to the cellar to fetch more."

He was angry at the reiteration of the word pay. They enter my café, he thought, they smash my windows, they order me about and think that all is well if they pay, pay, pay. It occurred to him that these men were intruders.

"Step to it," the officer said and turned and rebuked one of the men who had leant his rifle against the bar.

At the top of the cellar stairs the proprietor stopped. They were in darkness, but by the light from the bar he could just make out a body half-way down. He began to tremble violently, and it was some seconds before he could strike a match. The young German lay head downwards, and the blood from his head had dropped on to the step below. His eyes were open and stared back at the proprietor with the old despairing expression of life. The proprietor would not believe that he was dead. "Kamerad," he said bending down, while the match singed his fingers and went out, trying to recall some phrase in German, but he could only remember, as he bent lower still, "mein Bruder." Then suddenly he turned and ran up the steps, waved the match-box in the officer's face, and called out in a low hysterical voice to him and his men and to the customer stooping under the low green shade, "Cochons. Cochons." [13]

"What was that? What was that?" the officer exclaimed. "Did you say that he was your brother? It's impossible," and he frowned incredulously at the proprietor and rattled the coins in his pocket.

[13] Cochons: pigs.

STUDY QUESTIONS

1. The story takes place in a café in a working-class district of Paris, at a time when the government is vigorously engaged in putting down riots led by the French Communists. What are the proprietor's initial attitudes toward the French government and the Communists, respectively? Compare the proprietor's attitudes to those of the billiard player.
2. What assumption does the proprietor make about the young man and the woman who enter the café? Why does he later become more sympathetic toward them?
3. At first, the proprietor is relieved to find the riot police approaching his café. Presently, however, he is in conflict with them. What has changed his attitudes?
4. When he learns that the couple are German, the proprietor remembers a few German words and phrases, including *Kamerad* and *mein Bruder*. Later he repeats these German words as he bends over the dead body on the cellar stairs. Coming up the stairs, he calls out in French: "Cochons. Cochons." What change in his overall attitude has taken place? What internal conflict has he wrestled with?
5. What meaning does the writer develop through the use of conflict?

Edgar Allan Poe (1809–1849)

THE FACTS IN THE CASE OF M. VALDEMAR

Of course I shall not pretend to consider it any matter for wonder, that the extraordinary case of M. Valdemar has excited discussion. It would have been a miracle had it not—especially under the circumstances. Through the desire of all parties concerned, to keep the affair from the public, at least for the present, or until we had further opportunities for investigation—through our endeavors to effect this—a garbled or exaggerated account made its way into society, and became the source of many unpleasant misrepresentations; and, very naturally, of a great deal of disbelief.

It is now rendered necessary that I give the *facts*—as far as I comprehend them myself. They are, succinctly, these:

My attention, for the last three years, had been repeatedly drawn to the subject of Mesmerism;[1] and, about nine months ago, it occurred to me, quite suddenly, that in the series of experiments made hitherto, there had been a very remarkable and most unaccountable omission:—no person had as yet been mesmerized *in articulo mortis*.[2] It remained to be seen, first, whether, in such condition, there existed in the patient any susceptibility to the magnetic influence; secondly, whether, if any existed, it was impaired

[1] Mesmerism: hypnotism.
[2] *in articulo mortis*: in the process of dying.

or increased by the condition; thirdly, to what extent, or for how long a period, the encroachments of Death might be arrested by the process. There were other points to be ascertained, but these most excited my curiosity— the last in especial, from the immensely important character of its consequences.

In looking around me for some subject by whose means I might test these particulars, I was brought to think of my friend, M. Ernest Valdemar, the well-known compiler of the "Bibliotheca Forensica," [3] and author (under the *nom de plume*[4] of Issachar Marx) of the Polish versions of "Wallenstein" and "Gargantua." [5] M. Valdemar, who has resided principally at Harlem, N.Y., since the year of 1839, is (or was) particularly noticeable for the extreme spareness of his person—his lower limbs much resembling those of John Randolph:[6] and, also, for the whiteness of his whiskers, in violent contrast to the blackness of his hair—the latter, in consequence, being very generally mistaken for a wig. His temperament was markedly nervous, and rendered him a good subject for mesmeric experiment. On two or three occasions I put him to sleep with little difficulty, but was disappointed in other results which his peculiar constitution had naturally led me to anticipate. His will was at no period positively, or thoroughly, under my control, and in regard to *clairvoyance*,[7] I could accomplish with him nothing to be relied upon. I always attributed my failure at these points to the disordered state of his health. For some months previous to my becoming acquainted with him, his physicians had declared him in a confirmed phthisis.[8] It was his custom, indeed, to speak calmly of his approaching dissolution, as of a matter neither to be avoided nor regretted.

When the ideas to which I have alluded first occurred to me, it was of course very natural that I should think of M. Valdemar. I knew the steady philosophy of the man too well to apprehend any scruples from *him*; and he had no relatives in America who would be likely to interfere. I spoke to him frankly upon the subject; and, to my surprise, his interest seemed vividly excited. I say to my surprise; for, although he had always yielded his person freely to my experiments, he had never before given me any tokens of sympathy with what I did. His disease was of that character which would admit of exact calculation in respect to the epoch of its termination in death; and it was finally arranged between us that he would send for me about

---

[3] "Bibliotheca Forensica": library of medicine.

[4] *nom de plume*: pseudonym, pen name.

[5] "Wallenstein" and "Gargantua": the references are to a biography of Albrecht von Wallenstein, an Austrian general of the seventeenth century, and to a fictional work about the giant Gargantua by François Rabelais in 1535.

[6] John Randolph: American political figure and orator (1773–1833).

[7] *clairvoyance*: ability to perceive things out of the natural human range; extrasensory perception.

[8] phthisis: tuberculosis of the lungs.

twenty-four hours before the period announced by his physicians as that of his decease.

It is now rather more than seven months since I received, from M. Valdemar himself, the subjoined note:

"My Dear P——

"You may as well come *now*. D—— and F—— are agreed that I cannot hold out beyond to-morrow midnight; and I think they have hit the time very nearly.
Valdemar"

I received this note within half an hour after it was written, and in fifteen minutes more I was in the dying man's chamber. I had not seen him for ten days, and was appalled by the fearful alteration which the brief interval had wrought in him. His face wore a leaden hue; the eyes were utterly lustreless: and the emaciation was so extreme, that the skin had been broken through by the cheek-bones. His expectoration was excessive. The pulse was barely perceptible. He retained, nevertheless, in a very remarkable manner, both his mental power and a certain degree of physical strength. He spoke with distinctness—took some palliative medicines without aid—and, when I entered the room, was occupied in penciling memoranda in a pocket-book. He was propped up in the bed by pillows. Doctors D—— and F—— were in attendance.

After pressing Valdemar's hand, I took these gentlemen aside, and obtained from them a minute account of the patient's condition. The left lung had been for eighteen months in a semi-osseous[9] or cartilaginous[10] state, and was, of course, entirely useless for all purposes of vitality. The right, in its upper portion, was also partially, if not thoroughly, ossified, while the lower region was merely a mass of purulent tubercles,[11] running one into another. Several extensive perforations existed; and, at one point, permanent adhesion[12] to the ribs had taken place. These appearances in the right lobe were of comparatively recent date. The ossification had proceeded with very unusual rapidity; no sign of it had been discovered a month before, and the adhesion had only been observed during the three previous days. Independently of the phthisis, the patient was suspected of aneurism of the aorta;[13] but on this point the osseous symptoms rendered an exact diagnosis impossible. It was the opinion of both physicians that M. Valdemar would die about midnight on the morrow (Sunday). It was then seven o'clock on Saturday evening.

On quitting the invalid's bedside to hold conversation with myself, Doctors D—— and F—— had bidden him a final farewell. It had not been their

[9] semi-osseous: partly bony.
[10] cartilaginous: like cartilage.
[11] purulent tubercles: tuberculosis lesions containing pus.
[12] adhesion: union.
[13] aneurism of the aorta: blood-filled dilation of the main artery from the heart.

intention to return; but, at my request, they agreed to look in upon the patient about ten the next night.

When they had gone, I spoke freely with M. Valdemar on the subject of his approaching dissolution, as well as, more particularly, of the experiment proposed. He still professed himself quite willing and even anxious to have it made, and urged me to commence it at once. A male and a female nurse were in attendance; but I did not feel myself altogether at liberty to engage in a task of this character with no more reliable witnesses than these people, in case of sudden accident, might prove. I therefore postponed operations until about eight the next night, when the arrival of a medical student, with whom I had some acquaintance (Mr. Theodore L———l), relieved me from further embarrassment. It had been my design, originally, to wait for the physicians; but I was induced to proceed, first, by the urgent entreaties of M. Valdemar, and secondly, by my conviction that I had not a moment to lose, as he was evidently sinking fast.

Mr. L———l was so kind as to accede to my desire that he would take notes of all that occurred; and it is from his memoranda that what I now have to relate is, for the most part, either condensed or copied *verbatim*.[14]

It wanted about five minutes to eight when, taking the patient's hand, I begged him to state, as distinctly as he could, to Mr. L———l, whether he (M. Valdemar) was entirely willing that I should make the experiment of mesmerizing him in his then condition.

He replied feebly, yet quite audibly: "Yes, I wish to be mesmerized"— adding immediately afterward: "I fear you have deferred it too long."

While he spoke thus, I commenced the passes which I had already found most effectual in subduing him. He was evidently influenced with the first lateral stroke of my hand across his forehead; but, although I exerted all my powers, no further perceptible effect was induced until some minutes after ten o'clock, when Doctors D——— and F——— called, according to appointment. I explained to them, in a few words, what I designed and as they opposed no objection, saying that the patient was already in the death agony, I proceeded without hesitation—exchanging, however, the lateral passes for downward ones, and directing my gaze entirely into the right eye of the sufferer.

By this time his pulse was imperceptible and his breathing was stertorious,[15] and at intervals of half a minute.

This condition was nearly unaltered for a quarter of an hour. At the expiration of this period, however, a natural although a very deep sigh escaped from the bosom of the dying man, and the stertorious breathing ceased—that is to say, its stertoriousness was no longer apparent; the intervals were undiminished. The patient's extremities were of an icy coldness.

[14] *verbatim*: word for word.
[15] stertorious: (stertorous) labored; noisy.

At five minutes before eleven, I perceived unequivocal signs of the mesmeric influence. The glassy roll of the eye was changed for that expression of uneasy *inward* examination which is never seen except in cases of sleepwaking, and which it is quite impossible to mistake. With a few rapid lateral passes I made the lids quiver, as in incipient sleep, and with a few more I closed them altogether. I was not satisfied, however, with this, but continued the manipulations vigorously, and with the fullest exertion of the will, until I had completely stiffened the limbs of the slumberer, after placing them in a seemingly easy position. The legs were at full length; the arms were nearly so, and reposed on the bed at a moderate distance from the loins. The head was very slightly elevated.

When I had accomplished this, it was fully midnight, and I requested the gentlemen present to examine M. Valdemar's condition. After a few experiments, they admitted him to be in an unusually perfect state of mesmeric trance. The curiosity of both the physicians was greatly excited. Dr. D—— resolved at once to remain with the patient all night, while Dr. F—— took leave with a promise to return at daybreak. Mr. L——l and the nurses remained.

We left M. Valdemar entirely undisturbed until about three o'clock in the morning, when I approached him and found him in precisely the same condition as when Dr. F—— went away—that is to say, he lay in the same position; the pulse was imperceptible; the breathing was gentle (scarcely noticeable, unless through the application of a mirror to the lips); the eyes were closed naturally; and the limbs were as rigid and as cold as marble. Still, the general appearance was certainly not that of death.

As I approached M. Valdemar I made a kind of half effort to influence his right arm into pursuit of my own, as I passed the latter gently to and fro above his person. In such experiments with this patient, I had never perfectly succeeded before, and assuredly I had little thought of succeeding now; but to my astonishment, his arm very readily, although feebly, followed every direction I assigned it with mine. I determined to hazard a few words of conversation.

"M. Valdemar," I said, "are you asleep?" He made no answer, but I perceived a tremor about the lips, and was thus induced to repeat the question, again and again. At its third repetition, his whole frame was agitated by a very slight shivering; the eyelids unclosed themselves so far as to display a white line of a ball; the lips moved sluggishly, and from between them, in a barely audible whisper, issued the words:

"Yes:—asleep now. Do not wake me!—let me die so!"

I here felt the limbs, and found them as rigid as ever. The right arm, as before, obeyed the direction of my hand. I questioned the sleep-waker again:

"Do you still feel pain in the breast, M. Valdemar?"

The answer now was immediate, but even less audible than before:

"No pain—I am dying!"

I did not think it advisable to disturb him further just then, and nothing more was said or done until the arrival of Dr. F——, who came a little before sunrise, and expressed unbounded astonishment at finding the patient still alive. After feeling the pulse and applying a mirror to the lips, he requested me to speak to the sleep-waker again. I did so, saying:

"M. Valdemar, do you still sleep?"

As before, some minutes elapsed ere a reply was made; and during the interval the dying man seemed to be collecting his energies to speak. At my fourth repetition of the question, he said very faintly, almost inaudibly:

"Yes; still asleep—dying."

It was now the opinion, or rather the wish, of the physicians, that M. Valdemar should be suffered to remain undisturbed in his present apparently tranquil condition, until death should supervene—and this, it was generally agreed, must now take place within a few minutes. I concluded, however, to speak to him once more, and merely repeated my previous question.

While I spoke, there came a marked change over the countenance of the sleep-waker. The eyes rolled themselves slowly open, the pupils disappearing upwardly; the skin generally assumed a cadaverous[16] hue, resembling not so much parchment as white paper; and the circular hectic[17] spots which, hitherto, had been strongly defined in the centre of each cheek, *went out* at once. I use this expression, because the suddenness of their departure put me in mind of nothing so much as the extinguishment of a candle by a puff of the breath. The upper lip, at the same time, writhed itself away from the teeth, which it had previously covered completely; while the lower jaw fell with an audible jerk, leaving the mouth widely extended, and disclosing in full view the swollen and blackened tongue. I presume that no member of the party then present had been unaccustomed to death-bed horrors; but so hideous beyond conception was the appearance of M. Valdemar at this moment, that there was a general shrinking back from the region of the bed.

I now feel that I have reached a point of this narrative at which every reader will be startled into positive disbelief. It is my business, however, simply to proceed.

There was no longer the faintest sign of vitality in M. Valdemar; and concluding him to be dead, we were consigning him to the charge of the nurses, when a strong vibratory motion was observable in the tongue. This continued for perhaps a minute. At the expiration of this period, there issued from the distended and motionless jaws a voice—such as it would be madness in me to attempt describing. There are, indeed, two or three epithets which might be considered as applicable to it in part; I might say,

---

[16] cadaverous: corpselike.
[17] hectic: fevered.

for example, that the sound was harsh and broken and hollow; but the hideous whole is indescribable, for the simple reason that no similar sounds have ever jarred upon the ear of humanity. There were two particulars, nevertheless, which I thought then, and still think, might fairly be stated as characteristic of the intonation—as well adapted to convey some idea of its unearthly peculiarity. In the first place, the voice seemed to reach our ears —at least mine—from a vast distance, or from some deep cavern within the earth. In the second place, it impressed me (I fear, indeed, that it will be impossible to make myself comprehended) as gelatinous or glutinous matters impress the sense of touch.

I have spoken both of "sound" and of "voice." I mean to say that the sound was one of distinct—of even wonderfully, thrillingly distinct—syllabification. M. Valdemar *spoke*—obviously in reply to the question I had propounded to him a few minutes before. I had asked him, it will be remembered, if he still slept. He now said:

"Yes;—no;—I *have been* sleeping—and now—now—*I am dead.*"

No person present even affected to deny, or attempted to repress, the unutterable, shuddering horror which these few words, thus uttered, were so well calculated to convey. Mr. L——l (the student) swooned. The nurses immediately left the chamber, and could not be induced to return. My own impressions I would not pretend to render intelligible to the reader. For nearly an hour, we busied ourselves, silently—without the utterance of a word—in endeavors to revive Mr. L——l. When he came to himself, we addressed ourselves again to an investigation of M. Valdemar's condition.

It remained in all respects as I have last described it, with the exception that the mirror no longer afforded evidence of respiration. An attempt to draw blood from the arm failed. I should mention, too, that this limb was no further subject to my will. I endeavored in vain to make it follow the direction of my hand. The only real indication, indeed, of the mesmeric influence, was now found in the vibratory movement of the tongue, whenever I addressed M. Valdemar a question. He seemed to be making an effort to reply, but had no longer sufficient volition. To queries put to him by any other person than myself he seemed utterly insensible—although I endeavored to place each member of the company in mesmeric *rapport*[18] with him. I believe that I have now related all that is necessary to an understanding of the sleep-waker's state at this epoch. Other nurses were procured; and at ten o'clock I left the house in company with the two physicians and Mr. L——l.

In the afternoon we all called again to see the patient. His condition remained precisely the same. We had now some discussion as to the propriety and feasibility of awakening him; but we had little difficulty in agreeing that no good purpose would be served by so doing. It was evident that, so far,

[18] *rapport:* smoothly flowing relationship; harmony.

death (or what is usually termed death) had been arrested by the mesmeric process. It seemed clear to us all that to awaken M. Valdemar would be merely to insure his instant, or at least his speedy, dissolution.

From this period until the close of last week—*an interval of nearly seven months*—we continued to make daily calls at M. Valdemar's house, accompanied, now and then, by medical and other friends. All this time the sleep-waker remained *exactly* as I have last described him. The nurses' attentions were continual.

It was on Friday last that we finally resolved to make the experiment of awakening, or attempting to awaken him; and it is the (perhaps) unfortunate result of this latter experiment which has given rise to so much discussion in private circles—to so much of what I cannot help thinking unwarranted popular feeling.

For the purpose of relieving M. Valdemar from the mesmeric trance, I made use of the customary passes. These for a time were unsuccessful. The first indication of revival was afforded by a partial descent of the iris. It was observed, as especially remarkable, that this lowering of the pupil was accompanied by the profuse out-flowing of a yellowish ichor[19] (from beneath the lids) of a pungent and highly offensive odor.

It was now suggested that I should attempt to influence the patient's arm as heretofore. I made the attempt and failed. Dr. F—— then intimated a desire to have me put a question. I did so, as follows:

"M. Valdemar, can you explain to us what are your feelings or wishes now?"

There was an instant return of the hectic circles on the cheeks: the tongue quivered, or rather rolled violently in the mouth (although the jaws and lips remained rigid as before), and at length the same hideous voice which I have already described, broke forth:

"For God's sake!—quick!—quick!—put me to sleep—or, quick!—waken me!—quick!—*I say to you that I am dead!*"

I was thoroughly unnerved, and for an instant remained undecided what to do. At first I made an endeavor to recompose the patient; but, failing in this through total abeyance of the will, I retraced my steps and as earnestly struggled to awaken him. In this attempt I soon saw that I should be successful—or at least I soon fancied that my success would be complete—and I am sure that all in the room were prepared to see the patient awaken.

For what really occurred, however, it is quite impossible that any human being could have been prepared.

As I rapidly made the mesmeric passes, amid ejaculations of "dead! dead!" absolutely *bursting* from the tongue and not from the lips of the sufferer, his whole frame at once—within the space of a single minute, or less, shrunk—crumbled—absolutely *rotted* away beneath my hands. Upon

---

[19] ichor: fluid likened to blood.

the bed, before that whole company, there lay a nearly liquid mass of loathsome—of detestable putrescence.[20]

STUDY QUESTIONS

1. What kinds of "facts" does Poe present to make the story appear to be a real case history?
2. What has happened to M. Valdemar at the end of the story? Why?
3. Do you detect any humor in this story?
4. Describe the narrator. What reasons does he give for telling the story of Valdemar?
5. What conflicts are present in the story? To what extent does the narrator experience internal conflict? Is that conflict important to meaning?
6. What do you think that Poe is trying to tell us about living and dying?

Henry James (1843–1916)

PASTE

"I've found a lot more things," her cousin said to her the day after the second funeral; "they're up in her room—but they're things I wish *you'd* look at."

The pair of mourners, sufficiently stricken, were in the garden of the vicarage together, before luncheon, waiting to be summoned to that meal, and Arthur Prime had still in his face the intention, she was moved to call it rather than the expression, of feeling something or other. Some such appearance was in itself of course natural within a week of his stepmother's death, within three of his father's; but what was most present to the girl, herself sensitive and shrewd, was that he seemed somehow to brood without sorrow, to suffer without what she in her own case would have called pain. He turned away from her after this last speech—it was a good deal his habit to drop an observation and leave her to pick it up without assistance. If the vicar's widow, now in her turn finally translated, had not really belonged to him it was not for want of her giving herself, so far as he ever would take her; and she had lain for three days all alone at the end of the passage, in the great cold chamber of hospitality, the dampish greenish room where visitors slept and where several of the ladies of the parish had, without effect, offered, in pairs and successions, piously to watch with her. His personal connexion with the parish was now slighter than ever, and he had really not waited for this opportunity to show the ladies what he thought of

---

[20] putrescence: decaying, rotten matter.

them. She felt that she herself had, during her doleful month's leave from Bleet,[1] where she was governess, rather taken her place in the same snubbed order; but it was presently, none the less, with a better little hope of coming in for some remembrance, some relic, that she went up to look at the things he had spoken of, the identity of which, as a confused cluster of bright objects on a table in the darkened room, shimmered at her as soon as she had opened the door.

They met her eyes for the first time, but in a moment, before touching them, she knew them as things of the theatre, as very much too fine to have been with any verisimilitude things of the vicarage. They were too dreadfully good to be true, for her aunt had had no jewels to speak of, and these were coronets and girdles, diamonds, rubies and sapphires. Flagrant tinsel and glass, they looked strangely vulgar, but if after the first queer shock of them she found herself taking them up it was for the very proof, never yet so distinct to her, of a far-off faded story. An honest widowed cleric with a small son and a large sense of Shakespeare had, on a brave latitude of habit as well as of taste—since it implied his having in very fact dropped deep into the "pit"—conceived for an obscure actress several years older than himself an admiration of which the prompt offer of his reverend name and hortatory[2] hand was the sufficiently candid sign. The response had perhaps in those dim years, so far as eccentricity was concerned, even bettered the proposal, and Charlotte, turning the tale over, had long since drawn from it a measure of the career renounced by the undistinguished comédienne— doubtless also tragic, or perhaps pantomimic, at a pinch—or her late uncle's dreams. This career couldn't have been eminent and must much more probably have been comfortless.

"You see what it is—old stuff of the time she never liked to mention."

Our young woman gave a start; her companion had after all rejoined her and had apparently watched a moment her slightly scared recognition. "So I said to myself," she replied. Then to show intelligence, yet keep clear of twaddle: "How peculiar they look!"

"They look awful," said Arthur Prime. "Cheap gilt, diamonds as big as potatoes. These are trappings of a ruder age than ours. Actors do themselves better now."

"Oh now," said Charlotte, not to be less knowing, "actresses have real diamonds."

"Some of them." Arthur spoke dryly.

"I mean the bad ones—the nobodies too."

"Oh some of the nobodies have the biggest. But mamma wasn't of that sort."

"A nobody?" Charlotte risked.

[1] Bleet: presumably a country estate.
[2] hortatory: encouraging, urging.

"Not a nobody to whom somebody—well, not a nobody with diamonds. It isn't all worth, this trash, five pounds."

There was something in the old gewgaws[3] that spoke to her, and she continued to turn them over. "They're relics. I think they have their melancholy and even their dignity."

Arthur observed another pause. "Do you care for them?" he then asked. "I mean," he promptly added, "as a souvenir."

"Of you?" Charlotte threw off.

"Of me? What have I to do with it? Of your poor dead aunt who was so kind to you," he said with virtuous sternness.

"Well, I'd rather have them than nothing."

"Then please take them," he returned in a tone of relief which expressed somehow more of the eager than of the gracious.

"Thank you." Charlotte lifted two or three objects up and set them down again. Though they were lighter than the materials they imitated they were so much more extravagant that they struck her in truth as rather awkward heritage, to which she might have preferred even a matchbox or a penwiper. They were indeed shameless pinchbeck.[4] "Had you any idea she had kept them?"

"I don't at all believe she *had* kept them or knew they were there, and I'm very sure my father didn't. They had quite equally worked off any tenderness for the connexion. These odds and ends, which she thought had been given away or destroyed, had simply got thrust into a dark corner and been forgotten."

Charlotte wondered. "Where then did you find them?"

"In that old tin box"—and the young man pointed to the receptacle from which he had dislodged them and which stood on a neighbouring chair. "It's rather a good box still, but I'm afraid I can't give you *that*."

The girl took no heed of the box; she continued only to look at the trinkets. "What corner had she found?"

"She hadn't 'found' it," her companion sharply insisted; "she had simply lost it. The whole thing had passed from her mind. The box was on the top shelf of the old school-room closet, which, until one put one's head into it from a step-ladder, looked, from below, quite cleared out. The door's narrow and the part of the closet to the left goes well into the wall. The box had stuck there for years."

Charlotte was conscious of a mind divided and a vision vaguely troubled, and once more she took up two or three of the subjects of this revelation; a big bracelet in the form of a gilt serpent with many twists and beady eyes, a brazen belt studded with emeralds and rubies, a chain, of flamboyant architecture, to which, at the Theatre Royal Little Peddlington, Hamlet's

[3] gewgaws: trinkets.
[4] pinchbeck: something counterfeit or false.

mother must have been concerned to attach the portrait of the successor to Hamlet's father. "Are you very sure they're not really worth something? Their mere weight alone—!" she vaguely observed, balancing a moment a royal diadem[5] that might have crowned one of the creations of the famous Mrs. Jarley.[6]

But Arthur Prime, it was clear, had already thought the question over and found the answer easy. "If they had been worth anything to speak of she would long ago have sold them. My father and she had unfortunately never been in a position to keep any considerable value locked up." And while his companion took in the obvious force of this he went on with a flourish just marked enough not to escape her: "If they're worth anything at all—why you're only the more welcome to them."

Charlotte had now in her hand a small bag of faded figured silk—one of those antique conveniences that speak to us, in terms of evaporated camphor and lavender, of the part they have played in some personal history; but though she had for the first time drawn the string she looked much more at the young man than at the questionable treasure it appeared to contain. "I shall like them. They're all I have."

"All you have—?"

"That belonged to her."

He swelled a little, then looked about him as if to appeal—as against her avidity—to the whole poor place. "Well, what else do you want?"

"Nothing. Thank you very much." With which she bent her eyes on the article wrapped, and now only exposed, in her superannuated [7] satchel—a string of large pearls, such a shining circle as might once have graced the neck of a provincial Ophelia[8] and borne company to a flaxen wig. "This perhaps *is* worth something. Feel it." And she passed him the necklace, the weight of which she had gathered for a moment into her hand.

He measured it in the same way with his own, but remained quite detached. "Worth at most thirty shillings."

"Not more?"

"Surely not if it's paste."

"But *is* it paste?"

He gave a small sniff of impatience. "Pearls nearly as big as filberts?"

"But they're heavy," Charlotte declared.

"No heavier than anything else." And he gave them back with an allowance for her simplicity. "Do you imagine for a moment they're real?"

She studied them a little, feeling them, turning them round. "Mightn't they possibly be?"

---

[5] diadem: crown.

[6] Mrs. Jarley: fat, good-humored proprietress of Jarley's Wax Works in Charles Dickens' *Old Curiosity Shop.*

[7] superannuated: obsolete, overage.

[8] Ophelia: daughter of Polonius in *Hamlet.*

"Of that size—stuck away with that trash?"

"I admit it isn't likely," Charlotte presently said. "And pearls are so easily imitated."

"That's just what—to a person who knows—they're not. These have no lustre, no play."

"No—they *are* dull. They're opaque."

"Besides," he lucidly enquired, "how could she ever have come by them?"

"Mightn't they have been a present?"

Arthur stared at the question as if it were almost improper. "Because actresses are exposed—?" He pulled up, however, not saying to what, and before she could supply the deficiency had, with the sharp ejaculation of "No, they might n't!" turned his back on her and walked away. His manner made her feel she had probably been wanting in tact, and before he returned to the subject, the last thing that evening, she had satisfied herself on the ground of his resentment. They had been talking of her departure the next morning, the hour of her train and the fly[9] that would come for her, and it was precisely these things that gave him his effective chance. "I really can't allow you to leave the house under the impression that my stepmother was at *any* time of her life the sort of person to allow herself to be approached—"

"With pearl necklaces and that sort of thing?" Arthur had made for her somehow the difficulty that she could n't show him she understood him without seeming pert.

It at any rate only added to his own gravity. "That sort of thing, exactly."

"I didn't think when I spoke this morning—but I see what you mean."

"I mean that she was beyond reproach," said Arthur Prime.

"A hundred times yes."

"Therefore if she couldn't, out of her slender gains, ever have paid for a row of pearls—"

She couldn't in that atmosphere, ever properly have had one? Of course she couldn't. I've seen perfectly since our talk," Charlotte went on, "that that string of beads is n't even as an imitation very good. The little clasp itself does n't seem even gold. With false pearls, I suppose," the girl mused, "it naturally wouldn't be."

"The whole thing's rotten paste," her companion returned as if to have done with it. "If it were *not*, and she had kept it all these years hidden—"

"Yes?" Charlotte sounded as he paused.

"Why I shouldn't know what to think!"

"Oh I see." She had met him with a certain blankness, but adequately enough, it seemed, for him to regard the subject as dismissed, and there was no reversion to it between them before, on the morrow, when she had with difficulty made a place for them in her trunk, she carried off these florid survivals.

---

[9] fly: horse-drawn public carriage.

At Bleet she found small occasion to revert to them and, in an air charged with such quite other references, even felt, after she had laid them away, much enshrouded, beneath various piles of clothing, that they formed a collection not wholly without its note of the ridiculous. Yet she was never, for the joke, tempted to show them to her pupils, though Gwendolen and Blanche in particular always wanted, on her return, to know what she had brought back; so that without an accident by which the case was quite changed they might have appeared to enter on a new phase of interment. The essence of the accident was the sudden illness, at the last moment, of Lady Bobby, whose advent had been so much counted on to spice the five days' feast laid out for the coming of age of the eldest son of the house; and its equally marked effect was the dispatch of a pressing message, in quite another direction, to Mrs. Guy, who, could she by a miracle be secured— she was always engaged ten parties deep—might be trusted to supply, it was believed, an element of exuberance scarcely less potent. Mrs. Guy was already known to several of the visitors already on the scene, but she was n't yet known to our young lady, who found her, after many wires[10] and counterwires had at last determined the triumph of her arrival, a strange charming little red-haired black-dressed woman, a person with the face of a baby and the authority of a commodore. She took on the spot the discreet, the exceptional young governess into the confidence of her designs and, still more, of her doubts, intimating that it was a policy she almost always promptly pursued.

"To-morrow and Thursday are all right," she said frankly to Charlotte on the second day, "but I'm not half-satisfied with Friday."

"What improvement then do you suggest?"

"Well, my strong point, you know, is *tableaux vivants*." [11]

"Charming. And what is your favourite character?"

"Boss!" said Mrs. Guy with decision; and it was very markedly under that ensign that she had, within a few hours, completely planned her campaign and recruited her troop. Every word she uttered was to the point, but none more so than, after a general survey of their equipment, her final enquiry of Charlotte. She had been looking about, but half-appeased, at the muster of decoration and drapery. "We shall be dull. We shall want more colour. You've nothing else?"

Charlotte had a thought. "No—I've *some* things."

"Then why don't you bring them?"

The girl weighed it. "Would you come to my room?"

"No," said Mrs. Guy—"bring them tonight to mine."

So Charlotte, at the evening's end, after candlesticks had flickered through brown old passages bedward, arrived at her friend's door with the burden

---

[10] wire: telegram.

[11] *tableaux vivants*: "living pictures"; a famous scene posed by several participants in costume, a familiar party amusement.

of her aunt's relics. But she promptly expressed a fear. "Are they too garish?"

When she had poured them out on the sofa Mrs. Guy was but a minute, before the glass, in clapping on the diadem. "Awfully jolly—we can do Ivanhoe!" [12]

"But they're only glass and tin."

"Larger than life they are, *rather!*—which is exactly what's wanted for tableaux. *Our* jewels, for historic scenes, don't tell—the real thing falls short. Rowena must have rubies as big as eggs. Leave them with me," Mrs. Guy continued—"they'll inspire me. Good-night."

The next morning she was in fact—yet very strangely—inspired. "Yes, *I'll* do Rowena.[13] But I don't, my dear, understand."

"Understand what?"

Mrs. Guy gave a very lighted stare. "How you come to have such things."

Poor Charlotte smiled. "By inheritance."

"Family jewels?"

"They belonged to my aunt, who died some months ago. She was on the stage a few years in early life, and these are a part of her trappings."

"She left them to you?"

"No; my cousin, her stepson, who naturally has no use for them, gave them to me for remembrance of her. She was a dear kind thing, always so nice to me, and I was fond of her."

Mrs. Guy had listened with frank interest. "But it's *he* who must be a dear kind thing!"

Charlotte wondered. "You think so?"

"Is *he*," her friend went on, "also 'always so nice' to you?"

The girl, at this, face to face there with the brilliant visitor in the deserted breakfast-room, took a deeper sounding. "What is it?"

"Don't you know?"

Something came over her. "The pearls—?" But the question fainted on her lips.

"Doesn't *he* know?"

Charlotte found herself flushing. "They're *not* paste?"

"Haven't you looked at them?"

She was conscious of two kinds of embarrassment. "*You* have?"

"Very carefully."

"And they're real?"

Mrs. Guy became slightly mystifying and returned for all answer. "Come again, when you've done with the children, to my room."

Our young woman found she had done with the children that morning so promptly as to reveal to them a new joy, and when she reappeared before Mrs. Guy this lady had already encircled a plump white throat with the only

[12] Ivanhoe: historical novel by Sir Walter Scott (1771–1832), Scottish poet and novelist.
[13] Rowena: lady love of Ivanhoe, the central character of Scott's novel.

ornament, surely, in all the late Mrs. Prime's—the effaced Miss Bradshaw's —collection, in the least qualified to raise a question. If Charlotte had never yet once, before the glass, tied the string of pearls about her own neck, this was because she had been capable of no such stoop to approved "imitation", but she had now only to look at Mrs. Guy to see that, so disposed, the ambiguous objects might have passed for frank originals. "What in the world have you done to them?"

"Only handled them, understood them, admired them and put them on. That's what pearls want; they want to be worn—it wakes them up. They're alive, don't you see? How *have* these been treated? They must have been buried, ignored, despised. They were half-dead. Don't you *know* about pearls?" Mrs. Guy threw off as she fondly fingered the necklace.

"How *should* I? Do *you*?"

"Everything. These were simply asleep, and from the moment I really touched them—well," said their wearer lovingly, "it only took one's eye!"

"It took more than mine—though I did just wonder; and than Arthur's," Charlotte brooded. She found herself almost panting. "Then their value—?"

"Oh their value's excellent."

The girl, for a deep contemplative moment, took another plunge into the wonder, the beauty and the mystery, "Are you *sure*?"

Her companion wheeled round for impatience. "Sure? For what kind of an idiot, my dear, do you take me?"

It was beyond Charlotte Prime to say. "For the same kind as Arthur—and myself," she could only suggest. "But my cousin didn't know. He thinks they're worthless."

"Because of the rest of the lot? Then your cousin's an ass. But what—if, as I understand you, he gave them to you—has he to do with it?"

"Why if he gave them to me as worthless and they turn out precious—!"

"You must give them back? I don't see that—if he was such a noodle. He took the risk."

Charlotte fed, in fancy, on the pearls, which decidedly were exquisite, but which at the present moment somehow presented themselves much more as Mrs. Guy's than either as Arthur's or as her own. "Yes—he did take it, even after I had distinctly hinted to him that they looked to me different from the other pieces."

"Well then," said Mrs. Guy with something more than triumph—with a positive odd relief.

But it had the effect of making our young woman think with more intensity. "Ah you see he thought they could n't be different, because—so peculiarly—they shouldn't be."

"Shouldn't? I don't understand."

"Why how would she have got them?"—so Charlotte candidly put it. "She? Who?" There was a capacity in Mrs. Guy's tone for a sinking of persons—!

"Why the person I told you of: his stepmother, my uncle's wife—among whose poor old things, extraordinarily thrust away and out of sight, he happened to find them."

Mrs. Guy came a step nearer to the effaced Miss Bradshaw. "Do you mean she may have stolen them?"

"No. But she had been an actress."

"Oh well then," cried Mrs. Guy, "wouldn't that be just how?"

"Yes, except that she wasn't at all a brilliant one, nor in receipt of large pay." The girl even threw off a nervous joke. "I'm afraid she couldn't have been our Rowena."

Mrs. Guy took it up. "Was she very ugly?"

"No. She may very well, when young, have looked rather nice."

"Well then!" was Mrs. Guy's sharp comment and fresh triumph.

"You mean it was a present? That's just what he so dislikes the idea of her having received—a present from an admirer capable of going such lengths."

"Because she would n't have taken it for nothing? *Speriamo*[14]—that she wasn't a brute. The 'length' her admirer went was the length of the whole row. Let us hope she was just a little kind!"

"Well," Charlotte went on, "that she was 'kind' might seem to be shown by the fact that neither her husband, nor his son, nor I, his niece, knew or dreamed of her possessing anything so precious; by her having kept the gift all the rest of her life beyond discovery—out of sight and protected from suspicion."

"As if you mean"—Mrs. Guy was quick—"she had been wedded to it and yet was ashamed of it? Fancy," she laughed while she manipulated the rare beads, "being ashamed of *these!*"

"But you see she had married a clergyman."

"Yes, she must have been 'rum.'[15] But at any rate he had married *her*. What did he suppose?"

"Why that she had never been of the sort by whom such offerings are encouraged."

"Ah my dear, the sort by whom they're *not*—!" But Mrs. Guy caught herself up. "And her stepson thought the same?"

"Overwhelmingly."

"Was he then, if only her stepson—"

"So fond of her as that comes to? Yes; he had never known, consciously, his real mother, and, without children of her own, she was very patient and nice with him. And *I* liked her so," the girl pursued, "that at the end of ten years, in so strange a manner, to give her away—"

"Is impossible to you? Then don't!" said Mrs. Guy with decision.

---

[14] *Speriamo:* I should hope.
[15] 'rum': peculiar, unusual.

"Ah but if they're real I can't keep them!" Charlotte, with her eyes on them, moaned in her impatience. "It's too difficult."

"Where's the difficulty, if he has such sentiments that he'd rather sacrifice the necklace than admit it, with the presumption it carries with it, to be genuine? You've only to be silent."

"And keep it? How can *I* ever wear it?"

"You'd have to hide it, like your aunt?" Mrs. Guy was amused. "You can easily sell it."

Her companion walked round her for a look at the affair from behind. The clasp was certainly, doubtless intentionally, misleading, but everything else was indeed lovely. "Well, I must think. Why didn't *she* sell them? Charlotte broke out in her trouble.

Mrs. Guy had an instant answer. "Doesn't that prove what they secretly recalled to her? You've only to be silent!" she ardently repeated.

"I must think—I must think!"

Mrs. Guy stood with her hands attached but motionless. "Then you want them back?"

As if with the dread of touching them Charlotte retreated to the door. "I'll tell you tonight."

"But may I wear them?"

"Meanwhile?"

"This evening—at dinner."

It was the sharp selfish pressure of this that really, on the spot, determined the girl; but for the moment, before closing the door on the question, she only said: "As you like!"

They were busy much of the day with preparation and rehearsal, and at dinner that evening the concourse of guests was such that a place among them for Miss Prime failed to find itself marked. At the time the company rose she was therefore alone in the school-room, where, towards eleven o'clock she received a visit from Mrs. Guy. This lady's white shoulders heaved, under the pearls, with an emotion that the very red lips which formed, as if for the full effect, the happiest opposition of colour, were not slow to translate. "My dear, you should have seen the sensation—they've had a success!"

Charlotte, dumb a moment, took it all in. "It *is* as if they knew it—they're more and more alive. But so much the worse for both of us! I can't," she brought out with an effort, "be silent."

"You mean to return them?"

"If I don't I'm a thief."

Mrs. Guy gave her a long hard look: what was decidedly not of the baby in Mrs. Guy's face was a certain air of established habit in the eyes. Then, with a sharp little jerk of her head and a backward reach of her bare beautiful arms, she undid the clasp and, taking off the necklace, laid it on the table. "If you do you're a goose."

"Well, of the two—!" said our young lady, gathering it up with a sigh. And as if to get it, for the pang it gave, out of sight as soon as possible, she shut it up, clicking the lock, in the drawer of her own little table; after which, when she turned again, her companion looked naked and plain without it. "But what will you say?" it then occurred to her to demand.

"Downstairs—to explain?" Mrs. Guy was after all trying at least to keep her temper. "Oh I'll put on something else and say the clasp's broken. And you won't of course name *me* to him," she added.

"As having undeceived me? No—I'll say that, looking at the thing more carefully, it's my own private idea."

"And does he know how little you really know?"

"As an expert—surely. And he has always much the conceit of his own opinion."

"Then he won't believe you—as he so hates to. He'll stick to his judgement and maintain his gift, and we shall have the darlings back!" With which reviving assurance Mrs. Guy kissed her young friend for good-night.

She was not, however, to be gratified or justified by any prompt event, for, whether or no paste entered into the composition of the ornament in question, Charlotte shrank from the temerity of dispatching it to town by post. Mrs. Guy was thus disappointed of the hope of seeing the business settled—"by return," she had seemed to expect—before the end of the revels. The revels, moreover, rising to a frantic pitch, pressed for all her attention, and it was at last only in the general confusion of leave-taking that she made, parenthetically, a dash at the person in the whole company with whom her contact had been most interesting.

"Come, what will you take for them?"

"The pearls? Ah, you'll have to treat with my cousin."

Mrs. Guy, with quick intensity, lent herself. "Where then does he live?"

"In chambers in the Temple. You can find him."

"But what's the use, if *you* do neither one thing nor the other?"

"Oh I *shall* do the 'other,' " Charlotte said: "I'm only waiting till I go up. You want them so awfully?" She curiously, solemnly again, sounded her.

"I'm dying for them. There's a special charm in them—I don't know what it is: they tell so their history."

"But what do you know of that?"

"Just what they themselves say. It's all *in* them—and it comes out. They breathe a tenderness—they have the white glow of it. My dear," hissed Mrs. Guy in supreme confidence and as she buttoned her glove—"they're things of love!"

"Oh!" our young woman vaguely exclaimed.

"They're things of passion!"

"Mercy!" she gasped, turning short off. But these words remained, though indeed their help was scarce needed, Charlotte being in private face to face with a new light, as she by this time felt she must call it, on the dear dead kind colourless lady whose career had turned so sharp a corner in the middle. The pearls had quite taken their place as a revelation. She might have received them for nothing—admit that; but she couldn't have kept them so long and so unprofitably hidden, couldn't have enjoyed them only in secret, for nothing; and she had mixed them in her reliquary[16] with false things in order to put curiosity and detection off the scent. Over this strange fact poor Charlotte interminably mused: it became more touching, more attaching for her than she could now confide to any ear. How bad or how happy—in the sophisticated sense of Mrs. Guy and the young man at the Temple—the effaced Miss Bradshaw must have been to have had to be so mute! The little governess at Bleet put on the necklace now in secret sessions, she wore it sometimes under her dress; she came to feel verily a haunting passion for it. Yet in her penniless state she would have parted with it for money; she gave herself also to dreams of what in this direction it would do for her. The sophistry[17] of her so often saying to herself that Arthur had after all definitely pronounced her welcome to any gain from his gift that might accrue—this trick remained innocent, as she perfectly knew it for what it was. Then there was always the possibility of his—as she could only picture it—rising to the occasion. Mightn't he have a grand magnanimous moment?—mightn't he just say "Oh I couldn't of course have afforded to let you have it if I had known; but since you *have* got it, and have made out the truth by your own wit, I really can't screw myself down to the shabbiness of taking it back?"

She had, as it proved, to wait a long time—to wait till, at the end of several months, the great house of Bleet had, with due deliberation, for the season, transferred itself to town; after which, however, she fairly snatched at her first freedom to knock, dressed in her best and armed with her disclosure, at the door of her doubting kinsman. It was still with doubt and not quite with the face she had hoped that he listened to her story. He had turned pale, she thought, as she produced the necklace, and he appeared above all disagreeably affected. Well, perhaps there was reason, she more than ever remembered; but what on earth was one, in close touch with the fact, to do? She had laid the pearls on his table, where, without his having at first put so much as a finger to them, they met his hard cold stare.

"I don't believe in them," he simply said at last.

"That's exactly then," she returned with some spirit, "what I wanted to hear!"

She fancied that at this his colour changed; it was indeed vivid to her afterwards—for she was to have a long recall of the scene—that she had made him quite angrily flush. "It's a beastly unpleasant imputation, you

[16] reliquary: container for prized possessions.
[17] sophistry: reasoning that is superficially sound but actually illogical or misleading.

know!"—and he walked away from her as he had always walked at the vicarage.

"It's none of *my* making, I'm sure," said Charlotte Prime. "If you're afraid to believe they're real—"

"Well?"—and he turned, across the room, sharp round at her.

"Why it's not my fault."

He said nothing more, for a moment, on this; he only came back to the table. "They're what I originally said they were. They're rotten paste."

"Then I may keep them?"

"No. I want a better opinion."

"Than your own?"

"Than *your* own." He dropped on the pearls another queer stare; then, after a moment, bringing himself to touch them, did exactly what she had herself done in the presence of Mrs. Guy at Bleet—gathered them together, marched off with them to a drawer, put them in and clicked the key. "You say I'm afraid," he went on as he again met her; "but I shan't be afraid to take them to Bond Street." [18]

"And if the people say they're real—"

He had a pause and then his strangest manner. "They won't say it! They shan't!"

There was something in the way he brought it out that deprived poor Charlotte, as she was perfectly aware, of any manner at all. "Oh!" she simply sounded, as she had sounded for her last word to Mrs. Guy; and within a minute, without more conversation, she had taken her departure.

A fortnight later she received a communication from him, and toward the end of the season one of the entertainments in Eaton Square[19] was graced by the presence of Mrs. Guy. Charlotte was not at dinner, but she came down afterwards, and this guest, on seeing her, abandoned a very beautiful young man on purpose to cross and speak to her. The guest displayed a lovely necklace and had apparently not lost her habit of overflowing with the pride of such ornaments.

"Do you see?" She was in high joy.

They were indeed splendid pearls—so far as poor Charlotte could feel that she knew, after what had come and gone, about such mysteries. The poor girl had a sickly smile. "They're almost as fine as Arthur's."

"Almost? Where, my dear, are your eyes? They *are* 'Arthur's'!" After which, to meet the flood of crimson that accompanied her young friend's start: "I tracked them—after your folly, and, by miraculous luck, recognised them in the Bond Street window to which he had disposed of them."

"*Disposed* of them?" Charlotte gasped. "He wrote me that I had insulted

[18] Bond Street: elegant London shopping district.
[19] Eaton Square: fashionable London neighborhood.

his mother and that the people had shown him he was right—had pronounced them utter paste."

Mrs. Guy gave a stare. "Ah I told you he wouldn't bear it! No. But I had I assure you," she wound up, "to drive my bargain!"

Charlotte scarce heard or saw: she was full of her private wrong. "He wrote me," she panted, "that he had smashed them."

Mrs. Guy could only wonder and pity. "He's really morbid!" But it wasn't quite clear which of the pair she pitied: though the young person employed in Eaton Square felt really morbid too after they had separated and she found herself full of thought. She even went the length of asking herself what sort of a bargain Mrs. Guy had driven and whether the marvel of the recognition in Bond Street had been a veracious account of the matter. Hadn't she perhaps in truth dealt with Arthur directly? It came back to Charlotte almost luridly that she had had his address.

STUDY QUESTIONS

1. What is the initial incident in the story? Describe the relationships among the principal characters, including the deceased.
2. Is the story primarily about Arthur, his parents, Charlotte, or Mrs. Guy? Who, in other words, is the protagonist? Defend your choice.
3. Find specific information at the beginning of the story that reveals Arthur's character. How does his description of his late step-mother's stage jewelry further indicate what he is like?
4. The pearls have been hidden for many years. Why? How does it happen that they are not hidden for many more years after Charlotte takes possession of them?
5. Describe Charlotte's internal conflict when she discovers that the pearls are real. What arguments are advanced against returning the pearls to Arthur? Why does she decide not to keep them?
6. The pearls take on an almost mystical quality in the story. What is Mrs. Guy's role in creating that mystique? What does she suggest about their source, life, and significance? How does her information relate to the character of Arthur's step-mother? To Arthur himself?
7. What is the story's denouement? How does the ambiguity of the ending relate to the story's meaning?

Maricopa Indian Tale

THE CREATOR, THE SNAKE, AND THE RABBIT

After Cipas arranged that people should die, he said, "Even after they die, they should have life again." And he said that even after his death, he would have a spirit life.

Then he sat down to wait for all his people to talk. The Mission Indians were the first to talk. The Maricopa talked next. Then all the tribes spoke in turn. The Chemehuevi talked in the middle of the night, so their language is unintelligible to anybody else. All the tribes here had spoken. The white people were the very last to speak. It was said, that like a younger child, they were cry-babies. So the Creator did everything to soothe them, hence they are richer than any of the Indians. . . .

When everybody could speak, that is including rabbits and all other kinds of animals, he built a big house for them. This held all the beings he had created. When morning came they would all go out to play together; all the games of which they could think. Toward evening they would all go into the house. Then he also made a snake. It had no teeth. It was gentle. Its name was Kinyamás Kasur, meaning fragile and limp. They would take the snake and hit each other with it. The rabbit always got the snake and played with it. He would bring it out, so that they could play, hitting each other with it until it was half dead. . . .

[Once] early in the morning they all went out to play. The Creator was lying right by the door. The snake crawled up to him. The Creator asked him what he wanted. The snake said that he only crawled up because of his poor condition; he was not being treated right. He had life just like the others: he did not see why he was roughly treated by everyone in that house. The Creator told him to sit there and wait for the sun to rise. Then the Creator took some coals and chewed them into tiny bits. They both sat there; the snake facing the east as the sun rose. Then the Creator told him to open his mouth. This he did. Then the Creator put the coal and the sun rays together in it for teeth. The snake now had teeth, so he went back able to protect himself.

Toward evening when everybody returned to the house, they sent the rabbit again to get the snake. As she [sic] reached for the snake, she was bitten. She suffered with pain for just a short time and died at midnight. . . .

After the rabbit died they felt bad over their great loss. So instead of going out to play, they remained quiet mourning their sister. Then they began to wonder who had put teeth in the snake's mouth. They discovered who it was: their father, who had taken pity on the poor snake. Then they wondered why he did not feel sorry for the rabbit. Then they said they would kill their father, if only someone knew how. They thought he, too, ought to die.

Bullfrog was the one who knew how to do it. The frog sank into the ground and went under a slough[1] where the old man used to swim. If he went swimming again, the frog was to drink up all the water in the slough. He did this. As soon as the old man got out, he felt sick as he was going home.

---

[1] slough: backwater, pond, or creek.

[He tries to recover by lying in four places and by eating four remedies, but nothing helps.]

He said: "All these things I have tried in order to recover from my sickness, but they do no good. I have not been with you long enough to tell you all I know. Sickness must come to people just as it did to me." . . . Then he died on the fourth day.

When Cipas died he went under the earth. He lies there yet. Whenever he yawns a little and turns over, an earthquake is caused.

O. Henry (1862–1910)

THE COP AND THE ANTHEM

On his bench in Madison Square Soapy moved uneasily. When wild geese honk high of nights, and when women without sealskin coats grow kind to their husbands, and when Soapy moves uneasily on his bench in the park, you may know that winter is near at hand.

A dead leaf fell in Soapy's lap. That was Jack Frost's card. Jack is kind to the regular denizens of Madison Square, and gives fair warning of his annual call. At the corners of four streets he hands his pasteboard to the North Wind, footman of the mansion of All Outdoors, so that the inhabitants thereof may make ready.

Soapy's mind became cognizant of the fact that the time had come for him to resolve himself into a singular Committee of Ways and Means to provide against the coming rigor. And therefore he moved uneasily on his bench.

The hibernatorial ambitions of Soapy were not of the highest. In them were no considerations of Mediterranean cruises, of soporific[1] Southern skies or drifting in the Vesuvian Bay. Three months on the Island [2] was what his soul craved. Three months of assured board and bed and congenial company, safe from Boreas[3] and bluecoats,[4] seemed to Soapy the essence of things desirable.

For years the hospitable Blackwell's had been his winter quarters. Just as his more fortunate fellow New Yorkers had bought their tickets to Palm Beach and the Riviera each winter, so Soapy had made his humble arrangements for his annual hegira[5] to the Island. And now the time was come. On the previous night three Sabbath newspapers, distributed beneath his coat, about his ankles and over his lap, had failed to repulse the cold as he slept on his bench near the spurting fountain in the ancient square. So the Island

[1] soporific: causing sleep.
[2] Island: Blackwell's Island, in the East River in New York; former site of a city prison.
[3] Boreas: in Greek mythology, the north wind.
[4] bluecoats: policemen.
[5] hegira: flight.

loomed big and timely in Soapy's mind. He scorned the provisions made in the name of charity for the city's dependents. In Soapy's opinion the Law was more benign than Philanthropy. There was an endless round of institutions, municipal and eleemosynary,[6] on which he might set out and receive lodging and food accordant with the simple life. But to one of Soapy's proud spirit the gifts of charity are encumbered. If not in coin you must pay in humiliation of spirit for every benefit received at the hands of philanthropy. As Cæsar had his Brutus,[7] every bed of charity must have its toll of a bath, every loaf of bread its compensation of a private and personal inquisition. Wherefore it is better to be a guest of the law, which, though conducted by rules, does not meddle unduly with a gentleman's private affairs.

Soapy, having decided to go to the Island, at once set about accomplishing his desire. There were many easy ways of doing this. The pleasantest was to dine luxuriously at some expensive restaurant; and then, after declaring insolvency, be handed over quietly and without uproar to a policeman. An accommodating magistrate would do the rest.

Soapy left his bench and strolled out of the square and across the level sea of asphalt, where Broadway and Fifth Avenue flow together. Up Broadway he turned, and halted at a glittering café, where are gathered together nightly the choicest products of the grape, the silkworm, and the protoplasm.

Soapy had confidence in himself from the lowest button of his vest upward. He was shaven, and his coat was decent and his neat black, ready-tied four-in-hand [8] had been presented to him by a lady missionary on Thanksgiving Day. If he could reach a table in the restaurant unsuspected success would be his. The portion of him that would show above the table would raise no doubt in the waiter's mind. A roasted mallard duck, thought Soapy, would be about the thing—with a bottle of Chablis, and then Camembert,[9] a demi-tasse[10] and a cigar. One dollar for the cigar would be enough. The total would not be so high as to call forth any supreme manifestation of revenge from the café management; and yet the meat would leave him filled and happy for the journey to his winter refuge.

But as Soapy set foot inside the restaurant door the head waiter's eye fell upon his frayed trousers and decadent shoes. Strong and ready hands turned him about and conveyed him in silence and haste to the sidewalk and averted the ignoble fate of the menaced mallard.

Soapy turned off Broadway. It seemed that his route to the coveted Island was not to be an epicurean[11] one. Some other way of entering limbo[12] must be thought of.

[6] eleemosynary: charitable.
[7] Brutus: friend of Caesar who participated in Caesar's assassination.
[8] four-in-hand: necktie.
[9] Camembert: soft cheese.
[10] demi-tasse: small cup of coffee.
[11] epicurean: related to luxurious living.
[12] limbo: region of oblivion, neglect, or confinement.

At a corner of Sixth Avenue electric lights and cunningly displayed wares behind plate-glass made a shop window conspicuous. Soapy took a cobble-stone and dashed it through the glass. People came running around the corner, a policeman in the lead. Soapy stood still, with his hands in his pockets, and smiled at the sight of brass buttons.

"Where's the man that done that?" inquired the officer, excitedly.

"Don't you figure out that I might have had something to do with it?" said Soapy, not without sarcasm, but friendly, as one greets good fortune.

The policeman's mind refused to accept Soapy even as a clue. Men who smash windows do not remain to parley[13] with the law's minions.[14] They take to their heels. The policeman saw a man halfway down the block running to catch a car. With drawn club he joined in the pursuit. Soapy, with disgust in his heart, loafed along, twice unsuccessful.

On the opposite side of the street was a restaurant of no great pretensions. It catered to large appetites and modest purses. Its crockery and atmosphere were thick; its soup and napery thin. Into this place Soapy took his accusive shoes and telltale trousers without challenge. At a table he sat and consumed beefsteak, flapjacks, doughnuts and pie. And then to the waiter he betrayed the fact that the minutest coin and himself were strangers.

"Now, get busy and call a cop," said Soapy. "And don't keep a gentleman waiting."

"No cop for youse," said the waiter, with a voice like butter cakes and an eye like the cherry in a Manhattan cocktail. "Hey, Con!"

Neatly upon his left ear on the callous pavement two waiters pitched Soapy. He arose joint by joint, as a carpenter's rule opens, and beat the dust from his clothes. Arrest seemed but a rosy dream. The Island seemed very far away. A policeman who stood before a drug store two doors away laughed and walked down the street.

Five blocks Soapy travelled before his courage permitted him to woo capture again. This time the opportunity presented what he fatuously[15] termed to himself a "cinch." A young woman of a modest and pleasing guise was standing before a show window gazing with sprightly interest at its display of shaving mugs and inkstands, and two yards from the window a large policeman of severe demeanor leaned against a water plug.

It was Soapy's design to assume the rôle of the despicable and execrated "masher."[16] The refined and elegant appearance of his victim and the contiguity of the conscientious copy encouraged him to believe that he would soon feel the pleasant official clutch upon his arm that would insure his winter quarters on the right little, tight little isle.

---

[13] parley: talk.
[14] minions: followers or servants.
[15] fatuously: foolishly, stupidly.
[16] masher: slang for a man who forces amorous attentions on a woman.

Soapy straightened the lady missionary's ready-made tie, dragged his shrinking cuffs into the open, set his hat at a killing cant and sidled toward the young woman. He made eyes at her, was taken with sudden coughs and "hems," smiled, smirked and went brazenly through the impudent and contemptible litany[17] of the "masher." With half an eye Soapy saw that the policeman was watching him fixedly. The young woman moved away a few steps, and again bestowed her absorbed attention upon the shaving mugs. Soapy followed, boldly stepping to her side, raised his hat and said:

"Ah there, Bedelia! Don't you want to come and play in my yard?"

The policeman was still looking. The persecuted young woman had but to beckon a finger and Soapy would be practically en route for his insular haven. Already he imagined he could feel the cozy warmth of the stationhouse. The young woman faced him and, stretching out a hand, caught Soapy's coat sleeve.

"Sure, Mike," she said, joyfully, "if you'll blow me to a pail of suds. I'd have spoke to you sooner, but the cop was watching."

With the young woman playing the clinging ivy to his oak Soapy walked past the policeman overcome with gloom. He seemed doomed to liberty.

At the next corner he shook off his companion and ran. He halted in the district where by night are found the lightest streets, hearts, vows and librettos. Women in furs and men in greatcoats moved gaily in the wintry air. A sudden fear seized Soapy that some dreadful enchantment had rendered him immune to arrest. The thought brought a little of panic upon it, and when he came upon another policeman lounging grandly in front of a transplendent theatre he caught at the immediate straw of "disorderly conduct."

On the sidewalk Soapy began to yell drunken gibberish at the top of his harsh voice. He danced, howled, raved, and otherwise disturbed the welkin.[18]

The policeman twirled his club, turned his back to Soapy and remarked to a citizen:

" 'Tis one of them Yale lads celebratin' the goose egg they give to the Hartford College. Noisy; but no harm. We've instructions to leave them be."

Disconsolate, Soapy ceased his unavailing racket. Would never a policeman lay hands on him? In his fancy the Island seemed an unattainable Arcadia.[19] He buttoned his thin coat against the chilling wind.

In a cigar store he saw a well-dressed man lighting a cigar at a swinging light. His silk umbrella he had set by the door on entering. Soapy stepped inside, secured the umbrella and sauntered off with it slowly. The man at the cigar light followed hastily.

"My umbrella," he said, sternly.

[17] litany: religious ritual/prayer.
[18] welkin: the heavens.
[19] Arcadia: a region of ideal contentment.

"Oh, is it?" sneered Soapy, adding insult to petit larceny. "Well, why don't you call a policeman? I took it. Your umbrella! Why don't you call a cop? There stands one on the corner."

The umbrella owner slowed his steps. Soapy did likewise, with a presentiment that luck would again run against him. The policeman looked at the two curiously.

"Of course," said the umbrella man—"that is—well, you know how these mistakes occur—I—if it's your umbrella I hope you'll excuse me—I picked it up this morning in a restaurant—If you recognize it as yours, why—I hope you'll—"

"Of course it's mine," said Soapy, viciously.

The ex-umbrella man retreated. The policeman hurried to assist a tall blonde in an opera cloak across the street in front of a street car that was approaching two blocks away.

Soapy walked eastward through a street damaged by improvements. He hurled the umbrella wrathfully into an excavation. He muttered against the men who wear helmets and carry clubs. Because he wanted to fall into their clutches, they seemed to regard him as a king who could do no wrong.

At length Soapy reached one of the avenues to the east where the glitter and turmoil was but faint. He set his face down this toward Madison Square, for the homing instinct survives even when the home is a park bench.

But on an unusually quiet corner Soapy came to a standstill. Here was an old church, quaint and rambling and gabled. Through one violet-stained window a soft light glowed, where, no doubt, the organist loitered over the keys, making sure of his mastery of the coming Sabbath anthem. For there drifted out to Soapy's ears sweet music that caught and held him transfixed against the convolutions of the iron fence.

The moon was above, lustrous and serene; vehicles and pedestrians were few; sparrows twittered sleepily in the eaves—for a little while the scene might have been a country churchyard. And the anthem that the organist played cemented Soapy to the iron fence, for he had known it well in the days when his life contained such things as mothers and roses and ambitions and friends and immaculate thoughts and collars.

The conjunction of Soapy's receptive state of mind and the influences about the old church wrought a sudden and wonderful change in his soul. He viewed with swift horror the pit into which he had tumbled, the degraded days, unworthy desires, dead hopes, wrecked faculties and base motives that made up his existence.

And also in a moment his heart responded thrillingly to this novel mood. An instantaneous and strong impulse moved him to battle with his desperate fate. He would pull himself out of the mire; he would make a man of himself again; he would conquer the evil that had taken possession of him. There was time; he was comparatively young yet: he would resurrect his old eager ambitions and pursue them without faltering. Those solemn but sweet organ notes had set up a revolution in him. To-morrow he would go into the roaring downtown district and find work. A fur importer had once offered him a place as driver. He would find him to-morrow and ask for the position. He would be somebody in the world. He would——

Soapy felt a hand laid on his arm. He looked quickly around into the broad face of a policeman.

"What are you doin' here?" asked the officer.

"Nothin'," said Soapy.

"Then come along," said the policeman.

"Three months on the Island," said the Magistrate in the Police Court the next morning.

Bret Harte (1836–1902)

THE POSTMISTRESS OF LAUREL RUN

The mail stage had just passed Laurel Run,—so rapidly that the whirling cloud of dust dragged with it down the steep grade from the summit hung over the level long after the stage had vanished, and then, drifting away, slowly sifted a red precipitate over the hot platform of the Laurel Run post-office.

Out of this cloud presently emerged the neat figure of the postmistress with the mail-bag which had been dexterously flung at her feet from the top of the passing vehicle. A dozen loungers eagerly stretched out their hands to assist her, but the warning: "It's again the rules, boys, for any but her to touch it," from a bystander, and a coquettish shake of the head from the postmistress herself—much more effective than any official inter-dict—withheld them. The bag was not heavy,—Laurel Run was too recent a settlement to have attracted much correspondence,—and the young woman, having pounced upon her prey with a certain feline instinct, dragged it, not without difficulty, behind the partitioned inclosure in the office, and locked the door. Her pretty face, momentarily visible through the window, was slightly flushed with the exertion, and the loose ends of her fair hair, wet with perspiration, curled themselves over her forehead into tantalising little rings. But the window shutter was quickly closed, and this momentary but charming vision withdrawn from the waiting public.

"Guv'ment oughter have more sense than to make a woman pick mail-bags outer the road," said Jo Simmons sympathetically. " 'Tain't in her day's work anyhow; Guv'ment oughter hand 'em over to her like a lady; it's rich enough and ugly enough."

" 'Tain't Guv'ment; it's that stage company's airs and graces," inter-rupted a newcomer. "They think it mighty fine to go beltin' by, makin' everybody take their dust, just because *stoppin'* ain't in their contract. Why, if that expressman who chucked down the bag had any feelin's for a lady"—but he stopped here at the amused faces of his auditors.

"Guess you don't know much o' that expressman's feelin's, stranger," said Simmons grimly. "Why, you oughter see him just nussin' that bag like a baby as he comes tearin' down the grade, and then rise up and sorter heave it to Mrs. Baker ez if it was a five-dollar bokay! His feelin's for her! Why, he's give himself so dead away to her that we're looking for him to forget what he's doin' next, and just come sailin' down hisself at her feet."

Meanwhile, on the other side of the partition, Mrs. Baker had brushed the red dust from the padlocked bag, and removed what seemed to be a supplementary package attached to it by a wire. Opening it she found a handsome scent-bottle, evidently a superadded gift from the devoted expressman. This she put aside with a slight smile and the murmured word, "Foolishness." But when she had unlocked the bag, even its sacred interior was also profaned by a covert parcel from the adjacent postmaster at Burnt Ridge, containing a gold "specimen" brooch and some circus tickets. It was laid aside with the other. This also was vanity and—presumably—vexation of spirit.

There were seventeen letters in all, of which five were for herself—and yet the proportion was small that morning. Two of them were marked "Official Business," and were promptly put by with feminine discernment; but in another compartment than that holding the presents. Then the shutter was opened, and the task of delivery commenced.

It was accompanied with a social peculiarity that had in time become a habit of Laurel Run. As the young woman delivered the letters, in turn, to the men who were patiently drawn up in Indian file, she made that simple act a medium of privileged but limited conversation on special or general topics,—gay or serious as the case might be, or the temperament of the man suggested. That it was almost always of a complimentary character on their part may be readily imagined; but it was invariably characterised by an element of refined restraint, and, whether from some implied understanding or individual sense of honour, it never passed the bounds of conventionality or a certain delicacy of respect. The delivery was consequently more or less protracted, but when each man had exchanged his three or four minutes' conversation with the fair postmistress,—a conversation at times impeded by bashfulness or timidity, on his part solely, or restricted often to vague smiling,—he resignedly made way for the next. It was a formal levee,[1] mitigated by the informality of rustic tact, great good-humour, and infinite patience, and would have been amusing had it not always been terribly in earnest and at times touching. For it was peculiar to the place and the epoch, and indeed implied the whole history of Mrs. Baker.

She was the wife of John Baker, foreman of "The Last Chance," now

[1] levee: reception.

for a year lying dead under half a mile of crushed and beaten-in tunnel at Burnt Ridge. There had been a sudden outcry from the depths at high hot noontide one day, and John had rushed from his cabin—his young, foolish, flirting wife clinging to him—to answer that despairing cry of his imprisoned men. There was one exit that he alone knew which might be yet held open, among falling walls and tottering timbers, long enough to set them free. For one moment only the strong man hesitated between her entreating arms and his brothers' despairing cry. But she rose suddenly with a pale face, and said, "Go, John! I will wait for you here." He went, the men were freed—but she had waited for him ever since!

Yet in the shock of the calamity and in the after struggles of that poverty which had come to the ruined camp, she had scarcely changed. But the men had. Although she was to all appearances the same giddy, pretty Betsy Baker, who had been so disturbing to the younger members, they seemed to be no longer disturbed by her. A certain subdued awe and respect, as if the martyred spirit of John Baker still held his arm around her, appeared to have come upon them all. They held their breath as this pretty woman, whose brief mourning had not seemed to affect her cheerfulness or even playfulness of spirit, passed before them. But she stood by her cabin and the camp—the only woman in a settlement of forty men—during the darkest hours of their fortune. Helping them to wash and cook, and ministering to their domestic needs, the sanctity of her cabin was, however, always kept as inviolable as if it had been *his* tomb. No one exactly knew why, for it was only a tacit instinct; but even one or two who had not scrupled to pay court to Betsy Baker during John Baker's life, shrank from even a suggestion of familiarity towards the woman who had said that she would "wait for him there."

When brighter days came and the settlement had increased by one or two families, and laggard capital had been hurried up to relieve the still beleaguered and locked-up wealth of Burnt Ridge, the needs of the community and the claims of the widow of John Baker were so well told in political quarters that the post-office of Laurel Run was created expressly for her. Every man participated in the building of the pretty yet substantial edifice —the only public building of Laurel Run—that stood in the dust of the great highway, half a mile from the settlement. There she was installed for certain hours of the day, for she could not be prevailed upon to abandon John's cabin, and here, with all the added respect due to a public functionary, she was secure in her privacy.

But the blind devotion of Laurel Run to John Baker's relict[2] did not stop here. In its zeal to assure the Government authorities of the necessity for a post-office, and to secure a permanent competency to the postmistress, there was much embarrassing extravagance. During the first week the sale of

---

[2] relict: widow.

stamps at Laurel Run post-office was unprecedented in the annals of the Department. Fancy prices were given for the first issue; then they were bought wildly, recklessly, unprofitably, and on all occasions. Complimentary congratulation at the little window invariably ended with "and a dollar's worth of stamps, Mrs. Baker." It was felt to be supremely delicate to buy only the highest priced stamps, without reference to their adequacy; then mere *quantity* was sought; then outgoing letters were all over-paid and stamped in outrageous proportion to their weight and even size. The imbecility of this, and its probable effect on the reputation of Laurel Run at the General Post-office, being pointed out by Mrs. Baker, stamps were adopted as local currency, and even for decorative purposes on mirrors and the walls of cabins. Everybody wrote letters, with the result, however, that those *sent* were ludicrously and suspiciously in excess of those received. To obviate this, select parties made forced journeys to Hickory Hill, the next post-office, with letters and circulars addressed to themselves at Laurel Run. How long the extravagance would have continued is not known, but it was not until it was rumoured that, in consequence of this excessive flow of business, the Department had concluded that a post*master* would be better fitted for the place that it abated, and a compromise was effected with the General Office by a permanent salary to the postmistress.

Such was the history of Mrs. Baker, who had just finished her afternoon levee, nodded a smiling "good-bye" to her last customer, and closed her shutter again. Then she took up her own letters, but, before reading them, glanced, with a pretty impatience, at the two official envelopes addressed to herself, which she had shelved. They were generally a "lot of new rules," or notifications, or "absurd" questions which had nothing to do with Laurel Run and only bothered her and "made her head ache," and she had usually referred them to her admiring neighbour at Hickory Hill for explanation, who had generally returned them to her with the brief indorsement, "Purp stuff, don't bother," or, "Hog wash, let it slide." She remembered now that he had not returned the last two. With knitted brows and a slight pout she put aside her private correspondence and tore open the first one. It referred with official curtness to an unanswered communication of the previous week, and was "compelled to remind her of rule 47." Again those horrid rules! She opened the other; the frown deepened on her brow, and became fixed.

It was a summary of certain valuable money letters that had miscarried on the route, and of which they had given her previous information. For a moment her cheeks blazed. How dare they; what did they mean! Her waybills and register were always right; she knew the names of every man, woman, and child in her district; no such names as those borne by the missing letters had ever existed at Laurel Run; no such addresses had ever been sent from Laurel Run post-office. It was a mean insinuation! She would send in her resignation at once! She would get "the boys" to write an insulting letter to Senator Slocumb,—Mrs. Baker had the feminine idea of Government as a purely personal institution,—and she would find out who it was that had put them up to this prying, crawling impudence! It was probably that wall-eyed old wife of the postmaster at Heavy Tree Crossing, who was jealous of her. "Remind her of their previous unanswered communication," indeed! Where was that communication, anyway? She remembered she had sent it to her admirer at Hickory Hill. Odd that he hadn't answered it. Of course, he knew about this meanness—could he, too, have dared to suspect her! The thought turned her crimson again. He, Stanton Green, was an old "Laurel Runner," a friend of John's, a little "triflin' " and "presoomin'," but still an old loyal pioneer of the camp! "Why hadn't he spoke up?"

There was the soft, muffled fall of a horse's hoof in the thick dust of the highway, the jingle of dismounting spurs, and a firm tread on the platform. No doubt one of the boys returning for a few supplemental remarks under the feeble pretence of forgotten stamps. It had been done before, and she had resented it as "cayotin' round;" but now she was eager to pour out her wrongs to the first comer. She had her hand impulsively on the door of the partition, when she stopped with a new sense of her impaired dignity. Could she confess this to her worshippers? But here the door opened in her very face, and a stranger entered.

He was a man of fifty, compactly and strongly built. A squarely-cut goatee, slightly streaked with grey, fell straight from his thin-lipped but handsome mouth; his eyes were dark, humorous, yet searching. But the distinctive quality that struck Mrs. Baker was the blending of urban ease with frontier frankness. He was evidently a man who had seen cities and knew countries as well. And while he was dressed with the comfortable simplicity of a Californian mounted traveller, her inexperienced but feminine eye detected the keynote of his respectability in the carefully-tied bow of his cravat. The Sierrean throat was apt to be open, free, and unfettered.

"Good-morning, Mrs. Baker," he said, pleasantly, with his hat already in his hand. "I'm Harry Home, of San Francisco." As he spoke his eye swept approvingly over the neat inclosure, the primly-tied papers, and well-kept pigeon-holes; the pot of flowers on her desk; her china-silk mantle, and killing little chip hat and ribbons hanging against the wall; thence to her own pink, flushed face, bright blue eyes, tendriled clinging hair, and then —fell upon the leathern mail-bag still lying across the table. Here it became fixed on the unfortunate wire of the amorous expressman that yet remained hanging from the brass wards of the lock, and he reached his hand toward it.

But little Mrs. Baker was before him, and had seized it in her arms. She had been too preoccupied and bewildered to resent his first intrusion behind the partition, but this last familiarity with her sacred official property—albeit empty—capped the climax of her wrongs.

"How dare you touch it!" she said indignantly. "How dare you come in here! Who are you, anyway? Go outside, at once!"

The stranger fell back with an amused, deprecatory gesture, and a long silent laugh. "I'm afraid you don't know me, after all!" he said pleasantly. "I'm Harry Home, the Department Agent from the San Francisco office. My note of advice, No. 201, with my name on the envelope, seems to have miscarried too."

Even in her fright and astonishment it flashed upon Mrs. Baker that she had sent that notice, too, to Hickory Hill. But with it all the feminine secretive instinct within her was now thoroughly aroused, and she kept silent.

"I ought to have explained," he went on smilingly; "but you are quite right, Mrs. Baker," he added, nodding towards the bag. "As far as you knew, I had no business to go near it. Glad to see you know how to defend Uncle Sam's property so well. I was only a bit puzzled to know" (pointing to the wire) "if that thing was on the bag when it was delivered to you?"

Mrs. Baker saw no reason to conceal the truth. After all, this official was a man like the others, and it was just as well that he should understand her power. "It's only the expressman's foolishness," she said, with a slightly coquettish toss of her head. "He thinks it smart to tie some nonsense on that bag with the wire when he flings it down."

Mr. Home, with his eyes on her pretty face, seemed to think it a not inhuman or unpardonable folly. "As long as he doesn't meddle with the inside of the bag, I suppose you must put up with it," he said laughingly. A dreadful recollection, that the Hickory Hill postmaster had used the inside of the bag to convey *his* foolishness, came across her. It would never do to confess it now. Her face must have shown some agitation, for the official resumed with a half-paternal, half-reassuring air: "But enough of this. Now, Mrs. Baker, to come to my business here. Briefly, then, it doesn't concern you in the least, except so far as it may relieve you and some others, whom the Department knows equally well, from a certain responsibility, and, perhaps, anxiety. We are pretty well posted down there in all that concerns Laurel Run, and I think" (with a slight bow) "we've known all about you and John Baker. My only business here is to take your place to-night in receiving the "Omnibus Way Bag," that you know arrives here at 9.30, doesn't it?"

"Yes, sir," said Mrs. Baker hurriedly; "but it never has anything for us, except"—(she caught herself up quickly, with a stammer, as she remembered the sighing Green's occasional offerings) "except a notification from Hickory Hill post-office. It leaves there," she went on with an affectation of precision, "at half past eight exactly, and it's about an hour's run—seven miles by road."

"Exactly," said Mr. Home. "Well, I will receive the bag, open it, and dispatch it again. You can, if you choose, take a holiday."

"But," said Mrs. Baker, as she remembered that Laurel Run always made a point of attending her evening levee on account of the superior leisure it offered, "there are the people who come for letters, you know."

"I thought you said there were no letters at that time," said Mr. Home quickly.

"No—but—but"—(with a slight hysterical stammer) "the boys come all the same."

"Oh!" said Mr. Home dryly.

"And—O Lord!"— But here the spectacle of the possible discomfiture of Laurel Run at meeting the bearded face of Mr. Home, instead of her own smooth cheeks, at the window, combined with her nervous excitement, overcame her so that, throwing her little frilled apron over her head, she gave way to a paroxysm of hysterical laughter. Mr. Home waited with amused toleration for it to stop, and, when she had recovered, resumed. "Now, I should like to refer an instant to my first communication to you. Have you got it handy?"

Mrs. Baker's face fell. "No; I sent it over to Mr. Green, of Hickory Hill, for information."

"What!"

Terrified at the sudden seriousness of the man's voice, she managed to gasp out, however, that, after her usual habit, she had not opened the official letters, but had sent them to her more experienced colleague for advice and information; that she never could understand them herself,—they made her head ache, and interfered with her other duties,—but *he* understood them, and sent her word what to do. Remembering also his usual style of indorsement, she grew red again.

"And what did he say?"

"Nothing; he didn't return them."

"Naturally," said Mr. Home, with a peculiar expression. After a few moments' silent stroking of his beard, he suddenly faced the frightened woman.

"You oblige me, Mrs. Baker, to speak more frankly to you than I had intended. You have—unwittingly, I believe—given information to a man whom the Government suspects of peculation.[3] You have, without knowing it, warned the postmaster at Hickory Hill that he is suspected; and, as you might have frustrated our plans for tracing a series of embezzlements to their proper source, you will see that you might have also done great wrong to yourself as his only neighbour and the next responsible person. In plain words, we have traced the disappearance of money letters to a point when it lies between these two offices. Now, I have not the least hesitation in telling you that we do not suspect Laurel Run, and never have suspected it. Even the result of your thoughtless act, although it warned him, confirms our suspicion of his guilt. As to the warning, it has failed, or he has grown reckless, for another letter has been missed since. To-night, however, will settle all doubt in the matter. When I open that bag in this office to-night, and do not find a certain decoy letter in it, which was last checked at Heavy

[3] peculation: embezzlement.

Tree Crossing, I shall know that it remains in Green's possession at Hickory Hill."

She was sitting back in her chair, white and breathless. He glanced at her kindly, and then took up his hat. "Come, Mrs. Baker, don't let this worry you. As I told you at first, *you* have nothing to fear. Even your thoughtlessness and ignorance of rules have contributed to show your own innocence. Nobody will ever be the wiser for this; we do not advertise our affairs in the Department. Not a soul but yourself knows the real cause of my visit here. I will leave you here alone for a while, so as to divert any suspicion. You will come, as usual, this evening, and be seen by your friends; I will only be here when the bag arrives, to open it. Good-bye, Mrs. Baker; it's a nasty bit of business, but it's all in the day's work. I've seen worse, and, thank God, you're out of it."

She heard his footsteps retreat into the outer office and die out of the platform; the jingle of his spurs, and the hollow beat of his horse's hoofs that seemed to find a dull echo in her own heart, and she was alone.

The room was very hot and very quiet; she could hear the warping and creaking of the shingles under the relaxing of the nearly level sunbeams. The office clock struck seven. In the breathless silence that followed, a woodpecker took up his interrupted work on the roof, and seemed to beat out monotonously on her ear the last words of the stranger: Stanton Green —a thief! Stanton Green, one of the "boys" John had helped out of the falling tunnel! Stanton Green, whose old mother in the States still wrote letters to him at Laurel Run, in a few hours to be a disgraced and ruined man forever! She remembered now, as a thoughtless woman remembers, tales of his extravagance and fast living, of which she had taken no heed, and, with a sense of shame, of presents sent her, that she now clearly saw must have been far beyond his means. What would the boys say? What would John have said? Ah! what would John have *done!*

She started suddenly to her feet, white and cold as on that day that she had parted from John Baker before the tunnel. She put on her hat and mantle, and going to that little iron safe that stood in the corner, unlocked it and took out its entire contents of gold and silver. She had reached the door when another idea seized her, and opening her desk she collected her stamps to the last sheet, and hurriedly rolled them up under her cape. Then with a glance at the clock, and a rapid survey of the road from the platform, she slipped from it, and seemed to be swallowed up in the waiting woods beyond.

Once within the friendly shadows of the long belt of pines, Mrs. Baker kept them until she had left the limited settlement of Laurel Run far to the right, and came upon an open slope of Burnt Ridge, where she knew Jo Simmons' mustang, Blue Lightning, would be quietly feeding. She had often ridden him before, and when she had detached the fifty-foot reata[4] from his head-stall, he permitted her the further recognised familiarity of twining her fingers in his bluish mane and climbing on his back. The tool-shed of Burnt Ridge Tunnel, where Jo's saddle and bridle always hung, was but a canter farther on. She reached it unperceived, and—another trick of the old days —quickly extemporised a side-saddle from Simmons' Mexican tree, with its high cantle and horn bow, and the aid of a blanket. Then leaping to her seat, she rapidly threw off her mantle, tied it by its sleeves around her waist, tucked it under one knee, and let it fall over her horse's flanks. By this time Blue Lightning was also struck with a flash of equine recollection and pricked up his ears. Mrs. Baker uttered a little chirping cry which he re-membered, and the next moment they were both careering over the Ridge.

The trail that she had taken, though precipitate, difficult, and dangerous in places, was a clear gain of two miles on the stage road. There was less chance of her being followed or meeting any one. The greater cañons were already in shadow; the pines on the farther ridges were separating their masses, and showing individual silhouettes against the sky, but the air was still warm, and the cool breath of night, as she well knew it, had not yet begun to flow down the mountain. The lower range of Burnt Ridge was still uneclipsed by the creeping shadow of the mountain ahead of her. Without a watch, but with this familiar and slowly changing dial spread out before her, she knew the time to a minute. Heavy Tree Hill, a lesser height in the distance, was already wiped out by that shadowy index finger—half past seven! The stage would be at Hickory Hill just before half past eight; she ought to anticipate it, if possible,—it would stay ten minutes to change horses,—she *must* arrive before it left!

There was a good two-mile level before the rise of the next range. Now, Blue Lightning! all you know! And that was much,—for with the little chip hat and fluttering ribbons well bent down over the bluish mane, and the streaming gauze of her mantle almost level with the horse's back, she swept down across the long tableland like a skimming blue-jay. A few more bird-like dips up and down the undulations, and then came the long, cruel ascent of the Divide.

Acrid with perspiration, caking with dust, slithering in the slippery, im-palpable powder of the road, groggily staggering in a red dusty dream, coughing, snorting, head-tossing; becoming suddenly dejected, with slouch-ing haunch and limp legs on easy slopes, or wildly spasmodic and agile on sharp acclivities, Blue Lightning began to have ideas and recollections! Ah! she was a devil for a lark—this lightly-clinging, caressing, blarneying, coo-ing creature—up there! He remembered her now Ha! very well then. Hoop-la! And suddenly leaping out like a rabbit, bucking, trotting hard, ambling

---

[4] reata: lasso, rope.

lightly, "loping" on three legs and recreating himself,—as only a California mustang could,—the invincible Blue Lightning at last stood triumphantly upon the summit. The evening star had just pricked itself through the golden mist of the horizon line,—eight o'clock! She could do it now! But here, suddenly, her first hesitation seized her. She knew her horse, she knew the trail, she knew herself,—but did she know *the man* to whom she was riding? A cold chill crept over her, and then she shivered in a sudden blast; it was Night at last swooping down from the now invisible Sierras, and possessing all it touched. But it was only one long descent to Hickory Hill now, and she swept down securely on its wings. Half-past eight! The lights of the settlement were just ahead of her—but so, too, were the two lamps of the waiting stage before the post-office and hotel.

Happily the lounging crowd were gathered around the hotel, and she slipped into the post-office from the rear, unperceived. As she stepped behind the partition, its only occupant—a good-looking young fellow with a reddish moustache—turned towards her with a flush of delighted surprise. But it changed at the sight of the white, determined face and the brilliant eyes that had never looked once towards him, but were fixed upon a large bag, whose yawning mouth was still open and propped up beside his desk.

"Where is the through money letter that came in that bag?" she said quickly.

"What—do—you—mean?" he stammered, with a face that had suddenly grown whiter than her own.

"I mean that it's a *decoy*, checked at Heavy Tree Crossing, and that Mr. Home, of San Francisco, is now waiting at my office to know if you have taken it!"

The laugh and lie that he had at first tried to summon to mouth and lips never reached them. For, under the spell of her rigid, truthful face, he turned almost mechanically to his desk, and took out a package.

"Good God! you've opened it already!" she cried, pointing to the broken seal.

The expression on her face, more than anything she had said, convinced him that she knew all. He stammered under the new alarm that her despairing tone suggested. "Yes!—I was owing some bills—the collector was waiting here for the money, and I took something from the packet. But I was going to make it up by next mail—I swear it."

"How much have you taken?"

"Only a trifle. I"—

"How much?"

"A hundred dollars!"

She dragged the money she had brought from Laurel Run from her pocket, and counting out the sum, replaced it in the open package. He ran quickly to get the sealing-wax, but she motioned him away as she dropped the package back into the mail-bag. "No; as long as the money is found in the bag the package may have been broken *accidentally*. Now burst open one or two of those other packages a little—so;" she took out a packet of letters and bruised their official wrappings under her little foot until the tape fastening was loosened. "Now give me something heavy." She caught up a brass two-pound weight, and in the same feverish but collected haste wrapped it in paper, sealed it, stamped it, and, addressing it in a large printed hand to herself at Laurel Hill, dropped it in the bag. Then she closed it and locked it; he would have assisted her, but she again waved him away. "Send for the expressman, and keep yourself out of the way for a moment," she said curtly.

An attitude of weak admiration and foolish passion had taken the place of his former tremulous fear. He obeyed excitedly, but without a word. Mrs. Baker wiped her moist forehead and parched lips, and shook out her skirt. Well might the young expressman start at the unexpected revelation of those sparkling eyes and that demurely smiling mouth at the little window.

"Mrs. Baker!"

She put her finger quickly to her lips, and threw a word of unutterable and enigmatical meaning into her mischievous face.

"There's a big San Francisco swell takin' my place at Laurel to-night, Charley."

"Yes, ma'am."

"And it's a pity that the Omnibus Way Bag happened to get such a shaking up and banging round already, coming here."

"Eh?"

"I say," continued Mrs. Baker, with great gravity and dancing eyes, "that it would be just *awful* if that keerful city clerk found things kinder mixed up inside when he comes to open it. I wouldn't give him trouble for the world, Charley."

"No, ma'am, it ain't like you."

"So you'll be particularly careful on *my* account."

"Mrs. Baker," said Charley, with infinite gravity, "if that bag *should tumble off a dozen times* between this and Laurel Hill, I'd hop down and pick it up myself."

"Thank you! shake!"

They shook hands gravely across the window-ledge.

"And you ain't going down with us, Mrs. Baker?"

"Of course not; it wouldn't do,—for *I ain't here*,—don't you see?"

"Of course!"

She handed him the bag through the door. He took it carefully, but in spite of his great precaution fell over it twice on his way to the road, where from certain exclamations and shouts it seemed that a like miserable mischance attended its elevation to the boot. Then Mrs. Baker came back into the office, and, as the wheels rolled away, threw herself into a chair, and inconsistently gave way for the first time to an outburst of tears. Then her hand was grasped suddenly and she found Green on his knees before her. She started to her feet.

"Don't move," he said, with weak hysteric passion, "but listen to me, for God's sake! I am ruined, I know, even though you have just saved me from detection and disgrace. I have been mad!—a fool, to do what I have done, I know, but you do not know all—you do not know why I did it— you cannot think of the temptation that has driven me to it. Listen, Mrs. Baker. I have been striving to get money, honestly, dishonestly—any way, to look well in *your* eyes—to make myself worthy of you—to make myself rich, and to be able to offer you a home and take you away from Laurel Run. It was all for *you*, it was all for love of *you*, Betsy, my darling. Listen to me!"

In the fury, outraged sensibility, indignation, and infinite disgust that filled her little body at that moment, she should have been large, imperious, goddess-like, and commanding. But God is at times ironical with suffering womanhood. She could only writhe her hand from his grasp with childish contortions; she could only glare at him with eyes that were prettily and piquantly brilliant; she could only slap at his detaining hand with a plump and velvety palm, and when she found her voice it was high falsetto. And all she could say was, "Leave me be, looney, or I'll scream!"

He rose, with a weak, confused laugh, half of miserable affectation and half of real anger and shame.

"What did you come riding over here for, then? What did you take all this risk for? Why did you rush over here to share my disgrace—for *you* are as much mixed up with this now as *I* am—if you didn't calculate to share *everything else* with me? What did you come here for, then, if not for *me*?"

"What did *I* come here for?" said Mrs. Baker, with every drop of red blood gone from her cheek and trembling lip. "What—did—I—come here for? Well!—I came here for *John Baker's* sake! John Baker, who stood between you and death at Burnt Ridge, as I stand between you and damnation at Laurel Run, Mr. Green! Yes, John Baker, lying under half of Burnt Ridge, but more to me this day than any living man crawling over it—in—in"— oh, fatal climax—"in a month o' Sundays! What did I come here for? I came here as John Baker's livin' wife to carry on dead John Baker's work. Yes, dirty work this time, may be, Mr. Green! but his work and for *him* only— precious! That's what I came here for; that's what I *live* for; that's what I'm waiting for—to be up to *him* and his work always! That's me—Betsy Baker!"

She walked up and down rapidly, tying her chip hat under her chin again. Then she stopped, and taking her chamois purse from her pocket, laid it sharply on the desk.

"Stanton Green, don't be a fool! Rise up out of this, and be a man again.

Take enough out o' that bag to pay what you owe Gov'ment, send in your resignation, and keep the rest to start you in an honest life elsewhere. But light out o' Hickory Hill afore this time to-morrow."

She pulled her mantle from the wall and opened the door.

"You are going?" he said bitterly.

"Yes." Either she could not hold seriousness long in her capricious little fancy, or, with feminine tact, she sought to make the parting less difficult for him, for she broke into a dazzling smile. "Yes, I'm goin' to run Blue Lightning agin Charley and that way bag back to Laurel Run, and break the record."

It is said that she did! Perhaps owing to the fact that the grade of the return journey to Laurel Run was in her favour, and that she could avoid the long, circuitous ascent to the summit taken by the stage, or that, owing to the extraordinary difficulties in the carriage of the way bag,—which had to be twice rescued from under the wheels of the stage,—she entered the Laurel Run post-office as the coach leaders came trotting up the hill. Mr. Home was already on the platform.

"You'll have to ballast your next way bag, boss," said Charley, gravely, as it escaped his clutches once more in the dust of the road, "or you'll have to make a new contract with the company. We've lost ten minutes in five miles over that bucking thing."

Home did not reply, but quickly dragged his prize into the office, scarcely noticing Mrs. Baker, who stood beside him pale and breathless. As the bolt of the bag was drawn, revealing its chaotic interior, Mrs. Baker gave a little sigh. Home glanced quickly at her, emptied the bag upon the floor, and picked up the broken and half-filled money parcel. Then he collected the scattered coins and counted them. "It's all right, Mrs. Baker," he said gravely. "*He's* safe this time."

"I'm so glad!" said little Mrs. Baker, with a hypocritical gasp.

"So am I," returned Home, with increasing gravity, as he took the coin, "for, from all I have gathered this afternoon, it seems he was an old pioneer of Laurel Run, a friend of your husband's, and, I think, more fool than knave!" He was silent for a moment, clicking the coins against each other; then he said carelessly: "Did he get quite away, Mrs. Baker?"

"I'm sure I don't know what you're talking about," said Mrs. Baker, with a lofty air of dignity, but a somewhat debasing colour. "I don't see why *I* should know anything about it, or why he should go away at all."

"Well," said Mr. Home, laying his hand gently on the widow's shoulder, "well, you see, it might have occurred to his friends that the *coins were marked!* That is, no doubt, the reason why he would take their good advice and go. But, as I said before, Mrs. Baker, *you're* all right, whatever happens—the Government stands by *you!*"

William Carlos Williams (1883–1963)

THE USE OF FORCE

They were new patients to me, all I had was the name, Olson. Please come down as soon as you can, my daughter is very sick.

When I arrived I was met by the mother, a big startled looking woman, very clean and apologetic who merely said, Is this the doctor? and let me in. In the back, she added. You must excuse us, doctor, we have her in the kitchen where it is warm. It is very damp here sometimes.

The child was fully dressed and sitting on her father's lap near the kitchen table. He tried to get up, but I motioned for him not to bother, took off my overcoat and started to look things over. I could see that they were all very nervous, eyeing me up and down distrustfully. As often, in such cases, they weren't telling me more than they had to, it was up to me to tell them; that's why they were spending three dollars on me.

The child was fairly eating me up with her cold, steady eyes, and no expression to her face whatever. She did not move and seemed, inwardly, quiet; an unusually attractive little thing, and as strong as a heifer in appearance. But her face was flushed, she was breathing rapidly, and I realized that she had a high fever. She had magnificent blonde hair, in profusion. One of those picture children often reproduced in advertising leaflets and the photogravure[1] sections of the Sunday papers.

She's had a fever for three days, began the father and we don't know what it comes from. My wife has given her things, you know, like people do, but it don't do no good. And there's been a lot of sickness around. So we tho't you'd better look her over and tell us what is the matter.

As doctors often do I took a trial shot at it as a point of departure. Has she had a sore throat?

Both parents answered me together. No . . . No, she says her throat don't hurt her.

Does your throat hurt you? added the mother to the child. But the little girl's expression didn't change nor did she move her eyes from my face.

Have you looked?

I tried to, said the mother, but I couldn't see.

As it happens we had been having a number of cases of diphtheria[2] in the school to which this child went during that month and we were all, quite apparently, thinking of that, though no one had as yet spoken of the thing.

Well, I said, suppose we take a look at the throat first. I smiled in my best

[1] photogravure: illustrated "magazine" section of a newspaper.
[2] diphtheria: serious, highly contagious disease, a major symptom of which is an inflamed throat.

professional manner and asking for the child's first name I said, come on, Mathilda, open your mouth and let's take a look at your throat.

Nothing doing.

Aw, come on, I coaxed, just open your mouth wide and let me take a look. Look, I said opening both hands wide. I haven't anything in my hands. Just open up and let me see.

Such a nice man, put in the mother. Look how kind he is to you. Come on, do what he tells you to. He won't hurt you.

At that I ground my teeth in disgust. If only they wouldn't use the word "hurt" I might be able to get somewhere. But I did not allow myself to be hurried or disturbed but speaking quietly and slowly I approached the child again.

As I moved my chair a little nearer suddenly with one cat-like movement both her hands clawed instinctively for my eyes and she almost reached them too. In fact she knocked my glasses flying and they fell, though unbroken, several feet away from me on the kitchen floor.

Both the mother and father almost turned themselves inside out in embarrassment and apology. You bad girl, said the mother, taking her and shaking her by one arm. Look what you've done. The nice man . . .

For heaven's sake, I broke in. Don't call me a nice man to her. I'm here to look at her throat on the chance that she might have diphtheria and possibly die of it. But that's nothing to her. Look here, I said to the child, we're going to look at your throat. You're old enough to understand what I'm saying. Will you open it now by yourself or shall we have to open it for you?

Not a move. Even her expression hadn't changed. Her breaths however were coming faster and faster. Then the battle began. I had to do it. I had to have a throat culture for her own protection. But first I told the parents that it was entirely up to them. I explained the danger but said that I would not insist on a throat examination so long as they would take the responsibility.

If you don't do what the doctor says you'll have to go to the hospital, the mother admonished her severely.

Oh yeah? I had to smile to myself. After all, I had already fallen in love with the savage brat, the parents were contemptible to me. In the ensuing struggle they grew more and more abject, crushed, exhausted while she surely rose to magnificent heights of insane fury of effort bred of her terror of me.

The father tried his best, and he was a big man but the fact that she was his daughter, his shame at her behavior and his dread of hurting her made him release her just at the critical moment several times when I had almost achieved success, till I wanted to kill him. But his dread also that she might have diphtheria made him tell me to go on, go on though he himself was almost fainting, while the mother moved back and forth behind us raising and lowering her hands in an agony of apprehension.

Put her in front of you on your lap, I ordered, and hold both her wrists.

But as soon as he did the child let out a scream. Don't, you're hurting me. Let go of my hands. Let them go I tell you. Then she shrieked terrifyingly, hysterically. Stop it! Stop it! You're killing me!

Do you think she can stand it, doctor! said the mother.

You get out, said the husband to his wife. Do you want her to die of diphtheria?

Come on now, hold her, I said.

Then I grasped the child's head with my left hand and tried to get the wooden tongue depressor between her teeth. She fought, with clenched teeth, desperately! But now I also had grown furious—at a child. I tried to hold myself down but I couldn't. I know how to expose a throat for inspection. And I did my best. When finally I got the wooden spatula behind the last teeth and just the point of it into the mouth cavity, she opened up for an instant but before I could see anything she came down again and gripping the wooden blade between her molars she reduced it to splinters before I could get it out again.

Aren't you ashamed, the mother yelled at her. Aren't you ashamed to act like that in front of the doctor?

Get me a smooth-handled spoon of some sort, I told the mother. We're going through with this. The child's mouth was already bleeding. Her tongue was cut and she was screaming in wild hysterical shrieks. Perhaps I should have desisted and come back in an hour or more. No doubt it would have been better. But I have seen at least two children lying dead in bed of neglect in such cases, and feeling that I must get a diagnosis now or never I went at it again. But the worst of it was that I too had got beyond reason. I could have torn the child apart in my own fury and enjoyed it. It was a pleasure to attack her. My face was burning with it.

The damned little brat must be protected against her own idiocy, one says to one's self at such times. Others must be protected against her. It is social necessity. And all these things are true. But a blind fury, a feeling of adult shame, bred of a longing for muscular release are the operatives. One goes on to the end.

In a final unreasoning assault I overpowered the child's neck and jaws. I forced the heavy silver spoon back of her teeth and down her throat till she gagged. And there it was—both tonsils covered with membrane. She had fought valiantly to keep me from knowing her secret. She had been hiding that sore throat for three days at least and lying to her parents in order to escape just such an outcome as this.

Now truly she *was* furious. She had been on the defensive before but now she attacked. Tried to get off her father's lap and fly at me while tears of defeat blinded her eyes.

Peter DeVries (1910–   )

PIZZICATO[1] ON THE HEARTSTRINGS

Old Creighton's heavy tread on the staircase was long in making itself heard and Tom waited, very much ill at ease, while the monstrous clock in the corner aged away with a magnificent monotony, infallibly going on and on in a long metallic drip of seconds, seconds into minutes. The clock's manner of thus so precisely granulating time was but part of a general and somewhat appalling precision that the whole room had, the furniture of which— Empire[2] in every stick, sir—was chosen and ordered with a fixity and perfection that made the room more characteristic of the "period," it was to be feared, than the period itself. In this room, while the clock dripped moments, Tom sat nervously waiting for Creighton, the important lie shaped, carved, smoothed and ready on his lips.

Tom wondered how Creighton would be, speculated apprehensively on what his son's death had done to him. There were disturbing questions: Had he gone through Warren's personal effects yet? If he hadn't yet, he certainly would soon. Such an inordinate love, such an unreasonable doting affection as he had had for his son would certainly send him through books and papers, maybe letters, looking for some new morsel to devour. How much had Warren actually left behind which might crush old Creighton with disillusionment? Where was the diary when he died? Had he left it where it might easily be found? Had Creighton perhaps found the thing and, in his eagerness to read it, stumbled right into all the dynamite that it certainly must contain? Tom should surely get his hands on it tonight. "Mr. Creighton, before he died Warren gave me his diary." That was the important lie. Then he would somehow ask to take it home with him right away. It wasn't that Warren's life was a sham, not that at all. But such things as were in it would naturally shock a father such as Warren had.

The clock ticked away for a long time and still no Creighton. Now and then Tom heard faint sounds upstairs, muffled footsteps, and each time he heard them his heart would vault to his throat. He dreaded seeing Creighton.

He remembered the first time he'd met him. A grand shaggy fellow of sixty-eight with a graceful limp and a heavy facile stride, craggy features, a luxuriant bush of gray hair and an amiable roar, he had come plowing into the drawing room drowning down everybody with his bluff and resonant greetings. Creighton was respected and liked, the apotheosis[3] of manners, liked less because he was imposing and clever than because, despite being both of these, he was perfectly typical, representative, obvious; he had none of that excess of subtlety which always erects the barrier of jeal-

[1] pizzicato: music played by plucking instead of bowing a stringed instrument.
[2] Empire: early nineteenth-century French style of furniture.
[3] apotheosis: pinnacle or summit of perfection.

ousy between itself and consummate popularity. He was easily typed, described by a phrase. He was, surely, the uncle in English plays, terrifying the nephew's bright and much-heralded week-end visitor with his disarming and booming affability.[4] And when the party knotted into conversation groups he could be heard throwing out his line every time, "And I say it *is* important, young fellow; anything other than two studs[5] is aesthetically off." That sort of thing.

As he sat there waiting, Tom remembered how Creighton had made him shrink, how he had embarrassed him in all that crowd of people. It was right next to that chair there that he had been standing when Creighton, shaggy and incredible, had come limping down toward him, fast and smooth. Warren came over when he saw the two together, knowing perhaps that Tom would need help. Somehow they had gotten to talking about poetry and what he, Tom, liked. It was Creighton's favorite way of putting Warren's young friends on the spot. He candled [6] them that way, he said.

"Oh!" he boomed. "Swinburne,[7] eh? So! So you think Swinburne's quite the thing! Oho! You're still in that stage yet, eh? Lilies and languors and roses and raptures, eh?" he laughed, turning to the others in the room. "Oho! What do you think of my pagan here! Swinburne and the crimson things! That's what he likes. Better stick to Masefield and Wordsworth,[8] young fellow. Worst you'll get there is windburn and sunburn. But look out for Swinburne! Oho, look out for Swinburne! That's fatal. Oho!" And slapping Tom on the shoulder he had limped unconquerably off, getting out of earshot before Tom could even think of framing an answer, a technique by which he had thus far kept himself unfelled by anybody's repartee. It was his manner to retreat from his victories.

And later that evening he and Warren found themselves entangled with him again on the subject of "this generation," a subject on which he felt very loudly. "No, no, no, no!" he would roar. "We had the better generation! Not a lot of cynics and now-I-lay-me futilitarians.[9] Oho! No, sir! We were slow, but we were going some place. No, no, no, don't talk to me about this age of Picasso,[10] neurosis and Scriabin." [11] And he plowed his way out of the crowd into another.

---

[4] affability: friendliness.

[5] studs: ornamental fasteners for a dress shirt.

[6] candled: to check eggs by holding them up to a candle; hence, to check out a person's inner self.

[7] Swinburne: Algernon Charles Swinburne (1837–1909), English poet, considered shocking by the Victorians.

[8] Masefield and Wordsworth: John Masefield (1878–1967) and William Wordsworth (1770–1850), English poets whose romanticism would appeal to conservatives.

[9] futilitarians: persons who believe in the futility (uselessness) of human efforts and dreams.

[10] Picasso: Pablo Picasso (1881–1973), modern painter.

[11] Scriabin: Alexander Scriabin (1872–1915), Russian composer who used unusual musical sounds and harmonies to express a mystical and symbolic view of life.

How would the roaring old Creighton be tonight? At the funeral he was stony, still, shaggily and nobly alone, bowing his great gray head against everything, seemingly untouched by everything—the barely breathing organ, the preacher's tremolo[12] and shamefully rhetorical grieving, the sobbing of the vox humana,[13] the women weeping a storm about him and he unshaken like a rock. You didn't know how he felt. Of course he loved Warren, there was no mistake about that; but seeing it was his son's funeral he certainly should have shown *something*, some grief, some sign, especially with everybody else feeling so bad and the sympathetic women with their tears on tap, and him showing less than they—

Oh, but he did love Warren and this was a blow to him. Just think of how he had always bragged about Warren, what a model son he always said he was, how he told of Warren's devotion to his father and how he used to love his mother before she died. "Why, Warren couldn't hurt us. He simply couldn't. He's never mistreated us or hurt us or in any way wounded our emotions. No, sir, not Warren. Always gentle. Always! Never any pizzicato on our heartstrings. Oho!" And he laughed, putting his arm on the embarrassed Warren's shoulder. Like the time—

Tom's recollections were interrupted by very distinct footsteps. Yes, that was his walk. Slow now, but that limp gave it away. The noise moved to the head of the stairs, then came down slowly and muffled. And at last old Creighton appeared. He turned his leonine head and saw Tom. Tom rose even before he got into the drawing room.

"Good evening, Mr. Creighton," said Tom, conscious that he was pulling out his face to make it look appropriately solemn.

"Hello, Tom," said Creighton. His voice, modified now and shorn of at least three-quarters of its volume, was beautiful and low and grave as a cello. The overpowering stride was moderated to a slow but even limp. He was dressed in a great black suit.

"I don't know how you feel, Mr. Creighton, and whether you want visitors or not," Tom apologized.

"Oh. That's all right, Tom. Glad you called. The place is—enormously bleak now." A wistful smile curled out of one side of old Creighton's mouth.

"Yes, I guess it is," said Tom, conscious that his features were working faithfully to concoct an expression of compassion. He sighed with an infinite, sad finality and said, "Warren was a marvelous chap, Mr. Creighton. Warren was a marvelous chap."

Creighton, staring down to the rug, nodded slowly. "A great lad," he whispered. "You've lost a fine friend and I a splendid son." He held his head down and Tom, studying the gray mane and the rugged face with its jutting slab of a nose, knew that he hadn't read the diary.

Tom shifted and got ready to say it. "Mr. Creighton," he began. "Before he died, Warren gave me his diary."

[12] tremolo: a quavering tone of voice.
[13] vox humana: an organ stop imitating the human voice, usually with a tremolo.

The old head looked up slowly, the blue eyes pricked with curiosity. "Diary?" he said slowly. "Well! I didn't know Warren had been keeping a diary."

Perhaps my coming here was indiscreet, thought Tom when he heard that. Now maybe this will send him right after it. He summoned his most casual manner, "Yes, he's made a few jottings from time to time. Probably isn't complete at all. But I'd like it as a memento. You can imagine."

"Well!" Creighton had brightened. "Do you know where it is?"

"Well . . . no. I suppose it's in his room somewhere. But I'd be able to find it in a jiffy. I'd know just about where he'd keep it."

Creighton was silent again, looking down, this time reflectively. He looked up at last and said, "That's interesting, Tom. I'd like to read it."

Now, under the peril of the moment, Tom felt an exasperation with old Creighton for that blind and bland admiration, that assumptive, senseless parental pride. What should he say to this? He couldn't come right out and say no, it was his diary now and nobody else was going to look at it. It was a ticklish moment. He would have to be tactful, decent. He did finally manage to say the right thing—which in a moment like this would be the wrong thing. "Well . . . of course, whatever you say, Mr. Creighton. But a diary, you know, is—a pretty private thing—and maybe you'd think you were, well, treading on. . . ." He let the sentence dribble off.

Creighton smiled again. "There'd be nothing like that, of course," he said confidently. "Warren never kept anything secret from me, you know. Always frank and free with each other. Nooo . . . That would be all right."

Tom said nothing for a time. Neither did Creighton. He just sat still in the great chair, not only old but ancient, like his Empire furniture a charming anachronism, not at all of the present but evocative of a perished time, possessing, to Tom, precisely that air all his period furniture had of something able to live immortally unmolested now its day was up.

He turned to Tom and said, "If you think you have an idea of where it might be, let's go up and try to find it."

"Yes," Tom answered.

Following Creighton as he limped powerfully up the curving stairway, Tom decided there was but one thing for him to do: manage to get his hands on the diary and slip it into his pocket while the old fellow wasn't looking. Creighton went straight to the door of Warren's room, stood there a moment with his hand on the knob, turned it and swung the door lightly open.

It was a large beautifully furnished room, the walls stacked high with books. There was the little cabinet with its few precious books that Warren loved best of all. There was the cellaret always filled with richly tinkling bottles of choice liquor. There was the lounge where Tom would lay listening while Warren droned his verses, as he used to delight in doing.

"Well?" said Creighton. "Where would you look for it? I hate to think of pawing in such a raw way through all his things." His voice was low, dimmed with melancholy, and, Tom thought, a little careful. Oh, Creighton did feel deeply, really. Of course he did.

"Well, it might be in that drawer there," said Tom, believing it wouldn't, but stalling.

"Well, let's look then."

The two of them opened the drawer on Warren's desk and went through it. Nothing much in it—paper and a few pencils and an insignificant letter or two. "Nothing here," said Tom. "Suppose we try that cabinet." His heart hammering fearfully he went through the first two drawers, while Creighton looked on. The fellow irritated Tom standing there that way. Why didn't he go away and search somewhere himself? "Maybe you could look in the next room in his—" Tom began and then they both saw it. A square red book with a maroon leather cover and the word Diary stamped on it in gold letters.

"There it is," said Creighton quietly. He reached down and took it out.

Tom was furious with himself for having bungled it so. He should have asked to be let up by one of the servants when Creighton was out, or asked to be allowed to get a book of Warren's that he wanted and get it that way. Now he had messed it up.

"This is your diary, Tom," Creighton was saying as he ran the pages with his thumb with a light whirring sound, "but I'd just like to read it through once or twice. If you don't mind. Then you can come and get it say in about two days."

"Yes—all right," said Tom numbly. There was simply nothing else he could say.

Tom left that night feeling sick and miserable. He muttered curses at himself, quite audibly, as he walked down the long flagstone path toward the road. In the distance auto gears ground, a car turned a corner, headlights stroked a field and threw brief light on dying grass, then the noise faded and Tom thought of old Creighton and how he looked sitting down to read the diary.

Even before Tom reached the turn by the elm clump Creighton had settled himself in a chair to read the diary. How wonderful, how sweetly and sadly wonderful this would be. This diary, what an unexpectedly granted feast to a hungry heart. Slowly he opened the book, turning the covers like a man lifting the lid on a chest of treasures. . . .

Tom was afraid to return, dreading what the meeting would surely bring. He hesitated, he postponed. Finally, convincing himself that anything was better than this uncertainty, this waiting, he decided on the fourth evening after he had visited Creighton to go down immediately. He rang and the butler answered the door. "He isn't in, Tom, I believe he's sitting out in the garden. You might go back there."

He went around to the garden and when he opened the gate he saw

Creighton's great figure move bent and limping up the path. He hesitated a moment, then called. "Oh, hello, Mr. Creighton." Creighton turned hugely and watched Tom come toward him. He said nothing. When Tom came near he saw that Creighton's face was clouded and forbidding. Tom went sick inside, but he managed to say with some casualness, "Did you finish reading the diary, Mr. Creighton?"

Creighton looked at Tom for a moment, the great head like that of some magnificent and menacing animal. "Yes, I did." His voice was low, seemed broken.

"I suppose I may have it now?"

"The diary I have appropriately converted into ashes," said Creighton in a restrained rumble like distant thunder.

"Why—what—what do you mean?" said Tom, aware that he was not managing to get any surprise whatever into his voice.

Creighton went on, "The diary being what a diary is supposed to be, a record of a person's life, it will be easy for you to realize how I have been hurt. Shocked, horrified. Disillusioned," he added closing his eyelids wearily.

"Mr. Creighton, if you parents would only—"

"Hold your tongue!" said Creighton, his rumble none the less menacing because it was reduced to a whisper. "I'm disappointed enough, but I think if Warren had avoided your rotten influence—"

"Just what do you mean by that?"

"Just what I said. I don't doubt you wanted to get the diary out of the house, with what it might reveal about yourself."

"Mr. Creighton—"

"You get out! Go on, get out!"

"Just a minute. Not so fast—"

"Get out!"

Tom turned and walked out, feeling limp and wretched, without another word.

Creighton walked, trembling a little, to a bench by the rose arbor and settled himself on it slowly and wearily. He sighed out of his heart grown suddenly gray, folded his hands upon his knee, and looked about him. Against the wall was a cluster of hollyhock stalks, skinny and broken and ragged like mangled scarecrows. A new cold wind set to rustling the leaves above him. It was October and the garden was crisp and withered and full of whispers. And there were stars and stars, trembling—till the heaven was like a brimming bowl of jewels in an old man's hand. It was too cold out here; in just a minute he would go inside and sit down in a great chair and be like an old lady next to the fire, in whose hands the warm soft skein of yarn has, all of a sudden, become cruelly tangled. In just a minute he did go in. He limped over the path and up the stairs, and closed the door quietly behind him.

Philip Roth (1933–   )

THE CONVERSION OF THE JEWS

"You're a real one for opening your mouth in the first place," Itzie said. "What do you open your mouth all the time for?"

"I didn't bring it up, Itz, I didn't," Ozzie said.

"What do you care about Jesus Christ for anyway?"

"I didn't bring up Jesus Christ. He did. I didn't even know what he was talking about. Jesus is historical, he kept saying. Jesus is historical." Ozzie mimicked the monumental voice of Rabbi Binder.

"Jesus was a person that lived like you and me," Ozzie continued. "That's what Binder said—"

"Yeah? . . . So what! What do I give two cents whether he lived or not. And what do you gotta open your mouth!" Itzie Lieberman favored closed-mouthedness, especially when it came to Ozzie Freedman's questions. Mrs. Freedman had to see Rabbi Binder twice before about Ozzie's questions and this Wednesday at four-thirty would be the third time. Itzie preferred to keep *his* mother in the kitchen; he settled for behind-the-back subtleties such as gestures, faces, snarls and other less delicate barnyard noises.

"He was a real person, Jesus, but he wasn't like God, and we don't believe he is God." Slowly, Ozzie was explaining Rabbi Binder's position to Itzie, who had been absent from Hebrew School the previous afternoon.

"The Catholics," Itzie said helpfully, "they believe in Jesus Christ, that he's God." Itzie Lieberman used "the Catholics" in its broadest sense—to include the Protestants.

Ozzie received Itzie's remark with a tiny head bob, as though it were a footnote, and went on. "His mother was Mary, and his father probably was Joseph," Ozzie said. "But the New Testament says his real father was God."

"His *real* father?"

"Yeah," Ozzie said, "that's the big thing, his father's supposed to be God."

"Bull."

"That's what Rabbi Binder says, that it's impossible—"

"Sure it's impossible. That stuff's all bull. To have a baby you gotta get laid," Itzie theologized. "Mary hadda get laid."

"That's what Binder says: 'The only way a woman can have a baby is to have intercourse with a man.' "

"He said *that,* Ozz?" For a moment it appeared that Itzie had put the theological question aside. "He said that, intercourse?" A little curled smile shaped itself in the lower half of Itzie's face like a pink mustache. "What you guys do, Ozz, you laugh or something?"

"I raised my hand."

"Yeah? Whatja say?"

"That's when I asked the question."

Itzie's face lit up. "Whatja ask about—intercourse?"

"No, I asked the question about God, how if He could create the heaven and earth in six days, and make all the animals and the fish and the light in six days—the light especially, that's what always gets me, that He could make the light. Making fish and animals, that's pretty good—"

"That's damn good." Itzie's appreciation was honest but unimaginative: it was as though God had just pitched a one-hitter.

"But making light . . . I mean when you think about it, it's really something," Ozzie said. "Anyway, I asked Binder if He could make all that in six days, and He could *pick* the six days He wanted right out of nowhere, why couldn't He let a woman have a baby without having intercourse."

"You said intercourse, Ozz, to Binder?"

"Yeah."

"Right in class?"

"Yeah."

Itzie smacked the side of his head.

"I mean, no kidding around," Ozzie said, "that'd really be nothing. After all that other stuff that'd practically be nothing."

Itzie considered a moment. "What'd Binder say?"

"He started all over again explaining how Jesus was historical and how he lived like you and me but he wasn't God. So I said I under*stood* that. What I wanted to know was different."

What Ozzie wanted to know was always different. The first time he had wanted to know how Rabbi Binder could call the Jews "The Chosen People" if the Declaration of Independence claimed all men to be created equal. Rabbi Binder tried to distinguish for him between political equality and spiritual legitimacy, but what Ozzie wanted to know, he insisted vehemently, was different. That was the first time his mother had to come.

Then there was the plane crash. Fifty-eight people had been killed in a plane crash at La Guardia. In studying a casualty list in the newspaper his mother had discovered among the list of those dead eight Jewish names (his grandmother had nine but she counted Miller as a Jewish name); because of the eight she said the plane crash was "a tragedy." During free-discussion time on Wednesday Ozzie had brought to Rabbi Binder's attention this matter of "some of his relations" always picking out the Jewish names. Rabbi Binder had begun to explain cultural unity and some other things when Ozzie stood up at his seat and said that what he wanted to know was different. Rabbi Binder insisted that he sit down and it was then that Ozzie shouted that he wished all fifty-eight were Jews. That was the second time his mother came.

"And he kept explaining about Jesus being historical, and so I kept asking him. No kidding, Itz, he was trying to make me look stupid."

339

PHILIP ROTH

"So what he finally do?"

"Finally he starts screaming that I was deliberately simple-minded and a wise guy, and that my mother had to come, and this was the last time. And that I'd never get bar-mitzvahed [1] if he could help it. Then, Itz, then he starts talking in that voice like a statue, real slow and deep, and he says that I better think over what I said about the Lord. He told me to go to his office and think it over." Ozzie leaned his body towards Itzie. "Itz, I thought it over for a solid hour, and now I'm convinced God could do it."

Ozzie had planned to confess his latest transgression to his mother as soon as she came home from work. But it was a Friday night in November and already dark, and when Mrs. Freedman came through the door she tossed off her coat, kissed Ozzie quickly on the face, and went to the kitchen table to light the three yellow candles, two for the Sabbath and one for Ozzie's father.

When his mother lit the candles she would move her two arms slowly towards her, dragging them through the air, as though persuading people whose minds were half made up. And her eyes would get glassy with tears. Even when his father was alive Ozzie remembered that her eyes had gotten glassy, so it didn't have anything to do with his dying. It had something to do with lighting the candles.

As she touched the flaming match to the unlit wick of a Sabbath candle, the phone rang, and Ozzie, standing only a foot from it, plucked it off the receiver and held it muffled to his chest. When his mother lit candles Ozzie felt there should be no noise; even breathing, if you could manage it, should be softened. Ozzie pressed the phone to his breast and watched his mother dragging whatever she was dragging, and he felt his own eyes get glassy. His mother was a round, tired, gray-haired penguin of a woman whose gray skin had begun to feel the tug of gravity and the weight of her own history. Even when she was dressed up she didn't look like a chosen person. But when she lit candles she looked like something better; like a woman who knew momentarily that God could do anything.

After a few mysterious minutes she was finished. Ozzie hung up the phone and walked to the kitchen table where she was beginning to lay the two places for the four-course Sabbath meal. He told her that she would have to see Rabbi Binder next Wednesday at four-thirty, and then he told her why. For the first time in their life together she hit Ozzie across the face with her hand.

All through the chopped liver and chicken soup part of the dinner Ozzie cried; he didn't have any appetite for the rest.

On Wednesday, in the largest of the three basement classrooms of the synagogue, Rabbi Marvin Binder, a tall, handsome, broad-shouldered man

[1] bar-mitzvahed: ceremony initiating Jewish thirteen-year-old boy into the community.

of thirty with thick strong-fibered black hair, removed his watch from his pocket and saw that it was four o'clock. At the rear of the room Yakov Blotnik, the seventy-one-year-old custodian, slowly polished the large window, mumbling to himself, unaware that it was four o'clock or six o'clock, Monday or Wednesday. To most of the students Yakov Blotnik's mumbling, along with his brown curly beard, scythe nose, and two heel-trailing black cats, made of him an object of wonder, a foreigner, a relic, towards whom they were alternately fearful and disrespectful. To Ozzie the mumbling had always seemed a monotonous, curious prayer; what made it curious was that old Blotnik had been mumbling so steadily for so many years, Ozzie suspected he had memorized the prayers and forgotten all about God.

"It is now free-discussion time," Rabbi Binder said. "Feel free to talk about any Jewish matter at all—religion, family, politics, sports—"

There was silence. It was a gusty, clouded November afternoon and it did not seem as though there ever was or would be a thing called baseball. So nobody this week said a word about that hero from the past, Hank Greenberg[2]—which limited free discussion considerably.

And the soul-battering Ozzie Freedman had just received from Rabbi Binder had imposed its limitation. When it was Ozzie's turn to read aloud from the Hebrew book the rabbi had asked him petulantly why he didn't read more rapidly. He was showing no progress. Ozzie said he could read faster but that if he did he was sure not to understand what he was reading. Nevertheless, at the rabbi's repeated suggestion Ozzie tried, and showed a great talent, but in the midst of a long passage he stopped short and said he didn't understand a word he was reading, and started in again at a drag-footed pace. Then came the soul-battering.

Consequently when free-discussion time rolled around none of the students felt too free. The rabbi's invitation was answered only by the mumbling of feeble old Blotnik.

"Isn't there anything at all you would like to discuss?" Rabbi Binder asked again, looking at his watch. "No questions or comments?"

There was a small grumble from the third row. The rabbi requested that Ozzie rise and give the rest of the class the advantage of his thought.

Ozzie rose. "I forget it now," he said, and sat down in his place.

Rabbi Binder advanced a seat towards Ozzie and poised himself on the edge of the desk. It was Itzie's desk and the rabbi's frame only a dagger's-length away from his face snapped him to sitting attention.

"Stand up again, Oscar," Rabbi Binder said calmly, "and try to assemble your thoughts."

Ozzie stood up. All his classmates turned in their seats and watched as he gave an unconvincing scratch to his forehead.

"I can't assemble any," he announced, and plunked himself down.

[2] Hank Greenberg: famous Jewish baseball player.

"Stand up!" Rabbi Binder advanced from Itzie's desk to the one directly in front of Ozzie; when the rabbinical back was turned Itzie gave it five-fingers off the tip of his nose, causing a small titter in the room. Rabbi Binder was too absorbed in squelching Ozzie's nonsense once and for all to bother with titters. "Stand up, Oscar. What's your question about?"

Ozzie pulled a word out of the air. It was the handiest word. "Religion."

"Oh, now you remember?"

"Yes."

"What is it?"

Trapped, Ozzie blurted the first thing that came to him. "Why can't He make anything He wants to make!"

As Rabbi Binder prepared an answer, a final answer, Itzie, ten feet behind him, raised one finger on his left hand, gestured it meaningfully towards the rabbi's back, and brought the house down.

Binder twisted quickly to see what had happened and in the midst of the commotion Ozzie shouted into the rabbi's back what he couldn't have shouted to his face. It was a loud, toneless sound that had the timbre of something stored inside for about six days.

"You don't know! You don't know anything about God!"

The rabbi spun back towards Ozzie. "What?"

"You don't know—you don't—"

"Apologize, Oscar, apologize!" It was a threat.

"You don't—"

Rabbi Binder's hand flicked out at Ozzie's cheek. Perhaps it had only been meant to clamp the boy's mouth shut, but Ozzie ducked and the palm caught him squarely on the nose.

The blood came in a short, red spurt on to Ozzie's shirt front.

The next moment was all confusion. Ozzie screamed, "You bastard, you bastard!" and broke for the classroom door. Rabbi Binder lurched a step backwards, as though his own blood had started flowing violently in the opposite direction, then gave a clumsy lurch forward and bolted out the door after Ozzie. The class followed after the rabbi's huge blue-suited back, and before old Blotnik could turn from his window, the room was empty and everyone was headed full speed up the three flights leading to the roof.

If one should compare the light of day to the life of man: sunrise to birth; sunset—the dropping down over the edge—to death; then as Ozzie Freedman wiggled through the trapdoor of the synagogue roof, his feet kicking backwards bronco-style at Rabbi Binder's outstretched arms—at that moment the day was fifty years old. As a rule, fifty or fifty-five reflects accurately the age of late afternoons in November, for it is in that month, during those hours, that one's awareness of light seems no longer a matter of see-ing, but of hearing: light begins clicking away. In fact, as Ozzie locked shut the trapdoor in the rabbi's face, the sharp click of the bolt into the lock might momentarily have been mistaken for the sound of the heavier gray that had just throbbed through the sky.

With all his weight Ozzie kneeled on the locked door; any instant he was certain that Rabbi Binder's shoulder would fling it open, splintering the wood into shrapnel and catapulting his body into the sky. But the door did not move and below him he heard only the rumble of feet, first loud then dim, like thunder rolling away.

A question shot through his brain. "Can this be *me?*" For a thirteen-year-old who had just labeled his religious leader a bastard, twice, it was not an improper question. Louder and louder the question came to him—"Is it me? Is it me?"—until he discovered himself no longer kneeling, but racing crazily towards the edge of the roof, his eyes crying, his throat screaming, and his arms flying everywhichway as though not his own.

"Is it me? Is it me ME ME ME ME! It has to be me—but is it!"

It is the question a thief must ask himself the night he jimmies open his first window, and it is said to be the question with which bridegrooms quiz themselves before the altar.

In the few wild seconds it took Ozzie's body to propel him to the edge of the roof, his self-examination began to grow fuzzy. Gazing down at the street, he became confused as to the problem beneath the question: was it, is-it-me-who-called-Binder-a-bastard? or, is-it-me-prancing-around-on-the-roof? However, the scene below settled all, for there is an instant in any action when whether it is you or somebody else is academic. The thief crams the money in his pockets and scoots out the window. The bridegroom signs the hotel register for two. And the boy on the roof finds a streetful of people gaping at him, necks stretched backwards, faces up, as though he were the ceiling of the Hayden Planetarium.[3] Suddenly you know it's you.

"Oscar! Oscar Freedman!" A voice rose from the center of the crowd, a voice that, could it have been seen, would have looked like the writing on scroll. "Oscar Freedman, get down from there. Immediately!" Rabbi Binder was pointing one arm stiffly up at him; and at the end of that arm, one finger aimed menacingly. It was the attitude of a dictator, but one—the eyes confessed all—whose personal valet had spit neatly in his face.

Ozzie didn't answer. Only for a blink's length did he look towards Rabbi Binder. Instead his eyes began to fit together the world beneath him, to sort out people from places, friends from enemies, participants from spectators. In little jagged starlike clusters his friends stood around Rabbi Binder, who was still pointing. The topmost point on a star compounded not of angels but of five adolescent boys was Itzie. What a world it was, with those stars below, Rabbi Binder below . . . Ozzie, who a moment earlier hadn't been

---

[3] Hayden Planetarium: a building in New York City in which the movements of the stars, planets, etc. are represented by projection on the ceiling; a sort of planetary or astronomical museum.

able to control his own body, started to feel the meaning of the word control: he felt Peace and he felt Power.

"Oscar Freedman, I'll give you three to come down."

Few dictators give their subjects three to do anything; but, as always, Rabbi Binder only looked dictatorial.

"Are you ready, Oscar?"

Ozzie nodded his head yes, although he had no intention in the world— the lower one or the celestial one he'd just entered—of coming down even if Rabbi Binder should give him a million.

"All right then," said Rabbi Binder. He ran a hand through his black Samson[4] hair as though it were the gesture prescribed for uttering the first digit. Then, with his other hand cutting a circle out of the small piece of sky around him, he spoke. "One!"

There was no thunder. On the contrary, at that moment, as though "one" was the cue for which he had been waiting, the world's least thunderous person appeared on the synagogue steps. He did not so much come out the synagogue door as lean out, onto the darkening air. He clutched at the doorknob with one hand and looked up at the roof.

"Oy!"

Yakov Blotnik's old mind hobbled slowly, as if on crutches, and though he couldn't decide precisely what the boy was doing on the roof, he knew it wasn't good—that is, it wasn't-good-for-the-Jews. For Yakov Blotnik life had fractionated itself simply: things were either good-for-the-Jews or no-good-for-the-Jews.

He smacked his free hand to his in-sucked cheek, gently. "Oy, Gut" [5] And then quickly as he was able, he jacked down his head and surveyed the street. There was Rabbi Binder (like a man at an auction with only three dollars in his pocket, he had just delivered a shaky "Two!"); there were the students, and that was all. So far it-wasn't-so-bad-for-the-Jews. But the boy had to come down immediately, before anybody saw. The problem: how to get the boy off the roof?

Anybody who has ever had a cat on the roof knows how to get him down. You call the fire department. Or first you call the operator and you ask her for the fire department. And the next thing there is great jamming of brakes and clanging of bells and shouting of instructions. And then the cat is off the roof. You do the same thing to get a boy off the roof.

That is, you do the same thing if you are Yakov Blotnik and you once had a cat on the roof.

When the engines, all four of them, arrived, Rabbi Binder had four times given Ozzie the count of three. The big hook-and-ladder swung around the

[4] Samson: Hebrew hero whose great strength lay in his hair.
[5] "Oy, Gut!": "Oh, God!"

corner and one of the firemen leaped from it, plunging headlong towards the yellow fire hydrant in front of the synagogue. With a huge wrench he began to unscrew the top nozzle. Rabbi Binder raced over to him and pulled at his shoulder.

"There's no fire . . ."

The fireman mumbled back over his shoulder and, heatedly, continued working at the nozzle.

"But there's no fire, there's no fire . . ." Binder shouted. When the fireman mumbled again, the rabbi grasped his face with both his hands and pointed it up at the roof.

To Ozzie it looked as though Rabbi Binder was trying to tug the fireman's head out of his body, like a cork from a bottle. He had to giggle at the picture they made: it was a family portrait—rabbi in black skullcap,[6] fireman in red fire hat, and the little yellow hydrant squatting beside like a kid brother, bareheaded. From the edge of the roof Ozzie waved at the portrait, a one-handed, flapping, mocking wave; in doing it his right foot slipped from under him. Rabbi Binder covered his eyes with his hands.

Firemen work fast. Before Ozzie had even regained his balance, a big, round, yellowed net was being held on the synagogue lawn. The firemen who held it looked up at Ozzie with stern, feelingless faces.

One of the firemen turned his head towards Rabbi Binder. "What, is the kid nuts or something?"

Rabbi Binder unpeeled his hands from his eyes, slowly, painfully, as if they were tape. Then he checked: nothing on the sidewalk, no dents in the net.

"Is he gonna jump, or what?" the fireman shouted.

In a voice not at all like a statue, Rabbi Binder finally answered. "Yes, yes, I think so . . . He's been threatening to . . ."

Threatening to? Why, the reason he was on the roof, Ozzie remembered, was to get away; he hadn't even thought about jumping. He had just run to get away, and the truth was that he hadn't really headed for the roof as much as he'd been chased there.

"What's his name, the kid?"

"Freedman," Rabbi Binder answered. "Oscar Freedman."

The fireman looked up at Ozzie. "What is it with you, Oscar? You gonna jump, or what?"

Ozzie did not answer. Frankly, the question had just arisen.

"Look, Oscar, if you're gonna jump, jump—and if you're not gonna jump, don't jump. But don't waste our time, willya?"

Ozzie looked at the fireman and then at Rabbi Binder. He wanted to see Rabbi Binder cover his eyes one more time.

"I'm going to jump."

[6] black skullcap: ritual headcovering for Jewish males; yarmulke.

And then he scampered around the edge of the roof to the corner, where there was no net below, and he flapped his arms at his sides, swishing the air and smacking his palms to his trousers on the downbeat. He began screaming like some kind of engine, "Wheeeee . . . wheeeeee," and leaning way out over the edge with the upper half of his body. The firemen whipped around to cover the ground with the net. Rabbi Binder mumbled a few words to Somebody and covered his eyes. Everything happened quickly, jerkily, as in a silent movie. The crowd, which had arrived with the fire engines, gave out a long, Fourth-of-July fireworks oooh-aahhh. In the excitement no one had paid the crowd much heed, except, of course, Yakov Blotnik, who swung from the doorknob counting heads. "Fier und tsvansik . . . finf und tsvantsik[7] . . . Oy, Gut!" It wasn't like this with the cat.

Rabbi Binder peeked through his fingers, checked the sidewalk and net. Empty. But there was Ozzie racing to the other corner. The firemen raced with him but were unable to keep up. Whenever Ozzie wanted to he might jump and splatter himself upon the sidewalk, and by the time the firemen scooted to the spot all they could do with their net would be to cover the mess.

"Wheeeee . . . wheeeee . . ."

"Hey, Oscar," the winded fireman yelled, "What the hell is this, a game or something?"

"Wheeeee . . . wheeeee . . ."

"Hey, Oscar—"

But he was off now to the other corner, flapping his wings fiercely. Rabbi Binder couldn't take it any longer—the fire engines from nowhere, the screaming suicidal boy, the net. He fell to his knees, exhausted, and with his hands curled together in front of his chest like a little dome, he pleaded, "Oscar, stop it, Oscar. Don't jump, Oscar. Please come down . . . Please don't jump."

And further back in the crowd a single voice, a single young voice, shouted a lone word to the boy on the roof.

"Jump!"

It was Itzie. Ozzie momentarily stopped flapping.

"Go ahead, Ozz—jump!" Itzie broke off his point of the star and courageously, with the inspiration not of a wise-guy but of a disciple, stood alone. "Jump, Ozz, jump!"

Still on his knees, his hands still curled, Rabbi Binder twisted his body back. He looked at Itzie, then, agonizingly, back to Ozzie.

"Oscar, Don't jump! Please, Don't Jump . . . please please . . ."

"Jump!" This time it wasn't Itzie but another point of the star. By the time Mrs. Freedman arrived to keep her four-thirty appointment with Rabbi Binder, the whole little upside down heaven was shouting and pleading for

[7] Fier und tsvansik . . . : four and twenty; five and twenty.

Ozzie to jump, and Rabbi Binder no longer was pleading with him not to jump, but was crying into the dome of his hands.

Understandably Mrs. Freedman couldn't figure out what her son was doing on the roof. So she asked.

"Ozzie, my Ozzie, what are you doing? My Ozzie, what is it?"

Ozzie stopped wheeeeeing and slowed his arms down to a cruising flap, the kind birds use in soft winds, but he did not answer. He stood against the low, clouded, darkening sky—light clicked down swiftly now, as on a small gear—flapping softly and gazing down at the small bundle of a woman who was his mother.

"What are you doing, Ozzie?" She turned towards the kneeling Rabbi Binder and rushed so close that only a paper-thickness of dusk lay between her stomach and his shoulders.

"What is my baby doing?"

Rabbi Binder gaped at her but he too was mute. All that moved was the dome of his hands; it shook back and forth like a weak pulse.

"Rabbi, get him down! He'll kill himself. Get him down, my only baby . . ."

"I can't," Rabbi Binder said, "I can't . . ." and he turned his handsome head towards the crowd of boys behind him. "It's them. Listen to them."

And for the first time Mrs. Freedman saw the crowd of boys, and she heard what they were yelling.

"He's doing it for them. He won't listen to me. It's them." Rabbi Binder spoke like one in a trance.

"For them?"

"Yes."

"Why for them?"

"They want him to . . ."

Mrs. Freedman raised her two arms upward as though she were conducting the sky. "For them he's doing it!" And then in a gesture older than pyramids, older than prophets and floods, her arms came slapping down to her sides. "A martyr I have. Look!" She tilted her head to the roof. Ozzie was still flapping softly. "My martyr."

"Oscar, come down, *please*," Rabbi Binder groaned.

In a startlingly even voice Mrs. Freedman called to the boy on the roof. "Ozzie, come down, Ozzie. Don't be a martyr, my baby."

As though it were a litany, Rabbi Binder repeated her words. "Don't be a martyr, my baby. Don't be a martyr."

"Gawhead, Ozz—*be* a Martin!" It was Itzie. "Be a Martin, be a Martin," and all the voices joined in singing for Martindom, whatever *it* was. "Be a Martin, be a Martin . . ."

Somehow when you're on a roof the darker it gets the less you can hear. All Ozzie knew was that two groups wanted two new things: his friends were spirited and musical about what they wanted; his mother and the rabbi were even-toned, chanting, about what they didn't want. The rabbi's voice was without tears now and so was his mother's.

The big net stared up at Ozzie like a sightless eye. The big, cloudy sky pushed down. From beneath it looked like a gray corrugated board. Suddenly, looking up into that unsympathetic sky, Ozzie realized all the strangeness of what these people, his friends, were asking: they wanted him to jump, to kill himself; they were singing about it now—it made them that happy. And there was an even greater strangeness: Rabbi Binder was on his knees, trembling. If there was a question to be asked now it was not "Is it me?" but rather "Is it us? . . . Is it us?"

Being on the roof, it turned out, was a serious thing. If he jumped would the singing become dancing? Would it? What would jumping stop? Yearningly, Ozzie wished he could rip open the sky, plunge his hands through, and pull out the sun; and on the sun, like a coin, would be stamped JUMP or DON'T JUMP.

Ozzie's knees rocked and sagged a little under him as though they were setting him for a dive. His arms tightened, stiffened, froze, from shoulders to fingernails. He felt as if each part of his body were going to vote as to whether he should kill himself or not—and each part as though it were independent of *him*.

The light took an unexpected click down and the new darkness, like a gag, hushed the friends singing for this and the mother and rabbi chanting for that.

Ozzie stopped counting votes, and in a curiously high voice, like one who wasn't prepared for speech, he spoke.

"Mamma?"

"Yes, Oscar."

"Mamma, get down on your knees, like Rabbi Binder."

"Oscar—"

"Get down on your knees," he said, "or I'll jump."

Ozzie heard a whimper, then a quick rustling, and when he looked down where his mother had stood he saw the top of a head and beneath that a circle of dress. She was kneeling beside Rabbi Binder.

He spoke again. "Everybody kneel!" There was the sound of everybody kneeling.

Ozzie looked around. With one hand he pointed towards the synagogue entrance. "Make *him* kneel."

There was a noise, not of kneeling, but of body-and-cloth stretching. Ozzie could hear Rabbi Binder saying in a gruff whisper, ". . . or he'll *kill* himself," and when next he looked there was Yakov Blotnik off the doorknob and for the first time in his life upon his knees in the Gentile[8] posture of prayer.

[8] Gentile: non-Jew.

As for the firemen—it is not as difficult as one might imagine to hold a net taut while you are kneeling.

Ozzie looked around again; and then he called to Rabbi Binder.

"Rabbi?"

"Yes, Oscar."

"Rabbi Binder, do you believe in God?"

"Yes."

"Do you believe God can do Anything?" Ozzie leaned his head out into the darkness. "Anything?"

"Oscar, I think—"

"Tell me you believe God can do Anything."

There was a second's hesitation. Then: "God can do Anything."

"Tell me you believe God can make a child without intercourse."

"He can."

"Tell me!"

"God," Rabbi Binder admitted, "can make a child without intercourse."

"Mamma, you tell me."

"God can make a child without intercourse," his mother said.

"Make *him* tell me." There was no doubt who *him* was.

In a few moments Ozzie heard an old comical voice say something to the increasing darkness about God.

Next, Ozzie made everybody say it. And then he made them all say they believed in Jesus Christ—first one at a time, then all together.

When the catechizing was through it was the beginning of evening. From the street it sounded as if the boy on the roof might have sighed.

"Ozzie?" A woman's voice dared to speak. "You'll come down now?"

There was no answer, but the woman waited, and when a voice finally did speak it was thin and crying, and exhausted as that of an old man who has just finished pulling the bells.

"Mamma, don't you see—you shouldn't hit me. He shouldn't hit me. You shouldn't hit me about God, Mamma. You should never hit anybody about God—"

"Ozzie, please come down now."

"Promise me, promise me you'll never hit anybody about God."

He had asked only his mother, but for some reason everyone kneeling in the street promised he would never hit anybody about God.

Once again there was silence.

"I can come down now, Mamma," the boy on the roof finally said. He turned his head both ways as though checking the traffic lights. "Now I can come down . . ."

And he did, right into the center of the yellow net that glowed in the evening's edge like an overgrown halo.

READING SELECTIONS: POEMS

Edgar Lee Masters (1869–1950)

MRS. CHARLES BLISS

Reverend Wiley advised me not to divorce him
For the sake of the children,
And Judge Somers advised him the same.
So we stuck to the end of the path.
But two of the children thought he was right,   5
And two of the children thought I was right.
And the two who sided with him blamed me,
And the two who sided with me blamed him,
And they grieved for the one they sided with.
And all were torn with the guilt of judging,   10
And tortured in soul because they could not admire
Equally him and me.
Now every gardener knows that plants grown in cellars
Or under stones are twisted and yellow and weak.
And no mother would let her baby suck   15
Diseased milk from her breast.
Yet preachers and judges advise the raising of souls
Where there is no sunlight, but only twilight,
No warmth, but only dampness and cold—
Preachers and judges!   20

STUDY QUESTIONS

1. What biographical information is given about Mrs. Bliss in the poem?
2. What do you think is Mrs. Bliss's principal conflict? What information in the poem supports your assertion?
3. The poem is about a marriage and raising children as much as it is a character sketch. How would you describe the relationship between Mr. and Mrs. Bliss? What effect did their relationship have on the children?
4. Mrs. Bliss registers a strong complaint against preachers and judges. What is her argument, and how is it justified?
5. How does Mrs. Bliss's name relate to some of the ironies in the poem?

Edgar Lee Masters (1869–1950)

REV. LEMUEL WILEY

I preached four thousand sermons,
I conducted forty revivals,
And baptized many converts.
Yet no deed of mine
Shines brighter in the memory of the world,   5
And none is treasured more by me:
Look how I saved the Blisses from divorce,
And kept the children free from that disgrace,
To grow up into moral men and women,
Happy themselves, a credit to the village.   10

STUDY QUESTIONS

1. What is Rev. Wiley's principal trait?
2. What commentary on that trait is provided by Mrs. Bliss's statement?
3. What is Rev. Wiley's function in the conflict between Mr. and Mrs. Bliss?

Langston Hughes (1902–1967)

BALLAD OF THE LANDLORD

Landlord, landlord,
My roof has sprung a leak.
Don't you 'member I told you about it
Way last week?

Landlord, landlord,   5
These steps is broken down.
When you come up yourself
It's a wonder you don't fall down.

Ten Bucks you say I owe you?
Ten Bucks you say is due?   10
Well, that's Ten Bucks more'n I'll pay you
Till you fix this house up new.

What? You gonna get eviction orders?
You gonna cut off my heat?
You gonna take my furniture and   15
Throw it in the street?

Um-huh! You talking high and mighty.
Talk on—till you get through.
You ain't gonna be able to say a word
If I land my fist on you.   20

Police! Police!
Come and get this man!
He's trying to ruin the government
And overturn the land!

Copper's whistle!   25
Patrol bell!
Arrest.

Precinct Station.
Iron cell.
Headlines in press: 30

MAN THREATENS LANDLORD

. .

TENANT HELD NO BAIL

.

. .

JUDGE GIVES NEGRO 90 DAYS IN COUNTY JAIL

STUDY QUESTIONS

1. How many different voices are there in the poem? Identify the speakers and their lives.
2. The "Ballad of the Landlord" (like all ballads) tells a story. Summarize the action and identify the lines that present the rising action, climax, falling action, and resolution.
3. Is the conflict internal, external, or both? Identify the protagonist and antagonist of each conflict you identify.
4. What general meaning is expressed through the particular conflicts described in the poem?

Adrienne Rich (1929–   )

LIVING IN SIN

She had thought the studio would keep itself;
no dust upon the furniture of love.

Half heresy, to wish the taps less vocal,
the panes relieved of grime. A plate of pears,
a piano with a Persian shawl, a cat   5
stalking the picturesque amusing mouse
had risen at his urging.
Not that at five each separate stair would writhe
under the milkman's tramp; that morning light
so coldly would delineate the scraps   10
of last night's cheese and three sepulchral bottles;
that on the kitchen shelf among the saucers
a pair of beetle-eyes would fix her own—
Envoy from some village in the moldings . . .
Meanwhile, he, with a yawn,   15
sounded a dozen notes upon the keyboard,
declared it out of tune, shrugged at the mirror,
rubbed at his beard, went out for cigarettes;
while she, jeered by the minor demons,
pulled back the sheets and made the bed and found   20
a towel to dust the table-top,
and let the coffee-pot boil over on the stove.
By evening she was back in love again,
though not so wholly but throughout the night
she woke sometimes to feel the daylight coming   25
like a relentless milkman up the stairs.

STUDY QUESTIONS

1. The poem establishes several conflicting elements: the woman's view of living with her lover before and her present view; her feelings in daylight and in darkness; his attitude toward their life together and hers. How do these differences relate to internal and external conflict? How do they relate to meaning?

2. What is the point of view of the poem? In your response, consider the lack of names and how their omission relates to point of view.

3. To what does the sentence fragment that begins "Not that at five" (line 8) attach to make a complete sentence? Does this sentence add to the poem, especially in revealing conflict? Explain your response.

4. While "he" goes for cigarettes, "she" cleans the apartment "jeered by minor demons" (line 19). What are the demons? How does this phrase relate to conflict?

5. Is there a climax? A resolution? If so, what are they?

Thomas Hardy (1840–1928)

THE CURATE'S KINDNESS

A Workhouse Irony

I thought they'd be strangers aroun' me,
    But she's to be there!
Let me jump out o' wagon and go back and drown me
    At Pummery or Ten-Hatches Weir.

I thought: "Well, I've come to the Union—   5
    The workhouse at last—
After honest hard work all the week, and Communion
    O' Zundays, these fifty years past.

" 'Tis hard; but," I thought, "never mind it—
    There's gain in the end;   10
And when I get used to the place I shall find it
    A home, and may find there a friend.

"Life there will be better than t'other,
    For peace is assured.
The men in one wing and their wives in another   15
    Is strictly the rule of the Board."

Just then one young Pa'son arriving
    Steps up out of breath
To the side o' the wagon wherein we were driving
    To Union; and calls out and saith: 20

"Old folks, that harsh order is altered,
    Be not sick of heart!
The Guardians they poohed and they pished and they paltered
    When urged not to keep you apart.

" 'It is wrong,' I maintained, 'to divide them,   25
    Near forty years wed.'
'Very well, sir. We promise, then, they shall abide them
    In one wing together,' they said."

Then I sank—knew 'twas quite a foredone thing
    That misery should be   30
To the end! . . . To get freed of her there was the one thing
    Had made the change welcome to me.

To go there was ending but badly;
    'Twas shame and 'twas pain;

"But anyhow," thought I, "thereby I shall gladly   35
    Get free of this forty years' chain."

I thought they'd be strangers aroun' me,
    But she's to be there!
Let me jump out o' wagon and go back and drown me
    At Pummery or Ten-Hatches Weir.   40

STUDY QUESTIONS

1. As in the poem "Mrs. Charles Bliss," the central external conflict involves a marriage. Using specific information from the work, describe both sides of that conflict.
2. What internal conflict does the narrator experience?
3. Comment on the development and resolution of the external and internal conflicts in the poem. What role does the curate play in the resolution?
4. Hardy, like Masters, is making a commentary on "preachers." Precisely what does he suggest about them? Does the narrator's attitude towards the parson reflect that of the author? Justify your answer.

Amy Lowell (1874–1925)

PATTERNS

I walk down the garden-paths,
And all the daffodils
Are blowing; and the bright blue squills.
I walk down the patterned garden-paths
In my stiff, brocaded gown.   5
With my powdered hair and jewelled fan,
I too am a rare
Pattern. As I wander down
The garden-paths.

My dress is richly figured,   10
And the train
Makes a pink and silver stain
On the gravel, and the thrift
Of the borders.
Just a plate of current fashion,   15
Tripping by in high-heeled, ribboned shoes.
Not a softness anywhere about me,

3. squills: small, blue flowers; scilla.

Only whalebone and brocade.
And I sink on a seat in the shade
Of a lime-tree. For my passion   20
Wars against the stiff brocade.
The daffodils and squills
Flutter in the breeze
As they please.
And I weep;   25
For the lime-tree is in blossom
And one small flower has dropped upon my bosom.

And the plashing of waterdrops
In the marble fountain
Comes down the garden-paths.   30
The dripping never stops.
Underneath my stiffened gown
Is the softness of a woman bathing in a marble basin,
A basin in the midst of hedges grown
So thick, she cannot see her lover hiding,   35
But she guesses he is near,
And the sliding of the water
Seems the stroking of a dear
Hand upon her.
What is Summer in a fine brocaded gown!   40
I should like to see it lying in a heap upon the ground.
All the pink and silver crumpled up on the ground.

I would be the pink and silver as I ran along the paths,
And he would stumble after,
Bewildered by my laughter.   45
I should see the sun flashing from his sword-hilt and the buckles
      on his shoes.
I would choose
To lead him in a maze along the patterned paths,
A bright and laughing maze for my heavy-booted lover.
Till he caught me in the shade,   50
And the buttons of his waistcoat bruised my body as he clasped me
Aching, melting, unafraid.
With the shadows of the leaves and the sundrops,
And the plopping of the waterdrops,
All about us in the open afternoon—   55
I am very like to swoon
With the weight of this brocade,
For the sun sifts through the shade.

18. whalebone: used as stiffening in women's garments, particularly corsets.

Underneath the fallen blossom
In my bosom, 60
Is a letter I have hid.
It was brought to me this morning by a rider from the Duke.
"Madam, we regret to inform you that Lord Hartwell
Died in action Thursday se'nnight."
As I read it in the white, morning sunlight, 65
The letters squirmed like snakes.
"Any answer, Madam?" said my footman.
"No," I told him.
"See that the messenger takes some refreshment.
No, no answer." 70
And I walked into the garden,
Up and down the patterned paths,
In my stiff, correct brocade.
The blue and yellow flowers stood up proudly in the sun,
Each one. 75
I stood upright too,
Held rigid to the pattern
By the stiffness of my gown.
Up and down I walked,
Up and down. 80

In a month he would have been my husband.
In a month, here underneath this lime,
We would have broke the pattern;
He for me, and I for him,
He as Colonel, I as Lady, 85
On this shady seat.
He had a whim
That sunlight carried blessing.
And I answered, "It shall be as you have said."
Now he is dead. 90

In Summer and in Winter I shall walk
Up and down
The patterned garden-paths
In my stiff, brocaded gown. 95
The squills and daffodils
Will give place to pillared roses, and to asters, and to snow.
I shall go
Up and down,
In my gown. 100

64. se'nnight: seven days ago.

Gorgeously arrayed,
Boned and stayed.
And the softness of my body will be guarded from embrace
By each button, hook, and lace.
For the man who should loose me is dead,   105
Fighting with the Duke in Flanders,
In a pattern called a war.
Christ! What are patterns for?

106. Flanders: a region of northern France and southern Belgium, scene of bloody fighting in various wars.

STUDY QUESTIONS

1. Throughout the poem, the softness of a woman's body is contrasted with the stiffness of her brocaded gown. What internal conflict in the woman is represented by these external facts?
2. The woman is walking up and down in a formal garden, in which the paths are "patterned." Why does she place her sexual fantasies here in the garden instead of somewhere else—say, in her bedroom?
3. Comment on the possible meanings of the woman's final cry, "Christ! What are patterns for?" (line 108).

Walt Whitman (1819–1892)

COME UP FROM THE FIELDS FATHER

Come up from the fields father, here's a letter from our Pete,
And come to the front door mother, here's a letter from thy dear son.

Lo, 'tis autumn,
Lo, where the trees, deeper green, yellower and redder,
Cool and sweeten Ohio's villages with leaves fluttering in the moderate
     wind,   5
Where apples ripe in the orchards hang and grapes on the trellised vines,
(Smell you the smell of the grapes on the vines?
Smell you the buckwheat where the bees were lately buzzing?)
Above all, lo, the sky so calm, so transparent after the rain, and with wondrous clouds,
Below too, all calm, all vital and beautiful, and the farm prospers well. 10
Down in the fields all prospers well,
But now from the fields come father, come at the daughter's call,
And come to the entry mother, to the front door come right away.

Fast as she can she hurries, something ominous, her steps trembling,
She does not tarry to smooth her hair nor adjust her cap.   15

Open the envelope quickly,
O this is not our son's writing, yet his name is signed,
O a strange hand writes for our dear son, O stricken mother's soul!
All swims before her eyes, flashes with black, she catches the main words
    only,
Sentences broken, *gunshot wound in the breast, cavalry skirmish, taken to
    hospital,*   20
At present low, but will soon be better.

Ah now the single figure to me,
Amid all teeming and wealthy Ohio with all its cities and farms,
Sickly white in the face and dull in the head, very faint,
By the jamb of a door leans.   25

Grieve not so, dear mother (the just-grown daughter speaks through her sobs,
The little sisters huddle around speechless and dismayed),
See, dearest mother, the letter says Pete will soon be better.

Alas poor boy, he will never be better (nor may-be needs to be better, that
    brave and simple soul),
While they stand at home at the door he is dead already,   30
The only son is dead.

But the mother needs to be better,
She with thin form presently dressed in black,
By day her meals untouched, then at night fitfully sleeping, often waking,
In the midnight waking, weeping, longing with one deep longing,   35
O that she might withdraw unnoticed, silent from life escape and withdraw,
To follow, to seek, to be with her dear dead son.

STUDY QUESTIONS

1. Who is speaking in the poem? How many voices are there? Point out
   lines where you see each different voice.
2. Is there a single protagonist? Is the entire family the protagonist? Support your answer with references to the text. Who or what is the antagonist?
3. As specifically as you can, identify the conflict(s). Does the protagonist
   or antagonist win?
4. What effect is added to the poem by the contrast between the autumn
   harvest and the death of the son? Does this contrast affect the conflict?
5. Write a single sentence that expresses the meaning of the poem.

Michael Drayton (1563–1631)

SINCE THERE'S NO HELP

Since there's no help, come let us kiss and part.
Nay, I have done; you get no more of me,
And I am glad, yea, glad with all my heart,
That thus so cleanly I myself can free;
Shake hands for ever, cancel all our vows,   5
And when we meet at any time again,
Be it not seen in either of our brows
That we one jot of former love retain.
Now at the last gasp of Love's latest breath,
When, his pulse failing, Passion speechless lies,   10
When Faith is kneeling by his bed of death,
And Innocence is closing up his eyes,
Now if thou wouldst, when all have given him over,
From death to life thou mightst him yet recover.

STUDY QUESTIONS

1. In this sonnet, a love relationship is breaking up. One of the former lovers first states satisfaction with the end of the affair, and then offers to try to start over. Which partner has decided to end the relationship? Why does the speaker of the poem change his or her attitude?

2. In lines 9–14 the speaker describes a deathbed scene, as if the relationship itself were a dying person. In what tone of voice should these lines be read? What indirect hints earlier in the poem tend to prepare the reader for this tone of voice?

3. What internal conflict has the speaker of the poem experienced? What is the resolution of that conflict?

William Shakespeare (1564–1616)

TH' EXPENSE OF SPIRIT IN A WASTE OF SHAME (SONNET 129)

Th' expense of spirit in a waste of shame
Is lust in action; and till action, lust
Is perjur'd, murd'rous, bloody, full of blame,
Savage, extreme, rude, cruel, not to trust;
Enjoy'd no sooner but despised straight,   5

Past reason hunted, and no sooner had.
Past reason hated as a swallow'd bait
On purpose laid to make the taker mad;
Mad in pursuit and in possession so;
Had, having, and in quest to have, extreme;   10
A bliss in proof, and prov'd, a very woe;
Before, a joy propos'd; behind, a dream.
    All this the world well knows, yet none knows well
    To shun the heaven that leads men to this hell.

STUDY QUESTIONS

1. Since there is no identifiable speaker, the sonnet may be read as a philosophical or moral comment. However, it also contains a strong internal conflict. What elements are warring against each other?
2. The subject of the poem is lust, one of the "seven deadly sins," but Shakespeare's focus is primarily psychological rather than moral. That is, he describes lust through its effect on the person who experiences it. What, according to the first two lines of the poem, is his principal argument against lust?
3. "Before" and "after" are the two aspects of lust presented in the poem. List and explain all that is said about both states.
4. How does the final couplet relate to the conflict? Explain the references to heaven and hell, especially in light of the poem's psychological focus.

Robert Browning (1812–1889)

PORPHYRIA'S LOVER

The rain set early in tonight,
    The sullen wind was soon awake,
It tore the elm-tops down for spite,
    And did its worst to vex the lake:
    I listened with heart fit to break.   5
When glided in Porphyria; straight
    She shut the cold out and the storm,
And kneeled and made the cheerless grate
    Blaze up, and all the cottage warm;
    Which done, she rose, and from her form   10
Withdrew the dripping cloak and shawl,
    And laid her soiled gloves by, untied

Her hat and let the damp hair fall,
   And, last, she sat down by my side
   And called me. When no voice replied,   15
She put my arm about her waist,
   And made her smooth white shoulder bare,
And all her yellow hair displaced,
   And, stooping, made my cheek lie there,
   And spread, o'er all, her yellow hair,   20
Murmuring how she loved me—she
   Too weak, for all her heart's endeavor,
To set its struggling passion free
   From pride, and vainer ties dissever,
   And give herself to me for ever.   25
But passion sometimes would prevail,
   Nor could tonight's gay feast restrain
A sudden thought of one so pale
   For love of her, and all in vain:
   So, she was come through wind and rain.   30
Be sure I looked up at her eyes
   Happy and proud; at last I knew
Porphyria worshiped me; surprise
   Made my heart swell, and still it grew
   While I debated what to do.   35
That moment she was mine, mine, fair,
   Perfectly pure and good: I found
A thing to do, and all her hair
   In one long yellow string I wound
   Three times her little throat around,   40
And strangled her. No pain felt she;
   I am quite sure she felt no pain.
As a shut bud that holds a bee,
   I warily oped her lids: again
   Laughed the blue eyes without a strain.   45
And I untightened next the tress
   About her neck; her cheek once more
Blushed bright beneath my burning kiss:
   I propped her head up as before,
   Only, this time my shoulder bore   50
Her head, which droops upon it still:
   The smiling rosy little head,
So glad it has its utmost will,
   That all it scorned at once is fled,
   And I, its love, am gained instead!   55
Porphyria's love: she guessed not how

Her darling one wish would be heard.
And thus we sit together now,
    And all night long we have not stirred,
    And yet God has not said a word!   60

STUDY QUESTIONS

1. The poem presents a narrative about two characters. Which one is the protagonist? Defend your answer.
2. What is the dramatic situation that opens the poem?
3. What is the history of the relationship between Porphyria and her lover? What, at the beginning of the poem, is its future?
4. Trace the development of the principal conflict in the poem. What is the deciding factor in the resolution of that struggle?
5. What arguments does the narrator use to justify the murder of Porphyria? What do these arguments reveal about his character?
6. If you were the lawyer assigned to defend the narrator at his trial, what defense would you use?

Edgar Lee Masters (1869–1950)

HARRY WILMANS

I was just turned twenty-one,
And Henry Phipps, the Sunday-school superintendent,
Made a speech in Bindle's Opera House.
"The honor of the flag must be upheld," he said,
"Whether it be assailed by a barbarous tribe of Tagalogs   5
Or the greatest power in Europe."
And we cheered and cheered the speech and the flag he waved
As he spoke.
And I went to the war in spite of my father,
And followed the flag till I saw it raised   10
By our camp in a rice field near Manila,
And all of us cheered and cheered it.
But there were flies and poisonous things;
And there was the deadly water,
And the cruel heat,   15
And the sickening, putrid food;
And the smell of the trench just back of the tents
Where the soldiers went to empty themselves;
And there were the whores who followed us, full of syphilis;
And beastly acts between ourselves or alone,   20
With bullying, hatred, degradation among us,

And days of loathing and nights of fear
To the hour of the charge through the steaming swamp,
Following the flag,
Till I fell with a scream, shot through the guts.   25
Now there's a flag over me in Spoon River!
A flag! A flag!

Rudyard Kipling (1865–1936)

DANNY DEEVER

"What are the bugles blowin' for?" said Files-on-Parade.
"To turn you out, to turn you out," the Colour-Sergeant said.
"What makes you look so white, so white?" said Files-on-Parade.
"I'm dreadin' what I've got to watch," the Colour-Sergeant said.
 For they're hangin' Danny Deever, you can hear the Dead March play,
 The Regiment's in 'ollow square—they're hangin' him today; 6
 They've taken of his buttons off an' cut his stripes away,
 An' they're hangin' Danny Deever in the mornin'.

"What makes the rear-rank breathe so 'ard?" said Files-on-Parade.
"It's bitter cold, it's bitter cold," the Colour-Sergeant said. 10
"What makes that front-rank man fall down?" said Files-on-Parade.
"A touch o' sun, a touch o' sun," the Colour-Sergeant said.
 They are hangin' Danny Deever, they are marchin' of 'im round,
 They 'ave 'alted Danny Deever by 'is coffin on the ground;
 An' 'e'll swing in 'arf a minute for a sneakin' shootin' hound— 15
 O they're hangin' Danny Deever in the mornin'!

" 'Is cot was right-'and cot to mine," said Files-on-Parade.
" 'E's sleepin' out an' far to-night," the Colour-Sergeant said.
"I've drunk 'is beer a score o' times," said Files-on-Parade.
" 'E's drinkin' bitter beer alone," the Colour-Sergeant said. 20
 They are hangin' Danny Deever, you must mark 'im to 'is place,
 For 'e shot a comrade sleepin'—you must look 'im in the face;
 Nine 'undred of 'is county an' the Regiment's disgrace,
 While they're hangin' Danny Deever in the mornin'.

"What's that so black agin the sun?" said Files-on-Parade. 25
"It's Danny fightin' 'ard for life," the Colour-Sergeant said.
"What's that that whimpers over'ead?" said Files-on-Parade.
"It's Danny's soul that's passin' now," the Colour-Sergeant said.
 For they're done with Danny Deever, you can 'ear the quickstep play,
 The Regiment's in column, an' they're marchin' us away; 30
 Ho! the young recruits are shakin', an' they'll want their beer to-day,
 After hangin' Danny Deever in the mornin'!

Howard Nemerov (1920–   )

THE VACUUM

The house is so quiet now
The vacuum cleaner sulks in the corner closet,
Its bag limp as a stopped lung, its mouth
Grinning into the floor, maybe at my
Slovenly life, my dog-dead youth.   5

I've lived this way long enough,
But when my old woman died her soul
Went into that vacuum cleaner, and I can't bear
To see the bag swell like a belly, eating the dust
And the woolen mice, and begin to howl   10

Because there is old filth everywhere
She used to crawl, in the corner and under the stair.
I know now how life is cheap as dirt,
And still the hungry, angry heart
Hangs on and howls, biting at air.   15

Gwendolyn Brooks (1917–   )

THE BALLAD OF RUDOLPH REED

Rudolph Reed was oaken.
His wife was oaken too.
And his two good girls and his good little man
Oakened as they grew.

"I am not hungry for berries.   5
I am not hungry for bread
But hungry hungry for a house
Where at night a man in bed

"May never hear the plaster
Stir as if in pain.   10
May never hear the roaches
Falling like fat rain.

"Where never wife and children need
Go blinking through the gloom.
Where every room of many rooms   15
Will be full of room.

"Oh my home may have its east or west
Or north or south behind it.
All I know is I shall know it,
And fight for it when I find it." 20

It was in a street of bitter white
That he made his application.
For Rudolph Reed was oakener
Than others in the nation.

The agent's steep and steady stare 25
Corroded to a grin.
Why, you black old, tough old hell of a man,
Move your family in!

Nary a grin grinned Rudolph Reed,
Nary a curse cursed he, 30
But moved in his House. With his dark little wife,
And his dark little children three.

A neighbor would *look,* with a yawning eye
That squeezed into a slit.
But the Rudolph Reeds and the children three 35
Were too joyous to notice it.

For were they not firm in a home of their own
With windows everywhere
And a beautiful banistered stair
And a front yard for flowers and a back yard for grass? 40

The first night, a rock, big as two fists.
The second, a rock big as three.
But nary a curse cursed Rudolph Reed.
(Though oaken as man could be.)

The third night, a silvery ring of glass. 45
Patience ached to endure.
But he looked, and lo! small Mabel's blood
Was staining her gaze so pure.

Then up did rise our Rudolph Reed
And pressed the hand of his wife, 50
And went to the door with a thirty-four
And a beastly butcher knife.

He ran like a mad thing into the night.
And the words in his mouth were stinking.

By the time he had hurt his first white man   55
He was no longer thinking.

By the time he had hurt his fourth white man
Rudolph Reed was dead.
His neighbors gathered and kicked his corpse.
"Nigger—" his neighbors said.   60

Small Mabel whimpered all night long,
For calling herself the cause.
Her oak-eyed mother did no thing
But change the bloody gauze.

Conrad Aiken (1889–1973)

THE QUARREL

Suddenly, after the quarrel, while we waited,
Disheartened, silent, with downcast looks, nor stirred
Eyelid nor finger, hopeless both, yet hoping
Against all hope to unsay the sundering word:

While all the room's stillness deepened, deepened about us,   5
And each of us crept his thought's way to discover
How, with as little sound as the fall of a leaf,
The shadow had fallen, and lover quarreled with lover;

And while, in the quiet, I marveled—alas, alas—
At your deep beauty, your tragic beauty, torn   10
As the pale flower is torn by the wanton sparrow—
This beauty, pitied and loved, and now forsworn;

It was then, when the instant darkened to its darkest,—
When faith was lost with hope, and the rain conspired
To strike its gray arpeggios against our heartstrings,—   15
When love no longer dared, and scarcely desired:

It was then that suddenly, in the neighbor's room,
The music started: that brave quartette of strings
Breaking out of the stillness, as out of our stillness,
Like the indomitable heart of life that sings   20

When all is lost; and startled from our sorrow,
Tranced from our grief by that diviner grief,
We raised remembering eyes, each looked at other,
Blinded with tears of joy; and another leaf

Fell silently as that first; and in the instant   25
The shadow had gone, our quarrel became absurd;
And we rose, to the angelic voices of the music,
And I touched your hand, and we kissed, without a word.

15. arpeggios: musical chords played one note after another, instead of all at the same time.

Muriel Stuart (1889–)

IN THE ORCHARD

'I thought you loved me.' 'No, it was only fun.'
'When we stood there, closer than all?' 'Well, the harvest moon
Was shining and queer in your hair, and it turned my head.'
'That made you?' 'Yes.' 'Just the moon and the light it made
Under the tree?' 'Well, your mouth, too.' 'Yes, my mouth?'   5
'And the quiet there that sang like the drum in the booth.
You shouldn't have danced like that.' 'Like what?' 'So close,
With your head turned up, and the flower in your hair, a rose
That smelt all warm.' 'I loved you. I thought you knew
I wouldn't have danced like that with any but you.'   10
'I didn't know. I thought you knew it was fun.'
'I thought it was love you meant.' 'Well, it's done.' 'Yes, it's done.
I've seen boys stone a blackbird, and watched them drown
A kitten . . . it clawed at the reeds, and they pushed it down
Into the pool while it screamed. Is that fun, too?'   15
'Well, boys are like that . . . Your brothers . . .' 'Yes, I know.
But you, so lovely and strong! Not you! Not you!'
'They don't understand it's cruel. It's only a game.'
'And are girls fun, too?' 'No, still in a way it's the same.
It's queer and lovely to have a girl . . .' 'Go on.'   20
'It makes you mad for a bit to feel she's your own,
And you laugh and kiss her, and maybe you give her a ring,
But it's only in fun.' 'But I gave you everything.'
'Well, you shouldn't have done it. You know what a fellow thinks
When a girl does that.' 'Yes, he talks of her over his drinks   25
And calls her a—' 'Stop that now. I thought you knew.'
'But it wasn't with anyone else. It was only you.'
'How did I know? I thought you wanted it too.
I thought you were like the rest. Well, what's to be done?'
'To be done?' 'Is it all right?' 'Yes.' 'Sure?' 'Yes, but why?' 30
'I don't know. I thought you were going to cry.
You said you had something to tell me.' 'Yes, I know.

It wasn't anything really ... I think I'll go.'
'Yes, it's late. There's thunder about, a drop of rain
Fell on my hand in the dark. I'll see you again   35
At the dance next week. You're sure that everything's right?'
'Yes,' 'Well, I'll be going.' 'Kiss me ...' 'Good night.' ... 'Good night.'

Julius Lester (1939–   )

PARENTS

Linda failed to return home from a dance Friday night.
On Saturday
she admitted she had spent the night
with an Air Force lieutenant.

The Aults decided on a punishment   5
that would "wake Linda up."
They ordered her
to shoot the dog
she had owned about two years.
On Sunday,   10
the Aults and
Linda
took the dog into the desert
near their home.
They   15
had the girl
dig a shallow grave.
Then
Mrs. Ault
grasped the dog between her hands and   20
Mr. Ault
gave
his daughter
a .22 caliber pistol
and told her   25
to shoot the dog.

Instead,
the girl
put the pistol
to her right temple   30
and shot herself.

The police said
there were no charges
that could be filed
against the parents   35
except possibly

cruelty
to
animals.

Robert Frost (1874–1963)

THE VANISHING RED

He is said to have been the last Red Man
In Acton. And the Miller is said to have laughed—
If you like to call such a sound a laugh.
But he gave no one else a laugher's license.
For he turned suddenly grave as if to say,   5
'Whose business'—if I take it on myself,
Whose business—but why talk round the barn?—
When it's just that I hold with getting a thing done with.
You can't get back and see it as he saw it.
It's too long a story to go into now.   10
You'd have to have been there and lived it.
Then you wouldn't have looked on it as just a matter
Of who began it between the two races.

Some guttural exclamation of surprise
The Red Man gave in poking about the mill   15
Over the great big thumping shuffling millstone
Disgusted the Miller physically as coming
From one who had no right to be heard from.
'Come, John,' he said, 'you want to see the wheel-pit?'

He took him down below a cramping rafter,   20
And showed him, through a manhole in the floor,
The water in desperate straits like frantic fish,
Salmon and sturgeon, lashing with their tails.
Then he shut down the trap door with a ring in it
That jangled even above the general noise,   25
And came upstairs alone—and gave that laugh,
And said something to a man with a meal-sack
That the man with the meal-sack didn't catch—then.
Oh, yes, he showed John the wheel-pit all right.

George Gordon, Lord Byron (1788–1824)

WHEN WE TWO PARTED

When we two parted
  In silence and tears,
Half broken-hearted
  To sever for years,
Pale grew thy cheek and cold,   5
  Colder thy kiss;
Truly that hour foretold
  Sorrow to this.

The dew of the morning
  Sunk chill on my brow—   10
It felt like the warning
  Of what I feel now.
Thy vows are all broken,
  And light is thy fame:
I hear thy name spoken,   15
  And share in its shame.

They name thee before me,
  A knell to mine ear;
A shudder comes o'er me—
  Why wert thou so dear?   20
They know not I knew thee,
  Who knew thee too well:—
Long, long shall I rue thee,
  Too deeply to tell.

In secret we met—   25
  In silence I grieve,
That thy heart could forget,
  Thy spirit deceive.
If I should meet thee
  After long years,   30
How should I greet thee?—
  With silence and tears.

A. E. Housman (1859–1936)

IS MY TEAM PLOUGHING

"Is my team ploughing,
  That I was used to drive
And hear the harness jingle
  When I was man alive?"

Aye, the horses trample,   5
  The harness jingles now;
No change though you lie under
  The land you used to plough.

"Is football playing
  Along the river shore,   10
With lads to chase the leather,
  Now I stand up no more?"

Aye, the ball is flying,
  The lads play heart and soul;
The goal stands up, the keeper   15
  Stands up to keep the goal.

"Is my girl happy,
  That I thought hard to leave,
And has she tired of weeping
  As she lies down at eve?"   20

Aye, she lies down lightly,
  She lies not down to weep:
Your girl is well contented.
  Be still, my lad, and sleep.

"Is my friend hearty,   25
  Now I am thin and pine;
And has he found to sleep in
  A better bed than mine?"

Yes, lad, I lie easy,
  I lie as lads would choose;   30
I cheer a dead man's sweetheart,
  Never ask me whose.

9. football: rugby, a British game somewhat different from American football.

Ezra Pound (1885–1962)

SALUTATION

O Generation of the thoroughly smug
  and thoroughly uncomfortable,
I have seen fishermen picnicking in the sun,
I have seen them with untidy families,
I have seen their smiles full of teeth
  and heard ungainly laughter.

And I am happier than you are.   5
And they were happier than I am;
And the fish swim in the lake
    and do not even own clothing.

William Shakespeare (1564–1616)

NOT MARBLE,
NOR THE GILDED MONUMENTS
(SONNET 55)

Not marble nor the gilded monuments
Of princes shall outlive this pow'rful rhyme;
But you shall shine more bright in these contents
Than unswept stone besmear'd with sluttish time.
When wasteful war shall statues overturn,   5
And broils root out the work of masonry,
No Mars his sword nor war's quick fire shall burn
The living record of your memory.
'Gainst death and all-oblivious enmity
Shall you pace forth; your praise shall still find room   10
Even in the eyes of all posterity
That wear this world out to the ending doom.
   So till the judgment that yourself arise,
   You live in this, and dwell in lovers' eyes.

7. Mars: god of war.

William Shakespeare (1564–1616)

TIR'D WITH ALL THESE,
FOR RESTFUL DEATH I CRY
(SONNET 66)

Tir'd with all these, for restful death I cry:
As, to behold desert a beggar born,
And needy nothing trimm'd in jollity,
And purest faith unhappily forsworn,
And gilded honour shamefully misplace'd,   5
And maiden virtue rudely strumpeted,
And right perfection wrongfully disgrac'd,
And strength by limping away disabled,
And art made tongue-tied by authority,

And folly, doctor-like, controlling skill,   10
And simple truth miscall'd simplicity,
And captive good attending captain ill:
    Tir'd with all these, from these would I be gone,
    Save that to die, I leave my love alone.

6. strumpeted: sold, prostituted

William Shakespeare (1564–1616)

WHEN MY LOVE SWEARS THAT
SHE IS MADE OF TRUTH
(SONNET 138)

When my love swears that she is made of truth,
I do believe her, though I know she lies,
That she might think me some untutor'd youth,
Unlearned in the world's false subtleties.
Thus vainly thinking that she thinks me young,   5
Although she knows my days are past the best,
Simply I credit her false-speaking tongue:
On both sides thus is simple truth suppress'd.
But wherefore says she not she is unjust?
And wherefore say not I that I am old?   10
O, love's best habit is in seeming trust,
And age in love loves not to have years told.
    Therefore I lie with her, and she with me,
    And in our faults by lies we flattered be.

READING SELECTIONS: PLAYS

Susan Glaspell (1882–1948)

TRIFLES

Scene: *The kitchen in the now abandoned farmhouse of* JOHN WRIGHT, *a gloomy kitchen, and left without having been put in order—the walls covered with a faded wall paper.* D.R. *is a door leading to the parlor. On the* R. *wall above this door is a built-in kitchen cupboard with shelves in the* *upper portion and drawers below. In the rear wall at R., up two steps is a door opening onto stairs leading to the second floor. In the rear wall at L. is a door to the shed and from there to the outside. Between these two doors is an old-fashioned black iron stove. Running along the L. wall from the shed door is an old iron sink and sink shelf, in which is set a hand pump. Downstage of the sink is an uncurtained window. Near the window is an old wooden rocker. Center stage is an unpainted wooden kitchen table with straight chairs on either side. There is a small chair D.R. Unwashed pans under the sink, a loaf of bread outside the breadbox, a dish towel on the table—other signs of incompleted work. At the rear the shed door opens and the SHERIFF comes in followed by the COUNTY ATTORNEY and HALE. The SHERIFF and HALE are men in middle life, the COUNTY ATTORNEY is a young man; all are much bundled up and go at once to the stove. They are followed by the two women—the SHERIFF's wife, MRS. PETERS, first; she is a slight wiry woman, a thin nervous face. MRS. HALE is larger and would ordinarily be called more comfortable looking, but she is disturbed now and looks fearfully about as she enters. The women have come in slowly, and stand close together near the door.*

County Attorney (*at stove rubbing his hands*) This feels good. Come up to the fire, ladies.

Mrs. Peters (*after taking a step forward*) I'm not—cold.

Sheriff (*unbuttoning his overcoat and stepping away from the stove to right of table as if to mark the beginning of official business*) Now, Mr. Hale, before we move things about, you explain to Mr. Henderson just what you saw when you came here yesterday morning.

County Attorney (*crossing down to left of the table*) By the way, has anything been moved? Are things just as you left them yesterday?

Sheriff (*looking about*) It's just the same. When it dropped below zero last night I thought I'd better send Frank out this morning to make a fire for us—(*sits right of center table*) no use getting pneumonia with a big case on, but I told him not to touch anything except the stove—and you know Frank.

County Attorney Somebody should have been left here yesterday.

Sheriff Oh—yesterday. When I had to send Frank to Morris Center for that man who went crazy—I want you to know I had my hands full yesterday. I knew you could get back from Omaha by today and as long as I went over everything here myself—

County Attorney Well, Mr. Hale, tell just what happened when you came here yesterday morning.

Hale (*crossing down to above table*) Harry and I had started to town with a load of potatoes. We came along the road from my place and as I got here I said, "I'm going to see if I can't get John Wright to go in with me on a party telephone." I spoke to Wright about it once before and he put me off, saying folks talked too much anyway, and all he asked was peace and quiet—I guess you know about how much he talked himself; but I thought maybe if I went to the house and talked about it before his wife, though I said to Harry that I didn't know as what his wife wanted made much difference to John——

County Attorney Let's talk about that later, Mr. Hale. I do want to talk about that, but tell now just what happened when you got to the house.

Hale I didn't hear or see anything; I knocked at the door, and still it was all quiet inside. I knew they must be up, it was past eight o'clock. So I knocked again, and I thought I heard somebody say, "Come in." I wasn't sure, I'm not sure yet, but I opened the door—this door (*indicating the door by which the two women are still standing*) and there in that rocker —(*pointing to it*) sat Mrs. Wright.

(*They all look at the rocker* D.L.)

County Attorney What—was she doing?

Hale She was rockin' back and forth. She had her apron in her hand and was kind of—pleating it.

County Attorney And how did she—look?

Hale Well, she looked queer.

County Attorney How do you mean—queer?

Hale Well, as if she didn't know what she was going to do next. And kind of done up.

County Attorney (*takes out notebook and pencil and sits left of center table*) How did she seem to feel about your coming?

Hale Why, I don't think she minded—one way or other. She didn't pay much attention. I said, "How do, Mrs. Wright, it's cold, ain't it?" And she said, "Is it?"—and went on kind of pleating at her apron. Well, I was surprised; she didn't ask me to come up to the stove, or to set down, but just sat there, not even looking at me, so I said, "I want to see John." And then she—laughed. I guess you would call it a laugh. I thought of Harry and the team outside, so I said a little sharp: "Can't I see John?" "No," she says, kind o' dull like. "Ain't he home?" says I. "Yes," says she, "he's home." "Then why can't I see him?" I asked her, out of patience. " 'Cause he's dead," says she. "*Dead?*" says I. She just nodded her head, not getting a bit excited, but rockin' back and forth. "Why— where is he?" says I, not knowing what to say. She just pointed upstairs —like that. (*Himself pointing to the room above*). I started for the stairs, with the idea of going up there. I walked from there to here—then I says, "Why, what did he die of?" "He died of a rope round his neck," says she, and just went on pleatin' at her apron. Well, I went out and called Harry. I thought I might—need help. We went upstairs and there he was lyin'——

County Attorney I think I'd rather have you go into that upstairs, where you can point it all out. Just go on now with the rest of the story.

Hale Well, my first thought was to get that rope off. It looked ... (*stops, his face twitches*) ... but Harry, he went up to him, and he said, "No, he's dead all right, and we'd better not touch anything." So we went back downstairs. She was still sitting that same way. "Has anybody been notified?" I asked. "No," says she, unconcerned. "Who did this, Mrs. Wright?" said Harry. He said it business-like—and she stopped pleatin' of her apron. "I don't know," she says. "You don't *know?*" says Harry. "No," says she. "Weren't you sleepin' in the bed with him?" says Harry. "Yes," says she, "but I was on the inside." "Somebody slipped a rope round his neck and strangled him and you didn't wake up?" says Harry. "I didn't wake up," she said after him. We must 'a' looked as if we didn't see how that could be, for after a minute she said, "I sleep sound." Harry was going to ask her more questions but I said maybe we ought to let her tell her story first to the coroner, or the sheriff, so Harry went fast as he could to Rivers' place, where there's a telephone.

County Attorney And what did Mrs. Wright do when she knew that you had gone for the coroner?

Hale She moved from the rocker to that chair over there (*pointing to a small chair in the* D.R. *corner*) and just sat there with her hands held together and looking down. I got a feeling that I ought to make some conversation, so I said I had come in to see if John wanted to put in a telephone, and at that she started to laugh, and then she stopped and looked at me—scared. (*The* COUNTY ATTORNEY, *who has had his notebook out, makes a note*). I dunno, maybe it wasn't scared. I wouldn't like to say it was. Soon Harry got back, and then Dr. Lloyd came, and you, Mr. Peters, and so I guess that's all I know that you don't.

County Attorney (*rising and looking around*) I guess we'll go upstairs first—and then out to the barn and around there. (*To the* SHERIFF). You're convinced that there was nothing important here—nothing that would point to any motive?

Sheriff Nothing here but kitchen things.

(*The* COUNTY ATTORNEY, *after again looking around the kitchen, opens the door of a cupboard closet in* R. *wall. He brings a small chair from* R.—*gets up on it and looks on a shelf. Pulls his hand away, sticky.*)

County Attorney Here's a nice mess.

(*The women draw nearer* U.C.)

Mrs. Peters (*to the other woman*) Oh, her fruit; it did freeze. (*To the* LAWYER). She worried about that when it turned so cold. She said the fire'd go out and her jars would break.

Sheriff (*rises*) Well, can you beat the women! Held for murder and worryin' about her preserves.

County Attorney (*getting down from chair*) I guess before we're through she may have something more serious than preserves to worry about. (*Crosses down* R.C.)

Hale   Well, women are used to worrying over trifles.

(*The two women move a little closer together.*)

County Attorney (*with the gallantry of a young politician*)   And yet, for all their worries, what would we do without the ladies? (*The women do not unbend. He goes below the center table to the sink, takes a dipperful of water from the pail and pouring it into a basin, washes his hands. While he is doing this the* SHERIFF *and* HALE *cross to cupboard, which they inspect. The* COUNTY ATTORNEY *starts to wipe his hands on the roller towel, turns it for a cleaner place*). Dirty towels! (*Kicks his foot against the pans under the sink*). Not much of a housekeeper, would you say, ladies?

Mrs. Hale (*stiffly*)   There's a great deal of work to be done on a farm.

County Attorney   To be sure. And yet (*with a little bow to her*) I know there are some Dickson County farmhouses which do not have such roller towels.

(*He gives it a pull to expose its full length again.*)

Mrs. Hale   Those towels get dirty awful quick. Men's hands aren't always as clean as they might be.

County Attorney   Ah, loyal to your sex, I see. But you and Mrs. Wright were neighbors. I suppose you were friends, too.

Mrs. Hale (*shaking her head*)   I've not seen much of her of late years. I've not been in this house—it's more than a year.

County Attorney (*crossing to women* U.C.)   And why was that? You didn't like her?

Mrs. Hale   I liked her all well enough. Farmers' wives have their hands full, Mr. Henderson. And then——

County Attorney   Yes——?

Mrs. Hale (*looking about*)   It never seemed a very cheerful place.

County Attorney   No—it's not cheerful. I shouldn't say she had the home-making instinct.

Mrs. Hale   Well, I don't know as Wright had, either.

County Attorney   You mean that they didn't get on very well?

Mrs. Hale   No, I don't mean anything. But I don't think a place'd be any cheerfuller for John Wright's being in it.

County Attorney   I'd like to talk more of that a little later. I want to get the lay of things upstairs now.

(*He goes past the women to* U.R. *where steps lead to a stair door.*)

Sheriff   I suppose anything Mrs. Peters does'll be all right. She was to take in some clothes for her, you know, and a few little things. We left in such a hurry yesterday.

County Attorney   Yes, but I would like to see what you take, Mrs. Peters, and keep an eye out for anything that might be of use to us.

Mrs. Peters   Yes, Mr. Henderson.

(*The men leave by* U.R. *door to stairs. The women listen to the men's steps on the stairs, then look about the kitchen.*)

Mrs. Hale (*crossing* L. *to sink*)   I'd hate to have men coming into my kitchen, snooping around and criticizing.

(*She arranges the pans under sink which the* LAWYER *had shoved out of place.*)

Mrs. Peters   Of course it's no more than their duty.

(*Crosses to cupboard* U.R.)

Mrs. Hale   Duty's all right, but I guess that deputy sheriff that came out to make the fire might have got a little of this on. (*Gives the roller towel a pull*). Wish I'd thought of that sooner. Seems mean to talk about her for not having things slicked up when she had to come away in such a hurry. (*Crosses* R. *to* MRS. PETERS *at cupboard.*)

Mrs. Peters (*who has been looking through cupboard, lifts one end of a towel that covers a pan*)   She had bread set.

(*Stands still.*)

Mrs. Hale (*eyes fixed on a loaf of bread beside the breadbox, which is on a low shelf of the cupboard*)   She was going to put this in there. (*Picks up loaf, then abruptly drops it. In a manner of returning to familiar things*). It's a shame about her fruit. I wonder if it's all gone. (*Gets up on the chair and looks*). I think there's some here that's all right, Mrs. Peters. Yes—here; (*holding it toward the window*) this is cherries, too. (*Looking again*). I declare I believe that's the only one. (*Gets down, jar in her hand. Goes to the sink and wipes it off on the outside*). She'll feel awful bad after all her hard work in the hot weather. I remember the afternoon I put up my cherries last summer.

(*She puts the jar on the big kitchen table, center of the room. With a sigh, is about to sit down in the rocking chair. Before she is seated realizes what chair it is; with a slow look at it, steps back. The chair which she has touched rocks back and forth.* MRS. PETERS *moves to center table and they both watch the chair rock for a moment or two.*)

Mrs. Peters (*shaking off the mood which the empty rocking chair has evoked. Now in a businesslike manner she speaks*)   Well, I must get those things from the front room closet. (*She goes to the door at the* R., *but, after looking into the other room, steps back*). You coming with me, Mrs. Hale? You could help me carry them. (*They go in the other* *room; reappear,* Mrs. Peters *carrying a dress, petticoat and skirt,* Mrs. Hale *following with a pair of shoes).* My, it's cold in there.

(She puts the clothes on the big table, and hurries to the stove.)

Mrs. Hale *(right of center table examining the skirt)*   Wright was close. I think maybe that's why she kept so much to herself. She didn't even belong to the Ladies' Aid. I suppose she felt she couldn't do her part, and then you don't enjoy things when you feel shabby. I heard she used to wear pretty clothes and be lively, when she was Minnie Foster, one of the town girls singing in the choir. But that—oh, that was thirty years ago. This all you was to take in?

Mrs. Peters   She said she wanted an apron. Funny thing to want, for there isn't much to get you dirty in jail, goodness knows. But I suppose just to make her feel more natural. *(Crosses to cupboard).* She said they was in the top drawer in this cupboard. Yes, here. And then her little shawl that always hung behind the door. *(Opens stair door and looks).* Yes, here it is.

(Quickly shuts door leading upstairs.)

Mrs. Hale *(abruptly moving toward her)*   Mrs. Peters?

Mrs. Peters   Yes, Mrs. Hale? *(At* U.R. *door.)*

Mrs. Hale   Do you think she did it?

Mrs. Peters *(in a frightened voice)*   Oh, I don't know.

Mrs. Hale   Well, I don't think she did. Asking for an apron and her little shawl. Worrying about her fruit.

Mrs. Peters *(starts to speak, glances up, where footsteps are heard in the room above. In a low voice)*   Mr. Peters says it looks bad for her. Mr. Henderson is awful sarcastic in a speech and he'll make fun of her sayin' she didn't wake up.

Mrs. Hale   Well, I guess John Wright didn't wake when they was slipping that rope under his neck.

Mrs. Peters *(crossing slowly to table and placing shawl and apron on table with other clothing)*   No, it's strange. It must have been done awful crafty and still. They say it was such a—funny way to kill a man, rigging it all up like that.

Mrs. Hale *(crossing to left of* Mrs. Peters *at table)*   That's just what Mr. Hale said. There was a gun in the house. He says that's what he can't understand.

Mrs. Peters   Mr. Henderson said coming out that what was needed for the case was a motive; something to show anger, or—sudden feeling.

Mrs. Hale *(who is standing by the table)*   Well, I don't see any signs of anger around here. *(She puts her hand on the dish towel which lies on the table, stands looking down at table, one-half of which is clean, the other half messy).* It's wiped to here. *(Makes a move as if to finish work,* *then turns and looks at loaf of bread outside the breadbox. Drops towel. In that voice of coming back to familiar things*). Wonder how they are finding things upstairs. (*Crossing below table to* D.R.). I hope she had it a little more red-up[1] up there. You know, it seems kind of *sneaking*. Locking her up in town and then coming out here and trying to get her own house to turn against her!

Mrs. Peters   But, Mrs. Hale, the law is the law.

Mrs. Hale   I s'pose 'tis. (*Unbuttoning her coat*). Better loosen up your things, Mrs. Peters. You won't feel them when you go out.

(MRS. PETERS *takes off her fur tippet, goes to hang it on chair back left of table, stands looking at the work basket on floor near* D.L. *window*.)

Mrs. Peters   She was piecing a quilt.

(*She brings the large sewing basket to the center table and they look at the bright pieces,* MRS. HALE *above the table and* MRS. PETERS *left of it.*)

Mrs. Hale   It's a log cabin pattern. Pretty, isn't it? I wonder if she was goin' to quilt it or just knot it?

(*Footsteps have been heard coming down the stairs. The* SHERIFF *enters followed by* HALE *and the* COUNTY ATTORNEY.)

Sheriff   They wonder if she was going to quilt it or just knot it![2]

(*The men laugh, the women look abashed.*)

County Attorney (*rubbing his hands over the stove*)   Frank's fire didn't do much up there, did it? Well, let's go out to the barn and get that cleared up.

(*The men go outside by* U.L. *door.*)

Mrs. Hale (*resentfully*)   I don't know as there's anything so strange, our takin' up our time with little things while we're waiting for them to get the evidence. (*She sits in chair right of table smoothing out a block with decision*). I don't see as it's anything to laugh about.

Mrs. Peters (*apologetically*)   Of course they've got awful important things on their minds.

(*Pulls up a chair and joins* MRS. HALE *at the left of the table.*)

---

[1] red-up: neat, orderly.

[2] quilt: to stitch together two layers of cloth with padding between them; knot: to fasten separate pieces of cloth together with knots of yarn or thread spaced at regular intervals.

Mrs. Hale (*examining another block*) Mrs. Peters, look at this one. Here, this is the one she was working on, and look at the sewing! All the rest of it has been so nice and even. And look at this! It's all over the place! Why, it looks as if she didn't know what she was about!

(*After she has said this they look at each other, then start to glance back at the door. After an instant* Mrs. Hale *has pulled at a knot and ripped the sewing.*)

Mrs. Peters Oh, what are you doing, Mrs. Hale?

Mrs. Hale (*mildly*) Just pulling out a stitch or two that's not sewed very good. (*Threading a needle*). Bad sewing always made me fidgety.

Mrs. Peters (*with a glance at door, nervously*) I don't think we ought to touch things.

Mrs. Hale I'll just finish up this end. (*Suddenly stopping and leaning forward*). Mrs. Peters?

Mrs. Peters Yes, Mrs. Hale?

Mrs. Hale What do you suppose she was so nervous about?

Mrs. Peters Oh—I don't know. I don't know as she was nervous. I sometimes sew awful queer when I'm just tired. (Mrs. Hale *starts to say something, looks at* Mrs. Peters, *then goes on sewing*). Well, I must get these things wrapped up. They may be through sooner than we think. (*Putting apron and other things together*). I wonder where I can find a piece of paper, and string.

(*Rises.*)

Mrs. Hale In that cupboard, maybe.

Mrs. Peters (*crosses* R. *looking in cupboard*) Why, here's a birdcage. (*Holds it up*). Did she have a bird, Mrs. Hale?

Mrs. Hale Why, I don't know whether she did or not—I've not been here for so long. There was a man around last year selling canaries cheap, but I don't know as she took one; maybe she did. She used to sing real pretty herself.

Mrs. Peters (*glancing around*) Seems funny to think of a bird here. But she must have had one, or why would she have a cage? I wonder what happened to it?

Mrs. Hale I s'pose maybe the cat got it.

Mrs. Peters No, she didn't have a cat. She's got that feeling some people have about cats—being afraid of them. My cat got in her room and she was real upset and asked me to take it out.

Mrs. Hale My sister Bessie was like that. Queer, ain't it?

Mrs. Peters (*examining the cage*) Why, look at this door. It's broke. One hinge is pulled apart.

(*Takes a step down to* Mrs. Hale's *right.*)

Mrs. Hale (*looking too*) Looks as if someone must have been rough with it.

Mrs. Peters Why, yes.

(*She brings the cage forward and puts it on the table.*)

Mrs. Hale (*glancing toward* U.L. *door*) I wish if they're going to find any evidence they'd be about it. I don't like this place.

Mrs. Peters But I'm awful glad you came with me, Mrs. Hale. It would be lonesome for me sitting here alone.

Mrs. Hale It would, wouldn't it? (*Dropping her sewing*). But I tell you what I do wish, Mrs. Peters. I wish I had come over sometimes when *she* was here. I—(*looking around the room*)—wish I had.

Mrs. Peters But of course you were awful busy, Mrs. Hale—your house and your children.

Mrs. Hale (*rises and crosses* L.) I could've come. I stayed away because it weren't cheerful—and that's why I ought to have come. I—(*looking out* L. *window*) I've never liked this place. Maybe because it's down in a hollow and you don't see the road. I dunno what it is, but it's a lonesome place and always was. I wish I had come over to see Minnie Foster sometimes. I can see now—

(*Shakes her head.*)

Mrs. Peters (*left of table and above it*) Well, you mustn't reproach yourself, Mrs. Hale. Somehow we just don't see how it is with other folks until—something turns up.

Mrs. Hale Not having children makes less work—but it makes a quiet house, and Wright out to work all day, and no company when he did come in. (*Turning from window*). Did you know John Wright, Mrs. Peters?

Mrs. Peters Not to know him; I've seen him in town. They say he was a good man.

Mrs. Hale Yes—good; he didn't drink, and kept his word as well as most, I guess, and paid his debts. But he was a hard man, Mrs. Peters. Just to pass the time of day with him—— (*Shivers*). Like a raw wind that gets to the bone. (*Pauses, her eye falling on the cage*). I should think she would 'a' wanted a bird. But what do you suppose went with it?

Mrs. Peters I don't know, unless it got sick and died.

(*She reaches over and swings the broken door, swings it again, both women watch it.*)

Mrs. Hale You weren't raised round here, were you? (Mrs. PETERS *shakes her head*). You didn't know—her?

Mrs. Peters Not till they brought her yesterday.

Mrs. Hale She—come to think of it, she was kind of like a bird herself—

real sweet and pretty, but kind of timid and—fluttery. How—she—did —change. (*Silence; then as if struck by a happy thought and relieved to get back to everyday things. Crosses* R. *above* MRS. PETERS *to cupboard, replaces small chair used to stand on to its original place* D.R.). Tell you what, Mrs. Peters, why don't you take the quilt in with you? It might take up her mind.

Mrs. Peters Why, I think that's a real nice idea, Mrs. Hale. There couldn't possibly be any objection to it, could there? Now, just what would I take? I wonder if her patches are in here—and her things.

(*They look in the sewing basket.*)

Mrs. Hale (*crosses to right of table*) Here's some red. I expect this has got sewing things in it. (*Brings out a fancy box*). What a pretty box. Looks like something somebody would give you. Maybe her scissors are in here. (*Opens box. Suddenly puts her hand to her nose*). Why—— (MRS. PETERS *bends nearer, then turns her face away*). There's something wrapped up in this piece of silk.

Mrs. Peters Why, this isn't her scissors.

Mrs. Hale (*lifting the silk*) Oh, Mrs. Peters—it's—— (MRS. PETERS *bends closer.*)

Mrs. Peters It's the bird.

Mrs. Hale —But, Mrs. Peters—look at it! Its neck! Look at its neck! It's all—other side *to*.

Mrs. Peters Somebody—wrung—its—neck.

(*Their eyes meet. A look of growing comprehension, of horror. Steps are heard outside.* MRS. HALE *slips box under quilt pieces, and sinks into her chair. Enter* SHERIFF *and* COUNTY ATTORNEY. MRS. PETERS *steps* D.L. *and stands looking out of window.*)

County Attorney (*as one turning from serious things to little pleasantries*) Well, ladies, have you decided whether she was going to quilt it or knot it? (*Crosses to* C. *above table.*)

Mrs. Peters We think she was going to—knot it.

(SHERIFF *crosses to right of stove, lifts stove lid and glances at fire, then stands warming hands at stove.*)

County Attorney Well, that's interesting, I'm sure. (*Seeing the birdcage*). Has the bird flown?

Mrs. Hale (*putting more quilt pieces over the box*) We think the—cat got it.

County Attorney (*preoccupied*) Is there a cat?

(MRS. HALE *glances in a quick covert way at* MRS. PETERS.)

Mrs. Peters (*turning from window takes a step in*)   Well, not *now*. They're superstitious, you know. They leave.

County Attorney (*to* Sheriff Peters, *continuing an interrupted conversation*)   No sign at all of anyone having come from the outside. Their own rope. Now let's go up again and go over it piece by piece. (*They start upstairs*). It would have to have been someone who knew just the———

(Mrs. Peters *sits down left of table. The two women sit there not looking at one another, but as if peering into something and at the same time holding back. When they talk now it is in the manner of feeling their way over strange ground, as if afraid of what they are saying, but as if they cannot help saying it.*)

Mrs. Hale (*hesitatively and in hushed voice*)   She liked the bird. She was going to bury it in that pretty box.

Mrs. Peters (*in a whisper*)   When I was a girl—my kitten—there was a boy took a hatchet, and before my eyes—and before I could get there— (*Covers her face an instant*). If they hadn't held me back I would have— (*catches herself, looks upstairs where steps are heard, falters weakly*) —hurt him.

Mrs. Hale (*with a slow look around her*)   I wonder how it would seem never to have had any children around. (*Pause*). No, Wright wouldn't like the bird—a thing that sang. She used to sing. He killed that, too.

Mrs. Peters (*moving uneasily*)   We don't know who killed the bird.

Mrs. Hale   I knew John Wright.

Mrs. Peters   It was an awful thing was done in this house that night, Mrs. Hale. Killing a man while he slept, slipping a rope around his neck that choked the life out of him.

Mrs. Hale   His neck. Choked the life out of him.

(*Her hand goes out and rests on the bird-cage.*)

Mrs. Peters (*with rising voice*)   We don't know who killed him. We don't know.

Mrs. Hale (*her own feeling not interrupted*)   If there'd been years and years of nothing, then a bird to sing to you, it would be awful—still, after the bird was still.

Mrs. Peters (*something within her speaking*)   I know what stillness is. When we homesteaded in Dakota, and my first baby died—after he was two years old, and me with no other then———

Mrs. Hale (*moving*)   How soon do you suppose they'll be through looking for the evidence?

Mrs. Peters   I know what stillness is. (*Pulling herself back*). The law has got to punish crime, Mrs. Hale.

Mrs. Hale (*not as if answering that*)   I wish you'd seen Minnie Foster when she wore a white dress with blue ribbons and stood up there in the choir and sang. (*A look around the room*). Oh, I *wish* I'd come over here once in a while! That was a crime! That was a crime! Who's going to punish that?

Mrs. Peters (*looking upstairs*)   We mustn't—take on.

Mrs. Hale   I might have known she needed help! I know how things can be—for women. I tell you, it's queer, Mrs. Peters. We live close together and we live far apart. We all go through the same things—it's all just a different kind of the same thing. (*Brushes her eyes, noticing the jar of fruit, reaches out for it*). If I was you I wouldn't tell her her fruit was gone. Tell her it *ain't*. Tell her it's all right. Take this in to prove it to her. She—she may never know whether it was broke or not.

Mrs. Peters (*takes the jar, looks about for something to wrap it in; takes petticoat from the clothes brought from the other room, very nervously begins winding this around the jar. In a false voice*)   My, it's a good thing the men couldn't hear us. Wouldn't they just laugh! Getting all stirred up over a little thing like a—dead canary. As if that could have anything to do with—with—wouldn't they *laugh!*

(*The men are heard coming downstairs.*)

Mrs. Hale (*under her breath*)   Maybe they would—maybe they wouldn't.

County Attorney   No, Peters, it's all perfectly clear except a reason for doing it. But you know juries when it comes to women. If there was some definite thing. (*Crosses slowly to above table.* SHERIFF *crosses* D.R. MRS. HALE *and* MRS. PETERS *remain seated at either side of table*). Something to show—something to make a story about—a thing that would connect up with this strange way of doing it——

(*The women's eyes meet for an instant. Enter* HALE *from outer door.*)

Hale (*remaining* U.L. *by door*)   Well, I've got the team around. Pretty cold out there.

County Attorney   I'm going to stay awhile by myself. (*To the* SHERIFF). You can send Frank out for me, can't you? I want to go over everything. I'm not satisfied that we can't do better.

Sheriff   Do you want to see what Mrs. Peters is going to take in? (*The* LAWYER *picks up the apron, laughs.*)

County Attorney   Oh, I guess they're not very dangerous things the ladies have picked out. (*Moves a few things about, disturbing the quilt pieces which cover the box. Steps back*). No, Mrs. Peters doesn't need supervising. For that matter a sheriff's wife is married to the law. Ever think of it that way, Mrs. Peters?

Mrs. Peters   Not—just that way.

Sheriff (*chuckling*)   Married to the law. (*Moves to* D.R. *door to the other room*). I just want you to come in here a minute, George. We ought to take a look at these windows.

County Attorney (*scoffingly*) Oh, windows!

Sheriff We'll be right out, Mr. Hale.

(HALE *goes outside. The* SHERIFF *follows the* COUNTY ATTORNEY *into the other room. Then* MRS. HALE *rises, hands tight together, looking intensely at* MRS. PETERS, *whose eyes make a slow turn, finally meeting* MRS. HALE'S. *A moment* MRS. HALE *holds her, then her own eyes point the way to where the box is concealed. Suddenly* MRS. PETERS *throws back quilt pieces and tries to put the box in the bag she is carrying. It is too big. She opens box, starts to take bird out, cannot touch it, goes to pieces, stands there helpless. Sound of a knob turning in the other room.* MRS. HALE *snatches the box and puts it in the pocket of her big coat. Enter* COUNTY ATTORNEY *and* SHERIFF, *who remains* D.R.)

County Attorney (*crosses to* U.L. *door facetiously*) Well, Henry, at least we found out that she was not going to quilt it. She was going to—what is it you call it, ladies?

Mrs. Hale (*standing* C. *below table facing front, her hand against her pocket*). We call it—knot it, Mr. Henderson.

Curtain

Sophocles (496[?]–406 B.C.)
ANTIGONE
Translated by Elizabeth Wyckoff

CHARACTERS

Antigone	**Haemon**
Ismene	**Teiresias**
Chorus of Theban Elders	**A Messenger**
Creon	**Eurydice**
A Guard	

Scene: Thebes, before the royal palace. ANTIGONE *and* ISMENE *emerge from its great central door.*

Antigone   My sister, my Ismene, do you know
of any suffering from our father sprung
that Zeus does not achieve for us survivors?
There's nothing grievous, nothing free from doom,
not shameful, not dishonored, I've not seen.   5
Your sufferings and mine.
And now, what of this edict which they say
the commander has proclaimed to the whole people?
Have you heard anything? Or don't you know
that the foes' trouble comes upon our friends?   10
Ismene   I've heard no word, Antigone, of our friends.
Not sweet nor bitter, since that single moment
when we two lost two brothers
who died on one day by a double blow.
And since the Argive army went away   15
this very night, I have no further news
of fortune or disaster for myself.

Antigone   I knew it well, and brought you from the house
    for just this reason, that you alone may hear.
Ismene   What is it? Clearly some news has clouded you.   20
Antigone   It has indeed. Creon will give the one
    of our two brothers honor in the tomb;
    the other none.
    Eteocles, with just entreatment treated,
    as law provides he has hidden under earth   25
    to have full honor with the dead below.
    But Polyneices' corpse who died in pain,
    they say he has proclaimed to the whole town
    that none may bury him and none bewail,
    but leave him unwept, untombed, a rich sweet sight   30
    for the hungry birds' beholding.
    Such orders they say the worthy Creon gives
    to you and me—yes, yes, I say to *me*—
    and that he's coming to proclaim it clear
    to those who know it not.   35
    Further: he has the matter so at heart
    that anyone who dares attempt the act
    will die by public stoning in the town.
    So there you have it and you soon will show
    if you are noble, or fallen from your descent.   40
Ismene   If things have reached this stage, what can I do,
    poor sister, that will help to make or mend?
Antigone   Think will you share my labor and my act.
Ismene   What will you risk? And where is your intent?
Antigone   Will you take up that corpse along with me?   45
Ismene   To bury him you mean, when it's forbidden?
Antigone   My brother, and yours, though you may wish he were not.
    I never shall be found to be his traitor.
Ismene   O hard of mind! When Creon spoke against it!
Antigone   It's not for him to keep me from my own.   50
Ismene   Alas. Remember, sister, how our father
    perished abhorred, ill-famed.
    Himself with his own hand, through his own curse
    destroyed both eyes.
    Remember next his mother and his wife   55
    finishing life in the shame of the twisted strings.
    And third two brothers on a single day,
    poor creatures, murdering, a common doom
    each with his arm accomplished on the other.
    And now look at the two of us alone.   60
    We'll perish terribly if we force law

and try to cross the royal vote and power.
We must remember that we two are women
so not to fight with men.
And that since we are subject to strong power   65
we must hear these orders, or any that may be worse.
So I shall ask of them beneath the earth
forgiveness, for in these things I am forced,
and shall obey the men in power. I know
that wild and futile action makes no sense.   70

Antigone   I wouldn't urge it. And if now you wished
to act, you wouldn't please me as a partner.
Be what you want to; but that man shall I
bury. For me, the doer, death is best.
Friend shall I lie with him, yes friend with friend,   75
when I have dared the crime of piety.
Longer the time in which to please the dead
than that for those up here.
There shall I lie forever. You may see fit
to keep from honor what the gods have honored.   80

Ismene   I shall do no dishonor. But to act
against the citizens. I cannot.

Antigone   That's your protection. Now I go, to pile
the burial-mound for him, my dearest brother.

Ismene   Oh my poor sister. How I fear for you!   85

Antigone   For me, don't borrow trouble. Clear your fate.

Ismene   At least give no one warning of this act;
you keep it hidden, and I'll do the same.

Antigone   Dear God! Denounce me. I shall hate you more
if silent, not proclaiming this to all.   90

Ismene   You have a hot mind over chilly things.

Antigone   I know I please those whom I most should please.

Ismene   If but you can. You crave what can't be done.

Antigone   And so, when strength runs out, I shall give over.

Ismene   Wrong from the start, to chase what cannot be.   95

Antigone   If that's your saying, I shall hate you first,
and next the dead will hate you in all justice.
But let me and my own ill-counselling
suffer this terror. I shall suffer nothing
as great as dying with a lack of grace.   100

Ismene   Go, since you want to. But know this: you go
senseless indeed, but loved by those who love you.

(ISMENE *returns to the palace;* ANTIGONE *leaves by one of the side entrances.*
The CHORUS *now enters from the other side.*)

Chorus Sun's own radiance, fairest light ever shone on the gates of
  Thebes,
  then did you shine, O golden day's
  eye, coming over Dirce's stream   105
  on the Man who had come from Argos with all his armor
  running now in headlong fear as you shook his bridle free.

  He was stirred by the dubious quarrel of Polyneices.
  So, screaming shrill,
  like an eagle over the land he flew,   110
  covered with white-snow wing,
  with many weapons,
  with horse-hair crested helms.

He who had stood above our halls, gaping about our seven gates,
with that circle of thirsting spears.   115
Gone, without our blood in his jaws,
before the torch took hold on our tower-crown.
Rattle of war at his back; hard the fight for the dragon's foe.

  The boasts of a proud tongue are for Zeus to hate.
  So seeing them streaming on   120
  in insolent clangor of gold,
  he struck with hurling fire him who rushed
  for the high wall's top,
  to cry conquest abroad.

Swinging, striking the earth he fell   125
fire in hand, who in mad attack,
had raged against us with blasts of hate.
He failed. He failed of his aim.
For the rest great Ares dealt his blows about,
first in the war-team.   130

  The captains stationed at seven gates
  fought with seven and left behind
  their brazen arms as an offering
  to Zeus who is turner of battle.
  All but those wretches, sons of one man,   135
  one mother's sons, who sent their spears
  each against each and found the share
  of a common death together.

Great-named Victory comes to us
answering Thebe's warrior-joy.   140
Let us forget the wars just done
and visit the shrines of the gods.

All, with night-long dance which Bacchus will lead,
who shakes Thebe's acres.

(CREON *enters from the palace.*)

> Now here he comes, the king of the land,   145
> Creon, Menoeceus' son,
> newly named by the gods' new fate.
> What plan that beats about his mind
> has made him call this council-session,
> sending his summons to all?   150

Creon   My friends, the very gods who shook the state
with mighty surge have set it straight again.
So now I sent for you, chosen from all,
first that I knew you constant in respect
to Laius' royal power; and again   155
when Oedipus had set the state to rights,
and when he perished, you were faithful still
in mind to the descendants of the dead.
When they two perished by a double fate,
on one day struck and striking and defiled   160
each by his own hand, now it comes that I
hold all the power and the royal throne
through close connection with the perished men.
You cannot learn of any man the soul,
the mind, and the intent until he shows   165
his practise of the government and law.
For I believe that who controls the state
and does not hold to the best plans of all,
but locks his tongue up through some kind of fear,
that he is worst of all who are or were.   170
And he who counts another greater friend
than his own fatherland, I put him nowhere.
So I—may Zeus all-seeing always know it—
could not keep silent as disaster crept
upon the town, destroying hope of safety.   175
Nor could I count the enemy of the land
friend to myself, not I who know so well
that she it is who saves us, sailing straight,
and only so can we have friends at all.
With such good rules shall I enlarge our state.   180
And now I have proclaimed their brother-edict.
In the matter of the sons of Oedipus,
citizens, know: Eteocles who died,

defending this our town with champion spear,
is to be covered in the grave and granted   185
all holy rites we give the noble dead.
But his brother Polyneices whom I name
the exile who came back and sought to burn
his fatherland, the gods who were his kin,
who tried to gorge on blood he shared, and lead   190
the rest of us as slaves—
it is announced that no one in this town
may give him burial or mourn for him.
Leave him unburied, leave his corpse disgraced,
a dinner for the birds and for the dogs.   195
Such is my mind. Never shall I, myself,
honor the wicked and reject the just.
The man who is well-minded to the state
from me in death and life shall have his honor.

Chorus   This resolution, Creon, is your own,   200
in the matter of the traitor and the true.
For you can make such rulings as you will
about the living and about the dead.

Creon   Now you be sentinels of the decree.

Chorus   Order some younger man to take this on.   205

Creon   Already there are watchers of the corpse.

Chorus   What other order would you give us, then?

Creon   Not to take sides with any who disobey.

Chorus   No fool is fool as far as loving death.

Creon   Death is the price. But often we have known   210
men to be ruined by the hope of profit.

(*Enter, from the side, a* GUARD.)

Guard   Lord, I can't claim that I am out of breath
from rushing here with light and hasty step,
for I had many haltings in my thought
making me double back upon my road.   215
My mind kept saying many things to me:
"Why go where you will surely pay the price?"
"Fool, are you halting? And if Creon learns
from someone else, how shall you not be hurt?"
Turning this over, on I dilly-dallied.   220
And so a short trip turns itself to long.
Finally, though, my coming here won out.
If what I say is nothing, still I'll say it.
For I come clutching to one single hope
that I can't suffer what is not my fate.   225

Creon What is it that brings on this gloom of yours?
Guard I want to tell you first about myself.
  I didn't do it, didn't see who did it.
  It isn't right for me to get in trouble.
Creon Your aim is good. You fence the fact around.   230
  It's clear you have some shocking news to tell.
Guard Terrible tidings make for long delays.
Creon Speak out the story, and then get away.
Guard I'll tell you. Someone left the corpse just now,
  burial all accomplished, thirsty dust   235
  strewn on the flesh, the ritual complete.
Creon What are you saying? What man has dared to do it?
Guard I wouldn't know. There were no marks of picks,
  no grubbed-out earth. The ground was dry and hard,
  no trace of wheels. The doer left no sign.   240
  When the first fellow on the day-shift showed us,
  we all were sick with wonder.
  For he was hidden, not inside a tomb,
  light dust upon him, enough to turn the curse,
  no wild beast's track, nor track of any hound   245
  having been near, nor was the body torn.
  We roared bad words about, guard against guard,
  and came to blows. No one was there to stop us.
  Each man had done it, nobody had done it
  so as to prove it on him—we couldn't tell.   250
  We were prepared to hold to red-hot iron,
  to walk through fire, to swear before the gods
  we hadn't done it, hadn't shared the plan,
  when it was plotted or when it was done.
  And last, when all our sleuthing came out nowhere,   255
  one fellow spoke, who made our heads to droop
  low toward the ground. We couldn't disagree.
  We couldn't see a chance of getting off.
  He said we had to tell you all about it.
  We couldn't hide the fact.   260
  So he won out. The lot chose poor old me
  to win the prize. So here I am unwilling,
  quite sure you people hardly want to see me.
  Nobody likes the bringer of bad news.
Chorus Lord, while he spoke, my mind kept on debating.   265
  Isn't this action possibly a god's?
Creon Stop now, before you fill me up with rage,
  or you'll prove yourself insane as well as old.
  Unbearable, your saying that the gods

take any kindly forethought for this corpse. 270
Would it be they had hidden him away,
honoring his good service, his who came
to burn their pillared temples and their wealth,
even their land, and break apart their laws?
Or have you seen them honor wicked men? 275
It isn't so.
No, from the first there were some men in town
who took the edict hard, and growled against me,
who hid the fact that they were rearing back,
not rightly in the yoke, no way my friends. 280
These are the people—oh it's clear to me—
who have bribed these men and brought about the deed.
No current custom among men as bad
as silver currency. This destroys the state;
this drives men from their homes; this wicked teacher 285
drives solid citizens to acts of shame.
It shows men how to practise infamy
and knows the deeds of all unholiness.
Every least hireling who helped in this
brought about then the sentence he shall have. 290
But further, as I still revere great Zeus,
understand this, I tell you under oath,
if you don't find the very man whose hands
buried the corpse, bring him for me to see,
not death alone shall be enough for you 295
till living, hanging, you make clear the crime.
For any future grabbings you'll have learned
where to get pay, and that it doesn't pay
to squeeze a profit out of every source.
For you'll have felt that more men come to doom 300
through dirty profits than are kept by them.
Guard May I say something? Or just turn and go?
Creon Aren't you aware your speech is most unwelcome?
Guard Does it annoy your hearing or your mind?
Creon Why are you out to allocate my pain? 305
Guard The doer hurts your mind. I hurt your ears.
Creon You are a quibbling rascal through and through.
Guard But anyhow I never did the deed.
Creon And you the man who sold your mind for money!
Guard Oh! 310
How terrible to guess, and guess at lies!
Creon Go pretty up your guesswork. If you don't

show me the doers you will have to say
that wicked payments work their own revenge.
Guard   Indeed, I pray he's found, but yes or no,   315
taken or not as luck may settle it,
you won't see me returning to this place.
Saved when I neither hoped nor thought to be,
I owe the gods a mighty debt of thanks.

(CREON *enters the palace. The* GUARD *leaves by the way he came.*)

Chorus   Many the wonders but nothing walks stranger than man.   320
This thing crosses the sea in the winter's storm,
making his path through the roaring waves.
And she, the greatest of gods, the earth—
ageless she is, and unwearied—he wears her away
as the ploughs go up and down from year to year   325
and his mules turn up the soil.

Gay nations of birds he snares and leads,
wild beast tribes and the salty brood of the sea,
with the twisted mesh of his nets, this clever man.
He controls with craft the beasts of the open air,   330
walkers on hills. The horse with his shaggy mane
he holds and harnesses, yoked about the neck,
and the strong bull of the mountain.

Language, and thought like the wind
and the feelings that make the town,   335
he has taught himself, and shelter against the cold,
refuge from rain. He can always help himself.
He faces no future helpless. There's only death
that he cannot find an escape from. He has contrived
refuge from illnesses once beyond all cure.   340

Clever beyond all dreams
the inventive craft that he has
which may drive him one time or another to well or ill.
When he honors the laws of the land and the gods' sworn right
high indeed is his city; but stateless the man   345
who dares to dwell with dishonor. Not by my fire,
never to share my thoughts, who does these things.

(*The* GUARD *enters with* ANTIGONE.)

My mind is split at this awful sight.
I know her. I cannot deny
Antigone is here.   350

Alas, the unhappy girl,
her unhappy father's child.
Oh what is the meaning of this?
It cannot be you that they bring
for breaking the royal law,   355
caught in open shame.

Guard This is the woman who has done the deed.
We caught her at the burying. Where's the king?

(CREON *enters*.)

Chorus Back from the house again just when he's needed.
Creon What must I measure up to? What has happened?   360
Guard Lord, one should never swear off anything.
Afterthought makes the first resolve a liar.
I could have vowed I wouldn't come back here
after your threats, after the storm I faced.
But joy that comes beyond the wildest hope   365
is bigger than all other pleasure known.
I'm here, though I swore not to be, and bring
this girl. We caught her burying the dead.
This time we didn't need to shake the lots;
mine was the luck, all mine.   370
So now, lord, take her, you, and question her
and prove her as you will. But I am free.
And I deserve full clearance on this charge.
Creon Explain the circumstance of the arrest.
Guard She was burying the man. You have it all.   375
Creon Is this the truth? And do you grasp its meaning?
Guard I saw her burying the very corpse
you had forbidden. Is this adequate?
Creon How was she caught and taken in the act?
Guard It was like this: when we got back again   380
struck with those dreadful threatenings of yours,
we swept away the dust that hid the corpse.
We stripped it back to slimy nakedness.
And then we sat to windward on the hill
so as to dodge the smell.   385
We poked each other up with growling threats
if anyone was careless of his work.
For some time this went on, till it was noon.
The sun was high and hot. Then from the earth
up rose a dusty whirlwind to the sky,   390
filling the plain, smearing the forest-leaves,
clogging the upper air. We shut our eyes,

sat and endured the plague the gods had sent.
So the storm left us after a long time.
We saw the girl. She cried the sharp and shrill   395
cry of a bitter bird which sees the nest
bare where the young birds lay.
So this same girl, seeing the body stripped,
cried with great groanings, cried a dreadful curse
upon the people who had done the deed.   400
Soon in her hands she brought the thirsty dust,
and holding high a pitcher of wrought bronze
she poured the three libations for the dead.
We saw this and surged down. We trapped her fast;
and she was calm. We taxed her with the deeds   405
both past and present. Nothing was denied.
And I was glad, and yet I took it hard.
One's own escape from trouble makes one glad;
but bringing friends to trouble is hard grief.
Still, I care less for all these second thoughts   410
than for the fact that I myself am safe.
Creon   You there, whose head is drooping to the ground,
do you admit this, or deny you did it?
Antigone   I say I did it and I don't deny it.
Creon (*to the* GUARD)   Take yourself off wherever you wish to go   415
free of a heavy charge.
Creon (*to* ANTIGONE)   You—tell me not at length but in a word.
You knew the order not to do this thing?
Antigone   I knew, of course I knew. The word was plain.
Creon   And still you dared to overstep these laws?   420
Antigone   For me it was not Zeus who made that order.
Nor did that Justice who lives with the gods below
mark out such laws to hold among mankind.
Nor did I think your orders were so strong
that you, a mortal man, could over-run   425
the gods' unwritten and unfailing laws.
Not now, nor yesterday's, they always live,
and no one knows their origin in time.
So not through fear of any man's proud spirit
would I be likely to neglect these laws,   430
draw on myself the gods' sure punishment.
I knew that I must die; how could I not? ⸱
even without your warning. If I die
before my time, I say it is a gain.
Who lives in sorrows many as are mine   435
how shall he not be glad to gain his death?

And so, for me to meet this fate, no grief.
But if I left that corpse, my mother's son,
dead and unburied I'd have cause to grieve
as now I grieve not.   440
And if you think my acts are foolishness
the foolishness may be in a fool's eye.

Chorus   The girl is bitter. She's her father's child.
She cannot yield to trouble; nor could he.

Creon   These rigid spirits are the first to fall.   445
The strongest iron, hardened in the fire,
most often ends in scraps and shatterings.
Small curbs bring raging horses back to terms.
Slave to his neighbor, who can think of pride?
This girl was expert in her insolence   450
when she broke bounds beyond established law.
Once she had done it, insolence the second,
to boast her doing, and to laugh in it.
I am no man and she the man instead
if she can have this conquest without pain.   455
She is my sister's child, but were she child
of closer kin than any at my hearth,
she and her sister should not so escape
their death and doom. I charge Ismene too.
She shared the planning of this burial.   460
Call her outside. I saw her in the house,
maddened, no longer mistress of herself.
The sly intent betrays itself sometimes
before the secret plotters work their wrong.
I hate it too when someone caught in crime   465
then wants to make it seem a lovely thing.

Antigone   Do you want more than my arrest and death?

Creon   No more than that. For that is all I need.

Antigone   Why are you waiting? Nothing that you say
fits with my thought. I pray it never will.   470
Nor will you ever like to hear my words.
And yet what greater glory could I find
than giving my own brother funeral?
All these would say that they approved my act
did fear not mute them.   475
(A king is fortunate in many ways,
and most, that he can act and speak at will.)

Creon   None of these others see the case this way.

Antigone   They see, and do not say. You have them cowed.

Creon   And you are not ashamed to think alone?   480

Antigone No, I am not ashamed. When was it shame
  to serve the children of my mother's womb?
Creon It was not your brother who died against him, then?
Antigone Full brother, on both sides, my parents' child.
Creon Your act of grace, in his regard, is crime.   485
Antigone The corpse below would never say it was.
Creon When you honor him and the criminal just alike?
Antigone It was a brother, not a slave, who died.
Creon Died to destroy this land the other guarded.
Antigone Death yearns for equal law for all the dead.   490
Creon Not that the good and bad draw equal shares.
Antigone Who knows that this is holiness below?
Creon Never the enemy, even in death, a friend.
Antigone I cannot share in hatred, but in love.
Creon Then go down there, if you must love, and love   495
  the dead. No woman rules me while I live.

(ISMENE *is brought from the palace under guard.*)

Chorus Look there! Ismene is coming out.
  She loves her sister and mourns,
  with clouded brow and bloodied cheeks,
  tears on her lovely face.   500
Creon You, lurking like a viper in the house,
  who sucked me dry. I looked the other way
  while twin destruction planned against the throne.
  Now tell me, do you say you shared this deed?
  Or will you swear you didn't even know?   505
Ismene I did the deed, if she agrees I did.
  I am accessory and share the blame.
Antigone Justice will not allow this. You did not
  wish for a part, nor did I give you one.
Ismene You are in trouble, and I'm not ashamed   510
  to sail beside you into suffering.
Antigone Death and the dead, they know whose act it was.
  I cannot love a friend whose love is words.
Ismene Sister, I pray, don't fence me out from honor,
  from death with you, and honor done the dead.   515
Antigone Don't die along with me, nor make your own
  that which you did not do. My death's enough.
Ismene When you are gone what life can be my friend?
Antigone Love Creon. He's your kinsman and your care.
Ismene Why hurt me, when it does yourself no good?   520
Antigone I also suffer, when I laugh at you.
Ismene What further service can I do you now?

Antigone   To save yourself. I shall not envy you.

Ismene   Alas for me. Am I outside your fate?

Antigone   Yes. For you chose to live when I chose death.   525

Ismene   At least I was not silent. You were warned.

Antigone   Some will have thought you wiser. Some will not.

Ismene   And yet the blame is equal for us both.

Antigone   Take heart. You live. My life died long ago.
  And that has made me fit to help the dead.   530

Creon   One of these girls has shown her lack of sense
  just now. The other had it from her birth.

Ismene   Yes, lord. When people fall in deep distress
  their native sense departs, and will not stay.

Creon   You chose your mind's distraction when you chose   535
  to work out wickedness with this wicked girl.

Ismene   What life is there for me to live without her?

Creon   Don't speak of her. For she is here no more.

Ismene   But will you kill your own son's promised bride?

Creon   Oh, there are other furrows for his plough.   540

Ismene   But where the closeness that has bound these two?

Creon   Not for my sons will I choose wicked wives.

Ismene   Dear Haemon, your father robs you of your rights.

Creon   You and your marriage trouble me too much.

Ismene   You will take away his bride from your own son?   545

Creon   Yes. Death will help me break this marriage off.

Chorus   It seems determined that the girl must die.

Creon   You helped determine it. Now, no delay!
  Slaves, take them in. They must be women now.
  No more free running.   550
  Even the bold will fly when they see Death
  drawing in close enough to end their life.

(ANTIGONE *and* ISMENE *are taken inside.*)

Chorus   Fortunate they whose lives have no taste of pain.
  For those whose house is shaken by the gods
  escape no kind of doom. It extends to all the kin   555
  like the wave that comes when the winds of Thrace
  run over the dark of the sea.
  The black sand of the bottom is brought from the depth;
  the beaten capes sound back with a hollow cry.

  Ancient the sorrow of Labdacus' house, I know.   560
  Dead men's grief comes back, and falls on grief.
  No generation can free the next.
  One of the gods will strike. There is no escape.

So now the light goes out
for the house of Oedipus, while the bloody knife   565
cuts the remaining root. Folly and Fury have done this.

What madness of man, O Zeus, can bind your power?
Not sleep can destroy it who ages all,
nor the weariless months the gods have set. Unaged in time
monarch you rule of Olympus' gleaming light.   570
Near time, far future, and the pást,
one law controls them all:
any greatness in human life brings doom.

Wandering hope brings help to many men.
But others she tricks from their giddy loves,   575
and her quarry knows nothing until he has walked into flame.
Word of wisdom it was when someone said,
"The bad becomes the good
to him a god would doom."
Only briefly is that one from under doom.   580

(HAEMON *enters from the side.*)

    Here is your one surviving son.
    Does he come in grief at the fate of his bride,
    in pain that he's tricked of his wedding?
Creon   Soon we shall know more than a seer could tell us.
    Son, have you heard the vote condemned your bride?   585
    And are you here, maddened against your father,
    or are we friends, whatever I may do?
Haemon   My father, I am yours. You keep me straight
    with your good judgment, which I shall ever follow.
    Nor shall a marriage count for more with me   590
    than your kind leading.
Creon   There's my good boy. So should you hold at heart
    and stand behind your father all the way.
    It is for this men pray they may beget
    households of dutiful obedient sons,   595
    who share alike in punishing enemies,
    and give due honor to their father's friends.
    Whoever breeds a child that will not help
    what has he sown but trouble for himself,
    and for his enemies laughter full and free?   600
    Son, do not let your lust mislead your mind,
    all for a woman's sake, for well you know
    how cold the thing he takes into his arms
    who has a wicked woman for his wife.

What deeper wounding than a friend no friend?   605
Oh spit her forth forever, as your foe.
Let the girl marry somebody in Hades.
Since I have caught her in the open act,
the only one in town who disobeyed,
I shall not now proclaim myself a liar,   610
but kill her. Let her sing her song of Zeus
who guards the kindred.
If I allow disorder in my house
I'd surely have to licence it abroad.
A man who deals in fairness with his own,   615
he can make manifest justice in the state.
But he who crosses law, or forces it,
or hopes to bring the rulers under him,
shall never have a word of praise from me.
The man the state has put in place must have   620
obedient hearing to his least command
when it is right, and even when it's not.
He who accepts this teaching I can trust,
ruler, or ruled, to function in his place,
to stand his ground even in the storm of spears,   625
a mate to trust in battle at one's side.
There is no greater wrong than disobedience.
This ruins cities, this tears down our homes,
this breaks the battle-front in panic-rout.
If men love decently it is because   630
discipline saves their very lives for them.
So I must guard the men who yield to order,
not let myself be beaten by a woman.
Better, if it must happen, that a man
should overset me.   635
I won't be called weaker than womankind.
Chorus We think—unless our age is cheating us—
that what you say is sensible and right.
Haemon Father, the gods have given men good sense,
the only sure possession that we have.   640
I couldn't find the words in which to claim
that there was error in your late remarks.
Yet someone else might bring some further light.
Because I am your son I must keep watch
on all men's doing where it touches you,   645
their speech, and most of all, their discontents.
Your presence frightens any common man
from saying things you would not care to hear.

But in dark corners I have heard them say
how the whole town is grieving for this girl,　　　　　650
unjustly doomed, if ever woman was,
to die in shame for glorious action done.
She would not leave her fallen, slaughtered brother
there, as he lay, unburied, for the birds
and hungry dogs to make an end of him.　　　　　655
Isn't her real desert a golden prize?
This is the undercover speech in town.
Father, your welfare is my greatest good.
What loveliness in life for any child
outweighs a father's fortune and good fame?　　　　660
And so a father feels his children's faring.
Then, do not have one mind, and one alone
that only your opinion can be right.
Whoever thinks that he alone is wise,
his eloquence, his mind, above the rest,　　　　　665
come the unfolding, shows his emptiness.
A man, though wise, should never be ashamed
of learning more, and must unbend his mind.
Have you not seen the trees beside the torrent,
the ones that bend them saving every leaf,　　　　670
while the resistant perish root and branch?
And so the ship that will not slacken sail,
the sheet drawn tight, unyielding, overturns.
She ends the voyage with her keel on top.
No, yield your wrath, allow a change of stand.　　　675
Young as I am, if I may give advice,
I'd say it would be best if men were born
perfect in wisdom, but that failing this
(which often fails) it can be no dishonor
to learn from others when they speak good sense.　　680

Chorus　Lord, if your son has spoken to the point
you should take his lesson. He should do the same.
Both sides have spoken well.

Creon　At my age I'm to school my mind by his?
This boy instructor is my master, then?　　　　　685

Haemon　I urge no wrong. I'm young, but you should watch
my actions, not my years, to judge of me.

Creon　A loyal action, to respect disorder?

Haemon　I wouldn't urge respect for wickedness.

Creon　You don't think she is sick with that disease?　　690

Haemon　Your fellow-citizens maintain she's not.

Creon　Is the town to tell me how I ought to rule?

Haemon   Now there you speak just like a boy yourself.
Creon   Am I to rule by other mind than mine?
Haemon   No city is property of a single man.   695
Creon   But custom gives possession to the ruler.
Haemon   You'd rule a desert beautifully alone.
Creon (*to the* CHORUS)   It seems he's firmly on the woman's side.
Haemon   If you're a woman. It is you I care for.
Creon   Wicked, to try conclusions with your father.   700
Haemon   When you conclude unjustly, so I must.
Creon   Am I unjust, when I respect my office?
Haemon   You tread down the gods' due. Respect is gone.
Creon   Your mind is poisoned. Weaker than a woman!
Haemon   At least you'll never see me yield to shame.   705
Creon   Your whole long argument is but for her.
Haemon   And you, and me, and for the gods below.
Creon   You shall not marry her while she's alive.
Haemon   Then she shall die. Her death will bring another.
Creon   Your boldness has made progress. Threats, indeed!   710
Haemon   No threat, to speak against your empty plan.
Creon   Past due, sharp lessons for your empty brain.
Haemon   If you weren't father, I should call you mad.
Creon   Don't flatter me with "father," you woman's slave.
Haemon   You wish to speak but never wish to hear.   715
Creon   You think so? By Olympus, you shall not
    revile me with these tauntings and go free.
    Bring out the hateful creature; she shall die
    full in his sight, close at her bridegroom's side.
Haemon   Not at my side her death, and you will not   720
    ever lay eyes upon my face again.
    Find other friends to rave with after this.

(HAEMON *leaves, by one of the side entrances.*)

Chorus   Lord, he has gone with all the speed of rage.
    When such a man is grieved his mind is hard.
Creon   Oh, let him go, plan superhuman action.   725
    In any case the girls shall not escape.
Chorus   You plan for both the punishment of death?
Creon   Not her who did not do it. You are right.
Chorus   And what death have you chosen for the other?
Creon   To take her where the foot of man comes not.   730
    There shall I hide her in a hollowed cave
    living, and leave her just so much to eat
    as clears the city from the guilt of death.

There, if she prays to Death, the only god
of her respect, she may manage not to die. 735
Or she may learn at last and even then
how much too much her labor for the dead.

(CREON *returns to the palace.*)

Chorus Love unconquered in fight, love who falls on our havings.
You rest in the bloom of a girl's unwithered face.
You cross the sea, you are known in the wildest lairs. 740
Not the immortal gods can fly,
nor men of a day. Who has you within him is mad.

You twist the minds of the just. Wrong they pursue and are ruined.
You made this quarrel of kindred before us now.
Desire looks clear from the eyes of a lovely bride: 745
power as strong as the founded world.
For there is the goddess at play with whom no man can fight.

(ANTIGONE *is brought from the palace under guard.*)

Now I am carried beyond all bounds.
My tears will not be checked.
I see Antigone depart 750
to the chamber where all men sleep.
Antigone Men of my fathers' land, you see me go
my last journey. My last sight of the sun,
then never again. Death who brings all to sleep
takes me alive to the shore 755
of the river underground.
Not for me was the marriage-hymn, nor will anyone start the song
at a wedding of mine. Acheron is my mate.
Chorus With praise as your portion you go
in fame to the vault of the dead. 760
Untouched by wasting disease,
not paying the price of the sword,
of your own motion you go.
Alone among mortals will you descend
in life to the house of Death. 765
Antigone Pitiful was the death that stranger died,
our queen once, Tantalus' daughter. The rock
it covered her over, like stubborn ivy it grew.

758. Acheron: a mythological river in the world of the dead; hence the reference is to
Antigone's death.   767. Tantalus: in Greek mythology, a king was tortured by the
gods. His daughter, Niobe, was turned to stone but continued thereafter to weep for
the death of her children.

Still, as she wastes, the rain
and snow companion her.   770
Pouring down from her mourning eyes comes the water that soaks
    the stone.
My own putting to sleep a god has planned like hers.
Chorus   God's child and god she was.
    We are born to death.
    Yet even in death you will have your fame,   775
    to have gone like a god to your fate,
    in living and dying alike.
Antigone   Laughter against me now. In the name of our fathers' gods,
    could you not wait till I went? Must affront be thrown in my face?
    O city of wealthy men.   780
    I call upon Dirce's spring,
    I call upon Thebe's grove in the armored plain,
    to be my witnesses, how with no friend's mourning,
    by what decree I go to the fresh-made prison-tomb.
    Alive to the place of corpses, an alien still,   785
    never at home with the living nor with the dead.
Chorus   You went to the furthest verge
    of daring, but there you found
    the high foundation of justice, and fell.
    Perhaps you are paying your father's pain.   790
Antigone   You speak of my darkest thought, my pitiful father's fame,
    spread through all the world, and the doom that haunts our house,
    the royal house of Thebes.
    My mother's marriage-bed.
    Destruction where she lay with her husband-son,   795
    my father. These are my parents and I their child.
    I go to stay with them. My curse is to die unwed.
    My brother, you found your fate when you found your bride,
    found it for me as well. Dead, you destroy my life.
Chorus   You showed respect for the dead.   800
    So we for you: but power
    is not to be thwarted so.
    Your self-sufficiency has brought you down.
Antigone   Unwept, no wedding-song, unfriended, now I go
    the road laid down for me.   805
    No longer shall I see this holy light of the sun.
    No friend to bewail my fate.

(CREON *enters from the palace.*)

Creon   When people sing the dirge for their own deaths
    ahead of time, nothing will break them off

if they can hope that this will buy delay.   810
Take her away at once, and open up
the tomb I spoke of. Leave her there alone.
There let her choose: death, or a buried life.
No stain of guilt upon us in this case,
but she is exiled from our life on earth.   815
Antigone   O tomb, O marriage-chamber, hollowed out
house that will watch forever, where I go.
To my own people, who are mostly there;
Persephone has taken them to her.
Last of them all, ill-fated past the rest,   820
shall I descend, before my course is run.
Still when I get there I may hope to find
I come as a dear friend to my dear father,
to you, my mother, and my brother too.
All three of you have known my hand in death.   825
I washed your bodies, dressed them for the grave,
poured out the last libation at the tomb.
Last, Polyneices knows the price I pay
for doing final service to his corpse.
And yet the wise will know my choice was right.   830
Had I had children or their father dead,
I'd let them moulder. I should not have chosen
in such a case to cross the state's decree.
What is the law that lies behind these words?
One husband gone, I might have found another,   835
or a child from a new man in first child's place,
but with my parents hid away in death,
no brother, ever, could spring up for me.
Such was the law by which I honored you.
But Creon thought the doing was a crime,   840
a dreadful daring, brother of my heart.
So now he takes and leads me out by force.
No marriage-bed, no marriage-song for me,
and since no wedding, so no child to rear.
I go, without a friend, struck down by fate,   845
live to the hollow chambers of the dead.
What divine justice have I disobeyed?
Why, in my misery, look to the gods for help?
Can I call any of them my ally?
I stand convicted of impiety,   850
the evidence my pious duty done.

819. Persephone: a daughter of Zeus, taken by Pluto to the underworld as his queen.

Should the gods think that this is righteousness,
in suffering I'll see my error clear.
But if it is the others who are wrong
I wish them no greater punishment than mine.   855
Chorus   The same tempest of mind
    as ever, controls the girl.
Creon   Therefore her guards shall regret
    the slowness with which they move.
Antigone   That word comes close to death.   860
Creon   You are perfectly right in that.
Antigone   O town of my fathers in Thebe's land,
    O gods of our house.
    I am led away at last.
    Look, leaders of Thebes,   865
    I am last of your royal line.
    Look what I suffer, at whose command,
    because I respected the right.

(ANTIGONE *is led away. The slow procession should begin during the preceding passage.*)

Chorus   Danaë suffered too.
    She went from the light to the brass-built room,   870
    chamber and tomb together. Like you, poor child,
    she was of great descent, and more, she held and kept
    the seed of the golden rain which was Zeus.
    Fate has terrible power.
    You cannot escape it by wealth or war.   875
    No fort will keep it out, no ships outrun it.

    Remember the angry king,
    son of Dryas, who raged at the god and paid,
    pent in a rock-walled prison. His bursting wrath
    slowly went down. As the terror of madness went,   880
    he learned of his frenzied attack on the god.
    Fool, he had tried to stop
    the dancing women possessed of god,
    the fire of Dionysus, the songs and flutes.

    Where the dark rocks divide   885
    sea from sea in Thrace

869. Danaë: a maiden imprisoned in a stone tower by her father. There Zeus visited her
as a shower of golden rain, and she later gave birth to a son by him.   878. son of
Dryas: Lycurgus, who according to myth was punished for his opposition to the worship of Dionysus.   884. Dionysus: another name for Bacchus, the Greek god of wine,
revelry, and fertility, at whose festival the tragic dramas were performed.

is Salmydessus whose savage god
beheld the terrible blinding wounds
dealt to Phineus' sons by their father's wife.
Dark the eyes that looked to avenge their mother.   890
Sharp with her shuttle she struck, and blooded her hands.

Wasting they wept their fate,
settled when they were born
to Cleopatra, unhappy queen.
She was a princess too, of an ancient house,   895
reared in the cave of the wild north wind, her father.
Half a goddess but, child, she suffered like you.

(*Enter, from the side* Teiresias, *the blind prophet, led by a boy attendant.*)

Teiresias   Elders of Thebes, we two have come one road,
  two of us looking through one pair of eyes.
  This is the way of walking for the blind.   900
Creon   Teiresias, what news has brought you here?
Teiresias   I'll tell you. You in turn must trust the prophet.
Creon   I've always been attentive to your counsel.
Teiresias   And therefore you have steered this city straight.
Creon   So I can say how helpful you have been.   905
Teiresias   But now you are balanced on a razor's edge.
Creon   What is it? How I shudder at your words!
Teiresias   You'll know, when you hear the signs that I have marked
  I sat where every bird of heaven comes
  in my old place of augury, and heard   910
  bird-cries I'd never known. They screeched about
  goaded by madness, inarticulate.
  I marked that they were tearing one another
  with claws of murder. I could hear the wing-beats.
  I was afraid, so straight away I tried   915
  burnt sacrifice upon the flaming altar.
  No fire caught my offerings. Slimy ooze
  dripped on the ashes, smoked and sputtered there.
  Gall burst its bladder, vanished into vapor;
  the fat dripped from the bones and would not burn.   920
  These are the omens of the rites that failed,
  as my boy here has told me. He's my guide
  as I am guide to others.
  Why has this sickness struck against the state?

---

887. Salmydessus: a coastal town in Thrace.   889. Phineus: a blind prophet whose
second wife accused his sons of trying to seduce her; in response, Phineus blinded them.
891. shuttle: a thread-holding device used in weaving or sewing.

Through your decision. 925
All of the altars of the town are choked
with leavings of the dogs and birds; their feast
was on that fated, fallen Polyneices.
So the gods will have no offering from us,
not prayer, nor flame of sacrifice. The birds 930
will not cry out a sound I can distinguish,
gorged with the greasy blood of that dead man.
Think of these things, my son. All men may err
but error once committed, he's no fool
nor yet unfortunate, who gives up his stiffness 935
and cures the trouble he has fallen in.
Stubbornness and stupidity are twins.
Yield to the dead. Why goad him where he lies?
What use to kill the dead a second time?
I speak for your own good. And I am right. 940
Learning from a wise counsellor is not pain
if what he speaks are profitable words.

Creon Old man, you all, like bowmen at a mark,
have bent your bows at me. I've had my share
of seers. I've been an item in your accounts. 945
Make profit, trade in Lydian silver-gold,
pure gold of India; that's your chief desire.
But you will never cover up that corpse.
Not if the very eagles tear their food
from him, and leave it at the throne of Zeus. 950
I wouldn't give him up for burial
in fear of that pollution. For I know
no mortal being can pollute the gods.
O old Teiresias, human beings fall;
the clever ones the furthest, when they plead 955
a shameful case so well in hope of profit.

Teiresias Alas!
What man can tell me, has he thought at all . . .

Creon What hackneyed saw is coming from your lips?

Teiresias How better than all wealth is sound good counsel. 960

Creon And so is folly worse than anything.

Teiresias And you're infected with that same disease.

Creon I'm reluctant to be uncivil to a seer . . .

Teiresias You're that already. You have said I lie.

Creon Well, the whole crew of seers are money-mad. 965

Teiresias And the whole tribe of tyrants grab at gain.

Creon Do you realize you are talking to a king?

Teiresias I know. Who helped you save this town you hold?

Creon You're a wise seer, but you love wickedness.
Teiresias You'll bring me to speak the unspeakable, very soon.   970
Creon Well, speak it out. But do not speak for profit.
Teiresias No, there's no profit in my words for you.
Creon You'd better realise that you can't deliver
  my mind, if you should sell it, to the buyer.
Teiresias Know well, the sun will not have rolled its course   975
  many more days, before you come to give
  corpse for these corpses, child of your own loins.
  For you've confused the upper and lower worlds.
  You sent a life to settle in a tomb;
  you keep up here that which belongs below   980
  the corpse unburied, robbed of its release.
  Not you, nor any god that rules on high
  can claim him now.
  You rob the nether gods of what is theirs.
  So the pursuing horrors lie in wait   985
  to track you down. The Furies sent by Hades
  and by all gods will even you with your victims.
  Now say that I am bribed! At no far time
  shall men and women wail within your house.
  And all the cities that you fought in war   990
  whose sons had burial from wild beasts, or dogs,
  or birds that brought the stench of your great wrong
  back to each hearth, they move against you now.
  A bowman, as you said, I send my shafts,
  now you have moved me, straight. You'll feel the wound.   995
  Boy, take me home now. Let him spend his rage
  on younger men, and learn to calm his tongue,
  and keep a better mind than now he does.

(*Exit.*)

Chorus Lord, he has gone. Terrible prophecies!
  And since the time when I first grew grey hair   1000
  his sayings to the city have been true.
Creon I also know this. And my mind is torn.
  To yield is dreadful. But to stand against him.
  Dreadful to strike my spirit to destruction.
Chorus Now you must come to counsel, and take advice.   1005
Creon What must I do? Speak, and I shall obey.

---

986. Furies: three avenging goddesses: Alecto, Megaera, Tisiphone; Hades: another
name for Pluto, brother of Zeus who ruled the underworld.

Chorus   Go free the maiden from that rocky house.
   Bury the dead who lies in readiness.
Creon   This is your counsel? You would have me yield?
Chorus   Quick as you can. The gods move very fast   1010
   when they bring ruin on misguided men.
Creon   How hard, abandonment of my desire.
   But I can fight necessity no more.
Chorus   Do it yourself. Leave it to no one else.
Creon   I'll go at once. Come, followers, to your work.   1015
   You that are here round up the other fellows.
   Take axes with you, hurry to that place
   that overlooks us.
   Now my decision has been overturned
   shall I, who bound her, set her free myself.   1020
   I've come to fear it's best to hold the laws
   of old tradition to the end of life.

(*Exit.*)

Chorus   God of the many names, Semele's golden child,
   child of Olympian thunder, Italy's lord.
   Lord of Eleusis, where all men come   1025
   to mother Demeter's plain.
   Bacchus, who dwell in Thebes,
   by Ismenus' running water,
   where wild Bacchic women are at home,
   on the soil of the dragon seed.   1030

   Seen in the glaring flame, high on the double mount,
   with the nymphs of Parnassus at play on the hill,
   seen by Kastalia's flowing stream.
   You come from the ivied heights,
   from green Euboea's shore.   1035
   In immortal words we cry
   your name, lord, who watch the ways,
   the many ways of Thebes.

   This is your city, honored beyond the rest,
   the town of your mother's miracle-death.   1040

1023. *Semele's golden child:* Dionysus or Bacchus; Semele was a mortal whose union with Zeus produced Dionysus.   1025. *Eleusis:* a city in Attica with a great temple in honor of Demeter, the goddess of agriculture.   1027. *Bacchus:* another name for Dionysus.   1028. *Ismenus:* a river in Thebes.   1029: *Bacchic women:* women who worshiped Bacchus.   1032. *Parnassus:* a Greek mountain sacred to Apollo.   1033. *Kastalia:* a fountain on Mt. Parnassus.   1035. *Euboea:* an island in the Aegean Sea.

Now, as we wrestle our grim disease,
come with healing step from Parnassus' slope
or over the moaning sea.

Leader in dance of the fire-pulsing stars,
overseer of the voices of night,   1045
child of Zeus, be manifest,
with due companionship of Maenad maids
whose cry is but your name.

(*Enter one of those who left with* CREON, *as messenger.*)

Messenger   Neighbors of Cadmus, and Amphion's house,
there is no kind of state in human life   1050
which I now dare to envy or to blame.
Luck sets it straight, and luck she overturns
the happy or unhappy day by day.
No prophecy can deal with men's affairs.
Creon was envied once, as I believe,   1055
for having saved this city from its foes
and having got full power in this land.
He steered it well. And he had noble sons.
Now everything is gone.
Yes, when a man has lost all happiness,   1060
he's not alive. Call him a breathing corpse.
Be very rich at home. Live as a king.
But once your joy has gone, though these are left
they are smoke's shadow to lost happiness.
Chorus   What is the grief of princes that you bring?   1065
Messenger   They're dead. The living are responsible.
Chorus   Who died? Who did the murder? Tell us now.
Messenger   Haemon is gone. One of his kin drew blood.
Chorus   But whose arm struck? His father's or his own?
Messenger   He killed himself. His blood is on his father.   1070
Chorus   Seer, all too true the prophecy you told!
Messenger   This is the state of things. Now make your plans.

(*Enter, from the palace,* EURYDICE.)

Chorus   Eurydice is with us now, I see.
Creon's poor wife. She may have come by chance.
She may have heard something about her son.   1075

1047. Maenad maids: women who belonged to the cult of Dionysus.   1049. Cadmus:
founder of Thebes; Amphion: a son of Zeus who magically erected a wall around
Thebes.

Eurydice   I heard your talk as I was coming out
    to greet the goddess Pallas with my prayer.
    And as I moved the bolts that held the door
    I heard of my own sorrow.
    I fell back fainting in my women's arms.   1080
    But say again just what the news you bring.
    I, whom you speak to, have known grief before.
Messenger   Dear Lady, I was there, and I shall tell,
    leaving out nothing of the true account.
    Why should I make it soft for you with tales   1085
    to prove myself a liar? Truth is right.
    I followed your husband to the plain's far edge,
    where Polyneices' corpse was lying still
    unpitied. The dogs had torn him all apart.
    We prayed the goddess of all journeyings,   1090
    and Pluto, that they turn their wrath to kindness,
    we gave the final purifying bath,
    then burned the poor remains on new-cut boughs,
    and heaped a high mound of his native earth.
    Then turned we to the maiden's rocky bed,   1095
    death's hollow marriage-chamber.
    But, still far off, one of us heard a voice
    in keen lament by that unblest abode.
    He ran and told the master. As Creon came
    he heard confusion crying. He groaned and spoke: 1100
   "Am I a prophet now, and do I tread
    the saddest of all roads I ever trod?
    My son's voice crying! Servants, run up close,
    stand by the tomb and look, push through the crevice
    where we built the pile of rock, right to the entry.   1105
    Find out if that is Haemon's voice I hear
    or if the gods are tricking me indeed."
    We obeyed the order of our mournful master.
    In the far corner of the tomb we saw
    her, hanging by the neck, caught in a noose   1110
    of her own linen veiling.
    Haemon embraced her as she hung, and mourned
    his bride's destruction, dead and gone below,
    his father's actions, the unfated marriage.
    When Creon saw him, he groaned terribly,   1115
    and went toward him, and called him with lament:
   "What have you done, what plan have you caught up,

1077. Pallas: Pallas Athena, goddess of wisdom.

what sort of suffering is killing you?
Come out, my child, I do beseech you, come!"
The boy looked at him with his angry eyes,   1120
spat in his face and spoke no further word.
He drew his sword, but as his father ran,
he missed his aim. Then the unhappy boy,
in anger at himself, leant on the blade.
It entered, half its length, into his side.   1125
While he was conscious he embraced the maiden,
holding her gently. Last, he gasped out blood,
red blood on her white cheek.
Corpse on a corpse he lies. He found his marriage.
Its celebration in the halls of Hades.   1130
So he has made it very clear to men
that to reject good counsel is a crime.

(EURYDICE *returns to the house.*)

Chorus   What do you make of this? The queen has gone
 in silence. We know nothing of her mind.
Messenger   I wonder at her, too. But we can hope   1135
 that she has gone to mourn her son within
 with her own women, not before the town.
 She knows discretion. She will do no wrong.
Chorus   I am not sure. This muteness may portend
 as great disaster as a loud lament.   1140
Messenger   I will go in and see if some deep plan
 hides in her heart's wild pain. You may be right.
 There can be heavy danger in mute grief.

(*The* MESSENGER *goes into the house.* CREON *enters with his followers. They are carrying* HAEMON'S *body on a bier.*)

Chorus   But look, the king draws near.
 His own hand brings   1145
  the witness of his crime,
  the doom he brought on himself.
Creon   O crimes of my wicked heart,
 harshness bringing death.
 You see the killer, you see the kin he killed.   1150
 My planning was all unblest.
 Son, you have died too soon.
 Oh, you have gone away
  through my fault, not your own.
Chorus   You have learned justice, though it comes too late.   1155

Creon Yes, I have learned in sorrow. It was a god who struck,
who has weighted my head with disaster; he drove me to wild strange
ways,
his heavy heel on my joy.
Oh sorrows, sorrows of men.

(*Re-enter the* MESSENGER, *from a side door of the palace.*)

Messenger Master, you hold one sorrow in your hands   1160
but you have more, stored up inside the house.
Creon What further suffering can come on me?
Messenger Your wife has died. The dead man's mother in deed,
poor soul, her wounds are fresh.
Creon Hades, harbor of all,   1165
you have destroyed me now.
Terrible news to hear, horror the tale you tell.
I was dead, and you kill me again.
Boy, did I hear you right?
Did you say the queen was dead,   1170
slaughter on slaughter heaped?

(*The central doors of the palace begin to open.*)

Chorus Now you can see. Concealment is all over.

(*The doors are open, and the corpse of* EURYDICE *is revealed.*)

Creon My second sorrow is here. Surely no fate remains
which can strike me again. Just now, I held my son in my arms.
And now I see her dead.   1175
Woe for the mother and son.
Messenger There, by the altar, dying on the sword,
her eyes fell shut. She wept her older son
who died before, and this one. Last of all
she cursed you as the killer of her children.   1180
Creon I am mad with fear. Will no one strike
and kill me with cutting sword?
Sorrowful, soaked in sorrow to the bone!
Messenger Yes, for she held you guilty in the death
of him before you, and the elder dead.   1185
Creon How did she die?
Messenger Struck home at her own heart
when she had heard of Haemon's suffering.
Creon This is my guilt, all mine. I killed you, I say it clear.
Servants, take me away, out of the sight of men.   1190
I who am nothing more than nothing now.

Chorus   Your plan is good—if any good is left.
  Best to cut short our sorrow.
Creon   Let me go, let me go. May death come quick,
  bringing my final day.   1195
  O let me never see tomorrow's dawn.
Chorus   That is the future's. We must look to now.
  What will be is in other hands than ours.
Creon   All my desire was in that prayer of mine.
Chorus   Pray not again. No mortal can escape   1200
  the doom prepared for him.
Creon   Take me away at once, the frantic man who killed
  my son, against my meaning. I cannot rest.
  My life is warped past cure. My fate has struck me down.

(CREON *and his attendants enter the house.*)

Chorus   Our happiness depends   1205
  on wisdom all the way.
  The gods must have their due.
  Great words by men of pride
  bring greater blows upon them.
  So wisdom comes to the old.   1210

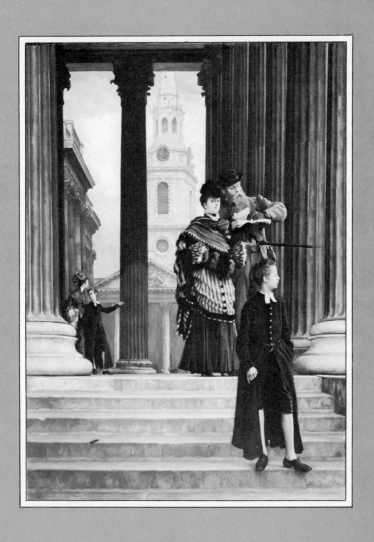

CHAPTER 3

SETTING
AND MEANING

People and their problems are, without doubt, central to most literature. People, however, exist in a particular time and place. In fact, where and when a person lives may account not only for "personality" but also for values, attitudes, and even problems in life. Consider yourself, for example. You are living today in the next-to-the-last decade of the twentieth century. It is a time of energy depletion and economic anxiety, of international crises and instant everything. In many ways, your life is affected by peculiarities of the time in which you live. Your daily schedule of activities—attending classes, studying, working, and relaxing—has an important influence on your life. Where you live is equally important in shaping your personality. Where were you born and raised: In the country? The city? The suburbs? Do you now live with your parents, in a dormitory or apartment, or in your own home? Alone? With others? Has your life been lived largely in one locale, or have you moved about a lot or traveled? The answers to all of these questions help to describe or identify you. In explaining who you are, then, you will necessarily take into account both time and place.

In literature, setting (time and place) can also exert a crucial influence on people and what they do. What constitutes setting and how it contributes to meaning will be made clear as we examine how time and place function in a narrative.

TIME

In literature there are four kinds of time: (1) *clock time*—the hour of the day; (2) *calendar time*—the date: day, month, year; or more generally a day of the week, or a time of a month; (3) *seasonal time*—spring, summer, autumn, winter, or a span in a year associated with a particular activity; (4) *historical time*—an era, such as Edwardian, Victorian, or Renaissance; the Great Depression, the Civil War, or peacetime.

Clock time can be used to provide suspense. Imagine that a gunfight is scheduled for high noon. As the seconds tick by, the passage of time heightens the effect of inexorably approaching danger. Clock time can also refer to an hour or period of the day that carries with it particular associations: the cocktail hour, quitting time, or night with its mystery and romance.

Calendar time can have equally specific associations. Monday might be washday, but also it is usually the first workday after the weekend; weekends are often periods of freedom from career; holidays, like Independence Day or Halloween, have special meanings for everyone.

Seasonal time usually connotes activities associated with the four seasons. Most of us think of youth, love, happiness, and new life in connection with spring; of cold and death in winter. Seasonal time can also relate to such specific activities as income tax preparation or school vacation. None of these, however, is necessarily related to a particular season of the year.

The broadest period of time is historic, since the span can range from years to centuries. Often historic time establishes a sociological or psychological framework for the action. Recognizing that "My Last Duchess" is set in the Renaissance helps the reader to understand the social concepts and economic conditions of the Duke and other characters in the poem. These concepts and conditions in turn affect or control, not only what is taking place, but also how we react to the people and events described.

Often, an author may include reference to several kinds of time in a single work. When the reader recognizes and understands these references, he or she has made some progress toward an intelligent reading of the work. Different kinds of time play an important part in the following short story.

I. L. Peretz (1851–1915)

IF NOT HIGHER

Early every Friday morning, at the time of the Penitential Prayers, the Rabbi of Nemirov would vanish.

He was nowhere to be seen—neither in the synagogue nor in the two Houses of Study nor at a *minyan*.[1] And he was certainly not at home. His door stood open; whoever wished could go in and out; no one would steal from the rabbi. But not a living creature was within.

Where could the rabbi be? Where should he be? In heaven, no doubt. A rabbi has plenty of business to take care of just before the Days of Awe. Jews, God bless them, need livelihood, peace, health, and good matches. They want to be pious and good, but our sins are so great, and Satan of the thousand eyes watches the whole earth from one end to the other. What he sees he reports; he denounces, informs. Who can help us if not the rabbi!

That's what the people thought.

But once a Litvak[2] came, and he laughed. You know the Litvaks. They think little of the Holy Books but stuff themselves with Talmud and law. So this Litvak points to a passage in the *Gemarah*[3]—it sticks in your eyes— where it is written that even Moses, our Teacher, did not ascend to heaven during his lifetime but remained suspended two and half feet below. Go argue with a Litvak!

So where can the rabbi be?

[1] *minyan*: a quorum for conducting Jewish public worship.
[2] Litvak: a Lithuanian Jew.
[3] *Gemarah*: part of the Talmud, a commentary on Jewish law.

"That's not my business," said the Litvak, shrugging. Yet all the while—what a Litvak can do!—he is scheming to find out.

That same night, right after the evening prayers, the Litvak steals into the rabbi's room, slides under the rabbi's bed, and waits. He'll watch all night and discover where the rabbi vanishes and what he does during the Penitential Prayers.

Someone else might have got drowsy and fallen asleep, but a Litvak is never at a loss; he recites a whole tractate[4] of the Talmud by heart.

At dawn he hears the call to prayers.

The rabbi has already been awake for a long time. The Litvak has heard him groaning for a whole hour.

Whoever has heard the Rabbi of Nemirov groan knows how much sorrow for all Israel, how much suffering, lies in each groan. A man's heart might break, hearing it. But a Litvak is made of iron; he listens and remains where he is. The rabbi, long life to him, lies on the bed, and the Litvak under the bed.

Then the Litvak hears the beds in the house begin to creak; he hears people jumping out of their beds, mumbling a few Jewish words, pouring water on their fingernails, banging doors. Everyone has left. It is again quiet and dark; a bit of light from the moon shines through the shutters.

(Afterward the Litvak admitted that when he found himself alone with the rabbi a great fear took hold of him. Goose pimples spread across his skin, and the roots of his earlocks[5] pricked him like needles. A trifle: to be alone with the rabbi at the time of the Penitential Prayers! But a Litvak is stubborn. So he quivered like a fish in water and remained where he was.)

Finally the rabbi, long life to him, arises. First he does what befits a Jew. Then he goes to the clothes closet and takes out a bundle of peasant clothes: linen trousers, high boots, a coat, a big felt hat, and a long wide leather belt studded with brass nails. The rabbi gets dressed. From his coat pocket dangles the end of a heavy peasant rope.

The rabbi goes out, and the Litvak follows him.

On the way the rabbi stops in the kitchen, bends down, takes an ax from under the bed, puts it in his belt, and leaves the house. The Litvak trembles but continues to follow.

The hushed dread of the Days of Awe hangs over the dark streets. Every once in a while a cry rises from some *minyan* reciting the Penitential Prayers, or from a sickbed. The rabbi hugs the sides of the streets, keeping to the shade of the houses. He glides from house to house, and the Litvak after him. The Litvak hears the sound of his heartbeats mingling with the sound of the rabbi's heavy steps. But he keeps on going and follows the rabbi to the outskirts of the town.

A small wood stands behind the town.

4 a whole tractate: discussion of an entire topic.
5 earlocks: a lock or curl of hair hanging in front of the ear.

The rabbi, long life to him, enters the wood. He takes thirty or forty steps and stops by a small tree. The Litvak, overcome with amazement, watches the rabbi take the ax out of his belt and strike the tree. He hears the tree creak and fall. The rabbi chops the tree into logs and the logs into sticks. Then he makes a bundle of the wood and ties it with the rope in his pocket. He puts the bundle of wood on his back, shoves the ax back into his belt, and returns to the town.

He stops at a back street beside a small broken-down shack and knocks at the window.

"Who is there?" asks a frightened voice. The Litvak recognizes it as the voice of a sick Jewish woman.

"I," answers the rabbi in the accent of a peasant.

"Who is I?"

Again the rabbi answers in Russian. "Vassil."

"Who is Vassil, and what do you want?"

"I have wood to sell, very cheap." And, not waiting for the woman's reply, he goes into the house.

The Litvak steals in after him. In the gray light of the early morning he sees a poor room with broken, miserable furnishings. A sick woman, wrapped in rags, lies on the bed. She complains bitterly, "Buy? How can I buy? Where will a poor widow get money?"

"I'll lend it to you," answers the supposed Vassil. "It's only six cents."

"And how will I ever pay you back?" said the poor woman, groaning.

"Foolish one," says the rabbi reproachfully. "See, you are a poor sick Jew, and I am ready to trust you with a little wood. I am sure you'll pay. While you, you have such a great and mighty God and you don't trust him for six cents."

"And who will kindle the fire?" said the widow. "Have I the strength to get up? My son is at work."

"I'll kindle the fire," answers the rabbi.

As the rabbi put the wood into the oven he recited, in a groan, the first portion of the Penitential Prayers.

As he kindled the fire and the wood burned brightly, he recited, a bit more joyously, the second portion of the Penitential Prayers. When the fire was set he recited the third portion, and then he shut the stove.

The Litvak who saw all this became a disciple of the rabbi.

And ever after, when another disciple tells how the Rabbi of Nemirov ascends to heaven at the time of the Penitential Prayers, the Litvak does not laugh. He only adds quietly, "If not higher."

All four kinds of time are involved in this story, and the reader must know what each signifies before he or she can begin to appreciate its effect on the tale. (Of course, some knowledge of European history and Jewish traditions is also needed in order to understand the Peretz story fully.)

1. Historical time: the story is set in an era before industrialization and modernization, when Russian peasants lived simple lives in simple villages. In such towns, the Jewish population lived totally segregated lives, their contact with Gentiles being limited to commerce or trade.
2. Seasonal time: reference to the need for fire suggests a season that may not be full summer.
3. Calendar time: the day is Friday, the evening of which begins the Jewish Sabbath, or "Day of Awe," as it is called in the text—a period of intense and carefully prescribed religious observance beginning at sundown Friday and continuing through Saturday sundown. "Days of Awe" could also very possibly refer to the time of preparation for the high holidays of early autumn.
4. Clock time: the principal events take place on Thursday evening and Friday morning.

What happens in the story, and how are time references significant in shaping events and our understanding of the work? Of primary import is the ritual associated with the Jewish Holy Day or Sabbath. In preparation for the Sabbath, members of the congregation recite the Penitential Prayers, separately or together. Usually the rabbi (or teacher) would be part of the communal observances; but during this time the Rabbi of Nemirov does something remarkable: he disappears. Instead of praying with the group, he performs a generous and caring act, the charity of which is increased by his anonymity. The rabbi dons the clothes of a peasant (not a Jew) and in this disguise chops wood and gives it to a poor woman in the village. Every week, the rabbi performs this deed, an act which exemplifies the neighborly love his tradition calls for, and in this way he earns a reward even greater than that accorded to Moses during his lifetime: during the time of the Penitential Prayers he is thought of as ascending to heaven, "if not higher." Thus understanding the various time settings in the story helps us to arrive at meaning, since in this case *when* the action occurs is directly related to the significance of what is happening.

PLACE

Like time, *place* can be a very important aspect of setting in any literary work. Place, of course, means the actual location in which the action occurs, but it includes the nonphysical as well as physical environments that characterize that location.

The location of a work may be very specifically described: a room in a building on a particular street in a particular town, city, or country. In most realistic fiction and drama, as well as in some poetry, such details are generally quite specific. In "If Not Higher," for example, the rabbi takes wood to a woman who lives on "a back street" in a "small broken-down shack" in the town of Nemirov. Although the description is brief, it gives a clear picture of the home of the woman whom the rabbi helps. Physical setting also includes such aspects of place as weather conditions: Is it raining or sunny? Cold or hot? Calm or stormy? In O. Henry's "The Cop and the Anthem" (pp. 310–315), for example, the coming of winter and the certain expectation of freezing weather in New York impels Soapy to seek the warmth of a prison cell for three months.

The nonphysical environment includes such cultural influences as education, social and economic class, or religious belief. These factors might be revealed by details about the physical properties present in the scene: books, pictures, furniture, or clothing—many of which relate to the backgrounds of their owners. The nonphysical environment may also be revealed through dialogue (both what is said and how it is said), a character's thoughts, statements by other characters or the narrator, or the behavior of the various characters. In Peretz' story the sick woman lives in a room "with broken, miserable furnishings." Added to these details that describe a climate of poverty is her question to the rabbi when he tells her the price of the wood is "only six cents." She asks him, "how will I ever pay you back? These and clues to the religious beliefs of Peretz' characters reveal the nonphysical environment in which they live.

The following story gives no place names; yet it offers many clues that help identify place and the nonphysical environment. Finding these clues is essential to understanding what the story is about.

Joyce Cary (1888–1957)

A SPECIAL OCCASION

The nursery door opened and Nurse's voice said in the sugary tone which she used to little girl guests, "Here you are, darling, and Tommy will show you all his toys." A little brown-haired girl in a silk party frock, sticking out all round her legs like a lampshade, came in at the door, stopped, and stared at her host. Tom, a dark little boy, aged five, also in a party suit, blue linen knickers, and a silk shirt, stared back at the girl. Nurse had gone into the night nursery, next door, on her private affairs.

Tom, having stared at the girl for a long time as one would study a curiosity, rare and valuable, but extremely surprising, put his feet together, made three jumps forward and said, "Hullo."

The little girl turned her head over one shoulder and slowly revolved on one heel, as if trying to examine the back of her own frock. She then stooped suddenly, brushed the hem with her hand, and said, "Hullo."

Tom made another jump, turned round, pointed out of the window, and said in a loud voice something like "twanky tweedle." Both knew that neither the gesture nor the phrase was meant to convey a meaning. They simply expressed the fact that for Tom this was an important and exciting, a very special occasion.

The little girl took a step forward, caught her frock in both hands as if about to make a curtsy, rose upon her toes, and said in a prim voice, "I beg your pardon."

They both gazed at each other for some minutes with sparkling eyes. Neither smiled, but it seemed that both were about to smile.

Tom then gave another incomprehensible shout, ran round the table, sat down on the floor and began to play with a clockwork engine on a circular track. The little girl climbed on a tricycle and pedaled round the floor. "I can ride your bike," she said.

Tom paid no attention. He was trying how fast the engine could go without falling off the track.

The little girl took a picture book, sat down under the table with her back to Tom, and slowly, carefully, examined each page. "It's got a crooked wheel," Tom said, "that's what it is." The little girl made no answer. She was staring at the book with round eyes and a small pursed mouth—the expression of a nervous child at the zoo when the lions are just going to roar. Slowly and carefully she turned the next page. As it opened, her eyes became larger, her mouth more tightly pursed, as if she expected some creature to jump out at her.

"Tom." Nurse, having completed her private business, came bustling in with the air of one restored to life after a dangerous illness. "Tom, you naughty boy, is this the way you entertain your guests? Poor little Jenny, all by herself under the table." The nurse was plump and middle-aged; an old-fashioned nanny.

"She's not by herself," Tom said.

"Oh Tom, that really is naughty of you. Where are all your nice manners? Get up, my dear, and play with her like a good boy."

"I am playing with her," Tom said, in a surly tone, and he gave Nurse a sidelong glance of anger.

"Now Tom, if you go on telling such stories, I shall know you are trying to be naughty. Get up now when I ask you." She stooped, took Tom by the arm, and lifted him up. "Come now, you must be polite, after you've asked her yourself and pestered for her all the week."

At this public disclosure, Tom instantly lost his temper and yelled, "I didn't—I didn't—I won't—I won't."

"Then I'll have to take poor little Jenny downstairs again to her mummy."

"No—no—no."

"Will you play with her then?"

"No, I hate her—I never wanted her."

At this the little girl rose and said, in precise indignant tones, "He *is* naughty, isn't he?"

Tom flew at her, and seized her by the hair; the little girl at once uttered a loud scream, kicked him on the leg, and bit his arm. She was carried screaming to the door by Nurse, who, from there, issued sentence on Tom, "I'm going straight to your father, as soon as he comes in." Then she went out, banging the door.

Tom ran at the door and kicked it, rushed at the engine, picked it up and flung it against the wall. Then he howled at the top of his voice for five minutes. He intended to howl all day. He was suffering from a large and complicated grievance.

All at once the door opened and the little girl walked in. She had an air of immense self-satisfaction as if she had just done something very clever. She said in a tone demanding congratulation, "I've come back."

Tom gazed at her through his tears and gave a loud sob. Then he picked up the engine, sat down by the track. But the engine fell off at the first push. He gave another sob, looked at the wheels, and bent one of them straight.

The little girl lifted her party frock behind in order not to crush it, sat down under the table, and drew the book onto her knee.

Tom tried the engine at high speed. His face was still set in the form of anger and bitterness, but he forgot to sob. He exclaimed with surprise and pleased excitement, "It's the lines too—where I trod on 'em."

The little girl did not reply. Slowly, carefully, she opened the book in the middle and gazed at an elephant. Her eyes became immense, her lips minute. But suddenly, and as it were, accidentally, she gave an enormous sigh of relief, a very special happiness.

To examine the aspects of place in this story, we can group particular details within the three categories defined earlier:

Location   The story takes place in a child's nursery. Specific details include the following. (1) This is the day nursery (playroom) of a five-year old boy. (2) The night nursery (child's bedroom) is next door. (3) The nursery is upstairs in the child's home, since the nurse must go "downstairs" to report the child's misbehavior.

Physical Environment   The atmosphere is comfortable, with some sense of excitement. It is a very special day. This atmosphere changes to one of hostility and disruption when Nurse is present. Specific details include the following. (1) "For Tom this was an important and exciting, a very special occasion." (2) When the nurse has left the room, the children gaze at each other "for some minutes with sparkling eyes." (3) The nurse bustles into the room, immediately changing the atmosphere: Tom speaks in "a surly tone"; loses his temper and yells; flies at Jenny; kicks the door; flings his engine against the wall; howls "at the top of his voice." (4) After Jenny returns alone to the room, she sighs with "a very special happiness."

Nonphysical Environment This is an upper or upper-middle class home, probably English. Specific details include the following. (1) The nurse is "an old-fashioned nanny"—an English term for a person hired to take primary responsibility for the young children of a household. (2) The nurse is evidently fully in charge of the child. She brings Jenny in with "the sugary tone which she used to little girl guests"; she says Tom had "pestered for her all the week." (3) Both children are beautifully dressed, the girl in "silk party frock" and the boy in "blue linen knickers, and a silk shirt." Knickers, loose pants that buckle at a cuff just below the knee, were popular for boys and men in the first half of this century both in Europe and the United States. The fact that knickers are worn helps to establish the general time of the action. The use of "frock," rather than dress, suggests England where the word is commonly used; linen and silk suggest economic status. (4) Both children, although only five, have already been taught etiquette. Jenny says "I beg your pardon" to Tom. Nurse asks Tom: "Where are all your nice manners?" and later tells him "you must be polite." The stress on manners helps suggest social class.

As the various details reveal, the nursery on the day of Jenny's visit is a pleasant, comfortable place for the children when they are alone. It is a child's world in which the kind of behavior expected by the adults around them doesn't matter. When the nurse, the adult who is responsible for teaching that kind of behavior, intrudes into that world, however, it is no longer pleasant or comfortable. The details about location, about physical and non-physical environments, help to clarify the conflicts between Tom and the nurse and Tom and Jenny. They are thus important to the overall meaning of the story.

THE USES OF SETTING

Sometimes, *time and place* in a work really don't matter very much, because setting is only a vague backdrop for action. In other works, however, the elements of setting are directly linked to mood or meaning, as is true of the following poem by Henry Reed.

Henry Reed (1914–   )

NAMING OF PARTS

To-day we have naming of parts. Yesterday,
We had daily cleaning. And to-morrow morning,
We shall have what to do after firing. But to-day,
To-day we have naming of parts. Japonica

Glistens like coral in all of the neighboring gardens,   5
    And to-day we have naming of parts.

This is the lower sling swivel. And this
Is the upper sling swivel, whose use you will see,
When you are given your slings. And this is the piling swivel,
Which in your case you have not got. The branches   10
Hold in the gardens their silent, eloquent gestures,
    Which in our case we have not got.

This is the safety-catch, which is always released
With an easy flick of the thumb. And please do not let me
See anyone using his finger. You can do it quite easy   15
If you have any strength in your thumb. The blossoms
Are fragile and motionless, never letting anyone see
    Any of them using their finger.

And this you can see is the bolt. The purpose of this
Is to open the breech, as you see. We can slide it   20
Rapidly backwards and forwards: we call this
Easing the spring. And rapidly backwards and forwards
The early bees are assaulting and fumbling the flowers:
    They call it easing the Spring.

They call it easing the Spring: it is perfectly easy   25
If you have any strength in your thumb: like the bolt,
And the breech, and the cocking-piece, and the point of balance,
Which in our case we have not got; and the almond-blossom
Silent in all of the gardens and the bees going backwards and forwards,
    For to-day we have naming of parts.   30

4. Japonica: an early flowering shrub, sometimes called "Japanese quince."

Clearly, the action takes place in a military camp, surrounded by homes and flower gardens. The first lines of each stanza appear to be the remarks of a trainer conducting a lesson in the use of a weapon. We can acquire some information about location and activity that will help us approach the poem by consulting a standard literary reference work. In this case, we will learn that Henry Reed, born in England, underwent military training early in World War II. Thus this poem, while it need not literally describe Reed's personal experiences (and many first-person narratives most certainly are *not* autobiographical) probably reflects that place and time. From any history of the war, we may learn that England was relatively unprepared, and basic training had to be rushed; in some instances, incomplete rifles or even dummy weapons were issued to recruits so that their training could begin.

In the poem, the trainer—probably a sergeant—is following a rigid schedule of lessons in the use of the rifle.

Details about time and place in the poem illustrate five ways in which setting can relate to meaning.

1. Setting may be used to create atmosphere and thus directly affect the reader's emotional experience. In "Naming of Parts" the monotony of military life is impressed upon us before we become aware of any particular characters or conflicts. Although we know almost nothing about the sergeant or the recruits, we feel a sense of oppression in the camp because the lesson itself is mechanical and dull. Mention of yesterday's and tomorrow's lessons informs us that we are in the middle of training, with little hope of a break in the routine. Japonica is in bloom in the "neighboring gardens," so we know the season is spring. The spring flowers and bees make life in the camp seem even duller by contrast. In "Naming of Parts," then, the atmosphere provides an important clue to meaning, since, as in many works (especially mysteries or horror stories), atmosphere directly affects the reader's feelings about what is happening.

2. Setting may have a direct effect on character and action: a person's attitudes, expectations, and behaviors may be to a large extent the result of the time and place in which he or she lives. Thus in "Naming of Parts," the sergeant plays the role assigned to him by the military. Whatever sort of person he may have been in civilian life, the pressures of wartime and the rigidity of the military make him impersonal and authoritarian. He does not treat the recruits as distinct persons, but rather as anonymous members of a group. While he may perfectly well be aware of the spring, as the men under his command are, he ignores the gardens and maintains a constant emphasis on the weapons being studied. He wishes to finish today's lesson today and keep on schedule: he has become just as mechanical as military life itself. In the same way, but perhaps to an even greater degree, the Rabbi of Nemirov, in "If Not Higher," is a product of his culture. His secret generosity toward the poor widow and the other Jews' reactions are the direct result of the situation of the Jews in this nineteenth-century Russian village.

3. An external force may enter a setting and change it significantly, with resultant conflicts for the persons present. The Japonica blossoms outside the training ground intrude upon the awareness of the recruits. The sergeant, therefore, must continually struggle to recall them to his explanation of the use of the rifle since the forces of spring divide the attention of the recruits. Similarly, in Joyce Cary's "A Special Occasion," as we have seen, the nursery is a comfortable setting for the children, really a child's world in which the boy and girl can play happily side by side. The intrusion of the nurse, however, with her adult sense of values, imposes standards of behavior that cause severe conflicts for the children.

4. The setting may itself be a major antagonist. If we think of the recruits (or the particular one of them who is speaking on their behalf) as the

protagonists, they are directly in conflict with the military itself. They wish to enjoy life, but are forced by circumstances to train for killing and to prepare themselves for death. They may very well be patriotic and perhaps eager to fight and win this war; nevertheless, they did not choose to live in a time of war, and they would prefer freedom and life to the necessarily rigid military discipline. This aspect of setting is perhaps even more clear in Eudora Welty's "A Worn Path," in which the conflict consists mainly of Phoenix Jackson's struggle against the physical distance she must travel and the social distance she must bridge in order to care for her grandson's needs.

5. Two settings in the same work may come into conflict with each other, frequently causing a parallel conflict in the character(s) who must live in both settings or else choose between them. The military camp and the neighboring gardens are in conflict with each other. The training necessary for fighting is in conflict with the immediate appeal of a beautiful spring day. The recruits must learn to use their weapons. They must, therefore, pull their attention back from spring and thoughts of love to the rifle lesson and thoughts of killing, but the setting outside the fence exerts an almost irresistible pull on them.

Clearly, these five ways in which setting may relate to meaning overlap, and any work may illustrate more than one of them. In "Naming of Parts," they all tend toward the same general meaning: life is preferable to death; peace preferable to war. Nevertheless, in a time of national emergency people may have to deal with the restrictions, impersonality, and dangers of the military life, even while they yearn for the more rewarding and natural life exemplified by flowers and bees and spring.

READING FOR SETTING

In some works setting is easily identified because the place and time are explicitly stated or the description of the scene makes them easy to recognize. In many works, however, you must look for clues to discover when and where the action occurs. In order to recognize and understand such clues, you will often find it helpful to begin by learning something about the author: the time and place in which he or she lived and other biographical information that may have influenced the work. Then note details that suggest setting, whether specific names and dates, or simply unique uses of language and vague references that hint at a particular location or historical or cultural environment. Unfamiliar words, places, names, and customs should be checked in a dictionary, atlas, encyclopedia, or other reference book. The following commentary and discussion illustrate all aspects of this process.

Archibald MacLeish (1892–)

MEMORIAL RAIN

for Kenneth MacLeish, 1894–1918

Ambassador Puser the ambassador
Reminds himself in French, felicitous tongue,
What these (young men no longer) lie here for
In rows that once, and somewhere else, were young . . .

> All night in Brussels the wind had tugged at my door: 5
> I had heard the wind at my door and the trees strung
> Taut, and to me who had never been before
> In that country it was a strange wind, blowing
> Steadily, stiffening the walls, the floor,
> The roof of my room. I had not slept for knowing   10
> He too, dead, was a stranger in that land
> And felt beneath the earth in the wind's flowing
> A tightening of roots and would not understand,
> Remembering lake winds in Illinois,
> That strange wind. I had felt his bones in the sand   15
> Listening.

> > *. . . Reflects that these enjoy*
> *Their country's gratitude, that deep repose,*
> *That peace no pain can break, no hurt destroy,*
> *That rest, that sleep . . .*   20

> > > At Ghent the wind rose.
> There was a smell of rain and a heavy drag
> Of wind in the hedges but not as the wind blows
> Over fresh water when the waves lag
> Foaming and the willows huddle and it will rain: 25
> I felt him waiting.

> > *. . . Indicates the flag*
> *Which (may he say) enisles in Flanders plain*
> *This little field these happy, happy dead*
> *Have made America . . .*   30

> > > In the ripe grain
> The wind coiled glistening, darted, fled,
> Dragging its heavy body: at Waereghem
> The wind coiled in the grass above his head:
> Waiting—listening . . .   35

. . . Dedicates to them
This earth their bones have hallowed, this last gift
A grateful country . . .

Under the dry grass stem
The words are blurred, are thickened, the words sift   40
Confused by the rasp of the wind, by the thin grating
Of ants under the grass, the minute shift
And tumble of dusty sand separating
From dusty sand. The roots of the grass strain,
Tighten, the earth is rigid, waits—he is waiting—   45

And suddenly, and all at once, the rain!

The living scatter, they run into houses, the wind
Is trampled under the rain, shakes free, is again
Trampled. The rain gathers, running in thinned
Spurts of water that ravel in the dry sand,   50
Seeping in the sand under the grass roots, seeping
Between cracked boards to the bones of a clenched hand:
The earth relaxes, loosens; he is sleeping,
He rests, he is quiet, he sleeps in a strange land.

A first reading of the poem indicates that the setting is in a Flanders cemetery where a memorial service for American war dead is taking place. The speaker of the poem is at the service, listening as Ambassador Puser dedicates the cemetery and thinking about Illinois, Brussels, Ghent, and Waereghem. Although the rain threatens throughout the ceremony, it comes only at the end.

The poem is dedicated to Kenneth MacLeish, who died in 1918. By researching the biography of the poet, we learn that Kenneth was the poet's younger brother, who grew up with him in Illinois. Kenneth joined the Air Force during World War I and was killed over France in 1918. He was buried, along with 367 other American servicemen also killed during that war, in Flanders Field, part of the district of Flanders in Belgium. Any map of Belgium will show that the district of Flanders includes the town of Waereghem and that Brussels and Ghent, other places named in the poem, are located in that country.

Research, therefore, provides a good starting point for approaching the poem, although the total experience and significance of this work, as indeed of most other works that have an autobiographical basis, go beyond the poet's response to his brother's death.

Keeping in mind this limitation of research, we can undertake a line-by-line analysis to discover details about setting:

Ambassador Puser the ambassador
Reminds himself in French, felicitous tongue,
What these (young men no longer) lie here for
In rows that once, and somewhere else, were
young . . .

A burial ground in a French-speaking country is the primary setting; the occasion is a ceremony of sufficient importance for an ambassador to speak.

All night in Brussels the wind had tugged at my
door:
I had heard the wind at my door and the trees
strung
Taut, and to me who had never been before
In that country it was a strange wind, blowing
Steadily, stiffening the walls, the floor,
The roof of my room. I had not slept for knowing
He too, dead, was a stranger in that land
And felt beneath the earth in the wind's flowing
A tightening of roots and would not understand,
Remembering lake winds in Illinois,
That strange wind. I had felt his bones in the sand
Listening.

Flashback to a room in Brussels. The narrator contrasts the wind in Brussels with the wind in Illinois. The wind in Brussels seems alien to him, and he suggests it is also alien to the dead soldier. Conflict between two settings: lake area of Illinois and Belgium. Another conflict is suggested between earlier time, when the dead soldier was young and alive, and the present.

. . . Reflects that these enjoy
Their country's gratitude, that deep repose,
That peace no pain can break, no hurt destroy,
That rest, that sleep . . .

The ambassador continues speaking of the dead in clichés.

At Ghent the wind rose.
There was a smell of rain and a heavy drag
Of wind in the hedges but not as the wind blows
Over fresh water when the waves lag
Foaming and the willows huddle and it will rain:
I felt him waiting.

Another flashback to that morning in the town of Ghent as he passed through. The wind there was unlike wind over fresh water (Illinois). Conflict between Illinois and Belgium restated.

. . . Indicates the flag
Which (may he say) enisles in Flanders plain
This little field these happy, happy dead
Have made America . . .

The dedication makes Flanders Field American. The primary setting now includes the American flag. Will it reduce conflict between settings?

In the ripe grain
The wind coiled glistening, darted, fled,
Dragging its heavy body: at Waereghem
The wind coiled in the grass above his head:
Waiting—listening . . .

Still another flashback to earlier that day. Details show Belgian setting more alien, rain still holding off—wind now snakelike. Ripe grain indicates calendar time: late summer.

...Dedicates to them *This earth their bones have hallowed, this last gift* *A grateful country...*	Puser formally dedicates the field, and the primary setting is now legally American. Will that reduce conflict between settings?
Under the dry grass stem The words are blurred, are thickened, the words sift Confused by the rasp of the wind, by the thin grating Of ants under the grass, the minute shift And tumble of dusty sand separating From dusty sand. The roots of the grass strain, Tighten, the earth is rigid, waits—he is waiting—	Increased concentration on negative aspects of the primary setting.
And suddenly, and all at once, the rain!	Intrusion of natural phenomenon into the setting.
The living scatter, they run into houses, the wind Is trampled under the rain, shakes free, is again Trampled. The rain gathers, running in thinned Spurts of water that ravel in the dry sand, Seeping in the sand under the grass roots, seeping Between cracked boards to the bones of a clenched hand: The earth relaxes, loosens; he is sleeping, He rests, he is quiet, he sleeps in a strange land.	The arrival of rain resolves the conflict between settings as the primary and secondary settings merge.

Thus, one way to understand the poem is to see how it grows around major conflicts involving both time and place. Illinois, where the wind blows over fresh water, is a remembered place and suggests a time when the soldier was alive. Belgium, where the rain threatens for at least two days before it comes, is the actual place where a service is held for the soldiers buried there. The difference between these settings seems to create conflict within the narrator, who is at first unable to accept the fact that an American soldier is buried on foreign soil. When the rain comes, it brings together the two settings. As the "clenched hand" of the dead man is reached by the soothing rain, in the imagination of the narrator, the narrator expresses his own release from internal conflict: hands of corpses do not, in fact, relax; only those of living people—in this case, the narrator—do. The joining of the two settings by the rain seems to suggest the power of nature in helping to overcome grief.

WRITING ABOUT SETTING

A paper intended to discuss setting must include a careful study of the specific setting of a work. Just what is the time of the action, and what aspects of time—clock, calendar, seasonal, historical—are important? What is the place: the geographical location, the cultural environment, the physical environment? If more than one setting is included, should time and place for each be explored? How does the setting affect the reader's experience or understanding of the work? Is setting primarily a device for providing atmosphere? Does the setting have an important influence on character and action? Does an intrusive force alter the setting, producing conflicts for the characters? Are there two settings that conflict with each other and so cause a parallel conflict within a major character? Once you have answered these questions, you will be able to discuss the meaning of a work in relation to setting. Then you will be ready to write a paper on setting, either a critical analysis of setting or a film treatment.

Option I: Critical Analysis of Setting

A critical essay is, as explained in earlier chapters, the most usual written response to a work because it allows a person to explore his or her understanding of a short story, poem, or play. Another reason why students as well as professional critics frequently use the critical essay is that it allows them to assess a writer's achievement. Making value judgments about literature must, of course, be done cautiously since a great deal of reading experience and study of literature are necessary for such judgments to be valid. However, most students can recognize works in which the characters and/or the conflicts are insufficiently developed to convey any significant meaning or where the reader's emotions are manipulated through sentimentality and trite language. Sentimentality is the use of more emotion than the situation deserves. It depends on *trite* language, the overused and conventional metaphors that were fresh at one time but have been repeated so often they are fresh no longer. It also involves words whose connotations stir emotion in sentimental people—words like *mother, baby, patriotism.* Consider, for example, the images and situation in the following verse:

> The wee, thin child, too weak to roam
> Stood trembling all that night
> Outside the warm and happy home
> With windows shining bright.
> He raised his eyes and tear-stained face   5
> To pray for God's eternal grace,
> And God, who saw him from above,
> Bent down and lifted him to love.

The child who is small, thin, weak, and trembling is conventional, meant to stir tears in the reader. The contrast between his situation and the brightly lighted house makes him all the more pathetic. No consideration is given to logic in that comparison, however. There are no reasons to explain why the child is outside or why the house is lighted all night when most houses are dark during the hours of sleep, nor why the home is "happy." The resolution of the situation is trite: the child's death is seen as an act of God's love. Thus readers' emotions are manipulated as they are moved from pity for the child to anger at the house to tears at the end. Literature that is *true* does not manipulate feelings, nor is it illogical; it stimulates emotional response by engaging the reader's mind, feelings, senses, and imagination.

In writing a critical essay about the use of setting in a literary work, you may confine your discussion to simple analysis of the importance of setting and its relation to the meaning of the work or you may include your assessment of the writer's achievement. In either case, the following guidelines will help you prepare for and write your paper.

1. Choose a work in this chapter and reread it carefully. Then follow the procedure explained in the section on "Reading for Setting."

a. Summarize what happens in the work and identify the primary setting.
b. Research the author, if this is appropriate, and the various clues to setting in the work.
c. Amplify your initial summary to include the information gained from your research.
d. Do a close analysis, breaking the work into smaller units and identifying each reference to time and place.
e. Determine the most important use of setting (see pp. 428–431, "The Uses of Setting").

2. Generalize from your analysis to a statement of the work's meaning. Clarify the importance of setting to the situation and resolution.

3. List references to setting to be used in your essay. Be sure to note the page number for stories or long poems, line number for short poems; act, scene, and line for most plays. Copy quoted material exactly as it appears in the work.

4. Write your introduction. Include the name of the work, the author, and introductory comments that establish the theme of the work and assess the writer's achievement if you wish to do so. Include a main-idea sentence. The *MIS* should indicate how the author uses setting and describe the structure of your paper.

5. Write the body of the essay, following the structure specified in the *MIS*. Use enough quotations, properly documented, to prove the points you make, but quote only enough to support your discussion.

6. Write the conclusion, expanding on the meaning of the work and perhaps restating some of the comments you made in the introduction (including your assessment if you made one).

7. Compose an appropriate title.

8. Put the essay aside to "cool" for a few days. Then reread it, checking and rewriting as necessary.

9. Prepare a clean copy for submission to your instructor.

OPTION I: SAMPLE ESSAY

And All at Once, The Rain!

The acceptance of loss, a familiar life crisis, is the theme of many literary works, yet seldom is it presented with as much emotional truth as in Archibald MacLeish's poem "Memorial Rain." The major problem for writers is to express depth of feeling without using clichés. The measure of his achievement is that MacLeish succeeds in expressing sentiment without sentimentality, involving the reader through tension created by tightly controlled conflict between the two major settings within the poem: America and Europe.

As the poem unfolds, the reader is taken back and forth between the two locales until the conflict is ultimately resolved. The American setting is unchanging throughout: always it is the lake area of Illinois, in some earlier time, perhaps a time when two brothers played on the dunes while wind blew "over fresh water" (line 24). It is remembered by the narrator like a snapshot, isolated in time and unchangeable in memory. Belgium, conversely, consists of several places, a journey from one town to another, ending at the military cemetery of Flanders Field. There the present action of the poem takes place, but the contrast created by the memory of America and the European experience creates suspense. As MacLeish balances each setting against the other, sustaining the tension of the poem, the conflict grows until the reader, like the narrator, feels the wind an enemy, "coiled in the grass" (line 34) over the graves. The landscape is so dry that even the "thin grating of ants under the grass" and the "tumble of dusty sand" (lines 41–43) seem to be heard. Everything in the Flanders setting is negative: The ambassador who speaks in a foreign language; the sand that suggests the passage of life; the snake-like wind; and the dryness that includes unreleased tears of grief as well as the lack of rain. When the rain finally does come, the conflicts between the Illinois scene and the cemetery end. As "the living scatter" (line 47), the rain "gathers, running in thinned / Spurts of water" (lines 49–50) into the sand and down to the coffin. "That strange wind" (line 15) is "trampled under the rain" (line 48). Finally, "The earth relaxes, loosens" (line 53), and the full realization of death comes. With it, however, healing tears also come, for finally the dead soldier "is quiet, he sleeps" (line 54).

"Memorial Rain" is a poem not easily forgotten because Archibald Mac-Leish takes the reader into the deepest stages of the grief that follows loss. The moving experience culminates in the reconciliation of tension. Flanders Field is no longer alien; for there the wind also brings rain, as it does in Illinois, and the dead can be at peace.

Option II: Set Design for Film Treatment

One way to demonstrate your full understanding of a work of literature is by designing a filmed version that illustrates the importance of setting in relation to meaning. A film treatment is a prose summary of what may later become a detailed shooting script. Such a summary includes detailed descriptions of the setting or settings, together with a general discussion of the use of actors, camera, sound, and any other important aspects of the finished film. It also includes a section relating to the use of camera and sound for one specific important incident in the work—the incident in which setting and meaning are most closely connected. In order to prepare a film treatment, you will have to think through not only how setting affects the meaning of the work you have in mind but also just what that setting looks like, and how to go about using picture and sound track to communicate meaning. Here are guidelines for writing a film treatment with emphasis on the setting.

1. Choose a work in which the author provides considerable information about both place and time, so that you have ample material on which to base your film treatment.

2. Follow steps 1 and 2 of the guidelines for the critical analysis to arrive at a clear understanding of the relation between setting and meaning.

3. Do additional research in standard reference works to gain a visual sense of the time and place. Architecture, costume, general geography, and so forth may be important in your film treatment, and you need to know enough to make what you describe reasonably authentic.

4. Imagine a film of the work. Let your visual senses have free play as you think what it might be like to watch the action in a movie theatre or on your television screen, instead of reading the words. Because most literature does not present every detail that appears in a film, you may need to include those implied by the action. You may even create additional details.

5. Write an introductory paragraph. Name the work and its author; state the general dramatic situation, briefly summarize the main action, describe the incident in which setting and meaning are most closely connected and suggest the nature of that meaning.

6. Write the body of your paper. Describe the setting(s) in detail and also discuss general treatment of camera and sound: Will there be flashbacks? Will the camera move from one setting to another? Will the camera concentrate on the general scene or on certain specific details within it? Will the soundtrack carry the live dialogue of the actors, or will there be a narrator's voice "over" the action? The organization of the body of your paper will depend on the nature of your film treatment. However, you should plan a series of paragraphs describing the principal setting and significant details within it. Additional paragraphs should describe how camera and sound will be used to reveal the conflicts connected with setting.

7. Write the concluding section of your paper. Show in some detail the treatment of the critical incident in which setting and meaning are most closely connected. End your paper with a statement of the meaning that you have found in the work and that you hope your film treatment will convey.

8. Let your paper rest a day or two before you proofread it and prepare a final fair copy for submission to your instructor.

OPTION II: SAMPLE FILM TREATMENT

Film Treatment for "Memorial Rain"

In "Memorial Rain," by Archibald MacLeish, the narrator attends the official dedication of Flanders Field, a cemetery in Belgium for American soldiers killed during World War I. The film treatment will present a man in his early thirties, who has come to the ceremony to commemorate the death of a soldier, perhaps the poet's brother, who is among the men buried there. As the narrator listens to the hollow-sounding words spoken at the dedication, he remembers happier times at his home in Illinois and feels his dead brother must be strangely out of place here in a foreign land. Only after a sudden shower breaks up the service is he able to think of his brother at peace under the grass.

A filmed realization of this poem would necessarily use Flanders Field and the occasion of the dedication service as its principal setting. The cemetery is stiff, formal, and foreign in feeling. Rows of crosses in rigid geometry stretch across a flat field toward a distant hedgerow, beyond which may be glimpsed wheat fields ready for cutting, with dashes of color from poppies and cornflowers; beyond these the spire of a village church stands against the leaden sky. In front of the rows of crosses is a large marble slab listing the names of the 368 soldiers buried here. A temporary platform has been erected before this slab, with chairs for dignitaries. On the ground immediately in front of the platform stand two color guards—Belgian on the right, American on the left—in World War I uniform. (Note: since this is some time between the two world wars, the American flag has 48 stars rather than 50.) Nearby, to one side, stand a few black early-twenties limousines, their uniformed chauffeurs standing at attention. Beyond them across a gravel road is a cluster of Belgian farmhouses.

The speaker's platform itself is draped with red-white-and-blue bunting. In a stiff row at the rear of the platform sit men of some local importance: paunchy, balding men in dark blue suits. One chair at the center is empty: its occupant has risen to stand before a microphone at the front of the platform. The microphone is a heavy metal stand topped by a ring about eight inches in diameter, with the actual microphone suspended on springs in the center of this ring. The speaker is dressed in a morning suit and wears the diagonal ribbon of an ambassador. He holds his top hat cradled in his left arm; his right hand holds a sheaf of manuscript from which he reads through pince-nez. A small crowd stands before the platform, consisting largely of local peasants awkward in their Sunday best, with here and there an American.

After taking in this general scene, with the ambassador's voice droning in French in the background, the camera closes in on one of the Americans, a bareheaded man in travel-rumpled seersucker. He is tense, ill at ease; he thrusts a clenched hand into his jacket pocket. This is the narrator: as he speaks the words of the poem (voice over, with the ambassador's voice fading out) the camera alternates between the ambassador and the young man himself, and we dissolve into flashbacks of his memories.

After showing the wind threatening rain in Brussels and Ghent, we come to the most important of the flashbacks: a beach area in Illinois. On a sandy bluff overlooking Lake Michigan, willow trees are bending in the wind. Two preadolescent boys in shorts and blouses run barefoot from the willows and down the steep sand bank. At the lake shore, waves are tumbling in. Rain begins and the boys gambol in it, turning their faces upward as they run on the beach. These scenes in flashback contrast sharply with the formality and aridity at Flanders Field, where a gust of wind stirs dust from the gravel at the narrator's feet.

At the end of the poem, a sudden downpour drives the company to shelter, the speaker and dignitaries to the limousines, the peasants to the farmhouses; but the narrator remains. In quick cuts we show the similarity after all between the rain and waves on Lake Michigan and the water streaming over the soil in Flanders Field. The narrator slowly lifts his face to the rain. He removes his fist from his jacket pocket and slowly opens it, palm up, to receive the downpour. It is his own hand that "relaxes, loosens," for at last he has been able to accept the fact of his brother's death and to feel that Flanders Field is not so completely foreign and strange as it had seemed.

READING SELECTIONS: STORIES

Charlotte Perkins Gilman (1860–1935)

THE YELLOW WALL-PAPER

It is very seldom that mere ordinary people like John and myself secure ancestral halls for the summer.

A colonial mansion, a hereditary estate. I would say a haunted house, and reach the height of romantic felicity—but that would be asking too much of fate!

Still I will proudly declare that there is something queer about it.

Else, why should it be let so cheaply? And why have stood so long untenanted?

John laughs at me, of course, but one expects that in marriage.

John is practical in the extreme. He has no patience with faith, an intense horror of superstition, and he scoffs openly at any talk of things not to be felt and seen and put down in figures.

John is a physician, and *perhaps*—(I would not say it to a living soul, of course, but this is dead paper and a great relief to my mind—) *perhaps* that is one reason I do not get well faster.

You see he does not believe I am sick!

And what can one do?

If a physician of high standing, and one's own husband, assures friends and relatives that there is really nothing the matter with one but temporary nervous depression—a slight hysterical tendency—what is one to do?

My brother is also a physician, and also of high standing, and he says the same thing.

So I take phosphates or phosphites—whichever it is, and tonics, and journeys, and air, and exercise, and am absolutely forbidden to "work" until I am well again.

Personally, I disagree with their ideas.

Personally, I believe that congenial work, with excitement and change, would do me good.

But what is one to do?

I did write for a while in spite of them; but it *does* exhaust me a good deal —having to be so sly about it, or else meet with heavy opposition.

I sometimes fancy that in my condition if I had less opposition and more society and stimulus—but John says the very worst thing I can do is to think about my condition, and I confess it always makes me feel bad.

So I will let it alone and talk about the house.

The most beautiful place! It is quite alone, standing well back from the road, quite three miles from the village. It makes me think of English places that you read about, for there are hedges and walls and gates that lock, and lots of separate little houses for the gardeners and people.

There is a *delicious* garden! I never saw such a garden—large and shady, full of box-bordered paths, and lined with long grape-covered arbors with seats under them.

There were greenhouses, too, but they are all broken now.

There was some legal trouble, I believe, something about the heirs and co-heirs; anyhow, the place has been empty for years.

That spoils my ghostliness, I am afraid, but I don't care—there is something strange about the house—I can feel it.

I even said so to John one moonlight evening, but he said what I felt was a *draught*, and shut the window.

I get unreasonably angry with John sometimes. I'm sure I never used to be so sensitive. I think it is due to this nervous condition.

But John says if I feel so, I shall neglect proper self-control; so I take pains to control myself—before him, at least, and that makes me very tired.

I don't like our room a bit. I wanted one downstairs that opened on the piazza and had roses all over the window, and such pretty old-fashioned chintz hangings! but John would not hear of it.

He said there was only one window and not room for two beds, and no near room for him if he took another.

He is very careful and loving, and hardly lets me stir without special direction.

I have a schedule prescription for each hour in the day; he takes all care from me, and so I feel basely ungrateful not to value it more.

He said we came here solely on my account, that I was to have perfect rest and all the air I could get. "Your exercise depends on your strength, my dear," said he, "and your food somewhat on your appetite; but air you can absorb all the time." So we took the nursery at the top of the house.

It is a big, airy room, the whole floor nearly, with windows that look all ways, and air and sunshine galore. It was nursery first and then playroom and gymnasium, I should judge; for the windows are barred for little children, and there are rings and things in the walls.

The paint and paper look as if a boys' school had used it. It is stripped off—the paper—in great patches all around the head of my bed, about as far as I can reach, and in a great place on the other side of the room low down. I never saw a worse paper in my life.

One of those sprawling flamboyant patterns committing every artistic sin.

It is dull enough to confuse the eye in following, pronounced enough to constantly irritate and provoke study, and when you follow the lame uncertain curves for a little distance they suddenly commit suicide—plunge off at outrageous angles, destroy themselves in unheard of contradictions.

The color is repellent, almost revolting; a smouldering unclean yellow, strangely faded by the slow-turning sunlight.

It is a dull yet lurid orange in some places, a sickly sulphur tint in others.

No wonder the children hated it! I should hate it myself if I had to live in this room long.

There comes John, and I must put this away,—he hates to have me write a word.

* * *

We have been here two weeks, and I haven't felt like writing before, since that first day.

I am sitting by the window now, up in this atrocious nursery, and there is nothing to hinder my writing as much as I please, save lack of strength.

John is away all day, and even some nights when his cases are serious.

I am glad my case is not serious!

But these nervous troubles are dreadfully depressing.

John does not know how much I really suffer. He knows there is no *reason* to suffer, and that satisfies him.

Of course it is only nervousness. It does weigh on me so not to do my duty in any way!

I meant to be such a help to John, such a real rest and comfort, and here I am a comparative burden already!

Nobody would believe what an effort it is to do what little I am able— to dress and entertain, and order things.

It is fortunate Mary is so good with the baby. Such a dear baby!

And yet I *cannot* be with him, it makes me so nervous.

I suppose John never was nervous in his life. He laughs at me so about this wall-paper!

At first he meant to repaper the room, but afterwards he said that I was letting it get the better of me, and that nothing was worse for a nervous patient than to give way to such fancies.

He said that after the wall-paper was changed it would be the heavy bedstead, and then the barred windows, and then that gate at the head of the stairs, and so on.

"You know the place is doing you good," he said, "and really, dear, I don't care to renovate the house just for a three months' rental."

"Then do let us go downstairs," I said, "there are such pretty rooms there."

Then he took me in his arms and called me a blessed little goose, and said he would go down cellar, if I wished, and have it whitewashed into the bargain.

But he is right enough about the beds and windows and things.

It is as airy and comfortable room as any one need wish, and, of course, I would not be so silly as to make him uncomfortable just for a whim.

I'm really getting quite fond of the big room, all but that horrid paper.

Out of one window I can see the garden, those mysterious deep-shaded arbors, the riotous old-fashioned flowers, and bushes and gnarly trees.

Out of another I get a lovely view of the bay and a little private wharf belonging to the estate. There is a beautiful shaded lane that runs down there from the house. I always fancy I see people walking in these numerous paths and arbors, but John has cautioned me not to give way to fancy in the least. He says that with my imaginative power and habit of story-making, a nervous weakness like mine is sure to lead to all manner of excited fancies, and that I ought to use my will and good sense to check the tendency. So I try.

I think sometimes that if I were only well enough to write a little it would relieve the press of ideas and rest me.

But I find I get pretty tired when I try.

It is so discouraging not to have any advice and companionship about my work. When I get really well, John says we will ask Cousin Henry and Julia down for a long visit; but he says he would as soon put fireworks in my pillow-case as to let me have those stimulating people about now.

I wish I could get well faster.

But I must not think about that. This paper looks to me as if it *knew* what a vicious influence it had!

There is a recurrent spot where the pattern lolls like a broken neck and two bulbous eyes stare at you upside down.

I get positively angry with the impertinence of it and the everlastingness. Up and down and sideways they crawl, and those absurd, unblinking eyes are everywhere. There is one place where two breadths didn't match, and the eyes go all up and down the line, one a little higher than the other.

I never saw so much expression in an inanimate thing before, and we all know how much expression they have! I used to lie awake as a child and get more entertainment and terror out of blank walls and plain furniture than most children could find in a toy-store.

I remember what a kindly wink the knobs of our big, old bureau used to have, and there was one chair that always seemed like a strong friend.

I used to feel that if any of the other things looked too fierce I could always hop into that chair and be safe.

The furniture in this room is no worse than inharmonious, however, for we had to bring it all from downstairs. I suppose when this was used as a playroom they had to take the nursery things out, and no wonder! I never saw such ravages as the children have made here.

The wall-paper, as I said before, is torn off in spots, and it sticketh closer than a brother—they must have had perseverance as well as hatred.

Then the floor is scratched and gouged and splintered, the plaster itself is dug out here and there, and this great heavy bed which is all we found in the room, looks as if it had been through the wars.

But I don't mind it a bit—only the paper.

There comes John's sister. Such a dear girl as she is, and so careful of me! I must not let her find me writing.

She is a perfect and enthusiastic housekeeper, and hopes for no better profession. I verily believe she thinks it is the writing which made me sick!

But I can write when she is out, and see her a long way off from these windows.

There is one that commands the road, a lovely shaded winding road, and one that just looks off over the country. A lovely country, too, full of great elms and velvet meadows.

This wall-paper has a kind of sub-pattern in a different shade, a particularly irritating one, for you can only see it in certain lights, and not clearly then.

But in the places where it isn't faded and where the sun is just so—I can see a strange, provoking, formless sort of figure, that seems to skulk about behind that silly and conspicuous front design.

There's sister on the stairs!

* * *

Well, the Fourth of July is over! The people are all gone and I am tired out. John thought it might do me good to see a little company, so we just had mother and Nellie and the children down for a week.

Of course I didn't do a thing. Jennie sees to everything now.

But it tired me all the same.

John says if I don't pick up faster he shall send me to Weir Mitchell in the fall.

But I don't want to go there at all. I had a friend who was in his hands once, and she says he is just like John and my brother, only more so!

Besides, it is such an undertaking to go so far.

I don't feel as if it was worth while to turn my hand over for anything, and I'm getting dreadfully fretful and querulous.

I cry at nothing, and cry most of the time.

Of course I don't when John is here, or anybody else, but when I am alone.

And I am alone a good deal just now. John is kept in town very often by serious cases, and Jennie is good and lets me alone when I want her to.

So I walk a little in the garden or down that lovely lane, sit on the porch under the roses, and lie down up here a good deal.

I'm getting really fond of the room in spite of the wall-paper. Perhaps *because* of the wall-paper.

It dwells in my mind so!

I lie here on this great immovable bed—it is nailed down, I believe—and follow that pattern about by the hour. It is as good as gymnastics, I assure you. I start, we'll say, at the bottom, down in the corner over there where it has not been touched, and I determine for the thousandth time that I *will* follow that pointless pattern to some sort of a conclusion.

I know a little of the principle of design, and I know this thing was not arranged on any laws of radiation, or alternation, or repetition, or symmetry, or anything else that I ever heard of.

It is repeated, of course, by the breadths, but not otherwise.

Looked at in one way each breadth stands alone, the bloated curves and flourishes—a kind of "debased Romanesque" with *delirium tremens*[1] go waddling up and down in isolated columns of fatuity.

But, on the other hand, they connect diagonally, and the sprawling outlines run off in great slanting waves of optic horror, like a lot of wallowing seaweeds in full chase.

The whole thing goes horizontally, too, at least it seems so, and I exhaust myself in trying to distinguish the order of its going in that direction.

They have used a horizontal breadth for a frieze,[2] and that adds wonderfully to the confusion.

There is one end of the room where it is almost intact, and there, when the crosslights fade and the low sun shines directly upon it, I can almost fancy radiation after all,—the interminable grotesques seem to form around a common centre and rush off in headlong plunges of equal distraction.

It makes me tired to follow it. I will take a nap I guess.

* * *

I don't know why I should write this.

I don't want to.

I don't feel able.

And I know John would think it absurd. But I *must* say what I feel and think in some way—it is such a relief!

But the effort is getting to be greater than the relief.

Half the time now I am awfully lazy, and lie down ever so much.

John says I mustn't lose my strength, and has me take cod liver oil and lots of tonics and things, to say nothing of ale and wine and rare meat.

Dear John! He loves me very dearly, and hates to have me sick. I tried to have a real earnest reasonable talk with him the other day, and tell him how I wish he would let me go and make a visit to Cousin Henry and Julia.

But he said I wasn't able to go, nor able to stand it after I got there; and I did not make out a very good case for myself, for I was crying before I had finished.

It is getting to be a great effort for me to think straight. Just this nervous weakness I suppose.

And dear John gathered me up in his arms, and just carried me upstairs and laid me on the bed, and sat by me and read to me till it tired my head.

He said I was his darling and his comfort and all he had, and that I must take care of myself for his sake, and keep well.

He says no one but myself can help me out of it, that I must use my will and self-control and not let any silly fancies run away with me.

---

[1] *delirium tremens*: severe hallucinations, anxiety, confusion, and trembling, usually associated with alcoholism.

[2] frieze: decorative border along the top of a wall.

There's one comfort, the baby is well and happy, and does not have to occupy this nursery with the horrid wall-paper.

If we had not used it, that blessed child would have! What a fortunate escape! Why, I wouldn't have a child of mine, an impressionable little thing, live in such a room for worlds.

I never thought of it before, but it is lucky that John kept me here after all, I can stand it so much easier than a baby, you see.

Of course I never mention it to them any more—I am too wise,—but I keep watch of it all the same.

There are things in that paper that nobody knows but me, or ever will.

Behind that outside pattern the dim shapes get clearer every day.

It is always the same shape, only very numerous.

And it is like a woman stooping down and creeping about behind that pattern. I don't like it a bit. I wonder—I begin to think—I wish John would take me away from here!

It is so hard to talk with John about my case, because he is so wise, and because he loves me so.

But I tried it last night.

It was moonlight. The moon shines in all around just as the sun does.

I hate to see it sometimes, it creeps so slowly, and always comes in by one window or another.

John was asleep and I hated to waken him, so I kept still and watched the moonlight on that undulating wall-paper till I felt creepy.

The faint figure behind seemed to shake the pattern, just as if she wanted to get out.

I got up softly and went to feel and see if the paper *did* move, and when I came back John was awake.

"What is it, little girl?" he said. "Don't go walking about like that—you'll get cold."

I thought it was a good time to talk, so I told him that I really was not gaining here, and that I wished he would take me away.

"Why, darling!" said he, "our lease will be up in three weeks, and I can't see how to leave before.

"The repairs are not done at home, and I cannot possibly leave town just now. Of course if you were in any danger, I could and would, but you really are better, dear, whether you can see it or not. I am a doctor, dear, and I know. You are gaining flesh and color, your appetite is better, I feel really much easier about you."

"I don't weigh a bit more," said I, "nor as much; and my appetite may be better in the evening when you are here, but it is worse in the morning when you are away!"

"Bless her little heart!" said he with a big hug, "she shall be as sick as she pleases! But now let's improve the shining hours by going to sleep, and talk about it in the morning!"

"And you won't go away?" I asked gloomily.

"Why, how can I, dear? It is only three weeks more and then we will take a nice little trip of a few days while Jennie is getting the house ready. Really dear you are better!"

"Better in body perhaps—" I began, and stopped short, for he sat up straight and looked at me with such a stern, reproachful look that I could not say another word.

"My darling," said he, "I beg of you, for my sake and for our child's sake, as well as for your own, that you will never for one instant let that idea enter your mind! There is nothing so dangerous, so fascinating, to a temperament like yours. It is a false and foolish fancy. Can you not trust me as a physician when I tell you so?"

So of course I said no more on that score, and we went to sleep before long. He thought I was asleep first, but I wasn't, and lay there for hours trying to decide whether that front pattern and the back pattern really did move together or separately.

* * *

On a pattern like this, by daylight, there is a lack of sequence, a defiance of law, that is a constant irritant to a normal mind.

The color is hideous enough, and unreliable enough, and infuriating enough, but the pattern is torturing.

You think you have mastered it, but just as you get well underway in following, it turns a back-somersault and there you are. It slaps you in the face, knocks you down, and tramples upon you. It is like a bad dream.

The outside pattern is a florid arabesque, reminding one of a fungus. If you can imagine a toadstool in joints, an interminable string of toadstools, budding and sprouting in endless convolutions—why, that is something like it.

That is, sometimes!

There is one marked peculiarity about this paper, a thing nobody seems to notice but myself, and that is that it changes as the light changes.

When the sun shoots in through the east window—I always watch for that first long, straight ray—it changes so quickly that I never can quite believe it.

That is why I watch it always.

By moonlight—the moon shines in all night when there is a moon—I wouldn't know it was the same paper.

At night in any kind of light, in twilight, candlelight, lamplight, and worst of all by moonlight, it becomes bars! The outside pattern I mean, and the woman behind it is as plain as can be.

I didn't realize for a long time what the thing was that showed behind, that dim sub-pattern, but now I am quite sure it is a woman.

By daylight she is subdued, quiet. I fancy it is the pattern that keeps her so still. It is so puzzling. It keeps me quiet by the hour.

I lie down ever so much now. John says it is good for me, and to sleep all I can.

Indeed he started the habit by making me lie down for an hour after each meal.

It is a very bad habit I am convinced, for you see I don't sleep.

And that cultivates deceit, for I don't tell them I'm awake—O no!

The fact is I am getting a little afraid of John.

He seems very queer sometimes, and even Jennie has an inexplicable look.

It strikes me occasionally, just as a scientific hypothesis,—that perhaps it is the paper!

I have watched John when he did not know I was looking, and come into the room suddenly on the most innocent excuses, and I've caught him several times *looking at the paper!* And Jennie too. I caught Jennie with her hand on it once.

She didn't know I was in the room, and when I asked her in a quiet, a very quiet voice, with the most restrained manner possible, what she was doing with the paper—she turned around as if she had been caught stealing, and looked quite angry—asked me why I should frighten her so!

Then she said that the paper stained everything it touched, that she had found yellow smooches on all my clothes and John's, and she wished we would be more careful!

Did not that sound innocent? But I know she was studying that pattern, and I am determined that nobody shall find it out but myself!

* * *

Life is very much more exciting now than it used to be. You see I have something more to expect, to look forward to, to watch. I really do eat better, and am more quiet than I was.

John is so pleased to see me improve! He laughed a little the other day, and said I seemed to be flourishing in spite of my wall-paper.

I turned it off with a laugh. I had no intention of telling him it was *because* of the wall-paper—he would make fun of me. He might even want to take me away.

I don't want to leave now until I have found it out. There is a week more, and I think that will be enough.

* * *

I'm feeling ever so much better! I don't sleep much at night, for it is so interesting to watch developments; but I sleep a good deal in the daytime.

In the daytime it is tiresome and perplexing.

There are always new shoots on the fungus, and new shades of yellow all over it. I cannot keep count of them, though I have tried conscientiously.

It is the strangest yellow, that wall-paper! It makes me think of all the yellow things I ever saw—not beautiful ones like buttercups, but old foul, bad yellow things.

But there is something else about that paper—the smell! I noticed it the moment we came into the room, but with so much air and sun it was not bad. Now we have had a week of fog and rain, and whether the windows are open or not, the smell is here.

It creeps all over the house.

I find it hovering in the dining-room, skulking in the parlor, hiding in the hall, lying in wait for me on the stairs.

It gets into my hair.

Even when I go to ride, if I turn my head suddenly and surprise it—there is that smell!

Such a peculiar odor, too! I have spent hours in trying to analyze it, to find what it smelled like.

It is not bad—at first, and very gentle, but quite the subtlest, most enduring odor I ever met.

In this damp weather it is awful. I wake up in the night and find it hanging over me.

It used to disturb me at first. I thought seriously of burning the house—to reach the smell.

But now I am used to it. The only thing I can think of that it is like is the *color* of the paper! A yellow smell.

There is a very funny mark on this wall, low down, near the mopboard. A streak that runs round the room. It goes behind every piece of furniture, except the bed, a long, straight, even *smooch*, as if it had been rubbed over and over.

I wonder how it was done and who did it, and what they did it for. Round and round and round—round and round and round!—it makes me dizzy!

* * *

I really have discovered something at last.

Through watching so much at night, when it changes so, I have finally found out.

The front pattern *does* move—and no wonder! The woman behind shakes it!

Sometimes I think there are a great many women behind, and sometimes only one, and she crawls around fast, and her crawling shakes it all over.

Then in the very bright spots she keeps still, and in the very shady spots she just takes hold of the bars and shakes them hard.

And she is all the time trying to climb through. But nobody could climb through that pattern—it strangles so; I think that is why it has so many heads.

They get through, and then the pattern strangles them off and turns them upside down, and makes their eyes white!

If those heads were covered or taken off it would not be half so bad.

* * *

I think that woman gets out in the daytime!

And I'll tell you why—privately—I've seen her!

I can see her out of every one of my windows!

It is the same woman, I know, for she is always creeping, and most women do not creep by daylight.

I see her in that long shaded lane, creeping up and down. I see her in those dark grape arbors, creeping all around the garden.

I see her on that long road under the trees, creeping along, and when a carriage comes she hides under the blackberry vines.

I don't blame her a bit. It must be very humiliating to be caught creeping by daylight!

I always lock the door when I creep by daylight. I can't do it at night, for I know John would suspect something at once.

And John is so queer now, that I don't want to irritate him. I wish he would take another room! Besides, I don't want anybody to get that woman out at night but myself.

I often wonder if I could see her out of all the windows at once.

But, turn as fast as I can, I can only see out of one at one time.

And though I always see her, she *may* be able to creep faster than I can turn!

I have watched her sometimes away off in the open country, creeping as fast as a cloud shadow in a high wind.

* * *

If only that top pattern could be gotten off from the under one! I mean to try it, little by little.

I have found out another funny thing, but I shan't tell it this time! It does not do to trust people too much.

There are only two more days to get this paper off, and I believe John is beginning to notice. I don't like the look in his eyes.

And I heard him ask Jennie a lot of professional questions about me. She had a very good report to give.

She said I slept a good deal in the daytime.

John knows I don't sleep very well at night, for all I'm so quiet!

He asked me all sorts of questions, too, and pretended to be very loving and kind.

As if I couldn't see through him!

Still, I don't wonder he acts so, sleeping under this paper for three months.

It only interests me, but I feel sure John and Jennie are secretly affected by it.

* * *

Hurrah! This is the last day, but it is enough. John to stay in town over night, and won't be out until this evening.

Jennie wanted to sleep with me—the sly thing! but I told her I should undoubtedly rest better for a night all alone.

That was clever, for really I wasn't alone a bit! As soon as it was moonlight and that poor thing began to crawl and shake the pattern, I got up and ran to help her.

I pulled and she shook, I shook and she pulled, and before morning we had peeled off yards of that paper.

A strip about as high as my head and half around the room.

And then when the sun came and that awful pattern began to laugh at me, I declared I would finish it to-day!

We go away to-morrow, and they are moving all my furniture down again to leave things as they were before.

Jennie looked at the wall in amazement, but I told her merrily that I did it out of pure spite at the vicious thing.

She laughed and said she wouldn't mind doing it herself, but I must not get tired.

How she betrayed herself that time!

But I am here, and no person touches this paper but me,—not *alive!*

She tried to get me out of the room—it was too patent! But I said it was so quiet and empty and clean now that I believed I would lie down again and sleep all I could; and not to wake me even for dinner—I would call when I woke.

So now she is gone, and the servants are gone, and the things are gone, and there is nothing left but that great bedstead nailed down, with the canvas mattress we found on it.

We shall sleep downstairs to-night, and take the boat home to-morrow.

I quite enjoy the room, now it is bare again.

How those children did tear about here!

This bedstead is fairly gnawed!

But I must get to work.

I have locked the door and thrown the key down into the front path.

I don't want to go out, and I don't want to have anybody come in, till John comes.

I want to astonish him.

I've got a rope up here that even Jennie did not find. If that woman does get out, and tries to get away, I can tie her!

But I forgot I could not reach far without anything to stand on!

This bed will *not* move!

I tried to lift and push it until I was lame, and then I got so angry I bit off a little piece at one corner—but it hurt my teeth.

Then I peeled off all the paper I could reach standing on the floor. It sticks horribly and the pattern just enjoys it! All those strangled heads and bulbous eyes and waddling fungus growths just shriek with derision!

I am getting angry enough to do something desperate. To jump out of the window would be admirable exercise, but the bars are too strong even to try.

Besides I wouldn't do it. Of course not. I know well enough that a step like that is improper and might be misconstrued.

I don't like to *look* out of the windows even—there are so many of those creeping women, and they creep so fast.

I wonder if they all come out of that wall-paper as I did?

But I am securely fastened now by my well-hidden rope—you don't get *me* out in the road there!

I suppose I shall have to get back behind the pattern when it comes night, and that is hard!

It is so pleasant to be out in this great room and creep around as I please!

I don't want to go outside. I won't, even if Jennie asks me to.

For outside you have to creep on the ground, and everything is green instead of yellow.

But here I can creep smoothly on the floor, and my shoulder just fits in that long smooch around the wall, so I cannot lose my way.

Why there's John at the door!

It is no use, young man, you can't open it!

How he does call and pound!

Now he's crying for an axe.

It would be a shame to break down that beautiful door!

"John dear!" said I in the gentlest voice, "the key is down by the front steps, under a plaintain leaf!"

That silenced him for a few moments.

Then he said—very quietly indeed, "Open the door, my darling!"

"I can't," said I. "The key is down by the front door under a plaintain leaf!"

And then I said it again, several times, very gently and slowly, and said it so often that he had to go and see, and he got it of course, and came in. He stopped short by the door.

"What is the matter?" he cried. "For God's sake, what are you doing!"

I kept on creeping just the same, but I looked at him over my shoulder.

"I've got out at last," said I, "in spite of you and Jane? And I've pulled off most of the paper, so you can't put me back!"

Now why should that man have fainted? But he did, and right across my path by the wall, so that I had to creep over him every time!

STUDY QUESTIONS

1. Describe the "colonial mansion" as completely as you can on the basis of details in the story.
2. Why is the text divided into sections separated by asterisks?
3. Trace the step-by-step development of the narrator's insanity. When does she begin having hallucinations? Why does she hide her writing from the others in the story?
4. To what extent does the yellow wall-paper cause the woman's mental breakdown? To what extent does she explain what is happening to her by imagining changes in the paper?
5. How far is John aware of his wife's deteriorating mental condition? In what ways does he actually contribute to her illness instead of helping to cure it?

P. G. Wodehouse (1881–1975)

HONEYSUCKLE COTTAGE

"Do you believe in ghosts?" asked Mr. Mulliner, abruptly.

I weighed the question thoughtfully. I was a little surprised, for nothing in our previous conversation had suggested the topic.

"Well," I replied, "I don't like them, if that's what you mean. I was once butted by one as a child."

"Ghosts. Not goats."

"Oh, ghosts? Do I believe in ghosts?"

"Exactly."

"Well, yes—and no."

"Let me put it another way," said Mr. Mulliner, patiently. "Do you believe in haunted houses? Do you believe that it is possible for a malign influence to envelop a place and work a spell on all who come within its radius?"

I hesitated.

"Well, no—and yes."

Mr. Mulliner sighed a little. He seemed to be wondering if I was always as bright as this.

"Of course," I went on, "one has read stories. Henry James's *Turn of The Screw*——"

"I am not talking about fiction."

"Well, in real life—— Well, look here, I once, as a matter of fact, did meet a man who knew a fellow——"

"My distant cousin James Rodman spent some weeks in a haunted house," said Mr. Mulliner, who, if he has a fault, is not a very good listener.

"It cost him five thousand pounds. That is to say, he sacrificed five thousand pounds by not remaining there. Did you ever," he asked, wandering, it seemed to me, from the subject, "hear of Leila J. Pinckney?"

Naturally I had heard of Leila J. Pinckney. Her death some years ago has diminished her vogue, but at one time it was impossible to pass a book-shop or a railway bookstall without seeing a long row of her novels. I had never myself actually read any of them, but I knew that in her particular line of literature, the Squashily Sentimental, she had always been regarded by those entitled to judge as pre-eminent. The critics usually headed their reviews of her stories with the words:—

ANOTHER PINCKNEY

or sometimes, more offensively:—

ANOTHER PINCKNEY! ! !

And once, dealing with, I think, *The Love Which Prevails*, the literary expert of the *Scrutinizer* had compressed his entire critique into the single phrase "Oh, God!"

"Of course," I said. "But what about her?"

"She was James Rodman's aunt."

"Yes?"

"And when she died James found that she had left him five thousand pounds and the house in the country where she had lived for the last twenty years of her life."

"A very nice little legacy."

"Twenty years," repeated Mr. Mulliner. "Grasp that, for it has a vital bearing on what follows. Twenty years, mind you, and Miss Pinckney turned out two novels and twelve short stories regularly every year, besides a monthly page of Advice to Young Girls in one of the magazines. That is to say, forty of her novels and no fewer than two hundred and forty of her short stories were written under the roof of Honeysuckle Cottage."

"A pretty name."

"A nasty, sloppy name," said Mr. Mulliner, severely, "which should have warned my distant cousin James from the start. Have you a pencil and a piece of paper?" He scribbled for a while, poring frowningly over columns of figures. "Yes," he said, looking, "if my calculations are correct, Leila J. Pinckney wrote in all a matter of nine million and one hundred and forty thousand words of glutinous sentimentality at Honeysuckle Cottage, and it was a condition of her will that James should reside there for six months in every year. Failing to do this, he was to forfeit the five thousand pounds."

"It must be great fun making a freak will," I mused. "I often wish I was rich enough to do it."

"This was not a freak will. The conditions are perfectly understandable.

James Rodman was a writer of sensational mystery stories, and his Aunt Leila had always disapproved of his work. She was a great believer in the influence of environment, and the reason why she inserted that clause in her will was that she wished to compel James to move from London to the country. She considered that living in London hardened him and made his outlook on life sordid. She often asked him if he thought it quite nice to harp so much on sudden death and blackmailers with squints. Surely, she said, there were enough squinting blackmailers in the world without writing about them.

"The fact that Literature meant such different things to these two had, I believe, caused something of a coolness between them, and James had never dreamed that he would be remembered in his aunt's will. For he had never concealed his opinion that Leila J. Pinckney's style of writing revolted him, however dear it might be to her enormous public. He held rigid views on the art of the novel, and always maintained that an artist with a true reverence for his craft should not descend to goo-ey love stories, but should stick austerely to revolvers, cries in the night, missing papers, mysterious Chinamen and dead bodies—with or without gash in throat. And not even the thought that his aunt had dandled him on her knee as a baby could induce him to stifle his literary conscience to the extent of pretending to enjoy her work. First, last, and all the time, James Rodman had held the opinion— and voiced it fearlessly—that Leila J. Pinckney wrote bilge.

"It was a surprise to him, therefore, to find that he had been left this legacy. A pleasant surprise, of course. James was making quite a decent income out of the three novels and eighteen short stories which he produced annually, but an author can always find a use for five thousand pounds. And, as for the cottage, he had actually been looking about for a little place in the country at the very moment when he received the lawyer's letter. In less than a week he was installed at his new residence."

James's first impressions of Honeysuckle Cottage were, he tells me, wholly favourable. He was delighted with the place. It was a low, rambling, picturesque old house with funny little chimneys and a red roof, placed in the middle of the most charming country. With its oak beams, its trim garden, its trilling birds and its rose-hung porch, it was the ideal spot for a writer. It was just the sort of place, he reflected whimsically, which his aunt had loved to write about in her books. Even the apple-cheeked old housekeeper who attended to his needs might have stepped straight out of one of them.

It seemed to James that his lot had been cast in pleasant places. He had brought down his books, his pipes, and his golf clubs, and was hard at work finishing the best thing he had ever done. *The Secret Nine* was the title of it; and on the beautiful summer afternoon on which this story opens he was in the study, hammering away at his typewriter, at peace with the world. The machine was running sweetly, the new tobacco he had bought the day before was proving admirable, and he was moving on all six cylinders to the end of a chapter.

He shoved in a fresh sheet of paper, chewed his pipe thoughtfully for a moment, then wrote rapidly:

For an instant Lester Gage thought that he must have been mistaken. Then the noise came again, faint but unmistakable—a soft scratching on the outer panel.

His mouth set in a grim line. Silently, like a panther, he made one quick step to the desk, noiselessly opened a drawer, drew out his automatic. After that affair of the poisoned needle, he was taking no chances. Still in dead silence, he tiptoed to the door; then, flinging it suddenly open, he stood there, his weapon poised.

On the mat stood the most beautiful girl he had ever beheld. A veritable child of Faërie.[1] She eyed him for a moment with a saucy smile; then with a pretty, roguish look of reproof shook a dainty forefinger at him.

"I believe you've forgotten me, Mr. Gage!" she fluted with a mock severity which her eyes belied.

James stared at the paper dumbly. He was utterly perplexed. He had not had the slightest intention of writing anything like this. To begin with, it was a rule with him, and one which he never broke, to allow no girls to appear in his stories. Sinister landladies, yes, and naturally any amount of adventuresses with foreign accents, but never under any pretext what may be broadly described as girls. A detective story, he maintained, should have no heroine. Heroines only held up the action and tried to flirt with the hero when he should have been busy looking for clues, and then went and let the villain kidnap them by some childishly simple trick. In his writing, James was positively monastic.

And yet here was this creature with her saucy smile and her dainty forefinger horning in at the most important point in the story. It was uncanny.

He looked once more at his scenario. No, the scenario was all right.

In perfectly plain words it stated that what happened when the door opened was that a dying man fell in and after gasping, "The beetle! Tell Scotland Yard that the blue beetle is——" expired on the hearthrug, leaving Lester Gage not unnaturally somewhat mystified. Nothing whatever about any beautiful girls.

In a curious mood of irritation, James scratched out the offending passage, wrote in the necessary corrections, and put the cover on the machine. It was at this point that he heard William whining.

The only blot on this paradise which James had so far been able to discover was the infernal dog, William. Belonging nominally to the gardener, on the very first morning he had adopted James by acclamation, and he maddened and infuriated James. He had a habit of coming and whining under the window when James was at work. The latter would ignore this as long

[1] Faërie: the imaginary land of fairies and enchantment.

as he could; then, when the thing became insupportable, would bound out of his chair, to see the animal standing on the gravel, gazing expectantly up at him with a stone in his mouth. William had a weak-minded passion for chasing stones; and on the first day James, in a rash spirit of camaraderie, had flung one for him. Since then James had thrown no more stones; but he had thrown any number of other solids, and the garden was littered with objects ranging from match boxes to a plaster statuette of the young Joseph prophesying before Pharaoh. And still William came and whined, an optimist to the last.

The whining, coming now at a moment when he felt irritable and unsettled, acted on James much as the scratching on the door had acted on Lester Gage. Silently, like a panther, he made one quick step to the mantelpiece, removed from it a china mug bearing the legend A Present From Clacton-on-Sea, and crept to the window.

And as he did so a voice outside said, "Go away, sir, go away!" and there followed a short, high-pitched bark which was certainly not William's. William was a mixture of Airedale, setter, bull terrier, and mastiff; and when in vocal mood, favoured the mastiff side of his family.

James peered out. There on the porch stood a girl in blue. She held in her arms a small fluffy white dog, and she was endeavouring to foil the upward movement toward this of the blackguard William. William's mentality had been arrested some years before at the point where he imagined that everything in the world had been created for him to eat. A bone, a boot, a steak, the back wheel of a bicycle—it was all one to William. If it was there he tried to eat it. He had even made a plucky attempt to devour the remains of the young Joseph prophesying before Pharaoh. And it was perfectly plain now that he regarded the curious wriggling object in the girl's arms purely in the light of a snack to keep body and soul together till dinner-time.

"William!" bellowed James.

William looked courteously over his shoulder with eyes that beamed with the pure light of a life's devotion, wagged the whiplike tail which he had inherited from his bull terrier ancestor and resumed his intent scrutiny of the fluffy dog.

"Oh, please!" cried the girl. "This great rough dog is frightening poor Toto."

The man of letters and the man of action do not always go hand in hand, but practice had made James perfect in handling with a swift efficiency any situation that involved William. A moment later that canine moron, having received the present from Clacton in the short ribs, was scuttling around the corner of the house, and James had jumped through the window and was facing the girl.

She was an extraordinarily pretty girl. Very sweet and fragile she looked as she stood there under the honeysuckle with the breeze ruffling a tendril of golden hair that strayed from beneath her coquettish little hat. Her eyes were very big and very blue, her rose-tinted face becomingly flushed. All wasted on James, though. He disliked all girls, and particularly the sweet, droopy type.

"Did you want to see somebody?" he asked, stiffly.

"Just the house," said the girl, "if it wouldn't be giving any trouble. I do so want to see the room where Miss Pinckney wrote her books. This is where Leila J. Pinckney used to live, isn't it?"

"Yes; I am her nephew. My name is James Rodman."

"Mine is Rose Maynard."

James led the way into the house, and she stopped with a cry of delight on the threshold of the morning room.

"Oh, how too perfect!" she cried. So this was her study?"

"Yes."

"What a wonderful place it would be for you to think in if you were a writer, too."

James held no high opinion of women's literary taste, but nevertheless he was conscious of an unpleasant shock.

"I am a writer," he said, coldly. "I write detective stories."

"I—I'm afraid"—she blushed—"I'm afraid I don't often read detective stories."

"You no doubt prefer," said James, still more coldly, "the sort of thing my aunt used to write."

"Oh, I love her stories!" cried the girl, clasping her hands ecstatically. "Don't you?"

"I cannot say that I do."

"What?"

"They are pure apple sauce," said James, sternly; "just nasty blobs of sentimentality, thoroughly untrue to life."

The girl stared.

"Why, that's just what's so wonderful about them, their trueness to life! You feel they might all have happened. I don't understand what you mean."

They were walking down the garden now. James held the gate open for her and she passed through into the road.

"Well, for one thing," he said, "I decline to believe that a marriage between two young people is invariably preceded by some violent and sensational experience in which they both share."

"Are you thinking of *Scent o' the Blossom*, where Edgar saves Maud from drowning?"

"I am thinking of every single one of my aunt's books." He looked at her curiously. He had just got the solution of a mystery which had been puzzling him for some time. Almost from the moment he had set eyes on her she had seemed somehow strangely familiar. It now suddenly came to him why it was that he disliked her so much. "Do you know," he said, "you might be one of my aunt's heroines yourself? You're just the sort of girl she used to love to write about."

Her face lit up.

"Oh, do you really think so?" She hesitated. "Do you know what I have been feeling ever since I came here? I've been feeling that you are exactly like one of Miss Pinckney's heroes."

"No, I say, really!" said James, revolted.

"Oh, but you are! When you jumped through that window it gave me quite a start. You were so exactly like Claude Masterson in *Heather o' the Hills*."

"I have not read *Heather o' the Hills*," said James, with a shudder.

"He was very strong and quiet, with deep, dark, sad eyes."

James did not explain that his eyes were sad because her society gave him a pain in the neck. He merely laughed scornfully.

"So now, I suppose," he said, "a car will come and knock you down and I shall carry you gently into the house and lay you——Look out!" he cried.

It was too late. She was lying in a little huddled heap at his feet. Round the corner a large automobile had come bowling, keeping with an almost affected precision to the wrong side of the road. It was now receding into the distance, the occupant of the tonneau,[2] a stout red-faced gentleman in a fur coat, leaning out over the back. He had bared his head—not, one fears, as a pretty gesture of respect and regret, but because he was using his hat to hide the number plate.

The dog Toto was unfortunately uninjured.

James carried the girl gently into the house and laid her on the sofa in the morning-room. He rang the bell and the apple-cheeked housekeeper appeared.

"Send for the doctor," said James. "There has been an accident."

The housekeeper bent over the girl.

'Eh, dearie, dearie!" she said. "Bless her sweet pretty face!"

The gardener, he who technically owned William, was routed out from among the young lettuces and told to fetch Doctor Brady. He separated his bicycle from William, who was making a light meal off the left pedal, and departed on his mission. Doctor Brady arrived and in due course he made his report.

"No bones broken, but a number of nasty bruises. And, of course, the shock. She will have to stay here for some time, Rodman. Can't be moved."

"Stay here! But she can't! It isn't proper."

"Your housekeeper will act as a chaperon."

The doctor sighed. He was a stolid-looking man of middle age with side whiskers.

"A beautiful girl, that, Rodman," he said.

"I suppose so," said James.

"A sweet, beautiful girl. An elfin child."

"A what?" cried James, starting.

[2] tonneau: the rear compartment of a limousine or other car.

This imagery was very foreign to Doctor Brady as he knew him. On the only previous occasion on which they had had any extended conversation, the doctor had talked exclusively about the effect of too much protein on the gastric juices.

"An elfin child; a tender, fairy creature. When I was looking at her just now, Rodman, I nearly broke down. Her little hand lay on the coverlet like some white lily floating on the surface of a still pool, and her dear, trusting eyes gazed up at me."

He pottered off down the garden, still babbling, and James stood staring after him blankly. And slowly, like some cloud athwart a summer sky, there crept over James's heart the chill shadow of a nameless fear.

It was about a week later that Mr. Andrew McKinnon, the senior partner in the well-known firm of literary agents, McKinnon & Gooch, sat in his office in Chancery Lane, frowning thoughtfully over a telegram. He rang the bell.

"Ask Mr. Gooch to step in here." He resumed his study of the telegram. "Oh, Gooch," he said when his partner appeared, "I've just had a curious wire from young Rodman. He seems to want to see me very urgently."

Mr. Gooch read the telegram.

"Written under the influence of some strong mental excitement," he agreed. "I wonder why he doesn't come to the office if he wants to see you so badly."

"He's working very hard, finishing that novel for Prodder & Wiggs. Can't leave it, I suppose. Well, it's a nice day. If you will look after things here I think I'll motor down and let him give me lunch."

As Mr. McKinnon's car reached the crossroads a mile from Honeysuckle Cottage, he was aware of a gesticulating figure by the hedge. He stopped the car.

"Morning, Rodman."

"Thank God, you've come!" said James. It seemed to Mr. McKinnon that the young man looked paler and thinner. "Would you mind walking the rest of the way? There's something I want to speak to you about."

Mr. McKinnon alighted; and James, as he glanced at him, felt cheered and encouraged by the very sight of the man. The literary agent was a grim, hard-bitten person, to whom, when he called at their offices to arrange terms, editors kept their faces turned so that they might at least retain their back collar studs. There was no sentiment in Andrew McKinnon. Editresses of society papers practised their blandishments on him in vain, and many a publisher had waked screaming in the night, dreaming that he was signing a McKinnon contract.

"Well, Rodman," he said, "Prodder & Wiggs have agreed to our terms. I was writing to tell you so when your wire arrived. I had a lot of trouble with them, but it's fixed at 20 per cent., rising to 25, and two hundred pounds advance royalties on day of publication."

"Good!" said James, absently. "Good! McKinnon, do you remember my aunt, Leila J. Pinckney?"

"Remember her? Why, I was her agent all her life."

"Of course. Then you know the sort of tripe she wrote."

"No author," said McKinnon, reprovingly, "who pulls down a steady twenty thousand pounds a year writes tripe."

"Well, anyway, you know her stuff."

"Who better?"

"When she died she left me five thousand pounds and her house, Honeysuckle Cottage. I'm living there now. McKinnon, do you believe in haunted houses?"

"No."

"Yet I tell you solemnly that Honeysuckle Cottage is haunted!"

"By your aunt?" said Mr. McKinnon, surprised.

"By her influence. There's a malignant spell over the place; a sort of miasma of sentimentalism. Everybody who enters it succumbs."

"Tut-tut! You mustn't have these fancies."

"They aren't fancies."

"You aren't seriously meaning to tell me——"

"Well, how do you account for this? That book you were speaking about, which Prodder & Wiggs are to publish—*The Secret Nine*. Everytime I sit down to write it a girl keeps trying to sneak in."

"Into the room?"

"Into the story."

"You don't want a love interest in your sort of book," said Mr. McKinnon, shaking his head. "It delays the action."

"I know it does. And every day I have to keep shooing this infernal female out. An awful girl, McKinnon. A soppy, soupy, treacly,[3] drooping girl with a roguish smile. This morning she tried to butt in on the scene where Lester Gage is trapped in the den of the mysterious leper."

"No!"

"She did, I assure you. I had to rewrite three pages before I could get her out of it. And that's not the worst. Do you know, McKinnon, that at this moment I am actually living the plot of a typical Leila May Pinckney novel in just the setting she always used! And I can see the happy ending coming nearer every day! A week ago a girl was knocked down by a car at my door and I've had to put her up, and every day I realise more clearly that sooner or later I shall ask her to marry me."

"Don't do it," said Mr. McKinnon, a stout bachelor. "You're too young to marry."

"So was Methuselah,"[4] said James, a stouter. " But all the same I know I'm going to do it. It's the influence of this awful house weighing upon me.

---

[3] treacly: cloying and sticky like treacle (molasses).

[4] Methuselah: a patriarch in the Book of Genesis, said to have lived 969 years.

I feel like an eggshell in a maelstrom. I am being sucked on by a force too strong for me to resist. This morning I found myself kissing her dog!"

"No!"

"I did! And I loathe the little beast. Yesterday I got up at dawn and plucked a nosegay of flowers for her, wet with the dew."

"Rodman!"

"It's a fact. I laid them at her door and went downstairs kicking myself all the way. And there in the hall was the apple-cheeked housekeeper regarding me archly. If she didn't murmur 'Bless their sweet young hearts!' my ears deceived me."

"Why don't you pack up and leave?"

"If I do I lose the five thousand pounds."

"Ah!" said Mr. McKinnon.

"I can understand what has happened. It's the same with all haunted houses. My aunt's subliminal ether[5] vibrations have woven themselves into the texture of the place, creating an atmosphere which forces the ego of all who come in contact with it to attune themselves to it. It's either that or something to do with the fourth dimension."

Mr. McKinnon laughed scornfully.

"Tut-tut!" he said again. "This is pure imagination. What has happened is that you've been working too hard. You'll see this precious atmosphere of yours will have no effect on me."

"That's exactly why I asked you to come down. I hoped you might break the spell."

"I will that," said Mr. McKinnon, jovially.

The fact that the literary agent spoke little at lunch caused James no apprehension. Mr. McKinnon was ever a silent trencherman.[6] From time to time James caught him stealing a glance at the girl, who was well enough to come down to meals now, limping pathetically; but he could read nothing in his face. And yet the mere look of his face was a consolation. It was so solid, so matter of fact, so exactly like an unemotional coconut.

"You've done me good," said James with a sigh of relief, as he escorted the agent down the garden to his car after lunch. "I felt all along that I could rely on your rugged common sense. The whole atmosphere of the place seems different now."

Mr. McKinnon did not speak for a moment. He seemed to be plunged in thought.

"Rodman," he said, as he got into his car, "I've been thinking over that suggestion of yours of putting a love interest into *The Secret Nine*. I think you're wise. The story needs it. After all, what is there greater in the world

[5] ether: a substance once thought to fill up all space, including the spaces between atoms.

[6] trencherman: a person who eats heartily.

than love? Love—love—aye, it's the sweetest word in the language. Put in a heroine and let her marry Lester Gage."

"If," said James, grimly, "she does succeed in worming her way in she'll jolly well marry the mysterious leper. But look here, I don't understand——"

"It was seeing that girl that changed me," proceeded Mr. McKinnon. And as James stared at him aghast, tears suddenly filled his hard-boiled eyes. He openly snuffled. "Aye, seeing her sitting there under the roses, with all that smell of honeysuckle and all. And the birdies singing so sweet in the garden and the sun lighting up her bonny face. The puir[7] wee lass!" he muttered, dabbing at his eyes. "The puir bonny wee lass! Rodman," he said, his voice quivering, "I've decided that we're being hard on Prodder & Wiggs. Wiggs has had sickness in his home lately. We mustn't be hard on a man who's had sickness in his home, hey, laddie? No, no! I'm going to take back that contract and alter it to a flat 12 per cent. and no advance royalties."

"What!"

"But you shan't lose by it, Rodman. No, no, you shan't lose by it, my manny. I am going to waive my commission. The puir bonny wee lass!"

The car rolled off down the road. Mr. McKinnon, seated in the back, was blowing his nose violently.

"This is the end!" said James.

It is necessary at this point to pause and examine James Rodman's position with an unbiased eye. The average man, unless he puts himself in James's place, will be unable to appreciate it. James, he will feel, was making a lot of fuss about nothing. Here he was, drawing daily closer and closer to a charming girl with big blue eyes, and surely rather to be envied than pitied.

But we must remember that James was one of Nature's bachelors. And no ordinary man, looking forward dreamily to a little home of his own with a loving wife putting out his slippers and changing the gramophone records, can realise the intensity of the instinct for self-preservation which animates Nature's bachelors in times of peril.

James Rodman had a congenital horror of matrimony. Though a young man, he had allowed himself to develop a great many habits which were as the breath of life to him; and these habits, he knew instinctively, a wife would shoot to pieces within a week of the end of the honeymoon.

James liked to breakfast in bed; and, having breakfasted, to smoke in bed and knock the ashes out on the carpet. What wife would tolerate this practice?

James liked to pass his days in a tennis shirt, grey flannel trousers, and slippers. What wife ever rests until she has inclosed her husband in a stiff

[7] puir: Scottish dialect for "poor."

collar, tight boots, and a morning suit and taken him with her to *thés musicales?* [8]

These and a thousand other thoughts of the same kind flashed through the unfortunate young man's mind as the days went by, and every day that passed seemed to draw him nearer to the brink of the chasm. Fate appeared to be taking a malicious pleasure in making things as difficult for him as possible. Now that the girl was well enough to leave her bed, she spent her time sitting in a chair on the sun-sprinkled porch, and James had to read to her— and poetry, at that; and not the jolly, wholesome sort of poetry the boys are turning out nowadays, either—good, honest stuff about sin and gas works and decaying corpses—but the old-fashioned kind with rhymes in it, dealing almost exclusively with love. The weather, moreover, continued superb. The honeysuckle cast its sweet scent on the gentle breeze; the roses over the porch stirred and nodded; the flowers in the garden were lovelier than ever; the birds sang their little throats sore. And every evening there was a magnificent sunset. It was almost as if Nature were doing it on purpose.

At last James intercepted Doctor Brady as he was leaving after one of his visits and put the thing to him squarely:

"When is that girl going?"

The doctor patted him on the arm.

"Not yet, Rodman," he said in a low, understanding voice. "No need to worry yourself about that. Mustn't be moved for days and days and days— I might almost say weeks and weeks and weeks."

"Weeks and weeks!" cried James.

"And weeks," said Doctor Brady. He prodded James roguishly in the abdomen. "Good luck to you, my boy, good luck to you," he said.

It was some small consolation to James that the mushy physician immediately afterward tripped over William on his way down the path and broke his stethoscope. When a man is up against it like James very little helps.

He was walking dismally back to the house after this conversation when he was met by the apple-cheeked housekeeper.

"The little lady would like to speak to you, sir," said the apple-cheeked exhibit, rubbing her hands.

"Would she?" said James, hollowly.

"So sweet and pretty she looks, sir—oh, sir, you wouldn't believe! Like a blessed angel sitting there with her dear eyes all a-shining."

"Don't do it!" cried James with extraordinary vehemence. "Don't do it!"

He found the girl propped up on the cushions and thought once again how singularly he disliked her. And yet, even as he thought this, some force against which he had to fight madly was whispering to him, "Go to her and take that little hand! Breathe into that little ear the burning words that will

---

[8] *thés musicales:* French, afternoon teas with musical entertainment.

make that little face turn away crimsoned with blushes!" He wiped a bead of perspiration from his forehead and sat down.

"Mrs. Stick-in-the-Mud—what's her name?—says you want to see me."

The girl nodded.

"I've had a letter from Uncle Henry. I wrote to him as soon as I was better and told him what had happened, and he is coming here to-morrow morning."

"Uncle Henry?"

"That's what I call him, but he's really no relation. He is my guardian. He and daddy were officers in the same regiment, and when daddy was killed, fighting on the Afghan frontier,[9] he died in Uncle Henry's arms and with his last breath begged him to take care of me."

James started. A sudden wild hope had waked in his heart. Years ago, he remembered, he had read a book of his aunt's entitled *Rupert's Legacy*, and in that book——

"I'm engaged to marry him," said the girl, quietly.

"Wow!" shouted James.

"What?" asked the girl, startled.

"Touch of cramp," said James. He was thrilling all over. That wild hope had been realised.

"It was daddy's dying wish that we should marry," said the girl.

"And dashed sensible of him, too; dashed sensible," said James, warmly.

"And yet," she went on, a little wistfully, "I sometimes wonder——"

"Don't!" said James. "Don't! You must respect daddy's dying wish. There's nothing like daddy's dying wish; you can't beat it. So he's coming here to-morrow, is he? Capital, capital! To lunch, I suppose? Excellent! I'll run down and tell Mrs. Who-Is-It to lay in another chop."

It was with a gay and uplifted heart that James strolled the garden and smoked his pipe next morning. A great cloud seemed to have rolled itself away from him. Everything was for the best of all possible worlds. He had finished *The Secret Nine* and shipped it off to Mr. McKinnon, and now as he strolled there was shaping itself in his mind a corking plot about a man with only half a face who lived in a secret den and terrorised London with a series of shocking murders. And what made them so shocking was the fact that each of the victims, when discovered, was found to have only half a face, too. The rest had been chipped off, presumably by some blunt instrument.

The thing was coming out magnificently, when suddenly his attention was diverted by a piercing scream. Out of the bushes fringing the river that ran beside the garden burst the apple-cheeked housekeeper.

"Oh, sir! Oh, sir! Oh, sir!"

[9] Afghan frontier: border region between Afghanistan and Northwest British India (now Pakistan), scene of repeated fighting between Afghans and British colonial troops.

"What is it?" demanded James, irritably.

"Oh, sir! Oh, sir! Oh, sir!"

"Yes, and then what?"

"The little dog, sir! He's in the river!"

"Well, whistle him to come out."

"Oh, sir, do come quick! He'll be drowned!"

James followed her through the bushes, taking off his coat as he went. He was saying to himself, "I will not rescue this dog. I do not like the dog. It is high time he had a bath, and in any case it would be much simpler to stand on the bank and fish for him with a rake. Only an ass out of a Leila J. Pinckney book would dive into a beastly river to save——"

At this point he dived. Toto, alarmed by the splash, swam rapidly for the bank, but James was too quick for him. Grasping him firmly by the neck, he scrambled ashore and ran for the house, followed by the housekeeper.

The girl was seated on the porch. Over her there bent the tall soldierly figure of a man with keen eyes and graying hair. The housekeeper raced up.

"Oh, miss! Toto! In the river! He saved him! He plunged in and saved him!"

The girl drew a quick breath.

"Gallant, damme! [10] By Jove! By gad! Yes, gallant, by George!" exclaimed the soldierly man.

The girl seemed to wake from a reverie.

"Uncle Henry, this is Mr. Rodman. Mr. Rodman, my guardian, Colonel Carteret."

"Proud to meet you, sir," said the colonel, his honest blue eyes glowing as he fingered his short crisp moustache. "As fine a thing as I ever heard of, damme!"

"Yes, you are brave—brave," the girl whispered.

"I am wet—wet," said James, and went upstairs to change his clothes.

When he came down for lunch, he found to his relief that the girl had decided not to join them, and Colonel Carteret was silent and proccupied. James, exerting himself in his capacity of host, tried him with the weather, golf, India, the Government, the high cost of living, first-class cricket, the modern dancing craze, and murderers he had met, but the other still preserved that strange, absent-minded silence. It was only when the meal was concluded and James had produced cigarettes that he came abruptly out of his trance.

"Rodman," he said, "I should like to speak to you."

"Yes?" said James, thinking it was about time.

"Rodman," said Colonel Carteret, "or rather, George—I may call you George?" he added, with a sort of wistful diffidence that had a singular charm.

---

[10] damme: variant of "damn me," a mild oath.

"Certainly," replied James, "if you wish it. Though my name is James."

"James, eh? Well, well, it amounts to the same thing, eh, what, damme, by gad?" said the colonel with a momentary return of his bluff soldierly manner. "Well, then, James, I have something that I wish to say to you. Did Miss Maynard—did Rose happen to tell you anything about myself in—er —connection with herself?"

"She mentioned that you and she were engaged to be married."

The colonel's tightly drawn lips quivered.

"No longer," he said.

"What?"

"No, John, my boy."

"James."

"No, James, my boy, no longer. While you were upstairs changing your clothes she told me—breaking down, poor child, as she spoke—that she wished our engagement to be at an end."

James half rose from the table, his cheeks blanched.

"You don't mean that!" he gasped.

Colonel Carteret nodded. He was staring out of the window, his fine eyes set in a look of pain.

"But this is nonsense!" cried James. "This is absurd! She—she mustn't be allowed to chop and change like this. I mean to say, it—it isn't fair———"

"Don't think of me, my boy."

"I'm not—I mean, did she give any reason?"

"Her eyes did."

"Her eyes did?"

"Her eyes, when she looked at you on the porch, as you stood there— young, heroic—having just saved the life of the dog she loves. It is you who have won that tender heart, my boy."

"Now listen," protested James, "you aren't going to sit there and tell me that a girl falls in love with a man just because he saves her dog from drowning?"

"Why surely," said Colonel Carteret, surprised. "What better reason could she have?" He sighed. "It is the old, old story, my boy. Youth to youth. I am an old man. I should have known—I should have foreseen—yes, youth to youth."

"You aren't a bit old."

"Yes, yes."

"No, no."

"Yes, yes."

"Don't keep on saying 'yes, yes'!" cried James, clutching at his hair. "Besides, she wants a steady old buffer[11]—a steady, sensible man of medium age—to look after her."

Colonel Carteret shook his head with a gentle smile.

[11] buffer: shock absorber, a person who protects another from petty annoyances.

"This is mere quixotry,[12] my boy. It is splendid of you to take this attitude; but no, no."

"Yes, yes."

"No, no." He gripped James's hand for an instant, then rose and walked to the door. "That is all I wished to say, Tom."

"James."

"James. I just thought that you ought to know how matters stood. Go to her, my boy, go to her, and don't let any thought of an old man's broken dream keep you from pouring out what is in your heart. I am an old soldier, lad, an old soldier. I have learned to take the rough with the smooth. But I think—I think I will leave you now. I—I should—should like to be alone for a while. If you need me you will find me in the raspberry bushes."

He had scarcely gone when James also left the room. He took his hat and stick and walked blindly out of the garden, he knew not whither. His brain was numbed. Then, as his powers of reasoning returned, he told himself that he should have foreseen this ghastly thing. If there was one type of character over which Leila J. Pinckney had been wont to spread herself, it was the pathetic guardian who loves his ward but relinquishes her to the younger man. No wonder the girl had broken off the engagement. Any elderly guardian who allowed himself to come within a mile of Honeysuckle Cottage was simply asking for it. And then, as he turned to walk back, a sort of dull defiance gripped James. Why, he asked, should he be put upon in this manner? If the girl liked to throw over this man, why should he be the goat?

He saw his way clearly now. He just wouldn't do it, that was all. And if they didn't like it they could lump it.

Full of a new fortitude, he strode in at the gate. A tall, soldierly figure emerged from the raspberry bushes and came to meet him.

"Well?" said Colonel Carteret.

"Well?" said James, defiantly.

"Am I to congratulate you?"

James caught his keen blue eye and hesitated. It was not going to be so simple as he had supposed.

"Well—er——" he said.

Into the keen blue eyes there came a look that James had not seen there before. It was the stern, hard look which—probably—had caused men to bestow upon this old soldier the name of Cold-Steel Carteret.

"You have not asked Rose to marry you?"

"Er—no; not yet."

The keen blue eyes grew keener and bluer.

"Rodman," said Colonel Carteret in a strange, quiet voice, "I have known that little girl since she was a tiny child. For years she has been all in all to me. Her father died in my arms and with his last breath bade me see that

[12] quixotry: idealistic, impractical attitudes or behavior, from *Don Quixote*.

no harm came to his darling. I have nursed her through mumps, measles—aye, and chicken pox—and I live but for her happiness." He paused, with a significance that made James's toes curl. "Rodman," he said, "do you know what I would do to any man who trifled with that little girl's affections?" He reached in his hip pocket and an ugly-looking revolver glittered in the sunlight. "I would shoot him like a dog."

"Like a dog?" faltered James.

"Like a dog," said Colonel Carteret. He took James's arm and turned him toward the house. "She is on the porch. Go to her. And if——" He broke off. "But tut!" he said in a kindlier tone. "I am doing you an injustice, my boy. I know it."

"Oh, you are," said James, fervently.

"Your heart is in the right place."

"Oh, absolutely," said James.

"Then go to her, my boy. Later on you may have something to tell me. You will find me in the strawberry beds."

It was very cool and fragrant on the porch. Overhead, little breezes played and laughed among the roses. Somewhere in the distance sheep bells tinkled, and in the shrubbery a thrush was singing its evensong.

Seated in her chair behind a wicker table laden with tea things, Rose Maynard watched James as he shambled up the path.

"Tea's ready," she called, gaily. "Where is Uncle Henry?" A look of pity and distress flitted for a moment over her flower-like face. "Oh, I—I forgot," she whispered.

"He is in the strawberry beds," said James in a low voice.

She nodded unhappily.

"Of course, of course. Oh, why is life like this?" James heard her whisper.

He sat down. He looked at the girl. She was leaning back with closed eyes, and he thought he had never seen such a little squirt in his life. The idea of passing his remaining days in her society revolted him. He was stoutly opposed to the idea of marrying anyone; but if, as happens to the best of us, he ever were compelled to perform the wedding glide,[13] he had always hoped it would be with some lady golf champion who would help him with his putting, and thus, by bringing his handicap down a notch or two, enable him to save something from the wreck, so to speak. But to link his lot with a girl who read his aunt's books and liked them; a girl who could tolerate the presence of the dog Toto; a girl who clasped her hands in pretty, childish joy when she saw a nasturtium in bloom—it was too much. Nevertheless, he took her hand and began to speak.

"Miss Maynard—Rose——"

She opened her eyes and cast them down. A flush had come into her cheeks. The dog Toto at her side sat up and begged for cake, disregarded.

---

[13] wedding glide: the slow, sliding step often used for processionals at weddings.

"Let me tell you a story. Once upon a time there was a lonely man who lived in a cottage all by himself——"

He stopped. Was it James Rodman who was talking this bilge?

"Yes?" whispered the girl.

"——but one day there came to him out of nowhere a little fairy princess. She——"

He stopped again, but this time not because of the sheer shame of listening to his own voice. What caused him to interrupt his tale was the fact that at this moment the tea table suddenly began to rise slowly in the air, tilting as it did so a considerable quantity of hot tea on to the knees of his trousers.

"Ouch!" cried James, leaping.

The table continued to rise, and then fell sideways, revealing the homely countenance of William, who, concealed by the cloth, had been taking a nap beneath it. He moved slowly forward, his eyes on Toto. For many a long day William had been desirous of putting to the test, once and for all, the problem of whether Toto was edible or not. Sometimes he thought yes, at other times no. Now seemed an admirable opportunity for a definite decision. He advanced on the object of his experiment, making a low whistling noise through his nostrils, not unlike a boiling kettle. And Toto, after one long look of incredulous horror, tucked his shapely tail between his legs and, turning, raced for safety. He had laid a course in a bee line for the open garden gate, and William, shaking a dish of marmalade off his head a little petulantly, galloped ponderously after him. Rose Maynard staggered to her feet.

"Oh, save him!" she cried.

Without a word James added himself to the procession. His interest in Toto was but tepid. What he wanted was to get near enough to William to discuss with him that matter of the tea on his trousers. He reached the road and found that the order of the runners had not changed. For so small a dog, Toto was moving magnificently. A cloud of dust rose as he skidded round the corner. William followed. James followed William.

And so they passed Farmer Birkett's barn, Farmer Giles's cow shed, the place where Farmer Willetts's pigsty used to be before the big fire, and the Bunch of Grapes public house, Jno. Biggs propr., licensed to sell tobacco, wines, and spirits. And it was as they were turning down the lane that leads past Farmer Robinson's chicken run that Toto, thinking swiftly, bolted abruptly into a small drain pipe.

"William!" roared James, coming up at a canter. He stopped to pluck a branch from the hedge and swooped darkly on.

William had been crouching before the pipe, making a noise like a bassoon into its interior; but now he rose and came beamingly to James. His eyes were aglow with chumminess and affection; and placing his forefeet on James's chest, he licked him three times on the face in rapid succession. And as he did so, something seemed to snap in James. The scales seemed to fall from James's eyes. For the first time he saw William as he really was, the authentic type of dog that saves his master from a frightful peril. A wave of emotion swept over him.

"William!" he muttered. "William!"

William was making an early supper off a half brick he had found in the road. James stooped and patted him fondly.

"William," he whispered, "you knew when the time had come to change the conversation, didn't you, old boy!" He straightened himself. "Come, William," he said. "Another four miles and we reach Meadowsweet Junction. Make it snappy and we shall just catch the up express, first stop London."

William looked up into his face and it seemed to James that he gave a brief nod of comprehension and approval. James turned. Through the trees to the east he could see the red roof of Honeysuckle Cottage, lurking like some evil dragon in ambush.

Then, together, man and dog passed silently into the sunset.

That (concluded Mr. Mulliner) is the story of my distant cousin James Rodman. As to whether it is true, that, of course, is an open question. I, personally, am of opinion that it is. There is no doubt that James did go to live in Honeysuckle Cottage and, while there, underwent some experience which has left an ineradicable mark upon him. His eyes to-day have that unmistakable look which is to be seen only in the eyes of confirmed bachelors whose feet have been dragged to the very brink of the pit and who have gazed at close range into the naked face of matrimony.

And, if further proof be needed, there is William. He is now James's inseparable companion. Would any man be habitually seen in public with a dog like William unless he had some solid cause to be grateful to him,— unless they were linked together by some deep and imperishable memory? I think not. Myself, when I observe William coming along the street, I cross the road and look into a shop window till he has passed. I am not a snob, but I dare not risk my position in Society by being seen talking to that curious compound.

Nor is the precaution an unnecessary one. There is about William a shameless absence of appreciation of class distinctions which recalls the worst excesses of the French Revolution. I have seen him with these eyes chivvy[14] a pomeranian[15] belonging to a Baroness in her own right from near the Achilles Statue to within a few yards of the Marble Arch.

And yet James walks daily with him in Piccadilly. It is surely significant.

STUDY QUESTIONS

1. Describe Aunt Leila's house. In what way does the cottage reflect its former inhabitant?

---

[14] chivvy: harry along.
[15] pomeranian: a breed of small, long-haired dogs.

2. How does the setting of this story add to your knowledge of a writer's habits?

3. How is the "psychological" environment of this story related to the physical setting?

4. Is this a "ghost" story? Why or why not?

5. How does setting contribute to humor, particularly in the contrast between the cottage as it is and as Rodman perceives it?

6. In this story do appearances influence characters' feelings? Discuss.

7. Show in detail how several minor characters—particularly the doctor, the agent, and the guardian—seem to come under the influence of Honeysuckle Cottage.

8. Indicate how the story seems to center on a conflict between the "real" and the sentimental. What is the focus of this conflict? Given Rodman's "literary" life, is the conflict as described an accurate or true one?

9. Does Wodehouse present us with a "happy" ending? In your discussion, make note of the role of the narrator.

James Purdy (1923–   )

DADDY WOLF

You aren't the first man to ask me what I am doing so long in the phone booth with the door to my flat open and all. Let me explain something, or if you want to use the phone, I'll step out for a minute, but I am trying to get Operator to re-connect me with a party she just cut me off from. If you're not in a big hurry would you let me just try to get my party again.

See I been home 2 days now just looking at them 2 or 3 holes in the linoleum in my flat, and those holes are so goddam big now—you can go in there and take a look—those holes are so goddam big that I bet my kid, if he was still here, could almost put his leg through the biggest one.

Maybe of course the rats don't use the linoleum holes as entrances or exits. They could come through the calcimine[1] in the wall. But I kind of guess and I bet the super for once would back me up on this, the rats are using the linoleum holes. Otherwise what is the meaning of the little black specks in and near each hole in the linoleum. I don't see how you could ignore the black specks there. If they were using the wall holes you would expect black specks there, but I haven't found a single one.

The party I was just talking to on the phone when I got cut off was surprised when I told her how the other night after my wife and kid left me I came in to find myself staring right head-on at a fat, I guess a Mama rat, eating some of my uncooked cream of wheat. I was so took by surprise that I did not see which way she went out. She ran, is all I can say, the minute I come into the room.

---

[1] calcimine: a white or tinted chalky wash, applied to plaster walls.

I had no more snapped back from seeing the Mama rat when a teeny baby one run right between my legs and disappeared ditto.

I just stood looking at my uncooked cream of wheat knowing I would have to let it go to waste.

It was too late that evening to call the super or anybody and I know from a lot of sad experience how sympathetic he would be, for the rats, to quote him, is a *un-avoidable probability* for whatever party decides to rent one of these you-know-what linoleum apartments.

If you want something better than some old you-know-what linoleum-floor apartments, the super says, *you got the map of Newyorkcity to hunt with.*

Rats and linoleum go together, and when you bellyache about rats, remember you're living on linoleum.

I always have to go to the hall phone when I get in one of these states, but tonight instead of calling the super who has gone off by now anyhow to his night job (he holds down 2 jobs on account of, he says, the high cost of chicken and peas), I took the name of the first party my finger fell on in the telephone book.

This lady answered the wire.

I explained to her the state I was in, and that I was over in one of the linoleum apartments and my wife and kid left me.

She cleared her throat and so on.

Even for a veteran, I told her, this is rough.

She kind of nodded over the phone in her manner.

I could feel she was sort of half-friendly, and I told her how I had picked her name out from all the others in the telephone book.

It was rough enough, I explained to her, to be renting an apartment in the linoleum district and to not know nobody in Newyorkcity, and then only the other night after my wife and kid left me this Mama rat was in here eating my uncooked cream of wheat, and before I get over this, her offspring run right between my legs.

This lady on the wire seemed to say *I see* every so often but I couldn't be sure on account of I was talking so fast myself.

I would have called the super of the building, I explained to her, in an emergency like this, but he has 2 jobs, and as it is after midnight now he is on his night job. But it would be just as bad in the daytime as then usually he is out inspecting the other linoleum apartments or catching up on his beauty sleep and don't answer the door or phone.

When I first moved into this building, I told her, I had to pinch myself to be sure I was actually seeing it right. I seen all the dirt before I moved in, but once I was in, I really SEEN: all the traces of the ones who had been here before, people who had died or lost their jobs or found they was the wrong race or something and had had to vacate all of a sudden before they could clean the place up for the next tenant. A lot of them left in such a hurry they just give you a present of some of their belongings and underwear along with their dirt. But then after one party left in such a hurry, somebody else from somewhere moved in, found he could not make it in Newyorkcity, and lit out somewhere or maybe was taken to a hospital in a serious condition and never returned.

I moved in just like the others on the linoleum.

Wish you could have seen it then. Holes everywhere and that most jagged of the holes I can see clear over here from the phone booth is where the Mama rat come through, which seems now about 3,000 years ago to me.

I told the lady on the phone how polite she was to go on listening and I hoped I was not keeping her up beyond her bedtime or from having a nightcap before she did turn in.

I don't object to animals, see. If it had been a Mama bird, say, which had come out of the hole, I would have had a start, too, as a Mama bird seldom is about and around at that hour, not to mention it not nesting in a linoleum hole, but I think I feel the way I do just because you think of rats along with neglect and lonesomeness and not having nobody near or around you.

See my wife left me and took our kid with her. They could not take any more of Newyorkcity. My wife was very scared of disease, and she had heard the radio in the shoe-repair store telling that they were going to raise the V.D. rate, and she said to me just a few hours before she left, *I don't think I am going to stay on here, Benny, if they are going to have one of them health epidemics.* She didn't have a disease, but she felt she would if the city officials were bent on raising the V.D. rate. She said it would be her luck and she would be no exception to prove the rule. She packed and left with the kid.

Did I feel sunk with them gone, but Jesus it was all I could do to keep on here myself. A good number of times at night I did not share my cream of wheat with them. I told them to prepare what kind of food they had a yen for and let me eat my cream of wheat alone with a piece of warmed-over oleo and just a sprinkle of brown sugar on that.

My wife and kid would stand and watch me eat the cream of wheat, but they was entirely indifferent to food. I think it was partly due to the holes in the linoleum, and them knowing what was under the holes of course.

We have only the one chair in the flat, and so my kid never had any place to sit when I was to home.

I couldn't help telling this party on the phone then about my wife and DADDY WOLF.

I was the one who told my wife about DADDY WOLF and the TROUBLE PHONE in the first place, but at first she said she didn't want any old charity no matter if it was money or advice or just encouraging words.

Then when things got so rough, my wife did call DADDY WOLF. I think the number is CRack 8-7869 or something like that, and only ladies can call. You phone this number and say *Daddy Wolf, I am a lady in terrible trouble. I am in one of the linoleum apartments, and just don't feel I can go on another day. Mama rats are coming in and out of their holes with their babies, and all we have had to eat in a month is cream of wheat.*

DADDY WOLF would say he was listening and to go on, and then he would ask her if she was employed anywhere.

DADDY WOLF, *yes and no. I just do not seem to have the willpower to go out job-hunting any more or on these house-to-house canvassing jobs that I have been holding down lately, and if you could see this linoleum flat, I think you would agree,* DADDY WOLF, *that there is very little incentive for me and Benny.*

Then my wife would go on about how surprised we had both been, though she was the only one surprised, over the high rate of V.D. in Newyorkcity.

You see, DADDY WOLF, *I won't hold a thing back, I have been about with older men in order to tide my husband over this rough financial situation we're in. My husband works in the mitten factory, and he just is not making enough for the three of us to live on. He has to have his cream of wheat at night or he would not have the strength to go back to his day-shift, and our linoleum apartment costs 30 smackers a week.*

I leave the kid alone here and go out to try and find work, DADDY WOLF, *but I'm telling you, the only job I can find for a woman of my education and background is this house-to-house canvassing of Queen Bee royal jelly[2] which makes older women look so much more appealing, but I hardly sell more than a single jar a day and am on my feet 12 hours at a stretch.*

The kid is glad when I go out to sell as he can have the chair to himself then. You see when I and his Daddy are home he either has to sit down on my lap, if I am sitting, or if his Daddy is sitting, just stand because I won't allow a little fellow like him to sit on that linoleum, it's not safe, and his Daddy will not let him sit on his lap because he is too dead-tired from the mitten factory.

That was the way she explained to DADDY WOLF on the TROUBLE PHONE, and that went on every night, night after night, until she left me.

DADDY WOLF always listened, I will give him credit for that. He advised Mabel too: *go to Sunday school and church and quit going up to strange men's hotel rooms. Devote yourself only to your husband's need, and you don't ever have to fear the rise in the V.D. rate.*

My wife, though, could just not take Newyorkcity. She was out selling that Queen Bee royal jelly every day, but when cold weather come she had only a thin coat and she went out less and less and that all added up to less cream of wheat for me in the evening.

It is funny thing about cream of wheat, you don't get tired of it. I think if I ate, say, hamburger and chop suey every night, I would get sick and tired of them. Not that I ever dine on them. But if I did, I would—get sick

[2] royal jelly: a highly nutritious secretion of the honeybee, which is fed to queen larvae.

and tired, I mean. But there's something about cream of wheat, with just a daub of warm oleo on it, and a sprinkle of brown sugar that makes you feel you might be eatin' it for the first time.

My wife don't care for cream of wheat nearly so much as I do.

Our kid always ate with the old gentleman down the hall with the skull-cap.[3] He rung a bell when it was supper time, and the kid went down there and had his meal. Once in a while, be brought back something or other for us.

It's funny talking to you like this, Mister, and as I told this lady I am waiting to get reconnected with on the phone, if I don't know any better I would think either one of you was DADDY WOLF on the TROUBLE PHONE.

Well, Mabel left me, then, and took the kid with her.

It was her silly fear of the V.D. rate that really made her light out. She could have stayed here indefinitely. She loved this here city at first. She was just crazy about Central Park.

Newyorkcity was just the place for me to find work in. I had a good job with the Singer sewing-machine people in one of their spare-parts rooms, then I got laid off and was without a thing for over 6 months and then was lucky to find this job at the mitten factory. I raise the lever that sews the inner lining to your mittens.

I don't think it is Mabel and the kid leaving me so much sometimes as it is the idea of that Mama rat coming through the holes in the linoleum that has got me so down-in-the-dumps today. I didn't even go to the mitten fac-tory this A.M., and I have, like I say, got so down-in-the-dumps I almost felt like calling DADDY WOLF myself on the TROUBLE PHONE like she did all the time. But knowing he won't talk to nobody but ladies, as a kind of next-best-thing I put my finger down haphazard on top of this lady's name in the phone book, and I sure appreciated having that talk with her.

See DADDY WOLF would only talk with my wife for about one and a half minutes on account of other women were waiting to tell him their troubles. He would always say *Go back to your affiliation with the Sunday school and church of your choice, Mabel, and you'll find your burdens lighter in no time.*

DADDY said the same thing to her every night, but she never got tired hearing it, I guess.

DADDY WOLF told Mabel she didn't have to have any fear at all of the V.D. rate on account of she was a married woman and therefore did not have to go out for that relationship, but if she ever felt that DESIRE coming over her when her husband was gone, to just sit quiet and read an uplifting book.

Mabel has not had time, I don't think, to write me yet, taking care of the kid and all, and getting settled back home, and I have, well, been so goddam

---

[3] skullcap: a close-fitting cap worn by Orthodox Jews.

worried about everything. They are talking now about a shut-down at the mitten factory so that I hardly as a matter of fact have had time to think about my wife and kid, let alone miss them. There is, as a matter of fact, more cream of wheat now for supper, and I splurged today and bought a 5-pound box of that soft brown sugar that don't turn to lumps, which I wouldn't ever have done if they was still here.

The old gent down the hall with the skullcap misses my kid, as he almost entirely kept the boy in eats.

He never speaks to me in the hall, the old man. They said, I heard this somewhere, he don't have linoleum on his floor, but carpets, but I have not been invited in to see.

This building was condemned two years ago, but still isn't torn down, and the old man is leaving as soon as he can find the right neighborhood for his married daughter to visit him in.

Wait a minute. No, I thought I seen some action from under that one hole there in the linoleum.

Excuse me if I have kept you from using the phone with my talk but all I can say is you and this lady on the phone have been better for me tonight than DADDY WOLF on the TROUBLE PHONE ever was for my wife.

Up until now I have usually called the super when I was in one of these down-moods, but all he ever said was *Go back where you and Mabel got your own people and roots, Benny. You can't make it here in a linoleum apartment with your background and education.*

He has had his eyes opened—the super. He has admitted himself that he never thought Mabel and me could stick it out this long. (He don't know she is gone.)

But I won't give up. I WILL NOT give up. Mabel let a thing like the hike in the V.D. rates chase her out. I tried to show her that that was just statistics, but she always was superstitious as all get-out.

I judge when this scare I've had about the Mama rat dies down and I get some sleep and tomorrow if I go back to the mitten factory I will then really and truly begin to miss Mabel and the kid. The old man down the hall already misses the kid. That kid ate more in one meal with him than Mabel and me eat the whole week together. I don't begrudge it to him, though, because he was growing.

Well, Mister, if you don't want to use the phone after all, I think I will try to have Operator re-connect me with that party I got disconnected from. I guess as this is the hour that Mabel always called DADDY WOLF I have just automatically caught her habit, and anyhow I sure felt in the need of a talk.

Do you hear that funny clicking sound? Here, I'll hold you the receiver so as you can hear it. Don't go away just yet: I think Operator is getting me that party again, so stick around awhile yet.

No, they cut us off again, hear? there is a bad connection or something.

Well, like I say, anyhow Mabel and the kid did get out of here, even if

it was superstition. Christ, when I was a boy I had every one of those diseases and it never did me no hurt. I went right into the army with a clean
bill of health, Korea, home again, and now Newyorkcity.

You can't bullshit me with a lot of statistics.

*Mabel, though, goddam it, I could knock the teeth down her throat, run-
ning out on me like this and taking the kid.*

WHERE IS THAT GODDAM OPERATOR?

Hello. Look, Operator, what number was that I dialed and talked so long.
Re-connect me please. That number I just got through talking with so long.
I don't know the party's name or number. Just connect me back, will you
please. This here is an emergency phone call, Operator.

STUDY QUESTIONS

1. Describe as precisely as you can the details of the physical environment:
   In what city does the story take place? In what kind of building is the
   speaker? Where in the building is he? What is his apartment like?
2. What biographical information does the speaker give about himself?
   How does the speaker's background relate to his physical environment?
3. The speaker calls his apartment a "linoleum apartment." What connotation does that phrase have for the reader by the end of the story? How
   important is that phrase to the element of setting?
4. The story was first published in 1961. Are there any clues in the story
   itself that indicate the approximate time of publication? Except for such
   specific references, how important is historical time? Or is the setting, as
   well as action and character, timeless? Explain your response.
5. Who or what is the antagonist in the story? Is it Daddy Wolf? The man
   who is waiting to use the phone? The lady who hangs up on the speaker?
   All of these people? Is it the setting itself? Support your answer by clear
   references to or quotes from the story.

Maxim Gorki (1868–1936)

TWENTY-SIX MEN AND A GIRL

A Poem

There were six-and-twenty of us—six-and-twenty living machines locked
up in a damp basement, where from morning till night we kneaded dough
and rolled it into pretzels and cracknels.[1] Opposite the windows of our basement was a bricked area, green and moldy with moisture. The windows were
protected from outside with a close iron grating, and the light of the sun

---

[1] cracknels: dry, brittle biscuits.

could not pierce through the windowpanes, covered as they were with flour dust.

Our employer had bars placed in front of the windows, so that we should not be able to give a bit of his bread to passing beggars, or to any of our fellows who were out of work and hungry. Our employer called us crooks, and gave us half-rotten tripe to eat for our midday meal, instead of meat. It was swelteringly close for us cooped up in that stone underground chamber, under the low, heavy, soot-blackened, cobwebby ceiling. Dreary and sickening was our life within its thick, dirty, moldy walls.

Unrefreshed, and with a feeling of not having had our sleep out, we used to get up at five o'clock in the morning; and at six, we were already seated, worn out and apathetic, at the table, rolling out the dough which our mates had already prepared while we slept. The whole day, from early morning until ten at night, some of us sat round that table, working up in our hands the unyielding dough, swaying to and fro so as not to grow numb; while the others mixed flour and water. And the whole day the simmering water in the kettle, where the pretzels were being cooked, sang low and sadly; and the baker's shovel scraped harshly over the oven floor, as he threw the slippery bits of dough out of the kettle on the heated bricks.

From morning till evening wood was burning in the oven, and the red glow of the fire gleamed and flickered over the walls of the bake-shop, as if silently mocking us. The giant oven was like the misshapen head of a monster in a fairy tale; it thrust itself up out of the floor, opened wide jaws, full of glowing fire, and blew hot breath upon us; it seemed to be ever watching out of its black air-holes our interminable work. Those two deep holes were like eyes—the cold, pitiless eyes of a monster. They watched us always with the same darkened glance, as if they were weary of seeing before them such slaves, from whom they could expect nothing human, and therefore scorned them with the cold scorn of wisdom.

In meal dust, in the mud which we brought in from the yard on our boots, in the hot, sticky atmosphere, day in, day out, we rolled the dough into pretzels, which we moistened with our own sweat. And we hated our work with a bitter hatred; we never ate what had passed through our hands, and preferred black bread to pretzels. Sitting opposite each other, at a long table —nine facing nine—we moved our hands and fingers mechanically during endlessly long hours, till we were so accustomed to our monotonous work that we ceased to pay any attention to our own motions.

We had all stared at each other so long, that each of us knew every wrinkle of his mates' faces. It was not long also before we had exhausted almost every topic of conversation; that is why we were most of the time silent, unless we were chaffing each other; but one cannot always find something about which to chaff another man, especially when that man is one's mate. Neither were we much given to finding fault with one another; how, indeed, could one of us poor devils be in a position to find fault with another, when we were all of us half dead and, as it were, turned to stone? For the heavy drudgery seemed to crush all feeling out of us. But silence is only terrible and fearful for those who have said everything and have nothing more to say to each other; for men, on the contrary, who have never begun to communicate with one another, it is easy and simple.

Sometimes, too, we sang; and this is how it happened that we began to sing: one of us would sigh deeply in the midst of our toil, like an overdriven horse, and then we would begin one of those songs whose gentle drawn-out melody seems always to ease the burden on the singer's heart.

At first one sang by himself, and we others sat in silence listening to his solitary song, which, under the heavy vaulted roof of the basement, died gradually away and became extinguished, like a little fire in the steppes,[2] on a wet autumn night, when the gray heaven hangs like a leaden roof over the earth. Then another would join in with the singer, and now two soft, sad voices would break into song in our narrow, dull hole of a basement. Suddenly others would join in, and the song would surge up like a wave, would grow louder and swell upward, till it would seem as if the damp, foul walls of our stone prison were widening out and opening. Then, all six-and-twenty of us would be singing; our loud, harmonious song would fill the whole shop; the song felt cramped, it was striking, as it were, against the walls in moaning sobs and sighs, moving our hearts with a soft, tantalizing ache, tearing open old wounds, and awakening longings.

The singers would sigh deeply and heavily; suddenly one would become silent and listen to the others singing, then let his voice flow once more in the common tide. Another would exclaim in a stifled voice, "Ah!" and would shut his eyes, while the deep, full sound waves would show him, as it were, a road, in front of him—a sunlit, broad road in the distance, which he himself, in thought, wandered along.

But the flame flickers once more in the huge oven, the baker scrapes incessantly with his shovel, the water simmers in the kettle, and the flicker of the fire on the wall dances as before in silent mockery. While in other men's words we sing out our dumb grief, the weary burden of live men robbed of the sunlight, the heartache of slaves.

So we lived, we six-and-twenty, in the vault-like basement of a great stone house, and we suffered each one of us, as if we had to bear on our shoulders the whole three stories of that house.

But we had something else good, besides the singing—something we loved, that perhaps took the place of the sunshine.

In the second story of our house there was established a gold-embroiderer's shop, and there, living among the other embroidery girls, was Tanya, a little maid-servant of sixteen. Every morning there peeped in through the glass door a rosy little face, with merry blue eyes; while a ringing, tender voice called out to us:

[2] steppes: a vast region of grassland.

"Little prisoners! Have you any pretzels, please, for me?"

At that clear sound we knew so well, we all used to turn round, gazing with good-natured joy at the pure girlish face which smiled at us so sweetly. The sight of the little nose pressed against the windowpane, and of the small white teeth gleaming between the half-open lips, had become for us a daily pleasure. Tumbling over each other we used to jump up to open the door, and she would step in, bright and cheerful, holding out her apron, with her head bent to one side, and a smile on her lips. Her thick, long chestnut braid fell over her shoulder and across her breast. We, ugly, dirty and misshapen as we were, looked up at her—the door was four steps above the floor— looked up at her with heads thrown back, wishing her good morning, and speaking strange, unaccustomed words, which we kept for her only. Our voices became softer when we spoke to her, our jests were lighter. For her —everything was different with us. The baker took from his oven a shovel- ful of the best and the brownest pretzels, and threw them deftly into Tanya's apron.

"Be off with you now, or the boss will catch you!" we warned her each time. She laughed roguishly, called out cheerfully: "Good-by, poor prison- ers!" and slipped away as quick as a mouse.

That was all. But long after she had gone we talked about her to one an- other with pleasure. It was always the same thing as we had said yesterday and the day before, because everything about us, including ourselves and her, remained the same—as yesterday—and as always.

Painful and terrible it is when a man goes on living, while nothing changes around him; and when such an existence does not finally kill his soul, then the monotony becomes with time, even more and more painful. Generally we spoke about women in such a way that sometimes it was loathsome to us ourselves to hear our rude, shameless talk. The women whom we knew deserved perhaps nothing better. But about Tanya we never let fall an evil word; none of us ever ventured so much as to lay a hand on her, even too free a jest she never heard from us. Maybe this was so because she never remained with us for long; she flashed on our eyes like a star falling from the sky, and vanished; and maybe because she was little and very beautiful, and everything beautiful calls forth respect, even in coarse people. And besides—though our life of drudgery had made us dull beasts, oxen, we were still men, and, like all men, could not live without worshiping something or other. Better than her we had none, and none but her took any notice of us, living in the basement—no one, though there were dozens of people in the house. And then, too—most likely, this was the chief thing— we all regarded her as something of our own, something existing as it were only by virtue of our pretzels. We took on ourselves in turns the duty of providing her with hot pretzels, and this became for us like a daily sacrifice to our idol, it became almost a sacred rite, and every day it bound us more closely to her. Besides pretzels, we gave Tanya a great deal of advice—to wear warmer clothes, not to run upstairs too quickly, not to carry heavy bundles of wood. She listened to all our counsels with a smile, answered them by a laugh, and never took our advice, but we were not offended at that; all we wanted was to show how concerned we were for her welfare.

Often she would apply to us with different requests, she asked us, for instance, to open the heavy door into the cellar, to chop wood: with delight and a sort of pride, we did this for her, and everything else she wanted.

But when one of us asked her to mend his solitary shirt for him, she said, with a laugh of contempt:

"What next! A likely idea!"

We made great fun of the queer fellow who could entertain such an idea, and—never asked her to do anything else. We loved her—all is said in that. Man always wants to give his love to someone, though sometimes he crushes, sometimes he sullies, with it. We were bound to love Tanya, for we had no one else to love.

At times one of us would suddenly begin to reason like this:

"And why do we make so much of the wench? What is there in her, eh? What a to-do we make about her!"

The man who dared to utter such words we promptly and coarsely cut short—we wanted something to love: we had found it and loved it, and what we twenty-six loved must be for each of us unshakable, as a holy thing, and anyone who acted against us in this was our enemy. We loved, maybe, not what was really good, but you see there were twenty-six of us, and so we always wanted to see what was precious to us held sacred by the rest.

Our love is not less burdensome than hate, and maybe that is just why some proud souls maintain that our hate is more flattering than our love. But why do they not run away from us, if it is so?

Besides our department, our employer had also a bakery where they made rolls; it was in the same house, separated from our hole only by a wall; but the bakers—there were four of them—held aloof from us, considering their work superior to ours, and therefore themselves better than us; they never used to come into our workroom, and laughed contemptuously at us when they met us in the yard. We, too, did not go to see them; this was forbidden by our employer, for fear that we should steal the fancy rolls. We did not like the bakers, because we envied them; their work was lighter than ours, they were paid more, and were better fed; they had a light, spacious workroom, and they were all so clean and healthy—and that made them hateful to us. We all looked gray and yellow; three of us had syphilis, several suffered from skin diseases, one was completely crippled by rheumatism. On holidays and in their leisure time the bakers wore pea-jackets and creaking boots, two of them had accordions, and they all used to go for strolls in the public park—we wore filthy rags and torn leather shoes or bast[3] slippers on

[3] bast: rope made from a woody fiber.

our feet, the police would not let us into the public park—could we possibly like the bakers?

And one day we learned that one of their men had gone on a spree, the master had sacked him and had already taken on another, and that this other was an ex-soldier, wore a satin waistcoat and a watch and gold chain. We were anxious to get a sight of such a dandy, and in the hope of catching a glimpse of him we kept running one after another out into the yard.

But he came of his accord into our workroom. Kicking at the door, he pushed it open, and leaving it ajar, stood in the doorway smiling, and said to us:

"God help the work! Good morning, mates!"

The frosty air, which streamed in through the open door, curled in streaks of vapor round his feet. He stood on the threshold, looked down upon us, and under his fair, twisted mustache gleamed big yellow teeth. His waistcoat was really something quite out of the common, blue-flowered, brilliant with shining little red stone buttons. He also wore a watch chain.

He was a fine fellow, this soldier; tall, healthy, rosy-cheeked, and his big, clear eyes had a friendly, cheerful glance. He wore on his head a white starched cap, and from under his spotlessly clean apron peeped the pointed toes of fashionable, well-blacked boots.

Our baker asked him politely to shut the door. The soldier did so without hurrying himself, and began to question us about the master. We explained to him, all speaking together, that our employer was a thorough-going brute, a crook, a knave, and a slave-driver; in a word, we repeated to him all that can and must be said about an employer, but cannot be repeated here. The soldier listened to us, twitched his mustache, and watched us with a friendly, open-hearted look.

"But haven't you got a lot of girls here?" he asked suddenly.

Some of us began to laugh deferentially, others leered, and one of us explained to the soldier that there were nine girls here.

"You make the most of them?" asked the soldier, with a wink.

We laughed, but not so loudly, and with some embarrassment. Many of us would have liked to have shown the soldier that we also were tremendous fellows with the girls, but not one of us could do so; and one of our number confessed as much, when he said in a low voice:

"That sort of thing is not in our line."

"Well, no; it wouldn't quite do for you," said the soldier with conviction, after having looked us over. "There is something wanting about you all. You don't look the right sort. You've no sort of appearance; and the women, you see, they like a bold appearance, they will have a well-set-up body. Everything has to be tip-top for them. That's why they respect strength. They want an arm like that!"

The soldier drew his right hand, with its turned-up shirt sleeve, out of his pocket, and showed us his bare arm. It was white and strong, and covered with shining golden wool.

"Leg and chest, all must be strong. And then a man must be dressed in the latest fashion, so as to show off his looks to advantage. Yes, all the women take to me. I don't call to them, I don't beckon them, yet with one accord, five at a time, they throw themselves at my head."

He sat down on a flour sack, and told at length all about the way women loved him, and how bold he was with them. Then he left, and after the door had creaked to behind him, we sat for a long time silent, and thought about him and his talk. Then we all suddenly broke silence together, and it became apparent that we were all equally pleased with him. He was such a nice, open-hearted fellow; he came to see us without any stand-offishness, sat down and chatted. No one else had ever come to us like that, and no one else had talked to us in that friendly sort of way. And we continued to talk of him and his coming triumph among the embroidery girls, who passed us by with contemptuous sniffs when they saw us in the yard, or who looked straight through us as if we had been air. But we admired them always when we met them outside, or when they walked past our windows; in winter, in fur jackets and toques[4] to match; in summer, in hats trimmed with flowers, and carrying colored parasols. Among ourselves, however, we talked about these girls in a way that would have made them mad with shame and rage, if they could have heard us.

"If only he does not get hold of little Tanya!" said the baker, suddenly, in an anxious tone of voice.

We were silent, for these words troubled us. Tanya had quite gone out of our minds, supplanted, put on one side by the strong, fine figure of the soldier.

Then began a lively discussion; some of us maintained that Tanya would never lower herself so; others thought she would not be able to resist him, and the third group proposed to break his ribs for him if he should try to annoy Tanya. And, finally, we all decided to watch the soldier and Tanya, and to warn the girl against him. This brought the discussion to an end.

Four weeks had passed by since then; during this time the soldier baked white rolls, walked out with the gold-embroidery girls, visited us often, but did not talk any more about his conquests; only twisted his mustache and licked his lips lasciviously.

Tanya called in as usual every morning for "little pretzels," and was as gay and as nice and friendly with us as ever. We certainly tried once or twice to talk to her about the soldier, but she called him a "goggle-eyed calf," and made fun of him all round, and that set our minds at rest. We saw how the gold-embroidery girls carried on with the soldier, and we were proud of our girl; Tanya's behavior reflected honor on us all; we imitated her, and began in our talks to treat the soldier with small consideration. She became dearer to us, and we greeted her with more friendliness and kindliness every morning.

[4] toques: small brimless hats.

One day the soldier came to see us, a bit drunk, and sat down and began to laugh. When we asked him what he was laughing about, he explained to us:

"Why, two of them—that Lydka girl and Grushka—have been clawing each other on my account. You should have seen the way they went for each other! Ha! ha! One got hold of the other one by the hair, threw her down on the floor of the passage, and sat on her! Ha! ha! ha! They scratched and tore each others' faces. It was enough to make one die with laughter! Why is it women can't fight fair? Why do they always scratch one another, eh?"

He sat on the bench, in fine fettle, fresh and jolly; he sat there and went on laughing. We were silent. This time he made an unpleasant impression on us.

"Well, it's a funny thing what luck I have with the women-folk! Eh? One wink, and it's all over with them! It's the d-devil!"

He raised his white arms covered with golden wool, and dropped them down on his knees. And his eyes seemed to reflect such frank astonishment, as if he were himself quite surprised at his good luck with women. His fat, red face glistened with delight and self-satisfaction, and he licked his lips more than ever.

Our baker scraped the shovel violently and angrily along the oven floor, and all at once he said sarcastically:

"There's no great strength needed to pull up fir saplings, but try a real pine-tree."

"Why—what do you mean by saying that to me?" asked the soldier.

"Oh, well . . ."

"What is it?"

"Nothing—it slipped out!"

"No, wait a minute! What's the point? What pine-tree?"

Our baker did not answer, working rapidly away with the shovel at the oven; flinging into it the half-cooked pretzels, taking out those that were done, and noisily throwing them on the floor to the boys who were stringing them on bast. He seemed to have forgotten the soldier and his conversation with him. But the soldier had all at once grown uneasy. He got up onto his feet, and went to the oven, at the risk of knocking against the handle of the shovel, which was waving spasmodically in the air.

"No, tell me, do—who is it? You've insulted me. I? There's not one could withstand me, n-no! And you say such insulting things to me?"

He really seemed genuinely hurt. He must have had nothing else to pride himself on except his gift for seducing women; maybe, except for that, there was nothing living in him, and it was only that by which he could feel himself a living man.

There are men to whom the most precious and best thing in their lives appears to be some disease of their soul or body. They fuss over it all their lives, and only living by it, suffering from it, they feed on it, they complain of it to others, and so draw the attention of their fellows to themselves. For that they extract sympathy from people, and apart from it they have nothing at all. Take from them that disease, cure them, and they will be miserable, because they have lost their one resource in life—they are left empty then. Sometimes a man's life is so poor, that he is driven instinctively to prize his vice and to live by it; one may say for a fact that often men are vicious out of boredom.

The soldier was offended, he went up to our baker and roared:

"No, tell me, do—who?"

"Tell you?" the baker turned suddenly to him.

"Well?"

"You know Tanya?"

"Well?"

"Well, there then! Only try."

"I?"

"You!"

"Her? Why, that's nothing to me—pooh!"

"We shall see!"

"You will see! Ha! ha!"

"She'll—"

"Give me a month!"

"What a braggart you are, soldier!"

"A fortnight! I'll prove it! Who is it? Tanya! Pooh!"

"Well, get out. You're in my way!"

"A fortnight—and it's done! Ah, you—"

"Get out, I say!"

Our baker, all at once, flew into a rage and brandished his shovel. The soldier staggered away from him in amazement, looked at us, paused, and softly, malignantly said, "Oh, all right, then!" and went away.

During the dispute we had all sat silent, absorbed in it. But when the soldier had gone, eager, loud talk and noise arose among us.

Someone shouted to the baker: "It's a bad job that you've started, Pavel!"

"Do your work!" answered the baker savagely.

We felt that the soldier had been touched to the quick, and that danger threatened Tanya. We felt this, and at the same time we were all possessed by a burning curiosity, most agreeable to us. What would happen? Would Tanya hold out against the soldier? And almost all cried confidently: "Tanya? She'll hold out! You won't catch her with your bare arms!"

We longed terribly to test the strength of our idol; we were forcibly trying to persuade each other that our divinity was a strong divinity and would come victorious out of this ordeal. We began at last to fancy that we had not worked enough on the soldier, that he would forget the dispute, and that we ought to pique his vanity further. From that day we began to live a different life, a life of nervous tension, such as we had never known before. We spent whole days in arguing together; we all grew, as it were, sharper; and got to talk more and better. It seemed to us that we were playing some sort of game with the devil, and the stake on our side was Tanya. And when we learned from the bakers that the soldier had begun "running after our Tanya," we felt a sort of delighted terror, and life was so interesting that we did not even notice that our employer had taken advantage of our preoccupation to increase our work by three hundred pounds of dough a day. We seemed, indeed, not even tired by our work. Tanya's name was on our lips all day long. And every day we looked for her with a certain peculiar impatience. Sometimes we pictured to ourselves that she would come to us, and it would not be the same Tanya as of old, but somehow different. We said nothing to her, however, of the dispute regarding her. We asked her no questions, and behaved as well and affectionately to her as ever. But even in this a new element crept in, alien to our old feeling for Tanya—and that new element was keen curiosity, keen and cold as a steel knife.

"Mates! Today the time's up!" our baker said to us one morning, as he set to work.

We were well aware of it without his reminder; but still we became alert.

"Have a good look at her. She'll be here directly," suggested the baker.

One of us cried out in a troubled voice, "Why! as though one could see anything! You need more than eyes."

And again an eager, noisy discussion sprang up among us. Today we were at last to discover how pure and spotless was the vessel into which we had poured all that was best in us. This morning, for the first time, it became clear to us that we really were playing for high stakes; that we might, indeed, through the exaction of this proof of purity, lose our divinity altogether.

All this time we had been hearing that Tanya was stubbornly and persistently pursued by the soldier, but not one of us had thought of asking her what she thought of him. And she came every morning to fetch her pretzels, and was the same toward us as ever.

This morning, too, we heard her voice outside: "You poor prisoners! Here I am!"

We opened the door hastily, and when she came in we all remained, contrary to our usual custom, silent. Our eyes fixed on her, we did not know what to say to her, what to ask her. And there we stood in front of her, a gloomy, silent crowd. She seemed to be surprised at this unusual reception; and suddenly we saw her turn white and become uneasy, then she asked, in a choking voice:

"Why are you—like this?"

"And you?" the baker flung at her grimly, never taking his eyes off her.

"What about me?"

"N-nothing."

"Well, then, give me the little pretzels quickly."

Never before had she bidden us hurry.

"There's plenty of time," said the baker, not stirring and not removing his eyes from her face.

Then, suddenly, she turned round and disappeared through the door.

The baker took his shovel and said, calmly turning away toward the oven:

"Well, that settles it! There's a soldier for you—the low cur!"

Like a flock of sheep we all pressed round the table, sat down silently, and began listlessly to work. Soon, however, one of us remarked:

"Perhaps, after all—"

"Shut up!" shouted the baker.

We were all convinced that he was a man of judgment, a man who knew more than we did about things. And at the sound of his voice we were convinced of the soldier's victory, and our spirits became sad and downcast.

At twelve o'clock—while we were eating our dinners—the soldier came in. He was as clean and as smart as ever, and looked at us—as usual—straight in the eyes. But we were all awkward in looking at him.

"Now then, honored sirs, would you like me to show you a soldier's prowess?" he said, chuckling proudly.

"Go out into the passage and look through the crack—do you understand?"

We went into the passage, and stood all pushing against one another, squeezed up to the cracks of the wooden partition of the passage that looked into the yard. We had not to wait long. Very soon Tanya, with hurried footsteps and an anxious face, walked across the yard, jumping over the puddles of melting snow and mud: she disappeared into the cellar. Then whistling, and not hurrying himself, the soldier followed in the same direction. His hands were thrust in his pockets; his mustaches were quivering.

Rain was falling, and we saw how its drops struck the puddles, and the puddles were wrinkled by them. The day was damp and gray—a very dreary day. Snow still lay on the roofs, but on the ground dark patches of mud had begun to appear. And the snow on the roofs too was covered by a layer of brownish dirt. The rain fell slowly with a depressing sound. It was cold and disagreeable for us waiting.

The first to come out of the cellar was the soldier; he walked slowly across the yard, his mustaches twitching, his hands in his pockets—the same as always.

Then—Tanya, too, came out. Her eyes—her eyes were radiant with joy and happiness, and her lips—were smiling. And she walked as though in a dream, staggering, with unsteady steps.

We could not bear this calmly. All of us at once rushed to the door, dashed out into the yard and—hissed at her, reviled her viciously, loudly, wildly.

She started at seeing us, and stood as though rooted in the mud under her feet. We formed a ring round her, and maliciously, without restraint, abused her with vile words, said shameful things to her.

We did this quietly, slowly, seeing that she could not get away, that she was hemmed in by us, and we could rail at her to our hearts' content. I don't know why, but we did not beat her. She stood in the midst of us, and turned her head this way and that, as she heard our insults. And we—more and more violently flung at her the filth and venom of our words.

The color had left her face. Her blue eyes, so happy a moment before, opened wide, her bosom heaved, and her lips quivered.

We in a ring round her avenged ourselves on her, for she had robbed us. She belonged to us, we had lavished on her our best, and though that best was beggar's crumbs, still there were twenty-six of us, she was one, and so there was no pain we could give her equal to her guilt! How we insulted her! She was still mute, still gazed at us with wild eyes, and a shiver ran through her.

We laughed, roared, yelled. Other people ran up from somewhere and joined us. One of us pulled Tanya by the sleeve of her blouse.

Suddenly her eyes flashed; deliberately she raised her hands to her head and straightening her hair she said loudly but calmly, straight in our faces:

"Ah, you miserable prisoners!"

And she walked straight at us, walked as directly as though we had not been before her, as though we were not blocking her way.

And hence none of us did actually block her way.

Walking out of our circle without turning round, she added loudly, with pride and indescribable contempt:

"Ah, you scum—brutes."

And—was gone, erect, beautiful, proud.

We were left in the middle of the yard, in the rain, under the gray sunless sky.

Then we went mutely away to our damp stone basement. As before— the sun never peeped in at our windows, and Tanya came no more. Never!

STUDY QUESTIONS

1. In some detail, describe the physical setting of the story. How does that setting affect the characters? The action of the story?
2. The narrator speaks for all twenty-six men. What effect does this have on the impact of the story?
3. Why does Tanya refuse to mend the worker's shirt?
4. Explain why the baker challenged the soldier. How do the twenty-six men react to the bet? Why?
5. After the baker wins the bet, why do the men treat Tanya so cruelly?
6. What have the men lost at the end of the story? Why?

Stephen Crane (1871–1900)

AN EPISODE OF WAR

The lieutenant's rubber blanket lay on the ground, and upon it he had poured the company's supply of coffee. Corporals and other representatives of the grimy and hot-throated men who lined the breastwork[1] had come for each squad's portion.

The lieutenant was frowning and serious at this task of division. His lips pursed as he drew with sword various crevices in the heap until brown squares of coffee, astoundingly equal in size, appeared on the blanket. He was on the verge of a great triumph in mathematics, and the corporals were thronging forward, each to reap a little square, when suddenly the lieutenant cried out and looked quickly at a man near him as if he suspected it was a case of personal assault. The others cried out also when they saw blood upon the lieutenant's sleeve.

He had winced like a man stung, swayed dangerously, and then straightened. The sound of his hoarse breathing was plainly audible. He looked sadly, mystically, over the breastwork at the green face of a wood, where now were many little puffs of white smoke. During this moment the men about him gazed statue-like and silent, astonished and awed by this catastrophe which happened when catastrophes were not expected—when they had leisure to observe it.

As the lieutenant stared at the wood, they too swung their heads, so that for another instant all hands, still silent, contemplated the distant forest as if their minds were fixed upon the mystery of a bullet's journey.

The officer had, of course, been compelled to take his sword into his left hand. He did not hold it by the hilt. He gripped it at the middle of the blade, awkwardly. Turning his eyes from the hostile wood, he looked at the sword as he held it there, and seemed puzzled as to what to do with it, where to put it. In short, this weapon had of a sudden become a strange thing to him. He looked at it in a kind of stupefaction, as if he had been endowed with a trident, a sceptre, or a spade.

Finally he tried to sheath it. To sheath a sword held by the left hand, at the middle of the blade, in a scabbard hung at the left hip, is a feat worthy of a sawdust ring. This wounded officer engaged in a desperate struggle with the sword and the wobbling scabbard, and during the time of it he breathed like a wrestler.

But at this instant the men, the spectators, awoke from their stone-like poses and crowded forward sympathetically. The orderly-sergeant[2] took the sword and tenderly placed it in the scabbard. At the time, he leaned nervously backward, and did not allow even his finger to brush the body of the

1 breastwork: temporary fortification.
2 orderly-sergeant: first sergeant.

lieutenant. A wound gives strange dignity to him who bears it. Well, men shy from this new and terrible majesty. It is as if the wounded man's hand is upon the curtain which hangs before the revelations of all existence—the meaning of ants, potentates, wars, cities, sunshine, snow, a feather dropped from a bird's wing; and the power of it sheds radiance upon a bloody form, and makes the other men understand sometimes that they are little. His comrades look at him with large eyes thoughtfully. Moreover, they fear vaguely that the weight of a finger upon him might send him headlong, precipitate the tragedy, hurl him at once into the dim, grey unknown. And so the orderly-sergeant, while sheathing the sword, leaned nervously backward.

There were others who proffered assistance. One timidly presented his shoulder and asked the lieutenant if he cared to lean upon it, but the latter waved him away mournfully. He wore the look of one who knows he is the victim of a terrible disease and understands his helplessness. He again stared over the breastwork at the forest, and then turning went slowly rearward. He held his right wrist tenderly in his left hand as if the wounded arm was made of very brittle glass.

And the men in silence stared at the wood, then at the departing lieutenant—then at the wood, then at the lieutenant.

As the wounded officer passed from the line of battle, he was enabled to see many things which as a participant in the fight were unknown to him. He saw a general on a black horse gazing over the lines of blue infantry at the green woods which veiled his problems. An aide galloped furiously, dragged his horse suddenly to a halt, saluted, and presented a paper. It was, for a wonder, precisely like an historical painting.

To the rear of the general and his staff a group, composed of a bugler, two or three orderlies, and the bearer of the corps standard, all upon maniacal horses, were working like slaves to hold their ground, preserve their respectful interval, while the shells boomed in the air about them, and caused their chargers to make furious quivering leaps.

A battery,[3] a tumultuous and shining mass, was swirling toward the right. The wild thud of hoofs, the cries of the riders shouting blame and praise, menace and encouragement, and, last, the roar of the wheels, the slant of the glistening guns, brought the lieutenant to an intent pause. The battery swept in curves that stirred the heart; it made halts as dramatic as the crash of a wave on the rocks, and when it fled onward, this aggregation of wheels, levers, motors, had a beautiful unity, as if it were a missile. The sound of it was a war-chorus that reached into the depths of man's emotion.

The lieutenant, still holding his arm as if it were of glass, stood watching this battery until all detail of it was lost, save the figures of the riders, which rose and fell and waved lashes over the black mass.

---

[3] battery: a company of artillerymen, together with their cannon, which are pulled by horses.

Later, he turned his eyes toward the battle where the shooting sometimes crackled like bush-fires, sometimes sputtered with exasperating irregularity, and sometimes reverberated like the thunder. He saw the smoke rolling upward and saw crowds of men who ran and cheered, or stood and blazed away at the inscrutable distance.

He came upon some stragglers, and they told him how to find the field hospital. They described its exact location. In fact, these men, no longer having part in the battle, knew more of it than others. They told the performance of every corps, every division, the opinion of every general. The lieutenant, carrying his wounded arm rearward, looked upon them with wonder.

At the roadside a brigade was making coffee and buzzing with talk like a girls' boarding-school. Several officers came out to him and inquired concerning things of which he knew nothing. One, seeing his arm, began to scold. "Why, man, that's no way to do. You want to fix that thing." He appropriated the lieutenant and the lieutenant's wound. He cut the sleeve and laid bare the arm, every nerve of which softly fluttered under his touch. He bound his handkerchief over the wound, scolding away in the meantime. His tone allowed one to think that he was in the habit of being wounded every day. The lieutenant hung his head, feeling, in this presence, that he did not know how to be correctly wounded.

The low white tents of the hospital were grouped around an old school-house. There was here a singular commotion. In the foreground two ambulances interlocked wheels in the deep mud. The drivers were tossing the blame of it back and forth, gesticulating and berating, while from the ambulances, both crammed with wounded, there came an occasional groan. An interminable crowd of bandaged men were coming and going. Great numbers sat under the trees nursing heads or arms or legs. There was a dispute of some kind raging on the steps of the school-house. Sitting with his back against a tree a man with a face as grey as a new army blanket was serenely smoking a corn-cob pipe. The lieutenant wished to rush forward and inform him that he was dying.

A busy surgeon was passing near the lieutenant. "Good-morning," he said, with a friendly smile. Then he caught sight of the lieutenant's arm and his face at once changed. "Well, let's have a look at it." He seemed possessed suddenly of a great contempt for the lieutenant. This wound evidently placed the latter on a very low social plane. The doctor cried out impatiently, "What mutton-head had tied it up that way anyhow?" The lieutenant answered, "Oh, a man."

When the wound was disclosed the doctor fingered it disdainfully. "Humph," he said. "You come along with me and I'll 'tend to you." His voice contained the same scorn as if he were saying, "You will have to go to jail."

The lieutenant had been very meek, but now his face flushed, and he looked into the doctor's eyes. "I guess I won't have it amputated," he said.

"Nonsense, man! Nonsense! Nonsense!" cried the doctor. "Come along, now. I won't amputate it. Come along. Don't be a baby."

"Let go of me," said the lieutenant, holding back wrathfully, his glance fixed upon the door of the old school-house, as sinister to him as the portals of death.

And this is the story of how the lieutenant lost his arm. When he reached home, his sisters, his mother, his wife, sobbed for a long time at the sight of the flat sleeve. "Oh, well," he said, standing shamefaced amid these tears, "I don't suppose it matters so much as all that."

STUDY QUESTIONS

1. What war is the setting of the action? Consider the fact that the lieutenant carries a sword, that he sees lines of "blue infantry," that the enemy are firing from "green woods," and the field hospital is located in tents around an old school-house.
2. Why does the lieutenant stand in full view of the enemy to divide the coffee grounds for the squads under his command?
3. What is the significance of the fact that stragglers not involved in the battle know more about what is happening than the troops who are actively engaged?
4. Why does the lieutenant lose status because of his wound?
5. As he approaches the field hospital, the lieutenant sees two ambulances loaded with wounded, with their wheels interlocked in the mud. Why is this detail significant?
6. What is the surgeon's attitude toward wounded soldiers? Why does he lie to the lieutenant?
7. The door of the old school-house is compared to "the portals of death." Discuss the aptness of this comparison.
8. At the close of the story, the sisters, mother, and wife of the lieutenant are shocked and grief-stricken at the loss of his arm. Why is his attitude by contrast, so calm and fatalistic?

William Faulkner (1897–1962)

THAT EVENING SUN

1

Monday is no different from any other weekday in Jefferson now. The streets are paved now, and the telephone and electric companies are cutting down more and more of the shade trees—the water oaks, the maples and locusts and elms—to make room for iron poles bearing clusters of bloated and ghostly and bloodless grapes, and we have a city laundry which makes the rounds on Monday morning, gathering the bundles of clothes into bright-colored, specially made motorcars: the soiled wearing of a whole week now flees apparitionlike behind alert and irritable electric horns, with a long diminishing noise of rubber and asphalt like tearing silk, and even the Negro women who still take in white people's washing after the old custom, fetch and deliver it in automobiles.

But fifteen years ago, on Monday morning the quiet, dusty, shady streets would be full of Negro women with, balanced on their steady, turbaned heads, bundles of clothes tied up in sheets, almost as large as cotton bales, carried so without touch of hand between the kitchen door of the white house and the blackened washpot beside a cabin door in Negro Hollow.

Nancy would set her bundle on top of her head, then upon the bundle in turn she would set the black straw sailor hat which she wore winter and summer. She was tall, with a high, sad face sunken a little where her teeth were missing. Sometimes we would go a part of the way down the lane and across the pasture with her, to watch the balanced bundle and the hat that never bobbed or wavered, even when she walked down into the ditch and up the other side and stooped through the fence. She would go down on her hands and knees and crawl through the gap, her head rigid, uptilted, the bundle steady as a rock or a balloon, and rise to her feet again and go on.

Sometimes the husbands of the washing women would fetch and deliver the clothes, but Jesus never did that for Nancy, even before Father told him to stay away from our house, even when Dilsey was sick and Nancy would come to cook for us.

And then about half the time we'd have to go down the lane to Nancy's cabin and tell her to come on and cook breakfast. We would stop at the ditch, because Father told us to not have anything to do with Jesus—he was a short black man, with a razor scar down his face—and we would throw rocks at Nancy's house until she came to the door, leaning her head around it without any clothes on.

"What yawl mean, chunking my house?" Nancy said. "What you little devils mean?"

"Father says for you to come on and get breakfast," Caddy said. "Father says it's over a half an hour now, and you've got to come this minute."

"I ain't studying no breakfast," Nancy said. "I going to get my sleep out."

"I bet you're drunk," Jason said. "Father says you're drunk. Are you drunk, Nancy?"

"Who says I is?" Nancy said. "I got to get my sleep out. I ain't studying no breakfast."

So after a while we quit chunking the cabin and went back home. When she finally came, it was too late for me to go to school. So we thought it was whiskey until that day they arrested her again and they were taking her to jail and they passed Mr. Stovall. He was the cashier in the bank and a deacon in the Baptist church, and Nancy began to say:

"When you going to pay me, white man? When you going to pay me, white man? It's been three times now since you paid me a cent—" Mr. Stovall knocked her down, but she kept on saying, "When you going to pay me, white man? It's been three times now since—" until Mr. Stovall kicked her in the mouth with his heel and the marshal caught Mr. Stovall back, and Nancy lying in the street, laughing. She turned her head and spat out some blood and teeth and said, "It's been three times now since he paid me a cent."

That was how she lost her teeth, and all that day they told about Nancy and Mr. Stovall, and all that night the ones that passed the jail could hear Nancy singing and yelling. They could see her hands holding to the window bars, and a lot of them stopped along the fence, listening to her and the jailer trying to make her stop. She didn't shut up until almost daylight, when the jailer began to hear a bumping and scraping upstairs and he went up there and found Nancy hanging from the window bar. He said that it was cocaine and not whiskey, because no nigger would try to commit suicide unless he was full of cocaine, because a nigger full of cocaine wasn't a nigger any longer.

The jailer cut her down and revived her, then he beat her, whipped her. She had hung herself with her dress. She had fixed it all right, but when they arrested her she didn't have on anything except a dress and so she didn't have anything to tie her hands with and she couldn't make her hands let go of the window ledge. So the jailer heard the noise and ran up there and found Nancy hanging from the window, stark naked, her belly already swelling out a little, like a little balloon.

When Dilsey was sick in her cabin and Nancy was cooking for us, we could see her apron swelling out; that was before Father told Jesus to stay away from the house. Jesus was in the kitchen, sitting behind the stove, with his razor scar on his black face like a piece of dirty string. He said it was a watermelon that Nancy had under her dress.

"It never come off of your vine, though," Nancy said.

"Off of what vine?" Caddy said.

"I can cut down the vine it did come off of," Jesus said.

"What makes you want to talk like that before these chillen?" Nancy said. "Whyn't you go on to work? You done et. You want Mr. Jason to catch you hanging around his kitchen, talking that way before these chillen?"

"Talking what way?" Caddy said. "What vine?"

"I can't hang around white man's kitchen," Jesus said. "But white man can hang around mine. White man can come in my house, but I can't stop him. When white man want to come in my house, I ain't got no house. I can't stop him, but he can't kick me outen it. He can't do that."

Dilsey was still sick in her cabin. Father told Jesus to stay off our place. Dilsey was still sick. It was a long time. We were in the library after supper.

"Isn't Nancy through in the kitchen yet?" Mother said. "It seems to me that she has had plenty of time to have finished the dishes."

"Let Quentin go and see," Father said. "Go and see if Nancy is through, Quentin. Tell her she can go on home."

I went to the kitchen. Nancy was through. The dishes were put away and the fire was out. Nancy was sitting in a chair, close to the cold stove. She looked at me.

"Mother wants to know if you are through," I said.

"Yes," Nancy said. She looked at me. "I done finished." She looked at me. "What is it?" I said. "What is it?"

"I ain't nothing but a nigger," Nancy said. "It ain't none of it my fault."

She looked at me, sitting in the chair before the cold stove, the sailor hat on her head. I went back to the library. It was the cold stove and all, when you think of a kitchen being warm and busy and cheerful. And with a cold stove and the dishes all put away, and nobody wanting to eat at that hour.

"Is she through?" Mother said.

"Yessum," I said.

"What is she doing?" Mother said.

"She's not doing anything. She's through."

"I'll go and see," Father said.

"Maybe she's waiting for Jesus to come and take her home," Caddy said.

"Jesus is gone." I said. Nancy told us how one morning she woke up and Jesus was gone.

"He quit me," Nancy said. "Done gone to Memphis, I reckon. Dodging them city po-lice for a while, I reckon."

"And a good riddance," Father said. "I hope he stays there."

"Nancy's scaired of the dark," Jason said.

"So are you," Caddy said.

"I'm not," Jason said.

"Scairy cat," Caddy said.

"I'm not," Jason said.

"You, Candace!" Mother said. Father came back.

"I am going to walk down the lane with Nancy," he said. "She says that Jesus is back."

"Has she seen him?" Mother said.

"No. Some Negro sent her word that he was back in town. I won't be long."

"You'll leave me alone, to take Nancy home?" Mother said. "Is her safety more precious to you than mine?"

"I won't be long," Father said.

"You'll leave these children unprotected, with that Negro about?"

"I'm going, too," Caddy said. "Let me go, Father."

"What would he do with them, if he were unfortunate enough to have them?" Father said.

"I want to go, too," Jason said.

"Jason!" Mother said. She was speaking to Father. You could tell that by the way she said the name. Like she believed that all day Father had been trying to think of doing the thing she wouldn't like the most, and that she knew all the time that after a while he would think of it. I stayed quiet, because Father and I both knew that Mother would want him to make me stay with her if she just thought of it in time. So Father didn't look at me. I was the oldest. I was nine and Caddy was seven and Jason was five.

"Nonsense," Father said. "We won't be long."

Nancy had her hat on. We came to the lane. "Jesus always been good to me," Nancy said. "Whenever he had two dollars, one of them was mine." We walked in the lane. "If I can just get through the lane," Nancy said, "I be all right then."

The lane was always dark. "This is where Jason got scaired on Halloween," Caddy said.

"I didn't," Jason said.

"Can't Aunt Rachel do anything with him?" Father said. Aunt Rachel was old. She lived in a cabin beyond Nancy's by herself. She had white hair and she smoked a pipe in the door, all day long; she didn't work any more. They said she was Jesus' mother. Sometimes she said she was and sometimes she said she wasn't any kin to Jesus.

"Yes you did," Caddy said. "You were scairder than Frony. You were scairder than T. P. even. Scairder than niggers."

"Can't nobody do nothing with him," Nancy said. "He say I done woke up the devil in him and ain't but one thing going to lay it down again."

"Well, he's gone now," Father said. "There's nothing for you to be afraid of now. And if you'd just let white men alone."

"Let what white men alone?" Caddy said. "How let them alone?"

"He ain't gone nowhere," Nancy said. "I can feel him. I can feel him now, in this lane. He hearing us talk, every word, hid somewhere, waiting. I ain't seen him, and I ain't going to see him again but once more, with that razor in his mouth. That razor on that string down his back, inside his shirt. And then I ain't going to be even surprised."

"I wasn't scaired," Jason said.

"If you'd behave yourself, you'd have kept out of this," Father said. "But it's all right now. He's probably in Saint Louis now. Probably got another wife by now and forgot all about you."

"If he has, I better not find out about it," Nancy said. "I'd stand there right over them, and every time he wropped [1] her, I'd cut that arm off. I'd cut his head off and I'd slit her belly and I'd shove—"

"Hush," Father said.

"Slit whose belly, Nancy?" Caddy said.

"I wasn't scaired," Jason said. "I'd walk right down this lane by myself."

---

[1] wropped: hugged, embraced.

"Yah," Caddy said. "You wouldn't dare to put your foot down in it if we were not here too."

2

Dilsey was still sick, so we took Nancy home every night until Mother said, "How much longer is this going on? I to be left alone in this big house while you take home a frightened Negro?"

We fixed a pallet in the kitchen for Nancy. One night we waked up, hearing the sound. It was not singing and it was not crying, coming up the dark stairs. There was a light in Mother's room and we heard Father going down the hall, down the back stairs, and Caddy and I went into the hall. The floor was cold. Our toes curled away from it while we listened to the sound. It was like singing and it wasn't like singing, like the sound that Negroes make.

Then it stopped and we heard Father going down the back stairs, and we went to the head of the stairs. Then the sound began again, in the stairway, not loud, and we could see Nancy's eyes halfway up the stairs, against the wall. They looked like cat's eyes do, like a big cat against the wall, watching us. When we came down the steps to where she was, she quit making the sound again, and we stood there until Father came back up from the kitchen, with his pistol in his hand. He went back down with Nancy and they came back with Nancy's pallet.

We spread the pallet in our room. After the light in Mother's room went off, we could see Nancy's eyes again. "Nancy," Caddy whispered, "are you asleep, Nancy?"

Nancy whispered something. It was oh or no. I don't know which. Like nobody had made it, like it came from nowhere and went nowhere, until it was like Nancy was not there at all; that I had looked so hard at her eyes on the stairs that they had got printed on my eyeballs, like the sun does when you have closed your eyes and there is no sun. "Jesus," Nancy whispered. "Jesus."

"Was it Jesus?" Caddy said. "Did he try to come into the kitchen?"

"Jesus," Nancy said. Like this: Jeeeeeeeeeeeeeeesus, until the sound went out, like a match or a candle does.

"It's the other Jesus she means," I said.

"Can you see us, Nancy?" Caddy whispered. "Can you see our eyes too?"

"I ain't nothing but a nigger," Nancy said. "God knows. God knows."

"What did you see down there in the kitchen?" Caddy whispered. "What tried to get in?"

"God knows," Nancy said. We could see her eyes. "God knows."

Dilsey got well. She cooked dinner. "You'd better stay in bed a day or two longer," Father said.

"What for?" Dilsey said. "If I had been a day later, this place would be to rack and ruin. Get on out of here now, and let me get my kitchen straight again."

Dilsey cooked supper too. And that night, just before dark, Nancy came into the kitchen.

"How do you know he's back?" Dilsey said. "You ain't seen him."

"Jesus is a nigger," Jason said.

"I can feel him," Nancy said. "I can feel him laying yonder in the ditch."

"Tonight?" Dilsey said. "Is he there tonight?"

"Dilsey's a nigger too," Jason said.

"You try to eat something," Dilsey said.

"I don't want nothing," Nancy said.

"I ain't a nigger," Jason said.

"Drink some coffee," Dilsey said. She poured a cup of coffee for Nancy. "Do you know he's out there tonight? How come you know it's tonight?"

"I know," Nancy said. "He's there, waiting. I know. I done lived with him too long. I know what he is fixing to do fore he know it himself."

"Drink some coffee," Dilsey said. Nancy held the cup to her mouth and blew into the cup. Her mouth pursed out like a spreading adder's, like a rubber mouth like she had blown all the color out of her lips with blowing the coffee.

"I ain't a nigger," Jason said. "Are you a nigger, Nancy?"

"I hellborn, child," Nancy said. "I won't be nothing soon. I going back where I come from soon."

3

She began to drink the coffee. While she was drinking, holding the cup in both hands, she began to make the sound again. She made the sound into the cup and the coffee sploshed out onto her hands and her dress. Her eyes looked at us and she sat there, her elbows on her knees, holding the cup in both hands, looking at us across the wet cup, making the sound.

"Look at Nancy," Jason said, "Nancy can't cook for us now. Dilsey's got well now."

"You hush up," Dilsey said. Nancy held the cup in both hands, looking at us, making the sound, like there were two of them: one looking at us and the other making the sound. "Whyn't you let Mr. Jason telefoam the marshal?" Dilsey said. Nancy stopped then, holding the cup in her long brown hands. She tried to drink some coffee again, but it sploshed out of the cup, onto her hands and her dress, and she put the cup down. Jason watched her.

"I can't swallow it," Nancy said. "I swallows but it won't go down me."

"You go down to the cabin," Dilsey said. "Frony will fix you a pallet and I'll be there soon."

"Won't no nigger stop him," Nancy said.

"I ain't a nigger," Jason said. "Am I, Dilsey?"

"I reckon not," Dilsey said. She looked at Nancy. "I don't reckon so. What you going to do, then?"

Nancy looked at us. Her eyes went fast, like she was afraid there wasn't time to look, without hardly moving at all. She looked at us, at all three of us at one time. "You remember that night I stayed in yawls' room?" she said. She told about how we waked up early the next morning, and played. We had to play quiet, on her pallet, until Father woke up and it was time to get breakfast. "Go and ask your maw to let me stay here tonight," Nancy said. "I won't need no pallet. We can play some more."

Caddy asked Mother. Jason went too. "I can't have Negroes sleeping in the bedrooms," Mother said. Jason cried. He cried until Mother said he couldn't have any dessert for three days if he didn't stop. Then Jason said he would stop if Dilsey would make a chocolate cake. Father was there.

"Why don't you do something about it?" Mother said. "What do we have officers for?"

"Why is Nancy afraid of Jesus?" Caddy said. "Are you afraid of Father, Mother?"

"What could the officer do?" Father said. "If Nancy hasn't seen him, how could the officers find him?"

"Then why is she afraid?" Mother said.

"She says he is there. She says she knows he is there tonight."

"Yet we pay taxes," Mother said. "I must wait here alone in this big house while you take a Negro woman home."

"You know that I am not lying outside with a razor," Father said.

"I'll stop if Dilsey will make a chocolate cake," Jason said. Mother told us to go out and Father said he didn't know if Jason would get a chocolate cake or not, but he knew what Jason was going to get in about a minute. We went back to the kitchen and told Nancy.

"Father said for you to go home and lock the door, and you'll be all right," Caddy said. "All right from what, Nancy? Is Jesus mad at you?" Nancy was holding the coffee cup in her hands again, her elbows on her knees and her hands holding the cup between her knees. She was looking into the cup. "What have you done that made Jesus mad?" Caddy said. Nancy let the cup go. It didn't break on the floor, but the coffee spilled out, and Nancy sat there with her hands still making the shape of the cup. She began to make the sound again, not loud. Not singing and not unsinging. We watched her.

"Here," Dilsey said. "You quit that, now. You get aholt of yourself. You wait here. I going to get Versh to walk home with you." Dilsey went out.

We looked at Nancy. Her shoulders kept shaking, but she quit making the sound. We stood there and watched her.

"What's Jesus going to do to you?" Caddy said. "He went away."

Nancy looked at us. "We had fun that night I stayed in yawls' room, didn't we?"

"I didn't," Jason said. "I didn't have any fun."

"You were alseep in Mother's room," Caddy said. "You were not there."

"Let's go down to my house and have some more fun," Nancy said.

"Mother won't let us," I said. "It's too late now."

"Don't bother her," Nancy said. "We can tell her in the morning. She won't mind."

"She wouldn't let us," I said.

"Don't ask her now," Nancy said. "Don't bother her now."

"She didn't say we couldn't go," Caddy said.

"We didn't ask," I said.

"If you go, I'll tell," Jason said.

"We'll have fun," Nancy said. "They won't mind, just to my house. I been working for yawl a long time. They won't mind."

"I'm not afraid to go," Caddy said. "Jason is the one that's afraid. He'll tell."

"I'm not," Jason said.

"Yes, you are," Caddy said. "You'll tell."

"I won't tell," Jason said. "I'm not afraid."

"Jason ain't afraid to go with me," Nancy said. "Is you, Jason?"

"Jason is going to tell," Caddy said. The lane was dark. We passed the pasture gate. "I bet if something was to jump out from behind that gate, Jason would holler."

"I wouldn't," Jason said. We walked down the lane. Nancy was talking loud.

"What are you talking so loud for, Nancy?" Caddy said.

"Who, me?" Nancy said. "Listen at Quentin and Caddy and Jason saying I'm talking loud."

"You talk like there was five of us here," Caddy said. "You talk like Father was here too."

"Who; me talking loud, Mr. Jason?" Nancy said.

"Nancy called Jason 'Mister,' " Caddy said.

"Listen how Caddy and Quentin and Jason talk," Nancy said.

"We're not talking loud," Caddy said. "You're the one that's talking like Father—"

"Hush," Nancy said, "hush, Mr. Jason."

"Nancy called Jason 'Mister' aguh—"

"Hush." Nancy said. She was talking loud when we crossed the ditch and stooped through the fence where she used to stoop through with the clothes on her head. Then we came to her house. We were going fast then. She opened the door. The smell of the house was like the lamp and the smell of Nancy was like the wick, like they were waiting for one another to begin to smell. She lit the lamp and closed the door and put the bar up. Then she quit talking loud, looking at us.

"What're we going to do?" Caddy said.

"What do yawl want to do?" Nancy said.

"You said we would have some fun," Caddy said.

There was something about Nancy's house; something you could smell besides Nancy and the house. Jason smelled it, even. "I don't want to stay here," he said. "I want to go home."

"Go home, then," Caddy said.

"I don't want to go by myself," Jason said.

"We're going to have some fun," Nancy said.

"How?" Caddy said.

Nancy stood by the door. She was looking at us, only it was like she had emptied her eyes, like she had quit using them. "What do you want to do?" she said.

"Tell us a story," Caddy said. "Can you tell a story?"

"Yes," Nancy said.

"Tell it," Caddy said. We looked at Nancy. "You don't know any stories."

"Yes," Nancy said. "Yes I do."

She came and sat in a chair before the hearth. There was a little fire there. Nancy built it up, when it was already hot inside. She built a good blaze. She told a story. She talked like her eyes looked, like her eyes watching us and her voice talking to us did not belong to her. Like she was living somewhere else, waiting somewhere else. She was outside the cabin. Her voice was inside and the shape of her, that Nancy that could stoop under a barbed wire fence with a bundle of clothes balanced on her head as though without weight, like a balloon, was there. But that was all. "And so this here queen come walking up to the ditch, where that bad man was hiding. She was walking up to the ditch, and she say, 'If I can just get past this here ditch,' was what she say . . ."

"What ditch?" Caddy said. "A ditch like that one out there? Why did a queen want to go into a ditch?"

"To get to her house," Nancy said. She looked at us. "She had to cross the ditch to get into her house quick and bar the door."

"Why did she want to go home and bar the door?" Caddy said.

4

Nancy looked at us. She quit talking. She looked at us. Jason's legs stuck straight out of his pants where he sat on Nancy's lap. "I don't think that's a good story," he said. "I want to go home."

"Maybe we had better," Caddy said. She got up from the floor. "I bet they are looking for us right now." She went toward the door.

"No," Nancy said. "Don't open it." She got up quick and passed Caddy. She didn't touch the door, the wooden bar.

"Why not?" Caddy said.

WILLIAM FAULKNER

"Come back to the lamp," Nancy said. "We'll have fun. You don't have to go."

"We ought to go," Caddy said. "Unless we have a lot of fun." She and Nancy came back to the fire, the lamp.

"I want to go home," Jason said. "I'm going to tell."

"I know another story," Nancy said. She stood close to the lamp. She looked at Caddy, like when your eyes look up at a stick balanced on your nose. She had to look down to see Caddy, but her eyes looked like that, like when you are balancing a stick.

"I won't listen to it," Jason said. "I'll bang on the door."

"It's a good one," Nancy said. "It's better than the other one."

"What's it about?" Caddy said. Nancy was standing by the lamp. Her hand was on the lamp, against the light, long and brown.

"Your hand is on that hot globe," Caddy said. "Don't it feel hot to your hand?"

Nancy looked at her hand on the lamp chimney. She took her hand away, slow. She stood there, looking at Caddy, wringing her long hand as though it were tied to her wrist with a string.

"Let's do something else," Caddy said.

"I want to go home," Jason said.

"I got some popcorn," Nancy said. She looked at Caddy and then at Jason and then at me and then at Caddy again. "I got some popcorn."

"I don't like popcorn," Jason said. "I'd rather have candy."

Nancy looked at Jason. "You can hold the popper." She was still wringing her hand; it was long and limp and brown.

"All right," Jason said. "I'll stay a while if I can do that. Caddy can't hold it. I'll want to go home again if Caddy holds the popper."

Nancy built up the fire. "Look at Nancy putting her hands in the fire," Caddy said. "What's the matter with you, Nancy?"

"I got popcorn," Nancy said. "I got some." She took the popper from under the bed. It was broken. Jason began to cry.

"Now we can't have any popcorn," he said.

"We ought to go home anyway," Caddy said. "Come on, Quentin."

"Wait," Nancy said, "wait. I can fix it. Don't you want to help me fix it?"

"I don't think I want any," Caddy said. "It's too late now."

"You help me, Jason," Nancy said. "Don't you want to help me?"

"No," Jason said. "I want to go home."

"Hush," Nancy said; "hush. Watch. Watch me. I can fix it so Jason can hold it and pop the corn." She got a piece of wire and fixed the popper.

"It won't hold good," Caddy said.

"Yes it will," Nancy said. "Yawl watch. Yawl help me shell some corn."

The popcorn was under the bed too. We shelled it into the popper and Nancy helped Jason hold the popper over the fire.

"It's not popping," Jason said. "I want to go home."

"You wait," Nancy said. "It'll begin to pop. We'll have fun then."

She was sitting close to the fire. The lamp was turned up so high it was beginning to smoke. "Why don't you turn it down some?" I said.

"It's all right," Nancy said. "I'll clean it. Yawl wait. The popcorn will start in a minute."

"I don't believe it's going to start," Caddy said. "We ought to start home, anyway. They'll be worried."

"No," Nancy said. "It's going to pop. Dilsey will tell um yawl with me. I been working for yawl long time. They won't mind if yawl at my house. You wait, now. It'll start any minute now."

Then Jason got some smoke in his eyes and he began to cry. He dropped the popper into the fire. Nancy got a wet rag and wiped Jason's face, but he didn't stop crying.

"Hush," she said. "Hush." He didn't hush. Caddy took the popper out of the fire.

"It's burned up," she said. "You'll have to get some more popcorn, Nancy."

"Did you put all of it in?" Nancy said.

"Yes," Caddy said. Nancy looked at Caddy. Then she took the popper and opened it and poured the cinders into her apron and began to sort the grains, her hands long and brown, and we watched her.

"Haven't you got any more?" Caddy said.

"Yes," Nancy said; "yes. Look. This here ain't burnt. All we need to do is—"

"I want to go home," Jason said. "I'm going to tell."

"Hush," Caddy said. We all listened. Nancy's head was already turned toward the door, her eyes filled with red lamplight. "Somebody is coming," Caddy said.

Then Nancy began to make that sound again, not loud, sitting there above the fire, her long hands dangling between her knees; all of a sudden water began to come out on her face in big drops, running down her face, carrying in each one a little turning ball of firelight like a spark until it dropped off her chin. "She's not crying," I said.

"I ain't crying," Nancy said. Her eyes were closed. "I ain't crying. Who is it?"

"I don't know," Caddy said. She went to the door and looked out. "We've got to go now," she said. "Here comes Father."

"I'm going to tell," Jason said. "Yawl made me come."

The water still ran down Nancy's face. She turned in her chair. "Listen. Tell him. Tell him we going to have fun. Tell him I take good care of yawl until in the morning. Tell him to let me come home with yawl and sleep on the floor. Tell him I won't need no pallet. We'll have fun. You member last time how we had so much fun?"

"I didn't have fun," Jason said. "You hurt me. You put smoke in my eyes. I'm going to tell."

5

Father came in. He looked at us. Nancy did not get up.

"Tell him," she said.

"Caddy made us come down here," Jason said. "I didn't want to."

Father came to the fire. Nancy looked up at him. "Can't you go to Aunt Rachel's and stay?" he said. Nancy looked up at Father, her hands between her knees. "He's not here," Father said. "I would have seen him. There's not a soul in sight."

"He in the ditch," Nancy said. "He waiting in the ditch yonder."

"Nonsense," Father said. He looked at Nancy. "Do you know he's there?"

"I got the sign," Nancy said.

"What sign?"

"I got it. It was on the table when I came in. It was a hog-bone, with blood meat still on it, laying by the lamp. He's out there. When yawl walk out that door, I gone."

"Gone where, Nancy?" Caddy said.

"I'm not a tattletale," Jason said.

"Nonsense," Father said.

"He out there," Nancy said. "He looking through that window this minute waiting for yawl to go. Then I gone."

"Nonsense," Father said. "Lock up your house and we'll take you on to Aunt Rachel's."

" 'Twon't do no good," Nancy said. She didn't look at Father now, but he looked down at her, at her long limp, moving hands. "Putting it off won't do no good."

"Then what do you want to do?" Father said.

"I don't know," Nancy said. "I can't do nothing. Just put it off. And that don't do no good. I reckon it belong to me. I reckon what I going to get ain't no more than mine."

"Get what?" Caddy said. "What's yours?"

"Nothing," Father said. "You all must get to bed."

"Caddy made me come," Jason said.

"Go on to Aunt Rachel's," Father said.

"It won't do no good," Nancy said. She sat down before the fire, her elbows on her knees, her long hands between her knees. "When even your own kitchen wouldn't do no good. When even if I was sleeping on the floor in the room with your chillen, and the next morning there I am, and blood—"

"Hush," Father said. "Lock your door and put out the lamp and go to bed."

"I scaired of the dark," Nancy said. "I scaired for it to happen in the dark."

"You mean you're going to sit right here with the lamp lighted?" Father said. Then Nancy began to make the sound again, sitting before the fire, her long hands between her knees. "Ah, damnation," Father said. "Come along, chillen. It's past bedtime."

"When yawl go home, I gone," Nancy said. She talked quieter now, and her face looked quiet, like her hands. "Anyway, I got my coffin money saved up with Mr. Lovelady." Mr. Lovelady was a short, dirty man who collected the Negro insurance, coming around to the cabins or the kitchens every Saturday morning, to collect fifteen cents. He and his wife lived at the hotel. One morning his wife committed suicide. They had a child, a little girl. He and the child went away. After a week or two he came back alone. We would see him going along the lanes and the back streets on Saturday mornings.

"Nonsense," Father said. "You'll be the first thing I'll see in the kitchen tomorrow morning."

"You'll see what you'll see, I reckon," Nancy said. "But it will take the Lord to say what that will be."

6

We left her sitting before the fire.

"Come and put the bar up," Father said. But she didn't move. She didn't look at us again, sitting quietly there between the lamp and the fire. From some distance down the lane we could look back and see her through the open door.

"What, Father?" Caddy said. "What's going to happen?"

"Nothing," Father said. Jason was on Father's back, so Jason was the tallest of all of us. We went down into the ditch. I looked at it, quiet. I couldn't see much where the moonlight and the shadows tangled.

"If Jesus *is* hid here, he can see us, can't he?" Caddy said.

"He's not there," Father said. "He went away a long time ago."

"You made me come," Jason said, high; against the sky it looked like Father had two heads, a little one and a big one. "I didn't want to."

We went up out of the ditch. We could still see Nancy's house and the open door, but we couldn't see Nancy now, sitting before the fire with the door open, because she was tired. "I just done got tired," she said. "I just a nigger. It ain't no fault of mine."

But we could hear her, because she began just after we came up out of the ditch, the sound that was not singing and not unsinging. "Who will do our washing now, Father?" I said.

"I'm not a nigger," Jason said, high and close above Father's head.

"You're worse," Caddy said, "you are a tattletale. If something was to jump out, you'd be scairder than a nigger."

"I wouldn't," Jason said.
"You'd cry," Caddy said.
"Caddy," Father said.
"I wouldn't!" Jason said.
"Scairy cat," Caddy said.
"Candace!" Father said.

STUDY QUESTIONS

1. Briefly describe the specifics of time and place in the story.
2. What details does Faulkner use to create distinct differences in his descriptions of the black and white environments of the story?
3. How do images of light and dark, black and white lend atmosphere to the narrative? What other contrasts contribute to setting?
4. What three distinct "worlds" does Faulkner create in "That Evening Sun"? What are the interrelationships of those "worlds"?
5. Fear seems to be a major theme of this story. How does Faulkner use environment to reflect that theme?
6. What is the relationship of dialogue to setting?
7. How is time important to the events in this story? What "kinds" of time do we become aware of?
8. What elements, other than dialogue, make this story particularly "Southern"?
9. How does Nancy's view of herself ("I ain't nothin' but a nigger") relate to setting? How does that view relate to the story's meaning?

Ray Bradbury (1920–)

THERE WILL COME SOFT RAINS

In the living room the voice-clock sang, *Tick-tock, seven o'clock, time to get up, time to get up, seven o'clock!* as if it were afraid that nobody would. The morning house lay empty. The clock ticked on, repeating and repeating its sounds into the emptiness. *Seven-nine, breakfast time, seven-nine!*

In the kitchen the breakfast stove gave a hissing sigh and ejected from its warm interior eight pieces of perfectly browned toast, eight eggs sunnyside up, sixteen slices of bacon, two coffees, and two cool glasses of milk.

"Today is August 4, 2026," said a second voice from the kitchen ceiling, "in the city of Allendale, California." It repeated the date three times for memory's sake. "Today is Mr. Featherstone's birthday. Today is the anniversary of Tilita's marriage. Insurance is payable, as are the water, gas, and light bills."

Somewhere in the walls, relays clicked, memory tapes glided under electric eyes.

Eight-one, tick-tock, eight-one o'clock, off to school, off to work, run, run, eight-one! But no doors slammed, no carpets took the soft tread of rubber heels. It was raining outside. The weather box on the front door sang quietly: "Rain, rain, go away; rubbers, raincoats for today . . ." And the rain tapped on the empty house, echoing.

Outside, the garage chimed and lifted its door to reveal the waiting car. After a long wait the door swung down again.

At eight-thirty the eggs were shriveled and the toast was like stone. An aluminum wedge scraped them into the sink, where hot water whirled them down a metal throat which digested and flushed them away to the distant sea. The dirty dishes were dropped into a hot washer and emerged twinkling dry.

Nine-fifteen, sang the clock, *time to clean.*

Out of warrens[1] in the wall, tiny robot mice darted. The rooms were acrawl with the small cleaning animals, all rubber and metal. They thudded against chairs, whirling their mustached runners, kneading the rug nap, sucking gently at hidden dust. Then, like mysterious invaders, they popped into their burrows. Their pink electric eyes faded. The house was clean.

Ten o'clock. The sun came out from behind the rain. The house stood alone in a city of rubble and ashes. This was the one house left standing. At night the ruined city gave off a radioactive glow which could be seen for miles.

Ten-fifteen. The garden sprinklers whirled up in golden founts, filling the soft morning air with scatterings of brightness. The water pelted window-panes, running down the charred west side where the house had been burned evenly free of its white paint. The entire west face of the house was black, save for five places. Here the silhouette in paint of a man mowing a lawn. Here, as in a photograph, a woman bent to pick flowers. Still farther over, their images burned on wood in one titanic instant, a small boy, hands flung into the air; higher up, the image of a thrown ball, and opposite him a girl, hands raised to catch a ball which never came down.

The five spots of paint—the man, the woman, the children, the ball— remained. The rest was a thin charcoaled layer.

The gentle sprinkler rain filled the garden with falling light.

Until this day, how well the house had kept its peace. How carefully it had inquired, "Who goes there? What's the password?" and, getting no answer from lonely foxes and whining cats, it had shut up its windows and drawn shades in an old-maidenly preoccupation with self-protection which bordered on a mechanical paranoia.

It quivered at each sound, the house did. If a sparrow brushed a window, the shade snapped up. The bird, startled, flew off! No, not even a bird must touch the house!

[1] warrens: crowded dwellings, narrow corridors.

The house was an altar with ten thousand attendants, big, small, servicing, attending, in choirs. But the gods had gone away, and the ritual of the religion continued senselessly, uselessly.

Twelve noon.

A dog whined, shivering, on the front porch.

The front door recognized the dog voice and opened. The dog, once huge and fleshy, but now gone to bone and covered with sores, moved in and through the house, tracking mud. Behind it whirred angry mice, angry at having to pick up mud, angry at inconvenience.

For not a leaf fragment blew under the door but what the wall panels flipped open and the copper scrap rats flashed swiftly out. The offending dust, hair, or paper, seized in miniature steel jaws, was raced back to the burrows. There, down tubes which fed into the cellar, it was dropped into the sighing vent of an incinerator which sat like evil Baal[2] in a dark corner.

The dog ran upstairs, hysterically yelping to each door, at last realizing, as the house realized, that only silence was here.

It sniffed the air and scratched the kitchen door. Behind the door, the stove was making pancakes which filled the house with a rich baked odor and the scent of maple syrup.

The dog frothed at the mouth, lying at the door, sniffing, its eyes turned to fire. It ran wildly in circles, biting at its tail, spun in a frenzy, and died. It lay in the parlor for an hour.

Two o'clock, sang a voice.

Delicately sensing decay at last, the regiments of mice hummed out as softly as blown gray leaves in an electrical wind.

Two-fifteen.

The dog was gone.

In the cellar, the incinerator glowed suddenly and a whirl of sparks leaped up the chimney.

Two thirty-five.

Bridge tables sprouted from patio walls. Playing cards fluttered onto pads in a shower of pips. Martinis manifested on an oaken bench with egg-salad sandwiches. Music played.

But the tables were silent and the cards untouched.

At four o'clock the tables folded like great butterflies back through the paneled walls.

Four-thirty.

The nursery walls glowed.

Animals took shape: yellow giraffes, blue lions, pink antelopes, lilac panthers cavorting in crystal substance. The walls were glass. They looked out

[2] Baal: a god widely worshiped in ancient times, regarded by the Old Testament writers as false and evil.

upon color and fantasy. Hidden films clocked through well-oiled sprockets, and the walls lived. The nursery floor was woven to resemble a crisp, cereal meadow. Over this ran aluminum roaches and iron crickets, and in the hot still air butterflies of delicate red tissue wavered among the sharp aroma of animal spoors![3] There was the sound like a great matted yellow hive of bees within a dark bellows, the lazy bumble of a purring lion. And there was the patter of okapi[4] feet and the murmur of a fresh jungle rain, like other hoofs, falling upon the summer-starched grass. Now the walls dissolved into distances of parched weed, mile on mile, and warm endless sky. The animals drew away into thorn brakes and water holes.

It was the children's hour.

Five o'clock. The bath filled with clear hot water.

Six, seven, eight o'clock. The dinner dishes manipulated like magic tricks, and in the study a *click.* In the metal stand opposite the hearth where a fire now blazed up warmly, a cigar popped out, half an inch of soft gray ash on it, smoking, waiting.

Nine o'clock. The beds warmed their hidden circuits, for nights were cool here.

Nine-five. A voice spoke from the study ceiling:

"Mrs. McClellan, which poem would you like this evening?"

The house was silent.

The voice said at last, "Since you express no preference, I shall select a poem at random." Quiet music rose to back the voice. "Sara Teasdale. As I recall, your favorite. . . .

> *"There will come soft rains and the smell of the ground,*
> *And swallows circling with their shimmering sound;*
>
> *And frogs in the pools singing at night,*
> *And wild plum-trees in tremulous white;*
>
> *Robins will wear their feathery fire*
> *Whistling their whims on a low fence-wire;*
>
> *And not one will know of the war, not one*
> *Will care at last when it is done.*
>
> *Not one would mind, either bird nor tree*
> *If mankind perished utterly;*
>
> *And Spring herself, when she woke at dawn,*
> *Would scarcely know that we were gone."* [5]

[3] spoors: droppings.

[4] okapi: an African mammal somewhat like a giraffe.

[5] " 'There Will Come Soft Rains,' " in Sara Teasdale, *Collected Poems* (New York: Macmillan, 1920).

The fire burned on the stone hearth and the cigar fell away into a mound of quiet ash on its tray. The empty chairs faced each other between the silent walls, and the music played.

At ten o'clock the house began to die.

The wind blew. A falling tree bough crashed through the kitchen window. Cleaning solvent, bottled, shattered over the stove. The room was ablaze in an instant!

"Fire!" screamed a voice. The house lights flashed, water pumps shot water from the ceilings. But the solvent spread on the linoleum, licking, eating under the kitchen door, while the voices took it up in chorus: "Fire, fire, fire!"

The house tried to save itself. Doors sprang tightly shut, but the windows were broken by the heat and the wind blew and sucked upon the fire.

The house gave ground as the fire in ten billion angry sparks moved with flaming ease from room to room and then up the stairs. While scurrying water rats squeaked from the walls, pistoled their water, and ran for more. And the wall sprays let down showers of mechanical rain.

But too late. Somewhere, sighing, a pump shrugged to a stop. The quenching rain ceased. The reserve water supply which had filled baths and washed dishes for many quiet days was gone.

The fire crackled up the stairs. It fed upon Picassos and Matisses[6] in the upper halls, like delicacies, baking off the oily flesh, tenderly crisping the canvases into black shavings.

Now the fire lay in beds, stood in windows, changed the colors of drapes!

And then, reinforcements.

From attic trapdoors, blind robot faces peered down with faucet mouths gushing green chemical.

The fire backed off, as even an elephant must at the sight of a dead snake. Now there were twenty snakes whipping over the floor, killing the fire with a clear cold venom of green froth.

But the fire was clever. It had sent flame outside the house, up through the attic to the pumps there. An explosion! The attic brain which directed the pumps was shattered into bronze shrapnel on the beams.

The fire rushed back into every closet and felt of the clothes hung there.

The house shuddered, oak bone on bone, its bared skeleton cringing from the heat, its wire, its nerves revealed as if a surgeon had torn the skin off to let the red veins and capillaries quiver in the scalded air. Help, help! Fire! Run, run! Heat snapped mirrors like the first brittle winter ice. And the voices wailed Fire, fire, run, run, like a tragic nursery rhyme, a dozen voices, high, low, like children dying in a forest, alone, alone. And the voices fading

---

[6] Picassos and Matisses: paintings by Pablo Picasso (1881–1973) and Henri Matisse (1869–1954), important European artists.

as the wires popped their sheathings like hot chestnuts. One, two, three, four, five voices died.

In the nursery the jungle burned. Blue lions roared, purple giraffes bounded off. The panthers ran in circles, changing color, and ten million animals, running before the fire, vanished off toward a distant steaming river. . . .

Ten more voices died. In the last instant under the fire avalanche, other choruses, oblivious, could be heard announcing the time, playing music, cutting the lawn by remote-control mower, or setting an umbrella frantically out and in the slamming and opening front door, a thousand things happening, like a clock shop when each clock strikes the hour insanely before or after the other, a scene of maniac confusion, yet unity; singing, screaming, a few last cleaning mice darting bravely out to carry the horrid ashes away! And one voice, with sublime disregard for the situation, read poetry aloud in the fiery study, until all the film spools burned, until all the wires withered and the circuits cracked.

The fire burst the house and let it slam flat down, puffing out skirts of spark and smoke.

In the kitchen, an instant before the rain of fire and timber, the stove could be seen making breakfasts at a psychopathic rate, ten dozen eggs, six loaves of toast, twenty dozen bacon strips, which, eaten by fire, started the stove working again, hysterically hissing!

The crash. The attic smashing into kitchen and parlor. The parlor into cellar, cellar into sub-cellar. Deep freeze, armchair, film tapes, circuits, beds, and all like skeletons thrown in a cluttered mound deep under.

Smoke and silence. A great quantity of smoke.

Dawn showed faintly in the east. Among the ruins, one wall stood alone. Within the wall, a last voice said, over and over again and again, even as the sun rose to shine upon the heaped rubble and steam:

"Today is August 5, 2026, today is August 5, 2026, today is . . ."

Fedor Sologub (1863–1927)

THE WHITE DOG

Maria Ivanovna had been working several years as pattern-maker in a ladies-tailoring establishment, where she had started as apprentice at an early age.

In the course of time she had become utterly weary of everything pertaining to her work, the patterns, the noise of the sewing-machines, the caprices of customers. . . . She was very irritable, and found fault with everybody. For the apprentices there was no respite from her scolding.

Now it was Tanyichka, the youngest of the working-girls, till recently an apprentice. Tanya did not answer, at first. Then in a gentle, placid voice that made everyone but Maria laugh, she said: "You are a perfect dog, Maria Ivanovna." The older girl, feeling shamefully affronted, exclaimed: "You're a dog yourself!"

Tanya kept on sewing. From time to time she stopped, and repeated calmly, "Yes, you are a dog; you're always barking; you have the muzzle of a dog, and the ears of a dog. Madam will chase you soon, you're such a mad cur, such a low beast."

Tanyichka was a plump, rosy, dainty miss, with a sweet innocent little face, in which cruel cunning was scarcely visible. She looked very naïve, and dressed like a simple apprentice. Her eyes shone bright from under her eyebrows, which arched prettily over her broad white forehead. Her dark chestnut hair was combed flat and smooth, and parted in the middle. Her voice was clear, sweet, seductive. From the distance one would have thought she was saying the most amiable things to Maria Ivanovna.

While the working-girls laughed, the apprentices only ventured to giggle, covering their mouths with their black aprons, and casting apprehensive glances at Maria, who was red with rage.

"You nasty little wretch!" she screamed, "I'll scratch your eyes out!"

Tanya in her bland voice replied: "Your paws aren't long enough. If you keep on barking and snapping, we'll have to muzzle you."

Maria was about to throw herself on the girl, when the mistress of the establishment, a large stout woman, entered, her skirts a-swish.

"Maria Ivanovna!" she exclaimed severely, "what is all this scandalous tumult about?"

"Will you permit her to call me a dog?" Maria answered in a voice trembling with anger.

"For no reason at all she started to yell at me," began Tanya plaintively; "she is forever scolding, no matter what I do."

The mistress looked at her harshly, and said: "Tanyichka, I know you. Do you mean to tell me you didn't begin it? Don't imagine that because you're a master-worker now you can run things here. If you don't put a stop to this fussing I'll tell your mother . . . she'll attend to you!"

Tanya flushed with vexation, but tried to preserve her air of gentle innocence. With perfect self-restraint she answered: "Forgive me, Erinna Petrovna; I'll never do it again. I always try not to provoke her, but she is so harsh. For the least little thing she is ready to pull my hair. I'm just as good a worker as she is. I'm not an errand-girl any more."

"Oh, getting quite important, I see," said the mistress ironically, approaching the girl. Two resounding slaps, accompanied by two exclamations of "Oh! Oh!" from Tanya, broke through the stillness of the room.

Almost sick with anger Maria wended her way homeward. Tanya had touched a very sore spot.

"So I'm a dog," she reflected. "Well, and if I am, is that any of her damned business? Do I study her to see whether she's a snake, or a fox, or anything? Do I sneak after her, and spy around, to see what sort of beast she is? To me she's Tatanya, that's all. There's plenty to be found wrong with everybody; a dog isn't the worst. . . .

It was a bright summer night. A cool, languid breeze stole across from the neighbouring fields to the peaceful streets of the town. The moon rose clear and full; such a moon as shines on wild desert-steppes whose inhabitants, their spirits oppressed with troubled memories of primeval days, howl and moan under its livid light. . . .

And with such a strangely troubled spirit, forgetful of her actual self, tortured with elemental longings, Maria choked back a savage cry that was struggling for utterance in her throat.

She began to undress, but stopped suddenly. What was the use? She knew well she would be unable to sleep.

She walked out of the room. In the corridor she felt the warm loose boards shaking and creaking, while little splinters and grains of sands tickled the soles of her feet.

On the piazza sat Granny Stepanita, a dark withered wrinkled little old woman. She was stooping forward, as if to bask in the light of the moon. Maria sat down on the steps near her, looking up at her sideways. She observed that the old woman's nose was long and curved, like the beak of a bird.

"An old crow," thought Maria, and smiled at the idea, while her eyes lighted up, and her heart felt less oppressed. The furrows of her wilted face vanished in the pale-green moonlight; she became young, nimble, merry, again, as in her girlhood days . . . before the moon's baleful power made her howl and moan at night under the windows of the bath-house. . . .

She moved closer to the old woman, and said gently:

"Granny Stepanita, I've been wanting to ask you a question for a long time."

The old woman turned toward Maria Ivanovna, and in a sharp, craving voice croaked: "Well, my pretty one, ask."

Maria laughed silently. A light breeze passed over her back, and she shivered. Again, in a low voice, she spoke to the old woman. "Granny, it seems to me . . . but I know it can't be true . . . how shall I say it? . . . Don't feel offended, please . . . I mean no harm". . . .

"Well, speak, little one; what is it?"

She looked at Maria with keen, piercing eyes and waited.

"I can't help fancying that you,—you won't feel offended, Granny? . . . you look like a crow."

The old woman turned away and nodded her head silently. She seemed to be recalling something; her head with its beak-like nose kept drooping forward and nodding. Maria thought she must be dozing, nodding, and dozing, and whispering ancient, very ancient, incantations.

In the courtyard it was still; neither dark nor light. Everything seemed as if under a spell, like a vision in a dream, yet too real to be only a dream. ... Everything was permeated with a strange witchery that oppressed the soul with painful yearning. Countless odours, undistinguishable by day, became sharp and distinct, evoking vague memories of ages long past.

Scarcely audible was the murmur of Stepana. "Yes, a crow, but without wings. And though I caw and caw no misfortune befalls anyone. I have the gift of prophecy, but they don't heed me. Only, when I see someone whom fate has doomed, I feel an irresistible desire to croak and caw". . . . She suddenly spread out her arms, and in a raucous voice screeched "Caw! Caw!"

Maria shivered.

"Granny, for whom are you cawing?" she asked.

"For you, my pretty one," she answered; "for you."

An uncanny fear settled on Maria, sitting there with the old woman.

She got up and returned to her room.

Then she sat down near the window and listened. Two voices were audible from beyond the courtyard.

"She barks and barks," muttered a harsh bass-voice.

"Did you see her, uncle?" rejoined a sweet tenor.

Maria thought it must be the blonde, freckled, curly-haired young fellow who lives in the same house.

There was a pause. But presently the harsh bass again blurted out.

"Sure I saw her; a large white dog, near the bath-house, baying at the moon."

To Maria it sounded like the voice of a black-bearded, low-browed, pig-eyed, heavy-legged fellow.

"What does she bark for?" asked the sweet-voiced tenor.

"Not for any good that I can see," blurted out the other; "and where she comes from I don't know either."

"But what if she's a soul from Purgatory?" the younger one asked.

"You must never turn back," the older one said.

Maria didn't quite understand what he meant, but she listened no further. Human speech mattered little to her now. For the moon showered its light full on her face, calling to her cruelly, irresistibly, with its every beam. Her yearning became so oppressively painful that she could remain seated no longer. She got up and undressed quickly. White, stark-naked, she walked into the corridor and opened the door.

No one was about. She hurried across the courtyard, then through the garden, till she reached the bath-house. The sharp tingle of the cold night-air and the chill ground under her feet quickened her blood.

She lay down in the grass on her belly, raised herself on her elbows, and turned her face toward the pallid moon. Then she uttered a prolonged moaning howl.

"Listen, uncle! do you hear her baying?" exclaimed the fair-haired one, shivering with fear.

"Howling again, damn her!" muttered the harsh bass.

Both rose from the bench where they had been sitting, and walked through the courtyard and garden toward the bath-house. The black-bearded fellow, armed with a rifle, led the way. The other followed timorously, looking back over his shoulder ever and anon.

Near the bath-house a white dog-like form lay cowering, baying at the moon. Her black-crested head was tilted full toward the moon's witching light. Her hind-paws were drawn under her, while her forepaws rested lightly on the ground.

In the fantastic pale-green moon-glow the dog looked enormous, monstrous, unearthly. The black shock of hair on the crown of her head wound sinuously down her back in an unbraided coil. Her tail was invisible, covered by her limbs, no doubt. From the distance her body looked curiously naked, dimly reflecting the livid moonlight. One could almost fancy it was a woman lying there, moaning and howling. The black-bearded fellow took aim; his companion crossed himself and murmured indistinctly.

There was a loud report. The dog sprang up on her hind paws, howling fearfully, and darted forward, the blood streaming over her naked body. . . . Not a dog but a woman. . . .

The two men, wild with terror, threw themselves on the ground, and began to howl. . . .

Mary Hunter Austin (1868–1934)

PAPAGO WEDDING

There was a Papago[1] woman out of Pantak who had a marriage paper from a white man after she had borne him five children, and the man himself was in love with another woman. This Shuler was the first to raise cotton for selling in the Gila Valley—but the Pimas and Papagoes had raised it long before that—and the girl went with him willingly. As to the writing of marriage, it was not then understood that the white man is not master of his heart, but is mastered by it, so that if it is not fixed in writing it becomes unstable like water and is puddled in the lowest place. The Sisters at San Xavier del Bac had taught her to clean and cook. Shuler called her Susie, which was nearest to her Papago name, and was fond of the children. He sent them to school as they came along, and had carpets in the house.

In all things Susie was a good wife to him, though she had no writing of marriage and she never wore a hat. This was a mistake which she learned from the sisters. They, being holy women, had no notion of the brujeria[2] which is worked in the heart of the white man by a hat. Into the presence

1 Papago: Indian tribe of the southwestern United States and northern Mexico.
2 brujeria: witchcraft, magic.

of their God also, without that which passes for a hat, they do not go. Even after her children were old enough to notice it, Susie went about the country with a handkerchief tied over her hair, which was long and smooth on either side of her face, like the shut wings of a raven.

By the time Susie's children were as tall as their mother, there were many white ranchers in the Gila country, with their white wives, who are like Papago women in this, that if they see a man upstanding and prosperous, they think only that he might make some woman happy, and if they have a cousin or a friend, that she should be the woman. Also the white ones think it so shameful for a man to take a woman to his house without a writing that they have no scruple to take him away from her. At Rinconada there was a woman with large breasts, surpassing well looking, and with many hats. She had no husband and was new to the country, and when Shuler drove her about to look at it, she wore each time a different hat.

This the Papagoes observed, and, not having visited Susie when she was happy with her man, they went now in numbers, and by this Susie understood that it was in their hearts that she might have need of them. For it was well known that the white woman had told Shuler that it was a shame for him to have his children going about with a Papago woman who had only a handkerchief to cover her head. She said it was keeping Shuler back from being the principal man among the cotton growers of Gila Valley, to have in his house a woman who would come there without a writing. And when the other white women heard that she had said that, they said the same thing. Shuler said, "My God, this is the truth, I know it," and the woman said that she would go to Susie and tell her that she ought to go back to her own people and not be a shame to her children and Shuler. There was a man from Pantak on the road, who saw them go, and turned in his tracks and went back, in case Susie should need him, for the Papagoes, when it is their kin against whom there is brujeria made, have in-knowing hearts. Susie sat in the best room with the woman and was polite. "If you want Shuler," she said, "you can have him, but I stay with my children." The white woman grew red in the face and went out to Shuler in the field where he was pretending to look after something, and they went away together.

After that Shuler would not go to the ranch except of necessity. He went around talking to his white friends. "My God," he kept saying, "what can I do, with my children in the hands of that Papago?" Then he sent a lawyer to Susie to say that if she would go away and not shame his children with a mother who had no marriage writing and no hat, he would give her money, so much every month. But the children all came in the room and stood by her, and Susie said, "What I want with money when I got my children and this good ranch?" Then Shuler said "My God!" again, and "What can I do?"

The lawyer said he could tell the Judge that Susie was not a proper person to have care of his children, and the Judge would take them away from Susie and give them to Shuler. But when the day came for Susie to come into court, it was seen that though she had a handkerchief on her hair, her dress was good, and the fringe of her shawl was long and fine. All the five children came also, with new clothes, well looking. "My God!" said Shuler, "I must get those kids away from that Papago and into the hands of a white woman." But the white people who had come to see the children taken away saw that although the five looked like Shuler, they had their mouths shut like Papagoes; so they waited to see how things turned out.

Shuler's lawyer makes a long speech about how Shuler loves his children, and how sorry he is in his heart to see them growing up like Papagoes, and water is coming out of Shuler's eyes. Then the Judge asks Susie if she has anything to say why her children shall not be taken away.

"You want to take these children away and giff them to Shuler?" Susie asks him. "What for you giff them to Shuler?" says Susie, and the white people are listening. She says, "Shuler's not the father of them. Thees children all got different fathers," says Susie. "Shuler—"

Then she makes a sign with her hand. I tell you if a woman makes that sign to a Papago he could laugh himself dead but he would not laugh off that. Some of the white people who have been in the country a long time know that sign and they begin to laugh.

Shuler's lawyer jumps up. . . . "Your Honour, I object——"

The Judge waves his hand. "I warn you the Court cannot go behind the testimony of the mother in such a case. . . ."

By this time everybody is laughing, so that they do not hear what the lawyer says. Shuler is trying to get out of the side door, and the Judge is shaking hands with Susie.

"You tell Shuler," she says, "if he wants people to think hees the father of thees children he better giff me a writing. Then maybe I think so myself."

"I will," said the Judge, and maybe two, three days after that he takes Shuler out to the ranch and makes the marriage writing. Then all the children come around Susie and say, "Now, Mother, you will have to wear a hat." Susie, she says, "Go, children, and ask your father." But it is not known to the Papagoes what happened after that.

Arna Bontemps (1902–1973)

A SUMMER TRAGEDY

Old Jeff Patton, the black share farmer, fumbled with his bow tie. His fingers trembled and the high, stiff collar pinched his throat. A fellow loses his hand for such vanities after thirty or forty years of simple life. Once a year, or maybe twice if there's a wedding among his kinfolks, he may spruce up, but generally fancy clothes do nothing but adorn the wall of the big room and feed the moths. That had been Jeff Patton's experience. He had not worn his stiff-bosomed shirt more than a dozen times in all his married life. His swallow-tailed coat lay on the bed beside him, freshly brushed and pressed, but it was as full of holes as the overalls in which he worked on weekdays. The moths had used it badly. Jeff twisted his mouth into a hideous toothless grimace as he contended with the obstinate bow. He stamped his good foot and decided to give up the struggle.

"Jennie," he called.

"What's that, Jeff?" His wife's shrunken voice came out of the adjoining room like an echo. It was hardly bigger than a whisper.

"I reckon you'll have to he'p me wid this heah bow tie, baby," he said meekly. "Dog if I can hitch it up."

Her answer was not strong enough to reach him, but presently the old woman came to the door, feeling her way with a stick. She had a wasted, dead-leaf appearance. Her body, as scrawny and gnarled as a string bean, seemed less than nothing in the ocean of frayed and faded petticoats that surrounded her. These hung an inch or two above the tops of her heavy unlaced shoes and showed little grotesque piles where the stockings had fallen down from her negligible legs.

"You oughta could do a heap mo' wid a thing like that'n me—beingst as you got yo' good sight."

"Looks like I oughta could," he admitted. "But my fingers is gone democrat on me. I get all mixed up in the looking glass an' can't tell wicha way to twist the devilish thing."

Jennie sat on the side of the bed, and old Jeff Patton got down on one knee while she tied the bow knot. It was a slow and painful ordeal for each of them in this position. Jeff's bones cracked, his knee ached, and it was only after a half dozen attempts that Jennie worked a semblance of a bow into the tie.

"I got to dress maself now," the old woman whispered. "These is ma old shoes an' stockings, and I ain't so much as unwrapped ma dress."

"Well, don't worry 'bout me no mo', baby," Jeff said. "That 'bout finishes me. All I gotta do now is slip on that old coat 'n ves' an' I'll be fixed to leave."

Jennie disappeared again through the dim passage into the shed room. Being blind was no handicap to her in that black hole. Jeff heard the cane placed against the wall beside the door and knew that his wife was on easy ground. He put on his coat, took a battered top hat from the bed post, and hobbled to the front door. He was ready to travel. As soon as Jennie could get on her Sunday shoes and her old black silk dress, they would start.

Outside the tiny log house, the day was warm and mellow with sunshine. A host of wasps were humming with busy excitement in the trunk of a dead sycamore. Gray squirrels were searching through the grass for hickory nuts, and blue jays were in the trees, hopping from branch to branch. Pine woods stretched away to the left like a black sea. Among them were scattered scores of log houses like Jeff's, houses of black share farmers. Cows and pigs wandered freely among the trees. There was no danger of loss. Each farmer knew his own stock and knew his neighbor's as well as he knew his neighbor's children.

Down the slope to the right were the cultivated acres on which the colored folks worked. They extended to the river, more than two miles away, and they were today green with the unmade cotton crop. A tiny thread of a road, which passed directly in front of Jeff's place, ran through these green fields like a pencil mark.

Jeff, standing outside the door, with his absurd hat in his left hand, surveyed the wide scene tenderly. He had been forty-five years on these acres. He loved them with the unexplained affection that others have for the countries to which they belong.

The sun was hot on his head, his collar still pinched his throat, and the Sunday clothes were intolerably hot. Jeff transferred the hat to his right hand and began fanning with it. Suddenly the whisper that was Jennie's voice came out of the shed room.

"You can bring the car round front whilst you's waitin'," it said feebly. There was a tired pause; then it added, "I'll soon be fixed to go."

"A'right, baby," Jeff answered. "I'll get it in a minute."

But he didn't move. A thought struck him that made his mouth fall open. The mention of the car brought to his mind with new intensity, the trip he and Jennie were about to take. Fear came into his eyes; excitement took his breath. Lord, Jesus!

"Jeff. . . . O Jeff," the old woman's whisper called.

He awakened with a jolt. "Hunh, baby?"

"What you doin'?"

"Nuthin. Jes studyin'. I jes been turnin' things round 'n round in ma mind."

"You could be gettin' the car," she said.

"Oh yes, right away, baby."

He started round to the shed, limping heavily on his bad leg. There were three frizzly chickens in the yard. All his other chickens had been killed or stolen recently. But the frizzly chickens had been saved somehow. That was fortunate indeed, for these curious creatures had a way of devouring "poison" from the yard and in that way protecting against conjure[1] and black luck and spells. But even the frizzly chickens seemed now to be in a stupor. Jeff thought they had some ailment; he expected all three of them to die shortly.

The shed in which the old T-model Ford stood was only a grass roof held up by four corner poles. It had been built by tremulous hands at a time

---

[1] conjure: magic.

when the little rattletrap car had been regarded as a peculiar treasure. And, miraculously, despite wind and downpour, it still stood.

Jeff adjusted the crank and put his weight upon it. The engine came to life with a sputter and bang that rattled the old car from radiator to tail light. Jeff hopped into the seat and put his foot on the accelerator. The sputtering and banging increased. The rattling became more violent. That was good. It was good banging, good sputtering and rattling, and it meant that the aged car was still in running condition. She could be depended on for this trip.

Again Jeff's thought halted as if paralyzed. The suggestion of the trip fell into the machinery of his mind like a wrench. He felt dazed and weak. He swung the car out into the yard, made a half turn, and drove around to the front door. When he took his hands off the wheel, he noticed that he was trembling violently. He cut off the motor and climbed to the ground to wait for Jennie.

A few minutes later she was at the window, her voice rattling against the pane like a broken shutter.

"I'm ready, Jeff."

He did not answer, but limped into the house and took her by the arm. He led her slowly through the big room, down the step, and across the yard.

"You reckon I'd oughta lock the do'?" he asked softly.

They stopped and Jennie weighed the question. Finally she shook her head.

"Ne' mind the door," she said. "I don't see no cause to lock up things."

"You right," Jeff agreed. "No cause to lock up."

Jeff opened the door and helped his wife into the car. A quick shudder passed over him. Jesus! Again he trembled.

"How come you shaking so?" Jennie whispered.

"I don't know," he said.

"You mus' be scairt, Jeff."

"No, baby, I ain't scairt."

He slammed the door after her and went around to crank up again. The motor started easily. Jeff wished that it had not been so responsive. He would have liked a few more minutes in which to turn things around in his head. As it was, with Jennie chiding him about being afraid, he had to keep going. He swung the car into the little pencil-mark road and started off toward the river, driving very slowly, very cautiously.

Chugging across the green countryside, the small battered Ford seemed tiny indeed. Jeff felt a familiar excitement, a thrill, as they came down the first slope to the immense levels on which the cotton was growing. He could not help reflecting that the crops were good. He knew what that meant, too; he had made forty-five of them with his own hands. It was true that he had worn out nearly a dozen mules, but that was the fault of old man Stevenson, the owner of the land. Major Stevenson had the old notion that one mule was all a share farmer needed to work a thirty-acre plot. It was an expensive notion, the way it killed mules from overwork but the old man held to it. Jeff thought it killed a good many share farmers as well as mules, but he had no sympathy for them. He had always been strong, and he had been taught to have no patience with weakness in men. Women or children might be tolerated if they were puny, but a weak man was a curse. Of course, his own children—

Jeff's thought halted there. He and Jennie never mentioned their dead children any more. And naturally, he did not wish to dwell upon them in his mind. Before he knew it, some remark would slip out of his mouth and that would make Jennie feel blue. Perhaps she would cry. A woman like Jennie could not easily throw off the grief that comes from losing five grown children within two years. Even Jeff was still staggered by the blow. His memory had not been much good recently. He frequently talked to himself. And, although he had kept it a secret, he knew that his courage had left him. He was terrified by the least unfamiliar sound at night. He was reluctant to venture far from home in the daytime. And that habit of trembling when he felt fearful was now far beyond his control. Sometimes he became afraid and trembled without knowing what had frightened him. The feeling would just come over him like a chill.

The car rattled slowly over the dusty road. Jennie sat erect and silent with a little absurd hat pinned to her hair. Her useless eyes seemed very large, very white in their deep sockets. Suddenly Jeff heard her voice, and he inclined his head to catch the words.

"Is we passed Delia Moore's house yet?" she asked.

"Not yet," he said.

"You must be drivin' mighty slow, Jeff."

"We just as well take our time, baby."

There was a pause. A little puff of steam was coming out of the radiator of the car. Heat wavered above the hood. Delia Moore's house was nearly half a mile away. After a moment Jennie spoke again.

"You ain't really scairt, is you, Jeff?"

"Nah, baby, I ain't scairt."

"You know how we agreed—we gotta keep on goin'."

Jewels of perspiration appeared on Jeff's forehead. His eyes rounded, blinked, became fixed on the road.

"I don't know," he said with a shiver, "I reckon it's the only thing to do."

"Hm."

A flock of guinea fowls, pecking in the road, were scattered by the passing car. Some of them took to their wings; others hid under bushes. A blue jay, swaying on a leafy twig, was annoying a roadside squirrel. Jeff held an even speed till he came near Delia's place. Then he slowed down noticeably.

Delia's house was really no house at all, but an abandoned store building converted into a dwelling. It sat near a crossroads, beneath a single black cedar tree. There Delia, a cattish old creature of Jennie's age, lived alone. She had been there more years than anybody could remember, and long ago had won the disfavor of such women as Jennie. For in her young days Delia had been gayer, yellower,[2] and saucier than seemed proper in those parts. Her ways with menfolks had been dark and suspicious. And the fact that she had had as many husbands as children did not help her reputation.

"Yonder's old Delia," Jeff said as they passed.

"What she doin'?"

"Jes sittin' in the do'," he said.

"She see us?"

"Hm," Jeff said. "Musta did."

That relieved Jennie. It strengthened her to know that her old enemy had seen her pass in her best clothes. That would give the old she-devil something to chew her gums and fret about, Jennie thought. Wouldn't she have a fit if she didn't find out? Old evil Delia! This would be just the thing for her. It would pay her back for being so evil. It would also pay her, Jennie thought, for the way she used to grin at Jeff—long ago, when her teeth were good.

The road became smooth and red, and Jeff could tell by the smell of the air that they were nearing the river. He could see the rise where the road turned and ran along parallel to the stream. The car chugged on monotonously. After a long silent spell, Jennie leaned against Jeff and spoke.

"How many bale o' cotton you think we got standin'?" she said.

Jeff wrinkled his forehead as he calculated.

" 'Bout twenty-five, I reckon."

"How many you make las' year?"

"Twenty-eight," he said. "How come you ask that?"

"I's jes thinkin'," Jennie said quietly.

"It don't make a speck o' difference though," Jeff reflected. "If we get much or if we get little, we still gonna be in debt to old man Stevenson when he gets through counting up agin us. It's took us a long time to learn that."

Jennie was not listening to these words. She had fallen into a trancelike meditation. Her lips twitched. She chewed her gums and rubbed her gnarled hands nervously. Suddenly, she leaned forward, buried her face in the nervous hands, and burst into tears. She cried aloud in a dry, cracked voice that suggested the rattle of fodder on dead stalks. She cried aloud like a child, for she had never learned to suppress a genuine sob. Her slight old frame shook heavily and seemed hardly able to sustain such violent grief.

"What's the matter, baby?" Jeff asked awkwardly. "Why you cryin' like all that?"

"I's jes thinkin'," she said.

---

[2] yellower: lighter-skinned, considered to be more attractive, more provocative.

"So you the one what's scairt now, hunh?"

"I ain't scairt, Jeff. I's jes thinkin' 'bout leavin' eve'thing like this—eve'thing we been used to. It's right sad-like."

Jeff did not answer, and presently Jennie buried her face again and cried.

The sun was almost overhead. It beat down furiously on the dusty wagon-path road, on the parched roadside grass and the tiny battered car. Jeff's hands, gripping the wheel, became wet with perspiration; his forehead sparkled. Jeff's lips parted. His mouth shaped a hideous grimace. His face suggested the face of a man being burned. But the torture passed and his expression softened again.

"You mustn't cry, baby," he said to his wife. "We gotta be strong. We can't break down."

Jennie waited a few seconds, then said, "You reckon we oughta do it, Jeff? You reckon we oughta go 'head an' do it, really?"

Jeff's voice choked; his eyes blurred. He was terrified to hear Jennie say the thing that had been in his mind all morning. She had egged him on when he had wanted more than anything in the world to wait, to reconsider, to think things over a little longer. Now she was getting cold feet. Actually, there was no need of thinking the question through again. It would only end in making the same painful decision once more. Jeff knew that. There was no need of fooling around longer.

"We jes as well to do like we planned," he said. "They ain't nothin' else for us now—it's the bes' thing."

Jeff thought of the handicaps, the near impossibility, of making another crop with his leg bothering him more and more each week. Then there was always the chance that he would have another stroke, like the one that had made him lame. Another one might kill him. The least it could do would be to leave him helpless. Jeff gasped—Lord Jesus! He could not bear to think of being helpless, like a baby, on Jennie's hands. Frail, blind Jennie.

The little pounding motor of the car worked harder and harder. The puff of steam from the cracked radiator became larger. Jeff realized that they were climbing a little rise. A moment later the road turned abruptly, and he looked down upon the face of the river.

"Jeff."

"Hunh?"

"Is that the water I hear?"

"Hm. Tha's it."

"Well, which way you goin' now?"

"Down this-a way," he said. "The road runs 'long 'side o' the water a lil piece."

She waited a while calmly. Then she said, "Drive faster."

"A'right, baby," Jeff said.

The water roared in the bed of the river. It was fifty or sixty feet below the level of the road. Between the road and the water there was a long smooth slope, sharply inclined. The slope was dry, the clay hardened by prolonged summer heat. The water below, roaring in a narrow channel, was noisy and wild.

"Jeff."

"Hunh?"

"How far you goin'?"

"Jes a lil piece down the road."

"You ain't scairt, is you, Jeff?"

"Nah, baby," he said trembling. "I ain't scairt."

"Remember how we planned it, Jeff. We gotta do it like we said. Brave-like."

"Hm."

Jeff's brain darkened. Things suddenly seemed unreal, like figures in a dream. Thoughts swam in his mind foolishly, hysterically, like little blind fish in a pool within a dense cave. They rushed again. Jeff soon became dizzy. He shuddered violently and turned to his wife.

"Jennie, I can't do it. I can't." His voice broke pitifully.

She did not appear to be listening. All the grief had gone from her face. She sat erect, her unseeing eyes wide open, strained and frightful. Her glossy black skin had become dull. She seemed as thin, as sharp and bony, as a starved bird. Now, having suffered and endured the sadness of tearing herself away from beloved things, she showed no anguish. She was absorbed with her own thoughts, and she didn't even hear Jeff's voice shouting in her ear.

Jeff said nothing more. For an instant there was light in his cavernous brain. The great chamber was, for less than a second, peopled by characters he knew and loved. They were simple, healthy creatures, and they behaved in a manner that he could understand. They had quality. But since he had already taken leave of them long ago, the remembrance did not break his heart again. Young Jeff Patton was among them, the Jeff Patton of fifty years ago who went down to New Orleans with a crowd of country boys to the Mardi Gras doings. The gay young crowd, boys with candy-striped shirts and rouged brown girls in noisy silks, was like a picture in his head. Yet it did not make him sad. On that very trip Slim Burns had killed Joe Beasley—the crowd had been broken up. Since then Jeff Patton's world had been the Greenbriar Plantation. If there had been other Mardi Gras carnivals, he had not heard of them. Since then there had been no time; the years had fallen on him like waves. Now he was old, worn out. Another paralytic stroke (like the one he had already suffered) would put him on his back for keeps. In that condition, with a frail blind woman to look after him, he would be worse off than if he were dead.

Suddenly Jeff's hands became steady. He actually felt brave. He slowed down the motor of the car and carefully pulled off the road. Below, the water of the stream boomed, a soft thunder in the deep channel. Jeff ran the car onto the clay slope, pointed it directly toward the stream, and put his foot heavily on the accelerator. The little car leaped furiously down the steep incline toward the water. The movement was nearly as swift and direct as a fall. The two old black folks, sitting quietly side by side, showed no excitement. In another instant the car hit the water and dropped immediately out of sight.

A little later it lodged in the mud of a shallow place. One wheel of the crushed and upturned little Ford became visible above the rushing water.

Ernest Hemingway (1899–1961)

OLD MAN AT THE BRIDGE

An old man with steel rimmed spectacles and very dusty clothes sat by the side of the road. There was a pontoon bridge across the river and carts, trucks, and men, women and children were crossing it. The mule-drawn carts staggered up the steep bank from the bridge with soldiers helping push against the spokes of the wheels. The trucks ground up and away heading out of it all and the peasants plodded along in the ankle deep dust. But the old man sat there without moving. He was too tired to go any farther.

It was my business to cross the bridge, explore the bridgehead beyond and find out to what point the enemy had advanced. I did this and returned over the bridge. There were not so many carts now and very few people on foot, but the old man was still there.

"Where do you come from?" I asked him.

"From San Carlos," he said, and smiled.

That was his native town and so it gave him pleasure to mention it and he smiled.

"I was taking care of animals," he explained.

"Oh," I said, not quite understanding.

"Yes," he said, "I stayed, you see, taking care of animals. I was the last one to leave the town of San Carlos."

He did not look like a shepherd nor a herdsman and I looked at his black dusty clothes and his gray dusty face and his steel rimmed spectacles and said, "What animals were they?"

"Various animals," he said, and shook his head. "I had to leave them."

I was watching the bridge and the African looking country of the Ebro Delta and wondering how long now it would be before we would see the enemy, and listening all the while for the first noises that would signal that ever mysterious event called contact, and the old man still sat there.

"What animals were they?" I asked.

"There were three animals altogether," he explained. "There were two goats and a cat and then there were four pairs of pigeons."

"And you had to leave them?" I asked.

"Yes. Because of the artillery. The captain told me to go because of the artillery."

"And you have no family?" I asked, watching the far end of the bridge where a few last carts were hurrying down the slope of the bank.

"No," he said, "only the animals I stated. The cat, of course, will be all right. A cat can look out for itself, but I cannot think what will become of the others."

"What politics have you?" I asked.

"I am without politics," he said. "I am seventy-six years old. I have come twelve kilometers now and I think now I can go no further."

"This is not a good place to stop," I said. "If you can make it, there are trucks up the road where it forks for Tortosa."

"I will wait a while," he said, "and then I will go. Where do the trucks go?"

"Towards Barcelona," I told him.

"I know no one in that direction," he said, "but thank you very much. Thank you again very much."

He looked at me very blankly and tiredly, then said, having to share his worry with some one, "The cat will be all right, I am sure. There is no need to be unquiet about the cat. But the others. Now what do you think about the others?"

"Why they'll probably come through it all right."

"You think so?"

"Why not," I said, watching the far bank where now there were no carts.

"But what will they do under the artillery when I was told to leave because of the artillery?"

"Did you leave the dove cage unlocked?" I asked.

"Yes."

"Then they'll fly."

"Yes, certainly they'll fly. But the others. It's better not to think about the others," he said.

"If you are rested I would go," I urged. "Get up and try to walk now."

"Thank you," he said and got to his feet, swayed from side to side and then sat down backwards in the dust.

"I was taking care of animals," he said dully, but no longer to me. "I was only taking care of animals."

There was nothing to do about him. It was Easter Sunday and the Fascists were advancing toward the Ebro. It was a gray overcast day with a low ceiling so their planes were not up. That and the fact that cats know how to look after themselves was all the good luck that old man would ever have.

READING SELECTIONS: POEMS

Edwin Arlington Robinson (1869–1935)

MR. FLOOD'S PARTY

Old Eben Flood, climbing alone one night
Over the hill between the town below
And the forsaken upland hermitage
That held as much as he should ever know
On earth again of home, paused warily.   5
The road was his with not a native near;
And Eben, having leisure, said aloud,
For no man else in Tilbury Town to hear:

"Well, Mr. Flood, we have the harvest moon
Again, and we may not have many more;   10
The bird is on the wing, the poet says,
And you and I have said it here before.
Drink to the bird." He raised up to the light
The jug that he had gone so far to fill,
And answered huskily: "Well, Mr. Flood,   15
Since you propose it, I believe I will."

Alone, as if enduring to the end
A valiant armor of scarred hopes outworn,
He stood there in the middle of the road
Like Roland's ghost winding a silent horn.   20
Below him, in the town among the trees,
Where friends of other days had honored him,
A phantom salutation of the dead
Rang thinly till old Eben's eyes were dim.

Then, as a mother lays her sleeping child   25
Down tenderly, fearing it may awake,
He set the jug down slowly at his feet
With trembling care, knowing that most things break;
And only when assured that on firm earth
It stood, as the uncertain lives of men   30
Assuredly did not, he paced away,
And with his hand extended paused again:

"Well, Mr. Flood, we have not met like this
In a long time; and many a change has come
To both of us, I fear, since last it was   35

We had a drop together. Welcome home!"
Convivially returning with himself,
Again he raised the jug up to the light;
And with an acquiescent quaver said:
"Well, Mr. Flood, if you insist, I might.   40

"Only a very little, Mr. Flood—
For auld lang syne. No more, sir; that will do."
So, for the time, apparently it did,
And Eben evidently thought so too;
For soon amid the silver loneliness   45
Of night he lifted up his voice and sang,
Secure, with only two moons listening,
Until the whole harmonious landscape rang—

"For auld lang syne." The weary throat gave out,
The last word wavered, and the song was done.   50
He raised again the jug regretfully
And shook his head, and was again alone.
There was not much that was ahead of him,
And there was nothing in the town below—
Where strangers would have shut the many doors   55
That many friends had opened long ago.

11. poet: the reference is to the *Rubaiyat of Omar Khayyam*, a group of Persian quatrains translated by Edward FitzGerald, stressing the brevity of life.   20. Roland:
nephew of Charlemagne who died in a desperate battle against the Moors in Spain;
just before his death he sounded a call for help, but help came too late.   42. auld
lang syne: Scottish phrase meaning "good past times"; words contained in a sentimental
old song.

STUDY QUESTIONS

1. Describe the setting of this poem. What sort of town is Tilbury? Where
   is Eben Flood's home in relation to Tilbury? What sort of road must he
   walk on the way home?
2. What has been the past relationship between Mr. Flood and people of
   the town of Tilbury? What is the relationship now?
3. On the basis of stanza 4, state Eben Flood's philosophy of life.
4. The song "For Auld Lang Syne" is a popular favorite at New Year's gath-
   erings. Discuss its significance at Mr. Flood's party.
5. Why do "only two moons" listen to the song? Just what happens at the
   "party"? Why?

Archibald MacLeish (1892–   )

THE END OF THE WORLD

Quite unexpectedly as Vasserot
The armless ambidextrian was lighting
A match between his great and second toe
And Ralph the lion was engaged in biting
The neck of Madame Sossman while the drum   5
Pointed, and Teeny was about to cough
In waltz-time swinging Jocko by the thumb—
Quite unexpectedly the top blew off:

And there, there overhead, there, there, hung over
Those thousands of white faces, those dazed eyes,   10
There in the starless dark the poise, the hover,
There with vast wings across the canceled skies,
There in the sudden blackness the black pall
Of nothing, nothing, nothing—nothing at all.

2. ambidextrian: literally, a person with two right hands; figuratively, a very handy person, able to use both hands well.   8. top: circus tent.

STUDY QUESTIONS

1. What is taking place in this poem? Describe the opening scene (lines 1–7) as specifically as you can. What intrudes in line 8 to alter the setting? How is the scene changed following this intrusion?
2. On one level, the action takes place at a circus, with freaks, animal trainers, and clowns performing. What may the circus and its performers actually represent?
3. MacLeish calls the poem "End of the World." To what extent is the setting "a world"? How does this title relate to the meaning of the work?
4. How important is time in the poem?

Gwendolyn Brooks (1917–   )

THE CHICAGO *DEFENDER* SENDS A MAN TO LITTLE ROCK: FALL, 1957

In Little Rock the people bear
Babes, and comb and part their hair
And watch the want ads, put repair

To roof and latch. While wheat toast burns
A woman waters multiferns.   5

Time upholds or overturns
The many, tight, and small concerns.

In Little Rock the people sing
Sunday hymns like anything,
Through Sunday pomp and polishing.   10

And after testament and tunes,
Some soften Sunday afternoons
With lemon tea and Lorna Doones.

I forecast
And I believe   15
Come Christmas Little Rock will cleave
To Christmas tree and trifle, weave,
From laugh and tinsel, texture fast.

In Little Rock is baseball; Barcarolle.
That hotness in July . . . the uniformed figures raw and   20
implacable and not intellectual,
Batting the hotness or clawing the suffering dust.
The Open Air Concert, on the special twilight green . . .
When Beethoven is brutal or whispers to ladylike air.
Blanket-sitters are solemn, as Johann troubles to lean   25
To tell them what to mean . . .

There is love, too, in Little Rock. Soft women softly
Opening themselves in kindness,
Or, pitying one's blindness,
Awaiting one's pleasure   30
In Azure
Glory with anguished rose at the root . . .
To wash away old semidiscomfitures.
They reteach purple and unsullen blue.
The wispy soils go. And uncertain   35
Half-havings have they clarified to sures.

In Little Rock they know
Not answering the telephone is a way of rejecting life,
That it is our business to be bothered, is our business
To cherish bores or boredom, be polite   40

19. Barcarolle: literally, a Venetian boat song; here, baseball is treated as if it were a
kind of dance form set to traditional music.   25. Johann: Johann Sebastian Bach
(1685–1750), the German composer.

To lies and love and many-faceted fuzziness.
I scratch my head, massage the hate-I-had.
I blink across my prim and pencilled pad.
The saga I was sent for is not down.
Because there is a puzzle in this town.   45
The biggest News I do not dare
Telegraph to the Editor's chair:
"They are like people everywhere."
The angry Editor would reply
In hundred harryings of Why.   50

And true, they are hurling spittle, rock,
Garbage and fruit in Little Rock.
And I saw coiling storm a-writhe
On bright madonnas. And a scythe
Of men harassing brownish girls.   55
(The bows and barrettes in the curls
And braids declined away from joy.)

I saw a bleeding brownish boy . . .

The lariat lynch-wish I deplored.

The loveliest lynchee was our Lord.   60

STUDY QUESTIONS

1. Brooks's poem responds to a specific time, place, and incident. In 1957 eight black students were integrated into Central High School in Little Rock, Arkansas. The protest of white parents and students became a riot in which three reporters and many black students and adults were beaten. Why does the speaker in the poem, a reporter for a Chicago newspaper, begin with the broad description of Little Rock given in the first eight stanzas? How does that purpose relate specifically to the fall of 1957?

2. What is the tone in the first eight stanzas? Support your answer by quoting phrases that reveal that tone. What does the tone suggest is the speaker's attitude toward Little Rock?

3. Note that the speaker refers to colors frequently. For example, color is implied in "wheat toast" and directly stated in "purple and unsullen blue." Find other examples. What is the purpose of these references? How do they relate to the setting?

4. In stanza 8, the narrator explains the problem of reporting the news to a faraway editor: "there is a puzzle in this town." How do the following stanzas explain that puzzle?

5. Is there a difference in language before and after stanza 8? Compare, for instance, the following words in stanza 9 with words in earlier stanzas:

"I saw coiling storm a-writhe / On bright madonnas." What action does
that sentence describe?

6. What is the cultural environment in Little Rock? Quote phrases that describe it. How does the cultural environment relate to the specific time in
the poem?

7. Review the introduction to this chapter, specifically "The Uses of Setting." What is the major use of setting in this poem?

Robert Frost (1874–1963)

THE WOOD-PILE

Out walking in the frozen swamp one gray day,
I paused and said, "I will turn back from here.
No, I will go on farther—and we shall see."
The hard snow held me, save where now and then
One foot went through. The view was all in lines   5
Straight up and down of tall slim trees
Too much alike to mark or name a place by
So as to say for certain I was here
Or somewhere else: I was just far from home.
A small bird flew before me. He was careful   10
To put a tree between us when he lighted,
And say no word to tell me who he was
Who was so foolish as to think what *he* thought.
He thought that I was after him for a feather—
The white one in his tail; like one who takes   15
Everything said as personal to himself.
One flight out sideways would have undeceived him.
And then there was a pile of wood for which
I forgot him and let his little fear
Carry him off the way I might have gone,   20
Without so much as wishing him good-night.
He went behind it to make his last stand.
It was a cord of maple, cut and split
And piled—and measured, four by four by eight.
And not another like it could I see.   25
No runner tracks in this year's snow looped near it.
And it was older sure than this year's cutting,
Or even last year's or the year's before.
The wood was gray and the bark warping off it
And the pile somewhat sunken. Clematis   30
Had wound strings round and round it like a bundle.
What held it, though, on one side was a tree

Still growing, and on one a stake and prop,
These latter about to fall. I thought that only
Someone who lived in turning to fresh tasks   35
Could so forget his handiwork on which
He spent himself, the labor of his ax,
And leave it there far from a useful fireplace
To warm the frozen swamp as best it could
With the slow smokeless burning of decay.   40

STUDY QUESTIONS

1. Describe the setting, giving as much detail about time and place as you can.
2. What elements in the setting make you aware that the poem includes a passage of time and movement in actual place?
3. At first reading, you may regard the narrator and the bird as the only life in the poem. Are there, however, other living elements present? If so, what are they?
4. Is the narrator upset by the abandonment of the pile of wood by some unknown woodcutter or not? Defend your answer.
5. How does the setting contribute to Frost's statement of meaning? Formulate a sentence that states that meaning.

Percy Bysshe Shelley (1792–1822)

OZYMANDIAS

I met a traveler from an antique land
Who said: Two vast and trunkless legs of stone
Stand in the desert . . . Near them, on the sand,
Half sunk, a shattered visage lies, whose frown,
And wrinkled lip, and sneer of cold command,   5
Tell that its sculptor well those passions read
Which yet survive, stamped on these lifeless things,
The hand that mocked them, and the heart that fed:
And on the pedestal these words appear:
"My name is Ozymandias, king of kings: 10
Look on my works, ye Mighty, and despair!"
Nothing beside remains. Round the decay
Of that colossal wreck, boundless and bare
The lone and level sands stretch far away.

Title. Ozymandias: Greek name for Ramses II, an Egyptian monarch of the thirteenth century B.C.

STUDY QUESTIONS

1. While the poem gives very little direct information about the kingdom over which Ozymandias ruled, reference books will show what Egypt was like at the time of Ramses II. Accumulate information for a detailed description.

2. In the centuries since the statue of Ozymandias was erected, much has changed. Describe the setting as it was seen by the "traveler from an antique land."

3. Why have these changes in setting taken place? What comment does the change make about the words on the pedestal of the statue?

Matthew Arnold (1822–1888)

DOVER BEACH

The sea is calm tonight,
The tide is full, the moon lies fair
Upon the straits;—on the French coast the light
Gleams and is gone; the cliffs of England stand,
Glimmering and vast, out in the tranquil bay.   5
Come to the window, sweet is the night-air!
Only, from the long line of spray
Where the sea meets the moon-blanched land,
Listen! you hear the grating roar
Of pebbles which the waves draw back, and fling.   10
At their return, up the high strand,
Begin, and cease, and then again begin,
With tremulous cadence slow, and bring
The eternal note of sadness in.

Sophocles long ago   15
Heard it on the Aegean, and it brought
Into his mind the turbid ebb and flow
Of human misery; we
Find also in the sound a thought,
Hearing it by this distant northern sea.   20

The Sea of Faith
Was once, too, at the full, and round earth's shore
Lay like the folds of a bright girdle furled.
But now I only hear
Its melancholy, long, withdrawing roar,   25
Retreating, to the breath

Of the night-wind, down the vast edges drear
And naked shingles of the world.

Ah, love, let us be true
To one another! for the world, which seems   30
To lie before us like a land of dreams,
So various, so beautiful, so new,
Hath really neither joy, nor love, nor light,
Nor certitude, nor peace, nor help for pain;
And we are here as on a darkling plain   35
Swept with confused alarms of struggle and flight,
Where ignorant armies clash by night.

11. strand: beach, shore.   15. Sophocles: Athenian tragic dramatist, died 406 B.C.
28. shingles: stony seashores.

STUDY QUESTIONS

1. What details of setting are contained in the first stanza of the poem?
2. To what element of setting is Arnold referring in the lines "the turbid ebb and flow / Of human misery"? How does the reference control the meaning of the line?
3. In stanza 3, Arnold considers the religious setting in England and the world. What is that setting, as he describes it? How does the religious setting relate to the geographical one?
4. What is Arnold's view of humanity? What is his answer to mankind's predicament and dilemma? Do you agree with his answer? Discuss.

Henry Wadsworth Longfellow (1807–1882)

THE TIDE RISES, THE TIDE FALLS

The tide rises, the tide falls,
The twilight darkens, the curlew calls;
Along the sea-sands damp and brown
The traveller hastens toward the town,
    And the tide rises, the tide falls.   5

Darkness settles on roofs and walls,
But the sea, the sea in the darkness calls;
The little waves, with their soft, white hands,
Efface the footprints in the sands,
    And the tide rises, the tide falls.   10

The morning breaks; the steeds in their stalls
Stamp and neigh, as the hostler calls;
The day returns, but nevermore
Returns the traveller to the shore,
    And the tide rises, the tide falls.   15

2. curlew: a large shore bird.   12. hostler: stableman at an inn.

STUDY QUESTIONS

1. What information about time and place is contained in the poem?
2. The poem describes a traveller's journey to a town. Do the person, the time, and the place have another, less literal meaning? What is it?
3. How do lines 8 and 9 relate to the poem's less literal meaning?
4. In what ways is the use of setting similar in this poem and in "Dover Beach"? How is it different?
5. Which of the two poems makes the more positive statement about life? Defend your answer.

William Butler Yeats (1865–1939)

THE WILD SWANS AT COOLE

The trees are in their autumn beauty,
The woodland paths are dry,
Under the October twilight the water
Mirrors a still sky;
Upon the brimming water among the stones   5
Are nine-and-fifty swans.

The nineteenth autumn has come upon me
Since I first made my count;
I saw, before I had well finished,
All suddenly mount   10
And scatter wheeling in great broken rings
Upon their clamorous wings.

I have looked upon those brilliant creatures,
And now my heart is sore.
All's changed since I, hearing at twilight,   15
The first time on this shore,
The bell-beat of their wings above my head,
Trod with a lighter tread.

Unwearied still, lover by lover,
    They paddle in the cold   20
Companionable streams or climb the air;
    Their hearts have not grown old;
Passion or conquest, wander where they will,
    Attend upon them still.

But now they drift on the still water   25
    Mysterious, beautiful;
Among what rushes will they build,
    By what lake's edge or pool
Delight men's eyes when I awake some day
    To find they have flown away?   30

STUDY QUESTIONS

1. Yeats spent many summers at Coole, a relatively remote area where he could feel in close touch with nature. What hints of the setting can you gain from the poem?
2. What changes have occurred in the setting in the nineteen years since the speaker first counted the swans? What changes have occurred in the speaker of the poem and in his attitudes?
3. The speaker of the poem imagines in lines 29 and 30 that the swans will some day leave. Is this to be understood literally, or is the speaker simply projecting onto nature his own expectation of death? Discuss.

Robert Browning (1812–1889)

LOVE AMONG THE RUINS

Where the quiet-colored end of evening smiles,
    Miles and miles,
On the solitary pastures where our sheep
    Half-asleep
Tinkle homeward through the twilight, stray or stop   5
    As they crop—
Was the site once of a city great and gay,
    (So they say)
Of our country's very capital, its prince
    Ages since   10
Held his court in, gathered councils, wielding far
    Peace or war.

Now,—the country does not even boast a tree,
    As you see,
To distinguish slopes of verdure, certain rills   15
    From the hills
Intersect and give a name to, (else they run
    Into one,)
Where the domed and daring palace shot its spires
    Up like fires   20
O'er the hundred-gated circuit of a wall
    Bounding all,
Made of marble, men might march on nor be pressed,
    Twelve abreast.

And such plenty and perfection, see, of grass   25
    Never was!
Such a carpet as, this summer-time, o'er spreads
    And embeds
Every vestige of the city, guessed alone,
    Stock or stone—   30
Where a multitude of men breathed joy and woe
    Long ago;
Lust of glory pricked their hearts up, dread of shame
    Struck them tame;

And that glory and that shame alike, the gold   35
    Bought and sold.
Now,—the single little turret that remains
    On the plains,
By the caper overrooted, by the gourd
    Overscored,   40
While the patching houseleek's head of blossom winks
    Through the chinks—
Marks the basement whence a tower in ancient time
    Sprang sublime,
And a burning ring, all round, the chariots traced   45
    As they raced,
And the monarch and his minions and his dames
    Viewed the games.

And I know, while thus the quiet-colored eve
    Smiles to leave   50

---

39. caper: a low prickly shrub.   41. houseleek: a common European plant found on old walls and roofs.

To their folding, all our many tinkling fleece
    In such peace,
And the slopes and rills in undistinguished gray
    Melt away—
That a girl with eager eyes and yellow hair   55
    Waits me there
In the turret whence the charioteers caught soul
    For the goal,
When the king looked, where she looks now, breathless, dumb
    Till I come.   60

But he looked upon the city, every side,
    Far and wide,
All the mountains topped with temples, all the glades'
    Colonnades,
All the causeys, bridges, aqueducts,—and then,   65
    All the men!
When I do come, she will speak not, she will stand,
    Either hand
On my shoulder, give her eyes the first embrace
    Of my face,   70
Ere we rush, ere we extinguish sight and speech
    Each on each.

In one year they sent a million fighters forth
    South and North,
And they built their gods a brazen pillar high   75
    As the sky,
Yet reserved a thousand chariots in full force—
    Gold, of course
Oh heart! oh blood that freezes, blood that burns!
    Earth's returns   80
For whole centuries of folly, noise and sin!
    Shut them in,
With their triumphs and their glories and the rest!
    Love is best.

STUDY QUESTIONS

1. The poem contrasts two settings. What details about the present setting are given?
2. Describe the city (past setting) as it once was. What aspects of its political and psychological bases are suggested by and included in the physical description?

3. What elements of the past setting survive? How do those elements connect past and present in the poem?
4. The central idea in the poem is very romantic. What is it? Do you think Browning fanciful or realistic? Defend your answer.
5. How does Browning's attitude toward life compare to Arnold's in "Dover Beach"?

John Keats (1795–1821)

THE EVE OF ST. AGNES

1

St. Agnes' Eve—Ah, bitter chill it was!
The owl, for all his feathers, was a-cold;
The hare limped trembling through the frozen grass,
And silent was the flock in woolly fold:
Numb were the Beadsman's fingers, while he told   5
His rosary, and while his frosted breath,
Like pious incense from a censer old,
Seemed taking flight for heaven, without a death,
Past the sweet Virgin's picture, while his prayer he saith.

2

His prayer he saith, this patient, holy man;   10
Then takes his lamp, and riseth from his knees,
And back returneth, meager, barefoot, wan,
Along the chapel aisle by slow degrees:
The sculptured dead, on each side, seem to freeze,
Emprisoned in black, purgatorial rails: 15
Knights, ladies, praying in dumb orat'ries,
He passeth by; and his weak spirit fails
To think how they may ache in icy hoods and mails.

3

Northward he turneth through a little door,
And scarce three steps, ere Music's golden tongue   20
Flattered to tears this aged man and poor;
But no—already had his deathbell rung:
The joys of all his life were said and sung:
His was harsh penance on St. Agnes' Eve:

5. Beadsman: a person hired to pray for the souls of others.

Another way he went, and soon among   25
  Rough ashes sat he for his soul's reprieve,
And all night kept awake, for sinner's sake to grieve.

4

That ancient Beadsman heard the prelude soft;
  And so it chanced, for many a door was wide,
From hurry to and fro. Soon, up aloft,   30
  The silver, snarling trumpets 'gan to chide:
  The level chambers, ready with their pride,
Were glowing to receive a thousand guests:
  The carvèd angels, ever eager-eyed,
  Stared, where upon their heads the cornice rests,   35
With hair blown back, and wings put cross-wise on their breasts.

5

At length burst in the argent revelry,
  With plume, tiara, and all rich array,
Numerous as shadows haunting fairily
  The brain, new stuffed, in youth, with triumphs gay   40
Of old romance. These let us wish away,
  And turn, sole-thoughted, to one Lady there,
  Whose heart had brooded, all that wintry day,
On love, and winged St. Agnes' saintly care,
As she had heard old dames full many times declare.   45

6

They told her how, upon St. Agnes' Eve,
  Young virgins might have visions of delight,
And soft adorings from their loves receive
  Upon the honeyed middle of the night,
If ceremonies due they did aright;   50
  As, supperless to bed they must retire,
  And couch supine their beauties, lily white;
  Nor look behind, nor sideways, but require
Of Heaven with upward eyes for all that they desire.

7

Full of this whim was thoughtful Madeline: 55
  The music, yearning like a god in pain,
She scarcely heard: her maiden eyes divine,
  Fixed on the floor, saw many a sweeping train

---

35. cornice: an ornamental molding.   37. argent: made of or resembling silver.

Pass by—she heeded not at all: in vain
Came many a tiptoe, amorous cavalier,   60
And back retired; not cooled by high disdain,
But she saw not: her heart was otherwhere:
She sighed for Agnes' dreams, the sweetest of the year.

8

She danced along with vague, regardless eyes,
Anxious her lips, her breathing quick and short: 65
The hallowed hour was near at hand: she sighs
Amid the timbrels, and the thronged resort
Of whispers in anger, or in sport;
'Mid looks of love, defiance, hate, and scorn,
Hoodwinked with faery fancy; all amort,   70
Save to St. Agnes and her lambs unshorn,
And all the bliss to be before to-morrow morn.

9

So, purposing each moment to retire,
She lingered still. Meantime, across the moors,
Had come young Porphyro, with heart on fire   75
For Madeline. Beside the portal doors,
Buttressed from moonlight, stands he, and implores
All saints to give him sight of Madeline,
But for one moment in the tedious hours,
That he might gaze and worship all unseen;   80
Perchance speak, kneel, touch, kiss—in sooth such things have been.

10

He ventures in: let no buzzed whisper tell:
All eyes be muffled, or a hundred swords
Will storm his heart, Love's fev'rous citadel:
For him, those chambers held barbarian hordes,   85
Hyena foemen, and hot-blooded lords,
Whose very dogs would execrations howl
Against his lineage; not one breast affords
Him any mercy, in that mansion foul,
Save one old beldame, weak in body and in soul.   90

11

Ah, happy chance! the aged creature came,
Shuffling along with ivory-headed wand,

67. timbrel: a small drum or tambourine, held in the hand.   70. amort: oblivious, paying no attention.   90. beldame: old woman.

To where he stood, hid from the torch's flame,
Behind a broad half-pillar, far beyond
The sound of merriment and chorus bland: 95
He startled her: but soon she knew his face,
And grasped his fingers in her palsied hand,
Saying, "Mercy, Porphyro! hie thee from this place;
They are all here to-night, the whole blood-thirsty race!

12

"Get hence! get hence! there's dwarfish Hildebrand; 100
He had a fever late, and in the fit
He cursed thee and thine, both house and land:
Then there's that old Lord Maurice, not a whit
More tame for his gray hairs—Alas me! flit!
Flit like a ghost away."—"Ah, Gossip dear, 105
We're safe enough; here in this arm-chair sit,
And tell me how"—"Good Saints; not here, not here;
Follow me, child, or else these stones will be thy bier."

13

He followed through a lowly arched way,
Brushing the cobwebs with his lofty plume, 110
And as she muttered "Well-a—well-a-day!"
He found him in a little moonlight room,
Pale, latticed, chill, and silent as a tomb.
"Now tell me where is Madeline," said he,
"O tell me, Angela, by the holy loom 115
Which none but secret sisterhood may see,
When they St. Agnes' wool are weaving piously."

14

"St. Agnes! Ah! it is St. Agnes' Eve—
Yet men will murder upon holy days:
Thou must hold water in a witch's sieve, 120
And be liege-lord of all the Elves and Fays,
To venture so: it fills me with amaze
To see thee, Porphyro!—St. Agnes' Eve!
God's help! my lady fair the conjuror plays
This very night: good angels her deceive! 125
But let me laugh awhile, I've mickle time to grieve."

105. Gossip: friend, confidant.   121. Fays: fairies.   126. mickle: much.

15

Feebly she laugheth in the languid moon,
While Porphyro upon her face doth look,
Like puzzled urchin on an aged crone
Who keepeth closed a wondrous riddle-book,   130
As spectacled she sits in chimney nook.
But soon his eyes grew brilliant, when she told
His lady's purpose; and he scarce could brook
Tears, at the thought of those enchantments cold,
And Madeline asleep in lap of legends old.   135

16

Sudden a thought came like a full-blown rose,
Flushing his brow, and in his pained heart
Made purple riot: then doth he propose
A stratagem, that makes the beldame start:
"A cruel man and impious thou art: 140
Sweet lady, let her pray, and sleep, and dream
Alone with her good angels, far apart
From wicked men like thee. Go, go!—I deem
Thou canst not surely be the same that thou didst seem."

17

"I will not harm her, by all saints I swear,"   145
Quoth Porphyro: "O may I ne'er find grace
When my weak voice shall whisper its last prayer,
If one of her soft ringlets I displace,
Or look with ruffian passion in her face:
Good Angela, believe me by these tears;   150
Or I will, even in a moment's space,
Awake, with horrid shout, my foemen's ears,
And beard them, though they be more fanged than wolves and bears."

18

"Ah! why wilt thou affright a feeble soul?
A poor, weak, palsy-stricken, churchyard thing,   155
Whose passing-bell may ere the midnight toll;
Whose prayers for thee, each morn and evening,
Were never missed."—Thus plaining, doth she bring
A gentler speech from burning Porphyro;

---

133. brook: hold back.   153. beard: confront boldly.   156. passing-bell: a bell
tolled to announce a death or funeral.

So woeful, and of such deep sorrowing,   160
  That Angela gives promise she will do
Whatever he shall wish, betide her weal or woe.

19

Which was, to lead him, in close secrecy,
Even to Madeline's chamber, and there hide
Him in a closet, of such privacy   165
That he might see her beauty unespied,
And win perhaps that night a peerless bride,
While legioned faeries paced the coverlet,
And pale enchantment held her sleepy-eyed.
Never on such a night have lovers met,   170
Since Merlin paid his Demon all the monstrous debt.

20

"It shall be as thou wishest," said the Dame:
"All cates and dainties shall be stored there
Quickly on this feast-night: by the tambour frame
Her own lute thou wilt see: no time to spare,   175
For I am slow and feeble, and scarce dare
On such a catering trust my dizzy head.
Wait here, my child, with patience; kneel in prayer
The while: Ah! thou must needs the lady wed,
Or may I never leave my grave among the dead."   180

21

So saying, she hobbled off with busy fear.
The lover's endless minutes slowly passed:
The dame returned, and whispered in his ear
To follow her; with aged eyes aghast
From fright of dim espial. Safe at last,   185
Through many a dusky gallery, they gain
The maiden's chamber, silken, hushed, and chaste,
Where Porphyro took covert, pleased amain.
His poor guide hurried back with agues in her brain.

22

Her falt'ring hand upon the balustrade,   190
  Old Angela was feeling for the stair,

---

162. betide her weal or woe: whether good or evil shall happen to her.   171. Merlin:
magician in King Arthur's court, severely punished by means of his own magic.   173.
cates: choice foods, delicacies.   188. amain: very much, exceedingly.   189. agues:
fevers.

When Madeline, St. Agnes' charmed maid,
Rose, like a missioned spirit, unaware:
With silver taper's light, and pious care,
She turned, and down the aged gossip led   195
To a safe level matting. Now prepare,
Young Porphyro, for gazing on that bed;
She comes, she comes again, like ring-dove frayed and fled.

23

Out went the taper as she hurried in;
Its little smoke, in pallid moonshine, died: 200
She closed the door, she panted, all akin
To spirits of the air, and visions wide:
No uttered syllable, or, woe betide!
But to her heart, her heart was voluble,
Paining with eloquence her balmy side;   205
As though a tongueless nightingale should swell
Her throat in vain, and die, heart-stifled, in her dell.

24

A casement high and triple-arched there was,
All garlanded with carven imag'ries
Of fruits, and flowers, and bunches of knotgrass,   210
And diamonded with panes of quaint device,
Innumerable of stains and splendid dyes,
As are the tiger-moth's deep-damasked wings;
And in the midst, 'mong thousand heraldries,
And twilight saints, and dim emblazonings,   215
A shielded scutcheon blushed with blood of queens and kings.

25

Full on this casement shone the wintry moon,
And threw warm gules on Madeline's fair breast,
As down she knelt for heaven's grace and boon;
Rose-bloom fell on her hands, together pressed,   220
And on her silver cross soft amethyst,
And on her hair a glory, like a saint:
She seemed a splendid angel, newly dressed,
Save wings, for heaven:—Porphyro grew faint:
She knelt, so pure a thing, so free from mortal taint.   225

214. heraldries: ceremonial designs.   216. scutcheon: coat of arms.   218. gules: in
heraldry, red.

26

Anon his heart revives: her vespers done,
Of all its wreathèd pearls her hair she frees;
Unclasps her warmèd jewels one by one;
Loosens her fragrant bodice; by degrees
Her rich attire creeps rustling to her knees: 230
Half-hidden, like a mermaid in sea-weed,
Pensive awhile she dreams awake, and sees,
In fancy, fair St. Agnes in her bed,
But dares not look behind, or all the charm is fled.

27

Soon, trembling in her soft and chilly nest,   235
In sort of wakeful swoon, perplexed she lay,
Until the poppied warmth of sleep oppressed
Her soothèd limbs, and soul fatigued away;
Flown, like a thought, until the morrow-day;
Blissfully havened both from joy and pain;   240
Clasped like a missal where swart Paynims pray;
Blinded alike from sunshine and from rain,
As though a rose should shut, and be a bud again.

28

Stol'n to this paradise, and so entranced,
Porphyro gazed upon her empty dress,   245
And listened to her breathing, if it chanced
To wake into a slumberous tenderness;
Which when he heard, that minute did he bless,
And breathed himself: then from the closet crept,
Noiseless as fear in a wide wilderness,   250
And over the hushed carpet, silent, stepped,
And 'tween the curtains peeped, where, lo!—how fast she slept.

29

Then by the bed-side, where the faded moon
Made a dim, silver twilight, soft he set
A table, and, half anguished, threw thereon   255
A cloth of woven crimson, gold, and jet:—
O for some drowsy Morphean amulet!
The boisterous, midnight, festive clarion,

226. anon: soon, presently.   241. missal: prayer book. swart Paynims: dark-skinned Pagans.   257. Morphean amulet: charm to induce sleep.

The kettle-drum, and far-heard clarinet,
  Affray his ears, though but in dying tone:—   260
The hall door shuts again, and all the noise is gone.

30

And still she slept an azure-lidded sleep,
  In blanchèd linen, smooth, and lavendered,
While he from forth the closet brought a heap
  Of candied apple, quince, and plum, and gourd;   265
With jellies soother than the creamy curd,
  And lucent syrops, tinct with cinnamon;
Manna and dates, in argosy transferred
  From Fez; and spicèd dainties, every one,
From silken Samarkand to cedared Lebanon.   270

31

These delicates he heaped with glowing hand
  On golden dishes and in baskets bright
Of wreathèd silver: sumptuous they stand
  In the retired quiet of the night,
Filling the chilly room with perfume light.—   275
  "And now, my love, my seraph fair, awake!
Thou art my heaven, and I thine eremite:
  Open thine eyes, for meek St. Agnes' sake,
Or I shall drowse beside thee, so my soul doth ache."

32

Thus whispering, his warm, unnerved arm   280
  Sank in her pillow. Shaded was her dream
By the dusk curtains:—'twas a midnight charm
  Impossible to melt as icèd stream:
The lustrous salvers in the moonlight gleam;
  Broad golden fringe upon the carpet lies: 285
It seemed he never, never could redeem
  From such a stedfast spell his lady's eyes;
So mused awhile, entoiled in woofèd phantasies.

33

Awakening up, he took her hollow lute—
  Tumultuous—and, in chords that tenderest be,   290

266. soother: sweeter, softer.   267. lucent: clear, luminous.   268. Manna: miraculous food. argosy: a rich merchant ship.   269. Fez: a city in Morocco.   270. Samarkand: a city in the Asian part of the USSR, known for cottons and silks. 276. seraph: one of the highest angels.   277. eremite: hermit, especially one devoted to religion.   284. salvers: trays for serving food or drink.   288. woofed: woven.

He played an ancient ditty, long since mute,
In Provence called, "La belle dame sans mercy":
Close to her ear touching the melody;—
Wherewith disturbed, she uttered a soft moan:
He ceased—she panted quick—and suddenly   295
Her blue affrayed eyes wide open shone:
Upon his knees he sank, pale as smooth-sculptured stone.

34

Her eyes were open, but she still beheld,
Now wide awake, the vision of her sleep:
There was a painful change, that nigh expelled   300
The blisses of her dream so pure and deep
At which fair Madeline began to weep,
And moan forth witless words with many a sigh;
While still her gaze on Porphyro would keep;
Who knelt, with joinèd hands and piteous eye,   305
Fearing to move or speak, she looked so dreamingly.

35

"Ah, Porphyro!" said she, "but even now
Thy voice was at sweet tremble in mine ear,
Made tuneable with every sweetest vow;
And those sad eyes were spiritual and clear: 310
How changed thou art! how pallid, chill, and drear!
Give me that voice again, my Porphyro,
Those looks immortal, those complainings dear!
Oh leave me not in this eternal woe,
For if thou diest, my Love, I know not where to go."   315

36

Beyond a mortal man impassioned far
At these voluptuous accents, he arose,
Ethereal, flushed, and like a throbbing star
Seen mid the sapphire heaven's deep repose:
Into her dream he melted, as the rose   320
Blended its odor with the violet—
Solution sweet: meantime the frost-wind blows
Like Love's alarum pattering the sharp sleet
Against the window-panes; St. Agnes' moon hath set.

292. Provence: a region of southern France, known for romantic love songs. La belle
dame sans mercy: the beautiful, merciless lady.

37

'Tis dark: quick pattereth the flaw-blown sleet: 325
"This is no dream, my bride, my Madeline!"
'Tis dark: the iced gusts still rave and beat:
"No dream, alas! alas! and woe is mine!
Porphyro will leave me here to fade and pine.—
Cruel! what traitor could thee hither bring?   330
I curse not, for my heart is lost in thine,
Though thou forsakest a deceivèd thing;—
A dove forlorn and lost with sick unprunèd wing."

38

"My Madeline! sweet dreamer! lovely bride!
Say, may I be for aye thy vassal blest?   335
Thy beauty's shield, heart-shaped and vermeil dyed?
Ah, silver shrine, here will I take my rest
After so many hours of toil and quest,
A famished pilgrim—saved by miracle.
Though I have found, I will not rob thy nest   340
Saving of thy sweet self; if thou think'st well
To trust, fair Madeline, to no rude infidel.

39

"Hark! 'tis an elfin-storm from faery land,
Of haggard seeming, but a boon indeed:
Arise—arise! the morning is at hand;—   345
The bloated wassailers will never heed:—
Let us away, my love, with happy speed;
There are no ears to hear, or eyes to see—
Drowned all in Rhenish and the sleepy mead:
Awake! arise! my love, and fearless be,   350
For o'er the southern moors I have a home for thee."

40

She hurried at his words, beset with fears,
For there were sleeping dragons all around,
At glaring watch, perhaps, with ready spears—
Down the wide stairs a darkling way they found.—   355
In all the house was heard no human sound.
A chain-drooped lamp was flickering by each door;

325. flaw-blown: blown by a brief, sudden gust of wind.   335. for aye: forever.
336. vermeil: brilliant red.   346. wassailers: carousers, revelers.   349. Rhenish:
Rhine wine. mead: a fermented drink made with honey.

The arras, rich with horseman, hawk, and hound,
    Fluttered in the besieging wind's uproar;
And the long carpets rose along the gusty floor.   360

41

They glide, like phantoms, into the wide hall;
Like phantoms, to the iron porch, they glide;
Where lay the Porter, in uneasy sprawl,
With a huge empty flagon by his side:
The wakeful bloodhound rose, and shook his hide,   365
But his sagacious eye an inmate owns:
By one, and one, the bolts full easy slide:—
The chains lie silent on the footworn stones;—
The key turns, and the door upon its hinges groans.

42

And they are gone: aye, ages long ago   370
These lovers fled away into the storm.
That night the Baron dreamt of many a woe,
And all his warrior-guests, with shade and form
Of witch, and demon, and large coffin-worm,
Were long be-nightmared. Angela the old   375
Died palsy-twitched, with meager face deform;
The Beadsman, after thousands aves told,
For aye unsought-for slept among his ashes cold.

358. arras: tapestry, wall-hanging.

STUDY QUESTIONS

1. An old tradition holds that if a young woman performs certain simple rituals on St. Agnes' Eve, she will dream of her future lover. Just what does Madeline do to prepare for her St. Agnes' Eve dream? How much of what follows is a dream? How much are we to understand is reality?
2. Define as closely as possible the time and place of the action.
3. The opening stanzas present a picture of cold, poverty, and death, in contrast to the richness and warmth of the festive gathering in the castle. What is the purpose of this contrast?
4. What is Porphyro's background and station in life? Why does Angela, the old woman, describe the men of the castle as barbarians and hyenas?
5. Stanza 24 describes the stained-glass window in Madeline's room, and stanza 25 mentions the colors of light that fall on Madeline as she kneels to pray. What are those colors and what is their significance?
6. Why does the poem end with the household all asleep, except for Angela and the Beadsman, who are dead?

William Wordsworth (1770–1850)

LINES: COMPOSED A FEW MILES ABOVE TINTERN ABBEY, ON REVISITING THE BANKS OF THE WYE DURING A TOUR, JULY 13, 1798

Five years have past; five summers, with the length
Of five long winters! and again I hear
These waters, rolling from their mountain-springs
With a soft inland murmur.—Once again
Do I behold these steep and lofty cliffs,   5
That on a wild secluded scene impress
Thoughts of more deep seclusion, and connect
The landscape with the quiet of the sky.
The day is come when I again repose
Here, under this dark sycamore, and view   10
These plots of cottage-ground, these orchard-tufts,
Which at this season, with their unripe fruits,
Are clad in one green hue, and lose themselves
'Mid groves and copses. Once again I see
These hedge-rows, hardly hedge-rows, little lines   15
Of sportive wood run wild: these pastoral farms,
Green to the very door; and wreaths of smoke
Sent up, in silence, from among the trees!
With some uncertain notice, as might seem
Of vagrant dwellers in the houseless woods,   20
Or of some hermit's cave, where by his fire
The hermit sits alone.

                  These beauteous forms,
Through a long absence, have not been to me
As is a landscape to a blind man's eye: 25
But oft, in lonely rooms, and 'mid the din
Of towns and cities, I have owed to them
In hours of weariness, sensations sweet,
Felt in the blood, and felt along the heart;
And passing even into my purer mind,   30
With tranquil restoration:—feelings too
Of unremembered pleasure: such, perhaps,
As have no slight or trivial influence
On that best portion of a good man's life,
His little, nameless, unremembered, acts   35
Of kindness and of love. Nor less, I trust,
To them I may have owed another gift,
Of aspect more sublime; that blessed mood,

In which the burthen of the mystery,
In which the heavy and the weary weight   40
Of all this unintelligible world,
Is lightened:—that serene and blessed mood,
In which the affections gently lead us on,—
Until, the breath of this corporeal frame
And even the motion of our human blood   45
Almost suspended, we are laid asleep
In body, and become a living soul:
While with an eye made quiet by the power
Of harmony, and the deep power of joy,
We see into the life of things.   50

                        If this
Be but a vain belief, yet, oh! how oft—
In darkness and amid the many shapes
Of joyless daylight; when the fretful stir
Unprofitable, and the fever of the world,   55
Have hung upon the beatings of my heart—
How oft, in spirit, have I turned to thee,
O sylvan Wye! thou wanderer thro' the woods,
How often has my spirit turned to thee!

        And now, with gleams of half-extinguished thought,   60
With many recognitions dim and faint,
And somewhat of a sad perplexity,
The picture of the mind revives again:
While here I stand, not only with the sense
Of present pleasure, but with pleasing thoughts   65
That in this moment there is life and food
For future years. And so I dare to hope,
Though changed, no doubt, from what I was when first
I came among these hills; when like a roe
I bounded o'er the mountains, by the sides   70
Of the deep rivers, and the lonely streams,
Wherever nature led: more like a man
Flying from something that he dreads, than one
Who sought the thing he loved. For nature then
(The coarser pleasures of my boyish days,   75
And their glad animal movements all gone by)
To me was all in all. I cannot paint
What then I was. The sounding cataract
Haunted me like a passion: the tall rock,

39. burthen: burden.   69. roe: deer

The mountain, and the deep and gloomy wood,   80
Their colors and their forms, were then to me
An appetite; a feeling and a love,
That had no need of a remoter charm,
By thought supplied, nor any interest
Unborrowed from the eye.—That time is past,   85
And all its aching joys are now no more,
And all its dizzy raptures. Not for this
Faint I, nor mourn nor murmur; other gifts
Have followed; for such loss, I would believe,
Abundant recompense. For I have learned   90
To look on nature, not as in the hour
Of thoughtless youth; but hearing oftentimes
The still, sad music of humanity.
Nor harsh nor grating, though of ample power
To chasten and subdue. And I have felt   95
A presence that disturbs me with the joy
Of elevated thoughts; a sense sublime
Of something far more deeply interfused,
Whose dwelling is the light of setting suns,
And the round ocean and the living air,   100
And the blue sky, and in the mind of man:
A motion and a spirit, that impels
All thinking things, all objects of all thought,
And rolls through all things. Therefore am I still
A lover of the meadows and the woods,   105
And mountains; and of all that we behold
From this green earth; of all the mighty world
Of eye, and ear—both what they half create,
And what perceive; well pleased to recognize
In nature and the language of the sense   110
The anchor of my purest thoughts, the nurse,
The guide, the guardian of my heart, and soul
Of all my moral being.

          Nor perchance,
If I were not thus taught, should I the more   115
Suffer my genial spirits to decay:
For thou art with me here upon the banks
Of this fair river; thou my dearest Friend,
My dear, dear Friend; and in thy voice I catch
The language of my former heart, and read   120
My former pleasures in the shooting lights
Of thy wild eyes. Oh! yet a little while
May I behold in thee what I was once,

My dear, dear Sister! and this prayer I make,
Knowing that Nature never did betray   125
The heart that loved her; 'tis her privilege,
Through all the years of this our life, to lead
From joy to joy: for she can so inform
The mind that is within us, so impress
With quietness and beauty, and so feed   130
With lofty thoughts, that neither evil tongues,
Rash judgments, nor the sneers of selfish men,
Nor greetings where no kindness is, nor all
The dreary intercourse of daily life,
Shall e'er prevail against us, or disturb   135
Our cheerful faith, that all which we behold
Is full of blessings. Therefore let the moon
Shine on thee in thy solitary walk;
And let the misty mountain winds be free
To blow against thee: and, in after years,   140
When these wild ecstasies shall be matured
Into a sober pleasure; when thy mind
Shall be a mansion for all lovely forms,
Thy memory be as a dwelling place
For all sweet sounds and harmonies; oh! then,   145
If solitude, or fear, or pain, or grief
Should be thy portion, with what healing thoughts
Of tender joy wilt thou remember me,
And these my exhortations! Nor, perchance—
If I should be where I no more can hear   150
Thy voice, nor catch from thy wild eyes these gleams
Of past existence—wilt thou then forget
That on the banks of this delightful stream
We stood together; and that I, so long
A worshiper of Nature, hither came   155
Unwearied in that service; rather say
With warmer love—oh! with far deeper zeal
Of holier love. Nor wilt thou then forget,
That after many wanderings, many years
Of absence, these steep woods and lofty cliffs,   160
And this green pastoral landscape, were to me
More dear, both for themselves and for thy sake!

STUDY QUESTIONS

1. Describe in your own words the landscape portrayed in this poem.
2. Explain in detail the "mental" environment of the poem.
3. What relationships of mind and nature does the poem present?
4. What is the "tone" of the poem? How does "tone" contribute to setting?
5. Is the passage of time significant to the environment in the poem? Explain.
6. What mental events does Wordsworth suggest that a landscape can trigger in a viewer? List in detail.
7. What three "environments" of youth are set forth here?
8. Does Wordsworth believe that we in part create what we see? Discuss.
9. Write a description of an environment that has had a significant effect on *your* life. In your description, consider the relationship between past and present, as Wordsworth does in his poem.

Norman Russell (1921–   )

indian school

in the darkness
of the house of the white brother
i go alone and am frightened
strange things touch me
i cannot breathe his air   5
or eat his tasteless food

on his walls
are pictures of the world
that his walls shut out
in his hands are leaves of words   10
from dead mens mouths

he speaks to me with only
the sounds of his mouth
for he is dumb and blind
as the staggering old bear   15
filled with many arrows
as the rocks that lie on the mountain

and in his odd robes
uglier
than any other creature i have ever seen   20

i am not wise enough to know
gods purpose in him.

Richard Wilbur (1921–   )

TO AN AMERICAN POET JUST DEAD

In the *Boston Sunday Herald* just three lines
Of no-point type for you who used to sing
The praises of imaginary wines,
And died, or so I'm told, of the real thing.

Also gone, but a lot less forgotten,   5
Are an eminent cut-rate druggist, a lover of Giving,
A lender, and various brokers: gone from this rotten
Taxable world to a higher standard of living.

It is out in the comfy suburbs I read you are dead,
And the soupy summer is settling, full of the yawns   10
Of Sunday fathers loitering late in bed,
And the ssshh of sprays on all the little lawns.

Will the sprays weep wide for you their chaplet tears?
For you will the deep-freeze units melt and mourn?
For you will Studebakers shred their gears   15
And sound from each garage a muted horn?

They won't. In summer sunk and stupefied
The suburbs deepen in their sleep of death.
And though they sleep the sounder since you died
It's just as well that now you save your breath.   20

2. no-point type: extremely small type—in printing, 1 point is 1/72 inch in size.
13. chaplet: a wreath or garland.

Alexander Pope (1688–1744)

EPISTLE TO MISS TERESA BLOUNT, ON HER LEAVING THE TOWN AFTER THE CORONATION

As some fond virgin, whom her mother's care
Drags from the town to wholesome country air,
Just when she learns to roll a melting eye,
And hear a spark, yet think no danger nigh;
From the dear man unwilling she must sever,   5
Yet takes one kiss before she parts forever:
Thus from the world fair Zephalinda flew,
Saw others happy, and with sighs withdrew;
Not that their pleasures caused her discontent,
She sighed not that they stayed, but that she went.   10
    She went to plain-work, and to purling brooks,

Old-fashioned halls, dull aunts, and croaking rooks;
She went from opera, park, assembly, play,
To morning walks, and prayers three hours a day;
To part her time 'twixt reading and bohea,   15
To muse, and spill her solitary tea,
Or o'er cold coffee trifle with the spoon,
Count the slow clock, and dine exact at noon;
Divert her eyes with pictures in the fire,
Hum half a tune, tell stories to the squire;   20
Up to her godly garret after seven,
Then starve and pray, for that's the way to Heaven.
  Some squire, perhaps, you take delight to rack,
Whose game is whisk, whose treat a toast in sack;
Who visits with a gun, presents you birds,   25
Then gives a smacking buss, and cries—"No words!"
Or with his hounds comes hallowing from the stable,
Makes love with nods and knees beneath a table:
Whose laughs are hearty, tho' his jests are coarse,
And loves you best of all things—but his horse.   30
  In some fair evening, on your elbow laid,
You dream of triumphs in the rural shade;
In pensive thought recall the fancied scene,
See coronations rise on every green;
Before you pass the imaginary sights   35
Of lords, and earls, and dukes, and gartered knights,
While the spread fan o'ershades your closing eyes;
Then give one flirt, and all the vision flies.
Thus vanish scepters, coronets, and balls,
And leave you in lone woods or empty walls.   40
  So when your slave, at some dear idle time,
(Not plagued with headaches, or the want of rhyme)
Stands in the streets, abstracted from the crew,
And while he seems to study, thinks of you;
Just when his fancy points your sprightly eyes,   45
Or sees the blush of soft Parthenia rise,
Gay pats my shoulder, and you vanish quite;
Streets, chairs, and coxcombs rush upon my sight;
Vexed to be still in town, I knit my brow,
Look sour, and hum a tune—as you may now.   50

Title. Coronation: that of George I (1714). 4. spark: a beau. 7. Zephalinda:
name adopted by Miss Blount. 11. plain-work: "Needlework, as distinguished from
embroidery" (Johnson's *Dictionary*). purling: rippling. 12. rooks: Old-World
crowlike birds. 15. bohea: expensive black tea. 24. sack: sherry. 26. buss:
kiss. 46. Parthenia: Martha Blount, Teresa's sister, and lifelong friend of Pope
47. Gay: John Gay (1685–1732), composer of *The Beggar's Opera*.

Thomas Hood (1798–1845)

PAST AND PRESENT

I remember, I remember
The house where I was born,
The little window where the sun
Came peeping in at morn;
He never came a wink too soon   5
Nor brought too long a day:
But now, I often wish the night
Had borne my breath away.

I remember, I remember
The roses, red and white,   10
The violets, and the lily-cups—
Those flowers made of light!
The lilacs where the robin built,
And where my brother set
The laburnum on his birthday,—   15
The tree is living yet!

I remember, I remember,
Where I was used to swing,
And thought the air must rush as fresh
To swallows on the wing;   20
My spirit flew in feathers then
That is so heavy now,
And summer pools could hardly cool
The fever on my brow.

I remember, I remember   25
The fir trees dark and high;
I used to think their slender tops
Were close against the sky:
It was a childish ignorance,
But now 'tis little joy   30
To know I'm farther off from Heaven
Than when I was a boy.

Christopher Marlowe (1564–1593)

THE PASSIONATE SHEPHERD TO HIS LOVE

Come live with me and be my love,
And we will all the pleasures prove

That valleys, groves, hills, and fields,
Woods, or steepy mountain yields.

And we will sit upon the rocks,   5
Seeing the shepherds feed their flocks
By shallow rivers, to whose falls
Melodious birds sing madrigals.

And I will make thee beds of roses
And a thousand fragrant posies,   10
A cap of flowers, and a kirtle
Embroidered all with leaves of myrtle;

A gown made of the finest wool
Which from our pretty lambs we pull,
Fair linéd slippers for the cold,   15
With buckles of the purest gold;

A belt of straw and ivy buds
With coral clasps and amber studs:
And if these pleasures may thee move,
Come live with me, and be my love.   20

The shepherds' swains shall dance and sing
For thy delight each May morning.
If these delights thy mind may move,
Then live with me and be my love.

8. madrigals: unaccompanied part songs.   11. kirtle: skirt or dress.

Sir Walter Raleigh (1552–1618)

THE NYMPH'S REPLY TO THE SHEPHERD

If all the world and love were young,
And truth in every shepherd's tongue,
These pretty pleasures might me move
To live with thee, and be thy love.

Time drives the flocks from field to fold,   5
When rivers rage, and rocks grow cold,
And Philomel becometh dumb,
The rest complains of cares to come.

The flowers do fade, and wanton fields
To wayward winter reckoning yields,   10
A honey tongue, a heart of gall,
Is fancy's spring, but sorrow's fall.

Thy gowns, thy shoes, thy beds of roses,
Thy cap, thy kirtle, and thy posies
Soon break, soon wither, soon forgotten,   15
In folly ripe, in reason rotten.

Thy belt of straw and ivy buds,
Thy coral clasps and amber studs,
All these in me no means can move
To come to thee, and be thy love.   20

But could youth last, and love still breed,
Had joys no date, nor age no need,
Then these delights my mind might move
To live with thee, and be thy love.

7. Philomel: nightingale.   14. kirtle: skirt or dress.

Henry Wadsworth Longfellow (1807–1882)

THE FIRE OF DRIFT-WOOD

Devereux Farm, near Marblehead

We sat within the farm-house old,
    Whose windows, looking o'er the bay,
Gave to the sea-breeze damp and cold
    An easy entrance, night and day

Not far away we saw the port,   5
    The strange, old-fashioned, silent town,
The lighthouse, the dismantled fort,
    The wooden houses, quaint and brown.

We sat and talked until the night,
    Descending, filled the little room;   10
Our faces faded from the sight,
    Our voices only broke the gloom.

We spake of many a vanished scene,
    Of what we once had thought and said,
Of what had been, and might have been,   15
    And who was changed, and who was dead;

And all that fills the hearts of friends,
    When first they feel, with secret pain,
Their lives henceforth have separate ends,
    And never can be one again;   20

The first slight swerving of the heart,
   That words are powerless to express,
And leave it still unsaid in part,
   Or say it in too great excess.

The very tones in which we spake   25
   Had something strange, I could but mark;
The leaves of memory seemed to make
   A mournful rustling in the dark.

Oft died the words upon our lips,
   As suddenly, from out the fire   30
Built of the wreck of stranded ships,
   The flames would leap and then expire.

And, as their splendor flashed and failed,
   We thought of wrecks upon the main,
Of ships dismasted, that were hailed   35
   And sent no answer back again.

The windows, rattling in their frames,
   The ocean, roaring up the beach,
The gusty blast, the bickering flames,
   All mingled vaguely in our speech;   40

Until they made themselves a part
   Of fancies floating through the brain,
The long-lost ventures of the heart,
   That send no answers back again.

O flames that glowed! O hearts that yearned!   45
   They were indeed too much akin,
The drift-wood fire without that burned,
   The thoughts that burned and glowed within.

John Keats (1795–1821)

TO AUTUMN

Season of mists and mellow fruitfulness,
   Close bosom-friend of the maturing sun;
Conspiring with him how to load and bless
   With fruit the vines that round the thatch-eves run;
To bend with apples the mossed cottage-trees,   5
   And fill all fruit with ripeness to the core;
      To swell the gourd, and plump the hazel shells

With a sweet kernel; to set budding more,
    And still more, later flowers for the bees,
    Until they think warm days will never cease,   10
        For summer has o'er-brimmed their clammy cells.

Who hath not seen thee oft amid thy store?
    Sometimes whoever seeks abroad may find
Thee sitting careless on a granary floor,
    Thy hair soft-lifted by the winnowing wind;   15
Or on a half-reaped furrow sound asleep,
    Drowsed with the fume of poppies, while thy hook
        Spares the next swath and all its twinèd flowers:
And sometimes like a gleaner thou dost keep
    Steady thy laden head across a brook;   20
    Or by a cider-press, with patient look,
        Thou watchest the last oozings hours by hours.

Where are the songs of Spring? Ay, where are they?
    Think not of them, thou hast thy music too,—
While barred clouds bloom the soft-dying day,   25
    And touch the stubble-plains with rosy hue;
Then in a wailful choir the small gnats mourn
    Among the river sallows, borne aloft
        Or sinking as the light wind lives or dies;
And full-grown lambs loud bleat from hilly bourn;   30
    Hedge-crickets sing; and now with treble soft
    The red-breast whistles from a garden-croft;
        And gathering swallows twitter in the skies.

4. thatch-eves: edges of a thatched roof.   28. sallows: willows.   30. bourn: pasture.   32. garden-croft: a small enclosed garden near a house.

John Crowe Ransom (1888–1974)

PIAZZA PIECE

—I am a gentleman in a dustcoat trying
To make you hear. Your ears are soft and small
And listen to an old man not at all,
They want the young man's whispering and sighing.
But see the roses on your trellis dying   5
And hear the spectral singing of the moon;
For I must have my lovely lady soon,
I am a gentleman in a dustcoat trying.

—I am a lady young in beauty waiting
Until my truelove comes, and then we kiss.   10

But what grey man among the vines is this
Whose words are dry and faint as in a dream?
Back from my trellis, Sir, before I scream!
I am a lady young in beauty waiting.

Jonathan Swift (1667–1745)

A DESCRIPTION OF A CITY SHOWER

Careful observers may foretell the hour
(By sure prognostics) when to dread a shower:
While rain depends, the pensive cat gives o'er
Her frolics, and pursues her tail no more.
Returning home at night, you'll find the sink   5
Strike your offended sense with double stink.
If you be wise, then go not far to dine;
You'll spend in coach hire more than save in wine.
A coming shower your shooting corns presage,
Old achès throb, your hollow tooth will rage.   10
Sauntering in coffeehouses is Dulman seen;
He damns the climate and complains of spleen.
    Meanwhile the South, rising with dabbled wings,
A sable cloud athwart the welkin flings,
That swilled more liquor than it could contain,   15
And, like a drunkard, gives it up again.
Brisk Susan whips her linen from the rope,
While the first drizzling shower is borne aslope:
Such is that sprinkling which some careless quean
Flirts on you from her mop, but not so clean: 20
You fly, invoke the gods; then turning, stop
To rail; she singing, still whirls on her mop.
Not yet the dust had shunned the unequal strife,
But, aided by the wind, fought still for life,
And wafted with its foe by violent gust,   25
'Twas doubtful which was rain and which was dust.
Ah! where must needy poet seek for aid,
When dust and rain at once his coat invade?
Sole coat, where dust cemented by the rain
Erects the nap, and leaves a mingled stain.   30
    Now in contiguous drops the flood comes down,
Threatening with deluge this devoted town.
To shops in crowds the daggled females fly,
Pretend to cheapen goods, but nothing buy.
The Templar spruce, while every spout's abroach,   35

Stays till 'tis fair, yet seems to call a coach.
The tucked up seamstress walks with hasty strides,
While streams run down her oiled umbrella's sides.
Here various kinds, by various fortunes led,
Commerce acquaintance underneath a shed.   40
Triumphant Tories and desponding Whigs
Forget their feuds, and join to save their wigs.
Boxed in a chair, the beau impatient sits,
While spouts run clattering o'er the roof by fits,
And ever and anon with frightful din   45
The leather sounds, he trembles from within.
So when Troy chairmen bore the wooden steed,
Pregnant with Greeks impatient to be freed
(Those bully Greeks, who, as the moderns do,
Instead of paying chairmen, ran them through),   50
Laocoön struck the outside with his spear,
And each imprisoned hero quaked for fear.
    Now from all parts the swelling kennels flow,
And bear their trophies with them as they go:
Filths of all hues and odors seem to tell   55
What street they sailed from by their sight and smell.
They, as each torrent drives with rapid force,
From Smithfield or St. 'Pulchre's shape their course,
And in huge confluence join at Snow Hill ridge,
Fall from the Conduit prone to Holborn Bridge.   60
Sweeping from butchers' stalls, dung, guts, and blood,
Drowned puppies, stinking sprats, all drenched in mud,
Dead cats, and turnip tops, come tumbling down the flood.

3. depends: threatens, is imminent.   5. sink: cesspool, sewer.   12. spleen: bad
temper, depression.   14. welkin: the heavens, the upper atmosphere.   19. quean:
prostitute, streetwalker.   20. flirts: flings, flicks.   33. daggled: bedraggled.   35.
Templar: lawyer. abroach: full of running water.   36. seems: pretends.   41. Tories, Whigs: political parties.   43. chair: an enclosed sedan chair, carried on poles.
46. leather: the roof of the sedan chair.   53. kennels: gutters.

William Wordsworth (1770–1850)

COMPOSED UPON WESTMINSTER BRIDGE, SEPTEMBER 3, 1802

Earth has not anything to show more fair:
Dull would he be of soul who could pass by
A sight so touching in its majesty;

This City now doth, like a garment, wear
The beauty of the morning; silent, bare,   5
Ships, towers, domes, theaters, and temples lie
Open unto the fields, and to the sky;
All bright and glittering in the smokeless air.
Never did sun more beautifully steep
In his first splendor, valley, rock, or hill;   10
Ne'er saw I, never felt, a calm so deep!
The river glideth at his own sweet will:
Dear God! the very houses seem asleep;
And all that mighty heart is lying still!

William Wordsworth (1770–1850)

I WANDERED LONELY AS A CLOUD

I wandered lonely as a cloud
  That floats on high o'er vales and hills,
When all at once I saw a crowd,
  A host, of golden daffodils,
Beside the lake, beneath the trees,   5
Fluttering and dancing in the breeze.

Continuous as the stars that shine
  And twinkle on the milky way,
They stretched in never-ending line
  Along the margin of a bay: 10
Ten thousand saw I at a glance,
Tossing their heads in sprightly dance.

The waves beside them danced; but they
  Out-did the sparkling waves in glee;
A poet could not but be gay,   15
  In such a jocund company;
I gazed—and gazed—but little thought
What wealth the show to me had brought:

For oft, when on my couch I lie
  In vacant or in pensive mood,   20
They flash upon that inward eye
  Which is the bliss of solitude;
And then my heart with pleasure fills,
And dances with the daffodils.

16. jocund: cheerful, lively.

William Wordsworth (1770–1850)

THE SOLITARY REAPER

Behold her, single in the field,
Yon solitary Highland lass!
Reaping and singing by herself;
Stop here, or gently pass!
Alone she cuts and binds the grain,   5
And sings a melancholy strain;
O listen! for the vale profound
Is overflowing with the sound.

No nightingale did ever chaunt
More welcome notes to weary bands   10
Of travellers in some shady haunt
Among Arabian sands.
A voice so thrilling ne'er was heard
In springtime from the cuckoo-bird,
Breaking the silence of the seas   15
Among the farthest Hebrides.

Will no one tell me what she sings?—
Perhaps the plaintive numbers flow
For old, unhappy, far-off things,
And battles long ago.   20
Or is it some more humble lay,
Familiar matter of today?
Some natural sorrow, loss, or pain,
That has been, and may be again?

Whate'er the theme, the maiden sang   25
As if her song could have no ending;
I saw her singing at her work,
And o'er the sickle bending—
I listened, motionless and still;
And, as I mounted up the hill,   30
The music in my heart I bore
Long after it was heard no more.

9. chaunt: chant.   16. Hebrides: islands west of Scotland.   18. numbers: measures, musical notes.   21. lay: poem, song.

Thomas Hardy (1840–1928)

THE MAN HE KILLED

"Had he and I but met
By some old ancient inn,
We should have sat us down to wet
Right many a nipperkin!

"But ranged as infantry,   5
And staring face to face,
I shot at him as he at me,
And killed him in his place.

"I shot him dead because—
Because he was my foe,   10
Just so: my foe of course he was;
That's clear enough: although

"He thought he'd 'list, perhaps,
Off-hand like—just as I—
Was out of work—had sold his traps—   15
No other reason why.

"Yes; quaint and curious war is!
You shoot a fellow down
You'd treat if met where any bar is,
Or help to half-a-crown."   20

4. nipperkin: small drinking vessel.   15. traps: tools of a trade.

Thomas Hardy (1840–1928)

NEUTRAL TONES

We stood by a pond that winter day,
And the sun was white, as though chidden of God,
And a few leaves lay on the starving sod;
   —They had fallen from an ash, and were gray.

Your eyes on me were as eyes that rove   5
Over tedious riddles of years ago;
And some words played between us to and fro
   On which lost the more by our love.

The smile on your mouth was the deadest thing
Alive enough to have strength to die;   10

And a grin of bitterness swept thereby
  Like an ominous bird a-wing. . . .

Since then, keen lessons that love deceives,
And wrings with wrong, have shaped to me
Your face, and the God-curst sun, and a tree,   15
  And a pond edged with grayish leaves.

Randall Jarrell (1914–1965)

SECOND AIR FORCE

Far off, above the plain the summer dries,
The great loops of the hangars sway like hills.
Buses and weariness and loss, the nodding soldiers
Are wire, the bare frame building, and a pass
To what was hers; her head hides his square patch   5
And she thinks heavily: My son is grown.
She sees a world: sand roads, tar-paper barracks,
The bubbling asphalt of the runways, sage,
The dunes rising to the interminable ranges,
The dim flights moving over clouds like clouds.   10
The armorers in their patched faded green,
Sweat-stiffened, banded with brass cartridges,
Walk to the line; their Fortresses, all tail,
Stand wrong and flimsy on their skinny legs,
And the crews climb to them clumsily as bears.   15
The head withdraws into its hatch (a boy's),
The engines rise to their blind laboring roar,
And the green, made beasts run home to air.
Now in each aspect death is pure.
(At twilight they wink over men like stars   20
And hour by hour, through the night, some see
The great lights floating in—from Mars, from Mars.)
How emptily the watchers see them gone.

They go, there is silence; the woman and her son
Stand in the forest of the shadows, and the light   25
Washes them like water. In the long-sunken city
Of evening, the sunlight stills like sleep
The faint wonder of the drowned; in the evening,
In the last dreaming light, so fresh, so old,
The soldiers pass like beasts, unquestioning,   30
And the watcher for an instant understands

What there is then no need to understand;
But she wakes from her knowledge, and her stare,
A shadow now, moves emptily among
The shadows learning in their shadowy fields   35
The empty missions.
               Remembering,
She hears the bomber calling, *Little Friend!*
To the fighter hanging in the hostile sky,
And sees the ragged flame eat, rib by rib,   40
Along the metal of the wing into her heart:
The lives stream out, blossom, and float steadily
To the flames of the earth, the flames
That burn like stars above the lands of men.

She saves from the twilight that takes everything   45
A squadron shipping, in its last parade—
Its dogs run by it, barking at the band—
A gunner walking to his barracks, half-asleep,
Starting at something, stumbling (above, invisible,
The crews in the steady winter of the sky   50
Tremble in their wired fur); and feels for them
The love of life for life. The hopeful cells
Heavy with someone else's death, cold carriers
Of someone else's victory, grope past their lives
Into her own bewilderment: The years meant *this?*   55

But for them the bombers answer everything.

READING SELECTIONS: PLAY

Oscar Wilde (1854–1900)
THE IMPORTANCE OF BEING EARNEST

CHARACTERS

John Worthing, J.P.[1]
Algernon Moncrieff
Rev. Canon Chasuble, D.D.

[1] J.P.: justice of the peace, a country gentleman of wealth and position.

Merriman, *butler*
Lane, *manservant*
Lady Bracknell
Hon. Gwendolen Fairfax
Cecily Cardew
Miss Prism, *governess*

THE SCENES OF THE PLAY
ACT I. *Algernon Moncrieff's Flat in Half-Moon Street, W.*[2]
ACT II. *The Garden at the Manor House, Woolton.*
ACT III. *Drawing-Room of the Manor House, Woolton.*
TIME. *The Present.*
PLACE. *London.*

ACT I

Scene: *Morning-room in* ALGERNON'S *flat in Half-Moon Street. The room is luxuriously and artistically furnished. The sound of a piano is heard in the adjoining room.*

LANE *is arranging afternoon tea on the table, and after the music has ceased,* ALGERNON *enters.*

Algernon Did you hear what I was playing, Lane?
Lane I didn't think it polite to listen, sir.
Algernon I'm sorry for that, for your sake. I don't play accurately—any-one can play accurately—but I play with wonderful expression. As far as the piano is concerned, sentiment is my forte. I keep science for Life.
Lane Yes, sir.
Algernon And, speaking of the science of Life, have you got the cucumber sandwiches cut for Lady Bracknell?
Lane Yes, sir.

(Hands them on a salver.)

Algernon *(Inspects them, takes two, and sits down on the sofa)* Oh! . . . by the way, Lane, I see from your book[3] that on Thursday night, when Lord Shoreman and Mr. Worthing were dining with me, eight bottles of champagne are entered as having been consumed.
Lane Yes, sir, eight bottles and a pint.
Algernon Why is it that at a bachelor's establishment the servants invariably drink the champagne? I ask merely for information.

[2] Half-Moon Street, W.: a fashionable street in the West End of London.
[3] book: household record book.

Lane   I attribute it to the superior quality of the wine, sir. I have often observed that in married households the champagne is rarely of a first-rate brand.

Algernon   Good Heavens! Is marriage so demoralizing as that?

Lane   I believe it *is* a very pleasant state, sir. I have had very little experience of it myself up to the present. I have only been married once. That was in consequence of a misunderstanding between myself and a young person.

Algernon (*Languidly*)   I don't know that I am much interested in your family life, Lane.

Lane   No, sir; it is not a very interesting subject. I never think of it myself.

Algernon   Very natural, I am sure. That will do, Lane, thank you.

Lane   Thank you, sir.

(LANE *goes out.*)

Algernon   Lane's views on marriage seem somewhat lax. Really, if the lower orders don't set us a good example, what on earth is the use of them? They seem, as a class, to have absolutely no sense of moral responsibility.

(*Enter* LANE.)

Lane   Mr. Ernest Worthing.

(*Enter* JACK. LANE *goes out.*)

Algernon   How are you, my dear Ernest? What brings you up to town?

Jack   Oh, pleasure, pleasure! What else should bring one anywhere? Eating as usual, I see, Algy!

Algernon (*Stiffly*)   I believe it is customary in good society to take some slight refreshment at five o'clock. Where have you been since last Thursday?

Jack (*Sitting down on the sofa*)   In the country.

Algernon   What on earth do you do there?

Jack (*Pulling off his gloves*)   When one is in town one amuses oneself. When one is in the country one amuses other people. It is excessively boring.

Algernon   And who are the people you amuse?

Jack (*Airily*)   Oh, neighbours, neighbours.

Algernon   Got nice neighbours in your part of Shropshire? [4]

Jack   Perfectly horrid! Never speak to one of them.

Algernon   How immensely you must amuse them!

(*Goes over and takes sandwich.*)

By the way, Shropshire is your county, is it not?

---

[4] Shropshire: a county in the west of England, some distance from London.

Jack Eh? Shropshire? Yes, of course. Hallo! Why all these cups? Why cucumber sandwiches? Why such reckless extravagance in one so young? Who is coming to tea?

Algernon Oh! merely Aunt Augusta and Gwendolen.

Jack How perfectly delightful!

Algernon Yes, that is all very well; but I am afraid Aunt Augusta won't quite approve of your being here.

Jack May I ask why?

Algernon My dear fellow, the way you flirt with Gwendolen is perfectly disgraceful. It is almost as bad as the way Gwendolen flirts with you.

Jack I am in love with Gwendolen. I have come up to town expressly to propose to her.

Algernon I thought you had come up for pleasure? . . . I call that business.

Jack How utterly unromantic you are!

Algernon I really don't see anything romantic in proposing. It is very romantic to be in love. But there is nothing romantic about a definite proposal. Why, one may be accepted. One usually is, I believe. Then the excitement is all over. The very essence of romance is uncertainty. If ever I get married, I'll certainly try to forget the fact.

Jack I have no doubt about that, dear Algy. The Divorce Court was specially invented for people whose memories are so curiously constituted.

Algernon Oh! there is no use speculating on that subject. Divorces are made in Heaven—(JACK *puts out his hand to take a sandwich.* ALGERNON *at once interferes.*) Please don't touch the cucumber sandwiches. They are ordered specially for Aunt Augusta.

(*Takes one and eats it.*)

Jack Well, you have been eating them all the time.

Algernon That is quite a different matter. She is my aunt. (*Takes plate from below.*) Have some bread and butter. The bread and butter is for Gwendolen. Gwendolen is devoted to bread and butter.

Jack (*Advancing to table and helping himself*) And very good bread and butter it is too.

Algernon Well, my dear fellow, you need not eat as if you were going to eat it all. You behave as if you were married to her already. You are not married to her already, and I don't think you ever will be.

Jack Why on earth do you say that?

Algernon Well, in the first place girls never marry the men they flirt with. Girls don't think it right.

Jack Oh, that is nonsense!

Algernon It isn't. It is a great truth. It accounts for the extraordinary number of bachelors that one sees all over the place. In the second place, I don't give my consent.

Jack Your consent!

Algernon My dear fellow, Gwendolen is my first cousin. And before I allow you to marry her, you will have to clear up the whole question of Cecily.

(*Rings bell.*)

Jack Cecily! What on earth do you mean? What do you mean, Algy, by Cecily? I don't know anyone of the name of Cecily.

(*Enter* LANE.)

Algernon Bring me that cigarette case Mr. Worthing left in the smoking-room the last time he dined here.
Lane Yes, sir.

(LANE *goes out.*)

Jack Do you mean to say you have had my cigarette case all this time? I wish to goodness you had let me know. I have been writing frantic letters to Scotland Yard [5] about it. I was very nearly offering a large reward.
Algernon Well, I wish you would offer one. I happen to be more than usually hard up.
Jack There is no good offering a large reward now that the thing is found.

(*Enter* LANE *with the cigarette case on a salver.* ALGERNON *takes it at once.* LANE *goes out.*)

Algernon I think that is rather mean of you, Ernest, I must say. (*Opens case and examines it.*) However, it makes no matter, for, now that I look at the inscription inside, I find that the thing isn't yours after all.
Jack Of course it's mine. (*Moving to him.*) You have seen me with it a hundred times, and you have no right whatsoever to read what is written inside. It is a very ungentlemanly thing to read a private cigarette case.
Algernon Oh! it is absurd to have a hard-and-fast rule about what one should read and what one shouldn't. More than half of modern culture depends on what one shouldn't read.
Jack I am quite aware of the fact, and I don't propose to discuss modern culture. It isn't the sort of thing one should talk of in private. I simply want my cigarette case back.
Algernon Yes; but this isn't your cigarette case. This cigarette case is a present from someone of the name of Cecily, and you said you didn't know anyone of that name.
Jack Well, if you want to know, Cecily happens to be my aunt.
Algernon Your aunt!
Jack Yes. Charming old lady she is, too. Lives at Tunbridge Wells. Just give it back to me, Algy.

[5] Scotland Yard: headquarters of the London police, especially the criminal investigation division.

Algernon (*Retreating to back of sofa*) But why does she call herself little Cecily if she is your aunt and lives at Tunbridge Wells? (*Reading*). 'From little Cecily with her fondest love.'

Jack (*Moving to sofa and kneeling upon it*) My dear fellow, what on earth is there in that? Some aunts are tall, some aunts are not tall. That is a matter that surely an aunt may be allowed to decide for herself. You seem to think that every aunt should be exactly like your aunt! That is absurd! For Heaven's sake give me back my cigarette case.

(*Follows* ALGERNON *round the room.*)

Algernon Yes. But why does your aunt call you her uncle? 'From little Cecily, with her fondest love to her dear Uncle Jack.' There is no objection, I admit, to an aunt being a small aunt, but why an aunt, no matter what her size may be, should call her own nephew her uncle, I can't quite make out. Besides, your name isn't Jack at all; it is Ernest.

Jack It isn't Ernest; it's Jack.

Algernon You have always told me it was Ernest. I have introduced you to everyone as Ernest. You answer to the name of Ernest. You look as if your name was Ernest. You are the most earnest looking person I ever saw in my life. It is perfectly absurd your saying that your name isn't Ernest. It's on your cards. Here is one of them. (*Taking it from case.*) 'Mr. Ernest Worthing, B 4, The Albany.' I'll keep this as a proof your name is Ernest if ever you attempt to deny it to me, or to Gwendolen, or to anyone else.

(*Puts the card in his pocket.*)

Jack Well, my name is Ernest in town and Jack in the country, and the cigarette case was given to me in the country.

Algernon Yes, but that does not account for the fact that your small Aunt Cecily, who lives at Tunbridge Wells, calls you her dear uncle. Come, old boy, you had much better have the thing out at once.

Jack My dear Algy, you talk exactly as if you were a dentist. It is very vulgar to talk like a dentist when one isn't a dentist. It produces a false impression.

Algernon Well, that is exactly what dentists always do. Now, go on! Tell me the whole thing. I may mention that I have always suspected you of being a confirmed and secret Bunburyist; and I am quite sure of it now.

Jack Bunburyist? What on earth do you mean by a Bunburyist?

Algernon I'll reveal to you the meaning of that incomparable expression as soon as you are kind enough to inform me why you are Ernest in town and Jack in the country.

Jack Well, produce my cigarette case first.

Algernon Here it is. (*Hands cigarette case.*) Now produce your explanation, and pray make it improbable.

(*Sits on sofa.*)

Jack My dear fellow, there is nothing improbable about my explanation at all. In fact it's perfectly ordinary. Old Mr. Thomas Cardew, who adopted me when I was a little boy, made me in his will guardian to his grand-daughter, Miss Cecily Cardew. Cecily, who addresses me as her uncle from motives of respect that you could not possibly appreciate, lives at my place in the country under the charge of her admirable governess, Miss Prism.

Algernon Where is that place in the country, by the way?

Jack That is nothing to you, dear boy. You are not going to be invited. . . . I may tell you candidly that the place is not in Shropshire.

Algernon I suspected that, my dear fellow! I have Bunburyed all over Shropshire on two separate occasions. Now, go on. Why are you Ernest in town and Jack in the country?

Jack My dear Algy, I don't know whether you will be able to understand my real motives. You are hardly serious enough. When one is placed in the position of guardian, one has to adopt a very high moral tone on all subjects. It's one's duty to do so. And as a high moral tone can hardly be said to conduce very much to either one's health or one's happiness, in order to get up to town I have always pretended to have a younger brother of the name of Ernest, who lives in the Albany, and gets into the most dreadful scrapes. That, my dear Algy, is the whole truth pure and simple.

Algernon The truth is rarely pure and never simple. Modern life would be very tedious if it were either, and modern literature a complete impossibility!

Jack That wouldn't be at all a bad thing.

Algernon Literary criticism is not your forte, my dear fellow. Don't try it. You should leave that to people who haven't been at a University. They do it so well in the daily papers. What you really are is a Bunburyist. I was quite right in saying you were a Bunburyist. You are one of the most advanced Bunburyists I know.

Jack What on earth do you mean?

Algernon You have invented a very useful younger brother called Ernest, in order that you may be able to come up to town as often as you like. I have invented an invaluable permanent invalid called Bunbury, in order that I may be able to do down into the country whenever I choose. Bunbury is perfectly invaluable. If it wasn't for Bunbury's extraordinary bad health, for instance, I wouldn't be able to dine with you at Willis's to-night, for I have been really engaged to Aunt Augusta for more than a week.

Jack I haven't asked you to dine with me anywhere to-night.

Algernon I know. You are absurdly careless about sending out invitations. It is very foolish of you. Nothing annoys people so much as not receiving invitations.

Jack You had much better dine with your Aunt Augusta.

Algernon I haven't the smallest intention of doing anything of the kind. To begin with, I dined there on Monday, and once a week is quite enough to dine with one's own relations. In the second place, whenever I do dine there I am always treated as a member of the family, and sent down[6] with either no woman at all, or two. In the third place, I know perfectly well whom she will place me next to, to-night. She will place me next Mary Farquhar, who always flirts with her own husband across the dinner-table. That is not very pleasant. Indeed, it is not even decent . . . and that sort of thing is enormously on the increase. The amount of women in London who flirt with their own husbands is perfectly scandalous. It looks so bad. It is simply washing one's clean linen in public. Besides, now that I know you to be a confirmed Bunburyist I naturally want to talk to you about Bunburying. I want to tell you the rules.

Jack I'm not a Bunburyist at all. If Gwendolen accepts me, I am going to kill my brother, indeed I think I'll kill him in any case. Cecily is a little too much interested in him. It is rather a bore. So I am going to get rid of Ernest. And I strongly advise you to do the same with Mr. . . . with your invalid friend who has the absurd name.

Algernon Nothing will induce me to part with Bunbury, and if you ever get married, which seems to me extremely problematic, you will be very glad to know Bunbury. A man who marries without knowing Bunbury has a very tedious time of it.

Jack That is nonsense. If I marry a charming girl like Gwendolen, and she is the only girl I ever saw in my life that I would marry, I certainly won't want to know Bunbury.

Algernon Then your wife will. You don't seem to realize, that in married life three is company and two is none.

Jack (*Sententiously*) That, my dear young friend, is the theory that the corrupt French Drama has been propounding for the last fifty years.

Algernon Yes; and that the happy English home has proved in half the time.

Jack For heaven's sake, don't try to be cynical. It's perfectly easy to be cynical.

Algernon My dear fellow, it isn't easy to be anything now-a-days. There's such a lot of beastly competition about. (*The sound of an electric bell is heard.*) Ah! that must be Aunt Augusta. Only relatives, or creditors, ever ring in that Wagnerian[7] manner. Now, if I get her out of the way for ten minutes, so that you can have an opportunity for proposing to Gwendolen, may I dine with you to-night at Willis's?

Jack I suppose so, if you want to.

[6] sent down: asked to escort to dinner.
[7] Wagnerian: in the manner of the grandiose dramatic operas of Richard Wagner (1813–1883).

Algernon   Yes, but you must be serious about it. I hate people who are not serious about meals. It is so shallow of them.

(*Enter* LANE.)

Lane   Lady Bracknell and Miss Fairfax.

(ALGERNON *goes forward to meet them. Enter* LADY BRACKNELL *and* GWENDOLEN.)

Lady Bracknell   Good afternoon, dear Algernon, I hope you are behaving very well.

Algernon   I'm feeling very well, Aunt Augusta.

Lady Bracknell   That's not quite the same thing. In fact the two things rarely go together.

(*Sees* JACK *and bows to him with icy coldness.*)

Algernon (*To* GWENDOLEN)   Dear me, you are smart!

Gwendolen   I am always smart! Aren't I, Mr. Worthing?

Jack   You're quite perfect, Miss Fairfax.

Gwendolen   Oh! I hope I am not that. It would leave no room for developments, and I intend to develop in many directions.

(GWENDOLEN *and* JACK *sit down together in the corner.*)

Lady Bracknell   I'm sorry if we are a little late, Algernon, but I was obliged to call on dear Lady Harbury. I hadn't been there since her poor husband's death. I never saw a woman so altered; she looks quite twenty years younger. And now I'll have a cup of tea, and one of those nice cucumber sandwiches you promised me.

Algernon   Certainly, Aunt Augusta.

(*Goes over to tea-table.*)

Lady Bracknell   Won't you come and sit here, Gwendolen?

Gwendolen   Thanks, mamma, I'm quite comfortable where I am.

Algernon (*Picking up empty plate in horror*)   Good heavens! Lane! Why are there no cucumber sandwiches? I ordered them specially.

Lane (*Gravely*)   There were no cucumbers in the market this morning, sir. I went down twice.

Algernon   No cucumbers!

Lane   No, sir. Not even for ready money.

Algernon   That will do, Lane, thank you.

Lane   Thank you, sir. (*Goes out.*)

Algernon   I am greatly distressed, Aunt Augusta, about there being no cucumbers, not even for ready money.

Lady Bracknell   It really makes no matter, Algernon. I had some crumpets with Lady Harbury, who seems to me to be living entirely for pleasure now.

Algernon   I hear her hair has turned quite gold from grief.

Lady Bracknell   It certainly has changed its colour. From what cause I, of course, cannot say. (ALGERNON *crosses and hands tea.*) Thank you. I've quite a treat for you to-night, Algernon. I am going to send you down with Mary Farquhar. She is such a nice woman, and so attentive to her husband. It's delightful to watch them.

Algernon   I am afraid, Aunt Augusta, I shall have to give up the pleasure of dining with you to-night after all.

Lady Bracknell (*Frowning*)   I hope not, Algernon. It would put my table completely out.[8] Your uncle would have to dine upstairs. Fortunately he is accustomed to that.

Algernon   It is a great bore, and, I need hardly say, a terrible disappointment to me, but the fact is I have just had a telegram to say that my poor friend Bunbury is very ill again. (*Exchanges glances with* JACK.) They seem to think I should be with him.

Lady Bracknell   It is very strange. This Mr. Bunbury seems to suffer from curiously bad health.

Algernon   Yes; poor Bunbury is a dreadful invalid.

Lady Bracknell   Well, I must say, Algernon, that I think it is high time that Mr. Bunbury made up his mind whether he was going to live or to die. This shilly-shallying with the question is absurd. Nor do I in any way approve of the modern sympathy with invalids. I consider it morbid. Illness of any kind is hardly a thing to be encouraged in others. Health is the primary duty of life. I am always telling that to your poor uncle, but he never seems to take much notice . . . as far as any improvement in his ailments goes. I should be much obliged if you would ask Mr. Bunbury from me, to be kind enough not to have a relapse on Saturday, for I rely on you to arrange my music for me. It is my last reception and one wants something that will encourage conversation, particularly at the end of the season when everyone has practically said whatever they had to say, which, in most cases, was probably not much.

Algernon   I'll speak to Bunbury, Aunt Augusta, if he is still conscious, and I think I can promise you he'll be all right by Saturday. Of course the music is a great difficulty. You see, if one plays good music, people don't listen, and if one plays bad music people don't talk. But I'll run over the programme I've drawn out, if you will kindly come into the next room for a moment.

Lady Bracknell   Thank you, Algernon. It is very thoughtful of you. (*Rising, and following* ALGERNON.) I'm sure the programme will be delightful, after a few expurgations.[9] French songs I cannot possibly allow. People

---

[8] put my table completely out: spoil the balance between men and women.

[9] expurgations: removal of material which might be considered obscene or offensive.

always seem to think that they are improper, and either look shocked, which is vulgar, or laugh, which is worse. But German sounds a thoroughly respectable language, and indeed, I believe is so. Gwendolen, you will accompany me.

Gwendolen Certainly, mamma.

(LADY BRACKNELL *and* ALGERNON *go into the music room,* GWENDOLEN *remains behind.*)

Jack Charming day it has been, Miss Fairfax.

Gwendolen Pray don't talk to me about the weather, Mr. Worthing. Whenever people talk to me about the weather, I always feel quite certain that they mean something else. And that makes me so nervous.

Jack I do mean something else.

Gwendolen I thought so. In fact, I am never wrong.

Jack And I would like to be allowed to take advantage of Lady Bracknell's temporary absence . . .

Gwendolen I would certainly advise you to do so. Mamma has a way of coming back suddenly into a room that I have often had to speak to her about.

Jack (*Nervously*) Miss Fairfax, ever since I met you I have admired you more than any girl . . . I have ever met since . . . I met you.

Gwendolen Yes, I am quite aware of the fact. And I often wish that in public, at any rate, you had been more demonstrative. For me you have always had an irresistible fascination. Even before I met you I was far from indifferent to you. (JACK *looks at her in amazement.*) We live, as I hope you know, Mr. Worthing, in an age of ideals. The fact is constantly mentioned in the more expensive monthly magazines, and has reached the provincial pulpits I am told: and my ideal has always been to love some one of the name of Ernest. There is something in that name that inspires absolute confidence. The moment Algernon first mentioned to me that he had a friend called Ernest, I knew I was destined to love you.

Jack You really love me, Gwendolen?

Gwendolen Passionately!

Jack Darling! You don't know how happy you've made me.

Gwendolen My own Ernest!

Jack But you don't really mean to say that you couldn't love me if my name wasn't Ernest?

Gwendolen But your name is Ernest.

Jack Yes, I know it is. But supposing it was something else? Do you mean to say you couldn't love me then?

Gwendolen (*Glibly*) Ah! that is clearly a metaphysical speculation, and like most metaphysical speculations has very little reference at all to the actual facts of real life, as we know them.

Jack Personally, darling, to speak quite candidly, I don't much care about the name of Ernest . . . I don't think the name suits me at all.

Gwendolen It suits you perfectly. It is a divine name. It has a music of its own. It produces vibrations.

Jack Well, really, Gwendolen, I must say that I think there are lots of other much nicer names. I think Jack, for instance, a charming name.

Gwendolen Jack? . . . No, there is very little music in the name Jack, if any at all, indeed. It does not thrill. It produces absolutely no vibrations. . . . I have known several Jacks, and they all, without exception, were more than usually plain. Besides, Jack is a notorious domesticity[10] for John! And I pity any woman who is married to a man called John. She would probably never be allowed to know the entrancing pleasure of a single moment's solitude. The only really safe name is Ernest.

Jack Gwendolen, I must get christened at once—I mean we must get married at once. There is no time to be lost.

Gwendolen Married, Mr. Worthing?

Jack (*Astounded*) Well . . . surely. You know that I love you, and you led me to believe, Miss Fairfax, that you were not absolutely indifferent to me.

Gwendolen I adore you. But you haven't proposed to me yet. Nothing has been said at all about marriage. The subject has not even been touched on.

Jack Well . . . may I propose to you now?

Gwendolen I think it would be an admirable opportunity. And to spare you any possible disappointment, Mr. Worthing, I think it only fair to tell you quite frankly beforehand that I am fully determined to accept you.

Jack Gwendolen!

Gwendolen Yes, Mr. Worthing, what have you got to say to me?

Jack You know what I have got to say to you.

Gwendolen Yes, but you don't say it.

Jack Gwendolen, will you marry me?

(*Goes on his knees.*)

Gwendolen Of course I will, darling. How long you have been about it! I am afraid you have had very little experience in how to propose.

Jack My own one, I have never loved anyone in the world but you.

Gwendolen Yes, but men often propose for practice. I know my brother Gerald does. All my girl-friends tell me so. What wonderfully blue eyes you have, Ernest! They are quite, quite, blue. I hope you will always look at me just like that, especially when there are other people present.

(*Enter* LADY BRACKNELL.)

Lady Bracknell Mr. Worthing! Rise, sir, from this semi-recumbent posture. It is most indecorous.

---

[10] domesticity: here, a household name, nickname.

Gwendolen   Mamma! (*He tries to rise; she restrains him.*) I must beg you to retire. This is no place for you. Besides, Mr. Worthing has not quite finished yet.
Lady Bracknell   Finished what, may I ask?
Gwendolen   I am engaged to Mr. Worthing, mamma.

(*They rise together.*)

Lady Bracknell   Pardon me, you are not engaged to anyone. When you do become engaged to some one, I, or your father, should his health permit him, will inform you of the fact. An engagement should come on a young girl as a surprise, pleasant or unpleasant, as the case may be. It is hardly a matter that she could be allowed to arrange for herself.... And now I have a few questions to put to you, Mr. Worthing. While I am making these inquiries, you, Gwendolen, will wait for me below in the carriage.
Gwendolen (*Reproachfully*)   Mamma!
Lady Bracknell   In the carriage, Gwendolen!

(GWENDOLEN *goes to the door. She and* JACK *blow kisses to each other behind* LADY BRACKNELL's *back.* LADY BRACKNELL *looks vaguely about as if she could not understand what the noise was. Finally turns round.*) Gwendolen, the carriage!

Gwendolen   Yes, mamma. (*Goes out, looking back at* JACK.)
Lady Bracknell (*Sitting down*)   You can take a seat, Mr. Worthing.

(*Looks in her pocket for note-book and pencil.*)

Jack   Thank you, Lady Bracknell, I prefer standing.
Lady Bracknell (*Pencil and note-book in hand*)   I feel bound to tell you that you are not down on my list of eligible young men, although I have the same list as the dear Duchess of Bolton has. We work together, in fact. However, I am quite ready to enter your name, should your answers be what a really affectionate mother requires. Do you smoke?
Jack   Well, yes, I must admit I smoke.
Lady Bracknell   I am glad to hear it. A man should always have an occupation of some kind. There are far too many idle men in London as it is. How old are you?
Jack   Twenty-nine.
Lady Bracknell   A very good age to be married at. I have always been of opinion that a man who desires to get married should know either everything or nothing. Which do you know?
Jack (*After some hesitation*)   I know nothing, Lady Bracknell.
Lady Bracknell   I am pleased to hear it. I do not approve of anything that tampers with natural ignorance. Ignorance is like a delicate exotic fruit; touch it and the bloom is gone. The whole theory of modern education is radically unsound. Fortunately in England at any rate, education pro-

duces no effect whatsoever. If it did, it would prove a serious danger to the upper classes, and probably lead to acts of violence in Grosvenor Square.[11] What is your income?

Jack   Between seven and eight thousand a year.

Lady Bracknell (*Makes a note in her book*)   In land, or in investments?

Jack   In investments, chiefly.

Lady Bracknell   That is satisfactory. What between the duties expected of one during one's lifetime, and the duties[12] exacted from one after one's death, land has ceased to be either a profit or a pleasure. It gives one position, and prevents one from keeping it up. That's all that can be said about land.

Jack   I have a country house with some land, of course, attached to it, about fifteen hundred acres, I believe; but I don't depend on that for my real income. In fact, as far as I can make out, the poachers[13] are the only people who make anything out of it.

Lady Bracknell   A country house! How many bedrooms? Well, that point can be cleared up afterwards. You have a town house, I hope? A girl with a simple, unspoiled nature, like Gwendolen, could hardly be expected to reside in the country.

Jack   Well, I own a house in Belgrave Square,[14] but it is let by the year to Lady Bloxham. Of course, I can get it back whenever I like, at six months' notice.

Lady Bracknell   Lady Bloxham? I don't know her.

Jack   Oh, she goes about very little. She is a lady considerably advanced in years.

Lady Bracknell   Ah, now-a-days that is no guarantee of respectability of character. What number in Belgrave Square?

Jack   149.

Lady Bracknell (*Shaking her head*)   The unfashionable side. I thought there was something. However, that could easily be altered.

Jack   Do you mean the fashion, or the side?

Lady Bracknell (*Sternly*)   Both, if necessary, I presume. What are your politics?

Jack   Well, I am afraid I really have none. I am a Liberal Unionist.[15]

Lady Bracknell   Oh, they count as Tories.[16] They dine with us. Or come in the evening, at any rate. Now to minor matters. Are your parents living?

Jack   I have lost both my parents.

[11] Grosvenor Square: a square in Mayfair, a fashionable district in London.
[12] duties: inheritance taxes.
[13] poachers: trespassers who hunt game on restricted land, such as a country estate.
[14] Belgrave Square: a very fashionable address in London.
[15] Liberal Unionist: member of the conservative branch of the Liberal political party.
[16] Tories: members of the Conservative political party.

Lady Bracknell Both? . . . That seems like carelessness. Who was your father? He was evidently a man of some wealth. Was he born in what the Radical papers call the purple of commerce, or did he rise from the ranks of the aristocracy?

Jack I am afraid I really don't know. The fact is, Lady Bracknell, I said I had lost my parents. It would be nearer the truth to say that my parents seem to have lost me . . . I don't actually know who I am by birth. I was . . . well, I was found.

Lady Bracknell Found!

Jack The late Mr. Thomas Cardew, an old gentleman of a very charitable and kindly disposition, found me, and gave me the name of Worthing, because he happened to have a first-class ticket for Worthing in his pocket at the time. Worthing is a place in Sussex. It is a seaside resort.

Lady Bracknell Where did the charitable gentleman who had a first-class ticket for this seaside resort find you?

Jack (*Gravely*) In a hand-bag.

Lady Bracknell A hand-bag?

Jack (*Very seriously*) Yes, Lady Bracknell. I was in a hand-bag—a somewhat large, black leather hand-bag, with handles to it—an ordinary hand-bag in fact.

Lady Bracknell In what locality did this Mr. James, or Thomas, Cardew come across this ordinary hand-bag?

Jack In the cloak-room at Victoria Station.[17] It was given to him in mistake for his own.

Lady Bracknell The cloak-room at Victoria Station?

Jack Yes. The Brighton line.

Lady Bracknell The line is immaterial. Mr. Worthing, I confess I feel somewhat bewildered by what you have just told me. To be born, or at any rate bred, in a hand-bag, whether it had handles or not, seems to me to display a contempt for the ordinary decencies of family life that remind one of the worst excesses of the French Revolution.[18] And I presume you know what that unfortunate movement led to? As for the particular locality in which the hand-bag was found, a cloak-room at a railway station might serve to conceal a social indiscretion—has probably, indeed, been used for that purpose before now—but it could hardly be regarded as an assured basis for a recognized position in good society.

Jack May I ask you then what you would advise me to do? I need hardly say I would do anything in the world to ensure Gwendolen's happiness.

Lady Bracknell I would strongly advise you, Mr. Worthing, to try and

[17] Victoria Station: railway terminal in London.

[18] French Revolution: revolt against monarchy and aristocracy between 1789 and 1799 in France. While it was democratic in concept, the Revolution involved mob tyranny and violence and, reputedly, "free love."

acquire some relations as soon as possible, and to make a definite effort to produce at any rate one parent, of either sex, before the season is quite over.

Jack Well, I don't see how I could possibly manage to do that. I can produce the hand-bag at any moment. It is in my dressing-room at home. I really think that should satisfy you, Lady Bracknell.

Lady Bracknell Me, sir! What has it to do with me? You can hardly imagine that I and Lord Bracknell would dream of allowing our only daughter —a girl brought up with the utmost care—to marry into a cloak-room, and form an alliance with a parcel? Good morning, Mr. Worthing!

(LADY BRACKNELL *sweeps out in majestic indignation.*)

Jack Good morning! (ALGERNON, *from the other room, strikes up the Wedding March.* JACK *looks perfectly furious, and goes to the door.*) For goodness' sake don't play that ghastly tune, Algy! How idiotic you are!

(*The music stops, and* ALGERNON *enters cheerily.*)

Algernon Didn't it go off all right, old boy? You don't mean to say Gwendolen refused you? I know it is a way she has. She is always refusing people. I think it is most ill-natured of her.

Jack Oh, Gwendolen is as right as a trivet.[19] As far as she is concerned, we are engaged. Her mother is perfectly unbearable. Never met such a Gorgon . . .[20] I don't really know what a Gorgon is like, but I am quite sure that Lady Bracknell is one. In any case, she is a monster, without being a myth, which is rather unfair. . . . I beg your pardon, Algy, I suppose I shouldn't talk about your own aunt in that way before you.

Algernon My dear boy, I love hearing my relations abused. It is the only thing that makes me put up with them at all. Relations are simply a tedious pack of people, who haven't got the remotest knowledge of how to live, nor the smallest instinct about when to die.

Jack Oh, that is nonsense!

Algernon It isn't!

Jack Well, I won't argue about the matter. You always want to argue about things.

Algernon That is exactly what things were originally made for.

Jack Upon my word, if I thought that, I'd shoot myself . . . (*A pause.*) You don't think there is any chance of Gwendolen becoming like her mother in about a hundred and fifty years, do you Algy?

Algernon All women become like their mothers. That is their tragedy. No man does. That's his.

[19] right as a trivet: OK, just right.
[20] Gorgon: in Greek mythology, a woman so ugly that men who looked at her turned to stone.

Jack   Is that clever?

Algernon   It is perfectly phrased! and quite as true as any observation in civilized life should be.

Jack   I am sick to death of cleverness. Everybody is clever now-a-days. You can't go anywhere without meeting clever people. The thing has become an absolute public nuisance. I wish to goodness we had a few fools left.

Algernon   We have.

Jack   I should extremely like to meet them. What do they talk about?

Algernon   The fools? Oh! about the clever people, of course.

Jack   What fools!

Algernon   By the way, did you tell Gwendolen the truth about your being Ernest in town, and Jack in the country?

Jack (*In a very patronising manner*)   My dear fellow, the truth isn't quite the sort of thing one tells to a nice, sweet, refined girl. What extraordinary ideas you have about the way to behave to a woman!

Algernon   The only way to behave to a woman is to make love to her, if she is pretty, and to someone else if she is plain.

Jack   Oh, that is nonsense.

Algernon   What about your brother? What about the profligate Ernest?

Jack   Oh, before the end of the week I shall have got rid of him. I'll say he died in Paris of apoplexy. Lots of people die of apoplexy, quite suddenly, don't they?

Algernon   Yes, but it's hereditary, my dear fellow. It's a sort of thing that runs in families. You had much better say a severe chill.

Jack   You are sure a severe chill isn't hereditary, or anything of that kind?

Algernon   Of course it isn't!

Jack   Very well, then. My poor brother Ernest is carried off suddenly in Paris, by a severe chill. That gets rid of him.

Algernon   But I thought you said that . . . Miss Cardew was a little too much interested in your poor brother Ernest? Won't she feel his loss a good deal?

Jack   Oh, that is all right. Cecily is not a silly, romantic girl, I am glad to say. She has got a capital appetite, goes long walks, and pays no attention at all to her lessons.

Algernon   I would rather like to see Cecily.

Jack   I will take very good care you never do. She is excessively pretty, and she is only just eighteen.

Algernon   Have you told Gwendolen yet that you have an excessively pretty ward who is only just eighteen?

Jack   Oh! One doesn't blurt these things out to people. Cecily and Gwendolen are perfectly certain to be extremely great friends. I'll bet you anything you like that half an hour after they have met, they will be calling each other sister.

Algernon   Women only do that when they have called each other a lot of other things first. Now, my dear boy, if we want to get a good table at Willis's, we really must go and dress. Do you know it is nearly seven?

Jack (*Irritably*)   Oh! it always is nearly seven.

Algernon   Well, I'm hungry.

Jack   I never knew you when you weren't. . . .

Algernon   What shall we do after dinner? Go to a theatre?

Jack   Oh no! I loathe listening.

Algernon   Well, let us go to the Club? [21]

Jack   Oh, no! I hate talking.

Algernon   Well, we might trot round to the Empire[22] at ten?

Jack   Oh, no! I can't bear looking at things. It is so silly.

Algernon   Well, what shall we do?

Jack   Nothing!

Algernon   It is awfully hard work doing nothing. However, I don't mind hard work where there is no definite object of any kind.

(*Enter* LANE.)

Lane   Miss Fairfax.

(*Enter* GWENDOLEN. LANE *goes out.*)

Algernon   Gwendolen, upon my word!

Gwendolen   Algy, kindly turn your back. I have something very particular to say to Mr. Worthing.

Algernon   Really, Gwendolen, I don't think I can allow this at all.

Gwendolen   Algy, you always adopt a strictly immoral attitude towards life. You are not quite old enough to do that.

(ALGERNON *retires to the fireplace.*)

Jack   My own darling!

Gwendolen   Ernest, we may never be married. From the expression on mamma's face I fear we never shall. Few parents now-a-days pay any regard to what their children say to them. The old-fashioned respect for the young is fast dying out. Whatever influence I ever had over mamma, I lost at the age of three. But although she may prevent us from becoming man and wife, and I may marry someone else, and marry often, nothing that she can possibly do can alter my eternal devotion to you.

Jack   Dear Gwendolen!

Gwendolen   The story of your romantic origin, as related to me by mamma, with unpleasing comments, has naturally stirred the deeper fibres of my nature. Your Christian name has an irresistible fascination.

---

[21] Club: a building where members and their guests gather for meals, conversation, etc.

[22] Empire: a musical comedy theater.

The simplicity of your character makes you exquisitely incomprehensible to me. Your town address at the Albany I have. What is your address in the country?

Jack   The Manor House, Woolton, Hertfordshire.[23]

(ALGERNON, *who has been carefully listening, smiles to himself, and writes the address on his shirt-cuff. Then picks up the Railway Guide.*[24])

Gwendolen   There is a good postal service, I suppose? It may be necessary to do something desperate. That, of course, will require serious consideration. I will communicate with you daily.

Jack   My own one!

Gwendolen   How long do you remain in town?

Jack   Till Monday.

Gwendolen   Good! Algy, you may turn round now.

Algernon   Thanks, I've turned round already.

Gwendolen   You may also ring the bell.

Jack   You will let me see you to your carriage, my own darling?

Gwendolen   Certainly.

Jack (*To* LANE, *who now enters*)   I will see Miss Fairfax out.

Lane   Yes, sir.

(JACK *and* GWENDOLEN *go off.* LANE *presents several letters on a salver to* ALGERNON. *It is to be surmised that they are bills, as* ALGERNON *after looking at the envelopes, tears them up.*)

Algernon   A glass of sherry, Lane.

Lane   Yes, sir.

Algernon   To-morrow, Lane, I'm going Bunburying.

Lane   Yes, sir.

Algernon   I shall probably not be back till Monday. You can put up my dress clothes, my smoking jacket, and all the Bunbury suits . . .

Lane   Yes, sir.

(*Handing sherry.*)

Algernon   I hope to-morrow will be a fine day, Lane.

Lane   It never is, sir.

Algernon   Lane, you're a perfect pessimist.

Lane   I do my best to give satisfaction, sir.

(*Enter* JACK. LANE *goes off.*)

Jack   There's a sensible, intellectual girl! the only girl I ever cared for in

---

[23] Hertfordshire: a county near London, a favored location for country estates.
[24] Railway Guide: the official time-table for rail passenger service.

my life. (ALGERNON *is laughing immoderately*.) What on earth are you so amused at?

Algernon   Oh, I'm a little anxious about poor Bunbury, that is all.

Jack   If you don't take care, your friend Bunbury will get you into a serious scrape some day.

Algernon   I love scrapes. They are the only things that are never serious.

Jack   Oh, that's nonsense, Algy. You never talk anything but nonsense.

Algernon   Nobody ever does.

(JACK *looks indignantly at him, and leaves the room.* ALGERNON *lights a cigarette, reads his shirt-cuff, and smiles.*)

(*Act-drop*)

ACT II

Scene: *Garden at the Manor House. A flight of gray stone steps leads up to the house. The garden, an old-fashioned one, full of roses. Time of year, July. Basket chairs, and a table covered with books, are set under a large yew tree.*

MISS PRISM *discovered seated at the table.* CECILY *is at the back watering flowers.*

Miss Prism (*Calling*)   Cecily, Cecily! Surely such a utilitarian occupation as the watering of flowers is rather Moulton's duty than yours? Especially at a moment when intellectual pleasures await you. Your German grammar is on the table. Pray open it at page fifteen. We will repeat yesterday's lesson.

Cecily (*Coming over very slowly*)   But I don't like German. It isn't at all a becoming language. I know perfectly well that I look quite plain after my German lesson.

Miss Prism   Child, you know how anxious your guardian is that you should improve yourself in every way. He laid particular stress on your German, as he was leaving for town yesterday. Indeed, he always lays stress on your German when he is leaving for town.

Cecily   Dear Uncle Jack is so very serious! Sometimes he is so serious that I think he cannot be quite well.

Miss Prism (*Drawing herself up*)   Your guardian enjoys the best of health, and his gravity of demeanour is especially to be commended in one so comparatively young as he is. I know no one who has a higher sense of duty and responsibility.

Cecily   I suppose that is why he often looks a little bored when we three are together.

Miss Prism Cecily! I am surprised at you. Mr. Worthing has many troubles in his life. Idle merriment and triviality would be out of place in his conversation. You must remember his constant anxiety about that unfortunate young man, his brother.

Cecily I wish Uncle Jack would allow that unfortunate young man, his brother, to come down here sometimes. We might have a good influence over him, Miss Prism. I am sure you certainly would. You know German, and geology, and things of that kind influence a man very much.

(CECILY *begins to write in her diary.*)

Miss Prism (*Shaking her head*) I do not think that even I could produce any effect on a character that according to his own brother's admission is irretrievably weak and vacillating. Indeed I am not sure that I would desire to reclaim him. I am not in favour of this modern mania for turning bad people into good people at a moment's notice. As a man sows so let him reap. You must put away your diary, Cecily. I really don't see why you should keep a diary at all.

Cecily I keep a diary in order to enter the wonderful secrets of my life. If I didn't write them down I should probably forget all about them.

Miss Prism Memory, my dear Cecily, is the diary that we all carry about with us.

Cecily Yes, but it usually chronicles the things that have never happened, and couldn't possibly have happened. I believe that Memory is responsible for nearly all the three-volume novels that Mudie[25] sends us.

Miss Prism Do not speak slightingly of the three-volume novel, Cecily. I wrote one myself in earlier days.

Cecily Did you really, Miss Prism? How wonderfully clever you are! I hope it did not end happily? I don't like novels that end happily. They depress me so much.

Miss Prism The good ended happily, and the bad unhappily. That is what Fiction means.

Cecily I suppose so. But it seems very unfair. And was your novel ever published?

Miss Prism Alas! no. The manuscript unfortunately was abandoned. I use the word in the sense of lost or mislaid. To your work, child, these speculations are profitless.

Cecily (*Smiling*) But I see dear Dr. Chasuble coming up through the garden.

Miss Prism (*Rising and advancing*) Dr. Chasuble! This is indeed a pleasure.

(*Enter* CANON CHASUBLE.)

Chasuble And how are we this morning? Miss Prism, you are, I trust, well?

[25] Mudie: a lending library.

Cecily Miss Prism has just been complaining of a slight headache. I think it would do her so much good to have a short stroll with you in the park, Dr. Chasuble.

Miss Prism Cecily, I have not mentioned anything about a headache.

Cecily No, dear Miss Prism, I know that, but I felt instinctively that you had a headache. Indeed, I was thinking about that, and not about my German lesson, when the Rector came in.

Chasuble I hope, Cecily, you are not inattentive.

Cecily Oh, I am afraid I am.

Chasuble That is strange. Were I fortunate enough to be Miss Prism's pupil, I would hang upon her lips. (Miss Prism *glares.*) I spoke metaphorically.—My metaphor was drawn from bees. Ahem! Mr. Worthing, I suppose, has not returned from town yet?

Miss Prism We do not expect him till Monday afternoon.

Chasuble Ah yes, he usually likes to spend his Sunday in London. He is not one of those whose sole aim is enjoyment, as, by all accounts, that unfortunate young man, his brother, seems to be. But I must not disturb Egeria[26] and her pupil any longer.

Miss Prism Egeria? My name is Lætitia, Doctor.

Chasuble (*Bowing*) A classical allusion merely, drawn from the Pagan authors. I shall see you both no doubt at Evensong.[27]

Miss Prism I think, dear Doctor, I will have a stroll with you. I find I have a headache after all, and a walk might do it good.

Chasuble With pleasure, Miss Prism, with pleasure. We might go as far as the schools and back.

Miss Prism That would be delightful. Cecily, you will read your Political Economy in my absence. The chapter on the Fall of the Rupee[28] you may omit. It is somewhat too sensational. Even these metallic problems have their melodramatic side.

(*Goes down the garden with* Dr. Chasuble.)

Cecily (*Picks up books and throws them back on table.*) Horrid Political Economy! Horrid Geography! Horrid, horrid German!

(*Enter* Merriman *with a card on a salver.*)

Merriman Mr. Ernest Worthing has just driven over from the station. He has brought his luggage with him.

Cecily (*Takes the card and reads it*) 'Mr. Ernest Worthing, B 4, The Albany, W.' Uncle Jack's brother! Did you tell him Mr. Worthing was in town?

[26] Egeria: from Roman mythology, a woman who advises or counsels others.
[27] Evensong: evening prayers, vespers.
[28] Fall of the Rupee: monetary standard of India, which collapsed as a result of British colonial policies.

Merriman Yes, Miss. He seemed very much disappointed. I mentioned that you and Miss Prism were in the garden. He said he was anxious to speak to you privately for a moment.

Cecily Ask Mr. Ernest Worthing to come here. I suppose you had better talk to the housekeeper about a room for him.

Merriman Yes, Miss.

(MERRIMAN *goes off.*)

Cecily I have never met any really wicked person before. I feel rather frightened. I am so afraid he will look just like everyone else.

(*Enter* ALGERNON, *very gay and debonair.*)

He does!

Algernon (*Raising his hat*) You are my little cousin Cecily, I'm sure.

Cecily You are under some strange mistake. I am not little. In fact, I believe I am more than usually tall for my age. (ALGERNON *is rather taken aback.*) But I am your cousin Cecily. You, I see from your card, are Uncle Jack's brother, my cousin Ernest, my wicked cousin Ernest.

Algernon Oh! I am not really wicked at all, cousin Cecily. You musn't think that I am wicked.

Cecily If you are not, then you have certainly been deceiving us all in a very inexcusable manner. I hope you have not been leading a double life, pretending to be wicked and being really good all the time. That would be hypocrisy.

Algernon (*Looks at her in amazement*) Oh! of course I have been rather reckless.

Cecily I am glad to hear it.

Algernon In fact, now you mention the subject, I have been very bad in my own small way.

Cecily I don't think you should be so proud of that, though I am sure it must have been very pleasant.

Algernon It is much pleasanter being here with you.

Cecily I can't understand how you are here at all. Uncle Jack won't be back till Monday afternoon.

Algernon That is a great disappointment. I am obliged to go up by the first train on Monday morning. I have a business appointment that I am anxious . . . to miss.

Cecily Couldn't you miss it anywhere but in London?

Algernon No: the appointment is in London.

Cecily Well, I know, of course, how important it is not to keep a business engagement, if one wants to retain any sense of the beauty of life, but still I think you had better wait till Uncle Jack arrives. I know he wants to speak to you about your emigrating.

Algernon About my what?

Cecily Your emigrating. He has gone up to buy your outfit.

Algernon I certainly wouldn't let Jack buy my outfit. He has no taste in neckties at all.

Cecily I don't think you will require neckties. Uncle Jack is sending you to Australia.

Algernon Australia! I'd sooner die.

Cecily Well, he said at dinner on Wednesday night, that you would have to choose between this world, the next world, and Australia.

Algernon Oh, well! The accounts I have received of Australia and the next world, are not particularly encouraging. This world is good enough for me, cousin Cecily.

Cecily Yes, but are you good enough for it?

Algernon I'm afraid I'm not that. That is why I want you to reform me. You might make that your mission, if you don't mind, cousin Cecily.

Cecily I'm afraid I've no time, this afternoon.

Algernon Well, would you mind my reforming myself this afternoon?

Cecily It is rather Quixotic[29] of you. But I think you should try.

Algernon I will. I feel better already.

Cecily You are looking a little worse.

Algernon That is because I am hungry.

Cecily How thoughtless of me. I should have remembered that when one is going to lead an entirely new life, one requires regular and wholesome meals. Won't you come in?

Algernon Thank you. Might I have a buttonhole[30] first? I never have any appetite unless I have a buttonhole first.

Cecily A Maréchal Niel? [31]

(*Picks up scissors.*)

Algernon No, I'd sooner have a pink rose.

Cecily Why?

(*Cuts a flower.*)

Algernon Because you are like a pink rose, cousin Cecily.

Cecily I don't think it can be right for you to talk to me like that. Miss Prism never says such things to me.

Algernon Then Miss Prism is a short-sighted old lady. (CECILY *puts the rose in his buttonhole.*) You are the prettiest girl I ever saw.

Cecily Miss Prism says that all good looks are a snare.

Algernon They are a snare that every sensible man would like to be caught in.

[29] Quixotic: capricious, romantic, like Don Quixote.
[30] buttonhole: flower to wear in the buttonhole on one's lapel.
[31] Maréchal Niel: a variety of yellow rose.

Cecily Oh! I don't think I would care to catch a sensible man. I shouldn't know what to talk to him about.

(*They pass into the house.* MISS PRISM *and* DR. CHASUBLE *return.*)

Miss Prism You are too much alone, dear Dr. Chasuble. You should get married. A misanthrope[32] I can understand—a womanthrope,[33] never!

Chasuble (*With a scholar's shudder*) Believe me, I do not deserve so neologistic a phrase. The precept as well as the practice of the Primitive Church[34] was distinctly against matrimony.

Miss Prism (*Sententiously*) That is obviously the reason why the Primitive Church has not lasted up to the present day. And you do not seem to realise, dear Doctor, that by persistently remaining single, a man converts himself into a permanent public temptation. Men should be more careful; this very celibacy leads weaker vessels astray.

Chasuble But is a man not equally attractive when married?

Miss Prism No married man is ever attractive except to his wife.

Chasuble And often, I've been told, not even to her.

Miss Prism That depends on the intellectual sympathies of the woman. Maturity can always be depended on. Ripeness can be trusted. Young women are green. (DR. CHASUBLE *starts.*) I spoke horticulturally. My metaphor was drawn from fruits. But where is Cecily?

Chasuble Perhaps she followed us to the schools.

(*Enter* JACK *slowly from the back of the garden. He is dressed in the deepest mourning, with crape hat-band and black gloves.*)

Miss Prism Mr. Worthing!

Chasuble Mr. Worthing?

Miss Prism This is indeed a surprise. We did not look for you till Monday afternoon.

Jack (*Shakes* MISS PRISM'S *hand in a tragic manner*) I have returned sooner than I expected. Dr. Chasuble, I hope you are well?

Chasuble Dear Mr. Worthing, I trust this garb of woe does not betoken some terrible calamity?

Jack My brother.

Miss Prism More shameful debts and extravagance?

Chasuble Still leading his life of pleasure?

Jack (*Shaking his head*) Dead!

Chasuble Your brother Ernest dead?

Jack Quite dead.

---

[32] misanthrope: person who hates mankind; man-hater.
[33] womanthrope: Miss Prism's own coinage, meaning woman-hater. The correct term is, of course, *misogynist*.
[34] Primitive Church: Christianity in its earliest beginnings.

Miss Prism What a lesson for him! I trust he will profit by it.

Chasuble Mr. Worthing, I offer you my sincere condolence. You have at least the consolation of knowing that you were always the most generous and forgiving of brothers.

Jack Poor Ernest! He had many faults, but it is a sad, sad blow.

Chasuble Very sad indeed. Were you with him at the end?

Jack No. He died abroad; in Paris, in fact. I had a telegram last night from the manager of the Grand Hotel.

Chasuble Was the cause of death mentioned?

Jack A severe chill, it seems.

Miss Prism As a man sows, so shall he reap.

Chasuble (*Raising his hand*) Charity, dear Miss Prism, charity! None of us are perfect. I myself am peculiarly susceptible to draughts. Will the interment take place here?

Jack No. He seemed to have expressed a desire to be buried in Paris.

Chasuble In Paris! (*Shakes his head.*) I fear that hardly points to any very serious state of mind at the last. You would no doubt wish me to make some slight allusion to this tragic domestic affliction next Sunday. (JACK *presses his hand convulsively.*) My sermon on the meaning of the manna[35] in the wilderness can be adapted to almost any occasion, joyful, or as in the present case, distressing. (*All sigh.*) I have preached it at harvest celebrations, christenings, confirmations, on days of humiliation and festal days. The last time I delivered it was in the Cathedral, as a charity sermon on behalf of the Society for the Prevention of Discontent among the Upper Orders. The Bishop, who was present, was much struck by some of the analogies I drew.

Jack Ah! that reminds me, you mentioned christenings I think, Dr. Chasuble? I suppose you know how to christen all right? (DR. CHASUBLE *looks astounded.*) I mean, of course, you are continually christening, aren't you?

Miss Prism It is, I regret to say, one of the Rector's most constant duties in this parish. I have often spoken to the poorer classes on the subject. But they don't seem to know what thrift is.

Chasuble But is there any particular infant in whom you are interested, Mr. Worthing? Your brother was, I believe, unmarried was he not?

Jack Oh, yes.

Miss Prism (*Bitterly*) People who live entirely for pleasure usually are.

Jack But it is not for any child, dear Doctor. I am very fond of children. No! the fact is, I would like to be christened myself, this afternoon, if you have nothing better to do.

Chasuble But surely, Mr. Worthing, you have been christened already?

Jack I don't remember anything about it.

Chasuble But have you any grave doubts on the subject?

[35] manna: the food miraculously received from heaven by the Israelites (Ex. 16).

Jack I certainly intend to have. Of course, I don't know if the thing would bother you in any way, or if you think I am a little too old now.

Chasuble Not at all. The sprinkling, and, indeed, the immersion of adults is a perfectly canonical practice.

Jack Immersion!

Chasuble You need have no apprehensions. Sprinkling is all that is necessary, or indeed I think advisable. Our weather is so changeable. At what hour would you wish the ceremony performed?

Jack Oh, I might trot round about five if that would suit you.

Chasuble Perfectly, perfectly! In fact I have two similar ceremonies to perform at that time. A case of twins that occurred recently in one of the outlying cottages on your own estate. Poor Jenkins the carter, a most hard-working man.

Jack Oh! I don't see much fun in being christened along with other babies. It would be childish. Would half-past five do?

Chasuble Admirably! Admirably! (*Takes out watch.*) And now, dear Mr. Worthing, I will not intrude any longer into a house of sorrow. I would merely beg you not to be too much bowed down by grief. What seem to us bitter trials are often blessings in disguise.

Miss Prism This seems to me a blessing of an extremely obvious kind.

(*Enter* Cecily *from the house.*)

Cecily Uncle Jack! Oh, I am pleased to see you back. But what horrid clothes you have got on! Do go and change them.

Miss Prism Cecily!

Chasuble My child! my child!

(Cecily *goes towards* Jack; *he kisses her brow in a melancholy manner.*)

Cecily What is the matter, Uncle Jack? Do look happy! You look as if you had toothache, and I have got a surprise for you. Who do you think is in the dining-room? Your brother!

Jack Who?

Cecily Your brother Ernest. He arrived about half an hour ago.

Jack What nonsense! I haven't got a brother.

Cecily Oh, don't say that. However badly he may have behaved to you in the past, he is still your brother. You couldn't be so heartless as to disown him. I'll tell him to come out. And you will shake hands with him, won't you, Uncle Jack?

(*Runs back into the house.*)

Chasuble These are very joyful tidings.

Miss Prism After we had all been resigned to his loss, his sudden return seems to me peculiarly distressing.

Jack My brother is in the dining-room? I don't know what it all means. I think it is perfectly absurd.

(Enter ALGERNON *and* CECILY *hand in hand. They come slowly up to* JACK.)

Jack   Good Heavens! *(Motions* ALGERNON *away.)*

Algernon   Brother John, I have come down from town to tell you that I am very sorry for all the trouble I have given you, and that I intend to lead a better life in the future.

*(*JACK *glares at him and does not take his hand.)*

Cecily   Uncle Jack, you are not going to refuse your own brother's hand?

Jack   Nothing will induce me to take his hand. I think his coming down here disgraceful. He knows perfectly well why.

Cecily   Uncle Jack, do be nice. There is some good in everyone. Ernest has just been telling me about his poor invalid friend Mr. Bunbury, whom he goes to visit so often. And surely there must be much good in one who is kind to an invalid, and leaves the pleasures of London to sit by a bed of pain.

Jack   Oh! he has been talking about Bunbury, has he?

Cecily   Yes, he has told me all about poor Mr. Bunbury, and his terrible state of health.

Jack   Bunbury! Well, I won't have him talk to you about Bunbury or about anything else. It is enough to drive one perfectly frantic.

Algernon   Of course I admit that the faults were all on my side. But I must say that I think that broher John's coldness to me is peculiarly painful. I expected a more enthusiastic welcome, especially considering it is the first time I have come here.

Cecily   Uncle Jack, if you don't shake hands with Ernest I will never forgive you.

Jack   Never forgive me?

Cecily   Never, never, never!

Jack   Well, this is the last time I shall ever do it.

(Shakes hands with ALGERNON *and glares.)*

Chasuble   It's pleasant, is it not, to see so perfect a reconciliation? I think we might leave the two brothers together.

Miss Prism   Cecily, you will come with us.

Cecily   Certainly, Miss Prism. My little task of reconciliation is over.

Chasuble   You have done a beautiful action to-day, dear child.

Miss Prism   We must not be premature in our judgments.

Cecily   I feel very happy.

(They all go off.)

Jack   You young scoundrel, Algy, you must get out of this place as soon as possible. I don't allow any Bunburying here.

(Enter MERRIMAN.)*

Merriman I have put Mr. Ernest's things in the room next to yours, sir. I suppose that is all right?

Jack What?

Merriman Mr. Ernest's luggage, sir. I have unpacked it and put it in the room next to your own.

Jack His luggage?

Merriman Yes, sir. Three portmanteaus, a dressing-case, two hat-boxes, and a large luncheon-basket.

Algernon I am afraid I can't stay more than a week this time.

Jack Merriman, order the dog-cart [36] at once. Mr. Ernest has been suddenly called back to town.

Merriman Yes, sir.

(*Goes back into the house.*)

Algernon What a fearful liar you are, Jack. I have not been called back to town at all.

Jack Yes, you have.

Algernon I haven't heard anyone call me.

Jack Your duty as a gentleman calls you back.

Algernon My duty as a gentleman has never interfered with my pleasures in the smallest degree.

Jack I can quite understand that.

Algernon Well, Cecily is a darling.

Jack You are not to talk of Miss Cardew like that. I don't like it.

Algernon Well, I don't like your clothes. You look perfectly ridiculous in them. Why on earth don't you go up and change? It is perfectly childish to be in deep mourning for a man who is actually staying for a whole week with you in your house as a guest. I call it grotesque.

Jack You are certainly not staying with me for a whole week as a guest or anything else. You have got to leave . . . by the four-five train.

Algernon I certainly won't leave you so long as you are in mourning. It would be most unfriendly. If I were in mourning you would stay with me, I suppose. I should think it very unkind if you didn't.

Jack Well, will you go if I change my clothes?

Algernon Yes, if you are not too long. I never saw anybody take so long to dress, and with such little result.

Jack Well, at any rate, that is better than being always over-dressed as you are.

Algernon If I am occasionally a little over-dressed, I make up for it by being always immensely over-educated.

Jack Your vanity is ridiculous, your conduct an outrage, and your presence in my garden utterly absurd. However, you have got to catch the

[36] dog-cart: a small open carriage drawn by a horse.

four-five, and I hope you will have a pleasant journey back to town. This Bunburying, as you call it, has not been a great success for you.

(*Goes into the house.*)

Algernon   I think it has been a great success. I'm in love with Cecily, and that is everything. (*Enter* CECILY *at the back of the garden. She picks up the can and begins to water the flowers.*) But I must see her before I go, and make arrangements for another Bunbury. Ah, there she is.

Cecily   Oh, I merely came back to water the roses. I thought you were with Uncle Jack.

Algernon   He's gone to order the dog-cart for me.

Cecily   Oh, is he going to take you for a nice drive?

Algernon   He's going to send me away.

Cecily   Then have we got to part?

Algernon   I am afraid so. It's a very painful parting.

Cecily   It is always painful to part from people whom one has known for a very brief space of time. The absence of old friends one can endure with equanimity. But even a momentary separation from anyone to whom one has just been introduced is almost unbearable.

Algernon   Thank you.

(*Enter* MERRIMAN.)

Merriman   The dog-cart is at the door, sir.

(ALGERNON *looks appealingly at* CECILY.)

Cecily   It can wait, Merriman . . . for . . . five minutes.

Merriman   Yes, Miss.

(*Exit* MERRIMAN.)

Algernon   I hope, Cecily, I shall not offend you if I state quite frankly and openly that you seem to me to be in every way the visible personification of absolute perfection.

Cecily   I think your frankness does you great credit, Ernest. If you will allow me I will copy your remarks into my diary.

(*Goes over to table and begins writing in diary.*)

Algernon   Do you really keep a diary? I'd give anything to look at it. May I?

Cecily   Oh, no. (*Puts her hand over it.*) You see, it is simply a very young girl's record of her own thoughts and impressions, and consequently meant for publication. When it appears in volume form I hope you will order a copy. But pray, Ernest, don't stop. I delight in taking down from dictation. I have reached 'absolute perfection.' You can go on. I am quite ready for more.

Algernon (*Somewhat taken aback*)   Ahem! Ahem!
Cecily   Oh, don't cough, Ernest. When one is dictating one should speak fluently and not cough. Besides, I don't know how to spell a cough.

(*Writes as* ALGERNON *speaks.*)

Algernon (*Speaking very rapidly*)   Cecily, ever since I first looked upon your wonderful and incomparable beauty, I have dared to love you wildly, passionately, devotedly, hopelessly.
Cecily   I don't think that you should tell me that you love me wildly, passionately, devotedly, hopelessly. Hopelessly doesn't seem to make much sense, does it?
Algernon   Cecily!

(*Enter* MERRIMAN.)

Merriman   The dog-cart is waiting, sir.
Algernon   Tell it to come round next week, at the same hour.
Merriman (*Looks at* CECILY, *who makes no sign*)   Yes, sir.

(MERRIMAN *retires.*)

Cecily   Uncle Jack would be very much annoyed if he knew you were staying on till next week, at the same hour.
Algernon   Oh, I don't care about Jack. I don't care for anybody in the whole world but you. I love you, Cecily. You will marry me, won't you?
Cecily   You silly boy! Of course. Why, we have been engaged for the last three months.
Algernon   For the last three months?
Cecily   Yes, it will be exactly three months on Thursday.
Algernon   But how did we become engaged?
Cecily   Well, ever since dear Uncle Jack first confessed to us that he had a younger brother who was very wicked and bad, you of course have formed the chief topic of conversation between myself and Miss Prism. And of course a man who is much talked about is always very attractive. One feels that must be something in him after all. I daresay it was foolish of me, but I fell in love with you, Ernest.
Algernon   Darling! And when was the engagement actually settled?
Cecily   On the 14th of February last. Worn out by your entire ignorance of my existence, I determined to end the matter one way or the other, and after a long struggle with myself I accepted you under this dear old tree here. The next day I bought this little ring in your name, and this is the little bangle with the true lovers' knot I promised you always to wear.
Algernon   Did I give you this? It's very pretty, isn't it?
Cecily   Yes, you've wonderfully good taste, Ernest. It's the excuse I've always given for your leading such a bad life. And this is the box in which I keep all your dear letters.

(Kneels at table, opens box, and produces letters tied up with blue ribbon.)

Algernon My letters! But my own sweet Cecily, I have never written you any letters.

Cecily You need hardly remind me of that, Ernest. I remember only too well that I was forced to write your letters for you. I wrote always three times a week, and sometimes oftener.

Algernon Oh, do let me read them, Cecily?

Cecily Oh, I couldn't possibly. They would make you far too conceited. *(Replaces box.)* The three you wrote me after I had broken off the engagement are so beautiful, and so badly spelled, that even now I can hardly read them without crying a little.

Algernon But was our engagement ever broken off?

Cecily Of course it was. On the 22nd of last March. You can see the entry if you like. *(Shows diary.)* 'To-day I broke off my engagement with Ernest. I feel it is better to do so. The weather still continues charming.'

Algernon But why on earth did you break it off? What had I done? I had done nothing at all. Cecily, I am very much hurt indeed to hear you broke it off. Particularly when the weather was so charming.

Cecily It would hardly have been a really serious engagement if it hadn't been broken off at least once. But I forgave you before the week was out.

Algernon *(Crossing to her, and kneeling.)* What a perfect angel you are, Cecily.

Cecily You dear romantic boy. *(He kisses her, she puts her fingers through his hair.)* I hope your hair curls naturally, does it?

Algernon Yes, darling, with a little help from others.

Cecily I am so glad.

Algernon You'll never break off our engagement again, Cecily?

Cecily I don't think I could break it off now that I have actually met you. Besides, of course, there is the question of your name.

Algernon Yes, of course. *(Nervously)*

Cecily You must not laugh at me, darling, but it had always been a girlish dream of mine to love some one whose name was Ernest. (ALGERNON *rises*, CECILY *also.*) There is some thing in that name that seems to inspire absolute confidence. I pity any poor married woman whose husband is not called Ernest.

Algernon But, my dear child, do you mean to say you could not love me if I had some other name?

Cecily But what name?

Algernon Oh, any name you like—Algernon—for instance . . .

Cecily But I don't like the name of Algernon.

Algernon Well, my own dear, sweet, loving little darling, I really can't see why you should object to the name of Algernon. It is not at all a bad name. In fact, it is rather an aristocratic name. Half of the chaps who get into the Bankruptcy Court are called Algernon. But seriously, Cecily . . .

(*Moving to her*) . . . if my name was Algy, couldn't you love me?

Cecily (*Rising*). I might respect you, Ernest. I might admire your character, but I fear that I should not be able to give you my undivided attention.

Algernon   Ahem! Cecily! (*Picking up hat.*) Your Rector here is, I suppose, thoroughly experienced in the practice of all the rites and ceremonials of the Church?

Cecily   Oh yes. Dr. Chasuble is a most learned man. He has never written a single book, so you can imagine how much he knows.

Algernon   I must see him at once on a most important christening—I mean on most important business.

Cecily   Oh!

Algernon   I shan't be away more than half an hour.

Cecily   Considering that we have been engaged since February the 14th, and that I only met you to-day for the first time, I think it is rather hard that you should leave me for so long a period as half an hour. Couldn't you make it twenty minutes?

Algernon   I'll be back in no time.

(*Kisses her and rushes down the garden.*)

Cecily   What an impetuous boy he is! I like his hair so much. I must enter his proposal in my diary.

(*Enter* Merriman.)

Merriman   A Miss Fairfax has just called to see Mr. Worthing. On very important business Miss Fairfax states.

Cecily   Isn't Mr. Worthing in his library?

Merriman   Mr. Worthing went over in the direction of the Rectory some time ago.

Cecily   Pray ask the lady to come out here; Mr. Worthing is sure to be back soon. And you can bring tea.

Merriman   Yes, Miss.

(*Goes out.*)

Cecily   Miss Fairfax! I suppose one of the many good elderly women who are associated with Uncle Jack in some of his philanthropic work in London. I don't quite like women who are interested in philanthropic work. I think it is so forward of them.

(*Enter* Merriman.)

Merriman   Miss Fairfax.

(*Enter* Gwendolen. *Exit* Merriman.)

Cecily (*Advancing to meet her*)   Pray let me introduce myself to you. My name is Cecily Cardew.

Gwendolen Cecily Cardew? (*Moving to her and shaking hands.*) What a very sweet name! Something tells me that we are going to be great friends. I like you already more than I can say. My first impressions of people are never wrong.

Cecily How nice of you to like me so much after we have known each other such a comparatively short time. Pray sit down.

Gwendolen (*Still standing up*) I may call you Cecily, may I not?

Cecily With pleasure?

Gwendolen And you will always call me Gwendolen, won't you.

Cecily If you wish.

Gwendolen Then that is all quite settled, is it not?

Cecily I hope so.

(*A pause. They both sit down together.*)

Gwendolen Perhaps this might be a favorable opportunity for my mentioning who I am. My father is Lord Bracknell. You have never heard of papa, I suppose?

Cecily I don't think so.

Gwendolen Outside the family circle, papa, I am glad to say, is entirely unknown. I think that is quite as it should be. The home seems to me to be the proper sphere for the man. And certainly once a man begins to neglect his domestic duties he becomes painfully effeminate, does he not? And I don't like that. It makes men so very attractive. Cecily, mamma, whose views on education are remarkably strict, has brought me up to be extremely short-sighted; it is part of her system; so do you mind my looking at you through my glasses?

Cecily Oh! not at all, Gwendolen. I am very fond of being looked at.

Gwendolen (*After examining* Cecily *carefully through a lorgnette[37]*) You are here on a short visit I suppose.

Cecily Oh no! I live here.

Gwendolen (*Severely*) Really? Your mother, no doubt, or some female relative of advanced years, resides here also?

Cecily Oh no! I have no mother, nor, in fact, any relations.

Gwendolen Indeed?

Cecily My dear guardian, with the assistance of Miss Prism, has the arduous task of looking after me.

Gwendolen Your guardian?

Cecily Yes, I am Mr. Worthing's ward.

Gwendolen Oh! It is strange he never mentioned to me that he had a ward. How secretive of him! He grows more interesting hourly. I am not sure, however, that the news inspires me with feelings of unmixed de-

---

[37] lorgnette: glasses mounted on a handle, carried by stylish women in preference to wearing standard eyeglasses.

light. (*Rising and going to her.*) I am very fond of you, Cecily; I have liked you ever since I met you! But I am bound to state that now that I know that you are Mr. Worthing's ward, I cannot help expressing a wish you were—well just a little older than you seem to be—and not quite so very alluring in appearance. In fact, if I may speak candidly——

Cecily Pray do! I think that whenever one has anything unpleasant to say, one should always be quite candid.

Gwendolen Well, to speak with perfect candour, Cecily, I wish that you were fully forty-two, and more than usually plain for your age. Ernest has a strong upright nature. He is the very soul of truth and honour. Disloyalty would be as impossible to him as deception. But even men of the noblest possible moral character are extremely susceptible to the influence of the physical charms of others. Modern, no less than Ancient History, supplies us with many most painful examples of what I refer to. If it were not so, indeed, History would be quite unreadable.

Cecily I beg your pardon, Gwendolen, did you say Ernest?

Gwendolen Yes.

Cecily Oh, but it is not Mr. Ernest Worthing who is my guardian. It is his brother—his elder brother.

Gwendolen (*Sitting down again*) Ernest never mentioned to me that he had a brother.

Cecily I am sorry to say they have not been on good terms for a long time.

Gwendolen Ah! that accounts for it. And now that I think of it I have never heard any man mention his brother. The subject seems distasteful to most men. Cecily, you have lifted a load from my mind. I was growing almost anxious. It would have been terrible if any cloud had come across a friendship like ours, would it not? Of course you are quite, quite sure that it is not Mr. Ernest Worthing who is your guardian?

Cecily Quite sure. (*A pause.*) In fact, I am going to be his.

Gwendolen (*Enquiringly*) I beg your pardon?

Cecily (*Rather shy and confidingly*) Dearest Gwendolen, there is no reason why I should make a secret of it to you. Our little county newspaper is sure to chronicle the fact next week. Mr. Ernest Worthing and I are engaged to be married.

Gwendolen (*Quite politely, rising*) My darling Cecily, I think there must be some slight error. Mr. Ernest Worthing is engaged to me. The announcement will appear in the 'Morning Post' on Saturday at the latest.

Cecily (*Very politely, rising*) I am afraid you must be under some misconception. Ernest proposed to me exactly ten minutes ago. (*Shows diary.*)

Gwendolen (*Examines diary through her lorgnette carefully*) It is certainly very curious, for he asked me to be his wife yesterday afternoon at 5:30. If you would care to verify the incident, pray do so. (*Produces diary of her own.*) I never travel without my diary. One should always have something sensational to read in the train. I am so sorry, dear Cecily, if it is any disappointment to you, but I am afraid *I* have the prior claim.

Cecily It would distress me more than I can tell you, dear Gwendolen, if it caused you any mental or physical anguish, but I feel bound to point out that since Ernest proposed to you he clearly has changed his mind.

Gwendolen (*Meditatively*) If the poor fellow has been entrapped into any foolish promise I shall consider it my duty to rescue him at once, and with a firm hand.

Cecily (*Thoughtfully and sadly*) Whatever unfortunate entanglement my dear boy may have got into, I will never reproach him with it after we are married.

Gwendolen Do you allude to me, Miss Cardew, as an entanglement? You are presumptuous. On an occasion of this kind it becomes more than a moral duty to speak one's mind. It becomes a pleasure.

Cecily Do you suggest, Miss Fairfax, that I entrapped Ernest into an engagement? How dare you? This is no time for wearing the shallow mask of manners. When I see a spade I call it a spade.

Gwendolen (*Satirically*) I am glad to say that I have never seen a spade. It is obvious that our social spheres have been widely different.

(*Enter* MERRIMAN, *followed by the footman. He carries a salver, table cloth, and plate stand.* CECILY *is about to retort. The presence of the servants exercises a restraining influence, under which both girls chafe.*)

Merriman Shall I lay tea here as usual, Miss?
Cecily (*Sternly, in a calm voice*) Yes, as usual.

(MERRIMAN *begins to clear and lay cloth. A long pause.* CECILY *and* GWENDOLEN *glare at each other.*)

Gwendolen Are there many interesting walks in the vicinity, Miss Cardew?

Cecily Oh! yes! a great many. From the top of one of the hills quite close one can see five counties.

Gwendolen Five counties! I don't think I should like that. I hate crowds.
Cecily (*Sweetly*) I suppose that is why you live in town?

(GWENDOLEN *bites her lip, and beats her foot nervously with her parasol.*)

Gwendolen (*Looking round*) Quite a well-kept garden this is, Miss Cardew?

Cecily So glad you like it, Miss Fairfax.
Gwendolen I had no idea there were any flowers in the country.
Cecily Oh, flowers are as common here, Miss Fairfax, as people are in London.

Gwendolen Personally I cannot understand how anybody manages to exist in the country, if anybody who is anybody does. The country always bores me to death.

Cecily Ah! This is what the newspapers call agricultural depression, is it not? I believe the aristocracy are suffering very much from it just at present. It is almost an epidemic amongst them, I have been told. May I offer you some tea, Miss Fairfax?

Gwendolen (*With elaborate politeness*) Thank you. (*Aside.*) Detestable girl! But I require tea!

Cecily (*Sweetly*) Sugar?

Gwendolen (*Superciliously*) No, thank you. Sugar is not fashionable any more.

(CECILY *looks angrily at her, takes up the tongs and puts four lumps of sugar into the cup.*)

Cecily (*Severely*) Cake or bread and butter?

Gwendolen (*In a bored manner*) Bread and butter, please. Cake is rarely seen at the best houses nowadays.

Cecily (*Cuts a very large slice of cake, and puts it on the tray*) Hand that to Miss Fairfax.

(MERRIMAN *does so, and goes out with footman.* GWENDOLEN *drinks the tea and makes a grimace. Puts down cup at once, reaches out her hand to the bread and butter, looks at it, and finds it is cake. Rises in indignation.*)

Gwendolen You have filled my tea with lumps of sugar, and though I asked most distinctly for bread and butter, you have given me cake. I am known for the gentleness of my disposition, and the extraordinary sweetness of my nature, but I warn you, Miss Cardew, you may go too far.

Cecily (*Rising*) To save my poor, innocent, trusting boy from the machinations of any other girl there are no lengths to which I would not go.

Gwendolen From the moment I saw you I distrusted you. I felt that you were false and deceitful. I am never deceived in such matters. My first impressions of people are invariably right.

Cecily It seems to me, Miss Fairfax, that I am trespassing on your valuable time. No doubt you have many other calls of a similar character to make in the neighbourhood.

(*Enter* JACK.)

Gwendolen (*Catching sight of him*) Ernest! My own Ernest!

Jack Gwendolen! Darling!

(*Offers to kiss her.*)

Gwendolen (*Drawing back*) A moment! May I ask if you are engaged to be married to this young lady?

(*Points to* CECILY.)

Jack (*Laughing*) To dear little Cecily! Of course not! What could have put such an idea into your pretty little head?

Gwendolen Thank you. You may.

(*Offers her cheek.*)

Cecily (*Very sweetly*) I knew there must be some misunderstanding, Miss Fairfax. The gentleman whose arm is at present around your waist is my dear guardian, Mr. John Worthing.

Gwendolen I beg your pardon?

Cecily This is Uncle Jack.

Gwendolen (*Receding*) Jack! Oh!

(*Enter* ALGERNON.)

Cecily Here is Ernest.

Algernon (*Goes straight over to* CECILY *without noticing anyone else*) My own love!

(*Offers to kiss her.*)

Cecily (*Drawing back*) A moment, Ernest! May I ask you—are you engaged to be married to this young lady?

Algernon (*Looking around*) To what young lady? Good heavens! Gwendolen!

Cecily Yes! to good heavens, Gwendolen, I mean to Gwendolen.

Algernon (*Laughing*) Of course not! What could have put such an idea into your pretty little head?

Cecily Thank you. (*Presenting her cheek to be kissed.*) You may. (ALGERNON *kisses her.*)

Gwendolen I felt there was some slight error, Miss Cardew. The gentleman who is now embracing you is my cousin, Mr. Algernon Moncrieff.

Cecily (*Breaking away from* ALGERNON) Algernon Moncrieff! Oh!

(*The two girls move towards each other and put their arms round each other's waist as if for protection.*)

Cecily Are you called Algernon?

Algernon I cannot deny it.

Cecily Oh!

Gwendolen Is your name really John?

Jack (*Standing rather proudly*) I could deny it if I liked. I could deny anything if I liked. But my name certainly is John. It has been John for years.

Cecily (*To* GWENDOLEN) A gross deception has been practised on both of us.

Gwendolen My poor wounded Cecily!

Cecily My sweet wronged Gwendolen!

Gwendolen (*Slowly and seriously*)   You will call me sister, will you not?

(*They embrace.* JACK *and* ALGERNON *groan and walk up and down.*)

Cecily (*Rather brightly*)   There is just one question I would like to be allowed to ask my guardian.

Gwendolen   An admirable idea! Mr. Worthing, there is just one question I would like to be permitted to put to you. Where is your brother Ernest? We are both engaged to be married to your brother Ernest, so it is a matter of some importance to us to know where your brother Ernest is at present.

Jack (*Slowly and hesitatingly*)   Gwendolen—Cecily—it is very painful for me to be forced to speak the truth. It is the first time in my life that I have ever been reduced to such a painful position, and I am really quite inexperienced in doing anything of the kind. However, I will tell you quite frankly that I have no brother Ernest. I have no brother at all. I never had a brother in my life, and I certainly have not the smallest intention of ever having one in the future.

Cecily (*Surprised*)   No brother at all?

Jack (*Cheerily*)   None!

Gwendolen (*Severely*)   Had you never a brother of any kind?

Jack (*Pleasantly*)   Never. Not even of any kind.

Gwendolen   I am afraid it is quite clear, Cecily, that neither of us is engaged to be married to anyone.

Cecily   It is not a very pleasant position for a young girl suddenly to find herself in. Is it?

Gwendolen   Let us go into the house. They will hardly venture to come after us there.

Cecily   No, men are so cowardly, aren't they?

(*They retire into the house with scornful looks.*)

Jack   This ghastly state of things is what you call Bunburying, I suppose?

Algernon   Yes, and a perfectly wonderful Bunbury it is. The most wonderful Bunbury I have ever had in my life.

Jack   Well, you've no right whatsoever to Bunbury here.

Algernon   That is absurd. One has a right to Bunbury anywhere one chooses. Every serious Bunburyist knows that.

Jack   Serious Bunburyist! Good heavens!

Algernon   Well, one must be serious about something, if one wants to have any amusement in life. I happen to be serious about Bunburying. What on earth you are serious about I haven't got the remotest idea. About everything, I should fancy. You have such an absolutely trivial nature.

Jack   Well, the only small satisfaction I have in the whole of this wretched business is that your friend Bunbury is quite exploded. You won't be able to run down to the country quite so often as you used to do, dear Algy. And a very good thing too.

Algernon   Your brother is a little off colour, isn't he, dear Jack? You won't be able to disappear to London quite so frequently as your wicked custom was. And not a bad thing either.

Jack   As for your conduct towards Miss Cardew, I must say that your taking in a sweet, simple, innocent girl like that is quite inexcusable. To say nothing of the fact that she is my ward.

Algernon   I can see no possible defence at all for your deceiving a brilliant, clever, thoroughly experienced young lady like Miss Fairfax. To say nothing of the fact that she is my cousin.

Jack   I wanted to be engaged to Gwendolen, that is all. I love her.

Algernon   Well, I simply wanted to be engaged to Cecily. I adore her.

Jack   There is certainly no chance of your marrying Miss Cardew.

Algernon   I don't think there is much likelihood, Jack, of you and Miss Fairfax being united.

Jack   Well, that is no business of yours.

Algernon   If it was my business, I wouldn't talk about it. (*Begins to eat muffins.*) It is very vulgar to talk about one's business. Only people like stockbrokers do that, and then merely at dinner parties.

Jack   How can you sit there, calmly eating muffins when we are in this horrible trouble, I can't make out. You seem to me to be perfectly heartless.

Algernon   Well, I can't eat muffins in an agitated manner. The butter would probably get on my cuffs. One should always eat muffins quite calmly. It is the only way to eat them.

Jack   I say it's perfectly heartless your eating muffins at all, under the circumstances.

Algernon   When I am in trouble, eating is the only thing that consoles me. Indeed, when I am in really great trouble, as anyone who knows me intimately will tell you, I refuse everything except food and drink. At the present moment I am eating muffins because I am unhappy. Besides, I am particularly fond of muffins.

(*Rising.*)

Jack (*Rising*)   Well, that is no reason why you should eat them all in that greedy way.

(*Takes muffins from* ALGERNON.)

Algernon (*Offering tea-cake*)   I wish you would have tea-cake instead. I don't like tea-cake.

Jack   Good heavens! I suppose a man may eat his own muffins in his own garden.

Algernon   But you have just said it was perfectly heartless to eat muffins.

Jack   I said it was perfectly heartless of you, under the circumstances. That is a very different thing.

Algernon   That may be. But the muffins are the same.

(*He seizes the muffin dish from* JACK.)

Jack   Algy, I wish to goodness you would go.

Algernon   You can't possibly ask me to go without having some dinner. It's absurd. I never go without my dinner. No one ever does, except vegetarians and people like that. Besides I have just made arrangements with Dr. Chasuble to be christened at a quarter to six under the name of Ernest.

Jack   My dear fellow, the sooner you give up that nonsense the better. I made arrangements this morning with Dr. Chasuble to be christened myself at 5:30, and I naturally will take the name of Ernest. Gwendolen would wish it. We can't both be christened Ernest. It's absurd. Besides, I have a perfect right to be christened if I like. There is no evidence at all that I ever have been christened by anybody. I should think it extremely probable I never was, and so does Dr. Chasuble. It is entirely different in your case. You have been christened already.

Algernon   Yes, but I have not been christened for years.

Jack   Yes, but you have been christened. That is the important thing.

Algernon   Quite so. So I know my constitution can stand it. If you are not quite sure about your ever having been christened, I must say I think it rather dangerous your venturing on it now. It might make you very unwell. You can hardly have forgotten that someone very closely connected with you was very nearly carried off this week in Paris by a severe chill.

Jack   Yes, but you said yourself that a severe chill was not hereditary.

Algernon   It usen't to be, I know—but I daresay it is now. Science is always making wonderful improvements in things.

Jack (*Picking up the muffin dish*)   Oh, that is nonsense, you are always talking nonsense.

Algernon   Jack, you are at the muffins again! I wish you wouldn't. There are only two left. (*Takes them.*) I told you I was particularly fond of muffins.

Jack   But I hate tea-cake.

Algernon   Why on earth then do you allow tea-cake to be served up for your guests? What ideas you have of hospitality!

Jack   Algernon! I have already told you to go. I don't want you here. Why don't you go!

Algernon   I haven't quite finished my tea yet! and there is still one muffin left.

(JACK *groans, and sinks into a chair.* ALGERNON *continues eating.*)

(*Act-Drop*)

ACT III

Scene: *Morning-room at the Manor House.*

GWENDOLEN *and* CECILY *are at the window, looking out into the garden.*

Gwendolen The fact that they did not follow us at once into the house, as anyone else would have done, seems to me to show that they have some sense of shame left.

Cecily They have been eating muffins. That looks like repentance.

Gwendolen (*After a pause*) They don't seem to notice us at all. Couldn't you cough?

Cecily But I haven't a cough.

Gwendolen They're looking at us. What effrontery!

Cecily They're approaching. That's very forward of them.

Gwendolen Let us preserve a dignified silence.

Cecily Certainly. It's the only thing to do now.

(*Enter* JACK *followed by* ALGERNON. *They whistle some dreadful popular air from a British Opera.*)

Gwendolen This dignified silence seems to produce an unpleasant effect.

Cecily A most distasteful one.

Gwendolen But we will not be the first to speak.

Cecily Certainly not.

Gwendolen Mr. Worthing, I have something very particular to ask you. Much depends on your reply.

Cecily Gwendolen, your common sense is invaluable. Mr. Moncrieff, kindly answer me the following question. Why did you pretend to be my guardian's brother?

Algernon In order that I might have an opportunity of meeting you.

Cecily (*To* GWENDOLEN) That certainly seems a satisfactory explanation, does it not?

Gwendolen Yes, dear, if you can believe him.

Cecily I don't. But that does not affect the wonderful beauty of his answer.

Gwendolen True. In matters of grave importance, style, not sincerity is the vital thing. Mr. Worthing, what explanation can you offer to me for pretending to have a brother? Was it in order that you might have an opportunity of coming up to town to see me as often as possible?

Jack Can you doubt it, Miss Fairfax?

Gwendolen I have the gravest doubts upon the subject. But I intend to crush them. This is not the moment for German scepticism.[38] (*Moving*

---

[38] scepticism: doubt, suspicion of generally accepted ideas, a philosophical movement popular in Germany in the nineteenth century and earlier elsewhere.

to Cecily.) Their explanations appear to be quite satisfactory, especially Mr. Worthing's. That seems to me to have the stamp of truth upon it.

Cecily   I am more than content with what Mr. Moncrieff said. His voice alone inspires one with absolute credulity.

Gwendolen   Then you think we should forgive them?

Cecily   Yes. I mean no.

Gwendolen   True! I had forgotten. There are principles at stake that one cannot surrender. Which of us should tell them? The task is not a pleasant one.

Cecily   Could we not both speak at the same time?

Gwendolen   An excellent idea! I nearly always speak at the same time as other people. Will you take the time from me?

Cecily   Certainly.

(Gwendolen *beats time with uplifted finger.*)

Gwendolen and **Cecily** (*Speaking together*)   Your Christian names are still an insuperable barrier. That is all!

Jack and **Algernon** (*Speaking together*)   Our Christian names! Is that all? But we are going to be christened this afternoon.

Gwendolen (*To* Jack)   For my sake you are prepared to do this terrible thing?

Jack   I am.

Cecily (*To* Algernon)   To please me you are ready to face this fearful ordeal?

Algernon   I am!

Gwendolen   How absurd to talk of the equality of the sexes! Where questions of self-sacrifice are concerned, men are infinitely beyond us.

Jack   We are.

(*Clasps hands with* Algernon.)

Cecily   They have moments of physical courage of which we women know absolutely nothing.

Gwendolen (*To* Jack)   Darling!

Algernon (*To* Cecily)   Darling!

(*They fall into each other's arms. Enter* Merriman. *When he enters he coughs loudly, seeing the situation.*)

Merriman   Ahem! Ahem! Lady Bracknell!

Jack   Good heavens!

(*Enter* Lady Bracknell. *The couples separate in alarm. Exit* Merriman.)

Lady Bracknell   Gwendolen! What does this mean?

Gwendolen   Merely that I am engaged to be married to Mr. Worthing, mamma.

Lady Bracknell Come here. Sit down. Sit down immediately. Hesitation of any kind is a sign of mental decay in the young, of physical weakness in the old. (*Turns to* JACK.) Apprised, sir, of my daughter's sudden flight by her trusty maid, whose confidence I purchased by means of a small coin, I followed her at once by a luggage train. Her unhappy father is, I am glad to say, under the impression that she is attending a more than usually lengthy lecture by the University Extension Scheme on the Influence of a permanent income on Thought. I do not propose to undeceive him. Indeed I have never undeceived him on any question. I would consider it wrong. But of course, you will clearly understand that all communication between yourself and my daughter must cease immediately from this moment. On this point, as indeed on all points, I am firm.

Jack I am engaged to be married to Gwendolen, Lady Bracknell!

Lady Bracknell You are nothing of the kind, sir. And now, as regards Algernon! . . . Algernon!

Algernon Yes, Aunt Augusta.

Lady Bracknell May I ask if it is in this house that your invalid friend Mr. Bunbury resides?

Algernon (*Stammering*) Oh! No! Bunbury doesn't live here. Bunbury is somewhere else at present. In fact, Bunbury is dead.

Lady Bracknell Dead! When did Mr. Bunbury die? His death must have been extremely sudden.

Algernon (*Airily*) Oh! I killed Bunbury this afternoon. I mean poor Bunbury died this afternoon.

Lady Bracknell What did he die of?

Algernon Bunbury? Oh, he was quite exploded.

Lady Bracknell Exploded! Was he the victim of a revolutionary outrage? I was not aware that Mr. Bunbury was interested in social legislation. If so, he is well punished for his morbidity.

Algernon My dear Aunt Augusta, I mean he was found out! The doctors found out that Bunbury could not live, that is what I mean—so Bunbury died.

Lady Bracknell He seems to have had great confidence in the opinion of his physicians. I am glad, however, that he made up his mind at the last to some definite course of action, and acted under proper medical advice. And now that we have finally got rid of this Mr. Bunbury, may I ask, Mr. Worthing, who is that young person whose hand my nephew Algernon is now holding in what seems to me a peculiarly unnecessary manner?

Jack That lady is Miss Cecily Cardew, my ward.

(LADY BRACKNELL *bows coldly to* CECILY.)

Algernon I am engaged to be married to Cecily, Aunt Augusta.

Lady Bracknell I beg your pardon?

Cecily Mr. Moncrieff and I are engaged to be married, Lady Bracknell.

Lady Bracknell (*With a shiver, crossing to the sofa and sitting down*) I do not know whether there is anything peculiarly exciting in the air of this particular part of Hertfordshire, but the number of engagements that go on seems to me considerably above the proper average that statistics have laid down for our guidance. I think some preliminary enquiry on my part would not be out of place. Mr. Worthing, is Miss Cardew at all connected with any of the larger railway stations in London? I merely desire information. Until yesterday I had no idea that there were any families or persons whose origin was a Terminus.[39]

(JACK *looks perfectly furious, but restrains himself.*)

Jack (*In a clear, cold voice*) Miss Cardew is the granddaughter of the late Mr. Thomas Cardew of 149, Belgrave Square, S.W.; Gervase Park, Dorking, Surrey; and the Sporran, Fifeshire, N.B.[40]

Lady Bracknell That sounds not unsatisfactory. Three addresses always inspire confidence, even in tradesmen. But what proof have I of their authenticity?

Jack I have carefully preserved the Court Guides of the period. They are open to your inspection, Lady Bracknell.

Lady Bracknell (*Grimly*) I have known strange errors in that publication.

Jack Miss Cardew's family solicitors are Messrs. Markby, Markby, and Markby.

Lady Bracknell Markby, Markby, and Markby! A firm of the very highest position in their profession. Indeed I am told that one of the Mr. Markbys is occasionally to be seen at dinner parties. So far I am satisfied.

Jack (*Very irritably*) How extremely kind of you, Lady Bracknell! I have also in my possession, you will be pleased to hear, certificates of Miss Cardew's birth, baptism, whooping cough, registration, vaccination, confirmation, and the measles; both the German and the English variety.

Lady Bracknell Ah! A life crowded with incident, I see; though perhaps somewhat too exciting for a young girl. I am not myself in favour of premature experiences. (*Rises, looks at her watch.*) Gwendolen! the time approaches for our departure. We have not a moment to lose. As a matter of form, Mr. Worthing, I had better ask you if Miss Cardew has any little fortune?

Jack Oh! about a hundred and thirty thousand pounds in the Funds.[41] That is all. Goodbye, Lady Bracknell. So pleased to have seen you.

[39] Terminus: railway station at the end of a line.

[40] Belgrave Square, etc.: elegant addresses; N.B. stands for North Britain—in other words, Scotland.

[41] Funds: highly regarded investment in government securities. The amount was equivalent to more than $600,000 at the time; today such a fortune would have much greater purchasing power.

Lady Bracknell (*Sitting down again*)   A moment, Mr. Worthing. A hundred and thirty thousand pounds! And in the Funds! Miss Cardew seems to me a most attractive young lady, now that I look at her. Few girls of the present day have any really solid qualities, any of the qualities that last, and improve with time. We live, I regret to say, in an age of surfaces. (*To* CECILY.) Come over here, dear. (CECILY *goes across*.) Pretty child! your dress is sadly simple, and your hair seems almost as Nature might have left it. But we can soon alter all that. A thoroughly experienced French maid produces a really marvellous result in a very brief space of time. I remember recommending one to young Lady Lancing, and after three months her own husband did not know her.

Jack (*Aside*)   And after six months nobody knew her.

Lady Bracknell (*Glares at* JACK *for a few moments. Then bends, with a practised smile, to* CECILY)   Kindly turn round, sweet child. (CECILY *turns completely round*.) No, the side view is what I want. (CECILY *presents her profile*.) Yes, quite as I expected. There are distinct social possibilities in your profile. The two weak points in our age are its want of principle and its want of profile. The chin a little higher, dear. Style largely depends on the way the chin is worn. They are worn very high, just at present. Algernon!

Algernon   Yes, Aunt Augusta!

Lady Bracknell   There are distinct social possibilities in Miss Cardew's profile.

Algernon   Cecily is the sweetest, dearest, prettiest girl in the whole world. And I don't care twopence about social possibilities.

Lady Bracknell   Never speak disrespectfully of Society, Algernon. Only people who can't get into it do that. (*To* CECILY.) Dear child, of course you know that Algernon has nothing but his debts to depend upon. But I do not approve of mercenary marriages. When I married Lord Bracknell I had no fortune of any kind. But I never dreamed for a moment of allowing that to stand in my way. Well, I suppose I must give my consent.

Algernon   Thank you, Aunt Augusta.

Lady Bracknell   Cecily, you may kiss me!

Cecily (*Kisses her*)   Thank you, Lady Bracknell.

Lady Bracknell   You may also address me as Aunt Augusta for the future.

Cecily   Thank you, Aunt Augusta.

Lady Bracknell   The marriage, I think, had better take place quite soon.

Algernon   Thank you, Aunt Augusta.

Cecily   Thank you, Aunt Augusta.

Lady Bracknell   To speak frankly, I am not in favour of long engagements. They give people the opportunity of finding out each other's character before marriage, which I think is never advisable.

Jack   I beg your pardon for interrupting you, Lady Bracknell, but this engagement is quite out of the question. I am Miss Cardew's guardian, and she cannot marry without my consent until she comes of age. That consent I absolutely decline to give.

Lady Bracknell Upon what grounds, may I ask? Algernon is an extremely, I may almost say an ostentatiously, eligible young man. He has nothing, but he looks everything. What more can one desire?

Jack It pains me very much to have to speak frankly to you, Lady Bracknell, about your nephew, but the fact is that I do not approve at all of his moral character. I suspect him of being untruthful.

(ALGERNON *and* CECILY *look at him in indignant amazement.*)

Lady Bracknell Untruthful! My nephew Algernon? Impossible! He is an Oxonian.[42]

Jack I fear there can be no possible doubt about the matter. This afternoon, during my temporary absence in London on an important question of romance, he obtained admission to my house by means of the false pretence of being my brother. Under an assumed name he drank, I've just been informed by my butler, an entire pint bottle of my Perrier-Jouet, Brut, '89; a wine I was specially reserving for myself. Continuing his disgraceful deception, he succeeded in the course of the afternoon in alienating the affections of my only ward. He subsequently stayed to tea, and devoured every single muffin. And what makes his conduct all the more heartless is, that he was perfectly well aware from the first that I have no brother, that I never had a brother, and that I don't intend to have a brother, not even of any kind. I distinctly told him so myself yesterday afternoon.

Lady Bracknell Ahem! Mr. Worthing, after careful consideration I have decided entirely to overlook my nephew's conduct to you.

Jack That is very generous of you, Lady Bracknell. My own decision, however, is unalterable. I decline to give my consent.

Lady Bracknell (*To* CECILY) Come here, sweet child. (CECILY *goes over.*) How old are you, dear?

Cecily Well, I am really only eighteen, but I always admit to twenty when I go to evening parties.

Lady Bracknell You are perfectly right in making some slight alteration. Indeed, no woman should ever be quite accurate about her age. It looks so calculating. . . . (*In a meditative manner.*) Eighteen, but admitting to twenty at evening parties. Well, it will not be very long before you are of age and free from the restraints of tutelage. So I don't think your guardian's consent is, after all, a matter of any importance.

Jack Pray excuse me, Lady Bracknell, for interrupting you again, but it is only fair to tell you that according to the terms of her grandfather's will Miss Cardew does not come legally of age till she is thirty-five.

---

[42] Oxonian: graduate of Oxford University.

Lady Bracknell That does not seem to me to be a grave objection. Thirty-five is a very attractive age. London society is full of women of the very highest birth who have, of their own free choice, remained thirty-five for years. Lady Dumbleton is an instance in point. To my own knowledge she has been thirty-five ever since she arrived at the age of forty, which was many years ago now. I see no reason why our dear Cecily should not be even still more attractive at the age you mention than she is at present. There will be a large accumulation of property.

Cecily Algy, could you wait for me till I was thirty-five?

Algernon Of course I could, Cecily. You know I could.

Cecily Yes, I felt it instinctively, but I couldn't wait all that time. I hate waiting even five minutes for anybody. It always makes me rather cross. I am not punctual myself, I know, but I do like punctuality in others, and waiting, even to be married, is quite out of the question.

Algernon Then what is to be done, Cecily?

Cecily I don't know, Mr. Moncrieff.

Lady Bracknell My dear Mr. Worthing, as Miss Cardew states positively that she cannot wait till she is thirty-five—a remark which I am bound to say seems to me to show a somewhat impatient nature—I would beg of you to reconsider your decision.

Jack But my dear Lady Bracknell, the matter is entirely in your own hands. The moment you consent to my marriage with Gwendolen, I will most gladly allow your nephew to form an alliance with my ward.

Lady Bracknell (*Rising and drawing herself up*) You must be quite aware that what you propose is out of the question.

Jack Then a passionate celibacy is all that any of us can look forward to.

Lady Bracknell That is not the destiny I propose for Gwendolen. Algernon, of course, can choose for himself. (*Pulls out her watch.*) Come dear; (Gwendolen *rises.*) we have already missed five, if not six, trains. To miss any more might expose us to comment on the platform.

(*Enter* Dr. Chasuble.)

Chasuble Everything is quite ready for the christenings.

Lady Bracknell The christenings, sir! Is not that somewhat premature?

Chasuble (*Looking rather puzzled, and pointing to* Jack *and* Algernon) Both these gentlemen have expressed a desire for immediate baptism.

Lady Bracknell At their age? The idea is grotesque and irreligious! Algernon, I forbid you to be baptised. I will not hear of such excesses. Lord Bracknell would be highly displeased if he learned that that was the way in which you wasted your time and money.

Chasuble Am I to understand then that there are to be no christenings at all this afternoon?

Jack I don't think that, as things are now, it would be of much practical value to either of us, Dr. Chasuble.

Chasuble I am grieved to hear such sentiments from you, Mr. Worthing. They savour of the heretical views of the Anabaptists,[43] views that I have completely refuted in four of my unpublished sermons. However, as your present mood seems to be one peculiarly secular, I will return to the church at once. Indeed, I have just been informed by the pew-opener that for the last hour and a half Miss Prism has been waiting for me in the vestry.

Lady Bracknell (*Starting*) Miss Prism! Did I hear you mention a Miss Prism?

Chasuble Yes, Lady Bracknell. I am on my way to join her.

Lady Bracknell Pray allow me to detain you for a moment. This matter may prove to be one of vital importance to Lord Bracknell and myself. Is this Miss Prism a female of repellent aspect, remotely connected with education?

Chasuble (*Somewhat indignantly*) She is the most cultivated of ladies, and the very picture of respectability.

Lady Bracknell It is obviously the same person. May I ask what position she holds in your household?

Chasuble (*Severely*) I am a celibate, madam.

Jack (*Interposing*) Miss Prism, Lady Bracknell, has been for the last three years Miss Cardew's esteemed governess and valued companion.

Lady Bracknell In spite of what I hear of her, I must see her at once. Let her be sent for.

Chasuble (*Looking off*) She approaches, she is nigh.

(*Enter* Miss Prism *hurriedly.*)

Miss Prism I was told you expected me in the vestry, dear Canon. I have been waiting for you there for an hour and three-quarters.

(*Catches sight of* Lady Bracknell, *who has fixed her with a stony glare.* Miss Prism *grows pale and quails. She looks anxiously round as if desirous to escape.*)

Lady Bracknell (*In a severe, judicial voice*) Prism! (Miss Prism *bows her head in shame.*) Come here, Prism! (Miss Prism *approaches in a humble manner.*) Prism! Where is that baby? (*General consternation. The Canon starts back in horror.* Algernon *and* Jack *pretend to be anxious to shield* Cecily *and* Gwendolen *from hearing the details of a terrible public scandal.*) Twenty-eight years ago, Prism, you left Lord Bracknell's house, Number 104, Upper Grosvenor Street, in charge of a perambulator that contained a baby, of the male sex. You never returned. A few weeks later, through the elaborate investigations of the Metropolitan police, the perambulator was discovered at midnight, standing by itself in a remote

---

[43] Anabaptists: a sect opposed to infant baptism.

corner of Bayswater. It contained the manuscript of a three-volume novel of more than usually revolting sentimentality. (MISS PRISM *starts in involuntary indignation.*) But the baby was not there! (*Everyone looks at* MISS PRISM.) Prism: Where is that baby?

(*A pause.*)

Miss Prism   Lady Bracknell, I admit with shame that I do not know. I only wish I did. The plain facts of the case are these. On the morning of the day you mention, a day that is for ever branded on my memory, I prepared as usual to take the baby out in its perambulator. I had also with me a somewhat old, but capacious hand-bag in which I had intended to place the manuscript of a work of fiction that I had written during my few unoccupied hours. In a moment of mental abstraction, for which I never can forgive myself, I deposited the manuscript in the bassinette, and placed the baby in the hand-bag.

Jack (*Who has been listening attentively*)   But where did you deposit the hand-bag?

Miss Prism   Do not ask me, Mr. Worthing.

Jack   Miss Prism, this is a matter of no small importance to me. I insist on knowing where you deposited the hand-bag that contained that infant.

Miss Prism   I left it in the cloak room of one of the larger railway stations in London.

Jack   What railway station?

Miss Prism (*Quite crushed*)   Victoria. The Brighton line.

(*Sinks into a chair.*)

Jack   I must retire to my room for a moment. Gwendolen, wait here for me.

Gwendolen   If you are not too long, I will wait here for you all my life.

(*Exit* JACK *in great excitement.*)

Chasuble   What do you think this means, Lady Bracknell?

Lady Bracknell   I dare not even suspect, Dr. Chasuble. I need hardly tell you that in families of high position strange coincidences are not supposed to occur. They are hardly considered the thing.

(*Noises heard overhead as if someone was throwing trunks about. Everyone looks up.*)

Cecily   Uncle Jack seems strangely agitated.

Chasuble   Your guardian has a very emotional nature.

Lady Bracknell   This noise is extremely unpleasant. It sounds as if he was having an argument. I dislike arguments of any kind. They are always vulgar, and often convincing.

Chasuble (*Looking up*)   It has stopped now.

(*The noise is redoubled.*)

Lady Bracknell I wish he would arrive at some conclusion.

Gwendolen This suspense is terrible. I hope it will last.

(*Enter* JACK *with a hand-bag of black leather in his hand.*)

Jack (*Rushing over to* MISS PRISM) Is this the hand-bag, Miss Prism? Examine it carefully before you speak. The happiness of more than one life depends on your answer.

Miss Prism (*Calmly*) It seems to be mine. Yes, here is the injury it received through the upsetting of a Gower Street omnibus in younger and happier days. Here is the stain on the lining caused by the explosion of a temperance beverage, an incident that occurred at Leamington. And here, on the lock, are my initials. I had forgotten that in an extravagant mood I had had them placed there. The bag is undoubtedly mine. I am delighted to have it so unexpectedly restored to me. It has been a great inconvenience being without it all these years.

Jack (*In a pathetic voice*) Miss Prism, more is restored to you than this hand-bag. I was the baby you placed in it.

Miss Prism (*Amazed*) You?

Jack (*Embracing her*) Yes . . . mother!

Miss Prism (*Recoiling in indignant astonishment*) Mr. Worthing! I am unmarried!

Jack Unmarried! I do not deny that is a serious blow. But after all, who has the right to cast a stone against one who has suffered? Cannot repentance wipe out an act of folly? Why should there be one law for men, and another for women? Mother, I forgive you.

(*Tries to embrace her again.*)

Miss Prism (*Still more indignant*) Mr. Worthing, there is some error. (*Pointing to* LADY BRACKNELL.) There is the lady who can tell you who you really are.

Jack (*After a pause*) Lady Bracknell, I hate to seem inquisitive, but would you kindly inform me who I am?

Lady Bracknell I am afraid that the news I have to give you will not altogether please you. You are the son of my poor sister, Mrs. Moncrieff, and consequently Algernon's elder brother.

Jack Algy's elder brother? Then I have a brother after all. I knew I had a brother! I always said I had a brother! Cecily,—how could you have ever doubted that I had a brother. (*Seizes hold of* ALGERNON.) Dr. Chasuble, my unfortunate brother. Miss Prism, my unfortunate brother. Gwendolen, my unfortunate brother. Algy, you young scoundrel, you will have to treat me with more respect in the future. You have never behaved to me like a brother in all your life.

Algernon Well, not till to-day, old boy, I admit. I did my best, however, though I was out of practice.

(*Shakes hands.*)

Gwendolen (*To* Jack) My own! But what own are you? What is your Christian name, now that you have become someone else?

Jack Good heavens! . . . I had quite forgotten that point. Your decision on the subject of my name is irrevocable, I suppose?

Gwendolen I never change, except in my affections.

Cecily What a noble nature you have, Gwendolen!

Jack Then the question had better be cleared up at once. Aunt Augusta, a moment. At the time when Miss Prism left me in the hand-bag, had I been christened already?

Lady Bracknell Every luxury that money could buy, including christening, had been lavished on you by your fond and doting parents.

Jack Then I was christened! That is settled. Now, what name was I given? Let me know the worst.

Lady Bracknell Being the eldest son you were naturally christened after your father.

Jack (*Irritably*) Yes, but what was my father's Christian name?

Lady Bracknell (*Meditatively*) I cannot at the present moment recall what the General's Christian name was. But I have no doubt he had one. He was eccentric, I admit. But only in later years. And that was the result of the Indian climate, and marriage, and indigestion, and other things of that kind.

Jack Algy! Can't you recollect what our father's Christian name was?

Algernon My dear boy, we were never even on speaking terms. He died before I was a year old.

Jack His name would appear in the Army Lists of the period, I suppose, Aunt Augusta?

Lady Bracknell The General was essentially a man of peace, except in his domestic life. But I have no doubt his name would appear in any military directory.

Jack The Army Lists of the last forty years are here. These delightful records should have been my constant study (*Rushes to bookcase and tears the books out*). M. Generals . . . Mallam, Maxbohm, Magley, what ghastly names they have—Markby, Migsby, Moss, Moncrieff! Lieutenant 1840, Captain, Lieutenant-Colonel, Colonel, General 1869, Christian names, Ernest John (*Puts book very quietly down and speaks quite calmly*). I always told you, Gwendolen, my name was Ernest, didn't I? Well, it is Ernest after all. I mean it naturally is Ernest.

Lady Bracknell Yes, I remember that the General was called Ernest. I knew I had some particular reason for disliking the name.

Gwendolen Ernest! My own Ernest! I felt from the first that you could have no other name!

Jack Gwendolen, it is a terrible thing for a man to find out suddenly that all his life he has been speaking nothing but the truth. Can you forgive me?

Gwendolen   I can. For I feel that you are sure to change.

Jack   My own one!

Chasuble (*To* Miss Prism)   Lætitia!

(*Embraces her.*)

Miss Prism (*Enthusiastically*)   Frederick! At last!

Algernon   Cecily! (*Embraces her*). At last!

Jack   Gwendolen! (*Embraces her*). At last!

Lady Bracknell   My nephew, you seem to be displaying signs of triviality.

Jack   On the contrary, Aunt Augusta, I've now realized for the first time in my life the vital Importance of Being Earnest.

(*Tableau*)[44]

(*Curtain*)

[44] *Tableau:* the actors hold their positions stiffly for a moment before the curtain falls.

CHAPTER 4

LANGUAGE AND MEANING

Language is used according to its purpose. In a laboratory report, for example, the writer generally tries to express an absolutely unambiguous and literal meaning. Whenever possible, numbers are used, and often a formula is substituted for a sentence. Vocabulary is precise, terms are carefully defined, and the entire document centers around the presentation and explanation of a scientific concept. In such a report, feelings are not appropriate, so the language must be "pure"; that is, it must be devoid of emotional content. Literature, on the other hand, is concerned with exploring some aspect of human experience. Such experience is rich, varied, and complicated. It usually involves powerful emotions that cannot be expressed in exact, literal language. Instead, feelings that are often difficult to put into words are described or evoked by language that suggests, rather than defines. Sometimes, words themselves carry emotional overtones that broaden or extend communication. "Keep cool," for instance, is meaningful precisely because the word *cool* has immediately accessible connotations. To try to express the same idea in technical language—"Stay at 17.6 centigrade"—would make the sentence merely silly. Similarly, such a sentence as "We hold these truths to be self-evident . . ." is deeply ambiguous. What, after all, is a "truth," and in what sense can anything be said to be "self-evident"? Yet the emotional values that attach to these words from the *Declaration of Independence* have had a profound effect on the world, perhaps even greater than that of the atom bomb made possible by Einstein's $E = MC^2$. In addition, the context of a word can increase or change its meaning. In most literature, particularly poetry, communication involves a process of compression and expansion: words are important for their own range of associations; but any word can take on new significance by being placed after, near, or between other words. For instance, one meaning of the word *characters* is letters of the alphabet. In "Parting, Without a Sequel," Ransom puts the word *character* side by side with *venomous*—and describes the "curve" as being hateful (the note mentioned in the poem is written "with characters venomous and hatefully curved"). Just six words in this particular combination tell the reader how the young woman felt when she wrote the letter and exactly what her communication was like. Of course, not all combinations of words are as easy to understand as this example. Sometimes, as you try to understand a work of literature, you will feel as if you are trying to solve a puzzle. Finding the solution will be easier in most cases if you understand specialized uses of language employed by writers of prose and poetry.

The most common ones are discussed in this chapter: imagery, figurative comparisons, symbol, allegory, and irony. Learning to identify their uses can help one to becoming a better reader. Not all literature makes use of every device (sometimes, a work may be devoid of figures altogether), but at other times recognizing and understanding a specialized use of language can be essential to seeing what a work is all about.

IMAGERY

Sometimes an author chooses to enhance description by appealing to the reader's senses of seeing, hearing, smelling, feeling, and tasting. Thus, he or she can employ *imagery*—words that are literal, concrete representations of sensory phenomena. For example, the author may use color (the red wheelbarrow), sound (the tolling bell), or texture (the smooth coin). Frequently, imagery is used to set a scene, as in prose fiction; but it can also be used to give meaning to a work. Both uses of imagery are employed in W. H. Auden's poem, "Musée des Beaux Arts":

W. H. Auden (1907–1973)

MUSÉE DES BEAUX ARTS

About suffering they were never wrong,
The Old Masters: how well they understood
Its human position; how it takes place
While someone else is eating or opening a window or just walking dully along;
How, when the aged are reverently, passionately waiting   5
For the miraculous birth, there always must be
Children who did not specially want it to happen, skating
On a pond at the edge of the wood:
They never forgot
That even the dreadful martyrdom must run its course   10
Anyhow in a corner, some untidy spot
Where the dogs go on with their doggy life and the torturer's horse
Scratches its innocent behind on a tree.

In Brueghel's *Icarus*, for instance: how everything turns away
Quite leisurely from the disaster; the ploughman may   15
Have heard the splash, the forsaken cry,
But for him it was not an important failure; the sun shone
As it had to on the white legs disappearing into the green
Water; and the expensive delicate ship that must have seen
Something amazing, a boy falling out of the sky,   20
Had somewhere to get to and sailed calmly on.

The title, freely translated from the French, means "museum of fine arts," but it also refers to the Musée Royaux des Beaux Arts in Brussels, which houses the Brueghel painting discussed in the second stanza. Through the title the author takes us into the museum where we are invited to look at life the way the "Old Masters" did—the phrase refers to the great European artists of the period from around 1500 to the early 1700s. First, Auden makes the observation that these painters understood an important aspect

of suffering: that it occurs to some people while others (and the world) continue life unheeding, "eating or opening a window or just walking dully along" (line 4). Auden follows this observation with two examples, both built up around images relating to other paintings in the museum. First, we have the "aged," waiting "reverently, passionately" (line 5) for the "miraculous birth" (the Nativity of Christ), while children are otherwise occupied, "skating / On a pond at the edge of the wood" (lines 7–8). In another picture we view a martyrdom, as someone is killed for his beliefs. Even such a dramatic event takes place "in a corner," the murder unheeded by dogs living their "doggy life" and the horse of the torturer, which "scratches its innocent behind on a tree" (lines 11, 12, 13).

The poem's principal example of unnoticed disaster is found in the painting "The Fall of Icarus" by Brueghel. This canvas is based on the myth of Daedalus and his son Icarus. In the legend, both father and son flew away from Crete on wings made of feathers and wax. Unfortunately, Icarus soared too close to the sun (against his father's advice) and his wings melted; he plunged into the sea and was drowned; but in the painting no one notices his fall: "everything turns away" (line 14). We see a ploughman on the left following his horse, staring at the ground. The image's "splash" and "forsaken cry" (line 16) suggest the sound of Icarus' plight; but the ploughman appears not to have heard them. The sun continues to shine on the meeting between "white legs" and "green / Water" (lines 18, 19); the old world continues to turn and life goes on as before. Thus, through a series of powerful visual and auditory images, Auden reproduces for the reader situations that involve seeing, hearing, and feeling. Since his imagery is both appropriate and evocative, it underlines and supports the meaning of the work while at the same time it increases the intensity of the reader's experience.

FIGURATIVE COMPARISONS

Although many of Auden's images are literal, the poem in its final lines depicts an "expensive delicate ship that must have seen" the fall, but "sailed calmly on." These words not only picture the ship for the reader; they also treat the ship as if it were capable of seeing and of having an emotional response to what it sees. Thus, the image suggests that the ship is somehow *like* a person. Since comparisons of this type are frequently used in literature, it is important to understand just how such use of language works.

All comparisons involve two objects or ideas: one is the actual topic of discussion; the other is a different object or idea that bears a significant similarity to the actual topic. Such comparisons may be intended literally or figuratively. The similarities may be actual (as when two objects that belong to the same general class are compared) or figurative (as when an object is compared to something markedly different, except for one unsuspected or unusual similarity). Here, for example, is a *literal* comparison:

A salamander in its larval stage is like a tiny snake.

This statement means what it says, no more or less. The reader who knows the general appearance of snakes but has no familiarity with salamanders can picture a long, slender body and tail, with no legs. Although the words are not scientifically precise, they can be taken literally, at *only* face value.

Figurative comparisons also call attention to similarities, but they usually mean something other than what they really say. In comparing persons to snakes, as in the following examples, the focus is not on physical appearance but rather on notions generally associated with snakes—danger, treachery, or powers of seduction. The comparison may be stated directly or simply implied by the context. Sometimes, too, only one of the two objects or ideas is mentioned, with the other expected to be understood.

The term *metaphor* is frequently used to indicate any of the three principal types of figurative comparison (simile, metaphor, and personification), but it is helpful to be able to distinguish among them.

Simile

In simile, a comparison is explicitly stated and generally uses the word *like* or *as* or an expression such as *bigger than*, or *redder than*.

Charles sits in the corner like a snake, poised and ready to strike.

The word *like* tells the reader that a comparison is being made between a person and a snake. However, we cannot assume that Charles has a long, slender, scaly body with no legs or that he is curled up in a position that prepares him to thrust his head forward and bite someone. Charles must be understood to be ready to speak out with "biting" words at the right moment, or perhaps even poised to leap up and lash out with his fists. Charles, then, is not physically like a snake; his behavior suggests the threat of danger, which we customarily attach to snakes.

At the last it [wine] biteth like a serpent, and stingeth like an adder.
[Prov. 33:32]

Wine does not literally bite or sting, though it may have a sharp flavor. Nevertheless, its effect can be like (simile) the poisonous bite of a snake, for it can cause serious harm to the unwary person.

Metaphor

When metaphor is used, a comparison between two objects or ideas is implied, not directly stated. Comparisons can be made in a number of ways without the explicit use of *like* or *as* or some other word. Three of the most common ways in which comparison can be implied are illustrated here:

1. Linking verbs, such as *is, are, was, were,* may be used to say that two objects or ideas are alike: "My so-called friend was a snake in the grass." The reader understands that the friend was a person who was comparable to a snake in behaving treacherously. Lady Macbeth's advice to her husband is to *seem* innocent as a flower (simile), but in fact to *be* dangerous and treacherous. "look like the innocent flower, / But be the serpent under 't" (*Macbeth*, I, v, 66–67). The linking verb "be" in her remark implies (metaphor) the figurative comparison, "behave like a serpent."

2. In the grammatical device called the appositive, the things to be compared are mentioned without the use of a linking verb. "Harold, the snake, is going out with somebody else." Again, the comparison suggests the notion of treachery.

3. Either of the two topics (or, rarely, both) may be omitted altogether, and merely understood from context. "Where's my serpent of old Nile?" (*Antony and Cleopatra*, I, v, 25): Cleopatra says that her lover sometimes speaks of her in this way. When he calls her his "serpent," he is emphasizing her likeness to a legendary serpent in having powers of seductive fascination. "There the grown serpent lies; the worm that's fled / Hath nature that in time will venom breed" (*Macbeth*, III, iv, 29–30): Banquo (like a grown serpent) has been a danger to Macbeth, but he has now been mur-

dered; his young son Fleance (like a worm that has fled) has escaped, and will eventually become a danger like his father. Neither Banquo nor Fleance is mentioned in the metaphors: the comparison is implied by the mention only of what the two men are compared to.

Personification

Personification treats an animal, an inanimate object, or an idea as if it were a person, capable of carrying out human behavior, implying a comparison between that and a person. In most of the examples above, as we have noted, persons are compared to snakes. However, if a snake were the actual topic of a passage, but figuratively compared to a person, we would have an instance of personification. "As it watched the rabbit, the boa constrictor tucked a bib under its chin." Boas do not wear bibs when eating; the implied comparison to a gluttonous person, however, emphasizes the predatory attitude of the snake. Look at these lines from "Eve," a poem by Christina Rossetti (1830–1894):

> Only the serpent in the dust,
> Wriggling and crawling,
> Grinned an evil grin, and thrust
> His tongue out with its fork.
> [Lines 67-70]

Serpents do not grin, nor do we have any right to regard them as having evil thoughts. This personification of a serpent is probably related to the story of the Garden of Eden in Genesis. Some readers, therefore, may point out that Satan (in a sense a person) disguised himself as a serpent in order to tempt Eve. Hence, in the view of such readers, the example above does not really *compare* a serpent to a person. However the passage is read, it is complex enough so that readers may have difficulty deciding just what it does mean.

One problem many readers experience with literature, in fact, results from overlooking or misinterpreting figurative comparisons that either provide important supplementary information about character, conflict, or setting or relate significantly to the meaning of the work as a whole. To see how to go about identifying and assessing the various kinds of comparisons, let us examine a story by Nathaniel Hawthorne (1804–1864):

YOUNG GOODMAN BROWN

Young Goodman Brown came forth at sunset into the street at Salem village; but put his head back, after crossing the threshold, to exchange a parting kiss with his young wife. And Faith, as the wife was aptly named, thrust her own pretty head into the street, letting the wind play with the pink ribbons of her cap while she called to Goodman Brown.

"Dearest heart," whispered she, softly and rather sadly, when her lips were close to his ear, "prithee put off your journey until sunrise and sleep in your own bed tonight. A lone woman is troubled with such dreams and such thoughts that she's afeard of herself sometimes. Pray tarry with me this night, dear husband, of all nights in the year."

"My love and my Faith," replied young Goodman Brown, "of all nights in the year, this one night must I tarry away from thee. My journey, as thou callest it, forth and back again, must needs be done 'twixt now and sunrise. What, my sweet, pretty wife, dost thou doubt me already, and we but three months married?"

"Then God bless you!" said Faith, with the pink ribbons; "and may you find all well when you come back."

"Amen!" cried Goodman Brown. "Say thy prayers, dear Faith, and go to bed at dusk, and no harm will come to thee."

So they parted; and the young man pursued his way until, being about to turn the corner by the meeting-house, he looked back and saw the head of Faith still peeping after him with a melancholy air, in spite of her pink ribbons.

"Poor little Faith!" thought he, for his heart smote him. "What a wretch am I to leave her on such an errand! She talks of dreams, too. Methought as she spoke there was trouble in her face, as if a dream had warned her what work is to be done tonight. But no, no; 't would kill her to think it. Well, she's a blessed angel on earth; and after this one night I'll cling to her skirts and follow her to heaven."

With this excellent resolve for the future, Goodman Brown felt himself justified in making more haste on his present evil purpose. He had taken a dreary road, darkened by all the gloomiest trees of the forest, which barely stood aside to let the narrow path creep through, and closed immediately behind. It was all as lonely as could be; and there is this peculiarity in such a solitude, that the traveller knows not who may be concealed by the innumerable trunks and the thick boughs overhead; so that with lonely footsteps he may yet be passing through an unseen multitude.

"There may be a devilish Indian behind every tree," said Goodman Brown to himself; and he glanced fearfully behind him as he added, "What if the devil himself should be at my very elbow!"

His head being turned back, he passed a crook of the road, and looking forward again, beheld the figure of a man, in grave and decent attire, seated at the foot of an old tree. He arose at Goodman Brown's approach and walked onward side by side with him.

"You are late, Goodman Brown," said he. "The clock of the Old South[1]

---

[1] Old South: Old South Church, Boston, Mass.

was striking as I came through Boston, and that is full fifteen minutes agone."

"Faith kept me back a while," replied the young man, with a tremor in his voice, caused by the sudden appearance of his companion, though not wholly unexpected.

It was now deep dusk in the forest, and deepest in that part of it where these two were journeying. As nearly as could be discerned, the second traveller was about fifty years old, apparently in the same rank of life as Goodman Brown, and bearing a considerable resemblance to him, though perhaps more in expression than features. Still they might have been taken for father and son. And yet, though the elder person was as simply clad as the younger, and as simple in manner too, he had an indescribable air of one who knew the world, and who would not have felt abashed at the governor's dinner table or in King William's[2] court, were it possible that his affairs should call him thither. But the only thing about him that could be fixed upon as remarkable was his staff, which bore the likeness of a great black snake, so curiously wrought that it might almost be seen to twist and wriggle itself like a living serpent. This, of course, must have been an ocular deception, assisted by the uncertain light.

"Come, Goodman Brown," cried his fellow-traveller, "this is a dull pace for the beginning of a journey. Take my staff, if you are so soon weary."

"Friend," said the other, exchanging his slow pace for a full stop, "having kept covenant by meeting thee here, it is my purpose now to return whence I came. I have scruples touching the matter thou wot'st of."

"Sayest thou so?" replied he of the serpent, smiling apart. "Let us walk on, nevertheless, reasoning as we go; and if I convince thee not thou shalt turn back. We are but a little way in the forest yet."

"Too far! too far!" exclaimed the goodman, unconsciously resuming his walk. "My father never went into the woods on such an errand, nor his father before him. We have been a race of honest men and good Christians since the days of the martyrs; and shall I be the first of the name of Brown that ever took his path and kept—"

"Such company, thou wouldst say," observed the elder person, interpreting his pause. "Well said, Goodman Brown! I have been as well acquainted with your family as with ever a one among the Puritans; and that's no trifle to say. I helped your grandfather, the constable, when he lashed the Quaker woman so smartly through the streets of Salem; and it was I that brought your father a pitch-pine knot, kindled at my own hearth, to set fire to an Indian village, in King Philip's war.[3] They were my good friends, both; and many a pleasant walk have we had along this path, and returned merrily after midnight. I would fain be friends with you for their sake."

2 King William: King of England (1687–1702).
3 King Philip's War: struggle between Massachusetts' colonists and Indians, 1675–1676.

"If it be as thou sayest," replied Goodman Brown. "I marvel they never spoke of these matters; or, verily, I marvel not, seeing that the least rumor of the sort would have driven them from New England. We are a people of prayer, and good works to boot, and abide no such wickedness."

"Wickedness or not," said the traveller with the twisted staff. "I have a very general acquaintance here in New England. The deacons of many a church have drunk the communion wine with me; the selectmen of divers towns make me their chairman; and a majority of the Great and General Court are firm supporters of my interest. The governor and I, too— But these are state secrets."

"Can this be so?" cried Goodman Brown, with a stare of amazement at his undisturbed companion. "Howbeit, I have nothing to do with the governor and council; they have their own ways, and are no rule for a simple husbandman like me. But, were I to go on with thee, how should I meet the eye of that good old man, our minister, at Salem village? Oh, his voice would make me tremble both Sabbath day and lecture day."

Thus far the elder traveller had listened with due gravity; but now burst into a fit of irrepressible mirth, shaking himself so violently that his snake-like staff actually seemed to wriggle in sympathy.

"Ha! ha! ha!" shouted he again and again; then composing himself, "Well, go on, Goodman Brown, go on; but, prithee, don't kill me with laughing."

"Well, then, to end the matter at once," said Goodman Brown, considerably nettled, "there is my wife, Faith. It would break her dear little heart; and I'd rather break my own."

"Nay, if that be the case," answered the other, "e'en go thy ways, Goodman Brown. I would not for twenty old women like the one hobbling before us that Faith should come to any harm."

As he spoke he pointed his staff at a female figure on the path, in whom Goodman Brown recognized a very pious and exemplary dame, who had taught him his catechism in youth, and was still his moral and spiritual adviser, jointly with the minister and Deacon Gookin.

"A marvel, truly, that Goody[4] Cloyse should be so far in the wilderness at nightfall," said he. "But with your leave, friend, I shall take a cut through the woods until we have left this Christian woman behind. Being a stranger to you, she might ask whom I was consorting with and whither I was going."

"Be it so," said his fellow-traveller. "Betake you to the woods, and let me keep the path."

Accordingly the young man turned aside, but took care to watch his companion, who advanced softly along the road until he had come within a staff's length of the old dame. She, meanwhile, was making the best of her way, with singular speed for so aged a woman, and mumbling some indis-

[4] Goody: abbreviation for *goodwife*.

tinct words—a prayer, doubtless—as she went. The traveller put forth his staff and touched her withered neck with what seemed the serpent's tail.

"The devil!" screamed the pious old lady.

"Then Goody Cloyse knows her old friend?" observed the traveller, confronting her and leaning on his writhing stick.

"Ah, forsooth, and is it your worship indeed?" cried the good dame. "Yea, truly is it, and in the very image of my old gossip, Goodman Brown, the grandfather of the silly fellow that now is. But—would your worship believe it?—my broomstick hath strangely disappeared, stolen, as I suspect, by that unhanged witch, Goody Cory, and that, too, when I was all anointed with the juice of smallage, and cinquefoil, and wolf's bane—"

"Mingled with fine wheat and the fat of a new-born babe," said the shape of old Goodman Brown.

"Ah, your worship knows the recipe," cried the old lady, cackling aloud. "So, as I was saying, being all ready for the meeting, and no horse to ride on, I made up my mind to foot it; for they tell me there is a nice young man to be taken into communion tonight. But now your good worship will lend me your arm, and we shall be there in a twinkling."

"That can hardly be," answered her friend. "I may not spare you my arm, Goody Cloyse; but here is my staff, if you will."

So saying, he threw it down at her feet, where, perhaps, it assumed life, being one of the rods which its owner had formerly lent to the Egyptian magi.[5] Of this fact, however, Goodman Brown could not take cognizance. He had cast up his eyes in astonishment, and, looking down again, beheld neither Goody Cloyse nor the serpentine staff, but his fellow-traveller alone, who waited for him as calmly as if nothing had happened.

"That old woman taught me my catechism," said the young man; and there was a world of meaning in this simple comment.

They continued to walk onward, while the elder traveller exhorted his companion to make good speed and persevere in the path, discoursing so aptly, that his arguments seemed rather to spring up in the bosom of his auditor, than to be suggested by himself. As they went he plucked a branch of maple, to serve for a walking-stick, and began to strip it of the twigs and little boughs, which were wet with evening dew. The moment his fingers touched them, they became strangely withered and dried up, as with a week's sunshine. Thus the pair proceeded, at a good free pace, until suddenly, in a gloomy hollow of the road, Goodman Brown sat himself down on the stump of a tree, and refused to go any farther.

"Friend," said he, stubbornly, "my mind is made up. Not another step will I budge on this errand. What if a wretched old woman do choose to go to the devil, when I thought she was going to Heaven! Is that any reason why I should quit my dear Faith, and go after her?"

---

[5] magi: reference to Moses and Aaron, who led the Israelites out of Egypt: Ex. 3:10–12.

"You will think better of this by and by," said his acquaintance, composedly. "Sit here and rest yourself awhile; and when you feel like moving again, there is my staff to help you along."

Without more words, he threw his companion the maple stick, and was as speedily out of sight as if he had vanished into the deepening gloom. The young man sat a few moments by the roadside, applauding himself greatly, and thinking with how clear a conscience he should meet the minister, in his morning walk, nor shrink from the eye of good old Deacon Gookin. And what calm sleep would be his, that very night, which was to have been spent so wickedly, but purely and sweetly now, in the arms of Faith! Amidst these pleasant and praiseworthy meditations, Goodman Brown heard the tramp of horses along the road, and deemed it advisable to conceal himself within the verge of the forest, conscious of the guilty purpose that had brought him thither, though now so happily turned from it.

On came the hoof tramps and the voices of the riders, two grave old voices, conversing soberly as they drew near. These mingled sounds appeared to pass along the road, within a few yards of the young man's hiding-place; but, owing doubtless to the depth of the gloom at that particular spot, neither the travellers nor their steeds were visible. Though their figures brushed the small boughs by the wayside, it could not be seen that they intercepted, even for a moment, the faint gleam from the strip of bright sky athwart which they must have passed. Goodman Brown alternately crouched and stood on tiptoe, pulling aside the branches and thrusting forth his head as far as he durst without discerning so much as a shadow. It vexed him the more, because he could have sworn, were such a thing possible, that he recognized the voices of the minister and Deacon Gookin, jogging along quietly, as they were wont to do, when bound to some ordination or ecclesiastical council. While yet within hearing, one of the riders stopped to pluck a switch.

"Of the two, reverend sir," said the voice like the deacon's, "I had rather miss an ordination dinner than tonight's meeting. They tell me that some of our community are to be here from Falmouth and beyond, and others from Connecticut and Rhode Island, besides several of the Indian powwows, who, after their fashion, know almost as much deviltry as the best of us. Moreover, there is a goodly young woman to be taken into communion."

"Mighty well, Deacon Gookin!" replied the solemn old tones of the minister. "Spur up, or we shall be late. Nothing can be done, you know, until I get on the ground."

The hoofs clattered again; and the voices, talking so strangely in the empty air, passed on through the forest, where no church had even been gathered or solitary Christian prayed. Whither, then, could these holy men be journeying so deep into the heathen wilderness? Young Goodman Brown caught hold of a tree for support, being ready to sink down on the ground, faint and overburdened with the heavy sickness of his heart. He looked up to the sky, doubting whether there really was a heaven above him. Yet there was the blue arch, and the stars brightening in it.

"With heaven above and Faith below, I will yet stand firm against the devil!" cried Goodman Brown.

While he still gazed upward into the deep arch of the firmament and had lifted his hands to pray, a cloud, though no wind was stirring, hurried across the zenith and hid the brightening stars. The blue sky was still visible, except directly overhead, where this black mass of cloud was sweeping swiftly northward. Aloft in the air, as if from the depths of the cloud, came a confused and doubtful sound of voices. Once the listener fancied that he could distinguish the accents of townspeople of his own, men and women, both pious and ungodly, many of whom he had met at the communion table, and had seen others rioting at the tavern. The next moment, so indistinct were the sounds, he doubted whether he had heard aught but the murmur of the old forest, whispering without a wind. Then came a stronger swell of those familiar tones, heard daily in the sunshine at Salem village, but never until now from a cloud of night. There was one voice of a young woman, uttering lamentations, yet with an uncertain sorrow, and entreating for some favor, which perhaps, it would grieve her to obtain; and all the unseen multitude, both saints and sinners, seemed to encourage her onward.

"Faith!" shouted Goodman Brown, in a voice of agony and desperation; and the echoes of the forest mocked him, crying, "Faith! Faith!" as if bewildered wretches were seeking her all through the wilderness.

The cry of grief, rage, and terror was yet piercing the night, when the unhappy husband held his breath for a response. There was a scream, drowned immediately in a louder murmur of voices, fading into far-off laughter, as the dark cloud swept away, leaving the clear and silent sky above Goodman Brown. But something fluttered lightly down through the air and caught on the branch of a tree. The young man seized it, and beheld a pink ribbon.

"My Faith is gone!" cried he, after one stupefied moment. "There is no good on earth; and sin is but a name. Come, devil; for to thee is this world given."

And, maddened with despair, so that he laughed loud and long, did Goodman Brown grasp his staff and set forth again, at such a rate that he seemed to fly along the forest path rather than to walk or run. The road grew wilder and drearier and more faintly traced, and vanished at length, leaving him in the heart of the dark wilderness, still rushing onward with the instinct that guides mortal man to evil. The whole forest was peopled with frightful sounds—the creaking of the trees, the howling of wild beasts, and the yell of Indians; while sometimes the wind tolled like a distant church bell, and sometimes gave a broad roar around the traveller, as if all Nature were laughing him to scorn. But he was himself the chief horror of the scene, and shrank not from its other horrors.

"Ha! ha! ha!" roared Goodman Brown when the wind laughed at him. "Let us hear which will laugh loudest. Think not to frighten me with your deviltry. Come witch, come wizard, come Indian powwow, come devil himself, and here comes Goodman Brown. You may as well fear him as he fears you."

In truth, all through the haunted forest there could be nothing more frightful than the figure of Goodman Brown. On he flew among the black pines, brandishing his staff with frenzied gestures, now giving vent to an inspiration of horrid blasphemy, and now shouting forth such laughter as set all the echoes of the forest laughing like demons around him. The fiend in his own shape is less hideous than when he rages in the breast of man. Thus sped the demoniac on his course, until, quivering among the trees, he saw a red light before him, as when the felled trunks and branches of a clearing have been set on fire, and throw up their lurid blaze against the sky, at the hour of midnight. He paused, in a lull of the tempest that had driven him onward, and heard the swell of what seemed a hymn, rolling solemnly from a distance with the weight of many voices. He knew the tune; it was a familiar one in the choir of the village meeting-house. The verse died heavily away, and was lengthened by a chorus, not of human voices, but of all the sounds of the benighted wilderness pealing in awful harmony together. Goodman Brown cried out, and his cry was lost to his own ear by its unison with the cry of the desert.

In the interval of silence he stole forward until the light glared full upon his eyes. At one extremity of an open space, hemmed in by the dark wall of the forest, arose a rock, bearing some rude, natural resemblance either to an altar or a pulpit, and surrounded by four blazing pines, their tops aflame, their stems untouched, like candles at an evening meeting. The mass of foliage that had overgrown the summit of the rock was all on fire, blazing high into the night and fitfully illuminating the whole field. Each pendant twig and leafy festoon was in a blaze. As the red light arose and fell, a numerous congregation alternately shone forth, then disappeared in shadow, and again grew, as it were, out of the darkness, peopling the heart of the solitary woods at once.

"A grave and dark-clad company," quoth Goodman Brown.

In truth they were such. Among them, quivering to and fro between gloom and splendor, appeared faces that would be seen next day at the council board of the province, and others which, Sabbath after Sabbath, looked devoutly heavenward, and benignantly over the crowded pews, from the holiest pulpits in the land. Some affirm that the lady of the governor was there. At least there were high dames well known to her, and wives of honored husbands, and widows, a great multitude, and ancient maidens, all of excellent repute, and fair young girls, who trembled lest their mothers should espy them. Either the sudden gleams of light flashing over the obscure field bedazzled Goodman Brown, or he recognized a score of the church members of Salem village famous for their especial sanctity. Good old Deacon Gookin had arrived, and waited at the skirts of that venerable saint, his revered pastor. But, irreverently consorting with these grave, reputable, and pious people, these elders of the church, these chaste dames and dewy virgins, there were men of dissolute lives and women of spotted fame, wretches given over to all mean and filthy vice, and suspected even of horrid crimes. It was strange to see that the good shrank not from the wicked, nor were the sinners abashed by the saints. Scattered also among their pale-faced enemies were the Indian priests, or powwows, who had often scared their native forest with more hideous incantations than any known to English witchcraft.

"But where is Faith?" thought Goodman Brown; and, as hope came into his heart, he trembled.

Another verse of the hymn arose, a slow and mournful strain, such as the pious love, but joined to words which expressed all that our nature can conceive of sin, and darkly hinted at far more. Unfathomable to mere mortals is the lore of fiends. Verse after verse was sung; and still the chorus of the desert swelled between like the deepest tone of a mighty organ; and with the final peal of that dreadful anthem there came a sound, as if the roaring wind, the rushing streams, the howling beasts, and every other voice of the unconcerted wilderness were mingling and according with the voice of guilty man in homage to the prince of all. The four blazing pines threw up a loftier flame, and obscurely discovered shapes and visages of horror on the smoke wreaths above the impious assembly. At the same moment the fire on the rock shot redly forth and formed a glowing arch above its base, where now appeared a figure. With reverence be it spoken, the figure bore no slight similitude, both in garb and manner, to some grave divine of the New England churches.

"Bring forth the converts!" cried a voice that echoed through the field and rolled into the forest.

At the word, Goodman Brown stepped forth from the shadow of the trees and approached the congregation, with whom he felt a loathful brotherhood by the sympathy of all that was wicked in his heart. He could have well-nigh sworn that the shape of his own dead father beckoned him to advance, looking downward from a smoke wreath, while a woman, with dim features of despair, threw out her hand to warn him back. Was it his mother? But he had no power to retreat one step, nor to resist, even in thought, when the minister and good old Deacon Gookin seized his arms and led him to the blazing rock. Thither came also the slender form of a veiled female, led between Goody Cloyse, that pious teacher of the catechism, and Martha Carrier, who had received the devil's promise to be queen of hell. A rampant hag was she. And there stood the proselytes beneath the canopy of fire.

"Welcome, my children," said the dark figure, "to the communion of your race. Ye have found this young your nature and your destiny. My children, look behind you!"

They turned; and flashing forth, as it were, in a sheet of flame, the fiend worshippers were seen; the smile of welcome gleamed darkly on every visage.

"There," resumed the sable form, "are all whom ye have reverenced from youth. Ye deemed them holier than yourselves, and shrank from your own sin, contrasting it with their lives of righteousness and prayerful aspirations heavenward. Yet here are they all in my worshipping assembly. This night it shall be granted you to know their secret deeds: how hoary-bearded elders of the church have whispered wanton words to the young maids of their households; how many a woman, eager for widows' weeds, has given her husband a drink at bedtime and let him sleep his last sleep in her bosom; how beardless youths have made haste to inherit their fathers' wealth; and how fair damsels—blush not, sweet ones—have dug little graves in the garden, and bidden me, the sole guest to an infant's funeral. By the sympathy of your human hearts for sin ye shall scent out all the places—whether in church, bedchamber, street, field, or forest—where crime has been committed, and shall exult to behold the whole earth one stain of guilt, one mighty blood spot. Far more than this. It shall be yours to penetrate, in every bosom, the deep mystery of sin, the fountain of all wicked arts, and which inexhaustibly supplies more evil impulses than human power —than my power at its utmost—can make manifest in deeds. And now, my children, look upon each other."

They did so, and, by the blaze of the hell-kindled torches, the wretched man beheld his Faith, and the wife her husband, trembling before that unhallowed altar.

"Lo, there ye stand, my children," said the figure, in a deep and solemn tone, almost sad with its despairing awfulness, as if his once angelic nature could yet mourn for our miserable race. "Depending upon one another's hearts, ye had still hoped that virtue were not all a dream. Now are ye undeceived. Evil is the nature of mankind. Evil must be your only happiness. Welcome again, my children, to the communion of your race."

"Welcome," repeated the fiend worshippers, in one cry of despair and triumph.

And there they stood, the only pair, as it seemed, who were yet hesitating on the verge of wickedness in this dark world. A basin was hollowed, naturally, in the rock. Did it contain water, reddened by the lurid light? or was it blood? or, perchance, a liquid flame? Herein did the shape of evil dip his hand and prepare to lay the mark of baptism upon their foreheads, that they might be partakers of the mystery of sin, more conscious of the secret guilt of others, both in deed and thought, than they could now be of their own. The husband cast one look at his pale wife, and Faith at him. What polluted wretches would the next glance show them to each other, shuddering alike at what they disclosed and what they saw!

"Faith! Faith!" cried the husband, "look up to heaven, and resist the wicked one."

Whether Faith obeyed he knew not. Hardly had he spoken when he found himself amid calm night and solitude, listening to a roar of the wind which died heavily away through the forest. He staggered against the rock, and felt it chill and damp; while a hanging twig, that had been all on fire, besprinkled his cheek with the coldest dew.

The next morning young Goodman Brown came slowly into the street of Salem village, staring around him like a bewildered man. The good old minister was taking a walk along the graveyard to get an appetite for breakfast and meditate his sermon, and bestowed a blessing, as he passed, on Goodman Brown. He shrank from the venerable saint as if to avoid an anathema.[6] Old Deacon Gookin was at domestic worship, and the holy words of his prayer were heard through the open window. "What God doth the wizard pray to?" quoth Goodman Brown. Goody Cloyse, that excellent old Christian, stood in the early sunshine at her own lattice, catechizing a little girl who had brought her a pint of morning's milk. Goodman Brown snatched away the child as from the grasp of the fiend himself. Turning the corner by the meeting-house, he spied the head of Faith, with the pink ribbons, gazing anxiously forth, and bursting into such joy at sight of him that she skipped along the street and almost kissed her husband before the whole village. But Goodman Brown looked sternly and sadly into her face, and passed on without a greeting.

Had Goodman Brown fallen asleep in the forest and only dreamed a wild dream of a witch-meeting?

Be it so if you will; but, alas! it was a dream of evil omen for young Goodman Brown. A stern, a sad, a darkly meditative, a distrustful, if not a desperate man did he become from the night of that fearful dream. On the Sabbath day, when the congregation were singing a holy psalm, he could not listen because an anthem of sin rushed loudly upon his ear and drowned all the blessed strain. When the minister spoke from the pulpit with power and fervid eloquence, and, with his hand on the open Bible, of the sacred truths of our religion, and of saint-like lives and triumphant deaths, and of future bliss or misery unutterable, then did Goodman Brown turn pale, dreading lest the roof should thunder down upon the gray blasphemer and his hearers. Often, waking suddenly at midnight, he shrank from the bosom of Faith; and at morning or eventide, when the family knelt down at prayer, he scowled and muttered to himself, and gazed sternly at his wife, and turned away. And when he had lived long, and was borne to his grave a hoary corpse, followed by Faith, an aged woman, and children and grandchildren, a goodly procession, besides neighbors not a few, they carved no hopeful verse upon his tombstone, for his dying hour was gloom.

A first quick reading of the story reveals that a man named Brown goes on a mysterious nighttime journey into the forest, where he comes into con-

---

[6] anathema: excommunication, curse.

tact with various forms of evil. He later returns to his village disillusioned and mistrustful of those whom he had previously loved and respected. Three questions will help you discover and understand instances of figurative comparison that may, at first, seem confusing.

1. Where *like* or *as* is used to make a comparison explicit, is that comparison literal or figurative? In "Young Goodman Brown" we are told, for example, that an old man whose appearance and behavior strongly suggest the devil begins stripping twigs away from a branch: "The moment his fingers touched them, they became strangely withered and dried up, as with a week's sunshine" (p. 637). Here the images of "withered" and "dried up" are strengthened by the comparison to twigs which have been left exposed to the sun for a full week. Dried up twigs are like dried up twigs, no matter what the cause of the drying, so that in spite of the supernaturally sudden effect the old man's touch has on the twigs, the comparison is literal. In the same story, however, several comparisons are figurative. One example is "the wind tolled like a distant churchbell" (p. 639). Of course, wind does not literally sound like a bell; but the comparison points to some characteristics it might share with a churchbell: hollowness of sound, ringing for the dead, and an ominous, rhythmic insistence. Hence this example illustrates a figurative comparison. Since the comparison is made explicit by the use of the word *like*, this is a simile.

2. Are there instances of words linked by *is* or *was*, where their relationship cannot be a literal one? Brown thinks, concerning his wife, "she's a blessed angel on earth" (p. 634), but we know that she is a living woman. The passage, then, must mean that she is *like* an angel in being sinless and a guide on the path to heaven. Thus it is a figurative comparison, which is implied rather than stated—a metaphor.

3. Are there particular words or expressions that, if taken literally, are inappropriate to the context? "The blue arch, and the stars brightening in it" does not appear to be literal; neither does "as if all Nature were laughing him to scorn." In each of these figures, one side of the comparison has been omitted, but can readily be supplied from context, so that the reader can mentally translate the first as a metaphor that means "the blue sky, shaped like an arch . . ." and the second as a personification, which might be paraphrased "as if Nature were like a person laughing him to scorn."

METONYMY/SYNECDOCHE

A metaphor such as "blue arch" may involve the substitution of one term (arch) for another (sky) for the purpose of implying a comparison. Some substitutions, however, do not compare but, instead, simply add emphasis or perhaps startle the reader with statements that are not literally true.

As Charles passed the broken window of the jewelry store, a serpent whispered to him, "Look how easy it would be to steal some watches!"

The voice Charles heard was not that of a person who sounded like a serpent (metaphor); nor was it an actual snake that somehow was like a person in being able to whisper (personification). It was the voice of temptation, the voice of evil in Charles's own nature or the voice of the devil. In other words, there is not truly a comparison but rather a substitution that makes use of the associations between serpents and temptation to sin.

In speaking of people Young Goodman Brown "had met at the communion table" (p. 639), Hawthorne employs a similar substitution. People may meet at the communion table, but they are much more likely literally to meet at church. The substitution serves to emphasize the presumed piety and goodness of these people. Similarly, near the end of the story, Brown shrinks "from the bosom of Faith" (p. 643). Since children and grandchildren attend Brown's funeral at the end of the story, we can assume that he maintains some sexual contact with his wife. What then is meant by the expression? Brown's mood after his night in the wilderness is one of withdrawal from human relationship, from human trust. By substituting "bosom" for "personal contact," the author emphasizes the tender, nurturing aspects of Faith. What Brown needs, in his revulsion at the knowledge of sinfulness in the world, is comfort and nurturance, but he is unable to accept these even from his wife. Thus the substitution of "bosom" for some other word enriches our understanding of what has happened to Brown.

The term *metonymy* refers to substitutions of this type, which call attention to associations between ideas. While *metonymy* is increasingly being used to refer to *all* such figures, some writers prefer the term *synecdoche* to designate those instances (like "bosom" for "woman") in which part of something stands for all of it: "As John lay on the desert sand, he felt scales passing slowly over his arm." John certainly felt scales, but the reference is to an entire snake, of which scales are only a part. *Synecdoche* can also mean (more rarely) the substitution of the whole for the part: "An army of ten thousand men battered down the gate of the castle." Presumably only a relative handful of soldiers actually destroyed the gate, although an entire army may have entered once the opening had been made.

Scholars who use *synecdoche* to mean either the part for the whole or the whole for the part limit the term *metonymy* to other kinds of substitutions, such as the container for its contents ("he drank the glass at one gulp"), a tool for the work it performs ("the pen is mightier than the sword") or an attribute for an object ("he saw his life spilling out of his severed hand").

Whatever term is used, associations and substitutions of these kinds can be particularly powerful agents in shaping the emotional content of a passage. Thus, "scales" for "snake" evokes feelings of fear and disgust, just as the substitution of "life" for "blood" elicits a response of terror and awe in the face of fast-approaching death. In this way, *metonymy* and *synecdoche*, like figures of comparison, define both effect and meaning in literature, as in the following verse:

> Stuffed shirts sit while sweatshirts slave;
> Idle tongues wag but the ravenous rave:
> A Rembrandt, a Rolls Royce, preferred stocks on tissue;
> A mortgage, life's ransom, a credit card issue.

SYMBOL

Frequently in a work of literature, an object is so treated that it stands not only for its physical self, but also for an abstract concept. In such an instance, the object becomes a symbol. Most symbols first appear as concrete objects—a forest or a rose, for instance—and, in the development of the work in which they are used, they take on a meaning that is both larger and deeper than themselves. A forest (in Hawthorne's "Young Goodman Brown") is a tangle of trees and undergrowth near Salem, but it comes to mean the confusion of dark places within the human soul; and a rose (as we shall see in Blake's "The Sick Rose") is first a flower, but it ultimately stands for innocence.

How does a reader discover a symbol and interpret its meaning? There are several clues that can serve as guides and clarify the process.

1. Sometimes an object is specifically identified as symbol, with the author making direct reference to a double significance—one literal, the other abstract. In "Young Goodman Brown," the protagonist learns that an old woman of Salem who had given him religious instruction is really a follower of the devil. After he comes to realize how good can mask evil, he says of her "That old woman taught me my catechism," and the author adds that "there was a world of meaning in this simple comment." Hawthorne thus calls the reader's attention to the literal and symbolic significance of "catechism," which suggests first the lessons in orthodox Puritan religion he had received from the woman, but grows to include his new belief in the devil and his pervasive influence in the world.

2. Often, a term will have two meanings, one of them concrete, one of them abstract, so an interchange of meaning is immediately possible. Such a term is *Faith* in "Young Goodman Brown," which is both the name of Brown's wife and a word that means religious belief. Thus, when Brown tells his diabolic companion in the forest that "Faith kept me back awhile," the reader is able to attach both concrete and abstract meanings to the word.

3. Reference to a myth can suggest a symbol either through a name, a description, an action, or a characteristic. When the speaker in "My Last

Duchess" tells his auditor to notice "Neptune . . . taming a sea-horse," the reader is presented with a name and an action. Neptune is a Roman god whose domain includes water, earthquakes, and horses. Because of his divinity and his demonstration of mastery of one of his subjects, he becomes a symbol of the Duke himself, just as the sea-horse being tamed represents the Duchess.

4. A reference (allusion) to people or events in history, again through names, descriptions, actions, or characteristics, can signify something abstract. In "Young Goodman Brown" Puritan abuse of Quakers is an allusion to religious intolerance, just as "King Philip's war" suggests racial prejudice. Thus both references have historic reality and also signify larger abstractions.

5. Some words or terms can represent real objects but traditionally imply larger ideas or associations. A rose, for instance, usually symbolizes beauty or love.

6. Sometimes, of course, such an object or action can be treated in a fantastic or unreal way. "The Sick Rose" is an example of such a treatment. A detailed examination of this poem shows how to identify and interpret a symbol that is used unconventionally.

William Blake (1757–1827)

THE SICK ROSE

O rose, thou art sick:
The invisible worm
That flies in the night,
In the howling storm,

Has found out thy bed   5
Of crimson joy,
And his dark secret love
Does thy life destroy.

At first, the poem would appear simply to be about a flower that a worm is destroying. The worm has several unusual attributes, however: it is invisible, it flies by night, and it comes in a howling storm. The flower is also unusual. First it is formally addressed in an apostrophe. While eighteenth-century poets often adopted a formal tone when referring to an inanimate object, they did not often talk about a "bed of crimson joy" (lines 5–6) in connection with a rose, nor did they usually describe an attack by a pest as a love affair. Finally, a rose eaten by a worm is only a rose eaten by a worm, so if Blake's poem were taken as a literal statement it would be mock heroic—taking a trivial subject, making too much of it, and creating humor in the process.

Far from inspiring humor, however, the poem suggests muted terror, and the reason for the terror can be discovered only when the concrete "rose" is interpreted to suggest abstractions like woman or beauty or innocence. Part of the difficulty (and part of the fascination) of dealing with symbols is that usually no one translation can be regarded as final or absolute—although an examination of the three suggested meanings for the rose will show that differences in aptness or even accuracy of application can exist. If the reader regards the rose as woman, much in the poem would support such a reading. The worm would represent the male and the love he brings; "crimson joy" could have a general sexual significance as well as suggest flow of blood, which would arise from loss of virginity or perhaps the menstrual cycle itself. The love of man for woman would be dangerous as well as joyful, diminishing and destroying her. Such a reading is not entirely satisfactory, however, because it is narrow, and because some of the facts of the poem, such as those about the worm's arrival, do not seem apt. If the rose is beauty, on the other hand, the poem becomes a more general statement about its destruction through time (the worm), which gradually eats away at beauty until nothing is left. One problem with this interpretation is that it is too broad. Time is an independent agency or factor whose operation is not entirely invisible. Perhaps, then, the best reading is to be found by identifying the rose as innocence—unaware, yearning for the experience that will destroy it. That experience (the worm, which carries with it the image of snake and its diabolical associations) means loss of innocence; it is fearsome; and it consumes its host and signifies the inevitable death of purity or sinlessness as corruption continues to its devastating conclusion. Because experience is itself a process, it is indeed invisible; and its operation can often be traumatic, insidious, deadly, yet at the same time gratifying and desired. This reading, of course, arises from the poem itself; but such an interpretation is given further credence by the title of the collection in which the poem first appeared: Songs of Innocence and Experience.

After a symbol has been identified and interpreted, discovering meaning in a work is largely a matter of replacing the literal reading with a more general one. Thus, "The Sick Rose" is on the lowest level about the destruction of a flower by an enemy that the rose somehow loves. Symbolically interpreted, the poem seems to say that the corruption of innocence by experience is an unavoidable, perhaps even sought-after, eventuality. Note, however, that such a transposition is possible only in those works in which development of a symbol or group of symbols is central to the story, poem, or play.

ALLEGORY

When people, places, and events in a narrative each represent a specific abstract concept and a symbolic equation can be made between them, the author has created an allegory. Usually, the people in an allegory are personifications (moral qualities, emotions, or ideas, given human form and sometimes names like "Greed," "Fellowship," or "Red Cross"). The principal event in an allegory is often a journey. The best-known allegories are lengthy works, such as Bunyan's *Pilgrim's Progress* or Spenser's *Faerie Queene*, but allegories may also be short. Often the dividing line between a work that is heavily symbolic and one that is allegorical is fine; but if the narrative deals with flat abstractions rather than complex human beings and if the symbolism is reducible to an equation that fits the entire work, the story, poem or play is probably an allegory. Such is the case with Hawthorne's "Young Goodman Brown." We have already mentioned various symbols in the story; but all of these (and more) are part of an allegorical construction. As with most allegories, characters in the narrative are primarily and merely personifications. The main event is a journey taken by a protagonist whose name is suggestive of Every Man on the start of the road from innocence to experience. Most of the action occurs in a forest that represents confusion in the human heart. On this journey, the persons, objects, and places have *both* literal and symbolic reality.

IRONY

Unlike figurative comparisons, which involve similarities, irony depends on differences—a contrast between what is said and what is meant; what seems to be true and what really is true; or what is expected to happen and what does, in fact, happen. The following are the three most frequently used types.

Verbal Irony Perhaps the easiest to detect, verbal irony contrasts what is said with what is meant. One form of verbal irony is sarcasm. When, for example, we say of someone we dislike, "Oh, I just love her," our tone of voice generally indicates that we don't mean what we say; in fact, we mean the opposite. Other times, what we say may simply be different from what we mean. In a literary work, understanding the context is necessary to recognizing verbal irony. For instance, in "Young Goodman Brown," Hawthorne notes that as Goody Cloyse hurries through the forest to the Black Mass, she is "mumbling some indistinct words—a prayer, doubtless" (pp. 636–637). If the teacher of catechism were within the limits of the town, the suggestion that she is praying would not be ironic, since she doubtless does pray there. Since, however, she is on her way to a meeting with the devil, the reader becomes aware of the true nature of the statement and may smile wryly at it.

Irony of Situation   This irony consists of a difference between what seems to be and what actually is, or between what is expected to happen and what does happen. The following poem by Edwin Arlington Robinson illustrates how such a contrast is established.

Edwin Arlington Robinson (1869–1935)

RICHARD CORY

Whenever Richard Cory went down town,
We people on the pavement looked at him:
He was a gentleman from sole to crown,
Clean favored, and imperially slim.

And he was always quietly arrayed,   5
And he was always human when he talked;
But still he fluttered pulses when he said,
"Good-morning," and he glittered when he walked.

And he was rich—yes, richer than a king—
And admirably schooled in every grace: 10
In fine, we thought that he was everything
To make us wish that we were in his place.

So on we worked, and waited for the light,
And went without the meat, and cursed the bread;
And Richard Cory, one calm summer night,   15
Went home and put a bullet through his head.

In this poem the speaker is clearly a member of the working class since he is one of the "people on the pavement" (line 2). He recognizes that Cory is "a gentleman" (line 3) not only because he is well bred ("admirably schooled in every grace"—line 10), but also because he is good-looking ("clean favored"—line 4), tastefully dressed ("quietly arrayed"—line 5), and "always human" (line 6) when he talks to those who are economically and socially in a lower class than himself. The speaker, as well as the other townspeople, admires Cory because he is everything admirable and not simply because he is "richer than a king" (line 9). Since Cory seems to have everything that makes life worth living, the people in the town assume that he is happy. The irony of the situation becomes apparent when Cory commits suicide. Contrary to the belief of the people, Cory is, in fact, so unhappy that he ends his life.

"Young Goodman Brown" also contains a number of examples of situational irony. Early in the story, for instance, as Brown sets off on his trip into the forest, he thinks: "after this one night I'll cling to her [Faith's] skirts and follow her to heaven" (p. 634). The actual situation, however, is very different, for when he returns from the forest he shrinks "from the bosom of Faith" (p. 643). Brown's attitude toward Faith before and after his trip itself illustrates situational irony. At first he considers her an "angel"; later he seems to consider her a devil, or at least a servant of the devil. His inability to recognize her humanness, and thus her capacity for both sin and virtue, is ironic. Faith is neither angel nor devil, as he thinks; she is woman.

Dramatic Irony   The third kind of irony results from the contrast between what a character believes to be the case and what, in fact, is true. For example, in "Young Goodman Brown" an ironical contrast exists between Brown's remark that, "We are a people of prayer, and good works to boot, and abide no such wickedness" (p. 636) and the facts of the situation, revealed just a few sentences earlier by the older companion: "I helped your grandfather, the constable, when he lashed the Quaker woman so smartly through the streets of Salem; and it was I that brought your father a pitch-pine knot, kindled at my own hearth, to set fire to an Indian village, in King Philip's war" (p. 635). Brown, although he hears these words, remains unaware of the contrast between the two statements, but the reader sees the difference between Brown's innocent—even naive—words and the facts, which Brown has not yet comprehended.

Another example of dramatic irony in Hawthorne's story is found in Brown's turning away from Faith because he sees her, finally, as evil and thus believes she is incapable of leading him to salvation (heaven). The reader recognizes that Faith, even though she is a mortal woman and thus imperfect, could lead him to salvation were he to join forces with her. In this case, then, there is again a difference between what the character believes and what the reader knows to be true. Note, though, that in this example the reader cannot recognize the irony until he or she has completed the story. The same is true in "Richard Cory," where not until the final line of the poem, when Cory's suicide is stated, is the contrast between the expected and the actual revealed. Thus, in both situational and dramatic irony the reader frequently must know all the facts of the work before the presence of irony can be recognized.

TONE

A significant part of the experience of literature—and therefore the totality of meaning generated—grows out of the impact the work has on the reader's senses, emotions, ideas, and/or attitudes. In other words, how the short story, poem, or play, makes the reader *feel* is as centrally connected to the effect as a whole as what it makes him or her *think*. How does a writer affect or control the reader's response? How does an author select and arrange materials and present them in such a way that a desired effect is achieved? One way is through *tone*, that is the attitude toward the subject and the reader implied in the work. While quite literally the *sound* of a voice, tone can be achieved in writing too, through rhythms, punctuation, choice of words and word order, all of which take the place of the accent and inflection of a speaker. Tone may be, among other possibilities, playful or serious, formal or informal, intimate or detached, condescending or sympathetic, ironic or straightforward. Irony, of course, is one major method through which an author establishes tone. In "Richard Cory," for example, Robinson uses irony to establish a certain distance between Cory and the townspeople, between their ideals and his representation of them. He further uses irony to bring Cory the superhuman to a very human level, just as he suggests through the same means the naivete and folly of the people who idolize him. But point of view can also contribute to tone. The first-person narrative creates an immediate intimacy between speaker and reader, while the third-person narrative can produce an effect of objectivity or almost absolute identity, depending on the author's desire to achieve or bridge distance.

Tone can also designate the mood or atmosphere of a work. Various devices can be used to create such a mood, including sentence structure, repetition, choice of detail (particularly in descriptions of setting or characters), imagery, figures of speech, or symbolism. In "Young Goodman Brown," details and figures combine to produce an atmosphere of gloom and mystery, both in the landscapes of Salem and the forest and in the people who inhabit these places. Sometimes, tone as attitude or tone as mood can be traced to a particular device; more often, it emerges as a position or color created by the total work. In either case, tone is directly related to effect, and thus to the meaning, of a work.

READING FOR LANGUAGE

Thus far, we have been examining various kinds of language use as they appear by themselves in stories or poems. To become a better reader, however, you should be able to recognize different figures, symbols, and ironies in a work, and you should discover how they combine to shape meaning in a work. As you apply your skills to the analysis of literature, you will find different problems in interpreting fiction and poetry.

Any reader able to understand the words will be likely to get something from almost any story, even if only a sense of the plot with its characters, conflicts, and settings. Awareness of specialized uses of language—simile and metaphor, for example—will increase the impact of the reading experience, since these devices add to the atmosphere and effect of the work. In some fiction, of course, recognizing symbolism or irony is the key to understanding the work. In stories where such devices are central, you must discover how they are employed before you can understand what the work is about. Much poetry is woven entirely out of figurative uses of language. Sometimes, an author can build a poem around an extended simile or metaphor. More often, the writer employs a series of interwoven images, figures, and symbols, sometimes layered with irony. Recognizing the significance of words and their context is the only way to understand such a work.

In analyzing fiction, a line-by-line approach is generally not practical. Instead, after a first reading, you should concentrate on two related procedures. First, find uses of figurative language in the text, underline them, and decide how these control or shape effect. Second, make marginal notes about symbolic or ironic usages and relate these to the overall significance of the work. Such a process is illustrated in the following notes on "Young Goodman Brown."

1. Read the work through to get a sense of the story line and summarize the principal events. In "Young Goodman Brown," the title character, setting aside the objections of his wife (named Faith), journeys at night into the wilderness where he encounters various representatives of evil and finally observes a Black Mass. Returning to the village, he finds himself disillusioned about human goodness and totally alienated from his fellow humans, including his wife.

2. Reread the work, this time underlining all images, similes, metaphors, personifications, and metonymies. In the margins, write briefly what the figure means. The following can be found in "Young Goodman Brown."

a. imagery: "a dreary road, darkened by all the gloomiest trees of the forest" (p. 634) "the creaking of trees, the howling of wild beasts, and the yell of Indians" (p. 639). These images increase the sense of mystery and terror.

b. figurative comparisons: "the wind tolled like a distant churchbell" (p. 639)—simile; "there was the blue arch, and the stars brightening in it" (p. 639)—metaphor; "as if all Nature were laughing him to scorn" (p. 639)—personification. The figures heighten the feeling of Brown's alienation and isolation.

c. metonymy: Brown shrinks from "the bosom of Faith" (p. 643)—bosom here representing her whole physical being, but especially the tender, nourishing, protective aspects of Faith.

3. Make note of irony or symbols in the work. In "Young Goodman Brown," examples of both can be found, but principally the work employs a system of symbols that establish an allegorical framework. In this frame-

work, Brown's trip into the forest symbolizes every man's movement from innocence to experience and awareness of evil. The forest, the people, and the Black Mass are the chief parts of this framework. The following details in the text expand on these elements:

a. The forest as journey into experience
   i. Imagery of the forest, as noted before.
   ii. "The road grew wilder and drearier, and more faintly traced, and vanished at length, leaving him in the heart of the dark wilderness, still rushing onward with the instinct that guides mortal man to evil" (p. 639).

b. People
   i. Wife "Faith" symbolizes faith.
   ii. The traveling companion is the devil, evil itself and specifically the evil present in Brown's own being. The following evidence supports this conclusion. First, he carries a staff with "the likeness of a great black snake" that seems to "twist and wriggle itself like a living serpent" (p. 635). Second, when he touches Goody Cloyse with the staff, she screams, "The devil." Finally, "the elder traveller exhorted his companion to make good speed and persevere in the path, discoursing so aptly, that his arguments seemed rather to spring up in the bosom of his auditor, than to be suggested by himself" (p. 637).

c. The Black Mass
   i. "Evil is the nature of mankind" (p. 642).
   ii. In the forest, there are an "altar or a pulpit" surrounded by "four blazing pines," like "candles" and a basin containing a red fluid like "blood" or "liquid flame."
   iii. The congregation at the Devil's worship service is made up of people who profess an alliance with heaven by appearing "Sabbath after Sabbath" looking "devoutly heavenward" in the churches about the land.
   iv. The hymn is a "slow and mournful strain such as the pious love, but joined to words which expressed all that our nature can conceive of sin, and darkly hinted at far more" (p. 641).
   v. Brown is invited to step forward, a "convert" to his "nature" and "destiny," a member of the communion of his race, after which he will be allowed to "behold the whole earth one stain of guilt, one mighty blood spot" (p. 642).
   vi. He tries to hold back: "Faith! Faith! . . . look up to heaven, and resist the wicked one" (p. 642).
   vii. The Black Mass disappears, and he finds the rock against which he staggered "chill and damp, while a hanging twig, that had been all on fire, besprinkled his cheek with the coldest dew" (p. 643).
   viii. He then becomes a "stern, a sad, a darkly meditative, a distrustful if not a desperate man" from the "night of that fearful dream" (p. 643).

4. After analyzing your notes and marginal comments, decide what the story means and how language use relates to that meaning. In "Young Goodman Brown," the author employs imagery and figurative comparisons to establish and maintain a mood of mystery and terror. To convey his meaning, he uses an allegorical framework in which the protagonist starts out on his journey to confront evil and is spiritually annihilated by the process.

Reading for language use in poetry involves a process that is not possible for most fiction. As before, first read the poem through once or twice to get a sense of what it is about:

William Shakespeare (1564–1616)

THAT TIME OF YEAR (Sonnet 73)

That time of year thou mayst in me behold
When yellow leaves, or none, or few, do hang
Upon those boughs which shake against the cold,
Bare ruin'd choirs where late the sweet birds sang.
In me thou see'st the twilight of such day   5
As after sunset fadeth in the west,
Which by and by black night doth take away,
Death's second self, that seals up all in rest.
In me thou see'st the glowing of such fire
That on the ashes of his youth doth lie,   10
As the death-bed whereon it must expire,
Consum'd with that which it was nourish'd by.
    This thou perceiv'st, which makes thy love more strong,
    To love that well which thou must leave ere long.

Clearly, the poet is describing a season, a time of day, and a fire. He is also applying what he says about these objects to himself; and, in turn, he is interested in conveying a message based on this comparison to another person. In this sonnet he makes use of three principal figures to suggest his time of life. As we look at each quatrain and the couplet we can see what these figures are and how meaning is conveyed through these devices:

That time of year thou may'st in me behold
When yellow leaves, or none, or few, do hang
Upon those boughs which shake against the cold,
Bare ruin'd choirs where late the sweet birds sang.

Time of year is a metaphor which refers to poet's age; the time is autumn. Why? Cold has come, and the boughs are bare or have only a few yellow leaves. The birds have flown away, so the branches no longer hold the song-birds. Note: "choir" to Shakespeare meant the place in the church that housed the singers. What can be personal about the cold? How does the idea of poet as singer of songs relate to a deserted choir?

In me thou see'st the twilight of such day
As after sunset fadeth in the west,
Which by and by black night doth take away,
Death's second self, that seals up all in rest.

Twilight is a metaphor which also relates to his Time of life, with the sun setting and the light fading. Black night, personified, is approaching, bringing sleep and rest. Question: What is death's second self?

In me thou see'st the glowing of such fire
That on the ashes of his youth doth lie,
As the death-bed whereon it must expire
Consum'd with that which it was nourish'd by.

Time of life is explained by the metaphor of a fire that has settled into embers, past its peak of heat (youth). The energy that feeds the fire is like life's energy: each person feeds on his life force and uses it up in the process. When it is entirely consumed, the person dies.

This thou perceiv'st, which makes thy love more strong,
To love that well which thou must leave ere long.

His listener is aware that the poet is getting old and must soon die; thus, he (the first 120 sonnets of the Shakespeare cycle are addressed to a man) will love the poet more appreciatively, since the listener will soon be separated from the beloved by time and death.

Thus the poem presents three extended metaphors for a "time of life": Autumn, evening, and ashes are compared to the poet's advancing years, each given specific reference, meaning, and life by the details with which each is presented. The sonnet also narrows its focus through the succession of quatrains: Season is the most expansive comparison; fire is the most concentrated. Similarly, the personal implications within the metaphors become progressively more pronounced, with fire (often a symbol for the life-force) a natural transition to the direct statement in the concluding couplet. That couplet is, however, ambiguous. The line-by-line commentary suggests one meaning, but others are possible. The poet could, for instance, be offering the "you" some advice: enjoy today and your youth while you can, because both will soon be gone. Whatever the significance of the couplet, however, the theme of the poem is a familiar one in poetry of the period.

WRITING ABOUT LANGUAGE

Writing about the ways in which a work of literature uses language in relation to meaning requires that you know the work very thoroughly before you attempt to write. Careful identification of such devices as imagery, figurative comparison, metonymy, symbol, and irony involves noting where each occurs in the work. Next explain or paraphrase each to make certain you understand what it means in itself and in relation to the whole work. Once you have arrived at such understanding, you will be better prepared to discuss the work in class or to express your response in writing. The following options give you a choice of three ways to do so.

Option I: Critical Analysis of Language

As in the previous chapters, the critical analysis of a work offers the most common and formal approach to responding to a literary work. Such a paper requires the use of exact quotations and specific references to support your own statements; thus your preparation should involve a very careful reading of the text, exact copying of quotations, and proper documentation. Also as before, the structure and content will be built into the main-idea sentence, which will serve as a structural guide for both writer and reader. The guidelines below outline the specific steps to follow in composing a formal analysis on the use of language in a literary work.

1. Study carefully the work you intend to analyze, making sure you understand all the facts.

2. Discover and note special uses of language in the work by following the steps outlined earlier in this chapter: (a) underline all figurative uses of language and make a note of their meanings (for poetry, do a line-by-line analysis); (b) identify symbols and/or irony and explain their meaning in the context of the work; and (c) relate the uses of language to the meaning of the work.

3. Determine the most important language uses in the work and list illustrations, noting page or line numbers (or act, scene, and lines for a play).

4. Write your introduction. Although you may organize the introduction in any way that presents the information coherently, be sure to include the

title of the work, the author's name, a brief summary of the principal events (if it is a story or narrative poem), and a main-idea sentence. Since the main-idea sentence establishes the focus and structure of your essay, it should identify the language use(s) you will discuss, the subdivisions of your topic, and a general statement of the work's meaning.

5. Write the body of the paper. In dealing with some works, a single symbol or other figure will be so central that the body of your paper will consist of only one paragraph. In other cases, two or three significant language uses will provide a natural division of your analysis. Whether the body has one or several paragraphs, expand the list you made in step 3, using quotations to link together and support your own general comments. Be sure to use transitions to help the reader move from one idea to another and from one paragraph to another.

6. Write your conclusion, being sure to explore in some detail just how the language use generates meaning. Check your list of quotations for any that you haven't used that might be useful at this point.

7. Decide on a title that relates to the language use you have discussed or to the meaning, or one that simply identifies the work on which your essay is based.

8. Check your paper and rewrite any parts that you feel are unclear or need further support or explanation. Be careful to eliminate superfluous quotations and check to be sure the quotations you do use are exactly as printed in the text. Also check spelling, punctuation, and page references. Finally, make a clean copy for submission to your instructor.

OPTION I: SAMPLE ESSAY—FICTION

Loss of Innocence

On the literal level, Hawthorne's "Young Goodman Brown" is about one man's night journey into the forest to participate in an initiation rite. Symbolically, however, "Young Goodman Brown" is the story of a man who abandons his belief in the reality of goodness when he encounters evil. Three symbols in the story are particularly important in establishing the allegorical framework: Brown's journey itself, the travelling companion who urges him on, and the ritual celebration he observes.

Because Young Goodman Brown is both person and symbol, representing Everyman, his action also has both literal and symbolic significance. His journey, which begins at dusk in Salem village, takes him into a dark forest, along "a dreary road, darkened by all the gloomiest trees of the forest" (p. 634). As the journey continues, however, the description makes more and more clear that the story is concerned not simply with an atmosphere of gloom but with the dark side of life: "The road grew wilder and drearier, and more faintly traced, and vanished at length, leaving him in the heart of the dark wilderness, still rushing onward, with the instinct that guides mortal man to evil" (p. 639). Gradually Brown becomes aware of the implications of his action and hesitates, sensing the confusion in his own heart and feeling the pull of his faith (also his wife's name) holding him back.

Brown is urged along on the journey by another symbolic character, a mysterious travelling companion who resembles both Brown's father and Satan. This companion carries a staff with "the likeness of a great black snake" that seems "to twist and wriggle itself like a living serpent" (p. 635). He encourages Brown through the forest in a manner that suggests that the voice of evil is part of Brown's own character: "the elder traveller exhorted his companion to make good speed and persevere in the path, discoursing so aptly, that his arguments seemed rather to spring up in the bosom of his auditor, than to be suggested by himself" (p. 637).

The climax of the action is the Black Mass in the forest, for at this point Brown is finally forced to see that "Evil is the nature of mankind" (p. 642). Once again, events have both a literal and symbolic reality. The setting parallels that of a Christian communion service. In the forest is an "altar or a pulpit" surrounded by "four blazing pines" like "candles" and a basin wherein, instead of wine, is a red fluid like "blood" or "liquid flame" (p. 642). These symbols of devotion to God, however, have been transformed into elements of devil worship. Around him, Brown sees a congregation, many of whom are members of his church, who sing what seems to be a hymn but expresses "all that our nature can conceive of sin, and darkly hinted at far more" (p. 641). In a baptismlike ritual Brown is asked by the minister/Satan to join his Faith as part of the "communion of his race" after which he will "behold the whole earth one stain of guilt, one mighty blood-spot" (p. 642). Although tempted, Brown makes one last effort, this time successful, to hold back: "Faith! Faith! . . . look up to heaven and resist the wicked one" (p. 642). With these words, he finds himself suddenly alone in the forest, unsure whether or not he had dreamed or imagined what had happened. He feels the rock against which he staggered "chill and damp, while a hanging twig, that had been all on fire, besprinkled his cheek with the coldest dew" (p. 643). Back in the village, he is forever unable to endure the society of former friends and even of his wife, having become a "stern, a sad, a darkly meditative, a distrustful, if not a desperate man" (p. 643).

By using people and events as symbols, Hawthorne suggests that like Brown all people must make a journey into their own hearts. In the process, they may discover that those they respected or loved are as tainted as they are, and that a blind reliance on faith cannot prevent them from going or protect them on their way from innocence to experience. Perhaps most important, however, they must be ready to accept their dual nature, recognizing in themselves an allegiance to heaven, which resides side by side with an affinity for the powers of evil. Otherwise, the story tells us, their lives will be like that of Goodman Brown, whose "dying hour was gloom" (p. 643).

OPTION I: SAMPLE ESSAY—POETRY

Life and Death

Through the use of two primary devices, metaphor and irony, Shakespeare explores the process and effects of aging in his sonnet "That Time of Year." The poem develops three major metaphors, each of which brings the awareness of death closer to the speaker. The somber tone, however, is lifted in the final two lines through the use of irony.

In the first quatrain, the speaker compares his stage in life to the time of year "When yellow leaves, or none, or few, do hang / Upon those boughs which shake against the cold" (lines 2–3). The season is late autumn, perhaps November, and suggests that the speaker is at the beginning of old age. The birds have flown south to warmer climates; the branches stand empty now, only "Bare ruin'd choirs" (line 4). The image of the empty "choirs," or nests, is a metaphor that may be interpreted in one of several ways: perhaps the speaker's house—the nest—is now empty of children ("the sweet birds") and so seems "bare" and "ruin'd"; perhaps the "bare ... choirs" represent the loss of the poet's ability to create (sing); or perhaps the reference suggests the inevitable physical deterioration of old age, along with shaking limbs and bent body. In any case, the loss that accompanies aging is evident, and the mood is one of sadness.

This mood continues and deepens in the second quatrain, in which the speaker compares his age to the beginning of night. Already he is in the period "after sunset," at "twilight," and realizes that this time will be soon taken away by "black night . . . Death's second self" (lines 7–8). The major metaphor here then compares his stage in life to a period within a day. The link between night and death strengthens this comparison and introduces the awareness of death's nearness. By personifying both night and death (night is "Death's second self"—line 8), the speaker reveals his hostility to both old age and death, who become a single antagonist. Death "seals up all" as the undertaker seals a casket. Because night (old age) is death's alter ego, and because it is much shorter than autumn, the metaphor of the second quatrain increases the mood of sadness and prepares the reader for the full recognition of death's inevitability, which comes in the third quatrain.

In the final metaphor the speaker compares his age to a dying fire. Nourished by wood or coal, a fire builds ashes until the ashes ultimately smother it. Stated simply, the metaphor implies that life, like a fire, is paradoxically both enhanced and destroyed by the act of living (burning). The speaker sees himself at the stage of life (fire) where he is still alive ("glowing") but lying "on the ashes of his youth" (line 10), which has become his "death-bed" (line 11). Thus, in this third metaphor, not only is death inevitable, but life is seen as even briefer than a time of year or day: it lasts only as long as a fire, burning in a fireplace.

"This thou perceiv'st," the final lines begin, and the purpose of the extended comparisons becomes clear. Since life is short, he says, it should be regarded as precious. This is the message he gives to the friend to whom the sonnet is addressed. But the intent of the message is ambiguous. First, the narrator may be observing that the awareness of approaching loss has made the speaker more loved by the listener, who values him more now because death may soon take him and, ironically, may even take the listener first ("love that well which *thou* must leave"). The line illustrates situational irony since the usual expectation is that aging decreases love. Such irony is also present in the second implied meaning, which is that all people ("thou"), seeing this one man's situation, should feel stronger love of their own lives because they realize life's brevity ("which makes thy love more strong, / To love that well which thou must leave ere long"). The recognition of death, then, should bring not despair but, rather, increased appreciation of life.

Thus through both metaphor and irony, Shakespeare's sonnet examines life and its relation to death. Although the tone is generally one of resignation, the conclusion suggests a perspective of acceptance and enjoyment of the life yet to be lived in those hours of "twilight" before the fire in the heart is totally extinguished.

Option II: Collage and Written Analysis

Literary works that express meaning primarily through a special use of language generally involve many visual images. One interesting way to show your understanding of such work is to construct a collage that will visually convey the writer's use of language to express meaning. You will first need to identify the objects or images most important to conveying meaning. Then you will need to find pictures that represent those objects or images. Since finding just the right pictures can be difficult, you may have to search extensively through magazines. Once you have found the pictures you need, however, you can then organize the collage so that it clearly expresses the work's meaning. A brief written analysis will accompany the collage to explain its arrangement and demonstrate your understanding of the work.

1. Choose a work that can be represented visually. A good choice for this assignment is any poem, story, or play that is rich in figurative language.

2. Reread the work, underlining the principal images and figures.

3. Determine which use of language is most important to meaning and summarize the meaning in a few words.

4. Find pictures, words, materials that represent or illustrate the use of language identified in step 3. For pictures, you may find it necessary to draw or cut your own—pink ribbon from pink paper, for instance. For words, you may use cut-out letters from magazines or newspapers.

5. On a suitably sized poster board, assemble your pictures, words, or other materials in a way that shows how images and figures are related to one another so that they convey the meaning of the work.

6. On a separate piece of paper, write the explanation of the collage you have constructed. Begin by naming the work you have chosen to examine. Then divide your paper into three parts. In the first, list the pictures, words, or materials you have selected and identify what each represents. In the second, explain images and figures and why you arranged them as you did. Finally, explore in some detail the meaning of the story, poem, or play you are analyzing.

OPTION II: SAMPLE COLLAGE

"Young Goodman Brown": Collage

1. Pictures and what they represent or symbolize:
   a. The devil and devil worshipers

      i. Face outline of devil, with fire and figures within the silhouette—Brown's companion on his journey.

      ii. Batlike forms above path in the wilderness—the terrors of darkness.

     iii. Hand, holding snakelike staff—the devil's grip and his sign.

     iv. Horses of the night—the bearers of the deacon and minister to the meeting.

      v. Mountain crags that could be a horse and witch on broomstick—the Witches' Sabbath.

     vi. Devil-worshipers around those crags—the Witches' Sabbath.

    vii. Ribbon—Faith's symbol.

  b. The wilderness

      i. Multitude of trees, bent, gnarled, dark, tangled—site of Brown's journey.

      ii. Mountain crag jutting into the "arch" of heaven—place of terror removed from hope and holiness.

     iii. Black trees silhouetted against sunset—site of Brown's journey.

  c. People

      i. Austere mother and child—humanity; Everyman.

      ii. Black figure next to tree in woods—Young Goodman Brown or the devil.

  d. The village

      i. Quiet New England town—where Brown comes from.

      ii. Cabin in the woods—where Brown lives.

2. Rationale for composition of collage:

The idea that governed the arrangement of images is the relationship between evil and wilderness, which the story explores through images and symbols. The evil is represented by the face of the devil on the far left, the hand clasping the snakelike staff, and the witch-like figures on the barren crags. The devil and his forces inhabit the wilderness, which is everywhere. The tangle of branches, the forbidding undergrowth suggest the density and the impenetrability of the woods/heart. Apparently isolated are the picturesque village and the little house—but these are surrounded by the forces of evil. The child is Young Goodman Brown, and what surrounds him is what he must somehow recognize and understand. The child is protected by his mother's arm, but both of them are held in the devil's grip, the symbolic snakelike staff close to the child's head, ready to exert its own powers of fascination. In addition, both mother and child are seen against a tremendous, rocklike protuberance silhouetted against what appears to be an "arch." Outlining the crag is blackness, and it is neither illuminated nor relieved by any light from above. The relationship between arch of sky and bloody crag and family unit indicates the vulnerability and the plight of humanity. Beneath them in the forest, Faith's ribbon (also symbolic) lies on the ground, which suggests that it has somehow been loosed by the devil's hand. The lines of black that move from side to side, the almost batlike shapes in the lower center that are part of those lines, the arrowhead that resembles a snake's head, seem also sections of the continuum, and the movement of flames from devil's head to burning trees to hand to arrowhead to corner to witchlike figure to the crags and the village is meant to suggest the motion of a pervasive evil that surrounds, almost to the point of overwhelming, humanity and its environment.

3. Exploration of theme:

Young Goodman Brown, representative of Everyman, must come to terms with pervasive evil. He cannot be shielded or held back by family considerations; nor should he postpone the journey that, allegorically at least, takes him into the wilderness of his own heart. Unfortunately, when he goes into the forest and hears that evil is part of the nature of mankind, he cannot accept what he learns. Forever afterwards, he is separated from the rest of humanity. Unable to reconcile his trip to his witches' sabbath with his desire for heaven, he remains loveless and alone; and his "dying hour" is "gloom."

Option III: The Sonnet

Several of the writing options in earlier chapters have encouraged you to use your creative talent in responding to a literary work: for example, a character sketch in Chapter 1, the personal essay in Chapter 2, and a film treatment in Chapter 3. Although each of these options required you to follow a prescribed structure, none was as formal and rigid as the sonnet, the third writing option for this chapter. Writing a sonnet involves following a relatively strict scheme for rhyme and rhythm within the limits of only about 140 syllables and fourteen lines. Maintaining such a narrow form while at the same time choosing language that creates images and generates rich meaning makes composing a sonnet a challenge for even professional poets. Yet this option can be an enjoyable experience for students who wish to test their ability to write poetry. Before you decide on this option, however, read the description of the sonnet form in step 3 and study several examples of sonnets included in this chapter.

1. Choose a work whose meaning you understand and can summarize in a single statement.

2. Think of a situation involving a character, conflict, and/or setting that generates the same meaning as the work you have chosen. Write a brief summary of that situation.

3. Decide whether the situation you have created could best be developed in an English or Italian sonnet. The English sonnet is divided into three quatrains (groups of four lines) and a concluding rhymed couplet (two lines). Usually the poet develops one idea or image in each quatrain, bringing them all together with a final summary or concluding comment in the couplet. The quatrains may be arranged chronologically or may have a logical or climactic order (see, for example, Shakespeare's Sonnet 73, "That Time of Year," p. 655). The Italian sonnet is divided into an octet (group of eight lines) and a concluding sestet (group of six lines). Often the poet outlines a situation in the octet and makes a comment on it in the sestet (see Wordsworth's "Composed upon Westminster Bridge," p. 568). The type of sonnet you choose should be determined by what you have to say.

4. If you have decided that your idea would be better handled in an English sonnet, begin to express each division of the topic in lines. Remember that all sonnets are written in iambic pentameter—lines of five feet, each consisting of an unstressed syllable followed by a stressed syllable. (Example: "That time of year thou mayst in me behold.") Also, the rhyme pattern of the English sonnet is abab cdcd efef gg, so that of the four lines in each quatrain, the first and third rhyme and the second and fourth rhyme. If, on the other hand, you have decided that the Italian sonnet is best suited to your topic, begin to formulate lines that will rhyme in the following pattern: abba, abba. The sestet should begin with a third sound, designated c, but you may organize the six lines in any pattern, such as cdecde or ccdede or cdcdee. In attempting to discover rhyming words, you may want to turn to a rhyming dictionary or a thesaurus.

5. When you have completed the poem, scan it to be sure that it is basically iambic pentameter (occasional variations of rhythm are allowed and may in fact strengthen the poem) and that the rhymes are not forced but instead say exactly what you want them to say. Rewrite any phrases or lines that don't achieve what you intend. Remember that metaphors and other figurative language add depth and allow the reader more interpretation.

6. When you are satisfied that the sonnet is the best that you can make it, decide on a title.

7. Prepare a glossary of any terms, names, or other references whose denotation or connotation is important in conveying the poem's meaning but which might be unfamiliar to the general reader. The glossary should include the line in which the word or phrase occurs, the word or phrase, and a brief statement of explanation.

8. Put your sonnet aside for a day or two. Then review and revise it.

9. Before submitting your sonnet, note at the top of your paper the title of the work your poem is based on and a statement summarizing the work's meaning.

OPTION III: SAMPLE SONNET

Work: "Young Goodman Brown" by Nathaniel Hawthorne
Meaning: People who cannot accept the reality of both good and evil may
          live lonely and loveless lives.

MR. SMITH

As strident sounds of Liszt's "Mephisto Waltz"
Made passing lovers shiver in the heat,
Young Smith proclaimed, "The world and love are false,"
From out his window, high above the street.
When summer evening settled into night,
Young Smith wrote down his words—he thought them rare—
Then shut the blinds and fumbled for the light
To pore through *Faust* for ones that could compare.
Throughout the night he sat with face set grim,
Black-leaded pencil poised above each page,
To prove that love's a word wrought out of whim
And good is naught—just sin and devils rage.
While he fumed thus alone in barren gloom,
The lovers kissed in nature's fragrant bloom.

Glossary

1. Liszt: Hungarian composer (1811–1886).
1. Mephisto: shortened form of Mephistopheles, the devil to whom Faust
   sold his soul.
8. *Faust:* a play by Goethe, German poet and dramatist (1749–1832).

READING   SELECTIONS: STORIES

Arthur C. Clarke (1917–)

THE NINE BILLION NAMES OF GOD

"This is a slightly unusual request," said Dr. Wagner, with what he hoped
was commendable restraint. "As far as I know, it's the first time anyone's
been asked to supply a Tibetan monastery with an Automatic Sequence

ARTHUR C. CLARKE

Computer. I don't wish to be inquisitive, but I should hardly have thought that your—ah—establishment had much use for such a machine. Could you explain just what you intend to do with it?"

"Gladly," replied the lama, readjusting his silk robes and carefully putting away the slide rule he had been using for currency conversions. "Your Mark V Computer can carry out any routine mathematical operation involving up to ten digits. However, for our work we are interested in *letters*, not numbers. As we wish you to modify the output circuits, the machine will be printing words, not columns of figures."

"I don't quite understand. . . ."

"This is a project on which we have been working for the last three centuries—since the lamasery[1] was founded, in fact. It is somewhat alien to your way of thought, so I hope you will listen with an open mind while I explain it."

"Naturally."

"It is really quite simple. We have been compiling a list which shall contain all the possible names of God."

"I beg your pardon?"

"We have reason to believe," continued the lama imperturbably, "that all such names can be written with not more than nine letters in an alphabet we have devised."

"And you have been doing this for three centuries?"

"Yes: we expected it would take us about fifteen thousand years to complete the task."

"Oh," Dr. Wagner looked a little dazed. "Now I see why you wanted to hire one of our machines. But exactly what is the *purpose* of this project?"

The lama hesitated for a fraction of a second, and Wagner wondered if he had offended him. If so, there was no trace of annoyance in the reply.

"Call it ritual, if you like, but it's a fundamental part of our belief. All the many names of the Supreme Being—God, Jehovah, Allah, and so on— they are only man-made labels. There is a philosophical problem of some difficulty here, which I do not propose to discuss, but somewhere among all the possible combinations of letters that can occur are what one may call the *real* names of God. By systematic permutation of letters, we have been trying to list them all."

"I see. You've been starting at AAAAAAA . . . and working up to ZZZZZZZZ. . . ."

"Exactly—though we use a special alphabet of our own. Modifying the electromatic typewriters to deal with this is, of course, trivial. A rather more interesting problem is that of devising suitable circuits to eliminate ridiculous combinations. For example, no letter must occur more than three times in succession."

[1] lamasery: a Lamaist monastery.

"Three? Surely you mean two."

"Three is correct: I am afraid it would take too long to explain why, even if you understood our language."

"I'm sure it would," said Wagner hastily. "Go on."

"Luckily, it will be a simple matter to adapt your Automatic Sequence Computer for this work, since once it has been programed properly it will permute each letter in turn and print the result. What would have taken us fifteen thousand years it will be able to do in a hundred days."

Dr. Wagner was scarcely conscious of the faint sounds from the Manhattan streets far below. He was in a different world, a world of natural, not man-made, mountains. High up in their remote aeries[2] these monks had been patiently at work, generation after generation, compiling their lists of meaningless words. Was there any limit to the follies of mankind? Still, he must give no hint of his inner thoughts. The customer was always right. . . .

"There's no doubt," replied the doctor, "that we can modify the Mark V to print lists of this nature. I'm much more worried about the problem of installation and maintenance. Getting out to Tibet, in these days, is not going to be easy."

"We can arrange that. The components are small enough to travel by air —that is one reason why we chose your machine. If you can get them to India, we will provide transport from there."

"And you want to hire two of our engineers?"

"Yes, for the three months that the project should occupy."

"I've no doubt that Personnel can manage that." Dr. Wagner scribbled a note on his desk pad. "There are just two other points—"

Before he could finish the sentence the lama had produced a small slip of paper.

"This is my certified credit balance at the Asiatic Bank."

"Thank you. It appears to be—ah—adequate. The second matter is so trivial that I hesitate to mention it—but it's surprising how often the obvious gets overlooked. What source of electrical energy have you?"

"A diesel generator providing fifty kilowatts at a hundred and ten volts. It was installed about five years ago and is quite reliable. It's made life at the monastery much more comfortable, but of course it was really installed to provide power for the motors driving the prayer wheels."

"Of course," echoed Dr. Wagner. "I should have thought of that."

The view from the parapet was vertiginous,[3] but in time one gets used to anything. After three months, George Hanley was not impressed by the two-thousand-foot swoop into the abyss or the remote checkerboard of fields in the valley below. He was leaning against the wind-smoothed stones

[2] aeries: high nests.
[3] vertiginous: dizzying.

and staring morosely at the distant mountains whose names he had never bothered to discover.

This, thought George, was the craziest thing that had ever happened to him. "Project Shangri-La," [4] some wit back at the labs had christened it. For weeks now the Mark V had been churning out acres of sheets covered with gibberish. Patiently, inexorably, the computer had been rearranging letters in all their possible combinations, exhausting each class before going on to the next. As the sheets had emerged from the electromatic typewriters, the monks had carefully cut them up and pasted them into enormous books. In another week, heaven be praised, they would have finished. Just what obscure calculations had convinced the monks that they needn't bother to go on to words of ten, twenty, or a hundred letters, George didn't know. One of his recurring nightmares was that there would be some change of plan, and that the high lama (whom they'd naturally called Sam Jaffe,[5] though he didn't look a bit like him) would suddenly announce that the project would be extended to approximately A.D. 2060. They were quite capable of it.

George heard the heavy wooden door slam in the wind as Chuck came out onto the parapet beside him. As usual, Chuck was smoking one of the cigars that made him so popular with the monks—who, it seemed, were quite willing to embrace all the minor and most of the major pleasures of life. That was one thing in their favor: they might be crazy, but they weren't bluenoses. Those frequent trips they took down to the village, for instance . . .

"Listen, George," said Chuck urgently. "I've learned something that means trouble."

"What's wrong? Isn't the machine behaving?" That was the worst contingency George could imagine. It might delay his return, and nothing could be more horrible. The way he felt now, even the sight of a TV commercial would seem like manna[6] from heaven. At least it would be some link with home.

"No—it's nothing like that." Chuck settled himself on the parapet, which was unusual because normally he was scared of the drop. "I've just found what all this is about."

"What d'ya mean? I thought we knew."

"Sure—we know what the monks are trying to do. But we didn't know *why*. It's the craziest thing—"

"Tell me something new," growled George.

"—but old Sam's just come clean with me. You know the way he drops in every afternoon to watch the sheets roll out. Well, this time he seemed rather excited, or at least as near as he'll ever get to it. When I told him that

---

[4] Shangri-La: Himalayan utopia in the book and film *Lost Horizon*.

[5] Sam Jaffe: character film actor who played the high lama of Shangri-La.

[6] manna: nourishment received by divine bounty.

we were on the last cycle he asked me, in that cute English accent of his, if I'd ever wondered what they were trying to do. I said, 'Sure'—and he told me."

"Go on: I'll buy it."

"Well, they believe that when they have listed all His names—and they reckon that there are about nine billion of them—God's purpose will be achieved. The human race will have finished what it was created to do, and there won't be any point in carrying on. Indeed, the very idea is something like blasphemy."

"Then what do they expect us to do? Commit suicide?"

"There's no need for that. When the list's completed, God steps in and simply winds things up . . . bingo!"

"Oh, I get it. When we finish our job, it will be the end of the world."

Chuck gave a nervous little laugh.

"That's just what I said to Sam. And do you know what happened? He looked at me in a very queer way, like I'd been stupid in class, and said, 'It's nothing as trivial as *that*.' "

George thought this over for a moment.

"That's what I call taking the Wide View," he said presently. "But what d'you suppose we should do about it? I don't see that it makes the slightest difference to us. After all, we already knew that they were crazy."

"Yes—but don't you see what may happen? When the list's complete and the Last Trump[7] doesn't blow—or whatever it is they expect—*we* may get the blame. It's our machine they've been using. I don't like the situation one little bit."

"I see," said George slowly. "You've got a point there. But this sort of thing's happened before, you know. When I was a kid down in Louisiana we had a crackpot preacher who once said the world was going to end next Sunday. Hundreds of people believed him—even sold their homes. Yet when nothing happened, they didn't turn nasty, as you'd expect. They just decided that he'd made a mistake in his calculations and went right on believing. I guess some of them still do."

"Well, this isn't Louisiana, in case you hadn't noticed. There are just two of us and hundreds of these monks. I like them, and I'll be sorry for old Sam when his lifework backfires on him. But all the same, I wish I was somewhere else."

"I've been wishing that for weeks. But there's nothing we can do until the contract's finished and the transport arrives to fly us out."

"Of course," said Chuck thoughtfully, "we could always try a bit of sabotage."

"Like hell we could! That would make things worse."

"Not the way I meant. Look at it like this. The machine will finish its run

---

[7] Last Trump: trumpet believed to announce the end of the world.

four days from now, on the present twenty-hours-a-day basis. The transport calls in a week. O.K.—then all we need to do is to find something that needs replacing during one of the overhaul periods—something that will hold up the works for a couple of days. We'll fix it, of course, but not too quickly. If we time matters properly, we can be down at the airfield when the last name pops out of the register. They won't be able to catch us then."

"I don't like it," said George. "It will be the first time I ever walked out on a job. Besides, it would make them suspicious. No, I'll sit tight and take what comes."

"I *still* don't like it," he said, seven days later, as the tough little mountain ponies carried them down the winding road. "And don't you think I'm running away because I'm afraid. I'm just sorry for those poor old guys up there, and I don't want to be around when they find what suckers they've been. Wonder how Sam will take it?"

"It's funny," replied Chuck, "but when I said good-by I got the idea he knew we were walking out on him—and that he didn't care because he knew the machine was running smoothly and that the job would soon be finished. After that—well, of course, for him there just isn't any After That. . . ."

George turned in his saddle and stared back up the mountain road. This was the last place from which one could get a clear view of the lamasery. The squat, angular buildings were silhouetted against the after-glow of the sunset: here and there, lights gleamed like portholes in the side of an ocean liner. Electric lights, of course, sharing the same circuit as the Mark V. How much longer would they share it? wondered George. Would the monks smash up the computer in their rage and disappointment? Or would they just sit down quietly and begin their calculations all over again?

He knew exactly what was happening up on the mountain at this very moment. The high lama and his assistants would be sitting in their silk robes, inspecting the sheets as the junior monks carried them away from the typewriters and pasted them into the great volumes. No one would be saying anything. The only sound would be the incessant patter, the never-ending rainstorm of the keys hitting the paper, the Mark V itself was utterly silent as it flashed through its thousands of calculations a second. Three months of this, thought George, was enough to start anyone climbing up the wall.

"There she is!" called Chuck, pointing down into the valley. "Ain't she beautiful!"

She certainly was, thought George. The battered old DC3 lay at the end of the runway like a tiny silver cross. In two hours she would be bearing them away to freedom and sanity. It was a thought worth savoring like a fine liqueur. George let it roll round his mind as the pony trudged patiently down the slope.

The swift night of the high Himalayas was now almost upon them. Fortunately, the road was very good, as roads went in that region, and they were both carrying torches. There was not the slightest danger, only a certain discomfort from the bitter cold. The sky overhead was perfectly clear, and ablaze with the familiar, friendly stars. At least there would be no risk, thought George, of the pilot being unable to take off because of weather conditions. That had been his only remaining worry.

He began to sing, but gave it up after a while. This vast arena of mountains, gleaming like whitely hooded ghosts on every side, did not encourage such ebullience. Presently George glanced at his watch.

"Should be there in an hour," he called back over his shoulder to Chuck. Then he added, in an afterthought: "Wonder if the computer's finished its run. It was due about now."

Chuck didn't reply, so George swung round in his saddle. He could just see Chuck's face, a white oval turned toward the sky.

"Look," whispered Chuck, and George lifted his eyes to heaven. (There is always a last time for everything.)

Overhead, without any fuss, the stars were going out.

STUDY QUESTIONS

1. What is the principal purpose of this story? In your opinion, is the purpose achieved? In what way?
2. Both Clarke and Bradbury are practitioners of a genre called science fiction. On the basis of this story, construct a definition of this form.
3. What is the basic philosophical premise of the story?
4. If the reader accepts that premise, does the story grow in a consistent and logical way? Explain.
5. What is the controlling language device in the story? How does this device contribute to or control meaning and effect?

Leo Tolstoy (1828–1910)

THE EMPTY DRUM

Emilyan, who worked out as a day-labourer, was crossing the meadow one day on his way to work, when he nearly stepped on a frog that hopped right in front of him. He just managed to avoid it. Suddenly he heard someone calling to him from behind. He looked round and saw a lovely girl who said to him:

"Why don't you marry, Emilyan?"

"How can I marry, my pretty maid? I have nothing in this world, and no one would have me."

"Well, then," said the maid, "take me for a wife."

The girl appealed to Emilyan. "I should like to," said he, "but where could we live?"

"Why worry about that?" said the girl. "All one has to do is to work hard and sleep less, and one can find food and clothing anywhere."

"Very well, let us get married, then," said he. "Where shall we go?"

"Let us go to the city."

And Emilyan and the girl went to the city. She took him to a small cottage on the outskirts of the city, and they were married and began keeping house.

One day the king, coming through the city, passed by Emilyan's cottage. Emilyan's wife came out to look at him. When the king saw her he was surprised. "Where did such a beauty come from?" he thought. He stopped his carriage, called Emilyan's wife and questioned her, "Who are you?"

"The wife of the peasant Emilyan," said she.

"How did you, such a beautiful woman, come to marry a peasant? You ought to be a queen."

"Thank you for your compliment," said she, "but I am well content with my husband."

The king talked with her awhile, and then rode on. He arrived at his palace, but Emilyan's wife was on his mind. He was sleepless throughout the night, scheming how to get her for himself. He could think of no way of doing it, and therefore summoned his servants and asked them to plan some way.

The king's servants said, "Have Emilyan come here as a workman, and we will work him to death. His wife will be left a widow, and you will then be able to have her."

The king heeded their counsel. He sent for Emilyan to come as a workman and to live at the palace with his wife.

The messengers came to Emilyan with the king's command. His wife said, "Go and work there during the day, but come home to me at night."

Emilyan went, and when he reached the palace, the king's steward questioned him, "Why have you come alone without your wife?"

"Why should I have her with me? She has her own home."

At the palace they gave Emilyan more work than two could have completed, and he began without hope of finishing it. But when evening came, lo and behold! it was all done. The steward saw that he had finished, and gave him four times the amount for the next day. Emilyan went home, and found everything there neat and in order; the stove was heated, the meal was being prepared, and his wife was sitting by the table sewing and awaiting his return. She welcomed him, set the table, gave him his supper, and then began to ask him about his work.

"Well," said he, "it's not so good. They gave me more than my strength was equal to. They will kill me with work."

"Don't worry about your work," said she. "Don't look behind nor before you to see how much has been done or how much you have left to be done. Just keep right on working, and all will be well."

So Emilyan went to sleep. The next morning he went to work again and toiled on without ever turning round. And lo and behold! it was all done by the evening, and in the twilight he returned home for the night.

Ever they kept increasing his tasks, and he nevertheless managed to get through in time to go home for the night. After a week had thus passed, the king's servants saw they could not overcome him with rough work, and they began assigning him to work that necessitated skill; but this availed little more. Carpentry, masonry, or roofing—no matter what—Emilyan finished in time to go home to his wife for the night. And a second week passed.

Then the king summoned his servants and said, "Why should I feed you for doing nothing? Two weeks have passed and I fail to see what you have done. You were going to kill Emilyan with work, but from my windows I can see him going home every evening, singing cheerfully. Is it your purpose to ridicule me?"

The servants began to make excuses. "We tried our very best to tire him out," they said, "but he found nothing too difficult. No work seemed to tire him. Then we had him do things requiring skill, thinking he lacked the wit for it, but he accomplished everything. Whatever task he is put to, he does with little effort. Either he or his wife must know magic. We are tired with it all, and try to think of something he cannot do. We have determined to have him build a cathedral in one day. Will you send for Emilyan and command him to build a cathedral opposite the palace in a single day? And if he does not succeed, let his head be cut off in punishment."

The king sent for Emilyan. "Attend well my command," said he. "Build me a new cathedral on the square opposite my palace, and have it all done by to-morrow evening. If it is ready I will reward you, and if you fail your head will be cut off."

Emilyan heard the king's command, turned round and went home. "Well," thought he, "my end is near." He came to his wife and said, "Get ready, wife, we must escape from here, or I shall surely be lost."

"What makes you so frightened?" she asked, "and why must we run away?"

"How can I help being frightened?" said he. "The king has ordered me to-morrow to build a cathedral, all in a single day. If I fail he will have my head cut off. The only thing to be done is to fly while there is time."

But his wife would not hear of this. "The king has many soldiers. They will catch us anywhere. We can't escape from him, but must obey him as long as you have the strength."

"But how can I obey him when I lack the strength?"

"Listen, little father, don't be worried. Eat your supper now and go to bed. Get up a little earlier in the morning and all will be well."

And Emilyan went to sleep. His wife wakened him next day.

"Go quickly," said she, "and build your cathedral. Here are nails and a hammer. There is enough work for the day."

Emilyan went to the city, and when he arrived at the square, a large cathedral, almost finished, stood there. Emilyan started to work, and by evening he completed it.

The king awoke and looked out from his window, and saw the cathedral already built, with Emilyan driving in the last nails. And the king was not pleased to see the cathedral. He was angered not to be able to punish Emilyan and take away his wife. And he called his servants again. "Emilyan has finished his task, and there is nothing to punish him for. Even this," he said, "was easy for him. A craftier plan must be devised, or I will punish you as well as him."

And the king's servants suggested that he should order Emilyan to construct a river round the palace, and have ships sailing on it. The king summoned Emilyan and explained his new task.

"If," said he, "you are able to erect a cathedral in one night, you should also be able to do this. See to it that it is ready to-morrow, or else your head will be cut off."

Emilyan despaired more than ever, and returned, disconsolate, to his wife.

"Why are you so downcast?" said his wife. "Have you some new task to perform?"

Emilyan told her. "We must escape," said he.

But his wife said, "You can't escape from the soldiers; they will catch us wherever we be. There is nothing but to obey."

"But how can I obey?"

"Well, little father," said she, "don't be so gloomy. Eat your supper now and go to bed. Get up early, and all will get done betimes."

And Emilyan went to sleep. The next morning his wife wakened him.

"Go," said she, "to the city. All is ready. At the wharf you will find just one mound. Take your spade and level it."

When Emilyan reached the city, he saw a river encircling the palace, with ships sailing about. And when the king awoke, he saw Emilyan levelling the mound. He was surprised, but not overjoyed at the sight of the river or the ships. He was merely annoyed at not being able to punish Emilyan. "There is no task that he cannot do. What shall we set him next?" And he summoned his servants to take counsel.

"Plan some task," said he, "beyond Emilyan's power. For whatever you have thus far schemed, he has accomplished, and I cannot take his wife from him."

The king's servants pondered a long time, and at last conceived a plan. They came to the king and said, "Summon Emilyan and say to him: 'Go somewhere, you don't know where, and bring back something, you don't know what.' Now there will be no escape for him, for wherever he goes, you can say he went to the wrong place, and whatever he brings, you can say he brought back the wrong thing. Then you can have him beheaded and have his wife."

This pleased the king. "That," he said, "is a brilliant thought." And the king sent for Emilyan and said to him, "Go somewhere you don't know where, and bring back something you don't know what. If you fail, I will cut your head off."

Emilyan went to his wife and told her what the king had said. His wife thought a while.

"Well," said she, "they have taught the king how to trap you. We must act wisely." She sat down, cudgeled her brain, and then spoke to her husband. "You will have to go far, to our grandmother—the old peasant woman —and you must ask her help. She will give you something, and you will take it at once to the palace; I shall be there. I cannot escape them now. They will take me by force, but not for long. If you follow our little grandmother, you will quickly rescue me."

The wife prepared her husband for the journey. She gave him a wallet as well as a spindle. "Give her this. By this she will know you are my husband." And then she showed him the road.

Emilyan set out. He arrived beyond the city and saw some soldiers drilling. Emilyan stopped to watch them. When the drill was over, the soldiers sat down to rest. Emilyan drew near and asked, "Do you know, my brothers, the direction to 'somewhere I don't know where', and where I can find 'something I don't know what'?"

The soldiers listened in amazement. "Who sent you on this quest?" asked they.

"The king," he replied.

"From the day we became soldiers, we have ourselves gone 'we don't know where,' and have sought 'we don't know what'. We surely cannot help you."

After he had rested a while, Emilyan continued on his way. He travelled on and on, and at last came to a forest where he found a hut. In the hut sat a little old woman—the old peasant woman—spinning flax and weeping. When the old woman saw Emilyan, she cried out to him, "What have you come for?"

Emilyan gave her the spindle and told her his wife had sent it. In answer to her questions, Emilyan began to tell her about his life: how he married the girl; how they had gone to live in the city; how he had drudged at the palace; how he had built the cathedral, and made a river with ships; and how the king had told him to go somewhere, he knew not where, and bring back something, he knew not what.

The little old woman heard his story, and then ceased weeping. She muttered to herself. Then she said to him, "Very well, my son, sit down and have something to eat."

Emilyan ate, and the little grandmother spoke to him. "Here is a little ball of thread; roll it before you, and follow it wherever it rolls. You will go far, till you get to the sea. There you will find a great city. You will enter the city and ask for a night's lodging at the last house. There you will find what you seek."

"But how shall I recognise it, granny?"

"When you see that which men obey sooner than father or mother, that will be it. Seize it and take it to the king. If the king will say it is not the right thing, answer him: 'If it is not the right thing, it must be broken'; then beat the thing and take it down to the river, smash it and pitch it into the water. Then you will recover your wife."

Emilyan said good-bye to the old woman, and rolled the little ball before him. It rolled on and on until it reached the sea, and by the sea was a great city, and at the end of the city was a large house. There Emilyan asked for shelter, and it was granted him. He went to sleep, and awoke early in the morning to hear a father calling his son and telling him to cut firewood. But the son would not obey. "It is too early," he said, "I have time enough." Then Emilyan heard the mother say, "Go, son your father's bones ache him; would you have him go? It is time to get up."

"There's time enough," the son muttered and went off to sleep again. Scarcely had he fallen asleep when there came a crashing noise in the street. The son jumped up, hastily put on his clothes and ran into the street. Emilyan jumped up also, and followed him to see what a son obeys more than his father or mother. He saw a man walking along the street carrying a round thing on which he beat with sticks. And *this* had made the thundering noise which the son had obeyed. Emilyan ran up closer and examined it; and saw it was round like a small tub, and skins were stretched over both ends. He asked what it was called.

"A drum," he was told.

Emilyan was astonished, and asked them to give him this object, but they refused. So Emilyan ceased asking, and walked along, following the drummer. He walked all day, and when the drummer lay down to sleep, Emilyan snatched the drum and ran off with it.

He ran and ran, and at last came back to his own city. He hoped to see his wife, but she was not at home. The day after he had gone away, they had taken her to the king. Emilyan went to the palace and told them to announce to the king that 'He, who went he knew not where, has returned, and brought back he knows not what.'

When they told the king, he asked Emilyan to return the next day.

But Emilyan insisted, "Tell the king I have come to-day, and have brought what he wanted. Let him come to me, or I will go to him."

The king came out. "Where have you been?" he asked.

"I don't know," Emilyan replied.

"What did you bring?"

Emilyan showed him the drum, but the king refused to look at it.

"That's not it."

"If it's not the right thing, it must be beaten," said Emilyan, "and the devil take it."

Emilyan came out of the palace and beat the drum, and as he did so, all the king's army ran to follow him, saluting Emilyan and awaiting his commands.

From the window the king began to shout to his army, forbidding them to follow Emilyan. But they did not heed the king and kept on following Emilyan.

When the king perceived this, he ordered Emilyan's wife returned to him, and asked Emilyan for the drum.

"I cannot do that," said Emilyan. "I must beat it, and then pitch the scraps into the river."

Emilyan went to the river, still carrying the drum and followed by the soldiers. At the bank of the river, Emilyan beat the drum into pieces and threw them into the water. And all the soldiers ran off in all directions. Then Emilyan took his wife and brought her home. And thenceforth the king ceased to worry him, and he lived happily ever after.

STUDY QUESTIONS

1. "The Empty Drum" is Tolstoy's adaptation of a folktale. What plot elements at the beginning of the story identify it as such?
2. Identify the principal conflict in the narrative.
3. What specific initial tasks does Emilyan receive from the king? How are they accomplished?
4. What is the nature of Emilyan's final assignment?
5. Explain specifically how the drum is discovered. What powers does the drum possess?
6. How does the drum prove to be both no answer and an answer to the king?
7. Discuss the symbolic nature of *one* of the early tasks.
8. What might the drum symbolize? In your answer, consider one critic's assertion that "The Empty Drum" is a story against war.
9. Considering the title, the tasks, and the ending, what else (other than war) could the story be about?

Guy de Maupassant (1850–1893)

THE JEWELRY

Having met the girl one evening, at the house of the office superintendent, M. Lantin became enveloped in love as in a net.

She was the daughter of a provincial tax collector, who had been dead for several years. Afterward she had come to Paris with her mother, who made regular visits to several *bourgeois*[1] families of the neighborhood, in hopes of being able to get her daughter married. They were poor and respectable, quiet and gentle. The young girl seemed to be the very ideal of that pure good woman to whom every young man dreams of entrusting his future. Her modest beauty had a charm of angelic shyness; and the slight smile that always dwelt about her lips seemed a reflection of her heart.

Everybody sang her praises; all who knew her kept saying: "The man who gets her will be lucky. No one could find a nicer girl than that."

M. Lantin, who was then chief clerk in the office of the Minister of the Interior, with a salary of 3,500 francs a year, asked for her hand, and married her.

He was unutterably happy with her. She ruled his home with an economy so adroit that they really seemed to live in luxury. It would be impossible to conceive of any attentions, tendernesses, playful caresses which she did not lavish upon her husband; and such was the charm of her person that, six years after he married her, he loved her even more than he did the first day.

There were only two points upon which he ever found fault with her—her love of the theatre, and her passion for false jewelry.

Her lady friends (she was acquainted with the wives of several small officeholders) were always bringing her tickets for the theatre; whenever there was a performance that made a sensation, she always had her loge[2] secured, even for first performances; and she would drag her husband with her to all these entertainments, which used to tire him horribly after his day's work. So at last he begged her to go to the theatre with some lady acquaintances who would consent to see her home afterward. She refused for quite a while—thinking it would not look very well to go out thus unaccompanied by her husband. But finally she yielded, just to please him; and he felt infinitely grateful to her for it.

Now this passion for the theatre at last evoked in her the desire of dress. It was true that her *toilette*[3] remained simple, always in good taste, but modest; and her sweet grace, her irresistible grace, ever smiling and shy, seemed to take fresh charm from the simplicity of her dresses. But she got into the habit of suspending in her pretty ears two big cut pebbles, fashioned in imitation of diamonds; and she wore necklaces of false pearls, bracelets of false gold, and haircombs studded with paste imitations of precious stones.

Her husband, who felt shocked by this love of tinsel and show, would often say: "My dear, when one has not the means to afford real jewelry, one should appear adorned with one's natural beauty and grace only—and these gifts are the rarest of jewels."

But she would smile sweetly and answer: "What does it matter? I like

---

[1] *bourgeois:* prosperous, middle class.
[2] loge: a comfortable, exclusive location for theatre seats.
[3] *toilette:* grooming, dress.

those things—that is my little whim. I know you are right; but one can't make oneself over again. I've always loved jewelry so much!"

And then she would roll the pearls of the necklaces between her fingers, and make the facets of the cut crystal flash in the light, repeating: "Now look at them—see how well the work is done. You would swear it was real jewelry."

He would then smile in his turn, and declare to her: "You have the tastes of a regular gypsy."

Sometimes, in the evening, when they were having a chat by the fire, she would rise and fetch the morocco box in which she kept her "stock" (as M. Lantin called it)—would put it on the tea table, and begin to examine the false jewelry with passionate delight, as if she experienced some secret and mysterious sensations of pleasure in their contemplation; and she would insist on putting one of the necklaces round her husband's neck, and laugh till she couldn't laugh any more, crying out: "Oh! how funny you look!" Then she would rush into his arms, and kiss him furiously.

One winter's night, after she had been to the Opera, she came home chilled through, and trembling. Next day she had a bad cough. Eight days after that, she died of pneumonia.

Lantin came close to following her into the tomb. His despair was so frightful that in one single month his hair turned white. He wept from morning till night, feeling his heart torn by inexpressible suffering, ever haunted by the memory of her, by the smile, by the voice, by all the charm of the dead woman.

Time did not assuage his grief. Often during office hours his fellow clerks went off to a corner to chat about this or that topic of the day—his cheeks might have been seen to swell up all of a sudden, his nose wrinkle, his eyes fill with water; he would pull a frightful face, and begin to sob.

He had kept his dead companion's room just in the order she had left it, and he used to lock himself up in it every evening to think about her. All the furniture, and even all her dresses, remained in the same place they had been on the last day of her life.

But life became hard for him. His salary, which, in his wife's hands, had amply sufficed for all household needs, now proved scarcely sufficient to supply his own few wants. And he asked himself in astonishment how she had managed always to furnish him with excellent wines and with delicate eating which he could not now afford at all with his scanty means.

He got a little into debt, like men obliged to live by their wits. At last one morning when he happened to find himself without a cent in his pocket, and a whole week to wait before he could draw his monthly salary, he thought of selling something; and almost immediately it occurred to him to sell his wife's "stock"—for he had always borne a secret grudge against the flash-jewelry that used to annoy him so much in former days. The mere sight of it, day after day, somewhat spoiled the sad pleasure of thinking of his darling.

He tried a long time to make a choice among the heap of trinkets she had left behind her; for up to the very last day of her life she had kept obstinately buying them, bringing home some new thing almost every night. And finally he resolved to take the big pearl necklace which she used to like the best of all, and which he thought ought certainly to be worth six or eight francs, as it was really very nicely mounted for an imitation necklace.

He put it in his pocket, and walked toward the office, following the boulevards, and looking for some jewelry store on the way, where he could enter with confidence.

Finally he saw a place and went in; feeling a little ashamed of thus exposing his misery, and of trying to sell such a trifling object.

"Sir," he said to the jeweler, "please tell me what this is worth."

The jeweler took the necklace, examined it, weighed it, took up a magnifying glass, called his clerk, talked to him in whispers, put down the necklace on the counter, and drew back a little bit to judge of its effect at a distance.

M. Lantin, feeling very much embarrassed by all these ceremonies, opened his mouth and began to declare: "Oh? I know it can't be worth much" . . . when the jeweler interrupted him by saying:

"Well, sir, that is worth between twelve and fifteen thousand francs; but I cannot buy it unless you can let me know exactly how you came by it."

The widower's eyes opened enormously, and he stood gaping, unable to understand. Then after a while he stammered out: "You said? . . . Are you sure?" The jeweler, misconstruing the cause of this astonishment, replied in a dry tone: "Go elsewhere if you like, and see if you can get any more for it. The very most I would give for it is fifteen thousand. Come back and see me again, if you can't do better."

M. Lantin, feeling perfectly idiotic, took his necklace and departed; obeying a confused desire to find himself alone and to get a chance to think.

But the moment he found himself in the street again, he began to laugh, and he muttered to himself: "The fool! Oh! what a fool! If I had only taken him at his word. Well, well! A jeweler who can't tell paste from real jewelry!"

And he entered another jewelry store, at the corner of the Rue de la Paix. The moment the jeweler set eyes on the necklace, he exclaimed: "Hello! I know that necklace well—it was sold here!"

M. Lantin, very nervous, asked:

"What's it worth?"

"Sir, I sold it for twenty-five thousand francs. I am willing to buy it back again for eighteen thousand, if you can prove to me satisfactorily, according to legal prescriptions, how you came into possession of it." This time, M. Lantin was simply paralyzed with astonishment. He said: "Well . . . but please look at it again, sir. I always thought until now that it was . . . was false."

The jeweler said: "Will you give me your name, sir?"

"Certainly. My name is Lantin; I am employed at the office of the Minister of the Interior. I live at No. 16, Rue des Martyrs."

The merchant opened the register, looked, and said: "Yes; this necklace was sent to the address of Madame Lantin, 16 Rue des Martyrs, on July 20, 1876."

And the two men looked into each other's eyes—the clerk wild with surprise; the jeweler suspecting he had a thief before him.

The jeweler resumed:

"Will you be kind enough to leave this article here for twenty-four hours only—I'll give you a receipt."

M. Lantin stuttered: "Yes—ah! certainly." And he went out, folding up the receipt, which he put in his pocket.

Then he crossed the street, went the wrong way, found out his mistake, returned by way of the Tuileries, crossed the Seine, found out he had taken the wrong road again, and went back to the Champs-Elysées without being able to get one clear idea into his head. He tried to reason, to understand. His wife could never have bought so valuable an object as that. Certainly not. But then, it must have been a present! ... A present from whom? What for?

He stopped and stood stock-still in the middle of the avenue.

A horrible suspicion swept across his mind. . . . She? . . . But then all those other pieces of jewelry must have been presents also! . . . Then it seemed to him that the ground was heaving under his feet; that a tree, right in front of him, was falling toward him; he thrust out his arms instinctively, and fell senseless.

He recovered his consciousness again in a drug store to which some bystanders had carried him. He had them lead him home, and he locked himself into his room.

Until nightfall he cried without stopping, biting his handkerchief to keep himself from screaming out. Then, completely worn out with grief and fatigue, he went to bed, and slept a leaden sleep.

A ray of sunshine awakened him, and he rose and dressed himself slowly to go to the office. It was hard to have to work after such a shock. Then he reflected that he might be able to excuse himself to the superintendent, and he wrote to him. Then he remembered he would have to go back to the jeweler's; and shame made his face purple. He remained thinking a long time. Still he could not leave the necklace there; he put on his coat and went out.

It was a fine day; the sky extended all blue over the city, and seemed to make it smile. Strollers were walking aimlessly about, with their hands in their pockets.

Lantin thought as he watched them passing: "How lucky the men are who have fortunes! With money a man can even shake off grief. You can go where you please, travel, amuse yourself! Oh! if I were only rich!"

He suddenly discovered he was hungry, not having eaten anything since the evening before. But his pockets were empty; and he remembered the necklace. Eighteen thousand francs! Eighteen thousand francs! That was a sum—that was!

He made his way to the Rue de la Paix and began to walk backward and forward on the sidewalk in front of the store. Eighteen thousand francs! Twenty times he started to go in; but shame always kept him back.

Still he was hungry—very hungry—and had not a cent. He made one brusque resolve, and crossed the street almost at a run, so as not to let himself have time to think over the matter; and he rushed into the jeweler's.

As soon as he saw him, the merchant hurried forward, and offered him a chair with smiling politeness. Even the clerks came forward to stare at Lantin, with gaiety in their eyes and smiles about their lips.

The jeweler said: "Sir, I made inquiries; and if you are still so disposed, I am ready to pay you down the price I offered you."

The clerk stammered: "Why, yes—sir, certainly."

The jeweler took from a drawer eighteen big bills, counted them, and held them out to Lantin, who signed a little receipt, and thrust the money feverishly into his pocket.

Then, as he was on the point of leaving, he turned to the ever-smiling merchant, and said, lowering his eyes: "I have some—I have some other jewelry, which came to me in the same—from the same inheritance. Would you purchase them also from me?"

The merchant bowed, and answered: "Why, certainly, sir—certainly. . . ." One of the clerks rushed out to laugh at his ease; another kept blowing his nose as hard as he could.

Lantin, impassive, flushed and serious, said: "I will bring them to you."

And he hired a cab to get the jewelry.

When he returned to the store, an hour later, he had not yet lunched. They examined the jewelry, piece by piece, putting a value on each. Nearly all had been purchased from that very house.

Lantin, now, disputed estimates made, got angry, insisted on seeing the books, and talked louder and louder the higher the estimates grew.

The big diamond earrings were worth 20,000 francs; the bracelets, 35,000; the brooches, rings, and medallions, 16,000; a set of emeralds and sapphires, 14,000; a solitaire, suspended from a gold neckchain, 40,000; the total value being estimated at 196,000 francs.

The merchant observed with mischievous good nature: "The person who owned these must have put all her savings into jewelry."

Lantin answered with gravity: "Perhaps that is as good a way of saving money as any other." And he went off, after having agreed with the merchant that an expert should make a counter-estimate for him the next day.

When he found himself in the street again, he looked at the Vendôme

Column[4] with the desire to climb it, as if it were a May pole. He felt jolly enough to play leapfrog over the Emperor's head, up there in the blue sky.

He lunched at Voisin's restaurant, and ordered wine at 20 francs a bottle.

Then he hired a cab and drove out to the Bois.[5] He looked at the carriages passing with a sort of contempt, and a wild desire to yell out to the passers-by: "I am rich, too—I am! I have 200,000 francs!"

The recollection of the office suddenly came back to him. He drove there, walked right into the superintendent's private room, and said: "Sir, I come to give you my resignation. I have just come into a fortune of *three* hundred thousand francs." The he shook hands all round with his fellow-clerks; and told them all about his plans for a new career. Then he went to dinner at the Café Anglais.

Finding himself seated at the same table with a man who seemed to him quite genteel, he could not resist the itching desire to tell him, with a certain air of coquetry, that he had just inherited a fortune of *four* hundred thousand francs.

For the first time in his life he went to the theatre without feeling bored by the performance; and he spent the night in revelry and debauch.

Six months after he married again. His second wife was the most upright of spouses, but had a terrible temper. She made his life very miserable.

STUDY QUESTIONS

1. Briefly outline the principal parts of the story, including the rising action, turning point, and denouement.
2. In Mme. Lantin, de Maupassant seems to be painting a portrait of the ideal wife. What are some of the details of that portrait?
3. Describe the marriage of M. and Mme. Lantin. Discover particular details that indicate their only apparent disagreements and their apparent great happiness together.
4. The central plot device in the story is an ironic twist for the husband and reader. In what ways does the author prepare for the surprise?
5. Find examples of all three kinds of irony in the story.
6. Does the story have any purpose other than to amuse? If so, what is it?
7. How is the last paragraph one more irony in a chain of ironies? How does the final irony relate to the meaning of the story? Comment on that meaning.
8. Both "The Jewels" and "Paste" are about moral values somehow altered by a revelation that what was false in material substance is real and that what is true in character is false. In what way are both stories similar? How do they differ? Which one would you say is more true to life? Why?

[4] Vendôme Column: a monument in Paris, in the form of a tall pillar.
[5] Bois: the Bois de Boulogne, a wooded park at the edge of Paris.

Bernard Malamud (1914–)

THE JEWBIRD

The window was open so the skinny bird flew in. Flappity-flap with its frazzled black wings. That's how it goes. It's open, you're in. Closed, you're out and that's your fate. The bird wearily flapped through the open kitchen window by Harry Cohen's top-floor apartment on First Avenue near the lower East River. On a rod on the wall hung an escaped canary cage, its door wide open, but this black-type longbeaked bird—its ruffled head and small dull eyes, crossed a little, making it look like a dissipated crow— landed if not smack on Cohen's thick lamb chop, at least on the table, close by. The frozen foods salesman was sitting at supper with his wife and young son on a hot August evening a year ago. Cohen, a heavy man with hairy chest and beefy shorts; Edie, in skinny yellow shorts and red halter; and their ten-year-old Morris (after her father)—Maurie, they called him, a nice kid though not overly bright—were all in the city after two weeks out, because Cohen's mother was dying. They had been enjoying Kingston, New York, but drove back when Mama got sick in her flat in the Bronx.

"Right on the table," said Cohen, putting down his beer glass and swatting at the bird. "Son of a bitch."

"Harry, take care with your langauge," Edie said, looking at Maurie who watched every move.

The bird cawed hoarsely and with a flap of its bedraggled wings—feathers tufted this way and that—rose heavily to the top of the open kitchen door, where it perched staring down.

"Gevalt,[1] a pogram!"[2]

"It's a talking bird," said Edie in astonishment.

"In Jewish," said Maurie.

"Wise guy," muttered Cohen. He gnawed on his chop, then put down the bone. "So if you can talk, say what's your business. What do you want here?"

"If you can't spare a lamb chop," said the bird, "I'll settle for a piece of herring with a crust of bread. You can't live on your nerve forever."

"This ain't a restaurant," Cohen replied. "All I'm asking is what brings you to this address?"

"The window was open," the bird sighed; adding after moment, "I'm running. I'm flying but I'm also running."

"From whom?" asked Edie with interest.

"Anti-Semeets."

"Anti-Semites?" they all said.

"That's from who."

---

[1] gevalt: a slang expression of anxiety or disgust.
[2] pogrom: an organized massacre of Jews.

"What kind of anti-Semites bother a bird?" Edie asked.

"Any kind," said the bird, "also including eagles, vultures, and hawks. And once in a while some crows will take your eyes out."

"But aren't you a crow?"

"Me? I'm a Jewbird."

Cohen laughed heartily. "What do you mean by that?"

The bird began dovening.[3] He prayed without Book or tallith,[4] but with passion. Edie bowed her head though not Cohen. And Maurie rocked back and forth with the prayer, looking up with one wide-open eye.

When the prayer was done Cohen remarked, "No hat,[5] no phylacteries?"[6]

"I'm an old radical."

"You're sure you're not some kind of a ghost or dybbuk?"[7]

"Not a dybbuk," answered the bird, "though one of my relatives had such an experience once. It's all over now, thanks God. They freed her from a former lover, a crazy jealous man. She's now the mother of two wonderful children."

"Birds?" Cohen asked slyly.

"Why not?"

"What kind of birds?"

"Like me. Jewbirds."

Cohen tipped back in his chair and guffawed. "That's a big laugh. I've heard of a Jewfish but not a Jewbird."

"We're once removed." The bird rested on one skinny leg, then on the other. "Please, could you spare maybe a piece of herring with a small crust of bread?"

Edie got up from the table.

"What are you doing?" Cohen asked her.

"I'll clear the dishes."

Cohen turned to the bird. "So what's your name, if you don't mind saying?"

"Call me Schwartz."

"He might be an old Jew changed into a bird by somebody," said Edie, removing a plate.

"Are you?" asked Harry, lighting a cigar.

"Who knows?" answered Schwartz. "Does God tell us everything?"

Maurie got up on his chair. "What kind of herring?" he asked the bird in excitement.

"Get down, Maurie, or you'll fall," ordered Cohen.

"If you haven't got matjes, I'll take schmaltz," said Schwartz.

[3] dovening: praying.

[4] tallith: prayer scarf or shawl.

[5] hat: skullcap, yarmulke; worn during prayer.

[6] phylacteries: leather boxes containing biblical passages worn during morning prayer.

[7] dybbuk: evil spirit or wandering soul of the dead.

"All we have is marinated, with slices of onion—in a jar," said Edie.

"If you'll open for me the jar I'll eat marinated. Do you have also, if you don't mind, a piece of rye bread—the spitz?"

Edie thought she had.

"Feed him out on the balcony," Cohen said. He spoke to the bird. "After that take off."

Schwartz closed both bird eyes. "I'm tired and it's a long way."

"Which direction are you headed, north or south?"

Schwartz, barely lifting his wings, shrugged.

"You don't know where you're going?"

"Where there's charity I'll go."

"Let him stay, papa," said Maurie. "He's only a bird."

"So stay the night," Cohen said, "but no longer."

In the morning Cohen ordered the bird out of the house but Maurie cried, so Schwartz stayed for a while. Maurie was still on vacation from school and his friends were away. He was lonely and Edie enjoyed the fun he had, playing with the bird.

"He's no trouble at all," she told Cohen, "and besides his appetite is very small."

"What'll you do when he makes dirty?"

"He flies across the street in a tree when he makes dirty, and if nobody passes below, who notices?"

"So all right," said Cohen, "but I'm dead set against it. I warn you he ain't gonna stay here long."

"What have you got against the poor bird?"

"Poor bird, my ass. He's a foxy bastard. He thinks he's a Jew."

"What difference does it make what he thinks?"

"A Jewbird, what a chuzpah.[8] One false move and he's out on his drumsticks."

At Cohen's insistence Schwartz lived out on the balcony in a new wooden birdhouse Edie had bought him.

"With many thanks," said Schwartz, "though I would rather have a human roof over my head. You know how it is at my age. I like the warm, the windows, the smell of cooking. I would also be glad to see once in a while the *Jewish Morning Journal* and have now and then a schnapps[9] because it helps my breathing, thanks God. But whatever you give me, you won't hear complaints."

However, when Cohen brought home a bird feeder full of dried corn, Schwartz said, "Impossible."

Cohen was annoyed. "What's the matter, crosseyes, is your life getting too good for you? Are you forgetting what it means to be migratory? I'll bet

[8] chuzpah: brash person.
[9] schnapps: one of various distilled liquors.

a helluva lot of crows you happen to be acquainted with, Jews or otherwise, would give their eyeteeth to eat this corn."

Schwartz did not answer. What can you say to a grubber yung? [10]

"Not for my digestion," he later explained to Edie. "Cramps. Herring is better even if it makes you thirsty. At least rainwater don't cost anything." He laughed sadly in breathy caws.

And herring, thanks to Edie, who knew where to shop, was what Schwartz got, with an occasional piece of potato pancake, and even a bit of soupmeat when Cohen wasn't looking.

When school began in September, before Cohen would once again suggest giving the bird the boot, Edie prevailed on him to wait a little while until Maurie adjusted.

"To deprive him right now might hurt his school work, and you know what trouble we had last year."

"So okay, but sooner or later the bird goes. That I promise you."

Schwartz, though nobody had asked him, took on full responsibility for Maurie's performance in school. In return for favors granted, when he was let in for an hour or two at night, he spent most of his time overseeing the boy's lessons. He sat on top of the dresser near Maurie's desk as he laboriously wrote out his homework. Maurie was a restless type and Schwartz gently kept him to his studies. He also listened to him practice his screechy violin, taking a few minutes off now and then to rest his ears in the bathroom. And they afterwards played dominoes. The boy was an indifferent checker player and it was impossible to teach him chess. When he was sick, Schwartz read him comic books though he personally disliked them. But Maurie's work improved in school and even his violin teacher admitted his playing was better. Edie gave Schwartz credit for these improvements though the bird pooh-poohed them.

Yet he was proud there was nothing lower than C minuses on Maurie's report card, and on Edie's insistence celebrated with a little schnapps.

"If he keeps up like this," Cohen said, "I'll get him in an Ivy League college for sure."

"Oh I hope so," sighed Edie.

But Schwartz shook his head. "He's a good boy—you don't have to worry. He won't be a shicker[11] or wifebeater, God forbid, but a scholar he'll never be, if you know what I mean, although maybe a good mechanic. It's no disgrace in these times."

"If I were you," Cohen said, angered, "I'd keep my big snoot out of other people's private business."

"Harry, please," said Edie.

"My goddamn patience is wearing out. That crosseyes butts into everything."

[10] grubber yung: rude young man.
[11] shicker: drunkard.

Though he wasn't exactly a welcome guest in the house, Schwartz gained a few ounces although he did not improve in appearance. He looked bedraggled as ever, his feathers unkempt, as though he had just flown out of a snowstorm. He spent, he admitted, little time taking care of himself. Too much to think about. "Also outside plumbing," he told Edie. Still there was more glow to his eyes so that though Cohen went on calling him crosseyes he said it less emphatically.

Liking his situation, Schwartz tried tactfully to stay out of Cohen's way, but one night when Edie was at the movies and Maurie was taking a hot shower, the frozen foods salesman began a quarrel with the bird.

"For Christ sake, why don't you wash yourself sometimes? Why must you always stink like a dead fish?"

"Mr. Cohen, if you'll pardon me, if somebody eats garlic he will smell from garlic. I eat herring three times a day. Feed me flowers and I will smell like flowers."

"Who's obligated to feed you anything at all? You're lucky to get herring."

"Excuse me, I'm not complaining," said the bird. "You're complaining."

"What's more," said Cohen, "even from out on the balcony I can hear you snoring away like a pig. It keeps me awake at night."

"Snoring," said Schwartz, "isn't a crime, thanks God."

"All in all you are a goddamn pest and free loader. Next thing you'll want to sleep in bed next to my wife."

"Mr. Cohen," said Schwartz, "on this rest assured. A bird is a bird."

"So you say, but how do I know you're a bird and not some kind of goddamn devil?"

"If I was a devil you would know already. And I don't mean because your son's good marks."

"Shut up, you bastard bird," shouted Cohen.

"Grubber yung," cawed Schwartz, rising to the tips of his talons, his long wings outstretched.

Cohen was about to lunge for the bird's scrawny neck but Maurie came out of the bathroom, and for the rest of the evening until Schwartz's bedtime on the balcony, there was pretended peace.

But the quarrel had deeply disturbed Schwartz and he slept badly. His snoring woke him, and awake, he was fearful of what would become of him. Wanting to stay out of Cohen's way, he kept to the birdhouse as much as possible. Cramped by it, he paced back and forth on the balcony ledge, or sat on the birdhouse roof, staring into space. In the evenings, while overseeing Maurie's lessons, he often fell asleep. Awakening, he nervously hopped around exploring the four corners of the room. He spent much time in Maurie's closet, and carefully examined his bureau drawers when they were left open. And once when he found a large paper bag on the floor, Schwartz poked his way into it to investigate what possibilities were. The boy was amused to see the bird in the paper bag.

"He wants to build a nest," he said to his mother.

Edie, sensing Schwartz's unhappiness, spoke to him quietly.

"Maybe if you did some of the things my husband wants you, you would get along better with him."

"Give me a for instance," Schwartz said.

"Like take a bath, for instance."

"I'm too old for baths," said the bird. "My feathers fall out without baths."

"He says you have a bad smell."

"Everybody smells. Some people smell because of their thoughts or because who they are. My bad smell comes from the food I eat. What does his come from?"

"I better not ask him or it might make him mad," said Edie.

In late November Schwartz froze on the balcony in the fog and cold, and especially on rainy days he woke with stiff joints and could barely move his wings. Already he felt twinges of rheumatism. He would have liked to spend more time in the warm house, particularly when Maurie was in school and Cohen at work. But though Edie was good-hearted and might have sneaked him in in the morning, just to thaw out, he was afraid to ask her. In the meantime Cohen, who had been reading articles about the migration of birds, came out on the balcony one night after work when Edie was in the kitchen preparing pot roast, and peeking into the birdhouse, warned Schwartz to be on his way soon if he knew what was good for him. "Time to hit the flyways."

"Mr. Cohen, why do you hate me so much?" asked the bird. "What did I do to you?"

"Because you're an A-number-one trouble maker, that's why. What's more, whoever heard of a Jewbird? Now scat or it's open war."

But Schwartz stubbornly refused to depart so Cohen embarked on a campaign of harassing him, meanwhile hiding it from Edie and Maurie. Maurie hated violence and Cohen didn't want to leave a bad impression. He thought maybe if he played dirty tricks on the bird he would fly off without being physically kicked out. The vacation was over, let him make his easy living off the fat of somebody else's land. Cohen worried about the effect of the bird's departure on Maurie's schooling but decided to take the chance, first, because the boy now seemed to have the knack of studying—give the black bird-bastard credit—and second, because Schwartz was driving him bats by being there always, even in his dreams.

The frozen foods salesman began his campaign against the bird by mixing watery cat food with the herring slices in Schwartz's dish. He also blew up and popped numerous paper bags outside the birdhouse as the bird slept, and when he had got Schwartz good and nervous, though not enough to leave, he brought a full-grown cat into the house, supposedly a gift for little Maurie, who had always wanted a pussy. The cat never stopped springing

BERNARD MALAMUD

up at Schwartz whenever he saw him, one day managing to claw out several
of his tailfeathers. And even at lesson time, when the cat was usually ex-
cluded from Maurie's room, though somehow or other he quickly found his
way in at the end of the lesson, Schwartz was desperately fearful of his life
and flew from pinnacle to pinnacle—light fixture to clothestree to door-top
—in order to elude the beast's wet jaws.

Once when the bird complained to Edie how hazardous his existence was,
she said, "Be patient, Mr. Schwartz. When the cat gets to know you better
he won't try to catch you any more."

"When he stops trying we will both be in Paradise," Schwartz answered.
"Do me a favor and get rid of him. He makes my whole life worry. I'm
losing feathers like a tree loses leaves."

"I'm awfully sorry but Maurie likes the pussy and sleeps with it."

What could Schwartz do? He worried but came to no decision, being
afraid to leave. So he ate the herring garnished with cat food, tried hard not
to hear the paper bags bursting like fire crackers outside the birdhouse at
night, and lived terror-stricken closer to the ceiling than the floor, as the
cat, his tail flicking, endlessly watched him.

Weeks went by. Then on the day after Cohen's mother had died in her
flat in the Bronx, when Maurie came home with a zero on an arithmetic test,
Cohen, enraged, waited until Edie had taken the boy to his violin lesson,
then openly attacked the bird. He chased him with a broom on the balcony
and Schwartz frantically flew back and forth, finally escaping into his birdhouse. Cohen triumphantly reached in and grabbing both skinny legs,
dragged the bird out, cawing loudly, his wings wildly beating. He whirled
the bird around and around his head. But Schwartz, as he moved in circles,
managed to sweep down and catch Cohen's nose in his beak, and hung on
for dear life. Cohen cried out in great pain, punched the bird with his fist,
and tugged at its legs with all his might, pulled his nose free. Again he
swung the yawking Schwartz around till the bird grew dizzy, then with a
furious heave, flung him into the night. Schwartz sank like stone into the
street. Cohen then tossed the birdhouse and feeder after him, listening at
the ledge until they crashed on the sidewalk below. For a full hour, broom
in hand, his heart palpitating and nose throbbing with pain, Cohen waited
for Schwartz to return but the broken-hearted bird didn't.

That's the end of that dirty bastard, the salesman thought and went in.
Edie and Maurie had come home.

"Look," said Cohen, pointing to his bloody nose swollen three times its
normal size, "what that sonofabitchy bird did. It's a permanent scar."

"Where is he now?" Edie asked, frightened.

"I threw him out and he flew away. Good riddance."

Nobody said no, though Edie touched a handkerchief to her eyes and
Maurie rapidly tried the nine times table and found he knew approximately
half.

In the spring when the winter's snow had melted, the boy, moved by a memory, wandered in the neighborhood, looking for Schwartz. He found a dead black bird in a small lot near the river, his two wings broken, neck twisted, and both bird-eyes plucked clean.

"Who did it to you, Mr. Schwartz?" Maurie wept.

"Anti-Semeets," Edie said later.

STUDY QUESTIONS

1. "The Jewbird" combines fantasy and realism. To what extent are the various elements of literature (character, conflict, and setting) realistic or fantastic in this story?
2. Is the Jewbird a convincing and sympathetic protagonist? Consider his character traits, his situation, and his actions.
3. When Schwartz arrives at the Cohens' apartment, they have just returned from vacation because Mr. Cohen's mother is dying. Schwartz is killed by Cohen the day after Cohen's mother dies. Is the relation in time between these events coincidental, or is Malamud making a comparison of some kind between the older Mrs. Cohen and Schwartz? If the latter, can you suggest what that relationship is?
4. The bird tells the family that he is running from "anti-Semeets." At the end of the story, Edie says he has been killed and desecrated by "anti-Semeets." Her statement implies that no escape was possible for the Jewbird. What does that suggest as to the meaning of "anti-Semeets" in the story? In what way is her statement ironic?
5. The action of the story suggests that the Jewbird is a symbol. What meanings of the bird as symbol are implied?
6. Consider the role of the Jewbird, his antagonists, their conflicts, and the resolution. What general statement about human existence is Malamud making?

Kurt Vonnegut, Jr. (1922–)

HARRISON BERGERON

The year was 2081, and everybody was finally equal. They weren't only equal before God and the law. They were equal every which way. Nobody was smarter than anybody else. Nobody was better looking than anybody else. Nobody was stronger or quicker than anybody else. All this equality was due to the 211th, 212th, and 213th Amendments to the Constitution, and to the unceasing vigilance of agents of the United States Handicapper General.

Some things about living still weren't quite right, though. April, for instance, still drove people crazy by not being springtime. And it was in that clammy month that the H-G men took George and Hazel Bergeron's fourteen-year-old son, Harrison, away.

It was tragic, all right, but George and Hazel couldn't think about it very hard. Hazel had a perfectly average intelligence, which meant she couldn't think about anything except in short bursts. And George, while his intelligence was way above normal, had a little mental handicap radio in his ear. He was required by law to wear it at all times. It was tuned to a government transmitter. Every twenty seconds or so, the transmitter would send out some sharp noise to keep people like George from taking unfair advantage of their brains.

George and Hazel were watching television. There were tears on Hazel's cheeks, but she'd forgotten for the moment what they were about.

On the television screen were ballerinas.

A buzzer sounded in George's head. His thoughts fled in panic, like bandits from a burglar alarm.

"That was a real pretty dance, that dance they just did," said Hazel.

"Huh?" said George.

"That dance—it was nice," said Hazel.

"Yup," said George. He tried to think a little about the ballerinas. They weren't really very good—no better than anybody else would have been, anyway. They were burdened with sashweights and bags of birdshot, and their faces were masked, so that no one, seeing a free and graceful gesture or a pretty face, would feel like something the cat drug in. George was toying with the vague notion that maybe dancers shouldn't be handicapped. But he didn't get very far with it before another noise in his ear radio scattered his thoughts.

George winced. So did two out of the eight ballerinas.

Hazel saw him wince. Having no mental handicap herself, she had to ask George what the latest sound had been.

"Sounded like somebody hitting a milk bottle with a ball peen hammer," said George.

"I'd think it would be real interesting, hearing all the different sounds," said Hazel, a little envious. "All the things they think up."

"Um," said George.

"Only," if I was Handicapper General, you know what I would do?" said Hazel. Hazel, as a matter of fact, bore a strong resemblance to the Handicapper General, a woman named Diana Moon Glampers. "If I was Diana Moon Glampers," said Hazel, "I'd have chimes on Sunday—just chimes. Kind of in honor of religion."

"I could think, if it was just chimes," said George.

"Well—maybe make 'em real loud," said Hazel. "I think I'd make a good Handicapper General."

"Good as anybody else," said George.

"Who knows better'n I do what normal is?" said Hazel.

"Right," said George. He began to think glimmeringly about his abnormal son who was now in jail, about Harrison, but a twenty-one-gun salute in his head stopped that.

"Boy!" said Hazel, "that was a doozy, wasn't it?"

It was such a doozy that George was white and trembling, and tears stood on the rims of his red eyes. Two of the eight ballerinas had collapsed to the studio floor, were holding their temples.

"All of a sudden you look so tired," said Hazel. "Why don't you stretch out on the sofa, so's you can rest your handicap bag on the pillows, honeybunch." She was referring to the forty-seven pounds of birdshot in a canvas bag, which was padlocked around George's neck. "Go on and rest the bag for a little while," she said. "I don't care if you're not equal to me for a while."

George weighed the bag with his hands. "I don't mind it," he said. "I don't notice it any more. It's just a part of me."

"You been so tired lately—kind of wore out," said Hazel. "If there was just some way we could make a little hole in the bottom of the bag, and just take out a few of them lead balls. Just a few."

"Two years in prison and two thousand dollars fine for every ball I took out," said George. "I don't call that a bargain."

"If you could just take a few out when you came home from work," said Hazel. "I mean—you don't compete with anybody around here. You just set around."

"If I tried to get away with it," said George, "then other people'd get away with it—and pretty soon we'd be right back to the dark ages again, with everybody competing against everybody else. You wouldn't like that, would you?"

"I'd hate it," said Hazel.

"There you are," said George. "The minute people start cheating on laws, what do you think happens to society?"

If Hazel hadn't been able to come up with an answer to this question George couldn't have supplied one. A siren was going off in his head.

"Reckon it'd fall all apart," said Hazel.

"What would?" said George blankly.

"Society," said Hazel uncertainly. "Wasn't that what you just said?"

"Who knows?" said George.

The television program was suddenly interrupted for a news bulletin. It wasn't clear at first as to what the bulletin was about, since the announcer, like all announcers, had a serious speech impediment. For about half a minute, and in a state of high excitement, the announcer tried to say, "Ladies and gentlemen—"

He finally gave up, handed the bulletin to a ballerina to read.

"That's all right—" Hazel said of the announcer, "he tried. That's the big thing. He tried to do the best he could with what God gave him. He should get a nice raise for trying so hard."

"Ladies and gentlemen—" said the ballerina, reading the bulletin. She must have been extraordinarily beautiful, because the mask she wore was hideous. And it was easy to see that she was the strongest and most graceful of all the dancers, for her handicap bags were as big as those worn by two-hundred-pound men.

And she had to apologize at once for her voice, which was a very unfair voice for a woman to use. Her voice was a warm, luminous, timeless melody. "Excuse me—" she said, and she began again, making her voice absolutely uncompetitive.

"Harrison Bergeron, age fourteen," she said in a grackle squawk, "has just escaped from jail, where he was held on suspicion of plotting to overthrow the government. He is a genius and an athlete, is under-handicapped, and should be regarded as extremely dangerous."

A police photograph of Harrison Bergeron was flashed on the screen upside down, then sideways, upside down again, then right side up. The picture showed the full length of Harrison against a background calibrated in feet and inches. He was exactly seven feet tall.

The rest of Harrison's appearance was Halloween and hardware. Nobody had ever borne heavier handicaps. He had outgrown hindrances faster than the H-G men could think them up. Instead of a little ear radio for a mental handicap, he wore a tremendous pair of earphones, and spectacles with thick wavy lenses. The spectacles were intended to make him not only half blind, but to give him whanging headaches besides.

Scrap metal was hung all over him. Ordinarily, there was a certain symmetry, a military neatness to the handicaps issued to strong people, but Harrison looked like a walking junkyard. In the race of life, Harrison carried three hundred pounds.

And to offset his good looks, the H-G men required that he wear at all times a red rubber ball for a nose, keep his eyebrows shaved off, and cover his even white teeth with black caps at snaggle-tooth random.

"If you see this boy," said the ballerina, "do not—I repeat, do not—try to reason with him."

There was the shriek of a door being torn from its hinges.

Screams and barking cries of consternation came from the television set. The photograph of Harrison Bergeron on the screen jumped again and again, as though dancing to the tune of an earthquake.

George Bergeron correctly identified the earthquake, and well he might have—for many was the time his own home had danced to the same crashing tune. "My God—" said George, "that must be Harrison!"

The realization was blasted from his mind instantly by the sound of an automobile collision in his head.

When George could open his eyes again, the photograph of Harrison was gone. A living, breathing Harrison filled the screen.

Clanking, clownish, and huge, Harrison stood in the center of the studio. The knob of the uprooted studio door was still in his hand. Ballerinas, technicians, musicians, and announcers cowered on their knees before him, expecting to die.

"I am the Emperor!" cried Harrison. "Do you hear? I am the Emperor! Everybody must do what I say at once!" He stamped his foot and the studio shook.

"Even as I stand here—" he bellowed, "crippled, hobbled, sickened—I am a greater ruler than any man who ever lived! Now watch me become what I *can* become!"

Harrison tore the straps of his handicap harness like wet tissue paper, tore straps guaranteed to support five thousand pounds.

Harrison's scrap-iron handicaps crashed to the floor.

Harrison thrust his thumbs under the bar of the padlock that secured his head harness. The bar snapped like celery. Harrison smashed his headphones and spectacles against the wall.

He flung away his rubber-ball nose, revealed a man that would have awed Thor, the god of thunder.

"I shall now select my Empress!" he said, looking down on the cowering people. "Let the first woman who dares rise to her feet claim her mate and her throne!"

A moment passed, and then a ballerina arose, swaying like a willow.

Harrison plucked the mental handicap from her ear, snapped off her physical handicaps with marvelous delicacy. Last of all, he removed her mask.

She was blindingly beautiful.

"Now—" said Harrison, taking her hand, "shall we show the people the meaning of the word dance? Music!" he commanded.

The musicians scrambled back into their chairs, and Harrison stripped them of their handicaps, too. "Play your best," he told them, "and I'll make you barons and dukes and earls."

The music began. It was normal at first—cheap, silly, false. But Harrison snatched two musicians from their chairs, waved them like batons as he sang the music as he wanted it played. He slammed them back into their chairs.

The music began again and was much improved.

Harrison and his Empress merely listened to the music for a while— listened gravely, as though synchronizing their heartbeats with it.

They shifted their weights to their toes.

Harrison placed his big hands on the girl's tiny waist, letting her sense the weightlessness that would soon be hers.

And then, in an explosion of joy and grace, into the air they sprang!

Not only were the laws of the land abandoned, but the law of gravity and the laws of motion as well.

They reeled, whirled, swiveled, flounced, capered, gamboled, and spun. They leaped like deer on the moon.

The studio ceiling was thirty feet high, but each leap brought the dancers nearer to it.

It became their obvious intention to kiss the ceiling.

They kissed it.

And then, neutralizing gravity with love and pure will, they remained suspended in air inches below the ceiling, and they kissed each other for a long, long time.

It was then that Diana Moon Glampers, the Handicapper General, came into the studio with a double-barreled ten-gauge shotgun. She fired twice, and the Emperor and the Empress were dead before they hit the floor.

Diana Moon Glampers loaded the gun again. She aimed it at the musicians and told them they had ten seconds to get their handicaps back on.

It was then that the Bergerons' television tube burned out.

Hazel turned to comment about the blackout to George. But George had gone out into the kitchen for a can of beer.

George came back in with the beer, paused while a handicap signal shook him up. And then he sat down again. "You been crying?" he said to Hazel.

"Yup," she said.

"What about?" he said.

"I forget," she said. "Something real sad on television."

"What was it?" he said.

"It's all kind of mixed up in my mind," said Hazel.

"Forget sad things," said George.

"I always do," said Hazel.

"That's my girl," said George. He winced. There was the sound of a riveting gun in his head.

"Gee—I could tell that one was a doozy," said Hazel.

"You can say that again," said George.

"Gee—" said Hazel, "I could tell that one was a doozy."

STUDY QUESTIONS

1. Describe the setting. When does the action take place? Where? What is the social and cultural environment? To what extent is the society described realistic?

2. Throughout the story people with any superior qualities wear handicaps to keep them from exercising those qualities. What may the various handicaps symbolize?

3. Harrison has an obvious external conflict with the laws and their enforcers. To what extent does he reveal internal conflict? Do any of the characters in the story reveal internal conflicts? Support your answers

with direct quotations or specific references. How is conflict (or the lack of it) related to irony?

4. Comment on the irony of the final conversation between George and Hazel. What kind of irony is illustrated?

5. In the society depicted in Vonnegut's story, what does *equality* mean? What meaning of equality is implied by the statement in the Declaration of Independence that "all men are created equal"?

6. Through the use of symbol and irony, what general statement does Vonnegut seem to be making about society? About individuals? To what extent is that statement important to people of the 1980s?

Sherwood Anderson (1876–1941)

THE EGG

My father was, I am sure, intended by nature to be a cheerful, kindly man. Until he was thirty-four years old he worked as a farmhand for a man named Thomas Butterworth whose place lay near the town of Bidwell, Ohio. He had then a horse of his own, and on Saturday evenings drove into town to spend a few hours in social intercourse with other farmhands. In town he drank several glasses of beer and stood about in Ben Head's saloon— crowded on Saturday evenings with visiting farmhands. Songs were sung and glasses thumped on the bar. At ten o'clock father drove home along a lonely country road, made his horse comfortable for the night, and himself went to bed, quite happy in his position in life. He had at that time no notion of trying to rise in the world.

It was in the spring of his thirty-fifth year that father married my mother, then a country school-teacher, and in the following spring I came wriggling and crying into the world. Something happened to the two people. They became ambitious. The American passion for getting up in the world took possession of them.

It may have been that mother was responsible. Being a schoolteacher she had no doubt read books and magazines. She had, I presume, read of how Garfield, Lincoln, and other Americans rose from poverty to fame and greatness, and as I lay beside her—in the days of her lying-in—she may have dreamed that I would some day rule men and cities. At any rate she induced father to give up his place as a farmhand, sell his horse, and embark on an independent enterprise of his own. She was a tall silent woman with a long nose and troubled gray eyes. For herself she wanted nothing. For father and myself she was incurably ambitious.

The first venture into which the two people went turned out badly. They rented ten acres of poor stony land on Grigg's Road, eight miles from Bidwell, and launched into chicken-raising. I grew into boyhood on the place and got my first impressions of life there. From the beginning they were impressions of disaster, and if, in my turn, I am a gloomy man inclined to see the darker side of life, I attribute it to the fact that what should have been for me the happy joyous days of childhood were spent on a chicken farm.

One unversed in such matters can have no notion of the many and tragic things that can happen to a chicken. It is born out of an egg, lives for a few weeks as a tiny fluffy thing such as you will see pictured on Easter cards, then becomes hideously naked, eats quantities of corn and meal bought by the sweat of your father's brow, gets diseases called pip, cholera, and other names, stands looking with stupid eyes at the sun, becomes sick and dies. A few hens and now and then a rooster, intended to serve God's mysterious ends, struggle through to maturity. The hens lay eggs out of which come other chickens and the dreadful cycle is thus made complete. It is all unbelievably complex. Most philosophers must have been raised on chicken farms. One hopes for so much from a chicken and is so dreadfully disillusioned. Small chickens, just setting out on the journey of life, look so bright and alert and they are in fact so dreadfully stupid. They are so much like people they mix one up in one's judgments of life. If disease does not kill them, they wait until your expectations are thoroughly aroused and then walk under the wheels of a wagon—to go squashed and dead back to their maker. Vermin infest their youth, and fortunes must be spent for curative powders. In later life I have seen how a literature has been built up on the subject of fortunes to be made out of the raising of chickens. It is intended to be read by the gods who have just eaten of the tree of the knowledge of good and evil. It is a hopeful literature and declares that much may be done by simple ambitious people who own a few hens. Do not be led astray by it. It was not written for you. Go hunt for gold on the frozen hills of Alaska, put your faith in the honesty of a politician, believe if you will that the world is daily growing better and that good will triumph over evil, but do not read and believe the literature that is written concerning the hen. It was not written for you.

I, however, digress. My tale does not primarily concern itself with the hen. If correctly told it will center on the egg. For ten years my father and mother struggled to make our chicken farm pay and then they gave up that struggle and began another. They moved into the town of Bidwell, Ohio, and embarked in the restaurant business. After ten years of worry with incubators that did not hatch, and with tiny—and in their own way lovely—balls of fluff that passed on into semi-naked pullethood and from that into dead henhood, we threw all aside and, packing our belongings on a wagon, drove down Grigg's Road toward Bidwell, a tiny caravan of hope looking for a new place from which to start on our upward journey through life.

We must have been a sad-looking lot, not, I fancy, unlike refugees fleeing from a battlefield. Mother and I walked in the road. The wagon that contained our goods had been borrowed for the day from Mr. Albert Griggs, a neighbor. Out of its sides stuck the legs of cheap chairs, and at the back of the pile of beds, tables, and boxes filled with kitchen utensils was a crate of live chickens, and on top of that the baby carriage in which I had been wheeled about in my infancy. Why we stuck to the baby carriage I don't know. It was unlikely other children would be born and the wheels were broken. People who have few possessions cling tightly to those they have. That is one of the facts that make life so discouraging.

Father rode on top of the wagon. He was then a bald-headed man of forty-five, a little fat, and from long association with mother and the chickens he had become habitually silent and discouraged. All during our ten years on the chicken farm he had worked as a laborer on neighboring farms and most of the money he had earned had been spent for remedies to cure chicken diseases, on Wilmer's White Wonder Cholera Cure or Professor Bidlow's Egg Producer or some other preparations that mother found advertised in the poultry papers. There were two little patches of hair on father's head just above his ear. I remember that as a child I used to sit looking at him when he had gone to sleep in a chair before the stove on Sunday afternoons in the winter. I had at that time already begun to read books and have notions of my own, and the bald path that led over the top of his head was, I fancied, something like a broad road, such a road as Caesar might have made on which to lead his legions out of Rome and into the wonders of an unknown world. The tufts of hair that grew above father's ears were, I thought, like forests. I fell into a half-sleeping, half-waking state and dreamed I was a tiny thing going along the road into a far beautiful place where there were no chicken farms and where life was a happy eggless affair.

One might write a book concerning our flight from the chicken farm into town. Mother and I walked the entire eight miles—she to be sure that nothing fell from the wagon and I to see the wonders of the world. On the seat of the wagon beside father was his greatest treasure. I will tell you of that.

On a chicken farm, where hundreds and even thousands of chickens come out of eggs, surprising things sometimes happen. Grotesques are born out of eggs as out of people. The accident does not often occur—perhaps once in a thousand births. A chicken is, you see, born that has four legs, two pairs of wings, two heads, or what not. The things do not live. They go quickly back to the hand of their maker that has for a moment trembled. The fact that the poor little things could not live was one of the tragedies of life to father. He had some sort of notion that if he could but bring into henhood or roosterhood a five-legged hen or a two-headed rooster his fortune would be made. He dreamed of taking the wonder about the county fairs and of growing rich by exhibiting it to other farmhands.

At any rate, he saved all the little monstrous things that had been born on our chicken farm. They were preserved in alcohol and put each in its own glass bottle. These he had carefully put into a box, and on our journey into town it was carried on the wagon seat beside him. He drove the horses with one hand and with the other clung to the box. When we got to our destination, the box was taken down at once and the bottles removed. All during our days as keepers of a restaurant in the town of Bidwell, Ohio, the grotesques in their little glass bottles sat on a shelf back of the counter. Mother sometimes protested, but father was a rock on the subject of his treasure. The grotesques were, he declared, valuable. People, he said, liked to look at strange and wonderful things.

Did I say that we embarked in the restaurant business in the town of Bidwell, Ohio? I exaggerated a little. The town itself lay at the foot of a low hill and on the shore of a small river. The railroad did not run through the town and the station was a mile away to the north at a place called Pickleville. There had been a cider mill and pickle factory at the station, but before the time of our coming they had both gone out of business. In the morning and in the evening busses came down to the station along a road called Turner's Pike from the hotel on the main street of Bidwell. Our going to the out-of-the-way place to embark in the restaurant business was mother's idea. She talked of it for a year and then one day went off and rented an empty store building opposite the railroad station. It was her idea that the restaurant would be profitable. Traveling men, she said, would be always waiting around to take trains out of town and town people would come to the station to await incoming trains. They would come to the restaurant to buy pieces of pie and drink coffee. Now that I am older I know that she had another motive in going. She was ambitious for me. She wanted me to rise in the world, to get into a town school and become a man of the towns.

At Pickleville father and mother worked hard, as they always had done. At first there was the necessity of putting our place into shape to be a restaurant. That took a month. Father built a shelf on which he put tins of vegetables. He painted a sign on which he put his name in large red letters. Below his name was the sharp command—"EAT HERE"—that was so seldom obeyed. A showcase was bought and filled with cigars and tobacco. Mother scrubbed the floor and the walls of the room. I went to school in the town and was glad to be away from the farm and from the presence of the discouraged, sad-looking chickens. Still I was not very joyous. In the evening I walked home from school along Turner's Pike and remembered the children I had seen playing in the town school yard. A troop of little girls had gone hopping about and singing. I tried that. Down along the frozen road I went hopping solemnly on one leg. "Hippity Hop To The Barber Shop," I sang shrilly. Then I stopped and looked doubtfully about. I was afraid of being seen in my gay mood. It must have seemed to me that I was doing a thing that should not be done by one who, like myself, had been raised on a chicken farm where death was a daily visitor.

Mother decided that our restaurant should remain open at night. At ten in the evening a passenger train went north past our door followed by a local freight. The freight crew had switching to do in Pickleville, and when the work was done they came to our restaurant for hot coffee and food. Sometimes one of them ordered a fried egg. In the morning at four they returned north-bound and again visited us. A little trade began to grow up. Mother slept at night and during the day tended the restaurant and fed our boarders while father slept. He slept in the same bed mother had occupied during the night and I went off to the town of Bidwell and to school. During the long nights, while mother and I slept, father cooked meats that were to go into sandwiches for the lunch baskets of our boarders. Then an idea in regard to getting up in the world came into his head. The American spirit took hold of him. He also became ambitious.

In the long nights when there was little to do, father had time to think. That was his undoing. He decided that he had in the past been an unsuccessful man because he had not been cheerful enough and that in the future he would adopt a cheerful outlook on life. In the early morning he came upstairs and got into bed with mother. She woke and the two talked. From my bed in the corner I listened.

It was father's idea that both he and mother should try to entertain the people who came to eat at our restaurant. I cannot now remember his words, but he gave the impression of one about to become in some obscure way a kind of public entertainer. When people, particularly young people from the town of Bidwell, came into our place, as on very rare occasions they did, bright entertaining conversation was to be made. From father's words I gathered that something of the jolly innkeeper effect was to be sought. Mother must have been doubtful from the first, but she said nothing discouraging. It was father's notion that a passion for the company of himself and mother would spring up in the breasts of the younger people of the town of Bidwell. In the evening bright happy groups would come singing down Turner's Pike. They would troop shouting with joy and laughter into our place. There would be song and festivity. I do not mean to give the impression that father spoke so elaborately of the matter. He was, as I have said, an uncommunicative man. "They want some place to go. I tell you they want some place to go," he said over and over. That was as far as he got. My own imagination has filled in the blanks.

For two or three weeks this notion of father's invaded our house. We did not talk much, but in our daily lives tried earnestly to make smiles take the place of glum looks. Mother smiled at the boarders and I, catching the infection, smiled at our cat. Father became a little feverish in his anxiety to please. There was, no doubt, lurking somewhere in him, a touch of the spirit of the showman. He did not waste much of his ammunition on the railroad men he served at night, but seemed to be waiting for a young man or woman from Bidwell to come in to show what he could do. On the counter in the restaurant there was a wire basket kept always filled with eggs, and it must have been before his eyes when the idea of being entertaining was born in his brain. There was something pre-natal about the way eggs kept themselves connected with the development of his idea. At any rate, an egg ruined his new impulse in life. Late one night I was awakened by a roar of anger coming from father's throat. Both mother and I sat upright in our beds. With trembling hands she lighted a lamp that stood on a table by her head. Downstairs the front door of our restaurant went shut with a bang and in a few minutes father tramped up the stairs. He held an egg in his hand and his hand trembled as though he were having a chill. There was a half-insane light in his eyes. As he stood glaring at us I was sure he intended throwing the egg at either mother or me. Then he laid it gently on the table beside the lamp and dropped on his knees beside mother's bed. He began to cry like a boy, and I, carried away by his grief, cried with him. The two of us filled the little upstairs room with our wailing voices. It is ridiculous, but of the picture we made I can remember only the fact that mother's hand continually stroked the bald path that ran across the top of his head. I have forgotten what mother said to him and how she induced him to tell her of what had happened downstairs. His explanation also has gone out of my mind. I remember only my own grief and fright and the shiny path over father's head glowing in the lamplight as he knelt by the bed.

As to what happened downstairs. For some unexplainable reason I know the story as well as though I had been a witness to my father's discomfiture. One in time gets to know many unexplainable things. On that evening young Joe Kane, son of a merchant of Bidwell, came to Pickleville to meet his father, who was expected on the ten-o'clock evening train from the South. The train was three hours late and Joe came into our place to loaf about and to wait for its arrival. The local freight train came in and the freight crew were fed. Joe was left alone in the restaurant with father.

From the moment he came into our place the Bidwell young man must have been puzzled by my father's actions. It was his notion that father was angry at him for hanging around. He noticed that the restaurant-keeper was apparently disturbed by his presence and he thought of going out. However, it began to rain and he did not fancy the long walk to town and back. He bought a five-cent cigar and ordered a cup of coffee. He had a newspaper in his pocket and took it out and began to read. "I'm waiting for the evening train. It's late," he said apologetically.

For a long time father, whom Joe Kane had never seen before, remained silently gazing at his visitor. He was no doubt suffering from an attack of stage fright. As so often happens in life he had thought so much and so often of the situation that now confronted him that he was somewhat nervous in its presence.

For one thing, he did not know what to do with his hands. He thrust one of them nervously over the counter and shook hands with Joe Kane. "How-de-do," he said. Joe Kane put his newspaper down and stared at him. Father's eyes lighted on the basket of eggs that sat on the counter and he began to talk. "Well," he began hesitatingly, "well, you have heard of Christopher Columbus, eh?" He seemed to be angry. "That Christopher Columbus was a cheat," he declared emphatically. "He talked of making an egg stand on its end. He talked, he did, and then he went and broke the end of the egg."

My father seemed to his visitor to be beside himself at the duplicity of Christopher Columbus. He muttered and swore. He declared it was wrong to teach children that Christopher Columbus was a great man when, after all, he cheated at the critical moment. He had declared he would make an egg stand on end and then, when his bluff had been called, he had done a trick. Still grumbling at Columbus, father took an egg from the basket on the counter and began to walk up and down. He rolled the egg between the palms of his hands. He smiled genially. He began to mumble words regarding the effect to be produced on an egg by the electricity that comes out of the human body. He declared that, without breaking its shell and by virtue of rolling it back and forth in his hands, he could stand the egg on its end. He explained that the warmth of his hands and the gentle rolling movement he gave the egg created a new center of gravity, and Joe Kane was mildly interested. "I have handled thousands of eggs," father said. "No one knows more about eggs than I do."

He stood the egg on the counter and it fell on its side. He tried the trick again and again, each time rolling the egg between the palms of his hands and saying the words regarding the wonders of electricity and the laws of gravity. When after a half-hour's effort he did succeed in making the egg stand for a moment, he looked up to find that his visitor was no longer watching. By the time he had succeeded in calling Joe Kane's attention to the success of his effort, the egg had again rolled over and lay on its side.

Afire with the showman's passion and at the same time a good deal disconcerted by the failure of his first effort, father now took the bottles containing the poultry monstrosities down from their place on the shelf and began to show them to his visitor. "How would you like to have seven legs and two heads like this fellow?" he asked, exhibiting the most remarkable of his treasures. A cheerful smile played over his face. He reached over the counter and tried to slap Joe Kane on the shoulder as he had seen men do in Ben Head's saloon when he was a young farmhand and drove to town on Saturday evenings. His visitor was made a little ill by the sight of the body of the terribly deformed bird floating in the alcohol in the bottle and got up to go. Coming from behind the counter, father took hold of the young man's arm and led him back to his seat. He grew a little angry and for a moment had to turn his face away and force himself to smile. Then he put the bottles back on the shelf. In an outburst of generosity he fairly compelled Joe Kane to have a fresh cup of coffee and another cigar at his expense. Then he took a pan and filling it with vinegar, taken from a jug that sat beneath the counter, he declared himself about to do a new trick. "I will heat this egg in this pan of vinegar," he said. "Then I will put it through the neck of a bottle without breaking the shell. When the egg is inside the bottle it will resume its normal shape and the shell will become hard again. Then I will give the bottle with the egg in it to you. You can take it about with you wherever you go. People will want to know how you got the egg in the bottle. Don't tell them. Keep them guessing. That is the way to have fun with this trick."

Father grinned and winked at his visitor. Joe Kane decided that the man who confronted him was mildly insane but harmless. He drank the cup of coffee that had been given him and began to read his paper again. When the egg had been heated in vinegar, father carried it on a spoon to the counter and going into a back room got an empty bottle. He was angry because his visitor did not watch him as he began to do his trick, but nevertheless went cheerfully to work. For a long time he struggled, trying to get the egg to go through the neck of the bottle. He put the pan of vinegar back on the stove, intending to reheat the egg, then picked it up and burned his fingers. After a second bath in the hot vinegar, the shell of the egg had been softened a little, but not enough for his purpose. He worked and worked and a spirit of desperate determination took possession of him. When he thought that at last the trick was about to be consummated, the delayed train came in at the station and Joe Kane started to go nonchalantly out at the door. Father made a last desperate effort to conquer the egg and make it do the thing that would establish his reputation as one who knew how to entertain guests who came into his restaurant. He worried the egg. He attempted to be somewhat rough with it. He swore and the sweat stood out on his forehead. The egg broke under his hand. When the contents spurted over his clothes, Joe Kane, who had stopped at the door, turned and laughed.

A roar of anger rose from my father's throat. He danced and shouted a string of inarticulate words. Grabbing another egg from the basket on the counter, he threw it, just missing the head of the young man as he dodged through the door and escaped.

Father came upstairs to mother and me with an egg in his hand. I do not know what he intended to do. I imagine he had some idea of destroying it, of destroying all eggs, and that he intended to let mother and me see him begin. When, however, he got into the presence of mother, something happened to him. He laid the egg gently on the table and dropped on his knees by the bed as I have already explained. He later decided to close the restaurant for the night and to come upstairs and get into bed. When he did so, he blew out the light and after much muttered conversation both he and mother went to sleep. I suppose I went to sleep also, but my sleep was troubled. I awoke at dawn and for a long time looked at the egg that lay on the table. I wondered why eggs had to be and why from the egg came the hen who again laid the egg. The question got into my blood. It has stayed there, I imagine, because I am the son of my father. At any rate, the problem remains unsolved in my mind. And that, I conclude, is but another evidence of the complete and final triumph of the egg—at least as far as my family is concerned.

STUDY QUESTIONS

1. Describe the structure of the story. What factors in the narrative contribute to unity or lack of it?
2. What figures of speech are used to describe the narrator's father's head? What significance might they have?
3. How does Anderson portray chickens? Does his description suggest symbolic values?
4. Does the title of the story suggest its real subject? Why or why not?
5. How does the reference to Columbus reflect the story's meaning?
6. In what way do the following relate to the theme of success/failure: the farm, the "treasure," the upended egg, and the egg in the bottle.
7. Find examples of irony. How do these examples affect the story's tone and meaning?
8. "In this tale, Anderson shows how the American Dream can become the American Nightmare." Comment.

Katherine Mansfield (1888–1923)

THE FLY

"Y'are very snug in here," piped old Mr. Woodifield, and he peered out of the great, green leather armchair by his friend the boss's desk as a baby peers out of its pram. His talk was over; it was time for him to be off. But he did not want to go. Since he had retired, since his . . . stroke, the wife and the girls kept him boxed up in the house every day of the week except Tuesday. On Tuesday he was dressed up and brushed and allowed to cut back to the City for the day. Though what he did there the wife and girls couldn't imagine. Made a nuisance of himself to his friends, they supposed. . . . Well, perhaps so. All the same, we cling to our last pleasures as the tree clings to its last leaves. So there sat old Woodifield, smoking a cigar and staring almost greedily at the boss, who rolled in his office chair, stout, rosy, five years older than he, and still going strong, still at the helm. It did one good to see him.

Wistfully, admiringly, the old voice added, "It's snug in here, upon my word!"

"Yes, it's comfortable enough," agreed the boss, and he flipped the *Financial Times* with a paper-knife. As a matter of fact he was proud of his room; he liked to have it admired, especially by old Woodifield. It gave him a feeling of deep, solid satisfaction to be planted there in the midst of it in full view of that frail old figure in the muffler.

"I've had it done up lately," he explained, as he had explained for the past—how many?—weeks. "New carpet," and he pointed to the bright red carpet with a pattern of large white rings. "New furniture," and he nodded towards the massive bookcase and the table with legs like twisted treacle. "Electric heating!" He waved almost exultantly towards the five transparent, pearly sausages glowing so softly in the tilted copper pan.

But he did not draw old Woodifield's attention to the photograph over the table of a grave-looking boy in uniform standing in one of those spectral photographers' parks with photographers' storm-clouds behind him. It was not new. It had been there for over six years.

"There was something I wanted to tell you," said old Woodifield, and his eyes grew dim remembering. "Now what was it? I had it in my mind when I started out this morning." His hands began to tremble, and patches of red showed above his beard.

Poor old chap, he's on his last pins, thought the boss. And, feeling kindly, he winked at the old man, and said jokingly, "I tell you what. I've got a little drop of something here that'll do you good before you go out into the cold again. It's beautiful stuff. It wouldn't hurt a child." He took a key off his watch-chain, unlocked a cupboard below his desk, and drew forth a dark, squat bottle. "That's the medicine," said he. "And the man from whom I got it told me on the strict Q. T. it came from the cellars at Windsor Castle."

Old Woodifield's mouth fell open at the sight. He couldn't have looked more surprised if the boss had produced a rabbit.

"It's whisky, ain't it?" he piped, feebly.

The boss turned the bottle and lovingly showed him the label. Whisky it was.

"D'you know," said he, peering up at the boss wonderingly, "they won't let me touch it at home." And he looked as though he was going to cry.

"Ah, that's where we know a bit more than the ladies," cried the boss, swooping across for two tumblers that stood on the table with the water-bottle, and pouring a generous finger into each. "Drink it down. It'll do you good. And don't put any water with it. It's sacrilege to tamper with stuff like this. Ah!" He tossed off his, pulled out his handkerchief, hastily wiped his moustaches, and cocked an eye at old Woodifield, who was rolling his in his chaps.

The old man swallowed, was silent a moment, and then said faintly, "It's nutty!"

But it warmed him; it crept into his chill old brain—he remembered.

"That was it," he said, heaving himself out of his chair. "I thought you'd like to know. The girls were in Belgium last week having a look at poor Reggie's grave, and they happened to come across your boy's. They're quite near each other, it seems."

Old Woodifield paused, but the boss made no reply. Only a quiver in his eyelids showed that he heard.

"The girls were delighted with the way the place is kept," piped the old voice. "Beautifully looked after. Couldn't be better if they were at home. You've not been across, have yer?"

"No, no!" For various reasons the boss had not been across.

"There's miles of it," quavered old Woodifield, "and it's all as neat as a garden. Flowers growing on all the graves. Nice broad paths." It was plain from his voice how much he liked a nice broad path.

The pause came again. Then the old man brightened wonderfully.

"D'you know what the hotel made the girls pay for a pot of jam?" he piped. "Ten francs! Robbery, I call it. It was a little pot, so Gertrude says, no bigger than a half-crown. And she hadn't taken more than a spoonful when they charged her ten francs. Gertrude brought the pot away with her to teach 'em a lesson. Quite right, too; it's trading on our feelings. They think because we're over there having a look around we're ready to pay anything. That's what it is." And he turned towards the door.

"Quite right, quite right!" cried the boss, though what was quite right he hadn't the least idea. He came round by his desk, followed the shuffling footsteps to the door, and saw the old fellow out. Woodifield was gone.

For a long moment the boss stayed, staring at nothing, while the grey-haired office messenger, watching him, dodged in and out of his cubby-hole like a dog that expects to be taken for a run. Then: "I'll see nobody for half an hour, Macey," said the boss. "Understand? Nobody at all."

"Very good, sir."

The door shut, the firm heavy steps recrossed the bright carpet, the fat body plumped down in the spring chair, and leaning forward, the boss covered his face with his hands. He wanted, he intended, he had arranged to weep. . . .

It had been a terrible shock to him when old Woodifield sprang that remark upon him about the boy's grave. It was exactly as though the earth had opened and he had seen the boy lying there with Woodifield's girls staring down at him. For it was strange. Although over six years had passed away, the boss never thought of the boy except as lying unchanged, unblemished in his uniform, asleep for ever. "My son!" groaned the boss. But no tears came yet. In the past, in the first months and even years after the boy's death, he had only to say those words to be overcome by such grief that nothing short of a violent fit of weeping could relieve him. Time, he had declared then, he had told everybody, could make no difference. Other men perhaps might recover, might live their loss down, but not he. How was it possible? His boy was an only son. Ever since his birth the boss had worked at building up this business for him; it had no other meaning if it was not for the boy. Life itself had come to have no other meaning. How on earth could he have slaved, denied himself, kept going all those years without the promise for ever before him of the boy's stepping into his shoes and carrying on where he left off?

And that promise had been so near being fulfilled. The boy had been in the office learning the ropes for a year before the war. Every morning they had started off together; they had come back by the same train. And what congratulations he had received as the boy's father! No wonder; he had taken to it marvellously. As to his popularity with the staff, every man jack of them down to old Macey couldn't make enough of the boy. And he wasn't in the least spoilt. No, he was just his bright, natural self, with the right word for everybody, with that boyish look and his habit of saying, "Simply splendid!"

But all that was over and done with as though it never had been. The day had come when Macey had handed him the telegram that brought the whole place crashing about his head. "Deeply regret to inform you . . ." And he had left the office a broken man, with his life in ruins.

Six years ago, six years . . . How quickly time passed! It might have happened yesterday. The boss took his hands from his face; he was puzzled. Something seemed to be wrong with him. He wasn't feeling as he wanted to feel. He decided to get up and have a look at the boy's photograph. But it wasn't a favorite photograph of his; the expression was unnatural. It was cold, even stern-looking. The boy had never looked like that.

At that moment the boss noticed that a fly had fallen into his broad inkpot, and was trying feebly but desperately to clamber out again. Help! help! said those struggling legs. But the sides of the inkpot were wet and slippery; it fell back again and began to swim. The boss took up a pen, picked the fly out of the ink, and shook it on to a piece of blotting-paper. For a fraction of a second it lay still on the dark patch that oozed round it. Then the front legs waved, took hold, and, pulling its small sodden body up, it began the immense task of cleaning the ink from its wings. Over and under, over and under, went a leg along a wing, as the stone goes over and under the scythe. Then there was a pause, while the fly, seeming to stand on the tips of its toes, tried to expand first one wing and then the other. It succeeded at last, and, sitting down, it began, like a minute cat, to clean its face. Now one could imagine that the little front legs rubbed against each other lightly, joyfully. The horrible danger was over; it had escaped; it was ready for life again.

But just then the boss had an idea. He plunged his pen back into the ink, leaned his thick wrist on the blotting-paper, and as the fly tried its wings down came a great heavy blot. What would it make of that? What indeed!

The little beggar seemed absolutely cowed, stunned, and afraid to move because of what would happen next. But then, as if painfully, it dragged itself forward. The front legs waved, caught hold, and, more slowly this time, the task began from the beginning.

He's a plucky little devil, thought the boss, and he felt a real admiration for the fly's courage. That was the way to tackle things; that was the right spirit. Never say die; it was only a question of . . . But the fly had again finished its laborious task, and the boss had just time to refill his pen, to shake fair and square on the new-cleaned body yet another dark drop. What about it this time? A painful moment of suspense followed. But behold, the front legs were again waving; the boss felt a rush of relief. He leaned over the fly and said to it tenderly, "You artful little b . . ." And he actually had the brilliant notion of breathing on it to help the drying process. All the same, there was something timid and weak about its efforts now, and the boss decided that this time should be the last, as he dipped the pen into the inkpot.

It was. The last blot on the soaked blotting-paper, and the draggled fly lay in it and did not stir. The back legs were stuck to the body; the front legs were not to be seen.

"Come on," said the boss. "Look sharp!" And he stirred it with his pen— in vain. Nothing happened or was likely to happen. The fly was dead.

The boss lifted the corpse on the end of the paper-knife and flung it into the waste-paper basket. But such a grinding feeling of wretchedness seized him that he felt positively frightened. He started forward and pressed the bell for Macey.

"Bring me some fresh blotting-paper," he said, sternly, "and look sharp about it." And while the old dog padded away he fell to wondering what it was he had been thinking about before. What was it? It was . . . He took out his handkerchief and passed it inside his collar. For the life of him he could not remember.

STUDY QUESTIONS

1. What are the literal events of the story? How does the incident of the fly relate to its narrative framework?
2. What kind of statement is "That's the medicine"? Why?
3. What does Mansfield achieve by repeating the word *photographers* in paragraph 5?
4. Language is used with explosive conciseness in the line "But it warmed him; it crept into his chill old brain—he remembered." Discuss, particularly the use of "remembered."
5. Does Mansfield use consistent imagery to characterize Max? If so, what is it?
6. What is the symbolism of the fly? Why can't the boss remember what he was thinking of after the fly dies?

7. Does the theme of this story deal with a sense of cosmic irony? Discuss.
8. What significant connections can you discover between this story and Blake's poem "The Fly" (p. 743)? Between this story and Gloucester's lines in *King Lear:*

> As flies to wanton boys, are we to th' gods,
> They kill us for their sport.
>
> [IV, i, 38–39]

Anton Chekhov (1860–1904)

THE DARLING

Olinka, daughter of a retired government-official, sat pensively on the porch facing the court-yard of her house. It was hot; the flies were an insistent nuisance, and she thought with pleasure of the approaching evening. Dark rain-clouds loomed up in the west, and a moist breeze blew, now and then.

In the middle of the yard stood Kukin, manager and owner of the Tivoli Pleasure-Garden, who lived as lodger in a wing of the house, and gazed at the sky.

"Rain again!" he exclaimed with vexation and disappointment in his tone; "day in and day out, nothing but rain, as if out of spite; it's enough to drive one to despair; it simply means ruin for me. Every day greater losses." He clapped his hands together in despair, and continued, turning to Olinka: "That's a life for you! ... You see, Olga Semyonovna, that's our miserable life ... it's enough to make one cry. A man gives up all his energy, labour, effort—suffers want, worries night and day trying to improve matters,—with what result? On the one hand, the public, stupid, barbarian; I give them the best operettas, féeries[1]—the most accomplished singers—as though they appreciate, or understand, anything.—What they really want is a cheap circus—trash. ... On the other hand there's the cursed weather. Rain almost every evening. ... from the first days of May through the whole month of June—it's awful—. The people stay away.—But I have to pay for my lease just the same—and the artists—

On the morrow, toward evening, again clouds began to lower, and Kukin's bitter complaints were interspersed with almost hysterical laughter.

"Good, good! let it rain! Let the whole Tivoli be drowned in a flood! myself, included!—me and my cursed luck— Let 'em *sue* me—that's right! Let 'em send me to Siberia—yes, to the scaffold! Ha, ha, ha, ha!"—

The next day was identical with the foregoing ones.

Olinka would listen to Kukin in grave silence, and at times she was even on the verge of tears. She finished by loving him for his misfortunes.

Kukin was short, thin, yellow-visaged, with a piping little tenor voice.

[1] féeries: religious pageants.

His face was nearly always a mask of despair. Nevertheless he wakened in Olinka a feeling of genuine, profound affection.

It was her nature to be always in love with someone or other. She could not live without loving. First it was her father; then an aunt who used to come to visit them occasionally. When she was in the High-school she was in love with her French-teacher. She was a quiet, good-hearted, girl, with soft gentle eyes. She was also quite robust. At sight of her plump rosy cheeks, and white neck, and her naïve, good-natured smile, men would say to themselves with a little grin, "Ah, yes, she's the goods!"

Other women could not help interrupting their conversation occasionally, and seize her hand, exclaiming fervidly, "*Du*-sheetsch-ka!" (darling-little-soul!).

The house in which she had lived from the day of her birth, belonged to her by right of inheritance, and was not far from the Tivoli-Garden. In the evening, and during the night, she could hear the music, and see the fireworks—it seemed to her as if Kukin was defying his ill-luck, and coming to close quarters with his inveterate enemy, the indifferent public. Her heart melted at the thought, and she could not sleep. When he returned home in the morning, she would tap on the window of her bedroom to attract his attention, and show him her smiling face through the curtains.

He proposed to her and she accepted him.

When her soft throat and well-rounded shoulders were close to him, he clapped his hands together gleefully and cried, "Dushitchka!"

He was happy. But on the day of the wedding, and later in the evening, it rained, and his face was eloquent with despair.

After the wedding they lived happily together. She acted as cashier in the box-office, and attended to the general management of the Garden. Her plump pink cheeks and naïve, amiable smile shone everywhere,—behind the glass-pane of the box-office, in the wings of the theatre, at the buffet.—She assured her friends that the stage was the most important, useful, and wonderful institution in society. "There is no enjoyment greater and more refined than the theatre; there can be no real education and culture without it", she would say. "But the public do not realise this", she would add; "all they want is cheap circuses. Yesterday we gave 'Faust',[2] and almost all the boxes were empty. But if Vanyichka[3] had given some trashy operetta, believe me the theatre would have been packed. To-morrow we are going to produce 'Orfeo'[4]—you'll come, won't you?"

Thus, whatever her husband said of the theatre she repeated. Like him she detested the public for its ignorance, and its indifference to good art. At rehearsal she corrected the actors and made suggestions to the musicians.

[2] *Faust:* opera by Charles Gounod, French composer (1818–1893).
[3] Vanyichka: familiar form of Ivan, Kukin's first name.
[4] *Orfeo:* opera by Christoph Gluck, German composer (1714–1787).

And when the newspapers gave an unfavorable criticism she actually wept, and went to the editors to plead for fairer treatment.

The actors were fond of her and called her "Dushitchka". If they cheated her out of little loans, occasionally, she did not complain to Kukin, but cried in secret.

In winter they were more prosperous. They leased the Municipal-Theatre for the season and sub-leased it to stock-companies and other troupes. Olinka grew stouter and was radiant with happiness. But Kukin kept growing thinner and yellower, and complained of financial losses, though business was fairly good all winter. At night he coughed, and she gave him medicinal-tea mixed with raspberries; she also rubbed him with alcohol and wrapped him in soft shawls.

"Poor dear," she would murmur lovingly; "poor, dear, Vanyichka"—

While he was away in Moscow, organising a company for the summer-season, she felt very lonely; she sat at her window and looked out into the court-yard, or gazed at the stars.

Kukin was delayed in Moscow, and wrote her to prepare the Tivoli for the summer.

Late one evening she heard a knocking at the gate-wicket. The sleepy kitchen-maid went stumbling to open it.

"I have a telegram for you; open!" a voice cried.

Olinka had received other telegrams from her husband, but this time she felt, for some inexplicable reason, almost palsied with nervousness. She opened the telegram with trembling hands, and read the following:

"Ivan Petrovitch died suddenly to-day! we await your wishes. Funeral takes place Tuesday."

"Oh Lord!" she cried, bursting into tears; "Vanyitchka! dear, dear Vanyitchka! —Why has such misfortune befallen me?!— Why did I ever come to love you?!—To whom have you left your Olinka! your poor unfortunate Olinka"—

Kukin was buried in Moscow on Tuesday. Olinka returned home the next day. No sooner did she enter her room than she threw herself on the bed and began to sob so violently that her neighbors heard her.

"Poor Duschitchka", they cried, crossing themselves; "Olga Duschitchka —how she takes on, poor thing"—

Three months later Olinka was on her way home from mass, in deep mourning. Besides her walked Vasilya Andreyitch, manager of Babakov's lumber-yard. He wore a straw hat, a white vest, and a gold chain, and looked more like a landed-proprietor than a merchant.

"Everything has its course, Olga Semyonovna", he was saying with dignified emotion; "if any of those who are dear to us pass away it is God's will; we must remember this and submit with resignation."

When they reached her house he took leave of her.

The rest of the day she was obsessed with the memory of his dignified voice, and she had scarcely closed her eyes when the vision of his black beard obtruded itself upon her.

He had made a deep impression on her, and she, evidently, had affected him likewise. Because, several days later, an elderly lady, a distant acquaintance of hers, came to have tea with Olinka; and no sooner were they both seated at the table than the visitor began to talk of Vasilya Andreyitch. She commended on his good-nature, and his strong stable qualities—the best woman in the world should deem herself lucky if she could marry such a man.

Three days later Andreyitch himself paid Olinka a visit. He stayed only a short while and spoke little, but Olinka, nevertheless, became so enamoured of him that she was feverish all night and could not sleep. In the morning she sent for the elderly lady.

They were presently engaged, and soon after, married.

After their marriage they lived happily. He sat, as usual, in his lumber-yard till noon. The he would go away on business and she took his place in the office, making out bills and attending to customers.

"Lumber has risen twenty per cent this year", she would tell them; "you see, in former years we dealt with the owners of the town-forest, but now Vasyichka must go as far as Mohilev to buy timber. And the taxes we have to pay! Lord, Lord!" . . . and she would put her hands to her cheeks and slowly shake her head from side to side.

It seemed to her as if she had been in the lumber-business for years and years; that the most important factor in civilisation is the forest; her voice was touchingly intimate as she spoke of logs and beams, rafters and planks and shingles . . . Her very thoughts were the echo of her husband's. If he thought that it was too hot in the house—or that business was bad, she thought the same.

Andreyitch did not like to go out much and she was also in perfect accord with him on this point.

"You are always indoors", her friends would say to her; "you ought to go out once in a while, to the theatre, or circus."

"Vasya and I have no time for the theatre," she would answer with dignity. "We have too much to do to waste time on such frivolous nonsense. What do people find in theatres to amuse them, anyway?"

Every Saturday night they would go to mass, and to early morning mass, on holidays; on the way home they would walk placidly, with pious tranquil faces, while her satin dress rustled genteelly. At home they drank tea, with preserves, and dumplings. In the office the samovar[5] was always prepared, and customers were invited to tea and crullers. Once a week the couple went to the Baths[6] and walked home together, flushed, radiant.

"We have nothing to complain of, thank God," she would tell her acquaintances; "may Heaven be as kind to others as to us" . . . .

[5] samovar: urn for making tea.
[6] Baths: public bathing houses.

When her husband was away on business in some distant province she felt very lonesome. She could not sleep at night and even cried.

Occasionally an army-veterinary, Smernin by name, would come to visit her in the evening. He was a lodger in a wing of the house. He told her stories, or played cards with her; this diverted her.

Most interesting of all, were the stories of his private life. He was married and had a little son, but was divorced from his wife because she had deceived him. Now, he said, he detested her. He was sending her forty roubles[7] a month for the child's bringing-up.

Olinka would sigh and shake her head at these tales, and she pitied Platonitch.

"Heaven help you!" she would exclaim at parting, lighting him to the stairs with a candle. "Thank you for keeping me company. . . . May God and the Blessed Virgin keep you!"

She would utter these sentiments in a solemn tone, just like her husband's. When the door had already shut behind him she would call him back and say to him: "Do you know, Vladimir Platonitch, you ought to make up with your wife. You ought to forgive her for your son's sake. . . . You know, he is probably beginning to understand". . . .

When her husband returned from his trip, she told him in low tones about the veterinary and his unhappy married-life. Both sighed, shook their heads, and spoke of the little son who must be longing for his father. And moved by a strange sudden impulse arising from the same current of thought, they both kneeled down before the holy-image, and bowed to the ground in prayer that they might beget children.

And so they lived in serene peace, in love and accord, for six years. One winter-day Vasilya Andreyitch was drinking tea in his lumber-yard. He went out to wait on a customer, and thus caught a cold. He became ill, and although the best physicians were called in, he died in about four months.

And again Olinka was a widow.

"How hast thou left me!" she sobbed as he was buried; "how shall I live without thee, miserable me!—Good-people, take pity on one that is lone and forsaken". . . .

She put on mourning and resolved nevermore to wear hat or gloves. She seldom left the house, and then went only to the church and her husband's grave. Her life was almost monastic.

When the six months had passed she doffed her mourning and opened wide the window shutters of her house. Occasionally she was seen marketing with her cook, but of her domestic existence little was known. They did notice, however, that she now sat in the garden, sometimes, drinking tea with the veterinary while the latter read the papers to her. And on happening to meet an acquaintance, once, she remarked to her: "In our town there is no veterinary supervision worth mentioning; that's why disease is so

---

[7] roubles: Russian silver coin, equivalent to approximately $1.11.

prevalent. You see, people get sick from bad milk—or catch diseases from infected cattle and horses. Yes, it's plain enough; domestic animals ought to be looked after quite as carefully as human beings."

She was repeating the veterinary's remarks, echoing, as was her nature, his thoughts and opinions. It was clear that she could not live without masculine friendship for even a year, and she now found her happiness in the wing of her house. Another would have been condemned for this, but of Olinka no one could think evil. For everything in her life was so simple and pure.

They tried to keep their union a secret, but did not succeed. For Olinka could not keep secrets. When Platonitch's friends, army-men, came to visit him she would speak about the epidemic among horned-beasts, as she poured out the tea, and of conditions in the town-slaughter-houses.

On hearing her speak in this fashion Platonitch felt greatly embarrassed. Even more so when his friends began to laugh. He seized her hands, in a rage, and muttered: "I told you—I've told you not to talk about things you don't know!"——

"But Valodytchka—then what shall I talk about?"

And, with her eyes full of tears, she put her arms around him, entreating him not to be angry with her.

And both of them were happy.

But her happiness did not endure. The veterinary left with his regiment and did not return, having been despatched to some distant far-Russian outpost.

Olinka was utterly forsaken. She became thin and ugly. Passers-by in the street no longer looked or smiled at her. Yes—her best years were behind her.

A new and strange life began for her, about which it is sad to think. Toward evening she would sit on the porch and fancy she was hearing the music in the Tivoli, and seeing the blazing sky-rockets. . . . But it excited no emotion in her. She would stare vacantly into the silent courtyard, thinking of nothing, wishing for nothing. At night she would go to sleep and dream only of the empty house and yard. She ate and drank mechanically. Worst of all she was now left opinionless. She observed everything around her without being able to make any comment or to form any opinion, and so could talk about nothing. What a terrible thing it must be to have no power of thinking out an opinion for one's self! . . . You see for instance, a bottle on a table . . . or the rain outside . . . or a peasant on his wagon—But why all these things, and what for—their meaning and significance,—not a trace of understanding, not a shadow of an opinion, for all the money in the world. When Kukin was alive, or Andreyitch, or the veterinary, it was different. But now her mind felt as empty as the court-yard, while her heart was overfilled with bitterness and sorrow.

The house grew blackened with the changing weather of years; the roof became rusty; the outhouse sunken-in; the whole courtyard overrun with weeds. Olinka herself grew old.

One hot July day, toward evening, someone knocked at the gate-wicket. As Olinka approached to open it she stopped, stupefied. Behind the wicket stood the veterinary, now gray, in civilian clothes.

"Darling mine!" she murmured with a quiver of joy. "From where has the Lord brought you?"

"I want to settle here for good," he answered; "I have resigned my commission, and have come here to lead an independent citizen's life, like other townspeople. It's time, too, for my son to go to the gymnasium,[8] he's grown up now—And do you know,—I have made up with my wife. . . .

"Where is she?" asked Olinka.

"She is with our son in a hotel, while I am looking around for an apartment."

"Why, my dear,—why not move into this house? I won't ask for any rent." . . . She grew very agitated and began to cry.

The very next day repairs were begun on the house; the walls were painted and whitewashed; Olinka, with arms akimbo, walked about busily overseeing all the activities. The old smile shone on her face, and she looked as though rejuvenated. Presently the veterinary's wife, a thin, plain, woman, with clipped hair and the look of a spoiled child, came. With her was Sascha, a boy of ten, small for his age, stout, with clear blue eyes and dimpled cheeks. No sooner had he entered the house than he began chasing the cat, and his merry laughter rang through the house. Olinka chatted with him, and gave him tea—her heart felt warm and pressed-together with joy, as if the lad were her own son, her own flesh and blood.

In the evening, as they sat in the dining-room, while he prepared his lessons, she looked at him and whispered pityingly: "Dove mine, pretty one, you are so smart, and white"——

He was studying aloud,—"An island is a body of land surrounded by water"—

"An island is a body of land surrounded by water"—she repeated after him. This was the first opinion she had uttered with decision after several years of silence and vacuity[9] of thought.

At supper she gave evidence of her renewed mental activity by speaking to Sascha's parents about the difficulties children now experienced in the gymnasium, but that a classic training is nevertheless better than a technical or commercial one, because from the gymnasium paths are open to the professions of medicine, engineering, etc. So Sascha began to attend the gymnasium.

His mother went to visit her sister in Kharkoff but did not come back.

[8] gymnasium: upper-grade public school.
[9] vacuity: emptiness.

His father rode off, somewhere, every day, and occasionally did not return for three days a time. It seemed to Olinka that they had abandoned the lad who must be dying of hunger. So she took him to her living-rooms and gave him one for his own use.

The boy is living with her now over half a year. She goes to his room every morning, and wakes him, calling: "Sascha! get up, darling, it is time for school."

He gets up, dresses, says his prayers, has his breakfast, and goes off to school, knapsack on his shoulder. She follows quietly behind and calls "Sascha!" he turns around and she gives him a candy.

"Go home, auntie", he says—I know how to get to school myself"—She stops and follows him only with her eyes till he is lost in the shadow of the entrance to the school-building.

How she loves him!—She would give him her life—this stranger-lad, with his dimples and blue eyes—Why?—who knows?—

On her way home from market she meets an acquaintance, who greets her smilingly.

"How are you, Duschitchka Olga? how are things, dear?"

After a few words in answer—: "Studying in the gymnasium is very hard these days. Just think: yesterday, in the first class, they had to learn a whole fable by heart. And a Latin translation. And a problem in mathematics. How can a little fellow be expected to learn all that?"

And she continues to talk about the teachers, and lessons, and textbooks, echoing Sascha in almost all his words.

Three o'clock they eat together. In the evening they do his lessons together. She puts him to bed, making the sign of the cross devoutly over him, and murmurs a prayer for the boy.

One day she suddenly hears a knock at the gate. She starts up in affright, thinking it may be a telegram from Kharkoff from Sascha's mother asking for the lad, perhaps . . . Oh God!—She is all a-tremble.

But it's only the veterinary—"Thank Heaven!" she murmurs.

STUDY QUESTIONS

1. The story consists largely of three separate episodes. What are they? How are they connected?
2. What is the principal linguistic device in the story? How does this use contribute to the story's shape and meaning?
3. Where does the author state precisely what Olinka's character is like? Note references to at least two different aspects of her personality.
4. In what ways might Chekhov be criticized for his portrait of a woman? Would such a criticism be justified? Defend your answer.
5. Much of the story grows around what some sociologists would describe

as a traditional European nineteenth-century attitude toward life in general as well as toward male and female roles. Using information from the text describe some of those attitudes.

6. What is the significance of the title?

Kate Chopin (1851–1904)

THE STORY OF AN HOUR

Knowing that Mrs. Mallard was afflicted with a heart trouble, great care was taken to break to her as gently as possible the news of her husband's death.

It was her sister Josephine who told her, in broken sentences; veiled hints that revealed in half concealing. Her husband's friend Richards was there, too, near her. It was he who had been in the newspaper office when intelligence of the railroad disaster was received, with Brently Mallard's name leading the list of "killed." He had only taken the time to assure himself of its truth by a second telegram, and had hastened to forestall any less careful, less tender friend in bearing the sad message.

She did not hear the story as many women have heard the same, with a paralyzed inability to accept its significance. She wept at once, with sudden, wild abandonment, in her sister's arms. When the storm of grief had spent itself she went away to her room alone. She would have no one follow her.

There stood, facing the open window, a comfortable, roomy armchair. Into this she sank, pressed down by a physical exhaustion that haunted her body and seemed to reach into her soul.

She could see in the open square before her house the tops of trees that were all aquiver with the new spring life. The delicious breath of rain was in the air. In the street below a peddler was crying his wares. The notes of a distant song which some one was singing reached her faintly, and countless sparrows were twittering in the eaves.

There were patches of blue sky showing here and there through the clouds that had met and piled one above the other in the west facing her window.

She sat with her head thrown back upon the cushion of the chair, quite motionless, except when a sob came up into her throat and shook her, as a child who has cried itself to sleep continues to sob in its dreams.

She was young, with a fair, calm face, whose lines bespoke repression and even a certain strength. But now there was a dull stare in her eyes, whose gaze was fixed away off yonder on one of those patches of blue sky. It was not a glance of reflection, but rather indicated a suspension of intelligent thought.

There was something coming to her and she was waiting for it, fearfully. What was it? She did not know; it was too subtle and elusive to name. But she felt it, creeping out of the sky, reaching toward her through the sounds, the scents, the color that filled the air.

Now her bosom rose and fell tumultuously. She was beginning to recognize this thing that was approaching to possess her, and she was striving to beat it back with her will—as powerless as her two white slender hands would have been.

When she abandoned herself a little whispered word escaped her slightly parted lips. She said it over and over under her breath: "free, free, free!" The vacant stare and the look of terror that had followed it went from her eyes. They stayed keen and bright. Her pulses beat fast, and the coursing blood warmed and relaxed every inch of her body.

She did not stop to ask if it were or were not a monstrous joy that held her. A clear and exalted perception enabled her to dismiss the suggestion as trivial.

She knew that she would weep again when she saw the kind, tender hands folded in death; the face that had never looked save with love upon her, fixed and gray and dead. But she saw beyond that bitter moment a long procession of years to come that would belong to her absolutely. And she opened and spread her arms out to them in welcome.

There would be no one to live for her during those coming years; she would live for herself. There would be no powerful will bending hers in that blind persistence with which men and women believe they have a right to impose a private will upon a fellow-creature. A kind intention or a cruel intention made the act seem no less a crime as she looked upon it in that brief moment of illumination.

And yet she had loved him—sometimes. Often she had not. What did it matter! What could love, the unsolved mystery, count for in face of this possession of self-assertion which she suddenly recognized as the strongest impulse of her being!

"Free! Body and soul free!" she kept whispering.

Josephine was kneeling before the closed door with her lips to the keyhole, imploring for admission. "Louise, open the door! I beg; open the door—you will make yourself ill. What are you doing, Louise? For heaven's sake open the door."

"Go away. I am not making myself ill." No; she was drinking in a very elixir of life through that open window.

Her fancy was running riot along those days ahead of her. Spring days, and summer days, and all sorts of days that would be her own. She breathed a quick prayer that life might be long. It was only yesterday she had thought with a shudder that life might be long.

She rose at length and opened the door to her sister's importunities. There was a feverish triumph in her eyes, and she carried herself unwittingly like a goddess of Victory. She clasped her sister's waist, and together they descended the stairs. Richards stood waiting for them at the bottom.

Some one was opening the front door with a latchkey. It was Brently Mallard who entered, a little travel-stained, composedly carrying his grip-sack and umbrella. He had been far from the scene of the accident, and did not even know there had been one. He stood amazed at Josephine's piercing cry; at Richards' quick motion to screen him from the view of his wife.

But Richards was too late.

When the doctors came they said she had died of heart disease—of joy that kills.

Guy de Maupassant (1850–1893)

THE NECKLACE

She was one of those pretty and charming girls who are sometimes, as if by a mistake of destiny, born in a family of clerks. She had no dowry, no expectations, no means of being known, understood, loved, wedded by any rich and distinguished man; and she let herself be married to a little clerk at the Ministry of Public Instruction.

She dressed plainly because she could not dress well, but she was as unhappy as though she had really fallen from her proper station, since with women there is neither caste nor rank; and beauty, grace, and charm act instead of family and birth. Natural fineness, instinct for what is elegant, suppleness of wit, are the sole hierarchy, and make from women of the people the equals of the very greatest ladies.

She suffered ceaselessly, feeling herself born for all the delicacies and all the luxuries. She suffered from the poverty of her dwelling, from the wretched look of the walls, from the worn-out chairs, from the ugliness of the curtains. All those things, of which another woman of her rank would never even have been conscious, tortured her and made her angry. The sight of the little Breton peasant[1] who did her humble housework aroused in her regrets which were despairing, and distracted dreams. She thought of the silent antechambers hung with Oriental tapestry, lit by tall bronze candelabra, and of the two great footmen in knee breeches who sleep in the big armchairs, made drowsy by the heavy warmth of the hot-air stove. She thought of the long salons[2] fitted up with ancient silk, of the delicate furniture carrying priceless curiosities, and of the coquettish perfumed boudoirs made for talks at five o'clock with intimate friends, with men famous and sought after, whom all women envy and whose attention they all desire.

When she sat down to dinner, before the round table covered with a tablecloth three days old, opposite her husband, who uncovered the soup tureen and declared with an enchanted air, "Ah, the good pot-au-feu![3] I don't

---

[1] Breton peasant: servant from the countryside in Brittany.
[2] salons: elegant parlors.
[3] pot-au-feu: a hearty soup often served in simple homes, not favored by the well-to-do.

know anything better than that," she thought of dainty dinners, of shining silverware, of tapestry which peopled the walls with ancient personages and with strange birds flying in the midst of a fairy forest; and she thought of delicious dishes served on marvelous plates, and of the whispered gallantries which you listen to with a sphinxlike smile, while you are eating the pink flesh of a trout or the wings of a quail.

She had no dresses, no jewels, nothing. And she loved nothing but that; she felt made for that. She would so have liked to please, to be envied, to be charming, to be sought after.

She had a friend, a former schoolmate at the convent, who was rich, and whom she did not like to go and see any more, because she suffered so much when she came back.

But one evening, her husband returned home with a triumphant air, and holding a large envelope in his hand.

"There," said he. "Here is something for you."

She tore the paper sharply, and drew out a printed card which bore these words:

"The Minister of Public Instruction and Mme. Georges Ramponneau request the honor of M. and Mme. Loisel's company at the palace of the Ministry on Monday evening, January eighteenth."

Instead of being delighted, as her husband hoped, she threw the invitation on the table with disdain, murmuring:

"What do you want me to do with that?"

"But, my dear, I thought you would be glad. You never go out, and this is such a fine opportunity. I had awful trouble to get it. Everyone wants to go; it is very select, and they are not giving many invitations to clerks. The whole official world will be there."

She looked at him with an irritated eye, and she said, impatiently:

"And what do you want me to put on my back?"

He had not thought of that; he stammered:

"Why, the dress you go to the theater in. It looks very well, to me."

He stopped, distracted, seeing that his wife was crying. Two great tears descended slowly from the corners of her eyes toward the corners of her mouth. He stuttered:

"What's the matter? What's the matter?"

But, by violent effort, she had conquered her grief, and she replied, with a calm voice, while she wiped her wet cheeks:

"Nothing. Only I have no dress and therefore I can't go to this ball. Give your card to some colleague whose wife is better equipped than I."

He was in despair. He resumed:

"Come, let us see, Mathilde. How much would it cost, a suitable dress, which you could use on other occasions, something very simple?"

She reflected several seconds, making her calculations and wondering also what sum she could ask without drawing on herself an immediate refusal and a frightened exclamation from the economical clerk.

Finally, she replied, hesitatingly:

"I don't know exactly, but I think I could manage it with four hundred francs."

He had grown a little pale, because he was laying aside just that amount to buy a gun and treat himself to a little shooting next summer on the plain of Nanterre, with several friends who went to shoot larks down there, of a Sunday.

But he said:

"All right. I will give you four hundred francs. And try to have a pretty dress."

The day of the ball drew near, and Mme. Loisel seemed sad, uneasy, anxious. Her dress was ready, however. Her husband said to her one evening:

"What is the matter? Come, you've been so queer these last three days."

And she answered:

"It annoys me not to have a single jewel, not a single stone, nothing to put on. I shall look like distress. I should almost rather not go at all."

He resumed:

"You might wear natural flowers. It's very stylish at this time of the year. For ten francs you can get two or three magnificent roses."

She was not convinced.

"No; there's nothing more humiliating than to look poor among other women who are rich."

But her husband cried:

"How stupid you are! Go look up your friend Mme. Forestier, and ask her to lend you some jewels. You're quite thick enough with her to do that."

She uttered a cry of joy:

"It's true. I never thought of it."

The next day she went to her friend and told of her distress.

Mme. Forestier went to a wardrobe with a glass door, took out a large jewel-box, brought it back, opened it, and said to Mme. Loisel:

"Choose, my dear."

She saw first of all some bracelets, then a pearl necklace, than a Venetian cross, gold and precious stones of admirable workmanship. She tried on the ornaments before the glass, hesitated, could not make up her mind to part with them, to give them back. She kept asking:

"Haven't you any more?"

"Why, yes. Look. I don't know what you like."

All of a sudden she discovered, in a black satin box, a superb necklace of diamonds, and her heart began to beat with an immoderate desire. Her hands trembled as she took it. She fastened it around her throat, outside her high-necked dress, and remained lost in ecstasy at the sight of herself.

Then she asked, hesitating, filled with anguish:

"Can you lend me that, only that?"

"Why, yes, certainly."

She sprang upon the neck of her friend, kissed her passionately, then fled with her treasure.

The day of the ball arrived. Mme. Loisel made a great success. She was prettier than them all, elegant, gracious, smiling, and crazy with joy. All the men looked at her, asked her name, endeavored to be introduced. All the attachés of the Cabinet wanted to waltz with her. She was remarked by the minister himself.

She danced with intoxication, with passion, made drunk by pleasure, forgetting all, in the triumph of her beauty, in the glory of her success, in a sort of cloud of happiness composed of all this homage, of all this admiration, of all these awakened desires, and of that sense of complete victory which is so sweet to a woman's heart.

She went away about four o'clock in the morning. Her husband had been sleeping since midnight, in a little deserted anteroom, with three other gentlemen whose wives were having a very good time. He threw over her shoulders the wraps which he had brought, modest wraps of common life, whose poverty contrasted with the elegance of the ball dress. She felt this, and wanted to escape so as not to be remarked by the other women, who were enveloping themselves in costly furs.

Loisel held her back.

"Wait a bit. You will catch cold outside. I will go and call a cab."

But she did not listen to him, and rapidly descended the stairs. When they were in the street they did not find a carriage; and they began to look for one, shouting after the cabmen whom they saw passing by at a distance.

They went down toward the Seine, in despair, shivering with cold. At last they found on the quay one of those ancient noctambulant coupés[4] which, exactly as if they were ashamed to show their misery during the day, are never seen round Paris until after nightfall.

It took them to their door in the Rue des Martyrs, and once more, sadly, they climbed up homeward. All was ended, for her. And as to him, he reflected that he must be at the Ministry at ten o'clock.

She removed the wraps, which covered her shoulders, before the glass, so as once more to see herself in all her glory. But suddenly she uttered a cry. She had no longer the necklace around her neck!

Her husband, already half undressed, demanded:

"What is the matter with you?"

She turned madly towards him:

"I have—I have—I've lost Mme. Forestier's necklace."

He stood up, distracted.

"What!—how?—impossible!"

And they looked in the folds of her dress, in the folds of her cloak, in her pockets, everywhere. They did not find it.

[4] coupés: small horse-drawn carriages.

He asked:

"You're sure you had it on when you left the ball?"

"Yes, I felt it in the vestibule of the palace."

"But if you had lost it in the street we should have heard it fall. It must be in the cab."

"Yes. Probably. Did you take his number?"

"No. And you, didn't you notice it?"

"No."

They looked, thunderstruck, at one another. At last Loisel put on his clothes.

"I shall go back on foot," said he, "over the whole route which we have taken to see if I can find it."

And he went out. She was waiting on a chair in her ball dress, without strength to go to bed, overwhelmed, without fire, without a thought.

Her husband came back about seven o'clock. He had found nothing.

He went to Police Headquarters, to the newspaper offices, to offer a reward; he went to the cab companies—everywhere, in fact, whither he was urged by the least suspicion of hope.

She waited all day, in the same condition of mad fear before this terrible calamity.

Loisel returned at night with a hollow, pale face; he had discovered nothing.

"You must write to your friend," said he, "that you have broken the clasp of her necklace and that you are having it mended. That will give us time to turn round."

She wrote at his dictation.

At the end of a week they had lost all hope.

And Loisel, who had aged five years, declared:

"We must consider how to replace that ornament."

The next day they took the box which had contained it, and they went to the jeweler whose name was found within. He consulted his book.

"It was not I, madame, who sold that necklace; I must simply have furnished the case."

Then they went from jeweler to jeweler, searching for a necklace like the other, consulting their memories, sick both of them with chagrin and anguish.

They found, in a shop at the Palais Royal, a string of diamonds which seemed to them exactly like the one they looked for. It was worth forty thousand francs. They could have it for thirty-six.

So they begged the jeweler not to sell it for three days yet. And they made a bargain that he should buy it back for thirty-four thousand francs, in case they found the other one before the end of February.

Loisel possessed eighteen thousand francs which his father had left him. He would borrow the rest.

He did borrow, asking a thousand francs of one, five hundred of another, five louis[5] here, three louis there. He gave notes, took up ruinous obligations, dealt with usurers and all the race of lenders. He compromised all the rest of his life, risked his signature without even knowing if he could meet it, and, frightened by the pains yet to come, by the black misery which was about to fall upon him, by the prospect of all the physical privations and of all the moral tortures which he was to suffer, he went to get the new necklace, putting down upon the merchant's counter thirty-six thousand francs.

When Mme. Loisel took back the necklace, Mme. Forestier said to her, with a chilly manner:

"You should have returned it sooner; I might have needed it."

She did not open the case, as her friend had so much feared. If she had detected the substitution, what would she have thought, what would she have said? Would she not have taken Mme. Loisel for a thief?

Mme. Loisel now knew the horrible existence of the needy. She took her part, moreover, all of a sudden, with heroism. That dreadful debt must be paid. She would pay it. They dismissed their servant; they changed their lodgings; they rented a garret under the roof.

She came to know what heavy housework meant and the odious cares of the kitchen. She washed the dishes, using her rosy nails on the greasy pots and pans. She washed the dirty linen, the shirts, and the dishcloths, which she dried upon a line; she carried the slops[6] down to the street every morning, and carried up the water, stopping for breath at every landing. And, dressed like a woman of the people, she went to the fruiterer, the grocer, the butcher, her basket on her arm, bargaining, insulted, defending her miserable money sou[7] by sou.

Each month they had to meet some notes, renew others, obtain more time.

Her husband worked in the evening making a fair copy of some tradesman's accounts, and late at night he often copied manuscript for five sous a page.

And this life lasted for ten years.

At the end of ten years, they had paid everything, everything, with the rates of usury, and the accumulations of the compound interest.

Mme. Loisel looked old now. She had become the woman of impoverished households—strong and hard and rough. With frowsy hair, skirts askew, and red hands, she talked loud while washing the floor with great swishes of water. But sometimes, when her husband was at the office, she sat down near the window, and she thought of that gay evening of long ago, of that ball where she had been so beautiful and so fêted.

What would have happened if she had not lost that necklace? Who

---

[5] louis: gold coin valued at twenty francs.

[6] slops: used wash water.

[7] sou: a very small coin, worth one-twentieth of a franc.

knows? Who knows? How life is strange and changeful! How little a thing is needed for us to be lost or to be saved!

But, one Sunday, having gone to take a walk in the Champs Elysées to refresh herself from the labor of the week, she suddenly perceived a woman who was leading a child. It was Mme. Forestier, still young, still beautiful, still charming.

Mme. Loisel felt moved. Was she going to speak to her? Yes, certainly. And now that she had paid, she was going to tell her all about it. Why not?

She went up.

"Good-day, Jeanne."

The other, astonished to be familiarly addressed by this plain goodwife, did not recognize her at all, and stammered:

"But—madam!—I do not know—You must be mistaken."

"No. I am Mathilde Loisel."

Her friend uttered a cry.

"Oh, my poor Mathilde! How you are changed!"

"Yes, I have had days hard enough, since I have seen you, days wretched enough—and that because of you!"

"Of me! How so?"

"Do you remember that diamond necklace which you lent me to wear at the ministerial ball?"

"Yes. Well?"

"Well, I lost it."

"What do you mean? You brought it back."

"I brought you back another just like it. And for this we have been ten years paying. You can understand that it was not easy for us, us who had nothing. At last it is ended, and I am very glad."

Mme. Forestier had stopped.

"You say that you bought a necklace of diamonds to replace mine?"

"Yes. You never noticed it, then! They were very like. "

And she smiled with joy which was proud and naïve at once.

Mme. Forestier, strongly moved, took her two hands.

"Oh, my poor Mathilde! Why, my necklace was paste. It was worth at most five hundred francs!"

Ambrose Bierce (1842–1914?)

OIL OF DOG

My name is Boffer Bings. I was born of honest parents in one of the humbler walks of life, my father being a manufacturer of dog-oil and my mother having a small studio in the shadow of the village church, where she disposed of unwelcome babes. In my boyhood I was trained to habits of industry; I not only assisted my father in procuring dogs for his vats, but was frequently employed by my mother to carry away the débris of her work in the studio. In performance of this duty I sometimes had need of all my natural intelligence for all the law officers of the vicinity were opposed to my mother's business. They were not elected on an opposition ticket, and the matter had never been made a political issue; it just happened so. My father's business of making dog-oil was, naturally, less unpopular, though the owners of missing dogs sometimes regarded him with suspicion, which was reflected, to some extent, upon me. My father had, as silent partners, all the physicians of the town, who seldom wrote a prescription which did not contain what they were pleased to designate as *Ol. can.*[1] It is really the most valuable medicine ever discovered. But most persons are unwilling to make personal sacrifices for the afflicted, and it was evident that many of the fattest dogs in town had been forbidden to play with me—a fact which pained my young sensibilities, and at one time came near driving me to become a pirate.

Looking back upon those days, I cannot but regret, at times, that by indirectly bringing my beloved parents to their death I was the author of misfortunes profoundly affecting my future.

One evening while passing my father's oil factory with the body of a foundling from my mother's studio I saw a constable who seemed to be closely watching my movements. Young as I was, I had learned that a constable's acts, of whatever apparent character, are prompted by the most reprehensible motives, and I avoided him by dodging into the oilery by a side door which happened to stand ajar. I locked it at once and was alone with my dead. My father had retired for the night. The only light in the place came from the furnace, which glowed a deep, rich crimson under one of the vats, casting ruddy reflections on the walls. Within the cauldron the oil still rolled in indolent ebullition, occasionally pushing to the surface a piece of dog. Seating myself to wait for the constable to go away, I held the naked body of the foundling in my lap and tenderly stroked its short, silken hair. Ah, how beautiful it was! Even at that early age I was passionately fond of children, and as I looked upon this cherub I could almost find it in my heart to wish that the small, red wound upon its breast—the work of my dear mother—had not been mortal.

It had been my custom to throw the babes into the river which nature had thoughtfully provided for the purpose, but that night I did not dare to leave the oilery for fear of the constable. "After all," I said to myself, "it cannot greatly matter if I put it into this cauldron. My father will never know the bones from those of a puppy, and the few deaths which may result from administering another kind of oil for the incomparable *ol. can.* are not important in a population which increases so rapidly." In short, I took the first step in crime and brought myself untold sorrow by casting the babe into the cauldron.

---

[1] *Ol. can.: olivum canis*, Latin for "oil of dog."

The next day, somewhat to my surprise, my father, rubbing his hands with satisfaction, informed me and my mother that he had obtained the finest quality of oil that was ever seen; that the physicians to whom he had shown samples had so pronounced it. He added that he had no knowledge as to how the result was obtained; the dogs had been treated in all respects as usual, and were of an ordinary breed. I deemed it my duty to explain— which I did, though palsied would have been my tongue if I could have foreseen the consequences. Bewailing their previous ignorance of the advantages of combining their industries, my parents at once took measures to repair the error. My mother removed her studio to a wing of the factory building and my duties in connection with the business ceased; I was no longer required to dispose of the bodies of the small superfluous, and there was no need of alluring dogs to their doom, for my father discarded them altogether, though they still had an honorable place in the name of the oil. So suddenly thrown into idleness, I might naturally have been expected to become vicious and dissolute, but I did not. The holy influence of my dear mother was ever about me to protect me from the temptations which beset youth, and my father was a deacon in a church. Alas, that through my fault these estimable persons should have come to so bad an end!

Finding a double profit in her business, my mother now devoted herself to it with a new assiduity. She removed not only superfluous and unwelcome babes to order, but went out into the highways and byways, gathering in children of a larger growth, and even such adults as she could entice to the oilery. My father, too, enamored of the superior quality of oil produced, purveyed for his vats with diligence and zeal. The conversion of their neighbors into dog-oil became, in short, the one passion of their lives—an absorbing and overwhelming greed took possession of their souls and served them in place of a hope in Heaven—by which, also, they were inspired.

So enterprising had they now become that a public meeting was held and resolutions passed severely censuring them. It was intimated by the chairman that any further raids upon the population would be met in a spirit of hostility. My poor parents left the meeting broken-hearted, desperate and, I believe, not altogether sane. Anyhow, I deemed it prudent not to enter the oilery with them that night, but slept outside in a stable.

At about midnight some mysterious impulse caused me to rise and peer through a window into the furnace-room, where I knew my father now slept. The fires were burning as brightly as if the following day's harvest had been expected to be abundant. One of the large cauldrons was slowly "walloping" with a mysterious appearance to self-restraint, as if it bided its time to put forth its full energy. My father was not in bed; he had risen in his nightclothes and was preparing a noose in a strong cord. From the looks which he cast at the door of my mother's bedroom I knew too well the purpose that he had in mind. Speechless and motionless with terror, I could do nothing in prevention or warning. Suddenly the door of my mother's apartment was opened, noiselessly, and the two confronted each other, both apparently surprised. The lady, also, was in her night clothes, and she held in her right hand the tool of her trade, a long, narrow-bladed dagger.

She, too, had been unable to deny herself the last profit which the unfriendly action of the citizens and my absence had left her. For one instant they looked into each other's blazing eyes and then sprang together with indescribable fury. Round and round the room they struggled, the man cursing, the woman shrieking, both fighting like demons—she to strike him with the dagger, he to strangle her with his great bare hands. I know not how long I had the unhappiness to observe this disagreeable instance of domestic infelicity, but at last, after a more than usually vigorous struggle, the combatants suddenly moved apart.

My father's breast and my mother's weapon showed evidences of contact. For another instant they glared at each other in the most unamiable way; then my poor, wounded father, feeling the hand of death upon him, leaped forward, unmindful of resistance, grasped my dear mother in his arms, dragged her to the side of the boiling cauldron, collected all his failing energies, and sprang in with her! In a moment, both had disappeared and were adding their oil to that of the committee of citizens who had called the day before with an invitation to the public meeting.

Convinced that these unhappy events closed to me every avenue to an honorable career in that town, I removed to the famous city of Otumwee, where these memoirs are written with a heart full of remorse for a heedless act entailing so dismal a commercial disaster.

D. H. Lawrence (1885–1930)

THE ROCKING-HORSE WINNER

There was a woman who was beautiful, who started with all the advantages, yet she had no luck. She married for love, and the love turned to dust. She had bonny children, yet she felt they had been thrust upon her, and she could not love them. They looked at her coldly, as if they were finding fault with her. And hurriedly she felt she must cover up some fault in herself. Yet what it was that she must cover up she never knew. Nevertheless, when her children were present, she always felt the centre of her heart go hard. This troubled her, and in her manner she was all the more gentle and anxious for her children, as if she loved them very much. Only she herself knew that at the centre of her heart was a hard little place that could not feel love, no, not for anybody. Everybody else said of her: "She is such a good mother. She adores her children." Only she herself, and her children themselves, knew it was not so. They read it in each other's eyes.

There were a boy and two little girls. They lived in a pleasant house, with a garden, and they had discreet servants, and felt themselves superior to anyone in the neighbourhood.

D. H. LAWRENCE

Although they lived in style, they felt always an anxiety in the house. There was never enough money. The mother had a small income, and the father had a small income, but not nearly enough for the social position which they had to keep up. The father went into town to some office. But though he had good prospects, these prospects never materialized. There was always the grinding sense of the shortage of money, though the style was always kept up.

At last the mother said: "I will see if I can't make something." But she did not know where to begin. She racked her brains, and tried this thing and the other, but could not find anything successful. The failure made deep lines come into her face. Her children were growing up, they would have to go to school. There must be more money, there must be more money. The father, who was always very handsome and expensive in his tastes, seemed as if he never would be able to do anything worth doing. And the mother, who had a great belief in herself, did not succeed any better, and her tastes were just as expensive.

And so the house came to be haunted by the unspoken phrase: There must be more money! There must be more money! The children could hear it all the time, though nobody said it aloud. They heard it at Christmas, when the expensive and splendid toys filled the nursery. Behind the shining modern rocking horse, behind the smart doll's-house, a voice would start whispering: "There must be more money! There must be more money!' And the children would stop playing, to listen for a moment. They would look into each other's eyes, to see if they had all heard. And each one saw in the eyes of the other two that they too had heard. "There must be more money! There must be more money!"

It came whispering from the springs of the still-swaying rocking horse, and even the horse, bending his wooden, champing head, heard it. The big doll, sitting so pink and smirking in her new pram, could hear it quite plainly, and seemed to be smirking all the more self-consciously because of it. The foolish puppy, too, that took the place of the Teddy bear, he was looking so extraordinarily foolish for no other reason but that he heard the secret whisper all over the house: "There must be more money!"

Yet nobody ever said it aloud. The whisper was everywhere, and therefore no one spoke it. Just as no one ever says: "We are breathing!" in spite of the fact that breath is coming and going all the time.

"Mother," said the boy Paul one day, "why don't we keep a car of our own? Why do we always use uncle's, or else a taxi?"

"Because we're the poor members of the family," said the mother.

"But why are we, mother?"

"Well—I suppose," she said slowly and bitterly, "it's because your father has no luck."

The boy was silent for some time.

"Is luck money, mother?" he asked, rather timidly.

"No, Paul. Not quite. It's what causes you to have money."

"Oh!" said Paul vaguely. "I thought when Uncle Oscar said filthy lucker, it meant money."

"Filthy lucre does mean money," said the mother. "But it's lucre, not luck."

"Oh!" said the boy. "Then what is luck, mother?"

"It's what causes you to have money. If you're lucky you have money. That's why it's better to be born lucky than rich. If you're rich, you may lose your money. But if you're lucky, you will always get more money."

"Oh! Will you? And is father not lucky?"

"Very unlucky, I should say," she said bitterly.

They boy watched her with unsure eyes.

"Why?" he asked.

"I don't know. Nobody ever knows why one person is lucky and another unlucky."

"Don't they? Nobody at all? Does nobody know?"

"Perhaps God. But He never tells."

"He ought to, then. And aren't you lucky, either, mother?"

"I can't be, if I married an unlucky husband."

"But by yourself, aren't you?"

"I used to think I was, before I married. Now I think I am very unlucky indeed."

"Why?"

"Well—never mind! Perhaps I'm not really," she said.

The child looked at her, to see if she meant it. But he saw, by the lines of her mouth, that she was only trying to hide something from him.

"Well, anyhow," he said stoutly, "I'm a lucky person."

"Why?" said his mother, with a sudden laugh.

He stared at her. He didn't even know why he had said it.

"God told me," he asserted, brazening it out.

"I hope He did, dear!" she said, again with a laugh, but rather bitter.

"He did, mother!"

"Excellent!" said the mother, using one of her husband's exclamations.

The boy saw she did not believe him; or, rather, that she paid no attention to his assertion. This angered him somewhat, and made him want to compel her attention.

He went off by himself, vaguely, in a childish way, seeking for the clue to "luck." Absorbed, taking no heed of other people, he went about with a sort of stealth, seeking inwardly for luck. He wanted luck, he wanted it, he wanted it. When the two girls were playing dolls in the nursery, he would sit on his big rocking horse, charging madly into space with a frenzy that made the little girls peer at him uneasily. Wildly the horse careered, the waving dark hair of the boy tossed, his eyes had a strange glare in them. The little girls dared not speak to him.

When he had ridden to the end of his mad little journey, he climbed down and stood in front of his rocking horse, staring fixedly into its lowered face.

Its red mouth was slightly open, its big eye was wide and glassy-bright.

"Now!" he would silently command the snorting steed. "Now, take me to where there is luck! Now take me!"

And he would slash the horse on the neck with the little whip he had asked Uncle Oscar for. He knew the horse could take him to where there was luck, if only he forced it. So he would mount again, and start on his furious ride, hoping at last to get there. He knew he could get there.

"You'll break your horse, Paul!" said the nurse.

"He's always riding like that! I wish he'd leave off!" said his elder sister Joan.

But he only glared down on them in silence. Nurse gave him up. She could make nothing of him. Anyhow he was growing beyond her.

One day his mother and his Uncle Oscar came in when he was on one of his furious rides. He did not speak to them.

"Hallo, you young jockey! Riding a winner?" said his uncle.

"Aren't you growing too big for a rocking horse? You're not a very little boy any longer, you know," said his mother.

But Paul only gave a blue glare from his big, rather close-set eyes. He would speak to nobody when he was in full tilt. His mother watched him with an anxious expression on her face.

At last he suddenly stopped forcing his horse into the mechanical gallop, and slid down.

"Well, I got there!" he announced fiercely, his blue eyes still flaring, and his sturdy long legs straddling apart.

"Where did you get to?" asked his mother.

"Where I wanted to go," he flared back at her.

"That's right, son!" said Uncle Oscar. "Don't you stop till you get there. What's the horse's name?"

"He doesn't have a name," said the boy.

"Gets on without all right?" asked the uncle.

"Well, he has different names. He was called Sansovino last week."

"Sansovino, eh? Won the Ascot. How did you know his name?"

"He always talks about horse races with Bassett," said Joan.

The uncle was delighted to find that his small nephew was posted with all the racing news. Bassett, the young gardener, who had been wounded in the left foot in the war and had got his present job through Oscar Cresswell, whose batman[1] he had been, was a perfect blade of the "turf." He lived in the racing events, and the small boy lived with him.

Oscar Cresswell got it all from Bassett.

"Master Paul comes and asks me, so I can't do more than tell him, sir," said Bassett, his face terribly serious, as if he were speaking of religious matters.

"And does he ever put anything on a horse he fancies?"

---

[1] batman: soldier-servant of British army officer.

"Well—I don't want to give him away—he's a young sport, a fine sport, sir. Would you mind asking him yourself? He sort of takes a pleasure in it, and perhaps he'd feel I was giving him away, sir, if you don't mind."

Bassett was serious as a church.

The uncle went back to his nephew, and took him off for a ride in the car.

"Say, Paul, old man, do you ever put anything on a horse?" the uncle asked.

The boy watched the handsome man closely.

"Why, do you think I oughtn't to?" he parried.

"Not a bit of it! I thought perhaps you might give me a tip for the Lincoln."

The car sped on into the country, going down to Uncle Oscar's place in Hampshire.

"Honour bright?" said the nephew.

"Honour bright, son!" said the uncle.

"Well, then, Daffodil."

"Daffodil! I doubt it, sonny. What about Mirza?"

"I only know the winner," said the boy. "That's Daffodil."

"Daffodil, eh?"

There was a pause. Daffodil was an obscure horse comparatively.

"Uncle!"

"Yes, son?"

"You won't let it go any further, will you? I promised Bassett."

"Bassett be damned, old man! What's he got to do with it?"

"We're partners. We've been partners from the first. Uncle, he lent me my first five shillings, which I lost. I promised him, honour bright, it was only between me and him; only you gave me that ten-shilling note I started winning with, so I thought you were lucky. You won't let it go any further, will you?"

The boy gazed at his uncle from those big, hot, blue eyes, set rather close together. The uncle stirred and laughed uneasily.

"Right you are, son! I'll keep your tip private. Daffodil, eh? How much are you putting on him?"

"All except twenty pounds," said the boy. "I keep that in reserve."

The uncle thought it a good joke.

"You keep twenty pounds in reserve, do you, you young romancer? What are you betting, then?"

"I'm betting three hundred," said the boy gravely. "But it's between you and me, Uncle Oscar! Honour bright?"

The uncle burst into a roar of laughter.

"It's between you and me all right, you young Nat Gould,"[2] he said, laughing. "But where's your three hundred?"

[2] Nat Gould: presumably a well-known gambler. The reference also may be to a member of the family of Jay Gould, an American millionaire.

"Bassett keeps it for me. We're partners."

"You are, are you! And what is Bassett putting on Daffodil?"

"He won't go quite as high as I do, I expect. Perhaps he'll go a hundred and fifty."

"What, pennies?" laughed the uncle.

"Pounds," said the child, with a surprised look at his uncle. "Bassett keeps a bigger reserve than I do."

Between wonder and amusement Uncle Oscar was silent. He pursued the matter no further, but he determined to take his nephew with him to the Lincoln races.

"Now, son," he said, "I'm putting twenty on Mirza, and I'll put five for you on any horse you fancy. What's your pick?"

"Daffodil, uncle."

"No, not the fiver on Daffodil!"

"I should if it was my own fiver," said the child.

"Good! Good! Right you are! A fiver for me and a fiver for you on Daffodil."

The child had never been to a race meeting before, and his eyes were blue fire. He pursed his mouth tight, and watched. A Frenchman just in front had put his money on Lancelot. Wild with excitement, he flayed his arms up and down, yelling "Lancelot! Lancelot!" in his French accent.

Daffodil came in first, Lancelot second, Mirza third. The child, flushed and with eyes blazing, was curiously serene. His uncle brought him four five-pound notes, four to one.

"What am I to do with these?" he cried, waving them before the boy's eyes.

"I suppose we'll talk to Bassett," said the boy. "I expect I have fifteen hundred now; and twenty in reserve; and this twenty."

His uncle studied him for some moments.

"Look here, son!" he said. "You're not serious about Bassett and that fifteen hundred, are you?"

"Yes, I am. But it's between you and me, uncle. Honour bright!"

"Honour bright all right, son! But I must talk to Bassett."

"If you'd like to be a partner, uncle, with Bassett and me, we could all be partners. Only, you'd have to promise, honour bright, uncle, not to let it go beyond us three. Bassett and I are lucky, and you must be lucky, because it was your ten shillings I started winning with . . ."

Uncle Oscar took both Bassett and Paul into Richmond Park for an afternoon, and there they talked.

"It's like this, you see, sir," Bassett said. "Master Paul would get me talking about racing events, spinning yarns, you know, sir. And he was always keen on knowing if I'd made or if I'd lost. It's about a year since, now, that I put five shillings on Blush of Dawn for him—and we lost. Then the luck turned, with that ten shillings he had from you, that we put on Singhalese.

And since that time, it's been pretty steady, all things considering. What do you say, Master Paul?"

"We're all right when we're sure," said Paul. "It's when we're not quite sure that we go down."

"Oh, but we're careful then," said Bassett.

"But when are you sure?" smiled Uncle Oscar.

"It's Master Paul, sir," said Bassett, in a secret, religious voice. "It's as if he had it from heaven. Like Daffodil, now, for the Lincoln. That was as sure as eggs."

"Did you put anything on Daffodil?" asked Oscar Cresswell.

"Yes, sir, I made my bit."

"And my nephew?"

Bassett was obstinately silent, looking at Paul.

"I made twelve hundred, didn't I, Bassett? I told uncle I was putting three hundred on Daffodil."

"That's right," said Bassett, nodding.

"But where's the money?" asked the uncle.

"I keep it safe locked up, sir. Master Paul he can have it any minute he likes to ask for it."

"What, fifteen hundred pounds?"

"And twenty! and forty, that is, with the twenty he made on the course."

"It's amazing!" said the uncle.

"If Master Paul offers you to be partners, sir, I would, if I were you; if you'll excuse me," said Bassett.

Oscar Cresswell thought about it.

"I'll see the money," he said.

They drove home again, and sure enough, Bassett came round to the garden-house with fifteen hundred pounds in notes. The twenty pounds reserve was left with Joe Glee, in the Turf Commission deposit.

"You see, it's all right, uncle, when I'm sure! Then we go strong, for all we're worth. Don't we, Bassett?"

"We do that, Master Paul."

"And when are you sure?" said the uncle, laughing.

"Oh, well, sometimes I'm absolutely sure, like about Daffodil," said the boy; "and sometimes I have an idea; and sometimes I haven't even an idea, have I, Bassett? Then we're careful, because we mostly go down."

"You do, do you! And when you're sure, like about Daffodil, what makes you sure, sonny?"

"Oh, well, I don't know," said the boy uneasily. "I'm sure, you know, uncle; that's all."

"It's as if he had it from heaven, sir," Bassett reiterated.

"I should say so!" said the uncle.

But he became a partner. And when the Leger was coming on, Paul was "sure" about Lively Spark, which was a quite inconsiderable horse. The boy insisted on putting a thousand on the horse, Bassett went for five hundred, and Oscar Cresswell two hundred. Lively Spark came in first, and the betting had been ten to one against him. Paul had made ten thousand.

"You see," he said, "I was absolutely sure of him."

Even Oscar Cresswell had cleared two thousand.

"Look here, son," he said, "this sort of thing makes me nervous."

"It needn't, uncle! Perhaps I shan't be sure again for a long time."

"But what are you going to do with your money?" asked the uncle.

"Of course," said the boy, "I started it for mother. She said she had no luck, because father is unlucky, so I thought if I was lucky, it might stop whispering."

"What might stop whispering?"

"Our house. I hate our house for whispering."

"What does it whisper?"

"Why—why"—the boy fidgeted—"why, I don't know. But it's always short of money, you know, uncle."

"I know it, son, I know it."

"You know people send mother writs, don't you, uncle?"

"I'm afraid I do," said the uncle.

"And then the house whispers, like people laughing at you behind your back. It's awful, that is! I thought if I was lucky . . ."

"You might stop it," added the uncle.

The boy watched him with big blue eyes that had an uncanny cold fire in them, and he said never a word.

"Well, then!" said the uncle. "What are we doing?"

"I shouldn't like mother to know I was lucky," said the boy.

"Why not, son?"

"She'd stop me."

"I don't think she would."

"Oh!"—and the boy writhed in an odd way—"I don't want her to know, uncle."

"All right, son! We'll manage it without her knowing."

They managed it very easily. Paul, at the other's suggestion, handed over five thousand pounds to his uncle, who deposited it with the family lawyer, who was then to inform Paul's mother that a relative had put five thousand pounds into his hands, which sum was to be paid out a thousand pounds at a time, on the mother's birthday, for the next five years.

"So she'll have a birthday present of a thousand pounds for five successive years," said Uncle Oscar. "I hope it won't make it all the harder for her later."

Paul's mother had her birthday in November. The house had been "whispering" worse than ever lately, and, even in spite of his luck, Paul could not bear up against it. He was very anxious to see the effect of the birthday letter, telling his mother about the thousand pounds.

When there were no visitors, Paul now took his meals with his parents, as he was beyond the nursery control. His mother went into town nearly every day. She had discovered that she had an odd knack of sketching furs and dress materials, so she worked secretly in the studio of a friend who was the chief "artist" for the leading drapers. She drew the figures of ladies in furs and ladies in silk and sequins for the newspaper advertisements. This young woman artist earned several thousand pounds a year, but Paul's mother only made several hundreds, and she was again dissatisfied. She so wanted to be first in something, and she did not succeed, even in making sketches for drapery advertisements.

She was down to breakfast on the morning of her birthday. Paul watched her face as she read her letters. He knew the lawyer's letter. As his mother read it, her face hardened and became more expressionless. Then a cold, determined look came on her mouth. She hid the letter under the pile of others, and said not a word about it.

"Didn't you have anything nice in the post for your birthday, mother?" said Paul.

"Quite moderately nice," she said, her voice cold and absent.

She went away to town without saying more.

But in the afternoon Uncle Oscar appeared. He said Paul's mother had had a long interview with the lawyer, asking if the whole five thousand could be advanced at once, as she was in debt.

"What do you think, uncle?" said the boy.

"I leave it to you, son."

"Oh, let her have it, then! We can get some more with the other," said the boy.

"A bird in the hand is worth two in the bush, laddie!" said Uncle Oscar.

"But I'm sure to know for the Grand National; or the Lincolnshire; or else the Derby. I'm sure to know for one of them," said Paul.

So Uncle Oscar signed the agreement, and Paul's mother touched the whole five thousand. Then something very curious happened. The voices in the house suddenly went mad, like a chorus of frogs on a spring evening. There were certain new furnishings, and Paul had a tutor. He was really going to Eton, his father's school, in the following autumn. There were flowers in the winter, and a blossoming of the luxury Paul's mother had been used to. And yet the voices in the house, behind the sprays of mimosa and almond blossom, and from under the piles of iridescent cushions, simply trilled and screamed in a sort of ecstasy: "There must be more money! Oh-h-h, there must be more money. Oh, now, now-w! Now-w-w—there must be more money—more than ever! More than ever!"

It frightened Paul terribly. He studied away at his Latin and Greek with his tutors. But his intense hours were spent with Bassett. The Grand National had gone by; he had not "known," and had lost a hundred pounds.

Summer was at hand. He was in agony for the Lincoln. But even for the Lincoln he didn't "know" and he lost fifty pounds. He became wild-eyed and strange, as if something were going to explode in him.

"Let it alone, son! Don't you bother about it!" urged Uncle Oscar. But it was as if the boy couldn't really hear what his uncle was saying.

"I've got to know for the Derby! I've got to know for the Derby!" the child reiterated, his big blue eyes blazing with a sort of madness.

His mother noticed how overwrought he was.

"You'd better go to the seaside. Wouldn't you like to go now to the seaside, instead of waiting? I think you'd better," she said, looking down at him anxiously, her heart curiously heavy because of him.

But the child lifted his uncanny blue eyes.

"I couldn't possibly go before the Derby, mother!" he said. "I couldn't possibly!"

"Why not?" she said, her voice becoming heavy when she was opposed. "Why not? You can still go from the seaside to see the Derby with your Uncle Oscar, if that's what you wish. No need for you to wait here. Besides, I think you care too much about these races. It's a bad sign. My family has been a gambling family, and you won't know till you grow up how much damage it has done. But it has done damage. I shall have to send Bassett away, and ask Uncle Oscar not to talk racing to you, unless you promise to be reasonable about it; go away to the seaside and forget it. You're all nerves!"

"I'll do what you like, mother, so long as you don't send me away till after the Derby," the boy said.

"Send you away from where? Just from this house?"

"Yes," he said, gazing at her.

"Why, you curious child, what makes you care about this house so much, suddenly? I never knew you loved it."

He gazed at her without speaking. He had a secret within a secret, something he had not divulged, even to Bassett or to his Uncle Oscar.

But his mother, after standing undecided and a little bit sullen for some moments, said:

"Very well, then! Don't go to the seaside till after the Derby, if you don't wish it. But promise me you won't let your nerves go to pieces. Promise you won't think so much about horse racing and events, as you call them!"

"Oh, no," said the boy casually. "I won't think much about them, mother. You needn't worry. I wouldn't worry, mother, if I were you."

"If you were me and I were you," said his mother, "I wonder what we should do!"

"But you know you needn't worry, mother, don't you?" the boy repeated.

"I should be awfully glad to know it," she said wearily.

"Oh, well, you can, you know. I mean, you ought to know you needn't worry," he insisted.

"Ought I? Then I'll see about it," she said.

Paul's secret of secrets was his wooden horse, that which had no name. Since he was emancipated from a nurse and a nursery-governess, he had had his rocking horse removed to his own bedroom at the top of the house.

"Surely, you're too big for a rocking horse!" his mother had remonstrated.

"Well, you see, mother, till I can have a real horse, I like to have some sort of animal about," had been his quaint answer.

"Do you feel he keeps you company?" she laughed.

"Oh, yes! He's very good, he always keeps me company, when I'm there," said Paul.

So the horse, rather shabby, stood in an arrested prance in the boy's bedroom.

The Derby was drawing near, and the boy grew more and more tense. He hardly heard what was spoken to him, he was very frail, and his eyes were really uncanny. His mother had sudden seizures of uneasiness about him. Sometimes, for half-an-hour, she would feel a sudden anxiety about him that was almost anguish. She wanted to rush to him at once, and know he was safe.

Two nights before the Derby, she was at a big party in town, when one of her rushes of anxiety about her boy, her first-born, gripped her heart till she could hardly speak. She fought with the feeling, might and main, for she believed in common sense. But it was too strong. She had to leave the dance and go downstairs to telephone to the country. The children's nursery-governess was terribly surprised and startled at being rung up in the night.

"Are the children all right, Miss Wilmot?"

"Oh, yes, they are quite all right."

"Master Paul? Is he all right?"

"He went to bed as right as a trivet. Shall I run up and look at him?"

"No," said Paul's mother reluctantly. "No! Don't trouble. It's all right. Don't sit up. We shall be home fairly soon." She did not want her son's privacy intruded upon.

"Very good," said the governess.

It was about one o'clock when Paul's mother and father drove up to their house. All was still. Paul's mother went to her room and slipped off her white fur coat. She had told her maid not to wait up for her. She heard her husband downstairs, mixing a whisky-and-soda.

And then, because of the strange anxiety at her heart, she stole upstairs to her son's room. Noiselessly she went along the upper corridor. Was there a faint nose? What was it?

She stood, with arrested muscles, outside the door, listening. There was a strange, heavy, and yet not loud noise. Her heart stood still. It was a soundless noise, yet rushing and powerful. Something huge, in violent, hushed motion. What was it? What in God's name was it? She ought to know. She felt that she knew the noise. She knew what it was.

Yet she could not place it. She couldn't say what it was. And on and on it went, like a madness.

Softly, frozen with anxiety and fear, she turned the door handle.

The room was dark. Yet in the space near the window, she heard and saw something plunging to and fro. She gazed in fear and amazement.

Then suddenly she switched on the light, and saw her son, in his green pyjamas, madly surging on the rocking horse. The blaze of light suddenly lit him up, as he urged the wooden horse, and lit her up, as she stood, blonde, in her dress of pale green and crystal, in the doorway.

"Paul!" she cried. "Whatever are you doing?"

"It's Malabar!" he screamed, in a powerful, strange voice. "It's Malabar."

His eyes blazed at her for one strange and senseless second, as he ceased urging his wooden horse. Then he fell with a crash to the ground, and she, all her tormented motherhood flooding upon her, rushed to gather him up.

But he was unconscious, and unconscious he remained, with some brain-fever. He talked and tossed, and his mother sat stonily by his side.

"Malabar! It's Malabar! Bassett, Bassett, I know it! It's Malabar!"

So the child cried, trying to get up and urge the rocking horse that gave him his inspiration.

"What does he mean by Malabar?" asked the heart-frozen mother.

"I don't know," said the father stonily.

"What does he mean by Malabar?" she asked her brother Oscar.

"It's one of the horses running for the Derby," was the answer.

And, in spite of himself, Oscar Cresswell spoke to Bassett, and himself put a thousand on Malabar: at fourteen to one.

The third day of the illness was critical: they were waiting for a change. The boy, with his rather long, curly hair, was tossing ceaselessly on the pillow. He neither slept nor regained consciousness, and his eyes were like blue stones. His mother sat, feeling her heart had gone, turned actually into a stone.

In the evening, Oscar Cresswell did not come, but Bassett sent a message, saying could he come up for one moment, just one moment? Paul's mother was very angry at the intrusion, but on second thought she agreed. The boy was the same. Perhaps Bassett might bring him to consciousness.

The gardener, a shortish fellow with a little brown moustache, and sharp little brown eyes, tiptoed into the room, touched his imaginary cap to Paul's mother, and stole to the bedside, staring with glittering, smallish eyes, at the tossing, dying child.

"Master Paul!" he whispered. "Master Paul! Malabar came in first all right, a clean win. I did as you told me. You've made over seventy thousand pounds, you have; you've got over eighty thousand. Malabar came in all right, Master Paul."

"Malabar! Malabar! Did I say Malabar, mother? Did I say Malabar? Do you think I'm lucky, mother? I knew Malabar, didn't I? Over eighty thousand pounds! I call that lucky, don't you, mother? Over eighty thousand pounds! I knew, didn't I know I knew? Malabar came in all right. If I ride my horse till I'm sure, then I tell you, Bassett, you can go as high as you like. Did you go for all you were worth, Bassett?"

"I went a thousand on it, Master Paul."

"I never told you, mother, that if I can ride my horse, and get there, then I'm absolutely sure—oh, absolutely! Mother, did I ever tell you? I'm lucky."

"No, you never did," said the mother.

But the boy died in the night.

And even as he lay dead, his mother heard her brother's voice saying to her: "My God, Hester, you're eighty-odd thousand to the good and a poor devil of a son to the bad. But, poor devil, poor devil, he's best gone out of a life where he rides his rocking horse to find a winner."

READING SELECTIONS: POEMS

William Blake (1757–1827)

THE TYGER

Tyger! Tyger! burning bright
In the forests of the night,
What immortal hand or eye
Could frame thy fearful symmetry?

In what distant deeps or skies   5
Burnt the fire of thine eyes?
On what wings dare he aspire?
What the hand dare seize the fire?

And what shoulder, and what art,
Could twist the sinews of thy heart?   10
And when thy heart began to beat,
What dread hand, and what dread feet?

What the hammer? what the chain?
In what furnace was thy brain?
What the anvil? what dread grasp   15
Dare its deadly terrors clasp?

When the stars threw down their spears,
And watered heaven with their tears,

Did he smile his work to see?
Did he who made the Lamb make thee?   20

Tyger! Tyger! burning bright
In the forests of the night,
What immortal hand or eye,
Dare frame thy fearful symmetry?

STUDY QUESTIONS

1. In this famous poem, Blake uses the tiger as a symbol. List the various characteristics of the tiger. What do these characteristics suggest the tiger symbolizes?
2. Compare Blake's reference to the forest in this poem with Hawthorne's use of the forest in "Young Goodman Brown." Do both writers use the image to symbolize the same idea? Explain your answer.
3. The images in the poem suggest a forge where the tiger is molded and cast in a furnace. How does the rhythm of the poem support this image?
4. The words "dread," "dare" and "fearful" are repeated several times in the poem. What is the purpose of these repetitions? What is their effect?
5. The first and last stanzas of the poem are identical except for one word. What word is different? Why?

William Blake (1757–1827)

THE FLY

Little Fly,
Thy summer's play
My thoughtless hand
Has brush'd away.

Am not I   5
A fly like thee?
Or art not thou
A man like me?

For I dance,
And drink, and sing,   10
Till some blind hand
Shall brush my wing.

If thought is life
And strength and breath,

And the want   15
Of thought is death;

Then am I
A happy fly,
If I live
Or if I die.   20

STUDY QUESTIONS

1. Blake's poem begins with an address to a fly. What is the condition of the fly, as suggested in the first stanza?
2. What does the poet mean in stanza 3 by the words "blind hand" and "wing"?
3. In what ways, according to the poet, are a fly and a person alike? How literal is this comparison?
4. The final two stanzas are a conditional (if . . . then. . . .) argument. State that argument in your own words. Is the argument valid? (If what follows the "if" is true, then what follows the "then" must also be true.)
5. Point out examples of personification and metaphor.

Alan Dugan (1923–   )

LOVE SONG: I AND THOU

Nothing is plumb, level or square:
    the studs are bowed, the joists
are shaky by nature, no piece fits
    any other piece without a gap
or pinch, and bent nails   5
    dance all over the surfacing
like maggots. By Christ
    I am no carpenter, I built
the roof for myself, the walls
    for myself, the floors   10
for myself, and got
    hung up in it myself. I
danced with a purple thumb
    at this house-warming, drunk
with my prime whiskey: rage.   15
    Oh I spat rage's nails
into the frame-up of my work:
    it held. It settled plumb,

level, solid, square and true
   for that one moment. Then   20
it screamed and went on through
   skewing as wrong the other way.
God damned it. This is hell,
   but I planned it, I sawed it,
I nailed it, and I   25
   will live in it until it kills me.
I can nail my left palm
   to the left-hand cross-piece but
I can't do everything myself.
   I need a hand to nail the right,   30
a help, a love, a you, a wife.

STUDY QUESTIONS

1. The poem is rich in metaphors relating to carpentry. What is the meaning of the various carpenter's terms—plumb, level, square, studs, joists? What has the speaker of the poem been building—that is, to what do all the metaphors refer?
2. Explain the metaphors in lines 13–15.
3. The last six lines suggest a crucifixion, as if the speaker of the poem has been very uncomfortable in his "house," but needs help to complete that suffering. Why does he use such terms as "love" and "wife" to describe the person who might help? In what ways and to what extent is this poem a "Love Song"?

Donald Finkel (1929–)

HUNTING SONG

The fox came lolloping, lolloping,
Lolloping. His tongue hung out
And his ears were high.
He was like death at the end of a string
When he came to the hollow   5
Log. Ran in one side
And out of the other. O
He was sly.

The hounds came tumbling, tumbling,
Tumbling. Their heads were low   10
And their eyes were red.

The sound of their breath was louder than death
When they came to the hollow
Log. They held at one end
But a bitch found the scent. O   15
They were mad.

The hunter came galloping, galloping,
Galloping. All damp was his mare
From her hooves to her mane.
His coat and his mouth were redder than death   20
When he came to the hollow
Log. He took in the rein
And over he went. O
He was fine.

The log, he just lay there, alone in   25
The clearing. No fox nor hound
Nor mounted man
Saw his black round eyes in their perfect disguise
(As the ends of a hollow
Log). He watched death go through him,   30
Around him and over him. O
He was wise.

STUDY QUESTIONS

1. What is the effect of the repeated stanza form, with something like a re-
   frain at the end? In each of the first three stanzas, an important verb is
   repeated: "lolloping," "tumbling," "galloping." Why is there no such
   repetition in stanza 4?
2. In what sense does death go through, around, and over the log (lines
   30–31)?
3. Why is the exclamation "O" spelled as it is instead of the more usual
   "Oh"?
4. Discuss the ironies of the last lines of each stanza.

Emily Dickinson (1830–1886)

EXULTATION IS THE GOING

Exultation is the going
Of an inland soul to sea,
Past the houses—past the headlands—
Into deep Eternity—

Bred as we, among the mountains,   5
Can the sailor understand
The divine intoxication
Of the first league out from land?

STUDY QUESTIONS

1. Dickinson begins with what seems to be a definition of the emotion of exultation presented to the reader as a metaphor. Specifically she compares exultation to the action of going far out on the ocean. What words in the first stanza suggest a deeper meaning? Why?
2. The second stanza asks a rhetorical question: can the sailor who, like us, was born and raised inland, understand the thrill we receive when we sail out to sea for the first time? Again she uses words that suggest deeper meanings. What words are they?
3. Consider the words you listed in response to the previous question. Did you include "sailor"? What connotations might that word have in light of your other answers?
4. What kind of inner experience or physical experience might cause exultation, as implied by the poem?

Emily Dickinson (1830–1886)

THE SOUL SELECTS HER OWN SOCIETY—

The Soul selects her own Society—
Then—shuts the Door—
To her divine Majority—
Present no more—

Unmoved—she notes the Chariots—pausing—   5
At her low Gate—
Unmoved—an Emperor be kneeling
Upon her Mat—

I've known her—from an ample nation—
Choose One—   10
Then—close the Valves of her attention—
Like Stone—

STUDY QUESTIONS

1. Dickinson personifies "Soul," making it a woman. What elements of setting help to characterize the woman?

2. What does "divine Majority" mean? Is the poet referring to numbers, age, both sorts of majority?
3. How does the word "Valves" relate to the major metaphor of the house? Is this word a poor choice or a good choice? Why?
4. What is the effect of the last line: "Like Stone—"?
5. What does the poem mean?

Emily Dickinson (1830–1886)

I HEARD A FLY BUZZ—WHEN I DIED

I heard a Fly buzz—when I died—
The Stillness in the Room
Was like the Stillness in the Air—
Between the Heaves of Storm—

The Eyes around—had wrung them dry—   5
And Breaths were gathering firm
For that last Onset—when the King
Be witnessed—in the Room—

I willed my Keepsakes—Signed away
What portion of me be   10
Assignable—and then it was
There interposed a Fly—

With Blue—uncertain stumbling Buzz—
Between the light—and me—
And then the Windows failed—and then   15
I could not see to see—

STUDY QUESTIONS

1. Describe the various details of setting in the poem as well as other details that establish the scene.
2. Describe the speaker.
3. Who is "the King" (line 7)?
4. Explain the metaphor in line 5. Cite other lines that illustrate metaphor and explain the comparison involved in each of them.
5. What are the possible meanings of "Windows" in line 15?
6. How accurate is the simile in lines 2–4?

George Herbert (1593–1633)

THE PULLEY

When God at first made man,
Having a glass of blessings standing by,
  "Let us," said he, "pour on him all we can.
Let the world's riches, which dispersèd lie,
    Contract into a span."   5

So strength first made a way;
Then beauty flowed, then wisdom, honor, pleasure.
  When almost all was out, God made a stay,
Perceiving that, alone of all his treasure,
    Rest in the bottom lay.   10

  "For if I should," said he,
"Bestow this jewel also on my creature,
  He would adore my gifts instead of me,
And rest in Nature, not the God of Nature;
    So both should losers be.   15

  "Yet let him keep the rest,
But keep them with repining restlessness.
  Let him be rich and weary, that at least,
If goodness lead him not, yet weariness
    May toss him to my breast."   20

STUDY QUESTIONS

1. What, according to the poet, does God not allow man to have? Why? In this context, explain the play on the word "rest."
2. What is the significance of the poem's title?
3. Discuss Herbert's distinction in the poem between "Nature" and the "God of Nature."
4. What is the meter and rhyme scheme of the poem?
5. Explain the meaning of the last couplet of stanza one. Is the poet's language here compact? Explain.
6. What meaning does the series of nouns in stanza two hold?
7. What is the central metaphor of the poem? One critic has said that this figure is stretched "almost beyond its bounds." Do you agree? Why?
8. What in man's nature does the poem attempt to explain? Is the answer a convincing one? Explain.

George Herbert (1593–1633)

THE COLLAR

I struck the board and cried, "No more;
    I will abroad!
What? shall I ever sigh and pine?
My lines and life are free, free as the road,
    Loose as the wind, as large as store.   5
        Shall I be still in suit?
Have I no harvest but a thorn
To let me blood, and not restore
What I have lost with cordial fruit?
        Sure there was wine   10
Before my sighs did dry it; there was corn
    Before my tears did drown it.
Is the year only lost to me?
    Have I no bays to crown it,
No flowers, no garlands gay? All blasted?   15
        All wasted?
  Not so, my heart; but there is fruit,
    And thou hast hands.
Recover all thy sigh-blown age
On double pleasures: leave thy cold dispute   20
Of what is fit and not. Forsake thy cage,
        Thy rope of sands,
Which petty thoughts have made, and made to thee
    Good cable, to enforce and draw,
        And be thy law,   25
  While thou didst wink and wouldst not see.
        Away! take heed;
        I will abroad.
Call in thy death's-head there; tie up thy fears.
        He that forbears   30
    To suit and serve his need,
        Deserves his load."
But as I raved and grew more fierce and wild
        At every word,
Methought I heard one calling, *Child!*   35
    And I replied, *My Lord.*

---

1. board: table.   5. store: full storehouse.   9. cordial: invigorating.   14. bays:
laurel wreaths, symbolizing honor.   29. death's-head: skull.   31. suit: learn, adapt.

STUDY QUESTIONS

1. Who and what is being addressed in the poem?
2. Why does the speaker repeat the idea, "I will abroad" (lines 2, 28)?
3. Explain the reference to a skull (line 29).
4. Find and explain as many metaphors as you can in which the speaker of the poem is in effect compared to something else.
5. How does language reflect the emotional state of the speaker?
6. What figure of speech is represented in lines 17 and 18?
7. What similarities in use of language and theme can you find in this poem and "The Pulley"?

Theodore Roethke (1908–1963)

THE WAKING

I wake to sleep, and take my waking slow.
I feel my fate in what I cannot fear.
I learn by going where I have to go.

We think by feeling. What is there to know?
I hear my being dance from ear to ear.   5
I wake to sleep, and take my waking slow.

Of those so close beside me, which are you?
God bless the Ground! I shall walk softly there,
And learn by going where I have to go.

Light takes the Tree; but who can tell us how?   10
The lowly worm climbs up a winding stair;
I wake to sleep, and take my waking slow.

Great Nature has another thing to do
To you and me; so take the lively air,
And, lovely, learn by going where to go.   15

This shaking keeps me steady. I should know.
What falls away is always. And is near.
I wake to sleep, and take my waking slow.
I learn by going where I have to go.

STUDY QUESTIONS

1. This poem is a villanelle, a very strict form in which lines 1 and 3 are repeated at definite times among the total of nineteen lines. To bear the

weight of such repetition these lines must have particular significance. What are some possible metaphors that might be indicated by "waking" and "sleep"? Should the first four words be read, "I wake up in order to sleep" or "I become awake to (aware of) the fact of sleep"? Or both?

2. Does line 3 imply, "The act of going where I have to go is a learning experience" or "In the process of going I find out where I must go"? Or both?

3. Roethke was trained as a biologist. What biological ideas may form the basis for the following metaphors: "Light takes the tree" (line 10); "The lowly worm climbs up a winding stair" (line 11); "Great Nature has another thing to do / To you and me" (lines 13–14).

4. Who is addressed as "you" in lines 7 and 14?

Robert Frost (1874–1963)

DIRECTIVE

Back out of all this now too much for us,
Back in a time made simple by the loss
Of detail, burned, dissolved, and broken off
Like graveyard marble sculpture in the weather,
There is a house that is no more a house   5
Upon a farm that is no more a farm
And in a town that is no more a town.
The road there, if you'll let a guide direct you
Who only has at heart your getting lost,
May seem as if it should have been a quarry—   10
Great monolithic knees the former town
Long since gave up pretense of keeping covered.
And there's a story in a book about it:
Besides the wear of iron wagon wheels
The ledges show lines ruled southeast-northwest,   15
The chisel work of an enormous Glacier
That braced his feet against the Arctic Pole.
You must not mind a certain coolness from him
Still said to haunt this side of Panther Mountain.
Nor need you mind the serial ordeal   20
Of being watched from forty cellar holes
As if by eye pairs out of forty firkins.
As for the woods' excitement over you
That sends light rustle rushes to their leaves,
Charge that to upstart inexperience.   25
Where were they all not twenty years ago?
They think too much of having shaded out

A few old pecker-fretted apple trees.
Make yourself up a cheering song of how
Someone's road home from work this once was,   30
Who may be just ahead of you on foot
Or creaking with a buggy load of grain.
The height of the adventure is the height
Of country where two village cultures faded
Into each other. Both of them are lost.   35
And if you're lost enough to find yourself
By now, pull in your ladder road behind you
And put a sign up CLOSED to all but me.
Then make yourself at home. The only field
Now left's no bigger than a harness gall.   40
First there's the children's house of make-believe,
Some shattered dishes underneath a pine,
The playthings in the playhouse of the children.
Weep for what little things could make them glad.
Then for the house that is no more a house,   45
But only a belilaced cellar hole,
Now slowly closing like a dent in dough.
This was no playhouse but a house in earnest.
Your destination and your destiny's
A brook that was the water of the house,   50
Cold as a spring as yet so near its source,
Too lofty and original to rage.
(We know the valley streams that when aroused
Will leave their tatters hung on barb and thorn.)
I have kept hidden in the instep arch   55
Of an old cedar at the waterside
A broken drinking goblet like the Grail
Under a spell so the wrong ones can't find it,
So can't get saved, as Saint Mark says they mustn't.
(I stole the goblet from the children's playhouse.)   60
Here are your waters and your watering place.
Drink and be whole again beyond confusion.

22. firkin: a small wooden barrel or cask.   57. Grail: the cup, according to legend,
used by Christ at the Last Supper, which became an object of knightly quest.

STUDY QUESTIONS

1. The first thirty-five lines of "Directive" describe a particular place at two
   different times: the present and a much earlier period. Describe the scene
   as it looks in each of those times.

2. What examples of personification, simile, and other figures of speech are present in lines 1–35? Does Frost seem to use one special figure more frequently than others? If so, can you suggest his reason?

3. Line 36 marks a turn in the poem. "If you're lost enough to find yourself," the speaker says, "Then make yourself at home." In what sense is he using the word "lost"? Quote other lines where the word is also used. Does "lost" mean the same thing in each of those lines? If not, what different meanings does it seem to have?

4. The poem is titled "Directive"; in line 8 the speaker identifies himself as the guide who will "direct" you, the reader, to an earlier time. Besides directions for locating a place, what other specific directions does he give the reader?

5. Frost calls this poem a parable—a simple story that illustrates a moral or religious message. Some of the words in the last fourteen lines have religious connotations, words like "destiny," "water," "goblet," and "saved." Others are Biblical or mythological allusions: "Grail," and "Saint Mark." Research these words; then consider how they relate to the preceding lines. What moral message does the poem seem to illustrate?

Robert Frost (1874–1963)

DESIGN

I found a dimpled spider, fat and white,
On a white heal-all, holding up a moth
Like a white piece of rigid satin cloth—
Assorted characters of death and blight
Mixed ready to begin the morning right,   5
Like the ingredients of a witches' broth—
A snow-drop spider, a flower like a froth,
And dead wings carried like a paper kite.

What had that flower to do with being white,
The wayside blue and innocent heal-all?   10
What brought the kindred spider to that height,
Then steered the white moth thither in the night?
What but design of darkness to appall?—
If design govern in a thing so small.

2. heal-all: a wildflower, usually blue, once used in folk medicine.

STUDY QUESTIONS

1. What is the literal "story" of this poem? What part of speech does the author primarily use to convey it?

2. The language in this poem is particularly direct and concise. What do these elements of diction have to do with the poem's being a sonnet?

3. Does imagery in "Design" create the atmosphere of a still life or a scene of action? Discuss.

4. What is the significance of the repetition of "white" in the poem? Does the word take on symbolic meaning? Discuss.

5. Notice that the first stanza of this poem is basically declarative and the second interrogative. Why?

6. Discuss the play on words in line 5.

7. Analyze the dramatic shift in imagery in line 13. Has Frost previously suggested such a shift in stanza 1? Is the closing couplet an ironic statement? Why?

William Shakespeare (1564–1616)

MY LOVE IS AS A FEVER, LONGING STILL
(SONNET 147)

My love is as a fever, longing still
For that which longer nurseth the disease,
Feeding on that which doth preserve the ill,
Th' uncertain sickly appetite to please.
My reason, the physician to my love,   5
Angry that his prescriptions are not kept,
Hath left me, and I desperate now approve
Desire is death, which physic did except.
Past cure I am, now reason is past care,
And frantic-mad with evermore unrest;   10
My thoughts and my discourse as madmen's are,
At random from the truth vainly express'd;
    For I have sworn thee fair, and thought thee bright,
    Who art as black as hell, as dark as night.

STUDY QUESTIONS

1. What is Shakespeare's image of reason? How does that image relate to his definition of love?

2. Which individual words in the poem indicate the speaker's state of mind?

3. What figure of speech is "Desire is death"? What does the figure mean? How does the figure relate to the Elizabethan notion of love?

4. How does Shakespeare use repetition in this poem? Why?

5. What is the relationship of line 1 to the last line of the poem?

6. Discuss Shakespeare's attitude toward love in this poem. What images express that attitude?

John Milton (1608–1674)

ON HIS BLINDNESS

When I consider how my light is spent
Ere half my days in this dark world and wide,
And that one talent which is death to hide
Lodged with me useless, though my soul more bent
To serve therewith my Maker, and present   5
My true account, lest he returning chide,
"Doth God exact day-labor, light denied?"
I fondly ask. But Patience, to prevent
That murmur, soon replies, "God doth not need
Either man's work or his own gifts. Who best   10
Bear his mild yoke, they serve him best. His state
Is kingly: thousands at his bidding speed,
And post o'er land and ocean without rest;
They also serve who only stand and wait."

STUDY QUESTIONS

1. Milton became totally blind in 1652 at the age of 44. He wrote this sonnet three years later. What is the major question he asks in the first seven
   lines?

2. In line 3 the poet refers to his "one talent." The allusion is to a biblical
   story in Matthew 25:14–30, in which a man gives five of his servants
   coins, called "talents," and asks each to use the money to make more.
   One servant, afraid to lose the money, buries it. The master calls him
   slothful, takes the coin from him and gives it to the one who has brought
   back the greatest profit. How does this allusion expand the meaning of
   the sonnet?

3. The word "fondly" in line 8 means "foolishly." Why does the poet consider his question foolish? What is the answer to the question posed in
   line 7?

4. Although this sonnet has the rhyme scheme of an Italian sonnet (abba,
   abba, cde, cde), Milton changed the structure so that this form is called
   Miltonian. How is it different from the 8-6 line division of the Italian
   sonnet?

5. Point out three examples of figurative language.

William Wordsworth (1770–1850)

THE WORLD IS TOO MUCH WITH US

The world is too much with us; late and soon,
Getting and spending, we lay waste our powers:
Little we see in Nature that is ours;
We have given our hearts away, a sordid boon!
The Sea that bares her bosom to the moon;   5
The winds that will be howling at all hours,
And are up-gathered now like sleeping flowers;
For this, for everything, we are out of tune;
It moves us not.—Great God! I'd rather be
A Pagan suckled in a creed outworn;   10
So might I, standing on this pleasant lea,
Have glimpses that would make me less forlorn;
Have sight of Proteus rising from the sea;
Or hear old Triton blow his wreathèd horn.

13. Proteus: legendary sea god who had the power to assume different shapes.
14. Triton: Greco-Roman demigod of the sea.

STUDY QUESTIONS

1. What does Wordsworth mean by his first statement? What is "the world" he refers to?
2. What is it he feels people of the modern age have lost?
3. What is the setting of the poem? Point out the lines that prove your answer.
4. Quote a line containing a simile, a line containing a personification, and a line containing a metaphor.
5. In the sestet, the poet declares he would rather be a pagan, believing in Greek sea gods, than to be out of tune with nature. Is he blaming Christianity for the loss of affinity with nature? Why or why not?

Gerard Manley Hopkins (1844–1889)

GOD'S GRANDEUR

The world is charged with the grandeur of God.
It will flame out, like shining from shook foil;
It gathers to a greatness, like the ooze of oil
Crushed. Why do men then now not reck his rod?

Generations have trod, have trod, have trod;   5
    And all is seared with trade; bleared, smeared with toil;
    And wears man's smudge and shares man's smell: the soil

Is bare now, nor can foot feel, being shod.
And for all this, nature is never spent;
    There lives the dearest freshness deep down things;   10
And though the last lights off the black West went
    Oh, morning, at the brown brink eastward, springs—
Because the Holy Ghost over the bent
    World broods with warm breast and with ah! bright wings.

STUDY QUESTIONS

1. Lines 1–3 include a cluster of metaphors and similes. What is the actual topic of these figurative comparisons? To what is it compared?
2. "Rod" (line 4) is a metonymy. What attribute of God does it stand for? The word *reck* in the same line may not be in your dictionary. Consider the meaning of the word *reckless* as a basis for defining "reck." What does *reck* mean as a verb in the context of line 4?
3. What is the effect of the repetitions in line 5?
4. What consonant sounds predominate in lines 7 and 8? What is their relation to the ideas being expressed?
5. The first eight lines of this sonnet present a question or problem. Define it in simple prose. What answer or solution is suggested by the final six lines?
6. What familiar symbol for the Holy Ghost is suggested by line 14?

Gerard Manley Hopkins (1844–1889)

(CARRION COMFORT)

Not, I'll not, (carrion comfort), Despair, not feast on thee;
Not untwist—slack they may be—these last strands of man
In me ór, most weary, cry *I can no more.* I can;
Can something, hope, wish day come, not choose not to be.
But ah, but O thou terrible, why wouldst thou rude on me   5
Thy wring-world right foot rock? lay a lionlimb against me? scan
With darksome devouring eyès my bruisèd bones? and fan,
O in turns of tempest, me heaped there; me frantic to avoid thee and flee?

Why? That my chaff might fly; my grain lie, sheer and clear.
Nay in all that toil, that coil, since (seems) I kissed the rod,   10
Hand rather, my heart lo! lapped strength, stole joy, would laugh, chéer.

Cheer whom though? The hero whose heaven-handling flung me, fóot tród
Me? or me that fought him? O which one? is it each one? That night, that
    year
Of now done darkness I wretch lay wrestling with (my God!) my God.

5. rude: roughly, violently.

STUDY QUESTIONS

1. Who (or what personified object or idea) is addressed in the first few
   lines? What action or attitude is compared to feasting on carrion comfort?
2. Who is addressed in lines 5 through 8?
3. Rearrange "why wouldst thou rude on me / Thy wring-world right foot
   rock?" in more normal word order. Which word is the verb?
4. Considering methods of threshing grain in use before modern technology
   (for example, in Biblical times) explain the metaphors of line 9.
5. Why does the speaker exclaim "(my God!)" in line 14? What realization
   or understanding has the speaker come to?

e. e. cummings (1894–1962)

WHO'S MOST AFRAID OF DEATH? THOU

who's most afraid of death? thou
                art of him
utterly afraid, i love of thee
(beloved) this

       and truly i would be   5
near when his scythe takes crisply the whim
of thy smoothness. and mark the fainting
murdered petals. with the caving stem.

But of all most would i be one of them

round the hurt heart which do so frailly cling . . . .)   10
i who am but imperfect in my fear

Or with thy mind against my mind, to hear
nearing our hearts' irrevocable play—
through the mysterious high futile day

an enormous stride   15
         (and drawing thy mouth toward
my mouth, steer our lost bodies carefully downward)

STUDY QUESTIONS

1. cummings's opening question seems very straightforward. It is followed, however, by an answer that may be difficult to understand, in part because the words are not in normal word order. For example, the usual word order of "thou / art of him / utterly afraid" would be "thou art utterly afraid of him." Read the sentences that make up cummings's answer; arrange the words in each of them in normal order and provide whatever punctuation you feel is necessary to help clarify meaning.

2. What words does cummings use that are associated with death? Identify examples of figurative language and indicate the type of figure that those words illustrate.

3. Death is a common symbol for sexual orgasm. Do you think that cummings is using death in that way anywhere in the poem? If so, what evidence is there to support your belief? Does cummings use death only as a sexual symbol, or does he also use it to mean "the end of life"? Support your answer with specific references to the poem itself.

4. What does the line "i who am but imperfect in my fear" suggest about the poet's attitude toward the death of his beloved? Toward his own death? Does it have any other implications as to the meaning of the poem?

5. Explain how the unusual word order in the poem extends meaning. For example, how many different ways might you read the following lines:

> but of all most would i be one of them
> round the hurt heart which do so frailly cling. . . .)

Walt Whitman (1819–1892)

WHEN LILACS LAST IN THE DOORYARD BLOOM'D

1

When lilacs last in the dooryard bloom'd,
And the great star early droop'd in the western sky in the night,
I mourn'd, and yet shall mourn with ever-returning spring.

Ever-returning spring, trinity sure to me you bring,
Lilac blooming perennial and drooping star in the west,   5
And thought of him I love.

2

O powerful western fallen star!
O shades of night—O moody, tearful night!
O great star disappear'd—O the black murk that hides the star!

O cruel hands that hold me powerless—O helpless soul of me!   10
O harsh surrounding cloud that will not free my soul.

3

In the dooryard fronting an old farm-house near the white-wash'd palings,
Stands the lilac-bush tall-growing with heart-shaped leaves of rich green,
With many a pointed blossom rising delicate, with the perfume strong I
    love,
With every leaf a miracle—and from this bush in the dooryard,   15
With delicate-color blossoms and heart-shaped leaves of rich green,
A sprig with its flower I break.

4

In the swamp in secluded recesses,
A shy and hidden bird is warbling a song.

Solitary the thrush,   20
The hermit withdrawn to himself, avoiding the settlements,
Sings by himself a song.

Song of the bleeding throat,
Death's outlet song of life, (for well dear brother I know,
If thou wast not granted to sing thou would'st surely die.)   25

5

Over the breast of the spring, the land, amid cities,
Amid lanes and through old woods, where lately the violets peep'd from the
    ground, spotting the gray debris,
Amid the grass in the fields each side of the lanes, passing the endless grass,
Passing the yellow-spear'd wheat, every grain from its shroud in the dark-
    brown fields uprisen,
Passing the apple-tree blows of white and pink in the orchards,   30
Carrying a corpse to where it shall rest in the grave,
Night and day journeys a coffin.

6

Coffin that passes through lanes and streets,
Through day and night with the great cloud darkening the land,
With the pomp of the inloop'd flags with the cities draped in black,   35
With the show of the States themselves as of crape-veil'd women standing,
With processions long and winding and the flambeaus of the night,
With the countless torches lit, with the silent sea of faces and the unbared
    heads,

12. palings: boards in a picket fence.   37. flambeaus: lighted torches.

With the waiting depot, the arriving coffin, and the sombre faces,
With dirges through the night, with the thousand voices rising strong and
    solemn,   40
With all the mournful voices of the dirges pour'd around the coffin,
The dim-lit churches and the shuddering organs—where amid these you
    journey,
With the tolling tolling bells' perpetual clang,
Here, coffin that slowly passes,
I give you my sprig of lilac.   45

7

(Nor for you, for one alone,
Blossoms and branches green to coffins all I bring,
For fresh as the morning, thus would I chant a song for you O sane and
    sacred death.

All over bouquets of roses,
O death, I cover you over with roses and early lilies,   50
But mostly and now the lilac that blooms the first,
Copious I break, I break the sprigs from the bushes,
With loaded arms I come, pouring for you,
For you and the coffins all of you O death.)

8

O western orb sailing the heaven,   55
Now I know what you must have meant as a month since I walk'd,
As I walk'd in silence the transparent shadowy night,
As I saw you had something to tell as you bent to me night after night,
As you droop'd from the sky low down as if to my side, (while the other
    stars all look'd on,)
As we wander'd together the solemn night, (for something I know not what
    kept me from sleep,)   60
As the night advanced, and I saw on the rim of the west how full you were
    of woe,
As I stood on the rising ground in the breeze in the cool transparent night,
As I watch'd where you pass'd and was lost in the netherward black of the
    night,
As my soul in its trouble dissatisfied sank, as where you sad orb,
Concluded, dropt in the night, and was gone.   65

9

Sing on there in the swamp,
O singer bashful and tender, I hear your notes, I hear your call,
I hear, I come presently, I understand you,

But a moment I linger, for the lustrous star has detain'd me,
The star my departing comrade holds and detains me.   70

10

O how shall I warble myself for the dead one there I loved?
And how shall I deck my song for the large sweet soul that has gone?
And what shall my perfume be for the grave of him I love?

Sea-winds blown from east and west,
Blown from the Eastern sea and blown from the Western sea, till there on
    the prairies meeting,   75
These and with these and the breath of my chant,
I'll perfume the grave of him I love.

11

O what shall I hang on the chamber walls?
And what shall the pictures be that I hang on the walls,
To adorn the burial-house of him I love?   80

Pictures of growing spring and farms and homes,
With the Fourth-month eve at sundown, and the gray smoke lucid and
    bright,
With floods of the yellow gold of the gorgeous, indolent, sinking sun, burn-
    ing, expanding the air,
With the fresh sweet herbage under foot, and the pale green leaves of the
    trees prolific,
In the distance the flowing glaze, the breast of the river, with a wind-dapple
    here and there,   85
With ranging hills on the banks, with many a line against the sky, and
    shadows,
And the city at hand with dwellings so dense, and stacks of chimneys,
And all the scenes of life and the workshops, and the workmen homeward
    returning.

12

Lo, body and soul—this land,
My own Manhattan with spires, and the sparkling and hurrying tides, and
    the ships,   90
The varied and ample land, the South and the North in the light, Ohio's
    shores and flashing Missouri,
And ever the far-spreading prairies cover'd with grass and corn.

Lo, the most excellent sun so calm and haughty,
The violet and purple morn with just-felt breezes,
The gentle soft-born measureless light,   95

The miracle spreading bathing all, the fulfill'd noon,
The coming eve delicious, the welcome night and the stars,
Over my cities shining all, enveloping man and land.

13

Sing on, sing on you gray-brown bird,
Sing from the swamps, the recesses, pour your chant from the bushes,   100
Limitless out of the dusk, out of the cedars and pines.

Sing on dearest brother, warble your reedy song,
Loud human song, with voice of uttermost woe.

O liquid and free and tender!
O wild and loose to my soul—O wondrous singer!   105
You only I hear—yet the star holds me, (but will soon depart,)
Yet the lilac with mastering odor holds me.

14

Now while I sat in the day and look'd forth,
In the close of the day with its light and the fields of spring, and the farmers
    preparing their crops,
In the large unconscious scenery of my land with its lakes and forests,   110
In the heavenly aerial beauty, (after the perturb'd winds and the storms,)
Under the arching heavens of the afternoon swift passing, and the voices of
    children and women,
The many-moving sea-tides, and I saw the ships how they sail'd,
And the summer approaching with richness, and the fields all busy with
    labor,
And the infinite separate houses, how they all went on, each with its meals
    and minutia of daily usages,   115
And the streets how their throbbings throbb'd, and the cities pent—lo, then
    and there,
Falling upon them all and among them all, enveloping me with the rest,
Appear'd the cloud, appear'd the long black trail,
And I knew death, its thought, and the sacred knowledge of death.

Then with the knowledge of death as walking one side of me,   120
And the thought of death close-walking the other side of me,
And I in the middle as with companions, and as holding the hands of com-
    panions,
I fled forth to the hiding receiving night that talks not,
Down to the shores of the water, the path by the swamp in the dimness,
To the solemn shadowy cedars and ghostly pines so still.   125

And the singer so shy to the rest receiv'd me,
The gray-brown bird I know receiv'd us comrades three,
And he sang the carol of death, and a verse for him I love.

From deep secluded recesses,
From the fragrant cedars and the ghostly pines so still,   130
Came the carol of the bird.

And the charm of the carol rapt me.
As I held as if by their hands my comrades in the night,
And the voice of my spirit tallied the song of the bird.

Come lovely and soothing death,   135
Undulate round the world, serenely arriving, arriving,
In the day, in the night, to all, to each,
Sooner or later delicate death.

Prais'd be the fathomless universe,
For life and joy, and for objects and knowledge curious,   140
And for love, sweet love—but praise! praise! praise!
For the sure-enwinding arms of cool-enfolding death.

Dark mother always gliding near with soft feet,
Have none chanted for thee a chant of fullest welcome?
Then I chant it for thee, I glorify thee above all,   145
I bring thee a song that when thou must indeed come, come unfalteringly.

Approach strong deliveress,
When it is so, when thou hast taken them I joyously sing the dead,
Lost in the loving floating ocean of thee,
Laved in the flood of thy bliss O death.   150

From me to thee glad serenades,
Dances for thee I propose saluting thee, adornments and feastings for thee,
And the sights of the open landscape and the high-spread sky are fitting,
And life and the fields, and the huge and thoughtful night.

The night in silence under many a star,   155
The ocean shore and the husky whispering wave whose voice I know,
And the soul turning to thee O vast and well-veil'd death,
And the body gratefully nestling close to thee.

Over the tree-tops I float thee a song,
Over the rising and sinking waves, over the myriad fields and the prairies
*   wide,*   160
Over the dense-pack'd cities all and the teeming wharves and ways,
I float this carol with joy, with joy to thee O death.

15

To the tally of my soul,
Loud and strong kept up the gray-brown bird,
With pure deliberate notes spreading filling the night.   165

Loud in the pines and cedars dim,
Clear in the freshness moist and the swamp-perfume,
And I with my comrades there in the night.

While my sight that was bound in my eyes unclosed,
As to long panoramas of visions.   170

And I saw askant the armies,
I saw as in noiseless dreams hundreds of battle-flags,
Borne through the smoke of the battles and pierc'd with missiles I saw them,
And carried hither and yon through the smoke, and torn and bloody,
And at last but a few shreds left on the staffs, (and all in silence,)   175
And the staffs all splinter'd and broken.

I saw battle-corpses, myriads of them,
And the white skeletons of young men, I saw them,
I saw the debris and debris of all the slain soldiers of the war,
But I saw they were not as was thought,   180
They themselves were fully at rest, they suffer'd not,
The living remain'd and suffer'd, the mother suffer'd,
And the wife and the child and the musing comrade suffer'd,
And the armies that remain'd suffer'd.

16

Passing the visions, passing the night,   185
Passing, unloosing the hold of my comrades' hands,
Passing the song of the hermit bird and the tallying song of my soul,
Victorious song, death's outlet song, yet varying ever-altering song,
As low and wailing, yet clear the notes, rising and falling, flooding the night,
Sadly sinking and fainting, as warning and warning, and yet again bursting
     with joy,   190
Covering the earth and filling the spread of the heaven,
As that powerful psalm in the night I heard from recesses,
Passing, I leave thee lilac with heart-shaped leaves,
I leave thee there in the door-yard, blooming, returning with spring.

I cease from my song for thee,   195
From my gaze on thee in the west, fronting the west, communing with thee,
O comrade lustrous with silver face in the night.

Yet each to keep and all, retrievements out of the night,
The song, the wondrous chant of the gray-brown bird,
And the tallying chant, the echo arous'd in my soul,   200
With the lustrous and drooping star with the countenance full of woe,
With the holders holding my hand nearing the call of the bird,
Comrades mine and I in the midst, and their memory ever to keep, for the
     dead I loved so well,

For the sweetest, wisest soul of all my days and lands—and this for his dear
  sake,
Lilac and star and bird twined with the chant of my soul,   205
There in the fragrant pines and the cedars dusk and dim.

STUDY QUESTIONS

1. "Lilacs" is Whitman's elegy to Abraham Lincoln, whose assassination in 1865 greatly moved the entire nation. The poem is structured around dominant symbols: the star, representing Lincoln; the lilacs, representing the poet's love; the thrush, representing the soul or spiritual life; and the cloud, representing death. In the first two sections, Whitman introduces three of these symbols. What is his initial attitude toward death? What is the mood of the speaker? Cite words or images that reveal his mood.
2. The speaker begins, in stanza 3, to move toward acceptance of death. What is the first action he takes? On what two levels of meaning does the breaking of the sprig of lilac operate?
3. In the fourth stanza, the thrush is introduced. Why is the bird described as "shy and hidden"? If the bird represents the spirit, is line 25, which states that the bird would die if it could not sing, appropriate? What does "sing" imply?
4. Stanzas 5–8 describe the journey of the train that carried Lincoln from Washington, D.C., to Springfield, Illinois. In these stanzas how does the speaker extend the elegy to others who are dead?
5. Throughout the poem Whitman varies the words that are symbols. What other word or words refer to death? To Lincoln? To love? To the spirit?
6. Following the funeral procession, the speaker again hears the thrush. What is his answer to the bird in stanza 9. Why?
7. In stanzas 10–13 the poet observes the world and reflects on it, while the bird waits. What human experience does this act compare to? How valid is the poet's experience?
8. Why is the thrush waiting in a swamp? Why does the poet go to find the bird at night in stanzas 14 and 15? Compare his nighttime experience in the swamp with the setting in stanza 16. What has happened?
9. In stanza 14 the bird sings to the speaker. What is the meaning of his song? Why does it lead the poet to the acceptance he was seeking?

Robert Lowell (1916–1977)

THE DRUNKEN FISHERMAN

Wallowing in this bloody sty,
I cast for fish that pleased my eye

(Truly Jehovah's bow suspends
No pots of gold to weight its ends);
Only the blood-mouthed rainbow trout   5
Rose to my bait. They flopped about
My canvas creel until the moth
Corrupted its unstable cloth.

A calendar to tell the day;
A handkerchief to wave away   10
The gnats; a conch unstuffed with storm
Pouching a bottle in one arm;
A whiskey bottle full of worms;
And bedroom slacks: are these fit terms
To mete the worm whose molten rage   15
Boils in the belly of old age?

Once fishing was a rabbit's foot—
O wind blow cold, O wind blow hot,
Let suns stay in or suns step out:
Life danced a jig on the sperm-whale's spout—   20
The fisher's fluent and obscene
Catches kept his conscience clean.
Children, the raging memory drools
Over the glory of past pools.

Now the hot river, ebbing, hauls   25
Its bloody waters into holes;
A grain of sand inside my shoe
Mimics the moon that might undo
Man and Creation too; remorse
Stinking, has puddled up its source;   30
Here tantrums thrash to a whale's rage.
This is the pot-hole of old age.

Is there no way to cast my hook
Out of this dynamited brook?
The Fisher's sons must cast about   35
When shallow waters peter out.
I will catch Christ with a greased worm,
And when the Prince of Darkness stalks
My bloodstream to its Stygian term . . .
On water the Man-Fisher walks.   40

39. Stygian: deathly; reference to River Styx, Greek mythical stream in world of the dead.

STUDY QUESTIONS

1. Describe the scene in stanza 1: where is the speaker; what is he doing; how successful is he in achieving his goal?
2. What words in the first stanza present an unpleasant image? Is that unpleasantness expected in view of your responses to the first question?
3. Is there a reference to the length of time involved in the action described in the first stanza? If so, how long is that time period?
4. In stanza 2 the poet lists familiar items—a calendar, a handkerchief, and the like—and asks if they are "fit terms / to mete the worm . . ." What associations does "worm" have? How does "worm" in this line relate to the "bottle full of worms"? How do both of these references to worms relate to "old age"?
5. In stanza 3 the poet describes the child's joy in fishing. How does that compare to the apparently old fisherman's feelings about fishing? What has happened to change that feeling?
6. List all the words you can find that either relate directly to time or symbolically suggest time.
7. In the final stanza, what does each of the following symbolize: the Fisher, the Prince of Darkness, the Man-Fisher? How do they relate to the line, "I will catch Christ"?
8. Is the poet angry at his own aging, at the corruption of nature, the corruption of modern society, or what?
9. Compare this poem to "Directive." What similarities do the two poems have? In what ways are they different? Are their meanings similar?

John Donne (1572–1631)

SONG: GO AND CATCH A FALLING STAR

Go and catch a falling star,
　　Get with child a mandrake root,
Tell me where all past years are,
　　Or who cleft the devil's foot,
Teach me to hear mermaids singing,　　　　　　　5
　　Or to keep off envy's stinging,
　　　　And find
　　　　What wind
Serves to advance an honest mind.

If thou be'st born to strange sights,　　　　　　　10
　　Things invisible to see,
Ride ten thousand days and nights,
　　Till age snow white hairs on thee,

Thou, when thou return'st, will tell me
    All strange wonders that befell thee,   15
        And swear
        No where
Lives a woman true and fair.

If thou find'st one, let me know
    Such a pilgrimage were sweet.   20
Yet do not; I would not go,
    Though at next door we might meet
Though she were true when you met her,
    And last till you write your letter,
        Yet she   25
        Will be
False, ere I come, to two or three.

2. mandrake root: large forked root of the mandragora herb, credited with human attributes and, according to superstition, able to promote conception.

STUDY QUESTIONS

1. Identify the speaker in the poem. To whom is he speaking?
2. How does diction work in the service of sound in this poem?
3. How is the first stanza hyperbolic? Why?
4. Discuss alliteration in the poem. Why do you think alliteration is particularly useful in a song?
5. What figure of speech does line 13 represent?
6. In one sentence, state the poem's principal argument. Do you agree? Why or why not?
7. Do Donne and modern songwriters share similarities in subject matter and theme? How?
8. Compare the attitudes toward love expressed in this poem and in Shakespeare's sonnets 18 and 130 (pp. 796 and 797). In what ways is the use of language in each similar? How different?

T. S. Eliot (1888–1965)

PRELUDES

I

The winter evening settles down
With smell of steaks in passageways.
Six o'clock.

The burnt-out ends of smoky days.
And now a gusty shower wraps   5
The grimy scraps
Of withered leaves about your feet
And newspapers from vacant lots;
The showers beat
On broken blinds and chimney-pots,   10
And at the corner of the street
A lonely cab-horse steams and stamps.
And then the lighting of the lamps.

II

The morning comes to consciousness
Of faint stale smells of beer   15
From the sawdust-trampled street
With all its muddy feet that press
To early coffee-stands.
With the other masquerades
That time resumes,   20
One thinks of all the hands
That are raising dingy shades
In a thousand furnished rooms.

III

You tossed a blanket from the bed,
You lay upon your back, and waited;   25
You dozed, and watched the night revealing
The thousand sordid images
Of which your soul was constituted;
They flickered against the ceiling.
And when all the world came back   30
And the light crept up between the shutters
And you heard the sparrows in the gutters,
You had such a vision of the street
As the street hardly understands;
Sitting along the bed's edge, where   35
You curled the papers from your hair,
Or clasped the yellow soles of feet
In the palms of both soiled hands.

IV

His soul stretched tight across the skies
That fade behind a city block,   40
Or trampled by insistent feet

At four and five and six o'clock;
And short square fingers stuffing pipes,
And evening newspapers, and eyes
Assured of certain certainties,   45
The conscience of a blackened street
Impatient to assume the world.
I am moved by fancies that are curled
Around these images, and cling:
The notion of some infinitely gentle   50
Infinitely suffering thing.

Wipe your hand across your mouth, and laugh,
The worlds revolve like ancient women
Gathering fuel in vacant lots.

STUDY QUESTIONS

1. Using examples, show how personification functions in this poem.
2. This poem not only uses images but might be considered to be *about* them. Discuss.
3. What techniques does Eliot use to create the scene?
4. List the sense information the poem presents. For what purpose?
5. Discuss the theme/passage of time in the poem. What figures of speech does Eliot use to portray it?
6. Discuss the poem's final simile and its relationship to the whole poem.
7. Does this poem address someone? If so, describe that person in your own words.
8. Discuss the dominant imagery of the poem. What vision of the world does it portray?
9. What is the purpose of the pronouns in the poem?
10. Discuss how "music" is put to use in the poem. Which figures of poetry does Eliot use to present it?
11. Discuss the title of the poem in relation to its meaning.

Osage Indian Lyric

THE WEAVER'S LAMENTATION

(Shrine Ritual)

You have left me to linger in hopeless longing,
Your presence had ever made me feel no want,
You have left me to travel in sorrow.

Left me to travel in sorrow; Ah! the pain,
Left me to travel in sorrow; Ah! the pain, the pain, the pain.   5

You have left me to linger in hopeless longing,
In your presence there was no sorrow,
You have gone and sorrow I shall feel, as I travel,
  Ah! the pain, the pain.

You have gone and sorrow I shall feel as I travel,   10
You have left me in hopeless longing.
In your presence there was no sorrow,
You have gone and sorrow I shall feel as I travel;
  Ah! the pain, the pain, the pain.

Content with your presence, I wanted nothing more,   15
You have left me to travel in sorrow; Ah! the pain, the pain, the pain!

Osage Indian Lyric

A SEQUENCE OF SONGS OF THE GHOST DANCE RELIGION

1

My children,
When at first I liked the whites,
I gave them fruits,
I gave them fruits.

2

Father have pity on me,   5
I am crying for thirst,
All is gone,
I have nothing to eat.

3

The father will descend,
The earth will tremble,   10
Everybody will arise,
Stretch out your hands.

4

The Crow—*Ehe'eye!*
I saw him when he flew down,
To the earth, to the earth.   15

He has renewed our life,
He has taken pity on us.

5

I circle around
The boundaries of the earth,
Wearing the long wing feathers,   20
As I fly.

6

I'yehé! my children—
My children,
We have rendered them desolate.
The whites are crazy—Ahe'yuhe'yu!   25

7

We shall live again,
We shall live again.

Zuñi Indian Lyric

PRAYER TO THE ANCIENTS AFTER HARVESTING

From where you stay quietly,
Your little wind-blown clouds,
Your fine wisps of clouds,
Your massed clouds you will send forth to sit down with us;
With your fine rain caressing the earth,   5
With all your waters
You will pass to us on our roads.
With your great pile of waters,
With your fine rain caressing the earth,
You will pass to us on our roads.   10
My fathers,
Add to your hearts.
Your waters,
Your seeds,
Your long life,   15
Your old age
You will grant to us.
Therefore I have added to your hearts,
To the end, my fathers,
My children: 20
You will protect us.

All my ladder-descending children
Will finish their roads;
They will grow old.
You will bless us with life.   25

Papago Indian Lyric

WAR SONG

   Is it for me to eat what food I have
And all day sit idle?
Is it for me to drink the sweet water poured-out
And all day sit idle?
Is it for me to gaze upon my wife   5
And all day sit idle?
Is it for me to hold my child in my arms
And all day sit idle?

   My desire was uncontrollable.
It was the dizziness [of battle];   10
I ground it to powder and therewith I painted my face.
It was the drunkenness of battle;
I ground it to powder and therewith I tied my hair in a war knot.
Then did I hold firm my well-strung bow and my smooth, straight-flying
     arrow.
To me did I draw my far-striding sandals, and fast I tied them.   15

   Over the flat land did I then go striding,
Over the embedded stones did I then go stumbling,
Under the trees in the ditches did I go stooping,
Through the trees on the high ground did I go hurtling,
Through the mountain gullies did I go brushing quickly.   20

   In four halts did I reach the shining white eagle, my guardian,
And I asked power.
Then favorable to me he felt
And did bring forth his shining white stone.
Our enemy's mountain he made white as with moonlight   25
And brought them close,
And across them I went striding.

   In four halts did I reach the blue hawk, my guardian,
And I asked power
The hawk favorable to me he felt   30
And did bring forth his blue stone.

Our enemy's waters he made white as with moonlight,
And around them I went striding.
There did I seize and pull up and make into a bundle
Those things which were my enemy's,   35
All kinds of seeds and beautiful clouds and beautiful winds.

Then came forth a thick stalk and a thick tassel,
And the undying seed did ripen.
This I did on behalf of my people.
Thus should you also think and desire,   40
All you my kinsmen.

Apache Indian Lyric

SONGS OF THE MASKED DANCERS

1

When the earth was made;
When the sky was made;
When my songs were first heard;
The holy mountain was standing toward me with life.

At the center of the sky, the holy boy walks four ways with life.   5
Just mine, my mountain became; standing toward me with life.
Gan children became; standing toward me with life.

When the sun goes down to the earth,
Where Mescal Mountain lies with its head toward the sunrise,
Black spruce became; standing up with me.   10

2

Right at the center of the sky the holy boy with life walks in four directions.
Lightning with life in four colors comes down four times.
The place which is called black spot with life;
The place which is called blue spot with life;
The place which is called yellow spot with life;   15
The place which is called white spot with life;
They have heard about me,
The black Gans dance in four places.
The sun starts down toward the earth.

3

The living sky black-spotted;   20
The living sky blue-spotted;
The living sky yellow-spotted;
The living sky white-spotted;

The young spruce as girls stood up for their dance in the way of life.
When my songs first were, they made my songs with words of jet.   25
Earth when it was made,
Sky when it was made,
Earth to the end,
Sky to the end,
Black Gan, black thunder, when they came toward each other,   30
The various bad things that used to be vanished.
The bad wishes which were in the world vanished.
The lightning of black thunder struck four times for them.
It struck four times for me.

4

When first my songs became,   35
When the sky was made,
When the earth was made,
The breath of the Gans on me made only of down;
When they heard about my life;
Where they got their life;   40

When they heard about me;
It stands.

5

The day broke with slender rain.
The place which is called "lightning's water stands,"
The place which is called "where the dawn strikes,"   45
Four places where it is called "it dawns with life,"
I land there.
The sky boys, I go among them.
He came to me with long life.
When he talked over my body with the longest life,   50
The voice of thunder spoke well four times.
Holy sky boy spoke to me four times.
When he talked to me my breath became.

7. Gan: Apache name for masked dancers.

Anne Sexton (1928–1975)

RINGING THE BELLS

And this is the way they ring
the bells in Bedlam
and this is the bell-lady
who comes each Tuesday morning

to give us a music lesson   5
and because the attendants make you go
and because we mind by instinct,
like bees caught in the wrong hive,
we are the circle of the crazy ladies
who sit in the lounge of the mental house   10
and smile at the smiling woman
who passes us each a bell,
who points at my hand
that holds my bell, E flat,
and this is the gray dress next to me   15
who grumbles as if it were special
to be old, to be old,
and this is the small hunched squirrel girl
on the other side of me
who picks at the hairs over her lip,   20
who picks at the hairs over her lip all day,
and this is how the bells really sound,
as untroubled and clean
as a workable kitchen,
and this is always my bell responding   25
to my hand that responds to the lady
who points at me, E flat;
and although we are no better for it,
they tell you to go. And you do.

2. Bedlam: popular name for the Hospital of St. Mary—a London insane asylum.

Gwendolyn Brooks (1917–   )

AN ASPECT OF LOVE, ALIVE IN THE ICE AND FIRE

LaBohem Brown

It is the morning of our love.

In a package of minutes there is this We.
How beautiful.
Merry foreigners in our morning,
we laugh, we touch each other,   5
are responsible props and posts.

A physical light is in the room.

Because the world is at the window
we cannot wonder very long.

You rise. Although   10
genial, you are in yourself again.
I observe
your direct and respectable stride.
You are direct and self-accepting as a lion
in African velvet. You are level, lean,   15
remote.

There is a moment in Camaraderie
when interruption is not to be understood.
I cannot bear an interruption.
This is the shining joy;   20
the time of not-to-end.

On the street we smile.
We go
in different directions
down the imperturbable street.   25

Erica Jong (1945–)

THE MAN UNDER THE BED

The man under the bed
The man who has been there for years waiting
The man who waits for my floating bare foot
The man who is silent as dustballs riding the darkness
The man whose breath is the breathing of small white butterflies   5
The man whose breathing I hear when I pick up the phone
The man in the mirror whose breath blackens silver
The boneman in closets who rattles the mothballs
The man at the end of the end of the line

I met him tonight   I always meet him   10
He stands in the amber air of a bar
When the shrimp curl like beckoning fingers
& ride through the air on their toothpick skewers
When the ice cracks & I am about to fall through
he arranges his face around its hollows   15
he opens his pupilless eyes at me

For years he has waited to drag me down
& now he tells me
he has only waited to take me home
We waltz through the street like death & the maiden   20
We float through the wall of the wall of my room

If he's my dream he will fold back into my body
His breath writes letters of mist on the glass of my cheeks
I wrap myself around him like the darkness
I breathe into his mouth   25
& make him real

Richard Wilbur (1921–　)

MIND

Mind in its purest play is like some bat
That beats about in caverns all alone,
Contriving by a kind of senseless wit
Not to conclude against a wall of stone.

It has no need to falter or explore;   5
Darkly it knows what obstacles are there,
And so may weave and flitter, dip and soar
In perfect courses through the blackest air.

And has this simile a like perfection?
The mind is like a bat. Precisely. Save   10
That in the very happiest intellection
A graceful error may correct the cave.

W. H. Auden (1907–1973)

THE UNKNOWN CITIZEN

(To JS/07/M/378 This Marble Monument Is Erected by the State)

He was found by the Bureau of Statistics to be
One against whom there was no official complaint,
And all the reports on his conduct agree
That, in the modern sense of an old-fashioned word, he was a saint,
For in everything he did he served the Greater Community.   5
Except for the War till the day he retired
He worked in a factory and never got fired,
But satisfied his employers, Fudge Motors Inc.
Yet he wasn't a scab or odd in his views,
For his Union reports that he paid his dues,   10
(Our report on his Union shows it was sound)
And our Social Psychology workers found
That he was popular with his mates and liked a drink.

The Press are convinced that he bought a paper every day
And that his reactions to advertisements were normal in every way.   15
Policies taken out in his name prove that he was fully insured,
And his Health-card shows he was once in hospital but left it cured.
Both Producers Research and High-Grade Living declare
He was fully sensible to the advantages of the Installment Plan
And had everything necessary to the Modern Man,   20
A phonograph, a radio, a car and a frigidaire.
Our researchers into Public Opinion are content
That he held the proper opinions for the time of year;
When there was peace, he was for peace; when there was war, he went.
He was married and added five children to the population,   25
Which our Eugenist says was the right number for a parent of his generation,
And our teachers report that he never interfered with their education.
Was he free? Was he happy? The question is absurd:
Had anything been wrong, we should certainly have heard.

Dylan Thomas (1914–1953)

DO NOT GO GENTLE INTO THAT GOOD NIGHT

Do not go gentle into that good night,
Old age should burn and rave at close of day;
Rage, rage against the dying of the light.

Though wise men at their end know dark is right,
Because their words had forked no lightning they   5
Do not go gentle into that good night.

Good men, the last wave by, crying how bright
Their frail deeds might have danced in a green bay,
Rage, rage against the dying of the light.

Wild men who caught and sang the sun in flight,   10
And learn, too late, they grieved it on its way
Do not go gentle into that good night.

Grave men, near death, who see with blinding sight
Blind eyes could blaze like meteors and be gay,
Rage, rage against the dying of the light.   15

And you, my father, there on the sad height,
Curse, bless, me now with your fierce tears, I pray.
Do not go gentle into that good night.
Rage, rage against the dying of the light.

Elinor Wylie (1885–1928)

VELVET SHOES

Let us walk in the white snow
  In a soundless space;
With footsteps quiet and slow,
  At a tranquil pace,
    Under veils of white lace.   5

I shall go shod in silk,
  And you in wool,
White as a white cow's milk,
  More beautiful
    Than the breast of a gull.   10

We shall walk through the still town
  In a windless peace;
We shall step upon white down,
  Upon silver fleece,
    Upon softer than these.   15

We shall walk in velvet shoes:
  Wherever we go
Silence will fall like dews
  On white silence below.
    We shall walk in the snow.   20

Robert Frost (1874–1963)

PROVIDE, PROVIDE

The witch that came (the withered hag)
To wash the steps with pail and rag
Was once the beauty of Abishag,

The picture pride of Hollywood.
Too many fall from great and good   5
For you to doubt the likelihood.

Die early and avoid the fate.
Or if predestined to die late,
Make up your mind to die in state.

Make the whole stock exchange your own!   10
If need be occupy a throne,
Where nobody can call *you* crone.

Some have relied on what they knew,
Others on being simply true.
What worked for them might work for you.   15

No memory of having starred
Atones for later disregard
Or keeps the end from being hard.

Better to go down dignified
With boughten friendship at your side   20
Than none at all. Provide, provide!

Robert Frost (1874–1963)

FIRE AND ICE

Some say the world will end in fire,
Some say in ice.
From what I've tasted of desire
I hold with those who favor fire.
But if it had to perish twice,   5
I think I know enough of hate
To say that for destruction ice
Is also great
And would suffice.

Lawrence Ferlinghetti (1919–   )

CONSTANTLY RISKING ABSURDITY

Constantly risking absurdity
                              and death
            whenever he performs
                         above the heads
                                      of his audience   5
        the poet like an acrobat
                   climbs on rime
                            to a high wire of his own making
and balancing on eyebeams
                            above a sea of faces   10
            paces his way
                  to the other side of day
      performing entrechats

                    and slight-of-foot tricks
and other high theatrics   15
                         and all without mistaking
          any thing
                         for what it may not be
      For he's the super realist
                              who must perforce perceive   20
              taut truth
                         before the taking of each stance or step
    in his supposed advance
                         toward that still higher perch
where Beauty stands and waits   25
                    with gravity
                         to start her death-defying leap
          And he
      a little charleychaplin man
                         who may or may not catch   30
          her fair eternal form
                    spreadeagled in the empty air
          of existence

13. entrechats: leaps in which the legs are repeatedly crossed.

Sylvia Plath (1932–1963)

THE COLOSSUS

I shall never get you put together entirely,
Pieced, glued, and properly jointed.
Mule-bray, pig-grunt and bawdy cackles
Proceed from your great lips.
It's worse than a barnyard.   5

Perhaps you consider yourself an oracle,
Mouthpiece of the dead, or of some god or other.
Thirty years now I have labored
To dredge the silt from your throat.
I am none the wiser.   10

Scaling little ladders with gluepots and pails of lysol
I crawl like an ant in mourning
Over the weedy acres of your brow
To mend the immense skull plates and clear
The bald, white tumuli of your eyes.   15

A blue sky out of the Oresteia
Arches above us. O father, all by yourself
You are pithy and historical as the Roman Forum.
I open my lunch on a hill of black cypress.
Your fluted bones and acanthine hair are littered   20

In their old anarchy to the horizon-line.
It would take more than a lightning-stroke
To create such a ruin.
Nights, I squat in the cornucopia
Of your left ear, out of the wind,   25

Counting the red stars and those of plum-color
The sun rises under the pillar of your tongue
My hours are married to shadow.
No longer do I listen for the scrape of a keel
On the blank stones of the landing.   30

Title: Colossus: huge statue of greater than heroic proportions.   15. tumuli: grave
mound.   16. Oresteia: a trilogy of Greek tragedies, written by Aeschylus, who died
in 456 B.C.   18. Roman Forum: open square in ancient Rome where judicial and
public business was conducted.   20. acanthine: thorny, prickly.

Sylvia Plath (1932–1963)

SPINSTER

Now this particular girl
During a ceremonious April walk
With her latest suitor
Found herself, of a sudden, intolerably struck
By the birds' irregular babel   5
And the leaves' litter.

By this tumult afflicted, she
Observed her lovers' gestures unbalance the air,
His gait stray uneven
Through a rank wilderness of fern and flower.   10
She judged petals in disarray,
The whole season, sloven.

How she longed for winter then!—
Scrupulously austere in its order
Of white and black   15
Ice and rock, each sentiment within border,
And heart's frosty discipline
Exact as a snowflake.

But here—a burgeoning
Unruly enough to pitch her five queenly wits   20
Into vulgar motley—
A treason not to be borne. Let idiots
Reel giddy in bedlam spring:
She withdrew neatly.

And round her house she set   25
Such a barricade of barb and check
Against mutinous weather
As no mere insurgent man could hope to break
With curse, fist, threat
Or love, either.   30

e. e. cummings (1894–1962)

I THANK YOU GOD FOR MOST THIS AMAZING

i thank You God for most this amazing
day:for the leaping greenly spirits of trees
and a blue true dream of sky;and for everything
which is natural which is infinite which is yes

(i who have died am alive again today,   5
and this is the sun's birthday;this is the birth
day of life and of love and wings:and of the gay
great happening illimitably earth)

how should tasting touching hearing seeing
breathing any—lifted from the no   10
of all nothing—human merely being
doubt unimaginable You?

(now the ears of my ears awake and
now the eyes of my eyes are opened)

e. e. cummings (1894–1962)

WHEN SERPENTS BARGAIN FOR THE RIGHT
TO SQUIRM

when serpents bargain for the right to squirm
and the sun strikes to gain a living wage—
when thorns regard their roses with alarm
and rainbows are insured against old age

when every thrush may sing no new moon in   5
if all screech-owls have not okayed his voice
—and any wave signs on the dotted line
or else an ocean is compelled to close

when the oak begs permission of the birch
to make an acorn—valleys accuse their   10
mountains of having altitude—and march
denounces april as a saboteur

then we'll believe in that incredible
unanimal mankind(and not until)

William Blake (1757–1827)

THE LAMB

Little Lamb, who made thee?
Dost thou know who made thee?
By the stream and o'er the mead;
Gave thee clothing of delight,
Softest clothing wooly bright;   5
Gave thee such a tender voice,
Making all the vales rejoice!
Little Lamb, who made thee?
Dost thou know who made thee?

Little Lamb, I'll tell thee,   10
Little Lamb, I'll tell thee!
He is callèd by thy name,
For he calls himself a Lamb;
He is meek and he is mild,
He became a little child;   15
I a child and thou a lamb,

We are callèd by his name.
Little Lamb, God bless thee.
Little Lamb, God bless thee.

William Blake (1757–1827)

THE LITTLE BLACK BOY

My mother bore me in the southern wild,
And I am black, but O! my soul is white;

White as an angel is the English child:
But I am black, as if bereaved of light.

My mother taught me underneath a tree,   5
And sitting down before the heat of day,
She took me on her lap and kissèd me,
And pointing to the east, began to say:

"Look on the rising sun: there God does live,
And gives his light, and gives his heat away;   10
And flowers and trees and beasts and men receive
Comfort in morning, joy in the noon day.

"And we are put on earth a little space
That we may learn to bear the beams of love;
And these black bodies and this sunburnt face   15
Is but a cloud, and like a shady grove.

"For when our souls have learned the heat to bear,
The cloud will vanish; we shall hear his voice,
Saying: 'Come out from the grove, my love and care,
And round my golden tent like lambs rejoice.' "   20

Thus did my mother say, and kissèd me;
And thus I say to little English boy:
When I from black and he from white cloud free,
And round the tent of God like lambs we joy,

I'll shade him from the heat till he can bear   25
To lean in joy upon our father's knee;
And then I'll stand and stroke his silver hair,
And be like him, and he will then love me.

William Blake (1757–1827)

THE CLOD AND THE PEBBLE

"Love seeketh not itself to please,
Nor for itself hath any care,
But for another gives its ease,
And builds a heaven in hell's despair."

So sung a little clod of clay,   5
Trodden with the cattle's feet,
But a pebble of the brook
Warbled out these metres meet:

"Love seeketh only Self to please,
To bind another to its delight,   10
Joys in another's loss of ease,
And builds a hell in heaven's despair."

Samuel Taylor Coleridge (1772–1834)

KUBLA KHAN

In Xanadu did Kubla Khan
A stately pleasure-dome decree:
Where Alph, the sacred river, ran
Through caverns measureless to man
    Down to a sunless sea.   5
So twice five miles of fertile ground
With walls and towers were girdled round:
And here were gardens bright with sinuous rills,
Where blossomed many an incense-bearing tree;
And here were forests ancient as the hills,   10
Enfolding sunny spots of greenery.

But oh! that deep romantic chasm which slanted
Down the green hill athwart a cedarn cover!
A savage place! as holy and enchanted
As e're beneath a waning moon was haunted   15
By woman wailing for her demon-lover!
And from this chasm, with ceaseless turmoil seething
As if this earth in fast thick pants were breathing,
A mighty fountain momently was forced:
Amid whose swift half-intermitted burst   20
Huge fragments vaulted like rebounding hail,
Or chaffy grain beneath the thresher's flail:
And 'mid these dancing rocks at once and ever
It flung up momently the sacred river.
Five miles meandering with a mazy motion   25
Through wood and dale the sacred river ran,
Then reached the caverns measureless to man,
And sank in tumult to a lifeless ocean:
And 'mid this tumult Kubla heard from far
Ancestral voices prophesying war!   30

    The shadow of the dome of pleasure
    Floated midway on the waves;
    Where was heard the mingled measure
    From the fountain and the caves.

It was a miracle of rare device,   35
A sunny pleasure-dome with caves of ice!

  A damsel with a dulcimer
  In a vision once I saw:
  It was an Abyssinian maid,
  And on her dulcimer she played,   40
  Singing of Mount Abora.
Could I revive within me
Her symphony and song,
To such a deep delight, 'twould win me,
That with music loud and long,   45
I would build that dome in air,
That sunny dome! those caves of ice!
And all who heard should see them there,
And all should cry, Beware! Beware!
His flashing eyes, his floating hair!   50
Weave a circle round him thrice,
And close your eyes with holy dread,
For he on honey-dew hath fed,
And drunk the milk of Paradise.

13. cedarn cover: cedar forest.

Emily Dickinson (1830–1886)

THE LIGHTNING IS A YELLOW FORK

    The Lightning is a yellow Fork
    From Tables in the sky
    By inadvertent fingers dropt
    The awful Cutlery

    Of mansions never quite disclosed   5
    And never quite concealed
    The Apparatus of the Dark
    To ignorance revealed.

Emily Dickinson (1830–1886)

IT DROPPED SO LOW—IN MY REGARD—

    It dropped so low—in my Regard—
    I heard it hit the Ground—

And go to pieces on the Stones
At bottom of my Mind—

Yet blamed the Fate that fractured it—*less*   5
Than I denounced Myself,
For entertaining Plated Wares
Upon my Silver Shelf—

Emily Dickinson (1830–1886)

"HOPE" IS THE THING WITH FEATHERS—

"Hope" is the thing with feathers—
That perches in the soul—
And sings the tune without the words—
And never stops—at all—

And sweetest—in the Gale—is heard—   5
And sore must be the storm—
That could abash the little Bird
That kept so many warm—

I've heard it in the chillest land—
And on the strangest Sea—   10
Yet, never, in Extremity,
It asked a crumb—of Me.

Emily Dickinson (1830–1886)

SUCCESS IS COUNTED SWEETEST

Success is counted sweetest
By those who ne'er succeed.
To comprehend a nectar
Requires sorest need.

Not one of all the purple Host   5
Who took the Flag today
Can tell the definition
So clear of Victory

As he defeated—dying—
On whose forbidden ear   10
The distant strains of triumph
Burst agonized and clear!

Robert Herrick (1591–1674)

TO THE VIRGINS, TO MAKE MUCH OF TIME

Gather ye rosebuds while ye may,
   Old Time is still a-flying;
And this same flower that smiles today
   Tomorrow will be dying.

The glorious lamp of heaven, the Sun,   5
   The higher he's a-getting,
The sooner will his race be run,
   And nearer he's to setting.

That age is best which is the first,
   When youth and blood are warmer;   10
But being spent, the worse, and worst
   Times still succeed the former.

Then be not coy, but use your time;
   And while ye may, go marry;
For having lost but once your prime,   15
   You may forever tarry.

Jonathan Swift (1667–1745)

THE PROGRESS OF BEAUTY

When first Diana leaves her bed
Vapors and steams her looks disgrace,
A frowzy dirty coloured red
Sits on her cloudy wrinkled face.

  But by degrees when mounted high   5
Her artificial face appears
Down from her window in the sky
Her spots are gone, her visage clears.

  'Twixt earthly females and the moon
All parallels exactly run;   10
If Celia should appear too soon
Alas, the nymph would be undone.

  To see her from her pillow rise
All reeking in a cloudy steam,
Cracked lips, foul teeth, and gummy eyes,   15
Poor Strephon, how would he blaspheme!

The soot or powder which was wont
To make her hair look black as jet,
Falls from her tresses on her front
A mingled mass of dirt and sweat.   20

Three colours, black, and red, and white,
So graceful in their proper place,
Remove them to a different light
They form a frightful hideous face,

For instance; when the lily slips   25
Into the precincts of the rose,
And takes possession of the lips,
Leaving the purple to the nose.

So Celia went entire to bed,
All her complexions safe and sound,   30
But when she rose, the black and red
Though still in sight, had changed their ground.

The black, which would not be confined
A more inferior station seeks
Leaving the fiery red behind,   35
And mingles in her muddy cheeks.

The paint by perspiration cracks,
And falls in rivulets of sweat,
On either side you see the tracks,
While at her chin the confluents met.   40

A skillful housewife thus her thumb
With spittle while she spins, anoints,
And thus the brown Meanders come
In trickling streams betwixt her joints.

But Celia can with ease reduce   45
By help of pencil, paint and brush
Each colour to its place and use,
And teach her cheeks again to blush.

She knows her early self no more
But filled with admiration, stands,   50
As other painters oft adore
The workmanship of their own hands.

Thus after four important hours
Celia's the wonder of her sex;
Say, which among the heavenly powers   55
Could cause such wonderful effects.

1. Diana: Roman goddess of the moon.

George Herbert (1593–1633)

LOVE (III)

Love bade me welcome: yet my soul drew back,
    Guilty of dust and sin.
But quick-eyed Love, observing me grow slack
    From my first entrance in,
Drew nearer to me, sweetly questioning   5
    If I lacked anything.

"A guest," I answered, "worthy to be here":
    Love said, "You shall be he."
"I, the unkind, ungrateful? Ah, my dear,
    I cannot look on thee."   10
Love took my hand, and smiling did reply,
    "Who made the eyes but I?"

"Truth, Lord; but I have marred them; let my shame
    Go where it does deserve."
"And know you not," says Love, "who bore the blame?"   15
    "My dear, then I will serve."
"You must sit down," says Love, "and taste my meat."
    So I did sit and eat.

George Herbert (1593–1633)

VIRTUE

Sweet day, so cool, so calm, so bright,
    The bridal of the earth and sky:
The dew shall weep thy fall tonight;
    For thou must die.

Sweet rose, whose hue, angry and brave,   5
    Bids the rash gazer wipe his eye:
Thy root is ever in its grave,
    And thou must die.

Sweet spring, full of sweet days and roses,
    A box where sweets compacted lie;   10
My music shows ye have your closes,
    And all must die.

Only a sweet and virtuous soul,
    Like seasoned timber, never gives;
But though the whole world turn to coal,   15
    Then chiefly lives.

John Donne (1572–1631)

THE FLEA

Mark but this flea, and mark in this,
How little that which thou deniest me is;
Me it sucked first, and now sucks thee,
And in this flea our two bloods mingled be;
Thou know'st that this cannot be said   5
A sin, or shame, or loss of maidenhead,
   Yet this enjoys before it woo,
     And pampered swells with one blood made of two,
     And this, alas, is more than we would do.

Oh stay, three lives in one flea spare,   10
Where we almost, nay more than married, are.
This flea is you and I, and this
Our marriage bed and marriage temple is;
Though parents grudge, and you, we are met,
And cloistered in these living walls of jet,   15
   Though use make you apt to kill me
   Let not to that, self-murder added be,
   And sacrilege, three sins in killing three.

Cruel and sudden, hast thou since
Purpled thy nail, in blood of innocence?   20
Wherein could this flea guilty be,
Except in that drop which it sucked from thee?
Yet thou triumph'st, and say'st that thou
Find'st not thy self nor me the weaker now;
   'Tis true, then learn how false fears be;   25
   Just so much honor, when thou yield'st to me,
   Will waste, as this flea's death took life from thee.

John Donne (1572–1631)

DEATH, BE NOT PROUD

Death, be not proud, though some have callèd thee
Mighty and dreadful, for thou art not so;
For those whom thou think'st thou dost overthrow
Die not, poor Death; nor yet canst thou kill me.
From rest and sleep, which but thy pictures be,   5
Much pleasure; then from thee much more must flow;
And soonest our best men with thee do go —
Rest of their bones and souls' delivery!

Thou'rt slave to fate, chance, kings, and desperate men,
And dost with poison, war, and sickness dwell;   10
And poppy or charms can make us sleep as well
And better than thy stroke. Why swell'st thou then?
One short sleep past, we wake eternally,
And Death shall be no more: Death, thou shalt die.

John Milton (1608–1674)

HOW SOON HATH TIME

How soon hath Time, the subtle thief of youth,
Stol'n on his wing my three-and-twentieth year!
My hasting days fly on with full career,
But my late spring no bud or blossom shew'th.
Perhaps my semblance might deceive the truth,   5
That I to manhood am arriv'd so near,
And inward ripeness doth much less appear,
That some more timely-happy spirits indu'th.
Yet it be less or more, or soon or slow,
It shall be still in strictest measure ev'n,   10
To that same lot, however mean or high,
Toward which Time leads me, and the will of Heav'n;
All is, if I have grace to use it so,
As ever in my great Taskmaster's eye.

William Shakespeare (1564–1616)

SHALL I COMPARE THEE TO A SUMMER'S DAY?
(SONNET 18)

Shall I compare thee to a summer's day?
Thou art more lovely and more temperate:
Rough winds do shake the darling buds of May,
And summer's lease hath all too short a date;
Sometime too hot the eye of heaven shines,   5
And often is his gold complexion dimm'd;
And every fair from fair sometimes declines,
By chance or nature's changing course untrimm'd:
But thy eternal summer shall not fade
Nor lose possession of that fair thou ow'st,   10
Nor shall Death brag thou wand'rest in his shade,

When in eternal lines to time thou grow'st;
   So long as men can breathe or eyes can see,
   So long lives this, and this gives life to thee.

8. untrimm'd: stripped of beauty.   10. ow'st: ownest.

William Shakespeare (1564–1616)

MY MISTRESS' EYES ARE NOTHING LIKE THE SUN (SONNET 130)

My mistress' eyes are nothing like the sun;
Coral is far more red than her lips' red;
If snow be white, why then her breasts are dun;
If hairs be wires, black wires grow on her head.
I have seen roses damask'd, red and white,   5
But no such roses see I in her cheeks;
And in some perfumes is there more delight
Than in the breath that from my mistress reeks.
I love to hear her speak, yet well I know
That music hath a far more pleasing sound;   10
I grant I never saw a goddess go;
My mistress, when she walks, treads on the ground:
   And yet, by heaven, I think my love as rare
   As any she beli'd with false compare.

5. damask'd: mingled red and white.   14. beli'd: belied.

Elizabeth Barrett Browning (1806–1861)

IF THOU MUST LOVE ME (SONNET 14)

If thou must love me, let it be for nought
Except for love's sake only. Do not say,
"I love her for her smile—her look—her way
Of speaking gently,—for a trick of thought
That falls in well with mine, and certes brought   5
A sense of pleasant ease on such a day;"—
For these things in themselves, Beloved, may
Be changed, or change for thee,—and love, so wrought,
May be unwrought so. Neither love me for
Thine own dear pity's wiping my cheeks dry: 10
A creature might forget to weep, who bore

Thy comfort long, and lose thy love thereby!
But love me for love's sake, that evermore
Thou may'st love on through love's eternity.

Elizabeth Barrett Browning (1806–1861)

HOW DO I LOVE THEE? (SONNET 43)

How do I love thee? Let me count the ways.
I love thee to the depth and breadth and height
My soul can reach, when feeling out of sight
For the ends of Being and Ideal Grace.
I love thee to the level of everyday's   5
Most quiet need, by sun and candlelight.
I love thee freely, as men strive for Right;
I love thee purely, as they turn from Praise.
I love thee with the passion put to use
In my old griefs, and with my childhood's faith.   10
I love thee with a love I seemed to lose
With my lost saints,—I love thee with the breath,
Smiles, tears, of all my life!—and, if God choose,
I shall but love thee better after death.

READING SELECTIONS : PLAYS

Fernando Arrabel (1932–   )

PICNIC ON THE BATTLEFIELD [1]

CHARACTERS

Zapo   *A soldier*
Monsieur Tépan   *The soldier's father*
Madame Tépan   *The soldier's mother*
Zépo   *An enemy soldier*
First Stretcher Bearer
Second Stretcher Bearer

[1] *Picnic on the Battlefield* premièred on April 25, 1959, in Paris, at the Théâtre de Lutèce, directed by Jean-Marie Serreau.

A battlefield. The stage is covered with barbed wire and sandbags.
The battle is at its height. Rifle shots, exploding bombs and machine guns
  can be heard.
ZAPO *is alone on the stage, flat on his stomach, hidden among the sandbags.*
  He is very frightened. The sound of the fighting stops. Silence.
ZAPO *takes a ball of wool and some needles out of a canvas workbag and*
  starts knitting a pullover, which is already quite far advanced. The field
  telephone, which is by his side, suddenly starts ringing.

Zapo Hallo, hallo . . . yes, Captain . . . yes, I'm the sentry of sector 47 . . .
  Nothing new, Captain . . . Excuse me, Captain, but when's the fighting
  going to start again? And what am I supposed to do with the hand-
  grenades? Do I chuck them in front of me or behind me? . . . Don't get
  me wrong, I didn't mean to annoy you . . . Captain, I really feel terribly
  lonely, couldn't you send me someone to keep me company? . . . Even if
  it's only a nanny-goat? (*The* CAPTAIN *is obviously severely reprimanding*
  him.) Whatever you say, Captain, whatever you say.

(ZAPO *hangs up. He mutters to himself. Silence. Enter* MONSIEUR *and*
MADAME TÉPAN, *carrying baskets as if they are going to a picnic. They*
address their son, who has his back turned and doesn't see them come in.)

Mons. T. (*Ceremoniously*) Stand up, my son, and kiss your mother on
  the brow. (ZAPO, *surprised, gets up and kisses his mother very respect-*
  fully on the forehead. He is about to speak, but his father doesn't give
  him a chance.) And now, kiss me.
Zapo But, dear Father and dear Mother, how did you dare to come all this
  way, to such a dangerous place? You must leave at once.
Mons. T. So you think you've got something to teach your father about
  war and danger, do you? All this is just a game to me. How many times—
  to take the first example that comes to mind—have I got off an underground train while it was still moving.
Mme. T. We thought you must be bored, so we came to pay you a little
  visit. This war must be a bit tedious, after all.
Zapo It all depends.
Mons. T. I know exactly what happens. To start with you're attracted by
  the novelty of it all. It's fun to kill people, and throw hand-grenades
  about, and wear uniforms—you feel smart, but in the end you get bored
  stiff. You'd have found it much more interesting in my day. Wars were
  much more lively, much more highly coloured. And then, the best thing
  was that there were horses, plenty of horses. It was a real pleasure; if the
  Captain ordered us to attack, there we all were immediately, on horseback, in our red uniforms. It was a sight to be seen. And then there were
  the charges at the gallop, sword in hand, and suddenly you found your-

self face to face with the enemy, and he was equal to the occasion too—with his horses—there were always horses, lots of horses, with their well-rounded rumps—in his highly-polished boots, and his green uniform.

Mme. T.   No no, the enemy uniform wasn't green. It was blue. I remember distinctly that it was blue.

Mons. T.   I tell you it was green.

Mme. T.   When I was little, how many times did I go out on to the balcony to watch the battle and say to the neighbour's little boy: 'I bet you a gum-drop the blues win.' And the blues were our enemies.

Mons. T.   Oh well, you must be right, then.

Mme. T.   I've always liked battles. As a child I always said that when I grew up I wanted to be a Colonel of dragoons. But my mother wouldn't hear of it, you know how she will stick to her principles at all costs.

Mons. T.   Your mother's just a half-wit.

Zapo   I'm sorry, but you really must go. You can't come into a war unless you're a soldier.

Mons. T.   I don't give a damn, we came here to have a picnic with you in the country and to enjoy our Sunday.

Mme. T.   And I've prepared an excellent meal, too. Sausage, hard-boiled eggs—you know how you like them!—ham sandwiches, red wine, salad, and cakes.

Zapo   All right, let's have it your way. But if the Captain comes he'll be absolutely furious. Because he isn't at all keen on us having visits when we're at the front. He never stops telling us: 'Discipline and hand-grenades are what's wanted in a war, not visits.'

Mons. T.   Don't worry, I'll have a few words to say to your Captain.

Zapo   And what if we have to start fighting again?

Mons. T.   You needn't think that'll frighten me, it won't be the first fighting I've seen. Now if only it was battles on horseback! Times have changed, you can't understand. (*Pause.*) We came by motor bike. No one said a word to us.

Zapo   They must have thought you were the referees.

Mons. T.   We had enough trouble getting through, though. What with all the tanks and jeeps.

Mme. T.   And do you remember the bottle-neck that cannon caused, just when we got here?

Mons. T.   You mustn't be surprised at anything in wartime, everyone knows that.

Mme. T.   Good, let's start our meal.

Mons. T.   You're quite right, I feel as hungry as a hunter. It's the smell of gunpowder.

Mme. T.   We'll sit on the rug while we're eating.

Zapo   Can I bring my rifle with me?

Mme. T.   You leave your rifle alone. It's not good manners to bring your rifle to table with you. (*Pause.*) But you're absolutely filthy, my boy. How on earth did you get into such a state? Let's have a look at your hands.

Zapo (*Ashamed, holding out his hands*)   I had to crawl about on the ground during the manoeuvres.

Mme. T.   And what about your ears?

Zapo   I washed them this morning.

Mme. T.   Well that's all right, then. And your teeth? (*He shows them.*) Very good. Who's going to give her little boy a great big kiss for clean-ing his teeth so nicely? (*To her husband*) Well, go on, kiss your son for cleaning his teeth so nicely. (M. Tépan *kisses his son.*) Because, you know, there's one thing I *will* not have, and that's making fighting a war an excuse for not washing.

Zapo   Yes, Mother.

(*They eat.*)

Mons. T.   Well, my boy, did you make a good score?

Zapo   When?

Mons. T.   In the last few days, of course.

Zapo   Where?

Mons. T.   At the moment, since you're fighting a war.

Zapo   No, nothing much. I didn't make a good score. Hardly ever scored a bull.

Mons. T.   Which are you best at shooting, enemy horses or soldiers?

Zapo   No, not horses, there aren't any horses any more.

Mons. T.   Well, soldiers then?

Zapo   Could be.

Mons. T.   Could be? Aren't you sure?

Zapo   Well you see ... I shoot without taking aim, (*pause*) and at the same time I say a Pater Noster for the chap I've shot.

Mons. T.   You must be braver than that. Like your father.

Mme. T.   I'm going to put a record on.

(*She puts a record on the gramophone—a pasodoble.[2] All three are sitting on the ground, listening.*)

Mons. T.   That really *is* music. Yes indeed, olé! (*The music continues. Enter an enemy soldier:* Zépo. *He is dressed like* Zapo. *The only differ-ence is the colour of their uniforms.* Zépo *is in green and* Zapo *is in grey.* Zépo *listens to the music openmouthed. He is behind the family so they can't see him. The record ends. As he gets up* Zapo *discovers* Zépo. *Both*

[2] *pasodoble:* a Spanish march tune.

put their hands up. M. *and* MME. TÉPAN *look at them in surprise.*) What's going on?

(ZAPO *reacts—he hesitates. Finally, looking as if he's made up his mind, he points his rifle at* ZÉPO.)

Zapo Hands up! (ZÉPO *puts his hands up even higher, looking even more terrified.* ZAPO *doesn't know what to do. Suddenly he goes quickly over to* ZÉPO *and touches him gently on the shoulder, like a child playing a game of 'tag'.*) Got you! (*To his father, very pleased.*) There we are! A prisoner!

Mons. T. Fine. And now what're you going to do with him?

Zapo I don't know, but, well, could be—they might make me a corporal.

Mons. T. In the meantime you'd better tie him up.

Zapo Tie him up? Why?

Mons. T. Prisoners always get tied up!

Zapo How?

Mons. T. Tie up his hands.

Mme. T. Yes, there's no doubt about that, you must tie up his hands, I've always seen them do that.

Zapo Right. (*To the prisoner.*) Put your hands together, if you please.

Zépo Don't hurt me too much.

Zapo I won't.

Zépo Ow! You're hurting me.

Mons. T. Now now, don't maltreat your prisoner.

Mme. T. Is that the way I brought you up? How many times have I told you that we must be considerate to our fellow-men?

Zapo I didn't do it on purpose. (*To* ZÉPO.) And like that, does it hurt?

Zépo No, it's all right like that.

Mons. T. Tell him straight out, say what you mean, don't mind us.

Zépo It's all right like that.

Mons. T. Now his feet.

Zapo His feet as well, whatever next?

Mons. T. Didn't they teach you the rules?

Zapo Yes.

Mons. T. Well then!

Zapo (*Very politely, to* ZÉPO) Would you be good enough to sit on the ground, please?

Zépo Yes, but don't hurt me.

Mme. T. You'll see, he'll take a dislike to you.

Zapo No he won't, no he won't. I'm not hurting you, am I?

Zépo No, that's perfect.

Zapo Papa, why don't you take a photo of the prisoner on the ground and me with my foot on his stomach?

Mons. T. Oh yes, that'd look good.

Zépo Oh no, not that!

Mme. T. Say yes, don't be obstinate.

Zépo No. I said no, and no it is.

Mme. T. But just a little teeny weeny photo, what harm could that do you? And we could put it in the dining room, next to the life-saving certificate my husband won thirteen years ago.

Zépo No—you won't shift me.

Zapo But why won't you let us?

Zépo I'm engaged. And if she sees the photo one day, she'll say I don't know how to fight a war properly.

Zapo No she won't, all you'll need to say is that it isn't you, it's a panther.

Mme. T. Come on, do say yes.

Zépo All right then. But only to please you.

Zapo Lie down flat.

(Zépo *lies down.* Zapo *puts a foot on his stomach and grabs his rifle with a martial air.*)

Mme. T. Stick your chest out a bit further.

Zapo Like this?

Mme. T. Yes, like that, and don't breathe.

Mons. T. Try and look like a hero.

Zapo What d'you mean, like a hero?

Mons. T. It's quite simple; try and look like the butcher does when he's boasting about his successes with the girls.

Zapo Like this?

Mons. T. Yes, like that.

Mme. T. The most important thing is to puff your chest out and not breathe.

Zépo Have you nearly finished?

Mons. T. Just be patient a moment. One . . . two . . . three.

Zapo I hope I'll come out well.

Mme. T. Yes, you looked very martial.

Mons. T. You were fine.

Mme. T. It makes me want to have my photo taken with you.

Mons. T. Now there's a good idea.

Zapo Right. I'll take it if you like.

Mme. T. Give me your helmet to make me look like a soldier.

Zépo I don't want any more photos. Even one's far too many.

Zapo Don't take it like that. After all, what harm can it do you?

Zépo It's my last word.

Mons. T. (*To his wife.*) Don't press the point, prisoners are always very sensitive. If we go on he'll get cross and spoil our fun.

Zapo Right, what're we going to do with him, then?

Mme. T. We could invite him to lunch. What do you say?

Mons. T.   I don't see why not.

Zapo (*To* Zépo)   Well, will you have lunch with us, then?

Zépo   Er . . .

Mons. T.   We brought a good bottle with us.

Zépo   Oh well, all right then.

Mme. T.   Make yourself at home, don't be afraid to ask for anything you want.

Zépo   All right.

Mons. T.   And what about you, did you make a good score?

Zépo   When?

Mons. T.   In the last few days, of course.

Zépo   Where?

Mons. T.   At the moment, since you're fighting a war.

Zépo   No, nothing much. I didn't make a good score, hardly ever scored a bull.

Mons. T.   Which are you best at shooting? Enemy horses or soldiers?

Zépo   No, not horses, there aren't any horses any more.

Mons. T.   Well, soldiers then?

Zépo   Could be.

Mons. T.   Could be? Aren't you sure?

Zépo   Well you see . . . I shoot without taking aim (*pause*), and at the same time I say an Ave Maria for the chap I've shot.

Zapo   An Ave Maria? I'd have thought you'd have said a Pater Noster.

Zépo   No, always an Ave Maria. (*Pause.*) It's shorter.

Mons. T.   Come come, my dear fellow, you must be brave.

Mme. T. (*To* Zépo)   We can untie you if you like.

Zépo   No, don't bother, it doesn't matter.

Mons. T.   Don't start getting stand-offish with us now. If you'd like us to untie you, say so.

Mme. T.   Make yourself comfortable.

Zépo   Well, if that's how you feel, you can untie my feet, but it's only to please you.

Mons. T.   Zapo, untie him.

(Zapo *unties him.*)

Mme. T.   Well, do you feel better?

Zépo   Yes, of course. I really am putting you to a lot of inconvenience.

Mons. T.   Not at all, just make yourself at home. And if you'd like us to untie your hands you only have to say so.

Zépo   No, not my hands, I don't want to impose upon you.

Mons. T.   No no, my dear chap, no no. I tell you, it's no trouble at all.

Zépo   Right . . . Well then, untie my hands too. But only for lunch, eh? I don't want you to think that you give me an inch and I take an ell.

Mons. T.   Untie his hands, son.

Mme. T. Well, since our distinguished prisoner is so charming, we're going to have a marvellous day in the country.

Zépo Don't call me your distinguished prisoner, just call me your prisoner.

Mme. T. Won't that embarrass you?

Zépo No no, not at all.

Mons. T. Well, I must say you're modest.

(*Noise of aeroplanes.*)

Zapo Aeroplanes. They're sure to be coming to bomb us. (Zapo *and* Zépo *throw themselves on the sandbags and hide. To his parents*) Take cover. The bombs will fall on you.

(*The noise of the aeroplanes overpowers all the other noises. Bombs immediately start to fall. Shells explode very near the stage but not on it. A deafening noise.*

Zapo and Zépo are cowering down between the sandbags. M. Tépan goes on talking calmly to his wife, and she answers in the same unruffled way. We can't hear what they are saying because of the bombing. Mme. Tépan goes over to one of the baskets and takes an umbrella out of it. She opens it. M. and Mme. Tépan shelter under it as if it were raining. They are standing up. They shift rhythmically from one foot to the other and talk about their personal affairs.

The bombing continues.

Finally the aeroplanes go away. Silence.

M. Tepan stretches an arm outside the umbrella to make sure that nothing more is falling from the heavens.)

Mons. T. (*to his wife*) You can shut your umbrella. (Mme. Tépan *does so. They both go over to their son and tap him lightly on the behind with the umbrella.*) Come on, out you come. The bombing's over.

(Zapo *and* Zépo *come out of their hiding place.*)

Zapo Didn't you get hit?

Mons. T. What d'you think could happen to your father? (*Proudly.*) Little bombs like that! Don't make me laugh!

(*Enter, left, two* Red Cross Soldiers. *They are carrying a stretcher.*)

1st Stretcher Bearer Any dead here?

Zapo No, no one around these parts.

1st Stretcher Bearer Are you sure you've looked properly?

Zapo Sure.

1st Stretcher Bearer And there isn't a single person dead?

Zapo I've already told you there isn't.

1st Stretcher Bearer No one wounded, even?

Zapo Not even that.

2nd Stretcher Bearer (*To the* 1st S. B.) Well, now we're in a mess! (*To* ZAPO *persuasively*.) Just look again, search everywhere, and see if you can't find us a stiff.

1st Stretcher Bearer Don't keep on about it, they've told you quite clearly there aren't any.

2nd Stretcher Bearer What a lousy trick!

Zapo I'm terribly sorry. I promise you I didn't do it on purpose.

2nd Stretcher Bearer That's what they all say. That no one's dead and that they didn't do it on purpose.

1st Stretcher Bearer Oh, let the chap alone!

Mons. T. (*Obligingly*) We should be only too pleased to help you. At your service.

2nd Stretcher Bearer Well, really, if things go on like this I don't know what the Captain will say to us.

Mons. T. But what's it all about?

2nd Stretcher Bearer Quite simply that the others' wrists are aching with carting so many corpses and wounded men about, and that we haven't found any yet. And it's not because we haven't looked!

Mons. T. Well yes, that really is annoying. (*To* ZAPO.) Are you quite sure no one's dead?

Zapo Obviously, Papa.

Mons. T. Have you looked under all the sandbags?

Zapo Yes, Papa.

Mons. T. (*Angrily*) Well then, you might as well say straight out that you don't want to lift a finger to help these gentlemen, when they're so nice, too!

1st Stretcher Bearer Don't be angry with him. Let him be. We must just hope we'll have more luck in another trench and that all the lot'll be dead.

Mons. T. I should be delighted.

Mme. T. Me too. There's nothing I like more than people who put their hearts into their work.

Mons. T. (*Indignantly, addressing his remarks to the wings*) Then is no one going to do anything for these gentlemen?

Zapo If it only rested with me, it'd already be done.

Zépo I can say the same.

Mons. T. But look here, is neither of you even wounded?

Zapo (*Ashamed*) No, not me.

Mons. T. (*To* ZÉPO) What about you?

Zépo (*Ashamed*) Me neither. I never have any luck.

Mme. T. (*Pleased*) Now I remember! This morning, when I was peeling the onions, I cut my finger. Will that do you?

Mons. T. Of course it will! (*Enthusiastically.*) They'll take you off at once!

1st Stretcher Bearer No, that won't work. With ladies it doesn't work.

Mons. T.   We're no further advanced, then.

1st Stretcher Bearer   Never mind.

2nd Stretcher Bearer   We may be able to make up for it in the other trenches.

(*They start to go off.*)

Mons. T.   Don't worry! If we find a dead man we'll keep him for you! No fear of us giving him to anyone else!

2nd Stretcher Bearer   Thank you very much, sir.

Mons. T.   Quite all right, old chap, think nothing of it.

(*The two* STRETCHER BEARERS *say goodbye. All four answer them. The* STRETCHER BEARERS *go out.*)

Mme. T.   That's what's so pleasant about spending a Sunday in the country. You always meet such nice people. (*Pause.*) But why are you enemies?

Zépo   I don't know, I'm not very well educated.

Mme. T.   Was it by birth, or did you become enemies afterwards?

Zépo   I don't know, I don't know anything about it.

Mons. T.   Well then, how did you come to be in the war?

Zépo   One day, at home, I was just mending my mother's iron, a man came and asked me: 'Are you Zépo?' 'Yes.' 'Right, you must come to the war.' And so I asked him: 'But what war?' and he said: 'Don't you read the papers then? You're just a peasant!' I told him I did read the papers but not the war bits. . . .

Zapo   Just how it was with me—exactly how it was with me.

Mons. T.   Yes, they came to fetch you too.

Mme. T.   No, it wasn't quite the same; that day you weren't mending an iron, you were mending the car.

Mons. T.   I was talking about the rest of it. (*To* ZÉPO.) Go on, what happened then?

Zépo   Then I told him I had a fiancée and that if I didn't take her to the pictures on Sundays she wouldn't like it. He said that that wasn't the least bit important.

Zapo   Just how it was with me—exactly how it was with me.

Zépo   And then my father came down and he said I couldn't go to the war because I didn't have a horse.

Zapo   Just what my father said.

Zépo   The man said you didn't need a horse any more, and I asked him if I could take my fiancée with me. He said no. Then I asked whether I could take my aunt with me so that she could make me one of her custards on Thursdays; I'm very fond of them.

Mme. T.   (*Realising that she'd forgotten it*)   Oh! The custard!

Zépo   He said no again.

Zapo   Same as with me.

Zépo   And ever since then I've been alone in the trench nearly all the time.

Mme. T.   I think you and your distinguished prisoner might play together this afternoon, as you're so close to each other and so bored.

Zapo   Oh no, Mother, I'm too afraid, he's an enemy.

Mons. T.   Now now, you mustn't be afraid.

Zapo   If you only knew what the General was saying about the enemy!

Mme. T.   What did he say?

Zapo   He said the enemy are very nasty people. When they take prisoners they put little stones in their shoes so that it hurts them to walk.

Mme. T.   How awful! What barbarians!

Mons. T.   (*Indignantly to* Zépo)   And aren't you ashamed to belong to an army of criminals?

Zépo   I haven't done anything. I don't do anybody any harm.

Mme. T.   He was trying to take us in, pretending to be such a little saint!

Mons. T.   We oughtn't to have untied him. You never know, we only need to turn our backs and he'll be putting a stone in our shoes.

Zépo   Don't be so nasty to me.

Mons. T.   What d'you think we *should* be, then? I'm indignant. I know what I'll do. I'll go and find the Captain and ask him to let me fight in the war.

Zapo   He won't let you, you're too old.

Mons. T.   Then I'll buy myself a horse and a sword and come and fight on my own account.

Mme. T.   Bravo! If I were a man I'd do the same.

Zépo   Don't be like that with me, Madame. Anyway I'll tell you something —our General told us the same thing about you.

Mme. T.   How could he dare tell such a lie!

Zapo   No—but the same thing really?

Zépo   Yes, the same thing.

Mons. T.   Perhaps it was the same man who talked to you both?

Mme. T.   Well if it was the same man he might at least have said something different. That's a fine thing—saying the same thing to everyone!

Mons. T.   (*To* Zépo, *in a different tone of voice*)   Another little drink?

Mme. T.   I hope you liked our lunch?

Mons. T.   In any case, it was better than last Sunday.

Zépo   What happened?

Mons. T.   Well, we went to the country and we put the food on the rug. While we'd got our backs turned a cow ate up all our lunch, and the napkins as well.

Zépo   What a greedy cow!

Mons. T.   Yes, but afterwards, to get our own back, we ate the cow.

(*They laugh.*)

Zapo (*To* Zépo)   They couldn't have been very hungry after that!

Mons. T.   Cheers!

(*They all drink.*)

Mme. T. (*To* ZÉPO)   And what do you do to amuse yourself in the trench?

Zépo   I spend my time making flowers out of rags, to amuse myself. I get terribly bored.

Mme. T.   And what do you do with the flowers?

Zépo   At the beginning I used to send them to my fiancée, but one day she told me that the greenhouse and the cellar were already full of them and that she didn't know what to do with them any more, and she asked me, if I didn't mind, to send her something else.

Mme. T.   And what did you do?

Zépo   I tried to learn to make something else, but I couldn't. So I go on making rag flowers to pass the time.

Mme. T.   Do you throw them away afterwards, then?

Zépo   No, I've found a way to use them now. I give one flower for each pal who dies. That way I know that even if I make an awful lot there'll never be enough.

Mons. T.   That's a good solution you've hit on.

Zépo (*Shyly*)   Yes.

Zapo   Well, what I do is knit, so as not to get bored.

Mme. T.   But tell me, are all the soldiers as bored as you?

Zépo   It all depends on what they do to amuse themselves.

Zapo   It's the same on our side.

Mons. T.   Then let's stop the war.

Zépo   How?

Mons. T.   It's very simple. (*To* ZAPO.) You just tell your pals that the enemy soldiers don't want to fight a war, and you (*to* ZÉPO) say the same to your comrades. And then everyone goes home.

Zapo   Marvellous!

Mme. T.   And then you'll be able to finish mending the iron.

Zapo   How is it that no one thought of such a good idea before?

Mme. T.   Your father is the only one who's capable of thinking up such ideas; don't forget he's a former student of the Ecole Normale, *and* a philatelist.

Zépo   But what will the sergeant-majors and corporals do?

Mons. T.   We'll give them some guitars and castanets to keep them quiet!

Zépo   Very good idea.

Mons. T.   You see how easy it is. Everything's fixed.

Zépo   We shall have a tremendous success.

Zapo   My pals will be terribly pleased.

Mme. T.   What d'you say to putting on the pasodoble we were playing just now, to celebrate?

Zépo   Perfect.

Zapo   Yes, put the record on, Mother.

(MME. TÉPAN *puts a record on. She turns the handle. She waits. Nothing can be heard.*)

Mons. T.   I can't hear a thing.
Mme. T.   Oh, how silly of me! Instead of putting a record on I put on a beret.

(*She puts the record on. A gay pasodoble is heard. ZAPO dances with ZÉPO, and MME. TÉPAN with her husband. They are all very gay. The field telephone rings. None of the four hears it. They go on dancing busily. The telephone rings again. The dance continues.*

The battle starts up again with a terrific din of bombs, shots and bursts of machine-gun fire. None of the four has seen anything and they go on dancing merrily. A burst of machine-gun fire mows them all down. They fall to the ground, stone dead. A shot must have grazed the gramophone; the record keeps repeating the same thing, like a scratched record. The music of the scratched record can be heard till the end of the play.

The two STRETCHER BEARERS enter left. They are carrying the empty stretcher.)

(*Sudden Curtain*)

STUDY QUESTIONS

1. Point to specific examples in the dialogue of literal and figurative language.
2. Considering the setting, would people talk the way these characters do? What is absurd about their language? What does the author achieve by this absurdity?
3. How does Arrabel create a sense of realism through the dialogue of the parents? How does he make the dialogue symbolic? Do Zépo and Zapo share this balance in their dialogue?
4. If the setting and dialogue of the play can be considered symbolic, what is being symbolized?
5. Why does Zapo capture Zépo by saying "You're it"? Discuss.
6. Is this play a comedy? What in the dialogue would make it seem to be?
7. What is compelling about the title of the play? Why?
8. Discuss how, in relation to the events of the play, the dialogue is ironic. How does the climax of the play relate to that irony?
9. What is the symbolic meaning of the play? How does Arrabel use language to create symbols? To create meaning?

Archibald MacLeish (1892–   )
THE FALL OF THE CITY

PREFACE

It took my generation of Americans two world wars to learn that an age had ended. When we went to the First World War in 1917 we believed in everything—in the war itself, in the Declaration of American Independence, in the revolution of mankind which that Declaration announced.

I remember an apple orchard above the Marne on a summer afternoon in 1918 and two New Mexico National Guardsmen, shuffling their feet in the long grass. They wanted to know why we were there—meaning by "there," not the orchard, but the Second Battle of the Marne.

I reminded them of President Wilson's words, "to make the world safe for democracy," and they nodded and walked off. They knew, and I knew, that democracy, the right to think as you pleased and say what you thought and govern yourself, was what every human being wanted—the one cause worth dying for in any country.

But twenty years later, when the Second World War was about to begin, no one would have used Mr. Wilson's words to answer that tragic question. Too many nations had walked away from freedom by that time and accepted tyranny in its place—Lenin's tyranny first . . . Mussolini's . . . Hitler's. And even in the United States the double talk of those who had lost heart had taken the place of Jefferson's honest English. "America first" meant, not that the old American commitment to human liberty came first, but that it didn't.

Our noble task was not to liberate France, which was already falling to Hitler, or to support Great Britain, which was near the end of its rope, but to look out for ourselves. And as for the rest of the world, if it preferred to live in police states rather than to persist in "the long labor of liberty," it was no concern of ours.

A courageous president and a magnificent army put an end to talk like that but we had glimpsed disaster and it was evident, even after we began to fight, that the great cause on which the Republic was founded was not a cause in which all mankind—even all Americans—believed. There were many who, left to themselves, would invent their conquerors and invite oppression as a way of life.

It was in the months of that realization that I wrote this play, using the everywhere of radio as a stage and all of history as a time—the imagined city of Tenochtitlán[1] where, before Cortez[2] conquered it, the dead woman appeared at noon at the tomb's door to prophesy: "The city of masterless men will take a master . . ."

I called it *The Fall of the City* and CBS produced it at the Seventh Regiment Armory in New York at seven o'clock on the evening of the eleventh of April, 1937, with Orson Welles, fresh from his actor's apprenticeship at the Gate Theatre in Dublin, as the Announcer and a crowd of high school students from New Jersey to fill the vast imagined square. It was, I have been told, the first verse play written for radio, but nobody knows how many listened to it—only that it was broadcast again a few months later from the Hollywood Bowl. But by that time Chamberlain[3] had gone to Germany and returned with "peace in our time" and the city had fallen . . . not to be raised again until the greatest of all wars was won.

A. MacL.

The Voice of the Studio Director (*Orotund,[4] professional*)

Ladies and gentlemen:
This broadcast comes to you from the city.
Listeners over the curving air have heard
From furthest-off frontiers of foreign hours—
Mountain Time: Ocean Time: of the islands: 5
Of waters after the islands—some of them waking
Where noon here is the night there: some
Where noon is the first few stars they see or the last one.

For three days the world has watched this city—
Not for the common occasions of brutal crime   10
Or the usual violence of one sort or another
Or coronations of kings or popular festivals:
No: for stranger and disturbing reasons—
The resurrection from death and the tomb of a dead woman.

Each day for three days there has come   15
To the door of her tomb at noon a woman buried!

---

[1] Tenochtitlán: now Mexico City, the capital of the Aztec nation, which welcomed Cortez and his troops without resistance.

[2] Cortez: Hernando Cortez (1485–1547), Spanish explorer, conqueror of Mexico.

[3] Chamberlain: Neville Chamberlain (1869–1940), British prime minister, who in the 1938 Munich Pact granted Germany's territorial claims to parts of Czechoslovakia. A year later, Germany invaded Poland, and Chamberlain led Britain into war.

[4] orotund: rich, pompous.

ARCHIBALD MAC LEISH

The terror that stands at the shoulder of our time
Touches the cheek with this: the flesh winces.
There have been other omens in other cities
But never of this sort and never so credible. 20
In a time like ours seemings and portents signify.
Ours is a generation when dogs howl and the
Skin crawls on the skull with its beast's foreboding.
All men now alive with us have feared.
We have smelled the wind in the street that changes weather. 25
We have seen the familiar room grow unfamiliar:
The order of numbers alter: the expectation
Cheat the expectant eye. The appearance defaults with us.

Here in this city the wall of the time cracks.

We take you now to the great square of this city . . . 30

(*The shuffle and hum of a vast patient crowd gradually rises: swells: fills the background.*)

The Voice of the Announcer (*Matter-of-fact*)
We are here on the central plaza.
We are well off to the eastward edge.
There is a kind of terrace over the crowd here.
It is precisely four minutes to twelve.
The crowd is enormous: there might be ten thousand: 35
There might be more: the whole square is faces.
Opposite over the roofs are the mountains.
It is quite clear: there are birds circling.
We think they are kites[5] by the look: they are very high . . .

The tomb is off to the right somewhere— 40
We can't see for the great crowd.
Close to us here are the cabinet ministers:
They stand on a raised platform with awnings.
The farmers' wives are squatting on the stones:
Their children have fallen asleep on their shoulders. 45
The heat is harsh: the light dazzles like metal.
It dazes the air as the clang of a gong does . . .
News travels in this nation:
There are people here from away off—
Horse-raisers out of the country with brooks in it: 50
Herders of cattle from up where the snow stays—
The kind that cook for themselves mostly:

[5] kites: small, swift birds of prey.

They look at the girls with their eyes hard
And a hard grin and their teeth showing . . .

It is one minute to twelve now: 55
There is still no sign: they are still waiting:
No one doubts that she will come:
No one doubts that she will speak too:
Three times she has not spoken.

(*The murmur of the crowd changes—not louder but more intense: higher.*)

The Voice of the Announcer (*Low but with increasing excitement*)
    Now it is twelve: now they are rising: 60
    Now the whole plaza is rising:
    Fathers are lifting their small children:
    The plumed fans on the platform are motionless . . .

    There is no sound but the shuffle of shoe leather . . .

    Now even the shoes are still . . .   65

    We can hear the hawks: it is quiet as that now . . .

    It is strange to see such throngs so silent . . .

    Nothing yet: nothing has happened . . .

    Wait! There's a stir here to the right of us:
    They're turning their heads: the crowd turns: 70
    The cabinet ministers lean from their balcony:
    There's no sound: only the turning . . .

(*A woman's voice comes over the silence of the crowd: it is a weak voice
but penetrating: it speaks slowly and as though with difficulty.*)

The Voice of the Dead Woman
    First the waters rose with no wind . . .
The Voice of the Announcer (*Whispering*)
    Listen: that is she! She's speaking!
The Voice of the Dead Woman
    Then the stones of the temple kindled   75
    Without flame or tinder of maize[6] leaves . . .
The Voice of the Announcer (*Whispering*)
    They see her beyond us: the crowd sees her . . .

---

[6] maize: Indian corn.

The Voice of the Dead Woman
    Then there were cries in the night haze:
    Words in a once-heard tongue: the air
    Rustling above us as at dawn with herons.   80

    Now it is I who must bring fear:
    I who am four days dead: the tears
    Still unshed for me—all of them: I
    For whom a child still calls at nightfall.

    Death is young in me to fear!   85
    My dress is kept still in the press in my bedchamber:
    No one has broken the dish of the dead woman.

    Nevertheless I must speak painfully:
    I am to stand here in the sun and speak:

(*There is a pause. Then her voice comes again loud, mechanical, speaking as by rote.*)

    The city of masterless men   90
    Will take a master.

    There will be shouting then:
    Blood after!

(*The crowd stirs. Her voice goes on weak and slow as before.*)

    Do not ask what it means: I do not know:
    Only sorrow and no hope for it.   95
The Voice of the Announcer
    She has gone . . . No, they are still looking.
The Voice of the Dead Woman
    It is hard to return from the time past. I have come
    In the dream we must learn to dream where the crumbling of
    Time like the ash from a burnt string has
    Stopped for me. For you the thread still burns: 100
    You take the feathery ash upon your fingers.
    You bring yourselves from the time past as it pleases you.

    It is hard to return to the old nearness . . .

    Harder to go again . . .
The Voice of the Announcer
                  She is gone.
    We know because the crowd is closing.   105

All we can see is the crowd closing.
We hear the releasing of held breath—
The weight shifting: the lifting of shoe leather.
The stillness is broken as surface of water is broken—
The sound circling from in outward.   110

(*The murmur of the crowd rises.*)

Small wonder they feel fear.
Before the murders of the famous kings—
Before imperial cities burned and fell—
The dead were said to show themselves and speak.
When dead men came disaster came. Presentiments   115
That let the living on their beds sleep on
Woke dead men out of death and gave them voices.
All ancient men in every nation knew this.

A Voice over the Crowd
Masterless men . . .

A Voice over the Crowd
When shall it be . . .   120

A Voice over the Crowd
Masterless men
Will take a master . . .

A Voice over the Crowd
What has she said to us . . .

A Voice over the Crowd
When shall it be . . .

A Voice over the Crowd
Masterless men   125
Will take a master.
Blood after . . .

A Voice over the Crowd
What has she said to us . . .

Voices Together
Blood after!

(*The voices run together into the excited roar of the crowd. The Announcer's voice is loud over it.*)

The Voice of the Announcer
They are milling around us like cattle that smell death.   130
The whole square is whirling and turning and shouting.
One of the ministers raises his arms on the platform.
No one is listening: now they are sounding drums:
Trying to quiet them likely: No! No!
Something is happening: there in the far corner: 135

A runner: a messenger: staggering: people are helping him:
People are calling: he comes through the crowd: they are quieter.
Only those on the far edge are still shouting:
Listen! He's here by the ministers now! He is speaking . . .

The Voice of the Messenger

There has come the conqueror! 140
I am to tell you.
I have raced over sea land:
I have run over cane land:
I have climbed over cone land.
It was laid on my shoulders 145
By shall and by shan't
That standing by day
And staying by night
Were not for my lot
Till I came to the sight of you. 150
Now I have come.

Be warned of this conqueror!
This one is dangerous!
Word has out-oared him.
East over sea-cross has 155
All taken—
Every country.
No men are free there.
Ears overhear them.
Their words are their murderers. 160
Judged before judgment
Tried after trial
They die as do animals:—
Offer their throats
As the goat to her slaughterer. 165
Terror has taught them this!

Now he is here!

He was violent in his vessel:
He was steering in her stern:
He was watching in her waist: 170
He was peering in her prow:
And he dragged her up
Nine lengths
Till her keel lodged
On this nation. 175

Now he is here
Waylaying and night-lying.
If they hide before dark
He comes before sunup.
Where hunger is eaten   180
There he sits down:
Where fear sleeps
There he arises.

I tell you beware of him!
All doors are dangers.   185
The warders of wealth
Will admit him by stealth.
The lovers of men
Will invite him as friend.
The drinkers of blood   190
Will drum him in suddenly.
Hope will unlatch to him:
Hopelessness open.

I say and say truly
To all men in honesty   195
Such is this conqueror!
Shame is his people.
Lickers of spittle
Their lives are unspeakable:
Their dying indecent.   200

Be well warned!
He comes to you slightly
Slanting and sprinting
Hinting and shadowing:
Sly is his hiding:—   205
A hard lot:
A later rider:

Watch! I have said to you!
The Voice of the Announcer
 They are leading him out: his legs give:
 Now he is gone in the crowd: they are silent: 210
 No one has spoken since his speaking:

 They stand still circling the ministers.
 No one has spoken or called out:—

There is no stir at all nor movement:
Even the farthest have stood patiently: 215
They wait trusting the old men:
They wait faithfully trusting the answer.
Now the huddle on the platform opens:
A minister turns to them raising his two arms . . .

The Voice of the Orator
Freemen of this nation!   220
The persuasion of your wills against your wisdom is not dreamed of.
We offer themes for your consideration.
What is the surest defender of liberty?
Is it not liberty?

A free people resists by freedom: 225
Not locks! Not blockhouses!

The future is a mirror where the past
Marches to meet itself. Go armed toward arms!
Peaceful toward peace! Free and with music toward freedom!
Face tomorrow with knives and tomorrow's a knife-blade.   230
Murder your foe and your foe will be murder!—
Even your friends suspected of false-speaking:
Hands on the door at night and the floorboards squeaking.

Those who win by the spear are the spear-toters.
And what do they win? Spears! What else is there?   235
If their hands let go they have nothing to hold by.
They are no more free than a paralytic propped against a tree is.

With the armored man the arm is upheld by the weapon:
The man is worn by the knife.

Once depend on iron for your freedom and your   240
Freedom's iron!
Once overcome your resisters with force and your
Force will resist you!—
You will never be free of force.
Never of arms unarmed   245
Will the father return home:
The lover to her loved:
The mature man to his fruit orchard
Walking at peace in that beauty—
The years of his trees to assure him.   250

Force is a greater enemy than this conqueror—
A treacherous weapon.
Nevertheless my friends there *is* a weapon!
Weakness conquers!

Against chainlessness who breaks?   255
Against wall-lessness who vaults?
Against forcelessness who forces?

Against the feather of the thistle
Is blunted sharpest metal.
No edge cuts seed-fluff.   260

This conqueror unresisted
Will conquer no longer: a posturer
Beating his blows upon burdocks—
Shifting his guard against shadows.
Snickers will sound among road-menders: 265
Titters be stifled by laundresses:
Coarse guffaws among chambermaids.
Reddened with rage he will roar.
He will sweat in his uniform foolishly.
He will disappear: no one hear of him!   270

There *is* a weapon my friends.
Scorn conquers!

The Voice of the Announcer (*The* Orator's *voice unintelligible under it*)
I wish you could all see this as we do—
The whole plaza full of these people—
Their colorful garments—the harsh sunlight—   275
The water-sellers swinging enormous gourds—
The orator there on the stone platform—
The temple behind him: the high pyramid—
The hawks overhead in the sky teetering
Slow to the windward: swift to the downwind—   280
The houses blind with the blank sun on them . . .

The Voice of the Orator
There is a weapon.
Reason and truth are that weapon.

Let this conqueror come!
Show him no hindrance!   285
Suffer his flag and his drum!
Words . . . win!

The Voice of the Announcer
　There's the shout now: he's done:
　He's climbing down: a great speech:
　They're all smiling and pressing around him:　　　　　　290
　The women are squatting in full sunlight:
　They're opening packages: bread we'd say by the look—
　Yes: bread: bread wrapped between corn leaves:
　They're squatting to eat: they're quite contented and happy:
　Women are calling their men from the sunny stones:　　　295
　There are flutes sounding away off:
　We can't see for the shifting and moving—
　Yes: there are flutes in the cool shadow:
　Children are dancing in intricate figures.

(*A drum and flute are heard under the voice.*)

　Even a few old men are dancing.　　　　　　　　　　　300
　You'd say they'd never feared to see them dancing.
　A great speech! really great!
　Men forget these truths in passion:
　They oppose the oppressors with blind blows:
　They make of their towns tombs: of their roofs burials:　305
　They build memorial ruins to liberty:
　But liberty is not built from ruins:
　Only in peace is the work excellent . . .

　That's odd! The music has stopped. There's something—
　It's a man there on the far side: he's pointing:　　　　310
　He seems to be pointing back through the farthest street:
　The people are twisting and rising: bread in their fists . . .
　We can't see what it is . . . Wait! . . . it's a messenger.
　It must be a messenger. Yes. It's a message—another.
　Here he is at the turn of the street trotting:　　　　　315
　His neck's back at the nape: he looks tired:
　He winds through the crowd with his mouth open: laboring:
　People are offering water: he pushes away from them:
　Now he has come to the stone steps: to the ministers:
　Stand by: we're edging in . . .　　　　　　　　　　　320

(*There are sounds of people close by: coughs: murmurs. The* ANNOUNCER'S *voice is lowered.*)

　Listen: he's leaning on the stone: he's speaking.
The Voice of the Messenger
　There has come . . . the conqueror . . .

I am to tell you . . .

I have run over corn land:
I have climbed over cone land: 325
I have crossed over mountains . . .

It was laid on my shoulders
By shall and by shan't
That standing by day
And staying by night   330
Were not for my lot
Till I came to the sight of you . . .

Now I have come.

I bear word:
Beware of this conqueror!   335

The fame of his story
Like flame in the winter grass
Widens before him.
Beached on our shore
With the dawn over shoulder   340
The lawns were still cold
When he came to the sheep meadows:—
Sun could not keep with him
So was he forward.

Fame is his sword.   345

No man opposing him
Still grows his glory.
He needs neither foeman nor
Thickset of blows to
Gather his victories—   350
Nor a foe's match
To earn him his battles.

He brings his own enemy!

He baggages with him
His closet antagonist—   355
His private opposer.
He's setting him up

At every road corner—
A figure of horror
With blood for his color: 360
Fist for his hand:
Reek where he stands:
Hate for his heat:
Sneers for his mouth:
Clouts[7] for his clothes: 365
Oaths if he speak:—
And he's knocking him down
In every town square
Till hair's on his blade
And blood's all about   370
Like dust in a drouth[8]
And the people are shouting
Flowers him flinging
Music him singing
And bringing him gold   375
And holding his heels
And feeling his thighs
Till their eyes start
And their hearts swell
And they're telling his praises   380
Like lays of the heroes
And chiefs of antiquity.

Such are his victories!
So does he come:
So he approaches . . .   385

(*A whisper rustles through the crowd.*)

No man to conquer
Yet as a conqueror
Marches he forward . . .

(*This whisper is louder.*)

Stands in your mountains . . .

(*A murmur of voices.*)

Soon to descend on you!   390

(*A swelling roar.*)

[7] Clouts: rags, patches.
[8] drouth: drought.

The Voice of the Announcer

That touched them! That frightened them!
Some of them point to the east hills:
Some of them mock at the ministers: "Freedom!"
"Freedom for what? To die in a rat trap?"
They're frantic with anger and plain fear.   395
They're sold out they say. You can hear them.
"Down with the government! Down with the orators!
"Down with liberal learned minds!
"Down with the mouths and the loose tongues in them!
"Down with the lazy lot! They've sold us!   400
"We're sold out! Talking has done for us!"
They're boiling around us like mullet[9] that smell shark.
We can't move for the mob: they're crazy with terror . . .

A Loud Voice (*Distant*)

God-lovers!
Think of your gods!   405

Earth-masters!
Taste your disasters!

Men!
Remember!

The Voice of the Announcer

There's a voice over the crowd somewhere.   410
They hear it: they're quieting down . . . It's the priests!
We see them now: it's the priests on the pyramid!
There might be ten of them: black with their hair tangled.
The smoke of their fire is flat in the quick wind:
They stand in the thick of the smoke by the stone of the victims: 415
Their knives catch in the steep sun: they are shouting:
Listen:—

Voices of the Priests

Turn to your gods rememberers!

A Single Voice

Let the world be saved by surrendering the world:
  Not otherwise shall it be saved.   420

Voices of the Priests

Turn to your gods rememberers!

A Single Voice

Let evil be overcome by the coming over of evil:
  Your hearts shall be elsewhere.

[9] mullet: a variety of marine fish that travel in schools.

Voices of the Priests
  Turn to your gods rememberers!
Voices of the Priests (*Antiphonally*)
  Turn to your gods!   425
    The conqueror cannot take you!

  Turn to your gods!
    The narrow dark will keep you!

  Turn to your gods!
    In god's house is no breaking!   430

  Turn to your gods!
    In god's silences sleep is!

  Lay up your will with the gods!
    Stones cannot still you!

  Lay up your mind with the gods!   435
    Blade cannot blind you!

  Lay up your heart with the gods!
    Danger departs from you!
The Voice of the Announcer
  It's a wonderful thing to see this crowd responding.
  Even the simplest citizens feel the emotion.   440
  There's hardly a sound now in the square. It's wonderful:
  Really impressive: the priests there on the pyramid:
  The smoke blowing: the bright sun: the faces—
A Single Voice
  In the day of confusion of reason when all is delusion:
  In the day of the tyrants of tongues when the truth is for hire: 445
  In the day of deceit when ends meet:
  Turn to your gods!

  In the day of division of nations when hope is derision:
  In the day of the supping of hate when the soul is corrupted:
  In the day of despair when the heart's bare: 450
  Turn to your gods!

(*A slow drum beat.*)

The Voice of the Announcer
  A kind of dance is beginning: a serpent of people:

A current of people coiling and curling through people:
A circling of people through people like water through water . . .

Chanting Voices (*To the drums*)

Out of the stir of the sun   455
Out of the shout of the thunder
Out of the hush of the star . . .
Withdraw the heart.

The Voice of the Announcer (*The chant and drums under*)

A very young girl is leading them:
They have torn the shawl from her bare breast: 460
They are giving her flowers: her mouth laughs:
Her eyes are not laughing . . .

Chanting Voices

Leave now the lovely air
To the sword and the sword-wearer—
Leave to the marksman the mark—   465
Withdraw the heart.

The Voice of the Announcer (*The chant and drums louder*)

She's coming . . . the drums pound . . . the crowd
Shrieks . . . she's reaching the temple . . . she's climbing it . . .
Others are following: five: ten . . .
Hundreds are following . . . crowding the stairway . . .   470
She's almost there . . . her flowers have fallen . . .
She looks back . . . the priests are surrounding her . . .

(*The drums suddenly stop: there is an instant's silence: then an angry
shout from the crowd.*)

The Voice of the Announcer

Wait! Wait! Something has happened!
One of the ministers: one of the oldest:
The general: the one in the feathered coat:—   475
He's driving them down with the staff of a banner:
He's climbed after them driving them down:
There's shouting and yelling enough but they're going:
He's telling them off too: you can hear him—

A Deep Voice (*Chatter of the crowd under it*)

Men! Old men! Listen!   480
Twist your necks on your nape bones!
The knife will wait in the fist for you.
There is a time for everything—
Time to be thinking of heaven:
Time of your own skins!   485

Cock your eyes to the windward!

Do you see smoke on those mountains?
The smoke is the smoke of towns.
And who makes it? The conqueror!
And where will he march now? Onward!⠀⠀⠀⠀⠀⠀⠀⠀⠀⠀490
The heel of the future descends on you!
The Voice of the Announcer
⠀⠀He has them now: even the priests have seen it:
⠀⠀They're all looking away here to the east.
⠀⠀There's smoke too: filling the valleys: like thunderheads!
The Voice of the General
⠀⠀You are foolish old men.⠀⠀⠀⠀⠀⠀⠀⠀⠀⠀495

⠀⠀You ought to be flogged for your foolishness.
⠀⠀Your grandfathers died to be free
⠀⠀And you—you juggle with freedom!
⠀⠀Do you think you're free by a law
⠀⠀Like the falling of apples in autumn?⠀⠀⠀⠀⠀⠀⠀⠀⠀⠀500

⠀⠀You thought you were safe in your liberties!
⠀⠀You thought you could always quibble!
⠀⠀You can't! You take my word for it.
⠀⠀Freedom's the rarest bird!
⠀⠀You risk your neck to snare it—⠀⠀⠀⠀⠀⠀⠀⠀⠀⠀505
⠀⠀It's gone while your eyeballs stare!

⠀⠀Those who'd lodge with a tyrant
⠀⠀Thinking to feed at his fire
⠀⠀And leave him again when they're fed are
⠀⠀Plain fools or were bred to it—⠀⠀⠀⠀⠀⠀⠀⠀⠀⠀510
⠀⠀Brood of the servile races
⠀⠀Born with the hangdog face . . .
The Voice of the Announcer
⠀⠀They're all pointing and pushing together:
⠀⠀The women are shouldering baskets: bread: children . . .
⠀⠀They smell smoke in the air: they smell terror . . .⠀⠀⠀⠀⠀⠀515
The Voice of the General (*Louder over the increasing sound*)
⠀⠀There's nothing in this world worse—
⠀⠀Empty belly or purse or the
⠀⠀Pitiful hunger of children—
⠀⠀Than doing the Strong Man's will!

⠀⠀The free will fight for their freedom.⠀⠀⠀⠀⠀⠀⠀⠀⠀⠀520
⠀⠀They're free men first. They feed
⠀⠀Meager or fat but as free men.

Everything else comes after—
Food: roof: craft—
Even the sky and the light of it!   525

(*The voices of the crowd rise to a tumult of sounds—drums: shouts: cries.*)

The Voice of the Announcer
    The sun is yellow with smoke . . . the town's burning . . .
    The war's at the broken bridge . . .
The Voice of the General (*Shouting*)
    You! Are you free? Will you fight?

There are still inches for fighting!

There is still a niche in the streets!   530

You can stand on the stairs and meet him!

You can hold in the dark of a hall!

You can die!

        —or your children will crawl for it!
The Voice of the Announcer (*Over the tumult*)
    They won't listen. They're shouting and screaming and circling.
    The square is full of deserters with more coming.   535
    Every street from the bridge is full of deserters.
    They're rolling in with the smoke blowing behind them.
    The plaza's choked with the smoke and the struggling of stragglers.
    They're climbing the platform: driving the ministers: shouting—
    One speaks and another: 540
The Voices of Citizens
    The city is doomed!
              There's no holding it!

Let the conqueror have it! It's his!

The age is his! It's his century!

Our institutions are obsolete.
He marches a mile while we sit in a meeting.   545

Opinions and talk!
Deliberative walks beneath the ivy and the creepers!

The age demands a made-up mind.
The conqueror's mind is decided on everything.

His doubt comes after the deed or never.   550

He knows what he wants for his want's what he knows.
He's gone before they say he's going.
He's come before you've barred your house.

He's one man: we are but thousands!

Who can defend us from one man?   555

Bury your arms! Break your standards!

Give him the town while the town stands!
The Voice of the Announcer
They're throwing their arms away: their bows are in bonfires.
The plaza is littered with torn plumes: spear-handles . . .
The Voices of Citizens
Masterless men!   560
Masterless men
Must take a master!

Order must master us!

Freedom's for fools:
Force is the certainty!   565

Freedom has eaten our strength and corrupted our virtues!

Men must be ruled!

Fools must be mastered!

Rigor and fast
Will restore us our dignity!   570

Chains will be liberty!
The Voice of the Announcer
The last defenders are coming: they whirl from the streets like
Wild leaves on a wind: the square scatters them.

Now they are fewer—ten together or five:
They come with their heads turned: their eyes back.   575

Now there are none. The street's empty—in shadow.
The crowd is retreating—watching the empty street:
The shouts die.

        The voices are silent.

              They're watching . . .

They stand in the slant of the sunlight silent and watching.
The silence after the drums echoes the drum beat.   580

Now there's a sound. They see him. They must see him!
They're shading their eyes from the sun: there's a rustle of whispering:
We can't see for the glare of it . . . Yes! . . . Yes! . . .
He's there in the end of the street in the shadow. We see him!
He looks huge—a head taller than anyone: 585
Broad as a brass door: a hard hero:
Heavy of heel on the brick: clanking with metal:
The helm closed on his head: the eyeholes hollow.

He's coming! . . .
        He's clear of the shadow! . . .
                The sun takes him.

They cover their faces with fingers. They cower before him.   590
They fall: they sprawl on the stone. He's alone where he's walking.
He marches with rattle of metal. He tramples his shadow.
He mounts by the pyramid—stamps on the stairway—turns—
His arm rises—his visor is opening . . .

(*There is an instant's breathless silence: then the voice of the* ANNOUNCER
low—almost a whisper.)
              There's no one! . . .
There's no one at all! . . .
        No one! . . .
             The helmet is hollow!   595
The metal is empty! The armor is empty! I tell you
There's no one at all there: there's only the metal:
The barrel of metal: the bundle of armor. It's empty!

The push of a stiff pole at the nipple would topple it.

They don't see! They lie on the paving. They lie in the   600
Burnt spears: the ashes of arrows. They lie there ...
They don't see or they won't see. They are silent ...

The people invent their oppressors: they wish to believe in them.
They wish to be free of their freedom: released from their liberty:—
The long labor of liberty ended!
                                    They lie there!   605

(*There is a whisper of sound. The* ANNOUNCER's *voice is louder.*)

Look! It's his arm! It is rising! His arm's rising!
They're watching his arm as it rises. They stir. They cry.
They cry out. They are shouting. They're shouting with happiness.
Listen! They're shouting like troops in a victory. Listen—
"The city of masterless men has found a master!"   610
You'd say it was they were the conquerors: they that had conquered.
A Roar of Voices
The city of masterless men has found a master!
The city has fallen!
The city has fallen!
The Voice of the Announcer (*Flat*)
The city has fallen ...   615

(*The End*)

CHAPTER 5

THE WHOLE WORK

In the preceding chapters, we have concentrated on one major element of literature at a time. Such an approach is possible with many works because character, conflict, setting, or figurative language may serve as the principal vehicle through which meaning is expressed. Nevertheless, most works of literature involve all four elements to some degree. Therefore a full statement of meaning can be arrived at only through an investigation of the various elements and their interaction.

Character, for example, can create conflict: two self-centered persons may have a very difficult time living together, while an unassuming and unselfish person might have no conflict with either one. Similarly, an individual may have two opposing traits: ambition and shyness in the same person can easily lead to internal conflicts. Conflict can also shape character; for example, personal response to conflict may lead to growth, as when a person becomes more courageous or more persevering through suffering. Setting, as we have seen, can place someone in conflict by thwarting his or her desires. Setting can also affect character, because each of us absorbs habits of behavior not only from the example of our parents but also from the socialization we experience in the larger setting in which we grow up. Finally, language is the vehicle through which the experience of literature is conveyed: it illuminates, either through literal narrative and imagery or through figurative means, the traits of characters, their conflicts, and the surroundings in which they live. In these and in a variety of other ways, the four elements we have examined separately actually interweave to generate meaning, even when one of them seems to predominate over the others.

In our study of "My Last Duchess," we focused on the character of the Duke. His particular traits are so clearly drawn that we are able to arrive at a general hypothesis that pride, arrogance, and a lack of respect for other humans can lead to brutally destructive behavior. However, the Duke does not operate in a vacuum. Setting, for example, has an important effect both on what happens in this poem and on how we understand it. Society has often given men great authority over their wives and daughters, but not many besides that of Renaissance Italy have allowed noblemen unlimited power, including the right to kill women who displeased them. Because the Duke's behavior seems to be accepted without comment by the society in which he lives, the reader is asked to judge the value system of the Renaissance, not merely that of a single person. In addition, some specialized uses of language enrich the poem's meaning. Reference to the bronze figure of Neptune taming a seahorse may symbolize the Duke's assumption of godlike power over those whose only purpose, as he thinks, is to serve his pleasure. Similarly, reference to the painting and the curtain that he keeps drawn over it can be interpreted to represent the total control over his Duchess that he was not able to achieve while she was alive. Among the various elements, probably conflict illuminates meaning most, by its interaction with character. We have come to some conclusions about the Duke's principal traits. Since everything we learn about the Duchess comes from his monologue, we must read cautiously, remembering that his pride may have led him to misjudge her. Clearly, nevertheless, her enjoyment of many simple things—her white mule, a bough of cherries, a painter's compliments to her beauty—brought her into direct conflict with the Duke. His wish was that she prefer his gift, a "nine-hundred-years-old name," to all others. Her nature led her to enjoy and appreciate many other gifts equally well, with the result that the Duke experienced internal conflict: he desired her to single him out for special thanks and respect, but he was unwilling to "stoop" to tell her what he expected. He resolves this conflict by controlling her behavior in another way that appears to him not to involve "stooping." In fact, having her put to death is a way of confirming his power and, therefore, of feeding his pride. Thus an examination of several elements in the poem broadens our awareness of just how his character traits lead him to a coolly calculated murder.

Similarly, our analysis of "John Gorham" was based almost completely on conflict and on the need of a person who has been humiliated in a quarrel to find some means of having the last word. Of the four literary elements we have examined, conflict is certainly dominant in this poem. Setting is hardly indicated at all, except that the frequent references to the moon imply a nighttime meeting out-of-doors. The most notable uses of figurative language involve metaphors: John Gorham calls Jane Wayland a butterfly and a cat; she states that she has never considered him a mouse. Clearly he thinks of her as flirtatious, a person who thrives on flitting from one admirer to another, playing with him as a cat plays with a mouse. She takes him at least somewhat seriously, though her initial reaction to him is to threaten to laugh. She does not seem to think of him as a helpless victim—a mouse. In any event, John Gorham appears to be a person with some determination: he has held on to his anger for a full year and now comes back to take his revenge. Some persons could shrug off a quarrel with a sweetheart or recover after a few days to fall in love with someone else. John Gorham, a slow, steady, serious person, feels his hurt deeply and can rid himself of it only by expressing his feelings directly. His character is such as to make the experience a particularly intense one; thus the interaction of character and conflict is important to a full appreciation of the poem.

As we noted in Chapter 3, the two major settings in "Memorial Rain" are central to the poem's meaning. In our interpretation, the dedication service in a foreign land is at first not adequate to enable the narrator to pass through grief to acceptance of death; the contrast between the Belgian cemetery and an Illinois lakefront illustrates a conflict going on within the mind of the speaker. Thus while we have few clues to the character of that speaker, we are very much aware of an internal struggle, a struggle revealed by the language and tone of the poem. The wind here is "strange," the trees "strung / Taut." In Belgium the wind is snakelike: it coils in the grass, it drags its heavy body along. Here it makes the earth rigid, like the buried soldiers. The descriptions suggest unease and anxiety, particularly as the speaker recalls the contrasting Illinois winds and the rains they bring. The comparison seems to heighten his own tensions and restlessness, which he in turn projects onto the dead soldier for whom he has come to this cemetery. Ultimately, the rain releases his tensions: we might see it as symbolizing his tears, which are possible only when the ambassador with his fine but empty speech has been driven to shelter. Thus, conflict and language in the poem both confirm and enrich the understanding arrived at through the study of setting.

Finally, the study of "Young Goodman Brown" primarily through the author's use of language leads to clear meaning, but that meaning too can be enlarged by an examination of other elements. Brown is a private, somewhat isolated person from the very beginning of the story, when he leaves on his night journey without telling his wife his purpose and why he must go by night instead of my day. He displays innocence in his initial insistence on the goodness of all the Puritans and is shocked to see Goody Cloyse, Deacon Gookin, and others he thought devout also journeying into the wilderness. In his final disillusionment he remains forever isolated and naive; his refusal to trust his fellow villagers or even his wife shuts him off from human comfort. At the same time, his conflicts reflect not only his own character but also the attractions that the two settings hold for him. He wishes to explore the wilderness, to know about the evil that is associated with it; at the same time, he wishes to remain connected to Faith and to the village, to live out his life without acknowledging the presence of evil in the village. His secret desire to know evil takes him into the forest. There he discovers that all the people he trusts most are in some degree tainted; hence, when he returns to the village, he can no longer associate with these people. While much of the meaning of the story is embodied in metaphors, metonymies, and symbols, an analysis of character, conflict, and setting contributes to that meaning. In other words, while the story may legitimately be examined almost entirely in terms of special language, it may be examined even more usefully as a whole, not isolating any one of its elements from the others.

Most longer works of literature, in fact, make such interrelated use of character, conflict, setting, and language that all of these must be examined as a totality before the reader can arrive at a full understanding of the text. Such is the case with the work in this chapter—Shakespeare's *Romeo and Juliet*. Before we approach the text itself, however, some outlines of various interpretations of the text and suggested methods of reading Shakespeare may help to prepare the reader for a more complete appreciation of the work as a whole.

THE PLAY: APPROACHES TO *ROMEO AND JULIET*

Romeo and Juliet, believed to have been written in 1595, is one of Shake-speare's earliest plays and the second of his ten tragedies. It tells the story of two young lovers, the only children of feuding families, who fall in love and marry in secret. Through misunderstandings and a series of disastrous events, their love leads directly to their death.

Like many other plays of the period, the story of the doomed lovers was based on a well-known tale. Earlier versions of the tragedy provided most of the characters and the major events of Shakespeare's drama. His changes, however, turned a familiar story into a great work of literary art. Shake-speare enhances the characterization so that even minor functional figures in earlier sources are made rich and complex. Mercutio, for example, once only a stock figure, becomes here one of the most interesting persons in the play and central to the tragedy. In addition, Shakespeare compresses the action into five days, which increases not only the suspense but also the sense of momentum, allowing no pause once the rising action begins. That compression thus strengthens unity, as does Shakespeare's use of balance: counterpoint. For example, a number of paired scenes in the drama involve similar events but have different outcomes, such as the two major scenes between Juliet and her nurse. In the first, the Nurse brings Juliet joy; in the second, she brings despair. Other scenes, like those involving fighting (act I, scene ii; act III, scene i; act V, scene ii), contribute to balance by their location in the action. A third unifying device is the recurrent use of a par-ticular image: the tomb as a metaphor for the bridal chamber, for example. All of these changes contribute not only to unity but also to the emotional intensity of the play, which is further increased by Juliet's extreme youth, the hatred between the families, the cynicism of the elders in contrast with the idealized love of the young people, and the pervasive irony of situation. Shakespeare, however, achieves his greatest emotional effect through the beauty of his lyric poetry. The declarations of love spoken by the young couple are unforgettable; the play is in fact one of the great love poems of all literature.

While love is at the heart of the drama, *Romeo and Juliet* is still a tragedy, for it is the story of two lovers whose union is doomed. The question read-ers are forced to ask is "Why?" Scholars disagree on the answer and offer different interpretations of the play, some of them grounded in commonly held Elizabethan beliefs, others derived more directly from the text itself. The following four approaches suggest, but of course do not exhaust, the range of possible readings and represent some ways students might con-sider exploring the play.

1. The first approach depends on recognition of the Elizabethan belief in astrology, the study of the effects of planets on human destiny. The posi-

tion of the planets at the time of one's birth and their movement from day to day influence personality, behavior, and even destiny. Fortune, the goddess who controls the movements of the planets, is seen as a fickle being who bestows good or bad luck according to her whim. The power of Fortune and the influence of the planets are mentioned several times in the play, most notably in the Prologue, where the central characters are described as "star-cross'd lovers" (line 6). If, as that description suggests, they were born under the power of malignant forces, their love cannot succeed; they are merely the innocent victims of forces whose influence they cannot escape.

2. The second approach places responsibility for the tragic events on human weakness; it requires recognition of the conflict between reason and passion in the drama. Elizabethans believed strongly that humans are essentially rational beings, superior to other forms of animal life by virtue of their unique ability to reason. Although Shakespeare's contemporaries recognized that all people are influenced by lower instincts of passion—like lust, greed, pride—they felt that the ability to control such weaknesses through the exercise of reason was the measure of one's character. If we look at the play from this point of view, we can see that in a number of key instances passion overrides reason. Failure to use reason therefore can be seen as a major cause of catastrophe and central to the tragedy.

3. Allied to the notion of the conflict between passion and reason is a third possible approach to the play, focusing on the potentially destructive power of love. *Romeo and Juliet* is concerned not merely with the passionate relationship between the two central characters. Parental and fraternal love, for instance, also fulfill important functions in the play. But romantic love is central to the story, and we must not forget that at the beginning, Romeo is deeply infatuated with a woman named Rosaline, whom he worships from a distance in the "courtly love" tradition. In courtly love, a beautiful woman is adored by a lover who regards himself as unworthy of her. Nevertheless, he requests that the beloved take pity on him; then, because she rejects him, he composes poems called complaints, extravagant compliments to her beauty. He becomes moody and physically ill from unrequited love, until (in some instances) his suit is finally successful and she yields to his embrace. Romeo is in the midst of the progress of this type of love toward Rosaline when he first meets Juliet; with her he goes through a different process, somewhat akin to the violent onset of a disease. This love occurs instantly, at first sight, contracted through the eyes. An immediate mutual obsession follows, and they are married the very next day. This kind of obsessive love is a frequent subject of the poetry of Shakespeare's day. Samuel Daniel wrote, "Love is a sickness, full of woe . . . ," and Shakespeare himself

wrote in Sonnet 147, "My love is as a fever. . . ." The play also contains a vocabulary associated with physical illness and malfunction to define the process of love. And since the love of Romeo and Juliet ultimately leads to their death, the play may be said to trace the progress of a debilitating and finally fatal disease.

4. A fourth way to examine the play relates to the Elizabethan acceptance of the doctrine of order. Living in a period when there was no separation between church and state, people in Europe regarded the universe as an ordered, hierarchical creation controlled by God; all humans were superior to other forms of earthly life. Within the human social structure, however, they recognized another hierarchy: the monarch was regarded as the supreme ruler of the country; his commands were the law of the land and must be obeyed if chaos was to be avoided. To maintain order, each segment of society depended on recognition of and obedience to authority. In the central unit of society, the family, the parents—and particularly the father—constituted the final authority. Yet that power carried with it certain responsibilities, primarily that of ruling the home by reason. The duty of children was to obey their parents' wishes, recognizing the superior wisdom of their elders. In *Romeo and Juliet*, all family members violate these rules. Shakespeare may be raising this question, then: "What happens when universal and societal orders are denied or flouted? What occurs when parents behave irrationally and children revolt? Can anything but tragedy result?"

As with all complex works of literature, interpretation of the play's meaning requires not only an awareness of the ideas that may have influenced the writer but also careful study of how these concepts are developed in the drama through character, conflict, setting, and language. The most important characters in *Romeo and Juliet* are of course the lovers. They are both young and are the children of well-to-do parents. There are, however, marked differences between them. Other less important characters also have distinctly drawn personalities. Benvolio and Tybalt are the cousins of Romeo and Juliet, respectively, and they share their families' mutual hostility. Yet they are also very different individuals: Tybalt, hot and fiery; Benvolio, generally calm and reasonable. Tybalt, in fact, is more like Mercutio in his hot temper, but he does not have Mercutio's love of fun. Unique character definition extends to the elder Montague and Capulet as well, who, although both of about the same age, station, and family situation, are very different in their reactions to situations. These uniquenesses of character relate directly to the way in which each member of the drama responds to the events that make up the action of the play.

Although the action arises ultimately from the feud, which we may call the central conflict since it affects everyone in the play, a number of lesser but vital external conflicts exist. Characters also experience internal conflicts, and these result from the kind of person each is and his or her need to interact with others as the plot unfolds.

Setting too is important in contributing to our understanding of the play. The time is the fifteenth or sixteenth century, during a period of five days in July, when the weather is hot and tempers are apt to flare. The place is Verona, a fairly large northern Italian city ruled by a prince. Ever present, whether it is night or day, are the planets: either the sun or the moon and various stars. Their influence on what happens within the setting is always felt.

Finally, the language of the play underscores and emphasizes character, conflict, and setting. How the various characters speak—their choice of words—reveals the kind of person each is and helps to establish, at least in part, the play's meaning.

READING THE WHOLE WORK

In previous chapters, we discussed a step-by-step process for the analysis of character, conflict, setting, and language in imaginative writing. Examining all four elements in literature simultaneously involves the same kind of process, but this time you first should look for lines or passages that relate to any of the four elements, singly or in combination, and then determine how they work together to produce the total effect. In analyzing a shorter work, discovering the elements and their interrelationship requires only close attention to detail and good notes to arrive at an interpretation that is firmly grounded in the text itself. Novellas, novels, long poems, and full-length dramas, however, present more material and therefore require a particular focus for critical analysis. Reading the whole work is even more complex when the author is Shakespeare.

Shakespeare's plays present some difficulties to modern readers. Many of his words are unusual or archaic. Then, too, his sentences (like those in most poetry) are not written in the usual order. One finds a subject here, a predicate there, and a large number of modifiers in between. As a result, most people do not sit down to read a Shakespearean play as they would a mystery novel or a best-seller by Michener. Of course, many people do see Shakespeare in performance, either live or on television. If the performance is well done, the experience will be significant and powerful, even if the viewer has no familiarity with the text. Even a good performance, however, will gain from prior study—such as the one you are about to begin.

As you approach the play, remember that whatever problems are presented by troublesome vocabulary or sentence structure, reading Shakespeare will be easier if you are aware of some of the stumbling blocks and how to avoid them. The following procedure offers one method for doing just that.

1. *Plunge right in for a first reading.* Open the book and force yourself to read as rapidly as possible the first time through. Try to get meaning from context, and push through the more complex passages.[1] Such a reading will give you a sense of the momentum and effect of the play. (Your instructor may suggest that you listen to a good recording of the play as you read along for the first time through.)

After a first reading of act I, scene ii, for example, the reader should come away with an increased awareness of the characters and complications that are developing. Capulet, head of one of the feuding families, has a young daughter named Juliet. Paris, a wealthy nobleman, is definitely interested in her as a marriage prospect. We learn also that Capulet is planning a party for that evening, and he invites Paris to compare his daughter with other young ladies who will be there. By one of the strange twists of fate that are common in this play, information about that party is given to Benvolio and Romeo. Benvolio is anxious to take Romeo's mind off his unsuccessful pursuit of Rosaline, and he challenges Romeo to attend the party, uninvited, for that purpose—even though the party is at the home of his family's enemy. Romeo accepts the challenge, but only for an opportunity to see Rosaline, who will also be there. Thus the scene builds on the momentum established in the beginning, except that the focus here is more personal. The reader also has some sense of how Romeo's character is being developed; in addition, he learns more about Capulet and Benvolio. The conflicts are becoming more clearly defined, and the influence of time and place on the action is beginning to assert itself.

2. *Reread the assignment.* This time read more slowly, and carefully work through complicated sections of the verse. It will help if you remember two things.

First, Shakespeare's plays are written largely in blank verse—unrhymed iambic pentameter; in the earlier plays like *Romeo and Juliet*, there are also long passages of heroic couplets (pairs of rhymed iambic pentameter lines). In either case, normal sentence patterns are often altered for the sake of rhythm, rhyme, or emphasis; key words are often omitted, and sentences extend for several lines. Look at the following passage, for example. After asking him to attend the party at his house that evening, Capulet says to Paris:

> Such comfort as do lusty young men feel
> When well-apparell'd April on the heel
> Of limping winter treads, even such delight

[1] In some passages of dialogue and in some stage directions, you will see words or phrases enclosed in brackets. These are glossed to indicate later additions or different readings in various editions of the play.

Among fresh female buds shall you this night
Inherit at my house.

[I, ii, 26–30]

In this statement, Capulet attempts to persuade Paris to attend his party
that evening by describing the pleasures he is sure to find there; but the
order of the sentence does not fit an ordinary pattern. At least part of the
reason for unorthodox word arrangement lies in Capulet's purpose, since he
is offering what amounts to a salesman's pitch to Paris. Thus he puts the
most mind-catching ideas first or in a position of emphasis: "such comfort,"
"this night" and "such delight." The passage is, of course, a good illustration of Shakespeare's skill as a poet and dramatist, a skill that allows him
to select the most appropriate words, arrange them for maximum effect, and
all the while augment the development of both characters and play. Because
of poetic and dramatic intent, the structure of Capulet's speech is intricate
and inverted, with the sense spread out over five lines. Thus no reader who
reads the passage (and others like it) as if each line contains a separate and
complete thought will get even a glimmer of understanding. The secret is
to read *sentences*, rearranging the words in your mind, finding subjects and
predicates, placing adjectival or adverbial elements in their proper places,
and if necessary filling in any missing words or elements. From these pieces,
properly arranged, the logic of the statement will emerge:

You shall inherit such comfort, even such delight this night among fresh female buds at my house as lusty young men do feel when well-apparell'd April
treads on the heel of limping winter.

Second, reading Shakespeare fairly and accurately also requires a knowledge of language discussed in the previous chapter. Readers could, if they
wished, find examples of almost every kind of figurative speech in Shakespeare—some of them simple to grasp, others that require both research
and reflection.

The passage just cited is not so involved as some others in the play, but
you must recognize the principal figures of speech in the text and comprehend their significance before you can arrive at meaning. Here Capulet
makes use of simile, personification, and metaphor to make his point. Paris's
pleasure in seeing the young ladies at the party is compared with the pleasures of experiencing spring after winter. Those pleasures are given importance not only by word arrangement but also by specifying what they are:
April and winter become persons. April, a well-dressed maiden, follows on
the heels of limping old man winter. The young ladies are called flowers,
specifically young buds, an implied comparison that also relates to the season of spring suggested by the reference to April. Through the use of these
images and figures, the statement becomes an elaborate compliment to
youth and beauty. And because the images and figures are somewhat familiar, their use also tells us something about the man who employs them:

Capulet tends to think in conventional ways. He is also eager to give praise when he thinks it is deserved, to be a good host, and to seem a desirable father-in-law to the rich and noble Paris.

As you work through the text, look for clues to character, conflict, setting, and language. Make notes in the margin like those given for act I, scene ii:

(*Enter* CAPULET, PARIS, *and the Clown, a* SERVANT).

Cap. But Montague is bound as well as I,
In penalty alike; and 'tis not hard, I think,
For men so old as we to keep the peace.

Conflict: reference to the feud between the families of Capulet and Montague and the threat of the Prince to take lives should there be a recurrence. Capulet is old, like his foe Montague; their age should make keeping the peace easier.

Par. Of honourable reckoning are you both;
And pity 'tis you liv'd at odds so long. 5

Conflict: the feud has apparently been going on for many years.

But now, my lord, what say you to my suit?

Complications leading to conflict: Paris seeks the hand of Juliet.

Cap. But saying o'er what I have said before.
My child is yet a stranger in the world;
She hath not seen the change of fourteen years.
Let two more summers wither in their pride, 10
Ere we may think her ripe to be a bride.

Character: Capulet seems unwilling to have his daughter marry too young; she should wait two years, until she is sixteen.
Language: Dramatic irony, since later he will rush the marriage to Paris. Also, personification of summer (line 10).

Par. Younger than she are happy mothers made.
Cap. And too soon marr'd are those so early made.
The earth hath swallow'd all my hopes but she;
She is the hopeful lady of my earth; 15
But woo her, gentle Paris, get her heart,
My will to her consent is but a part;
An she agree, within her scope of choice
Lies my consent and fair according voice.
This night I hold an old accustom'd feast, 20
Whereto I have invited many a guest,

Character: Juliet is Capulet's only surviving child (line 14).
Setting: daughters are not free to marry as they wish; the father's word is law (lines 17–19).
Setting: the season is one in which Capulet traditionally gives a party.
Language: simile, metaphor,

Such as I love; and you, among the store
One more, most welcome, makes my number
  more.
At my poor house look to behold this night
Earth-treading stars that make dark heaven
  light.   25
Such comfort as do lusty young men feel
When well-apparell'd April on the heel
Of limping winter treads, even such delight
Among fresh female buds shall you this night
Inherit at my house. Hear all, all see,   30
And like her most whose merit most shall be;
Which [on] more view of, many, mine being one,
May stand in number, though in reckoning none.
Come, go with me. (*To* Servant.) Go, sirrah,
  trudge about
Through fair Verona; find those persons out 35
Whose names are written there, and to them say
My house and welcome on their pleasure stay.

(*Exeunt* Capulet *and* Paris.)

Serv. Find them out whose names are written here! It is written that the shoemaker should meddle with his yard and the tailor with his last, the fisher with his pencil and the painter with his nets; but I am sent to find those persons whose names are here writ, and can never find what names the writing person hath here writ. I must to the learned.—In good time. 45

(*Enter* Benvolio *and* Romeo.)

Ben. Tut, man, one fire burns out another's burn-
  ing,
  One pain is less'ned by another's anguish;
Turn giddy, and be holp by backward turning;
  One desperate grief cures with another's
  languish.
Take thou some new infection to thy eye,   50
And the rank poison of the old will die.
Rom. Your plaintain-leaf is excellent for that.
Ben. For what, I pray thee?
Rom.   For your broken shin.
Ben. Why, Romeo, art thou mad?
Rom. Not mad, but bound more than a madman
  is;   55
Shut up in prison, kept without my food,
Whipp'd and tormented and—God-den good
  fellow.

and personification. Young women are compared to stars that walk the earth, giving light to darkness (line 25). April and winter are personified (lines 27–28); young ladies and budding blossoms are compared (line 29). Young men will feel as delighted in seeing the ladies at the party as they feel when spring arrives.

Character: Capulet uses conventional figures, but he wants to be a good host, give praise when it is due, and properly impress Paris, a would-be suitor for his daughter's hand in marriage.

Setting: only the wealthy are educated; Capulet should have known he has given a servant a task he cannot perform.

Language: metaphors relating to love: one fire burning out another; giddiness prompted by turning in another direction replacing that caused by earlier spinning. Note particularly the use of disease and eye imagery. A new infection will replace the old one, but it is an infection connected with the eyes. A belief of the time *(setting)* was that love formed and grew through sight of the beloved.

Character: Romeo is tortured by his frustration, almost to the point of madness.

Serv. God gi' god-den. I pray, sir, can you read?	*Character:* Romeo may be upset over love, but he can still jest with the servant. He almost goes too far, but he finally speaks to the point and agrees to read that which the servant cannot.
Rom. Ay, mine own fortune in my misery. 59	
Serv. Perhaps you have learn'd it without book. But, I pray, can you read anything you see?	
Rom. Ay, if I know the letters and the language.	
Serv. Ye say honestly. Rest you merry!	
Rom. Stay, fellow; I can read. 64	*Conflict:* among the guests at the party will be Rosaline.
(*Reads.*) "Signior Martino and his wife and daughters; County Anselme and his beauteous sisters; the lady widow of Vitruvio; Signior Placentio and his lovely nieces; Mercutio and his brother Valentine; mine uncle Capulet, his wife, and daughters; my fair niece Rosaline; Livia; Signior Valentio and his cousin Tybalt; Lucio and the lively Helena." A fair assembly: whither should they come?	
Serv. Up.	

Rom. Whither? To supper?	*Conflict:* reference to the feud; the servant invites them to the party if they do not belong to the enemy household.
Serv. To our house. 75	
Rom. Whose house?	
Serv. My master's.	
Rom. Indeed, I should have ask'd you that before.	*Character:* Benvolio offers his friend some good advice.
Serv. Now I'll tell you without asking. My master is the great rich Capulet; and if you be not of the house of Montagues, I pray, come and crush a cup of wine. Rest you merry! 81	*Conflict:* Rosaline is identified as the young lady loved by Romeo.
(*Exit.*)	
Ben. At this same ancient feast of Capulet's Sups the fair Rosaline whom thou so loves. With all the admired beauties of Verona. Go thither; and with unattainted eye 85 Compare her face with some that I shall show, And I will make thee think thy swan a crow.	*Language:* Benvolio insists that in comparison with the other young ladies, Rosaline will be a crow instead of the swan Romeo thinks her to be.

Rom. When the devout religion of mine eye Maintains such falsehood, then turn tears to fires. And these, who, often drown'd, could never die, Transparent heretics, be burnt for liars! 91 One fairer than my love! The all-seeing sun Ne'er saw her match since first the world begun.	*Character:* Romeo insists he will never make such a judgment. *Language:* a very complicated series of comparisons. First, Romeo compares his love with a religion. He asserts that if he were to betray his faith (love), the tears he sheds would turn to fires and burn his eyes for being heretics (deniers of true faith). He also indicates that though he has

drowned his eyes with tears, they did not die. The reference here is to the tradition of courtly love, in which an elaborate ritual of love was codified into a near-religion. Reference is made again to the belief that sight is the base of love. The sun is personified in a compliment to Rosaline.

Ben. Tut, you saw her fair, none else being by,
Herself pois'd with herself in either eye;   95
But in that crystal scales let there be weigh'd
Your lady's love against some other maid
That I will show you shining at this feast,
And she shall scant show well that now seems best.
Rom. I'll go along no such sight to be shown,
But to rejoice in splendour of mine own.   101

(Exeunt.)

Language: eyes become crystal scales, and Benvolio advises Romeo to weigh Rosaline with other beauties in those scales. *Character:* Romeo once more insists he will never swerve from his devotion to his lady.

In summary, we may analyze the scene thus:

Character   Capulet offers his age as a reason why the peace should be easy to maintain; he seems genuinely concerned about the well-being of his only daughter, Juliet, and is eager to host a good party and be hospitable to his guests, especially Paris, a would-be suitor of Juliet. Paris is still a mystery. Two lines don't really tell us anything. Romeo's trait of appearing to be in love with love, as well as with Rosaline, seems to be reinforced. He also shows a facility for witticisms and enjoys bantering with Benvolio. In the first scene of the play, Benvolio established himself as a peacemaker. That characteristic is also demonstrated by his attempts to help cure Romeo of his lovesickness.

Conflict   The first reference in the scene is to the feud, the overriding external conflict that underlies all the important action in the play. Further conflicts include both the possibility that Paris's suit will somehow interfere with or complicate the Romeo-Juliet alliance and the difficulties Romeo is having with Rosaline about their relationship.

Setting   Reference is made to the time of the annual Capulet feast. Also part of the setting are ideas of that era about the nature of love and the dependency of daughters.

Language Capulet's speeches are formal and straightforward. His images and figures are like his character—relatively conventional and unimaginative. Both Romeo and Benvolio make liberal use of figurative language, but Romeo's are far more complicated and involved. Most of their images relate to love, an indication that the subject is one that has captured their imagination.

William Shakespeare

THE TRAGEDY OF
ROMEO AND JULIET

[Dramatis Personæ

ESCALUS, Prince of Verona.

PARIS, a young nobleman, kinsman to the prince.

MONTAGUE, CAPULET, } heads of two houses at variance with each other.

An old man, of the Capulet family.

ROMEO, son to Montague.

MERCUTIO, kinsman to the prince, and friend to Romeo.

BENVOLIO, nephew to Montague, and cousin to Romeo.

TYBALT, nephew to Lady Capulet.

FRIAR LAURENCE, FRIAR JOHN, } Franciscans.

BALTHASAR, servant to Romeo.

ABRAHAM, servant to Montague.

SAMPSON, GREGORY, } servants to Capulet.

PETER, servant to Juliet's nurse.

An Apothecary.

Three Musicians.

Page to Paris; *another Page.*

An Officer.

LADY MONTAGUE, wife to Montague.

LADY CAPULET, wife to Capulet.

JULIET, daughter to Capulet.

Nurse to Juliet.

Chorus.

Citizens of Verona; several Men and Women, kinsfolk to both houses; Maskers, Guards, Watchmen, and Attendants.

Scene   *Verona; Mantua.*]

PROLOGUE

Two households, both alike in dignity,
    In fair Verona, where we lay our scene,

From ancient grudge break to new mutiny,
 Where civil blood makes civil hands unclean.
From forth the fatal loins of these two foes   5
 A pair of star-cross'd lovers take their life;
Whose misadventur'd piteous overthrows
 Doth with their death bury their parents' strife.
The fearful passage of their death-mark'd love,
 And the continuance of their parents' rage,   10
Which, but their children's end, nought could remove,
 Is now the two hours' traffic of our stage;
The which if you with patient ears attend,
What here shall miss, our toil shall strive to mend.

ACT I

Scene I. [*Verona. A public place.*]

(*Enter* SAMPSON *and* GREGORY, *of the house of Capulet, with swords and bucklers.*)

Sam. Gregory, on my word, we'll not carry coals.
Gre. No, for then we should be colliers.
Sam. I mean, an we be in choler, we'll draw.
Gre. Ay, while you live, draw your neck out of collar.
Sam. I strike quickly, being mov'd.   5
Gre. But thou art not quickly mov'd to strike.
Sam. A dog of the house of Montague moves me.
Gre. To move is to stir, and to be valiant is to stand; therefore, if thou art mov'd, thou run'st away.
Sam. A dog of that house shall move me to stand. I will take the wall of any man or maid of Montague's.   11
Gre. That shows thee a weak slave; for the weakest goes to the wall.
Sam. 'Tis true; and therefore women, being the weaker vessels, are ever thrust to the wall; therefore I will push Montague's men from the wall, and thrust his maids to the wall.   15
Gre. The quarrel is between our masters and us their men.
Sam. 'Tis all one, I will show myself a tyrant. When I have fought with the men, I will be [cruel] with the maids; I will cut off their heads.

Prol., 3. mutiny: discord.   6. star-cross'd: doomed by the stars.
Act. I, sc. i, 1. carry coals: submit to insult.   5. mov'd: angered.   10. take the wall.
Keeping to the side of the walk next to the wall was the pedestrian's best protection in the dirty streets of Shakespeare's day. To "take the wall" could be insulting, just as to yield it was courteous.   18. [cruel] Q₄. *civil* Q₂.

Gre. The heads of the maids?

Sam. Ay, the heads of the maids, or their maidenheads; take it in what
sense thou wilt.   21

Gre. They must take it in sense that feel it.

Sam. Me they shall feel while I am able to stand; and 'tis known I am a
pretty piece of flesh.

Gre. 'Tis well thou art not fish; if thou hadst, thou hadst been poor John.
Draw thy tool; here comes [two] of the house of Montagues.   26

(*Enter two other serving-men* [ABRAHAM *and* BALTHASAR].)

Sam. My naked weapon is out. Quarrel! I will back thee.

Gre. How! turn thy back and run?

Sam. Fear me not.

Gre. No, marry; I fear thee!   30

Sam. Let us take the law of our sides; let them begin.

Gre. I will frown as I pass by, and let them take it as they list.

Sam. Nay, as they dare. I will bite my thumb at them; which is disgrace
to them, if they bear it.

Abr. Do you bite your thumb at us, sir?   35

Sam. I do bite my thumb, sir.

Abr. Do you bite your thumb at us, sir?

Sam. [*Aside to Gre.*]   Is the law of our side, if I say ay?

Gre. No.

Sam. No, sir, I do not bite my thumb at you, sir; but I bite my thumb, sir.

Gre. Do you quarrel, sir?   41

Abr. Quarrel, sir? No, sir.

Sam. But if you do, sir, I am for you. I serve as good a man as you.

Abr. No better.

Sam. Well, sir.   45

(*Enter* BENVOLIO.)

Gre. Say "better"; here comes one of my master's kinsmen.

Sam. Yes, better, sir.

Abr. You lie.

Sam. Draw, if you be men. Gregory, remember thy [swashing] blow.
                                                         [*They fight.*

Ben. Part, fools!   50
Put up your swords; you know not what you do.
                                              [*Beats down their swords.*]

(*Enter* TYBALT.)

25. poor John: salt hake.   26. [two] Q_1. = Om. Q_2.   46. here . . . kinsmen. Tybalt
is sighted.   49. [swashing] Q_4: crushing.   *washing* Q_2.

Tyb. What, art thou drawn among these heartless hinds?
  Turn thee, Benvolio, look upon thy death.
Ben. I do but keep the peace. Put up thy sword,
  Or manage it to part these men with me.   55
Tyb. What, drawn, and talk of peace! I hate the word
  As I hate hell, all Montagues, and thee.
  Have at thee, coward!   [*They fight.*

(*Enter three or four* Citizens [*and* Officers], *with clubs or partisans.*)

Off. Clubs, bills, and partisans! Strike! Beat them down!
  Down with the Capulets! down with the Montagues!   60

(*Enter* Capulet *in his gown, and* Lady Capulet.)

Cap. What noise is this? Give me my long sword, ho!
La. Cap. A crutch, a crutch! why call you for a sword?
Cap. My sword, I say! Old Montague is come,
  And flourishes his blade in spite of me.

(*Enter* Montague *and* Lady Montague.)

Mon. Thou villain Capulet,—Hold me not, let me go.   65
La. Mon. Thou shalt not stir one foot to seek a foe.

(*Enter* Prince Escalus, *with his train.*)

Prin. Rebellious subjects, enemies to peace,
  Profaners of this neighbour-stained steel,—
  Will they not hear?—What, ho! you men, you beasts,
  That quench the fire of your pernicious rage   70
  With purple fountains issuing from your veins,
  On pain of torture, from those bloody hands
  Throw your mistemper'd weapons to the ground,
  And hear the sentence of your moved prince.
  Three civil brawls, bred of an airy word,   75
  By thee, old Capulet, and Montague,
  Have thrice disturb'd the quiet of our streets,
  And made Verona's ancient citizens
  Cast by their grave beseeming ornaments
  To wield old partisans, in hands as old,   80
  Cank'red with peace, to part your cank'red hate;
  If ever you disturb our streets again

---

52. heartless hinds: cowardly servants.   59. Clubs: a cry of the London apprentices,
who wielded clubs. bills: battle-axes. partisans: pikes or spears with two-edged knives
affixed.   64. spite: defiance.   68. neighbour-stained: stained with neighbor's blood.
73. mistemper'd: angry.   81. Cank'red: (1) rusted, (2) malignant.

Your lives shall pay the forfeit of the peace.
For this time, all the rest depart away.
You, Capulet, shall go along with me;   85
And, Montague, come you this afternoon,
To know our farther pleasure in this case,
To old Free-town, our common judgement-place.
Once more, on pain of death, all men depart.

               [Exeunt [all but Montague, Lady Montague, and Benvolio].

Mon.   Who set this ancient quarrel new abroach?   90
   Speak, nephew, were you by when it began?

Ben.   Here were the servants of your adversary,
   And yours, close fighting ere I did approach.
   I drew to part them. In the instant came
   The fiery Tybalt, with his sword prepar'd,   95
   Which, as he breath'd defiance to my ears,
   He swung about his head and cut the winds,
   Who, nothing hurt withal, hiss'd him in scorn.
   While we were interchanging thrusts and blows,
   Came more and more and fought on part and part,   100
   Till the Prince came, who parted either part.

La. Mon.   O, where is Romeo? Saw you him to-day?
   Right glad I am he was not at this fray.

Ben.   Madam, an hour before the worshipp'd sun
   Peer'd forth the golden window of the east,   105
   A troubled mind [drave] me to walk abroad;
   Where, underneath the grove of sycamore
   That westward rooteth from [the city's] side,
   So early walking did I see your son.
   Towards him I made, but he was ware of me   110
   And stole into the covert of the wood.
   I, measuring his affections by my own,
   Which then most sought where most might not be found,
   Being one too many by my weary self,
   Pursued my humour not pursuing his,   115
   And gladly shunn'd who gladly fled from me.

Mon.   Many a morning hath he there been seen,
   With tears augmenting the fresh morning's dew,
   Adding to clouds more clouds with his deep sighs;
   But all so soon as the all-cheering sun   120
   Should in the farthest east begin to draw

90. set ... abroach: tap and leave running.   106. [drave] F. *drive* Q₂.   108. [the
city's] Q₁. *this city* Q₂.   112. affections: inclinations.   113. where ... found: the
most unfrequented place.

The shady curtains from Aurora's bed,
Away from light steals home my heavy son,
And private in his chamber pens himself,
Shuts up his windows, locks fair daylight out,   125
And makes himself an artificial night.
Black and portentous must this humour prove
Unless good counsel may the cause remove.

Ben.   My noble uncle, do you know the cause?
Mon.   I neither know it nor can learn of him.   130
Ben.   Have you importun'd him by any means?
Mon.   Both by myself and many other friends;
But he, his own affections' counsellor,
Is to himself—I will not say how true—
But to himself so secret and so close,   135
So far from sounding and discovery,
As is the bud bit with an envious worm
Ere he can spread his sweet leaves to the air
Or dedicate his beauty to the [sun].
Could we but learn from whence his sorrows grow,   140
We would as willingly give cure as know.

(*Enter* ROMEO.)

Ben.   See, where he comes! So please you, step aside;
I'll know his grievance, or be much deni'd.
Mon.   I would thou wert so happy by thy stay
To hear true shrift. Come, madam, let's away.   145
                                        [*Exeunt* [*Montague and Lady.*]
Ben.   Good morrow, cousin.
Rom.   Is the day so young?
Ben.   But new struck nine.
Rom.   Ay me! sad hours seem long.
Was that my father that went hence so fast?
Ben.   It was. What sadness lengthens Romeo's hours?
Rom.   Not having that which, having, makes them short.   150
Ben.   In love?
Rom.   Out—
Ben.   Of love?
Rom.   Out of her favour, where I am in love.
Ben.   Alas, that love, so gentle in his view,   155
Should be so tyrannous and rough in proof!
Rom.   Alas, that love, whose view is muffled still,

137. envious: malicious.   139. [sun] (Theobald). *same* Q₂.   145. shrift: confession.   155. view: looks.   156. proof: experience.

Should, without eyes, see pathways to his will!
Where shall we dine? O me! What fray was here?
Yet tell me not, for I have heard it all. 160
Here's much to do with hate, but more with love.
Why, then, O brawling love! O loving hate!
O anything, of nothing first [create]!
O heavy lightness! serious vanity!
Mis-shapen chaos of [well-seeming] forms! 165
Feather of lead, bright smoke, cold fire, sick health!
Still-waking sleep, that is not what it is!
This love feel I, that feel no love in this.
Dost thou not laugh?

Ben. No, coz, I rather weep.

Rom. Good heart, at what?

Ben. At thy good heart's oppression. 170

Rom. Why, such is love's transgression.
Griefs of mine own lie heavy in my breast,
Which thou wilt propagate to have it prest
With more of thine. This love that thou hast shown
Doth add more grief to too much of mine own. 175
Love is a smoke made with the fume of sighs;
Being purg'd, a fire sparkling in lovers' eyes;
Being vex'd, a sea nourish'd with [lovers'] tears.
What is it else? A madness most discreet,
A choking gall, and a preserving sweet. 180
Farewell, my coz.

Ben. Soft! I will go along.
An if you leave me so, you do me wrong.

Rom. Tut, I have [left] myself; I am not here.
This is not Romeo; he's some otherwhere.

Ben. Tell me in sadness, who is that you love? 185

Rom. What, shall I groan and tell thee?

Ben. Groan! why, no;
But sadly tell me who.

Rom. [Bid a] sick man in sadness [make] his will,—
Ah, word ill urg'd to one that is so ill!
In sadness, cousin, I do love a woman. 190

Ben. I aim'd so near when I suppos'd you lov'd.

Rom. A right good mark-man! And she's fair I love.

Ben. A right fair mark, fair coz, is soonest hit.

---

163. [create] Q$_1$. *created* Q$_2$. 165. [well-seeming] Q$_4$. *well-seeing* Q$_2$. 173. to
have: *by having.* 178. [lovers'] (Pope). *a lovers* Q$_1$. *loving* Q$_2$. 183. [left]
(Allen conj.). *lost* Q$_2$. 185. sadness: *seriousness.* 188. [Bid a] . . . [make] Q$_1$.
A . . . makes Q$_2$.

Rom.   Well, in that hit you miss. She'll not be hit
   With Cupid's arrow; she hath Dian's wit;   195
   And, in strong proof of chastity well arm'd,
   From Love's weak childish bow she lives [unharm'd].
   She will not stay the siege of loving terms,
   Nor bide th' encounter of assailing eyes,
   Nor ope her lap to saint-seducing gold.   200
   O, she is rich in beauty, only poor
   That, when she dies, with beauty dies her store.
Ben.   Then she hath sworn that she will still live chaste?
Rom.   She hath, and in that sparing make huge waste;
   For beauty starv'd with her severity   205
   Cuts beauty off from all posterity.
   She is too fair, too wise, wisely too fair,
   To merit bliss by making me despair.
   She hath forsworn to love, and in that vow
   Do I live dead that live to tell it now.   210
Ben.   Be rul'd by me, forget to think of her.
Rom.   O, teach me how I should forget to think.
Ben.   By giving liberty unto thine eyes;
   Examine other beauties.
Rom.   'Tis the way
   To call hers, exquisite, in question more.   215
   These happy masks that kiss fair ladies' brows,
   Being black, puts us in mind they hide the fair;
   He that is strucken blind cannot forget
   The precious treasure of his eyesight lost.
   Show me a mistress that is passing fair,   220
   What doth her beauty serve, but as a note
   Where I may read who pass'd that passing fair?
   Farewell! Thou canst not teach me to forget.
Ben.   I'll pay that doctrine, or else die in debt.

                                         [Exeunt.

Scene II.   [*A street.*]

(*Enter* CAPULET, PARIS, *and the* Clown [*a* SERVANT].)

Cap.   But Montague is bound as well as I,
   In penalty alike; and 'tis not hard, I think,
   For men so old as we to keep the peace.

195. wit: mind, purpose.   196. proof: armor.   197. [unharm'd] Q_1. *uncharm'd* Q_2.   198. stay: bide.   202. store: riches.   215. in . . . more: into greater consideration.   224. pay . . . doctrine: teach that lesson.

Par. Of honourable reckoning are you both;
    And pity 'tis you liv'd at odds so long.   5
    But now, my lord, what say you to my suit?
Cap.   But saying o'er what I have said before.
    My child is yet a stranger in the world;
    She hath not seen the change of fourteen years.
    Let two more summers wither in their pride,   10
    Ere we may think her ripe to be a bride.
Par.   Younger than she are happy mothers made.
Cap.   And too soon marr'd are those so early made.
    [The] earth hath swallow'd all my hopes but she;
    She is the hopeful lady of my earth;   15
    But woo her, gentle Paris, get her heart,
    My will to her consent is but a part;
    An she [agree], within her scope of choice
    Lies my consent and fair according voice.
    This night I hold an old accustom'd feast,   20
    Whereto I have invited many a guest,
    Such as I love; and you, among the store
    One more, most welcome, makes my number more.
    At my poor house look to behold this night
    Earth-treading stars that make dark heaven light.   25
    Such comfort as do lusty young men feel
    When well-apparell'd April on the heel
    Of limping winter treads, even such delight
    Among fresh [female] buds shall you this night
    Inherit at my house. Hear all, all see,   30
    And like her most whose merit most shall be;
    Which [on] more view of, many, mine being one,
    May stand in number, though in reckoning none.
    Come, go with me. [*To Servant.*] Go, sirrah, trudge about
    Through fair Verona; find those persons out   35
    Whose names are written there, and to them say
    My house and welcome on their pleasure stay.

                         [*Exeunt [Capulet and Paris]*].

Serv.   Find them out whose names are written here! It is written that the
    shoemaker should meddle with his yard and the tailor with his last, the
    fisher with his pencil and the painter with his nets; but I am sent to find
    those persons whose names are here writ, and can never find what names
    the writing person hath here writ. I must to the learned.—In good time.

Sc. ii. 4. reckoning: repute.   14. [The] Q₄. Om. Q₂.   15. earth: body, or world.
18. [agree] F. *agreed* Q₂.   29. [female] Q₁. *fennell* Q₂.   30. Inherit: possess.
32. [on] Q₄. *one* Q₂.

(*Enter* BENVOLIO *and* ROMEO.)

Ben. Tut, man, one fire burns out another's burning,
   One pain is less'ned by another's anguish;
  Turn giddy, and be holp by backward turning;   45
   One desperate grief cures with another's languish.
  Take thou some new infection to thy eye,
  And the rank poison of the old will die.
Rom. Your plaintain-leaf is excellent for that.
Ben. For what, I pray thee?
Rom.   For your broken shin.   50
Ben. Why, Romeo, art thou mad?
Rom. Not mad, but bound more than a madman is;
  Shut up in prison, kept without my food,
  Whipp'd and tormented and—God-den, good fellow.
Serv. God gi' god-den. I pray, sir, can you read?   55
Rom. Ay, mine own fortune in my misery.
Serv. Perhaps you have learn'd it without book. But, I pray, can you read
  anything you see?
Rom. Ay, if I know the letters and the language.
Serv. Ye say honestly. Rest you merry!   60
Rom. Stay, fellow; I can read.
(*Reads.*) "Signior Martino and his wife and daughters; County Anselme
  and his beauteous sisters; the lady widow of Virtruvio; Signior Placentio
  and his lovely nieces; Mercutio and his brother Valentine; mine uncle
  Capulet, his wife, and daughters; my fair niece Rosaline; Livia; Signior
  Valentio and his cousin Tybalt; Lucio and the lively Helena." A fair as-
  sembly: whither should they come?
Serv. Up.
Rom. Whither? To supper?
Serv. To our house.   70
Rom. Whose house?
Serv. My master's.
Rom. Indeed, I should have ask'd you that before.
Serv. Now I'll tell you without asking. My master is the great rich Capu-
  let; and if you be not of the house of Montagues, I pray, come and crush
  a cup of wine. Rest you merry!   [*Exit.* 76
Ben. At this same ancient feast of Capulet's
  Sups the fair Rosaline whom thou so loves,
  With all the admired beauties of Verona.
  Go thither; and with unattainted eye   80

---

45. backward: in the reverse direction.   54. God-den: good evening.   75. crush:
drink.   77. ancient: customary.   80. unattainted: unprejudiced.

Compare her face with some that I shall show,
And I will make thee think thy swan a crow.
Rom.   When the devout religion of mine eye
   Maintains such falsehood, then turn tears to [fires];
And these, who, often drown'd, could never die,   85
   Transparent heretics, be burnt for liars!
One fairer than my love! The all-seeing sun
Ne'er saw her match since first the world begun.
Ben.   Tut, you saw her fair, none else being by,
Herself pois'd with herself in either eye;   90
But in that crystal scales let there be weigh'd
Your lady's love against some other maid
That I will show you shining at this feast,
And she shall scant show well that now seems best.
Rom.   I'll go along no such sight to be shown,   95
But to rejoice in splendour of mine own.   [*Exeunt.*]

Scene III.   [*A room in Capulet's house.*]

(*Enter* LADY CAPULET *and* NURSE.)

La. Cap.   Nurse, where's my daughter? Call her forth to me.
Nurse   Now, by my maidenhead at twelve year old.
   I bade her come. What, lamb! What, ladybird!
   God forbid!—Where's this girl? What, Juliet!

(*Enter* JULIET.)

Jul.   How now! Who calls?
Nurse   Your mother.
Jul.   Madam, I am here.   5
   What is your will?
La. Cap.   This is the matter.—Nurse, give leave a while,
   We must talk in secret.—Nurse, come back again;
   I have remem'bred me, thou's hear our counsel.
   Thou know'st my daughter's of a pretty age.   10
Nurse   Faith, I can tell her age unto an hour.
La. Cap.   She's not fourteen.
Nurse   I'll lay fourteen of my teeth,—
   And yet, to my teen be it spoken, I have but four,—

84. [fires] (Pope). *fire* Q$_2$.   85. these: i.e., my eyes.   90. pois'd: balanced.
Sc. iii, 4. God forbid: i.e., that anything is wrong.   2–78. Q$_2$ prints the Nurse's
speeches in prose and in italics.   9. thou's: thou shalt.   12. lay: wager.   13.
teen: sorrow.

She's not fourteen. How long is it now
To Lammas-tide?
La. Cap.　　　　　　A fortnight and odd days.　　　　15
Nurse　Even or odd, of all days in the year,
　Come Lammas-eve at night shall she be fourteen.
　Susan and she—God rest all Christian souls!—
　Were of an age. Well, Susan is with God;
　She was too good for me. But, as I said,　　　　20
　On Lammas-eve at night shall she be fourteen;
　That shall she, marry; I remember it well.
　'Tis since the earthquake now eleven years,
　And she was wean'd,—I never shall forget it—
　Of all the days of the year, upon that day;　　　　25
　For I had then laid wormwood to my dug,
　Sitting in the sun under the dove-house wall;
　My lord and you were then at Mantua;—
　Nay, I do bear a brain;—but, as I said,
　When it did taste the wormwood on the nipple　　　　30
　Of my dug and felt it bitter, pretty fool,
　To see it tetchy and fall out wi' the dug!
　Shake, quoth the dove-house; 'twas no need, I trow,
　To bid me trudge.
　And since that time it is eleven years;　　　　35
　For then she could stand high-lone; nay, by the rood,
　She could have run and waddled all about;
　For even the day before, she broke her brow;
　And then my husband—God be with his soul!
　'A was a merry man—took up the child.　　　　40
　"Yea," quoth he, "dost thou fall upon thy face?
　Thou wilt fall backward when thou hast more wit;
　Wilt thou not, Jule?" and, by my holidame,
　The pretty wretch left crying and said, "Ay."
　To see, now, how a jest shall come about!　　　　45
　I warrant, an I should live a thousand years,
　I never should forget it. "Wilt thou not, Jule?" quoth he;
　And, pretty fool, it stinted and said, "Ay."
La. Cap.　Enough of this; I pray thee, hold thy peace.
Nurse　Yes, madam; yet I cannot choose but laugh　　　　50
　To think it should leave crying and say, "Ay."
　And yet, I warrant, it had upon it brow

15. Lammas-tide: August 1st.　29. bear a brain: i.e., have a great memory.　32. tetchy: fretful.　36. high-lone: quite alone. rood: cross.　43. holidame: i.e., halidom, holiness.　48. stinted: ceased.

A bump as big as a young cock'rel's stone;
A perilous knock; and it cried bitterly.
"Yea," quoth my husband, "fall'st upon thy face?   55
Thou wilt fall backward when thou comest to age;
Wilt thou not, Jule?" It stinted and said, "Ay."
Jul.   And stint thou too, I pray thee, nurse, say I.
Nurse   Peace, I have done. God mark thee to his grace!
Thou wast the prettiest babe that e'er I nurs'd.   60
An I might live to see thee married once,
I have my wish.
La. Cap.   Marry, that "marry" is the very theme
I came to talk of. Tell me, daughter Juliet,
How stands your dispositions to be married?   65
Jul.   It is an [honour] that I dream not of.
Nurse   An [honour]! were not I thine only nurse,
I would say thou hadst suck'd wisdom from thy teat.
La. Cap.   Well, think of marriage now; younger than you,
Here in Verona, ladies of esteem,   70
Are made already mothers. By my count,
I was your mother much upon these years
That you are now a maid. Thus then in brief:
The valiant Paris seeks you for his love.
Nurse   A man, young lady! Lady, such a man   75
As all the world—why, he's a man of wax.
La. Cap.   Verona's summer hath not such a flower.
Nurse   Nay, he's a flower; in faith, a very flower.
La. Cap.   What say you? Can you love the gentleman?
This night you shall behold him at our feast;   80
Read o'er the volume of young Paris' face
And find delight writ there with beauty's pen;
Examine every married lineament
And see how one another lends content,
And what obscur'd in this fair volume lies   85
Find written in the margent of his eyes.
This precious book of love, this unbound lover,
To beautify him, only lacks a cover.
The fish lives in the sea, and 'tis much pride
For fair without the fair within to hide.   90
That book in many's eyes doth share the glory,
That in gold clasps locks in the golden story;

---

53. cock'rel's: a young cock's.   66, 67. [honour] Q_1. *houre* Q_2.   76. man of wax:
as handsome as a wax figure.   83. married: harmonious.   86. margent: margin.
89. The . . . sea: i.e., the lover is yet uncaught.

So shall you share all that he doth possess,
By having him, making yourself no less.
Nurse No less! nay, bigger; women grow by men.   95
La. Cap. Speak briefly, can you like of Paris' love?
Jul. I'll look to like, if looking liking move;
But no more deep will I endart mine eye
Than your consent gives me strength to make [it] fly.

(*Enter* SERVANT.)

Serv. Madam, the guests are come, supper serv'd up, you call'd, my young
lady ask'd for, the nurse curs'd in the pantry, and everything in extremity. I must hence to wait; I beseech you, follow straight.   [*Exit.*
La. Cap. We follow thee. Juliet, the County stays.   103
Nurse Go, girl, seek happy nights to happy days.   [*Exeunt.*

Scene IV. [*A street.*]

(*Enter* ROMEO, MERCUTIO, BENVOLIO, *with five or six other* Maskers, Torch-
bearers.)

Rom. What, shall this speech be spoke for our excuse?
Or shall we on without apology?
Ben. The date is out of such prolixity.
We'll have no Cupid hoodwink'd with a scarf.
Bearing a Tartar's painted bow of lath,   5
Scaring the ladies like a crow-keeper;
[Nor no without-book prologue, faintly spoke
After the prompter, for our entrance;]
But let them measure us by what they will,
We'll measure them a measure and be gone.   10
Rom. Give me a torch. I am not for this ambling;
Being but heavy, I will bear the light.
Mer. Nay, gentle Romeo, we must have you dance.
Rom. Not I, believe me. You have dancing shoes
With nimble soles; I have a soul of lead   15
So stakes me to the ground I cannot move.
Mer. You are a lover; borrow Cupid's wings,
And soar with them above a common bound.

99. [it] Q₁. Om. Q₂.   103. stays: waits.
Sc. iv, 1. speech. Maskers used to be preceded by one who made a speech.   4. hood-
wink'd: blindfolded.   6. crow-keeper: scarecrow.   7–8. [Nor . . . entrance] Q₁. Om.
Q₂.   10. measure: dance.

Rom.   I am too sore enpierced with his shaft
    To soar with his light feathers, and so bound   20
    I cannot bound a pitch above dull woe.
    Under love's heavy burden do I sink.
[Mer.]   And, to sink in it, should you burden love;
    Too great oppression for a tender thing.
Rom.   Is love a tender thing? It is too rough,   25
    Too rude, too boist'rous, and it pricks like thorn.
Mer.   If love be rough with you, be rough with love;
    Prick love for pricking, and you beat love down.—
    Give me a case to put my visage in,   *[Puts on a mask.]*
    A visor for a visor! what care I   30
    What curious eye doth quote deformities?
    Here are the beetle brows shall blush for me.
Ben.   Come, knock and enter; and no sooner in,
    But every man betake him to his legs.
Rom.   A torch for me; let wantons light of heart   35
    Tickle the senseless rushes with their heels,
    For I am proverb'd with a grandsire phrase:
    I'll be a candle-holder, and look on.
    The game was ne'er so fair, and I am [done].
Mer.   Tut, dun's the mouse, the constable's own word.   40
    If thou art Dun, we'll draw thee from the mire
    Or, save your reverence, love, wherein thou stickest
    Up to the ears. Come, we burn daylight, ho!
Rom.   Nay, that's not so.
Mer.   I mean, sir, in delay
    We waste our lights in vain, [like] lights by day.   45
    Take our good meaning, for our judgement sits
    Five times in that ere once in our [five] wits.
Rom.   And we mean well in going to this mask;
    But 'tis no wit to go.
Mer.   Why, may one ask?
Rom.   I dream'd a dream to-night.
Mer.   And so did I.   50

23. [Mer.] Q_4.   *Horatio* Q_2.   29. case: mask.   30. visor . . . visor: mask for a mask-like (i.e., ugly) face.   31. quote: notice.   36. rushes. Rushes were used as floor covering.   37. grandsire phrase: old proverb, viz., "A good candle-holder (i.e., on-looker) proves a good gamester" (l. 38). Another seems to be echoed in l. 39: "He is wise who gives over (is done) when the game is fairest."   39. [done] Q_1. *dum* Q_2. *dun* Q_3.   40. dun's the mouse. A stock phrase apparently meaning "keep still."   41. Dun. Alluding to an old Christmas game, "Dun is in the mire." A heavy log represent-ing a horse stuck in the mud is hauled out by the players.   42. Or . . . love. Many edd. read *Of this sir-reverence love*, from Q_1.   45. [like] (Johnson). *lights* Q_2. 47. [five] (Wilbraham conj.).   *fine* Q_2.

Rom.   Well, what was yours?
Mer.   That dreamers often lie.
Rom.   In bed asleep, while they do dream things true.
Mer.   O, then, I see Queen Mab hath been with you.
   She is the fairies' midwife, and she comes
   In shape no bigger than an agate-stone   55
   On the fore-finger of an alderman,
   Drawn with a team of little atomies
   Over men's noses as they lie asleep;
   Her waggon-spokes made of long spinners' legs,
   The cover of the wings of grasshoppers,   60
   Her traces of the smallest spider web,
   Her collars of the moonshine's wat'ry beams.
   Her whip of cricket's bone, the lash of film,
   Her waggoner a small grey-coated gnat,
   Not half so big as a round little worm   65
   Prick'd from the lazy finger of a [maid];
   Her chariot is an empty hazel-nut
   Made by the joiner squirrel, or old grub,
   Time out o' mind the fairies' coachmakers.
   And in this state she gallops night by night   70
   Through lovers' brains, and then they dream of love;
   On courtiers' knees, that dream on curtsies straight;
   O'er lawyers' fingers, who straight dream on fees;
   O'er ladies' lips, who straight on kisses dream,
   Which oft the angry Mab with blisters plagues,   75
   Because their breath with sweetmeats tainted are.
   Sometime she gallops o'er a courtier's nose,
   And then dreams he of smelling out a suit;
   And sometimes comes she with a tithe-pig's tail
   Tickling a parson's nose as 'a lies asleep,   80
   Then he dreams of another benefice.
   Sometime she driveth o'er a soldier's neck,
   And then dreams he of cutting foreign throats,
   Of breaches, ambuscadoes, Spanish blades,
   Of healths five fathom deep; and then anon   85
   Drums in his ear, at which he starts and wakes,
   And being thus frighted swears a prayer or two
   And sleeps again. This is that very Mab
   That plats the manes of horses in the night,
   And bakes the elf-locks in foul sluttish hairs,   90

53–91. O . . . bodes. So Q₁. Prose Q₂.   66. [maid] Q₁. *man* Q₂.   79. tithe-pig's:
pig paid as part of parish dues.   90. elf-locks: hair tangled by elves.

Which, once untangled, much misfortune bodes.
This is the hag, when maids lie on their backs,
That presses them and learns them first to bear,
Making them women of good carriage.
This is she—
Rom.   Peace, peace, Mercutio, peace!   95
Thou talk'st of nothing.
Mer.   True, I talk of dreams,
Which are the children of an idle brain,
Begot of nothing but vain fantasy,
Which is as thin of substance as the air
And more inconstant than the wind, who wooes   100
Even now the frozen bosom of the north,
And, being anger'd, puffs away from thence,
Turning his [face] to the dew-dropping south.
Ben.   This wind you talk of blows us from ourselves.
Supper is done, and we shall come too late.   105
Rom.   I fear, too early; for my mind misgives
Some consequence yet hanging in the stars
Shall bitterly begin his fearful date
With this night's revels, and expire the term
Of a despised life clos'd in my breast   110
By some vile forfeit of untimely death.
But He that hath the steerage of my course
Direct my [sail]! On, lusty gentlemen!
Ben.   Strike, drum.   *[They march about the stage.*
[Exeunt.]

Scene V.   *[A hall in Capulet's house.]*

([Musicians *waiting.*] *Enter* Serving-men, *with napkins.*)

[1.] Serv.   Where's Potpan, that he helps not to take away? He shift a trencher! He scrape a trencher!

[2.] Serv.   When good manners shall lie all in one or two men's hands, and they unwash'd too, 'tis a foul thing.   4

[1.] Serv.   Away with the joint-stools, remove the court-cupboard, look to the plate. Good thou, save me a piece of marchpane; and, as thou loves me, let the porter let in Susan Grindstone and Nell. Antony and Potpan!

2. Serv.   Ay, boy, ready.

---

103. [face] Q_1. *side* Q_2. dew-dropping: rainy.   113. [sail] Q_1. *sute* Q_2.
Sc. v, 5. joint-stools: folding stools. court-cupboard: sideboard.   6. marchpane: marzipan, cake made of almond paste.

[1.] Serv.   You are look'd for and call'd for, ask'd for and sought for, in the great chamber.   10
3. Serv.   We cannot be here and there too. Cheerly, boys; be brisk a while, and the longer liver take all.   [*They retire.*]

(*Enter* [CAPULET, *with* JULIET, TYBALT, *and others of his house, meeting*] *the* Guests, ROMEO, *and other* Maskers.)

Cap.   Welcome gentlemen! Ladies that have their toes
Unplagu'd with corns will walk [a bout] with you.
Ah, my mistresses, which of you all   15
Will now deny to dance? She that makes dainty,
She, I'll swear, hath corns. Am I come near ye now?
Welcome, gentlemen! I have seen the day
That I have worn a visor and could tell
A whispering tale in a fair lady's ear,   20
Such as would please; 'tis gone, 'tis gone, 'tis gone.
You are welcome, gentlemen! Come, musicians, play.
                                                    [*Music plays, and they dance.*
A hall, a hall! give room! and foot it, girls.
More light, you knaves; and turn the tables up,
And quench the fire, the room is grown too hot.   25
Ah, sirrah, this unlook'd-for sport comes well.
Nay, sit, nay, sit, good cousin Capulet,
For you and I are past our dancing days.
How long is't now since last yourself and I
Were in a mask?
2. Cap.   By'r lady, thirty years.   30
Cap.   What man! 'tis not so much, 'tis not so much.
'Tis since the nuptial of Lucentio,
Come Pentecost as quickly as it will,
Some five and twenty years; and then we mask'd.
2. Cap.   'Tis more, 'tis more. His son is elder, sir;   35
His son is thirty.
Cap.   Will you tell me that?
His son was but a ward two years ago.
Rom. [*To a Serving-Man.*]   What lady's that which doth enrich the hand
Of yonder knight?
Serv.   I know not, sir.   40
Rom.   O, she doth teach the torches to burn bright!
It seems she hangs upon the cheek of night
As a rich jewel in an Ethiop's ear;

14. [a bout] (Daniel).   *about* Q₂. To "walk a bout" is to tread a measure.   23. A hall: make room.

Beauty too rich for use, for earth too dear!
So shows a snowy dove trooping with crows,   45
As yonder lady o'er her fellows shows.
The measure done, I'll watch her place of stand,
And, touching hers, make blessed my rude hand.
Did my heart love till now? Forswear it, sight!
For I ne'er saw true beauty till this night.   50

Tyb. This, by his voice, should be a Montague.
Fetch me my rapier, boy. What dares the slave
Come hither, cover'd with an antic face,
To fleer and scorn at our solemnity?
Now, by the stock and honour of my kin,   55
To strike him dead I hold it not a sin.

Cap. Why, how now, kinsman! wherefore storm you so?

Tyb. Uncle, this is a Montague, our foe,
A villain that is hither come in spite
To scorn at our solemnity this night.   60

Cap. Young Romeo is it?

Tyb.   'Tis he, that villain Romeo.

Cap. Content thee, gentle coz, let him alone,
'A bears him like a portly gentleman;
And, to say truth, Verona brags of him
To be a virtuous and well-govern'd youth.   65
I would not for the wealth of all this town
Here in my house do him disparagement;
Therefore be patient, take no note of him;
It is my will, the which if thou respect,
Show a fair presence and put off these frowns,   70
An ill-beseeming semblance for a feast.

Tyb. It fits, when such a villain is a guest.
I'll not endure him.

Cap.   He shall be endur'd.
What, goodman boy! I say he shall; go to!
Am I master here, or you? Go to!   75
You'll not endure him! God shall mend my soul!
You'll make a mutiny among my guests!
You will set cock-a-hoop! You'll be the man!

Tyb. Why, uncle, 'tis a shame.

Cap.   Go to, go to;
You are a saucy boy. Is't so, indeed?   80
This trick may chance to scathe you; I know what.
You must contrary me! Marry, 'tis time.—

---

54. fleer: mock. solemnity: feast.   63. portly: dignified.   78. set cock-a-hoop:
throw things into disorder.

Well said, my hearts!—You are a princox; go;
Be quiet, or—More light, more light!—for shame!
I'll make you quiet.—What, cheerly, my hearts! 85
Tyb. Patience perforce with wilful choler meeting
Makes my flesh tremble in their different greeting.
I will withdraw; but this intrusion shall
Now seeming sweet convert to bitt'rest gall. [*Exit.*
Rom. [*To* JULIET.] If I profane with my unworthiest hand 90
This holy shrine, the gentle [fine] is this:
My lips, two blushing pilgrims, ready stand
To smooth that rough touch with a tender kiss.
Jul. Good pilgrim, you do wrong your hand too much,
Which mannerly devotion shows in this; 95
For saints have hands that pilgrims' hands do touch,
And palm to palm is holy palmers' kiss.
Rom. Have not saints lips, and holy palmers too?
Jul. Ay, pilgrim, lips that they must use in prayer.
Rom. O, then, dear saint, let lips do what hands do; 100
They pray, grant thou, lest faith turn to despair.
Jul. Saints do not move, though grant for prayers' sake.
Rom. Then move not while my prayer's effect I take.
Thus from my lips, by thine, my sin is purg'd. [*Kissing her.*]
Jul. Then have my lips the sin that they have took. 105
Rom. Sin from my lips? O trespass sweetly urg'd!
Give me my sin again. [*Kissing her again.*
Jul.   You kiss by the book.
Nurse Madam, your mother craves a word with you.
Rom. What is her mother?
Nurse   Marry, bachelor,
Her mother is the lady of the house, 110
And a good lady, and a wise and virtuous.
I nurs'd her daughter, that you talk'd withal;
I tell you, he that can lay hold of her
Shall have the chinks.
Rom.   Is she a Capulet?
O dear account! my life is my foe's debt. 115
Ben. Away, be gone; the sport is at the best.
Rom. Ay, so I fear; the more is my unrest.
Cap. Nay, gentlemen, prepare not to be gone;
We have a trifling foolish banquet towards.

---

83. princox: saucy boy.   86. perforce: enforced.   90–103. These lines make a sonnet in the Shakespearean form.   91. [fine] (Theobald). *sin* Q₂.   92. ready Q₁.
did readie Q₂.   107. by the book: methodically.   114. chinks: money.   115. my
foe's debt: i.e., in the power of my foe.   119. towards: coming.

Is it e'en so? Why, then, I thank you all;   120
I thank you, honest gentlemen; good-night.
More torches here! Come on then, let's to bed.
Ah, sirrah, by my fay, it waxes late;
   I'll to my rest.   [*All but Juliet and Nurse begin to go out.*]
Jul. Come hither, nurse. What is yond gentleman?
Nurse The son and heir of old Tiberio.   125
Jul. What's he that now is going out of door?
Nurse Marry, that, I think, be young Petruchio.
Jul. What's he that follows here, that would not dance?
Nurse I know not.
Jul. Go, ask his name.—If he be married,   130
   My grave is like to be my wedding-bed.
Nurse His name is Romeo, and a Montague;
   The only son of your great enemy.
Jul. My only love sprung from my only hate!
   Too early seen unknown, and known too late!   135
   Prodigious birth of love it is to me
   That I must love a loathed enemy.
Nurse What's this? what's this?
Jul.   A rhyme I learn'd even now
   Of one I danc'd withal.   [*One calls within,* "Juliet."
Nurse   Anon, anon!   140
   Come, let's away; the strangers all are gone.   [*Exeunt.*

ACT II

[Prologue]

([Enter] Chorus.)

[**Chor.**] Now old Desire doth in his death-bed lie,
   And young Affection gapes to be his heir;
That fair for which love groan'd for and would die,
   With tender Juliet [match'd] is now not fair.
Now Romeo is belov'd and loves again,   5
   Alike bewitched by the charm of looks,
But to his foe suppos'd he must complain,
   And she steal love's sweet bait from fearful hooks.
Being held a foe, he may not have access

136. Prodigious: ominous.
Act II, Prol., 4. [match'd] F. *match* Q₂.

To breathe such vows as lovers use to swear;   10
And she as much in love, her means much less
   To meet her new-beloved anywhere.
But passion lends them power, time means, to meet,
Temp'ring extremities with extreme sweet.   *[Exit.]*

Scene I.   *[A lane by the wall of Capulet's orchard.]*

(*Enter* ROMEO, *alone.*)

Rom.   Can I go forward when my heart is here?
  Turn back, dull earth, and find thy centre out.
          [He climbs the wall, and leaps down within it.]

(*Enter* BENVOLIO *with* MERCUTIO.)

Ben.   Romeo! my cousin Romeo!
Mer.   He is wise;
  And, on my life, hath stol'n him home to bed.
Ben.   He ran this way, and leap'd this orchard wall.   5
  Call, good Mercutio.
[Mer.]   Nay, I'll conjure too.
  Romeo! humours! madman! passion! lover!
  Appear thou in the likeness of a sigh!
  Speak but one rhyme, and I am satisfied;
  Cry but "Ay me!" [pronounce] but "love" and ["dove"];   10
  Speak to my gossip Venus one fair word,
  One nick-name for her purblind son and [heir],
  Young [Adam] Cupid, he that shot so [trim],
  When King Cophetua lov'd the beggar-maid!
  He heareth not, he stirreth not, he moveth not;   15
  The ape is dead, and I must conjure him.
  I conjure thee by Rosaline's bright eyes,
  By her high forehead and her scarlet lip,
  By her fine foot, straight leg, and quivering thigh,
  And the demesnes that there adjacent lie,   20
  That in thy likeness thou appear to us!
Ben.   An if he hear thee, thou wilt anger him.
Mer.   This cannot anger him; 'twould anger him

Sc. i, 2. dull earth. Romeo means himself.   6. [Mer.] Q_1. Continued to Benvolio Q_2.
10. [pronounce] Q_1. *provaunt* Q_2. ["dove"] Q_1. *day* Q_2.   11. gossip: friend.
12. purblind: totally blind. [heir] Q_1. *her* Q_2.   13. [Adam] (Upton conj.). *Abraham* Q_2.   Adam is Adam Bell, famous archer of the old ballads. [trim] Q_1. *true* Q_2.
Trim is the word used in the ballad of King Cophetua.

To raise a spirit in his mistress' circle,
Of some strange nature, letting it there stand   25
Till she had laid it and conjur'd it down.
That were some spite; my invocation
Is fair and honest; in his mistress' name
I conjure only but to raise up him.

Ben.   Come, he hath hid himself among these trees   30
To be consorted with the humorous night.
Blind is his love and best befits the dark.

Mer.   If Love be blind, Love cannot hit the mark.
Now will he sit under a medlar tree
And wish his mistress were that kind of fruit   35
As maids call medlars, when they laugh alone.
O, Romeo, that she were, O, that she were
An open [*et cetera*], thou a poperin pear!
Romeo, good-night; I'll to my truckle-bed;
This field-bed is too cold for me to sleep.   40
Come, shall we go?

Ben.   Go, then; for 'tis in vain
To seek him here that means not to be found.

> [*Exeunt* [*Ben. and Mer.*].

Scene II.   [*Capulet's orchard.* ROMEO *advances from the wall.*]

Rom.   He jests at scars that never felt a wound.

> [*Juliet appears above at her window.*]

But, soft! what light through yonder window breaks?
It is the east, and Juliet is the sun.
Arise, fair sun, and kill the envious moon,
Who is already sick and pale with grief   5
That thou, her maid, art far more fair than she.
Be not her maid, since she is envious;
Her vestal livery is but sick and green,
And none but fools do wear it; cast it off.
It is my lady, O, it is my love!   10
O, that she knew she were!
She speaks, yet she says nothing; what of that?
Her eye discourses; I will answer it.—
I am too bold, 'tis not to me she speaks.

---

27. spite: vexation.   31. humorous: damp.   34. medlar: a fruit like an apple.
38. [*et cetera*] Q$_1$. or Q$_2$. poperin: a Flemish variety of pear.   39. truckle-bed:
small bed (made to slip under a larger).

Two of the fairest stars in all the heaven,   15
Having some business, [do] entreat her eyes
To twinkle in their spheres till they return.
What if her eyes were there, they in her head?
The brightness of her cheek would shame those stars,
As daylight doth a lamp; her eyes in heaven   20
Would through the airy region stream so bright
That birds would sing and think it were not night.
See, how she leans her cheek upon her hand!
O, that I were a glove upon that hand,
That I might touch that cheek!
Jul.   Ay me!
Rom.   She speaks!   25
O, speak again, bright angel! for thou art
As glorious to this night, being o'er my head,
As is a winged messenger of heaven
Unto the white-upturned wond'ring eyes
Of mortals that fall back to gaze on him   30
When he bestrides the lazy-[pacing] clouds
And sails upon the bosom of the air.
Jul. O Romeo, Romeo! wherefore art thou Romeo?
Deny thy father and refuse thy name;
Or, if thou wilt not, be but sworn my love,   35
And I'll no longer be a Capulet.
Rom. [*Aside.*] Shall I hear more, or shall I speak at this?
Jul. 'Tis but thy name that is my enemy;
Thou art thyself, though not a Montague.
What's Montague? It is nor hand, nor foot,   40
Nor arm, nor face, [nor any other part]
Belonging to a man. O, be some other name!
What's in a name? That which we call a rose
By any other word would smell as sweet;
So Romeo would, were he not Romeo call'd,   45
Retain that dear perfection which he owes
Without that title. Romeo, doff thy name,
And for thy name, which is no part of thee,
Take all myself.
Rom.   I take thee at thy word.
Call me but love, and I'll be new baptiz'd;   50
Henceforth I never will be Romeo.

Sc. ii, 16. [do] F. *to* Q₂.   32. [pacing] Q₁. *puffing* Q₂.   42. [nor ... part] Q₁.
Om. Q₂.   41. O ... name. After *face* in l. 41 Q₂.   Q₁ omits 42.   44. word Q₂.
name Q₁.   46. owes: possesses.

Jul. What man art thou that thus bescreen'd in night
So stumblest on my counsel?
Rom.   By a name
I know not how to tell thee who I am.
My name, dear saint, is hateful to myself,   55
Because it is an enemy to thee;
Had I it written, I would tear the word.
Jul. My ears have yet not drunk a hundred words
Of thy tongue's uttering, yet I know the sound.
Art thou not Romeo, and a Montague?   60
Rom. Neither, fair maid, if either thee dislike.
Jul. How cam'st thou hither, tell me, and wherefore?
The orchard walls are high and hard to climb,
And the place death, considering who thou art,
If any of my kinsmen find thee here.   65
Rom. With love's light wings did I o'erperch these walls;
For stony limits cannot hold love out,
And what love can do, that dares love attempt;
Therefore thy kinsmen are no stop to me.
Jul. If they do see thee, they will murder thee.   70
Rom. Alack, there lies more peril in thine eye
Than twenty of their swords! Look thou but sweet,
And I am proof against their enmity.
Jul. I would not for the world they saw thee here.
Rom. I have night's cloak to hide me from their eyes;   75
And but thou love me, let them find me here.
My life were better ended by their hate,
Than death prorogued, wanting of thy love.
Jul. By whose direction found'st thou out this place?
Rom. By Love, that first did prompt me to inquire;   80
He lent me counsel and I lent him eyes.
I am no pilot; yet, wert thou as far
As that vast shore [wash'd] with the farthest sea,
I should adventure for such merchandise.
Jul. Thou know'st the mask of night is on my face,   85
Else would a maiden blush bepaint my cheek
For that which thou hast heard me speak to-night.
Fain would I dwell on form, fain, fain deny
What I have spoke; but farewell compliment!
Dost thou love me? I know thou wilt say "Ay,"   90
And I will take thy word; yet, if thou swear'st,

61. dislike: displease.   78. prorogued: postponed.   83. [wash'd] Q₄.   *washeth* Q₂.
89. compliment: convention.

Thou mayst prove false. At lovers' perjuries,
They say, Jove laughs. O gentle Romeo,
If thou dost love, pronounce it faithfully;
Or if thou think'st I am too quickly won,   95
I'll frown and be perverse and say thee nay,—
So thou wilt woo; but else, not for the world.
In truth, fair Montague, I am too fond,
And therefore thou mayst think my ['haviour] light;
But trust me, gentleman, I'll prove more true   100
Than those that have [more cunning] to be strange.
I should have been more strange, I must confess,
But that thou overheard'st, ere I was ware,
My true love's passion; therefore pardon me,
And not impute this yielding to light love,   105
Which the dark night hath so discovered.
Rom.   Lady, by yonder blessed moon I vow
That tips with silver all these fruit-tree tops—
Jul.   O, swear not by the moon, the inconstant moon,
That monthly changes in her circled orb,   110
Lest that thy love prove likewise variable.
Rom.   What shall I swear by?
Jul.   Do not swear at all;
Or, if thou wilt, swear by thy gracious self,
Which is the god of my idolatry,
And I'll believe thee.
Rom.   If my heart's dear love—   115
Jul.   Well, do not swear. Although I joy in thee,
I have no joy of this contract to-night;
It is too rash, too unadvis'd, too sudden,
Too like the lightning, which doth cease to be
Ere one can say it lightens. Sweet, good-night!   120
This bud of love, by summer's ripening breath,
May prove a beauteous flower when next we meet.
Good-night, good-night! as sweet repose and rest
Come to thy heart as that within my breast!
Rom.   O, wilt thou leave me so unsatisfied?   125
Jul.   What satisfaction canst thou have to-night?
Rom.   Th' exchange of thy love's faithful vow for mine.
Jul.   I gave thee mine before thou didst request it;
And yet I would it were to give again.
Rom.   Wouldst thou withdraw it? For what purpose, love?   130

99. ['haviour] *haviour* Q₁. *behaviour* Q₂.   101. [more cunning] Q₁. *coying* Q₂.
strange: reserved, distant.   107. vow Q₂. *swear* Q₁.

Jul.   But to be frank, and give it thee again.
And yet I wish but for the thing I have.
My bounty is as boundless as the sea,
My love as deep; the more I give to thee,
The more I have, for both are infinite.   135

                                                [Nurse] calls within.

I hear some noise within; dear love, adieu!
Anon, good nurse; Sweet Montague, be true.
Stay but a little, I will come again.   *[Exit, above.]*
Rom.   O blessed, blessed night! I am afeard,
Being in night, all this is but a dream,   140
Too flattering-sweet to be substantial.

(Re-enter JULIET, *above.)*

Jul.   Three words, dear Romeo, and good-night indeed.
If that thy bent of love be honourable,
Thy purpose marriage, send me word to-morrow,
By one that I'll procure to come to thee,   145
Where and what time thou wilt perform the rite;
And all my fortunes at thy foot I'll lay
And follow thee my lord throughout the world.
[Nurse.] *(Within.)*   Madam!
Jul.   I come, anon.—But if thou mean'st not well,   150
I do beseech thee—
[Nurse.] *(Within.)*   Madam!
Jul.   By and by, I come:—
To cease thy suit, and leave me to my grief.
To-morrow will I send.
Rom.   So thrive my soul—
Jul.   A thousand times good-night!   *[Exit [above].*   155
Rom.   A thousand times the worse, to want thy light.
Love goes toward love, as schoolboys from their books,
But love from love, toward school with heavy looks.

                                                         [Retiring.]

(Re-enter JULIET, *above.)*

Jul.   Hist! Romeo, hist! O, for a falconer's voice,
To lure this tassel-gentle back again!   160
Bondage is hoarse, and may not speak aloud;
Else would I tear the cave where Echo lies,
And make her airy tongue more hoarse than [mine],

131. frank: generous.   143. bent: inclination.   149, 151. [Nurse] (Capell).   Om.
Q₂.   152. By and by: immediately.   160. tassel-gentle: male hawk.   163. [mine]
Q₄.   Om. Q₂.

With repetition of my [Romeo's name.]
Romeo!
Rom.   It is my soul, that calls upon my name.   165
How silver-sweet sound lovers' tongues by night,
Like softest music to attending ears!
Jul. Romeo!
Rom.   My [dear]?
Jul.   What o'clock to-morrow
Shall I send to thee?
Rom.   By the hour of nine.
Jul. I will not fail: 'tis twenty year till then.   170
I have forgot why I did call thee back.
Rom. Let me stand here till thou remember it.
Jul. I shall forget, to have thee still stand there,
Rememb'ring how I love thy company.
Rom. And I'll still stay, to have thee still forget,   175
Forgetting any other home but this.
Jul. 'Tis almost morning, I would have thee gone;—
And yet no farther than a wanton's bird,
That lets it hop a little from [her] hand,
Like a poor prisoner in his twisted gyves,   180
And with a [silk] thread plucks it back again,
So loving-jealous of his liberty.
Rom. I would I were thy bird.
Jul.   Sweet, so would I;
Yet I should kill thee with much cherishing.
Good-night, good-night! Parting is such sweet sorrow,   185
That I shall say good-night till it be morrow.

                                                        [*Exit, above.*]

Rom. Sleep dwell upon thine eyes, peace in thy breast!
Would I were sleep and peace, so sweet to rest!
Hence will I to my ghostly [father's] cell,
His help to crave, and my dear hap to tell.   190
                                                        [*Exit.*

Scene III.   [*Friar Laurence's cell.*]

(*Enter* FRIAR [LAURENCE], *with a basket.*)

Fri. L.   The grey-ey'd morn smiles on the frowning night,
Chequ'ring the eastern clouds with streaks of light,

164. [Romeo's name] Q$_1$. Om. Q$_2$.   168. [dear] Q$_4$. *Neece* Q$_2$.   179. [her] Q$_1$.
his Q$_2$.   180. gyves: fetters.   181. [silk] Q$_1$. *silken* Q$_2$.   188. After *rest* Q$_2$
inserts iii. 1–4.   189. ghostly: spiritual. [father's] Q$_1$. *Friers close* Q$_2$.   190.
dear hap: good fortune.

And flecked darkness like a drunkard reels
From forth day's path and Titan's [fiery] wheels.
Now, ere the sun advance his burning eye,   5
The day to cheer and night's dank dew to dry,
I must up-fill this osier cage of ours
With baleful weeds and precious-juiced flowers.
The earth, that's nature's mother, is her tomb;
What is her burying grave, that is her womb;   10
And from her womb children of divers kind
We sucking on her natural bosom find:
Many for many virtues excellent,
None but for some, and yet all different.
O, mickle is the powerful grace that lies   15
In plants, herbs, stones, and their true qualities;
For nought so vile that on the earth doth live
But to the earth some special good doth give,
Nor aught so good but, strain'd from that fair use,
Revolts from true birth, stumbling on abuse.   20
Virtue itself turns vice, being misapplied;
And vice [sometime's] by action dignified.

(*Enter* ROMEO.)

Within the infant rind of this weak flower
Poison hath residence and medicine power;
For this, being smelt, with that part cheers each part;   25
Being tasted, [slays] all senses with the heart.
Two such opposed kings encamp them still
In man as well as herbs, grace and rude will;
And where the worser is predominant,
Full soon the canker death eats up that plant.   30
Rom.   Good morrow, father.
Fri. L.   *Benedicite!*
What early tongue so sweet saluteth me?
Young son, it argues a distempered head
So soon to bid good morrow to thy bed.
Care keeps his watch in every old man's eye,   35
And where care lodges, sleep will never lie;
But where unbruised youth with unstuff'd brain
Doth couch his limbs, there golden sleep doth reign;
Therefore thy earliness doth me assure
Thou art up-rous'd with some distemp'rature;   40

Sc. iii, 4. [fiery] Q₁. *burning* Q₂.   7. osier cage: willow basket.   22. [sometime's]
(Capell). *sometimes* Q₁. *sometime* Q₂.   25. that part: i.e., the odor.   26. [slays]
F. *stays* Q₂.   30. canker: canker-worm.   33. distempered: sick.

Or if not so, then here I hit it right,
Our Romeo hath not been in bed to-night.
Rom.   That last is true; the sweeter rest was mine.
Fri. L.   God pardon sin! Wast thou with Rosaline?
Rom.   With Rosaline, my ghostly father? No!   45
I have forgot that name, and that name's woe.
Fri. L.   That's my good son; but where hast thou been, then?
Rom.   I'll tell thee ere thou ask it me again.
I have been feasting with mine enemy,
Where on a sudden one hath wounded me   50
That's by me wounded; both our remedies
Within thy help and holy physic lies.
I bear no hatred, blessed man, for, lo,
My intercession likewise steads my foe.
Fri. L.   Be plain, good son, and homely in thy drift;   55
Riddling confession finds but riddling shrift.
Rom.   Then plainly know my heart's dear love is set
On the fair daughter of rich Capulet.
As mine on hers, so hers is set on mine;
And all combin'd, save what thou must combine   60
By holy marriage. When and where and how
We met, we woo'd, and made exchange of vow,
I'll tell thee as we pass; but this I pray,
That thou consent to marry us to-day.
Fri. L.   Holy Saint Francis, what a change is here!   65
Is Rosaline, that thou didst love so dear,
So soon forsaken? Young men's love then lies
Not truly in their hearts, but in their eyes.
Jesu Maria, what a deal of brine
Hath wash'd thy sallow cheeks for Rosaline!   70
How much salt water thrown away in waste,
To season love, that of it doth not taste!
The sun not yet thy sighs from heaven clears,
Thy old groans yet [ring] in mine ancient ears;
Lo, here upon thy cheek the stain doth sit   75
Of an old tear that is not wash'd off yet.
If e'er thou wast thyself and these woes thine,
Thou and these woes were all for Rosaline.
And art thou chang'd? Pronounce this sentence then:
Women may fall, when there's no strength in men.   80
Rom.   Thou chid'st me oft for loving Rosaline.
Fri. L.   For doting, not for loving, pupil mine.

56. shrift: absolution.   74. [ring] Q₄.   ringing Q₂.

Rom. And bad'st me bury love.
Fri. L.   Not in a grave,
  To lay one in, another out to have.
Rom. I pray thee, chide me not. Her I love now   85
  Doth grace for grace and love for love allow;
  The other did not so.
Fri. L.   O, she knew well
  Thy love did read by rote that could not spell.
  But come, young waverer, come, go with me,
  In one respect I'll thy assistant be;   90
  For this alliance may so happy prove
  To turn your households' rancour to pure love.
Rom. O, let us hence; I stand on sudden haste.
Fri. L. Wisely and slow; they stumble that run fast.   [*Exeunt.*

Scene IV. [*A street.*]

(*Enter* BENVOLIO *and* MERCUTIO.)

Mer. Where the devil should this Romeo be?
  Came he not home to-night?
Ben. Not to his father's; I spoke with his man.
Mer. Why, that same pale hard-hearted wench, that Rosaline,
  Torments him so, that he will sure run mad.   5
Ben. Tybalt, the kinsman of old Capulet,
  Hath sent a letter to his father's house.
Mer. A challenge, on my life.
Ben. Romeo will answer it.
Mer. Any man that can write may answer a letter.   10
Ben. Nay, he will answer the letter's master, how he dares, being dared.
Mer. Alas, poor Romeo! he is already dead; stabb'd with a white wench's
  black eye; run through the ear with a love song; the very pin of his heart
  cleft with the blind bow-boy's butt-shaft: and is he a man to encounter
  Tybalt?   15
Ben. Why, what is Tybalt?
Mer. More than prince of cats. O, he's the courageous captain of compliments. He fights as you sing prick-song; keeps time, distance, and
  proportion; he rests his minim rests, one, two, and the third in your
  bosom: the very butcher of a silk button; a duellist, a duellist; a gentle-

---

88. rote: memory.   93. stand on: insist on.
Sc. iv, 13. pin: peg in center of a target.   14. butt-shaft: blunt arrow.   17. prince
of cats. The king of the cats in *Reynard the Fox* was called Tibalt.   18. prick-song:
music sung from written notes.

man of the very first house, of the first and second cause. Ah, the immortal *passado!* the *punto reverso!* the *hai!*   22

Ben. The what?

Mer. The pox of such antic, lisping, affecting [fantasticoes]; these new
tuners of accent! "By Jesu, a very good blade! a very tall man! a very
good whore!" Why, is not this a lamentable thing, grandsire, that we
should be thus afflicted with these strange flies, these fashion-mongers,
these [*perdona-mi's*], who stand so much on the new form, that they
cannot sit at ease on the old bench? O, their bones, their bones!

(*Enter* ROMEO.)

Ben. Here comes Romeo, here comes Romeo.   30

Mer. Without his roe, like a dried herring: O flesh, flesh, how art thou
fishified! Now is he for the numbers that Petrarch flowed in. Laura to his
lady was a kitchen-wench (marry, she had a better love to be-rhyme her);
Dido a dowdy; Cleopatra a gipsy; Helen and Hero hildings and harlots;
Thisbe, a grey eye or so, but not to the purpose. Signior Romeo, *bonjour!*
There's a French salutation to your French slop. You gave us the counterfeit fairly last night.   37

Rom. Good morrow to you both. What counterfeit did I give you?

Mer. The slip, sir, the slip; can you not conceive?

Rom. Pardon, good Mercutio, my business was great; and in such a case
as mine a man may strain courtesy.   41

Mer. That's as much as to say, such a case as yours constrains a man to
bow in the hams.

Rom. Meaning, to curtsy.

Mer. Thou hast most kindly hit it.   45

Rom. A most courteous exposition.

Mer. Nay, I am the very pink of courtesy.

Rom. Pink for flower.

Mer. Right.

Rom. Why, then is my pump well flower'd.   50

Mer. Sure wit! Follow me this jest now till thou hast worn out thy pump,
that, when the single sole of it is worn, the jest may remain, after the
wearing, solely singular.

Rom. O single-sol'd jest, solely singular for the singleness!

Mer. Come between us, good Benvolio; my wits faint.   55

21. first house: best school (of fencing). of . . . cause: i.e., very ready to quarrel. A
satirical reference to the manuals which codified the reasons for quarreling.   22. *passado:* forward thrust; *punto reverso:* back-handed thrust; *hai:* home thrust.   24.
[fantasticoes] Q₁; coxcombs. *phantacies* Q₂.   25. tall: brave.   28. [*perdona-
mi's*] Q₄: pardon me's (Ital.). *pardons mees* Q₂. form: (1) fashion, (2) bench.
29. bones. Pun on *bons* (Fr.).   32. numbers: verses.   34. hildings: good-for-
nothings.   36. slop: loose breeches (French fashion).   38–39. counterfeit . . . slip.
Counterfeit coins were called *slips*.   45. kindly: naturally.   54. singleness: silliness.

Rom. Switch and spurs, switch and spurs; or I'll cry a match.

Mer. Nay, if our wits run the wild-goose chase, I am done, for thou hast more of the wild-goose in one of thy wits than, I am sure, I have in my whole five. Was I with you there for the goose?

Rom. Thou wast never with me for anything when thou wast not there for the goose.   61

Mer. I will bite thee by the ear for that jest.

Rom. Nay, good goose, bite not.

Mer. Thy wit is a very bitter sweeting; it is a most sharp sauce.

Rom. And is it not, then, well serv'd in to a sweet goose?   65

Mer. O, here's a wit of cheveril, that stretches from an inch narrow to an ell broad!

Rom. I stretch it out for that word "broad"; which added to the goose, proves thee far and wide a broad goose.

Mer. Why, is not this better now than groaning for love? Now art thou sociable, now art thou Romeo, now art thou what thou art, by art as well as by nature; for this drivelling love is like a great natural, that runs lolling up and down to hide his bauble in a hole.

Ben. Stop there, stop there.

Mer. Thou desir'st me to stop in my tale against the hair.   75

Ben. Thou wouldst else have made thy tale large.

Mer. O, thou art deceiv'd; I would have made it short; for I was come to the whole depth of my tale, and meant, indeed, to occupy the argument no longer.

Rom. Here's goodly gear!   80

(*Enter* NURSE *and her man* [PETER].)

   A sail, a sail!

Mer. Two, two; a shirt and a smock.

Nurse Peter!

Peter Anon!

Nurse My fan, Peter.   85

Mer. Good Peter, to hide her face; for her fan's the fairer face.

Nurse God ye good morrow, gentlemen.

Mer. God ye good den, fair gentlewoman.

Nurse Is it good den?

Mer. 'Tis no less, I tell ye; for the bawdy hand of the dial is now upon the prick of noon.   91

Nurse Out upon you! what a man are you!

Rom. One, gentlewoman, that God hath made [for] himself to mar.

57. wild-goose chase: a cross-country riding game, in which the leader could pick whatever course he chose and the others had to follow. The object was to capture the lead. 64. sweeting: a variety of apple.   66. cheveril: kid leather.   67. ell: 45 inches. 72. natural: idiot.   75. hair: i.e., grain.   76. large: i.e., with a pun on sense of *gross, lewd.*   80. gear: matter.   93. [for] Q_1. Om. Q_2.

Nurse By my troth, it is well said; "for himself to mar," quoth 'a! Gentle-
men, can any of you tell me where I may find the young Romeo?   95
Rom. I can tell you; but young Romeo will be older when you have found
him than he was when you sought him. I am the youngest of that name,
for fault of a worse.
Nurse You say well.
Mer. Yea, is the worst well? Very well took, i' faith; wisely, wisely.   100
Nurse If you be he, sir, I desire some confidence with you.
Ben. She will indite him to some supper.
Mer. A bawd, a bawd, a bawd! So ho!
Rom. What hast thou found?   104
Mer. No hare, sir; unless a hare, sir, in a lenten pie, that is something
stale and hoar ere it be spent.   [*Sings.*]
> "An old hare hoar,
>   And an old hare hoar,
> Is very good meat in lent;
>   But a hare that is hoar   110
>   Is too much for a score,
> When it hoars ere it be spent."

Romeo, will you come to your father's? We'll to dinner thither.
Rom. I will follow you.
Mer. Farewell, ancient lady; farewell, [*singing*] "lady, lady, lady."   115
                                          [*Exeunt Mercutio and Benvolio.*
Nurse I pray you, sir, what saucy merchant was this, that was so full of
his ropery?
Rom. A gentleman, nurse, that loves to hear himself talk, and will speak
more in a minute than he will stand to in a month.
Nurse An 'a speak anything against me, I'll take him down, and 'a were
lustier than he is, and twenty such Jacks; and if I cannot, I'll find those
that shall. Scurvy knave! I am none of his flirt-gills; I am none of his
skains-mates.—And thou must stand by too, and suffer every knave to
use me at his pleasure!   124
Peter I saw no man use you at his pleasure; if I had, my weapon should
quickly have been out. I warrant you, I dare draw as soon as another
man, if I see occasion in a good quarrel, and the law on my side.
Nurse Now, afore God, I am so vex'd that every part about me quivers.
Scurvy knave! Pray you, sir, a word: and as I told you, my young lady
bid me inquire you out; what she bid me say, I will keep to myself. But
first let me tell ye, if ye should lead her [into] a fool's paradise, as they
say, it were a very gross kind of behaviour, as they say; for the gentlewoman is young, and, therefore, if you should deal double with her,

---

101. confidence: blunder for *conference*.   102. indite: Benvolio's intentional mala-
propism for *invite*.   103. So ho: hunter's cry when sighting a hare.   117. ropery:
roguery.   121. Jacks: saucy fellows.   122. flirt-gills: flirting women.   123.
skains-mates. A derogatory term not occurring elsewhere.   131. [into] Q₁. *in* Q₂.

truly it were an ill thing to be off'red to any gentlewoman, and very weak
dealing.   135

Rom.   Nurse, commend me to thy lady and mistress. I protest unto thee—

Nurse   Good heart, and, i' faith, I will tell her as much. Lord, Lord, she
will be a joyful woman.

Rom.   What wilt thou tell her, nurse? Thou dost not mark me.

Nurse   I will tell her, sir, that you do protest; which, as I take it, is a
gentlemanlike offer.   141

Rom.   Bid her devise
Some means to come to shrift this afternoon;
And there she shall at Friar Laurence' cell
Be shriv'd and married. Here is for thy pains.   145

Nurse   No, truly, sir; not a penny.

Rom.   Go to; I say you shall.

Nurse   This afternoon, sir? Well, she shall be there.

Rom.   And stay, good nurse;—behind the abbey wall
Within this hour my man shall be with thee,   150
And bring thee cords made like a tackled stair;
Which to the high top-gallant of my joy
Must be my convoy in the secret night.
Farewell; be trusty, and I'll quit thy pains.
Farewell; commend me to thy mistress.   155

Nurse   Now God in heaven bless thee! Hark you, sir.

Rom.   What say'st thou, my dear nurse?

Nurse   Is your man secret? Did you ne'er hear say,
"Two may keep counsel, putting one away"?

Rom.   [I] warrant thee, my man's as true as steel.   160

Nurse   Well, sir; my mistress is the sweetest lady—Lord, Lord! when
'twas a little prating thing,—O, there is a nobleman in town, one Paris,
that would fain lay knife aboard; but she, good soul, had as lief see a
toad, very toad, as see him. I anger her sometimes and tell her that Paris
is the properer man; but, I'll warrant you, when I say so, she looks as
pale as any clout in the versal world. Doth not rosemary and Romeo
begin both with a letter?   167

Rom.   Ay, nurse; what of that? Both with an R.

Nurse   Ah, mocker! that's the dog's name. R is for the—No; I know it
begins with some other letter—and she hath the prettiest sententious of
it, of you and rosemary, that it would do you good to hear it.   171

Rom.   Commend me to thy lady.

Nurse   Ay, a thousand times. Peter!   *[Exit Romeo.]*

Pet.   Anon!

Nurse   Before, and apace.   *[Exeunt.*

---

151. tackled stair: rope ladder.   152. top-gallant: summit.   153. convoy: convey-
ance.   160. [I] F$_2$. Om. Q$_2$.   165. properer: handsomer.   166. clout: rag. versal: universal.   170. sententious: blunder for *sentences*, i.e., proverbs.

Scene V.   [*Capulet's orchard.*]

(*Enter* JULIET.)

Jul.   The clock struck nine when I did send the nurse;
In half an hour she promis'd to return.
Perchance she cannot meet him: that's not so.
O, she is lame! Love's heralds should be thoughts,
Which ten times faster [glide] than the sun's beams   5
Driving back shadows over louring hills;
Therefore do nimble-pinion'd doves draw Love,
And therefore hath the wind-swift Cupid wings.
Now is the sun upon the highmost hill
Of this day's journey, and from nine till twelve   10
Is three long hours, yet she is not come.
Had she affections and warm youthful blood,
She would be as swift in motion as a ball;
My words would bandy her to my sweet love,
And his to me;   15
But old folks, [marry,] feign as they were dead,
Unwieldy, slow, heavy and pale as lead.

(*Enter* NURSE [*and* PETER].)

O God, she comes! O honey nurse, what news?
Hast thou met with him? Send thy man away.
Nurse   Peter, stay at the gate.   [*Exit Peter.*   20
Jul.   Now, good sweet nurse,—O Lord, why look'st thou sad?
Though news be sad, yet tell them merrily;
If good, thou sham'st the music of sweet news
By playing it to me with so sour a face.
Nurse   I am a-weary, give me leave a while.   25
Fie, how my bones ache! What a jaunce have I [had]!
Jul.   I would thou hadst my bones, and I thy news.
Nay, come, I pray thee, speak; good, good nurse, speak.
Nurse   Jesu, what haste! Can you not stay a while?
Do you not see that I am out of breath?   30
Jul.   How art thou out of breath, when thou hast breath
To say to me that thou art out of breath?
Th' excuse that thou dost make in this delay
Is longer than the tale thou dost excuse.
Is thy news good, or bad? Answer to that;   35

Sc. v, 5. [glide] F$_4$. *glides* Q$_2$.   14. bandy: toss.   16. [marry] (Johnson).   *many*
Q$_2$.   26. jaunce: jaunt.   [had] F. Om. Q$_2$.

Say either, and I'll stay the circumstance.
Let me be satisfied, is't good or bad?

Nurse Well, you have made a simple choice; you know not how to choose
a man. Romeo! no, not he. Though his face be better than any man's, yet
his leg excels all men's; and for a hand, and a foot, and a body, though
they be not to be talk'd on, yet they are past compare. He is not the
flower of courtesy, but, I'll warrant him, as gentle as a lamb. Go thy
ways, wench; serve God. What, have you din'd at home?

Jul. No, no! But all this did I know before.
What says he of our marriage? What of that?   45

Nurse Lord, how my head aches! What a head have I!
It beats as it would fall in twenty pieces.
My back o' t' other side,—O, my back, my back!
Beshrew your heart for sending me about
To catch my death with jauncing up and down!   50

Jul. I' faith, I am sorry that thou art not well.
Sweet, sweet, sweet nurse, tell me, what says my love?

Nurse Your love says, like an honest gentleman, and a courteous, and
a kind, and a handsome, and, I warrant, a virtuous,—Where is your
mother?   55

Jul. Where is my mother! why, she is within;
Where should she be? How oddly thou repliest!
"Your love says, like an honest gentleman,
'Where is your mother?' "

Nurse   O God's lady dear!
Are you so hot? Marry, come up, I trow;   60
Is this the poultice for my aching bones?
Henceforward do your messages yourself.

Jul. Here's such a coil!—Come, what says Romeo?

Nurse Have you got leave to go to shrift today?

Jul. I have.   65

Nurse Then hie you hence to Friar Laurence' cell;
There stays a husband to make you a wife.
Now comes the wanton blood up in your cheeks;
They'll be in scarlet straight at any news.
Hie you to church; I must another way,   70
To fetch a ladder, by the which your love
Must climb a bird's nest soon when it is dark.
I am the drudge and toil in your delight,
But you shall bear the burden soon at night.
Go; I'll to dinner; hie you to the cell.   75

Jul. Hie to high fortune! Honest nurse, farewell.   [*Exeunt.*

---

36. stay the circumstance: wait for details.   63. coil: fuss.

Scene VI.   [*Friar Laurence's cell.*]

(*Enter* FRIAR LAURENCE *and* ROMEO.)

Fri. L.   So smile the heavens upon this holy act,
    That after-hours with sorrow chide us not!
Rom.   Amen, amen! but come what sorrow can,
    It cannot countervail th' exchange of joy
    That one short minute gives me in her sight.   5
    Do thou but close our hands with holy words,
    Then love-devouring Death do what he dare;
    It is enough I may but call her mine.
Fri. L.   These violent delights have violent ends,
    And in their triumph die, like fire and powder,   10
    Which as they kiss consume. The sweetest honey
    Is loathsome in his own deliciousness
    And in the taste confounds the appetite:
    Therefore love moderately; long love doth so;
    Too swift arrives as tardy as too slow.   15

(*Enter* JULIET.)

    Here comes the lady. O, so light a foot
    Will ne'er wear out the everlasting flint.
    A lover may bestride the gossamer
    That idles in the wanton summer air,
    And yet not fall; so light is vanity.   20
Jul.   Good even to my ghostly confessor.
Fri. L.   Romeo shall thank thee, daughter, for us both.
Jul.   As much to him, else is his thanks too much.
Rom.   Ah, Juliet, if the measure of thy joy
    Be heap'd like mine, and that thy skill be more   25
    To blazon it, then sweeten with thy breath
    This neighbour air, and let rich music's tongue
    Unfold the imagin'd happiness that both
    Receive in either by this dear encounter.
Jul.   Conceit, more rich in matter than in words,   30
    Brags of his substance, not of ornament.
    They are but beggars that can count their worth;
    But my true love is grown to such excess
    I cannot sum up sum of half my wealth.
Fri. L.   Come, come with me, and we will make short work;   35
    For, by your leaves, you shall not stay alone
    Till Holy Church incorporate two in one.   [*Exeunt.*

Sc. vi, 4. countervail: equal.   13. confounds: destroys.   26. blazon: proclaim.
30. Conceit: imagination.

ACT III

Scene I. [*A public place.*]

(*Enter* MERCUTIO, BENVOLIO, *and men.*)

Ben. I pray thee, good Mercutio, let's retire.
The day is hot, the Capulets abroad,
And, if we meet, we shall not scape a brawl,
For now, these hot days, is the mad blood stirring.   4

Mer. Thou art like one of these fellows that, when he enters the confines of a tavern, claps me his sword upon the table and says, "God send me no need of thee!" and by the operation of the second cup draws him on the drawer, when indeed there is no need.

Ben. Am I like such a fellow?   9

Mer. Come, come, thou art as hot a Jack in thy mood as any in Italy, and as soon moved to be moody, and as soon moody to be moved.

Ben. And what to?

Mer. Nay, an there were two such, we should have none shortly, for one would kill the other. Thou! why, thou wilt quarrel with a man that hath a hair more or a hair less in his beard than thou hast. Thou wilt quarrel with a man for cracking nuts, having no other reason but because thou hast hazel eyes. What eye but such an eye would spy out such a quarrel? Thy head is as full of quarrels as an egg is full of meat, and yet thy head hath been beaten as addle as an egg for quarrelling. Thou hast quarrell'd with a man for coughing in the street, because he hath wakened thy dog that hath lain asleep in the sun. Didst thou not fall out with a tailor for wearing his new doublet before Easter? with another for tying his new shoes with old riband? And yet thou wilt tutor me for quarrelling!

Ben. An I were so apt to quarrel as thou art, any man should buy the fee-simple of my life for an hour and a quarter.   25

Mer. The fee-simple! O simple!

(*Enter* TYBALT, PETRUCHIO, *and others.*)

Ben. By my head, here comes the Capulets.

Mer. By my heel, I care not.

Tyb. Follow me close, for I will speak to them.
Gentlemen, good den; a word with one of you.   30

Act III, sc. i, 8. drawer: tapster.   11. moody: angry.   25. fee-simple: absolute possession.

Mer. And but one word with one of us?
Couple it with something; make it a word and a blow.
Tyb. You shall find me apt enough to that, sir, an you will give occasion.
Mer. Could you not take some occasion without giving?
Tyb. Mercutio, thou consortest with Romeo,—   35
Mer. Consort! what, dost thou make us minstrels? An thou make minstrels of us, look to hear nothing but discords. Here's my fiddlestick; here's that shall make you dance. 'Zounds, consort!
Ben. We talk here in the public haunt of men.
Either withdraw unto some private place,   40
Or reason coldly of your grievances,
Or else depart; here all eyes gaze on us.
Mer. Men's eyes were made to look, and let them gaze;
I will not budge for no man's pleasure, I.

(*Enter* ROMEO.)

Tyb. Well, peace be with you, sir; here comes my man.   45
Mer. But I'll be hang'd, sir, if he wear your livery.
Marry, go before to field, he'll be your follower;
Your worship in that sense may call him "man."
Tyb. Romeo, the love I bear thee can afford
No better term than this: thou art a villain.   50
Rom. Tybalt, the reason that I have to love thee
Doth much excuse the appertaining rage
To such a greeting. Villain am I none;
Therefore farewell; I see thou know'st me not.
Tyb. Boy, this shall not excuse the injuries   55
That thou hast done me; therefore turn and draw.
Rom. I do protest I never injur'd thee,
But love thee better than thou canst devise
Till thou shalt know the reason of my love;
And so, good Capulet,—which name I tender   60
As dearly as mine own,—be satisfied.
Mer. O calm, dishonourable, vile submission!
Alla stoccata carries it away.   [*Draws.*]
Tybalt, you rat-catcher, will you walk?
Tyb. What wouldst thou have with me?   65
Mer. Good king of cats, nothing but one of your nine lives; that I mean to make bold withal, and, as you shall use me hereafter, dry-beat the rest of the eight. Will you pluck your sword out of his pilcher by the ears? Make haste, lest mine be about your ears ere it be out.

38. 'Zounds: by God's wounds.   47. field: i.e., for duelling.   63. *Alla stoccata:* "with the thrust"—meaning Tybalt. Cf. II.iv.19–27.   carries it away: wins.   67. dry-beat: thrash without drawing blood.   68. pilcher: scabbard.

Tyb. I am for you.   [*Drawing.*]

Rom. Gentle Mercutio, put thy rapier up.   71

Mer. Come, sir, your *passado.*   [*They fight.*]

Rom. Draw, Benvolio; beat down their weapons.

Gentlemen, for shame, forbear this outrage!

Tybalt, Mercutio, the Prince expressly hath   75

Forbid this bandying in Verona streets.

Hold, Tybalt! Good Mercutio!

> [*Tybalt under Romeo's arm thrusts Mercutio, and flies.*

Mer.   I am hurt.

A plague o' both [your] houses! I am sped.

Is he gone, and hath nothing?

Ben.   What, art thou hurt?

Mer. Ay, ay, a scratch, a scratch; marry, 'tis enough.   80

Where is my page? Go, villain, fetch a surgeon.   [*Exit Page.*]

Rom. Courage, man; the hurt cannot be much.

Mer. No, 'tis not so deep as a well, nor so wide as a church-door; but 'tis
enough, 'twill serve. Ask for me to-morrow, and you shall find me a
grave man. I am pepper'd, I warrant, for this world. A plague o' both
your houses! 'Zounds, a dog, a rat, a mouse, a cat, to scratch a man to
death! a braggart, a rogue, a villain, that fights by the book of arithmetic!
Why the devil came you between us? I was hurt under your arm.

Rom. I thought all for the best.

Mer. Help me into some house, Benvolio,   90

Or I shall faint. A plague o' both your houses!

They have made worms' meat of me. I have it,

And soundly too. Your houses!   [*Exeunt [Mercutio and Benvolio].*

Rom. This gentleman, the Prince's near ally,

My very friend, hath got this mortal hurt   95

In my behalf; my reputation stain'd

With Tybalt's slander,—Tybalt, that an hour

Hath been my cousin! O sweet Juliet,

Thy beauty hath made me effeminate

And in my temper soft'ned valour's steel!   100

(*Re-enter* BENVOLIO.)

Ben. O Romeo, Romeo, brave Mercutio's dead!

That gallant spirit hath aspir'd the clouds,

Which too untimely here did scorn the earth.

---

78. [your] (Dyce). Om. Q₂; *the* F. sped: done for. 94. ally: kinsman. 102. aspir'd: mounted to.

Rom. This day's black fate on moe days doth depend;
This but begins the woe others must end.   105
Ben. Here comes the furious Tybalt back again.

(*Re-enter* TYBALT.)

Rom. [Alive], in triumph! and Mercutio slain!
Away to heaven, respective lenity,
And [fire-eyed] fury be my conduct now!
Now, Tybalt, take the "villain" back again   110
That late thou gav'st me; for Mercutio's soul
Is but a little way above our heads,
Staying for thine to keep him company.
Either thou, or I, or both, must go with him.
Tyb. Thou, wretched boy, that didst consort him here,   115
Shalt with him hence.
Rom.   This shall determine that.

                                   [*They fight; Tybalt falls.*

Ben. Romeo, away, be gone!
The citizens are up, and Tybalt slain.
Stand not amaz'd; the Prince will doom thee death
'f thou art taken. Hence, be gone, away!   120
Rom. O, I am fortune's fool!
Ben.   Why dost thou stay?   [*Exit Romeo.*

(*Enter* CITIZENS.)

[A] Cit. Which way ran he that kill'd Mercutio?
Tybalt, that murderer, which way ran he?
Ben. There lies that Tybalt.
[A] Cit.   Up, sir, go with me;
I charge thee in the Prince's name, obey.   125

(*Enter* PRINCE, MONTAGUE, CAPULET, *their* WIVES, *and all.*)

Prin. Where are the vile beginners of this fray?
Ben. O noble Prince, I can discover all
The unlucky manage of this fatal brawl.
There lies the man, slain by young Romeo,
That slew thy kinsman, brave Mercutio.   130
La. Cap. Tybalt, my cousin! O my brother's child!
O Prince! O cousin! husband! O, the blood is spilt
Of my dear kinsman! Prince, as thou art true,

---

104. moe: more.   107. [Alive] Q₁. *He gan* Q₂.   108. respective: considerate.
109. [fire-eyed] Q₁. *fier end* Q₂; *fire and* F. conduct: guide.   119. amaz'd: stupefied.   127. discover: reveal.   128. manage: conduct.

For blood of ours, shed blood of Montague.

O cousin, cousin!   135

Prin. Benvolio, who began this bloody fray?

Ben. Tybalt, here slain, whom Romeo's hand did slay!

Romeo that spoke him fair, bid him bethink

How nice the quarrel was, and urg'd withal

Your high displeasure; all this, uttered   140

With gentle breath, calm look, knees humbly bow'd,

Could not take truce with the unruly spleen

Of Tybalt deaf to peace, but that he tilts

With piercing steel at bold Mercutio's breast,

Who, all as hot, turns deadly point to point,   145

And, with a martial scorn, with one hand beats

Cold death aside, and with the other sends

It back to Tybalt, whose dexterity

Retorts it. Romeo he cries aloud,

"Hold, friends! friends, part!" and, swifter than his tongue,   150

His [agile] arm beats down their fatal points,

And 'twixt them rushes; underneath whose arm

An envious thrust from Tybalt hit the life

Of stout Mercutio, and then Tybalt fled;

But by and by comes back to Romeo,   155

Who had but newly entertain'd revenge,

And to't they go like lightning, for, ere I

Could draw to part them, was stout Tybalt slain,

And, as he fell, did Romeo turn and fly.

This is the truth, or let Benvolio die.   160

La Cap. He is a kinsman to the Montague;

Affection makes him false; he speaks not true.

Some twenty of them fought in this black strife,

And all those twenty could but kill one life.

I beg for justice, which thou, Prince, must give;   165

Romeo slew Tybalt, Romeo must not live.

Prin. Romeo slew him, he slew Mercutio;

Who now the price of his dear blood doth owe?

[Mon.] Not Romeo, Prince, he was Mercutio's friend;

His fault concludes but what the law should end,   170

The life of Tybalt.

Prin.   And for that offence

Immediately we do exile him hence.

I have an interest in your [hate's] proceeding,

---

139. nice: foolish.   151. [agile] Q_1. *aged* Q_2.   169. [Mon.] Q_4. *Capu* Q_2.   173.
[hate's] Q_1. *hearts* Q_2.

My blood for your rude brawls doth lie a-bleeding;
But I'll amerce you with so strong a fine   175
That you shall all repent the loss of mine.
[I] will be deaf to pleading and excuses;
Nor tears nor prayers shall purchase out abuses;
Therefore use none. Let Romeo hence in haste,
Else, when he's found, that hour is his last.   180
Bear hence this body and attend our will.
Mercy but murders, pardoning those that kill.

[*Exeunt.*

Scene II.   [*Capulet's orchard.*]

(*Enter* JULIET, *alone.*)

Jul.   Gallop apace, you fiery-footed steeds,
Towards Phœbus' lodging; such a waggoner
As Phaethon would whip you to the west,
And bring in cloudy night immediately.
Spread thy close curtain, love-performing night,   5
That runaway's eyes may wink, and Romeo
Leap to these arms untalk'd of and unseen!
Lovers can see to do their amorous rites
By their own beauties; or, if love be blind,
It best agrees with night. Come, civil night,   10
Thou sober-suited matron, all in black,
And learn me how to lose a winning match,
Play'd for a pair of stainless maidenhoods.
Hood my unmann'd blood, bating in my cheeks,
With thy black mantle, till strange love grow bold,   15
Think true love acted simple modesty.
Come, night; come, Romeo; come, thou day in night;
For thou wilt lie upon the wings of night,
Whiter than new snow [on] a raven's back.
Come, gentle night, come, loving, black-brow'd night,   20
Give me my Romeo; and, when [he] shall die,
Take him and cut him out in little stars,

175. amerce: punish by fine.   177. [I] Q_1. *It* Q_2.
Sc. ii, 6. runaway's. Unexplained and probably corrupt. There is no apostrophe in the
early texts. The stars, sun, moon, Phaeton, Cupid, and many others have been suggested
as the runaway. wink: close.   9. By Q_4. *And* by Q_2.   10. civil: grave.   14.
Hood: cover; unmann'd: untamed; bating: fluttering. Terms from falconry. The hawk
was blindfolded to keep it quiet.   19. [on] F_2. *upon* Q_2.   21. [he] Q_4. *I* Q_2.

And he will make the face of heaven so fine
That all the world will be in love with night
And pay no worship to the garish sun.   25
O, I have bought the mansion of a love,
But not possess'd it, and, though I am sold,
Not yet enjoy'd. So tedious is this day
As is the night before some festival
To an impatient child that hath new robes   30
And may not wear them. O, here comes my nurse,

(*Enter* Nurse, *with cords.*)

And she brings news; and every tongue that speaks
But Romeo's name speaks heavenly eloquence.
Now, nurse, what news? What hast thou there? The cords
That Romeo bid thee fetch?

Nurse   Ay, ay, the cords.   35
                                        [*Throws them down.*]

Jul.   Ay me! what news? Why dost thou wring thy hands?
Nurse   Ah, well-a-day! he's dead, he's dead, he's dead!
   We are undone, lady, we are undone!
   Alack the day! he's gone, he's kill'd, he's dead!
Jul.   Can heaven be so envious?
Nurse   Romeo can,   40
   Though heaven cannot. O Romeo, Romeo!
   Who ever would have thought it? Romeo!
Jul.   What devil art thou, that dost torment me thus?
   This torture should be roar'd in dismal hell.
   Hath Romeo slain himself? Say thou but ay,   45
   And that bare vowel *I* shall poison more
   Than the death-darting eye of cockatrice.
   I am not I, if there be such an ay;
   Or those eyes shut, that makes thee answer ay.
   If he be slain, say ay; or if not, no.   50
   Brief sounds determine [of] my weal or woe.
Nurse   I saw the wound, I saw it with mine eyes,—
   God save the mark!—here on his manly breast.
   A piteous corse, a bloody piteous corse!
   Pale, pale as ashes, all bedaub'd in blood,   55
   All in gore-blood; I swounded at the sight.
Jul.   O, break, my heart! poor bankrupt, break at once!
   To prison, eyes, ne'er look on liberty!

47. cockatrice: fabulous animal which killed by its glance.   49. those eyes: i.e.,
Romeo's.   51. [of] F. Om. Q_2.

Vile earth, to earth resign; end motion here;
And thou and Romeo press [one] heavy bier!   60

Nurse   O Tybalt, Tybalt, the best friend I had!
O courteous Tybalt! honest gentleman!
That ever I should live to see thee dead!

Jul.   What storm is this that blows so contrary?
Is Romeo slaught'red, and is Tybalt dead?   65
My dearest cousin, and my dearer lord?
Then, dreadful trumpet, sound the general doom!
For who is living, if those two are gone?

Nurse   Tybalt is gone, and Romeo banished;
Romeo that kill'd him, he is banished.   70

Jul.   O God! did Romeo's hand shed Tybalt's blood?

Nurse   It did, it did; alas the day, it did!

Jul.   O serpent heart, hid with a flow'ring face!
Did ever dragon keep so fair a cave?
Beautiful tyrant! fiend angelical!   75
[Dove-feather'd] raven! wolvish ravening lamb!
Despised substance of divinest show!
Just opposite to what thou justly seem'st,
A [damned] saint, an honourable villain!
O nature, what hadst thou to do in hell,   80
When thou didst bower the spirit of a fiend
In mortal paradise of such sweet flesh?
Was ever book containing such vile matter
So fairly bound? O, that deceit should dwell
In such a gorgeous palace!

Nurse   There's no trust,   85
No faith, no honesty in men; all perjur'd,
All forsworn, all naught, all dissemblers.
Ah, where's my man? Give me some *aqua vitæ*;
These griefs, these woes, these sorrows make me old.
Shame come to Romeo!

Jul.   Blister'd be thy tongue   90
For such a wish! he was not born to shame.
Upon his brow shame is asham'd to sit;
For 'tis a throne where honour may be crown'd
Sole monarch of the universal earth.
O, what a beast was I to chide at him!   95

Nurse   Will you speak well of him that kill'd your cousin?

Jul.   Shall I speak ill of him that is my husband?

---

60. [one] Q₄. *on* Q₂.   76. [Dove-feather'd] (Theobald). *Ravenous dovefeatherd*
Q₂.   78. Just: exact.   79. [damned] Q₄. *dimme* Q₂.   81. bower: lodge.

Ah, poor my lord, what tongue shall smooth thy name,
When I, thy three-hours wife, have mangled it?
But, wherefore, villain, didst thou kill my cousin? 100
That villain cousin would have kill'd my husband.
Back, foolish tears, back to your native spring;
Your tributary drops belong to woe,
Which you, mistaking, offer up to joy.
My husband lives that Tybalt would have slain; 105
And Tybalt's dead that would have slain my husband.
All this is comfort; wherefore weep I then?
Some word there was, worser than Tybalt's death,
That murd'red me; I would forget it fain;
But, O, it presses to my memory 110
Like damned guilty deeds to sinners' minds:
"Tybalt is dead, and Romeo—banished."
That "banished," that one word "banished,"
Hath slain ten thousand Tybalts. Tybalt's death
Was woe enough, if it had ended there; 115
Or, if sour woe delights in fellowship
And needly will be rank'd with other griefs,
Why follow'd not, when she said, "Tybalt's dead,"
Thy father, or thy mother, nay, or both,
Which modern lamentation might have mov'd? 120
But with a rear-ward following Tybalt's death,
"Romeo is banished," to speak that word,
Is father, mother, Tybalt, Romeo, Juliet,
All slain, all dead. "Romeo is banished!"
There is no end, no limit, measure, bound, 125
In that word's death; no words can that woe sound.
Where is my father and my mother, nurse?
Nurse   Weeping and wailing over Tybalt's corse.
Will you go to them? I will bring you thither.
Jul.   Wash they his wounds with tears? Mine shall be spent, 130
When theirs are dry, for Romeo's banishment.
Take up those cords. Poor ropes, you are beguil'd,
Both you and I, for Romeo is exil'd.
He made you for a highway to my bed,
But I, a maid, die maiden-widowed. 135
Come, cords, come, nurse; I'll to my wedding-bed;
And death, not Romeo, take my maidenhead!

117. needly: necessarily.   120. modern: ordinary.   126. sound: (1) express, (2) fathom.

Nurse   Hie to your chamber. I'll find Romeo
  To comfort you; I wot well where he is.
  Hark ye, your Romeo will be here at night.   140
  I'll to him; he is hid at Laurence' cell.
Jul.   O, find him! Give this ring to my true knight,
  And bid him come to take his last farewell.

[Exeunt.

Scene III.   [Friar Laurence's cell.]

(Enter Friar Laurence, Romeo [following].)

Fri. L.   Romeo, come forth; come forth, thou fearful man:
  Affliction is enamour'd of thy parts,
  And thou art wedded to calamity.
Rom.   Father, what news? What is the Prince's doom?
  What sorrow craves acquaintance at my hand,   5
  That I yet know not?
Fri. L.   Too familiar
  Is my dear son with such sour company.
  I bring thee tidings of the Prince's doom.
Rom.   What less than dooms-day is the Prince's doom?
Fri. L.   A gentler judgment vanish'd from his lips,   10
  Not body's death, but body's banishment.
Rom.   Ha, banishment! Be merciful, say "death";
  For exile hath more terror in his look,
  Much more than death. Do not say "banishment"!
Fri. L.   Here from Verona art thou banished.   15
  Be patient, for the world is broad and wide.
Rom.   There is no world without Verona walls,
  But purgatory, torture, hell itself.
  Hence "banished" is banish'd from the world,
  And world's exile is death; then "banished"   20
  Is death mis-term'd. Calling death "banishment,"
  Thou cut'st my head off with a golden axe,
  And smil'st upon the stroke that murders me.
Fri. L.   O deadly sin! O rude unthankfulness!
  Thy fault our law calls death; but the kind prince,   25
  Taking thy part, hath rush'd aside the law,
  And turn'd that black word "death" to "banishment."
  This is dear mercy, and thou seest it not.

Sc. iii, 1. fearful: full of fear.   10. vanish'd: issued.   17. without: outside.

Rom.   'Tis torture, and not mercy. Heaven is here,
    Where Juliet lives; and every cat and dog   30
    And little mouse, every unworthy thing,
    Live here in heaven and may look on her;
    But Romeo may not. More validity,
    More honourable state, more courtship lives
    In carrion-flies than Romeo; they may seize   35
    On the white wonder of dear Juliet's hand
    And steal immortal blessing from her lips,
    Who, even in pure and vestal modesty,
    Still blush, as thinking their own kisses sin;
    But Romeo may not; he is banished.   40
    This may flies do, when I from this must fly;
    They are free men, but I am banished:
    And say'st thou yet that exile is not death?
    Hadst thou no poison mix'd, no sharp-ground knife,
    No sudden mean of death, though ne'er so mean,   45
    But "banished" to kill me?—"Banished"?
    O friar, the damned use that word in hell;
    Howling attends it. How hast thou the heart,
    Being a divine, a ghostly confessor,
    A sin-absolver, and my friend profess'd,   50
    To mangle me with that word "banished"?
Fri. L.   [Thou] fond mad man, hear me a little speak.
Rom.   O, thou wilt speak again of banishment.
Fri. L.   I'll give thee armour to keep off that word;
    Adversity's sweet milk, philosophy,   55
    To comfort thee, though thou art banished.
Rom.   Yet "banished"? Hang up philosophy!
    Unless philosophy can make a Juliet,
    Displant a town, reverse a prince's doom,
    It helps not, it prevails not. Talk no more.   60
Fri. L.   O, then I see that madmen have no ears.
Rom.   How should they, when that wise men have no eyes?
Fri. L.   Let me dispute with thee of thy estate.
Rom.   Thou canst not speak of that thou dost not feel.
    Wert thou as young as I, Juliet thy love,   65
    An hour but married, Tybalt murdered,
    Doting like me and like me banished,
    Then mightst thou speak, then mightst thou tear thy hair,

---

33. validity: worth.   40–43. But ... death. In Q₂ the order of the lines is 41, 43, 40,
(41), 42. (41) reads *Flies may do this*, etc.   45. mean ... mean: means ... base.   52.
[Thou] Q₁. *Then* Q₂. fond: foolish.   63. dispute: discuss. estate: situation.

And fall upon the ground, as I do now,
Taking the measure of an unmade grave.   [*Knocking within.*   70
Fri. L.   Arise; one knocks. Good Romeo, hide thyself.
Rom.   Not I; unless the breath of heart-sick groans,
  Mist-like, infold me from the search of eyes.   [*Knocking.*
Fri. L.   Hark, how they knock! Who's there? Romeo, arise;
  Thou wilt be taken.—Stay a while!—Stand up;   [*Knocking.*   75
  Run to my study.—By and by!—God's will,
  What simpleness is this!—I come, I come!   [*Knocking.*
  Who knocks so hard? Whence come you? What's your will?

(*Enter* Nurse.)

Nurse   Let me come in, and you shall know my errand.
  I come from Lady Juliet.
Fri. L.   Welcome, then.   80
Nurse   O holy friar, O, tell me, holy friar,
  Where is my lady's lord, where's Romeo?
Fri. L.   There on the ground, with his own tears made drunk.
Nurse   O, he is even in my mistress' case,
  Just in her case! O woeful sympathy!   85
  Piteous predicament! Even so lies she,
  Blubb'ring and weeping, weeping and blubb'ring.
  Stand up, stand up; stand, an you be a man.
  For Juliet's sake, for her sake, rise and stand;
  Why should you fall into so deep an O?   90
Rom.   Nurse!
Nurse   Ah sir! ah sir! Death's the end of all.
Rom.   Spak'st thou of Juliet? How is it with her?
  Doth not she think me an old murderer,
  Now I have stain'd the childhood of our joy   95
  With blood remov'd but little from her own?
  Where is she? and how doth she? and what says
  My conceal'd lady to our cancell'd love?
Nurse   O, she says nothing, sir, but weeps and weeps;
  And now falls on her bed; and then starts up,   100
  And Tybalt calls; and then on Romeo cries,
  And then down falls again.
Rom.   As if that name,
  Shot from the deadly level of a gun,
  Did murder her, as that name's cursed hand
  Murder'd her kinsman. O, tell me, friar, tell me,   105
  In what vile part of this anatomy

90. O: i.e., groan.   98. conceal'd: secretly married.

Doth my name lodge? Tell me, that I may sack
The hateful mansion.

     [He offers to stab himself, and the Nurse snatches the dagger away.

Fri. L.   Hold thy desperate hand!
Art thou a man? Thy form cries out thou art;
Thy tears are womanish; thy wild acts denote   110
The unreasonable fury of a beast.
Unseemly woman in a seeming man,
And ill-beseeming beast in seeming both,
Thou hast amaz'd me! By my holy order,
I thought thy disposition better temper'd.   115
Hast thou slain Tybalt? Wilt thou slay thyself,
And slay thy lady that in thy life [lives],
By doing damned hate upon thyself?
Why rail'st thou on thy birth, the heaven, and earth?
Since birth, and heaven, and earth, all three do meet   120
In thee at once, which thou at once wouldst lose.
Fie, fie, thou sham'st thy shape, thy love, thy wit;
Which, like a usurer, abound'st in all,
And usest none in that true use indeed
Which should bedeck thy shape, thy love, thy wit.   125
Thy noble shape is but a form of wax,
Digressing from the valour of a man;
Thy dear love sworn but hollow perjury,
Killing that love which thou hast vow'd to cherish;
Thy wit, that ornament to shape and love,   130
Mis-shapen in the conduct of them both,
Like powder in a skilless soldier's flask,
Is set a-fire by thine own ignorance,
And thou dismemb'red with thine own defence.
What, rouse thee, man! thy Juliet is alive,   135
For whose dear sake thou wast but lately dead:
There art thou happy. Tybalt would kill thee,
But thou slewest Tybalt: there art thou happy.
The law that threat'ned death becomes thy friend
And turns it to exile: there art thou happy.   140
A pack of blessings light upon thy back;
Happiness courts thee in her best array;
But, like a misbehav'd and sullen wench,
Thou [pout'st upon] thy fortune and thy love.
Take heed, take heed, for such die miserable.   145

117. [lives] F$_4$.   *lies* Q$_2$.   123. Which: who.   134. defence: weapon.   144.
[pout'st upon] Q$_5$. *puts up* Q$_2$.

Go, get thee to thy love, as was decreed;
Ascend her chamber; hence, and comfort her.
But look thou stay not till the watch be set,
For then thou canst not pass to Mantua,
Where thou shalt live till we can find a time   150
To blaze your marriage, reconcile your friends,
Beg pardon of the Prince, and call thee back
With twenty hundred thousand times more joy
Than thou went'st forth in lamentation.
Go before, nurse; commend me to thy lady;   155
And bid her hasten all the house to bed,
Which heavy sorrow makes them apt unto.
Romeo is coming.
Nurse O Lord, I could have stay'd here all the night
To hear good counsel. O, what learning is!   160
My lord, I'll tell my lady you will come.
Rom. Do so, and bid my sweet prepare to chide.
                              [*Nurse offers to go in, and turns again.*
Nurse Here, sir, a ring she bid me give you, sir.
Hie you, make haste, for it grows very late.
Rom. How well my comfort is reviv'd by this!   [*Exit Nurse.* 165
Fri. L. Go hence; good-night; and here stands all your state:
Either be gone before the watch be set,
Or by the break of day disguis'd from hence.
Sojourn in Mantua; I'll find out your man,
And he shall signify from time to time   170
Every good hap to you that chances here.
Give me thy hand; 'tis late. Farewell; good-night.
Rom. But that a joy past joy calls out on me,
It were a grief, so brief to part with thee.
Farewell.   [*Exeunt.* 175

Scene IV.   [*A room in Capulet's house.*]

(*Enter* CAPULET, LADY CAPULET, *and* PARIS.)

Cap. Things have fallen out, sir, so unluckily
That we have had no time to move our daughter.
Look you, she lov'd her kinsman Tybalt dearly,
And so did I. Well, we were born to die.
'Tis very late, she'll not come down to-night;   5

151. blaze: announce.   166. here ... state: i.e., this is the situation.   174. brief:
hastily.

I promise you, but for your company,
I would have been a-bed an hour ago.
Par. These times of woe afford no times to woo.
Madam, good-night; commend me to your daughter.
La. Cap. I will, and know her mind early tomorrow;   10
To-night she's mewed up to her heaviness.
Cap. Sir Paris, I will make a desperate tender
Of my child's love. I think she will be rul'd
In all respects by me; nay, more, I doubt it not.
Wife, go you to her ere you go to bed;   15
Acquaint her here of my son Paris' love;
And bid her—mark you me?—on Wednesday next—
But, soft! what day is this?
Par.   Monday, my lord.
Cap. Monday! ha, ha! Well, Wednesday is too soon,
O' Thursday let it be,—o' Thursday, tell her,   20
She shall be married to this noble earl.
Will you be ready? Do you like this haste?
We'll keep no great ado,—a friend or two;
For, hark you, Tybalt being slain so late,
It may be thought we held him carelessly,   25
Being our kinsman, if we revel much;
Therefore we'll have some half a dozen friends,
And there an end. But what say you to Thursday?
Par. My lord, I would that Thursday were tomorrow.
Cap. Well, get you gone; o' Thursday be it, then.   30
Go you to Juliet ere you go to bed;
Prepare her, wife, against this wedding-day.
Farewell, my lord. Light to my chamber, ho!
Afore me! it is so very late that we
May call it early by and by. Good-night.   [*Exeunt.*   35

Scene V. [*Capulet's orchard.*]

(*Enter* Romeo *and* Juliet, *aloft.*)

Jul. Wilt thou be gone? it is not yet near day.
It was the nightingale, and not the lark,
That pierc'd the fearful hollow of thine ear;
Nightly she sings on yond pomegranate-tree.
Believe me, love, it was the nightingale.   5

Sc. iv, 11. mewed: shut.   12. desperate tender: bold offer.

WILLIAM SHAKESPEARE

Rom. It was the lark, the herald of the morn,
No nightingale. Look, love, what envious streaks
Do lace the severing clouds in yonder east.
Night's candles are burnt out, and jocund day
Stands tiptoe on the misty mountain tops. 10
I must be gone and live, or stay and die.
Jul. Yond light is not day-light, I know it, I;
It is some meteor that the sun exhales
To be to thee this night a torch-bearer
And light thee on thy way to Mantua; 15
Therefore stay yet; thou need'st not to be gone.
Rom. Let me be ta'en, let me be put to death;
I am content, so thou wilt have it so.
I'll say yon grey is not the morning's eye,
'Tis but the pale reflex of Cynthia's brow; 20
Nor that is not the lark, whose notes do beat
The vaulty heaven so high above our heads.
I have more care to stay than will to go.
Come, death, and welcome! Juliet wills it so.
How is't, my soul? Let's talk; it is not day. 25
Jul. It is, it is. Hie hence, be gone, away!
It is the lark that sings so out of tune,
Straining harsh discords and unpleasing sharps.
Some say the lark makes sweet division;
This doth not so, for she divideth us. 30
Some say the lark and loathed toad change eyes;
O, now I would they had chang'd voices too,
Since arm from arm that voice doth us affray,
Hunting thee hence with hunt's-up to the day.
O, now be gone; more light and light it grows. 35
Rom. More light and light; more dark and dark our woes!

(*Enter* Nurse [*from the chamber*].)

Nurse Madam!
Jul. Nurse?
Nurse Your lady mother is coming to your chamber.
The day is broke; be wary, look about. [*Exit.* 40
Jul. Then, window, let day in, and let life out.
Rom. Farewell, farewell! One kiss, and I'll descend. [*He goeth down.*
Jul. Art thou gone so? Love, lord, ay, husband, friend!
I must hear from thee every day in the hour,

Sc. v, 20. Cynthia's: the moon's.   23. care: desire.   28. sharps: high notes.   29.
division: melody.   34. hunt's-up: a song to waken hunters.

For in a minute there are many days. 45
O, by this count I shall be much in years
Ere I again behold my Romeo!
Rom. [*From below.*]   Farewell!
I will omit no opportunity
That may convey my greetings, love, to thee. 50
Jul.   O, think'st thou we shall ever meet again?
Rom.   I doubt it not; and all these woes shall serve
For sweet discourses in our times to come.
Jul.   O God, I have an ill-divining soul!
Methinks I see thee, now thou art [below], 55
As one dead in the bottom of a tomb.
Either my eyesight fails, or thou look'st pale.
Rom.   And trust me, love, in my eye so do you;
Dry sorrow drinks our blood. Adieu, adieu!
Jul.   O Fortune, Fortune! all men call thee fickle; 60
If thou art fickle, what dost thou with him
That is renown'd for faith? Be fickle, Fortune;
For then, I hope, thou wilt not keep him long,
But send him back.

(*Enter* LADY CAPULET.)

La. Cap.   Ho, daughter! are you up? 65
Jul.   Who is't that calls? It is my lady mother.
Is she not down so late, or up so early?
What unaccustom'd cause procures her hither?
La. Cap.   Why, how now, Juliet?
Jul.   Madam, I am not well.
La Cap.   Evermore weeping for your cousin's death? 70
What, wilt thou wash him from his grave with tears?
An if thou couldst, thou couldst not make him live;
Therefore, have done. Some grief shows much of love,
But much of grief shows still some want of wit.
Jul.   Yet let me weep for such a feeling loss. 75
La. Cap.   So shall you feel the loss, but not the friend
Which you weep for.
Jul.   Feeling so the loss,
I cannot choose but ever weep the friend.
La. Cap.   Well, girl, thou weep'st not so much for his death,
As that the villain lives which slaughter'd him. 80
Jul.   What villain, madam?
La. Cap.   That same villain, Romeo.

54. ill-divining: foreboding evil.   55. [below] Q_1. *so low* Q_2.   59. Dry sorrow.
Sorrow was believed to dry up the blood.   75. feeling: affecting.

Jul. [*Aside.*]   Villain and he be many miles asunder.—
God pardon [him]! I do, with all my heart;
And yet no man like he doth grieve my heart.
La. Cap.   That is, because the traitor murderer lives.   85
Jul.   Ay, madam, from the reach of these my hands.
Would none but I might venge my cousin's death!
La. Cap.   We will have vengeance for it, fear thou not;
Then weep no more. I'll send to one in Mantua,
Where that same banish'd runagate doth live,   90
Shall give him such an unaccustom'd dram
That he shall soon keep Tybalt company;
And then, I hope, thou wilt be satisfied.
Jul.   Indeed, I never shall be satisfied
With Romeo, till I behold him—dead—   95
Is my poor heart, so for a kinsman vex'd.
Madam, if you could find out but a man
To bear a poison, I would temper it
That Romeo should, upon receipt thereof,
Soon sleep in quiet. O, how my heart abhors   100
To hear him nam'd, and cannot come to him
To wreak the love I bore my cousin [Tybalt]
Upon his body that hath slaughter'd him!
La. Cap.   Find thou the means, and I'll find such a man.
But now I'll tell thee joyful tidings, girl.   105
Jul.   And joy comes well in such a needy time.
What are they, [I] beseech your ladyship?
La. Cap.   Well, well, thou hast a careful father, child;
One who, to put thee from thy heaviness,
Hath sorted out a sudden day of joy   110
That thou expects not nor I look'd not for.
Jul.   Madam, in happy time, what day is that?
La. Cap.   Marry, my child, early next Thursday morn
The gallant, young, and noble gentleman,
The County Paris, at Saint Peter's Church,   115
Shall happily make thee there a joyful bride.
Jul.   Now, by Saint Peter's Church and Peter too,
He shall not make me there a joyful bride.
I wonder at this haste that I must wed
Ere he that should be husband comes to woo.   120
I pray you, tell my lord and father, madam,
I will not marry yet; and, when I do, I swear,

83. [him] Q₄. Om. Q₂.   84. like: as much as.   95. dead. Juliet intends this word
to make sense both with what precedes and what follows it.   102. [Tybalt] F₂. Om.
Q₂.   107. [I] Q₄. Om. Q₂.

It shall be Romeo, whom you know I hate,
Rather than Paris. These are news indeed!
La. Cap.   Here comes your father; tell him so yourself,   125
And see how he will take it at your hands.

(*Enter* CAPULET *and* NURSE.)

Cap.   When the sun sets, the [air] doth drizzle dew;
But for the sunset of my brother's son
It rains downright.
How now! a conduit, girl? What, still in tears?   130
Evermore show'ring? In one little body
Thou counterfeits a bark, a sea, a wind:
For still thy eyes, which I may call the sea,
Do ebb and flow with tears; the bark thy body is,
Sailing in this salt flood; the winds, thy sighs,   135
Who, raging with thy tears, and they with them,
Without a sudden calm, will overset
Thy tempest-tossed body. How now, wife!
Have you delivered to her our decree?
La. Cap.   Ay, sir; but she will none, she gives you thanks.   140
I would the fool were married to her grave!
Cap.   Soft! take me with you, take me with you, wife.
How! will she none? Doth she not give us thanks?
Is she not proud? Doth she not count her blest,
Unworthy as she is, that we have wrought   145
So worthy a gentleman to be her bride?
Jul.   Not proud you have; but thankful that you have.
Proud can I never be of what I hate;
But thankful even for hate that is meant love.
Cap.   How how, how how, chop-logic! What is this?   150
"Proud," and "I thank you," and "I thank you not;"
And yet "not proud." Mistress minion, you,
Thank me no thankings, nor proud me no prouds,
But fettle your fine joints 'gainst Thursday next,
To go with Paris to Saint Peter's Church,   155
Or I will drag thee on a hurdle thither.
Out, you green-sickness carrion! Out, you baggage!
You tallow-face!

127. [air] Q₄. *earth* Q₂.   130. conduit: water-pipe.   145. wrought: secured.
146. bride. Used of either man or woman in Shakespeare's day.   150. chop-logic:
sophist.   152. minion: spoiled child.   154. fettle: prepare.   156. hurdle: con-
veyance for criminals.   157. green-sickness: anemia (suggesting Juliet's paleness).

La. Cap.   Fie, fie! what, are you mad?

Jul.   Good father, I beseech you on my knees,

  Hear me with patience but to speak a word.   160

Cap.   Hang thee, young baggage! disobedient wretch!

  I tell thee what: get thee to church o' Thursday,

  Or never after look me in the face.

  Speak not, reply not, do not answer me!

  My fingers itch. Wife, we scarce thought us blest   165

  That God had lent us but this only child;

  But now I see this one is one too much,

  And that we have a curse in having her.

  Out on her, hilding!

Nurse   God in heaven bless her!

  You are to blame, my lord, to rate her so.   170

Cap.   And why, my lady Wisdom? Hold your tongue,

  Good prudence; smatter with your gossips, go.

Nurse   I speak no treason.

[Cap.]   O, God ye god-den.

[Nurse]   May not one speak?

Cap.   Peace, you mumbling fool!

  Utter your gravity o'er a gossip's bowl;   175

  For here we need it not.

La. Cap.   You are too hot.

Cap.   God's bread! it makes me mad.

  Day, night, hour, tide, time, work, play,

  Alone, in company, still my care hath been

  To have her match'd; and having now provided   180

  A gentleman of noble parentage,

  Of fair demesnes, youthful and nobly [train'd],

  Stuff'd, as they say, with honourable parts,

  Proportion'd as one's thought would wish a man;

  And then to have a wretched puling fool,   185

  A whining mammet, in her fortune's tender

  To answer, "I'll not wed; I cannot love,

  I am too young; I pray you, pardon me."

  But, an you will not wed, I'll pardon you.

  Graze where you will, you shall not house with me.   190

  Look to't, think on't, I do not use to jest.

  Thursday is near; lay hand on heart, advise.

---

172. smatter: chatter.   173. [Cap.] Q_4. Given to Nurse in Q_2.   182. demesnes: estates. [train'd] Q_1. *liand* Q_2. *allied* F.   186. mammet: doll. in . . . tender: when good fortune is offered her.   192. advise: consider.

An you be mine, I'll give you to my friend;
An you be not, hang, beg, starve, die in the streets,
For, by my soul, I'll ne'er acknowledge thee,   195
Nor what is mine shall never do thee good.
Trust to't, bethink you; I'll not be forsworn.   [*Exit.*
Jul.   Is there no pity sitting in the clouds,
That sees into the bottom of my grief?
O, sweet my mother, cast me not away!   200
Delay this marriage for a month, a week;
Or, if you do not, make the bridal bed
In that dim monument where Tybalt lies.
La. Cap.   Talk not to me, for I'll not speak a word.
Do as thou wilt, for I have done with thee.   [*Exit.*
Jul.   O God!—O nurse, how shall this be prevented?
My husband is on earth, my faith in heaven;
How shall that faith return again to earth,
Unless that husband send it me from heaven
By leaving earth? Comfort me, counsel me!   210
Alack, alack, that heaven should practise stratagems
Upon so soft a subject as myself!
What say'st thou? Hast thou not a word of joy?
Some comfort, nurse.
Nurse   Faith, here it is.
Romeo is banish'd; and all the world to nothing   215
That he dares ne'er come back to challenge you;
Or, if he do, it needs must be by stealth.
Then, since the case so stands as now it doth,
I think it best you married with the County.
O, he's a lovely gentleman!   220
Romeo's a dishclout to him. An eagle, madam,
Hath not so green, so quick, so fair an eye
As Paris hath. Beshrew my very heart,
I think you are happy in this second match,
For it excels your first; or if it did not,   225
Your first is dead; or 'twere as good he were
As living here and you no use of him.
Jul.   Speak'st thou from thy heart?
Nurse   And from my soul too; else beshrew them both.
Jul.   Amen!   230
Nurse   What?
Jul.   Well, thou hast comforted me marvellous much.
Go in; and tell my lady I am gone,

227. here: i.e., in this world.

Having displeas'd my father, to Laurence' cell,
To make confession and to be absolv'd.   235
Nurse Marry, I will; and this is wisely done.   [*Exit.*]
Jul. Ancient damnation! O most wicked fiend!
Is it more sin to wish me thus forsworn,
Or to dispraise my lord with that same tongue
Which she hath prais'd him with above compare   240
So many thousand times? Go, counsellor;
Thou and my bosom henceforth shall be twain.
I'll to the friar, to know his remedy;
If all else fail, myself have power to die.   [*Exit.*

ACT IV

Scene I. [*Friar Laurence's cell.*]

(*Enter* FRIAR LAURENCE *and* PARIS.)

Fri. L. On Thursday, sir? The time is very short.
Par. My father Capulet will have it so,
And I am nothing slow to slack his haste.
Fri. L. You say you do not know the lady's mind.
Uneven is the course, I like it not.   5
Par. Immoderately she weeps for Tybalt's death,
And therefore have I little [talk'd] of love,
For Venus smiles not in a house of tears.
Now, sir, her father counts it dangerous
That she do give her sorrow so much sway,   10
And in his wisdom hastes our marriage
To stop the inundation of her tears;
Which, too much minded by herself alone,
May be put from her by society.
Now do you know the reason of this haste.   15
Fri. L. [*Aside.*]   I would I knew not why it should be slow'd.
Look, sir, here comes the lady toward my cell.

(*Enter* JULIET.)

Par. Happily met, my lady and my wife!
Jul. That may be, sir, when I may be a wife.
Par. That may be must be, love, on Thursday next.   20

Act IV, sc. i, 5. Uneven: irregular.   7. [talk'd] Q₅. *talke* Q₂.

Jul.   What must be shall be.
Fri. L.   That's a certain text.
Par.   Come you to make confession to this father?
Jul.   To answer that, I should confess to you.
Par.   Do not deny to him that you love me.
Jul.   I will confess to you that I love him.   25
Par.   So will ye, I am sure, that you love me.
Jul.   If I do so, it will be of more price,
  Being spoke behind your back, than to your face.
Par.   Poor soul, thy face is much abus'd with tears.
Jul.   The tears have got small victory by that,   30
  For it was bad enough before their spite.
Par.   Thou wrong'st it, more than tears, with that report.
Jul.   That is no slander, sir, which is a truth;
  And what I spake, I spake it to my face.
Par.   Thy face is mine, and thou hast sland'red it.   35
Jul.   It may be so, for it is not mine own.
  Are you at leisure, holy father, now;
  Or shall I come to you at evening mass?
Fri. L.   My leisure serves me, pensive daughter, now.
  My lord, we must entreat the time alone.   40
Par.   God shield I should disturb devotion!
  Juliet, on Thursday early will I rouse ye;
  Till then, adieu; and keep this holy kiss.   [*Exit.*
Jul.   O, shut the door! and when thou hast done so,
  Come weep with me, past hope, past care, past help!   45
Fri. L.   O Juliet, I already know thy grief;
  It strains me past the compass of my wits.
  I hear thou must, and nothing may prorogue it,
  On Thursday next be married to this County.
Jul.   Tell me not, friar, that thou hear'st of this,   50
  Unless thou tell me how I may prevent it.
  If, in thy wisdom, thou canst give no help,
  Do thou but call my resolution wise,
  And with this knife I'll help it presently.
  God join'd my heart and Romeo's, thou our hands;   55
  And ere this hand, by thee to Romeo's seal'd,
  Shall be the label to another deed,
  Or my true heart with treacherous revolt
  Turn to another, this shall slay them both.
  Therefore, out of thy long-experienc'd time,   60
  Give me some present counsel, or, behold,

---

41. shield: forbid.   45. care Q$_2$. *cure* Q$_1$.   57. label: seal.

'Twixt my extremes and me this bloody knife
Shall play the umpire, arbitrating that
Which the commission of thy years and art
Could to no issue of true honour bring.   65
Be not so long to speak; I long to die
If what thou speak'st speak not of remedy.
Fri. L.   Hold, daughter! I do spy a kind of hope,
Which craves as desperate an execution
As that is desperate which we would prevent.   70
If, rather than to marry County Paris,
Thou hast the strength of will to [slay] thyself,
Then is it likely thou wilt undertake
A thing like death to chide away this shame,
That cop'st with Death himself to scape from it;   75
And, if thou dar'st, I'll give thee remedy.
Jul.   O, bid me leap, rather than marry Paris,
From off the battlements of any tower,
Or walk in thievish ways, or bid me lurk
Where serpents are; chain me with roaring bears,   80
Or hide me nightly in a charnel-house,
O'er-cover'd quite with dead men's rattling bones,
With reeky shanks and yellow chapless skulls;
Or bid me go into a new-made grave
And hide me with a dead man in his [shroud],—   85
Things that, to hear them told, have made me tremble;
And I will do it without fear or doubt,
To live an unstain'd wife to my sweet love.
Fri. L.   Hold, then. Go home, be merry, give consent
To marry Paris. Wednesday is to-morrow.   90
To-morrow night look that thou lie alone;
Let not the nurse lie with thee in thy chamber.
Take thou this vial, being then in bed,
And this [distilled] liquor drink thou off;
When presently through all thy veins shall run   95
A cold and drowsy humour; for no pulse
Shall keep his native progress, but surcease;
No warmth, no [breath] shall testify thou livest;
The roses in thy lips and cheeks shall fade
To [paly] ashes, thy eyes' windows fall,   100

62. extremes: extremities.   64. commission: authority.   72. [slay] Q_1.   *stay* Q_2.
75. cop'st with: wouldest encounter.   79. thievish: full of thieves.   81. hide
Q_2.   *shut* Q_1.   83. reeky: foul smelling. chapless: jawless.   85. [shroud] Q_4.
Om. Q_2.   94. [distilled] Q_1.   *distilling* Q_2.   98. [breath] Q_1.   *breast* Q_2.   100.
[paly] Q_5.   *many* Q_2.

Like death when he shuts up the day of life;
Each part, depriv'd of supple government,
Shall, stiff and stark and cold, appear like death:
And in this borrowed likeness of shrunk death
Thou shalt continue two and forty hours,   105
And then awake as from a pleasant sleep.
Now, when the bridegroom in the morning comes
To rouse thee from thy bed, there art thou dead.
Then, as the manner of our country is,
[In] thy best robes uncovered on the bier   110
Thou shall be borne to that same ancient vault
Where all the kindred of the Capulets lie.
In the mean time, against thou shalt awake,
Shall Romeo by my letters know our drift,
And hither shall he come; and he and I   115
Will watch thy waking, and that very night
Shall Romeo bear thee hence to Mantua.
And this shall free thee from this present shame;
If no inconstant toy, nor womanish fear,
Abate thy valour in the acting it.   120

Jul.   Give me, give me! O, tell not me of fear!

Fri. L.   Hold; get you gone, be strong and prosperous
In this resolve. I'll send a friar with speed
To Mantua, with my letters to thy lord.

Jul.   Love give me strength! and strength shall help afford.   125
Farewell, dear father!   [*Exeunt.*

Scene II.   [*Hall in Capulet's house.*]

(*Enter* CAPULET, LADY CAPULET, NURSE, *and* SERVING-MEN, *two or three.*)

Cap.   So many guests invite as here are writ.   [*Exit 1. Servant.*]
Sirrah, go hire me twenty cunning cooks.

[2.] Serv.   You shall have none ill, sir; for I'll try if they can lick their
fingers.

Cap.   How canst thou try them so?   5

[2.] Serv.   Marry, sir, 'tis an ill cook that cannot lick his own fingers;
therefore he that cannot lick his fingers goes not with me.

Cap.   Go, be gone.   [*Exit 2. Servant.*]
We shall be much unfurnish'd for this time.

110. [In] *Is* Q₂. bier. After l. 110 Qq Ff print a line "Be borne to burial in thy
kindreds grave," probably an unerased alternative for l. 111.   113. against: in preparation for the time when.   119. toy: whim.

What, is my daughter gone to Friar Laurence?   10
Nurse Ay, forsooth.
Cap. Well, he may chance to do some good on her.
A peevish self-will'd harlotry it is.

(*Enter* JULIET.)

Nurse See where she comes from shrift with merry look.
Cap. How now, my headstrong! where have you been gadding?   15
Jul. Where I have learn'd me to repent the sin
Of disobedient opposition
To you and your behests, and am enjoin'd
By holy Laurence to fall prostrate here
And beg your pardon. Pardon, I beseech you!   20
Henceforward I am ever rul'd by you.
Cap. Send for the County; go tell him of this.
I'll have this knot knit up to-morrow morning.
Jul. I met the youthful lord at Laurence' cell
And gave him what becomed love I might,   25
Not stepping o'er the bounds of modesty.
Cap. Why, I am glad on't; this is well; stand up.
This is as 't should be. Let me see the County;
Ay, marry, go, I say, and fetch him hither.
Now, afore God! this reverend holy friar,   30
All our whole city is much bound to him.
Jul. Nurse, will you go with me into my closet
To help me sort such needful ornaments
As you think fit to furnish me to-morrow?
La. Cap. No, not till Thursday; there is time enough.   35
Cap. Go, nurse, go with her; we'll to church to-morrow.
                              [*Exeunt Juliet and Nurse.*

La. Cap. We shall be short in our provision;
'Tis now near night.
Cap.   Tush, I will stir about,
And all things shall be well, I warrant thee, wife;
Go thou to Juliet, help to deck up her.   40
I'll not to bed to-night; let me alone;
I'll play the housewife for this once. What, ho!
They are all forth. Well, I will walk myself
To County Paris, to prepare up him
Against to-morrow. My heart is wondrous light,   45
Since this same wayward girl is so reclaim'd.   [*Exeunt.*

Sc. ii, 13. peevish: refractory. harlotry: wench.   25. becomed: fitting.

Scene III.   [*Juliet's chamber.*]

(*Enter* JULIET *and* NURSE.)

Jul.   Ay, those attires are best; but, gentle nurse,
  I pray thee, leave me to myself to-night;
  For I have need of many orisons
  To move the heavens to smile upon my state,
  Which, well thou know'st, is cross and full of sin.   5

(*Enter* LADY CAPULET.)

La. Cap.   What, are you busy, ho? Need you my help?
Jul.   No, madam; we have cull'd such necessaries
  As are behoveful for our state to-morrow.
  So please you, let me now be left alone,
  And let the nurse this night sit up with you;   10
  For, I am sure, you have your hands full all,
  In this so sudden business.
La. Cap.   Good-night.
  Get thee to bed, and rest; for thou hast need.
                         [*Exeunt* [*Lady Capulet and Nurse*].
Jul.   Farewell! God knows when we shall meet again.
  I have a faint cold fear thrills through my veins,   15
  That almost freezes up the heat of life.
  I'll call them back again to comfort me.
  Nurse!—What should she do here?
  My dismal scene I needs must act alone.
  Come, vial.   20
  What if this mixture do not work at all?
  Shall I be married then to-morrow morning?
  No, no; this shall forbid it. Lie thou there.   [*Laying down her dagger.*]
  What if it be a poison, which the friar
  Subtly hath minist'red to have me dead,   25
  Lest in this marriage he should be dishonour'd
  Because he married me before to Romeo?
  I fear it is; and yet, methinks, it should not,
  For he hath still been tried a holy man.
  How if, when I am laid into the tomb,   30
  I wake before the time that Romeo
  Come to redeem me? There's a fearful point!
  Shall I not then be stifled in the vault,
  To whose foul mouth no healthsome air breathes in,

Sc. iii, 5. cross: perverse.   8. behoveful: needful.   29. still: ever. tried: proved.

And there die strangled ere my Romeo comes?   35
Or, if I live, is it not very like
The horrible conceit of death and night,
Together with the terror of the place,—
As in a vault, an ancient receptacle,
Where, for this many hundred years, the bones   40
Of all my buried ancestors are pack'd;
Where bloody Tybalt, yet but green in earth,
Lies fest'ring in his shroud; where, as they say,
At some hours in the night spirits resort;—
Alack, alack, is it not like that I,   45
So early waking,—what with loathsome smells,
And shrieks like mandrakes' torn out of the earth,
That living mortals, hearing them, run mad;—
O, if I wake, shall I not be distraught,
Environed with all these hideous fears,   50
And madly play with my forefathers' joints,
And pluck the mangled Tybalt from his shroud,
And, in this rage, with some great kinsman's bone
As with a club, dash out my desperate brains?
O, look! methinks I see my cousin's ghost   55
Seeking out Romeo, that did spit his body
Upon a rapier's point. Stay, Tybalt, stay!
Romeo, [I come! This do I] drink to thee.

     [*She falls upon her bed, within the curtains.*

Scene IV. [*Hall in Capulet's house.*]

(*Enter* Lady Capulet *and* Nurse.)

La. Cap. Hold, take these keys and fetch more spices, nurse.
Nurse They call for dates and quinces in the pastry.

(*Enter* Capulet.)

Cap. Come, stir, stir, stir! the second cock hath crow'd,
 The curfew-bell hath rung, 'tis three o'clock.
 Look to the bak'd meats, good Angelica;   5
 Spare not for cost.

---

37. conceit: idea. 47. mandrakes'. The root of the mandrake plant was believed to
utter a shriek when pulled up. 58. [I come! This do I] Q₁. *Romeo, Romeo, heeres
drinke, I* Q₂.
Sc. iv, 2. pastry: pastry-room, pantry. 5. bak'd meats: meat pies.

Nurse   Go, you cot-quean, go,
Get you to bed. Faith, you'll be sick to-morrow
For this night's watching.
Cap.   No, not a whit! What! I have watch'd ere now
All night for lesser cause, and ne'er been sick.   10
La. Cap.   Ay, you have been a mouse-hunt in your time;
But I will watch you from such watching now.

                              [*Exeunt Lady Capulet and Nurse.*

Cap.   A jealous-hood, a jealous-hood!

(*Enter three or four* [SERVING-MEN,] *with spits, logs, and baskets.*)

                              Now, fellow,
What's there?
[1. Serv.]   Things for the cook, sir; but I know not what.   15
Cap.   Make haste, make haste. [*Exit 1. Serv.*] Sirrah, fetch drier logs:
Call Peter, he will show thee where they are.
[2. Serv.]   I have a head, sir, that will find out logs,
And never trouble Peter for the matter.
Cap.   Mass, and well said; a merry whoreson, ha!   20
Thou shalt be logger-head. [*Exit 2. Serv.*] Good [faith], 'tis day.
The County will be here with music straight,
For so he said he would. I hear him near.   [*Music within.*
Nurse! Wife! What, ho! What, nurse, I say!

(*Re-enter* NURSE.)

Go waken Juliet, go and trim her up;   25
I'll go and chat with Paris. Hie, make haste,
Make haste; the bridegroom he is come already.
Make haste, I say.   [*Exeunt.*]

Scene V.   [*Juliet's chamber.*]

(*Enter* NURSE.)

Nurse   Mistress! what, mistress! Juliet!—Fast, I warrant her, she.—
Why, lamb! why, lady! fie, you slug-a-bed!
Why, love! I say, madam! sweetheart! why, bride!
What, not a word? You take your penny-worths now;
Sleep for a week; for the next night, I warrant,   5
The County Paris hath set up his rest

6. cot-quean: man who plays housewife.   11. mouse-hunt: woman-chaser.   13.
jealous-hood: jealous person.   15. [1. Serv.] (Capell). *Fel.* (i.e., Fellow) Q₂.   18.
[2. Serv.] (Capell). *Fel.* Q₂.   21. logger-head: blockhead. [faith] Q₄. *father* Q₂.
Sc. v, 1. Fast: i.e., fast asleep.   6. set … rest: resolved.

That you shall rest but little. God forgive me!
Marry, and amen, how sound is she asleep!
I needs must wake her. Madam, madam, madam!
Ay, let the County take you in your bed;   10
He'll fright you up, i' faith. Will it not be?   [*Draws back the curtains.*]
What, dress'd, and in your clothes! and down again!
I must needs wake you. Lady! lady! lady!
Alas, alas! Help, help! my lady's dead!
O, well-a-day, that ever I was born!   15
Some *aqua vitæ*, ho! My lord! my lady!

(*Enter* LADY CAPULET.)

La. Cap.   What noise is here?
Nurse   O lamentable day!
La. Cap.   What is the matter?
Nurse   Look, look! O heavy day!
La. Cap.   O me, O me! My child, my only life,
Revive, look up, or I will die with thee!   20
Help, help! Call help.

(*Enter* CAPULET.)

Cap.   For shame, bring Juliet forth; her lord is come.
Nurse   She's dead, deceas'd, she's dead; alack the day!
La. Cap.   Alack the day, she's dead, she's dead, she's dead!
Cap.   Ha! let me see her. Out, alas! she's cold;   25
Her blood is settled, and her joints are stiff;
Life and these lips have long been separated.
Death lies on her like an untimely frost
Upon the sweetest flower of all the field.
Nurse   O lamentable day!
La. Cap.   O woeful time!   30
Cap.   Death, that hath ta'en her hence to make me wail,
Ties up my tongue, and will not let me speak.

(*Enter* FRIAR LAURENCE *and* PARIS, *with* MUSICIANS.)

Fri. L.   Come, is the bride ready to go to church?
Cap.   Ready to go, but never to return.—
O son! the night before thy wedding-day   35
Hath Death lain with thy wife. There she lies,
Flower as she was, deflowered by him.
Death is my son-in-law, Death is my heir;
My daughter he hath wedded. I will die

And leave him all; life, living, all is Death's.   40
Par.   Have I thought [long] to see this morning's face,
    And doth it give me such a sight as this?
La. Cap.   Accurs'd, unhappy, wretched, hateful day!
    Most miserable hour that e'er Time saw
    In lasting labour of his pilgrimage!   45
    But one, poor one, one poor and loving child,
    But one thing to rejoice and solace in,
    And cruel Death hath catch'd it from my sight!
Nurse   O woe! O woeful, woeful, woeful day!
    Most lamentable day, most woeful day,   50
    That ever, ever, I did yet behold!
    O day! O day! O day! O hateful day!
    Never was seen so black a day as this.
    O woeful day, O woeful day!
Par.   Beguil'd, divorced, wronged, spited, slain!   55
    Most detestable Death, by thee beguil'd,
    By cruel cruel thee quite overthrown!
    O love! O life! not life, but love in death!
Cap.   Despis'd, distressed, hated, martyr'd, kill'd!
    Uncomfortable time, why cam'st thou now   60
    To murder, murder our solemnity?
    O child! O child! my soul, and not my child!
    Dead art thou! Alack! my child is dead;
    And with my child my joys are buried.
Fri. L.   Peace, ho, for shame! Confusion's [cure] lives not   65
    In these confusions. Heaven and yourself
    Had part in this fair maid; now heaven hath all,
    And all the better is it for the maid.
    Your part in her you could not keep from death,
    But heaven keeps his part in eternal life.   70
    The most you sought was her promotion,
    For 'twas your heaven she should be advanc'd;
    And weep ye now, seeing she is advanc'd
    Above the clouds, as high as heaven itself?
    O, in this love, you love your child so ill   75
    That you run mad, seeing that she is well.
    She's not well married that lives married long;
    But she's best married that dies married young.
    Dry up your tears, and stick your rosemary
    On this fair corse; and, as the custom is,   80

41. thought [long] Q_3: longed. *thought love* Q_2.   65. [cure] (Theobald). *care* Q_2.
79. rosemary: an herb (symbolic of remembrance).

[In all] her best array bear her to church;
For though [fond] nature bids us all lament,
Yet nature's tears are reason's merriment.
Cap.   All things that we ordained festival,
Turn from their office to black funeral;   85
Our instruments to melancholy bells,
Our wedding cheer to a sad burial feast,
Our solemn hymns to sullen dirges change,
Our bridal flowers serve for a buried corse,
And all things change them to the contrary.   90
Fri. L.   Sir, go you in; and, madam, go with him;
And go, Sir Paris; every one prepare
To follow this fair corse unto her grave.
The heavens do lour upon you for some ill;
Move them no more by crossing their high will.   95
                    [*Exeunt* [*Capulet, Lady Capulet, Paris, and Friar*].
[1.] Mus.   Faith, we may put up our pipes and be gone.
Nurse   Honest good fellows, ah, put up, put up; For, well you know, this
is a pitiful case.   [*Exit.*
[1.] Mus.   Ay, by my troth, the case may be amended.

(*Enter* [PETER].)

Pet.   Musicians, O, musicians, "Heart's ease, Heart's ease!" O, an you
will have me live, play "Heart's ease."   101
[1.] Mus.   Why "Heart's ease"?
Pet.   O, musicians, because my heart itself plays "My heart is full [of
woe]." O, play me some merry dump to comfort me.
[1.] Mus.   Not a dump we; 'tis no time to play now.   105
Pet.   You will not, then?
[1.] Mus.   No.
Pet.   I will then give it you soundly.
[1.] Mus.   What will you give us?
Pet.   No money, on my faith, but the gleek; I will give you the minstrel.
[1.] Mus.   Then will I give you the serving-creature.   111
Pet.   Then will I lay the serving-creature's dagger on your pate. I will carry
no crotchets; I'll *re* you, I'll *fa* you. Do you note me?
[1.] Mus.   An you *re* us and *fa* us, you note us.
[2.] Mus.   Pray you, put up your dagger, and put out your wit.   115

81. [In all] Q$_1$. *And in* Q$_2$.   82. [fond] F$_2$. *some* Q$_2$.   100. s.d. [PETER] Q$_4$.
Will Kemp Q$_2$. Kemp, the low comedian in Shakespeare's company, apparently acted
Peter.   103. [of woe] Q$_4$. Om. Q$_2$.   105. dump: mournful tune.   110. gleek:
gibe.   112. carry: endure.   113. crotchets: (1) whims, (2) quarter notes.   115.
put out: exert.

Pet. Then have at you with my wit! I will dry-beat you with an iron wit, and put up my iron dagger. Answer me like men:

"When griping griefs the heart doth wound,
[And doleful dumps the mind oppress,]
Then music with her silver sound"— 120

why "silver sound"? Why "music with her silver sound"? What say you, Simon Catling?

[1.] Mus. Marry, sir, because silver hath a sweet sound.

Pet. [Pretty!] What say you, Hugh Rebeck?

2. Mus. I say, "silver sound," because musicians sound for silver. 125

Pet. [Pretty] too! What say you, James Soundpost?

3. Mus. Faith, I know not what to say.

Pet. O, I cry you mercy; you are the singer; I will say for you. It is "music with her silver sound," because musicians have no gold for sounding:

"Then music with her silver sound 130
With speedy help doth lend redress." [*Exit.*

1. Mus. What a pestilent knave is this same!

2. Mus. Hang him, Jack! Come, we'll in here, tarry for the mourners, and stay dinner. [*Exeunt.*

ACT V

Scene I. [*Mantua. A street.*]

(*Enter* ROMEO.)

Rom. If I may trust the flattering truth of sleep,
My dreams presage some joyful news at hand.
My bosom's lord sits lightly in his throne,
And all this day an unaccustom'd spirit
Lifts me above the ground with cheerful thoughts. 5
I dreamt my lady came and found me dead—
Strange dream, that gives a dead man leave to think!—
And breath'd such life with kisses in my lips
That I reviv'd and was an emperor.
Ah me! how sweet is love itself possess'd, 10
When but love's shadows are so rich in joy!

---

116. Then . . . wit. So Q_4. Cont. to 2. *Mus.* in Q_2. 119. [And . . . oppress] Q_1.
Om. Q_2. 124, 126. [Pretty] (Pope). *Prates* Q_2. 128. singer. Peter's joke is that
as a singer the musician can only *sing*, not *say.*
Act V, sc. i, 3. bosom's lord: heart.

(*Enter* BALTHASAR, *his man, booted.*)

   News from Verona!—How now, Balthasar!
   Dost thou not bring me letters from the friar?
   How doth my lady? Is my father well?
   How [fares my] Juliet? that I ask again;   15
   For nothing can be ill, if she be well.
Bal.   Then she is well, and nothing can be ill.
   Her body sleeps in Capel's monument,
   And her immortal part with angels lives.
   I saw her laid low in her kindred's vault,   20
   And presently took post to tell it you.
   O, pardon me for bringing these ill news,
   Since you did leave it for my office, sir.
Rom.   Is it [even] so? Then I [defy] you, stars!
   Thou know'st my lodging; get me ink and paper   25
   And hire post-horses; I will hence to-night.
Bal.   I do beseech you, sir, have patience.
   Your looks are pale and wild, and do import
   Some misadventure.
Rom.   Tush, thou art deceiv'd:
   Leave me, and do the thing I bid thee do.   30
   Hast thou no letters to me from the friar?
Bal.   No, my good lord.
Rom.   No matter; get thee gone
   And hire those horses; I'll be with thee straight.   [*Exit Balthasar.*
   Well, Juliet, I will lie with thee to-night.
   Let's see for means. O mischief, thou art swift   35
   To enter in the thoughts of desperate men!
   I do remember an apothecary,—
   And hereabouts 'a dwells,—which late I noted
   In tatt'red weeds, with overwhelming brows,
   Culling of simples; meagre were his looks,   40
   Sharp misery had worn him to the bones;
   And in his needy shop a tortoise hung,
   An alligator stuff'd, and other skins
   Of ill-shap'd fishes; and about his shelves
   A beggarly account of empty boxes,   45
   Green earthen pots, bladders and musty seeds,
   Remnants of packthread and old cakes of roses
   Were thinly scattered, to make up a show.

---

15. [fares my] Q_1. *doth my Lady* Q_2.   24. [even] F. *in* Q_2. [defy] Q_1. *denie* Q_2.
40. simples: medicinal herbs.

Noting this penury, to myself I said,
"An if a man did need a poison now,   50
Whose sale is present death in Mantua,
Here lives a caitiff wretch would sell it him."
O, this same thought did but forerun my need;
And this same needy man must sell it me.
As I remember, this should be the house.   55
Being holiday, the beggar's shop is shut.
What, ho! apothecary!

(*Enter* APOTHECARY.)

Ap.   Who calls so loud?
Rom.   Come hither, man. I see that thou art poor.
  Hold, there is forty ducats. Let me have
  A dram of poison, such soon-speeding gear   60
  As will disperse itself through all the veins
  That the life-weary taker may fall dead,
  And that the trunk may be discharg'd of breath
  As violently as hasty powder fir'd
  Doth hurry from the fatal cannon's womb.   65
Ap.   Such mortal drugs I have; but Mantua's law
  Is death to any he that utters them.
Rom.   Art thou so bare and full of wretchedness,
  And fear'st to die? Famine is in thy cheeks,
  Need and oppression starveth in thy eyes,   70
  Contempt and beggary hangs upon thy back;
  The world is not thy friend nor the world's law;
  The world affords no law to make thee rich;
  Then be not poor, but break it, and take this.
Ap.   My poverty, but not my will, consents.   75
Rom.   I [pay] thy poverty, and not thy will.
Ap.   Put this in any liquid thing you will,
  And drink it off; and, if you had the strength
  Of twenty men, it would dispatch you straight.
Rom.   There is thy gold, worse poison to men's souls,   80
  Doing more murder in this loathsome world,
  Than these poor compounds that thou mayst not sell.
  I sell thee poison; thou hast sold me none.
  Farewell! Buy food, and get thyself in flesh.

63. trunk: body.   67. utters: sells.   76. [pay] Q_1. *pray* Q_2.

Come, cordial and not poison, go with me   85
To Juliet's grave; for there must I use thee.   [*Exeunt.*

Scene II.   [*Verona. Friar Laurence's cell.*]

(*Enter* FRIAR JOHN.)

Fri. J.   Holy Franciscan friar! brother, ho!

(*Enter* FRIAR LAURENCE.)

Fri. L.   This same should be the voice of Friar John.
Welcome from Mantua! What says Romeo?
Or, if his mind be writ, give me his letter.
Fri. J.   Going to find a bare-foot brother out,   5
One of our order, to associate me,
Here in this city visiting the sick,
And finding him, the searchers of the town,
Suspecting that we both were in a house
Where the infectious pestilence did reign,   10
Seal'd up the doors and would not let us forth,
So that my speed to Mantua there was stay'd.
Fri. L.   Who bare my letter, then, to Romeo?
Fri. J.   I could not send it,—here it is again,—
Nor get a messenger to bring it thee,   15
So fearful were they of infection.
Fri. L.   Unhappy fortune! By my brotherhood,
The letter was not nice but full of charge
Of dear import, and the neglecting it
May do much danger. Friar John, go hence;   20
Get me an iron crow, and bring it straight
Unto my cell.
Fri. J.   Brother, I'll go and bring it thee.   [*Exit.*
Fri. L.   Now must I to the monument alone;
Within this three hours will fair Juliet wake.   25
She will beshrew me much that Romeo
Hath had not notice of these accidents;
But I will write again to Mantua.
And keep her at my cell till Romeo come;
Poor living corse, clos'd in a dead man's tomb!   [*Exit.*   30

85. cordial: restorative.
Sc. ii, 8. searchers: i.e., health officers.   18. nice: trivial.   charge: importance.   21.
crow: crowbar.   26. beshrew: censure.

Scene III. [*A churchyard; in it a tomb belonging to the Capulets.*]

(*Enter* PARIS, *and his* PAGE *with flowers and sweet water* [*and a torch*].)

Par. Give me thy torch, boy. Hence, and stand aloof.
    Yet put it out, for I would not be seen.
    Under yond [yew-tree] lay thee all along,
    Holding [thine] ear close to the hollow ground;
    So shall no foot upon the churchyard tread,   5
    Being loose, unfirm, with digging up of graves,
    But thou shalt hear it. Whistle then to me,
    As signal that thou hear'st something approach.
    Give me those flowers. Do as I bid thee, go.
Page [*Aside.*]   I am almost afraid to stand alone   10
    Here in the churchyard; yet I will adventure.   [*Retires.*]
Par.   Sweet flower, with flowers thy bridal bed I strew,—
    O woe! thy canopy is dust and stones—
    Which with sweet water nightly I will dew,
    Or, wanting that, with tears distill'd by moans.   15
    The obsequies that I for thee will keep
    Nightly shall be to strew thy grave and weep.   [*The Page whistles.*
    The boy gives warning something doth approach.
    What cursed foot wanders this way to-night,
    To cross my obsequies and true love's rite?   20
    What, with a torch! Muffle me, night, a while.   [*Retires.*]

(*Enter* ROMEO *and* [BALTHASAR], *with a torch, a mattock, and a crow of iron.*)

Rom.   Give me that mattock and the wrenching iron.
    Hold, take this letter; early in the morning
    See thou deliver it to my lord and father.
    Give me the light. Upon thy life I charge thee,   25
    Whate'er thou hear'st or seest, stand all aloof,
    And do not interrupt me in my course.
    Why I descend into this bed of death
    Is partly to behold my lady's face,
    But chiefly to take thence from her dead finger   30
    A precious ring, a ring that I must use
    In dear employment; therefore hence, be gone.
    But if thou, jealous, dost return to pry
    In what I farther shall intend to do,
    By heaven, I will tear thee joint by joint   35

Sc. iii, 3. [yew-tree] Q_1. *young trees* Q_2. all along: prone.   4. [thine] Q_1. *thy* Q_2.
14. sweet: perfumed.   22. s.d. [BALTHASAR] Q_1. *Peter* Q_2.   33. jealous: suspicious.

And strew this hungry churchyard with thy limbs.
The time and my intents are savage-wild,
More fierce and more inexorable far
Than empty tigers or the roaring sea.
[**Bal.**]   I will be gone, sir, and not trouble ye.   40
Rom.   So shalt thou show me friendship. Take thou that;
Live, and be prosperous; and farewell, good fellow.
[**Bal.**] [*Aside.*]   For all this same, I'll hide me hereabout.
His looks I fear, and his intents I doubt.   [*Retires.*]
Rom.   Thou detestable maw, thou womb of death,   45
Gorg'd with the dearest morsel of the earth,
Thus I enforce thy rotten jaws to open,
And, in despite, I'll cram thee with more food!   [*Opens the tomb.*]
Par.   This is that banish'd haughty Montague,
That murd'red my love's cousin, with which grief,   50
It is supposed, the fair creature died;
And here is come to do some villainous shame
To the dead bodies. I will apprehend him.   [*Comes forward.*]
Stop thy unhallowed toil, vile Montague!
Can vengeance be pursued further than death?   55
Condemned villain, I do apprehend thee.
Obey, and go with me; for thou must die.
Rom.   I must indeed; and therefore came I hither.
Good gentle youth, tempt not a desperate man.
Fly hence, and leave me; think upon these gone,   60
Let them affright thee. I beseech thee, youth,
Put not another sin upon my head,
By urging me to fury: O, be gone!
By heaven, I love thee better than myself;
For I come hither arm'd against myself.   65
Stay not, be gone; live, and hereafter say
A madman's mercy bid thee run away.
Par.   I do defy thy [conjurations]
And apprehend thee for a felon here.
Rom.   Wilt thou provoke me? Then have at thee, boy!   [*They fight.*
[**Page**]   O Lord, they fight! I will go call the watch.   [*Exit.*]
Par.   O, I am slain! [*Falls.*] If thou be merciful,
Open the tomb, lay me with Juliet.   [*Dies.*]
Rom.   In faith, I will. Let me peruse this face.
Mercutio's kinsman, noble County Paris!   75
What said my man, when my betossed soul

40, 43. [Bal.] Q₄.   *Pet.* Q₂.   68. [conjurations] Q₁.   *commiration* Q₂.   71. [Page.]
Q₄.   Om. Q₂.   *Pet.* F.

Did not attend him as we rode? I think
He told me Paris should have married Juliet.
Said he not so? Or did I dream it so?
Or am I mad, hearing him talk of Juliet,   80
To think it was so? O, give me thy hand,
One writ with me in sour misfortune's book!
I'll bury thee in a triumphant grave.
A grave? O, no! a lantern, slaught'red youth,
For here lies Juliet, and her beauty makes   85
This vault a feasting presence full of light.
Death, lie thou there, by a dead man interr'd.   [*Laying Paris in the tomb.*]
How oft when men are at the point of death
Have they been merry! which their keepers call
A lightning before death. O, how may I   90
Call this a lightning? O my love! my wife!
Death, that hath suck'd the honey of thy breath,
Hath had no power yet upon thy beauty.
Thou art not conquer'd; beauty's ensign yet
Is crimson in thy lips and in thy cheeks,   95
And death's pale flag is not advanced there.
Tybalt, li'st thou there in thy bloody sheet?
O, what more favour can I do to thee,
Than with that hand that cut thy youth in twain
To sunder his that was thine enemy?   100
Forgive me, cousin! Ah, dear Juliet,
Why art thou yet so fair? Shall I believe
That unsubstantial Death is amorous,
And that the lean abhorred monster keeps
Thee here in dark to be his paramour?   105
For fear of that, I still will stay with thee,
And never from this [palace] of dim night
Depart again. Here, here will I remain
With worms that are thy chamber-maids; O, here
Will I set up my everlasting rest,   110
And shake the yoke of inauspicious stars
From this world-wearied flesh. Eyes, look your last!
Arms, take your last embrace! and, lips, O you
The doors of breath, seal with a righteous kiss
A dateless bargain to engrossing death!   115
Come, bitter conduct, come, unsavoury guide!

86. presence: presence-chamber.   89. keepers: nurses.   107. [palace] Q₁. *pallat*
Q₂. After this line, and before l. 108, Q₂ and F insert: "Depart againe, come lye thou
in my arme,/Heer's to thy health, where ere thou tumblest in./O true Appothecarie!/
Thy drugs are quicke. Thus with a kisse I die."   115. dateless: eternal.   engrossing:
monopolizing.

Thou desperate pilot, now at once run on
The dashing rocks thy sea-sick weary bark!
Here's to my love! [*Drinks.*] O true apothecary!
Thy drugs are quick. Thus with a kiss I die.   [*Dies.*]   120

(*Enter* FRIAR LAURENCE, *with lantern, crow, and spade.*)

Fri. L.   Saint Francis be my speed! how oft to-night
  Have my old feet stumbled at graves! Who's there?
Bal.   Here's one, a friend, and one that knows you well.
Fri. L.   Bliss be upon you! Tell me, good my friend,
  What torch is yond, that vainly lends his light   125
  To grubs and eyeless skulls? As I discern,
  It burneth in the Capels' monument.
Bal.   It doth so, holy sir; and there's my master,
  One that you love.
Fri. L.   Who is it?
Bal.   Romeo.
Fri. L.   How long hath he been there?
Bal.   Full half an hour.   130
Fri. L.   Go with me to the vault.
Bal.   I dare not, sir.
  My master knows not but I am gone hence;
  And fearfully did menace me with death
  If I did stay to look on his intents.
Fri. L.   Stay, then; I'll go alone. Fear comes upon me: 135
  O, much I fear some ill unthrifty thing.
Bal.   As I did sleep under this [yew]-tree here,
  I dreamt my master and another fought,
  And that my master slew him.
Fri. L.   Romeo!   [*Advances.*]
  Alack, alack, what blood is this, which stains   140
  The stony entrance of this sepulchre?
  What mean these masterless and gory swords
  To lie discolour'd by this place of peace?   [*Enters the tomb.*]
  Romeo! O, pale! Who else? What, Paris too?
  And steep'd in blood? Ah, what an unkind hour   145
  Is guilty of this lamentable chance!
  The lady stirs.   [*Juliet rises.*
Jul.   O comfortable friar! where is my lord?
  I do remember well where I should be,
  And there I am. Where is my Romeo?   [*Noise within.*]   150

---

136. unthrifty: unlucky (which F reads).   137. [yew] (Pope). *yong* Q₂.   148. comfortable: comforting.

Fri. L. I hear some noise. Lady, come from that nest
Of death, contagion, and unnatural sleep,
A greater power than we can contradict
Hath thwarted our intents. Come, come away.
Thy husband in thy bosom there lies dead;   155
And Paris too. Come, I'll dispose of thee
Among a sisterhood of holy nuns.
Stay not to question, for the watch is coming;
Come, go, good Juliet [*Noise again*], I dare no longer stay.

               [*Exit Fri. Lau.*

Jul. Go, get thee hence, for I will not away.   160
What's here? A cup, clos'd in my true love's hand?
Poison, I see, hath been his timeless end.
O churl! drunk all, and left no friendly drop
To help me after? I will kiss thy lips;
Haply some poison yet doth hang on them,   165
To make me die with a restorative.
Thy lips are warm.

(*Enter* WATCH, *with the* PAGE *of Paris*.)

[1.] Watch. Lead, boy; which way?
Jul. Yea, noise? Then I'll be brief. O happy dagger!

           [*Snatching Romeo's dagger.*]
This is thy sheath (*Stabs herself*); there rust, and let me die.   170
        [*Falls [on Romeo's body, and dies*].
[Page] This is the place; there, where the torch doth burn.
[1.] Watch. The ground is bloody; search about the churchyard.
Go, some of you, whoe'er you find attach.   [*Exeunt some.*]
Pitiful sight! here lies the County slain;
And Juliet bleeding, warm, and newly dead,   175
Who here hath lain this two days buried.
Go, tell the Prince; run to the Capulets;
Raise up the Montagues; some others search.   [*Exeunt others.*]
We see the ground whereon these woes do lie;
But the true ground of all these piteous woes   180
We cannot without circumstance descry.

(*Re-enter [some of the* WATCH, *with*] BALTHASAR.)

[2.] Watch. Here's Romeo's man; we found him in the churchyard.
[1.] Watch. Hold him in safety till the Prince come hither.

---

162. timeless: untimely. 168. [1.] *Watch.* For the speeches of the 1st Watch, the
headings of Q₂ are *Watch* or *Chief Watch;* for those of the 2d Watch and 3d Watch,
Watch. 171. [Page] (Capell). *Watch boy* Q₂. 173. attach: arrest.

(*Re-enter another* WATCHMAN, *with* FRIAR LAURENCE.)

[3.] Watch.   Here is a friar, that trembles, sighs, and weeps.
We took this mattock and this spade from him,   185
As he was coming from this churchyard's side.
[1.] Watch.   A great suspicion. Stay the friar too.

(*Enter the* PRINCE [*and* Attendants].)

Prince   What misadventure is so early up,
That calls our person from our morning rest?

(*Enter* CAPULET, LADY CAPULET, *and others.*)

Cap.   What should it be, that [they] so shriek abroad?   190
La. Cap.   Oh! the people in the street cry Romeo,
Some Juliet, and some Paris; and all run,
With open outcry, toward our monument.
Prince   What fear is this which startles in [our] ears?
[1.] Watch.   Sovereign, here lies the County Paris slain;   195
And Romeo dead; and Juliet, dead before,
Warm and new kill'd.
Prince   Search, seek, and know how this foul murder comes.
[1.] Watch.   Here is a friar, and slaughter'd Romeo's man,
With instruments upon them, fit to open   200
These dead men's tombs.
Cap.   O heavens! O wife, look how our daughter bleeds!
This dagger hath mista'en,—for, lo, his house
Is empty on the back of Montague,—
And it mis-sheathed in my daughter's bosom!   205
La. Cap.   O me! this sight of death is as a bell,
That warns my old age to a sepulchre.

(*Enter* MONTAGUE [*and others*].)

Prince   Come, Montague; for thou art early up
To see thy son and heir [more early] down.
Mon.   Alas, my liege, my wife is dead to-night;   210
Grief of my son's exile hath stopp'd her breath.
What further woe conspires against mine age?
Prince   Look, and thou shalt see.
Mon.   O thou untaught! what manners is in this,
To press before thy father to a grave?   215
Prince   Seal up the mouth of outrage for a while,
Till we can clear these ambiguities,

190. [they] F. *is* Q$_2$.   194. [our] (Johnson conj.). *your* Q$_2$.   203. house: scabbard.   209. [more early] Q$_1$. *now earling* Q$_2$.   216. outrage: outcry.

And know their spring, their head, their true descent;
And then will I be general of your woes
And lead you even to death. Meantime forbear,   220
And let mischance be slave to patience.
Bring forth the parties of suspicion.
Fri. L.   I am the greatest, able to do least,
Yet most suspected, as the time and place
Doth make against me, of this direful murder;   225
And here I stand, both to impeach and purge
Myself condemned and myself excus'd.
Prince   Then say at once what thou dost know in this.
Fri. L.   I will be brief, for my short date of breath
Is not so long as is a tedious tale.   230
Romeo, there dead, was husband to that Juliet;
And she, there dead, [that] Romeo's faithful wife.
I married them; and their stol'n marriage-day
Was Tybalt's dooms-day, whose untimely death
Banish'd the new-made bridegroom from this city,   235
For whom, and not for Tybalt, Juliet pin'd.
You, to remove that siege of grief from her,
Betroth'd and would have married her perforce
To County Paris. Then comes she to me,
And, with wild looks, bid me devise some mean   240
To rid her from this second marriage,
Or in my cell there would she kill herself.
Then gave I her, so tutor'd by my art,
A sleeping potion; which so took effect
As I intended, for it wrought on her   245
The form of death. Meantime I writ to Romeo,
That he should hither come as this dire night.
To help to take her from her borrowed grave,
Being the time the potion's force should cease.
But he which bore my letter, Friar John,   250
Was stay'd by accident, and yesternight
Return'd my letter back. Then all alone
At the prefixed hour of her waking,
Came I to take her from her kindred's vault;
Meaning to keep her closely at my cell,   255
Till I conveniently could send to Romeo;
But when I came, some minutes ere the time
Of her awak'ning, here untimely lay
The noble Paris and true Romeo dead.

232. [that] Q₄.   *thats* Q₂.   247. as this: this very.   255. closely: secretly.

She wakes; and I entreated her come forth   260
And bear this work of heaven with patience.
But then a noise did scare me from the tomb;
And she, too desperate, would not go with me,
But, as it seems, did violence on herself.
All this I know; and to the marriage   265
Her nurse is privy; and, if aught in this
Miscarried by my fault, let my old life
Be sacrific'd, some hour before his time,
Unto the rigour of severest law.
Prince We still have known thee for a holy man.   270
   Where's Romeo's man? What can he say to this?
Bal. I brought my master news of Juliet's death;
   And then in post he came from Mantua
   To this same place, to this same monument.
   This letter he early bid me give his father,   275
   And threat'ned me with death, going in the vault,
   If I departed not and left him there.
Prince Give me the letter; I will look on it.
   Where is the County's page, that rais'd the watch?
   Sirrah, what made your master in this place?   280
Page He came with flowers to strew his lady's grave;
   And bid me stand aloof, and so I did.
   Anon comes one with light to ope the tomb,
   And by and by my master drew on him;
   And then I ran away to call the watch.   285
Prince This letter doth make good the friar's words,
   Their course of love, the tidings of her death.
   And here he writes that he did buy a poison
   Of a poor 'pothecary, and therewithal
   Came to this vault to die, and lie with Juliet.   290
   Where be these enemies? Capulet! Montague!
   See, what a scourge is laid upon your hate,
   That Heaven finds means to kill your joys with love.
   And I for winking at your discords too
   Have lost a brace of kinsmen. All are punish'd.   295
Cap. O brother Montague, give me thy hand.
   This is my daughter's jointure, for no more
   Can I demand.
Mon.   But I can give thee more;
   For I will raise her statue in pure gold;
   That whiles Verona by that name is known,   300

297. jointure: marriage portion.

There shall no figure at such rate be set
As that of true and faithful Juliet.
Cap.   As rich shall Romeo's by his lady's lie,
Poor sacrifices of our enmity!
Prince   A glooming peace this morning with it brings;   305
    The sun, for sorrow, will not show his head.
Go hence, to have more talk of these sad things;
    Some shall be pardon'd, and some punished:
For never was a story of more woe
Than this of Juliet and her Romeo.   [*Exeunt.*   310

301. rate: value.

WRITING ABOUT THE WHOLE WORK

In previous chapters you have approached your critical essay by focusing on one element—character, conflict, setting, or language. By carefully studying the use of that element in the work, you arrived at a statement of meaning. In this assignment you are given two options for writing, both focusing on an examination of all four elements as they contribute to meaning. The first of these is a critical essay; the second is a set of director's notes, an option presented in Chapter I and here expanded to include the literary elements in addition to character. These options are explained in the guidelines that follow.

Option I: The Critical Essay

In writing about the whole work, you may wish to examine one character, the conflicts he or she experiences, and the importance of setting and special language as they relate to that character. From such an examination you will arrive at a partial statement of the meaning of the work. On the other hand, you may wish to begin your analysis by identifying a theme in the work; examining how one of the characters, in conjunction with the other elements of the work, is related to that theme; and moving finally to a theme statement. A *theme* is a word or phrase that expresses the topic or one of the topics of a work. For example, women's rights, grief, and young love are all common themes in literature. A *theme statement* is a statement of meaning: it expresses what the work seems to say about the theme. Some men believe women give up their rights when they marry ("My Last Duchess"); overcoming grief may depend on an act of nature ("Memorial Rain"); young love sometimes ends in tragedy (*Romeo and Juliet*). A long and complex work (and sometimes even a short one) can have a number of themes, any of which may be developed through one or more characters. The guidelines that follow are designed to assist you in writing a critical essay on theme in *Romeo and Juliet* as it is revealed through a single character. A similar procedure may be used to examine theme in regard to two or more related characters (the two fathers, for instance). Of course, the process of discovering and writing about theme through a focus on character(s) may be applied to any other work you may study.

1. Identify a theme in the work that seems to you to be one of its major concerns.
2. From among the characters who are in some way related to this theme, choose one and write a statement that expresses the relationship.

3. Go through the work, underlining (perhaps using different colored markers for each element) the evidence to support your theme statement: character traits, conflicts, setting, and language that emphasize that character's relation to the theme.

4. Make a list of quotations that support your theme statement. As you do so, note the relevant act, scene, and line numbers, and be sure that you quote accurately. Add to your list any other information you think you might need, such as location of the scene or who is being spoken to, as well as additional quotations you may find useful in your introduction or conclusion.

5. Group your information and quotations according to the elements they illustrate. Those pertaining to character traits belong in one group, conflict in another group, and so forth.

6. Revise your theme statement as necessary and write a main-idea sentence that includes the theme statement and indicates the structure of your paper.

7. Write an introduction that includes, as always, the title of the work, the author, and your main-idea sentence.

8. Expand your list of quotations and information and incorporate them into your own discussion to compose the body of your paper. You will probably want to organize the body into four sections, one for each of the four elements you will be discussing. Use transitional sentences to link all paragraphs.

9. Write the conclusion. Since the paper will be quite long (it should be six to ten pages in length), a brief summation of your major points will be helpful to your reader. You may also wish to generalize from the particular character you have discussed to other characters in the work and to explore further the implications of the theme statement.

10. Go over your first draft carefully, rewriting as needed. Check all quotes and references to the work to make sure that they are accurate. If possible, put the work aside for a few days, so that you can become more objective about its style and content. Then rewrite as necessary.

11. Decide on a title for your essay and make a clean copy for submission to your instructor.

OPTION I: SAMPLE ESSAY

The Fiery Passion

In *Romeo and Juliet,* Shakespeare follows the course of two young people who fall in love despite the enmity between their families. They are ruled by their hearts, not their minds, and to some extent become victims of their unreasoning passion for one another. The trait of surrendering to passion is shared by many characters in the play; however, the one who seems to illustrate this tendency to the greatest degree is Tybalt, Juliet's cousin. Although he appears only in the first half of the drama, he is central to the action and in some ways precipitates the final catastrophe. Through Tybalt's character, his conflicts, and the setting and language that relate to him, Shakespeare reveals that giving passion full control can be not only devastating but even fatal.

Tybalt appears in only three scenes, but he makes a lasting impression on the reader and profoundly influences the course of this drama. Part of his impact is due to his singleness of purpose as it relates to his principal trait. Tybalt is described as "fiery" (I, i, 95), and indeed his character is like a comet that flames into life, startles the beholder, and dominates the heavens until it burns itself out. In the opening scene, after encountering Benvolio's attempt to break up a fight between Montague's and Capulet's servants, Tybalt does not even pause to assess the situation and learn what really is happening. Rather, he immediately challenges Benvolio to fight: "Turn thee, Benvolio, look upon thy death" (I, i, 53). When Benvolio protests, explaining his sword is drawn to keep the peace, not break it, Tybalt calls him a liar and a coward (I, i, 58). Although the arrival of the Prince stops the fight, his warning that their "lives shall pay the forfeit" (I, i, 83) for another street fight fails to cool Tybalt's need for battle. He is again ready to fight when he discovers Romeo at Capulet's party that same evening: "Fetch me my rapier, boy," he orders as he recognizes the masked Romeo, "cover'd with an antic face" (I, v, 52–53), like the others at the ball. Only the quick and decisive interference of Capulet prevents bloodshed, but Tybalt does not for one moment relinquish his desire for vengeance. Instead, he sends a challenge to Romeo and spends the next morning looking through the streets of Verona for his enemy. This desire for vengeance is so strong that he ignores laws of hospitality. He does not act according to his reputation for civilized behavior: Mercutio has described him as a "courageous captain of compliments . . . a gentleman of the very first house" (II, iv, 17–21). All considerations of law, custom, or public opinion are thrust aside as he rushes headlong to his own doom in the climax of the play.

The climax itself not only resolves Tybalt's conflicts but arises from them. All of his conflicts are external; they are altercations, both verbal and physical. At no point in the play does Tybalt reveal any internal struggle: his lust for violence dominates him throughout the action. The sword fights discussed above illustrate his tendency to fight rather than think. He is also prone to argue, as he does in the scene with Capulet during the party. Capulet orders Tybalt to let Romeo alone " 'A bears him like a portly gentleman" (I, v, 62–63), and reminds his nephew that it is not appropriate to scowl at a feast. Tybalt's quick retort is, "It fits, when such a villain is a guest. / I'll not endure him" (I, v, 72–73). The argument between them goes on for thirty-four lines until Tybalt finally yields for the moment to his uncle's authority. Most of the time, however, he couples words and blows, and for him any dispute is best settled by taking out his sword and putting a stop to talk with his rapier's point. For most of the people in the play, the feud is an unfortunate fact of life. For Tybalt, the feud seems heaven-sent, for it offers him a series of opportunities to indulge his delight in personal combat. He hates even the word *peace,* and his view of life seems limited to a never ending quest for quarrels. He lives by the sword, and true to the axiom, he dies the same way.

Tybalt's character and conflicts relate directly to setting. He lives in an age when mastery of the sword is expected of young gentlemen and challenging a foe to duel to the death is a common way to resolve a grievance. Street fights, however, are not. Moreover, the Prince has clearly stated that he will tolerate no more fighting in the city streets. When Tybalt challenges Romeo, Benvolio warns him that both the time and place are inappropriate: "here all eyes gaze on us" (III, i, 42). Romeo too declares it an outrage, "bandying in Verona streets" (III, i, 76), and refuses to fight. However, Mercutio's death draws Romeo into the conflict and causes other citizens to take the law into their own hands: "Which way ran he that kill'd Mercutio? / Tybalt, that murderer, which way ran he?" (III, i, 122–123). Only the arrival of the Prince restores order. The use of setting to emphasize Tybalt's failure to use reason can also be seen at Capulet's party since the place is inappropriate for Tybalt's attempted assault on Romeo.

Various uses of time illustrate Tybalt's hotheadedness in other ways. For example, Tybalt lives only two of the five days of the play. As time seems to speed by, he speeds forward toward his fatal encounter with Romeo. What the Chorus says in the Prologue to Act II, in reference to Romeo and Juliet, is equally true for Tybalt in his pursuit of Romeo: "passion lends them power, time means, to meet" (13). Another important factor of setting is the time of year; the month is July, when the "mad blood [is] stirring" (III, i, 4). The "hot days" are like the hot passions that dominate Tybalt and other characters. Thus various aspects of place and time contribute in several important ways to the theme of the play as it is developed through Tybalt.

Tybalt's character and conflicts are also made explicit in figurative language relating to him. We have already noted Benvolio's description of Tybalt's nature as "fiery." When the Prince upbraids both Benvolio and Tybalt for fighting, he charges that they "quench the fire of . . . pernicious rage" by drawing blood from one another (I, i, 70). Knowing Benvolio's moderate temperament, the reader recognizes that the charge is unfair to him but is an apt description of Tybalt, the instigator of the brawl, who has already revealed his hot temper and what feeds it: "I hate hell, all Montagues, and thee [Benvolio]" (I, i, 57). His stalking through the streets searching for his prey relates to a second metaphor associated with him, that of a domestic animal, particularly a cat. Mercutio calls him "king of cats" emphasizing his feline behavior: capricious, aloof, relentless, and deadly, waiting for the crucial moment, and then pouncing on his prey. Despite the uproar he creates with Mercutio's death, despite the danger to himself, Tybalt returns to the scene for the kill that is his obsession, appropriate to the "rat-catcher" he is called. As Mercutio lies dying from his wounds, he extends his comparison of Tybalt to include a menagerie: "Zounds, a dog, a rat, a mouse, a cat, to scratch a man to death!" (III, i, 86–87). The metaphors suggest that while Tybalt is trained to live peaceably with people, his civility is only a veneer covering the wild animal inside. The comparison not only provides an illustration of metaphor but also of irony: the discrepancy between what seems to be true (education and socialization alter basic instincts) and what is, in fact, true (they do not). This use of irony is only one of many in relation to Tybalt, for irony is the most pervasive use of language in connection with him.

For example, following the fight with Benvolio, the Prince warns, "If ever you disturb our streets again / Your lives shall pay the forfeit for the peace" (I, i, 82–83). He means, of course, that his sentence for the crime will be death, and reasonable persons would obey and behave so as to avoid that penalty. Tybalt, however, goes on to commit the crime and loses his life in consequence even before the Prince can judge and condemn him. This unexpected reversal illustrates situational irony. The second duel involves dramatic irony, for the reader knows that Romeo's reluctance to fight is due to his new relationship with Tybalt; they are at this point members of the same family. Unknowingly, Tybalt urges a relative to duel and dies at the hands of that family member. A second instance of dramatic irony can be seen in Juliet's vision when she is preparing to take the potion: "O, look! methinks I see my cousin's ghost / Seeking out Romeo, that did spit his body / Upon a rapier's point" (IV, iii, 55–57). Although Tybalt does not come back from death to strike Romeo a death blow, the blow that killed Tybalt accomplished the same end, for Romeo's death can be traced directly back to it. Thus Juliet's vision is ironic for the reader, who knows the inevitable progress of the plot to its final outcome.

While Tybalt is certainly not the only character in *Romeo and Juliet* who is ruled by emotions, the revelation of his character through conflict and setting reveal him to be central to the theme of unreasoning passion. The results of that fiery temper and the irony related to those results suggest Shakespeare's statement on that theme: passion not moderated by reason can have only dire results. For Tybalt and for so many others in the play, the result is death. For others, equally guilty of failure to use reason, it is the loss of those they love. Although a small consolation for the loss of life, the golden statues to be erected in memory of Romeo and Juliet will at least attest to their lives and love. For Tybalt, there is nothing but the tomb.

Option II: Director's Notes on a Character:
Conflict, Setting, and Language

In the first chapter, director's notes were one way of approaching the study of a character in a literary work. The assignment called for a paper in which the writer assumed the role of director of a staged version of a short story, poem, or play and described the background, appearance, and behavior of a particular character as he or she would be represented by an actor. In many short works, such as "My Last Duchess," a single character may be the central focus of the reader's interest, and therefore director's notes for that character may encompass much of the content and meaning of the work.

Longer works of literature are usually much more complex. *Romeo and Juliet*, for example, involves the interactions among a group of characters, including not merely the two lovers but also at least half a dozen secondary characters who play important parts in bringing about the final tragedy. Furthermore, it is not only the traits of these various characters that produce action; they exist in a total context of conflict, setting, and language, from which meaning may be derived. Thus it would not be satisfactory to study only the traits of eight or more characters in an attempt to define the meaning of the play. Obviously, on the other hand, to examine that many characters together with their conflicts, the setting, and language in the play would be an impossible assignment. However, if you concentrate on only one character and at the same time discuss all four elements and their interrelationship, you will at least approach an understanding of the work as a whole, since any character exists within the context of the whole. It will be necessary to have a detailed knowledge of the entire work before attempting such a paper.

Thus, while the guidelines for this assignment are similar to those for the director's notes in Chapter I, some important modifications and additions are included to integrate discussion of conflict, setting, and language with close examination of one character.

1. Choose a single character who plays a significant role in the action, preferably *not* Romeo or Juliet.
2. Imagine a staged version of the play, either in a theater or on film, and

consider how your subject would appear. To do this, think about the meaning of the play and how the character you are describing is related to that meaning. Write down your ideas about this relationship. Your notes on your chosen character and on the play in general will provide the basis for the first section of your director's notes.

3. Find information in the play about the background, stage appearance, stage action, major traits, and significant conflicts of the character you are studying. Note the relationship between the character's behavior and the setting. Note, too, those metaphors and other specialized uses of language that describe the character or that the character uses in the play. Finally, choose a key scene or two in which your character appears, and study just how actions and speeches in these scenes relate to the overall meaning of the play. It may at times be necessary for you to invent or imagine details of appearance, action, and so forth, where these are not explicitly stated in the work itself. If you do, be sure that what you say is consistent with the tone and substance of what the author has written. Use quotations from the play to support or amplify your interpretations, giving act, scene, and line numbers for each citation.

4. Organize your specific information from the play according to the following division:
   a. background biographical information: facts about age, achievements, and situation in life pertinent to understanding this character;
   b. dominant traits controlling the character's behavior;
   c. stage appearance: physical description, voice, costume;
   d. stage action: movement and behavior, gestures, mannerisms;
   e. conflicts: how behavior reflects external and internal struggles, how words and actions define the conflicts;
   f. setting: what it is and what effect it has on conflicts;
   g. language: figurative language used by others to describe this character, habitual ways of using language in the character's own speech that help to define his or her traits, conflicts, and their relation to meaning;
   h. key scene(s): just how the character functions in an important scene or two, and within the context of that scene or scenes, how character, conflict, setting, and language combine to generate meaning.

5. Write a general introductory paragraph for your director's notes, exploring the overall meaning of the play and stating briefly how your selected character relates to that meaning.

6. Develop the notes you have compiled in steps 3 and 4 into a numbered group of paragraphs, following the division of the material established in step 4.

7. After letting your first draft cool for a few days, polish it in detail and write a final fair copy. You may use the name of your character as a title.

OPTION II: SAMPLE DIRECTOR'S NOTES

Tybalt

I. A number of themes are present in Shakespeare's *Romeo and Juliet*. Much of the tragedy, for example, seems to result from breakdowns in the social or world order. The Prince's authority is ignored as the servants and young dandies of the two feuding families continually engage in street brawls. The two lovers marry without permission, fearing that their parents will withhold approval. Capulet, insisting on Juliet's immediate marriage to Paris, gives what seem unreasonable orders even in the context of his authority as father and head of a household. Another apparent theme is that fate or bad luck is the cause of the tragic events. Shakespeare's own Prologue to the play speaks of "star-cross'd lovers" (line 6)—an astrological reference to the destructive fate that lies in store for them. The fact that Friar Laurence's letter never reaches Romeo (V, ii) can be attributed to ill fortune, entirely outside the control of the major characters. However, the letter need never have been sent. Juliet did not need to take the potion; Romeo did not have to be banished; Capulet did not have to insist on Juliet's marriage to Paris; the lovers did not have to marry in secret. Moreover, these acts are not simply the results of the operation of fate. They are also unreasoned behavior and relate to yet another theme in the play, the theme of the conflict between reason and passion. If the characters kept reason in control instead of yielding to their passions of the moment, there would be no tragedy. Reasonable parents would find a way to patch up the quarrel between the two families. Reasonable young lovers would discuss their plans with their parents and try to win support or at least acceptance. Reasonable young men would stay on friendly terms and confine their rivalry to relatively harmless games and contests. But since passion prevails in the play, a series of hasty actions leads to the final tragedy. All of the principal characters share this characteristic, but one illustrates particularly vividly the total abandonment of reason and the constant dominance of passion. This is Tybalt, the most determined and vigorus prosecutor of the family feud between the Capulets and the Montagues.

II. Tybalt is nephew to Capulet, cousin to Juliet. In his late teens or early twenties, he is young enough to be addressed as "goodman boy" by his uncle (I, v, 74) but old enough in turn to call Romeo a "wretched boy" (III, i, 115). The favored male child in a wealthy and proud family, he has lived in relative idleness, with little opportunity or need to learn responsibility. He has, however, devoted himself to fine clothes, a swaggering manner, and great skill in swordplay. These give him a sense of superiority over his peers and a cockiness that he makes no attempt to conceal. Having been a somewhat spoiled child, he is reluctant to obey orders and does so only with a display of sullenness. Within the family, however, he is generally regarded with both esteem and affection; after his death, the nurse cries out,

> O Tybalt, Tybalt, the best friend I had!
> O courteous Tybalt! honest gentleman!
> That ever I should live to see thee dead!
>   [III, ii, 61–63]

Juliet refers to him as "my dearest cousin" (III, ii, 66).

III. Tybalt's principal trait is habitual anger and violence. He is described by Benvolio as "fiery" (I, i, 95) and "furious" (III, i, 106). Although he appears only briefly, in three scenes, he is much talked about, and both his actions and the comments of others confirm that he is quick to anger and slow to forgive. He turns to his sword and dagger at the least excuse; fighting is his approach to problem solving, and he never appears to consider moral, legal, or philosophical issues of any kind in his lust for battle.

IV. Tybalt is moderately tall, well muscled, but not conspicuously athletic. His lean face, with a long nose and thin lips, suggests aristocracy and seems frozen in a sneer. His voice is slightly high pitched, and he speaks in a very precise, rapid-fire style. His doublet and hose are flamboyant, brightly colored, with exaggeratedly puffed sleeves and a smooth, tight fit from thigh to ankle. At the party, he is unarmed and wears particularly vivid colors. On the street, he adds a brigandine (a corset-like piece of leather armor) and a cloak thrown with studied carelessness over one shoulder. The feather on his hat is noticeably longer than that worn by the other young men but is dashing, rather than grotesque. The hangers that carry his sword and dagger are elegant and rich-looking, although the weapons inside are very practical.

V. Tybalt's style of duelling, as described by Mercutio, suggests a lithe grace like that of a dancer: "He fights as you sing prick-song; keeps time, distance, and proportion; he rests his minim rests, one, two, and the third in your bosom . . ." (II, iv, 18–20). There is an insidious quality in his movement as well: he moves quickly, quietly, like a cat (Mercutio calls him "More than prince of cats": II, iv, 17). He swaggers proudly; he delivers insults from a stance just out of sword's reach but moves in aggressively once he has drawn his rapier. His hands are habitually on the handles of his weapons or near them, on his hips. He gestures broadly, more often with a sword than with his arm alone. Benvolio describes him as having swung his sword "about his head and cut the winds" (I, i, 97). Yet Tybalt is not a caricature —he is stylish and knows it; he is dangerous and knows that, too.

VI. Tybalt's conflicts are simple, direct, and external. Untroubled by any moral reservations about feuding, he is ready at any moment to attack all Montagues, their servants, and their friends. He thinks the worst of his enemies; when he comes upon Benvolio trying to stop a fight among the servants, Tybalt assumes that Benvolio is an active participant: "What, drawn, and talk of peace!" Without reason, he hates "all Montagues" (I, i, 56–57).

This hatred brings him into physical conflict successively with Benvolio, Mercutio (a friend of Romeo, though not actually a member of the family), and Romeo. It also brings him into an angry dispute with his uncle, who wishes to be a good host, calmly accepting the presence of Romeo, a Montague, as an uninvited guest at his annual feast. Tybalt knows no way to resolve conflict except by fighting; when Capulet refuses to allow him to fight Romeo at the party, Tybalt stalks off angrily. He is not so rash as to offer direct disobedience to his uncle, but he promptly sends a written challenge to Romeo.

VII. The setting is Verona, in northern Italy, during the Renaissance. The Prince is considered the representative of God's power in the temporal realm: his commands are to be obeyed. Heads of households, especially among the wealthy nobility, obey the Prince and in turn give orders to their own wives and children. The Prince has ordered all fighting in the streets to cease (I, i, 67–89); this edict old Capulet wishes to obey; further, he wishes to be gracious and courteous as a host, saying with respect to Romeo, "I would not for the wealth of all this town / Here in my house do him disparagement" (I, v, 66–67). Thus Tybalt's anger is frustrated by the constraints of the setting, and his mood becomes more and more violent. At the same time, it is July and, as the wise Benvolio points out:

> The day is hot, the Capulets abroad,
> And, if we meet, we shall not scape a brawl,
> For now, these hot days, is the mad blood stirring.
> [III, i, 2–4]

In effect, Tybalt's anger and need for violence are increased both by the restraining hand of the society in which he lives and by the oppressive weather.

VIII. The language of the play underscores Tybalt's attitudes and outlook. Mercutio's metaphors for Tybalt—"More than prince of cats" (II, iv, 17), "rat-catcher" (III, i, 64), and "king of cats" (III, i, 66)—are first of all an insulting play on Tybalt's name, which is similar to that of the cat in the fables of *Reynard the Fox*. The comparison with a tomcat is apt, since it calls attention to Tybalt's aggressive behavior, his constant snarling and fighting. Tybalt's own vocabulary also focuses on his passions. In his very first speech in the play, he threatens Benvolio with death (I, i, 53); in his next, he uses the word *hate* twice (I, i, 56–57). In a play revolving around love, Tybalt uses the word *love* ironically: "Romeo, the love I bear thee can afford / No better term than this: thou art a villain" (III, i, 49–50). His angry passions are revealed constantly in his language.

IX. Two scenes in particular illustrate Tybalt's hotheadedness, his characteristic yielding to passion instead of following the restraints of reason. These are Act I, scene v, at the Capulet party and Act III, scene i, on the streets of Verona, where Tybalt kills Mercutio and later is himself killed by

Romeo. In both, Tybalt's behavior is consistent with his character but quite inappropriate in the setting. At the party, a finely dressed company have gathered at the invitation of the gracious old Capulet. There is food and drink, musicians are playing, dancing begins. This is obviously a time for courteous behavior. However, when the masked Romeo speaks about Juliet's beauty, Tybalt reacts violently:

> This, by his voice, should be a Montague.
> Fetch me my rapier, boy. . . .
> To strike him dead I hold it not a sin.
>
> [I, v, 51–56]

His remarks lead Capulet to ask, "wherefore storm you so?" (line 57); and when Capulet recommends patience, saying that frowns do not suit the occasion, Tybalt bursts out, "It fits, when such a villain is a guest. / I'll not endure him" (lines 72–73). Tybalt's anger moves Capulet to scold him, calling him a "saucy boy" (line 80) and a "princox"—an impertinent, insolent fellow (line 83). But Tybalt cannot accept either reason or authority. He angrily stalks from the room, muttering threats. As we presently learn, he sends a letter challenging Romeo to a duel. He cannot wait for an answer, however, for in Act III, scene i, we find him searching the streets for Romeo, in spite of the Prince's edict forbidding fighting in Verona. In addition, the hot July weather increases the danger of a general brawl if any fighting starts. Nevertheless, Tybalt's grudge against Romeo overrides all other considerations, and he can think of no way to settle their difference other than by violence. He scarcely responds to Mercutio's needling, since he is completely preoccupied with his desire to fight Romeo. On Romeo's entrance, Tybalt calls him a "villain" (III, i, 50)—the proper style for starting a quarrel. It is Romeo's peaceful and gentle response that stirs Mercutio to draw his sword and start fighting Tybalt. Even while Romeo is trying to part them, Tybalt lunges under Romeo's arm and kills Mercutio. Though he runs off immediately, Tybalt is still hot for Romeo's blood, and promptly returns "in triumph" to satisfy his blood lust (line 107). This time, as he continues to follow the passions of the moment instead of listening to the dictates of reason, he loses. The result is not only his own death but a series of disasters that strike down most of the principals in the tragedy. Looked at from the point of view of Tybalt, that tragedy is partially his own doing, as his anger and rashness lead him only to the grave.

APPENDIX: GUIDELINES FOR DOCUMENTATION OF SOURCES

The following sample notes and bibliography entries satisfy the requirements of the *MLA Handbook for Writers of Research Papers, Theses, and Dissertations* (New York: Modern Language Association, 1977) and are therefore suitable models for documentation done in most colleges and universities. In all cases, students should follow the particular directions or modifications of instructors for whom papers are being written. In any event, the student should always observe the two primary rules of documentation:

1. references must be clear and exact;
2. form must be consistent.

Footnotes and Endnotes

Footnotes   Type single-spaced at the bottom of the page on which the reference is made. Quadruple-space after the final line of your text and to the first footnote line; double-space between footnotes. Observe the usual marginal rules of one inch on either side of the note, and do not go below your one-inch margin at the bottom of the page. If the note is too long to be contained within the bottom margin, continue it on the next page. Single-space after the last text line on the new page, type a solid line from the left margin to the right, and complete your note. New notes for this page are entered directly after your continued note. The first line of each footnote should be indented five spaces; the number of the note is raised one-half space above the line; and a space should be left before the note itself begins. Using commas to separate items, except where noted below, type information in the following order:

1. The full name of the author (or authors) should be given as it appears on the title page of your source. If there are more than three authors, give the complete name of the first author only, followed by "et al." (an abbreviation of the Latin term *et alii*, meaning "and others"). When an editor or editors are quoted instead of an author, these names should appear in this position, followed by a comma and the abbreviation "ed." ("editor," plural "eds."). See notes 3 and 17 below.

2. When quoting excerpted material, list the title (if any) of the selection or chapter quoted, enclosed in quotation marks (see notes 9, 12, 18, and 20 below).

3. The third entry is the underlined title of the complete work in which the selection or chapter appears. If you are quoting from a titled selection or chapter in this work, the source title is preceded by "in." If you are not quoting from a titled chapter or selection, the title of the book appears immediately after the author (see note 1 below).

4. After the source title, enter the name or names of editors, translators, and compilers. The name is preceded by the appropriate abbreviation: "ed.," "trans.," or "comp." (Do not use "eds." if there is more than one editor cited: here the abbreviation stands for "edited by," not "editor.") When the editor has been quoted and thus placed in first position in the note, omit the name here. (See notes 18, 19, and 21 below.) This information and that in item 5 are also found on the title page.

5. List the edition used, if it is not the first, in abbreviated form. If the edition is revised, add this information: for example, "4th ed., rev." (See note 17 below.) If the edition is a reprint, follow the instructions in item 6.

6. The next entry consists of the place of publication, publisher (in a shortened form), and date of publication of the source. In parentheses, list the city where the work was published (and the abbreviated name of the state if the city is very small), followed by a colon; the name of the publisher, followed by a comma, and the date of publication (see note 1 below). If the work is a reprint, in parentheses list the first publication date, followed by a semicolon; the abbreviation "rpt."; and then the publication place, publisher, and date of the reprint edition (see note 4 below). This information is found on the back of the title page. A comma follows the parentheses, but there is no punctuation between the preceding element and the opening parenthesis.

7. Enter the volume number of the source, if it has more than one volume, in capital Roman numerals. Precede the numeral with the abbreviation "Vol." if you are citing the entire volume or if you are citing specific pages in the volume but other information appears between the volume number and the page numbers. Omit "Vol." when specific page numbers follow the volume number immediately. (See note 15 below; compare with note 8, where additional information intervenes between volume and page numbers.)

8. Page numbers in Arabic numerals are the last item in the footnote. Precede the number with "p." (plural "pp."). List only the pages actually quoted in your text.

Encyclopedias, journals, newspapers, and other forms of periodicals include additional information, such as journal volume (if any) and number. The place of publication and publisher are omitted. When month of publication is included, it is abbreviated unless the name of the month is only one syllable long. Notes 10, 12, 13, 14, and 20 below illustrate such entries. If no author is listed, the article title begins the note.

For subsequent references to a work already documented in an earlier footnote, use "Ibid." if the second reference is exactly the same as the first and follows it immediately. "Ibid." is an abbreviation of the Latin term *ibidem*, meaning "identical." If all information is the same except the page quoted, include the new page number, as in note 2 below. When one or more notes separate two references to the same work, and the work you are quoting is the only one you are using by that author, the second reference needs only the author's last name and the page number referred to (if your notes include works by two authors with identical last names, give the author's full name). If you quote from two or more works by the same author, in your second reference to any of them, give the author's last name and a shortened title of the work (see note 7 below).

Endnotes If your instructor prefers endnotes, enter them on a separate page at the end of your essay, preceding your bibliography. Endnotes are typed in exactly the same format as footnotes; however, they should be double-spaced both within and between notes. Beginning two inches from the top edge of the sheet, title the page "Notes" (of course omitting the quotation marks used here), and quadruple-space to the first line of the notes. Observe usual marginal rules of one inch on both sides and at the top and bottom of endnote pages.

[1] Louis A. Allison, *Writing Your Term Paper* (Boston: Houghton Mifflin, 1967), p. 211.

[2] Ibid., p. 59.

[3] Edward C. Lathem and Lawrance Thompson, eds., *Robert Frost: Poetry and Prose* (New York: Holt, 1972), p. xii.

[4] Narcissus Creech, *Collected Poems of Narcissus Creech*, ed. Harmon R. A. Kurth (1927; rpt. Edgarsville, Md.: Gazelle, 1968), p. 174.

[5] Louis A. Allison, *Library Resources for the Layman* (Boston: Houghton Mifflin, 1970), p. 8.

[6] Lathem and Thompson, p. 48.

[7] Allison, *Library Resources*, p. 36.

[8] Lawrance Thompson, *The Years of Triumph*, Vol. II of *Robert Frost* (New York: Holt, 1971), p. 145.

[9] William Smithers, "Symbolists in the Nineteenth Century," in *Famous Literary Essays* (New York: Macmillan, 1951), pp. 301–02.

[10] Graham Goulder Hough, "Keats, John," *Encyclopaedia Britannica*, 1973 ed.

[11] Ibid.

[12] John L. Kern, "Erica," *Writer's Digest*, June 1981, p. 20.

[13] "Better Read Than Dead," *Life*, 29 Dec. 1972, p. 51.

[14] Helen Vendler, "The Poetry of Autobiography," *New York Times*, 14 Aug. 1977, Sec. 7, p. 24, col. 1.

[15] Thompson, *Robert Frost*, II, 540.

[16] "William Shakespeare," *World Book Encyclopedia*, 1962 ed., XVI, 269.

[17] Walter Blair et al., eds., *The Literature of the United States*, 3rd ed. (New York: Scott, Foresman, 1966), II, 15.

[18] Margaret Walker, "Jubilee," in *Right On: An Anthology of Black Literature*, ed. Bradford Chambers et al. (New York: Mentor, 1970), p. 31.

[19] Jean-Paul Sartre, *The Reprieve*, trans. Eric Sutton (New York: Bantam, 1968), p. 91.

[20] Robert O. Stephens, "Hemingway's Old Man and the Iceberg," *Modern Fiction Studies*, 7 (1961–62), p. 297.

[21] Leo Stoller, "Thoreau's Doctrine of Simplicity," in *Thoreau: A Collection of Critical Essays*, ed. Sherman Paul (Englewood Cliffs, N.J.: Prentice-Hall, 1962), p. 38.

Bibliography

A bibliography is a list of the sources you made reference to or quoted from in your paper. You may also include major works that you consulted but did not refer to, especially when those works might be important resources for your readers. Bibliography references are not numbered.

Note that the order of items in a bibliography entry is the same as for notes. The punctuation, however, differs. Each major item is separated by periods (followed by two spaces); place of publication, publisher, and date use the same internal punctuation as in footnotes but omit the parentheses. Items following a period begin with a capital letter, even if the first word in the item is an abbreviation that would not be capitalized in a footnote ("Ed.," not "ed."). Volume and page numbers are given only for multi-volume books and selections in books and periodicals, where there would be no reason to refer your reader to the entire work. These numbers are separated from each other by commas, as in notes. A final period completes both note and bibliography entries.

Another difference between bibliography and note entries concerns author listings and the placement of bibliography entries on the page. Author names are reversed, with a comma following the last name, and sources are listed alphabetically by author's last name. If no author is mentioned in the source, the work is listed alphabetically by the first word of the book or selection title (when the first word is an article, alphabetization is done according to the first letter of the second word). If a work has more than one author, only the first author's name is reversed, with a comma following both parts; other authors appear in normal order. Should the bibliography contain more than one work by an author, the works are grouped together in the author's proper alphabetical location; within this group, these works may be alphabetized by title or listed chronologically, as you prefer. The first entry includes the author's full name. Subsequent entries by the same author omit his or her name and substitute a line of ten hyphens, followed by a period and two spaces.

The first line of each reference begins at the left margin, and additional lines are indented five spaces. Otherwise bibliography entries are double-spaced and positioned on the page in exactly the same way as endnotes, with the title "Bibliography" at the head of the first page. Examine carefully each of the following examples.

Allison, Louis A. *Library Resources for the Layman.* Boston: Houghton Mifflin, 1970.

———. *Writing Your Term Paper.* Boston: Houghton Mifflin, 1967.

"Better Read Than Dead." *Life,* 29 Dec. 1972, p. 51.

Blair, Walter, et al., eds. *The Literature of the United States.* 3rd ed. New York: Scott, Foresman, 1966. Vol. II.

Creech, Narcissus. *Collected Poems of Narcissus Creech.* Ed. Harmon R. A. Kurth. 1927; rept. Edgarsville, Md.: Gazelle, 1968.

Hough, Graham Goulder. "Keats, John." *Encyclopaedia Britannica.* 1973 ed.

Kern, John L. "Erica." *Writer's Digest,* June 1981, pp. 20–23.

Lathem, Edward C., and Lawrance Thompson, eds. *Robert Frost: Poetry and Prose.* New York: Holt, 1972.

Sartre, Jean-Paul. *The Reprieve*. Trans. Eric Sutton. New York: Bantam, 1968.

Smart, Genevieve. *Poetic Ventures: A Criticism*. Kanesville, Ohio: Leader Press, 1937.

————, and Margaret Brent. *Some Studies in Modern Literary Criticism*. Kanesville, Ohio: Leader Press, 1940.

Smithers, William. "Symbolists in the Nineteenth Century." In *Famous Literary Essays*. New York: Macmillan, 1951.

Stephens, Robert O. "Hemingway's Old Man and the Iceberg." *Modern Fiction Studies*, 7 (1961–62), 295–304.

Stoller, Leo. "Thoreau's Doctrine of Simplicity." In *Thoreau: A Collection of Critical Essays*. Ed. Sherman Paul. Englewood Cliffs, N.J.: Prentice-Hall, 1962, pp. 37–53.

Thompson, Lawrance. *The Years of Triumph*. Vol. II of *Robert Frost*. New York: Holt, 1971.

Vendler, Helen. "The Poetry of Autobiography." *New York Times*, 14 Aug. 1977, Sec. 7, pp. 1, 24–25.

Walker, Margaret. "Jubilee." In *Right On: An Anthology of Black Literature*. Ed. Bradford Chambers et al. New York: Mentor, 1970.

"William Shakespeare." *World Book Encyclopedia*. 1962 ed.

GLOSSARY OF LITERARY TERMS

Allegory: a work in which a group of interrelated metaphors or symbols take on a total pattern of meaning. In the medieval play *Everyman*, for example, all of the characters are personified abstractions, including "Good Deeds," "Knowledge," "Beauty," "Strength," etc.; the overall concern of the play is with the question of who will accompany "Everyman" on his way to death and beyond, to God's judgment. In less strictly constructed allegories, the meanings of the various metaphors and symbols may be more loosely connected than in this one-to-one situation. See Chapter 4.

Alliteration: use of the same initial letter or initial sound for emphasis or other special effect; for example, the repetition of *b*, *w*, and *br* sounds in "Because the Holy Ghost over the bent / World broods with warm breast and with ah! bright wings."

Allusion: reference to historical, literary, or mythological characters or events to enrich or illuminate meaning, as in "He stood there in the middle of the road / Like Roland's ghost winding a silent horn."

Anapest, anapestic: see Meter.

Antagonist: a person or force against whom or which the protagonist (main character) struggles in an external conflict. See Chapter 2.

Apostrophe: direct address to an inanimate object, an animal, or a dead person as if the addressee were able to hear and understand the speaker: "O Rose, thou art sick!" See Chapter 4.

Assonance: repetition of a vowel sound for poetic effect, as in the long *i* sounds in "If her eyes have not blinded thine. . . ."

Atmosphere: the general mood or emotional quality of a work, created through details related to weather, time of day, the physical setting, etc. See Chapter 3.

Ballad: a poem that tells a story, often in a series of four-line stanzas alternating iambic tetrameter with iambic trimeter and rhyming *abcb*.

Blank verse: poetry consisting of unrhymed iambic pentameter, usually not divided into stanzas:

> Five years have past; five summers, with the length
> Of five long winters! and again I hear
> These waters, rolling from their mountain-springs
> With a soft inland murmur.—Once again
> Do I behold these steep and lofty cliffs. . . .

Character: a person in a work of fiction, poetry, or drama; also, the particular combination of traits that make up an identifiable and more or less predictable person. Characters may be dynamic or static: a dynamic character changes in one or more traits as a result of the events of a narrative; a static character remains unchanged, exhibiting exactly the same traits at the end of the work as at the beginning. See Chapter 1.

Characterization: the means by which an author reveals traits of character to the reader. Direct characterization refers to explicit statements (often made by a third-person narrator) about traits or habits of behavior. Indirect characterization occurs when specific actions or remarks or other clues in the work allow the reader to infer traits. See Chapter 1.

Climax: the moment of greatest tension in a story, poem, or play, when the central conflict is about to be resolved. See Chapter 2.

Comedy: a work (frequently a play) in which problems are overcome and conflicts successfully resolved, so that there is a "happy ending." Comedies typically include humorous or even ridiculous material but may be quite serious in intent.

Complication: a new or changed situation which introduces additional conflicts or intensifies previous ones. See Chapter 2.

Conflict: a struggle or contest between two opposing forces in a work. In *external conflict*, a character struggles against some outer force, such as another character, a force of nature, or society. In *internal conflict*, a character faces a choice between two inner needs, drives, desires, or moral standards. See Chapter 2.

Connotation: the emotional associations commonly connected to a word, as distinguished from denotation, the basic literal meaning of the word. *Woman* and *lady*, for example, both have the denotation of an adult female person. *Lady*, however, has connotations connected with elegant and courteous behavior, delicacy, and the like, or perhaps even snobbery or superiority of attitude.

Consonance: repetition of consonant sounds other than initial consonants. The phrase "And wears man's smudge and shares man's smell" includes both alliteration and consonance, as well as internal rhyme (*wears-shares*).

Couplet: two consecutive lines of verse, sharing the same meter and frequently rhyming: "This thou perceivest, which makes thy love more strong, / To love that well which thou must leave ere long." See Chapter 4.

Dactyl, dactylic: see meter.

Deciding factor: the event, attitude, or situation that leads to the resolution of a conflict. See Chapter 2.

Denotation: the basic or literal meaning of a word, as opposed to connotation.

Denouement: the final unraveling of the plot and its complications, after the climax. See Chapter 2.

Dialogue: conversation among characters in a literary work, sometimes used as a narrative point of view. See Chapter 1.

Direct characterization: see Characterization.

Dynamic character: see Character.

Elizabethan sonnet: English sonnet; see Sonnet.

English sonnet: see Sonnet.

External conflict: see Conflict.

Falling action: that part of the plot following the climax or turning point. See Chapter 2.

Fantasy: a work containing strange or unrealistic material beyond what is likely in real life.

Farce: a type of comedy stressing broad humor, ridiculous situations, and often practical jokes.

Figurative comparison: comparison of two essentially unlike topics, to call attention to some specific similarity. The basic types are (1) *simile,* an explicit comparison using "like" or "as" or some other expression of comparison: "O my luv is like a red, red rose"; (2) *metaphor,* a comparison not directly stated but implied by the context: "The Sea of Faith / Was once, too, at the full"; (3) *personification:* treatment of an idea, an inanimate object, or an animal as if it were a person: "The Sea that bares her bosom to the moon." The term "metaphor" may be used generally to refer to all three types of figurative comparison. See Chapter 4.

First-person point of view: see Point of view; see also Chapter 1.

Flashback: a shift in time sequence back to an earlier event or series of events. See Chapter 2.

Flat character: a character with only one or two clear traits, not "rounded."

Foot: see Meter.

Foreshadowing: hints or suggestions of coming events in a narrative or play.

Free verse: poetry without a definite, regular pattern of meter or, frequently, rhyme.

Hyperbole: extreme exaggeration or overstatement for poetic effect.

Iamb, iambic: see Meter.

Image, imagery: descriptive language used to produce sensory experiences in the mind of the reader. See Chapter 4.

Indirect characterization: see Characterization.

Initial situation: the conflict or relationship that sets a plot in motion. See Chapter 2.

Internal conflict: see Conflict.

Irony: a discrepancy between the apparent meaning of a passage and the reader's actual understanding. *Dramatic irony* refers to a contrast between what a character says and what the reader understands to be true. *Situational irony* occurs when events turn out in a way contrary to expectation. *Verbal irony* refers to a contrast between what is actually said and what is meant by the speaker. See Chapter 4.

Italian sonnet: see Sonnet.

Limited point of view: see Point of view; see also Chapter 1.

Literal comparison: a comparison intended to be understood literally, in contrast to figurative comparisons. See Chapter 4.

Melodrama: a narrative or dramatic work in which good and evil are sharply contrasted, frequently containing oversimplified, flat characters and sensational events.

Metaphor: see Figurative comparison.

Meter: the rhythmic pattern of accents in poetry. A metrical "foot" is usually one accented syllable accompanied by one or two unaccented syllables. The most common types of foot are

1. *iamb*, two syllables, with the second accented: "today";
2. *trochee*, two syllables, with the first accented: "traffic";
3. *anapest*, three syllables, with the third accented: "in the house";
4. *dactyl*, three syllables, with the first accented: "galloping";
5. *spondee*, two syllables, both accented: "hard times."

A line of verse is metrically labeled according to the basic type of foot it contains and its total number of feet. The most frequently used line lengths are

1. *trimeter*, three feet: "Had he / and I / but met" (iambic trimeter);
2. *tetrameter*, four feet: " 'Twas the night / before Christ/mas and all / through the house" (anapestic tetrameter);
3. *pentameter*, five feet: "When I / consid/er how / my light / is spent" (iambic pentameter).

Metonymy: substitution of a closely associated term for an idea or object: "He drinks a *six-pack* every evening," instead of "He drinks six beers every evening." Although the term "metonymy" is being used increasingly to refer to all substitutions of this general type, some writers distinguish between strict metonymy and "synecdoche," which is the specific substitution of the part for the whole ("Our barn is designed to hold twenty *head* of cattle") or vice versa ("On December 7, 1941, *Japan* bombed Pearl Harbor"). See Chaper 4.

Mood: see Atmosphere.

Myth: a narrative about gods or heroes, embodying some basic religious belief or explanation of a phenomenon not otherwise understood.

Narrator: the speaker or teller of a series of events in a narrative.

Objective point of view: see Point of view; see also Chapter 1.

Omniscient point of view: see Point of view; see also Chapter 1.

Parable: a story that is intended to teach a lesson. Many illustrations exist in the Bible. In Milton's poem "On His Blindness," reference is made to the parable of the talents (see study questions for that poem on p. 756).

Paradox: a statement that seems contradictory but is in fact understandable and even true. The final two lines of John Crowe Ransom's poem "Parting Without a Sequel" are "she stood there hot as fever / And cold as any icicle." To be both hot and cold at the same time seems impossible, but the suggestion of deep and conflicting emotions existing together is a valid one (see the analysis of this poem in Chapter 2).

Paraphrase: a restatement of a work of literature (or part of it) that retains the original attitude, information, and point of view, phrased in different words. For a poem, this is usually line by line; for prose, it is sentence by sentence. A condensed restatement of a work is called a précis.

Pentameter: see Meter; see also Chapter 1.

Persona: the speaker of a literary work, thus the voice or mask through which the author speaks (not the author's own voice); it is most recognizable in first-person narrative and in satire (see Satire). Through the persona, the author in part establishes tone (see Tone).

Personification: the attribution of human characteristics to animals, objects, or ideas: "Passion speechless lies." See Chapter 4.

Petrarchan sonnet: Italian sonnet. See Sonnet.

Place: see Setting; see also Chapter 3.

Plot: the arrangement of the events that make up the action of a narrative work or a play. See Chapter 2.

Point of view: method of presenting a literary situation; therefore, the speaker in a work of prose fiction or a poem. Point of view is subdivided as follows: *first person*—a character in the work relates the events; *third person*—events are told by someone not among the characters, whose point of view may be *omniscient* (all-knowing), *limited* (knowing only the thoughts and feelings of a single character), or *objective* (knowing only what can be seen and heard); and *dialogue*—no one tells the events: the entire work is conveyed through conversation among characters. Occasionally a literary work can be written in the *second person*; and in some very complex, extended works (mostly modern), different points of view will appear in various sections. See Chapter 1.

Précis: a rephrased condensation of a literary work (or part of it) that retains the structure, all details of information, emphasis, and point of view of the original.

Problem play: a drama that examines a social issue.

Prologue: the introductory section, usually to a play or a long poem, that gives the background of the action about to take place.

Protagonist: the major character in a literary work through whose experience readers view the central conflict. See Antagonist; see also Chapter 2.

Quatrain: a four-line stanza or other portion of a poem.

Realism: literature that depicts the familiar world, with recognizable settings, characters, and conflicts.

Resolution: the outcome of a conflict. See Chapter 2.

Rhyme: the patterned repetition of similar-sounding words. This repetition can occur as *end rhyme,* at the end of lines; or as *internal rhyme,* within a single line. They may be *exact* rhymes ("moon"/"June"); *eye* rhymes ("food"/"good"), which look as if they should rhyme on the page but are pronounced somewhat differently; or *slant* rhymes ("fight"/ "fate"), which begin and end with the same sounds but contain very different internal sounds. Rhymes that are one-syllable words or stress the final syllable ("turn"/"burn," "withstand"/"underhand") are sometimes called *masculine* rhyme. Those that are of more than one syllable and accent the first syllable ("dying"/"lying") are sometimes called *feminine* rhymes.

Rhythm: the arrangement of stressed and unstressed syllables in poetry. See Meter.

Rising action: the series of complications within a plot that increase the conflict and lead to the climax. See Chapter 2.

Rounded character: a complex character; one who is fully developed. See Chapter 1.

Sarcasm: a bitter statement, often biting; a form of verbal irony. See Chapter 4.

Satire: a literary work that ridicules in order to criticize a vice, social condition, or folly.

Second-person point of view: see Point of view.

Setting: the physical environment, including place and time, of the action; and the nonphysical environment that includes cultural influences on the events and/or the characters themselves. See Chapter 3.

Shakespearean sonnet: the English sonnet. See Sonnet.

Simile: see Figurative comparison; see also Chapter 4.

Situational irony: see Irony; see also Chapter 4.

Soliloquy: a speech in a play by an actor who either is or thinks he or she is alone on the stage; generally the character is thinking aloud; however, the soliloquy may be a direct address by the character to the audience.

Sonnet: a poem fourteen lines in length, written in iambic pentameter with a fixed rhyme scheme. The two major forms are the English sonnet, with a rhyme scheme of *abab, cdcd, efef, gg,* thus consisting of three quatrains and a concluding couplet; and the Italian sonnet, with a rhyme scheme of *abbaabba, cdecde* (or any other combination of the *c, d,* and *e* rhymes), which is thus made up of an *octet* (a group of eight lines) and a *sestet* (a group of six lines). The sonnet usually consists of only one stanza, although some poets divide the English sonnet into stanzas representing the constituent quatrains and the couplet. See Writing Option III in Chapter 4.

Speaker: the narrating voice in a work of literature. See Persona and Point of view; see also Chapter 1.

Spondee: See Meter.

Stage direction: an author's commentary within a play that gives actors and readers information about dialogue and movement.

Stanza: a unit within a poem consisting of a group of lines whose number, meter, and rhyme scheme are repeated in one or more units. Stanzas are sometimes numbered by the poet; often they are only separated by spaces.

Static character: see Character.

Stream of consciousness: a narrative technique in which the thoughts of the narrator are presented in the disorganized manner of free association, so that the work (or part of it) consists of what the character thinks.

Structure: the organization of a literary work.

Style: the writer's choice of language and its organization.

Symbol: an object, person, or action that suggests deeper meanings to the reader, particularly representing ideas. See Chapter 4.

Synecdoche: see Metonymy; see also Chapter 4.

Syntax: the grammatical relationship among words in a phrase or sentence.

Tetrameter: see Meter.

Theme: the subject or topic of a work: for example, pride, old age, young love. See Chapter 5.

Theme statement: a statement summarizing what a literary work is saying about its theme; sometimes referred to as the *thesis* of a work. See Chapter 5.

Third-person point of view: see Point of view; see also Chapter 1.

Time: an essential part of the setting of a literary work; it includes clock time, calendar time, and historical time. See Chapter 2.

Tone: a manner of speaking that expresses attitude (for example, sarcasm, melancholy). In literature tone is established by characters and/or the narrator.

Tragedy: a work (frequently a play) that ends in catastrophe for the hero, often brought about by a flaw in character (known as a "tragic flaw"), such as an excess of pride, but usually involving misfortune or bad luck as well. See Chapter 5.

Trimeter: see Meter.

Trochee: see Meter.

Type character: a character who represents a single quality, such as greed or cruelty; frequently mythic.

Understatement: a kind of verbal irony that expresses less than what is actually meant: "Death lasts a long time."

Verbal irony: see Irony; see also Chapter 4.

INDEX OF AUTHORS
AND TITLES *

* Italicized numbers indicate pages on which authors' works are reprinted in full.